# THE QUEST FOR
# MODERN ASSAM

Celebrating 35 Years of
Penguin Random House India

# ADVANCE PRAISE FOR THE BOOK

'*The Quest for Modern Assam* compellingly demonstrates the centrality of Assam to the modern history of South Asia. Drawing on years of deep research, it seamlessly blends social, political, economic, environmental and cultural history to present a richly readable portrait of one of the most fascinating (as well as most troubled) states of the Indian Union. This is a model work of historical scholarship that sets new standards in the field. It will have a transformative impact on how we understand modern Assam and the Indian Republic itself'—**Ramachandra Guha**, historian and biographer

'*The Quest for Modern Assam* is a remarkable accomplishment by the foremost scholar of north-eastern India and one of the most eminent historians of modern India. Arupjyoti Saikia shows how various wars and regional political strife left their deep imprint on Assam. His magisterial study exhibits authoritative command of its sources and provides a brisk and lively narrative that ranges across topics including agriculture, environment, energy industries, migration and infrastructure. It is destined to become the definitive work on the politics and society of Assam in the latter half of the twentieth century. Scholars of South and South-east Asia, and students of nation-building in the age of decolonization and the Cold War more generally, will surely find this work immensely valuable'—**K. Sivaramakrishnan**, Dinakar Singh Professor of Anthropology and professor, School of the Environment, Yale University

'Based on meticulous research, this instant classic provides a comprehensive portrait of Assam between the Second World War and the 2000s. With the historian's eye for revealing detail, Arupjyoti Saikia explains the region's multifaceted and conflicted trajectory like no one else. We learn how turbulent ecological, economic and demographic processes constantly compelled Assam's inhabitants to rethink and rework their cultural and political identities. This solid study of an oft-misunderstood state makes essential reading for anyone interested in India's modern history'—**Willem van Schendel**, professor of history, University of Amsterdam and International Institute of Social History, the Netherlands

'Arupjyoti Saikia's book provides necessary nuance to standard historical works on a critical period of Assam's political history at a time when simplistic narratives are hazing the clarity of a sharp historical analysis. This is an informed and accessible work of modern history, based on solid academic scholarship, and an indispensable companion for lay readers and specialists alike'—**Gunnel Cederlöf**, professor of history, Linnaeus University

'This is that rare work that combines a panoramic sweep with archival depth. Dr Saikia does more, much more than give us a sophisticated and nuanced view of the unfolding of political and social change in Assam in the late twentieth century. He also sets a standard for political histories of post-independent India and South Asia. A book not to be missed'—**Mahesh Rangarajan**, professor of environmental studies and history, Ashoka University

'Saikia's book is the most well-researched, comprehensive history of contemporary Assam ever written. After taking note of the enormous impact of the Second World War—unlike anything in the rest of India—Saikia presents in detail the immense variety of political, social and cultural formations of Assam and its hill districts. He, then, examines critically the struggles for identity and exclusion that mark the more recent period. A spectacular achievement'—**Partha Chatterjee**, Professor Emeritus, Anthropology and of Middle Eastern, South Asian and African Studies, Columbia University

'*The Quest for Modern Assam* is an outstanding history of Assam since the 1940s, broadly conceived, deeply researched and deftly presented. Arupjyoti Saikia deploys his formidable command of the political and economic, social and cultural, environmental and international histories of the region to offer a compelling account. The book sets new standards for the writing of India's contemporary history, especially from the vantage point of the states'—**Srinath Raghavan**, professor of international relations and history, Ashoka University

'Sophisticated, subtle and woven with illuminating dexterity, there's none better than Arupjyoti Saikia to tell the turbulent tale of Assam's post-Independence journey. *The Quest for Modern Assam* affirms Assam as a critical region, historically and in the histories to come. Filled with twists and turns, this is India's eastside story'—**Jelle J.P. Wouters**, associate professor of anthropology and sociology, Royal Thimphu College, Bhutan

'*The Quest for Modern Assam* is a detailed and extremely readable work that examines the history of Assam in the second half of the twentieth century. While engaging with the idea of Assamese modernity, Arupjyoti Saikia skilfully delves into the various contingencies that helped in the creation of modern Assam. Beginning with the Second World War and its impact on the region, the author capably addresses the political issues that emerged in the region against a backdrop of the ever-changing and ever-evolving economic, environmental and demographic challenges that the state has encountered. The book will be most interesting for all those who would like to have a handle on the politics of north-east India especially in the post-Independence period. It offers interesting insights and provides fresh details even to events and circumstances that are more well known'—**Joy L.K. Pachuau**, professor of history, Centre for Historical Studies, Jawaharlal Nehru University

'*The Quest for Modern Assam* gives us a deeply researched, wide-ranging and insightful history of modern Assam. Alive with the drama of political struggles, Saikia brings to life the people who have made modern Assam and brings to light many unsung heroes. This book will also be essential reading far beyond India as an exemplary study of how much we gain when we study nations not from their heartlands but from their edges and borders'—**Sunil Amrith**, Renu and Anand Dhawan Professor of History, Yale University

# THE QUEST FOR MODERN ASSAM

## *A History*
### 1942–2000

**ARUPJYOTI SAIKIA**

SUPPORTED BY

An imprint of Penguin Random House

ALLEN LANE

USA | Canada | UK | Ireland | Australia
New Zealand | India | South Africa | China | Singapore

Allen Lane is part of the Penguin Random House group of companies whose addresses can be found at global.penguinrandomhouse.com

Published by Penguin Random House India Pvt. Ltd
4th Floor, Capital Tower 1, MG Road,
Gurugram 122 002, Haryana, India

First published in Allen Lane by Penguin Random House India 2023

Copyright © Arupjyoti Saikia 2023

All rights reserved

10 9 8 7 6 5 4 3 2 1

The views and opinions expressed in this book are the author's own and the facts are as reported by him which have been verified to the extent possible, and the publishers are not in any way liable for the same.

ISBN 9780670095704

Typeset in Adobe Garamond Pro by Manipal Technologies Limited, Manipal
Printed at Thomson Press India Ltd, New Delhi

This book is sold subject to the condition that it shall not, by way of trade or otherwise, be lent, resold, hired out, or otherwise circulated without the publisher's prior consent in any form of binding or cover other than that in which it is published and without a similar condition including this condition being imposed on the subsequent purchaser.

www.penguin.co.in

*To Nizan and his generation,
who will take the story forward*

'Close on the heels of our youth came the fury of the Second World War. Followed soon after by the revolt of '42. And then, freedom arrived, attended by the terror of India's Partition and the taint of communalism bringing refugees, inflation and famine, the deluge of floods, erosion and the Great Quake of the fifties. The shadow of an apocalypse gradually cast itself over our national life, our language and letters, and shaped our very existence.'

—Mahim Bora, Preface to *Ronga-Jiya*, 1978
tr. Rakhee Kalita Moral

'. . . and just like that
a familiar village sight
metamorphosed before our very eyes . . .

for some came Autumn,
Spring for a few,
for some a Summer of scorching suns . . .'

—Jiban Narah, 'Painting an Old World Anew', 2023
tr. Anindita Kar

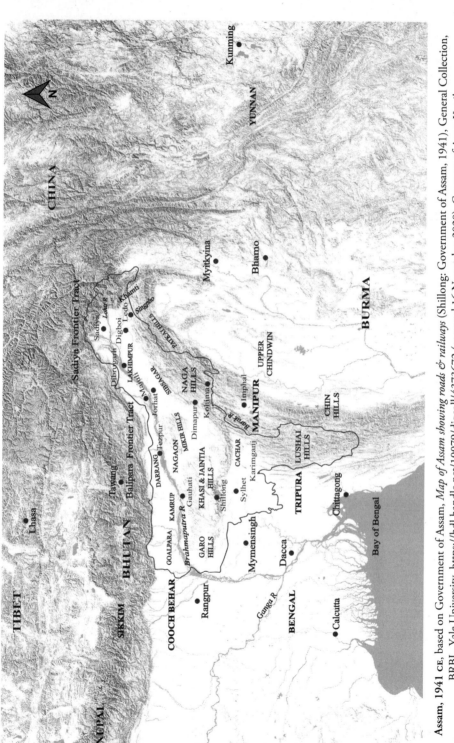

**Assam, 1941 CE**, based on Government of Assam, *Map of Assam showing roads & railways* (Shillong: Government of Assam, 1941), General Collection, BRBL, Yale University, https://hdl.handle.net/10079/digcoll/4373672 (accessed 16 November 2020). Courtesy of Ayon Kopil. This illustration is not drawn to scale and is a historical representation of the area for illustrative purposes only. The boundaries shown on the illustration are neither authentic nor correct.

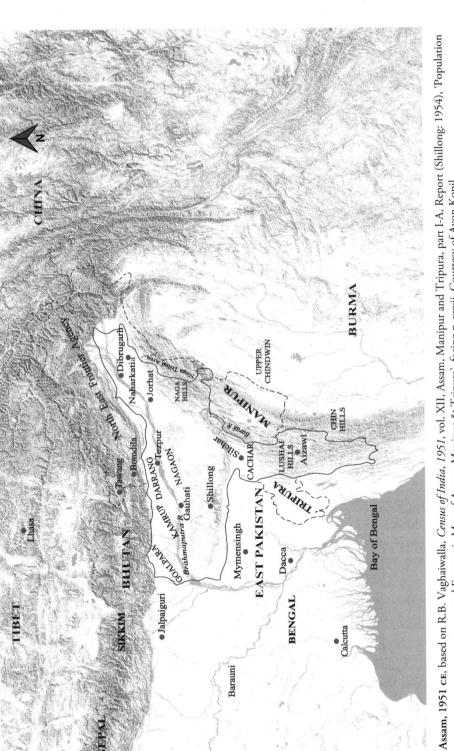

**Assam, 1951 CE**, based on R.B. Vaghaiwalla, *Census of India, 1951*, vol. XII, Assam, Manipur and Tripura, part I-A, Report (Shillong; 1954). 'Population and Economic Map of Assam, Manipur & Tripura', facing p. xxvii. Courtesy of Ayon Kopil.

This illustration is not drawn to scale and is a historical representation of the area for illustrative purposes only. The boundaries shown on the illustration are neither authentic nor correct.

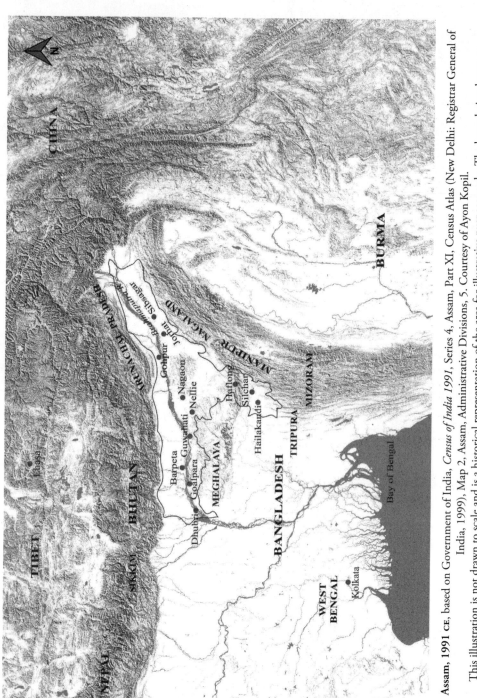

**Assam, 1991 CE**, based on Government of India, *Census of India 1991*, Series 4, Assam, Part XI, Census Atlas (New Delhi: Registrar General of India, 1999), Map 2, Assam, Administrative Divisions, 5. Courtesy of Ayon Kopil. This illustration is not drawn to scale and is a historical representation of the area for illustrative purposes only. The boundaries shown on the illustration are neither authentic nor correct.

# Contents

*A Note on the Spellings, Transliteration, Citations and Illustrations*    xv
*Prologue*    xvii

1. The Empire in Disarray    1
2. Bumpy Road to Independence    40
3. Birth Pangs    79
4. Assam in a Federal India    116
5. Domestic Woes    161
6. In Search of the Modern    211
7. Trouble in the Eastern Himalayas    258
8. Unfolding Crises in the Highlands    307
9. Atop a Volcano    352
10. The Battle Continues    377
11. Economic and Political Storms    406
12. Waves of Popular Protest    437
13. Moving towards the Millennium    495

*Epilogue*    539
*Acknowledgements*    547

| | |
|---|---:|
| *Timeline (Late Eighteenth Century–2000 CE)* | 555 |
| *Assam: List of Premiers (1937–50) and Chief Ministers (1950–2001)* | 563 |
| *Abbreviations and Acronyms* | 565 |
| *Notes* | 567 |
| *Glossary* | 779 |
| *Further Readings on Assam before 1947* | 783 |
| *Select Bibliography* | 789 |
| *Index* | 839 |

# A Note on the Spellings, Transliteration, Citations and Illustrations

This book uses current names of places that were earlier transliterated differently, such as Gauhati, Durrung, Nowgong, etc. Exceptions are made for historically used spellings of places, including institutions, such as Gauhati University. I have also used the older names for many places, for example Calcutta, Bombay, etc., which correspond to the time that I have written about.

There are many variant spellings of Assamese/Bengali names of individuals who have found a place in this book; as far as possible, the spellings used were preferred by the persons themselves, except in the case of individuals or authors cited in works.

In the case of references to works written in Indian languages (mainly Assamese and Bengali), the English transliterations are phonetic except in the case of those works with pre-existing English transliterations. All translations into English are my own unless otherwise stated.

This book uses the most commonly known endonyms for various indigenous communities except for quoted matter where exonyms appear in the original.

The cited archival sources are not listed in the bibliography. Such references, along with the newspapers and online repositories, are mentioned with complete details in the notes.

The maps are for purposes of illustration only and are not to scale. They have been redrawn based on original historical works, which have been cited in each case.

# Prologue

Where can we begin a chronicle of contemporary Assam? At what point in the region's history was there a decisive break from earlier times? For this book, I have considered 1944 as a key moment: this is when the Japanese and the British Indian Army fought a crucial battle in the hilly frontiers of India's North-east. Assam was among a handful of Indian states that were reshaped as geopolitical entities in their own right by World War II. In 1942, as Japan occupied Burma, thousands of Indians fled from the atrocities of the imperial army into British India's North-east, and Assam became a highly vulnerable and strategic frontier province. The hilly regions that had been lightly governed so far now came under stricter state control.

After the war, the Allied armies withdrew, but the years leading to India's independence were chaotic. Long before talks about the modalities of the British withdrawal from India took shape, many in the remote North-eastern hills had expressed very different ideas about their future. Several influential British officials believed that the tribal districts of Assam could remain under British administration after India's independence. Though these ideas did not materialize, they had far-reaching impacts on the aspirations of the people of some of these districts.

In August 1947, at the time of Independence and Partition, Assam ranked fifth among Indian states in terms of area, comprising 85,000 square miles of land that constituted approximately 7 per cent of India's total territory. Just a month earlier, Assam's geography had been strikingly different. A referendum held in Sylhet, the south-western-most district of Assam, in July 1947, saw voters choosing to join Pakistan. In August, as Sir Cyril Radcliffe announced his Partition Award, Assam's geography was changed with the stroke of his pen. Assam was a landlocked province; consequent to its access to the sea being blocked by the changed political boundaries and as a result of being connected by a 'chicken neck' to the rest of India, the commercial outlets for the region's agricultural, forest and mineral products were imperilled. It took several years before new trade routes were developed, and Assam could hardly escape the consequences, both economic and political.

Members from Assam in India's Constituent Assembly tried to raise their voices to express concern regarding their new-found economic and political destiny. But these voices were too feeble and too belated to make a difference. The only relief came as the Constituent Assembly allowed Gopinath Bardoloi, Assam's premier, to draft a lengthy report on the political destiny of Assam's tribal population. Eventually, this report became the Sixth Schedule of the Indian Constitution, a special provision assigning more legislative and administrative powers to local communities. This little-known instrument of the Indian Constitution held the possibility of political empowerment for many; its full potential remains untapped to this day.

With the mass migration caused by Partition, largely empty rural and urban spaces of Assam were slowly filled by Bengali-speaking traders and farmers. For the Congress-led state government in Shillong, these were unwelcome guests; a strong anti-Bengali sentiment, which had already existed for some decades, began to take deeper roots among much of the Assamese-speaking population as the new settlers seemed a huge burden for a struggling state. Prime Minister Jawaharlal Nehru had to persuade, and even reprimand, the Assamese leaders to appreciate the crisis all of India was facing. Though the Assamese government machinery did extend its support to refugees, there was a certain lack of compassion and sensitivity. The new settlers did become citizens. However, a major language-based fault line developed, which did not bode well for the future. In the process, once language became the marker of regional nationalism, what was one's mother tongue became a politically significant question.

If that was not enough, the massive Assam–Tibet earthquake of 15 August 1950 brought devastation of an insurmountable level. With a magnitude of 8.6 on the Richter scale, the earthquake jolted the mighty Brahmaputra, raising the riverbed by several feet. In Assam, 1500 people were feared killed. What was not reported was the earthquake's massive devastation of the rice fields and how it permanently changed the Brahmaputra Valley's flooding pattern. The earthquake's epicentre was in Assam's loosely administered North-Eastern Frontier Agency, known as NEFA. The natural disaster necessitated quick relief operations, and this led to the establishment of the Indian government machinery and control of these areas.

Assam as a state in 1947 was not marked by coherence or unity, either culturally, ecologically, politically or administratively. The challenges of governing such a complex geographical mosaic became apparent soon enough. The emergence of Assam as a constituent unit of federal India was to prove a challenge for the state-level leadership. The Assamese-speaking ruling elite tried to assert its control over the complex cultural and environmental landscape: the Lushai Hills, the Naga Hills, the Garo, Khasi and Jaintia ranges, the Barak Valley and many other areas inhabited by different ethnic and linguistic groups. Not all residents of the new Assam identified themselves as Assamese (Assomiya). Many expressly articulated vastly different sub-nationalisms.

The leadership failed to adequately address the popular aspirations in the hill districts. The superior attitude of many Assamese officials and politicians was resented by groups with distinct identities and cultures. In the 1950s, Nehru advised Assamese leaders to listen to the voices from the hills. Nehru's close aide Verrier Elwin, the Oxford-trained anthropologist, helped the Indian government shape Assam's future, keeping in view the sensitive nature of its tribal areas. This attempt failed; it was viewed as patronizing by the hill leaders, and it only deepened the resentment of the Assamese elites against New

Delhi. Meanwhile, the tribal elites' anger against Assamese cultural and political dominance began to assume various shapes.

The people in the hills, who spoke different languages, felt strongly against the Assamese ruling elite for the latter's refusal to appreciate their ways of life. Waves of protest, often violent and with the support of a large majority of the people, swept through the hills, much to the concern of the Assamese leaders. Meanwhile, the linguistic reorganization of the country led to the restructuring and emergence of several new Indian states in the decade of 1956–66. Though Assam stoutly resisted Delhi's attempt to redraw its political boundaries, years of protracted people's movements in the tribal districts finally gave birth to the Indian states of Nagaland (1963), and Meghalaya and Mizoram in 1972. The contraction in area and the decrease in the population of the 'united Assam' of 15 August 1947 were viewed as tragedies by the Assamese ruling elite and middle classes. Assamese leaders felt that Delhi had conspired against Assam and its people; that distrust never went away. Assam had literally been cut to size.

The relationship between Assam and India's Union government grew even more strained for other reasons. Assam bore the brunt of the war between India and China in 1962, both militarily and psychologically. When the Chinese army occupied the state's northern highlands, Assam's inhabitants felt betrayed by Nehru's government. Even prior to this in the 1950s, Assam's people felt disappointed and dejected that its economic development was not given due priority. In 1953, the Assam Oil Company's drillers found oil at 9700 feet, the deepest ever in India. This oil reserve could support the production of 2.5 million tonnes of oil a year. Most people in Assam thought this would bring jobs and prosperity to the state, given that India had embarked on a programme of rapid industrialization. However, in 1956, the Indian government, supported by the private oil companies, decided to establish a refinery in Calcutta, rather than in Assam, to process this crude oil. Though Assam got a second oil refinery in 1961 after a war of words and violent street protests in urban areas, its economic condition hardly improved. India's new wave of industrialization had a limited impact on the state's economy. In addition, the failure of several state-sponsored flood control projects had catastrophic consequences for agriculture. Between 1947 and 1970, Assam's per capita income declined. By the last quarter of the twentieth century, Assam was among the noticeably impoverished Indian states.

By the 1960s, with the departure of the British plantation owners and capitalists, Assam's economy, trade and finance came to be predominantly controlled by Marwari traders and, to some extent, by Hindu Bengalis. The Assamese, Naga, Mizo or Khasi had very little stakes in commerce. The number of unemployed Assamese increased, with fierce competition for government jobs. Bhupen Hazarika's 1968 song about the youth earning a meagre livelihood by driving autorickshaws evoked a sense of utter helplessness among the educated Assamese. The people's financial insecurity and unhappiness took the form of political restlessness.

In the 1980s, Assam's political landscape was heavily marked by widespread popular unrest. Those who joined the protests believed that their cultural identity and political leverage were at stake because of those whom they called *bideshi* (foreigners). The bideshi included businesspeople, traders and jobseekers from other Indian states as well as from Nepal and Burma/Myanmar, apart from the political and environmental refugees from East Pakistan/Bangladesh. These streams of non-Assamese migrants had been absorbed over the decades into the social, political and economic structures of Assam. After years of protracted political negotiations and sustained popular protests, the Union government agreed to detect and deport illegal foreigners staying in Assam. This aggravated the state's political troubles.

Even as popular unrest reached every nook and corner of Assam, a few young men and women from urban and rural Assamese families joined hands in the hope of fulfilling their dream of a sovereign, independent Assam. Other groups from amongst the tribal population followed in their footsteps with their own demands. By the early 1990s, the Union government, threatened by the growing incidence of attacks by rebels on business and commercial enterprises, decided to declare an all-out war on separatists. Some of the top rebel leaders went into exile in Bangladesh, Burma or Bhutan. As the armed conflict with the

Indian Union continued, many of the rebels were fatigued by their life in the jungles, lost hope and even started questioning their ideologies. In the decade of the 2010s, the Indian government succeeded in bringing back most of the key rebel leaders to India. A page had turned in Assam's history, but now new questions arose about Assam, its past and its possible future scenario.

Assam's post-Independence journey is essentially seen in most works as influenced by two major political developments: first, the state's quest to become a linguistically coherent, political and cultural unit within the political milieu of the Indian Union; and second, the abiding fear among the Assamese of losing out to 'outsiders' in a fiercely competitive economic, cultural and political environment. But beyond this standard narrative, there is a set of complex events, with deep processes and interconnected developments, which shaped Assam's fate in the second half of the twentieth century. These events were influenced by Assam's distant pasts and troubled histories when dealing with its linguistic, environmental and geostrategic situations. All these elements played a role in the series of catastrophic political developments in Assam, as well as in its economic underdevelopment.

The landscape of the state of Assam at Independence was broadly characterized by two valleys divided by a series of fragmented hill ranges including the Shillong Plateau. The state is bound by the towering eastern Himalayas to the north and the Patkai and Arakan Hills to the east. Of the two valleys, the larger is formed by the river Brahmaputra, which flows from east to west before entering Bangladesh. This narrow, flooded alluvial valley, characterized by a modest gradient, has a maximum width of 90 kilometres. This east–west valley is criss-crossed by numerous other rivers, most of them tributaries of the Brahmaputra, which come down from the surrounding hills and mountains. Long spells of heavy rainfall between April and September and the melting of the Himalayan snows ensure that these rivers are always full. With a tropical climate and receiving heavy rainfall, Assam is characterized by humid summers and mild winters. The Brahmaputra passes through many climatic and vegetation zones. Each bit of the valley presents an experience of geomorphological transformations shaping the relationship between humans and nature. Literary minds, over the centuries, have reflected on this volatile relationship; for instance, the Vaishnavite saint-scholar Sankardeva (died 1568 CE) wrote of the monsoon as an elegant aesthetic occasion.[1] The smaller valley, to the south of the Shillong Plateau, is formed by the Barak River, which originates in Manipur. Protected in the east and south-east by the Patkai mountain ranges, which are characterized by steep slopes, thick forests, conical peaks and deep valleys, the river flows south-west through a vast patch of flat landscape into Bangladesh, where it is rechristened Meghna. The Brahmaputra merges with the Ganga after leaving Assam and flows into the Meghna. Both the Brahmaputra and the Barak are major pointers to Assam's geographical distinction. The Brahmaputra bisects the valley diagonally from east to west, and the people usually refer to themselves as residents of upper, central or lower Assam.

Assam's environmentally impulsive landscape is central to its character. The state's boundaries of agriculture and human settlement patterns have changed continually. Sedentary and shifting cultivation have marched hand in hand with its rich and diverse biota. Like the Brahmaputra, which is a great conveyer belt for Himalayan sediments flowing into the Bay of Bengal, Assam was a major thoroughfare for merchants, pilgrims and itinerant populations until modern nation states enforced restrictions. Over the centuries, complex and multiform political and economic systems arose across the region's hills, plains and lowlands and were founded and built on this fluid environment.

More than 50 languages (this number would vary depending on the source), rooted in the Indo-Aryan, Tibeto-Burman, Dravidian and Austro-Asiatic language families, are spoken in Assam and its neighbourhood.[2] In this highly multilingual environment, community cultures overlapped and remained in a state of fluidity. Contrary to the long-held idea of the region being landlocked and geographically isolated, Assam was a part of an extensive network of overland commercial activities between India, China and South-east Asia.

~

Assam's diverse landscape housed differently equipped state systems, but the most powerful rulers established themselves in the plains. For a large part of the second millennium, until the early nineteenth century, political control of the Brahmaputra Valley was commanded by the powerful Ahom dynasty. In the sixteenth century, the Koch dynasty gained military and political dominance over parts of Assam, until it was restricted to Koch Bihar (British Cooch Behar) by the renewed ascendancy of Ahom political power in the seventeenth century. Other kingdoms of varying military, political and economic strength grew across the larger region of Assam. The Ahom kingdom's endurance was based on a complex bureaucratic and military system and a highly secured rice economy enabled by the state, which built moderate-sized embankments and water tanks. By the early seventeenth century, the people of the Ahom kingdom were organized to pay taxes in the form of labour; in return, every individual was given a fixed area of agricultural land, approximately equivalent to 3 acres, invariably in the meticulously engineered and embanked rice-growing landscape of Upper Assam. Under this system, called *Paik* or *Pyke*, every three or four individuals, organized into a labour squad, provided labour in rotation to the ruler; while one of them worked for the government, the rest attended to household needs. These peasant-labourers also formed the standing militia of the kingdom. An extensive range of artisans, including gold washers, elephant catchers, etc., paid their taxes in kind. Some others served as bonded labour to the noble or royal households. As the state's requirements increased during the Burmese wars in 1817–26, the Ahom king introduced newer taxes in cash.

Much of the military might, state infrastructure and population of the Ahom kingdom were spread over the plains. The hills were largely beyond its political and military control. The Ahom kingdom's relations with the hill rulers were founded on diplomatic negotiations, occasional military raids and bartering of commodities, for instance, rice or dry fish from the plains being exchanged for salt procured from the hills. The foothills across the northern and southern frontiers of the kingdom were the sites of such diplomatic negotiations and commodity exchanges, as well as of intense clashes over resources and labour.

Protected to a large extent from the Chinese and the Burmese kingdoms by the mountain and hill ranges to its north and east, Assam had long resisted the threat of the Mughal Empire from the south and west. The latter nevertheless continued to show an enduring interest in the region's elephants and other forest products. During the seventeenth century, the Mughal Empire first annexed the western part of the valley, and, in 1662, defeated the Ahom rulers in the east. But this was only a temporary win; given Assam's volatile environment of rivers and hills, it could never be effectively controlled by outside powers, no matter how strong. The relentless monsoon and thick vegetation ensured that the Mughal military often had to retreat. The natural environment remained a significant force determining the political sovereignty of this region through the centuries. In the twentieth century, Assam's strategic geopolitical location as a frontier state of India turned out to be equally decisive.

By the early nineteenth century, due to decades of civil and external wars (1760s to 1820s), which led to parts of Assam coming under the control of Burma, Assam's finances and its extensive peasant agriculture, which was its mainstay, were in complete disarray. The British East India Company (EIC) was able to secure a territory rich in natural resources, including timber and elephants, vital for the consolidation of the British Empire. European traders had eyed this region with interest since the 1750s, and by the beginning of the nineteenth century, EIC traders were engaged in a highly profitable trade in forest and mineral resources with Assam and its neighbourhood. Finally, the EIC acquired this region after defeating Burma in the First Anglo-Burmese War (1824–26). It took control of Guwahati in July 1824 and the whole of Assam, Cachar and Manipur in 1826. Further annexation and consolidation of EIC rule in Assam and surrounding territories happened slowly. The annexation of Upper Assam—territories that had been restored to the control of the Ahom king by the EIC in 1833 after a series of rebellions by Ahom princes and nobles—was completed by 1838. More areas were added to Assam: the territories further east, held by other smaller kingdoms, such as Matak, Singpho and Khamti, were annexed by 1843. These areas held extraordinary promise for tea plantations, besides being strategically important locations as they provided access to China. However, there was serious opposition from the local populations in the annexed areas.[3] In the south, the kingdom of Cachar, vital for communication between Manipur and Sylhet, and seen by the EIC as providing a safe passage for the Burmese military into areas of Bengal, was annexed between 1832 and 1853. The Khasi and Jaintia Hills were also brought under its control in 1835. The assumption of power directly by the British Crown in 1858 hastened the conquest of many more remote areas; areas such as the Khasi and Jaintia Hills (1835), Naga Hills (1866–78), Garo Hills (1872) and Lushai Hills (1890) were annexed through a combination of low-intensity military expeditions and diplomatic and political negotiations. These areas were initially administered by the Bengal government.

In 1874, by a grand design of bringing together areas across diverse landscapes and cultures, a separate province of Assam was formed by merging Goalpara, Cachar, Garo, Khasi and Jaintia Hills and Naga Hills. The new province was put under the control of a senior British bureaucrat designated as chief commissioner. Bengal's Sylhet district was added to the Assam province in September 1874, and, finally, Lushai Hills was added in 1898. To the north, in the far eastern Himalayas, the vast, sparsely populated tracts lying between Tibet, China and Burma were indirectly controlled by the colonial government through its officials posted in Assam.

Acquisition of these territories came with its problems. The EIC's biggest concern was to integrate and collect taxes from these vastly spread-out lands, which bore diverse geographical features and fostered many bureaucratic and revenue regimes. For some decades, British colonialists would describe the political economy in this region as being strikingly disorderly. Ambitious British officials and cartographers made repeated excursions to fix the outer boundaries of this territory. On their part, the inhabitants of Assam had mixed reactions to the EIC's rule. The hill residents, who were described by the British government as stateless and wandering people, fought against the advancing armies of the colonial government. Frequent military raids were conducted by the British to subjugate the highlands, but the conquest remained incomplete. Equally challenging for the colonial government was Assam's monsoonal climate.[4] Floods, changing river courses, river siltation and the rapid growth of vegetation regularly erased the footprints of colonialists as they tried to assert their claims in the newly secured territories.

The colonial government embarked on several ambitious projects. With great speed, the colonialists tried to discipline the peasants of the lowlands to pay rent, imposed controls on their agricultural practices and converted forested lands into government-owned reserve forests. David Scott, the first EIC official appointed to govern these newly annexed territories, introduced moderate revenue reforms and changes into the system of revenue collection. Pykes were freed from working for the Ahom king and nobles in Upper Assam (who petitioned against this) and asked to pay taxes in cash.[5] In Lower Assam, which had a long history of interaction with Bengal, Scott's radical changes had two outcomes: the idea of private property was firmly put in place and the EIC was assured of collection of revenue, though the execution of this was an overwhelming task.

While the senior British officials in Bengal were ideologically divided among themselves about the level of intervention in Assam, those posted in Assam had to manage more daunting and practical obstacles, such as absconding peasants, floods and even its remoteness from Calcutta; travel time between Calcutta and Goalpara was no less than 25 days.[6] In 1847, steamers plying between Calcutta and Guwahati were introduced on the Brahmaputra. After a series of bureaucratic experiments, in 1867, the colonial government introduced the *ryotwari* system—where land was settled directly with individual peasant cultivators—in most of Assam. Cachar and Goalpara were already under the Permanent Settlement of Bengal of 1793. Under this system, landlords controlled their lands, which were tilled by poor peasants who had no legal rights and who ended up paying excessive rent. A significant proportion of the population spread across the plains and the hills, however, continued to practise their shifting cultivation.

Things moved fast in the last decades of the nineteenth century as the colonial government introduced a series of bureaucratic mechanisms and laws to affirm its full control over minerals, forests and lands. However, the imperial project to survey and settle lands with peasants and ensure a steady collection of revenue was a complex process. Peasants, informed by their experience in the volatile watery landscape—where floods, changing river courses and deposition of sand by the rivers always posed risks to their crops and livestock—refused to take long-term land leases and be part of a fixed taxation system. By the early twentieth century, the work was only partially completed; a large number of peasants still eluded the official records.

~

But the British colonists' most significant fortune came from an earlier event: the EIC military officials' acquaintance with wild tea plants in the forests of Upper Assam immediately before and during the Anglo-Burmese War of 1824–26. Among those who played a role in the British discovery of treasure from the wild was Maniram Dutta Barbhandar Barua. He was an influential and enterprising Assamese noble who believed that the British had rescued Assam from the 'sea of the Burmese trouble' and felt that they should rule for a million years.[7] In 1823, Maniram introduced Robert Bruce, the merchant and military official of the EIC who was on a trade mission to the region and eventually came to be on the payroll of the Ahom king, to Beesa Gaum, the Singpho chief.[8] In the latter's territory in Upper Assam, tea grew in the wild and in abundance. Tea was a part of the culinary culture of the Singphos and other tribes who lived and exercised sovereign control over the vast areas between Burma and Assam, but it was not on the list of products exported from this region.[9] Elderly local inhabitants believed that tea plants had been introduced to these areas by their predecessors, who had migrated much earlier from farther east.[10] By the nineteenth century, Britain was desperately searching for an alternative source of tea, as the cost of Chinese tea had risen with the entry of the Dutch and Americans in the tea trade. Assam's prospective tea cultivation could be an answer for Britain. Assam's ruler Purandar Singha, who would be the last Ahom king, also saw the promise in

Assam tea.[11] When tea tracts were discovered in his territory, he divided these equally between himself and the EIC and requested the Company to provide him labour and other support in return. Francis Jenkins, the head of the EIC administration in Assam, readily agreed.[12]

There was some uncertainty about the genuineness of Assam's tea plant, but by the mid-1830s its equivalence with the Chinese tea plant was verified. William Griffith, the EIC botanist, enthusiastically confirmed that the tea plant was possibly 'one of the commonest plants of [a] large portion of Upper Assam'.[13] Early experimental cultivation at the initiative of the EIC, with the assistance of local entrepreneurs, proved a success. Unlike China, where small peasant cultivators remained at the centre of the tea economy, Assam started commercial production of tea on plantations in the late 1830s. In 1839, members of the Tea Committee, which had been formed in 1834 to authenticate the quality of the Assamese tea plant, established the Assam Company, the first enterprise in the world to establish tea estates. At the same time, several Bengal-based EIC merchants and officials, including Dwarkanath Tagore, one of Bengal's pioneering industrialists, founded the Bengal Provincial Tea Company. This later merged with the Assam Company, and Tagore was made one of the directors. For the next two decades, the Assam Company became a near-monopoly in tea cultivation in Assam. In 1840, it became a joint-stock company. A few aspiring Assamese entrepreneurs attempted but failed to secure a place in this capitalist project: Maniram was one among them having established two such gardens, but he was condemned to death in 1858 for his role in the Indian Rebellion of 1857.[14]

With financial support from Britain and upon securing adequate skills in tea production, British planters made a beeline to acquire millions of acres of land in Assam: in 1861, 160 plantations were held by 62 companies and individuals in Upper Assam alone. The colonial government passed favourable laws and extended military aid to take over more areas from rebellious populations. The lands granted to the planters under special leases were mostly highlands that were covered with timber. These were cleared to make room for tea cultivation. In the 1860s, Assam tea became a highly prized commodity, eagerly sought by British households. Planters expanded tea cultivation to more areas; by 1870–71, an estimated 3.6 per cent of Assam's total area was under the control of tea planters.[15] By 1900, Assam produced 141 million pounds of tea, an estimated 71 per cent of British India's total tea output. India's contribution to Britain's consumption of tea for this period was a whopping 55 per cent. Britain fundamentally transformed Assam into a producer of tea for the mass market, and Assam tea, which accounted for the major portion of the tea produced in India, became a household name in England. However, the commodity hardly evoked passion and thirst in nineteenth-century Assam, except as a source of lower-rank jobs on plantations for some.

Early tea cultivation was undertaken with support from Chinese workers, who soon fell out with the planters. Planters' attempts to attract the local population—from an otherwise 'sparingly cultivated' Assam 'with a scanty population'[16]—to work on their plantations also failed. Most rural people chose to work on their self-owned farmland, as dealing in agricultural products was more profitable than working on the tea plantations. More importantly, this choice offered a freedom that could hardly be matched by the demands for rigorous work on tea plantations. Planters, learning from experiences in other parts of the world, also knew that migrant workers who were away from their families would be more docile and submissive. With little hope of finding a mass labour force locally, the planters opted to recruit workers from outside: an estimated 3 million workers were brought in between the 1860s and 1947, mostly from poverty-stricken areas of central and eastern India. Brought as indentured labour and made to sign a penal contract, they were subjected to horrific treatment. The planters acquired policing rights to punish errant workers. Except for occasional deserters, most stayed back in Assam. Workers who were not found good enough by the planters had to leave the tea estates and survived through the meagre production of food on patches of land either rented from wealthy Assamese landowners or cleared in a neighbouring forest. For the next several generations, these people remained in a wretched condition, unable to free themselves from the clutches of poverty. The massive project of tea plantations had also ushered in an era of environmental disruptions because of the large-scale clearance of forests: one recent estimate points out that as many as 10 million trees were felled in the district of Sibsagar between the 1830s and 1924–25.[17] The tea plantations, thus, led to the fragmentation of the forests, a shrinking habitat for fauna along with increased hunting for sport, leading to a decrease in the population of large mammals. Meanwhile, the plantation workers suffered from malnutrition, and epidemics swept away the lives of thousands.

British exploration of Assam also brought news of traces of petroleum deposits in Upper Assam. After several decades of experimentation and deliberation, the commercial scope of these finds was validated. Extraction of crude oil began in 1881, followed by a basic process of refining.[18] Several British tea planters in Assam took part in this venture, which finally led to the formation of the Assam Oil Company in 1899. Industrial refining of the crude oil had to wait until the establishment of a refinery by the Assam Oil Company at Digboi in Upper Assam in 1901.

~

During much of the nineteenth century and the first few decades of the twentieth century, Assam's destiny came to be inseparably linked to the capitalist desires of Britain, just as her fate had been linked to the imperial rivalries among Britain, China and Burma in the early nineteenth century. Colonial rule had brought global capitalism into Assam, its natural resources were commodified, and techno-bureaucratic rules were put in place to govern a province whose people were presumed uncontrollable. As the British Indian Empire's fuzzy north-eastern frontier province, Assam was a gatekeeper against the ambitious Chinese army. As a classic instance of colonizaton, Assam's timber, crops, plants, animals and minerals helped the empire thrive, but its people received little economic benefit. The colonial government converted vast tracts of forest lands, mainly bearing hard and soft woods and grasses, into government-owned reserved forests. By the mid-1940s, approximately 10 per cent of Assam's total area came under the direct or indirect control of the Forest Department, the wing of the colonial government tasked with managing forest affairs. Revenue earned from the sale of timber was never below 5 per cent of the total revenue deposited each year—approximately 5.85 per cent during 1939–40—in the imperial treasury. Limestone, coal, petroleum and elephants too joined the list of exploited resources and were exported from Assam. Assam turned out to be one of the most prized provinces of British India.[19]

As Assam was integrated into a pan-Indian British colonial administrative structure, the province's population faced a series of bureaucratic, social and economic experiments, some of which were initiated by the missionaries who were spreading Christianity alongside imparting education. One measure that would have long-term consequences was the EIC administration's decision to introduce Bengali in elementary education and as the official language for lower courts in Assam in 1836. The EIC officials' preference for Bengali was based on several factors: first, they were uncertain about the distinct linguistic status of Assamese, presuming its many linguistic similarities with Bengali as proof of Assamese being a variant of Bengali. Besides, Bengali, apart from English, had already acquired stability as a language for governance and was, therefore, deemed suitable for official purposes in Assam too. A relentless campaign against this step was begun by a tiny group of Assamese scholars and American Baptist missionaries. They persuasively made a case for the distinct literary and linguistic tradition of the Assamese, but it took 36 years before Bengali was officially replaced by Assamese. This happened in 1873, as Assam waited to be declared a separate province in 1874.

More drama was unfolding in Assam's vast floodplains, with the beginning of the cultivation of jute. The jute industry had flourished in Bengal, controlled by British capital, since the mid-nineteenth century. By the end of the century, the demand for raw jute for these industries had increased exponentially, and part of this began to be met by jute produced in the fertile floodplains of the Brahmaputra. Batches of peasants were resettled in these places from rural East Bengal, and previously unploughed lands in the watery floodplains were reclaimed to produce jute. These peasants, the majority being followers of Islam, were victims of the ecological ravaging of their homelands, or had suffered the tyranny of the landlords (zamindars) of eastern Bengal and the viciousness of moneylenders. By 1947, Assam produced approximately one-third of India's jute, for supply to Bengal's jute industries. Meanwhile, a significant portion of Assam's population, approximately 12–15 per cent between 1901 and 1931, comprised 'immigrants' from other Indian provinces.[20]

Despite this massive reordering of Assam's agricultural economy and demography, land settlement processes remained incomplete. In the 1940s, a significant number of people remained without a land title, and very few bothered to secure such rights. If the volatile and dynamic floodplain landscape and old traditions of shifting agriculture stood against settlement processes, another reason was the slow decline in power of the colonial land revenue bureaucracy. The unwieldy task of land settlement became increasingly associated with Assam's electoral politics, and in the Congress's scheme of free India, land reform, not land revenue, would secure an important place.

India's anti-colonial struggle struck deep roots across Assam's valleys through the 1920s and 1930s, as Gandhian slogans ignited hundreds of thousands to be part of India's freedom movement. Some refused to pay revenue, many opposed the tea planters, some defied the zamindars, others resisted the colonial forestry programme. In the hills, where a nationalist upsurge of the Gandhian kind was largely absent, the colonial machinery was already facing hostility. Several communities of Assam's hills, who have remained unnoticed in most of the rich scholarship on India's anti-colonial struggle, bravely resisted the march of the empire from the early twentieth century. The empire had earlier faced violent opposition from Assam's peasants and others at regular intervals (for instance, during 1861 and 1893–94), who challenged the extraction of land revenue and resisted the expansion of tea cultivation into people's *jhum* (shifting cultivation) lands.

Political changes that were introduced as India moved towards freedom, for instance, the introduction of separate electorates for Muslims through the Government of India Act, 1935, sparked bitter exchanges between different groups. Hindus and Muslims constituted approximately 42 and 32 per cent, respectively, of Assam's population in 1941, and the fragile political environment saw further deterioration when linguistic identities subsumed religious identities. From 1936 to 1947, Assam experienced an intense and acrimonious political contestation, seeing six governments with a brief period of Governor's rule in between. Of the six governments, two were headed by the Congress and four by the Muslim League.[21] These political battles would continue to play out in the life of twentieth- and twenty-first-century Assam, as will be seen in the chapters of this book.

~

In independent India, the Union government's relationship with Assam was founded on continuous promise and hope. Contrary to the wishes of Jawaharlal Nehru and Vallabhbhai Patel, the pioneers of modern India's national unification programme, Assam and its neighbourhood continued to question the idea of India. Assam's political rebels and the Assamese elite gave the Indian state a tough time. To explain this uneasy relationship, we need to narrate the ups and downs and the twists and turns in Assam's political, cultural, intellectual and economic landscape in the second half of the twentieth century. How did the region evolve and relate to the rest of India, politically and culturally? Was there a different experience of nation-making in Assam? Has India come to terms with living with these politically and culturally volatile spaces? Were the terms of the relationship between the Union and the state a one-way imposition or were they a genuine attempt at fair dialogue between partners in a new federalism? The promises that remained unrealized resulted in an unending wariness between India and Assam and the other North-eastern states. So was the lingering mistrust between Assam and the other smaller, less populated and less politically influential North-eastern states.

Assam's political journey after India's independence, therefore, is a narrative that is deeply troubled and tense. Even after several decades of Independence, this tension persists, often taking different forms.

An account of this tense relationship is provided in the following chapters, alongside consideration of several related questions. How did the events between 1942 and 1944, both domestic and global, fundamentally reshape Assam's destiny? What was the political and economic fallout of India's independence and Partition in this part of the country? How did Assam negotiate for its future during the framing of India's Constitution? How can one read the broad political history of Assam—that of the Assamese and the countervailing forces (state and Union) that one encounters—through the prism of economic and social developments in the state? How did India's international relations determine the destiny of modern Assam? Did the political events and cultural processes in the second half of the twentieth-century Assam free it from being viewed largely as a troubled borderland state of India? Did its internal partitions enabling the formation of new states resolve the issues of its dissatisfied tribal and ethnic minorities? The book addresses these questions, often drawing on hitherto unexamined archival records. Readers may find some of the answers here as they traverse the diverse landscapes of Assam during the long decades between the 1940s and 2000.

Assam's increasing importance in South Asian scholarship stems from the episodic and volcanic political troubles in the state. A growing body of academic and other studies on Assam and its political life since 1947 bears witness to this.[22] The state's catastrophic political mess, however, has often forestalled a nuanced historical understanding of its journey in recent times. One needs to take into consideration the multiple and simultaneous strands to get a clear picture of Assam of this period.

Barring occasional and refreshing exceptions, historians have generally refrained from writing complex biographies of Indian states in the post-colonial period. Of the many reasons for this neglect, I can refer to two. The first is people's close involvement with significant political and other developments, which is crucial for keeping alive India's democratic experiments. As contemporary historians have been engrossed in mega political events—wars, fall of governments, rise and fall of political parties and social conflicts—there was little opportunity to reflect on these historical developments until a period of time had passed. The second is that it is only recently that one has begun to get access to archival records of the post-Independence era. The task of organizing the official central and state archives of the period after 1947 is still at a rudimentary stage. The laborious process of making these rich records available has now gained momentum. Future historians will be luckier as more archival records become available. In addition to the official archives, a great deal of information is available from a wide range of literary and other materials, both in Indian languages and in English.

This book discusses and debates Assam's complex and troubled history since the early 1940s. It shows how interconnected layers of political, environmental, economic and cultural processes shaped the making of the idea of Assam during this tumultuous period. The book also aims to familiarize the readers with how a political and cultural region was formed in post-Independence India and how a state had to walk a difficult terrain to be a part of India's complex nation-making process. The notion of modern Assam, as it evolved politically and culturally since the 1940s, drew upon numerous pasts and varied histories in the shaping of its regional identity. The book also traces the development of the state apparatus in Assam, and how different elite segments captured this arena through electoral and other processes. It demonstrates how the post-Independence state apparatus and bureaucratic machinery came to be significantly controlled by the Assamese speakers, who, ironically laboured under the belief that Assam should hold on to its colonial territorial imagination. Much of Assam's political upheaval between the 1960s and 1990s was an outcome of both the early and more recent historical processes.

The following chapters move from the 1940s to recent times, from the British Indian province of Assam—that is, all of present-day North-east India, minus Sikkim, Manipur and Tripura—to the present-day truncated Assam, minus Nagaland, Mizoram, Meghalaya and Arunachal Pradesh. While writing this book, I have been aware of the wide range of methodological problems faced by historians in dealing with a new, smaller territorial unit and comparing it with the older, larger one. I have tried to make sense of how newer political circumstances rebuilt the state's territorial and cultural boundaries and regional identities.

A basic requirement for writing a definitive history of modern Assam is familiarity with the majority of the numerous languages spoken in the state. This book unfortunately relies on the knowledge of only a fraction of them. Also, while my intention was to add fresh layers of thought, based on rich archives, to what previous commentators have already written about the period covered here, it is obvious that I cannot claim to have examined all the developments that shaped modern Assam; I have focused only on what I considered the major ones. Moreover, the pre-1940s historical processes—which played a role in shaping the post-1947 regional identity—have not been discussed in detail except where relevant. For interested readers, the bibliography includes a separate list that provides a comprehensive understanding of Assam in earlier times.[23] This book has been written to shed light on Assam's past in newer ways that, in turn, will show fresh ways of viewing its present.

# 1

# The Empire in Disarray

The last months of the British Empire in India are often seen as a time of high political drama. Whether it was the powerful resistance crafted by Gandhi's Quit India Movement or the dogged negotiations of the Congress with the British, it was a time of rapidly unfolding events. The *Transfer of Power* and *Towards Freedom* volumes record these political negotiations.[1] Assam did not have any of the grand buildings of Delhi, London or Shimla. Yet, it was the theatre of some intriguing drama of its own at this time of the Empire in retreat. It was a time of anxiety and enigma in Assam.

The crisis began to unfold from the last weeks of 1941, when Japanese forces began bombing southern Burma. Till the time they were forced out at the end of the monsoon of 1945, India's north-eastern region, including the Bay of Bengal, was devastated by military operations. The drama unfolding in Burma brought to an end Britain's authority over India's eastern frontier, which, ironically, it had established after an epic war against the Burmese more than a century earlier.

The outbreak of World War II posed challenges unforeseen. The war left deep scars on the region and had lasting political, economic and social after-effects. Within weeks of Burma's occupation by the Japanese forces, Assam's vulnerability became clear. The impenetrable mountains had long been seen as a fortified frontier. The indomitable tribes of Assam's hill districts were not seen as a threat. Once the war arrived on the eastern frontier, things came apart and fast. The war dramatically brought Assam to the centre stage of imperial Britain's geopolitics. Percival Griffiths, the official historian of the Indian tea industry, wrote, 'Up to 1941 Assam was a sleepy backwater in which only the oil and tea industries made serious demands on rail and river transport, but after the entry of Japan into the War, Assam was transformed into an area of large-scale military operations.'[2]

Assam's critical importance in World War II is now being increasingly recognized—and not just by historians. In 2013, the National Army Museum in London chose the Battle of Kohima of 1944 over the more celebrated battles of D-Day and Waterloo as 'Britain's greatest battle ever'. This was a recognition of that battle's political and historical impact, the challenges the troops faced and the strategy and tactics that were employed.[3] The British perception and acknowledgement of the significance of the Battle of Kohima/Imphal was important. But the war's tremendous political, societal and psychological impact on Assam and her people was to be pivotal. That impact has been immortalized in influential Assamese literary classics.[4]

~

The Japanese forces swept through South-east Asia into Burma in the early months of 1942. The first air raid in Rangoon took place on 23 December 1941. There were more attacks during Christmas. These took the British government by surprise.[5] In January 1942, the Japanese occupied Rangoon and soon proceeded to capture its hinterlands, known as the rice bowl of the British Empire. Support for the Japanese came from the Aung San-led Burma Independence Army, and the Subhas Chandra Bose-led Indian National Army (INA) too joined the Japanese forces.

There were more than a million people of Indian origin in Burma at the time. A powerful anti-Indian political atmosphere had led to bloody riots in 1930. Bitterness about Indians had been building up among Burmese nationalists from at least the 1920s.[6] Indians, who had been seeking their fortunes in Burma since the nineteenth century, faced the wrath of the Burmese especially after the nationalists intensified political and economic campaigns against them in the aftermath of the global economic depression.

As chaos engulfed Burma, the Indian and European populations faced serious challenges from both the Japanese as well as the Burmese nationalists. As the Japanese gradually captured Burma, the British government launched arrangements for the evacuation of its people. Civic amenities collapsed, hunger and disease engulfed the country. Left to their fate, Indians began to stream out of Rangoon and central Burma. The early batches of mostly Europeans and a few rich and lucky Indians managed to get berths in ships and planes to travel to India. But not everyone was lucky. The great Indian flight from Burma had begun towards the end of 1941, before the Japanese occupation, and it acquired a significant scale over the months that followed.

The imperial government trusted the Patkai hills to act as a buffer between Assam and its neighbours, and, initially, it was believed that the fall of Rangoon would not pose any imminent danger to the Empire's eastern frontier. Ursula Bower, an English anthropologist who was living among the Nagas when the war broke out, wrote, 'All through the winter of 1941–42, however, the war seemed to be a long way off . . . shut off behind the high wall of the Barail.'[7]

The Eastern Command of the British Indian Army lacked adequate intelligence of these landscapes beyond their punitive expeditions against Assam's hill tribesmen.[8] These vast landscapes were largely free from direct imperial state control and, as historical scholarship shows, were part of extensive pre-modern trade linkages between interdependent areas.[9] While linguistic and topographical diversities were the hallmarks of these areas, the consolidation of global capital in Assam also isolated and territorialized Patkai's inhabitants.[10] We will discuss this in greater detail later.

The British forces had begun to retreat from Burma towards the end of April 1942;[11] as they withdrew to Calcutta, they destroyed most of the oil and mining installations, along with tens of thousands of boats and motor vehicles. The majority of the demoralized troops who arrived in Assam were wounded, and the military camps in Guwahati struggled with insufficient medical facilities. As Burma crumbled, there was chaos everywhere. 'Commander-less soldiers, civilian officials, army-less commanders, hordes of refugees, individual planes and plane crews, all falling back in confusion before the Japanese advance, were choking . . . highways, railways, airlines . . . and communications.'[12]

With the collapse of British authority in Burma, more than 1,00,000 European and Indian refugees fled northwards from Rangoon and other coastal lowlands, across the sea routes into the Chittagong Hills of eastern Bengal. But the Japanese advance soon sealed the sea and air routes in the south and south-west, and the refugees now had to choose other routes.[13] Crossing the Patkai—using three different routes—was the only choice, but the toughest one. They had to walk through the densely forested Chindwin Valley to enter India. Depending on local exigencies, these evacuees climbed the Patkai to arrive in either Manipur or Assam. While some descended through the Burmese border outpost of Tamu, others crossed the passes at Pangsau, Chaukan or even further south through the Hukawng Valley to reach railheads in eastern Assam. The route to Burma through the Naga hills was crisscrossed by tracks used by local villagers to keep their kinship networks intact and occasionally for elephant trade.[14] These difficult routes were known to the British surveyors, foresters, itinerant traders and, more intimately, to the local tribes. They were hardly designed for large-scale human movement. The evacuees had to face torrential rain, negotiate rivers without bridges, climb over slippery mountainsides and cross impenetrable jungles. Thousands, including old men and women, children and infants, walked, crawled and skidded along the treacherous paths.[15] When they exhausted their meagre stocks of food, they sometimes ended up consuming poisonous fruits. 'The butterflies in Assam that year were the most beautiful on record. They added to the sense of the macabre as they flitted amongst the corpses.'[16] A few lucky ones had maps to guide them through the difficult terrain.[17] These causalities of the war, many Telegu, Hindi and Tamil speakers, have recently been given long overdue attention by historians. However, their stories of suffering, of death and of survival await raconteurs.

The numbers of those who fled Burma reached a staggering 6,00,000 by July 1942, of which Assam received nearly two-thirds.[18] Unlike the Chinese, who had an effective evacuation plan that ensured very few casualties, as many as 80,000 Indians perished on the way.[19] Wavell, India's viceroy, lamented that 'no large-scale migration of people can surely ever have taken place in worse condition'.[20] The closest resemblance to this tragedy would be staged a few years later when, before leaving, the British decided to divide India. The stream of refugees from Burma began to dry up towards the end of 1942. Wavell's lament masks the racial chasm in the way refugees of culture were treated by the ruling race during the war. If the Japanese scored a military victory, the British officialdom in retreat did much to undermine any idea of so-called 'fair play'.

The travails of the Burma evacuees were recorded by Debendranath Acharya in the Assamese literary classic *Jangam*, but they have otherwise largely vanished from Assamese public memory.[21] The numbers of those who began to trickle across India's eastern frontier from March 1942 can hardly be estimated accurately. With the onset of the monsoon, some could not make it to India and were left behind to face uncertain futures in hilly hamlets.[22] As the civilian escapees traversed the 134-mile stretch of the Manipur Road from Imphal to Dimapur, the small wayside station on the Assam Bengal Railway line turned into a huge camp and supply dump through which, over the next four years, moved thousands of men and women and masses of stores and munitions.[23] The British Government of India (BGOI), grappling with a surge of nationalist discontent, was ill-prepared for this extraordinary humanitarian crisis. The local governments of Assam and Manipur struggled to arrange food and medical support in the shelter camps, which were described as 'primitive' by *The Times*, alongside ensuring the regular movement of trains.[24] The evacuees were afflicted by malaria, but they mercifully escaped the havoc of cholera as the Assam Medical Service arranged for the distribution of anti-cholera serum.[25] Several types of malaria treatment were later put into place.

Historians have criticized the British Indian government's inept handling of the evacuation crisis, which was 'riddled with assumptions about race, nutrition, and fitness'.[26] Along with many others, like the Ramakrishna Mission, medical teams of the Congress and other faceless people, Assam's resourceful European tea planters—who had at their disposal the extraordinary physical labour of their garden workers—extended a wide range of logistical support.[27] 'But of all voluntary help so splendidly given, none deserve the high praise that should be given to the Indian Tea Association,' applauded one official report.[28] Their efforts, however, could not rise above their racial biases.[29]

The financing of military expenditure led to severe inflation, with a six-fold increase in notes in circulation between 1939 and 1945.[30] The choking of transport facilities by the military resulted in a shortage of materials, which impacted traders. The rich and powerful, including the Marwari traders, were able to get help from influential bodies like the Chambers of Commerce. The Indian business magnate G.D. Birla, a valued associate of Gandhi, closely monitored the relief programmes for the refugee traders in Assam and Bengal.[31] Congress volunteers and the Marwari Association worked together in Guwahati and elsewhere.[32] But racial discrimination by British officials in the refugee camps and the way in which arrangements were made for railway travel were widely reported. Hridya Nath Kunzru of the Servants of India Society, which was involved in various relief and social works, privately visited Manipur to find out about such discrimination. His report drew wide attention.[33] The arrival of the Burma evacuees and the fear of an imminent Japanese attack caused panic in Assam. Large numbers of Marwari and other Hindi-speaking traders from northern India who had settled in small towns in Assam chose to leave.

Among the evacuees from Burma was Purnakanta Buragohain, an Assamese trader, who had been there for a decade when war broke out in Rangoon. Buragohain, who was at a China–Burma border outpost, quickly decided to return to India. His diary provides a graphic account of his negotiations with local communities in Burma for a protected passage to Manipur.[34] Unlike the majority of evacuees, his journey was not through an unfamiliar landscape. He procured an elephant and, with his cash securely bundled up, moved out of northern Burma in the last week of March 1942. Buragohain's route was dotted by thin settlements of the Singpho, Naga, Kachin and Shan, whose languages he could speak and with whose culinary practices he was familiar. He made his way through forests, finding places on the way to rest and procure food. He came across scattered settlements belonging to Assamese people whose forefathers had settled here in the early nineteenth century, when they were taken captive during the First Anglo-Burmese War. The 13-foot-tall elephant grass did not hamper his progress; rather, his elephant feasted on it. Buragohain was not the only refugee who received help from the local ethnic communities or the Buddhist monasteries.[35] But he was one of the lucky few who reached home early and gave a few public talks in Assam on the war.

~

By mid-1942, the British Empire, battered by war, faced another crisis. Like everywhere else in India, Gandhi's 8 August 1942 call of Quit India drew huge political and moral support in Assam.[36] The spread of the Quit India Movement in India's eastern war zone was especially worrisome for the government. Winston Churchill, the British Prime Minister, speaking in parliament in September 1942, charged the Congress with undermining 'the defence of India against the Japanese invader who stands on the frontiers of Assam'.[37] He accused the Congress of colluding with Japanese fifth columnists to target communications of the Indian forces in Bengal and on the Assam frontier.

The government in Assam was headed by Muhammad Saadulla of the Muslim League. Saadulla, who had stepped down as Assam's premier in December 1941,[38] once again formed a ministry in August 1942.[39] In the early 1940s, the Assam government, along with that of Bengal, was considered by many as the most ineffective and demoralized in India.[40] The Muslim League had already committed itself to the British war effort, and Saadulla received support from other non-Congress members.[41] A Muslim League leader warned that Gandhi's refusal to support the BGOI was 'an open invitation for the Japanese' to Assam, which was being bombed.[42] The League had no intention of endorsing Gandhi's call. Jinnah had already labelled Quit

India 'a manifestation of an angered and desperate mentality'.[43] The Assam government formed a National War Front and Village Defence Parties as a counterweight to the Congress organization. Meanwhile, the BGOI declared the Congress an unlawful body. This resulted in a mass uprising through the length and breadth of the country.

The protests in Assam began a few days later, but given its proximity to the war front, any form of instability was bound to hurt the Empire. A panicky Assam government arrested the former premier Gopinath Bardoloi after he returned from a session of the All India Congress Committee (AICC). News of the arrest was dispatched by Reuters and aired by Rome Radio and Berlin Radio, the centres of Axis power. As the Allied forces struggled to reorganize after the setbacks in Burma, Congress volunteers, including the Shanti Sena, which had approximately 20,000 members, and the members of All India Spinners' Association, All India Village Industries Association, etc., targeted the symbols of the Empire: planters' bungalows, railways, bridges, schools, clubhouses of tea gardens, roads, military communication systems, houses and granaries of lower-rank land revenue officials and grain traders, post offices, etc.[44]

The Allied war effort became a special target of the protestors. A no-rent movement was planned in 1942 in Upper Assam, where the exodus from Burma had brought about a new political consciousness among the people.[45] Extensive arson and sabotage followed. Most parts of the Assam Bengal Railway in Assam passed through forested landscape, which provided an opportunity for such acts of vandalism.[46] Several instances of derailment were reported; one especially daring attempt was the targeting of a special military train in central Assam on 24 November 1942. The sabotage of the railways diverted traffic to steamers.[47] There were attempts to stop the military from procuring supplies from the local markets, tea garden workers were asked not to join the services of the war, there were stray attacks on military stores and garrison engineers' offices and an attempt to set ablaze the military aerodrome at Tezpur.[48] These daring and adventurous acts by the Congress volunteers, who were largely drawn from peasant households, to hijack and overthrow the war effort were poignantly narrated in

*Mrityunjoy*, the celebrated Assamese literary classic by Birendra Kumar Bhattacharya.[49]

As in the rest of India, thousands of students, peasants and women came out in the streets to be part of processions.[50] The lower strata of rural society participated widely, and, in some places, they were joined by the urban working classes.[51] Many gardens continued to report clashes between workers and planters.[52] Popular political action was in the main loosely coordinated, and most actions originated at the local level. Whenever a top-ranking Congress leader was arrested, local leaders leapt forward to inspire the masses. Anti-imperialism and patriotism shaped the political environment. Massive popular support stalled, for a while, the state's efforts to make arrests. Weeks later, the provincial head of police admitted that 'there was an atmosphere of rebellion' in the central part of the province.[53] Employees of the state, like those in the railways or in the police, were forced to wear various symbols of anti-imperialism like Gandhi caps or to sing *Vande Mataram*.[54]

The arrests of the frontline Congress leaders were followed by arrests of leading writers and other members of the intelligentsia. Traders who had stopped supplying provisions to the military and government officials were also arrested. The bazaars that had sprung up without the state's approval were raided by police. Several newspapers were fined, and censorship was imposed. The repression was unprecedented: thousands were arrested, one was sent to the gallows and many died. Andrew Clow, the governor of Assam, admitted that the 'determined attempts to burn bridges had only been quelled with military aid and after several fatalities'.[55] On another occasion, Clow wrote to Delhi about how the troops (police and military) 'enjoyed the exercise' of brutal repression.[56] Peasant organizations with even moderate ideological moorings were banned. Many bravely faced bayonets and bullets, and some died fearlessly. Kanaklata Barua, a teenager who was shot dead while leading a large procession of villagers to hoist the national flag on a police station, emerged as a symbol of resistance against the Empire. As the police atrocities came to be strongly condemned, the government considered punishing Bengal's newspapers for quoting the verdict of an Indian judge who described the police action as 'indiscriminate, uncontrolled and cowardly'.[57] Those were highly politically charged and chaotic moments.

Inspiring leadership for every conceivable form of political resistance was provided by some charismatic Assamese, including women such as Chandraprabha Saikiani and Pushpalata Das.[58] While some leaders were put behind bars, others went underground to ensure that the political momentum continued. The retreat of the colonial government also meant the rise of the people's government. With the entire national leadership of the Congress as well as most of their local counterparts in jail, the people, temporarily, got a taste of power. Some localities organized panchayats and ceremoniously conducted their parallel governments, much to the annoyance of the BGOI.[59] These parallel governments pronounced judgements in local disputes, and the heavily indebted peasantry firmly backed the Congress call for no rent.[60] In some places, the no rent campaign was a major success, and revenue officials were unable to collect taxes until early 1943.[61] The Muslim League ministry was not sympathetic towards the indebted, and in November 1942, the BGOI amended The Assam Debt Conciliation Act, 1936, to ensure the recovery of loans from debtors.[62]

Many areas saw Gandhi's satyagrahas being replicated, and local leaders, women, peasants and the tribal population helped to galvanize the movement in different capacities. However, the Barak Valley, despite reports of widespread incidences of sabotages, did not feel similar reverberations of the Quit India Movement; probably it was more focused on the war in its eastern neighbourhood.[63] Also, not everyone was aligned with the movement: there was no large-scale participation by Muslim peasants. Muslim leaders, including Saadulla, believed that Gandhi and other Congress leaders would not coerce Muslims into participating in the Quit India Movement.[64] There were instances of Muslim peasants challenging Congress volunteers' attempts to regulate the sale of agricultural products.[65] In the Brahmaputra Valley, several Assamese government officials who worked to quash the movement were monetarily compensated.[66] But while the Muslim League, the dominant political voice of the Muslims of the province, headed the government, its pan-Indian adversary Jamiat Ulema-e-Hind (JUH) actively supported the movement in Sylhet.[67] Many lower-rank officials, who were unsure about their stance in the early stages of the movement, slowly came to be absorbed into it. Some revenue collectors refused to collect rent, some resigned from their jobs and actively participated in the movement.

The majority of the Indian communists under the banner of the Communist Party of India (CPI), given their ideological loyalty to the USSR, decided not to support the Quit India Movement, which would have meant taking an anti-war position. Thanks to its pro-Soviet stand and the USSR's war-time alliance with England, the CPI was declared legal in July 1943. This gave the CPI the opportunity to fight its own ideological opponents, including a radical group that would soon be named the Revolutionary Communist Party of India (RCPI), which was largely confined to Assam and Bengal. The CPI's general secretary, P.C. Joshi, targeted the followers of RCPI, who were very well-organized and strong in Assam as the splinter faction of the 'fifth columnists'.[68] Joshi claimed that his party's cadres 'succeeded in isolating the actual fifth columnists from misguided patriots' in some places of Assam.[69] But other communist and socialist groups understood the power of the mass uprising and decided to get absorbed in it.[70] Some groups on the left, such as the Congress Socialists and RCPI, saw a great opportunity to carry out low-intensity armed attacks to paralyze the state machinery.[71] All these, the government knew well, would not seriously challenge the might of the state. An upbeat government official described the communists as verbose.[72]

As the Quit India passions ran high, the Assam government, worried about the combined fallout of political unrest and war, came down heavily on the protestors.[73] The brutal crackdown resulted in several deaths. Local Congress units were banned, and their leaders were arrested.[74] Spiritual leader Pitambar Deva Goswami, the head of a Vaishnavite *math* or religious seminary, who was known for his liberal views and had great influence on the people, was targeted. For years, Goswami had been closer to the Hindu Mahasabha, both ideologically and organizationally.[75] But while the Mahasabha did not endorse

Gandhi's call for 'Do or Die',[76] this did not stop Goswami from becoming a part of this mass uprising.[77] Neither did the Mahasabha have any significant presence in Assam's political landscape.[78] The government imprisoned Goswami, restricted rations to his disciples and, at one point, considered sending him out of the state.[79]

A punitive tax, intended primarily to create fear while securing loyalty to the embattled empire, was imposed, and a wide range of prohibitions were enforced across the province.[80] But prohibitory orders, fines and raids could not ensure the security of state properties. Not everyone was fined, and not everyone bowed down before the strong arm of the state. Only 55 per cent of the total fines imposed could be collected.[81] At least one poor peasant from Lower Assam was shot dead for refusing to pay the fine. Often, no one came forward to bid in auctions to buy confiscated properties. Not everyone was, thus, punished. Officially excluded from this punitive taxation were the Muslim peasants, so-called Hindu lower castes and families of serving soldiers. The Congress had brought the *Nadiyals*, the fishermen, under its fold already—and they were among the radical loyalists of the movement who were not excluded.[82] The BGOI tried to discourage awarding military war contracts to supporters of the movement.[83] Shaken by the collective fines (3 per cent of Assam's land revenue collection for that year), the villagers, in some cases, cooperated to rebuild bridges, etc., but the BGOI remained suspicious.[84] As the masses successfully evaded intelligence operatives, the BGOI branded its own machinery as 'insufficiently active' or 'inadequate'. Some volunteers abandoned Gandhi caps to avoid police attention; some dug trenches and erected gates to secure themselves. The detention of political leaders continued well into 1944, as the Assam government expressed doubts whether 'such potential leaders [could] be released until the war threat [was] withdrawn altogether from Assam's borders'.[85]

This resistance began to lose intensity after the summer of 1943 after it had scored a significant political victory. The Congress's anti-war messaging haunted the BGOI to the extent that it imposed a partial ban on the screening of a pro-Russian movie, *Mission to Moscow*.[86] Quit India had greatly demoralized the BGOI. While imprisoned,

Gandhi survived a 21-day fast that ended on 3 March 1943. He was released 14 months later in May 1944. Congress leaders in Assam, too, were released, and the bans on the Congress and the RCPI were lifted gradually.[87] Meanwhile, the war loomed even closer to Assam's easternmost districts.

~

The Japanese conquest of Burma was completed in May 1942. America entered the war in December 1941, following the Japanese attack on the US naval base at Pearl Harbour, Hawaii. Early in 1943, the Allied forces had two gigantic tasks: to defend India's fragile eastern frontier and to regain Burma. The Manipur and Arakan fronts were the responsibility of Britain, while the eastern Assam front was America's responsibility. By May 1943, the Allied forces were clinging perilously to the north-eastern borders of India against the advancing Japanese forces.[88] The whole swathe from northern Burma to New Guinea was firmly under Japanese control.

Meanwhile, in August 1943, the leaders of Britain, the US and Canada met in the Canadian city of Quebec.[89] They acknowledged that their Asian war effort was greatly undermined by the dismal communication links between Calcutta, Assam's airfields and the frontline further to the east. It was agreed that the volume of air cargo to China from Assam's airfields would be increased and the newly built road from Ledo in Assam would be extended to Myitkyina in Burma and to Kunming in China. Further, a gasoline pipeline would be constructed from Assam to Kunming and from Calcutta to Assam. It was decided that China would supply air transport command, an American-operated barge line on the Brahmaputra would bring supplies forward from the Calcutta port to bases in Assam and the capacity of the Bengal and Assam railways would be enhanced. Between 1942 and 1944, there was a sevenfold increase in military stores, including aviation fuel supplied by the Joint Steamer Company.[90]

From 1943, the American armed forces, along with their defence equipment, came to have a strong presence in eastern India. American

A Japanese leaflet which was airdropped into Assam in 1944 and which reads: 'As slaves of the British, hunger and death rule. After Independence, happiness and peace rule'

army camps were established in several places in Assam, including Tezpur and Dibrugarh.[91] The Allied forces converted Assam and Manipur into a highly militarized zone, with an estimated 600,000 Indian, British, West African, Chinese and American soldiers defending the border.[92] From mid-November 1943, American troops began to assist in the operation of the Bengal and Assam railways.[93] Feeding the huge numbers of military personnel nutritious, preferably non-vegetarian, food was a challenge. The Hindu Assamese objected to the slaughter of cattle on religious grounds, and after failed attempts to bring animals from other parts of India through the Brahmaputra Valley, supplies were moved from Silchar to Imphal. This ad hoc arrangement ultimately gave way to tinned food for the troops.[94]

The valley's west–east lifeline, the Assam Trunk Road, only a tenth of which was metalled and whose bridges had a load capacity of only 4 tonnes, had received bitumen surfacing over its entire length in 1942. The metalling project would have required perhaps a million tonnes of road stone and a considerable labour force. Construction of the Ledo Road had begun in December 1942. Built at a cost of $150 million (approximately equivalent to Rs 150 billion in 2020), this longer than 1700-kilometre legendary road, renamed Stilwell Road after the American General Joseph Stilwell who led the Allied forces in the China-Burma-India theatre, began at the upper end of the Brahmaputra Valley and was one of the railheads of the Assam Bengal Railway. Spiralling across the Patkai up to 9000 feet, the road from Ledo to Myitkyina in Burma would link up with the Burma Road, which led to Kunming in China. Despite the use of heavy earth-moving equipment, work progressed slowly. The human cost was great: 1100 of the 17,000 Afro-American soldiers who were engaged in the construction of the road lost their lives, earning the road the ill fame of costing 'a man a mile'. However, it could carry more tonnage of military supplies to China than the amount that could be airlifted from Ledo to Kunming across the portion of the eastern Himalayas, which pilots of the Allied military transport aircraft had nicknamed 'The Hump'. Kunming received the first batch of trucks in January 1945. By the time the war came to an end in August, 26,000 trucks had arrived there.

War preparations also enhanced the demand for petroleum. Assam had oilfields and a small refinery that produced a little more than 5000 metric tonnes of petroleum per day, which was not enough to meet the heavy demand.[95] The Assam Oil Company provided motor gasoline and high-speed diesel. Even as newer British and American military vehicles continued to arrive in Assam, most became inoperative soon, either due to the absence of locally available repairing skills or the lack of sufficient fuel supply from the Digboi Refinery. This necessitated massive overhauling of the oil supply system in Bengal and Assam. American engineers built a 6-inch pipeline from Calcutta, where a tanker unloading terminal was also built, to Tinsukia near Ledo. Once completed, an estimated 75,000 tonnes of petroleum products were emptied into a large storage terminal every month. Two more 4-inch pipelines, constructed parallel to the Ledo Road, pumped out these petroleum products to Kunming at a rate of 8000 barrels every 24 hours.[96] These pipelines would play a vital role in supplying aviation gasoline to the newly constructed airfields along the Ledo Road. Another such pipeline was constructed through southern Assam to Imphal.[97] In March 1944, a 4-inch pipeline was completed from Chandranathpur in Silchar to Dimapur, following the alignment of the Akhaura–Lumding railway link, delivering 15,000 tonnes per month.

The railway network too was not adequate for wartime needs. Assam was connected to Bengal by 2 metre-gauge, single-track lines with rudimentary telegraph and signal systems. The river ports on the Brahmaputra were linked to both rail and road systems. But the railways were meant primarily for the transport of agricultural and forest produce, such as tea and jute, and were unsuitable for transporting heavy military equipment. As war approached, some improvements were made both in the signalling systems and in the ferrying capacity of the river. The monsoon of 1942 and the events around Quit India caused major disruptions, but things improved in the following year. In April 1944, the American Military Railway Service (MRS), with its makeshift headquarters in Guwahati, took over the operation of the Assam Bengal Railway.[98] The number of freight wagons was more than doubled from 14,000 to 35,085, most of which were imported from the US. Trains moved faster, and war-time monitoring ensured that they were run more professionally.

The arrival of American technology noticeably improved the communication system of the Assam Bengal Railway. But it could not conquer the Brahmaputra, the principal mode of communication. Although steam-powered shipping services had been around for a hundred years, it was still at least a seven-day journey from Dibrugarh, the farthest upstream navigable port in eastern Assam, to Calcutta. The return journey, against the flow of the mighty river, took longer. Night navigation, crucial for military operations, was virtually impossible. The rapidly changing course of the river and the densely distributed sandbars posed other formidable challenges.[99] At Amingaon, where the railway terminal ended, ferries had to transport railway cars with much difficulty.[100] After the MRS took over the operations of the Assam Bengal Railway, the ferries, in the spring of 1944, could transfer 415 wagons per day. A new port was built near Jorhat to serve Dimapur, which eventually connected to the war's frontline in the Naga Hills and Manipur. Assam's western town of Dhubri came to have a new port, where freight, including fuel and lubricants brought by the railways from mainland India, was unloaded.

Further south of the Ledo Road, the ancient routes across the Patkai were quickly overhauled. These re-engineered roads directly facilitated the forward march of the British Indian troops to the centre of the Japanese-occupied Assam hills. A large number of workers recruited from Assam's tea plantations worked to ensure that the ancient land routes across Burma, Manipur and Assam became fit for military purposes. These workers, the unsung heroes of World War II, braved the challenges of incessant rain, Japanese air attacks and the crippling absence of heavy earth-moving machinery. Their hard work paid off, and, in May 1943, the Allied forces completed a 265-kilometre road from eastern Manipur to Tiddim in Burma's Chin Hills.[101] This strategic road allowed the Allied forces to confront advancing Japanese troops from the Indian side.

The Assam tea planters' role in World War II is well recorded. *The Times* wrote, 'What in these circumstances they [the military] would have done without the tea planters of Assam it is difficult to say.'[102] But no less significant was the role of the plantation workers. The planters conscripted from their estates more than 40,000 labourers to help build roads and airfields and to work as porters for the military.[103] Dibrugarh, a prosperous plantation town, would see the fast expansion of a small, existing all-weather airstrip into a major airfield. This rapid upgradation was part of the American strategy to airlift military cargo to China, with supply planes flying over the Hump to Kunming.[104] The upgraded Dinjan Airfield outside Dibrugarh allowed the American-built Douglas DC-3s—which were developed into the Douglas C-47 (Dakota) military transport aircraft—to be used effectively by the Allies. In all, 13 new all-weather airfields came up in places where there were agricultural fields in eastern Assam.[105] To carry out these massive construction works, a dedicated engineering organization called the General Reserve Engineer Force (GREF) was formed.[106]

~

Indian workers walking along a military runway in fields in Sadiya, Assam, 1943

From May 1942, Japanese raids on eastern Assam and eastern Bengal became frequent, and they continued into late 1943. There was a devastating air raid on Manipur, and it seemed as though Japanese occupation was imminent. Singapore Radio had quoted Nehru as saying that Assam faced a major threat of being bombed and asking people to remain alert.[107] As the threat became a reality, Assam's Congress leaders appealed to the people to organize 'themselves in their fight against the Japanese invasion'.[108] As one of the most serious moments of militarization of this region in modern times unfolded, places like Guwahati also felt the impact of air raids, albeit in minor ways, causing panic. Guwahati, which was not yet Assam's capital but a major economic and cultural centre, was rife with rumours of impending bombing. The Cotton College, the hub of the province's educational and intellectual activities, was taken over by the Allied Army. A Bengali newspaper believed that the heroic Naga, inhabiting India's eastern wall, would resist the advancing Japanese.[109] In Manipur, the government instructed villagers to hide their property and food from the advancing Japanese troops.[110] Meanwhile, the Congress leadership appealed to the people not to extend support to the Japanese. Occupation by the Japanese would delay the prospects of freedom by a few more decades—this was the Congress's message to the masses.[111]

Things began to change from the middle of 1943 as communication links between Bengal, Assam and Burma improved considerably. In September, the South-east Asia Command, which had come into existence in the previous month, and the BGOI planned their strategy for the recapture of Burma. Large numbers of Assamese, as well as Tamilians, Bengalis and Telugus, were recruited into the British Indian Army to meet the increased need for personnel.[112] The challenge in South-east Asia marked the death knell of the martial race theory, which had for long determined BGOI's military recruitment policy. The inclusion of Assam in the South-east Asia Command put the province, along with Bihar, Orissa and Bengal, ahead of Indian Standard Time by an hour.[113]

The Japanese military occupation of Burma was led by Lieutenant General Renya Mutaguchi. Early in January 1944, the Japanese government permitted Mutaguchi to 'occupy and secure a strategic zone in Northeast India in the area of Imphal'.[114] Imphal was a major supply base of the British Indian Army. Its capture would serve three purposes for the Japanese: prevent the Allied invasion of Burma, stop air supplies to China and secure a base to conduct air attacks deep inside India. As the Japanese troops began their westward move across the Chindwin River—the main tributary of the Irrawaddy in Burma—towards India's north-eastern frontier, their goals were to occupy the valley of Imphal and establish a strong defence around eastern Assam. In March, Mutaguchi launched a full-scale attack on Imphal, the tiny capital city of Manipur, and the Naga Hills of Assam. The Japanese forces were logistically strong and had the support of an additional 1,00,000 troops of the INA. By the end of the month, the Japanese had cut off the Imphal–Kohima road and quickly isolated the hilltop town of Kohima. By mid-April 1944, all but the central ridge was captured. The village of Ukhrul became the focal point of the war and came to be remembered as the place where the Battle of Imphal was fought.[115]

As Japanese troops advanced to the highest point in Kohima, the Naga families fled. The Japanese watched and waited.[116] They tried to cajole the Nagas to join them, citing racial affinity and promising to drive out the British. In the previous months, a few Naga villagers had joined the Japanese forces, but most of them had subsequently returned.[117] One Naga leader, however, stood out in this extraordinary time: Angami Zapu Phizo, who would in the years to come pose a formidable challenge to the government of independent India. Phizo, whose earlier application to join the British Army had been rejected[118] and who had been struggling for a livelihood in Burma, enlisted himself as a corporal in Bose's INA. He was hopeful about the Japanese promise of independence from the British.[119] Phizo would be arrested after the defeat of the Japanese and go on to be imprisoned in Rangoon. Many Kukis too, who had been conscripted by the British for the war, joined the INA and extended support to the Japanese forces. They recalled the humiliations suffered during the Anglo-Kuki War of 1917–19, and they hoped that the arrival of the Japanese would lead to the fall of the British imperial authority.[120] Massive Japanese propaganda, promising economic prosperity for India and predicting the imminent collapse of British power, clouded the political atmosphere of north-eastern India. Some of the posters and leaflets dropped by Japanese aircraft would find their way to the British war museum. The Allies responded with propaganda of their own, which included attacks on the Congress. The INA, notwithstanding their help to the Japanese forces, did not face condemnation in Assam. Following the war, Bardoloi said, 'Free India would have hailed them [INA soldiers, who fought alongside the Japanese] as heroes instead of trying them.'[121]

The Japanese taught the Nagas their alphabet and national anthem, and the Nagas carried paddy, tobacco and hay, and even pounded rice for the Japanese forces.[122] However, the Japanese took away their food stocks and fed entire fields of produce to the horses. Trees were left with no leaves, forests were devastated. The early bonhomie with the Japanese waned,[123] and the Nagas began to extend support to the Allied forces in many ways: they misguided or captured Japanese soldiers and provided the Allies with intelligence.[124] Field Marshal William Slim,

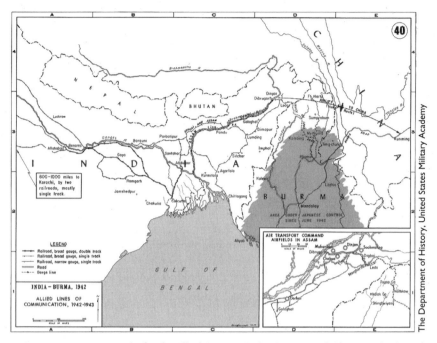

Communication networks for the Allied Army in India, Burma, and China, 1942–43

the British commander of the Fourteenth Army, had this to say: 'These were the gallant Nagas whose loyalty, even in the most depressing times of the invasion, had never faltered. Despite floggings, torture, execution, and the burning of their villages, they refused to aid the Japanese in any way to betray our troops.'[125]

As Allied reinforcements of men, tanks and guns streamed into Kohima,[126] they could, despite the onset of monsoon, mount pressure on the Japanese.[127] Between July 1944 and August 1945, Assam's hill districts and Burma were recouped by the Allied forces. Led by William Slim, but mostly comprising Indians, the Allied troops fought bloody battles on the high passes of Assam and north Burma.[128] They inflicted a crushing land defeat on the Japanese. Mutaguchi's forces lost more than 50,000 men in what is considered their greatest defeat in the war.[129] 'The Japanese army thrown against Imphal and Kohima was a kind of mass suicide squad,' wrote historians Bayly and Harper.[130]

Discarded Japanese equipment somewhere near Imphal, Manipur

As the Japanese troops retreated, they left behind a trail of gloom and misery. Most villagers did not have a harvest that winter. Bombs had destroyed their homes. An estimated 2,00,000 people of the Naga Hills and Manipur had fled to escape the brutality of the Japanese troops.[131] To deny the Japanese access to water and food, the Allied forces had poisoned water bodies and burnt paddy stocks and houses in Manipur. Military camps were set up in parts of eastern Assam, and Naga or Meiti villages were used for war operations. Homes and agricultural plots were seized or relocated.[132] In Imphal, as many as 20,000 houses were occupied by the Allied army.

In the Naga Hills and in Manipur, rehabilitation began quickly. While the Indian government spelt out the modalities of relief and rehabilitation, such measures were directly supervised by the Assam government. It was decided that relief—mostly in kind—should be 'fair and adequate but without undue extravagance' so that 'the people will rebuild their own houses, clear and repair their watercourses, and arrange for the resumption of cultivation' without incurring any labour cost. Partial support came in the form of food, building materials, agricultural tools, seeds and livestock.[133] But an ineffective bureaucracy and the changing political scenario delayed the implementation of many relief programmes. As villagers slowly returned to what remained of their homes, disputes arose. The war victims petitioned the Assam government; but as their claims were delayed or rejected, anger and bitter political debates arose.[134]

With the war on the eastern frontier, Assam's economy and resources had come under great pressure. 'The clerical and professional classes are having to tighten their belts everyday . . . there has been a distinct upsetting of the economic balance.'[135] Very few got new opportunities for employment in either the military or civilian spheres. The oil refinery at Digboi was taken over by the Allied forces, and Assam received a trifling sum in return from the South-east Asia Command.[136] Towns and civilian populations had to be guarded, massive publicity campaigns were to be created, refugees and arriving armies had to be fed. A part of Assam's civil defence was maintained by the Assam Rifles and the newly raised Assam Regiment. Large numbers from Naga, Kuki, Chin or other hill tribes were conscripted for the war, and some were recruited as the Viceroy's commissioned officers. Finances had to be organized for them. Assam also paid for several combat aircraft.[137] Budgets remained in deficit, but the government had few other options. Land revenue, the primary source of government earnings, had reached a tipping point. Saadulla, the premier of Assam, withdrew the existing practice of remission of land revenue, and this, along with the business done by the Forest Department, a new tax on petrol and contributions to the Assam War Fund, helped to partly bridge the deficit. Assam had an impressive financial graph during 1937–38 and 1946–47, when both revenue collection and expenditure increased by more than 100 per cent.[138] But the war resulted in budget deficits in both Assam and Bengal.[139]

The presence of the Allied military further burdened and traumatized the people of Assam. Prices of everyday items went up manifold. Some gained quick profits, but, in general, it was a worrying situation. Clow, Assam's governor, wrote, 'Civil morale suffers in

Lakhimpur from the disturbances involved by numerous requisitions of land, and in large parts of the province from the locust-like habits of the forces, which render housing and supplies of all kinds very hard for civilians to procure.'[140] War had initially caused widespread panic, but most people had become resigned to living in a war zone. 'Military activity is now taken so much for granted that when in one village where I was talking to the villagers, an amphibious jeep driven by an apparently nude negro went through, I was among the few who turned to look at it,' wrote Clow.[141]

The legacy of war included environmental stress as well.[142] In 1942, the respected science journal *Nature* had predicted that 'war may prove [to be] the salvation of these Assam hill districts, since it would seem apparent that for military purposes communications are being opened up in what has heretofore been a wild mass of more or less inaccessible hill tracts.'[143] This prediction did soon come true; however, it came at a cost. The war, which alone created demands for 'millions of tent poles', exerted an extraordinary and unprecedented burden on Assam's forests. Assam's Forest Department worked in close coordination with the military to accelerate the felling of trees. The war opened the doors for a new era of timber-based industry.[144] Within a short span of time, millions of trees, mainly the tall hardwoods of Upper Assam (dipterocarps), apart from shrubs, thatching grass and bamboo were cut down or uprooted. A major new operation was the pruning of forests at high elevations for the manufacture of softwood boxes. The value of the materials supplied from Assam's forests increased by an estimated 745 per cent between 1941 and 1945.[145] More sawmills were established to ensure war supply. The construction of roads, such as the Ledo Road, new railways and airfields across the Patkai resulted in the destruction of large swathes of forests in Upper Assam. New settlements arose along the new transport arteries,[146] and some refugees squatted on Forest Department lands. A major impact was felt on the paper industry. In rural India, plantain leaves came to be used as a substitute for paper, which was in short supply.

The breakdown of controls against the poaching of wildlife in eastern Assam during the war is also well recorded. Roads cut through ecologically fragile mountain environments inevitably leave deep scars. They also open up remote terrains to large-scale movements of population from the lowlands, resulting in further deforestation. In the case of the Ledo Road, this effect was limited, as the post-Independence Indian government closed the India–Burma frontier for some 30 years. But the war did create unprecedented access to the Burmese uplands, contributing to the pressure on the region's species-rich wildlife habitat. The Indian government's unwillingness to make this route available for the movement of the civilian population for political reasons[147] allowed the forest to quickly reclaim the road. In 1957, the British filmmaker Tim Slessor, driving from Ledo to Myitkyina as part of the Oxford and Cambridge Far Eastern Expedition, found tall grasses and a thick green jungle all along this road.[148] Horses left behind by the Allied troops had found a home in the wild in the Patkai foothills.

Despite the serious challenges, most British capitalist ventures in Assam significantly improved their profits. Account books of the plantation companies swelled, and river navigation companies doubled their incomes. Tea was not associated with the question of hunger, but the population in Britain could not do without it. So, by 1940, the BGOI and the Indian tea industry had agreed that 'Britain must be adequately supplied with tea, there must be no profiteering, and the mechanism of the International Tea Agreement must, as far as possible, be kept in operation'. Percival Griffiths estimated that in the last four years of the war, the Indian tea industry witnessed an increase of 20 per cent in the average annual production of tea over the pre-war figure.[149] The BGOI imposed an Excess Profits Tax on profits earned beyond the approximate maximum average calculated for the years 1935–37.[150] Meanwhile, tea garden workers, with experience gained working in military projects at moderately higher wages and improved working conditions during the war, began to view jobs in collieries and tea gardens with contempt.

By 1942, the Japanese occupation of Burma had disrupted the supply of rice to Assam's tea gardens. The problem was aggravated by the complete takeover of Assam's transport system by the military. To overcome the general food crisis, the Assam government in that year appointed Steel Brothers & Company as official agents to purchase and distribute rice in Assam. Another concern was the smuggling of food from Assam into Bengal. Often the police resorted to firing to stop such smuggling from taking place.[151] Rural and urban discrepancies became apparent. A year later, the BGOI, which believed that Steel Brothers & Company often supplied poor-quality rice, made the commitment that a part of the company's procurement would be done by the tea industry. The Indian Tea Association appointed officers to purchase and distribute grains in Assam. Till 1944, the system worked efficiently, and Griffiths recorded that it 'stood between the plantation labour force and starvation'. At the same time, however, many tea gardens began to procure rice locally, and malnourished plantation workers were encouraged to grow improved strains of the grain. H.A. Antrobus, the official historian of the Assam Company, noted that food supplies were diverted to the needs of the Allied forces, while the 'labourer was suffering from malnutrition brought about by an unbalanced diet'.[152] The food crisis also impacted the rich in some ways. Gopinath Bardoloi, the former premier, postponed the wedding of his daughter.[153]

As expected, the railway and steamer companies made war-time profits. Jute producers benefitted too, as prices spiralled manifold.[154] Some well-connected individuals—as depicted in a range of literary works—secured contracts for the construction of military barracks, roadways, airstrips, bridges, hospitals and refugee camps, as well as for the supply of bamboos, thatch, etc.[155] Contractors and workers came from outside, much to the displeasure of the tiny Assamese bourgeoisie, to take advantage of these new economic opportunities.[156] Hem Barua, who would later become a parliamentarian, captured the mood aptly when he observed that 'as war loomed large in the sky of Assam', the Assamese gained a new sense of trade and commerce.[157] Some of those who made money invested in the tea industry. Between 1943 and 1952, there was a five-fold increase in Assamese ownership of tea plantations, and the interest in ownership spiked as there were clear indications of the flight of foreign capital after 1945.[158] War also brought sudden financial prosperity, however trifling, to Assam's towns. Guwahati witnessed a dramatic increase in industrial and trading activities, leading to growth in employment; of a population of 44,000 in 1945, the number employed in trade and industries increased from 5918 in 1938 to 9931 during 1945–46.[159]

War left its scars on society. It transformed the 'geographical vacuum' in India's North-east into a 'live' frontier,[160] dramatically changing the lives of all those who belonged there. The presence of large numbers of Allied troops had led to endless strife with the local people. Petty controversies between locals and Allied soldiers over liquor and prices in the marketplaces were widely reported. Further, the molestation, rape and murder of women by soldiers destroyed many families.[161] These horrific experiences, new to the people in the region, found place in later literary works. In Birendra Kumar Bhattacharya's *Yaruingam*, Sharengla, the female protagonist, was captured by Japanese soldiers and briefly stayed with one of the Japanese soldiers.[162]

This was also the beginning of the militarization of the area. The volume of modern weapons left behind here after the war was hard to estimate. Some of these weapons were brought home by villagers as trophies, others lay buried or rusted. Some American soldiers clandestinely sold their weapons to private buyers.[163] Loss or pilferage of military weapons and property with the active participation of soldiers had begun even before the war ended,[164] and these fell into the hands of communist guerrillas or political rebels and insurgents in the post-war era.

~

Assam's ethnic and tribal communities were patronizingly described in the European press as simple, primitive folks, cheerful and patient.[165] However, not every description of these communities, who found themselves in the crossfire between the contending parties in the war, was condescending. A collection of paintings by Anthony Gross, the British printmaker, painter and war artist, memorably depicts the north-eastern tribes—Nagas, Chins, Kachins—fighting on the war front.[166] At this crucial juncture, warfare and anthropology came to intersect in curious ways. Edmund Leach, the young British anthropologist who

Field Marshal Claude Auchinleck, the British Army Commander with Naga troops in 1946

had trained with Bronislaw Malinowski and Raymond Firth, arrived in Burma for ethnographic research in 1939. As war broke out, he used his linguistic and ethnographic skills to organize Kachin guerrilla bands against the Japanese troops.[167] Others like A.G. McCall, the superintendent of Lushai Hills, or the young British anthropologist Ursula Graham Bower, raised territorial troops like the Lushai Hills Total Defence Scheme or the Watch and Ward Scheme. Equipped with basic military training, these organizations raised the morale of the population, ensured the loyalty of local communities and kept the Allied troops' intelligence operations intact.[168] In doing so, British strategic policy sowed seeds of long-term conflict as militarized highland societies with distinct ethnonationalism became allies of an imperial power fighting for survival.

As discussed earlier, as the early Japanese overtures to the Indian tribes turned into assaults on their food, cattle and villages, the tribal people fought back. They guided Allied patrols through difficult terrain, carried their wounded soldiers, built roads for them and provided them food from their own meagre stocks.[169] When the Japanese troops attacked the Naga Hills, Bower was living with the Nagas, studying them, photographing them and collecting material for her book. After briefly running a canteen for the troops at one of the stations on the Assam Bengal Railway, Bower became a useful partner to the British. She trained the Nagas to scout the jungles for Japanese troops, helping gather military intelligence.[170] Some Nagas organized themselves against the Japanese.[171] Officers of the US army reported that the Nagas helped them in creating warning networks that the Japanese couldn't get through without detection.[172] The Kachins and Chins of the Indo-Burmese border fought the Japanese with their indigenous weapons and also acted as intelligence providers.[173] The Khasis served as porters.[174] As the war was drawing to a close, the BGOI awarded the Naga Viceroy's Commissioned Officers (VCOs) for their role during the Burma operations.[175] The war also ensured the participation of tribal women in various capacities. In 1944, when the Countess of Carlisle, chief commander of the Women's Auxiliary Corps of India, toured eastern India, she met Nepalese girls working as military intelligence providers, frontline girls at Ledo and Khasi girls engaged at air force camps in Calcutta.[176] The men and women trained in logistics, weaponry and even combat support would in many cases emerge as political actors in the troubled politics of border regions of post-1947/1948 India and Burma.

The wartime demand for food for soldiers and refugees, and the snapping of India's crucial rice dependency on Burma contributed to the Bengal famine. As millions began to die, the BGOI organized the first-ever food production conference in Delhi in April 1942. Speaking at the conference, Nalini Ranjan Sarkar, member in charge of health in the Viceroy's Council, confessed that 'the virtual cessation of rice imports from Burma has caused an appreciable gap in the total supply of rice for home consumption.'[177] A massive 'Grow More Food' campaign was started across the country. Meanwhile, poor masses from the intensely famine-stricken rural eastern Bengal started to arrive in Assam's floodplains.[178] While Assam's Muslim League ministry encouraged the incoming peasants from Bengal to clear land for agriculture, the All-India Hindu Mahasabha adopted a resolution opposing the influx of Muslim peasants into Assam.[179] By the end of 1943, government officials began to notice that 'every possible piece of land for cultivation' was taken up; between 1937 and 1946, land under cultivation increased from 4.88 million acres to 5.33 million acres.[180] Huge amounts of vegetables also made their way into military markets, as some rice fields were converted into vegetable gardens. As pressure for land settlement increased from agrarian communities, the government advised that if there was not enough suitable land for settlement, the answer should be intensive cultivation of existing agricultural land as well as bringing tracts of forest land under cultivation.

The Assam government undertook a massive programme of requisition of private properties as a part of its war efforts. This met with some acts of resistance, which became etched in the public mind through several powerful literary works. In Jyotiprasad Agarwala's classic play *Lovita*, for instance, the eponymous female protagonist refuses to vacate her family land for the military. She demands an alternative for her people and is furious when it is not provided. 'If the government does not know the needs of its people who else will know?' she boldly asks a police officer.[181]

~

For the Empire, the war signalled the arrival of an era of vulnerability. Indians saw British imperial authority and legitimacy crumbling before their eyes. In its final days, a radical new proposal was put forward by the British for India's north-east frontier. The proposal, born out of London's strategic and administrative wartime experience, designed by their senior-most officials and championed by the governor of Assam, floated the idea of a new unit under the Crown that would merge Burma and the highlands of north-east India. The scheme, which was eventually shelved, arose as British officials in Assam pondered over the future of the tribal areas that constituted 40 per cent of the territory of the province. Would the fate of the tribes be assigned to a government of the Assamese or would they be given freedom from being ruled by the Assamese? Would they be with independent India or outside of it? The British were not alone in considering these questions. In 1943, the eminent Indian sociologist G.S. Ghurye published a lengthy treatise titled *The Aborigines—'So-Called'—And Their Future*, outlining his vision of the destiny of India's tribal population.[182] While Ghurye strongly recommended the integration of the tribes of Central India into the larger ambit of Hindu India, he did not prescribe the same for the tribes of Assam. Barring some differences, his ideas largely matched those of the British officials.

Between 1941 and 1947, four reports around these anxieties were drafted and read by senior British officials.[183] The earliest of these was written by Assam's Governor Robert Reid (1937–42).[184] Reid, an ICS officer of the 1907 batch, had a long career in Bengal, Assam and Bihar. During his governorship, he had travelled extensively across Assam and had thoroughly enjoyed those visits. Reid recommended that the contiguous frontier areas of Assam and Burma be made into a British colony. This combined territory—including the modern-day Indian states of Tripura, Manipur, Mizoram, Nagaland, Arunachal Pradesh and Meghalaya, the Chin and Shan states of Burma and the Chittagong Hill District of Bangladesh—would be directly administered under the supervision of the British Crown. Reid proposed that the officials from the Burma Frontier Service could run the administration, and finance could be handled by the imperial authorities with additional support from the federal and local governments of India.

Some of these possibilities had been spelt out even earlier. The idea that these areas should be carved out of India and Burma goes back to 1928. That the hill areas should remain beyond the ambit of the plains of Assam was clearly recommended in the Assam government's memorandum to the Indian Statutory Commission in that year.[185] These areas 'should be excluded from the Province of Assam in the new constitution . . . These areas have nothing in common with the rest of the Province'.[186] J.H. Hutton, who served as the administrator of the Naga Hills and was also a distinguished anthropologist, often underlined that the tribal population in Assam's hill districts shared little with the Assamese-speaking population. He emphasized the considerable cultural gap between the dominant Assamese-speaking people and Assam's tribal-language-speaking population. Also, Reid recalled that Leo Amery, the secretary of state for India between 1940 and 1945, had said in a BBC broadcast on 3 March 1941, 'Burma belongs not to India, but to the easternmost of the great southward projection of the main bulk of Asia, the Indo-Chinese peninsula.' Divide and rule seemed to be giving way to the unstated idea of fragment and quit.

What led Robert Reid to take such a radical view of the future of the hill tracts of Assam? Reid had no doubt that 'when one emerges from the hills into the plains of Assam, one enters a different world, whereas the boundaries between our hills and the Burma hills is artificial as it is imperceptible'. Christianity had spread rapidly in the hills, and Christians were not to be drawn into 'the struggle between Hindus and Muslims'. The fate of the population living in the hills, Reid warned, 'cannot be left to Indian political leaders with neither the knowledge, interest nor any feelings for these areas'. Reid was horrified by the idea of either the Congress or the Muslim League controlling the future of these areas: 'Palpably outrageous though they are, the claims of Congress to include the hills of Assam in a Hindu Raj and of the Muslim League to make them part of Pakistan are seriously meant. To allow them is to abandon every undertaking on behalf of minorities that has so solemnly been made.' The hill people, he said, 'are not, by a hundred years, ready to take their place in a democratic constitution, or to compete with the sophisticated Indian politician for place and power, and personally I have no doubt whatever that to allow them in any way to be involved in Indian politics and with no safeguards such as now exist, would spell disaster for them'.[187] These 'areas do not, and cannot form part of India', he asserted and had little doubt that 'they will not get a square deal from an autonomous Indian government and the sequel would be rebellion, bloodshed, and ultimate ruin'. The charter was for continual imperial dominion of a strategic region premised on ethno-geographical markers.

But the idea of detaching this complex geography from the Indian political milieu goes back farther, to the previous century. The process of granting immunity to imperial regulations in these 'excluded' or 'partially excluded' areas began in the early nineteenth century. One of the earliest experiments, in 1822, was to exempt the Garo Hills in Assam's south-west from the rules and regulations applicable in the province of Bengal. As British rule began to take firm root after the First Anglo-Burmese War of 1824–26, the hilly regions beyond the floodplains of the Brahmaputra, inhabited by various ethnic groups speaking the Tibeto-Burman languages, were introduced into the region in stages, thereby broadening this centre and giving shape to the province of Assam. This process was not smooth and frequently met with resistance. The hill communities and those living in the floodplains were interdependent and interconnected socially, politically, economically and culturally.

As British rule expanded, those interconnections were disrupted. Soon, British speculative private capital, often in complicity with India's Marwari traders, was marching into Assam's frontier hills. Between 1881 and 1901, the perimeters of tea plantations increased by 118 per cent, often after hilly forests were brutally shorn and their inhabitants ousted. Rubber (*Ficus elastica*), ivory and timber were sold in global markets.[188] As inhabitants of those areas fought back, the conflicts intensified. But since it was important to keep up the imperial image of liberal governance alongside ensuring the safety of British capital and long-term stability of British rule, as well as retaining control over resources, innovative systems of governance were framed. The modalities of governance that were spelt out in August 1873 envisaged intricate administrative, juridical and political ideas for the region. The passage of the Bengal Eastern Frontier Regulation was a momentous intervention that imagined an 'Inner Line' separating the plains from the hills, the civilized from the seemingly savage, the modern from the primitive, which would also be the territorial frontier of the colonial capital.[189] British subjects from the plains were barred from entering the hills without an official permit and were restricted to pursuing only commercial activities. The residents of the hills would be free from the laws and regulations of British India and would be governed by their own customs. Subsequent legislation in 1874 and 1880 reinforced this segregation.

Most recent studies have shown that the Inner Line effected a dramatic transformation in the hills.[190] In an arrangement of indirect governance, traditional chiefs were rechristened as agents to collect house tax and maintain order on behalf of the Empire. Posts of political officers were created to supervise the actions of the chiefs, and many of the incumbents became exemplary ethnographers of these communities. Backed by the Raj, several western Christian missionaries began proselytizing activities, leading to unprecedented transformation. By the early twentieth century, these systems of governance came to be deeply embedded in the hills. When the British government began experimenting with limited transfer of power through constitutional reforms, Assam's geography beyond the Inner Line remained outside the scope of these experiments. The Government of India Act of 1919 put these areas, known as 'Backward Tracts', beyond the jurisdiction of the provincial government. The Government of India Act of 1935 referred to them as 'Excluded Areas' or 'Partially Excluded Areas',[191] which were to be governed directly by Assam's governor. The administration was financed by Assam's treasury.[192] The western frontier of Burma had followed a similar trajectory after the Second Anglo-Burmese War.[193] It was against this background that Reid proposed in 1941 to combine the loosely administered frontier areas of Assam and the contiguous frontier areas of Burma into a British colony.

Reid's confidential note passed through several hands, including those of Viceroy Linlithgow and Secretary of State Amery, and caused excitement as well as apprehension. One senior British official said, '[I]t is infinitely better than anything else that I have seen from Reid's pen.'[194] While many officers managing Assam's eastern Himalayan localities were uninterested, Linlithgow was hopeful. Years previously, Reid had hosted the unusually tall viceroy in Shillong and ensured that a long bed was brought in from Calcutta for him.

Amery, too, was pleased with the idea proposed by Reid. He shared it with the historian Reginald Coupland, Beit Professor of Colonial

History at the University of Oxford. Coupland was then writing the *Report on the Constitutional Problem in India*. Coupland's *The Future of India*, which was published in 1943, revealed the plan to separate the tribal areas of India and Burma and give them a different government in future, much to Reid's delight.[195] 'There is one major area,' wrote Coupland, 'which seems to call for special treatment—the hill tracts on the eastern frontier of Assam,' which 'adjoin similar hill tracts on the north-west frontier of Burma. The inhabitants of both areas are alike in race and culture. They are not Indians or Burmans, but of Mongol stock. In no sense did they belong to the Indian or Burman "nation" . . . Both share a common neighbour—China—and that demands a common frontier policy. These considerations have inspired a suggestion that the two areas might be united in a single territory.'[196] Racial views, cultural markers and unique geography, as much as the 'Two Nation Theory', proved handy for an Empire in retreat.

By July 1944, the Allied forces had secured the north-eastern frontier. While the strategic vulnerability of India's North-east was out in the open, would Coupland's proposition make any dent in the imperial outlook? The Indian and British governments brought the idea of a Crown colony back to the discussion table. The Burma officials responsible for the frontier areas (known as Scheduled Areas) opposed the idea from the beginning.[197] Reginald Dorman-Smith, the governor of Burma, however, approved of the idea and would have liked to bring these areas under the direct administration of the governor of Burma and the governor-general of India.

Viceroy Wavell, who was then in the thick of negotiations for the transfer of power and was fairly well-acquainted with Indian political waters, knew that the Coupland Plan (which we should more accurately term the 'Reid–Coupland Plan') would invite disaster. He spelt out his apprehensions to Amery, writing that this would not be accepted by Indian nationalist politicians and that, as an idea, it was 'quite impracticable'.[198] Wavell, however, did not object to the creation of a separate province, to be brought under either the Indian or the Burmese government. Amery saw reason in the viceroy's apprehensions and in September wrote to Wavell that Britain was 'under no solemnly recorded obligation' to undertake such messy work involving finance and administrative responsibility.[199]

The resignation of Winston Churchill as Britain's Prime Minister in July 1945 put an end to the possibility of another partition at the India–Burma frontier. The province of Burma had already been separated from British India in 1937, leaving behind a trail of economic and political quandaries. Amery was succeeded as secretary of state for India and Burma by Frederick Pethick-Lawrence, a socialist and a member of the Labour Party. Pethick-Lawrence had visited Guwahati in 1926 and had attended the Congress session that year. He was intimately acquainted with India's nationalist aspirations.[200] Wavell and he had similar views on this question.

~

At the time the Coupland Plan fizzled out, the situation in Assam was fast becoming fuzzy. The idea of Pakistan was taking definite shape, but the provincial boundaries of India had not been fixed. At this critical juncture, two more reports surfaced on the fate of Assam's hills, written by J.P. Mills and Andrew Clow.[201] J.P. Mills, the advisor to Assam's Governor for tribal affairs, was an influential figure on the question of the tribes of India. He served in Assam for several years and wrote an immensely influential ethnographic work on the Nagas. In 1948, he began teaching at the School of Oriental and African Studies, and soon thereafter became the president of the Royal Anthropological Institute. Mills wrote that 'the Mongolians of Eastern India cannot as yet be incorporated in India.' He recorded a number of reasons to justify his claim, which included: 'the plainsmen have never conquered the hill tribes and could not control them in the future' and 'the hillmen have served' the British Indian government 'magnificently in the war and we cannot leave them to their fate'. Mills, however, cautioned that this arrangement would only be in place till they were 'able to stand on their own feet and take their chance in the Indian political field'. Mills also prophesied something that went on to haunt future generations, regarding the boundaries demarcating the tribal-inhabited 'excluded areas' and administered areas. An exact boundary between these distinctive geographies, in the eyes of the imperial masters, was missing until then. Mills proposed three options, out of which he thought the exclusion of all the hills from Assam was the best. The excluded areas would be accorded special treatment, would be ruled indirectly and would be allowed to develop their own time-tested self-rule institutions until they were eventually united with Assam. Mills also made it clear that this separation would not cause any inconvenience to Assam.

Andrew Clow, a career civil servant, had arrived in Assam in May 1942 to succeed Reid. Initially reluctant to come to Assam at a time of war, he stayed on until 1947.[202] Clow agreed with Reid and Mills on their anthropological view of the hill population, but he drafted a lengthier proposal that also moved away from theirs. The views incorporated in this report were part of his long correspondence with higher authorities, including Wavell. Clow, aware of the fact that the Indian nationalists 'would probably oppose a partition' of Assam, portrayed the idea of Crown colony as a 'primitive type' that was certain to create problems for India's defence.[203] He stressed that Assam's 'hills and plains are linked by geography, by economic necessities, by administrative history and arrangements and by a *lingua franca*'. The hills should look towards Assam rather than Burma for 'economic progress', adding that 'the extension of Burma into the middle of the Assam plains would be most undesirable'. In case of any misfortune emanating from the Indian political situation, the hill population would get 'the largest measure of responsibility they are capable of discharging'. Clow provided his solution: present-day Arunachal and a major part of the Naga Hills along with areas taken from Burma should be formed into a separate unit where the enhanced authority of the tribal institutions should be the foundation of its government. This would only be a temporary measure. The rest of the hills should be merged with Assam, and 'the ultimate aim should be a single province'. Clow's adamant rebuttal of Reid's scheme was more than enough to put a nail in its coffin. In 1946, the Indian government formally rejected all these ideas.[204]

The idea of separation of the hills from the future control of Assam went against the wishes of the Assamese.[205] The new Congress government in Assam, which had taken office in 1946, fiercely contested the scheme, though Premier Bardoloi was personally sympathetic to the predicament of Assam's tribal communities. As independence approached, the tribal question began to take shape very differently from the views of the British administrators. The Indian leaders were largely sensitive to this delicate situation. The Constituent Assembly of India, which was tasked with the responsibility of spelling out the future of India, asked a team of senior members to visit these hill districts. The Indian leaders also knew very well that they could not afford to push for a quick takeover of these areas. Some of those sensitivities were shared by none other than Nehru. In a letter to T. Sakhrie, secretary of the Naga National Council, in 1946, Nehru spelt out the future of the hills: 'I do not want them to be swamped by people from other parts of the country who might go there to exploit them to their own advantage.'[206] However, the Naga political leaders became restless and negotiated aggressively with the Congress. A number of Khasi leaders, on the other hand, thought India was a good option for them. After Independence, Tripura, Manipur and the Khasi states signed the Instrument of Accession with the Indian government. Tripura and Manipur were accorded Union Territory status, but several areas were empowered with the unique provision of the District Council, which we discuss in more detail in a later chapter.

As political aspirations in the hills and plains evolved along different trajectories, many people from the hills saw no problem with the Crown colony proposal. But others detected an imperial design behind this. A year after Independence, the best-known Naga leader, Phizo, wrote from his prison cell in Calcutta to Governor-General C. Rajagopalachari that the idea of the Crown colony was 'hatched by [the] Naga Hill Administration who were always clever and stout-hearted British aristocrats', and would be a 'master stroke for a few cunning British schemers'. He reminded Rajagopalachari that the Naga leaders opposed the scheme 'because it would go against the interest of other Eastern people'.

The idea of the hills as a distinct entity would continue to haunt the political life of India's North-east for a long time, even as the region became entangled with political developments in China, Burma and Tibet. The integration of the North-east into the Indian nation would remain an uneasy idea for decades to come. When the Chinese communists were on the verge of unleashing a political revolution in China, Sardar Patel, India's Home Minister, had to assure the Indian parliament that his government had taken 'appropriate steps' for Assam's security.[207] Very few will disagree that much of this perception of Assam's strategic vulnerability was a legacy of the trauma of World War II.

# 2

# Bumpy Road to Independence

As World War II reached India's eastern frontier, Assam's place in the Muslim League's geographical schema of Pakistan became clearer. There had been whispers regarding this possibility among some Muslim leaders in Assam and Bengal. According to the 1941 Census, one-third of Assam's population was Muslim. A significant number were recent settlers from Bengal and were spread over the floodplains of Lower Assam. The prospect of Assam's inclusion in the future state of Pakistan brought both fear and excitement among its people. Amidst this, the Census enumeration of 1941 sparked massive political debates[1]—especially regarding the redefinition of who constituted Hindus—further intensifying the drawing of battle lines between the Congress and the Muslim League.[2]

On 30 and 31 January 1941, Sylhet hosted the annual conference of the Assam Provincial Muslim League. Presided over by Bengal's powerful premier Fazlul Huq, the meeting called for a revival of the lost glory of the Muslims in India. Referring to the impending Census enumeration, Huq declared that the 'numerical strength of the community' would guide its 'destiny'.[3] Moving one step ahead of Huq, Muhammad Saadulla, Assam's premier, had hinted at the possibility of the inclusion of Assam in Pakistan.[4] In February 1941, a leaked document spelt out the Muslim League's idea of a physically demarcated and sovereign state of Pakistan.[5] Pakistan would include the four north-western provinces, including Delhi, and Bengal and Assam in the east.

~

At the heart of the struggle between the Congress and the Muslim League lay the deeply contested subject of land settlement. Guided by electoral needs and competitive welfare schemes, the Assam government undertook several land settlement programmes from 1938 for pieces of land with an upper ceiling of 30 bighas. The modalities of distribution varied considerably and were dependent on which party was in power and the social, religious and political background of beneficiary peasants. A Muslim League-led government—with the support of several Hindu lawmakers not affiliated to the Congress—was in power for the most part in pre-Independence Assam. The beneficiaries of its land settlement programme were the province's native poor as well as those who had migrated from Bengal before 1938. (By 1931, an estimated 5,75,000 Bengal-born peasants had settled in Assam.)[6] These land settlement schemes were censured by the Congress and Assamese public opinion. The Brahmaputra Valley's political narrative, thus, began to be centred around the question of land. Despite adverse public opinion, a gigantic bureaucratic exercise, involving large numbers of revenue officials, politicians and petitions from peasants, helped settle hundreds and thousands of poor peasants in these floodplains.

Between 1934–35 and 1944–45, approximately 1.1 million acres of land were newly added to the net areas under cultivation in the floodplains of the Brahmaputra.[7] The areas that were opened up for cultivation included former grazing lands for cattle and buffaloes, Reserved Forests and other uncultivated government lands. Pressure on state-owned forest lands increased exponentially from the 1930s when the government decided to make room for peasant settlement. Foresters, in the recent past, had struggled against the expanding of agricultural lands into forests, but the coming of the provincial ministries had accelerated this process. The most vulnerable were the Unclassed State Forests (USFs), which were patches of forest land governed by the revenue administration before they came under the direct custody of the forest department. In 1940–41, approximately 24 per cent of Assam's total land area was classified in this category. After decades of being exploited for commercial prospects and contributing a significant share to the province's revenue, the USFs were no longer lucrative for the forest department. 'This is of no economic importance,' wrote one commentator in 1942.[8] Another described it as a 'wasting asset'.[9] As pressure mounted to deforest extensive government-owned forested tracts for agriculture, the Assam government amended the Assam Forest Regulation of 1891 in 1943 to allow peasant settlements. Between 1940 and 1946, an estimated one-tenth of the USFs were converted into peasant landholdings.[10]

The prospect of owning a piece of land brought in fresh waves of Bengali-speaking peasants who were ravaged by decades of famine, poverty and environmental degradation and economically oppressed by their landlords and moneylenders in eastern Bengal. The lawmakers in Bengal had repeatedly sought opening up of Assam to their distressed poor, and as famine raged in Bengal, the Assam government acceded to this demand in August 1943. The destitute victims of the Bengal famine started to arrive in Assam's western districts from mid-1943. One official report indicated that even in November 1943, when this population flow began to reduce, approximately 450 people were still entering Assam daily.[11] The flow of migrants from Bengal moderately declined by about the mid-1940s, and their population in Assam stood at approximately 8,33,288 in 1951.[12] Most of them were Muslims from the district of Mymensingh in East Bengal, which produced jute for Bengal's British-owned jute industries. Of course, not everyone who migrated to Assam got a share in the land; officially only 15 per cent received land between 1941 and 1944, but this figure was seriously disputed.[13]

Sandwiched between the government and the peasants in search of land were Assam's Nepali dairy farmers. Early groups of Nepalis, who had arrived there as part of the EIC's military campaigns, had settled in the Brahmaputra Valley early in the nineteenth century.[14] If a minuscule number of them were absorbed by the imperial bureaucracy, the majority made a new life by excelling in dairy farming in the fertile alluvial floodplains. From a few hundred in the 1870s, their population rose to 1,00,000 in the mid-twentieth century. Despite early hostilities from the forest conservators, dairy farming became an integral part of Assam's economy. The Nepali cattle grazers came to occupy a unique place in Assam's social and agrarian landscape. Collections of grazing fees rose from a modest Rs 2000 in 1888–89 to Rs 3.55 lakh in 1917–18. The government encouraged the Nepalis to expand the frontiers of their pasture lands to increase the number of grazers. In 1917, an estimated half a million acres of land were specially demarcated for pastures. By 1940, the valley's grassy floodplains housed an estimated 5 million cattle and buffaloes.[15] However, if the government levied taxes on grazing, the Assamese and Marwari trader-cum-moneylenders entered into a usurious trade relationship with the Nepalis. In the 1930s, several of these grazing pastures also changed hands, often illegally in the official view, and became a part of the Bengali settlers' landscape. Between 1926–27 and 1942–43, one-third of such pastures were either lost to river erosion or transferred to the Bengali peasant settlers.[16]

The dynamics of land settlement changed rapidly when World War II arrived in India's North-east, with pressure from many directions. When famine engulfed Bengal, Muslim organizations and the Bengal government intensified their pressure on the Muslim League-led government in Assam to do away with what was known as the Line System, namely an administrative measure to separate new Bengali-speaking settlers from the indigenous Assamese.[17] The Government of India's wartime 'Grow More Food' campaign, discussed in the previous chapter, had already given further impetus to land distribution initiatives. The Bengal government, too, faced pressure, as the region's Muslim organizations strongly rebuked the Bengal provincial Muslim League for their 'utter callousness and absolute indifference to the harrowing distress that thousands of destitute immigrants have been subjected to in Assam who have collected there in search of food and have been roaming from place to place half-naked and half-starved without any support and sympathy from local authorities'.[18] Maulana

Abdul Hamid Khan, a Muslim League member from Lower Assam, popularly known as Bhashani, was one of the strongest advocates of the Bengal peasants' rights in Assam. Known for his left-leaning political views, Bhashani, certainly the most charismatic leader of Assam's poor Bengali Muslim peasants in the 1940s, dreamt of a prosperous Assam that actualized the land settlement programme.[19]

Till the early months of 1944, Premier Saadulla had not encouraged land settlement for the Bengali peasants, and the Muslim League was unhappy about this. Land reclamation under peasant holding in the Brahmaputra Valley between 1936–37 and 1942–43 increased only moderately—3,47,530 acres, which was an approximate increase of 9 per cent.[20] The third annual conference of the Assam Provincial Muslim League was held in the first week of April 1944 at Barpeta in Lower Assam, whose floodplains had seen a proliferation of several thousand settlements of Bengali peasants. Jinnah was unable to attend the conference, and Choudhry Khaliquzzaman, a prominent Muslim League leader from Lucknow, presided over the meeting. Around the same time, in April 1944, M.A. Rashid, a member of the Muslim League from Lower Assam, wrote to Jinnah complaining against Saadulla:[21] 'Can he say that he gave a smooth running to the immigrants of Assam?' According to Rashid, the Assam premier lacked the courage and strength to allow the immigrants to settle; he had also not abolished the Line System. Jinnah, then in Srinagar, assured Rashid that his concerns would 'certainly receive' his 'very careful attention . . . but the question of how to tackle it properly still remains'.[22] If Saadulla's conservative colleagues were apprehensive about his intentions, the Assam Governor, Andrew G. Clow, had his own share of concerns. Till now, Saadulla had been firmly in control of his government despite his temptation to resign. Clow wrote how Saadulla, whom he considered not the best candidate to govern an Indian province, had told him that he 'would rather be a living rat than a dead lion'. He was not a man to give up, Clow admitted in February 1943, and he found it 'impossible to watch people doing indifferently what he thinks he can do well himself'.[23] Weeks later, Saadulla caved in as he realized that he was losing his grip over his ministry, that his colleagues in the League were stronger now and that the pressure from the Bengal government was mounting,[24] besides which he faced continued resistance from the immigrants and persistent pressure from the central government to encourage the 'Grow More Food' campaign.

After a visit to Assam in December 1943, Viceroy Wavell highlighted that Assam's 'chief political problem is the desire of the Moslem ministers to increase this immigration into the uncultivated government lands under the slogan of "Grow More Food", but what they are really after is "grow more Moslems"'.[25] Senior British officials in the 1930s and 1940s repeatedly expressed their concern at the political and social implications of the continuous flow of peasants from the districts of East Bengal. That this had only served to strengthen the League's claim on Assam was admitted by several, including Robert Reid, Clow's predecessor as Governor of Assam. The 'more Muhammadens you have in Assam, the stronger the case for Pakistan', he commented in 1944.[26] Clow wrote in 1943,

> The immigrant question is, for most Hindus, the big cloud on the horizon. The easygoing and peace-loving Assamese have good reason to fear that they will be largely ousted by the upending and prolific stream of Mymensinghis, who will bring prosperity for a time, but may ultimately, by sheer numbers, reduce the countryside to the standards of Mymensingh.[27]

His viceroy agreed: 'The native Assamese are lazy and likely to be ousted by more push[y] but less attractive Bengali Moslems.'[28]

Amidst this intensifying political battle, in April 1944, C. Rajagopalachari, the ex-premier of Madras and by now out of favour with the Congress, with approval from Gandhi, conveyed to Jinnah the need for a political resolution of the Hindu–Muslim political question. He hinted at accepting the Muslim League's idea of Pakistan.[29] Rajaji's acceptance of the idea of Pakistan was, however, conditional: after the war and the British transfer of power to Indians, a commission would demarcate 'contiguous districts in the Northwest and East of India, wherein the Muslim population is in absolute majority'.³⁰ In this demarcated area, a plebiscite would be held to decide 'the issue of separation from Hindustan'. However, for this to happen, the Muslim League would need to endorse the demand for Indian independence and cooperate with the Congress to form a national government. Gandhi and Jinnah met and exchanged letters in the following months. Gandhi wrote to Jinnah explaining his reluctant and conditional approval to divide the country.³¹ The Rajaji–Gandhi–Jinnah dialogues sparked off protests in Punjab and Bengal, including those by the Hindu Mahasabha and the Akalis.³² Jinnah, too, was not persuaded by these promises and said that Gandhi's consent to the division of India into Pakistan and Hindustan did not come from his 'heart'.³³ Jinnah pressured Gandhi to accept the Muslim League's two-nation theory and also that 'sovereign Muslim states must be composed substantially of the British Indian provinces now regarded as Muslim (e.g., Sind, Baluchistan in the north-west, the North-West Frontier Province and the Punjab, and Assam and Bengal in the north-east)'.³⁴ Jinnah also spoke to international audiences about his idea of Pakistan.³⁵ Despite the pressure created by Jinnah, the negotiations fell apart.

The C.R. formula refuelled Assam's panic at the prospect of being included in Pakistan. Ex-premier Gopinath Bardoloi, now out from prison, sought an assurance from Rajaji against any such a possibility. The latter replied that Bardoloi should 'rest assured all the facts will be kept in view'.³⁶ Others like the firebrand Assamese public figure Ambikagiri Raychowdhury warned Gandhi against this.³⁷ Meanwhile, as the Gandhi–Jinnah dispute raged, several influential personalities formed a committee to seek reconciliation. Chaired by Tej Bahadur Sapru and with members like the philosopher S. Radhakrishnan, industrialist John Mathai and academic Sachchidananda Sinha amongst others, the committee's report would become an inspiration for the future Constitution of India. In the course of its deliberations, the committee received several letters from Assam, including that of Bardoloi to Rajaji and another sent by Rohini Kumar Chaudhuri.³⁸ Its report indicated that the 'inclusion of Assam with the Eastern Zone of Pakistan does not appear to be justified by facts'.³⁹

Apart from the Assam unit of the Communist Party of India, endorsement of the principle of self-determination advocated by the C.R. formula came from the All Assam Ahom Association.[40] Formed in 1893 as Ahom Sabha, the Association was initially a moderate force representing the political aspirations of Assam's longest-serving ruling dynasty till the end of the 1930s. This moderate outlook of the Association changed swiftly from 1941 onwards, as it metamorphosed into a political entity, secured legislative representation and began to push for the idea of a separate minority identity. The Association's new ambitions were unmistakably spelt out by Surendranath Buragohain, a bright lawyer turned lawmaker. The Association admired Rajaji's formula of the principle of self-determination in the hope of achieving its dream of creating a sovereign state of Assam.[41]

On the other hand, the thought of Assam's inclusion in East Pakistan fired the imagination of Bengal's Muslim intelligentsia.[42] In 1944, Mujibur Rahman Khan, a prolific journalist and a literary personality, published his *Eastern Pakistan: Its Population, Delimitation, and Economics* as the Gandhi–Jinnah talks were underway. Spelling out East Pakistan's political, economic and territorial goals, Khan gave his reasons for proposing the inclusion of Assam: 'Eastern Bengal districts are literally expanding to Assam'. Khan's ideas were seriously contested by the Assamese intelligentsia, who believed the Congress leadership had been unfamiliar with Assam's special circumstances in the past. A quick response came from Harendranath Barua, a lawyer and, later, a journalist, who often disagreed with the Congress. Barua's *Reflections on Assam cum Pakistan* was a lengthy rebuttal of the Muslim League's demands.[43] Bardoloi thought this work 'has marshalled only the most essential and unassailable facts of history and has relied on undisputable authority to prove' why 'Assam cannot be included in any state of Pakistan'.[44] Barua's apprehensions were, however, assuaged when Rajendra Prasad, who would be the first President of independent India, gave a more detailed rebuttal to the idea of including Assam in Pakistan.[45] His insights were crucial in shaping the Congress stand on Assam.

Jinnah's demand for a separate Pakistan gained further momentum after Rajaji's formula fell through. Meanwhile, the bitter political battle on the question of Assam's land settlement turned chaotic. In 1945, the Congress, through political negotiations, succeeded in reining in the government to place a restraint on the free distribution of land. The Muslim League-led government outlined that future land distribution would be regulated through the official machinery, no newcomers would be encouraged and Assamese sons of the soil would get preference. Among the Bengali-speaking population, only those who arrived before 1938 would be entitled to land. The government also promised to evict all unlawful settlers. But on the ground, ways were found around this official policy.

In August 1945, Wavell announced elections for the Indian central and provincial legislative assemblies. If for the Muslim League it was a test of their popular claims for the demand of Pakistan, the Congress had to prove that it had support across religious and ethnic groups. For the Muslim League, Punjab was the main battleground[46], and Assam was not far behind. Elections took place in January 1946.[47] Of the 14 per cent of the total population of Assam who were eligible to vote—a limited franchise based on wealth but including many new beneficiaries of the wartime redistribution of wealth—a little more than half voted (52.3 per cent of the general and 53.1 per cent of the Muslim electorate). A fairly large number of women voters, 56 per cent, exercised their right.[48]

The Congress, led by Bardoloi, had a well-organized political machinery and was aggressively pursuing linguistic nationalism as one of its election planks. It was lucky to have both Gandhi and Nehru visit Assam to galvanize support.[49] On the other side, the Muslim League was confident about the loyalty of the Muslim voters, and they even surmised that the 'aboriginals and the tribal population' did not owe their allegiance to the Hindus, which made them believe that Assam was a Muslim-majority province.[50] The results were as expected. The League won a majority of the Muslim seats, while the Congress won the general and most of the reserved seats.[51] The Congress far outstripped the ultra-nationalist Ahom Association in securing the support of the ethnic Assamese. The League was jubilant with the election results: 'Assam Muslims have given the clearest verdict in favour of this in the last elections.'[52] A section of the Muslims, however, voted differently. They were inspired by the political and social ideas of Jamiat Ulema-e-Hind (JUH), whose leader, Maulana Hussain Ahmad Madani, consistently opposed the ideas of the Muslim League.[53] The JUH remained steadfastly close to the Congress, both ideologically and electorally.[54] The former won two seats in Sylhet and one in Cachar.[55] A European planter backed by the Congress contested a European seat but was defeated heavily. The communists and the Ahom Association combined got less than 1 per cent of the vote.[56]

~

The Bardoloi-led government was sworn in on 1 February 1946, with the Muslim League as a strong voice in the opposition. Saadulla extended an olive branch to Bardoloi, but his colleagues did not. Jinnah visited Shillong in the first week of March[57] and reiterated his dream of the inclusion of Assam in Pakistan. When the members of the League met in Delhi in April 1946, Saadulla spoke his mind: 'Assam's physical situation is such that it leaves no alternative to Assam but to join Pakistan.'[58] The Muslim League demanded that all of Assam be included in East Pakistan without partitioning the province or excluding any area based on language, culture or land tenure.

The premier's hands were full as he assumed charge. Days previously, Bardoloi had overtly denounced the idea of the Assam hills as a Crown colony (see Chapter 1): 'I can hardly understand how such a plan could be entertained by anybody.'[59] His government also had to take a tough stand on the recent settlers, and the first major task was to carry out evictions, which the government began enforcing by early May 1946.[60] Meanwhile, Patel was in constant touch with Wavell to ensure the situation in Assam did not go out of control. Before the eviction drive snowballed into a major political crisis, there were other political challenges that had to be tackled. On 19 February 1946, Lord Pethick-Lawrence, secretary of state for India, announced a special mission to India. Three British Cabinet ministers—Pethick-Lawrence, Stafford Cripps and A.V. Alexander—would hold discussions with Indian leaders to set up an apparatus for framing the constitutional structure for independent India. The Mission arrived in Delhi on 24 March, and the next few weeks witnessed intense political discussions. At the viceroy's summer capital in Shimla, the Mission listened to politicians, governors of provinces, lawyers, newsmen, top functionaries of the Congress, Muslim League leaders and also leaders of the Indian provinces, including the Sikh political and religious leader, Tara Singh. Both Bardoloi and Khan Abdul Ghaffar Khan from the North-West Frontier Province (NWFP) were interviewed by the Cabinet Mission on 1 April. Wavell, temperamentally sceptical of Indian leaders, was impressed by Bardoloi's 'forcible and quicker intelligence' but found his personality unpleasing. Battered by a series of domestic problems, including a devastating flood and strikes by telecom and postal employees, Bardoloi had to convince the Cabinet Mission about Assam's unique situation. He presented a detailed history of Assam, apprised the Mission that the Centre took away all the profits from Assam's oil and tea and reassured them that there was no truth in the League's claim that Assam was full of uncultivated lands, and that the hill people would like to remain under the Assam government.[61] When Bardoloi, who 'cared neither for prizes nor for the dictates of his party's high command',[62] proudly declared that Assam had always been a 'great independent kingdom before the British came', Wavell politely reminded him that the British Empire had rescued Assam from Burmese rule.[63] A day later, on 2 April, Saadulla, who was not in his best form and 'was not very clear on the main issue', insisted on the inclusion of the entire province of Assam in East Pakistan: Assam, he said, 'was largely dependent on Bengal for many of its civilised amenities'. An Assam removed from the protection of Bengal would have to maintain a police force to keep itself safe against 'raids from the hill tribes', Saadulla concluded.[64]

On 12 May, Jinnah issued a statement that the six Muslim-majority provinces (Bengal and Assam, in the north-east, and the Punjab, NWFP, Sindh and Baluchistan in the north-west) would constitute a separate

Gopinath Bardoloi, Assam premier speaking to journalists after his meeting with the British Cabinet Mission in New Delhi in 1946

constitution-making unit to decide on all subjects except foreign affairs, defence, and defence-related communication.[65] The Mission rejected this proposal, and after protracted negotiations between the League and the Congress, made its offer. At 7 p.m. on 16 May, the Mission announced through a global broadcast the offer of an independent Indian Union supported by a complex constitutional mechanism. What was envisaged was a three-tier government structure.[66] There would be a minimal Union government at the top, vested with powers of foreign affairs, defence and communication. Below that would be the provinces and the princely states. The second tier would merge into the next tier comprising three zones: Section A consisting of the Hindu-majority provinces, Section B consisting of the Muslim-dominated areas of the north-west and the north-east and Section C consisting of the Hindu-dominated areas in the rest of India, including Assam and Bengal. The Union government at the top would bind these structures together into a loose federation. Each Provincial Legislative Assembly was to elect a total number of seats proportional to its population. Group C would have 70 seats (36 Muslims and 34 Hindus), where Assam's total seats would be 10 (seven Hindus and three Muslims). After 10 years, any province could seek reconsideration of the terms of the constitution. A Constituent Assembly representing a cross-section of the population of India, 'as broad based and accurate' as possible, would decide the details of the constitution. An elaborate method of assuring representation of all the communities was outlined, with due consideration given to the representation of the states as well as the provinces.

Jinnah found the Cabinet Mission Plan attractive 'because it gave him the assurance of being able to control Groups B and C. It was only because of this that he accepted it', wrote George Abell, private secretary to Wavell, to Mountbatten in April 1947.[67] The Congress leadership in Assam could not reconcile itself to being grouped with Bengal, which would be Muslim-majority with 33 seats reserved for Muslims. Whatever the constitutional nitty-gritty of the proposal, that Assam was to be a junior partner to Bengal in this scheme of constitutional arrangement was sure to immediately spark off an adverse reaction in Assam. Wavell had sensed such trouble. He noticed that, as the statement was finalized on 16 May 1946, Nehru was perceptibly worried about the merger of Assam and Bengal. Nehru, Wavell thought, had forced himself to believe that, given their territorial proximity, there were very few options.[68] Within days, Bardoloi rushed to Delhi to assert Assam's opposition to the idea of grouping with Bengal, though he concurred with the larger scheme.[69]

~

For a long time, before the advent of the British, Assam and Bengal had enjoyed a healthy exchange of ideas through traders, scholars, pilgrims and religious preachers. However, a competitive relationship between the two began to firmly take root towards the closing decades of the nineteenth century. Economic opportunities, linguistic pride and cultural rivalries, among other factors, contributed to this hostility. But not everyone was influenced by this competitive nationalistic pride. Appreciation of each other's cultural and economic milieu continued; many Assamese benefitted from the booming economic enterprises of colonial Bengal. Pragyasundari Devi, who belonged to the Tagore family of Calcutta, married Lakshminath Bezbaroa, Assam's cultural doyen. In her celebrated recipe book, *Amish o Niramish Aahar*, published in 1902, a few of her meticulously detailed Bengali recipes were blended with Assamese cuisine. The comradeship between the Bengalis and Assamese flourished in other ways too. Ashutosh Mukherjee, one of Bengal's scholarly doyens who infused new pride into India's literary history, spearheaded a literary movement in which Assamese was given significant attention. The result was the publication of the multi-volume *History of Assamese Literature*.[70] But the twentieth century's electoral politics, appeal to linguistic nationalism and Bengal's assumed role as the custodian of eastern India's economic fate displaced that mutual respect and comradeship. Added to these was the political crisis that unfolded due to the land settlement programme and the rise of provincial electoral politics. Assam now saw Bengal as her forceful opponent.

The Cabinet Mission Plan left enormous scope for ambiguity, which was actually a matter of relief for the Assamese leaders. They sought further clarification on the prospective implications of the plan from Gandhi and other Congress leaders. Was it compulsory to be included in a group with Bengal? Would Bengal have a say in matters of Assam? And was the colonial decision to maintain Assam and Bengal as a single economic unit simply a means to serve the interests of the British Empire?[71] After a lengthy correspondence, it became clear that Bengal would indeed have a say in Assam's matters and that both states would be part of the same group, though in the margin of a letter from Gandhi about this, Wavell noted, 'The answer must be a very definite and decided "No".'[72] Assam was not alone; NWFP and the Sikhs, too, joined the voices of opposition. Master Tara Singh wrote to Pethick-Lawrence stating that bringing 'the whole province of Assam where the non-Muslims are in overwhelming majority' under Muslim domination was 'evidently done to placate the Muslims'.[73] Bardoloi, fast emerging as the trusted leader of a linguistic community, made Assam's opposition clear. By May 1946, the Assam Provincial Congress Committee expressed apprehensions about the grouping of Assam with Bengal.[74] It argued that such a grouping would undermine Assam's identity as a 'distinct unit in the Indian Union' and convert the political majority into a minority.[75] Fault lines within the Congress on the issue of grouping Assam with Bengal now became apparent. Many Hindu Congress leaders, including Assam's home minister, Basanta Kumar Das, who came from the Surma Valley, favoured the grouping with Bengal.[76] Bengal was happy that the Mission proposal had saved it from imminent partition. Huseyn Shaheed Suhrawardy, Bengal's premier who consistently campaigned for a united Bengal, warned the viceroy that 'Assam would try to go out of the Bengal group at the earliest', though Bengal would have an 'economic stranglehold' on Assam.[77] A section of Bengal's Hindu leaders, belonging to both the Congress and the Hindu Mahasabha, and also nationalist Muslim leaders, however, extended their moral support to Assam.[78]

Assam's Congress leadership aggressively reached out to the national leadership. Intense bargaining started between the leaders of the All-India Congress Committee (AICC) and the Assam Congress.[79] Maulana Abul Kalam Azad had best captured Assam's staunch opposition to this plan, writing that 'they [Assam] said that if Bengal and Assam were grouped together, the whole region would be dominated by Muslims'. On 14 June, Azad wrote to Wavell that 'the Frontier Province and Assam have expressed themselves with considerable force against any compulsory grouping'.[80] The Assam Congress seized this opportunity to mobilize public opinion against the proposal, and the anti-grouping popular protests—which were joined by peasants, workers, students, leaders of the tribal communities and others—spread across the Brahmaputra Valley.[81] For several weeks, Assam's political landscape remained animated with anti-Cabinet Mission political activities. The battle was fought on the turf of constitutionalism and the political future of Assam. The Asom Jatiya Mahasabha (initially known as the Asom Sangrakhini Sabha), the communists and the Congress socialists joined hands with the Congress.[82] Numerous meetings took place, and hundreds of telegrams opposing Assam's inclusion in Section C were sent to the AICC. Emboldened by the popular mood, the Assam Congress leadership lost no opportunity to challenge the Cabinet Mission Plan. The Muslim League's support for the inclusion of Assam in a group to be dominated by Bengal further hardened the adamant position taken by Assam; the NWFP and the Sikhs were also against this. Jinnah knew that they 'could not be forced to do so'.[83]

Meanwhile, B.N. Rau prepared an outline for the secretariat of the future Constituent Assembly. Rau made it clear that each provincial secretariat required specific expertise: 'No one will be able to draft a satisfactory constitution for Assam without intimate knowledge of its sharply contrasted valley, its excluded and partially excluded areas.'[84] Assam's spirited public campaign took a wider political form when, on 16 July 1946, a special session of the Assam Legislative Assembly, which was yet to elect Assam's representatives to the Constituent Assembly, gave an opportunity to the Congress-led government to adopt a resolution refusing to join Section C.[85] The Congress lawmakers also vowed to draft a separate constitution for Assam—as a step towards achieving its cherished dream of full provincial autonomy. The carefully worded resolution read, 'Assam has an undoubted claim to have the Constitution of the province framed and settled by its own representatives elected to the Constitution Assembly. Assam would not be part of any section as planned by the Cabinet Mission.'[86] Saadulla, though he stood by his party and defended the connection of Assam with Bengal for keeping its economic linkages intact, skilfully extended his support for the ideals enshrined in the resolution.[87] Bardoloi, as he summed up the debate, cited Saadulla's repeated references to 'the integrity and dignity' of Assam and 'its right to be considered in terms of equality with any other Province'.[88]

Assamese public figures stood solidly behind the Congress but also appealed to the people to remain vigilant. In a lengthy essay in the widely circulated *Dainik Assamiya*, Harendranath Barua warned the Assamese not to be assured only by the Congress's commitment to Assam's refusal to be part of any specific section and its right of self-determination.[89] Debeswar Sarmah, speaker of the Assam Legislative

Assembly, sent a strongly worded telegram to the British government in November: 'Assam cannot and shall not accept undemocratic and anti-national position of her future constitution being framed by Bengal . . . shall struggle for true provincial autonomy inside framework of one whole Indian constitution.' His telegram also asked the British 'not to balkanize India to placate Jinnah'.[90]

But not everyone in Assam agreed with the Congress's stand.[91] The prospect of joining Pakistan or not joining India appealed to many Ahoms, who were largely sceptical of the Hindu domination in Assam's political machinery, during 1944–46, but in a contested and limited way.[92] Surendranath Buragohain, a lawmaker, wrote to Jinnah that if the 'League respects aspirations of Assam's minorities, I hope Assam's backing may later be available to the League to set up another Union, provided Assam's sovereign right to secede or opt out from it is guaranteed'.[93] Meanwhile, several tribal communities strongly articulated their position regarding their political future, contrary to the wishes of the Assamese political leaders. In the nineteenth century, the British Empire had formulated a highly complex system of governance in the areas inhabited by these communities. These areas remained largely untouched by British rule, and there was limited penetration of British capital. Yet, most parts remained within Assam's administrative ambit. By virtue of this, and also because of the historical linkages which were largely snapped during the earlier decades, the Assamese-speaking population aspired to retain their cultural and political control over these territories. As Independence approached, political activities in these areas created panic among Assamese leaders.

Some others outside the body politic also sensed that there were problems with this grouping proposal for Assam. One of them was the British anthropologist, Verrier Elwin, who had made India his home and had started working among Indian tribal communities. It was his emphatic defence of the tribal people and their world view that familiarized urban Indians with a world hitherto unknown to them. In 1946, Elwin was the second-in-command of the newly established Anthropological Survey of India. He had not yet visited Assam. As Assam's anti-grouping movement became known across India, Elwin sent a scathing letter to the *Times of India*, opposing both the popular notion that the tribes of Assam wanted to be included in Pakistan and that they were anxious to be grouped with Bengal.[94] This was not the case, Elwin said, quoting J.H. Hutton's presidential address to the Royal Anthropological Institute. Hutton, whom Elwin considered the 'greatest authority [on] the Naga tribes', said that the tribes of Assam have an intense love for independence, 'nor has it been lost on them that Mr Jinnah has claimed the whole of Assam for his Pakistan, and his movement is one with which they have not the remotest sympathy'.[95] These developments, however, did little to affect the political fate of Assam in the immediate term. Neither did this help the two-nation theory gain any further ground in Assam.

Meanwhile, their task unfulfilled, the Cabinet Mission left for England at the end of June. On 10 August 1946, the Congress Working Committee (CWC) accepted the Cabinet scheme, barring some proposals. Assam sent 10 members to the Constituent Assembly—seven from Congress and three from the League. Their nominations were a matter of intense public scrutiny. The next few months were eventful; ups and downs in the mood of the Assam Congress were easily noticeable. As events began to unfold dramatically and contrary to the expectations of Assam, the Nehru-led interim government and the Constituent Assembly were formed. Assam tried hard to win support from the AICC. A visit by Ram Manohar Lohia, the socialist leader to Assam, in the last week of August 1946 boosted the morale of the Assamese leadership. The CWC was largely of the view that the Congress 'should not reopen the question of grouping'. Meanwhile, Nehru moved fast to give concrete shape to the proposals of the Cabinet Mission Plan. His interim government was sworn in on 2 September 1946.

Despite being isolated, Assam, the NWFP and the Sikhs persisted with their demands. When Patel dined with Wavell on 5 September 1946, he expressed his apprehension about Assam being placed in Section C, where it 'might be overwhelmed' by Muslims.[96] Wavell assured him that the Muslims would only have a narrow majority. To placate Assam's opposition, Maulana Azad wrote to the viceroy opposing the participation of European members in the Constituent Assembly.

The viceroy agreed as the Europeans in the Bengal Assembly declared their intention to not seek representation. Azad refused to make any more concessions and said, 'Jawaharlal agreed with me that the fears of the Assamese leaders were unjustified and tried hard to impress them with his views.' Senior Congress leaders like Rajendra Prasad and C. Rajagopalachari, too, felt that Assam's fear was 'unrealistic'.[97]

Nehru and others continued to assure the Assamese leaders of support. On 17 September 1946, Nehru wrote to Ambikagiri Raychowdhury, the general secretary of the Asom Jatiya Mahasabha, saying that 'it is for the province to agree or not to agree' on the question of forming groups. Days later, he reiterated a similar stand to Bardoloi. Nehru made it clear that 'in no event are we going to agree to a province like Assam being forced against its will to do anything . . . Whatever they (developments in the Constituent Assembly) might be, if Assam is strong enough nothing can happen to Assam that it does not like'.[98] Jinnah took strong objection to Nehru's stand. He wrote to the viceroy that 'in this highly surcharged and explosive atmosphere, even to think of the proposed Constituent Assembly . . . is neither advisable nor possible'.[99]

To help Assam overcome its fear of being dominated by Bengal, the Mission proposed that it would refer this dispute to a federal court. The Congress saw it as a way out of this deadlock. Meanwhile, much to Nehru's relief, the League also joined his government towards the end of October 1946. They, however, refrained from joining the Constituent Assembly, which was to assemble from 9 December. On 21 November 1946, Jinnah took the final decision to dissociate the League from the Constituent Assembly. In the meantime, much to the worry of Assam, on 6 December 1946, Wavell made it clear that Assam could not opt out of the grouping until after the new elections.[100]

When the Constituent Assembly assembled for the first time on 9 December 1946, the question of Assam loomed large. On 18 December, J.J.M. Nichols Roy, the towering tribal leader, spelt out Assam's refusal to be part of Section C with Bengal. Over several weeks, Assam secured support for its position from many others. 'I see in particular no justification whatsoever for compelling Assam to form a common government with Bengal—for any purpose,' said Hridya Nath Kunzru. Patel, too, remained decidedly with Assam. On 15 December, Patel wrote a strongly worded letter to Stafford Cripps: 'If you think that Assam can be coerced to accept the domination of Bengal, the sooner you rid of that disillusion the better.'[101] But the boldest moral support to Assam came from none other than Gandhi, which was a matter of concern for the AICC leadership. He held a series of meetings with anxious Assamese leaders, encouraged them to remain true to their conviction and opposed the Cabinet Mission Plan. On 15 December, two senior Congress leaders met Gandhi in Srirampur, the centre of his famous Noakhali tour, seeking his advice on this matter. 'I do not need a single minute to come to a decision, for on this I have a mind,' an exasperated Gandhi told his guests.[102] 'Whether you have that courage, grit and the gumption, I do not know. You alone can say that. But if you can make that declaration, it will be a fine thing. As soon as the time comes for the Constituent Assembly to go into Sections, you will say, "Gentlemen, Assam retires".' Gandhi reminded his guests that he had the same piece of advice for the Sikhs as well. He also told them that the arbitration in the federal court would go against Assam's wishes.

Gandhi's advice worried many Muslims across India. They believed that it not only contradicted his own suggestion to the League to join the Constituent Assembly but also his advocacy of Hindu–Muslim unity. Gandhi, however, did not change his opinion. 'Why should Assam be absorbed in Bengal against its will or the Frontier Province or the Sikhs into the Punjab and Sind?'[103] Gandhi advised Assam to take 'care of itself' and 'the rest of India will be able to look after itself'.

Gandhi's strong censure compelled the Congress to soften its stand on Assam. On 22 December 1946, Nehru submitted a confidential draft to the CWC, where he clearly stated, 'It is well known that the proposal in regard to grouping affected injuriously two provinces especially, namely Assam and the North West Frontier Province, as well as the Sikhs in the Punjab.'[104] He added, 'The time may come when Assam will have to fight; that fight will not be single-handed but will be waged with the whole of India behind them.' He said that he was quite 'alive to the dangers' that confronted them (including the mass migration of Bengali Muslims into Assam), and that Assam should take 'a positive and constructive approach'.

In the first week of January 1947, the AICC gave a public statement, which stated, among other things, 'There must be no interference whatsoever by any external authority, and no compulsion of any province or part of a province by another province.'[105] Assam's strong opposition to the Cabinet Mission Plan and the Muslim League's equal emphasis on Assam's acceptance of the grouping remained the bone of contention. Azad wrote that 'nobody can understand why the League placed so much emphasis on the question of Assam, when Assam was not a Muslim majority province'. As pressure mounted in Assam and Punjab, Azad had to write to the viceroy about the relentless opposition against the grouping. 'The Frontier province and Assam have expressed themselves with considerable force against any compulsory grouping.'[106]

When Lord Louis Mountbatten, whose arrival in India in April 1947 as the new viceroy intensified the negotiations for the transfer of power, enquired as to why Assam was so resolutely against the Cabinet Mission arrangement, Clow explained that of Assam's 10 million people, 3.5 million were Hindus and 2.5 million Muslims; the rest, he said, were divided between Scheduled Castes and Tribes. The weak representation of the tribal population in the legislature had given the Congress an electoral majority. If Assam were to sit in the same section as Bengal, the Congress would be outnumbered; and if the tribal population was to be given seats in the legislature on a pro rata basis, the Congress would be outnumbered by the joint effort of tribals and Muslims.[107] Mountbatten understood the concerns of Assam. Writing to Patel on 16 May 1947, he agreed that . . .

> there always was inherent in this plan the risk that a provincial constitution might be rigged by the majority in a Section; in the case of Assam, there undoubtedly has been a fear on the part of the present Assam ministry that a constitution devised for Assam by Section C would be such as would in effect put them out of office.[108]

Meanwhile, he had had a series of meetings with Jinnah and Nehru, among others. When Mountbatten privately informed Nehru that Jinnah would ask for the partition of Assam, the latter said that 'this was a perfectly reasonable request and could easily be agreed to'.[109]

By May 1947, the Cabinet Mission Plan collapsed. This was undeniably a victory for the Assam government.[110] What was critical on the eve of Independence was the increasing clamour for regional economic and political freedom. The Assamese leaders' anti-grouping agitation was also founded on this political premise. In the Constituent Assembly, Assam's representative eloquently spelt out these ideas. In 1947, the editorial of *Abahon,* a respected liberal Assamese literary magazine, spoke of how every unit of the Union of India had the right to work independently, depending on their needs.[111] Meanwhile, as the Cabinet Mission Plan turned to dust, the prospect of Partition became clear.

~

Between March 1946 and May 1947, Assam witnessed a catastrophic political battle that ran parallel to the crisis arising out of the Cabinet Mission Plan. Bengali Muslim peasants had clashed with the police from the time Bardoloi's government, after being elected in February 1946, quickly set the tone for an aggressive policy of eviction. Within the first few months of coming to power, the government evicted a couple of thousand settlers from government-owned grazing reserves, including tribal people and caste Hindu peasant families. Most of the land remained free for a brief period before being occupied again.[112] Clashes between Bengali settlers and the Assamese peasantry had been localized in earlier decades; now they became widespread.

The economic integration of Bengali settlers and Assamese peasants was only partial. Sections of the settlers had to borrow money from the Assamese or the Marwari grain traders. Some Assamese landowners welcomed the newcomers as sharecroppers. The Marwari and Assamese traders were the primary buyers of the new settlers' produce, which eventually reached the Bengal markets.

But this complex economic relationship could not be converted into political trust. As the pro-Pakistan movement spread rapidly across East Bengal,[113] it soon overwhelmed Assam's western districts. In their fiery speeches, the leaders of the League projected Assam's unoccupied and unploughed lands as a future haven for Bengali Muslim peasants. Popular mobilization to reclaim government-owned uncultivated lands spread like wildfire. The frenzied pro-Pakistan movement in Assam belonged not to the urbane Saadulla but to the rustic Maulana Abdul Hamid Khan, popularly known as Bhashani. For several years, Bhashani had challenged Saadulla's political leadership. With communist political leanings that saw him fight for poor Muslim peasants against exploitative zamindars in East Bengal, Bhashani's popularity saw a meteoric rise.[114] By 1944, Bhashani, described in one report as 'progressively more and more fiery' and the undisputed leader of the poor Muslim peasants, became the president of the Muslim League in Assam. Choudhry Khaliquzzaman, the Muslim League leader, visited Lower Assam in April 1944 to preside over the League's conference at Barpeta and experienced for himself this blistering orator. Khaliquzzaman had no knowledge of the Bengali in which Bhashani spoke to the restless audiences, but he could very well understand that 'the Maulana spoke . . . in perfect oratorical style . . . could only guess at the trend of his speech . . . he seemed to be emitting fire and warming up the illiterate masses to fever heat'.[115] Soon, Bhashani's political campaign became entangled with sectarian politics, and he campaigned aggressively for the inclusion of Assam in Pakistan.[116] Bhashani wrote, 'Pakistan is our only demand, history justifies it, numbers confirm it, justice claims it, destiny demands it, posterity awaits it, plebiscite verdicts it.' To defend the cause of the immigrant peasants, he had to counter the demands and criticisms of the Assamese peasants. It was for this reason that the majority of Assamese peasants and nationalists felt that Bhashani propagated communal politics. As he aggressively spoke for a merger of Assam with Pakistan, his politics was condemned by the Assamese nationalists.

The previous Saadulla-led government, too, had carried out a moderate programme of eviction of Bengali peasants from government lands towards the end of 1944. This had invited the wrath of Bhashani and his followers, and the government had been forced to stop. An all-party conference was convened in December 1944, and a vaguely worded official policy statement of January 1945 gave political legitimacy to the eviction of recent settlers from Bengal.[117] However, the Congress rejected this on the ground that it would fall short of evicting the peasants. The next few months saw hectic political parleying and a reconstitution of the Muslim League ministry, which now had a wider social and political representation including a key Congress nominee. Finally, another government policy statement on 13 July 1945 spelt out a mechanism of evicting unlawful immigrant settlers who had encroached on government lands post-1938.[118]

The Bardoloi government's eviction programme gave great stimulus to the Muslim League's popularity amongst the Muslim peasants. The League decided to retaliate by organizing innumerable meetings, processions and hartals, provoking its followers to rebuild broken houses, reoccupy paddy fields or take into possession more government lands.[119] The Muslim League in Bengal joined in solidarity. Their lawmakers raised this issue in the Assembly.[120] However, the government refused to soften its stand, with the result that the Bengali peasants became more resolute than ever to support the Muslim League. They were united across class and communal lines, and they vociferously demanded Assam's inclusion in Pakistan.[121] When Saadulla, as leader of the Muslim League in Assam, sat across the table with the Cabinet Mission, he had this looming crisis on his mind. In the face of pressure from Congress lawmakers, who were nervous about the prospect of Assam's merger with Pakistan, the Bardoloi government took a conciliatory approach.

Some reprieve came with the monsoons of 1946. The recently evicted peasants reoccupied their lands in most places, and their fields were green with jute and paddy again. But more confrontation was looming. In the wake of the deadlock arising out of the Cabinet Mission Plan and his inability to score a victory over the Congress, Jinnah appealed to millions of his followers to observe 16 August 1946 as a day of complete hartal,[122] declaring this as 'the most historic act in our history'. Saadulla and some other leaders of the League renounced the titles conferred on them by the imperial government. Jinnah's goal was to secure a bargain with the Congress for greater representation of Muslims in Nehru's interim government. On that fateful day, Calcutta witnessed horrific and brutal killings. Between 16 and 19 August, the city was overwhelmed by a wave of increasing religious polarization and murders,[123] termed the Great Calcutta Killings. Among the victims were the young left-leaning Assamese poet, Amulya Barua, and an Assamese student, Ananda Phukan.[124]

Ravaged by floods, Assam escaped similar violence. Supporters of the League briefly closed down Fancy Bazar, the busiest market in Guwahati.[125] Other shops and markets in the city also remained closed. Thousands marched in the streets of Guwahati shouting slogans of '*larke lenge Pakistan* (we will wrest Pakistan by force)'. This invited the wrath of the urban Assamese.[126] In Sylhet, supporters of the League and the JUH clashed.[127] Guwahati remained tense, as stories spread about the Calcutta violence. The situation was less tense in Upper Assam among Assamese-speaking Muslims.[128] Communists belonging to the Revolutionary Communist Party of India (RCPI) tried to maintain normalcy.[129] Anyway, despite a brief stand-off by the supporters of the League, neither did social relations between Hindus and Muslims or Bengalis and Assamese collapse nor did everyday social interactions and cultural exchanges disappear.

Away from Guwahati, Bhashani's pro-Pakistan campaign gained frantic momentum in the numerous rural bazaars frequented by Bengali Muslim peasants. In his blistering speeches, Bhashani challenged the government and exhorted Muslim peasants to economically boycott non-Muslims. While there was frequent retaliation too— in some places, Nepali milkmen refused to supply milk to Muslim customers[130]—Bhashani travelled widely, met Muslim League activists asking them to resist eviction and encouraged a new wave of migration from the Mymensingh district. For Bhashani, it was an opportunity for the Muslim League in Assam to reiterate the goals of justice for poor peasants and Assam's union with Pakistan.[131]

The Noakhali riots broke out in East Bengal in October 1946, and the news spread to Assam. In this highly polarized environment,

Muslim peasants heeded the call of their leaders. Many started arriving in Assam 'in boats and trains' and 'forcibly squatted over any vacant land', Bardoloi told Patel in a telegram on 15 November 1946.[132] He feared a 'military emergency'. Bardoloi announced his government's intention to begin evictions at this crucial time. As 1946 was nearing its end, peasants across the valley were in the middle of harvesting their winter crops. The first fortnight of November 1946 was 'extremely uneasy'.[133] The leaders of the League knew that the government was adamant on carrying out eviction; there was public pressure from the Assamese. Clashes between the tribal people and the Bengali peasants were also reported from Lower Assam.[134] Sensing trouble, and also to prepare for a stronger resistance, many prospective evictees evacuated and sold their harvested kharif crops. But this did not prevent the inflow of more peasants from Bengal to claim land in Assam.

A massive confrontation loomed between the Muslim peasants and the government. G.E.B. Abell, private secretary to Wavell, enquired of Patel whether the Assam government was not inviting further trouble by 'this dangerous action'. Patel advised Abell to persuade the Muslim League not to encourage further encroachment on land in Assam.[135] Sensing trouble ahead, in mid-November 1946, Bardoloi promulgated the draconian Assam Maintenance of Public Order Ordinance. The early months of 1947 witnessed the simultaneous increase in eviction as well as resistance by re-encroachment. Undeterred by the government's high-handed actions and to boost the morale of its cadres and followers, the Muslim League decided to launch a civil disobedience movement. It sought help from the Muslim National Guard, the Muslim League's paramilitary affiliate, to ensure tough resistance and commissioned volunteers from Bengal.

Towards the end of April 1947, an attempt at a compromise between the government and the League fell through.[136] 'There is no more land to spare and those who say there is, must be thinking of the bed of the Brahmaputra,' said Bardoloi who had toughened his stand.[137] As the confrontation between the League and the government intensified, the soft-spoken Saadulla condemned the eviction as 'mendacious in parts, misleading in general and malicious as a whole'.[138] Police intelligence claimed some 450 public meetings and 180 huge processions were organised to strengthen communal solidarity from March to May. Top leaders of the League appealed to Muslim peasants to grab all wastelands, even at the risk of sacrificing their lives. *Killa*s (makeshift forts) were built on some of these lands, which acted as centres of resistance activities. Several peasants died after the military fired near Tezpur in May 1947. The Muslim peasants became more skilful in the art of resistance and played hide-and-seek with the police. The settlers often abandoned their huts on hearing that the police were approaching only to return soon after the police left.

The Leaguers were happy with the strong and determined resistance that was being put up. The Shillong-based reporter of *Dawn*, the mouthpiece of the Muslim League, claimed that the resistance proceeded 'with the speed of Morocco desert wind, which has already shaken the sandy structure of the Bardoloi ministry'.[139] The peasants in Bengal were tormented by zamindari exploitation, and there was little land available there for expanding families. But the land promised to them in Assam, too, was not free of problems. They frequently fell prey to tricksters, and some of them eventually became sharecroppers to rich Assamese and Bengali Muslim landowners.

The resistance to eviction helped build a pro-Pakistan popular euphoria. Clashes involving Bengali settlers, Assamese peasants, Nepali grazers and the tribal people became frequent, though they remained localized. The Asom Jatiya Mahasabha mobilized Assamese peasants to build a counter-resistance.[140] The Sabha's towering leader, Ambikagiri Raychowdhury, gave fiery speeches exhorting Assamese villagers to form self-defence groups to protect themselves.[141]

However, the pro-Pakistan mobilization had very limited appeal for the Assamese Muslim peasants. These were descendants of Muslims who had come to Assam during the seventeenth-century Mughal–Ahom wars or earlier and had settled here, adopting Assamese cultural practices. Their presence in the pro-Pakistan meetings was negligible. In fact, the Assamese Muslims were apprehensive about the political goals of the Muslim League. A public meeting of Assamese Muslim peasants in Jorhat in April 1947, presided over by Pitambar Deva Goswami, the *satradhikar* of the Garmur Satra, a powerful leader of the Assamese

Hindu peasants and a Hindu Mahasabha sympathizer,[142] lamented the fact that the Assam government had not distributed land to the landless Assamese Muslim peasants. Another resolution described how East Bengali Muslim peasants, who had recently settled in Assam, were a social nuisance to both Assamese Hindus and Muslims.

The Bardoloi government's eviction drive was enforced with full state authority. Crops and homes of thousands were damaged. As the Muslim peasants faced the ruthless assault of the police or military patrol, the flow of newcomers slowed, and many were forced to return to Bengal. Leaders of the Muslim National Guard threatened to retaliate, and their speeches were full of provocative polemics. The Bardoloi government received a moderate rebuke from Gandhi himself, who was asked about the evictions at a prayer meeting in the NWFP on 22 January 1947.[143] Refusing to see a communal angle in this crisis, Gandhi asserted that based on what he had seen in Assam in 1946, this was not a Hindu–Muslim question. Gandhi reiterated that he could not endorse the forcible occupation of government lands—however, he acknowledged that the Assam government would be 'guilty of crime against humanity' if it had evicted lawful residents. While official records are clueless about whether any of those evicted were—in Gandhi's language—lawful settlers, Gandhi was ready to hear another perspective so that he could advise an impartial commission of enquiry.

The political unrest did not remain confined to rural areas. As Muslim peasants retaliated, Marwari traders and policemen became their targets. The situation in towns like Guwahati or Goalpara, government intelligence noted, was 'explosive', with 'mass disobedience' against prohibitory orders.[144] Bardoloi wrote to his counterpart in Bengal to discourage the flow of volunteers of the National Guard into Assam.[145] In the border areas of Bengal, Hindus of Mankachar town fled to the neighbouring Garo Hills.[146] A symbolic Pakistani killa set up near the Assam–Bengal border attracted thousands. To reassure their followers and as a show of strength, the League declared 10 March 1947 as anti-eviction day. The League threatened to send more followers from Bengal to Assam in March 1947, but by April, Mountbatten noted that the plan had been aborted.[147]

Meanwhile, hectic negotiations took place between the government and the Muslim League. Both Saadulla and Bardoloi began to understand the gravity of the situation. At one point, B. N. Rau, the constitutional advisor to the Indian government, had to mediate between the two: 'The situation (in Assam) was extremely tense.'[148] As an outcome of this mediation, the Muslim League was supposed to discontinue their civil disobedience, but the League's local committee did not agree to this.[149]

Violent clashes between peasants and police continued until May 1947.[150] On 3 June, the British government announced the plan for India's independence, which conceded the formation of Pakistan.[151] The Muslim League formally withdrew the anti-eviction movement on 11 June, as the chances of Assam becoming a part of Pakistan had died out.[152] A few Muslim Leaguers, though, continued to entertain stray hopes of Assam's inclusion in Pakistan for some time.[153]

~

Along with the announcement that India would be divided came a declaration of referendums to be held in NWFP and in Sylhet—a district of south-western Assam, with an area of 14,000 square kilometres—which would decide for themselves whether they would become a part of India or Pakistan.[154] If the referendum in Sylhet favoured joining East Bengal, a boundary commission would demarcate the 'Muslim majority areas of the Sylhet district and the contiguous Muslim majority areas of the adjoining districts, which will then be transferred to Eastern Bengal'.[155] At a press conference on 4 June 1947, Mountbatten made it clear that 'the idea was that [if] Assam was to be partitioned, then Sylhet and possibly contiguous areas, in which there is a definite Muslim majority should be separated'.[156]

Bardoloi, who was in Delhi then, quickly endorsed the Sylhet referendum plan. Earlier, when Bardoloi met Mountbatten on 1 May, he had confided that he did not mind losing Sylhet.[157] Given his recent experience in the Constituent Assembly's Tribal Advisory Committee, which was tasked with framing the constitutional mechanism to govern

India's tribal-dominated areas, Bardoloi also urged Mountbatten 'to include a small portion of the Mymensingh district which is contiguous to Garo Hills with a population of fifty to sixty thousand of Garo people' on the same principle of conceding to the 'Muslim League . . . such areas of Assam with Muslim majorities as are contiguous to East Bengal'.[158]

On 7 June, Mountbatten instructed Assam's Governor, Akbar Hydari, to take steps for this referendum.[159] Hydari, worried about the outbreak of communal violence, decided on two important steps: that the existing electoral rolls would be used to conduct the referendum and that symbols would be used for the two choices. The 3 June statement, however, had kept the idea of Sylhet's referendum shrouded in ambiguity. The British government left it to the Bengal legislature to finally approve the idea of the partition of Bengal. That endorsement came on 20 June. On that day, the East Bengal section of the Bengal Legislative Assembly voted for the amalgamation of Sylhet with East Bengal by 105 to 34 votes.[160] The Sylhet referendum was to be held on 6 and 7 July 1947 to decide if the district would join Pakistan.

Sylhet, comprising one-tenth of Assam's total area of 1,42,322 square kilometres, had a many-layered history. It had been governed as a part of Bengal since 1765, when the British East India Company acquired *dewani* rights over it. Beginning in 1874, its boundaries were redrawn several times. Sylhet's sprawling lowlands were regularly inundated by floods, which shaped the local economy. Sandwiched between Assam and Bengal, Sylhet had a dynamic history of population movement. The people of this region 'had close ties both with Bengal to the west and Assam to the east'.[161] While these ties were varyingly further reinforced or disrupted during the nineteenth century, the relationship with the cultural elites of Bengal was deeply fraught. Bipin Chandra Pal, the prominent Indian nationalist, who hailed from Sylhet, regretted that people from Dhaka looked down upon the Sylhetis.[162] Sylhet, with its own distinctive linguistic and literary culture, uniquely shaped by its Sylheti-Nagri script, waged a bitter struggle for its identity.[163]

The birth of Assam as a provincial unit of British India in 1874 was shaped by a range of considerations. The first was the need of arranging the widely dispersed tea plantation areas—distributed between the Sylhet, Cachar and Brahmaputra Valley districts—into one single unit of governance. Planters' interests remained predominant in the affairs of Assam for a long time. This led Bampfylde Fuller, the chief commissioner of Assam (1902–05), to describe the province as truly reflecting the 'character of an English colony'.[164]

Since 1874, there had been growing voices of unhappiness in Sylhet at being appended to Assam, and the district witnessed turbulent times, swinging like a pendulum between the attempts made by Assamese and Bengali speakers to each secure maximum benefits for themselves. Much later, M.S. Aney, a member of the Imperial Legislative Assembly, wrote that 'a deep injury, a deep wound had been inflicted on them [the Bengali-speakers of Sylhet]'.[165] The Hindu zamindars were appalled at the moral and social backwardness of the Assamese.[166] Sylhet's Hindu landlords rose in protest in 1882, when Assam's chief commissioner, William Ward, proposed a uniform set of land laws in conformity with Assam's dominant ryotwari settlement system.[167] Decades later, in 1905, Sylhet became a district of the newly formed East Bengal and Assam province, and when this new province was dismantled in 1911, Sylhet once again became a district of Assam. Since then, the political elite had made frequent demands seeking Sylhet's amalgamation with Bengal. The Hindu and Muslim populations were divided about this. Occasional rifts and anxieties persisted because Sylhet remained with Assam.

In the 1920s and 1930s, the question of the reunion of Sylhet with Bengal resurfaced several times, shaped by the prospects of social, economic and political opportunities in a communally divided environment. In 1926, the Assam Legislative Council passed a resolution favouring Sylhet's transfer to Bengal. Two years later, Padmanath Bhattacharya, the well-known Sanskritist and antiquarian who was then teaching at Guwahati's Cotton College, wrote to the Simon Commission demanding Sylhet's immediate reunion with Bengal.[168] The Muslims, comprising 60 per cent of the population in Sylhet, wanted to stay with Assam. In 1930, the Assam government, in its memorandum submitted to the Indian Statutory Commission, favoured Sylhet's transfer from Assam: 'The Government of Assam have no wish to disparage sentiment nor to underrate its strength in determining a country's history, and, provided no other interests were at stake, they would not oppose the transfer, if convinced that it was the desire of the people.'[169] The loss of Sylhet would, however, mean that Assam could no longer be a Governor's province, which alone entitled an Indian province to have its own legislature. The Assamese elite wanted to let go of Sylhet, but they wanted to retain the benefit of having a legislature.

Over the years, Sylhet had also developed a strained relationship with the Assamese intelligentsia. The latter openly disapproved of Sylhet remaining in Assam, but still wanted to hold on to Goalpara, the westernmost district of Assam. The Assamese intelligentsia feared that the Sylhetis would extract concessions from the government on the basis of their linguistic minority status. In 1874, when a survey was carried out to ascertain the linguistic backgrounds of government employees, the Assamese and the Bengalis were almost equal.[170] But over the decades, and particularly after Sylhet became a part of Assam, the Bengalis began to swell in number. Bengali Hindus held an indomitable sway over government jobs, and of the approximately 6000 government jobs in Assam, the Sylhetis' share was more than one-third in 1931.[171]

In 1935, Jnananath Bora, an Assamese advocate in the Calcutta High Court and author of several works on Assam's economic and political future, spoke before a motley group of Assamese in Calcutta on the need for separation of Sylhet from Assam. His long address, published as *Srihatta Bicched* (Separation of Sylhet),[172] made a strong case. Bora marshalled official figures to show that Sylhet was only a burden on Assam's resources. Sylhet had remained with Assam partly because the Assamese leaders were anxious to preserve Assam's status as a major province with a legislature.[173] However, not everyone from among the Assamese intelligentsia shared Bora's view. Decades earlier, Benudhar Rajkhowa, a civil servant and an Assamese linguist, claimed that the 'ancient literature of Sylhet is Assamese, that the Sylheti dialect has sprung from the Assamese language and that the people of Sylhet are really Assamese',[174] though he agreed that these peculiarities of the Sylheti language no more held true in present times. Lakshminath Bezbaroa, a literary icon of Assam, agreed that Sylheti was a corrupt form of Assamese and argued that 'The Sylheti friends' attempts to become a Bengali is only a matter of convenience'.[175] Further, Lakshminath reminded his readers in 1937, 'Sylhetis live in a borderland, in an ambiguous space, one can side with this or that way at one's will.'[176]

The news of the referendum came as a shock to the Hindu population of Sylhet. They were worried about joining the ruined state of East Bengal and the Muslim-controlled future East Pakistan. The Hindu elite made last-minute attempts to delegitimize the Muslim League's claim for the inclusion of Sylhet in Pakistan, appealing for public funds to mobilize popular support for Sylhet remaining in Assam.[177] A 'false step may lead to a disaster of the first magnitude', they warned their fellow community members.[178] 'By forcible inclusion of the district of Sylhet in the possible Pakistan State of Eastern Bengal, the nationalist aspirations of the people will be smothered, and door will be barred to the large Hindu minority, nearly half of the population, to progress culturally, politically and economically,' lamented Jnananjan Pal, son of Bipin Chandra Pal.[179] Another Bengal resident, R.N. Choudhury, anxiously wrote to Patel that the referendum was 'very ill-timed in as much as the Muslim feelings in Sylhet have been worked up to a white heat of communal frenzy on the issue of eviction of Muslim encroachers from certain Upper Assam districts'.[180] Rohini Kumar Chaudhuri, the Assamese Congressman, had also written to Sardar Patel to postpone the referendum. Choudhury was of the opinion that, given the political climate, the voice of the Hindus of Sylhet would not be heard. A few public meetings in the Brahmaputra Valley also campaigned for the retention of Sylhet in Assam. Leaders of the lower castes warned their community members that they would be deprived of their rights in Pakistan.[181]

While distress calls kept coming to him, Patel made it clear that 'it was impossible to escape from the referendum'.[182] He equally clearly instructed Bardoloi to try his best and 'not remain indifferent' to 'securing votes in favour of the retention of Sylhet in Assam'.[183] Patel was of the opinion that '45 per cent of Hindus are in Sylhet and some of the Muslims are also desiring to remain inside', and thus believed that Sylhet would vote to be with India.

However, unlike their stance in the 1930s, the large majority of Sylhet's Muslim leadership was now solidly behind the idea of joining Pakistan. Jinnah had received this feedback, and he appealed to all the Muslims of Sylhet to 'vote solidly in favour of Sylhet's amalgamation' with Pakistan.[184] Sylhet's sky was already clouded with communalism. In April 1947, violent protests had broken out here against the Bardoloi ministry's eviction programme in the valley.[185] Forceful eviction and state repression against Muslim squatters in Assam became the major plank in the referendum. Clashes took place between Congress ministers and supporters of the JUH and the Muslim League.

Some prominent Indian Muslim leaders thought it would not be a bad thing if Sylhet voted against joining Pakistan, as Assam would, in the near future, anyway become a part of East Bengal as the Muslim population of the province would grow.[186] 'It is reasonable to expect that in the course of the next few years the number of Muslims in the Province shall be equal to the number of caste Hindus and that, thereafter, the Muslims will be the largest single community in the Province,' Nawab Hamidullah of Bhopal wrote to Jinnah with reference to Assam. If 'Sylhet and its surrounding Muslim-majority areas decide to continue as part of Assam, there is every prospect that with passing years Assam will grow closer to East Bengal and that at no distant date the two will decide either to form one Province or to form one group'. However, if 'Sylhet decided to join East Bengal . . . this would mean that Assam would for all time have been abandoned as a part of Pakistan', the Nawab argued.

While the Hindu and Muslim leaders of Bengal and Sylhet campaigned for their respective causes, the wider spectrum of Assamese leaders remained aloof to the referendum. For the large majority of Assamese leaders, the prospect of Sylhet's departure from Assam was a great relief,[187] as long as Assam did not become part of Pakistan and could be spared the burden of political and cultural domination by its sizeable Bengali population. Premier Bardoloi was somewhat an exception, though more than a year before he had told the Cabinet Mission that 'Assam would be quite happy to hand over Sylhet to East Bengal'.[188] As far back as 1944, Governor Andrew Clow, too, had envisaged that, as Sylhet belonged 'linguistically and culturally' to Bengal, there was every chance of Assam losing this district in the event of 'redistribution of the provincial boundaries'.[189] Some of Bardoloi's ministerial colleagues were possibly more candid. Though Bishnu Ram Medhi made a reluctant appeal to Sylhetis to remain in India, Governor Hydari wrote to Mountbatten that Bardoloi's ministers including 'Medhi and the others do not mind if Sylhet goes to eastern Bengal'.[190] Bardoloi himself, quite likely alone except for colleagues like Rohini Kumar Choudhury, and slightly changing his earlier stand, expressed the view that Hindu areas of Sylhet should remain with India.[191] On 8 July, Bardoloi telegrammed Patel that he, along with another senior Congress leader, Prabhu Dayal Himatsingka, had done their 'utmost', but the results were still uncertain.

Though the referendum was to be based on the 1946 electoral rolls, special constituencies of planters, industrialists and teagarden workers were debarred from participating in this referendum. The earliest suggestion that they should be debarred from voting came from Liaquat Ali Khan[192] and was agreed upon by the Reform Commission.[193] This came as a bit of a surprise to the viceroy's office, which sought further explanation. While the total number of votes of the first two groups was rather small (868), of the approximately 2,00,000 workers in the 221 tea gardens of Sylhet, the electoral rolls of 1946 included 11,449 eligible voters.[194] These workers, who were recruited from different Indian provinces and were generally non-Muslims, were denied franchise for their alleged non-indigeneity.[195] K.V.K. Sundaram, the able official from the Reform Commission, who later rose to become India's chief election commissioner, reasoned that these workers were a 'floating population with little or no stake' in the political life of Sylhet.[196] To put it simply, they could not stake claim to participation in the political life of Sylhet. Sylhet's Hindu leaders as also the local Congress fought against this principle till the eve of the referendum.[197] Knowing that a reduced electorate could upset the verdict, they demanded that these workers be allowed to participate in the referendum.[198] Two days before the referendum, Basanta Kumar Das, Assam's home minister, urgently cabled the British Prime Minister, Clement Attlee, demanding that each vote for remaining with India be counted as two votes.[199] Nehru, too, registered a mild protest with Mountbatten against the tea-plantation workers being considered non-eligible for the referendum.[200] Purnendu Gupta of the Indian National Trade Union Congress, who hailed from Sylhet, had already warned Patel about the fate of approximately 0.2 million tea garden labourers in the event of Sylhet deciding to join Pakistan.

The workers in Assam's tea plantations were long-suffering. During the war, their lives were at stake even as the plantation owners reaped profits and earned laurels. A number of tea gardens had to be closed down during the war.[201] The crisis in the gardens only deepened in the months leading up to Independence. Workers in the tea garden were restless, and they demanded higher wages and better conditions. There were some clashes between planters and workers; one European manager in Dibrugarh had died in the last week of June 1947 when violence broke out over rations.[202] 'There were,' the official historian of the Assam Tea Company wrote, 'many occasions where trouble was averted by only the narrowest margin.'[203] The troubles of Sylhet's plantation workers were compounded by their omission from the referendum. On 20 June 1947, Patel made it clear that no 'further changes can be made in regard to the electoral rolls'.[204]

The referendum, thus, took place in a politically charged environment. In the 239 polling stations, arrangements were made for 5,47,000 voters, of which 3,11,000 were Muslim, and 2,36,000 Hindu.[205] There were heavy rains on both days of the referendum.[206] Sylhet was a low-lying area, prone to flooding, and there was water everywhere. Campaigners would miss no opportunity to blame the rains and floods for any outcome of the plebiscite. Sylhetis living away from the area arrived in batches in boats, and many more arrived by train. On those two days, shops closed earlier than usual, and mobile military patrolling was seen at frequent intervals. But the rain did not stop 'unending streams of demonstrators, carrying flags of different organisations, pour[ing] into the town'.[207] 'In spite of the weather, the streets were crowded, and animated scenes were witnessed at the polling stations,' another report mentioned.[208] Labourers from the gardens staged protests on not being allowed to vote.[209]

Sporadic violence broke out. While both the Congress and the Muslim League were accused of forcing their followers to vote, the latter's use of force was widely reported.[210] The Congress, along with the Communist Party of India and the All Assam Manipuri Congress, appealed to voters to choose to remain in India.[211] Volunteers of the Muslim National Guard and the Hindustan National Guard, organizations affiliated with the League and the Hindu Mahasabha, respectively, aroused feelings of panic among people on either side. Accusations of malpractice came from both the Muslim League and the Congress. Mountbatten was of the opinion that some of the charges 'might have some substance', but others were of a trivial nature. Jinnah objected to the symbol of an axe being used on the ballot paper for joining East Bengal, as he said it symbolized injury to oneself. He also perceived H.C. Stock, who was appointed commissioner of the referendum, as anti-Muslim, for he had been a prisoner of war in Turkey during World War I.[212]

Governor Hydari, whose government passed the Assam (Sylhet) Referendum Offence Ordinance, 1947, denied all reports of breakdown of law and order.[213] Hydari confided to Mountbatten that such allegations largely stemmed from the realization that the referendum would result in Sylhet joining Pakistan:[214] Both Jinnah and Nehru demanded an enquiry into these allegations. Nehru was convinced that the referendum process saw 'intimidation, false impersonation, and incursion of Muslim National Guards from Bengal',[215] but he agreed that such instances could not 'materially affect the result'. *Dawn* continued to report about the massive malpractices and harassment of Muslims by Hindu leaders, as well as tampering with ballot boxes.

The strong probability that Sylhet would choose to join Pakistan was well known. In April 1947, during the Governor's conference, Clow had stated that Sylhet would vote 'probably in favour of Pakistan'.[216] Observers outside India, too, had predicted a pro-Pakistan sweep.[217] 'It may be assumed that the Sylhet district will go with eastern Bengal into the Muslim area,' wrote *The Times*, London, on 24 June.[218]

Governor Hydari telegrammed Nehru about the results of the referendum on 14 July 1947, and he also shared the news with the press. Of the total votes, 77.33 per cent, that is, 4,23,660 votes, were valid. Of the valid votes, 2,39,619 and 1,84,041 respectively were for and against joining East Bengal.[219] Thus, more than 56 per cent voted for Sylhet's amalgamation with East Pakistan.[220] In only one of the five subdivisions, South Sylhet, the people had voted overwhelmingly to remain with Assam. When Mountbatten declared the results on 15 July, the fault line was clear. The outcome was in accordance with the linguistic and religious profile of the district.

The results, though expected, unnerved the Hindu leaders; 'the Hindus of Sylhet in all fairness cannot be called upon to abide by the result of this spurious referendum', warned R.N. Choudhury, the Congress leader.[221] But more was in store for the Hindus, as people turned on each other. Muslim tenants humiliated and assaulted Hindu landlords, or their properties were burnt.[222] An exasperated Gandhi condemned the post-referendum violence in Sylhet. 'The referendum there is over but harassment of the people continues. Why have the Muslims there gone crazy? Nationalist Muslims are being killed.'[223]

A section of the Muslims, who were Indian nationalists, had voted in favour of remaining with India. When Mountbatten announced his 3 June 1947 plan, this tiny section was relieved because the Cabinet Mission Plan had been abandoned.[224] They were inspired by the political and social ideas of the JUH, whose leader, Maulana Hussain Ahmad Madani, had appealed to his disciples to oppose Sylhet's amalgamation with East Bengal.[225] Those who campaigned against joining East Pakistan drew attention to a range of challenges they would encounter in Pakistan.[226]

The Sylhet referendum also cast a shadow on the fate of Cachar. Cachar's inhabitants, both Muslim and Hindu, were in general unwilling to be a part of Pakistan. The (Hidimba) Dimasa-Kacharis, whose history of settlement in Cachar predates that of the Bengali speakers, and who were, a long time ago, political masters of the valley, argued before the Bengal Boundary Commission of their strong unwillingness to be a part of Pakistan. 'The original inhabitants of Cachar were mostly Cacharis or Manipuris or aboriginal and animist tribes such as the Kukis, Nagas, and Mikirs who still live in the hills of the north Cachar sub-division.'[227] Assam's Congress leaders shared their sentiment.

The Indian Independence Bill, too, did not carry good news for the Sylheti Hindus. Mountbatten's 3 June statement mentioned that Sylhet's Muslim-majority areas would merge with Pakistan, but the bill proposed something more, which B.N. Rau, the legal advisor to the Constituent Assembly, found flawed.[228] The bill provided that in case Sylhet joined East Bengal, the province of Assam would cease to exist.[229] Similarly, Bengal would cease to exist, and two new provinces—West Bengal and East Bengal—would come into being. The Muslim League interpreted that if the Sylhet referendum resulted in a pro-East Bengal verdict, 'adjoining districts' would also be partitioned.[230] The Congress opposed this provision.[231] The British cabinet agreed to amend this provision of the bill.[232]

Sylhet's merger with Pakistan remained a fraught political subject in post-Partition India. Its incorporation into East Pakistan assured the district of a stock of rice and a significant decline in the prices of tea, which affected the people's livelihoods.[233] Though free from any serious political violence, the Sylheti people's sense of loss of their original homeland, and the subsequent political and economic insecurity in their new homeland, resulted in post-Partition trauma.

# 3

# Birth Pangs

The India Independence Bill of 1947, introduced on 14 July, declared that all of Sylhet would become a part of East Bengal. The same day, the verdict of the Sylhet referendum was announced in favour of Sylhet joining Pakistan. Sylhet's departure posed two problems. Which areas of Sylhet would go to East Pakistan? Would there be a separate boundary commission? The 14 July pronouncement was contrary to Mountbatten's 3 June declaration, under which, in case the Sylhet referendum went in favour of leaving India, a boundary commission would be set up to demarcate the areas of Sylhet that would go to Pakistan, as in the case of Bengal and Punjab. On being alerted by Assam's premier, Bardoloi, and B.N. Rau, the constitutional advisor, Nehru wrote to Mountbatten about this ambiguity.[1] Though the viceroy admitted that there was a contradiction, he left it to the Bengal Boundary Commission to decide on the matter.[2] This commission was to demarcate the Muslim-majority areas of Sylhet and the adjoining districts.[3]

Assam had already sought a separate commission to decide its boundary. Governor Akbar Hydari had conveyed to Mountbatten that the commission appointed for Bengal was not acceptable to Assam.[4] Bardoloi, who was also consulted by Mountbatten, was unhappy about a common commission for Assam and Bengal. He reminded Nehru that Assam could not expect to get a fair deal. And Nehru concurred: 'There is, as a matter of fact, a longstanding difference of opinion between the Bengalees and the Assamese, quite apart from any of them being Hindus or Muslims,'[5] and 'The Boundary Commission consists of eminent Calcutta High Court Judges who naturally will be inclined to view the question more from the point of view of Bengal than of Assam.'[6]

Mountbatten rejected Assam's demand for a separate boundary commission, as he thought it would further delay the process of demarcation.[7] In late June, he finalized the terms of reference of the Bengal Boundary Commission to also include demarcation of 'the Muslim majority areas of Sylhet district and contiguous Muslim majority areas of adjoining districts'.[8] On 30 June, Mountbatten announced the formation of the Bengal Boundary Commission,[9] headed by Cyril Radcliffe and including Justices Bijan Kumar Mukherjea, Charu Chandra Biswas, Abu Saleh Muhammad Akram and S.A. Rahman. Many Congress leaders, including Rabindra Nath Aditya from Sylhet, expressed their displeasure at this turn of events.[10]

~

The first meeting of the commission took place on 9 July at Alipur. The members were divided on communal lines. Two members—Justices Akram and Rahman—felt that the commission could attach to East Bengal 'any Muslim majority areas of any part of Assam that could be described as contiguous to East Bengal'.[11] The other two—Justices Mukherjea and Biswas—disagreed and argued that the commission's jurisdiction was limited to Sylhet and 'contiguous Muslim majority areas (if any) of other districts of Assam that adjoined Sylhet'. Radcliffe, with hesitation and in consultation with Mountbatten, concurred with the later opinion:[12]

> In my view, the question is limited to the districts of Sylhet and Cachar, since of the other districts of Assam that can be said to adjoin Sylhet neither the Garo Hills nor the Khasi and Jaintia Hills nor the Lushai Hills have anything approaching a Muslim majority of population in respect of which a claim could be made.

The government of East Bengal argued that 'the whole of the District of Sylhet at least must be transferred to East Bengal', but the commission rejected this view too.

From 4 August 1947, the commission held meetings in Calcutta for three days to listen to the counsels of the Government of East Bengal, the Muslim League, the Government of Assam, the Assam Provincial Congress Committee and the Assam Provincial Hindu Mahasabha.[13] In a lengthy memorandum to the commission, the Nikhil Cachar Haidimba Barman Samiti exhorted it 'not to include an inch of land of Cachar district in the Pakistan state'.[14] Planters, communist leaders and labour unions of Sylhet demanded that Sylhet's tea belt remain with Assam.[15] Radcliffe was not personally present but was supplied with the daily records of the Calcutta proceedings. The commission then met in Delhi for the final deliberations.

On 17 August, two days after Independence, the award was finally published, under which Assam would retain the four thanas (a thana is an area under the jurisdiction of a police station) of Patharkandi, Ratabari, Karimganj and Badarpur.[16] These thanas were crucial to protecting southern Assam's plantation economy and also Assam's link with Tripura.[17] Radcliffe had found that eight of the 35 thanas in Sylhet had non-Muslim majorities. Of these, two were surrounded by Muslim thanas, while the remaining six were part of two subdivisions on the southern border of Sylhet. Radcliffe concluded that 'some exchange of territories must be effected if a workable division is to result. Some of the non-Muslim thanas must go to East Bengal and some Muslim territory and Hailakandi must be retained by Assam'.[18] Sylhet's departure also resulted in an Arbitral Tribunal of 1947 awarding a 15 per cent share of the assets of Assam to East Pakistan.[19]

Angry Congress leaders from Sylhet read many inherent ambiguities in the award and looked to the home minister, Vallabhbhai Patel, to reverse this turn of events.[20] One of them, Rabindranath Choudhury, wrote to Patel: 'Is it a meaningless fury signifying nothing? One man, Sir Cyril, from 3000 miles afar, comes as arbiter of destinies of millions and draws up a whimsical line on the map propped up by worthless arguments—and that is that. Everybody has to submit to it. What a pity!'[21] Patel promised them that the concerns of Sylheti Hindus would be placed before the cabinet for discussion. In December 1947, Choudhury sent another memorandum to Patel asking if something could be done 'for retrieving nearly 37% of the district of Sylhet by a new and very probable interpretation of the Award of the Sylhet Boundary Commission'.[22] It was not only the Hindus who found themselves in a tricky situation; the retention of Muslim-dominated Karimganj in Assam worried the Muslims as well.

~

Weeks before Partition, indeed, the Assam government frantically wrote to the Government of India expressing their fear that 'there would be no direct link between the road system in Assam and other parts of Indian Union'.[23] Making this nightmare a reality, Radcliffe's Partition Award mutilated Assam's geography. Its western frontier came to have limited access to mainland India—whether through road, river or railway routes. The existing railway routes to Bengal now passed through East Pakistan, and the road links to northern Bengal were poor. The vibrant river route was also disrupted; like the railways, this too had to pass through East Pakistan territory. People who found themselves across the newly created border also worried about their political future. Some 50,000 to 60,000 people from the Garo community living in Bengal's Mymensingh district, which was contiguous to the Garo Hills in Assam, had demanded before a subcommittee formed by the Constituent Assembly that their areas be merged with Assam. Bardoloi, Assam's premier and the head of this committee, had also written to Mountbatten endorsing this demand. However, the commission refused to concede to this demand, and the Garos living in the lowlands came to be part of East Pakistan. Over the years, East Pakistan would witness the birth of Garo identity politics.[24]

Assam had long been crucially dependent on the geography of East Bengal to sustain its trade and commerce. Partition, as we will see later, destabilized this dependency, suddenly redefining the multifaceted economic, cultural and ecological commonalities shared by Bengal and Assam over the centuries. The Brahmaputra River had the foremost role to play in defining these commonalities, having been vital in crafting the trade dynamics between the two regions. By the nineteenth century, the Assam–Bengal relationship had already taken a new form when Assam's commodity production became dependent on the Calcutta-based financial and business organizations. Calcutta's managing agencies, jute mills and ports in the Bay of Bengal became a crucial link between Assam and the British Empire. Circulation of human resources in the service of the British Empire further complicated the existing relationship. Sociocultural enmities between Assamese- and Bengali-speaking urban intelligentsia developed even as economic dependency on each other was further reinforced.

Some leading personalities from Assam considered visiting North Bengal to meet their counterparts there regarding the possibility of some of these districts being included in the new state of Assam. Sponsors of the mission argued that these areas of North Bengal, such as Jalpaiguri, Dinajpur and Darjeeling, had been a part and parcel of Assam until the nineteenth century and had social, cultural and linguistic affinities with the province.[25] These areas were for long frequented by Assamese Brahmins who provided priestly services there under the *jajmani* system. A section of the Assamese literary elite and others wanted Cooch Behar's merger with Assam.[26] Cooch Behar meant more than a mere territory; many fondly recalled that the rise of Assamese Vaishnavism and Vaishnavite literary culture had found much of its early patronage from this princely state.[27] Early in the twentieth century, many scholars reached out to the royal library in Cooch Behar and other places for a glimpse into the early modern Assamese literary heritage; a leading scholar prepared a bibliography of those literary works.[28] Cooch Behar's merger with Bengal in 1949 caused an uproar among this group and others in Assam, which included the firebrand leader Ambikagiri Raychowdhury,[29] whose anger led a senior official from Cooch Behar to pronounce him a 'fanatic anti-Bengali'.[30] Others—like Rabindra Nath Aditya—urged that Assam should not allow Chittagong, which adjoined the Lushai Hills district and was the crucial port for the province's economy, to slip off its radar. Indeed, even Nehru considered seeking the merger of Chittagong with Assam.[31]

~

At Independence, Assam, occupying one-fifteenth of India's total land surface, was approximately 2,07,200 square kilometres and ranked fifth in size among the Indian states. A 960-kilometre-long border separated the state from East Pakistan. The border was fluid, dotted with rivers, river islands, hills and marshy lands. 'Most of it lies along the foot of the hills . . . there are practically no roads over the hills . . . a good part of the border is the river which is so wide and full of subsidiary channels and islands that it was difficult to draw a line,' wrote Bishnu Ram Medhi, the successor to Gopinath Bardoloi as Assam's chief minister (1950–57), to Nehru.[32] The Brahmaputra, with its expansively wide and constantly fluctuating channels, formed part of this border, Medhi reminded Nehru.

This muddy and riverine border with East Pakistan led to regular trouble, as disputes over territory soon surfaced. There were claims and counterclaims about the territorial jurisdiction of India and East Pakistan, and the actual demarcation could not take place for several months due to rains. Clashes along the border and reports and rumours of harassment of citizens on both sides also became common. For several years, the major tension was regarding the forest patches in the border areas of Cachar in the southern district of Assam. In January and February 1948, Prime Minister Nehru repeatedly cabled Liaquat Ali Khan, his counterpart in Pakistan, condemning the East Pakistan government for attempting to 'encroach' into the Patharia Hills Reserved Forest in southern Assam's Karimganj, which had been part of the Sylhet district before Partition.[33] East Pakistan denied any such wrongdoing.[34] This was the first relatively major incident of this kind on the eastern borders, and it turned out to be a serious source of diplomatic unease. The Assam government also claimed that the Pakistani army had flag marches in these areas, and Nehru demanded that Pakistan withdraw its forces, warning that failure to do so would lead to India having to take action.³⁵ In the first week of February 1948, Nehru spelt out the government's stand on this increasing hostility on India's eastern frontier, with the Pakistani military having seized a little more than 100 square kilometres of Indian territory in Assam. Like many stretches in Bengal, the exact boundary line running through Patharia Hill Reserved Forest in Cachar, along Sylhet and Assam, remained fuzzy after the Radcliffe Commission's award.³⁶ Local skirmishes, mostly between peasants and security personnel, on both sides became frequent. Patharia remained in dispute largely owing to the possibility of oil deposits being present there. The Burmah Oil Company had earlier carried out prospecting there. In 1950, the Indo-Pakistan Boundary Disputes Tribunal, chaired by the Swedish judge, Algot Bagge, retained the status quo and allowed India to carry on prospecting for oil on her side.³⁷

Such incidents remained at the forefront of public rhetoric on both sides as uncertainty about the borders continued. Allegations of East Pakistani fishermen encroaching into Assam or Assam's telegraph men intentionally cutting down telephone lines of East Pakistan were commonly heard.³⁸ More such incidents were reported from the Sylhet and Dawki borders. As allegations intensified, the Indian government rushed military equipment to Assam.

People on either side of the newly created border were somewhat perplexed about their fate, with frequent rumours being spread, including speculation about the possible merger of India and Pakistan.³⁹ Political leaders and officials regularly visited border areas to assert their political presence.⁴⁰ The Assam government expressed apprehension following reports of the hoisting of Pakistani flags in areas of Assam bordering East Pakistan. It sent troops to these areas to dispel any sense of its loss of control. Infrastructure development in hitherto unadministered areas, mostly hill and tribal habitats, was discussed widely.

In March 1948, before he left office and departed for England, Mountbatten, along with his two daughters, made a quick visit to Assam, Manipur, West Bengal and Burma. In Guwahati, he prophesied that Assam would become one of the richest Indian states once the Brahmaputra's resources could be tapped for cheap hydropower production.[41] This visit dispelled all rumours of a merger, and in April 1948, India and Pakistan signed an agreement to 'discourage any propaganda for the amalgamation of India and Pakistan or portions thereof'.[42]

As India began the process of integration of the states, the Khasi and Jaintia hills posed a complex problem. The integration of the Khasi chieftainships or 'states' with the Indian union, 25 in number, did not prove to be easy, albeit on a smaller scale as compared to princely states like Jodhpur, Hyderabad, etc.[43] Some Khasi states like Cherrapunji, which at one time received the highest rainfall in the world, were still in touch with officials of Sylhet.[44] The Siem, traditional chief, of Cherrapunji was drawn to Pakistan as his private properties were in Sylhet, but he acceded to India. Much to Bardoloi's unease,[45] the state of Nongstoin, rich in mineral resources, openly expressed its desire to join Pakistan.[46] Its chief advisor had fled to Pakistan. Another state, Rambrai, also refused to join India. Many voiced their support for the merger too; a loosely organized platform called Khasi Jaintia Federated State National Conference—whose ranks were filled by Congress leaders—was one of them.[47] The Bardoloi ministry was relieved when both these Khasi states finally signed the Instrument of Accession in March 1948.[48] However, for another couple of years, communist leaders from Mymensingh, who had a powerful presence in the Garo Hills, remained a matter of concern for the governments of both India and Pakistan.[49]

Assam's fears regarding the boundary issue were voiced by Bardoloi, who wrote to Nehru in February 1948 saying, 'It is necessary to point out that the border troubles, particularly those in Assam, must not be taken as an isolated problem . . . [T]hey cannot be considered negligible for [especially] a place like Assam.'[50] Nehru held a different view; while he appreciated the seriousness of the troubles at the border, he felt that Assam needed to think ahead. Nehru assured Bardoloi that Assam 'has a bright future and it seems to me that the only way to tackle our problems is to do so constructively through development schemes and not negatively'. But the boundary disputes refused to die down. As the *Times of India* reported, 'It was a little difficult to say exactly the spot where the boundary ended unless one consulted maps and surveys.'[51] There were regular meetings and exchanges between officials to demarcate the boundary between Assam and East Pakistan.[52] Disputes remained in the Mizo hills, Goalpara and Cachar borders. Hilly forested tracts and rivers made the task of boundary-making extremely complicated. Though the disputes seemed to have become less tense with time, negotiations for settlement were underway even as late as in 1955, when Indian and Pakistani officials met in Shillong.[53]

One obvious outcome of the lack of boundary demarcation was that the cultivable agricultural land along the borders lay fallow for several years. In the East Khasi Hills and Sylhet, these obstacles could not be overcome until the governments of India and Pakistan signed a pact in 1955 to liberalize the visa and passport system so that farmers on both sides could move freely.[54] Illegal cattle trade as well as cattle rustling were a recurrent source of dispute. In a gesture of 'goodwill', in 1955, both sides acknowledged the problem of cattle lifting, and in one such instance, the Sylhet administration handed over a draft of Rs 3000 as a payoff for cattle lifted from East Khasi Hills and transported to Sylhet.[55]

The attempts to regularize human movement across Bengal, Assam, Tripura and East Pakistan raised several issues. From 1948, a permit system was in place between West Pakistan and India, and a formal passport and visa system was introduced in 1952. The introduction of a passport system in West Pakistan created a great deal of 'panic and insecurity' across India's eastern borders, leading to 'alarming' levels of exodus from both sides. Bishnu Ram Medhi reminded Patel of the need to regulate the flow of people from East Pakistan by introducing a permit system and establishing checkpoints.[56] Border traffic was unregulated on the eastern borders until 15 October 1952, when the passport and visa system was introduced to regulate traffic between India and East Pakistan.[57] A special visa, valid for five years, was introduced for people on either side who lived within 16 kilometres of the border. This category of visa holders did not need to pass through a checkpoint or register themselves with the police. District magistrates were allowed to grant such special visas to the 'people living in the border areas between the two Bengals and Assam and Tripura [*sic*]'.[58] These groups of people mostly included cultivators and small artisans who were substantially dependent on cross-border economic exchanges.

The bureaucratic processes aimed at regulating human mobility further worsened the economic prospects of cultivators, traders and others. Lack of economic opportunities fuelled cross-border movement of people, and this, in turn, strengthened the Assamese political opposition against in-migration. By 1950, this came to be debated under the shadow of 'citizenship'. With the introduction of the passport/visa system, an increasing flow of people into Assam, particularly into Cachar, the southernmost district, became noticeable. The Census of 1951 estimated the figure at a little less than 0.1 million.[59] This number was soon contested by different organizations that hinted at a much higher figure.[60]

The official process of issuing passports and visas took a long time. Tea planters in Tripura, unaccustomed to such bureaucratic high-handedness, were the first to express their uneasiness with the new system. They found that it gave rise to transport difficulties, particularly in procuring coal from the Pakistan-run East Bengal Railways.[61] Urgent restoration of transport links between Bengal and Assam came as a breather to the Assam tea planters. The fate of millions of small peasants producing jute was, however, different. A small-scale jute mill would be established in Assam in the 1950s, but that did not help stabilize the jute economy.

In addition, families that had been split across the borders were affected, as more restrictions were imposed on those needing to cross the borders on a regular basis. Splitting of families meant the division of immovable properties, including agricultural lands. Farmers had to take permission from both sides to carry back their agricultural produce. In 1950, cultivators were allowed to carry approximately 1400 kg of paddy across the Assam–East Pakistan and Tripura–East Pakistan borders.[62] This system continued well into 1954.

As both India and Pakistan took control over their respective borders, little was done to preserve pre-Partition connections. This meant that everyday family relationships, and ownership of agricultural fields and commons along the border acquired new meanings, hardly comprehensible to the thousands of inhabitants. Assam was also deprived of access to the major ports of Chittagong and Calcutta (the route to the latter lay through East Pakistan), and the Brahmaputra lost its centrality as an artery of trade. Most hill areas remained geographically isolated. The economic challenges for Assam never dissipated, and the deep dislocations in communications and transport still await redress today.

~

In the massive cross-border migrations that followed Partition, the eastern states' experience was different from the western ones. While the influx of Hindu and Sikh refugees in India's north-west was more or less balanced by the exodus of Muslims to West Pakistan, in the east, a corresponding efflux from India had not balanced the influx from East Pakistan. This was the assessment of a report by the Ministry of Rehabilitation in New Delhi.[63]

Several factors contributed to the comparatively lower number of emigrant Muslims from India's east, most importantly the lesser degree of communal violence compared to the situation in Punjab. The memories of the Noakhali communal violence and the Great Calcutta Killings of 1946 were still fresh and may have acted as a deterrent to further outbreaks of violence. Unlike in the west, where mass migration took place within a short span of time, in the east, the exodus took place slowly and over an extended period of time. The migrants also did not take a definite route nor any particular mode of transport, which would allow them to become easy targets for their opponents.

As previous chapters have shown, the question of migration was not new to Assam and had been a contentious one since the early decades of the century. By the 1920s, anti-immigration protests had become a powerful ideological force voiced mainly by Assamese Hindu leaders; though it was not unusual for tribal leaders to unite with them. Such resistance had forced the British government to introduce regulatory mechanisms; for instance, the settlement of the East Bengali jute cultivators in the Brahmaputra Valley was regulated through the highly controversial Line System, discussed in the previous chapter.[64] As we have seen, by the time this administrative mechanism was withdrawn by the Muslim League-led Assam government in 1938, it had succeeded in acting as a prelude to the birth of Muslim identity politics. In the weeks following Partition, a section of Muslim peasants, who had settled in Lower Assam, went back to East Pakistan.[65] The lands vacated by these peasants were reclaimed by the Assamese peasants. Meanwhile, the Muslim League in Assam was abolished in March 1948.[66]

A number of Hindus from East Bengal had already begun to trickle into Assam from the beginning of October 1946, when communal violence troubled Noakhali in Bengal; but, at that point, it was not considered a major crisis. However, closer to Independence, the *Dainik Assamiya* worriedly reported that the local population had expressed displeasure at the arrival of Hindu peasant refugees from East Bengal, approximately 12,000 in number, to the small towns of North Kamrup. Unlike earlier years, most refugees were Hindus, and not all of them were in search of land. The Assam government carried out a census in July 1949, which indicated that there were 1,14,500 persons who had arrived after the Partition.[67] The flow of refugees continued even as the tense political climate of Partition abated, and, in 1950, London's *The Times* reported that '10,000 Hindus are leaving East Bengal every day and almost as many Muslims are pouring in'.[68] More than half of the total refugee population came during the months from February to April in 1950. The refugees in Assam had reached a figure of 2,72,075 by the early months of 1951.[69] Many Muslims who had fled Assam in 1947 came back during 1950. One estimate claimed that during the second fortnight of September 1950, an estimated 15,500 Muslims entered Assam.[70] Assam's Chief Minister Medhi considered this a 'carefully calculated plan engineered by powerful interests in East Bengal'. According to him, 2,00,000 Muslims had left Assam, and 80 per cent of them returned. By 1957, an official report claimed that 'so far 1,28,500 families of displaced persons have come over to this state for permanent rehabilitation . . .'[71] A later assessment suggested that approximately 5 million people had moved from East Bengal to

India between 1946 and 1964—mostly Hindu Bengalis—of which an estimated 13 per cent moved to Assam.[72] It must be noted here that a large number of refugees did not report at the check-posts, avoided direct routes for fear of confiscation of their valuables, etc. Demographers could not arrive at any conclusive estimate.[73]

Indian officials who prepared the 1951 Census reported that most refugees came from Sylhet followed by Mymensingh and Dacca (Dhaka).[74] Independent surveys hinted at Comilla as another place from where refugees arrived.[75] The Census Report of 1951 also noted that in 1949, the refugees were 'middle classes—intellectuals', who were following the proceedings of the Constituent Assembly of Pakistan and were generally worried about the fate of the Hindu population in Pakistan, or 'richer classes who could afford to come away'.[76] The later refugees were mostly petty traders, small peasants or government employees.

As the question of East Bengali refugees and the future of minorities in both countries became a highly contested political question, the governments of India and Pakistan signed the Nehru–Liaquat Agreement on 8 April 1950. For some, this was like 'a glimpse of blue sky in the overcast atmosphere of Indo-Pakistani relations', but many in Bengal were unhappy.[77] The objectives of this carefully drafted agreement were to quell the refugee-related political disquiet in eastern India and East Pakistan and to partially restore the pre-Partition economic relations between the two. Reaching out to the refugee population, the agreement promised that there would be 'freedom of movement and protection in transit', 'freedom to carry movable property, an end to harassment caused by customs officials, and if anyone returned before the end of 1950', the government would ensure that the person would get back their immovable property. The agreement might have succeeded in restoring confidence among the minority populations in both the countries; by the end of 1950, it was being reported that there was a slowdown of the inflow of refugees.

Why did Hindus move out of East Pakistan? R.B. Vaghaiwalla, census superintendent in Assam in 1951, explained a very complex social and political situation in this way: 'In Pakistan the wholesale opting out of experienced non-Muslim officers and their replacement by junior inexperienced Muslim officers, greatly weakened the administrative machinery and created a general feeling of insecurity and lack of confidence in the bona fides of the new State.' Vaghaiwalla further explained that other factors, such as 'the lessening of prospects for Hindus in government, and administrative services, in business and trade which in these days of control depend largely on permits, licenses, and government sympathy and encouragement', apart from the prospect of Pakistan becoming an Islamic state, caused the exodus of Hindus.[78] This official view only partly explains the larger political and humanitarian crisis that accompanied India's Partition. These regions and their people have not yet recovered from the fall-out of the Partition, as has been persuasively documented by other writers.[79]

The arrival of refugees, largely Hindus, from East Pakistan would add another layer to Assam's anti-immigrant political narrative. The newcomers surfaced in official correspondence not as migrants but as 'infiltrators' from a hostile East Pakistan, while the popular narrative failed to differentiate between a refugee and an immigrant. The earliest batches of refugees in Assam were not given any official document as proof of them being refugees. Those who arrived in the early 1950s were expected to pass through 'border camps' and were issued registration certificates. However, not everyone crossed over through these camps or received such certificates. Without any special support from the Assam government, the refugees began to scatter themselves 'almost imperceptibly among the local residents especially of those areas which had already some Bengali population'.[80] Former Bengal government employees and many others who were economically better off explored private avenues to seek employment or a place to live in. Family ties or personal acquaintances became useful in this moment of crisis. Social organizations, such as the Ramakrishna Mission, Marwari Relief Society and the Shillong Refugee Aid Society, each with their own cultural ethos, became active in relief work. The railway colonies, which were already predominantly populated by Bengali-speaking people, attracted a lot of refugees. About 50,000 refugees were found staying in the main railway colonies of Assam by 1948.[81]

Even before the refugee crisis became apparent, the Hindu Bengali employees of the Assam government in Sylhet, who opted for India, presented a challenge for the government of Assam. Accommodating them within the existing job schemes was a serious issue, given the history of competition between Assamese- and Bengali-speaking job seekers. Besides government jobs, a significant part of Assam's trade, and the economy in general, was in the hands of Bengalis and Marwaris. On more than one occasion, Gandhi had referred to the non-Assamese control of trade and government jobs and how the Assamese disliked this.[82] The educated Assamese felt that their only option available was to seek government jobs, and this too, they feared, would become increasingly difficult with the influx of the refugees. On 22 August 1947, the Assam government announced that the Sylhetis could not be absorbed into government jobs as this would be 'in excess of their requirements or create blocks to local recruitment'.[83] The Bengal press denounced this stand,[84] and as pressure mounted, by July 1948, the Assam government offered employment to 1153 of the 1496 government employees from Sylhet who had already been released from their duties by the government of East Bengal.[85]

As refugees poured in, the availability of land became an important concern. The Assam government expressed its inability to provide any more land or any further support to refugees, and in this, it had strong public backing. Sucheta Kripalani, an AICC member who had headed a Congress fact-finding team to look into refugee rehabilitation in Assam and a Bengali herself, recalled in 1974 the lack of compassion on the part of the Assam government: refugees were

> living in huge camps, mostly in forest like areas, in great distress, suffering from all kinds of diseases (and) not getting adequate food, medical attention, in spite of all that the state government was doing. But the state government did not have much heart in the work that they were doing.[86]

The Assam government, backed by the Asom Jatiya Mahasabha, bitterly opposed the Indian government's proposal to settle refugees in the state.[87] Despite pressure from various quarters, the Congress government in Assam had decided that under no circumstances was land to be given to non-indigenous people.[88] On several occasions, Bardoloi wrote to Jawaharlal Nehru of his government's helplessness in arranging for land for the newcomers. Pro-Hindu and exclusivist Assamese nationalist leaders resolutely opposed any further land settlements for the migrant population, while left-wing peasant organizations vociferously demanded land for landless local families. The mood among urban Hindu Assamese families was captured by a forthright editorial in the sole English daily published from Guwahati, the *Assam Tribune*:

> Since independence, the attack is being carried on from two flanks. First, there are the Muslim immigrants whose love and attachment to Pakistan are as strong as ever. There is no evidence of a change of heart and yet they are finding it much easier to migrate to this province under the shelter of the secular state policy of the government of India. Then there are Hindu immigrants who apparently want to create a Bengal in this province.[89]

The Bardoloi ministry came under attack from Nehru for its 'narrow-minded policy'. Nehru's stance was understandable. His government was involved in handling one of the biggest humanitarian crises in modern history: the settlement of millions of refugees on Indian soil.[90] Whatever may have been Assam's internal challenges, in Nehru's view, the larger goal of the nation was more important. However, for Assam, migration had for some time been an extremely sensitive issue, politically and culturally. Since the 1920s, the settlement of people from outside Assam had often caused tension among the Assamese population. For every government in Assam after 1936, whether led by the Muslim League or the Congress, the settlement of 'outsiders' was the hardest fought political subject. Bardoloi's response to Nehru's appeal was to give a comprehensive picture of the per-capita availability of land along with the complex sociopolitical landscape surrounding the uncultivated government lands available for distribution.[91]

Nehru possibly saw the situation on the eastern borders of India as different from that in the west. He thought that persuasion and diplomacy with the East Pakistani leadership was the best way out. Nehru promised Akbar Hydari, Assam's Governor, all possible support, saying that he did not want any 'barrier to free movement but a large influx of people should certainly be avoided'. Nehru also wrote to Bardoloi expressing his concern at the 'double immigration of Hindus and Muslims into Assam' but advised that 'there should be no bar to individuals coming'. Nehru, however, felt that Bardoloi was justified in stopping large groups from arriving without the approval of the Assam government.[92]

In order to ease migrations into Assam, the first of several Inter-Dominion conferences took place in Calcutta in April 1948. While the Assam chief minister was sceptical about the possible outcome of these conferences, the possibilities of the introduction of a permit system were raised, and Nehru continued to appeal for a reasonable stand on this subject.

In early 1949, Mohanlal Saxena, the Union rehabilitation minister, visited Assam to discuss the situation of the refugees there. The Bardoloi ministry promised that 'they would do their best to rehabilitate such refugees as have not been absorbed in the province as quickly as possible'.[93] This assurance served as a trigger for the Asom Jatiya Mahasabha to kick off an agitation opposing any such plan. Newspaper reports in the *Times of India* quoted Ambikagiri Raychowdhury, the chief of the Mahasabha and a fierce orator, blaming the Assam government for pursuing a 'weak-kneed policy and sacrificing the whole future of the Assamese people by accepting the harmful suggestions from the Centre'.[94] The Assam government, sensing opposition to the rehabilitation programme in the province, expressed its inability to offer any large-scale land settlement programme to the Bengali Hindu refugees, and, in a press release of 9 May 1949, flatly denied the assurances it had given to the Union minister.

The question of refugee rehabilitation brought the Union government and the Assam government into open confrontation.[95] Nehru was unwilling to brook any opposition from Assam. Almost a year after Saxena's failed mission, in May 1950, an exasperated Nehru, stressed by similar problems on India's western frontier, wrote to Bardoloi,

> You say that there is no further land available in Assam. This is a question of fact which can easily be determined. It is patent, however, that if land is not available in Assam, it is still less available in the rest of India which is very heavily populated, barring the deserts and mountains. What then are we to do with the millions of refugees we have to deal with?[96]

The West Bengal government, backed by its intelligentsia, was of the view that the burden of the refugees needed to be shared by West Bengal's adjoining states.[97] The economist Radhakamal Mukherjee estimated that land amounting to 17.3 million acres in Assam was lying fallow, and Bengali refugees, who possessed the 'sturdy spirit of individualism, courage and enterprise', should be settled in Bengal's contiguous areas. 'East Bengali farmers fought the tiger and the crocodile,' Mukherjee proudly stated, 'to overcome the hazards of the forest and the flood to make East Bengal the granary of rice as well as jute in India and one of the most flourishing gardens of Asia.'[98]

Assam's Congress leadership argued that before land and other resources were shared with the refugees, Assam's local population, who were landless and needy, had to be provided for.[99] This defence was given credibility by the fact that Assam had a history of striving to provide land for its landless peasants.[100] Bishnu Ram Medhi, then revenue minister who was soon to succeed Bardoloi as the chief minister, was more than vocal in this regard and used all his resources to fight the pressure from the Centre. Despite the Assam government's resistance, Nehru demanded the dignified rehabilitation of refugees, thereby angering the Assamese leaders. Patel was firmer, insisting that the government had 'to give priority to refugees, even against local sentiment'.[101] Patel even rebuked Bardoloi for his insensitivity to the country's humanitarian crisis.[102] As for Medhi, Patel commented that he 'has been the protagonist of the view that no surplus land was available in Assam'.¹⁰³ Medhi, Patel knew, had also resisted the appointment of Bengali officers in the refugee rehabilitation work.¹⁰⁴ In 1949, the Assam government had turned down the Union government's offer of building a township near Pandu in Guwahati, citing internal security and the communist political orientation of Hindu Bengalis as reasons.¹⁰⁵

As the Assam government was opposing the refugee rehabilitation programme, the Union Ministry of Rehabilitation assumed responsibility for it. Meanwhile, the Assam government's Department of Relief and Rehabilitation too began operations from May 1950. A month later, Bardoloi stated that Assam had taken responsibility for rehabilitating 2,25,000 refugees. Of these, 10,000 had been allotted land in areas 'from which Muslim immigrants were evicted', apart from settling a few in tea gardens and Reserved Forests.¹⁰⁶ This, however, did not help the Bardoloi government much. It was caught between pressure from the Assamese and tribal populations, who demanded land, and refugees who demanded greater support. A worried Bardoloi wrote to Patel, saying that if the Assam government had to accept the demands of the refugees 'as superior to those of the local people, or even at par with them', the Assam Congress 'should decide not to contest [the] next election'.¹⁰⁷

In 1950, the Union Ministry of Rehabilitation roped in the Indian Tea Association (ITA) to hand over a small portion of unused land from its gardens to be distributed among the refugees. This did not go down well with Assam's Congress leadership, which forced the ITA to go back on what it had promised.¹⁰⁸ After hectic parleying, it was agreed that only 50 per cent of land acquired from the Assam tea estates would be given to refugees; the other half would go to the Assamese landless. The Assam government had already passed the Assam Land (Requisition and Acquisition) Act, 1948, primarily intended to facilitate the taking over of extra lands from tea estates.¹⁰⁹ However, this Act was of little help to the government in acquiring unused land from the powerful planters.

While the settling of refugees was an important issue, rehabilitation required infrastructure, housing and means of livelihood, which, too, began at a rather slow pace. Provision of cultivable lands, building of urban colonies, establishment of new markets and arrangement of financial loans emerged as key features of the government's initiatives. New townships came up in Guwahati, Goalpara and Shillong. A small number of farmers were given land in Kamrup, Goalpara and Cachar. Homes were established in Nagaon, Guwahati and Rupsi to take care of destitute women, children and the elderly. The able-bodied among them were taught crafts like spinning and weaving, paddy husking, preparation of puffed rice, pottery making, gardening and cow-keeping.[110]

There were cases of mismanagement too. In 1953, the ITA, due to mounting pressure from various quarters, and with a weaker lobbying capacity at this time, promised 3 acres of land each to 3500 families of 'displaced persons who have recently come from East Pakistan'. The total cost of the rehabilitation of these families was estimated at Rs 17,45,000, and the ITA would receive Rs 1,00,000 from the Assam government as compensation for the land. As the scheme took off, it could hardly fulfil its promises. This led to serious accusations against the ITA. Complaints of offers of unfit land, or of ITA not having actual ownership of enough land and increasing hostility from the tea garden workers complicated matters further.

These families were mostly cultivators of jute and paddy. 'The refugees were dumped by truck on jungle-covered knolls,' wrote a reporter in the *Times of India*. 'They could at best construct huts perched on hilltops and hope for the land they had been promised. Very few families got land worth cultivating, not to speak of three acres each, and then it was said that the land was not fit for jute or paddy.'[111]

Apprehensions about settling refugees in a state already burdened with migration in the previous decades, however, slowly weakened, and the state became more proactive later in the 1950s. The Assam government took over the task of administration of refugee rehabilitation in February 1953. By 1957, there was moderate progress thanks to efforts to dispense with the frustrating bureaucratic red-tapism at least to some extent. An official from Assam proudly stated that government reception centres were opened, in the first stage, in the 'bordering districts of Cachar, Goalpara, and United Khasi Hills'.[112] Worried about a backlash in Assamese public opinion, the Assam government however kept the rehabilitation programme a low-key affair. Financial support was given in small sums to small batches of refugees for a range of petty economic activities, including housing, shops and small business ventures. Such financial stringency drew criticism from the Indian government. 'Payment of loans in small driblets either as a measure of security or even as a token gesture of good will is unwise in as much as the amounts so paid are invariably frittered away,' a union official reminded.[113] Most refugees found it difficult to see a ray of hope as they struggled to survive on paltry incomes.

~

When Mountbatten met Bardoloi in May 1947, the latter had said he would 'like Bengal to remain unified and join Hindustan, since this would give Assam the very access to the rest of Hindustan'. If Bengal remained unified and joined Pakistan, it would 'virtually strangle Assam'.[114] Early in 1942, the two major railway companies, the Eastern Bengal Railway and Assam Bengal Railway, which connected Assam with Bengal and transported her coal, oil, tea and jute, had been merged to form the Bengal and Assam Railway. The former, which ran through the fertile Brahmaputra Valley, had played a major role in facilitating the movement of workers and peasants into Assam from faraway places. The latter, initially running through the foothills of the Barail Range and then further south, linked Assam with the port of Chittagong and many parts of Eastern Bengal. In 1940–41, the Assam Bengal Railway alone had carried more than 16 million passengers.[115] During the war, these railways, as discussed in Chapter 1, were important carriers of both soldiers and supplies. But the wartime modernization of technology and improvement in efficiency collapsed at the time of Partition, when Assam's railway connection with Bengal, including Bengal's northern districts, was snapped. Railway coaches and wagons lay unused, becoming temporary homes for refugees. The Assam Bengal Railway steamer companies had connected Assam with

Bengal and beyond,[116] but, in August 1947, Assam lost its access to Chittagong and Calcutta ports.

Post-Partition, Assam was connected to the rest of India only through the Siliguri 'chicken-neck' corridor in West Bengal, hardly 20-kilometre wide, jammed between Nepal and East Pakistan. By the end of 1949, the Pakistan Railway stopped all goods in transit to and from Assam.[117] As the Brahmaputra flowed through Assam into East Pakistan, river trade also virtually collapsed during this period. Assam's political leadership had anticipated this crisis and made a desperate attempt to avoid it. In November 1947, Assam Governor Akbar Hydari, Chief Minister Bardoloi and Revenue Minister Bishnu Ram Medhi met government officials and political leaders in Delhi. The Union government decided to undertake an urgent restoration of communications with Assam, recognizing that the state could not depend on Pakistan's goodwill to remain connected with India. Meanwhile, the air and postal services to Assam had also come to a halt in August 1947. All these events massively impacted the export of tea and the trade in jute.

Work to establish a telecommunication network between Assam and the rest of India began in July 1947,[118] and direct telephone and telegraph links were restored in April 1948. Assam had acquired several airports during the war, but, except for Guwahati and Tezpur, these were meant only for light aircraft.[119] After the resumption of the direct air link between Calcutta and Guwahati, letters and postcards began to arrive by airmail in December 1947.[120] In 1949, goods began to be airlifted between Calcutta and Guwahati.[121] There was a non-scheduled chartered air service between Calcutta and Guwahati via northern Bengal (Bagdogra).[122] Other airstrips across the north-east also came to be used. Planters secured their machinery, vehicles, textiles and groceries, including tobacco, by air. The cargoes of return flights included tea. These flights were reminiscent of the Hump route to China during the war. Air traffic increased moderately, and with their wartime experience of flying in difficult situations, Indian, Australian and American pilots found employment.[123] However, with the Indo-Pakistan War engulfing India's western frontier, Pakistan objected to flights over its airspace, and in August 1948, it banned most flights between Assam and the rest of India.

Building a direct rail link between western Assam and the districts of northern West Bengal was a challenge. The engineers of the Indian Railways had before them a gigantic task to design and execute this railway in the shortest possible time.[124] Establishment of such links was a priority for political and security reasons, unlike in earlier times when economic profit and business viability had played a key role. At the same time, the paddy trade in the newly formed North Dinajpur district and the mineral resources of the Garo hills were incentives to build links. Financial support for this railway was promised in the first budget of independent India.[125]

This was a project of a different scale and magnitude, for which India's railway engineers shouldered responsibility independently, free of their old colonial superiors. They had to assemble resources and support from a wide range of expertise and bureaucracy. Despite the lack of technical personnel, the work on the railway line began early in 1948 and was completed in two years. The Assam Bengal Railway had to build tracks over a distance of 227 kilometres between Assam's Fakiragram and Bihar's Kishanganj. More than 33,000 workers toiled in an inhospitable landscape dotted with rivers, waterbodies and marshlands. Most of the workers came from the United Provinces, Bihar, Madras and Bombay, apart from local agricultural labourers. In addition, 6000 grade-IV employees and 735 officers were engaged for the task. Most of the officers were Hindu Bengali refugees from East Bengal. Known as the Assam Rail Link project, the chief project engineer was the 44-year-old Karnail Singh, an engineering graduate from the Roorkee Engineering College. Singh had already completed a similar arduous job on the western border.

The most difficult task was to construct bridges across the torrential rivers Teesta, Torsa, Sankosh and Raidak. New engineering innovations had to be developed to overcome these challenges from these tropical rivers. A wide range of machinery was used. A total of 379 bridges, of different sizes and lengths, had to be constructed in this stretch of the Himalayan foothills with dense jungles and innumerable rivulets and water bodies. The railways moved 5.6 million cubic metres of earth. The engineering feat that the Indian Railways achieved in such a short time received praise in the Indian media. The *Statesman* commented, 'Turbulent rivers bridged, jungles cleared and the monsoon outwitted. These would have been achievements at any time, but that they should have been efficiently accomplished in a period of post-war malaise and shortages, and of post-partitional disruption, is notably impressive.'[126] A later article in the widely respected *Economic Weekly* commented, 'Of the engineering projects completed during the post-war period, none has been so remarkable as the Assam Rail Link.'[127]

By the end of 1949, this stretch of railway line was complete, and goods trains began to run from 8 December. The distance between Assam and Calcutta was greater on this new route, but the Indian government insisted on retaining the pre-1947 rate of freight, keeping in mind the demands of the tea-plantation lobby. Passenger trains ran from 26 January 1950, coinciding with India's first Republic Day. Soon this rail link also transported Indian troops to Assam's borders with East Pakistan.[128] This new link between Assam and the rest of India played a crucial role in defining new regional aspirations, in addition to providing relief to the ailing state economy and tea exports. And more than this, Patel recognized the symbolic significance of this unification project when he wrote to N. Gopalaswami Ayyangar saying, 'We shall have drawn Assam closer to us and the opening up of this communication would, I am sure, form a very vital link in the consolidation of our country.'[129]

~

While one-fourth of Assam's revenue came from taxes on land, its economy was well-integrated with global markets. The state was more than a hinterland for the metropolitan industrial economy. The Reserve Bank of India assessed that of the total foreign capital invested in India at the time of Independence, a little over a quarter was in tea and jute, which together constituted half of India's exports.[130] Assam's commercial and banking institutions were largely controlled by Calcutta-based managing agencies and by Bengali or Marwari financiers. The Bank of Assam, with its headquarters in Shillong, and the only scheduled bank in Assam, was under the management of Bengali financiers.[131] Historian Amalendu Guha estimated that fewer than 15 such managing agencies, which regulated more than 200 joint-stock companies (both sterling and rupee), were the dominant factor in Assam's economy.[132] Planters still owned 1.5 million acres of land and employed half a million workers. In 1949–50, foreign companies still controlled 85 per cent of the area under tea and half the paid-up capital in the plantation industries generally. Assam's share in the production of tea and jute was 53 per cent and 23 per cent respectively in 1950.[133] The scale of foreign investment becomes even greater when we consider the collieries, oil refinery, railways and timber industry.[134] However, a little more than 95 per cent of the population still lived in villages and toiled in the fields.[135]

In October 1947, the Assam government asked for central assistance of Rs 100 million for speeding up welfare works and another Rs 100 million as an annual grant from the excise duty earned from petrol, tea and jute in the state.[136] Bardoloi lamented that Assam had not received its due economic share from the new federal structure, nor was it empowered to impose fresh taxes.[137]

The price of consumer goods rose sharply across India immediately after Independence. The general index of wholesale prices, which stood at 244.1 in August 1947, rose to 302.2 in November 1947 and to 389.6 in July 1948.[138] The prices of essential commodities had, in fact, begun to rise after 1944.[139] Assam was not as badly hit as some other parts of the country, but the earthquake of 1950 worsened the situation.

Assam's trade and commerce suffered greatly due to Partition, especially the export of tea. In 1950, the province, as mentioned earlier, produced 53 per cent of the country's tea, the bulk of which was exported through the port of Calcutta. For several months, there was an almost complete cessation of Assam's trade.[140]

The planters had for long branded their enterprises as agricultural pursuits and avoided being taxed.[141] This privilege was challenged by Indian nationalists, and when the Bardoloi ministry first came to power in 1937, a century after the first consignment of tea from Assam was sold in London, it passed an act which compelled the planters to pay income tax.[142] This angered the European planters, though the move received support from a few Assamese tea planters who were willing to bear this tax burden. At the height of the nationalist struggle, it was a symbolic move to earn the goodwill of the masses. The British planters continued to fight ugly political and legal battles to resist paying taxes until after Independence, some of which required the intervention of the privy council.[143] In 1944, the Indian government also imposed excise and export duties on tea. In 1952–53, the planters finally paid an estimated Rs 10 million as income tax, approximately 7 per cent of Assam's gross revenue.[144]

By the time of Independence, there was also a glimmer of hope for the plantation workers. Years of organized political mobilization by the communists had made the workers conscious of their deplorable working conditions. In May 1947, the Congress formed the Indian National Trade Union Congress to win over the workers and prevent them from drifting any further towards the communists. The benefits of heightened political awareness amongst the tea garden workers would become visible soon thereafter.

On the eve of Independence, the Congress government had conveyed its intention to nationalize the British-owned industries at the earliest.[145] In 1948, the Indian government announced its Industrial Policy Resolution.[146] This was a signal for a mixed economy, enforcing exclusive state ownership in some sectors, but allowing private sector enterprises to continue in others. A year later, Nehru announced that foreign firms could earn and repatriate profits. Tea planters escaped any major impact, except that restrictions were imposed on the import of machinery. The planters had long imported machinery and auxiliary items like tea chests, so they were unhappy, but they had few options. 'Companies have to make do with many items manufactured in India the quality of which is inferior to the imported article, and the price no less,' wrote H.A. Antrobus, the official historian of the Assam Company.[147] In 1948, the Assam government curtailed the land revenue exemption hitherto enjoyed by the tea planters.[148]

The production of jute, the other important commodity in Assam, too was severely affected by Partition. The production of jute involved millions of small farmers, and any ups and downs in the economy impacted them adversely. Before Partition, in 1945–46, Assam produced 6 per cent of India's total jute, West Bengal produced 9 per cent and East Bengal 80 per cent. Jute was the highest earner for Assam, more than tea; the profits from jute production helped Assam pay for cloth, pulses and consumer goods.[149]

Raw jute from Assam was transported to mills in Calcutta. In the early years of the 1860s, the hydraulic pressure mills in the city pressed raw jute, which would be shipped to mills in Dundee (Scotland) for the production of jute cloth that was used as packaging material. From the 1870s, the situation changed, and the Calcutta mills also began to produce jute cloth. Post-Partition, in order to reach Calcutta, raw jute shipments had to cross the border twice—once into East Pakistan and then back into India. Apart from the ban on the export of jute from East Pakistan to India, there were regular reports of Pakistan withholding the transit rights of jute sent from Assam to Calcutta via river routes.[150] The desperate tea and jute suppliers used air services to send their products to Calcutta. In 1950, 30 aircraft were in regular service to transport both jute and tea.

Independent India's domestic requirement of raw jute was 7.05 million bales, while Assam and West Bengal produced only 1.6 million bales.[151] This massive deficit of raw jute led the Indian government to initiate schemes for the expansion of areas under jute cultivation as well as the intensification of its cultivation, besides imposing a ban on the export of jute seeds. In 1949, fertilizers and seeds were supplied to farmers in Assam, and an additional 50,000 acres came under jute cultivation.[152] As a result, there was a 76 per cent increase in jute acreage in Assam between 1947 and 1955.[153] However, despite such efforts, there were fluctuations in international prices following the Pakistan government's increasing attempts to regulate the unauthorized movement of jute from East Pakistan to India, and jute producers in both Assam and West Bengal suffered heavily. Moreover, in 1949, the Indian government withdrew the right of some provinces, including Assam, to a share in the revenue from export duties on jute and jute products. Export duties on jute along with the earnings from tea exports had contributed a major part of state revenues, and this retraction would significantly impact Assam's economic health. Faced with bitter opposition from these provinces in the Constituent Assembly, the Union government agreed to give grants-in-aid in lieu of export duties on jute.[154]

That Partition would hurt the lucrative jute industry in India's east had been prophesied in 1943 in the pages of the *Geographical Journal*.[155] In 1949, India and Britain devalued their currency, while Pakistan did not. As India refused to accept Pakistani currency at its unrevised value, trade between the two countries came to a temporary halt, and the transportation of jute from Assam was again hampered.[156] While India struggled to rejuvenate the battered industry by expanding production to new areas as well as intensifying production in existing areas, for Pakistan, jute became a crucial agricultural product that would support the new nation's ambitious industrialization and economic modernization programmes.[157]

Early in 1950, as western Assam witnessed massive communal violence and an outflow of Muslims to East Pakistan, many of them jute cultivators, a worried Nehru wrote to Bardoloi: 'I am concerned... about jute cultivation in Goalpara district.'[158] He offered a piece of advice:

> I feel convinced that the only right way to solve this is for you to send the Hindu refugees who have come to Cachar district to Goalpara. I understand that very few Hindu refugees have come direct to Goalpara, though a vast Muslim population have left it. In Cachar few Muslims have left, but a very large number of Hindus have come in, so that it would be desirable in any event to send some of these Hindu refugees from Cachar to Goalpara and to encourage them to do jute cultivation for the time being at least.

The primary problem for both the tea and jute producers was the broken transport linkages. The Standstill Agreement signed between India and

Pakistan immediately after Independence, under which goods moving from one country to the other would be exempt from customs duty, was terminated in March 1948. As a result, many customs check-posts came up. All these rendered the transport of tea along pre-Partition routes difficult, if not impossible. Moreover, there was a shortage of railway wagons, and the Pakistan railway system gave priority to the transport of jute over Indian tea. Besides, a number of railway employees had opted for India, and others who took their place were not familiar with the bulk handling of tea. Planters in North Bengal looked for new routes, but the choice was severely limited for Assam, since there was no direct rail link with India. Thus, when the new Assam Bengal Railway became operational, it was a boon for Assam's tea planters. The planters nevertheless succeeded in boosting their profits; though the cost of production of tea doubled between 1943 and 1948, so did the price, and it continued to rise.[159]

Everyday economic activity across the new border also received a serious setback. Partition entailed changes in the production structure and marketing pattern. Rice supply to Assam fell, forcing many to depend on tapioca, a root that had been imported into India long ago.[160] The supply of coal and limestone from the Khasi and Garo Hills to East Bengal (now East Pakistan) declined, and labourers working in these mines lost their regular employment. The hill population's traditional access to agricultural lands in the foothills of East Bengal came to an end. Minerals, vegetables, fruits and a wide range of horticultural products from the Khasi and Jaintia Hills no longer had access to their earlier markets.[161] Vegetables and fruits produced in these areas had for long enjoyed a lucrative market in Bengal through Sylhet, with urban households in Calcutta greatly favouring oranges produced in the Khasi Hills. The 'miles and miles of orange groves' seen by P.R.T. Gurdon, the widely travelled British official, a few decades before slowly shrank after Partition.[162] Before Partition, 12,00,000 maunds of oranges grown in the Khasi and Jaintia Hills would be supplied to Bengal, but this came down to 2,40,000 maunds in 1948–49 and 12,000 maunds in 1949–50, and this fall in demand was also true for other fruits, potatoes, bay leaf, betel leaf, areca nuts and limestone.[163] Thus, the earnings of hill farmers fell sharply.[164] Several official reports noted the sharp decline in the general living standards of the people of the border areas.[165] It was also noted that 'the rich buildings in the border area villages, which are now tottering away, bear eloquent testimony to the past prosperity of the border economy'.[166] Thousands of labourers lost their jobs in orchards. Many years later, P.R. Kyndiah, a veteran Khasi politician, lamented the decline of the orange trade: '[In] the old days before 1947 . . . there was a saying . . . that the border people are so rich and well off that you can pluck gold out of the tree leaves, that is, the golden oranges. That time has gone with the coming of Independence followed by Partition.'[167] Khasi villages adjoining Sylhet faced serious difficulty in procuring rice and neither could they sell off their oranges.[168]

Maintaining and expanding the road network in the border areas was a challenging task for the government, given the difficult terrain, high costs and very short window for the 'working season' because of the long monsoon. A year after Independence, the Assam government had partially restored road links with Cachar and the isolated Garo hills,[169] but such efforts could hardly restore the broken economic links. In 1950, Medhi worriedly wrote to Patel that 'border hats [markets] have not yet been revived'.[170] But the new borders could not completely end the economic interdependence between the people they separated. The widespread growth in unregulated everyday economic transactions became a headache for the governments.[171] Several years later, Khasi political leaders, including the experienced Khasi politician J.J.M. Nichols Roy, complained about this situation.[172]

With the disruption in supply links, food shortages became common in Assam. Omeo Kumar Das, Assam's food minister, went on a fast in June 1948 citing his inability to address the crisis. Meanwhile, the government decontrolled rice, leading to a sharp rise in its price. On 27 June 1948, rice was sold in Shillong for Rs 65 per maund. The *Times of India* reported that due to the price rise, families in Shillong could eat only one meal a day. The government claimed that this crisis had resulted from the failure of the price fixation system. Most cultivators refused to part with their stocks in expectation of a further rise in prices. Rice husking mills stopped working due to the non-availability of paddy in the rural markets.[173] Added to the crisis was the declining rice yields in the Brahmaputra Valley, which had begun to experience major floods more frequently after the 1950 earthquake.[174] The intensity of the floods had deepened with the construction of embankments.[175] The government responded by remitting revenue and extending financial relief to farmers.

Broken trade and commercial networks forced organizations, including the Hindu Mahasabha, to plead for mutual goodwill between India and East Pakistan. At the same time, there were calls for economic sanctions against East Pakistan; at a public meeting held in Shillong, speakers from various groups, including members of the Forward Bloc, deplored the fact that 'by practically discontinuing trade with India, the government of Pakistan had driven people living on the border to the verge of starvation'.[176]

~

The question of Indian citizenship was discussed from the time India's Constituent Assembly first met in December 1946. In April 1947, a report suggested that 'every person born in the Union or naturalized according to its laws and subject to the jurisdiction thereof shall be a citizen of the Union.'[177] Days after Independence, the Constituent Assembly began to discuss the subject of power-sharing between the Union and the state governments. The Nehru–Patel government wanted a powerful centre, contrary to the wishes of the Indian provinces and their leaders. As the Union government kept the subject of citizenship exclusively to itself, Assam's representatives felt cornered.[178]

For decades, Assam's political concerns had been dominated by the issue of migration into the region. From 1948, the Assam government began writing to the Indian government expressing apprehensions about the arrival of increasing numbers of refugees and demanding that this flow should be stopped.[179] A permit system—like that on India's western border, though not as strict—between Assam and East Pakistan could be a way out, as senior Assam officials regularly advised their political masters. Much to the unhappiness of the Assam government, a confidential note of the Union government, however, emphasized that a permit system must allow for 'exemptions and less formal authorisations'.[180] With respect to the migration of Muslims from East Pakistan, Assam officials expressed anxiety that 'as there are various unrecognized routes and there is a long border unprotected by natural barriers, it is difficult to check all influx, as the visitors will be sheltered by other Muslims'.[181] 'The only way to check influx of Muslims from the East Pakistan is to get an ordinance,' suggested the head of Assam police.

The Indian government dithered on introducing a permit system or an ordinance, for this would have serious repercussions. The government feared that any such restrictions would create trouble and curb the 'freedom of movement of a large number of persons, who, even in their ordinary avocations, had to pass between East Pakistan and either Assam or West Bengal'.[182] Instead, the government suggested that it could introduce a legal mechanism to 'expel from Assam any foreign nationals who entered that State and whose continuance was likely to cause disturbance to its economy'.[183] Assam agreed to this. However, as the introduction of any such mechanism required legislative approval, the Union government drafted a bill for this purpose in December 1949.

The proposed bill to empower the Assam government to expel anyone who was not deemed to be a citizen was not taken up for discussion, thereby necessitating the promulgation of an ordinance in January 1950. The Influx from Pakistan (Control) Ordinance, intended to regulate the flow of refugees from West Pakistan, was already in place as a template. While there was some political clarity over who was an Indian citizen,[184] confusion still persisted over how to distinguish between a refugee and a migrant. Historians of Indian citizenship have little doubt that religious distinction easily subsumed these categories. But a legal interpretation of the meaning of citizenship would come only in 1955.

Lengthy discussions on the Undesirable Immigrants (Expulsion from Assam) Bill—the Act had dropped 'undesirable'—began on

8 February 1950.[185] Citizenship being exclusively a subject in the Union List, the central government had to clarify that the powers under this new legislation were only being delegated to officials in Assam. By differentiating between refugees and illegal migrants, the bill spelt out Assam's political climate:

> During the last few months, a serious situation has arisen in Assam due to immigration from East Bengal. Such large migration is disturbing the economy of the state, besides giving rise to a serious law and order problem. The Bill seeks to confer necessary powers on the Central Government to deal with the situation.[186]

Mindful of India's difficulties on her western borders and in Kashmir, Gopalaswami Ayyangar, who introduced the bill clarified,

> Members from the United Provinces, West Bengal, Punjab, Assam and Orissa unequivocally demanded that Assam, given its complex history of migration and its impact on the political life of the province, must be safeguarded against the menace of refugees. The government succumbed to these pressures and at one time even admitted that the refugee influx to Assam bore characteristics . . . which might justify the inferences that it was a planned one.[187]

Further, he said,

> I am afraid that [a] certain over-zealous friend in Assam [referring to Rohini Kumar Chaudhuri] will consider many of the Hindu refugees on the same footing and consider that their stay in Assam is "detrimental to the interests of India". I want it to be clearly, definitely and expressly understood that the Assam Government will not eject those friends of ours who have come to Assam, who are genuine refugees and who have come seeking refuge in India.

When the bill was taken up for discussion, as many as 15 members spoke at length on the very first day, raising the question of Indian citizenship.

Among the many who defended the bill aggressively, Bhupinder Singh Mann from Punjab did not conceal his hostility towards Pakistan and strongly criticized the government for not showing enough concern for Assam.[188] He further questioned the Assam government's ability to deal with the problem: 'I doubt very much that this weak-kneed and negligent Assam government will become powerful with the aid of this measure and be able to evict them.'

Mann's castigation did not go down well with the Assamese members. Kuladhar Chaliha, a prominent Congress leader from Assam, cautioned that he was 'making sweeping remarks'. Sucheta Kripalani, who with her extensive recent experience in refugee settlements, understood the challenges that refugees were facing, reminded fellow lawmakers that Assam's eastern boundary was 'unsettled and [in] chaotic condition'. Rohini Kumar Chaudhuri, one of the vocal Congressmen from Assam, however, made it clear that a distinction should be made between genuine refugees from East Pakistan and other migrants who were not victims of Partition. Assam was not hostile to the Hindu refugees, said Chaliha, '[W]e should make it clear that the term "immigrant" does not apply to refugees at all.' Dev Kant Barooah, another prominent Assamese Congressman, who was also well known for his literary distinction, said, 'We must draw a line between these two types of people—people of Pakistani origin and nationality who owe no loyalty to our country and to our state, and people who, for their love of India and patriotism have been persecuted in Pakistan and have taken shelter in Assam.'[189]

Barooah regretted that his parliamentary colleagues knew very little about Assam: 'I am quite grateful that people here know that the capital of Assam is Shillong and not Bangkok.' He and his Assamese colleagues made it known that there must be a distinction between 'genuine' refugees and those who were part of the pre-Partition inflow. While different members may have had their methods and procedures for identifying refugees and migrants, they shared one common idea: the non-Hindu population, which primarily included Muslims, that had migrated to Assam in 1947 and after, were not entitled to Indian citizenship and needed to be expelled. However, there were some MPs who felt that given Assam's low population density and the availability of land, it should continue to welcome people for settlement. A. C. Guha from Bengal was confident that 'according to physical laws a vacuum is not to be tolerated'.[190]

More discussions took place on 10 February and 13 February. The Assamese members were more aggressive and emotive. Rohini Kumar Chaudhuri squarely blamed Nehru's government for continuing to allow migrants from Pakistan; it 'was not due to any "cowardice" on the part of the people of Assam that Pakistanis have been able to enter that Province'.[191] The rhetoric of two and a half days of animated parliamentary debate was largely dominated by members from the Hindi–Urdu speaking zone, with rare interventions from those belonging to southern India, while Nehru conspicuously abstained from any discussion. The Immigrants (Expulsion from Assam) Act, 1950—widely known as the Assam Expulsion Act—came into effect on 1 March 1950. While the Act empowered the government to expel non-Indian citizens, it barred the application of its provisions to bona fide refugees fleeing Pakistan.

As the legal framework to expel non-citizens from Assam was given final shape, localized clashes, largely between Hindus and Muslims, continued to surface in the interiors of Lower Assam. Some local Hindu leaders sent petitions to the Assam government seeking retribution against their Muslim neighbours for the latter's presumed loyalty to Pakistan.[192] Following weeks of intense communal polarization, bloody riots broke out in remote villages of Lower Assam—mostly in Goalpara and Kamrup—in the later part of February 1950. Violence ensued between groups of Santhals—who had settled there decades earlier—and Muslims, several of whom had come from East Pakistan, but there was 'little, hardly any, killing' Nehru informed his chief ministers.[193] 'For a whole week, they had rioted unimpeded because that part of Goalpara is so remote that hardly anybody knew about it,' wrote Taya Zinkin, a journalist, who came across many of these refugees in East Bengal.[194] She, however, noted that 'the riots were not so much anti-Muslim as anti-the-men-of-the-plains, who had driven the Santhals into the hills over the years'. Bardoloi charged 'Bengali refugees and communists [from Bengal]' with instigating the violence against the Santhals. Nehru, anguished and taken aback by these riots, telegrammed Bardoloi about the serious fall out of 'this large-scale destruction and looting and driving away of thousands of Muslims'.[195] As large numbers of families living in these areas, variously estimated between 40,000 to 1,00,000 persons, fled to East Pakistan, Nehru's Pakistani counterpart Liaquat Ali Khan spoke his mind in Pakistan's Constituent Assembly.[196] On 10 March, Khan telegrammed Nehru to take a 'far more effective and energetic action by your civil and armed forces than has hitherto been taken for protection of minority community'.[197] A visibly worried Nehru admitted to Rajendra Prasad that the relationship 'between India and Pakistan is very tense'.[198]

The Immigrants (Expulsion from Assam) Act, 1950, did not remain in force for long. Within days, it invited trouble for many Bengali Muslims, and when an old resident was asked to leave his residence in an Upper Assam town within three days, Nehru was furious. Writing to Bardoloi on 10 April 1950, Nehru asked him to suspend the enforcement of the Act.[199] Two days before that, Nehru and his counterpart in Pakistan, Liaquat Ali Khan, had signed an agreement to defuse cross-border uneasiness and to rehabilitate the refugees. Khan had wanted the Act to be referred to in the agreement, but Nehru did not oblige, though he wanted the spirit of the agreement to remain intact.[200] Soon thereafter, Assam's political compulsions to chase away the 'illegal' migrants took a back seat as the state had other issues to tackle. Writing to Patel in October 1950, Medhi acknowledged that 'the Act has become a dead letter'.[201] Some years later, E.H. Pakyntein, Assam's census superintendent in 1961, cautiously noted that Assam had applied the Act 'with wise restraint and great discrimination'; the number of cases instituted 'did not exceed a low three-figure category' over the previous decade.[202]

Meanwhile, despite the energetic debates in the Constituent Assembly to conclusively shape the idea of citizenship, the Indian government was yet to arrive at a conclusive legal definition of an Indian citizen. The existing legal framework of citizenship set out by the Foreigners Act, 1946 defined a 'foreigner' as a person who was not a natural-born British subject or had not been granted a certificate of naturalization as a British subject under any law in force in India. A change in this definition was made in 1957 when India defined a 'foreigner' as a person who was not a citizen of India, and this brought Pakistani nationals under the category of 'foreigner'.

The definition of Indian citizenship acquired concrete form during the census enumeration of 1951, as the Ministry of Home Affairs instructed census officials to prepare a National Register of Citizens (NRC) for all the provinces of India on the basis of census data. The NRC, which the Union government planned to regularly update, did not, however, include the names of post-Partition refugees from Pakistan.[203] The government held that this not-to-be-published register would serve as a permanent administrative record and a suitable framework for the maintenance of electoral rolls and conducting of various statistical surveys.[204] The respective district administrations became the custodians of these registers. For Assam, this register came to be invested with immense political meaning, though the census process was itself not foolproof, and Vaghaiwalla, Assam's census superintendent in 1951, wrote about the difficulties faced during the final preparation of the NRC, stating that the reports were 'written by unqualified or ill-educated enumerators'.[205] A majority of people were unaware of the importance of this register as a legal record that could be used to prove citizenship. Other states silently allowed the NRC to slip into hibernation, but, in the early 1960s, the Assam government took advantage of it to identify 'illegal migrants'. A decade later, there arose political demands to appropriately use this as an effective instrument of citizenship. Both the National Register of Citizens and the decadal population census would play an important role in Assam's electoral politics through the later decades of the twentieth century, as the controversy of citizenship refused to disappear from the state's political landscape.

## 4

## Assam in a Federal India

When India's Constituent Assembly was formed in 1946, Assam had 10 nominees: seven from the Congress and three from the Muslim League.[1] When Partition and the Sylhet referendum necessitated the reconstitution of Bengal's, Punjab's and Assam's seats in the Constituent Assembly, Assam was allotted eight seats, of which six belonged to the Congress.[2] These members had decades of experience in governance and in public life—as former heads of the province, barristers, ministers or lawmakers. Among the Constituent Assembly's more than 300 members, the representatives from Assam had their distinct voice, their own political, social and economic priorities. Their opinions counted despite their being so few in number. While Gopinath Bardoloi, the premier of the province, would take over as head of the committee to decide the political future of the tribal population, Muhammad Saadulla, Assam's erstwhile premier from the Muslim League, who joined the Constituent Assembly on 14 July 1947, was appointed as a member of the Drafting Committee of the Indian Constitution.

In the early months, Assam's members intervened in the debate only occasionally, rejecting the Cabinet Mission's grouping formula. They expressed worries about the separation of Sylhet. Here, Assam found itself alone, as the politico-religious narrative surrounding Sylhet with its underlying emotions would ultimately determine the course of events. In Tezpur, Omeo Kumar Das had seen hope in the Constituent Assembly of which he was to be a member, as he called for a socialist economy as a way to root out all social problems.[3] Assam shot into the limelight when in April 1947 the Assembly debated on the interim report of a committee on fundamental rights that was chaired by Vallabhbhai Patel. Integral to this was the question of the rights of the tribes of India, and Assam got special attention from members like Jaipal Singh, the vocal tribal leader from the Bihar province. While the political future of Assam's tribal population, trapped in a complicated and ill-defined bureaucratic political framework, was hotly debated, some members surreptitiously drew attention to the increase in the tribal Christian population. Assam's tribal population was fortunate that Reverend James Joy Mohan Nichols Roy was a strong defender of their rights in the Constituent Assembly.[4]

Assam's members equally partook in defining shared ideals and approving imageries to represent the new nation. Saadulla welcomed the symbolic significance of the national flag, as he felt it would contribute to demolishing prejudices against the Muslims in the country. Aware of the sneering campaign against the Muslim members of the Assembly, Saadulla spoke out:

> In my opinion the Flag symbolizes the evolution of our aspirations, the fulfilment of our struggles and the ultimate result of all our sacrifices. If I may be permitted to draw an analogy from nature, the saffron represents the condition of the earth, the scorched condition caused by the torrid heat of the Indian Sun . . . the saffron colour should remind us that we should keep ourselves on that high plane of renunciation which has been the realm of our *Sadhus* and saints, *Pirs* and *Pandits* . . . as an old inhabitant of the furthest and the smallest province of the Indian Union, I salute this Flag as a symbol of India's freedom.[5]

Back home, many wished Prime Minister Nehru would include a representative from Assam in his ministry, but this did not happen.[6] These leaders predicted that Assam was going to be a 'problem province' in the decades to come. Mohammad Tayyebulla, the Congress president in Assam who had recently been in dispute with Bardoloi, gifted two books to Patel authored by historian Suryya Kumar Bhuyan as proof that Assam always 'took interest in all-India affairs'.[7] Ambikagiri telegrammed Patel asking him not to appoint any Bengali or Punjabi officers in 'railways and post and telegraph departments' in Assam, though he was open to the idea of appointing 'Madrasi officers' if there was no suitable Assamese candidate.[8]

On occasion, Assam's members, or more so the populace of the province, some of whom were closely following the happenings in the Constituent Assembly, felt offended by other choices. Tagore's *Jana Gana Mana* was formally declared as India's national anthem by the Constituent Assembly on 24 January 1950 after a precarious journey.[9] The anthem's missing reference to Assam had already caused public protest in Assam in 1948, the popular disapproval being endorsed by *Dainik Assamiya,* an influential daily newspaper.[10] Those demonstrations had invited the wrath of Nehru.[11] Anyway, decades earlier in 1928, Assamese leaders, determined not to be marginalized in the nationalist movement, had adopted as their 'jatiya sangeet' (national anthem) a song—*O Mor Aponar Desh*—composed by the illustrious literary figure of Assam, Lakshminath Bezbaroa. Lakshminath, infuriated by what he perceived as the sidelining of his province, even suggested, '[W]e don't need Vande Mataram,'[12] expressing the Assamese leadership's contested view on the emerging idea of India.[13]

Away from the grand narratives of the nation-making process, Assam's members were not far behind in partaking in lighter moments in the Assembly debates. Rohini Kumar Chaudhuri, one of the vocal members who had no inhibitions in expressing his opinions against political rights for women, cautioned his fellow members 'to take care of their ear-drums' as he was 'a loud-speaker' and when he used the microphone 'the sound might become perilous for their ears'. Kuladhar Chaliha, the veteran Congress leader from Assam, insisted on Sanskrit as India's national language and wanted to change the anglicized spelling of *Assam* to *Asom*.[14] Chaliha also stressed that India must 'make a Constitution which is not only fool-proof, but also knave-proof'.[15]

These brief snapshots from the tumultuous years between 1946 and 1950 are not, however, representative of how Assam negotiated its key political aspirations in the Constituent Assembly. How different was Assam's experience from that of other Indian provinces, say Bengal or Punjab? Could the province secure a special position as desired by its members? In fact, Assam's contribution to the making of the Indian Constitution was in several senses unique. To understand this, we have to carefully leaf through the pages of the *Constituent Assembly Debates*.

~

On 15 July 1947, Patel presented the *Report on the Principles of a Model Provincial Constitution*.[16] Days later, on 21 July, Nehru submitted the *Report of the Union Constitution Committee*.[17] Both these reports affirmed India's move towards a parliamentary and federal form of government. As lengthy discussions on the principles underlying the future Constitution of India carried on over several days in the Assembly, Assam endeavoured to make known its unique position vis-à-vis geography and population. Despite its contribution to India's anti-imperial movement, it found itself at odds with the new scheme of the Constitution. Its members, largely familiar with the wider Indian political landscape, collectively lamented the lack of interest in Assam among other members. The uneasy political relations between the League and the Congress had not yet eased. When Saadulla wanted one member per 2,00,000 population in Assam's legislative bodies, Omeo Kumar Das, one of the key leaders of the Congress in Assam,[18] vehemently opposed it.[19] Das wanted Assam's upper house to be abolished, and he insisted that its 'backward communities' must be given a chance to be elected to the province's legislature, a view shared by his colleague, Nichols Roy.[20] The latter demanded a higher number of representatives from areas inhabited by hill tribes, which could enable the voices of the people to be heard. For him, 'one lakh per-member' would cause 'great and terrible hardship to the people of hills'. To defend himself, he cited the cases of the Lushai Hills and North Cachar; the former had a population of little over a lakh and a half distributed over 20,000 square kilometres.[21] Bardoloi further urged that in the case of provincial representation, the treatment of the people in the plains must be different from that of the people in tribal areas. Rohini Kumar Chaudhuri specifically raised the case of representation of the Shillong territory and the population residing in the Khasi and Jaintia Hills. Saadulla defended his Congress colleagues on most matters, and, a few days after the Sylhet referendum, he reminded the others that 'Assam was the Cinderella of all Indian Provinces . . .' and that the separation of Sylhet and [thereby making Assam a smaller province] would demote it further.[22] But Assam's appeal hardly drew any sympathy. One exception was Jaipal Singh. He shared the same political and social trajectory as his colleagues from Assam, where 'the problem of hilliness, inaccessibility, sparseness of population and all similar physical difficulties have been pointed out'.[23] Singh said he came 'from the Chota Nagpur Plateau, Jharkhand, which is equally mountainous, equally inaccessible as some of the territories that have been described by my friend Mr. Gopinath Bardoloi from Assam'. Patel also received representation from others in Assam, including an army sergeant from North Cachar Hills, who was posted in Punjab and who acknowledged that he was 'fully aware of the impropriety on [his] part in writing to' Patel. He wrote supporting the special cases of Assam's smaller population's rightful representation in the legislature.[24]

Patel did not like this outcry for special treatment. He retorted that

> some friend from Assam . . . seems to have developed a sense of inferiority complex, that Assam must always have some special treatment. It is a matter for congratulation that women have come forward to say that they do not want any special treatment. But at the same time, it is a matter of regret that men have not yet come up to that standard.[25]

This terse rebuke from a Congress leader, who was coequal in stature to Prime Minister Nehru, resulted in all the amendments being withdrawn that were initiated by members of the Assembly from Assam when the

*Report on the Principles of a Model Provincial Constitution* was taken up for discussion in July 1947.

Concern for the preservation of provincial political rights was not unique to Assam; such ideas swept across other provinces.[26] Days after Independence, when the Assembly began to discuss the subject of the distribution of power between the Union and provinces, Assam waited for its chance to seek its rights in federal India. Aware of domestic challenges, including the increasingly uneasy relationship with tribal groups, the Assamese members did not see a chance for a debate on provincial autonomy but only on power-sharing between the union and the provinces. On their home turf, however, they were swayed by the rising popular mood, which clamoured for more rights for their province in India's future federal constitutional scheme. Assam's public intellectuals consistently voted for a stronger province over the next couple of decades.[27] Proud of their linguistic and historical heritage, its writers, public figures and politicians were worried that Assam's distinctiveness would be subsumed by a pan-India identity. They were equally worried that Assamese aspirations to gain a foothold in the regional economy would not be successful because of the rising power of capitalists from other provinces. Several historians' popular writings, including those of Suryya Kumar Bhuyan, which made the Assamese aware of their proud place in India's history, helped to reinforce these aspirations and anxieties.[28]

Provincial autonomy, defined as a centrifugal tendency by a leading political scientist, was the ultimate aspiration of many leading Assamese and was thoroughly embedded in the provincial politics of Assam.[29] With the coming of the Government of India Act of 1935, which redefined the scope of provincial autonomy, several Assamese writers made their intentions clear. Illustrative of such ideas was a series of articles by Jnananath Bora. Bora was no unfamiliar name in Assam's public life. A lawyer at the Calcutta High Court, a vocal Assamese public figure, an advocate of federalism and also the author of *A Plea for Sanskrit as National Language*, Bora expressed unhappiness at Assam's increasing economic impoverishment. Critiquing the provincial autonomy as encapsulated in the Act of 1935, Bora argued that this would not serve the cause of Assam.[30] The recent history of separation of Burma from British India was, for him, the best model of such autonomy. Bora was enthusiastic about the new political developments in Burma, an erstwhile British Indian province that had followed a similar path to that of Assam. Bora thought Assam could learn from Burma's example. Such ideas were boldly articulated on the eve of Independence and immediately after. Ambikagiri Raychowdhury, who missed no occasion to express his views, was known for his relentless public opinion against the migration of new settlers. It was Raychowdhury who said that 'Assam for Assamese is the battle cry of all the true sons of Assam'.[31] He reiterated his claim for Assam's provincial autonomy as the Constituent Assembly began to discuss the Union powers. Speaking at a meeting of his own organization, the Asom Jatiya Mahasabha, he made an emotive appeal: 'Assam should come out of the Indian Union and become an independent country like Burma or any other country.'[32] Some of his followers were even more forthright. Celebrating the idea of smaller sovereign states, they dreamt of Assam 'perhaps [to] be one of the strongest little states in the whole of East'. They also asserted that 'Assam's sovereignty was a fact of ages ago and it should be of future'.[33] These views were essentially Assam's outpouring against a powerful Union, her protest against the new settlers and her bid for autonomy that would enable the province to take advantage of the new economic opportunities of the mid-twentieth century.[34] Similar sentiments surfaced repeatedly and rang loudly on the eve of Independence.[35] Assam's representatives in the Assembly, too, voiced these ideas, but they could hardly influence the course of the debates in the face of the majority view. When such political views were denounced as provincialism, *Dainik Assamiya* proudly pronounced their stand in favour of 'provincial nationalism'.[36] Even after the Constitution was adopted, the campaign for provincialism continued. In 1955, Jnananath Bora voiced the views of many of his fellow Assamese: 'If provincialism means simply love for one's own state, that will ever remain along with the existence of the states and it is natural and desirable.'[37]

The reports presented by Patel and Nehru gave shape to the powers of the Union government and the nature of federalism in India. In July and August 1947, when the Assembly briefly debated on the reports of the Union Constitution Committee and Union Powers Committee,[38] Assam could hardly make her case for autonomy. In fact, Bardoloi along with the prime ministers of Bombay and the United Provinces agreed to the principle of federation with a strong Centre.[39] While many were concerned that a strong Centre would mean weak provinces, it did not stop the larger principle of a strong Centre from being adopted. Omeo Kumar Das, the lone Assamese voice in this round of debate in the Constituent Assembly, made his opinion clear: 'Strengthen the centre we must, confronted as we are with a situation which is volcanic . . . but we should not weaken the Provinces.'[40] Assam had little doubt that its weakened position was not related to political power but emerged out of poor provincial finances. Raising the need for the preservation of Assam's unique culture, an angry Das said, 'If Assam which is the homeland of the Assamese people . . . cannot be protected . . . I think I have no justification to come to this House. Assamese people have a culture distinct from other provinces.' Das finished his brief speech by reminding his fellow members that the 'Assamese people have a language which is a separate language and which though Sanskritic in origin has got Tibetan and Burman influences'.

The press in Assam—both Assamese and English—closely followed the debates in Delhi. The *Assam Tribune*, a powerful English language daily, by then almost a decade old, remained a watchdog.[41] It regularly reported on what was happening on the floor of the Assembly and ensured the rise of a powerful popular narrative that consistently backed Assam's stakes in the future Indian federal structure.

The Provincial Constitution Committee of the Constituent Assembly recommended that members of the Assembly from each province would vote separately to decide on whether the legislature in their province should have an upper house. The Assamese members decided to do away with their upper house, the Assam Legislative Council.[42]

What was Assam's vision for a powerful province? Would such a province guarantee equal rights to her people across class, caste and religion? What would be the future of the minority populations in this constitutional framework? The constitution-makers had debated extensively on the question of the rights of India's minorities 10 days into Partition. The Committee on Minorities, chaired by Patel, had submitted its report in August 1947, which dealt with 'political safeguards' for the minorities.[43] The lengthy debate saw little participation by members, except for Rohini Kumar Chaudhuri's appeal for reservation of jobs for the Assamese in Assam. But back home, the leaders were vocal. Rupnath Brahma, the influential tribal leader from Assam, wrote to the Minority Committee seeking adequate provisions in the framework of the Constitution for the tribal population living in the plains of Assam.[44] Bardoloi proposed to the Advisory Committee on Fundamental Rights, Minorities and Tribal and Excluded Areas that in Assam, as no community had any 'absolute majority over others', the right of minorities to contest general seats should not be applied.[45]

No matter how vigorously the representatives of Assam contested for the rights of their own communities and tribal or religious minorities, their contribution in the debates regarding the rights of women, untouchables and caste was minimal as compared to the other members of the Constituent Assembly. Regarding the last two issues, the justification for their disengagement could be that Assam had not faced the direct brunt of these forms of discrimination as much as the other members of the Assembly did. The representatives from Assam also disassociated themselves from the most controversial subject in the Assembly, which was language: the language to be spoken in the House, the language in which the Constitution would be written, the language that would be given that singular designation of 'national', and consequently the battle over the choices of Hindustani, Hindi and English.

Assam had sizeable populations of religious minorities. A large majority of hill residents and a few in the plains had embraced Christianity decades ago. In the nineteenth century, the American Baptists, Welsh Presbyterians, Irish Roman Catholics and Italian Jesuits had taken their message to the villages. In 1941, of Assam's 11 million population, about half a million practised Christianity.[46] While they enjoyed a rare prominence in the hills, Christians in the plains were mostly from poor tribal families and workers in the tea gardens. However, the missionaries had deeply influenced the social and cultural lives of their followers: they recorded the hill languages in the Roman script, and the schools and hospitals established by them had an impeccable record of providing succour to the needy and the sick. The new religion gave people a new political identity too.

The idea of religious freedom cropped up in April and May 1947 when the Assembly debated the interim report on fundamental rights. In fact, two early draft reports had treated conversion guardedly.[47] As part of these debates, on 1 May 1947, K.M. Munshi, a key architect of the report, introduced a clause into the interim report on fundamental rights. This read, 'Any conversion from one religion to another of any person brought about by fraud, coercion or undue influence or of a minor under the age of 18 shall not be recognized by law.'[48] Nichols Roy, a Khasi Christian, rose to oppose it: '. . . I am against this very principle of forcing the youths by not allowing them to exercise their religious conviction according to their consciences.' More acrimonious exchanges followed. If Purushottam Das Tandon welcomed Munshi's proposal, saying that 'we Congressmen deem it very improper to convert from one religion to another', Ambedkar insisted that Munshi drop this amendment. Rajendra Prasad, the president of the Assembly, suggested that the clause be sent back to the Advisory Committee for further deliberations but not before Patel's advisory came in, which stated that 'There is no point in introducing any element of heat in this controversy. It is well known in this country that there are mass conversions', but 'we have to live in this country and find a solution to build up a nation'.[49] While the right to convert prevailed, the uneasy relationship between the missionaries and the Indian government surfaced in the hill districts of Assam soon afterwards, as discussed in a later chapter.

What about the Muslims? While the Constituent Assembly unanimously disapproved of reservations for Muslims, Saadulla had to walk a slippery path when the ban on cow slaughter was debated.[50] In November 1948, when among other things, a new clause proposed that the government take steps for the prohibition of cow slaughter,

Saadulla intervened to make his views known: 'I have every sympathy and appreciation for their feelings; for, I am [a] student of comparative religions. I know that the vast majority in the Hindu nation revere the cow as their goddess and therefore they cannot brook the idea of seeing it slaughtered.'[51] While he acknowledged the religious sentiments of his fellow countrymen, he politely cautioned that these possible restrictions could lead to unnecessary economic strain. He gave an example from his time as Assam's premier, during World War II, when the provincial government had passed a law prohibiting the slaughter of milch cattle or cattle which could be used for draught to conserve these resources.

> But, wonder of wonders, I personally found that droves of cattle were being taken to the military depots for being slaughtered not by Muslims, but by Hindus who had big 'sikhas' on their heads. When I saw this during my tours I asked those persons why, in spite of their religion and in spite of Government orders, were they taking the cattle to be slaughtered. They said: 'Sir, these are all unserviceable cattle. They are all dead-weight on our economy. We want to get ready cash in exchange for them.'[52]

~

Assam's determination to speak up became noticeable when the Assembly had to sort out the complex subject of fiscal federalism in August 1949. The structure of revenue-sharing between the provinces and the Union government had been spelt out in the Government of India Act of 1935, following the Otto Niemeyer Committee's recommendation. Niemeyer, the British banker who influenced the financial policies of several countries, was not convinced about Assam's demand for special rights over her products, including oil.[53] His formula did not go down well with the leaders of Assam, which read the report 'with profound disappointment'.[54] The Constituent Assembly formed an expert committee headed by noted Indian economist N.R. Sarkar to give suggestions on the financial relations between the Union and provincial governments amongst other questions. The Sarkar Committee received inputs from the provincial governments. The Assam government made a representation to the committee against the current situation under which Bengal was getting the benefit of taxes on incomes generated in Assam: 'Large amounts of income accrue in Assam but are assessed in Calcutta which is headquarters of the concerned companies.'[55] Assam asked for 75 per cent of the excise duty on oil and the export duty on tea produced in the state.[56] Both Bengal and Bihar asked for 75 per cent of the export duty from jute and jute products, but strangely Assam did not do the same. A considerate Sarkar Committee recognized the reasons behind Assam's grievances; it agreed to 'larger fixed subventions than now' for Assam and Orissa and also recommended an amendment in the Constitution for an annual grant of Rs 1.5 million (5 per cent of India's total share of 28 million rupees as share of export duty on jute for 1946–47) in lieu of jute export duty. The Drafting Committee agreed to a grant from the jute export duty for a period of 10 years to Assam.

The Constituent Assembly took up the question of financial power-sharing, covered in Articles 247 to 260 of the Draft Constitution, for discussion on 5 August 1949. The tone of the day's discussion was set by Orissa's ex-premier, Bishwanath Das. A towering figure in provincial politics, Das was no novice in matters of finance. Das volleyed the harshest words against the finance department for being apathetic to the needs of the Indian provinces and their welfare programmes. Bardoloi's anger against the finance department was also palpable as he apprised the Assembly about Assam's inability to undertake any substantial welfare work because of the 'planters' raj' and post-Partition financial challenges. Assam had numerous worries—its international borders needed support, the people in the hills needed more care, and it also had to meet the challenges of the rising popularity of the communists. Bardoloi saw little hope for Assam, given the proposed scheme of financial devolution. 'When passing the clauses on Fundamental Rights, we thought that poverty, distress, disease and ignorance will be dispelled from the face of India. Now I want to ask: How are you going to do it?'[57] He demanded a 50 per cent share (scaling down what his government had proposed to the Sarkar Committee) of the excise duty on petroleum and kerosene and also a greater share from the export duty on tea.

In the Drafting Committee meeting held on 27 March 1948, Saadulla pressed for the acceptance of amendments moved by Bardoloi in matters of distribution of resources between the Union and the states. The Drafting Committee, however, did not agree to Saadulla's proposal.[58]

Bardoloi's colleagues J.J.M. Nichols Roy and Rohini Kumar Chaudhuri, too, voiced their concerns. Their central aim was to secure a greater share of export duty earned from tea. Nichols Roy demanded greater consideration for smaller states like Assam and said that such states required more funds for rural development and for better transport. He also asked for the excise duty on tea to be reinstated so that the state government could get their due share, but he did not push beyond what the Drafting Committee had proposed for jute. Chaudhuri too asked for Assam's rightful share in the duty on tea export. He indignantly told the house: 'If you want to retain Assam, if you want to have a peaceful India, if you want to protect the frontiers of India, then you must bestow more care and thought on that province.'[59] The prominent Congress leader Kuladhar Chaliha, too, spoke against the financial arrangements between the provinces and the Centre. In mid-1949, an aggressive Chaliha decided to challenge Ambedkar's view: 'You are doing something which will have a disintegrating effect and will accentuate differences instead of solving them. If you take too much power for the Centre the provinces will try to break away from you.' Chaliha further challenged the centralization of power:

> How can a man in Madras understand the feelings [and] the sentiments of a man in Assam or Bengal? You seem to think that all the best qualities are possessed by people here in the Centre. But the provinces charge you with taking too much power and reducing them to a municipal body without any initiative left in them. You think you possess better qualities than the men in the provinces, but I know there are people there who are much better than you are.[60]

Assam got more opportunities to portray its dismal economic condition as the discussion on fiscal federalism progressed. When India's Department of External Affairs circulated a pamphlet on Assam's frontier areas, Saadulla, now a member of the Drafting Committee, drew the members' attention to this. He described Assam's condition 'as that of [a] poor man's hut' and knew that the members had no 'inclination to go through these pamphlets'. He, therefore, took more time than Bardoloi and others to give the committee a detailed sketch of Assam's finances based on his vast experience in the Assam government. He took issue with Bengal for taking away Assam's wealth—'pouring oil on the oily head'. He said that most managing agencies' headquarters were located in Calcutta and that the income tax 'which is paid in Calcutta goes to the credit of Bengal'. He sought equitable and proportionate distribution of revenue for all states. When the Drafting Committee met the provincial premiers in July 1949, Bardoloi and his finance minister demanded export duty proceeds for articles produced in the province.

After days of discussions, the Assembly agreed upon the principles of financial sharing, not differing much though from the existing Act of 1935 [which itself was crafted on the principles of extraordinary fiscal centralism]: the Centre would retain the right to collect all the proceeds from some taxes (customs duty or company tax), while others would either be shared with the states (taxes on income or excise) or would be claimed exclusively by the states (land, property and sales tax).[61] However, the Union Finance Ministry vetoed any sharing of jute export duty with the provinces.[62] All of these had effectively ensured that the sort of fiscal federalism advocated by the Constituent Assembly fundamentally contradicted Assam's claims for federal autonomy.

~

The economic disparity between Assam and other provinces and the inability of Assamese people to secure any gains and establish a foothold in emerging commercial and business enterprises had haunted the Assamese bourgeoisie for several decades. Examples of Assamese businessmen venturing out of their home turf were rare; Bholanath Borooah and Lakshminath Bezbaroa, who ventured into business in timber, among other things, in Bengal, were exceptions. Borooah's annual turnover in 1901 was Rs 7,49,212, which was not bad compared to his contemporaries in Bengal.[63] Several public figures expressed their sense of unfair competition by the 1920s. Writing in 1925, Jnananath Bora underlined that the development of a province meant that trade, commerce and agriculture must be in the hands of its people, along with progress in language and literature.[64] He referred to the pattern of economic development of Madras, Bombay and Bengal as examples.

The blueprint of fiscal federalism was laid down in the 1919 reforms under which the revenues from income tax and customs duty were allocated to the Government of India, while the provinces were to earn revenue from sources like land and forests. At that time, Assam did not face any serious hardships as revenue from both contributed—an estimated 47 per cent of the total revenue during 1916–17—significantly to her income, but her representatives in the imperial legislative council protested against this financial arrangement.[65]

The reforms of 1919, which provided a classification of the central and provincial subjects, came in the aftermath of World War I. The Government of India, having experienced an alarming increase in its expenditure due to the war, considered the financial situation 'as one [causing] grave anxiety'. It was felt that the Centre would face a deficit and that the provinces needed to provide a share of their incomes to overcome this shortfall.[66] Lord Meston, the erstwhile finance member in the Viceroy's Council, who headed a small committee, was asked to assess this share of the provinces. Assam's initial contribution to the Centre's deficit was stipulated at an annual sum of Rs 1.5 million. What was the basis of such provincial contributions? The Meston Committee agreed that the guiding principle should be the 'capacity to contribute'.[67] Though the committee did not visit Assam, it made an elaborate inquiry into the financial condition of the provinces and finally recommended a fixed ratio for each. Assam's share was fixed at

2.5 per cent of its income, while Bengal would contribute 19 per cent of its income.

The provinces protested against this award.[68] Except for Burma, the annual budgets of all the Indian provinces (1921–22) faced a deficit following the Meston Award.[69] Not vocal initially, Assam's scathing critique of the Meston Award found place in its memorandum to the Indian Statutory Commission, which was drafted by none other than Saadulla, then the finance member in the Council. The financial contribution from the imperial treasury to Assam as per the Meston Award came to an end during 1928–29. The Assam government admitted that the 'limit of taxation has been reached in the case of the rural and even the urban population'.[70] The 'province ought to get a larger return from its industries. The tea industry contributes some 12 lakhs to the province in the form of land revenue, and the oil wells and coal mines together some 2.5 lakhs'. Assam also highlighted its unfair loss from incomes accrued in the province from petroleum and tea.

After being the worst hit by the worldwide economic depression, some hope emerged for Assam when the report of the Federal Finance Commission of 1932 recognized that 'Assam appears to present one peculiar feature, not present in the same degree in any other province, namely, that it is comparatively undeveloped and can't itself afford to raise the capital necessary for its development'.[71] The commission, headed by British parliamentarian Eustace Percy, advised a grant (subvention) to adjust the deficit budget of the province. Meanwhile, Assam's share of revenue increased, but this was largely due to the expansion of land settlement. Readjustment of provincial finance came to be widely discussed during the Third Round Table Conference in 1932.[72] Bengal demanded that the export duty on jute, which had been introduced in 1916 and exclusively went to the Central treasury, be assigned as provincial revenue.

The imperial government partly conceded this demand as the Government of India Act of 1935 acknowledged the rights of India's jute-growing provinces to a share of export duty from jute, and from 1934–35, a share of export duty from jute was assigned to Bengal,

Assam and Orissa. The Percy Committee's suggestion was given a concrete shape in Niemeyer's recommendation. The Niemeyer Award, largely as a measure of relief for European planters in Assam and jute mills owners in Bengal withered by the Depression, assigned 62.5 per cent of revenue from the jute export duty to the jute-growing provinces. Assam was to get Rs 3 million as a grant. An angry Saadulla called this the 'cruelest joke that could be perpetrated upon a poor province'.[73] He said,

> Take petroleum and kerosene. Assam is the only province which produces that very valuable commodity in the dominion of India. We get only a paltry sum of Rs 5 lakhs of royalty [from] the crores of rupees worth of crude oil that is pumped out [of] the bowels of mother earth . . .

Thus, the question of how the resources of the government were to be shared between the Centre and the provinces continued to haunt India.[74]

Niemeyer's admission that Assam was essentially a 'deficit province and must undoubtedly receive assistance' would be quoted by Assamese leaders for a long time to come.[75] In the mid-40s, nationalist leaders aggressively blamed Assam's tea economy for the economic ills of the province. To recapitulate, in 1942, 84 per cent of Assam's tea estates were controlled by European managing-agency houses, some operating from Calcutta and some from London. Thirteen such leading houses operating from Calcutta controlled three-fourths of India's tea production in 1939.[76]

Jute and tea were the two principal commodities in India's export trade both before and after the war. During 1937–38, jute's share was 24 per cent, while that of tea was 14 per cent. While the share of tea remained almost the same for the year 1947–48, jute's share increased to 39 per cent.[77] In 1947, Assam still had a surplus state budget.[78] But one-fourth of her earnings came from land revenue, 11 per cent from excise tax and 10 per cent from forests. A small share was earned from customs duty, which included a tax imposed on jute. At Independence, a tiny fraction of Assam's population—0.12 per cent—paid income tax.[79] Though this percentage was higher than that of Bengal, most of the taxpayers were tea planters. Nevertheless, despite its annual deficit budget, Assam's income had increased from Rs 3.2 million to Rs 7.2 million between 1936–37 (when the Government of India Act, 1935 came into effect) and 1946–47. A major share of this increase came from the enhanced income from forests, land revenue, income from tea and its share of export duty from jute.[80]

In 1947, with independent India in effective 'nationalized' control of former imperial assets and with no incentive for provincial concessions, an expert committee on the Financial Provisions of the Union Constitution endorsed the cessation of sharing export duty. When the Constituent Assembly started sorting out the thorny subject of resource-sharing, the Centre reworked the provincial share in jute export duty to 20 per cent.[81] The Constitution stipulated that the provincial share in income tax would be recommended by the Finance Commission. During the interim period, till the early 1950s, Assam was to get 3 per cent of the revenue earned from the income tax compared to 13 or 12 per cent for Bihar and West Bengal respectively.[82] Many in Assam considered such a financial arrangement as a continuity of colonial rule.

As the Constituent Assembly debated on the modalities for India's federal finance, Assam's economy saw a steep fall. The total revenue of the province declined from Rs 71.9 million in 1946–47 to Rs 66.2 million in the next financial year. This was owing to both the loss of Sylhet and the disruption in the economy owing to British withdrawal. The 1950s and 1960s saw the further contraction of grants and contributions from the Union government,[83] and Assam's own revenue earnings (principally consisting of land revenue, excise and agricultural income tax) declined from 53 per cent in 1951–52 to 35 per cent in 1965–66.[84] The export earnings from jute, now considered grants-in-aid in the official vocabulary, also slowly diminished.

~

> The future of the Assam hill-tribes when India gains independence is one of considerable difficulty.[85]

The Cabinet Mission had underlined the need for India's Constituent Assembly to pay special attention to the future of India's tribal population.[86] This task was entrusted by the Constituent Assembly to a small team: the Advisory Committee on Fundamental Rights of Citizens, Minorities, and Tribal Areas and Excluded Areas, headed by Patel. Early in February 1947, the Advisory Committee set up three subcommittees to devise mechanisms for the future governance of the tribes of Assam, the NWFP and Baluchistan and the rest of India. Partition warranted that only two of these areas remained relevant for India. Assam's premier Gopinath Bardoloi was to head the subcommittee that would recommend future forms of governance for the tribal areas of Assam. The five other members included two of his ministerial colleagues Rupnath Brahma and J.J.M. Nichols Roy, A.V. Thakkar, who was known for his work among the tribals in the Bombay Presidency, Aliba Imti, the formidable Naga leader and first head of the Naga National Council (NNC), and R.K. Ramadhyani, ICS. More members were nominated later from each of the tribal communities.

Bardoloi and his colleagues were convinced that conditions in Assam were of a wholly different nature, 'not to be found elsewhere' in India. The governance of these areas required special attention. The political presence of the Indian government in Assam's northern frontier—more of which we will discuss in a later chapter—was weak.[87] Tibetan tax collectors still had a visible presence in the far north.

Many members of the subcommittees carried their own preconceived notions of conditions in the tribal areas. The tribal areas were marked by the absence of 'civilising facilities as roads, schools, dispensaries, and water supply', the teams agreed.[88] The tribals were 'simple people' and always vulnerable to forces of business or moneylenders. So, they sounded a note of caution, the 'sudden disruption of the tribal customs and ways by exposure to the impact of a more complicated and sophisticated manner of life is capable of doing great harm'.[89] This was a change from the long-held views of British colonial officials, who insisted on a policy of isolation. Many Assamese writers too shared the colonial views, which usually distinguished the tribes of Assam into two clearly disconnected categories depending on their geographical distribution: hills and plains.[90] The plains tribes were considered to be more in tune with an advanced economy. Workers on tea plantations, many of whom were on the list of tribes elsewhere in the country, were not treated as tribals in Assam.

In the early months of 1947, the Bardoloi Committee undertook extensive visits to most of the areas in the hill districts of Assam. They listened to and received petitions from large numbers of Assam's tribal representatives.[91] Two members from each tribal community were nominated by the committee. These visits were noticeably different from the British officials' annual tours, as they instilled a sense of confidence, and many tribal people fearlessly articulated their political aspirations. It was an extraordinary and exciting experience of constitution-making on the eve of Independence, one that most other parts of India could hardly experience. There was occasional role reversal too, wherein British officials were interviewed by the committee members. A pamphlet written in English outlining the prospects and possibilities of this constitutional scheme was also shared with the people (possibly translated by local officials). A circulated questionnaire spelt out the intention of the visitors: 'We have no plan of our own. We want your views because you know best what your own needs are.'[92] The visitors told their hosts that they were there to understand the latter's special needs so that those could be incorporated in the future Indian constitution. As Bardoloi and his team spoke to a cross section of the population, the pain and anger amongst Assam's tribal population became quite evident. Most talked about their poverty, landlessness and the sense of helplessness they feared as a result of the aggression of non-tribals, which was both economic and political in nature. When Bardoloi's team spoke to a few Karbi individuals, they asked for legal protection of their land from being taken over by others.

In the third week of April 1947, the Bardoloi Committee, accompanied by B.N. Rau, arrived at its first stop in Aizawl, the headquarters of the Lushai district in the south-eastern-most part of Assam. Bardoloi assured the tribal leaders:

> The first thing I have to say is if you think we have come with any set views, we must disabuse you of that idea. You have already had a note from us. The British Government have made it perfectly clear that from June 1948, they will not be here. It is we who shall have to look to our own . . . and therefore it is our duty that we should put our heads together to see how we can do so. Certain problems are very evident.[93]

Anxiety clouded those conversations, which took place across the Lushai and the neighbouring outlying districts of Assam that lined the Patkai Hills along the western frontiers of Burma. As a result of several decades of intense imperial military and bureaucratic exercises, the Lushai Hills had come to be administered as part of Assam since 1898.[94] The penetration of British rule did not necessarily displace the traditional chiefs and their powers. A deputed British official took these chiefs into confidence and ran the affairs of the government. By the time World War II gripped these areas, the chiefs had begun to lose their control. The Assam government was worried about the administration of this vast geographic expanse and its highly politically conscious ethnic communities with their customary ways.

Disputes arose about which organization would be a true representative of the diverse Mizo people—the Mizo Union or the District Conference. The Bardoloi Committee preferred the Mizo Union, led largely by the educated elite and those ideologically opposed to the Lushai chiefs.[95] Formed in 1946, the Mizo Union also popularized the term 'Mizo' as opposed to the 'Lushai'. The latter represented the dominant clans and chiefs with support from the British officials, while the Mizo Union commanded support across various other clans. Members of the District Conference were unhappy that it was being taken for granted that they would join the Indian Union. The following excerpt of a conversation between the visiting Bardoloi team and the members of the District Conference gives an idea of the confrontation.[96]

Rev. Zairema: *[Y]ou are really taking it for granted that we want to join the Indian Union. That means we are not free to choose.*

Miss Lalziki Sallo: *You want to know what our idea is—whether we join the Indian Union or what we do?*

B. N. Rau: *We want to know what special provision you need within the Indian Union.*

Bardoloi: *That is the only way in which we can look at things. You can choose but we are not capable of going into that question.*

B. N. Rau: *We are not taking it for granted that you remain in the Union. We have only been asked to enquire about the circumstances in which you can remain a part of the Indian Union.*

The Bardoloi Committee also questioned Major MacDonald, the superintendent of the Lushai Hills who was stoutly against the Mizo Union.[97] MacDonald was more than blunt when in 1946 he had proposed a scheme for the future governance of the Mizo Hills under which the Indian government would take control only of matters related to defence. When Bardoloi enquired from him about the minds of the people in the Lushai Hills, he sarcastically replied that 'they might join Burma'.[98] He thought that the financial assistance that the Lushai Hills district was getting was not sufficient and that it would be best to give the Mizos financial support and allow them to run their own affairs.

Unlike their staunch Church leaders, the Mizo Union saw many possibilities for themselves within the framework of the Constituent Assembly. But Mizo opinion was clearly divided—a small section wanted to join Burma, while an emerging middle class vowed to join India.[99] A team of non-Mizos, consisting of Marwari, Nepali and Bengali traders and settlers, wanted conducive trade relations with India. A team of Mizo women said that 'some of the customary laws in respect of women are not good for their improvement'.[100] They made a radical demand: 'We want adult franchise i.e., every man or woman more than 18, should have the right of vote and we would like at least 2 or 3 members of the [40-member] Council to be women.' They also demanded special assistance for female education, including medical studies.

For the next few weeks, Bardoloi and his team were able to speak to British officials, journalists and editors, members of women's unions, tribal leaders, community headmen, lawyers, members of organizations like the Ahom Association and the Hindu Mahasabha, Congress leaders and hundreds of individuals. Talking to the tribal people took the members of the committee on an anthropological journey and proved an eye-opener for many of them as they learnt about tribal dress, food, religion, customs and beliefs. A Singpho person told them,

> We have grown into ignorant men, we do not want our sons to do the same . . . we must have schools, we must have roads, we must have hospitals and all that. But we cannot contribute any money for all this work . . . we do not also want other people who are non-Kachins to live with us.[101]

Assamese-speaking Ahom families, who were also Buddhists and living in the southern part of present-day Arunachal Pradesh, had something different to tell: 'We are feeling the pinch of land for wet cultivation, therefore lots of people from outside the Province should not come to us.' They wanted land for their landless fellow community people, and wanted educational facilities, but wished to be free from the burden of taxation in the initial days of Independence. Several Singphos made a demand for 'schools to be opened in our midst for our children to learn things and get educated'. A Naga from the Namsang area said, 'We have had no occasion of enmity with the Assamese people and our relations with them are very good.' Other individuals concurred, 'We are backward and we have no educated people amongst us. If you send doctors or any missionaries to educate us, we shall certainly not ill-treat them.'[102] And, 'Beyond our inner line, we should remain independent, but we would like to remain in friendship with the people of Assam and the Assamese Government'.[103] Three Kacharis demanded preferential treatment in the local administration. A team of Kaibartas (fishermen by profession) did not want to remain under their political officer and wanted their localities exempted from the present arrangement of excluded areas; their per-capita land holding was small, and they did not want outsiders. The Nepali grazers wanted to join the Indian Union, two Muslims did not want any outsiders to own land 'as the land in this area is already not sufficient'. Marwari traders spoke the least, but they admitted that their 'aspirations are not in any way different from those of the local people'.[104] Most advocated elected local bodies as primary units of governance, unlike the powerful traditional bodies. They aspired for elected bodies with a strong sense of autonomy. Several Khamti people, reminding the committee about an early nineteenth-century treaty with the British East India Company, wanted to 'create a small state' where preference would be given to their own people, followed by the Assamese.[105]

Many other tribal delegates whom the advisory team met also repeatedly referred to the political agreements with the East India Company concluded in the early nineteenth century.[106] A few Adi people narrated that Tibetan officials visited them regularly, of whom 'some are good and some are bad'.[107] But they said they would not allow 'any new Assamese, Bengalies, Marwaries [sic] or any other people, not even the British'.[108] All argued that taxes collected inside their territories should belong to their village councils.

> If all the expenditure we are talking about cannot be met from our own revenue, then the difference shall have to be made up by the provincial government or by the Central Government. This is the opinion of all of us. The Mishmis will want exactly what we have asked for. This is the desire of our Kebangs. It is for the money that we can get from you that we want to keep friendship with you.

They wanted the *Posa* system to continue.[109]

Not all these areas were exclusive to any one ethnic community; the demographic composition and social life in the foothills were highly fluid in nature, receiving and welcoming people of varied ethnic backgrounds and speaking many languages. Instances were numerous when the committee would come across groups of people who had settled there recently: for instance the workers from the tea plantations who had completed their contracts, or had retired, were part of those social landscapes, earning a livelihood from those diverse economic landscapes.

At the picturesque hamlet of Haflong, the committee was told on 12 May by a mixed population of Kuki, Naga, Karbi and Dimasa that '[s]o far, we have been absolutely in the dark. We want more light'. They asked for education, better health facilities and also improved communication, as otherwise they were unable to sell their produce. They demanded 'improved methods of agriculture to be introduced with the aid of the Government'. They also provided a simple arithmetic of revenue: '[T]he revenue realised from this portion of the country is small to meet these improvements. Therefore it is our earnest request to Government that more money should be spent in this area.'[110] Further, 'we do not wish that permission should be given to others to take up land here'.[111] And 'we do not want industries to be set up by outsiders. We want the Government to provide the facilities for us to start such industries. The capital for the industries should not be from outside. It should be from the Government and from the people themselves'.[112] Here, Zeme Nagas complained that Bengali was taught along with English in schools, but they did not want the former; 'the common language should be Hindustani'.[113] Another carefully worded memorandum of all the communities demanded that begging should be stopped, and 'foreigners' should not be allowed to settle in or participate in the political process.[114]

~

Across the eastern Himalayas, in the Balipara Frontier Tract, a group of 'Bhutias and Buguns' from the north bank of the Brahmaputra walked for five days to depose before the committee.[115] They reminded the visiting team that they were 'the original inhabitants' and that they did not have 'any tradition saying that we came either from the south or from the north'.[116] They spoke about their regular commercial trips to places across Assam and their social relations with other tribes. Many of them 'are our old friends. We eat together'. Bardoloi put the position to them: 'British will leave our country and the natives—we, the blackmen, will have to take up the rule in these wide areas. Whom would you like to be ruled by?'

Bardoloi asked them directly, 'Would you like to rule yourselves?' Their reaction was equally candid: 'We are not literate and we know very little of what sort of change is coming. We think the existing state of affairs will continue and so we want to continue as we are. Please explain to us the nature of the coming change?' When Bardoloi insisted on knowing from them whether they had any objection to other people living with them, they replied saying,

> We have been very friendly with the Assamese in times past. With the coming of the British, they said that we should remain friendly with them and that they would give us certain moneys (sic) and pretty cloth, and certain other things. If our old friendly relations with Assam are revived, we shall only be too happy about it. We shall certainly remain as your friends and it is for you to decide the manner in which that relationship should be continued, and it is for you to decide everything for us. If you continue to give us the *posa*, it will be good for us.

Some others were more doubtful. A team of 50 Akas told the visitors, 'We hear that the British Government are [*sic*] going to quit India and give it to the Indians. We do not know how the Indians propose to treat us.'[117]

Often there were animated and nuanced discussions on a wide range of constitutional subjects in areas then described as partially excluded areas. Among the issues discussed were seat-sharing arrangements in the legislature and the future of traditional and customary institutions. The Khasis declared that they did not want the restoration of a king and proposed a Federated State National Council as a governing unit of all the Khasi people.[118] The members of this council would be elected through adult franchise and would include women representatives; their traditional chiefs (called *Syiem*) would have no place there. The Khasi representative demanded protection of their customs and rights including their rights over land. R.K. Ramadhyani, who was the secretary of the committee, agreed saying, 'Protection is conceded. You will have protection from exploitation. You will have freedom to run your own social systems.'[119]

A week after the Sylhet referendum, the committee interviewed Ambikagiri Raychowdhury, the firebrand Assamese nationalist in Shillong,[120] who steadfastly fought against allotment of land for Bengali settlers. He explained to Bardoloi that his idea of the Assamese people was wide-ranging. 'Assamese means all indigenous people of Assam and outsiders who have cast their lot with the good and bad of the Assamese people or those who have identified themselves with the interests of the people of Assam . . . consider the people of the Hills as Assamese.' Raychowdhury sought 'full autonomy' for excluded and partially excluded areas. Behind the curtain of his eagerness to bequest equality of political rights to the ethnic communities of the Assam hills, his sense of cultural authority was clear, and not all his contemporaries shared his stance.[121] Raychowdhury's generosity, he made it known, came out of his sense of kindness. The well-being of the tribal residents of the hills should be specially provided for in the budget of Assam, he said. Besides,

> there are also tribal people in the plains. They are also entitled to protection and safeguards. We are prepared to give the same concessions and advantages to these people, but not [along] line[s] of separate electorates. They should be given seats in the legislature according to their population. The tribal people in the plains are being ousted by outsiders. They want special protection.

His opinions were possibly a source of satisfaction for Bardoloi, who would face more opposition from his own party colleagues as we will see below. Raychowdhury, meanwhile, telegrammed Aliba Imti Ao, president of the NNC, expressing his support to the Nagas' stand for self-determination.[122]

The committee also spoke to the well-known anthropologist, Biraja Sankar Guha,[123] the first Indian to receive a doctoral degree in anthropology.[124] Born in Shillong, Guha had been educated at Harvard University and had studied the dramatic transformation of native American tribes, before turning to the physical characteristics and cultural institutions of the many tribes of Assam. He became the first director of the newly established Anthropological Survey of India and had submitted a detailed report as adviser to the committee. He was asked by Bardoloi for his opinion on the view that tribes should be kept more or less secluded, away from contact with the outside world. This was a view held by anthropologist Verrier Elwin, the erstwhile Oxford professor, as discussed in a later chapter. Guha's blunt answer was, 'I do not agree with this view because it is impossible in this world to keep anybody completely secluded and because seclusion means going down. Civilisation has been built up by contact and intermixture between races and cultures.'[125] Besides, tribes in Assam were not isolated, for they had for long deeply interacted with others in Assam. But he qualified this understanding with the sophistication and alertness of a professional anthropologist, stating that

> It is essential ... to preserve the tribal authority and social structure and adjustments made on the basis of their indigenous institutions. Their own internal autonomy and tribal structure must be maintained and no one can deny that there are many things in their life, such as the position of women and the republican form of government which the so-called progressive peoples of India have not got.

Guha also advocated the tribal method of jhum cultivation.

> Besides it must not be forgotten that civilisation, like domestication of animals, often leads to emasculation, and material and intellectual progress if it leads to physical deterioration and emasculation is not a substitute for a sturdy people ... In short the tribes must

not be completely left to themselves but should be integrated to the general life of the province and the Country at large, but there must not be any exploitation and the tribal life should be adjusted from within.

He explained the cultural and intellectual meaning of the practice of head hunting, which according to him had not stopped even with the arrival of Christianity. 'The tribes must be very closely associated with the Provincial Government because . . . the people forming it are best able to understand them and their needs. It should form the connecting link between the tribal autonomous areas and the people of the province.' Without doubt, for Bardoloi and his colleagues, interaction with Guha was a different and meaningful experience.

Not everyone was willing to think in a similar way. Rabindra Nath Aditya, a senior Congressman, believed that jhum was uneconomical and caused floods in the plains of Assam. Aditya's unease with granting greater autonomy to the tribal areas was evident; he thought that the general policies for the hill areas should be framed by Assam, with limited autonomy to those areas. 'We are prepared to give them representation in the Legislature.'[126] The Khasi leader Nichols Roy was quick to remind him that the hill people were the owners of the lands and, therefore,

> It is not for the legislature or for the people of Assam to give them the rights but they already have the rights . . . they only surrender certain rights to the legislature or to the province of Assam for the sake of helping them to develop themselves according to their own ways [sic].[127]

Aditya thought that this was an 'untenable position'.

~

The Bardoloi Committee met the Naga leaders in Kohima in the third week of May 1947. That stop was expectedly thorny.[128] Prime Minister

Nehru, while speaking at the Constituent Assembly, had highlighted the prevalence of head hunting among the Nagas,[129] stating that 315 heads had been taken in the short period since the end of the war. For many in the Constituent Assembly, it was an eye-opener. The mistrust between Bardoloi's team and the Nagas was clear early on. In the first-ever public meeting to interact with the Naga leaders, Bardoloi spoke in Assamese. The Naga leaders protested and asked Bardoloi to speak both in Assamese and in English: 'Some members have not understood what the Chairman said. It may be better if you speak [in] both [languages].'[130] The reason might have been simple enough: Assamese was the general *lingua franca*, but possibly many Nagas spoke a different dialect and could not understand the Assamese spoken by Bardoloi. Further, by insisting on English, they subtly but firmly rejected assimilation into Assam. This was a prelude to the unfolding political trouble waiting for Bardoloi and the future government of India.

The Naga Hills had been restless for years. Throughout much of the nineteenth century, the Nagas and other hill residents had resisted the expansion of the British into the foothills. The legal and bureaucratic Inner Line provision had hardly stopped this resistance. 'Nagas raided [a tea garden] last night, burnt factories, bungalow and murdered manager,' a telegram from a panicky planter described one such moment of 1880.[131] While workers at the tea gardens frequently refused to work in plantations in the foothills, merchants and planters sought stronger measures from the government for their safety, and the British colonial officials responded through the occasional armed expedition.[132] Things had hardly improved since then. In 1929, the Simon Commission was told by a group of Naga leaders (headmen and government officials), known as the Naga Club, to leave them 'alone to determine for ourselves as in ancient times'. The World War disrupted life and resulted in a new political churning in the hill districts of Assam. Wartime contracts and sudden evacuation of a significant number of Hindi- and Bengali-speaking traders from Burma gave limited opportunities to the hill population to engage in petty economic activities. The slow growth of private ownership of property, in place of community ownership, led to a heightened political consciousness.[133] In 1946, the Naga National Council (NNC) was formed. Angami Zapu Phizo, who became its fourth president in 1950, wanted a sovereign Naga state. As discussed in Chapter 1, he had sided with the Japanese forces and the INA during the war.

Weeks prior to the committee's visit, on 29 March 1947, the Naga leaders had sent off a memorandum to the British government that explained their differences with the people in the plains of Assam and in the rest of India. In conclusion, it asked the question, 'Ought the British Government, or the Government of India throw this society into the heterogeneous mixture of other Indian races?' It further noted that a

> constitution drawn by people who have no knowledge of the Naga Hills and the Naga People will be quite unsuitable and unacceptable to the Naga People. Thrown among forty crores of Indian people, the one million Nagas with their unique system of life will be wiped out of existence. Hence this earnest plea of the Nagas for a separate form of an Interim Government to enable them to grow to a fuller stature.

The memorandum had one request: 'Setting up an Interim Government of the Naga People with financial provisions for a period of 10 years, at the end of which the Naga People will be left to choose any form of Government under which they themselves choose to live.'[134]

The Secretary of State for India and Burma, Pethick-Lawrence, saw this memorandum and sought the advice of Henry Knight, who was acting as the Governor of Assam. Knight's advice was not to take this seriously, as the NNC was a 'self-constituted body of the more conservative educated Nagas'; he added that 'the real problem underlying the memorandum is the preservation of the Naga Hill's economic equilibrium until the bulk of the Nagas are educated enough to compete with the free and independent Indian voter', though it is difficult to see how this is to be attained; some form of interim self-government with some control by the central Indian government seems inevitable. Mere incorporation into Assam might lead either to the collapse of the Naga economy and to famine or to the relapse of the Nagas into head-hunting isolation.[135]

When Mountbatten took over as viceroy of India in March 1947, he wrote to the secretary of state that 'the placing of the hill tribes under a central India Government would mean that they would be subject to politicians at Delhi, who would be even more unaware of their needs than the politicians in Assam, and to whom they would have no access'. Mountbatten's advice was that 'if they can be brought with suitable safeguards within the framework of the Assam constitution, they can themselves expect some share in the Government there and will have access to and influence over the Government'. He rejected the economic-equilibrium argument, but he agreed that as these hilly areas had no surplus revenue, they had to be financially supported. 'It affects in the same or only a slightly less degree all the excluded and partially excluded areas of Assam . . . the main problem is the protection of these people from exploitation and the preservation of their way [of] living.'[136]

In early January 1947, Burmese leader U Aung San spoke of autonomy for the hillmen of Burma and of a transfer of power to the frontier tribes.[137] In his view, 'The British people owe as great a debt as ever one people is likely to owe to another' to these hill communities.[138] Clow, the former Governor of Assam, was not interviewed by the committee, but, nevertheless, he gave his opinion on the Naga crisis. He thought that 'it was not practicable for any Naga peoples, or even for all of them, to form a separate state, or even a separate Province.' Clow, who had already helped put the last nail in the coffin of the Crown colony idea, had no doubt that if such a thing were to happen, the Nagas would 'always remain poor and backward'. His advice, therefore, was that 'they should aim at reaching an accommodation with the people of the Plains [sic] of Assam which would be of mutual benefit to both'. He also agreed that the Assamese leaders were well aware of the differences between the plains and the hills, and that the latter's best practices would be preserved. Clow advised the Nagas to cooperate with other hill people too. 'The Hill peoples of Assam have had long experience in pure democracy.' The 'Naga people can contribute to the maintenance of democracy in India. They can have a share in the Government of their own Hills . . . ultimately [they] would make a valuable contribution to the Government as a whole'.[139]

When the Bardoloi Committee met the Naga leaders in Kohima in May 1947, political mobilization in the Naga Hills had reached a heightened stage. Days before, the Kohima Tribal Council had demanded the return of a few forest patches from one of Assam's districts, a fair demarcation of the Naga Hills, and opposed any dilution of the existing laws.[140] They bluntly emphasized that the 'Nagas shall reserve to themselves the right to allow or disallow outsiders into their land'.[141] The NNC leaders told Bardoloi and his colleagues that they must understand 'the desire of the people on the question of how their land should be governed when the British power withdraws from India'.[142] Bardoloi must have been anxious not to open a Pandora's box. He explained, 'We all desire independence and as much as it is possible for us to work out, but the meaning of independence should not be to mean isolation.' Bardoloi made it clear that they could not discuss the question of independence.[143] Unlike in other places, Bardoloi had to explain to his Naga audiences that independence from India was hardly a logical idea; no one could remain isolated in modern times was his most preferred sermon. Neither were the Naga leaders willing to give space to Bardoloi. He had to persuade them to submit their 'wishes and desires within the framework of what is possible' for the Constituent Assembly.[144] Bardoloi did notice signs of fissures within the Naga people—between the radicals and moderates. While the Naga Nationalist Council, the radical faction amongst the Nagas, was opposed to the views presented by the Bardoloi Committee, a section of moderates also 'put forward their views'.[145]

On 20 May 1947, the NNC handed over a short note to the committee demanding an interim government for 10 years.[146] 'By the ten-year interim Government we just mean a Government that has been defined by ourselves in our memorandum and further elucidation of the case has been just submitted now.'[147] Bardoloi complained that NNC's memorandum was not addressed to the committee but rather to His Majesty's government through the Prime Minister of India. The committee disagreed with the NNC's claim to be the sole representative body of all the people in the Naga Hills. Aliba Imti, who had been co-opted as a member of the committee, said,

> I am always for a free Naga people. I am always for an independent Naga people ... So here today I wish that I am not a member and I want to speak on behalf of the Naga people. But the constitution of the Committee and principle do not allow me that.[148]

Convinced that the NNC was no more interested in pursuing an engagement with it, the committee ended their interaction with the Naga leaders. Before the report of the committee had been submitted, the political disagreements with the Naga leaders came out in the open.

The Bardoloi Committee's intense engagement with the Naga leaders was followed by another mission led by Akbar Hydari, the Governor of Assam, in July 1947. Hydari was upbeat about arriving at a consensus with the Naga leaders 'in respect of their future relationship' with Assam and the Indian government.[149] Leaders of the NNC and the Governor of Assam had already tried to sort out a political settlement earlier in June 1947. In July, both sides agreed to an interim political solution, but it failed to work as the NNC insisted on complete independence after the interim period of 10 years. Unhappy, on 14 August 1947, the People's Independence League, a breakaway faction of the NNC, drafted a cable to the United Nations declaring Naga independence; however, this was not sent.[150]

~

Modern state machinery had eluded the tribes of Assam for long; the colonial period had hardly affected them. Early in the twentieth century, several pieces of legislation, including the Chin Hills Regulation of 1896 and the Bengal Eastern Frontier Regulation of 1873 had shaped the life of the people in the hill districts of Assam. The rights of communities enshrined in the Chin Hills Regulation came to be embedded in twentieth-century governance frameworks of the hill districts.[151] The idea of keeping the hill districts of Assam out of the purview of the constitutional provisions of the Government of India Act of 1935 began to take shape in 1919.[152] The notions inherited from the nineteenth century and the financial considerations of the early twentieth century shaped those ideas. The Indian Statutory Commission also received support from the Government of Assam in a similar direction.

> These areas have nothing in common with the rest of the province. There is no sympathy on either side, and the union is an artificial one, resented by both parties. The backward tracts are, with certain safeguards, brought within the reforms and the control of a Council in which they cannot be effectively represented. On the other hand, the Council and indeed the rest of the province generally resent the burden which the administration of these areas placed on the provincial revenues and fear that their political growth and material development are impeded or may be impeded by their being yoked to the backward tracts.

The government of Assam insisted that the

> backward tracts have not and cannot for many years hope to have effective representation in the Council, and because they must be allowed to develop on their ideas and be protected against exploitation and the subversion of their rules and customs by a different civilization which would be unsuited to them in the present state of their development, and in which they would be unable at present to distinguish the good from the evil.

Accordingly came the assertion for the administration of these areas solely by British officers. 'The tribes would, in fact, resent as a breach of faith, and might refuse to submit to any other authority.' The government also insisted that '[T]he the progress of Indianization in, and the provincialization of, the services will make it impossible to provide the officers required for these areas from the Assam cadres, unless special provision is made for them and the cost of administration is not debited to provincial revenues.' 'The backward tracts should be excluded from the province of Assam and be administered by the Governor-in-Council, as agent for the Governor-General in Council, and at the cost of the central revenues', the Assam government concluded.[153]

Political ideas produced during the Indian Statutory Commission's operations soon found their way into the making of the Government of India Act, 1935. Most Indian leaders remained lukewarm to the life and times of India's tribal population. The British parliament discussed the question of governance of these areas again during the framing of the Government of India Bill. The Act reinforced these provisions on a firm footing.[154] When the British lawmakers discussed the Sixth Schedule of the Government of India Bill in May 1935, they still carried with them racial biases. Edward Cadogan, the British politician from the Conservative Party, speaking on this, claimed how he was

> one of the few . . . of this House who have had conversation with the head hunters of Kohima in their own jungle . . . Presumably the District Commissioner had informed the tribal chieftain that my head was of no intrinsic value as he evinced no disposition to transfer it from my shoulders to his head hunter's basket which was slung over his back and was, I think, the only garment he affected.[155]

Cadogan insisted that he recounted this narrative 'to prove that these little tribesmen are more sophisticated in their own particular way than perhaps the Committee may imagine. They have a very shrewd suspicion that something is being done to take away from them their immemorial rights and customs'.

Would the scenario change dramatically now? Would universal franchise be extended into these areas? The Assam government was opposed to such an idea and wanted the hill areas to attain more political maturity first.[156] However, the inhabitants of these areas wanted to be a part of this exercise, and the Bardoloi Committee agreed partially. With the exception of Sadiya, Balipara and Tirap (forming modern Arunachal Pradesh), the others would participate in electoral democracy. They would form a part of the autonomous district councils. Denying franchise to the inhabitants of Arunachal Pradesh was, according to historian Ornit Shani, a result of preconceived notions while also keeping in mind India's security considerations.[157] The committee proposed that (1) modern Meghalaya, Nagaland, Mizoram, the North Cachar Hills and the Mikir Hills (excluding certain plains areas) be made autonomous districts, with wide-ranging powers vested in the district councils for the administration and development of these areas; (2) the Sadiya and Balipara Frontier Tracts, the Tirap Frontier Tract and the Naga Tribal Area should be non-autonomous areas, and responsibility for their all-round administration and development should be vested in the Governor of Assam; and (3) the tribals in the plains of Assam should be recognized as minorities and be entitled to all the privileges due to minorities, including representation in legislatures and in the services and that their land should be protected. The district council was an administrative innovation which found its place under the Sixth Schedule of the Constitution. Meanwhile, immediately after Independence, Bardoloi spelt out promises of equal rights to the tribal population in Assam, constituting approximately one-fifth of its population.[158]

~

Bardoloi's team submitted their rather lengthy report on 28 July 1947. Though it would not be of interest to the public who were otherwise enthusiastic to read about India's constitution-making process, *Amrita Bazar Patrika* could not ignore the sum and substance of the report, which stated that 'tribes should continue to form part and parcel of Assam and urged the need for closer and friendlier relations between the people of the province and the tribal people'.[159] For Bardoloi, most hill people demonstrated a fair sense of political consciousness and exhibited a desire for 'independent status'. This exercise, one of the many firsts in the constitution-making process, generated widespread public interest. In the Lushai Hills, a conference, held chiefly to consolidate the views of traditional chiefs, proposed a model constitution, which suggested that the district should govern itself except in matters of defence. The Naga Hills proposed an 'interim government of the Naga people', which would work under a benevolent 'guardian power'. The latter would provide funds for development and defence. Ten years later, the Naga Hills would decide 'what they would do with themselves'. Other areas also came up with similar model constitutions with varying degrees of political aspirations. Some wanted control over land, some over taxation or the justice system and so on. All these autonomous councils would have the right to frame laws in matters of land (except reserved forests), canals or water courses, jhum and village or town matters. The council would also have the liberty to either permit or prohibit the drinking of rice beer.

Bardoloi's report did not face any major challenge before it became a part of the draft constitution, and in February 1948, most of its suggestions were incorporated into the Sixth Schedule of the Constitution.[160] Patel's Advisory Committee, too, accepted all the recommendations with minimal amendments.[161] The Drafting Committee discussed it further in October 1948. But it was only a year later, in the first week of September 1949, that the Assembly took up the issue of tribes for extensive discussion, followed by a discussion on the Sixth Schedule of the Indian Constitution for the next two days. A wide range of perceptions and biases shaped the contours of those discussions. Brajeshwar Prasad, the Congressman from Gaya in Bihar who had earlier eloquently participated in debates on issues of citizenship, Centre–State relations and also public health, wanted the tribal areas to be governed as centrally administered areas rather than by the Assam government. As conflicts between different groups in Assam had reached a serious stage, 'therefore these problems should be left into the hands of the experts, social workers, doctors, teachers, engineers, psychologists, professors, philosophers, and sociologists, and no politicians should be allowed to meddle in this affair'.[162] He did not approve of legislative power being given to the tribal people (in the form of autonomous councils) either: 'The responsibilities of parliamentary life can be shouldered by those who are competent, wise, just and literate. To vest wide political powers into the hands of tribals is the surest method of inviting chaos, anarchy and disorder throughout the length and breadth of this country.' Kuladhar Chaliha, too, was clearly hostile and harsh in his assessment:

> The Nagas are a very primitive and simple people and they have not forgotten their old ways of doing summary justice when they have a grievance against anyone. If you allow them to rule us or run the administration it will be a negation of justice or administration and it will be something like anarchy.[163]

Chaliha, along with Rohini Kumar Chaudhuri, both veteran Congressmen from Assam, were most vocal and made known their strongest opposition to the idea of the Sixth Schedule.[164] Rights of doing trade or ownership of property by non-tribals in tribal areas, including that of Shillong, became a major source of contention. They moved umpteen amendments, most of which did not receive support from other members from Assam as well as other provinces of India. B.R. Ambedkar, law minister and the chairman of the Drafting Committee of the Constitution, wearily admitted that they wanted 'something more than what I can give. You are like hungry David Copperfield asking for more gruel'. Bardoloi had to persuade his fellow Assembly members by giving them a sense of the larger political circumstances—wartime sufferings, promises made by the British officials, the role of the Christian missionaries—which went into the making of the Sixth Schedule. He outlined those social institutions amongst the Assam tribes which bore powerful democratic characteristics. 'One of the things which I felt was very creditable [about] these tribes was the manner in which they settle their disputes,' Bardoloi told the Assembly.[165]

As most members were opposed to the idea of special political provisions for the tribes, Nichols Roy defended his people saying, 'To say that these tribesmen will be inimical to or they would raid Assam or go over to Tibet if this Sixth Schedule is introduced in these areas is rather surprising.'[166] An equally strong defence came from Jaipal Singh:

> I have been shocked by the amount of venom that has been poured forth this morning by some of the members against what they imagine the tribal people of Assam are going to do, if this or that is passed by this House . . . there are various kinds of hostilities.

Singh, however, agreed that the constitutional set-up provided 'an opportunity to forget the past and to make a happy beginning, in the beginning of which the hill people have given us their assurance'.[167] Appreciating the Bardoloi Committee for accommodating 'the wishes of those hill tribes', he acknowledged that the hill tribal people 'have climbed down' from their earlier stand. 'There is no question of keeping the hill tracts permanently in water-tight compartments . . . India cannot isolate itself from the rest of the world, nor can the hill tribes.' Jaipal Singh especially noted the massive transformation that had taken place since World War II (which has been discussed in chapter 1). 'Now ideas have penetrated the tracts, these mountainous tracts that were previously inaccessible. The position has completely changed. There is a new outlook. It is no good trying to think of the Naga as the eternal head-hunter.' Singh urged his fellow members to read the anthropologist Christoph von Fürer-Haimendorf's *The Naked Nagas* to 'understand these people even if they have not been to the Naga Hills'. According to him, it was important to comprehend the mind of the Nagas. A.V. Thakkar, a Gandhian social worker, came to the rescue of Jaipal Singh saying, 'I am very much ashamed at the ignorance we are all showing about the knowledge of the tribals, in Assam especially.'[168]

Ambedkar always made sure that the Assembly did not deliberate on matters which were beyond its scope, but his was perhaps one of the longest interventions on Assam.

> With regard to the tribals in Assam . . . [t]heir roots are still in their own civilization and their own culture. They have not adopted, mainly or in a large part, either the modes or the manners of the Hindus who surround them. Their laws of inheritance, their laws of marriage, customs and so on are quite different from that of the Hindus. I think that is the main distinction which influenced us to have a different sort of scheme for Assam from the one we have provided for other territories. In other words, the position of the tribals of Assam, whatever may be the reason for it, is somewhat analogous to the position of the Red Indians in the United States as against the white emigrants there.

Ambedkar's firm support, backed by Patel and Nehru, ensured that Chaudhuri's and Chaliha's disapproval failed to work.

After three days of gruelling debate, the Constituent Assembly finally adopted the Sixth Schedule on 7 September 1949. The partly tweaked Sixth Schedule stipulated that the executive authority of the Governor would extend to both tribal and non-tribal areas; the authority of the Assam legislature and the Parliament, too, would remain, except for moneylending, land alienation or judicial functions, which would be exercised by the village councils. These areas would not be immune to the high court and the Supreme Court. Laws made by the Parliament or the Assam legislature would be inapplicable unless the Governor notified them as otherwise. These areas would have legislative representation in the Parliament and in the Assam legislature.

It was not only on the floor of the Assembly where the lawmakers tried to spin the story. In the Drafting Committee meetings, too, there were disgruntled members when consensus on the rights of tribals was arrived at, and acrimony between disagreeing members did not escape the attention of the Indian press.[169] The Assamese intelligentsia was clearly divided. Some were solidly behind Bardoloi, while others lost no opportunity to pour out their venom. The latter's caste and cultural prejudices and their desire to control the economic and political affairs of Assam shaped their political position.

The Assamese connection with the province's hill districts had many facets. Some took adventurous journeys to the hill towns to study with their teachers who had been transferred from their hometowns to Kohima.[170] Towns and villages in the foothills had become major sites of trade and commerce under British rule.[171] Annual fairs held in the foothills facilitated and regulated these trading relations.[172] In the lower reaches of the Naga Hills, Dimapur developed as a vibrant township doing brisk trade, and more profitably during the war. Many residents from here expressed their willingness to be part of Assam.

The new constitutional arrangement left many perplexed and disturbed. In March 1948, a Mizo man wrote to the *Guardian* stating that the Mizos were 'greatly surprised to see the British leaving the Lushais without leaving concrete provisions for their future destiny'.[173] The letter concluded that 'it seems inevitable that we shall somehow or other desire to link ourselves with Burmese people who are more akin to us by custom and heredity', stressing that 'such desire would not be a mere whim nor would it be meant as an act of disloyalty to the new India'. In late 1947, Indian and British writers had already exchanged angry letters in the *Manchester Guardian* on the fate of Assam's hill people under the new Indian government.[174] The British man who initiated the exchanges thought that Assam's hill men had fought bravely against the Japanese during World War II and deserved better than what the British government had done. 'Naga headhunters were a constant source of terror to Japanese patrols in the Naga Hills area,' he wrote.[175] The gentleman cited discussions on the possibility of granting independence to the Kachins, Karens and Chins—the tribal population of Burma—and expressed regret that in the events leading up to Indian Independence, 'no publicity was given to the views and wishes of those tribes on the Assam-Burma border whose case closely resembles that of their Burmese counterparts'. In response, two Indian writers aggressively blamed the British for the poor condition of the tribes of India's North-east. One of them asked if the Englishmen still wanted to rule India's North-east. 'What would Mr. Bowman want his Government to do—give them self-rule or make the plea of special protection an excuse for British rule to continue?'[176]

Though many British colonial officials held similar nostalgic views of India's North-east, the expatriates were mostly silent. London's *Times*, normally vocal about India matters, did not report this constitutional development. The only exception to this silence came in May 1950, when the anthropologist Christoph von Fürer-Haimendorf, then teaching at the School of Oriental and African Studies, delivered the George Birdwood Memorial Lecture at the Royal Society of Arts in London. He spoke on the fate of Indian tribes in the new political structure of India. He had spent several years in the northern frontier of Assam as an anthropologist, and later, during his brief stint in the External Affairs Department of the Indian government, he was posted in the very same areas of Assam. Fürer-Haimendorf agreed that the making of the Sixth Schedule proved that Indian legislators were awake to 'their responsibility' towards India's tribal population, whose future depended on 'the vision and goodwill of their more progressive compatriots'.[177] He was equally sure that though change in the lives of tribal communities in the North-east was inevitable, they would 'persist in their distinctive way of life more stubbornly than any other tribal community of India'. He explained that this was because of the 'culture-pattern' of the 'Mongoloid, Tibeto-Burman-speaking hillmen', who had their roots outside the 'orbit of Indian civilisation'.

Bringing Assam's hill areas into the ambit of a modern state machinery had always been opposed. In 1939, in a conference held on the administration of the 'partially excluded areas', 'one of the first proposals made was that they should all be placed under the jurisdiction of the High Court'—which was strongly opposed by the Khasi leaders, including J.J.M. Nichols Roy. J.P. Mills, secretary to the Governor of Assam and erstwhile commissioner of the Naga Hills, wrote to E.S. Hyde, the British official posted in Bastar, Central India, that 'there has never been any question of placing the Excluded areas under the Calcutta High Court'. Mills told his colleague, 'I should think it would be impossible to find stronger evidence than this that people who really understand so-called primitive tribes would never willingly agree to High Court jurisdiction.'[178]

While the question of protection and welfare of the ethnic communities, no doubt, shaped the course of the Sixth Schedule, India's national security concerns also significantly influenced those political debates on the future of Indian tribes. The rise of the Communist Party to political power in China similarly became a matter of serious worry for the Indian government. There was a sense of unease among the Indian officials as they highlighted the role of the communists on both sides, Burma and India.[179] The 'Communists are now trying to fish in the troubled waters of the north eastern hills,' wrote H.V.R. Iyengar, a senior ICS official in the Ministry of Home Affairs. Iyengar warned that the communists had been trying to mobilize the hill population on 'racial and ethnic[al] grounds'.[180] Moreover, he highlighted the Ahom Revivalist Movement, the Ahom leader Surendranath Buragohain's interaction with various Kachin chiefs, the Burmese attempt to establish contact with the Ahom leaders in Assam and Lushai's increasing political contacts with the Burmese tribal leaders.

The Burmese government also recruited people from the Lushai Hills into the Chin Regiment of Burma. Indian officials were aware that many Indians were 'apparently attracted by the promise of regular employment in the Chin Regiments'.

> It is obviously undesirable that Indian Lushais should receive military training by the Burmese government. If and when they eventually return to their own home in India, they may form a nucleus of men trained in the use of modern weapons. The ease with which arms can be smuggled over the border will make them a potential menace later on.[181]

Indian embassy officials in Burma, however, discounted any political motive behind such recruitment and emphasized the mere economic reasons. 'Most of the recruits slip across the border and apply to the recruiting officer when he goes on tour in the Chin Hills. They claim to be residents of villages on the Burma side of the border, and join the army either as Chins and Gurkhas,' said one official. Much to the worry of the Indian government, in May 1949, clashes had broken out between the Burmese government and rebels in the Chin Hills near the Assam–Burma border.[182] This border would remain porous over the decades into the twenty-first century, as several communities of Assam's hills were dispersed on either side of it.

The Sixth Schedule only defined the territories and forms of government for India's tribal population. But there was also a realization that there should be more discussions on the list of communities that should be considered as tribes in the Scheduled list, particularly those who lived in the plains of Assam or did not inhabit the 'specified tribal areas'. An existing list was drawn from Section 91 of the Government of India Act, 1935. Biraja Sankar Guha, director of the Anthropological Survey of India and advisor to the Government of India on tribal affairs, suggested to the Constituent Assembly that the existing provisions were 'not comprehensive enough in protecting the aboriginal population inhabiting such regions as were outside the scope of the "Excluded" or "Partially Excluded Areas"'. He suggested a revision of the Eighth Schedule of the Draft Constitution of India—by incorporating more tribes into this list—which listed the recognized Indian aboriginal tribes so that it becomes 'comprehensive and uniform'.[183] The Assam government's response, unlike that of many other Indian provinces, was lukewarm.[184] The fallout of this was catastrophic as we will see in the later chapters.

# 5

# Domestic Woes

As Assam negotiated its future position in the larger scheme of India's political framework, there was turmoil within. The Bardoloi government faced several pressing domestic issues. Besides the contentious question of land redistribution, low agrarian productivity and incomes, poor infrastructure and the struggle for control over the state's resources, such as oil, the Naga demand for independence intensified and became a cause of national concern. The first shock, however, came from a section of the rural population who had infused great dynamism into anti-imperialist mass politics in earlier years. The spectacular rise of communists in Assam's countryside posed a challenge to the Congress. Their popularity saw a phenomenal increase post-Independence, largely among the rural poor, which included sharecroppers and landless labourers.

Official accounts of 1951 present a grim picture of Assam's agrarian situation. Out of its population of 9 million, three-quarters were entirely supported by agriculture. Of these, 58 per cent (about 5.2 million) were peasant landowners who owned slightly more land than was needed for their subsistence. They tended their land, often with family members, and, occasionally, with the help of a few seasonal workers. Others, an estimated 13 per cent (1.1 million), who had less land than they needed to support themselves, rented an extra plot or made themselves available as temporary farmhands. Less than 1 per cent, many of whom lived in the towns, earned income solely by leasing out their lands. Many families derived additional income from crafts, which connected these rural families to a wider commercial network. Unlike the zamindari system of neighbouring Bengal, multiple forms of legal rights existed over land in Assam. If a majority of lands came under the ryotwari system, the hill dwellers retained their customary traditions of ownership and practised various modes of shifting cultivation. In the non-hilly vast plains of Assam, one-fifth of those dependent on agriculture were sharecroppers who cultivated land rented from others.[1] They were not rich; some three-quarters of them possessed tiny plots of less than 0.13 hectare. Many people were worse off with no land and heavily burdened by debt. On the other hand, a tiny fraction—1 per cent—of the population lived off the rents collected from their landed property. Communist ideology naturally held an appeal for Assam's impoverished peasants.

~

Ruth Fischer, the co-founder of the Austrian Communist Party, once said that the Indian communists could not build a nation-wide organization, on the one hand, because of their heavy reliance on 'rationalism, the French Enlightenment and Western Marxism', and, on the other, owing to Gandhi's spectacular success in the anti-imperialist struggle, which had brought him the support of India's masses.[2] But things began to change after 1942, as two decades of defending the economic rights of the agrarian poor had helped the communists gain an impressive foothold in rural India. In the northern districts of Bengal, sharecroppers had long refused to toe the line of the powerful zamindars.[3] In the princely state of Hyderabad, too, the sharecroppers were united against the zamindars. Assam was not far behind.[4] The large labour force in the tea gardens—half a million in 1944—were on daily wages[5] and not beyond the reach of unionism.[6] As the economic distress of the mid-1940s worsened the agrarian situation, the communists violently turned Assam's rural world upside down in 1947. They persuaded the sharecroppers, who so far had been forced to hand over roughly half of their total produce to the landlords, either to refuse to give anything or to give a drastically reduced portion. They also encouraged the rural population to reclaim government-owned land, including forests.

Towards the end of 1947, most landlords bore the brunt of sharecroppers' direct refusal to hand over any part of their produce. The Bardoloi government passed a law that, on paper, accepted the demands of the sharecroppers backed by the communists, but it did not show any promptness to implement it. As the sharecroppers continued to resist the landlords, the Assam government allowed the Assam Adhiar Rights and Protection Act of 1948 to be enforced in areas on the southern bank of the Brahmaputra, in Kamrup, in June but kept the other districts beyond its purview. While the passing of the law resulted in the jubilance of the sharecroppers, it did not end the rural discontent. The landlords were not ready to come to terms with the angry sharecroppers, and landless peasants could not effectively thrust themselves onto the government's lands. The landlords, most of whom hailed from Assamese Hindu families and who were firmly in control of the political machinery and land revenue bureaucracy, ensured that the land reforms were unsuccessful. Two decades later, when an official of the Indian planning commission visited Assam to take stock of the implementation of the land reform laws, he found that 'even the lower revenue staff' were 'themselves unaware of the provisions of the law', while the 'people were generally completely ignorant' of them.[7]

While the Congress, with its vast organization, had a firm grip on the state machinery, it could not stop the Communist Party of India (CPI) from stepping up its anti-landlord mobilization. In the second party congress of the CPI in Calcutta in 1948, two of its leaders—Puran Chand Joshi and Bhalchandra Trimbak Ranadive—strongly disagreed on whether the party should work within the constitutional framework of the new Indian state or aspire to be a revolutionary party. Joshi, then the general secretary of the party and an admirer of Gandhi,[8] thought that the party must support Nehru's government, given that the CPI lacked popular support and had secured a low vote share in the provincial assembly elections held in 1946.[9] Joshi's views, however, had few takers, and the leadership passed into the hands of his radical comrade, Ranadive.

According to Ranadive, the time for revolution had arrived.[10] He denounced India's independence from the British Empire as false, which in Hindi went, '*Yeh azaadi jhoothi hai* (This freedom is not real).' Under his leadership, the CPI embarked on armed struggles in Telangana, West Bengal, Tripura and Travancore–Cochin between October 1948 and March 1950, with the call to replace the Indian state with a republic of workers, peasants and the oppressed middle classes.[11] In West Bengal, the party was banned in March 1948, a move considered by Nehru's government as a panic reaction 'in spite of virulent propaganda'.[12] Having escaped an all-India ban, the CPI continued to mobilize in Assam. The party's Assam unit did not want to follow Ranadive's ideological position, and it was reorganized in 1949.[13]

The Revolutionary Communist Party of India (RCPI), which had broken away from the CPI in 1934, was organizationally confined to a few places in India, but it had a wider influence in Assam. Their principal ideologue was Saumyendranath Tagore. Tagore closely interacted with European communist leaders during his stay in Western Europe between 1927 and 1934. In 1933, he wrote to his grand-uncle, the Nobel Prize-winning poet Rabindranath Tagore, criticising him for his inability to appreciate the increasing dangers of political steps taken by Hitler in Germany.[14] When he returned from Europe in 1934, his disagreement with the Indian communist leaders became open, and he formed the Communist League, which was renamed the Revolutionary Communist Party of India in 1940.[15] Tagore's RCPI, meanwhile, succeeded in attracting many from amongst the younger generation in Assam to his fold. Tagore, who felt that the ideas of the Russian revolutionary Leon Trotsky were more apt in the Indian context than those of Joseph Stalin, was also unconvinced about carrying out a revolutionary upsurge in India,[16] unlike his ideological opponents such as Pannalal Dasgupta[17] in Bengal, who planned to overthrow the Government of India. Pannalal had many years of experience in organizing extremist activities in Bengal. Assam, for him, was a fertile ground for a restaging of the revolution in China, where an alliance of communist guerrillas with peasants was to capture political power in 1949.[18] While these competing ideas took many twists and turns, Pannalal parted ways with Saumyendranath, and the Assam unit of RCPI remained with the latter.[19]

In Assam, the communists had been active long before Independence and made significant gains in 1938. The communists relentlessly pressured the government to abolish landlordism,[20] and it succeeded in mobilizing workers from rice mills, oil pressing mills, steamer workers, tea gardens, the Digboi oil refinery and the match factory, among other places. Labour unions flourished; there were frequent strikes of short durations over wage disputes.[21] The strikes, whose frequency had increased, in tea gardens often took a violent form.[22]

Early in 1947, Assam's chief secretary, Harold George Dennehy, had spelt out his government's intention to keep track of any communist-minded individuals.[23] By 1949, as the communists became successful in mobilizing the rural population, more so in remote areas, including places like the Garo hills, panic gripped the Assam administration.[24] The Bardoloi government was determined to win back the disgruntled rural population and overcome the communist threat. Bardoloi assured Nehru that though the communists were still popular 'among the tribal people and the students', the Congress party machinery had dealt with them successfully.[25] In mid-1949, the government began to arrest or detain rebellious sharecroppers and their communist leaders under the Assam Maintenance of Public Order Act of 1947.[26] By July, they had arrested nearly 400 communists, including their prominent leaders who had gone underground. Parts of Assam were declared as disturbed areas.[27] Defiant villages were put under police surveillance, intelligence gathering was intensified and a punitive tax was imposed on the villages.[28] Occasionally, as in the July 1949 clashes during a programme organized by the Indian People's Theatre Association (IPTA), a cultural wing of the CPI, at Naliapool in Dibrugarh (a tea garden-dominated township), violent clashes erupted between the Communists and the police and state machinery.[29] Violent acts on both sides invited censure from even left-leaning public figures.[30] When he heard of these violent clashes, a young Assamese wrote in his diary, 'Hell.'³¹ State repression further intensified. 'We have won the first round in our fight against the Communists, who are out to spread chaos and disruption in the province,' Bishnuram Medhi, Bardoloi's powerful cabinet colleague, declared in July 1949.³²

Anti-communist state action gained greater significance as communist China invaded Tibet in 1950 and made its presence felt in Burma. Bardoloi frequently briefed Nehru not just about the rising communist activities in Assam, but also about the threat from across the northern and eastern borders. The 'communist menace from the side of Burma is assuming a threatening attitude', Bardoloi wrote to Nehru.³³ Patel, too, wrote to Nehru about prospective 'communist threats' to India's security along India's 'northern and north-eastern frontiers where, for supplies of arms and ammunition, they can safely depend on [the] communist arsenals in China'.³⁴ There were widespread rumours, further aggravated by inputs from India's intelligence officials, of the infiltration of communists from Burma and China, which Nehru had to deny.³⁵

By 1950, the state machinery was deeply unsettled by communist activities. An alert Bardoloi undertook an extensive tour of Assam to overcome the 'vile propaganda' of the communists 'for ousting all government authority' in many places.³⁶ 'Communist problems are quite acute,' Patel worriedly acknowledged.³⁷ The government measures could not wear out the communists nor reduce their popularity. They had become a 'potent force', conceded Assam's erstwhile Governor, Sri Prakasa, in June 1950.³⁸ In many places, landlords could not collect rent from sharecroppers. Policemen and socially powerful or wealthy merchants were killed.³⁹ In Robin Hood-style, the communist rebels often took money from the rich and redistributed it among the poor, who were officially described as 'sympathizers of the Communists'.

As the communists remained popular in the countryside, the landlords, a major source of support for the Congress, pressured the government. In July 1950, the RCPI was banned.⁴⁰ The Assam government dithered on banning the CPI.⁴¹ In August that year, parts of Upper Assam were declared disturbed areas. A British government secret official record noted that the party 'was planning subversive activities on a wide scale' and there was evidence of 'guerilla training'.[42] According to Assam's Governor, 'Its members are believed to have been responsible for murders, robberies, and intimidation' in tribal areas.[43] In the same year, anti-communist state repression reached its peak. Armed police, equipped with wide-ranging powers, hunted down communist leaders and their followers across the state. The landlords too, armoured with the state machinery, evicted sharecroppers or took the help of the police to secure their rents. Surendranath Buragohain, a union minister, confirmed that the 'murderous activities' of the communist leaders were now 'checked'.[44]

But the massive state repression failed to demoralize the communists and their committed followers. As the sharecroppers remained united, tied by ethnic and caste factors, the communists retained their grip across rural Assam well into the 1950s and even later. Early in 1951, a contemporary observer remarked that Assam had become 'communist infested'.[45] Most RCPI leaders went underground and continued to receive support from the villagers in their hideouts. Communist leaders like Bishnu Rabha were able to delay or evade arrest as villagers protected them. The lure of rewards could not persuade people to give up their charismatic leaders.[46] Communist leaders recounted their roller-coaster existence at that time, when villagers, mostly tribal peasants, outsmarted the police by resorting to lying and trickery and helped their leaders to escape arrest. These underground accounts became part of folklore.

As the communists intensified their actions against the landlords and the state machinery, their scathing verbal attacks were popularized through pamphlets. Decades of repressive social and economic relations between Assamese Hindu landowners and their tribal sharecroppers broke down. A perceptive Assamese novel of 1952 captured this broken relationship brilliantly. The father of the novel's protagonist, an Assamese Hindu landowner, ranted, 'They [tribal sharecroppers] should be shot down.' When the protagonist had asked their sharecropper's daughter why they had not paid the rent, she had countered, 'How do I know? The people asked us not to pay.'[47]

Meanwhile, the number of arrested communists swelled. About 1250 activists or followers of RCPI were arrested between 1950 and 1951;[48] some among them were prosecuted. Implicit help came from Congress workers, who provided the police with intelligence. Weapons were seized from communist hideouts in the southern hilly neighbourhood of Guwahati, which were described in the press as secret camps to establish a 'red regime'.[49] Communist propaganda material was proscribed, and a month-long ban was imposed on public meetings and processions.[50] By early 1951, the police took back more than 2500 square kilometres of land from communist control.[51] Yet, there were more areas where the communists were considered local heroes and were offered steadfast support. In Guwahati's neighbourhoods, communist workers had stolen paddy from rich landlords and dispensed them to hungry families. 'Looting of rice and other heinous crimes are still going on there,' reported an Assamese daily.[52]

As police surveillance and suppression increased, many communist leaders took refuge deep inside forests. In Upper Assam, personnel of the Assam Rifles, a unit of the Indian Army, encircled more than 2500 square kilometres to prevent the escape of Khagen Barbarua, a widely popular leader who became a member of the Legislative Assembly years later.[53] The *Statesman* described how the police 'had barricaded roads and dug trenches around the hideout'.[54] But the communists continued to pose a threat to the state. The government has 'during the past year been endeavouring to combat the red menace within their border areas but the communist activities have not been yet suppressed', reported the *Times of India*.[55]

By the end of 1951, after suffering months of repression, and despite the silent victories of villagers, the communists sought ways to reconcile themselves with the Indian state. As a result of ideological disputes that caused a split in the party, they decided to discard aggressive political action.[56] Communist leader Bishnu Rabha and several others acknowledged their organizational mistakes.[57] Some others accepted that theirs had been acts of revolutionary adventurism. As they took cognizance of their strategic mistakes and made a fresh appraisal of Assam's agrarian relations, a senior communist leader later wrote that in most parts of Assam 'there were no rich landlords' and asked: '[If] we give only one-fifth of the produce how will they [petty landlords] survive.'[58] The CPI decided to participate in the country's first general elections. The leaders were upbeat about their popularity and recent successes across rural India. They felt that since 'the growth of the mass movement has not kept pace with the growth of discontentment' with Nehru's government, they 'must fight the parliamentary elections'.[59] In the first general election to the Assam Legislative Assembly of 1952, the CPI contested 18 seats. Though it won only one seat, it got an impressive 13.75 per cent of the total votes polled in the constituencies contested.[60] The socialists and communists together got 22 per cent of the total votes polled, as against the 43.48 per cent votes for the Congress. Gaurisankar Bhattacharyya, CPI's general secretary, won from a seat in Guwahati, securing more than one-third of the votes polled.

Following political negotiations between RCPI leaders and the government in August 1952, the government annulled the ban on the party in October.[61] While the election results indicated that the CPI was not far behind the Congress, the communists had lost significant organizational strength. Most communist leaders realized that, in the process of mobilizing the sharecroppers, they had lost the critical support of a majority of the Assamese small peasants. The election had briefly stopped the communists' rural mobilization, and newly formed Congress-led organizations encouraged distressed peasants to seek relief from their landlords and the government. To demonstrate its pro-peasant position, the government formed land settlement advisory committees. However, being dominated by rich landowners, the government also gave reprieve to the rich landlords and tea planters.

The communist- and socialist-led peasant organizations were convinced about the success of the peasant movement. They believed that the payment of rent amounting to 50 per cent of the produce to the landlords had completely stopped, the landlords had failed to enter the villages or evict their sharecroppers, the sharecroppers had retained their lands, the village panchayats had become paramount, the state administration had receded and the contractors of the forest department were working in the hill forests after taking permission from the panchayats. They also believed that the expectations of the peasants had been met to a certain extent. For instance, a boatman who was an erstwhile supporter of the Congress Socialist Party (CSP), who had helped in their political activities in the neighbourhoods of Guwahati, later reclaimed land in northern Kamrup with the help of the CSP. In a couple of years, he had cultivated it to produce crops, though, of course, this land was without tenurial security.[62] Like many across other districts, he remembered the tumultuous days of political action, which helped them in their pursuit of freedom from an oppressive social structure.

Shortly thereafter, the communists, especially the RCPI, welcomed the immigrant peasants and Hindu refugees into their fold. The communists and socialists were increasingly seen as helping common people, hearing them out in matters of local civic governance. They demanded the establishment of fair price shops, the conversion of annually leased land to permanent lease land and the distribution of land among the landless. They won the local board elections. At the same time, they did not lose sight of the fact that they had mobilized the sharecroppers and occasionally succeeded in stopping rent to the landowners.[63] The communists' movement against unequal tenancy in the countryside brought a ray of hope for the poor besides giving the left parties a decisive, though limited, electoral advantage. But years of struggle did not put an end to tenancy; rather in 1961, it rose sharply to 37 per cent of the total agrarian population.[64]

The rise in political consciousness among the working class, including workers in the tea gardens, rickshaw-pullers, postal employees and railway workers, was noticeable. Workers of the steamer companies in the Brahmaputra demanded the nationalization of this industry.[65] The clashes in the tea gardens intensified. There was a growing demand for the implementation of the suggestions of the Plantation Inquiry Commission of 1956. Bitter clashes between the planters and workers were reported. In 1957, a manager of the tea estate in Darrang died in one such clash. Outside the tea industry, the situation was equally grim. Employees of the printing presses of Dibrugarh went on strike demanding higher wages.[66]

~

One of the hardest jobs for Nehru's government was to deliver on many of the Congress's pre-Independence promises on agrarian reform. Some Indian provinces had initiated piecemeal land reforms by the late 1940s. To bring parity in those efforts, and to understand the post-reform situation, the Congress formed an Agrarian Reforms Committee (ARC) in 1948.[67] Headed by the noted Gandhian economist J.C. Kumarappa, the ARC visited Assam in July of that year. The first person that the committee spoke to was Umakanta Goswami, who was teaching at Cotton College and was the father of the celebrated Assamese litterateur Mamoni Raisom Goswami. The latter's well-known Assamese novel *Datal Hatir Uye Khowa Haoda* was based on tumultuous events occurring during the 1940s on the landed estates owned by her parents. Others interviewed were Jagadish Medhi, Kamakhya Ram Barooah, Dinanath Medhi and Haladhar Bhuyan, whose views represented that of the tiny Assamese power elite. As the committee heard the views of a cross-section of the Assamese people, it emerged that the overall mood was against sharecropping; there was a demand for a ceiling on landholding. Most people were familiar with the massive rural mobilization against sharecropping in Assam. Many public figures and those from well-to-do families, who did not necessarily endorse communist political ideas, still took a harsh view of sharecropping: 'I do not want subletting of the land as a rule but for the time being it must continue.'[68] Public opinion was against the zamindari system too: 'Zamindars have got land without much sacrifice and do little by way of investment for their improvement',[69] and 'if somebody has got some land, he should either cultivate it or he should be urged to give it up. There should be no tenant'.[70] Others agreed that excess land in the tea gardens should be taken away. Many stressed the need for greater efficiency in farming—apparently sharing their displeasure against jhum—in the hills. Most insisted that attention be paid to river training, though they admitted its impracticality in controlling floods, which they recognized as a reason behind Assam's agrarian stagnancy.

Kumarappa's visit gave the Assam government much-needed ideological and political backing to push for the abolition of zamindari.[71] The Assam Legislative Assembly had passed the Assam State Acquisition of Zamindaris Bill on 28 March 1949 to abolish the zamindari system in two districts of Assam, but it had to wait for presidential confirmation till July 1951 for it to become an Act. Meanwhile, the Assam Management of Estates Act was passed in 1949 with a view to protecting the natural wealth of the estates, forests, fisheries, etc.[72] The powerful zamindars, like many of their counterparts across India, challenged the legality of this law but lost their case in 1954 in the Supreme Court.[73]

The Act came into force in April 1954 after getting the go-ahead from India's highest court. A year later, the government brought all zamindari property under its control. Meanwhile, tenants of zamindars, who were being mobilized by the communists, and who had long dreamt of such a step, demanded that their rights as tenants be secured.[74] Most tenants in the zamindari estates of Goalpara belonged to the tribal communities (Bodo, Koch, Rabha or Garo). From the early 1940s onwards, zamindars had allowed settlers from neighbouring Bengal too.[75] However, the settlers hardly benefitted from zamindari abolition as land rights were not transferred to them. By early 1957, of the nearly 7,00,000 hectares of land under zamindari in Assam, an estimated one-third was taken over by the government with compensation of approximately Rs 50 million paid to the intermediaries.[76] The Act incorporated a complex mathematical formula to calculate the compensation to be given to the zamindars, but there was no elaborate description of the methods of transfer of rights to the would-be owners. The compensation was to be paid in cash and in bonds. Angry zamindars ejected their tenants, rampantly cut down forests and fraudulently leased out wastelands. This continued even as the zamindars challenged the 1949 law on the management of estates.

The Goalpara zamindars stood on a different footing from those in Cachar. The district had been added to Assam in 1874, and since then, these areas had uneasy relations with Assam. In the first half of the century, the zamindars fought for their cultural and social identity and tried to carefully develop a relationship with the Assamese literary intelligentsia. The Goalpara zamindars' wish to join Bengal remained a formidable political idea well into the mid-twentieth century. In 1925, Prabhat Chandra Barua, an influential zamindar of Goalpara, made it clear that 'in case Sylhet is transferred to Bengal, it would be difficult to resist the claims of Goalpara'.[77] By the middle of the twentieth century, after years of fraught cultural and intellectual battles, these old preferences were delicately positioned alongside Goalpara's erstwhile landlords' defence of Assamese linguistic and nationalistic aspirations.

Goalpara witnessed extraordinary discontentment among the lower classes, including tenants who toiled in the fields, in the early twentieth century. The zamindars faced serious challenges as tenants made concerted attempts to secure their rights. Mass mobilization, violent clashes and court cases became rampant. Kalicharan Brahma, one of the pioneering religious reformers of the Bodo ethnic community, which formed a sizable section of tenants, mobilized these tenants, seeking legal safeguards in terms of their tenurial rights and against excessive rent extraction. A.J. Laine, the British colonial official who was specially deputed to investigate these growing disputes, recorded that between 1907 and 1917, there were 5782 rent suits in Goalpara.[78] In their southern neighbourhood, the Garos ferociously resisted many attempts by zamindars to acquire their lands.[79] The charismatic Garo leader Sonaram Sangma fought a lengthy legal and political battle against the zamindars. A law in 1929 gave some relief to the tenants but further angered the zamindars.[80] Meanwhile, the Gandhian mass mobilization enthused many of the tenants. Their political battles, often scattered and isolated, took a sharp turn in the early 1940s when agrarian relations underwent striking changes. Haats and a bazaar were looted by the tribal population during the Quit India Movement of 1942. By this time, the demographic composition of the agrarian society had undergone dramatic changes with the settlement of peasants from East Bengal. Abdul Hamid Khan Bhashani politically mobilized them during the peak of the pro-Pakistan movement.[81] The communist and socialists made an entry into these areas and met with partial success and partial failure. Well into the second half of the century, this anti-landlord discontentment and protests did not acquire any significant sectarian form.

The Goalpara zamindars were not far behind in protecting their privileges. They tried to win over the Assamese nationalist leaders, putting aside their petty social rivalries, and took up Assamese linguistic and literary causes. They may well have lost their zamindari privileges, but they manipulated legal procedures to keep a significant share of their erstwhile property in their custody through fictitious titles. Complicated legal procedures, well-entrenched in the Goalpara Tenancy Act of 1929, barred tenants from becoming owners of land for several decades. However, all over Assam, there was very little sympathy for the landlords, who attributed their downfall to the 'sinful acts' of the communists. Theirs was largely a story of decadence, and many succeeded in taking advantage of legal loopholes to hold on to their properties. Some took up petty industrial and commercial ventures; one zamindar heir, Pratima Barua Pandey, became a celebrated folk singer. But most disappeared from public memory.

A researcher who carried out field investigations in these areas during 1960–61 confirmed that landlords, whether large or petty, had fallen 'from the zenith of their past status and prominence in social life'.[82] But many of their now free tenants found it difficult to negotiate their new legal status. This researcher was told by erstwhile tenants about their bitter experience with government revenue officials. The majority of the tribal population in the erstwhile zamindaris were bound by the red tape of revenue officials, as a result of which they were not entitled to any legal rights. The researcher also found that revenue officials often fabricated false records either 'perfunctorily or deliberately' for personal gain. Another survey conducted in 1970–71 found that a little over 78 per cent of families held less than 2 hectares of land each. The number of families that owned more than 50 hectares of land stood at 20.[83] While big landlordism had apparently declined, it had metamorphosed into other forms, though now, tenants did not shy away from asserting their claims.[84] But this did not happen without some help from the state.

The communist leaders were critical of such ineffective land reform programmes. The CPI censured the legislation in Assam as 'worse than similar acts in other provinces'.[85] In 1964, the Congress party conceded that in most zamindari areas 'up-to-date records-of-rights worth the name were not available'.[86] A revenue bureaucracy, trained primarily to collect revenue and protect the rights of the landlords, was unable to manage their new task, and it would take them a very long time to change. A Planning Commission official in the mid-1960s found that countless bureaucratic and legal hurdles had denied faceless tenants access to legal rights and ownership for years.[87] More than 35,700 lawsuits were filed by tenants in 1964 to ensure their rights were protected,[88] but these disputes would not be resolved until the next decade.

~

Three pieces of legislation had come into existence between 1948 and 1959 to fulfil the Gandhian promises of land reform.[89] These laws took on the economically and socially powerful, and addressed the massive agrarian discontent discussed above. They combined two socialistic goals: to decimate the might of landed proprietors, including the tea planters, and redistribute the land according to the principles of social justice.

One of the Acts—the Assam Land (Requisition and Acquisition) Act, 1948—was primarily targeted at the massive tea estates, less than a third of which were actually under tea cultivation in 1947.[90] The Congress government had for years contemplated such an idea. The powerful tea planters tried to prevent the law from coming into effect by taking it to court. When the government decided to take away 1000 bighas of the oldest tea company, the Assam Company's Cherideo Purbut Tea Estate, for redistribution among 'landless, indigenous, and actual cultivators', the company fought back on two grounds. It contested the constitutional validity of this law as it preceded the

Indian Constitution and said that these lands were already under cultivation following the ideals of the government's own 'Grow More Food' campaign. The judges did not agree.[91] Patches of land were, thus, quickly redistributed among landless Assamese, ostensibly to preempt any 'directive from the Government of India that such lands must be reserved for the Bengali-Hindu refugees'.[92]

An Act that fixed the upper limit that a resident could own at 20 hectares created a significant impact. In 1951, families whose lands exceeded this area constituted less than 1 per cent of the total.[93] The Assamese rich landowning families and tea planters managed to stave off its execution until the Supreme Court upheld its validity in 1961. By the end of the 1960s, some 2000 landowners and more than a 100 tea planters had to part with an estimated 36,000 hectares of land.[94]

The third Act brought religious institutions under the ambit of this ceiling.[95] Some rich and influential religious heads sold off their properties in anticipation of the arrival of the new law. 'Hearing that some ceiling is on the way, gosains are selling off their land,' whispers a character in the novel *Datal Hatir Uye Khowa Haoda*.[96]

Though these Acts were radical on the surface, their implementation was tardy and complicated. 'Pace of progress ... has not been as quick as expected owing to the lengthy procedure prescribed under the Act,' an official document recorded.[97] Many landowners were able to dodge the law and deceitfully transfer or redistribute their lands among their family members under fictitious names to evade its acquisition by the state.[98]

The hope of getting surplus land for redistribution fell 'far short of original expectation'. The government admitted that its 'land reforms measures are revolutionary in nature, but they lack all the elements of revolution'.[99] Legal and political challenges thwarted effective implementation of agrarian reform legislation. Many of these legislative initiatives took shape due to widespread popular agitation. Over the years, rich and powerful politicians, businessmen and rich landowners partnered with the bureaucracy to make the laws ineffective. In 1971, a government enquiry, which investigated cases of manipulation of ceiling laws, including by Congress politician F.A. Ahmed (later President of

India), agreed that 'the inadequacy of the administrative machinery together with the all-pervasive influence of the rich have combined to defeat the basic purpose of one of the most primary land reform legislations'.[100] The land reforms gained some political momentum again in the mid-1970s during the Emergency. Then the biggest losers were the tea gardens; the government filed as many as 761 lawsuits against planters between 1975 and 1977 under the ceiling law. Of the total land acquired by the government under this law, 70 per cent were held by the planters.[101]

Since 1948, the Assam government had begun settling landless people in remote forested areas by opening up Reserved Forests. One such example was the Kaki Land Reclamation Project in central Assam. When it was opened for settlement, the area had poor communications, scarcity of water and a general unhealthy atmosphere, which dampened the 'pioneering spirit of the early settlers who were not much hopeful to reclaim the deep forest area without state aid'. In 1952, the government obtained technology and machinery which, coupled with German expertise, helped in massive forest clearance and flattening of the earth. In 1954, when a correspondent visited this site, he found 'unprecedented enthusiasm among the four hundred settlers . . . determined to create a "Brave New World" for them[selves]'. A German expert stationed there 'killed an eighteen-foot python in the area and stopped the commotion that prevailed in this otherwise peaceful area', the reporter noted. A young settler, who had been uprooted by a recent devastating flood, met the reporter with his prized catch—a barking deer. 'What was once a dense jungle is now gradually being cleared by the sixteen tractors and bulldozers.' The journalist was hopeful that 'a visit to the area will convince even the bitterest critic of the Government that they (government) are very serious [about] land reforms, and they are engaged in a gigantic fight to settle the uprooted humanity, caused by floods and other natural calamities'.[102]

For years before Independence, Assam's tribal population, across the vast floodplains, waged a political and cultural struggle demanding respect and equal status with their caste Hindu Assamese neighbours, a share in the emerging legislative domain and legal protection to retain their lands. If, in 1927, a Bodo author complained about how the Bodos had not been given due respect by the Assamese,[103] during 1928–29, the tribal and lower-caste leaders, claiming that they did not 'bind [themselves] to the chariot wheels of the big Hindu community',[104] sent a memorandum to the Simon Commission seeking measures for social improvement and autonomous legislative rights.[105] From 1933 onwards, the Tribal League was at the forefront of the growing collective awareness, with an impressive presence among many tribal and lower caste communities. The Congress reached out to them, and between 1937 and 1946, lawmakers backed by the Tribal League won elections and became key allies of the pre-Independence governments. Their leaders, among them Bhimbor Deuri (1903–47) and Rupnath Brahma (1902–68), had remarkable legislative careers and campaigned relentlessly for legal and political measures to ensure that poor tribals did not lose their land. By the 1930s, disputes between tribal peasants and the new settlers from Bengal became intensely political—even though arguments on both sides were often alleged to be shrouded in 'fictions and fairy tales'.[106] Political pressure from the tribal leaders led to a significant move by the government in 1939, when it proposed that the allocation of 'prohibited areas' would be 'inhabited predominantly by backward and tribal classes'.[107] But the War and fast-changing political developments delayed the process till 1945.[108] In 1946, the Tribal League joined the newly formed Bardoloi government.[109] In 1947, the government created legal provisions to create protected areas exclusively for the tribal population, termed as tribal belts and blocks. Between 1947 and 1951, 31 such protected sites were constituted across Lower Assam and elsewhere, spread over more than 15,000 square kilometres and equivalent to one-fifth of the state. These extensive sites were carved out without dislocating any major economic infrastructure.

The actual process of ascribing legal rights to residents of tribal belts did not however take any firm shape. Soon, these areas began to shrink with urban expansion and the spread of industrial or irrigation infrastructure. Rich, urban, non-tribal families disagreed with the idea of protected sites, as these areas fast emerged as places of economic and cultural importance. Government officials felt the same. When Guwahati began to expand in the 1960s, one city planner warned that the idea of tribal belts would 'simply frustrate the aims of the Master Plan'.[110] In early 1965, a petition by a group of angry residents of Guwahati stated that 'the tribal-belts [are] being made at the expense of national interests of integration and solidarity'.[111] A decade later, an official enquiry committee agreed that 'nowhere' had the provisions of the Act 'been sincerely implemented'.[112] Assam's Tribal Research Institute carried out enquiries in the 1980s and came to the conclusion that little less than a fifth of the tribal families from these protected areas had already moved out or had been forced to do so.[113]

As these tribal belts and blocks were given an official shape and pattern, villages with 50 per cent tribal population—approximately 25 per cent of the total land in the valley—were earmarked for them.[114] This special provision of land settlement—though intended to keep these areas free from non-tribal landlords, among others—could not jeopardize the interests of the Assamese landlords. Further, lands earmarked for tribal settlements were in remote and less fertile areas, and were, thus, insignificant from the perspective of, say, the state's Forest Department. The interests of capitalist enterprises like the tea plantations remained legally protected. Two fundamental causes of tribal land alienation were overlooked: the predominance of traders and moneylenders in the tribal economy and the lack of tenurial security of tribal sharecroppers. The legal mechanism was, thus, not a strong deterrent to creating a land market. A dynamic forestry programme and bureaucratic and political manipulation of land settlement initiatives, over a period of time, further made these legal protections ineffective. Outside the tribal belts and blocks, the Forest Department continued to confine the tribal peasants to a limited habitat and limited share in land for cultivation. By the late 1950s, not only the Indian forestry programme but also a series of development programmes further weakened the original principle of the policy of land settlement with tribal peasants.[115] In the late 1960s, the government began allowing urbanization or industrialization in these protected areas as part of a plan to develop Guwahati as the capital of Assam.[116] Speculative land purchase forced many tribal families to retreat further. Many of them became footloose workers in Guwahati's urban landscape. Dissent began to be voiced, and decades later—in the 1970s—it became a critical ideological pillar for a renewed phase of ethnic movements.

~

If Assam's land reforms rocked its political landscape, they had a severe effect on its economy as well. Before this crisis could begin to be handled, a deadly earthquake brought disaster of an unimaginable magnitude. On Independence Day in 1950, this earthquake that measured 8.75 in the Richter scale jolted the mighty Brahmaputra, raising the river's bed by several feet. Some 1500 people were feared killed. What was less widely reported was the earthquake's massive devastation of the rice fields, and how it permanently changed the Brahmaputra Valley's flooding pattern.[117] The natural disaster also gave the Government of India, in the process of relief work, a chance to fully assert its control over Assam's loosely administered Northeastern Frontier Hills (known as NEFA).[118] This gave a jolt to Assam's ambitions of provincial autonomy and angered Assamese leaders, whose plans of cultural and political control over this vast hilly stretch were scotched. But this hardly mattered to the residents of these hills, who hardly were equal partners in the scheme. The new state faced uncertain times, even as there were genuine hopes of a better future.

Even as Assam recovered from the devastation of the earthquake, it waited fearfully for the monsoon of 1951. 'Trembling and praying, Assam expects yet another calamity. The onset of the monsoon, it is feared, may touch off an unprecedented flood in the quake-scarred north-eastern region.'[119] That year, heavy floods inundated more than 10,000 square kilometres in the Brahmaputra Valley. 'As the rivers overflowed their banks after a long and heavy downpour, the inhabitants of low-lying river valleys knew what was coming and evacuated to safer areas.'[120] There were reports of how several tributaries of the Brahmaputra changed course, caused massive inundation and destroyed rice crops. With the severely disrupted supply of essential

Cracks in Upper Assam Trunk Road during the earthquake of 1950

food items to tea gardens not yet restored, the raging waters of many tributaries of the Brahmaputra lashed against the crumbling transport infrastructures at many places. A large number of villages were swept away.

Meanwhile, Partition-induced snags in the transportation of agricultural products were being slowly overcome. The new railway track, acclaimed as an example of 'great engineering skill and ingenuity',[121] added to the length of travel from Assam. At Independence, Assam had been promised an annual financial grant from the Centre for governance of her tribal areas, and more financial help was promised for law and order in these areas and for its transport infrastructure. This grant had not required any vote in the Parliament.[122]

Jawaharlal Nehru crossing an improvised bamboo-pole bridge at Dholla, Upper Assam. An existing 70-feet steel bridge collapsed as a result of the August 1950 earthquake.

The wartime 'Grow More Food' campaign had only marginally increased the expansion of acreage and total output of rice,[123] and this slow pace continued after Independence. Despite sluggish industrial growth and the majority of the population being heavily dependent on agriculture, the net area sown increased only slightly between 1947 and 1954 from 4.8 million acres to 5.1 million acres. In the newly cultivated areas, there was a sizeable increase in the area under rice production.[124] In order to increase agrarian productivity, the Assam government embarked on a massive programme of embankment of rivers and drainage of low-lying areas. In the absence of an engineering college, technical help was taken from the Assam Civil Engineering Schools.

The state government sponsored public welfare programmes that were directed towards the expansion of general education.[125] The number of students increased threefold between 1950 and 1965.[126] But much of this educational expansion was confined to the urban plains. The hill districts, with the exception of the Mizo hills, and the Muslim-dominated areas remained far behind. Officially, there were a little over 25,000 villages; close to 10,000 of these had no schools, and another 9449 had schools having only a single teacher. During 1960–61, of the 1869 villages in one of the large hill districts, 1360 had no schools.[127] In 1961, Assam had 13,066 people with a university degree, of which just 585 belonged to the tribal communities; of the 1790 technical graduates, only 29 came from the tribal communities. The American political scientist Myron Weiner described this expansion in the number of people with education in the cities as a significant indicator of 'a large middle class' in Assam. The number of people looking for non-agricultural employment opportunities increased. The situation was still not seen as worrisome: while economist K.N. Raj's calculation showed that Assam's per capita income dropped from Rs 343 in 1949–50 to Rs 323 in 1958–59, it was still ahead of the all-India estimate of Rs 281 and also ahead of Bihar, Uttar Pradesh and Orissa.[128] Per capita income generation from manufacturing stood at Rs 1.10, much lower than the all-India figure of Rs 9.6 in 1951.[129] The majority of Assam's population had no access to electricity; compared to the all-India average of 18 kWh of electricity consumption, Assam's per capita consumption was 0.6 kWh.[130] Despite being a storehouse of mineral resources, Assam's industrial expansion during India's First Five-Year Plan was unbelievably low; compared to an all-India average 6 per cent expenditure on this sector, Assam spent only a meagre 0.5 per cent of her total expenses on industry.[131]

A majority of Assamese speakers lived and earned their livelihoods within their home state. The Census of 1961 found that a mere 0.3 per cent of Assamese speakers lived outside their state.[132] Many of them were in their immediate vicinity of NEFA, Manipur or Nagaland. In terms of geographical mobility, the Assamese were far behind other Indians. For instance, 7 per cent of Tamil-speaking people lived outside their province. The colonial legacy of managing agencies of big companies as a major source of employment continued for some time. Educated Assamese youth under the banner of Guwahati University Students' Advisory Board asked the managerial agencies of foreign companies working in Assam to reserve higher-ranking jobs for Assamese students. All 'recruitments should be done locally' was their slogan.[133] 'Unfortunately, the foreign-owned industries have not adequately Indianized their superior staff,' said an editorial in the *Assam Tribune*.[134] There was a call to the government to 'exercise the powers at its disposal to make the foreign firms see justice'.

The British railway companies had shifted their repairing workshops out of Assam.[135] Outside of the well-organized petroleum and tea plantations, recruitment in other industries was poor. The oil industry had employed around 8000 persons in 1946.[136] The much older tea industries employed 5,49,000 workers in 1953, fewer than in 1947.[137] Some people were employed in petty industrial establishments—sawmills, rice and oil mills, engineering workshops or printing presses—mostly owned by non-Assamese entrepreneurs. The number of these industries increased slowly between 1951 and 1962 from 842 to 1362. They employed fewer than 100 people per 2500 square kilometres compared to over 100 and up to 1000 people in the southern and central Indian states.[138] State support for industrialization took off moderately towards the end of the 1950s. Surveys were conducted to assess the potential of industrialization or establishment of industrial estates to house factories. A bicycle factory, a sugar mill, a spun-silk mill and a cotton ginning mill were established before the outbreak of the war with China in 1962 derailed this process. Privately owned factories like rice, oil and flour mills absorbed a little less than 4 per cent of Assam's industrial workers in 1961. A small-scale experiment had been undertaken to establish a sugar mill in Bokajan in 1948 but had to be shut down the next year because it could not get financial support from the Union government.[139]

Meanwhile, the price of consumer goods rose exponentially across India immediately after Independence. Prices of essential commodities had begun to rise after 1944, and it never subsided.[140] The general index number of wholesale prices, which stood at 244.1, rose to 302.2 in November 1947 and further to 389.6 in July 1948.[141] But with only a limited number of people dependent on consumer goods, Assam did not face major hardships outside of its urban population.

The crop that suffered the most was jute. This golden fibre was never to recover from the economic debacle caused by the political crisis of Partition. Apart from damage caused by pests and insects, floods swept away almost one-eighth of the jute growing area of the valley.[142] In 1945–46, Assam and West Bengal had produced 5,05,000 (~6 per cent) and 7,20,000 (~9 per cent) bales of jute respectively produced in British India, while East Bengal produced 62,35,000 (~80 per cent) bales. The profits earned from jute helped fix Assam's balance of payments deficit arising out of imports of cloth, pulses and consumer goods.[143] The massive deficit of raw jute for the Calcutta jute mills following the disruption in transport networks after Partition led to a government-sponsored scheme of expansion of areas under jute cultivation in the frontier areas of India, including Assam. A scheme was initiated in 1949, leading to a 20 per cent increase in the jute acreage of Assam between 1948 and 1955.

The 'Grow More Food' campaign redirected the research of several agricultural research stations and farms across Assam. These organizations had been in existence since the last decade of the nineteenth century and were interested in the possibility of increasing and producing new and improved varieties of paddy, wheat, potato and ginger, along with the introduction of irrigation works. The Upper Shillong Farm was established in 1897. The Titabar rice farm began to function from 1921, and in 1950, an estimated 1199 types of paddy were under observation there. Some farms tried to experiment with *Bao* and *Boro* varieties of paddy cultivation. Both types could grow in low-lying areas. In Assam's hill districts, there was unease around the popular practice of shifting cultivation or jhum. In the lower hills of NEFA, some communities had partially taken to permanent cultivation.[144] The British colonial officials and inhabitants of the hills differed on jhum, which continued as a mode of agriculture.[145] The cultural world and everyday lives of the hill people were largely shaped by the rhythms of jhum. Only a year before Independence, Assam had passed the Naga Hills Jhum Regulation, which reinforced customary rights over jhum lands. Nehru himself held the view that jhum should be discouraged, but many in his government disagreed, including Elwin. In 1951, M.D. Chaturvedi, India's inspector general of forests, cautioned that one must recognize jhum as an 'agricultural practice evolved as reflex to the physiographic character of the land'.[146] Nehru wanted to send experts to Assam to devise an alternative for jhum. Assam, however, resisted.[147] Later research confirmed that jhum added to the increased diversity of plant life, but statist views persisted, and extensive modelling or laboratory-based studies were carried out to deny the worth of jhum.[148]

~

Early in the 1950s, India had to take a call on the question of the economic feasibility of developing its own large-scale petroleum refineries rather than importing petroleum products from Middle Eastern countries. Till then, India's only oil-producing fields were in Assam. Between 1938 and 1940, the Assam Oil Company (AOC, established in 1899) was given mining concessions in various parts of Assam, apart from its exclusive rights in Digboi, over an area of 13,778 square kilometres. On the eve of the war, the oil industry faced severe labour unrest, and a series of strikes disrupted production.[149] This resulted in conflict between the provincial Congress government and imperial interests. The AOC sought to gain political clout and privileges as enjoyed by the tea-plantation lobby but was not successful in securing its position.

The setting up of an Indian oil refinery was Assam's economic dream in the 1950s. Like its colonial counterpart, the tea plantations, the oil sector also remained crucially dependent on imperial capital. The Government of India reacted slowly, keeping a watchful eye on the international flow of capital into the oil industry. With the gradual increase in American oil interest in India, the British oil companies were forced to increase their exploration activities aggressively.

Early in the 1950s, India was largely dependent on the import of petroleum products. India's annual consumption was nearly 24.5 million metric tonnes (MMT) in 1954, partly fulfilled by Assam's crude oil output. In the early 1950s, Assam had been able to produce 2.6 MMT annually, an increase from 2 MMT in 1931.[150] In 1954, Standard Vacuum Oil (Esso) from USA installed a refinery at Trombay near Bombay with an annual capacity of 11.3 MMT to refine imported crude oil.[151] Two more refineries would come up soon in Bombay and Vishakhapatnam. This only slightly narrowed the gap between production and requirement. Meanwhile, exploration for new fields had also begun. The Government of India tried to pursue a policy of 'developing oil resources under the exclusive control of the state'. Many felt that India's oil industry would be better off under the public sector, but the government did not have the political mechanism for effective control over mineral oil.[152] Three global oil marketing companies—Burmah Shell (BOC), Caltex and Anglo-Persian Oil Company—enjoyed a substantial monopoly in crude oil production and manufacturing of petroleum products. These companies had a powerful grip over the oil economy, and the Government of India had no means to control them.

An alliance with BOC had given the AOC some protection in the Indian market. The AOC was termed an indigenous industry, and this entitled it to some tariff concessions from the Government of India.[153] By 1949, the AOC had become a wholly owned subsidiary of BOC.[154]

After Independence, Assam stood her ground in the Constituent Assembly, and in sharp contrast to the Union government's point of view, it remained firm on its demand to negotiate independently with the AOC for oil exploration.[155] In 1951, the company was granted permission for more exploration in Naharkatiya in Upper Assam. The AOC was technically equipped with newer methods to identify oil deposits and undertook surveys covering several thousand square kilometres to assess the valley's petroleum deposits.[156] By the end of 1953, new oilfields were discovered, and, months later, the AOC declared their commercial worth.[157] The new discoveries, whose output was expected to touch 2.5 million tonnes per year, could offset India's requirements partially. An upbeat Assam government gave licences to the AOC for more exploration.[158] In 1956, most of the 11 wells in Upper Assam's oil fields produced crude oil, and only one was a gas producer. The Naharkatiya oil fields also began to supply crude oil to the Digboi refinery.[159] At this point, Assam's oil fields were supplying 8 per cent of India's total requirement. Although Assam agreed to relinquish its rights over its petroleum resources, it insisted on ensuring the participation of Indian capital in this venture. While the AOC had exclusively exercised a right to undertake oil exploration in Assam, other global companies followed. Shell Oil and Standard Vacuum Oil, two American companies, began exploration in Assam and West Bengal in 1951.[160]

Concurrently, Nehru's government was moving towards securing more government participation in India's oil industry. An Indian company was planned, but this turned out to be more complicated than what had been anticipated.[161] The Assam government, as a signal of departure from the colonial practice of granting long-term leases to mineral companies, had reduced the lease period. As the Union government bargained hard to give shape to the Indian company, including nationalization of capital and employees, in Assam, the Assam government and its publicists passionately debated on whether or not the Government of India should be allowed to mine oil in Assam. At one point, Keshav Dev Malaviya, Union minister of mines and oil, had indicated that a refinery could well be set up in Assam.[162] However, when the Government of India consulted its technical experts on where crude oil from Assam should be refined, Calcutta was the place that was suggested, as the experts were of the opinion that without a mass consumer base, Assam could not be a choice for setting up a refinery. Calcutta was also the preferred choice of the AOC.[163] The AOC had 'taken up a very difficult attitude and insisted on the refinery being near Calcutta' Nehru informed Fazal Ali, the Assam Governor in June 1957.[164]

While Nehru insisted that his government would not be 'dictated' to by the AOC, he made it clear that 'nor could we accept the proposal to have the refinery in Assam, when the military opinion was dead against it'.[165] Being eastern India's financial and commercial capital and with a vast consumer market, Calcutta could provide a backdrop similar to that of India's upcoming coastal refineries in Bombay and Visakhapatnam, where crude oil imported from the Middle East was refined. The surplus could be sold in the rich Gangetic upland markets.[166] Malaviya was well aware of the AOC's advantages in such a deal, though his choice of location for a refinery was Barauni in Bihar.[167] Easier transport logistics meant that products from Barauni could be distributed to northern India at a lower price than from the Bombay and Visakhapatnam refineries. Any political fallout in Assam from such a decision could be handled by setting up a plant in Assam for the manufacture of nitrogenous fertiliser from natural gas.[168] In addition, the Government of India could not ignore Assam's location as a strategic frontier. Writing to the Governor of Assam, Fazal Ali, Nehru emphasized that the Indian defence chiefs had refused to undertake protection of the refinery if it was situated in Assam. 'This strong and definite statement by those responsible for our defence and security could not be ignored.'[169]

With the increasing debate over Indian oil resources, a committee was formed to look into the rights of the government and the various contested oil policies.[170] The committee, whose view was based on considerations of economic feasibility, suggested that crude oil from Assam should be processed and refined at another location. It suggested Calcutta as the favoured site with Barauni as the next option. A site in western Assam, too, could be considered, but only if circumstances compelled the government to do so.[171]

It soon became public knowledge that Assam was not the favoured location for the public-sector refinery, for reasons both strategic and technical, and India's Second Five-Year Plan finally turned Assam's hopes to dust.[172] This inevitably resulted in bitterness and political turmoil in Assam. The public cried foul over the 'flimsy and untenable' grounds for the decision, and political parties came together to protest. Street demonstrations, strikes and aggressive public debates took place and were largely endorsed by political parties, including the Congress. The communists and socialists helped in popular mobilization for the movement to demand that the refinery should be established in Assam. The press in Assam remained solidly behind the movement. A newly formed All Assam Oil Refinery Action Committee, whose most visible faces were socialist leaders Hareswar Goswami and Hem Barua, was an immediate success. A general strike called by the Action Committee on 28 August 1956 was a huge success, but it was accompanied by widespread violence. The Assam government tried to play down the crisis by announcing that a decision on a refinery outside Assam had not yet been taken.[173] This was not quite true, as a day earlier, when Malaviya spoke in Guwahati, he had virtually dismissed any chance of the refinery being awarded to Assam.

Meanwhile, some amendments were made in the terms of the lease rights that the AOC (as a subsidiary of BOC) exercised. The primary objective of the company would be to develop the oil field. The AOC had to form a rupee company, and a prescribed percentage of the equity would be reserved for Indians in case oil was found. This agreed percentage was fixed at 33.5, and the Government of India had decided to take up this shareholding interest itself.[174] Accordingly, in the new joint rupee company, the AOC was to invest two-thirds of the equity capital.[175] In December 1956, after months of intense negotiations, the Government of India and the AOC finally announced the formation of an Indian oil company, which would explore and produce crude oil in Assam.[176]

The All Assam Oil Refinery Action Committee united all sections of the population. Meetings, processions and strikes drew extensive support. A secret official communique showed that even tea garden workers, who had little to benefit from the economic outcomes of the refinery, extended their support.[177] Most of Assam's lawmakers, too, supported the view that a refinery in Assam was both technically and commercially possible, and they argued that a refinery could lift the province out of its economic stagnation. Goswami, the socialist leader, reprimanded those who thought that the demand for a refinery was parochial. 'If it is parochial, I will suffer to be parochial rather than to live in a house where I have no rights over my belongings.'[178] The message was clear: crude oil sourced in Assam would not be sent to a refinery in another state. Assam must have a refinery of its own. The Congress government in the state began to feel the popular pressure and publicly expressed its commitment to a refinery in Assam.

In June 1957, the Union government reconfirmed its decision to set up the Barauni refinery for Assam's crude oil.[179] Assam was outraged, engulfed by a 'sense of frustration and resentment'.[180] Angry

Assamese leaders rushed to Delhi to meet Nehru. Medhi received a strongly worded message from Nehru reminding him that 'important decisions cannot depend on pure sentiment or political pressures'.[181] Refusing to bow down, on 13 June 1957, Medhi telegrammed Nehru that a refinery in Assam was 'technically and economically feasible' and the 'consequences of denying' this would be 'far reaching'.[182] The very next day, he warned Nehru that the Congress government would not be able to 'continue to function with the entire population completely alienated'.[183] When the Umtru Hydro Electric Project was commissioned in July 1957, it was boycotted by many.[184] The Assam government, which by now supported the popular movement, hired a French expert to advise them on the possibility of a refinery in Assam.[185] Assam was yet to settle down politically after the massive communist mobilization of the late 1950s. After days of public meetings and popular demonstrations, a general strike was called on 29 July.[186] A confidential official report admitted that the strike was 'spontaneous'.[187] The press, which stood steadfastly behind the popular unrest, termed the strike as a 'historic and unique event'.[188] 'People of different shades, castes and creed joined' the strike in which the 'student community was [at] the forefront', and 'shops, public and private institutions remained closed'.

In mid-July 1957, the Union government had hinted at setting up a refinery in Assam, but this only partially cooled tempers. 'We have told [the Assam government] that there is no question of ruling out a location in Assam,' Nehru conceded on 27 July 1957.[189] Popular protests continued, and so did state retaliation. According to an official report, speakers across Assam generally emphasized that theirs was a movement of 'the people for establishing their right against illegal exploitation of wealth' of Assam.[190] Finally, in August 1957, the Union government gave in and announced, in the way modern political negotiations typically work around an impasse, the appointment of an 11-member expert committee, which had a French and a Romanian member, to decide on the location of the refinery.[191] The committee would consider both economic and strategic issues in determining the site. But Assam was not convinced and could not be pacified. Assamese leaders intensified their campaign. Nehru made a visit to Assam in October in a bid to reason with the Assam leadership. Nehru apparently insisted that a refinery site should be decided on the basis of economic feasibility alone.[192] He believed that the idea of development was apolitical and that the programme of industrialization involved planning by experts on rational and scientific grounds: the location of a refinery was a technical, financial and security question, not a political question. A press statement made Nehru's views clear: 'Questions involving technical and other complicated aspects can only be decided by cool and dispassionate thinking and consultation.'[193] Nehru succeeded in persuading Assam's leaders to see the larger point. He agreed that Assam must be put on the path of industrialization and that 'Assam is fortunate in the fresh discoveries of oil'; while emphasizing that 'this acquisition of Assam's wealth should be utilized to the best advantage as well of the rest of India', he also made it clear that 'a solid foundation should be laid for the rapid development of this oil business in Assam so that the people of Assam might be the first to prosper under it and other industries should grow up'.

The Union government, meanwhile, engaged the American Foster Wheeler Corporation to study the feasibility of establishing two refineries, and this finally resolved the issue. In November, the decision was announced to establish two refineries, one at Guwahati and the other at Barauni.[194] The organizational structure that sustained the year-long movement was dissolved, and those who had been arrested were released.

Work on the Guwahati refinery began soon thereafter.[195] Built with technological and financial help from the Romanian government, the new industrial set-up, known as Guwahati refinery, became functional from January 1962.[196] Digboi refinery's capacity was 0.55 million tonnes, Guwahati's was 0.75 million tonnes and Barauni's was 2 million tonnes.[197] Out of the total cost of US $33.6 million, Romania provided $11.76 million at 2.5 per cent interest, and 50 Romanian technocrats assisted in the construction work.[198] The Union government had already sought the help of the Soviet Union to build the Bihar and Cambay (Gujarat) refineries.

Jawaharlal Nehru inaugurated the Guwahati Oil Refinery at Noonmati at Guwahati on 1 January 1962

The Union government took a loan of Rs 175 million from the UK government to meet the cost of constructing a pipeline to transport crude oil to Guwahati and further to Barauni.[199] The work was undertaken in two stages: in the first stage, 434 kilometres from Upper Assam to Noonmati, and in the next, 724 kilometres between Guwahati and Barauni. The 35–40 cm, 1158-kilometre-long pipeline could pump 152 metric tonnes (MT) of crude oil per day; several pumping stations ensured the flow of crude up to 304 MT per day from Assam's Naharkatiya and Moran oilfields.[200] Soon thereafter, 2.75 million tonnes of crude oil were transported from Naharkatiya oilfields to Noonmati, and 2 million tonnes from Noonmati to Barauni per year.

The pipeline passed through diverse landscapes: paddy fields, tea gardens, forests, hills, swamps and rivers. The most daunting challenge was presented by the Brahmaputra and 77 other rivers. Covering the

Foundation stone of the first bridge on the Brahmaputra in Guwahati was laid on 10 January 1960. The picture is a close-up of a complete sinking well in the river.

Brahmaputra alone cost Rs 1 crore. Pumping stations were erected at intervals of approximately 144 kilometres along the pipeline to keep the oil flowing. The *New York Times* mentioned that Assam's oilfields were now linked with the subcontinents' 'highly industrialised areas'. In future, additional pumps could help carry another 304 MT of oil, if found.[201]

The construction of the oil pipeline was an example of India's employment of high-end technology and its major international engineering partnerships. The electric resistance 35-cm pipes were manufactured at the Rourkela Hindustan Steel Plant with technological input from Germany; 40-cm pipes were imported from the United Kingdom. The first phase of the pipeline—between Naharkatiya and Noonmati—was commissioned in 1962 with a capacity of 1,50,000 tonnes per year. In 1963, the final section of the Guwahati–Barauni pipeline was completed. The construction was undertaken by the

British-owned Burmah Oil Company Pipelines Ltd, and the main contractors were Mannesmann and Saipem, a German and Italian combine. The German company, Mannesmann, which was the largest European tube-making company of the time, had previous experiences of laying water pipes in Rourkela and high-pressure tubes in Bokaro and Durgapur steel plants.[202] Mannesmann trained Indian welders and technicians to lay the lines, while the more specialized work was completed by the German and Italian engineers.

As the pipeline was laid, a war of words briefly arose between the Union government and the Assam government. Two issues broadly shaped the disquiet: the question of Assam's stake in the development of its natural resources as well as its share of royalties from the crude oil. In 1959, the Government of India invited foreign oil companies to lead the highly complex and challenging task of oil exploration within the country. The AOC, by then a subsidiary of the BOC, formed Oil India Limited (OIL) in 1959 to explore for oil in Assam. The Union government had a one-third share in this new company, and the AOC, with a two-thirds share, provided the finance to build the pipeline. After two years of intense financial negotiations, in 1961, the Government of India allowed the OIL to explore an additional 1800 square miles in Assam.[203] The newly discovered crude oil was to be refined in Assam and Bihar.

The tussle between Assam and the Union government over revenue to be earned from crude oil continued for some time to come.[204] Assam earned revenue from petroleum either in the form of royalties paid by the petroleum producing companies—a practice originating in the late nineteenth century[205]—or through taxes on petroleum products sold within Assam. The crude oil royalty was fixed as a percentage of the *well-head* value—the retail sale prices of crude oil. While globally, the standard share was 15–20 per cent, the AOC parted with only 5 per cent to Assam.[206] After Independence, in 1949, the Union government permitted Assam to receive a royalty rate of 10 per cent of the prices of crude. Yet, ambiguity persisted on how to fix the prices of crude oil. Further, as petroleum, like tea and jute, was largely sold outside the state, Assam earned little from the sale, except for a share of the revenue from sales tax earned by the Union government as decided by India's Finance Commission. The Assam government sought to take legislative measures to impose tax on the sale of jute, tea, etc., though the Indian Constitution clearly restricted states from collecting tax from the sale of these exported commodities.[207] When this constitutional restriction took a legislative form in the Central Sales Act of 1956, Assam's hope of gaining from the sale of petroleum products was ended. The state renewed its insistence on raising the share of royalty from crude oil.

However, in 1961, the Union government—as it signed a new agreement with Assam Oil Company and Burmah Oil Company on behalf of Oil India Limited, now with equal financial stake—reduced Assam's royalty share by more than half.[208] In response, an angry Assam government, much to the annoyance of Nehru, refused to grant permission to OIL to explore for deposits in Assam, insisting that, as owner of its natural resources, Assam should fix the royalty. This dispute drew global attention, and Assam was seen as obstructing India's much-needed development of the oil industry. Nehru criticized Chief Minister Bimala Prasad Chaliha 'rather strongly on the attitude of the Assam Government in regard to this business of oil exploration etc.', calling it 'most unfortunate and irritating'. Nehru wrote to his minister for natural resources that it would be 'absurd for [them] to spend time, energy and money over the development of Assam'.[209] The Union government suspended oil exploration in Assam in 1962.[210] Assam, opposing Delhi's centralizing move, appealed for arbitration in India's Supreme Court. Nehru, fearing further deterioration in federal relations, was agreeable to such an arbitration, but his cabinet was not. Morarji Desai, the Union finance minister, was asked to propose a new formula for Assam's share of crude oil royalty and sales tax.[211] As the Indo-China War broke out in October 1962, and the Chinese threat to Assam's oil fields loomed large, Nehru's government had little option but to agree to a higher share for Assam.[212]

This was only a short-term reprieve for Assam's economy, as the state increasingly lost its bargaining power with the Union government to seek more compensation for the commercial exploitation of her natural resources. Oil emerged as one of the key natural resources, which came to be endowed with claims of exclusive Assamese rights. There was a move to expand the capacity of the Digboi refinery to include the establishment of crude oil-based industries like fertilizers, petrochemicals and synthetic rubber.[213] Discoveries of new oil deposits led to the rise of popular demands for establishment of another refinery in the mid-1960s.[214]

While oil became the symbol of Assam's quest for a new federal politics, there was also the question of employment generation. The oil industry brought prosperity to a few households, as the oilfield townships symbolized the rise of a tiny Assamese economic and social elite.[215] The highly technology-centred oil refineries and allied industries needed skilled personnel and failed to create substantial local employment. An enquiry in 1969 revealed that the Oil and Natural Gas Commission, which started its oil drilling activities in 1959 in Assam, had 3788 employees in Assam, of which 437 were categorized as officers.[216] Of this latter number, only 44 were born in Assam. Other ranks fared better, but the general lack of employment opportunities caused popular discontentment. Besides, the establishment of refinery and oil-drilling industries created many a micro-history of displacement among the poorer classes, most of whom belonged to the tribal communities and who would not be among the gainers from modern Assam's industrialization and urbanization processes.[217] Many had to move out of their homes to faraway places—like Reserved Forests, etc.—to benefit from the government's poorly planned rehabilitation schemes.[218]

~

Horace G. Alexander, the British Quaker and friend of Gandhi's, wrote in 1951 that 'the most difficult [and] immediate problem confronting Assam government is posed by the Nagas'.[219] Alexander also noted that Assam's borders with China, Burma and Tibet were a big challenge. 'For a small state, with a few outstanding political leaders, this amounts to an excessive burden of problems. Assam is bound to rely a good deal on Delhi, but Delhi is far away.'[220] Alexander prophesied that Assam would be happier 'when peace and order are re-established in the northern half of Burma. Will that happen soon? Or will Communist agents prevent it? To such questions there can be no confident answer'. There were others too, who believed that the impending crisis in the eastern Himalayas and the Patkai arch arose from the Naga desire to unite their brethren with those in communist-dominated western Burma.[221]

Weeks after their stormy meeting with the Bardoloi Committee (discussed in Chapter 4), the Naga leaders had met the Assam Governor, Akbar Hydari, on 26 June 1947 when the latter was visiting Kohima.[222] They handed over a memorandum of demands to the Governor, and over the next few days, Hydari had detailed discussions with them. The outcome was the signing of an agreement in Kohima—to be remembered as the Nine Point Agreement.[223] Largely drawn on the basis of the Government of India Act of 1935, this agreement outlined how power would be shared between the Indian state and the Naga National Council (NNC) after the departure of the British. The laws passed by either the Assam or the Central legislature would not be applicable without the NNC's consent. The NNC would exercise control over forests and agriculture, and land could not be transferred to non-Nagas without the NNC's consent. The NNC would also impose and collect taxes on land, houses, etc. One of the last clauses of the agreement, which subsequently became a source of dispute, stipulated that after a period of 10 years, 'the NNC will be asked whether they require' this agreement to 'be extended for a further period or a new agreement regarding the future of the Naga people arrived at'.[224] The Bardoloi team was still in the middle of their sessions in Shillong in 1947, when they agreed in general to the 'substance of the proposed arrangements'. Hydari also sent a copy of the agreement to Nehru.[225]

Towards the end of 1947 and early in 1948, some of these ideas were incorporated into the draft Constitution, but this did not satisfy the Naga leaders. In June 1948, the Assam government gave a written assurance reaffirming its commitment to this agreement, and Bardoloi and Hydari issued a joint declaration, which stated that the draft Constitution was in 'no way inconsistent with the agreement'.[226]

Among the various clauses in the agreement between Hydari and the NNC, there was a promise of transferring Reserved Forests that were detached from the Naga hill districts back to the Naga hills. But the government did not honour this commitment, and these forested areas were 'colonised by Assamese'.[227] As the AOC's recent oil drilling in Nichuguard, located in the Naga foothills, made these areas contested sites for both the Government of India and the NNC, Britain's high commissioner in India wrote to his government in a secret communique that 'Naga hopes are not entirely unjustified'.[228]

The NNC was a small group, largely a product of the political and economic transformation of the Naga hills during and after the War. It had considerable influence, though opinion was divided about its real strength. According to the former Assam Governor Andrew Clow, the NNC was 'self-constituted' and popular among the 'more educated Nagas, particularly among the Angami and Ao tribes'.

The NNC representatives led by A.Z. Phizo met Gandhi in Delhi on 19 July 1947. It is not clear how this meeting was arranged, but a few days later, Gandhi wrote to Ram Manohar Lohia that he had met the Naga leaders and understood what was going on in their minds.[229] A later account indicates that they had submitted their points of discussion in advance to Pyarelal, Gandhi's secretary.[230] It seems that the Naga leaders confided in Gandhi about their intention to declare independence on 15 August 1947, and Gandhi retorted, 'Why not immediately?' As their conversation progressed, Gandhi explained the meaning of independence:

> You have opened a very large subject. Independence, yes. But if you say you will be independent of the whole world, you cannot do it. I am independent in my own home. If I become independent of Delhi, I would be crushed to atoms. I have not stored food. I have to get it from Delhi.

When Gandhi asked them about their source of cloth, the Naga leaders replied that they wore 'foreign cloth'. Gandhi, who was furious hearing this reply, said, 'Then you are slaves of foreigners. Will you go naked if the foreigners do not give you cloth? What of your food?' The Nagas replied that they grew enough food, but Gandhi was not convinced. 'You cannot be in complete isolation.' The Naga leaders tried to convince him that they did not want isolation. Gandhi assured them, 'Then no army will deprive you of your freedom. Those days are gone.' When they said, 'We will be friends with all,' Gandhi replied, 'Then you are safe so far as India is concerned. India has shed blood for her own freedom. Is she going to deprive others of their freedom?' Personally, I believe you all belong to me, to India. But if you say you don't, no one can force you.' Gandhi also told them that '[if I] come there I will teach you the art of spinning and weaving. You grow cotton and yet you import cloth. Learn all the handicrafts. That's the way to peaceful independence. If you use rifles and guns and tanks, it is a foolish thing.' The Naga leaders gave him their word.[231]

The NNC was also in contact with the secretariat at the Constituent Assembly. It continued to press for an agreement by which the Nagas would be free after a period of 10 years to decide on their future. However, nothing came of this demand. In December 1948, the NNC sent another memorandum to the Constituent Assembly proposing the creation of a centrally administered administrative unit to be called the North-East Frontier Agency. They also made known their disapproval of the nascent idea of the Sixth Schedule of the draft Constitution.[232] Another widely distributed memorandum seeking 'independence and sovereignty' followed. Meanwhile, the NNC was troubled by an internal rift. An Indian home ministry account suggests that Phizo resigned in 1948, opposing the moderate policy of his comrades. He was briefly arrested. In June 1949, the NNC made it known that they could not accept the Indian Constitution.[233] They continued to express unhappiness with 'mere local autonomy'. The next year, 1950, they reached out to the United Nations, but their petition was not included in the agenda for the General Assembly. Phizo returned to the NNC and was elected its president in December 1950.[234] He had a brief meeting with Assam Chief Minister Bishnuram Medhi in December, but the Assam government took a tough stance against the NNC. By 1950, the Naga hills was officially declared a 'disturbed area', and the Nagas were identified as 'the only . . . people in India who have refused to accept the Constitution'.[235] When in October 1950, the ornithologist S. Dillon Ripley from Yale University arrived in Assam to collect bird species, he wanted to travel to Mount Saramati, the easternmost areas of the Naga hills. 'One has to pass through the unadministered tribal area. No one can travel through that area without an escort of the Assam Rifles,' wrote the Assam Governor.

By early 1950s, acting like a parallel state, the NNC interfered with the drilling exploration at Nichuguard. The BOC was told to abandon their work and Nagas were urged not to work for the company—an appeal that most community members adhered to. The BOC was threatened that they would be 'called upon to compensate the Nagas fully, when the latter became independent, for any loss or damage caused to the land, forests, and fields, and for all the oil extracted from Naga territory'.[236] The Nagas' ability to extract submission—through extraction of rent—from other tribes had already been noticed by British officials.[237] While the NNC continued to assert that it did not recognize the Indian Constitution, no one was sure how much popular support it had. In January 1951, Phizo wrote to the president of India expressing the NNC's desire to hold a plebiscite to decide on the future of the Naga hills.[238] The modus operandi would be simple: any Naga could come to the plebiscite offices to record their opinion. Many in Parliament and in the Assam government viewed this with apprehension and called on the Union government to restrain the Naga leaders from going ahead. In February 1951, the Union government instructed Chief Minister Medhi to take action against Phizo for any violence.

In May 1951, Phizo proposed a political gathering of all Naga groups to sort out the future course of action. Indian intelligence was worried, but Nehru apparently did not pay heed to the warning.[239] The Assam government, too, did not take it seriously. S.M. Datta, the deputy chief of India's Intelligence Bureau, thought that given the 'high divisive influences amongst the Nagas', any move to unite them would be futile, but a 'miracle might happen'. Phizo had also met Nehru when the latter came to Assam in 1949. Nehru advised Phizo to accept the Constitution in good sprit.

The conference in May was also attended by Datta. Proving his predictions wrong, most of the clans came together to hold a plebiscite to decide 'whether the Naga Hills District should ask for independence or should remain within the Indian Union'.[240] 'Phizo conceded that their demand for independence could be diluted to the extent that Defence and Foreign Affairs would remain with the Government of India.'[241]

The Constitution gave the Nagas an autonomous district council and three lawmakers in the Assam Legislative Assembly. The NNC boycotted India's elections in 1951–52, and Phizo toured the Naga villages extensively, 'moving from village to village, holding village-wise plebiscite'. The NNC succeeded in instilling in the Nagas a sense of Naga nationality. By the middle of 1952, Phizo declared that '99 per cent of the people of Naga Hills District had supported the demand for an independent Naga State'.[242] The plebiscite's decision was conveyed by Phizo to the president, and he wanted the Government of India to honour it. In August 1952, Phizo declared that the NNC would have 'no truck with India', and he launched a civil disobedience movement. National and official celebrations were boycotted, and their sabotage was intensified. The 'Nagas are definitely non-cooperative and even to some extent hostile', said Nehru.[243] As the Government of India mounted pressure, Phizo escaped to Burma in 1952, after a brief period of remaining underground.

But despite all that was happening, Nehru was not visibly perturbed. 'I do not think we need trouble ourselves much,' he conveyed to Medhi, Assam's chief minister, in October 1952.[244] When Nehru had met Phizo for the first time in 1949, his impression was that he 'was a crank and need not be taken seriously'.[245] During their second interaction a year later, Phizo continued to insist that after 10 years of the Constitution, the Nagas should be allowed to secede. Nehru did not agree. He had no patience for Phizo and the NNC's demand for independence. 'I met this man twice and formed a poor opinion of him. His demand on behalf of the Nagas is for independence,' Nehru wrote in 1952. He shared this sentiment with U Nu, his Burmese counterpart: 'A man of the name Zapu Phizo has been demanding complete independence for that area. It is obvious that we cannot think of an independent country, tiny in size, just on our border.' Early in 1953, when U Nu met Nehru again, he agreed to Phizo's extradition to India.[246]

Handling Assam and its people remained a challenge for Nehru. He agreed that the tribes of Assam 'are different from the others and should be considered rather separately'.[247] They 'lack the feeling of oneness with the rest of India . . ., are greatly afraid that their small numbers will be swamped by others and that they would lose their distinctive customs and culture, apart from suffering economically'. Nehru was also sceptical because, he said, 'in the past, they have largely dealt with British officers or foreign missionaries, who have, no doubt, instilled in them a feeling of slight contempt for Indians as weak people and who have, at the same time, made them a little afraid of the mass of India.' When field workers from the department of anthropology of the Union government visited the interiors of the Naga hills to study their 'social and religious institutions and patterns of life', they had to come back 'due to oppositions from the Naga tribes'.[248]

The NNC remained in touch with the erstwhile colonial masters, although some British officials had turned against the Naga independence movement.[249] After Independence, British officials posted in new positions in India knew well that 'unless very skillfully handled', the Nagas would 'resist any future political arrangement which subordinates them too openly to the tutelage of the Assamese'.[250] The NNC addressed a letter to the British high commissioner in Delhi recounting the 'psychological animosity' between Indians and Nagas 'that makes their association as citizens of the same country impossible'.[251] In 1953, the NNC sent a memorandum to the British Prime Minister,[252] which created some anxiety in the British foreign office. A senior official opined that the 'notion of an independent or semi-independent state in the hills between India and Burma' was always 'advocated by the frontier officers and missionaries'. His measured conclusion was that 'economically as well as politically such a state could not survive except as a dependency of India or Burma'.[253] On the other hand, the British high commissioner in India was largely sympathetic to the NNC's appeal:

> With the memories of the Nagas' war record, it is difficult for us not to feel some sympathy for the aspirations of these tribesmen, and it is certainly flattering to learn that they would still prefer their affairs to be supervised by the British political officers rather than by [the] more "democratic" Indian regime.[254]

Bipinpal Das, then general secretary of the Socialist Party of India and author of *The Naga Problem*, recounted that much of the early deterioration in relations with the Naga leadership was due to the policies of the Assam government.[255] Initially, when the trouble started, the Assam government did not see Phizo as a powerful enough force to take him seriously. They did not agree to the Naga demand for special status, which they felt would invite similar demands from other hill districts. Medhi blamed everything on the colonial past. He wrote to Nehru:

> The separatist tendencies in the tribal areas, which have taken a virulent form in the Naga Hills and culminated in the absurd demand of the Naga National Council for independence, are directly attributable to the British policy of keeping the tribal areas separate and isolated from the rest of India and Assam[256]

In March 1953, when Nehru was visiting the Naga hill districts and Manipur with his counterpart from Burma, the NNC wanted to read out a statement at a public meeting where the two prime ministers would be on the dais. Medhi pre-empted such a possibility and did not permit the Nagas to give Nehru a memorandum. So, when Nehru arrived at the venue in Kohima, the Nagas walked out in protest.

Clashes began to escalate from 1954. The Government of India was facing trouble in Kashmir and Goa, diplomatic and military challenges from Pakistan and disturbances on the Tibetan frontier. This had compelled the government to allow the Assam government to take care of Nagaland. When the States Reorganisation Commission wanted to hear out the public opinion in 1954, Phizo demanded independence for the Naga lands.[257] Meanwhile, the Naga rebels were divided on

Jawaharlal Nehru in a village near Kohima in 1953

the ways to achieve independence. One group, under Theyiechüthie Sakhrie, the secretary of the NNC, wanted to find a solution for Nagaland within the framework of the Indian Constitution; the other, led by Phizo, wanted secession from India. As mentioned in Chapter 4, activists in the Naga hills declared independence on 14 August 1947. In 1954, Phizo—after drafting a constitution for a sovereign Naga country—announced the formation of the People's Sovereign Republic of Free Nagaland. Two years later, he was to declare the formation of a Federal Government of Nagaland.[258]

In August 1955, Nehru announced in Parliament the government's plan to send a battalion of the Indian Army to the Naga hills.[259] Military operations began in February 1956.[260] Sensitive as he was to the question of using military power in the newly created nation-state, Nehru made it clear that the military 'will act in close consultation with the local civil authorities and will be withdrawn as soon as these violent elements have been rounded up'. He also underlined that 'there is no change in our policy of non-interference with their social customs and tribal culture'. A contemporary account from Assam regretted that 'the decision has been so long in coming'.²⁶¹ A leading newspaper, while questioning the government for allowing 'so much dangerous weed to grow under their feet', described the political situation in the Naga hills as a 'veritable reign of terror, reminiscent of the Mau Mau trouble in East Africa . . . unleashed by the terrorist groups'.²⁶²

With the geography in their favour and equipped with stocks of arms, the Naga rebels took on the Indian Army. The *Guardian* reported that Phizo freely used 'a portion of an arms dump abandoned by the Allies and Japanese'.²⁶³ 'The armed forces have a very difficult and delicate task . . . the terrain . . . the jungle and the absence of communications all favour the rebels. The army cannot live off the land and has, therefore, to maintain long and difficult lines of supply,' wrote the *Times of India*.²⁶⁴ In the second week of June 1956, Phizo's forces virtually captured Kohima and continued to hold it for three days, causing great embarrassment to the Government of India.²⁶⁵ Government officials were kidnapped, and Indian security convoys were ambushed.

If the public in the rest of India was largely unaware of this sudden turn of events in the Naga hills, Assam was tormented by it. The Assam government raised a militia,²⁶⁶ 'composed of loyal Nagas who [were] prepared to fight the hostiles' and who were trained by the Indian Army, promulgated stringent laws to curb civil liberties and arrested activists. Villages were segregated and regrouped to create fear and make the presence of the state felt. Intelligence mechanisms were beefed up.

As the military operations began, turmoil ensued. Speaking in Parliament a year later, Nehru admitted that 'many villages have been burnt there', for some of which, he indicated, the Naga rebels were responsible. He said that he considered it 'fantastic for that little corner between China and Burma and India to be called an independent State'.

> The Government of India's prestige does not arise when we are dealing with our own countrymen. The Government of India is too big for its prestige to suffer in such small ways. But we cannot take a

step which will be misunderstood, misinterpreted, and criticised by our own colleagues among the Nagas.[267]

The Union government, aided by the Assam government, sought to quell the Naga rebels. Bhola Nath Mullik, head of India's Intelligence Bureau (1950–64), recounted that despite mounting pressure from three brigades of the Indian Army, 'the Nagas fought on with great determination'.[268] As the Government of India pressed on, the Naga rebels remained active on the ground with traditional weapons bought from the markets in the foothills or procured by raiding shops of non-Nagas in Dimapur and by forcing lower-rank staff in the forest department to guide them through the interiors.[269] Early in 1957, the government said, 'the hard core with the best guns . . . are gradually gaining in experience and efficiency as guerillas. As such it may be harder for the army to get them and they are likely to indulge in more ruthlessness to keep themselves going.' A section of Nagas, however, had 'made no secret of the fact that they are Indian citizens' and wanted 'some separate administration' for their development.[270] As the violent clashes between the NNC and the government's forces continued, there were kidnappings of village headmen, sabotage of trains, sniping, firing, ambushes and abductions of pro-government officials and raids and forays for collection of food. The Ao Nagas did not succumb easily: 'Villagers of the regrouped villages in the Ao area have kept portions of their paddy and other foodstuffs concealed in jungles which are to be obtained by hostiles.'[271] The army's retaliation resulted in losses; one of the leading Naga public figures, Dr Harielungbe Haralu, was killed in 1956. Sakhrie, considered a moderate amongst the Naga leaders, was also killed by the radicals. A contemporary eyewitness stated that such 'political murders' would torment the Naga hills for decades to come.[272]

Many interpreted Phizo's demand for independence 'as nothing more than a desire to escape association with Assam'.[273] The Nagas and Assamese speakers had a long history of intimacy laced with hostility, and the Nagas' dislike of Assamese and Indian officers was well-known.[274]

> In fact it [the Indian government] is reluctant to admit that it is the Naga attitude to the Assamese that is at the root of all the trouble. If the Army appears to be taking more time than it should in dealing with the situation, the responsibility must be borne largely by the Assam civil authorities.[275]

The superintendent of Census of 1961 noted that the hill tribes, including those in Assam,

> have strictly preserved their own identity . . . so much so, that neither the ignorance of the enumerators nor the "tyranny" of a superior local dominant language can minimize the existence of their own mother tongue. Formerly, there was a tendency among the plains tribals to identify their language with that of a predominant local language, but in 1961 there is a reassertion of their identity.[276]

Nehru conceded that 'Assamization has perhaps been injudiciously pursued'.[277] The Asam Sahitya Sabha repeatedly said that it wanted to popularize the Assamese language and literature in the hill districts of Assam.[278] The Assam government provided financial support to the Sabha to enable them to do this.[279] In 1953, the Sabha praised a government proposal to allow tribal teachers to learn the Assamese language.[280] The Sabha also took steps to introduce Assamese primers for lower classes in the schools of Kohima. Two members of the Sabha, Praphulladatta Goswami and Bhabananda Dutta, the latter a Marxist, showed some sensitivity and led the Sabha to adopt a resolution to publish a vocabulary of tribal words of everyday use.[281]

In June 1957, a conference of Ao villages was held at Mokokchung, in which it was agreed to form Naga Special Police squads in each village, and villagers were urged to not share rations with the rebels.[282] A peace mission was started by the Reverend Longri Ao. The Assam Christian Council and National Christian Council of India, too, initiated programmes: 'Cash grants, foodgrains, salt, blankets, pulses, milk powder, seeds, etc., are being distributed as measures of relief and rehabilitation.'[283]

Through 1957, the political crisis in the Naga hills deepened. 'Sniping, ambush[ing] both Police and Army convoys, collecting funds and rations etc., were the main features of the period,' according to senior officials in the Assam government.[284] In mid-1957, Nehru, speaking in the Parliament, hinted at the possibility of the creation of a Naga state.[285] The Government of India was trying to regain its lost political space and seeking a middle path. But a large majority of the Nagas still did not believe the government. In August 1957, the All-Tribes Naga Conference, mainly attended by Nagas who espoused liberal political views, expressed their anxieties, but they supported the idea of a separate state outside Assam but within the Indian Union. The Assamese press and others, including the socialists and communists, warned that such a step would lead to the further disintegration of Assam. Rather, they suggested more autonomy within the framework of the Sixth Schedule. Non-Naga traders were worried about the prospect of the prosperous Dimapur town becoming a part of the proposed Naga state.[286] When delegates from this conference, the Kohima Convention as it is known, met Nehru in September 1957, the latter signalled his government's willingness to the idea of conceding a separate state within India for the Nagas.[287]

On 30 November 1957, after two years of intense hostility, the Government of India decided to form a separate unit of the Naga Hills Tuensang Area by welding together the Naga hills district and Tuensang frontier division. The Tuensang division, the northernmost territories of present-day Nagaland, first became a part of NEFA and was subsequently merged with the Naga hills district. This area came to be separately administered from the end of 1957 till the formal birth of Nagaland in 1963. The transitional unit would be ruled by the Governor of Assam, directly under India's ministry of external affairs. The Naga rebels were granted amnesty. P.N. Luthra, development commissioner of NEFA, took over as commissioner of this centrally administered unit.[288] Meanwhile, in 1958, Burmese newspapers reported seeing Phizo's men on Burma's western frontier in the Burmese Naga villages. They 'are terrorizing neighbouring Burmese Naga villages', reported the Indian embassy in Rangoon.[289] In 1960, Phizo escaped to London via Zurich for fear of being prosecuted. The Naga political narrative now took a new turn, about which much has been written.

The Union government's decision to form a separate state of Nagaland did not go down well with several political parties in Assam; people at large did not like the idea either. It invited trouble for Medhi, who had to resign. He was appointed as the Governor of Madras, the first Assamese to hold this high position. The RCPI thought that such a move would encourage other hill tribes to make similar demands, and it called upon the people of Assam to launch a united struggle to resist the Government of India's contemplated move in the wider interest of national unity.

# 6

# In Search of the Modern

One of the first tasks of Gopinath Bardoloi's government was to fulfil Assam's desire to have a university of its own. The Gauhati University Act was passed by Assam's legislature in September 1947.[1] The fact that this was barely within a month of India becoming independent indicates how central the university was to the project of modern Assam. Assam had two government-funded colleges and a few private colleges run with the help of private donations and student fees. But these were all affiliated to the University of Calcutta, which conferred the degrees. Cotton College, established in 1901 and named after Assam's top official, Henry Cotton, was widely considered to be the pinnacle of higher education.[2] It had very high standards of teaching in both the sciences and humanities, and it left a deep and long-lasting imprint on the minds of its students. The other college, Murari Chand College, was located in Sylhet. It, too, had many accomplished teachers and researchers and drew students from the Brahmaputra Valley.

Well into the 1900s, Assam's students would struggle to pursue further education after their matriculation.[3] Those who could afford it enrolled themselves in colleges outside the province, many of which were in Calcutta. This trend began in the mid-nineteenth century, and the city became a second home for these students. They not only attended their courses but, as importantly, absorbed metropolitan Calcutta's thriving sociocultural and intellectual ambience, which, coupled with Assam's traditions of scholarship, went a long way in shaping the ideals of a new generation of leadership. Against the backdrop of rising nationalist consciousness, students became the torchbearers of surging Assamese nationalist awareness. Their extensive efforts to consolidate and re-energize their nationalist aspirations also included literary activities. Often the tone and tenor of their ideas were pitted against the powerful Bengali literary and cultural world. But firing up the nationalist imagination was not their only goal. Some pursued further studies at European universities, where they read the basic sciences, law, history and the classics. Many returned to their home state and found jobs to their satisfaction as medical practitioners, lawyers, engineers, educationists, traders or government employees.

~

The idea of a university in Assam began gaining ground in the late 1910s.[4] Concerns over administrative inconvenience and demands from the Assamese educated classes drove the political debate on establishing a university in the province. Many lawmakers and publicists considered the university as a tool that would help the Assamese people achieve their aspirations, and the idea of the province having its own university was seen as being inherent in the idea of provincial autonomy that was encapsulated in the Montagu–Chelmsford Reforms of 1919. Yet, financial considerations, and the fact that only a few colleges expressed the desire to be affiliated with a provincial university rather than with Calcutta University, prevented the idea from making quick progress.[5]

The idea gained widespread popular support in the mid-1930s. In 1935, as the Government of India Act was drafted and the movement for provincial autonomy became more popular, the Assamese historian Suryya Kumar Bhuyan prepared a note explaining why a university was needed in Assam. Bhuyan's note argued that '[T]he absence of a University in Assam has served as a serious obstacle in the realization' of the goal of 'political advancement in India', which was none other than 'complete autonomy in every province'.[6] Bhuyan also noted that the 'syllabus of the Calcutta University is chiefly formulated to meet the ideals and needs of Bengal students; but the students of Assam being different on many vital points from those of Bengal the syllabus satisfies but partially [their] ideals and needs'. The public sentiment was clear: 'There is no university to represent Assamese culture and civilization.' The London University-trained historian was giving an articulate voice to the widespread public sentiment. The university had symbolic importance well beyond the constituency of higher education.

On 22 May 1935, as Assamese students in Calcutta celebrated Assam University Day,[7] Assamese scholars and others continued to push the idea of a separate university, Bhuyan being one among them.[8] Many agreed that, given the increasing rivalry between Assam and Bengal, the University of Calcutta failed to fulfil the aspirations of the Assamese, being 'specially adjusted to suit the requirements of the province of Bengal'. Bhuyan asked, 'Why have not the anomalous relations between Assam and the Calcutta University been [able to] put a stop to by the establishment of a separate University in the province? . . . No University is successful if its roots do not penetrate the life of the people.' Assamese students had succeeded in reaching out to India's leading scientists and scholars to support their cause. One of them, the Nobel Laureate C.V. Raman, agreed that 'the natural desire of the Assamese people to have a university of their own will, I am sure, receive universal support'. The Sanskritist and Indologist from Assam, Krishna Kanta Handiqui, who studied modern history at Oxford University, asserted that the 'establishment of regional universities on a linguistic basis has been a prominent educational feature of our times'. Others prepared an elaborate scheme outlining the academic courses and programmes for the future university.[9] Parallel to this, the idea of a university in Assam, however, was contested by a few in Bengal; a young historian wrote a lengthy essay in the *Modern Review* highly critical of the idea.[10] Anyway, Assamese nationalism had long sought to emerge from Bengal's deep shadow. This aspiration was now being realized through the establishment of a university.

A majority of the Assamese lawmakers firmly shared the public sentiment, and so did Assam's hill leaders, who stood by the Assamese public opinion. Political and bureaucratic initiatives began to take shape in 1940. Assam's premier Saadulla tasked historian Bhuyan to prepare the blueprint for the university. A bill for a separate university for Assam—which did not mention the location of this university—was introduced in the provincial assembly in 1941.[11] The Assamese leaders wanted the university to be established in the Brahmaputra Valley, while popular public opinion in Sylhet—driven mainly by a competitive economic and cultural environment—was against this.[12] Disapproval of this bill for a university came from Bardoloi, but for other reasons. He insisted that a 'right type of university' must be established in Guwahati.[13] Bardoloi, then in prison and deeply doubtful about the government's political steps, reminded his countrymen that 'it is very important that our educated young men should be men with full knowledge of the needs and necessities of our masses and means to satisfy them'. The lack of political consensus and war-time financial contingency did not favour the legislation.

An unfavourable political atmosphere, however, could not halt the campaign for a university in Assam. A trust board—comprising Assamese philanthropists, political leaders and scholars, among others—was formed in 1944. Over the years, it collected funds worth Rs 6 lakh, with donations pouring in from a cross-section of society.[14] A sprawling and picturesque location outside the city was selected by the trust board. Maheswar Neog, a trust board member, felt it desirable that the university should remain free of urban influence.[15] For Neog and others, a university would provide the Assamese with 'real strength' and a 'true weapon' to accomplish its goal as a nation.[16] Guwahati was also considered as the 'centre of the localities inhabited by almost all the tribal people of the hills and plains'.[17] As the university began to take a concrete shape, the trust board communicated with several Indian universities as well as Ceylon University for guidance on its plan and structure.

The birth of its first university on 1 January 1948 was a joyous moment for Assam. Bhuyan proposed master's classes on the culture and civilization of Assam, a course that was expected to 'constitute a special feature of the Gauhati university'.[18] The course outline had papers on Assam's tribes and races, social and religious history, Assamese literature, folk literature, Assam's archaeology and its economic resources. This course had the sanction of leading scholars and also the premier, Bardoloi.[19] It would show that 'Assam's civilization is not a growth of the namby-pamby order; it has evolved out of the twin threads of Aryan and Non-Aryan culture', Bhuyan was confident. The course would form part of the training of future public servants and would inspire Assam's philanthropists to donate to the cause, which would empower the university materially. Bhuyan was of the firm opinion that 'state aid should be accepted on an irreducible minimum basis and, if possible, it should be eliminated for, however autonomous a university may be, a patron-state will always try to exercise some degree of interference'. But the hopes held out by this proposed course turned to dust with the appointment of K.K. Handiqui as the first vice-chancellor of the university.

Handiqui was picked by Bardoloi from a list of several probables. Handiqui's uncompromising attitude was well-known. He had espoused his vision for a university on earlier occasions when he said that the German ideal was the most desired goal for an academic institution.[20] 'Germany was doing in the intellectual sphere what England was doing in the political,' Handiqui wrote in 1928, referring to the French philosopher and orientalist Ernest Renan.[21] Handiqui further quoted Renan, 'Whenever in Germany one speaks of a scholar, it is at once asked: in which university is he? . . . when one speaks of a professor, it is at once asked: what has he written, what has he accomplished in the domain of science?' When Handiqui gave his first convocation address in 1951, he emphasized both these aspects, but he added that 'the proper function of a university is to teach'.[22]

The first task of the university was to conduct examinations, which had so far been held by the University of Calcutta. While the idea of a university for Assam had not gone down well with Calcutta University, and its vice-chancellor, P.N. Banerjee, had expressed his displeasure to Bardoloi, it soon extended administrative support.[23] Despite some initial hiccups, in 1949–50, more than 800 students were enrolled in the Gauhati University. A few classes on economics and labour problems were taken by visiting foreign teachers. Master's classes began in subjects including history, philosophy, economics, Assamese, mathematics, statistics and botany. As the university began to find its feet, two other academic programmes were given high priority—medical and agricultural science. In 1961, the university had 1468 students; by 1963, the university and its affiliated colleges had enrolled more than 30,000 students.[24] But towards the end of the 1950s, the university had got embroiled in a wide range of controversies—including financial mismanagement and unfair appointment of teachers. A commission appointed to look into these issues described 'the moral atmosphere' of the university as 'very depressing'.[25]

Though Bhuyan's proposed course on Assam's civilization and culture did not materialize, the university did not ignore regional needs. Handiqui agreed that the university should 'harmonise and give due recognition to the legitimate interests of all such groups who, in their turn, are expected to regard the University as their own'. The university gave importance to regional linguistic aspirations; of the many subjects passionately taught and pursued, Assamese language and literature was foremost. Anyway, as we will see below, the rise of modern education in Assam played a crucial role in enabling cultural expressions and the possibilities for linguistic solidarities to emerge.

~

Was Assam, with its rich and glorious history, sufficiently well known to the rest of India and the world? What was the place of Assam in the civilizational history of India? These were the questions that had long troubled the Assamese. Since the early nineteenth century, after a series of 'discoveries', Assam had become fairly well known in the English-speaking world for its different varieties of tea and mineral resources.[26] Despite this, in 'the histories of India, Assam is barely mentioned', lamented historian Edward Gait in the early twentieth century.[27] Four decades later, in 1946, an Oxford University Press pamphlet voiced a similar opinion. Written by two British officials posted in Assam, the pamphlet reconfirmed what Gait had written earlier: 'Despite its long history, going back to the days of the Mahabharata war, Assam remains largely unknown even to the rest of India.'[28] Assam's own writers and others too, including merchants and pioneer capitalists, had earlier made efforts to introduce Assam to the wider world. Some works were largely envisioned for those Europeans who wanted to pursue commerce in Assam during the time of rising anti-colonial mobilization. *Hints for Europeans*, first published in 1925, with Bengal and Assam as its special focus, was meant for those who 'on their first arrival in India' needed to be made aware of the complexities of its culture. The book warned that 'by general consent, the use of the words "native" and "coolie" were to be avoided by Europeans in India, as they are considered to offend the sensibilities of the educated Indian'.[29]

Given the new political environment, the Assamese became more proactive in presenting their past to the world. One example was Dimbeswar Neog's *Introduction to Assam*. Published in 1947, with a preface by Premier Bardoloi, it was intended to help Assam secure a space within new-born India's imagination.[30] Neog's introduction spelt out a brief political, cultural and linguistic narrative of his province, and it included detailed references. Using references to Hindu epics or inscriptions, he did all he could to claim a distinctive place for Assam in the history of the Indian civilization. Vaishnavism, which had struck deep roots in Assam, was established on the basis of reading and writing—and Assamese literary and religious history were closely intertwined.

Neog's was not the only contribution. In May 1954, Suniti Kumar Chatterji, the leading Indian linguist and a familiar name in India's intellectual circles for his pioneering work *The Origin and Development of the Bengali Language*, delivered the first Banikanta Kakati Memorial Lecture in Guwahati. Banikanta Kakati had carried out his research on the origin and growth of the Assamese language under Chatterji's guidance to become one of the leading Indian linguists of the early twentieth century. The teacher was asked to give the first memorial lecture in the name of his former student, whom he considered to be among the 'front rank[ing] of linguistics and investigators of history and culture who have added luster to Indian scholarship . . . '.[31] Chatterji did not fail Kakati's admirers. In three lectures on the place of Assam in the history and civilization of India, the noted scholar offered, in his own style, a bird's-eye view of Assam's long journey. 'The whole of India was brought within the pale of Puranic geography (including that of the Mahabharata), and Assam naturally was no exception to it,' Chatterji told his Assamese audience.[32] He reminded them that 'Assam, with its checkered history, has taken her share in the evolution of the civilization of India'.[33]

This search for antiquity and heritage was not a recent pursuit. Consciousness of a rich history of Assamese language and literature arose in the 1880s. The last decades of the nineteenth century witnessed a wider public movement for the collection of old manuscripts and standardization of the written Assamese language. Calcutta-based Assamese students began pursuing such standardization in the 1880s, and a civic public forum, Barpeṭā Hitasādhinī Sabhā, consisting of government officials, traders and literary scholars, was formed in the 1890s in Lower Assam, with a similar intention.[34] The search for antiquity in Bengal had already given birth to centres of cultural scholarship including the Bangiya Sahitya Parishad and the Varendra Anusandhan Samiti among others. By the 1910s, similar-minded scholars in Assam assembled under the umbrella organization Kamarupa Anusandhan Samiti (KAS). Formed in 1912, the members of the Samiti undertook the combined task of discovery and assemblage of facets of Assam's cultural heritage,[35] collecting old Assamese manuscripts, exploring ancient ruins and publishing their research. These antiquarian scholars were famous in their own right as Sanskritists, poets and historians. Within a short time, they amassed an extensive body of artefacts embodying the Assamese historical journey. The KAS flourished in the years to come; it proudly announced several accomplished scholars as honorary members, including the director-general of the Archaeological Survey of India, Sir John Marshall, who oversaw the excavation of Mohenjo-daro and Harappa.[36] Its tiny compound stored a 'brilliant assortment of historical articles', including 'curios, images, inscribed stones, martial weapons, regalia, and tokens of currency'.[37] Twenty-one years later, it began to publish a journal in English—*Journal of the Assam Research Society*—which published some of the finest historical writings on the ancient life of Assam. In its first volume, J.P. Mills, the British ICS official and an outstanding anthropologist, had foreseen that the task before the KAS was 'to push further and further back into past the division between history and prehistory'.[38]

Of the many immediate outcomes of the KAS's initiative was the publication of an anthology of inscriptions on ancient Assam in 1931. The author of this masterly work, mainly aimed at scholars in metropolitan Calcutta, was the Sanskritist Padmanath Bhattacharya.[39] This work successfully disputed many of the imperial historians' assumptions about the political lineage of ancient Assam. More works, containing painstaking scholarship and explaining the ancient lineage of Assam, were published in the next two decades.[40] The search for the ancient gained institutional and scholarly support after the 1950s, resulting in the publication of three more volumes between 1974 and 1981.[41] These newer works presented inscriptions as the earliest evidence of the growth of the Assamese script and the embodiment of Assamese literary history, which I will discuss shortly.

Having failed in their attempts to garner state support for the establishment of a museum in Guwahati, Assam's antiquarians and historians took the initiative to set up, in 1917, a museum to showcase the cultural heritage of ancient Assam. This museum was meant mainly for scholars and the occasional interested layperson, but not for the public at large. Its tiny building housed a wealth of old Assamese and Sanskrit manuscripts and newly retrieved inscriptions. The custodian of this museum was the KAS. Years later, in 1940, this collection was moved from its 'very cramped and unsuitable quarters' to the Provincial Museum in Guwahati, which was thrown open to the public.[42] By that time, the pursuit of the historical past had gained a distinctive place in the Assamese cultural imagination, leading to the establishment of this larger museum. The past was established in order to help buttress the claims of the present.

In 1953, this private initiative received official sanction when it was taken over by the state government.[43] By the mid-1950s, the Assam State Museum was propagating the idea of Assam. The more than 80,000 people who visited the museum annually were greeted by a 'large-sized rhinoceros as they [entered] the . . . building'.[44] The building housed 'a fair collection of antiquities, such as stone and metal sculptures dating from circa 8th to the 16th century AD', and stone inscriptions, which reaffirmed Assam's ancient political lineage and created 'an almost unbroken genealogy of the Assam Kings from the middle of the 4th century AD to the 12th century AD'.[45] The museum reinforced the idea of Assamese identity and its Hindu past; the ethnic tribal communities were not given significance in this limited framework of Assamese history. The eight-century-long genealogy was invoked to convey a legacy of political cohesion, unity and stability.

If the antiquarians got credit for shaping an outline of ancient Assam or painting a picture of its glorious past, historians were not far behind. Traditionalists as well as those trained in the western canon of historical research and writing had taken the initial steps to introduce Assamese history to the English-speaking world;[46] others enthralled Assamese readers with highly imaginative prose on their heroes, rich local histories or their family histories.[47] Suryya Kumar Bhuyan, who was equally accessible to Assamese and English readers, obtained a doctorate in history from the University of London in 1938 and returned to teach English literature at Cotton College. His passion for historical research was driven by an unqualified nationalistic spirit; he had proudly proclaimed in 1926 that the 'past of Assam is flooded with the stories of heroes, great religious leaders, and others'.[48]

Compared to his English works, Bhuyan's Assamese historical writings were aimed at a more general readership and were full of moral lessons for the larger well-being of the nation and the Assamese people. Two inter-related processes went into the success of Bhuyan's project: his rediscovery of a pre-British Assamese tradition of statecraft and his accounts of pre-colonial Assamese heroes on a par with other great Indian political heroes. Bhuyan repeatedly reminded his readers of the uniqueness and glory of Assam's past, and he engaged them with stories of Assam's heroes. The Ahom state was no less than the Mughal Empire in diplomacy and statecraft, he argued. Some of his heroes were not only great military personnel, but they were superb strategists and diplomats as well. Bhuyan portrayed Lachit Barphukan, the seventeenth-century Ahom military general who fought and won wars against the Mughals, as a patriotic Assamese warrior and a 'great hero' who resisted 'the mighty power' of the Mughal army. Lachit Barphukan's example should be a source of inspiration to 'my countrymen in Assam and my friends in the rest of India', Bhuyan reminded his readers.[49] His edited *buranji*s, or chronicles, presented the tribal kingdoms as petty structures playing a marginal role in the making of the Ahom polity. In most of his writings, Bhuyan preached moral lessons (as in a conventional folktale) aimed at, in his own words, re-strengthening the 'confidence of the Assamese', and his biographies of heroes combined literary flair and historical knowledge for the purpose of nation-building. Bhuyan was not alone in this endeavour of educating Assamese readers; his illustrious contemporary Benudhar Sarma also wrote popular accounts of Assamese historical heroes or contemporary political figures.[50]

A folio from *Kamrupar Buranji*

~

Gauhati University's ambitious programme of teaching Assamese language and literature had many parallel developments. The most important initiative of this time was a series of publications on Assamese literary history.[51] A project of writing histories of Assamese language and literature had been underway since the mid-nineteenth century. Generations of Assamese scholars fondly remembered the young Anandaram Dhekial Phukan's masterly memorandum to the EIC official A.J. Moffatt Mills as one of the finest specimens of Assamese literary history.[52] As the nineteenth century progressed, the early Assamese nationalists repeatedly invoked Assam's rich literary history. Following a series of such works, a major cultural mission was undertaken from the early twentieth century onward to reinforce this project. Though mostly published between the 1910s and 1960s, this project continued subsequently and reassured Assamese litterateurs that their cherished language and literature held a significant place in India's literary history.[53]

An account of the long evolutionary history, including the growth and development, of the Assamese script was published in 1936 by Sarbeswar Sarma Kataki, a veteran member of the KAS. Kataki traced the earliest specimen of the Assamese script to the seventh century AD: 'The Assamese script is found in unbroken continuity covering a period of about 1300 years.'[54] Kataki's conclusion was based on the discovery in 1912 of a copper-plate inscription dating back to 610 AD from the time of the Assamese king Bhaskaravarman.[55] Kataki concluded that the Assamese script emerged from the Brahmi script, one of the principal sources of Indian language scripts, and he said that further archaeological discoveries could push this date earlier. Kataki's theory was in part a response to the prevalent idea—given currency by Bengal's celebrated literary historian Dinesh Chandra Sen and archaeologist R.D. Banerji—that the Assamese script was a variation of the Bengali script.[56] However, historians of the Assamese script would have to wait some time for Kataki's theory to be widely accepted.

A major part of the nineteenth century was spent disputing the claims of leading Bengali scholars and writers, including Rabindranath Tagore, about Assamese being a dialect of Bengali. The debates continued into the following century, occasionally sparking off passionate exchanges in the pages of literary journals. When Rabindranath suggested in 1898 in the widely acclaimed Bengali literary journal *Bharati* that Assamese and Oriya were merely dialects of Bengali, similar to the language spoken by the people of Chittagong, which too was a variant of

Bengali, the Assamese literary doyen, Lakshminath Bezbaroa, retorted that Rabindranath was poorly informed.[57]

In the first few decades of the twentieth century, Assamese scholars also began to probe the question of the origin of the Asamiya language. An important question discussed was how much of the origin of Assamese is owed to Sanskrit? Linguists generally agreed that Vedic Sanskrit had branched in two broad directions: one took the shape of classical Sanskrit and largely remained a popular literary language; the other, increasingly described as Prakrit, fulfilled both literary and colloquial requirements. The evolution of Indo-Aryan languages, such as Hindi, Bengali, Marathi, etc., meandered through Prakrit, a term reserved for a compendium of tongues extensively used in different parts of India from the fourth or fifth century BC to the eighth century AD. The majority of linguists agreed that before 100 AD, Prakrit had evolved from being the language of the masses into three different orders of literary languages: Magadhi, Maharashtri and Shauraseni. The Irish linguist-administrator George Abraham Grierson believed that it was from the Magadhi branch that early Assamese evolved. These tongues thereafter developed into Apabhramsa and matured into the various modern Indo-Aryan languages that are spoken today.[58]

What was the position of Assamese among the Indo-Aryan languages? Assamese scholars in the nineteenth century generally subscribed to the view that the Assamese language was one of the direct branches of the Indo-Aryan family.[59] This idea was concretized between 1903 and 1935 in the works of Grierson and the linguist Banikanta Kakati.[60] Though, not everyone concurred; Suniti Kumar Chatterji, the acclaimed linguist, had, however, in 1912, rebuffed the idea that Assamese had originated from Sanskrit: 'Sanskrit is not the mother of Assamese rather, sister of mother only.'[61] A small group of scholars directed their attention to the role of Prakrit in the evolution of Assamese.[62] Their view was that Assamese owed its origin to two different shades of Prakrit.[63] That Assamese may have directly descended from the Indo-Aryan family was a view that was sure to receive much appreciation, but it was not accepted by many scholars.[64] One of them, Kaliram Medhi, not only explained how Assamese originated from a combined background of both Sauraseni and Magadhi Prakrit, but he opined that even the Tibeto-Burman languages spoken by many tribes 'left permanent marks in the Assamese language'.[65]

While these scholars debated and probed into the origin of the Asamiya language, some others continued to concentrate on the evolutionary patterns of the Asamiya script and the fact that it was an ancient language. These scholars' analysis of the rise of the Assamese language and script was linked to their passion for the language and its antiquity. Their conviction was reaffirmed by the extensive reinterpretations of the inscriptions and readings of old manuscripts. If the former were seen as proof of the ancientness of the Assamese script, the latter embodied the evolution of the several modern branches of the script. A large number of manuscripts written between the fifteenth and eighteenth centuries were now read using advances made in India's textual studies tradition. Knowledge of the older variety of scripts brought additional rewards. Those who were trained in all three styles of the Assamese script—Gargaya, Kaitheli and Bamunia—could read and discover the richness of the old Assamese texts.

The discovery of two fifth-century inscriptions in 1955 and 1972 helped scholars to antedate the origin of the Assamese script by two centuries.[66] Those who, including that of T.P. Verma, the palaeographer from the University of Banaras, considered this to be the earliest evidence of the rise of the Asamiya script argued that the parentage of the early Assamese script could be traced to the family of Indian scripts known as Kutila, which developed as a proto-regional script from Brahmi.[67] Later scholars did not disagree with Verma's position. Others, however, had suggested that there was little evidence to prove that the Assamese script originated from Brahmi.[68]

As the language probe was guided by nationalistic passions, a young Assamese language researcher named Golok Chandra Goswami, who had been initiated into modern linguistics at the University of California, Berkeley in 1956–58 and who had also studied linguistics at the Deccan College Post-Graduate and Research Institute, Pune, completed his thesis on the phonology and morphology of the Assamese language from Gauhati University. Goswami began to publish his findings from 1966, and they marked a significant departure from the work of his Assamese grammarian predecessors.⁶⁹ Goswami, who had trained as a linguist and was unhappy in the company of prescriptive grammarians, insisted that Sanskrit was not the mother of Assamese, but its great-grandmother. Far-reaching 'changes and innovations of the Aryan tongue were the results of a fusion of Aryan and extra-Aryan speakers into a common fold and medium, viz. Assamese'.⁷⁰ Goswami was more interested in understanding the structure of the language and insisted that the abundant presence of so many non-Aryan languages around the Assamese landscape made it decidedly different from many other Indo-Aryan languages. Many features of the alphabet, for example, the absence of the Sanskrit [*t*], or the presence of [*x*] or the conjunction (*sandhi*) in Assamese are different from Sanskrit and other Indian languages. Goswami's insights—by establishing the long-sought distinctiveness of the Assamese language—unknowingly rescued the new generation of émigré Assamese speakers, who had to constantly defend their tongue that was oddly different from that of Hindi speakers.

~

The long political and economic shock of the 1940s, described in Chapters 1 and 2 earlier, had to be absorbed by Assamese writers too.⁷¹ Assamese prose began to see a change in the 1940s, and several key elements of the earlier forms were done away with.⁷² Novelists discarded the romantic literary style, described by critics as having fuzzy plots in an undefined time and space, full of metaphors, vernacular styles, as well as idealistic characterizations.⁷³ The new literary style of the '40s saw realistic prose derived from harsh social realities and imagined freedom. It was characterized by a balanced use of both formal and colloquial words. Authors like Banikanta Kakati, Kaliram Medhi and Bhabananda Dutta, who came from varied backgrounds—linguistics, philosophy, anthropology and religious studies—liked their prose to be simple, compact, logical and factual. Kakati tilted towards a functional narrative style; Dutta's powerful prose was based on imagination and logical reasoning and was free of provocative political rhetoric.[74] Complexity in prose gave way to simplicity, textured with empiricism. Reasoned conviction about empiricism paved the way for the rise of a modern discipline that replaced the tradition of history-writing based on ancient pride.[75] Historians agreed that strong, spontaneous and flawless prose could help the Assamese to look at their past intelligently.[76]

There had been an equally gigantic shift in the Assamese literary style earlier in the twentieth century, when leading Assamese authors had begun to include mundane rural forms of language as an integral element of their writings. In 1924, Lakshminath Bezbaroa, president of the Asam Sahitya Sabha, warned against the frequent use of Sanskrit words.[77] Even earlier, from the mid-nineteenth century (coinciding with the coming of print in the Assamese language) until the early twentieth century, Assamese writers and their missionary patrons had tried to infuse writings with idioms and colloquial phrases that were heavily drawn from the social world of Upper Assam.[78] In the long run, this would help, it was thought, to ensure that the Assamese style remained distinctive and free from any Bengali influence. The emerging style—called the standard *ujaniya* Asamiya or *manyabhasa*—hardly found any resonance with the residents of Lower Assam, and, early in the twentieth century, it faced resistance from a group of scholars and writers from this region.[79] These scholars reminded the votaries of standard Asamiya about the 'autonomy, dignity, and fundamental differences' of the old Kamrupiya with *ujaniya* Asamiya (the standard variety). In 1911, one of them asserted that the language of *Namghosha*, the powerful sixteenth-century text composed by Madhavdeva, Sankardeva's most prominent disciple, was the finest specimen of Asamiya *sadhubhasa* of the bygone era.[80] Some of them, however, wished for a national language, *sarbajanin* Asamiya, which would be comprehensible to all. Banikanta Kakati recommended Bezbaroa's style as the national literary style.[81] The authors of the 1940s, who were mostly aware of this contestation, wanted to overcome it.

The resultant prose was tighter than in the earlier periods and saw the useful appropriation of and search for *Tatsom* and *Tadvob* words (complex derivatives from the Sanskrit).[82] Earlier generations of authors had viewed such words with caution—words that were in frequent use in the competitive world of the Bengali language. This new prose style, in conformity with Sanskrit-based words and their derivatives, rescued Assamese prose from several decades of emotive search for the Assamese soul in restrictively localized cultural milieus.[83]

Assamese authors' response to the hopes of freedom in the 1940s was the publication of a new-age literary journal named *Jayantee*. Though first published in 1938, its publication had ceased during the War. The revived journal was ideologically Left leaning after 1945. Condemning writings based on romanticism, *Jayantee* announced the arrival of an age of progressive idealism.[84] Assamese literary journals had always played a powerful role in influencing the literary tastes of Assamese readers. Literary historians identified periods of Assamese literary history with the names of leading journals of those times. If the earlier periods were identified as the age of *Orunodoi, Banhi* or *Jonaki, Jayantee* found a significant place in the mid-twentieth century, carrying out the finest experiments in the new style in Assamese poetry.

By the mid-twentieth century, Assamese poets had left behind the ideals of romanticism perfected in the writings of their predecessors.[85] The literary style of the new generation was spontaneous, free and rhythmic, and it was informed by social awareness and a disdain for bourgeoisie individualism. Some of their verses freely denounced the capitalist economy. A poet who was associated with these experiments argued that spontaneous prose was proof of oratorical skill.[86] The spontaneity and free verse of the poems inspired younger generations—as a contemporary critic expressed it, their dreams took flight.[87] They were free from dogma, read Bengal's influential poets like Jibanananda Das, Buddhadeva Bose and Bishnu Dey while also appreciating other poets of India and the world.[88] Their experiments with words, styles or forms did not stop in the 1950s.[89]

~

By the turn of the nineteenth century, the Assamese language by and large secured recognition as an Indo-Aryan language. From the 1850s, Assamese scholars canonized Sankardeva and the rich corpus of Assamese Vaishnava literature through extensive production of biographies and works of literary criticism. The Vaishnava corpus was a source of inspiration for the Assamese scholars, and many considered it a pillar of their national literature and the quintessence of Assamese culture.[90] In the twentieth century, this joyous encounter continued to receive sustenance. Biographical literature on Sankardeva and his apostles was still a part of the everyday religious life of Assamese Vaishnavism. Inherited through a complex process of community performances reminiscing the life and times of the Vaishnavite saints, these literary works, and also oral traditions, had lived through many ups and downs of Assam's cultural and environmental journey. Earlier scholars had ensured that a small section of these works made their way into printed form, but a large corpus remained unpublished and untouched by the lens of textual criticism. Such works gained wider support after the 1950s. Most Assamese writers devoted their attention to the study of this genre of Assamese literary texts.[91] Banikanta Kakati, being one of them, spent significant time on a distinctive literary criticism of Sankardeva and other Vaishnavite scholars' writings.[92]

The search for Assamese linguistic identity took place alongside the rise of scholarship on Vaishnavism. The latter's twentieth-century rebirth was critical in influencing Assamese linguistic identity; indeed, many considered it of utmost importance to the Assamese identity.[93] While key Vaishnava texts were made available in print from the second half of the nineteenth century, the early twentieth century witnessed a significant proliferation in the reproduction of religious manuscripts. Between 1911 and 1914, Lakshminath published two authoritative biographies of Sankardeva and Madhavdeva,[94] which were free of excessive hagiographical focus. The transition from the pre-print phase of Vaishnava devotion to the new era of print gave a fresh lease of life to Assamese Vaishnavism.[95] Similar was the case of popular narratives on India's religious reform movements. In the first decades of the century, the celebrated Assamese literary magazine *Banhi* and several others regularly published dispassionate debates on these reform movements. It was fairly clear that the Assamese public debates on these subjects were not in conformity with what was going on elsewhere in India. A socio-religious movement challenging the orthodoxies of the Assamese Vaishnava satras had swept parts of Assam since the late 1920s.[96]

From 1960 onwards, a team of scholars from Gauhati University, which included Sanskritists and linguists, began work on an Assamese translation of the Mahabharata from the original Sanskrit, and the first volume was published in 1962.[97] Both the Hindu epics had been translated into Assamese at various times from the fourteenth century onwards. Madhava Kandali's masterly fourteenth-century translation of the Ramayana in verse captivated generations of listeners and readers. From the early twentieth century, some of these translations were printed as part of old Assamese literature.[98]

Sankardeva's teachings, morals and literary works also attracted the attention of literary figures who were followers of Islam. In 1987, the award-winning writer Syed Abdul Malik wrote one of the most widely read fictional biographies of Sankardeva.[99] The Assamese literati also acknowledged that Persian vocabularies considerably enriched the Assamese language.[100] This was a result of the considerable influences of Persian culture in pre-modern India as well as the eagerness of provincial rulers to profit from Mughal political and economic institutions, which was not unique to Assam.[101] The ideals of cultural cosmopolitanism remained the hallmark of literary works well into the 1970s.

~

The mid-twentieth century was a time for clarity and consolidation of the idea of the Assamese classical past. The rediscovery and celebration of the past—some of which had begun in the last decades of the nineteenth century—came to be centred around Assamese Vaishnavite classical literature. As said earlier, this project of rediscovery of the Assamese literary and cultural heritage, largely through the works of scholars who were male and belonged to upper-caste families, was further hastened when Assamese began to be taught at the University of Calcutta as part of its Indian language courses since 1919.[102] Since then, the scholarly publication of a wide range of Vaishnavite literary works continued to receive the patronage of scholars and publishers.[103]

Assamese writers were pledged to furthering the cause of the motherland, and modernization and enrichment of their literary tradition were part of their pledge. The majority drew ideological inspiration from a mix of their vernacular world and western literary thinking. They had inherited a rich scribal culture that had prospered before the nineteenth century.[104] Some of them were proud owners of *puthi*s, manuscripts of various kinds, including Vaishnavite religious texts, ayurvedic works and folk literature drawn from a multi-religious cultural milieu. Possession of these puthis was proof of their social capital.

Literary historians did not use the word 'classical' to identify a special body of literary works of the earlier period. Their preferred word was *Purani*, literally translated as 'old' and figuratively as 'golden age'. In this body of *Purani Asamiya Sahitya* (old Assamese literature), which included the rich Vaishnava literature, Assamese buranjis and folk literature, they recognized the exemplary character of the Assamese literary past.[105] In the early twentieth century, Assamese readers had often considered these works as 'trivial books of verses read by ordinary villagers'.[106] Banikanta Kakati rediscovered and elevated their literary merit through a series of essays. Kakati and his contemporaries saw that these works needed to be reappraised and made available to a wider readership of modern Assamese people. They enthused Assamese readers morally, culturally and as a nation, and their rediscovery benefited book publishers, readers and the Assamese as a *jati* (a cohesive community).[107]

The most celebrated example of this was the editing and printing of biographical accounts of Vaishnava saints. Widely popular as an oral tradition and a sacred heritage among the followers of Assamese Vaishnavism, it was recited as part of everyday religious activities. Before beginning its life in print, it was among the thousands of manuscripts lying in secret corners of family homes or religious places. The anonymously authored *Katha-guru-carita*, a wide-ranging account of Assam's Vaishnava saints, which was believed to have been composed from oral traditions in the eighteenth century and received as a gift by Banikanta Kakati from his religious preceptor, was edited and published in 1952.[108] Considered the finest specimen in the tradition of old Assamese prose and a 'work of immense national interest',[109] the printed edition became part of Gauhati University's Assamese literature syllabus. The university's manuscript library acquired carita manuscripts. Maheswar Neog, now a teacher in the Assamese department, carried with him to class both the printed edition and few folios of the manuscript. The caritas emerged as a lens through which Assam's classical past was scrutinized. Marking a courageous departure from the powerful tradition of hagiography, literary historians used methods of textual criticism to study these caritas or used them as an archive to understand Assam's material transformation in the earlier centuries. Over the years, their works elevated these biographical works into Assamese canonical texts.[110] The caritas were also increasingly considered the true heirs to the ancient inscriptions—'they threw light on the dark age post Kamarupa-Sasanavali'[111]—giving greater clarity to the historical lineage of the Assamese language.

A folio from *Katha Guru Carit*

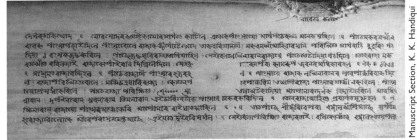

A folio from *Katha Guru Carit*

Another illustrative example was the *ankiya nat*, the one-act drama, a key performative component of Assamese Vaishnavite religious life. Scripts of these dramas—their performances being known as *bhaona* or *bhawana*—formed part of the vast manuscript collection and were also edited and published by scholars.[112] Most emphasized the influence and power of these drama forms on the Assamese mind. The bhawana represents the 'sentiment and temperament of the Assamese people', wrote the cultural historian and the novelist Birinchi Kumar Barua in 1940. The rich body of scholarship on Vaishnavite religious works and its unending popular appeal refortified Assam's curiosity about its classical literary heritage and unambiguously acknowledged the importance of the everyday cultural traditions in the making of modern Assamese literary history.[113]

The search for, and collection of, ancient Assamese manuscripts (*puthi*s) remained at the forefront of Assamese nationalistic imagination for a major part of the twentieth century. The moral authority derived from these texts provided a crucial rallying point to secure a distinguished place for Assam in India's cultural history. It was seen as fundamental to being Assamese. The government should spare some resources for these activities rather than wasting money on hill–plains cultural unity, the historian Benudhar Sarma said angrily in 1953.[114] Anyway, the Assamese literati remarkably grappled with their classical heritage but sought to move it forward in new directions.

~

The journey of Assamese cinema began in 1935 with the film *Joymoti*.[115] Based on a historical legend around the royal political rivalries of seventeenth-century Assam, seen through the eyes of the female protagonist Joymoti, this film was directed by Jyotiprasad Agarwala, who belonged to a Marwari merchant family. His great-grandparents had migrated to Assam, following in the footsteps of the British East India Company. Trained in Germany as a cinematographer, Jyotiprasad was well known by the 1940s as an idealist, poet, theatre personality, music composer, author, singer, composer and a non-conformist political activist and public intellectual.[116] His cinematic narrative, based on Lakshminath Bezbaroa's 1915 novel, viewed India's anti-colonial political struggle, which encompassed the ideals of satyagraha, through the prism of an Assamese historical legend.[117] While for its actors, the film's cinematic features and centrality within the larger Assamese nationalist political imagination was no doubt significant, it did not appeal to critics and the audience. One of the earliest reviews of the film said the 'team of players' was 'absolutely ignorant of films'.[118] A financial disaster, the film was largely a social and political statement for the writer-artist who went to jail several times for his anti-colonial political stand. Though *Joymoti* was often considered an avant-garde film, laying the foundation of Assamese cinema, it struggled to resonate with Assamese tastes.[119]

A limited number of movies were made in Assamese in the 1940s. Some drew upon historical themes from the Assamese literary world, others fell back on social issues or patriotism; many more would soon follow in the footsteps of popular Hindi films.[120] A few—*Siraj* (1948) for instance—probed social stereotypes and expressed a longing for an equal society. Jyotiprasad, himself, was convinced of the 'educative value' of cinema in the nation-making process. Writing to an official who was responsible for the administration of Assam's northern hills, he noted that 'the majority of Hill brothers and sisters' were waiting to get 'the sense of Freedom, Education and vast foreign knowledges for their uplift' and needed to be 'educated by all means by exhibiting Films possessing educative value'.[121]

Financial support for early Assamese cinema came in part from Assamese tea planters. Cinema halls were not only for male audiences; women viewers had special seats shielded by curtains.[122] From 1950, Marwari mercantile houses began to participate in the process of cinema production as well as distribution through their trade networks.[123] They also owned the majority of cinema halls. The halls showed Assamese, Bengali and Hindi movies. Popular Hindi films like *Do Bigha Zamin* drew huge audiences.

Music, too, saw some radical developments in Assam, as several musicians experimented with replacing the 'classical Assamese tune with the modern'.[124] These new songs were 'clearly cut off from the past both in matter and tune', wrote a historian.[125] The modern journey of Assamese songs in the late nineteenth century was tumultuous, often criticized for its 'blind imitation of Bengali songs both in language and tune'. The era of experimentation had begun decades earlier. Both *raag*-based music and folk music were part of Lakshmiram Barooah's magnum opus *Sangeet Kosha*—an anthology comprising the *raags* and tunes of 422 songs—published in 1907.[126] Bengal's Dwijendralal Ray and Rabindranath continued to exercise influence for another quarter century. Thereafter, 'a rich variety' of 'tunes of folk-songs' gave a new turn to Assamese songs.[127] The new songs, some of which were 'artistically woven into the playlets', were regularly aired on All India Radio and became part of Assamese movies. These developments helped to define Assamese cultural sensibilities. Years later, the musical tastes for *raag* and folk music came together in the All Assam Music Conference, which saw leading Indian classical musicians, including the shehnai maestro Bismillah Khan, perform in Guwahati.[128] Cultural activists were in search of Assamese classical musical forms that could place them on a par with other Indian classical musical traditions. Ambikagiri's appeal for Borgeet and Rupnath Brahma's focus on Bodo songs drew attention to temple dance forms.

Prior to 1947, the All India Radio (AIR) station in Calcutta aired a 30-minute daily programme for Assamese listeners, which largely included news and snapshots of Assamese literary or cultural history, etc.[129] The Shillong–Gauhati station began to air daily programmes in three slots from 1948. Home Minister Vallabhbhai Patel sent a message on the day of the inauguration, saying that this public service would cater to popular regional tastes.[130] Catering to the tastes and redefining the sensibilities of Assamese listeners, but not necessarily creating a mass culture, these radio programmes were significant steps in Assam's new, technologically empowered cultural journey. A blend of news programmes, music programmes with modern songs by leading and upcoming Assamese singers as well as Assamese folk songs, Hindi film songs and Indian classical music, lectures on Assam's history and literature, Hindi language lessons and a programme meant for the rural population was offered.¹³¹ The Shillong station would cater exclusively to the capital region and its immediate hilly neighbourhood, while the Brahmaputra Valley would be served by a separate station. The Guwahati station began independent transmission from 1950 and soon became an important platform for the Assamese cultural elite to articulate their aspirations. The two stations were connected to each other by telephone, and programmes were broadcast by both. Mehra Masani, of the London School of Economics and hailing from a Parsi family, was selected as the first station director of AIR in Assam.¹³² Assamese literary scholars wrote scripts, songs and plays for the radio programmes. With the rise of political consciousness in the Assam hills, radio programmes offered special slots for each hill region, including NEFA, Lushai hills, etc.¹³³ The radio network in India covered only a fifth of its population in 1951, and the population with access to radio in Assam was small.¹³⁴ The numbers of radio listeners began to grow slowly; several stores frequently advertised new models of radio sets produced by Murphy or Philips.

~

Some of Assam's literary heroes found national recognition through the newly established Sahitya Akademi (National Academy of Letters).¹³⁵ From 1955 onwards, the Akademi's annual awards strengthened the Assamese literary world's relationship with the Indian nation-state.¹³⁶ The Akademi published translations of Assamese literary works in other Indian languages. In June 1957, the Union government established the National Book Trust to publish the classical literature of India and translations of standard Indian or foreign works into various Indian languages. The Assamese press welcomed it as 'a landmark in the cultural renaissance of free India'.¹³⁷

Translation was a powerful cultural and political project; it could be seen as a process of social reform. Through the translation and reading of a pan-Indian Hindu text in a local language, for instance, pan-Indian cultural traditions penetrate into the local society. In parallel, the Assam government set up its own publication board in 1957. It produced an extensive body of work—original, translated or editions of old manuscripts—aided by new printing technology and endowed with an aesthetic sense, catering to a generation of Assamese readers. The books delivered a new literary experience to thousands of homes. The state-sponsored publisher soon became a cultural icon, reinforcing the Assamese cultural history project.

While western modernity coupled with a deep reverence for their cultural and literary tradition shaped their perspectives, a section of Assam's intellectuals and scholars were equally influenced by the global communist movement. They did not have much interest in China, but Russia's political transformation charmed a section of the Assamese intelligentsia. The linguist Kakati and philosopher Dutta were greatly inspired by Soviet communism. Filmmaker Agarwala befriended Indian communists. The young historian Amalendu Guha visited Moscow in 1957 and was impressed by the living standards of Russian peasants and workers.[138] Russian literary works were translated for the masses. *Soviet Desh*, a well-designed and well-produced literary monthly magazine in Assamese that carried mainly Soviet political propaganda, reached many Assamese people.[139]

The foremost cultural influence of the communists was through organizational enterprises of IPTA, a Communist Party of India organization born in 1943 during World War II. The Assam chapter of IPTA was formed in 1947. Inspired by the left movement and in keeping with its goal of cultural reawakening, it beckoned several Assamese artists to break away from their high literary tradition to give a new political meaning to their writing.[140] Championing the songs of faceless people and giving voice to the accounts of their hopes and sorrows, IPTA inspired Jyotiprasad Agarwala to become the first president of the organization's Assam branch, until he was removed from this position in 1949 as many within IPTA considered him as bourgeois.[141] Others, including Bhupen Hazarika and Hemanga Biswas, enthralled and politically inspired masses with their songs.

~

Several Assamese collections of proverbs, popular sayings and folktales were published in the late nineteenth and early twentieth centuries,[142] and they found popularity among an increasingly large Assamese reading public. As the Assamese modernist literary project advanced, folk and classical literature walked hand in hand. The study of Assamese rural and tribal life received serious scholarly attention within the institutional space of Gauhati University. A centre of collection and archive for folklore was established in 1955—a momentous decision for Gauhati University, which was considered an institution whose thrust was towards classical studies. Scholars like Verrier Elwin and Christoph von Führer-Haimendorf had already conducted extensive studies of folk traditions and tribal myths in India's North-east.

The department was initially established as a repository of folklore, with the intention of acquiring a 'comprehensive collection of the oral literature and traditions of the tribes and people of Assam', under the aegis of the department of anthropology.[143] Birinchi Kumar Barua, a celebrated novelist and cultural and literary historian, was the first leader of this archival centre. Barua had a brief stint at the Indiana University in 1963, further exploring advances in folkloristics.[144]

The leaders of the university's folklore studies initially focused on two major areas: Assam's tribal life and rural and rustic societies. They also diligently studied folk oral-literary traditions alongside the Assamese classical literary traditions. Their scholarship recognized the deep penetration of the Hindu epic tradition into the oral traditions of Assam. These folklorists understood that non-Sanskrit and non-Assamese literary archives could help re-evaluate the social and intellectual landscape of Assam. Praphulladatta Goswami, a leading folklorist of his time who encouraged studies on the cultural life of tribal societies, saw this as a major step in the democratic process of nation-building in post-Independence India. Goswami's comradeship with scholars from tribal communities resulted in the emphasis on academic studies of tribal life. During the following two decades, the department consistently encouraged studies of the tribal cultural world. A 1972 publication of folktales of the Bodos became a major landmark.[145] Scholarly studies on folklore began to look at varied local forms of religious and other cultural practices, which would normally be ignored in the canonical works.

Just as the popularization of the collection and study of an extensive corpus of folklore gained momentum from the 1940s,[146] so did the urban popularity of the rural festival of Bihu.[147] In 1948, the Sikh and Hindu Assamese populations jointly celebrated the Khalsa (Baisakhi) and Bohag Bihu festivals.[148] Muslims, too, participated in the cultural activities of Bihu. Urban Bihu celebrations, a combination of sports (boat racing) and cultural programmes, including the performance of Bihu dance and songs, made sporadic appearances in the first half of the century.[149] From the mid-twentieth century, they became a regular phenomenon, and in 1966, there were 13 different programmes within Guwahati city itself.[150] Most of the Bihu programmes that year were inaugurated by major political leaders.

In the meantime, the first half of the twentieth century saw a growth, albeit a slow one, in Assam's urban population from 12,000 in 1900 to 43,000 in 1951. The main growth was in the capital city of Shillong; it was much slower in other towns. These towns were mainly inhabited by salaried employees, professionals, traders, a few industrial workers and some poor people. Most people were still rooted in rural agrarian life; many earned an income from their land, receiving either rent or supplies of food products from these properties. This new urban population, which was yet to cut the umbilical cord to its origins in village society, brought rural folk traditions into the urban setting. This was a pan-India phenomenon, not unique to Assam. These imported rural cultures acquired new forms and styles in conformity with the taste and sensibilities of city dwellers.

The carnivalesque dimension of this popular rural festival remained a source of unease for the urban Assamese intelligentsia in the nineteenth century; some even wanted to outlaw Bihu.[151] Gunabhiram Barua, considered a torchbearer of the Assamese renaissance of the nineteenth century, wanted to purge the festival of its carnivalesque elements.[152] Towards the end of the nineteenth century, the hostilities of the cultural elite eventually began to give way to accommodation. *Miri Jiyori*, a major literary work of 1894, stood in solidarity with the rural revellers, as it portrayed both the rich and the poor taking part in Bihu revelry.[153] Such voices of support became louder despite resistance from the 'educated' in the next few decades.[154] Lakshminath Bezbaroa not only derided the critics but applauded Bihu festivities as a testimony of Assam's allegiance to the ancient Aryan civilization.[155] When the historian Nakul Chandra Bhuyan published a motley collection in 1923, a time when 'it was almost obscene for a decent young man to dabble in such songs',[156] he purged the rustic words and replaced them with new ones, which were most often Sanskritized. In 1923, the province's education minister highlighted that 'though these songs appeared stale and commonplace having no place beyond affording certain vulgar enjoyment to the rural youths of Assam', they were truly 'the chief stocks in trade of Assam literature'.[157]

By the mid-1950s the cultural elite began to describe Bohag Bihu as the most important festival of Assam; others described it as a manifestation of the collective political will of the Assamese.[158] Various dance forms of the ethnic and tribal communities of Assam were included in the Bihu programmes. In 1954, the Latasil Bihu programme, one of the first of its kind, had curated a mosaic of dance programmes representing Mishing, Bodo, Sattriya and Manipuri dance forms, among others.[159] By the 1950s, the AIR station in Guwahati had programmes of Bihu songs, including special programmes for Bodo and Mishing Bihu.[160]

As the Bihu festival was absorbed by the urban milieu—at a time when 'the symbolic significance of old rituals and festivals were lost'—it 'acquired a sort of elitist character', wrote Praphulladatta Goswami.[161] But these songs became a source of 'inspiration for the present', Goswami noted.[162] Historian Benudhar Sarma observed that Bihu had helped divided factions in Assam to unite in the past, and it served as an inspiration for the present generation.[163]

Other festivals of a deeply communitarian religious nature, such as Durga Puja, Eid, Christmas, gave a secular character to urban lives. Some nineteenth-century community celebrations took newer forms to invoke nationalism and unity. The *Sankardeva tithi*, where devotees performed an annual ritual for Sankardeva, was one such celebration that gained wide popularity. Till the 1950s, occasions like *tithi*s (death rituals) were not recognized as public holidays; rather, they were confined to a particular community's cultural calendar.[164]

~

From the mid-twentieth century, Assam witnessed the publication of a wide spectrum of Assamese literary works. The introduction of the systematic study of Assamese language and literature as part of the university curriculum since the early decades of the twentieth century remained an additional driving force. Of these numerous works, some stood out and received the attention of readers and literary critics.

Literary critics customarily identify the dawning of a new age in Assamese literature with the publication of Birinchi Kumar Barua's Assamese novel *Jivanar Batat* (On the Path of Life), published in 1944. *Jivanar Batat* was about the social and moral predicaments of contemporary Assamese society. Dominated by powerful women characters, and deeply embedded both in the Assamese cultural milieu and its contemporary political and economic landscape, this novel was a morale booster for Assamese readers and remained a bestseller for decades. Booksellers publicized it widely,[165] critics welcomed it, and commendations continued to pour in. One of the earliest reviews declared it the 'book of the year' and added that 'every aspect of Assamese life and culture from the kitchen to public life is made alive by the author's masterly dealing with the facts'.[166] Banikanta Kakati hailed it as the only 'Assamese work of fiction that will bear translating into an International Language like English' because of its 'artistry and local colour'.[167] 'The local colour, humour and pathos in which it abounds easily appeal to the various categories of reading public; but what generally eludes attention is the fine organization of all these ingredients into a moral centrality,' wrote a later critic in 1966.[168] Another literary critic saw objectivity, restraint and maturity as the hallmarks of Barua's literary prose.[169] A distinguished literary critic declared that the failure of the novel to profoundly influence ordinary Assamese readers was an unfortunate state of affairs for modern Assamese literature.[170]

Meanwhile, with an increasing rate of literacy, officially 27.4 per cent in 1961, and an increase in the numbers of college-going students—from an estimated 4515 in 1947–48 to 31,000 in 1961–62—the reading public had expanded.[171] In 1951, there was only one Assamese daily, with an approximate circulation of 3000, against 4.9 million Assamese speakers.[172] By 1971, this increased significantly to 41 Assamese language newspapers, though still low in comparison to 769 Bengali and 3116 Hindi newspapers.[173]

This was also the new age of Assamese literary criticism. As a literary critic, Kakati had already refashioned the contours of Assamese literary modernity. With his sharp commentaries on the history of the Assamese literary tradition, his corpus of literary criticism became the foundation for a new era in the Assamese literary journey. When he breathed his last in 1952, Kakati's scholarship had already left a strong imprint in the fields of historical and anthropological investigation into Assam's religious life.[174] He stressed on the need for re-examining the central presumption of Assam's Hindu past. He gave the example of various words—for instance, Pragjyotishpur, the ancient name of Assam—that had non-Aryan roots. Kakati was also deeply influenced by the ideas of Russian and Chinese socialism. But it was essentially his historical-anthropological investigation into religious orders and the milieu of Assam that unsettled many colonial assumptions.

Along with the rediscovery of the Assamese classical literary world, new Assamese literary and cultural heroes were identified. Some of them acquired an enduring eminence, and their influence on the collective Assamese mind never diminished. One of the first to get the status of a hero was Lakshminath Bezbaroa, whose birth centenary was widely celebrated in 1968. An editorial in the *Assam Tribune* provides an idea of his stature: 'In the fierce battles that had to be waged for the preservation of our cultural identity, Bezbaroa filled the same proud position of leadership which Lachit did centuries earlier in the field of Saraighat against the invading Mughuls.'[175] He was the 'crowning glory of an age', it reiterated.

As literary production in Assamese and its use as the language of governance achieved spectacular progress, many speakers of tribal languages of Assam quietly grew worried, as they could foresee trouble. In an age of growing self-determination among ethnic groups, one could hardly expect the tribals to adopt Assamese as their language and discard their own.[176] Rising ethnic political and cultural consciousness, and the fluid linguistic landscape, made the promotion of Assamese as the exclusive language of the Assam state a daunting task towards the end of the '50s. Meanwhile, the visualization of the varied forms of Hindu religious practices as predominant cultural forms of the region contributed to the tribal communities and practitioners of non-Aryan linguistic and religious practices being dislocated from the centre stage of Assamese society and culture.

~

The renaissance in Assamese cultural and literary history took a violent political turn in the summer of 1960. Clouds had been gathering over Assam's political landscape for years. Passions ran high over language in many parts of India. The idea of the mother tongue, *matribhasa*, as the medium of instruction in educational institutions or as the language of official correspondence had gained wide acceptance amongst India's regional language speakers in the 1950s. In 1954, Gujarati became the medium of instruction in Gujarat University.[177] In 1953, the Union government had formed the Andhra state after conceding the demands of Telugu speakers. It also constituted the States Reorganisation Commission in the same year to look into similar demands from other parts of India. In Assam, except for a brief period from 1937 to 1947 when the Assamese–Bengali conflict took a competitive communal form around questions of land and sharing of political power, the tussle was mostly over language.

Compared with the animated political moments in many parts of India, the Commission encountered an unusually low-key response in Assam. Assam 'would welcome the merger, if possible, of Cooch-Behar, Manipur, and Tripura . . . '[178] Its hill districts dreamt of separate statehood or even independence from India. West Bengal's demand for the inclusion of Goalpara on the ground of 'considerable presence of Muslim population', who it claimed spoke Bengali, was rejected by the Commission: 'Such historical connection as there has been between Goalpara and West Bengal has been intermittent and tenuous.'[179] The Commission also disagreed with Nehru's idea of a tribal policy in the North-east. It is 'neither necessary nor desirable to confer on the tribes any immunity from external contacts to such an extent as to hamper their development'.[180] The Commission was hostile to the idea of an Inner Line, and although it agreed that Partition had dealt a significant blow to the economy of the hill regions, it took a tough stand on the demand for a separate hill state. 'The creation of a new hill state will . . . accentuate these distinctions,' the Commission concluded. Another proposal that caused ripples across political circles was the idea of creating a 'Purbachal' state by amalgamating Cachar, Tripura, Mizo hills, Naga hills, Manipur and NEFA.[181] This idea had originated in 1948, the principal sponsor being the Cachar States Reorganization Committee, but it was dismissed.[182] The Commission believed that Assam would prosper economically and culturally only 'if two conditions are fulfilled . . . that the state of Assam is compact, rich and resourceful, and that there exists within this state, mutual tolerance and goodwill'.[183]

The colonial bureaucracy had tried to accommodate the complex and highly fluid language situation, with officials being expected to learn tribal languages and textbooks being printed in these languages. Throughout the late 1940s and 1950s, Assamese political leaders, public intellectuals and litterateurs pushed to make Assamese the official language and the language of instruction for the state.[184] With Independence and the arrival of the state apparatus under the full command of the Assamese elite, the Assam government conceded to such demands as early as 1947, but not without offending many communities.[185] In 1950, the Asam Sahitya Sabha made it amply clear that it wanted the government's patronage to make Assamese the language of the state.

> Assam has got the status of state in the Indian dominion but the threat to her language and literature has not disappeared. Assamese is

yet to be the state language. To strengthen Assam's unity, there must be careful steps to expand and popularize the Assamese language and literature in the vastly spread out tribal areas.[186]

Weeks after India's celebration of its first Republic Day, the Sabha adopted a cautiously worded resolution in March 1950, urging the Assam government to declare Assamese as 'the State (official) language of Assam and as the medium of instruction in all the high schools of Assam, with the exception of the high schools of Khasi, Jaintia and Garo Hills districts'.[187] Such propositions were always firmly opposed by the hill peoples.[188]

Meanwhile, the question of Hindi as official language of India had gained further legitimacy, consequent to the report submitted by India's first Official Language Commission in 1956. One of the members of the Commission was the writer Birinchi Kumar Barua. The Commission's push for Hindi did not go unchallenged, however. When the Commission arrived in Assam to gather evidence, a prominent Assamese judge made it clear that 'I for myself have not much acquaintance with Hindi, nor do I suppose that it will be very useful as a Court language here. I consider the regional languages to be best adopted for use in courts up to the High Court stage'.[189] The All India Language Conference which took place in Calcutta in 1958, organized at the initiative of C. Rajagopalachari and attended by representatives of Assam, witnessed the pronounced declaration of this mounting challenge against Hindi. 'Elder statesmen, jurists, scientists, creative writers, educationists, industrialists, journalists, senior military officers belonging to different regions came forward' to express their opposition, the All India Language Conference reported.[190] As opposition to Hindi grew, the Commission recognized that 'In the field of the States' administration, the successors [of English] would be the respective regional languages'.

Assam had no disagreement on the role of Hindi as India's *lingua franca* but 'not at the cost of our own language—Assamese', warned the noted scholar Birendra Kumar Bhattacharya in 1958.[191] Others, however, saw hope in the use of the Devanagari script for the Assamese language. A tiny group of scholars and politicians, including the folklorist Prapulladatta Goswami, pushed for changing the Assamese script to Devanagari.[192]

In 1959, Madras adopted Tamil as its state language, and the trend of adopting regional languages as state languages followed. The year 1960 would see two states—Maharashtra and Gujarat—being born out of the new political language movement. This was when the Sabha intensified pressure on Chief Minister Bimala Prasad Chaliha and his government to take similar steps in Assam, though proceeding with caution, given Assam's complex linguistic situation. The Sabha agreed that it would be 'much easier' to make Assamese the 'medium of correspondence' in the Brahmaputra Valley districts and in the 'civil secretariat', and it advised the government to accept communication 'in Bengali in Cachar district, in Khasi in the Khasi & Jaintia Hills, in Garo in Garo Hills and in Lushai in Mizo districts', adding that 'steps may be taken for translating such communication into Assamese'.[193] The Assam Congress, while agreeing with the Sabha's views, had asked that the government 'should be given some latitude and time to make its own decision on a vital matter'.[194]

~

The political momentum to declare Assamese as the state's official language had started building from April 1959. The Sabha's annual literary festival, which was attended by literary stalwarts and celebrities, drew large crowds. Spread over several days, the programme included impressive seminars and talks on Assamese literature, history and science as well as carefully orchestrated cultural entertainment. That year, the Sabha adopted nine resolutions, three of which were dedicated to the contested political future of the Assamese language.[195] One of the resolutions demanded that the Union government introduce Assamese as the medium of instruction in the NEFA region (discussed further in the next chapter). Another insisted that the Assam government compulsorily teach Assamese in non-Assamese-medium schools. The Sabha demanded that the government should declare Assamese as an official language in 1960. To build popular support and pressure the government, the Sabha organized Assam Rajya Bhasa Demand Days in September 1959 and March 1960. The political opponents of the Congress, barring the All Party Hill Leaders Conference, mounted pressure on the government in the legislative assembly.[196] The Assam government, aware of the political fallout of such a move, chose to tread with caution. '[The] Government would prefer to wait till they get the same demand from the non-Assamese speaking population for declaration of Assamese as a state language,' Chaliha said.[197] He warned that 'if this issue is decided only on the basis of majority or minority, Government is afraid that its object would be defeated'. The announcement of the official position resulted in tension and discontent, the signs of which were evident everywhere.

The tribal members in the legislative assembly expressed their disapproval of the proposal that Assamese be declared the state language. The hills had a large number of educational institutions, largely run by Christian missionaries, and had a clear advantage in choosing English. Assamese was the language of social interaction and may have been required by people to carry out trade transactions, but they realized that it would not help them in employment or public debate. Some Bengali speakers took out a street procession in Shillong and abused the Assamese language, which was widely denounced in the Assamese press.[198] The move to declare Assamese as the official language of the state had the support of large sections of the Assamese literary class, who saw it as a means to curb the widespread use of Bengali.[199] A letter to the editor complained that the Indian Railways was using Bengali words on tickets.[200]

In February 1960, two lawmakers from the Opposition demanded in the Assembly that Assam's capital should be shifted from Shillong to Guwahati, and Assamese should be declared the state language.[201] Chaliha's refusal to agree to this politically challenging demand was widely condemned by the public, and it even caused discontent within the Congress party.[202] Months previously, Mahendra Mohan Choudhury, the Assam Congress president, had written to the Asam Sahitya Sabha, extending support to their idea.[203] An angry Sabha organized State

Language Day on 11 March 1960. Chaliha was denounced as 'odd and thoughtless' by the votaries of the demand.[204] In Guwahati, Ambikagiri, who gave up his pension in protest, asked in a fiery speech why the Assamese national feeling had not still awakened.[205] Others endorsed him; Raghunath Choudhary, a well-known poet and writer, appealed for direct action to achieve this. Public pressure throughout March, however, did not help. Chaliha, who was elected from the Bengali-dominated Cachar, insisted that Assam needed to listen to its linguistic minorities.[206] Public meetings and publication of popular essays in defence of Assamese as state language continued.[207] Tactical support came from Marwari traders, Sikh residents and even the Brahmaputra Valley's Hindu Bengali speakers.[208] 'We express our fullest support to Assamese as the state language of the state of Assam. It is the *de facto* state language . . .,' said a letter from the Valley's Bengali speakers.

As the Opposition saw an opportunity to corner the government, the Congress party tried to retain its popular support. On 22 April 1960, the Congress in Assam adopted a series of resolutions extending support to Assamese as the state official language,[209] while not losing sight of the objections raised by the tribal speakers and the Bengali speakers and also including the earlier rider that Assamese would not be imposed on Cachar and the hill districts. While this meant that Assamese would be accepted as the official language only when the people of the hill districts and Cachar were ready to adopt it, it also meant that the residents of these areas were expected, sooner or later, to accept Assamese. This could satisfy no one.

Popular mobilization and localized clashes between Assamese and Bengali sections of the urban population began in late May 1960. Protests, mainly in the form of street demonstrations,[210] saw a spike, spearheaded by Assamese-speaking students demanding Assamese as the state language. Garos, Mizos, Jaintias, Bengalis and Nagas organized a demonstration in Shillong on 21 May, where slurs were allegedly used against the Assamese language and signboards in Assamese were removed and thrown into dumps. This promptly inflamed passions in the Brahmaputra Valley.[211] Students and the urban literary elite joined hands with the advocates of the official language campaign. Support came from tea garden workers, industrial workers' unions[212] and from the Valley's Bengali speakers too.[213] Opposition political parties, such as the Praja Socialist Party and the communists, joined hands. From the third week of June, the urban demonstrations mutated into actions of loot, arson and attack on government properties.[214] In the face of great public pressure, Chaliha announced on 23 June 1960 that his government would bring in legislation to make Assamese the official language, but he still remained sensitive to his earlier position.[215]

Months of simmering tension exploded into full-blown communal violence in several parts of the Brahmaputra Valley and spread like wildfire by July 1960. Earlier, as Assamese and Bengali speakers clashed, a curfew had been imposed in Guwahati city on the night of 30 June. Similar violence was seen in other towns as well.[216] Bengali newspapers were burnt, stray assaults on Bengali speakers were reported in the first few days of July, and they started fleeing to West Bengal.[217] Calcutta-based newspaper reports on Assam's violent situation invited wrath in Assam, which instantaneously 'flared up riots in Guwahati'.[218] A crowd injured the district magistrate, while others set on fire houses of Bengali-speaking families.[219] A teenage student, Ranjit Borpujari, died in police firing on 4 July in the residential part of the iconic Cotton College.[220] The next day, the newspapers carried pictures of the student's dead body, which triggered anger among the Assamese and fear among the Bengalis. On 5 July, Guwahati was 'a deserted city'. 'The din and bustle of busy life here has been transformed as if by magic into a dead silence . . . The sole occupants of the scene being the police and military men with guns fixed with bayonets,' said an eyewitness account.[221] 'Such a grim atmosphere was never witnessed before in this Gauhati, not even in those cruel days of the Second World War,' said another.[222] Riots soon spread to the rural areas. The Army was called in. By the end of July, an estimated 55,000 were homeless, 7000 homes were burned and dozens were killed.[223] Between 4 and 7 July, rioters had attacked poor Bengali-speaking families in Goreswar, a north bank locality.[224] The *Times of India* described the situation as an 'insanity fair': 'The people of Assam seem to be in the grip of madness'.[225]

The riots were censured as *Bongal Kheda Andolan*—a movement to drive out Bengalis. An official enquiry committee later indicted the government machinery for the situation.[226] Several thousand huts—8000 to 9000 in one estimate—were burnt down in the Brahmaputra Valley. The official enquiry report blamed the 'incompetence' of the bureaucracy for the rapid spread of violence.[227] The 'administration had collapsed'. As mob frenzy reigned supreme and Hindu Bengalis were outnumbered, thousands fled to Bengal.[228] A distinguished economist who was witness to the events conceded that 'the agitation in Assam was only against Bengalis and that too against Hindu Bengalis who have been unsympathetic to other people'.[229] The scale and intensity of the arson and rioting were aggravated because the lower ranks of the police shared the popular passions. The government appeared fragile—Chaliha fell ill, and one of his cabinet colleagues, and also chief secretary of the Congress, was attending a conference in faraway Kashmir. The 'State was deprived of guidance at [a] political level', said a team of parliamentarians.[230]

Most of the victims were poor Hindu Bengali families living on paltry incomes. Sweet-makers' utensils, clothes, ornaments and food stocks were stolen; a Bengali worker's savings of Rs 150 was taken away; a shopkeeper's stock register was burnt; another's children (who ironically were studying in Assamese-medium schools) were mercilessly beaten up.[231] Jewellery shops were gutted, and granaries were broken into. There was some intercommunity support: a Bengali tailor in Upper Assam who fled on a boat reported to police, 'They followed me but the Miri people protected me and after spending six days there, they dropped me at Dhansiri.'[232] An IPTA cultural troupe that included Bhupen Hazarika, the future cultural icon of Assam, and the celebrated Bengali folk singer Hemanga Biswas, tried to comfort besieged victims.[233]

Assamese and Bengali newspapers entered into a cultural war; Nehru was amazed at their 'emotional narrow approach'. 'If I read them, even my blood curdles at the things they write,' he said.[234] As anti-Bengali violence raged in the Brahmaputra Valley, anti-Assamese sentiment gripped Bengal.[235] Assamese students abstained from attending classes in Calcutta. Assam's leader of Opposition, Hareswar Goswami, was chased by an angry mob at a North Bengal railway station, leading to the death of several people.[236] Calcutta, which was already burdened with massive workers' strikes in July, observed a general strike on 16 July, which brought the city to a complete halt. As Assamese and Bengalis fought in the streets, Nirad C. Chaudhuri, the influential Bengali writer, sharpened the polarization, saying that the political battles were the result of economic and social rivalry, 'caused by movements of population from province to province and akin to many other countries'. Describing all Assamese as descendants of the Mongoloid Ahom, Chaudhuri concluded that 'they [the Assamese] had accepted Hindu culture from Bengal, and no [one] but a madman will say that their language is not a dialectal offshoot of Bengali'. Chaudhuri, however, conceded that 'the episode left both the sides more embittered and alienated than before'.[237] Not everyone among the Assamese literary elite was at odds with Bengali society or vice versa in the 1950s.[238] A contemporary account described how 'many Bengalis [were] thriving as doctors, lawyers, teachers, clerks and occasionally as traders' in Assam.[239] Many of them found solace in Rabindra Sangeet, others enthusiastically read Calcutta-based Bengali newspapers.

Nehru gave permission for the Gandhian Vinoba Bhave to undertake a 1500-kilometre walk to Assam, which began in September, on a peace mission. He himself had arrived in the state on a three-day visit along with his daughter Indira on 17 July and had been visibly shaken. On 1 September 1960, he initiated a political debate on the crisis. 'There can be absolutely no doubt that what has happened in Assam is a grievous tragedy,' Nehru said, as he tried to regain confidence in his hold over provincial politics.[240] He had little doubt that disgruntled Congress leaders from Assam had added fuel as the state burnt, and observed that the 'prestige [of the Congress party] has gone down very much because of these occurrences'.[241] Describing the Assamese–Bengali cultural war as an 'upheaval' of atavism, he asked N. Sanjiva Reddy, the Congress president, to conduct an inquiry.[242]

When Nehru arrived in Guwahati on 17 July, he had made his position clear:

> I am in full agreement with you that Assamese should be the State language. But you cannot have it with *lathis* and making people homeless. A language is like a delicate plant which has to be nurtured carefully so that it comes into full bloom in the natural course of time. If you catch hold of it, throttle it and shout 'you must grow up quicker', the plant will wither away.[243]

His meeting with the members of the Assam Congress did not go well. Nehru accused his party men of not doing enough, and said he had 'conclusive evidence that unhealthy rivalry existed within the Assam Congress'.[244] Nehru returned from Assam an unhappy man: 'Can I hold on to my sanity or not?'[245] He worriedly conceded that the events at Assam had 'shaken the foundation of the country'.

~

Towards the end of September 1960, the Assam government again faced pressure to go ahead with the Assam Official Language Bill. An upset Nehru, who had just returned from Pakistan after signing the Indus Waters Treaty, warned Chaliha that such a step 'may lead, ultimately, to the splitting up of the present Assam State'. 'I think that the people who are trying to hustle this matter are not acting wisely or even in their own interest,' he said, adding, '[W]hile Assamese should be made the State language that by itself is not enough. Undoubtedly, Assam is a bi-lingual State even apart from the Hill areas and we should recognize this fact.'[246]

The Assam government's move was angrily rejected by the hill leaders.[247] A joint platform predicted that this would lead to their assimilation into Assamese society and eventually dissolve their identities. 'Such assimilation and disintegration are against the deepest sentiments of the Hill people'.[248] Their counterparts in the Parliament, too, were steadfastly opposed to the idea. 'We do not need to learn Assamese in order to be civilised,' came a retort from a lawmaker from the Mizo hills.[249] 'We the tribal people of Assam now feel that we have no future.' Instead of 'giving us scholarship for technical education they give us handsome scholarship to learn Assamese'. 'Today, whereas an Assamese officer will not have to learn any tribal language before he gets confirmation and promotion, the tribal officers have to learn Assamese; if they are stationed in the plains of Assam, they have to learn Assamese.'

Many rounds of political negotiations could not appease Cachar. The Bengali speakers united under the umbrella of the All-Assam Bengali Conference and proposed that Assam would be a bilingual state.[250] Nehru had to persuade Chaliha that the 'Cachar people are greatly exercised on the language question' and advised him not to employ any 'strong arm methods' to suppress them.[251] After the loss of Sylhet, a section of the Bengali political and literate class viewed the rise of post-Independence Assam with suspicion. Many Assamese speakers too wanted the disintegration of Assam to carve out a state for themselves and to allow Cachar to be a separate state.[252] 'Assam now spends Rs 5 crores per year on the Hills. By separating the hills, this money can be utilized for the development of the valley,'[253] many argued.

As the rift widened, the Bengali speakers were convinced that widespread violence was part of a larger and premeditated design to drive them out from Assam. They referred to two Assamese popular literary works as proof of this plan.[254] Newly published, these books did not have a mass readership, and their protagonists dwelt on ideas far removed from the question of language. These works, however, epitomized the social and economic anxieties of rural Assam, which reconfirmed the anxieties of many. The decadal census of 1961, the process for which had begun as the language riots raged, showed 57 per cent of the population were Assamese speakers, compared to only 17 per cent Bengali speakers.[255] Unlike the numerically weaker position of the Assamese speakers in earlier censuses, this dramatic upscaling of the proportionate share was largely a product of Assam's territorial reorganization at Independence. The number, which had not increased much since 1951, was seen with suspicion by Bengali speakers.[256] Speakers of Bodo, Khasi, Garo or Mizo, which belonged to Indo-Tibetan and Austric groups of languages, were far behind. These numerically weaker sections had no common language. Among those who declared Assamese as their mother tongue were migrant Bengali Muslims and migrant workers of tea plantations. What language did the Muslim migrants speak at home? 'In fairness to them . . . all Muslim immigrants from East Bengal do not speak the soft-spoken Bengali of Nadiya. What they really speak is a rough dialect of Bengali which they call "Bhatiali".' However, when 'they come to Assam, these Muslim immigrants honestly try to know the Assamese language and send their children to schools where the Assamese language is the medium of instruction'.[257] This official position was agreed upon and welcomed by a section of the Assamese elite.[258] A census official explained this choice: the 'knowledge of Assamese language helps them to become "indigenous"', which was a critical criterion to own a small plot of land. Unlike them, the 'Bengali Hindus always returned Bengali and nothing else'. Prior to the 1931 census, enumerators had described the language of the tea garden workers and their families—a mix of Hindustani, Assamese and Bengali, which was called 'coolie-*bat*' by planters—as Bengali. This changed as the Assamese enumerators became aware of their numerical strength, and these workers were generally designated as Assamese speakers in the 1951 census.

Chaliha was worried even as he was preparing to go ahead with the bill in October 1960 and was in constant touch with Nehru. 'I can quite realise your difficulty, and I have admired the way you have faced these agitations. Sometimes I have found that the Assam Congress or your own legislature party have shown weakness in such matters,' Nehru reassured Chaliha.[259] 'I can understand the desire of people in Assam to further the use of the Assamese language . . . But the way agitations are started and often supported by young schoolboys disturbs me for the future of Assam.' As the bill came up for discussion, a tense Nehru wrote to Assam's Governor that 'the people of Assam Valley have shown and are showing no wisdom at all and by their narrow-minded outlook are injuring the whole future of Assam.'[260] Govind Ballabh Pant, India's then home minister, also tried to mediate briefly by offering both Assamese and Hindi as the official languages of Assam, but this suggestion found few takers.[261]

Assamese speakers were united behind the agitation. A contemporary observer had this to say: 'Congress and non-Congress leaders, politicians of all shades of opinion, those on the Right and on the Left, Hindus, Muslims, poets, priests, men of letters, sober educationists, unruly students—all have wonderfully cooperated.'[262] But it was the Assamese students who led from the front and were the backbone of the agitation. Worried about their future, they thought of political action as the way out. Some of them were idealists, some regionalists, and many were inspired by the political leadership of their brethren elsewhere in the world. By the late 1950s, there was significant political restlessness in the university. The official inquiry commission of 1962, appointed to investigate corruption and other malpractices in the university, had to also enquire into the 'general state of discipline'.[263] The Commission noted 'the outburst of indiscipline among the students'.[264] Among the reasons for this situation, they referred to the opinion of departmental heads that 'the University is "putting less and less emphasis on studies"'. A parliamentary delegation described the impressive organizational strength of the agitating students:

> The students in Assam are well-organised. They have their Central Organisation at Gauhati to which District organisations and other institutional unions of students are affiliated. The youthful imagination of the students had already been inflamed by the language agitation . . . They organized processions, meetings, and hartals and soon they began to dominate the situation throwing the political parties into background.[265]

~

Amidst the failure of an all-party conference to reach an agreement, widespread opposition from Bengalis and tribal leaders (two of whom, Williamson Sangma and Lalmuia, resigned from their ministries) and with the backing of the Congress party, Chaliha was able to introduce the Assam Official Language Bill on 10 October 1960.[266] Several Assamese cultural organizations gave a call to offer prayers by lighting a diya (*chaki-banti*) on the day the Language Bill was to be introduced in the Assembly.[267]

But the idea of allowing Bengali for Cachar, a key aspect of the new bill, rocked the state again.[268] The bill also allowed the use of English for official purposes till the coming of Hindi as another state language. This infuriated the Assamese much more than the Bengalis.[269] Amidst severe criticism, further debates took place in the Assembly when it met to discuss the bill on 18 October. The gallery was full of visitors. The bill's complete Assamese translation was published in local dailies, signifying the importance of public scrutiny of this legislative instrument.[270] Public meetings condemned the Congress as a turncoat. A private member's alternative language bill could not be introduced. In a newspaper article titled 'Mrityur Sesh Muhurtat Abedan' (Appeal from the death bed), Ambikagiri made a passionate appeal to the Assamese speakers to pressure their elected representatives not to go ahead with the government's bill.[271] On 24 October 1960, the bill was finally accepted minutes before 10 at night,[272] even as Chaliha's cabinet colleague, Moinul Hoque Choudhury, abstained from the debate. The Assembly was greeted with slogans, banners and protests. That day, the lawmakers could not go home for their lunch break.

After the bill was passed, there was a deceptive lull. The Sabha held its annual literary festival in the last week of October. Speakers hailed the victory of the language movement; Padmadhar Chaliha, a veteran litterateur, likened the Assamese language to the roar of a lion; others denied the accusation that the Assamese were being imperialists.[273] Nehru wrote to a Congress lawmaker from Cachar that 'if we cannot pull together, then we go to pieces'.[274]

The resistance of the hill population took a definitive political turn by early 1961. When a worried delegation of Assam's hill leaders met Nehru and Lal Bahadur Shastri, the newly appointed home minister, on 17 May 1961, they repeated their refusal to accept Assamese as the state language and wanted a 'clear break' between the hills and Assam.[275] The Bengali speakers, meanwhile, readied themselves for a political confrontation. A vast majority of those who had fled Assam were yet to come home, as the memories of 1960 were kept alive.[276]

The Bengali speakers continued to stand their ground and, under the umbrella of Gana Sangram Parisad, began popular mobilization to have Bengali declared as an additional state language. The Parisad gave a call for a strike on 19 May. As passions ran high, Cachar came to a complete halt. In Silchar, a large crowd freed their arrested comrades from police custody.[277] When the police retaliated, 11 of the protestors died. Popular mobilization continued, and more protestors died in June. The Assam government declared parts of Cachar as disturbed areas, allowing the military wider powers over the civil administration in matters of law and order.

When Home Minister Shastri visited Cachar after 19 May, he was greeted by 'young boys and girls standing on either side of the road with absolute silence, but with placards of protest in their hands'.[278] After days of hectic negotiations, Shastri managed to persuade Chaliha's government to agree to amend the Act so that there would be no chance of Bengali being replaced as the official language of Cachar in the future.[279] Also, English would continue to be used along with Assamese for official purposes; all government publications would have an English version, even if they were first written in Assamese. Chaliha also made clear his government's willingness to write these changes into law. Shastri's scheme, seen by Assamese scholars as the ultimate blow to the possibility of Assamese being firmly established in Cachar,[280] meant that Assam would continue to have two languages: 'Assamese in terms of law and English or Hindi in terms of practice.'[281]

For years, the advocates of Assamese continued to appeal to the government to put the Assam Official Language Act into practice. Such demands also came from senior members of the Congress, including the well-known writer Dev Kant Borooah, who headed Assam's Official Language Implementation Committee in 1964.[282] The Bengali and tribal language speakers, too, continued to press their demands, albeit in a lower tone. Much to the unhappiness of a small group of people who wanted the Act to be implemented in October 1964, the month in which Sankardeva's birth anniversary is normally celebrated, the Assam government decided to make Assamese the official language from August 1964.[283] But it was no easy task; a delegation of worried

Garo villagers was assured by the government that they could conduct their village proceedings in Garo.[284] The Bodo Sahitya Sabha organized a well-attended public meeting on 16 November 1964 to reiterate their demand for education in the Bodo language.[285] Thankfully, the peace was not disrupted following the Act's implementation. 'Psychologically, the people of Assam seemed to have regretted the ugly incidents of July 1960.'[286] But meanwhile, Assam faced trouble from other sources.

# 7

# Trouble in the Eastern Himalayas

In 1950, a secret note from the British Commonwealth Office described Assam as unique among the Indian states for two reasons. First, it was a frontier state with few similarities to others like Bihar, UP, Punjab or Rajasthan. Second, the 'absence of ethnic and linguistic, cultural, religious, or administrative uniformity', the report claimed, deprived Assam of 'any political compactness' and, thus, of strength, 'since, where external dangers threaten internal unity is a pre-requisite of strength'.[1] This British government intelligence soon proved correct as Assam faced a tumultuous encounter on its northern borders.

Prior to British occupation, Assamese rulers had secured their access to the eastern Himalayas through diplomatic and military means.[2] The *posa* system, involving the payment of taxes to hill dwellers in return for their support of the Assamese rulers' control up to the foothills, was continued by the colonialists as well as by the post-colonial Indian state.[3] The family of Yeshe Dorjee Thongchi, a distinguished name in the Assamese literary world, who was born in NEFA, continued to receive its token share of posa in the 1950s.[4] Throughout the nineteenth century and well into the early decades of the twentieth, the colonial officials did not directly govern the hill areas while also ensuring that their inhabitants were not completely isolated.[5] Marwari traders in Assam, for instance, had established and consolidated lucrative trade networks with the local people in the eastern Himalayas, and the

Leader of the Sherdukpen Sat Rajas in NEFA arriving on horseback on the plains of Assam to receive posa (annual payments) from the government

colonial government extended support to such commercial activities through various means, including holding annual trade fairs across the Himalayan foothills.[6] Prized products from the eastern Himalayas included *Coptis teeta* (popularly known as Mishmi Teeta) and Aconite root, which were used for medicinal purposes, and the musk bag of the musk deer.[7] The dried rhizomes of *Coptis teeta* were used extensively in nineteenth-century Indian pharmaceuticals and European practices as a febrifuge and 'for restoring appetite and increasing digestive powers'.[8] Haribilash Agarwala, prominent amongst the Marwari traders and also the grandfather of the filmmaker Jyoti Prasad Agarwala, earned millions through an extensive trade in India rubber.[9]

~

J.P. Mills, Adviser to the Governor of Assam for Tribal Areas, with Sherdukpen Sat Rajas at their winter camp near Charduar, Assam, where the latter presented Mills with a gift

Until 1914, the idea of a firm international border in the northeastern Himalayas was hardly taken seriously.[10] The Simla Conference of 1914—which brought together officials of the British Indian government and the governments of China and Tibet—outlined a border between British India and China, but the latter, preoccupied with domestic political troubles, never ratified this border. China rather insisted that the region between the border—known as McMahon Line, after the British official Henry McMahon who led the negotiation on behalf of the British, or Maikema Hongxian in Chinese—and the Assam plains belonged to it and called it South Tibet.[11] In 1922, the Chinese leader Sun Yat-sen proposed a train line to the Assam frontier.[12] Meanwhile, since 1914, the Indian government also started encouraging the colonial officers stationed in Assam's northern frontier hills to learn the Chinese language in order to effectively control these lightly administered areas.[13]

Japan's entry into World War II suddenly heightened the strategic importance of the eastern Himalayas.[14] The snow peaks central to the McMahon Line had till then been surveyed only from a distance, but in 1944, expeditions were undertaken to reach this line and establish effective control over these areas, which was a herculean task. British officers undertook winter excursions to the remotest borders to reaffirm the presence of the imperial state. These officials' accounts shaped the idea of a romantic frontier besides playing a crucial role in the consolidation, however fragile, of frontier governance.[15] Christoph von Fürer-Haimendorf, the Austrian anthropologist who spent several months here at that time, later recounted the difficulty in accessing those obscure areas. He was specially deputed to the Indo-Tibetan border to prepare the 'ground for the extension of administrative control over' these areas.[16] This area of 48,000 square kilometres, home to half a million people speaking 50 different languages and dialects, was without a single bridle path, and the 'only bridges were flimsy structures of bamboo and cane suspended from the branches of trees'.[17] Most inhabitants of these areas were till then 'unused to any sort of authority' except that of their tribal leaders in some places. They did not 'relish the idea of bowing to an outside power which might interfere with their old way of life and curtail their cherished independence'.[18]

A rudimentary modern government began to make its presence felt in these remote areas in the wake of India's Independence when the North-East Frontier Tracts (NEFT) were appended to the Assam administration. Assam's preparedness to govern these areas was constrained by a limited politico-bureaucratic apparatus and experiences, and in the next few years, these tracts underwent several territorial modifications. In 1951, the Indian government transferred the plain areas from NEFT to Assam, while the hill tracts along with a portion of the Naga Hills were re-designated as North-East Frontier Agency (NEFA) in 1954.[19] The position of the Inner Line changed, and several localities went from Assam to NEFA or vice versa. By the early 1950s, the headquarters of the NEFA administration had moved to the interior from the foothills of Assam. Doctors, teachers and other officials posted there experienced days of adventure before reaching their destination. The residents had always challenged such penetration by the Indian state; an Assamese described his encounter with an armed group in 1949.[20] There were other challenges too. The British officials had been aware of the Tibetan influence in these areas, which was largely an outcome of centuries of trade, pilgrimage and pastoral activities.[21] During 1949–50, the Assam government frequently expressed worry about possible Chinese communist influence in the lightly administered NEFT.[22]

A NEFA district headquarter

The experiment of allowing the Assam government to administer these areas on behalf of the Indian government was brief. When the Sixth Schedule was being framed, these areas still remained outside mainstream governance. The Constituent Assembly, after a brief discussion, reverted to the old system, whereby the Assam Governor was to act independently of the Assam government while administering these areas,[23] which were designated as Part B Tribal Areas under the Sixth Schedule. The rudimentary forms of governance based on the models left behind by the colonial state were retained. Bardoloi appointed three young Assamese as political officers of NEFA, and

> a few bright young men from respected and educated families of tribals in the hill districts were also recruited, partly in the interests of

ultimate integration, partly as it was expected that tribal officers from the hills would find less difficulty in adjusting themselves to the hard life involved in frontier service.[24]

Enhancing the number of Assamese in the bureaucracy was seen as a step towards integrating NEFA into Assam.[25] Firm control of trading activities with help from a supportive bureaucracy was also a source of satisfaction to the Assamese bourgeoisie.[26] But these were temporary measures.

Assam gradually realized the impossibility of its hope that NEFA would become an integral part of the state. Unlike the other hill districts, there was no representative from the NEFA areas in the Assam Legislative Assembly. The President of India could nominate a member to the Parliament, but this was seen by Assam as an impediment to NEFA's future integration with Assam. Moreover, the Governor became the ultimate authority and administered these areas directly under the Central government's guidance and support, including financial support. This worried the Assam government. Yet, the Governor's power to 'exclude any tribal area' from being designated as NEFA was seen by Assamese leaders as a possibility for bringing these areas directly under the Assam government.[27]

The Chinese occupation of Tibet in 1950 quickly changed India's standpoint on the north-eastern frontier region. As the renamed NEFA's governance took a political-bureaucratic form, there was an abrupt disjunction of the control of NEFA from Assam. Assam's political leaders were enraged. In early March 1952, the Assam Congress passed a resolution saying this arrangement was a recipe for 'isolation and disintegration'.[28] Medhi, the chief minister, wrote to Nehru in March 1952, 'the Government and the people of Assam are vitally interested in the affairs of the Agency.'[29] Medhi remained passionate in asserting that NEFA 'really forms a part of the State and the scheme of the Constitution is to assimilate these areas progressively within the framework of the administration of the state'.[30] The government of Assam had 'a constitutional obligation to take over the administration of the Frontier Tracts in progressive stages, in the light of circumstances as they develop', Medhi wrote.

The administration of the new-born NEFA was looked after by the Ministry of External Affairs, and the Governor had the power to act independently of the advice of the Assam government. An officer from the Assam cadre in the Indian Administrative Service was to advise the Governor, and Nari Rustomji (originally of the Indian Civil Service) was appointed as the first adviser. Rustomji had to 'walk to get from one place to another, as the hill tracks were not yet fit for even ponies or mules to negotiate'. However, as he and other officials were not 'on a lightning tip-and-run visit by jeep or helicopter', they were 'rewarded with a glimpse into tribal life', as they could 'chat at length with the tribal guides and village headmen'.[31]

NEFA was spread over approximately 56,000 square kilometres in 1951. 'It is not possible at this stage even to form a firm and reasonably accurate estimate of the population,' wrote the Census superintendent for that year.[32] The first ever census in NEFA began in 1960, when enumerators visited scattered hamlets and even played the role of amateur anthropologists.[33] These vast areas had been a major source of timber, firewood, cane, bamboo and elephants for Assam since the early decades of the century. In fact, Marwari traders had been doing brisk trade with NEFA residents since the late nineteenth century. They established their trading depots across the Himalayan foothills,[34] except in parts of the landscape that were impenetrable, and 'thrived on trade with the tribal people'.[35] With better transportation after the war years, the extraction of forest resources in NEFA had increased manifold. Much of the trade in these products was controlled by Marwari or Punjabi entrepreneurs, though more enterprises came to be owned by Assamese entrepreneurs during World War II. But NEFA residents themselves did not have a major role in this emerging economy. In the 1950s, the Inner Line Regulation was relaxed to allow the inflow of traders and their mercantile activities.[36] Bazars and shops sprang up, and commodity products found their way into these hilly areas. By this time, a few locals had begun to earn a living as employees in new construction activities. Many of the contractors were Punjabis who had, by then, sufficient experience of living and earning in the central Himalayas. A 1951 account summarized how 'practically all trade in the town of Sadiya', a foothill town home to the headquarters of NEFA, was 'in the hands of the Marwaris, who are the only people in the district possessing capital, enterprise and business instincts.'[37] When J.D. Baveja, an Indian government official, visited one of the five NEFA headquarters, he was 'surprised to see a large number of Marwari and Punjabi traders'.[38] These developments were unpalatable for Nehru. He was horrified when he heard of 'cheap textiles and other totally unnecessary articles' being sold in some shops.[39] By now, these traders were, however, 'so rooted that it was not possible to get rid of them'.[40] Even in November 1962, when Indira Gandhi visited Pasighat, she was met by panicked Marwari and Bihari merchants seeking protection of their tiny town from the Chinese forces that had entered NEFA.[41]

With flexible Inner Line Regulation, private speculation in timber trade prospered across NEFA.[42] Trade in timber became a major component of state-making in NEFA. Sprawling timber industries came to dominate the foothills in the north-eastern most corner of the Valley. The timber trade was monopolized by the Assam Saw Mills and Timber Company, an erstwhile British commercial interest owned by a Marwari business venture since the 1950s, with its headquarters in Calcutta.[43] This company extracted more than 20,000 cubic metre per year of hollock (*Terminalia myriocarpa*) and hollong (*Dipterocarpus retusus*) timber alone to make veneer for tea boxes.[44] At Independence, in the spirit of the new Constitution, regulations were put in place to restrict this massive inflow of private merchants and industrial capital into NEFA. The government brought in the Balipara, Tirap, Sadiya Frontier Tract Jhum Land Regulation in 1947, marking a major entry of the state apparatus into these tracts. This legal apparatus confirmed the NEFA residents' claim on their jhum lands. It produced the twin results of restricting the flow of private capital and of making the presence of the state more visible. As many as 13 forests were declared Reserved Forests by the mid-1950s, which sparked opposition from NEFA residents.[45]

~

Prime Minister Nehru's sympathetic appreciation of Assam's tribal world repeatedly found place in his public statements or correspondence with the Assam government.[46] After one of his visits to these areas in October 1952, Nehru told his officials that his 'whole conception of what are called the tribal folk has changed'.[47] At a public gathering, he appealed: 'My only advice to you is to love the tribal people. Do not hate them. Do not consider them lower than yourselves. Try to learn their way of life, their language and culture.'[48] His ideas were not welcomed by the Assamese leaders. Medhi was apprehensive that the Union government's policies 'will have the effect of isolating the hill people and plains people in Assam and lead to fresh difficulties and repercussion in the future'. Medhi also blamed Nehru's isolationist policy, which he said had led to an 'unsatisfactory state of affairs' in the Naga hills. Nehru was not impressed by Medhi's stand.

India may have gained significantly from the grand project of integration of princely states immediately after Independence, but it was clear that the eastern Himalayas, and to a large extent Assam's other hill districts, remained largely outside the political imagination of the Indian state. Nehru wrote: 'My ideas were not clear at all, but I felt that we should avoid two extreme courses: one was to treat them as anthropological specimens for study and the other was to allow them to be engulfed by the masses of Indian humanity.'[49]

By 1952, the Assam Congress leaders had already begun to express their unhappiness about the structure of the NEFA administration and the fact that it was beyond the political scope of Assam.[50] This view was largely supported by Assamese public opinion.[51] The *Assam Tribune* still referred to the residents of these areas as 'unsophisticated and backward people'. As pressure from Assam mounted for integration of NEFA with the state, Nehru refused to change his position. He visited NEFA in October 1952 and again in March–April of the following year. Now having greater clarity about this area, he believed that conditions 'in these tribal areas [were] so different that [the] Government considered it necessary that the administration of these areas should be kept apart and should be under the *direct control of the Central Government*' (emphasis added).⁵² For Nehru, things were still 'fluid' in NEFA. Nehru was convinced that . . .

> They are *sui generis* and any attempt on our part to apply all our normal rules and regulations to them will be unfortunate . . . With care, it might be made to take the right shape. But it is equally easy for it to take the wrong shape, if we delay or if we take [a] wrong step.

In the spring of 1953, Nehru sent T.N. Kaul, a Union government officer who had been put in charge of NEFA, to visit the region so that 'he could bring to bear somewhat wider experience' on its governance.⁵³ Kaul's understanding was based on his research on the governance of tribes in the USSR. His report, which would be a guiding force for the Nehru government's approach to NEFA for some time to come, proposed a specialized administrative cadre, outside the steel frame of the Indian Administrative Service. The report, which highlighted the region's economic backwardness and lack of infrastructure for transport, communication and education, was disapproved by Medhi forthwith. He accused Kaul of making a hurried visit and said that 'his observations and inferences appear to be based on [an] inadequate appreciation of the local conditions'.⁵⁴ Though Medhi was fast losing any hope of acquiring NEFA, he reminded Nehru that 'the Assamese people are composed of tribals and non-tribals' and the Assamese language is 'a composite structure of words borrowed from Sanskrit, Persian, and tribal languages'. He blamed the missionaries for causing division: 'The charge that the Assamese officers are trying to Assamise the tribal areas appear to be based upon a bogie deliberately raised by the missionaries in their attempt to camouflage their anti-Indian activities.'⁵⁵ Medhi underlined a developmental model largely following the Nehruvian plan, but he insisted on an 'interdependent economy in which the hills and plains play [their] full part'.⁵⁶ However, some observers thought that, despite pressure from many quarters to integrate NEFA with Assam, Medhi was apparently unsure of his government's capacity to govern NEFA.⁵⁷ In July 1953, Nehru made it clear that he could not 'say that the NEFA will be completely integrated with the state of Assam at a later stage'.⁵⁸ NEFA was now important from a defence perspective.

Towards the end of 1953, Nehru sent the British-born Indian anthropologist Verrier Elwin to Shillong to advise the Governor on the tribal affairs of Assam. Nehru and Elwin did not differ much in their outlook on India's tribal question. Owing to his opinion that 'tribal people should be segregated from the normal plainsmen because they should not be contaminated with the views of plainsmen in any part of India', Elwin's appointment did not go down well with many in India's political circles.⁵⁹ In the next few years, Elwin travelled extensively to every part of NEFA, mostly on foot. He covered over 3000 kilometres, describing it as a pilgrimage, spending time with people of different communities and collecting a great volume of artefacts for a museum that he set up in his Shillong residence. His visit was very different from those of Francis Kingdon-Ward, the British botanist whose interests were mainly confined to natural history, or the British political officers who spent time in getting to know these areas, but always as rulers. Elwin's travels led him to discover many exclusive treasures. In Tawang, he spent his days in the Buddhist monasteries and was shown a 'fine library', whose collection included eight volumes of Buddhist scriptures called Getompa, three of them lettered in gold.⁶⁰ As his stay in NEFA neared three years, Elwin wrote *A Philosophy for NEFA*, based on his interaction with the people of the region.

In 1953, the Indian government announced a plan to revamp NEFA's governance, and the presence of the state machinery began to be significantly enhanced in key areas—transport and communication, health, education, cottage industry and agriculture.⁶¹ A sum of approximately 30 million rupees was granted for NEFA in the First Five-Year Plan.⁶² The implementation of the objectives of the plan was worked out for NEFA.⁶³ Emphasis on improved methods of agriculture became one of the key aspects of this state-making process. The move evoked sharp opposition from political parties across the ideological spectrum in Assam. Many saw it as further confirmation of their fear of complete separation of NEFA from Assam, and Nehru's assurances could hardly convince them.⁶⁴ The CPI said that NEFA would become 'a military preserve to fulfil the needs and requirements of the policies of the Anglo-American Imperialists'.[65] A hurriedly formed All Assam Disintegration Resistance Committee was able to muster strong public support.[66]

Things began to move quickly as there began an era of Indianization of NEFA's economic and bureaucratic structures, including a revamp of existing educational institutes and medical facilities. Still, only 48 per cent of NEFA residents had been vaccinated against smallpox till 1964.[67] A few hundreds of kilometres of roads were constructed despite environmental challenges.[68] The Hindustani Talimi Sangh, a Gandhian organization mandated to impart Basic National Education, gave ideological orientation to the educational programmes in NEFA.[69] School teachers were given multiple roles, one of which was to help the residents learn 'advanced' methods of agriculture—and they always carried with them the basic tools used by Indian farmers. Students were taught to cultivate cauliflower and tomatoes, which were unknown to the local population who were only familiar with the local flora and fauna. In January 1954, a batch of Naga teachers from the southernmost area of NEFA (the Naga tribal area) was taken on a pan-India tour. They visited many places, including the Digboi refinery, the AIR station in Guwahati, various sites of Calcutta, Chittaranjan Locomotive Works in Asansol, Tatanagar, the Damodar Valley Project, the Sindri fertilizer factory in Bihar (now Jharkhand) and the monuments in Agra, and they ended the tour by attending the Republic Day parade in New Delhi.[70]

One of the first Assamese to join NEFA (then NEFT) as a senior education officer had been Indira Miri. She was born into a so-called lower-caste, middle class Assamese family in Guwahati and had lost her mother at a young age.[71] Her father made sure she received a good education, in Calcutta, after which she got a degree in education from Guwahati and trained under Maria Montessori in Ahmedabad on a government scholarship. She then got a scholarship to pursue a master's degree at Edinburgh University followed by a three months' training at Oxford University. She returned in 1947 to take up the post in the Assamese town of Sadiya. She worked among the tribals for 10 years and became known and respected for her efforts to promote education among them. Many from Assam followed in her footsteps.[72]

The Indianization of NEFA took many forms. India's developmental programme included, for instance, the introduction of wet-rice cultivation in the foothills and in the valleys.[73] Communities had to be persuaded to accept newer designs of agricultural tools and advanced practices in farming. Until then, only a few in NEFA, like the Apatani communities, had perfected the art of wet-rice cultivation. The anthropologist Fürer-Haimendorf noted how an Apatani 'tends every square yard of his land with loving care and the greatest ingenuity'.[74] The NEFA landscape and climate, however, did not allow the extension of wet-rice cultivation to many places, and such experiments produced mixed results.[75] Moreover, the NEFA residents never considered this to be essential to their subsistence economy. Still, the Union government's effort did have some effect. When a radio broadcaster asked Elwin about 'what has been the impact of the new administration on the people' in NEFA, he wittily responded that they were 'taking to wet-rice cultivation'.[76]

State-making also meant airdropping foodstuff (primarily for Indian officials) and setting up skeleton communication systems, including post and telegraph.[77] Nehru, as external affairs minister, had to persuade his parliamentary colleagues about the effectiveness of his government in NEFA. He repeatedly reminded them about 'various degrees of administration' and the constant challenges faced by government officials in NEFA.[78] A major task of these officials was to keep intact the essence of tribal life—one of the central premises of Nehruvian policy. Incidentally, Indianization had earlier taken place at a different level with the immersion of some of Gandhi's ashes in Parshuram Kund, an important Hindu pilgrimage centre in the present-day Lohit district of Arunachal Pradesh.

In 1954, the government promulgated the North East Frontier Areas Regulation to ensure further integration of the region into the machinery of the Indian Union. Reterritorialization was essential to consolidating and expanding the reach of the Indian Union on the governed areas. Six districts were created to enable more effective administration.[79] The hill tracts were given new names: Kameng, Subansiri, Siang, Lohit, Tirap and Tuensang.[80] There were more visits by leaders; President Rajendra Prasad toured for 10 days in early 1954.[81] Appointments in the NEFA bureaucracy were regulated by Delhi. In 1954, six political officers were appointed as a prelude to the Indian Frontier Administrative Service (IFAS). None among the Assamese candidates was selected as a political officer; a few, though, were appointed as junior officers.[82] This bureaucratic restructuring was seen by Assamese leaders as a 'systematic campaign in NEFA to drive away the Assam people from service in this organization', though this was not true.[83] The Assamese intelligentsia protested strongly. 'The Government of India's assurance that the ultimate end of its frontier policy is to secure the democratic integration of the NEFA areas with Assam is a mere eyewash,' wrote the *Assam Tribune*.[84]

The IFAS, as T.N. Kaul, the senior official from the Union government, saw it, would comprise 'special types of officials and workers who [would] go and mix with [the tribals] socially, live and eat with them and endear themselves to them by serving their real interests'.[85] The recruitment of a separate cadre for NEFA broke with the convention of assigning a few officials from the Assam cadre of the IAS to NEFA. Medhi warned that the IFAS officials would be of a different frame of mind altogether and that 'the cumulative effect of these steps would be the complete isolation of the Agency areas from the state of Assam'.[86] According to the Government of India, 'initiative, imagination, resourcefulness and a broad sympathy with and understanding of the tribal people and their customs' in addition to being 'mentally and physically fit' were essential qualities for IFAS officials.[87] The IFAS assumed a formal pattern and was inaugurated in 1956.[88] Elwin was to train the new recruits.[89] The early IFAS batches had cadres mainly from a military background. Indira Miri noticed this, but she agreed that Elwin's influence helped them to acquire a more sympathetic attitude.[90] Rustomji thought that 'it was far-fetched to imagine that a six-week lecture course could transform a soldier, a sailor, or an airman, however competent, into a tribal administrator'.[91] He added, however, '[Many of] the officers of NEFA prior to the constitution of the I.F.A.S. were rough diamonds, lacking in grace, but they fitted in with the landscape and were content to remain [a] part of it until the end of their service.'

The Indian government began an era of anthropological investigation but with the clear purpose of smoothening governance issues. While NEFA was a suitable place for the anthropologist's tribal experiment, Elwin made it clear that he was not in favour of complete isolation of the tribes; one had to be patient. 'When a man breaks a long fast, he is not immediately given a full meal; he takes a sip of orange juice,' he wrote in his *Philosophy for NEFA*, which set out his principles for NEFA's governance.[92] The Assamese intelligentsia, however, had strong words against Elwin's book. The writer Birendra Kumar Bhattacharya said it supported tribalism, its ideas were drawn from British officials and scholars and did not fit the Indian reality. Reassertion of the earlier policy of separation of plains and hills was a wrong understanding of Assam's past, and the isolation of NEFA would be detrimental to Indian democracy, Bhattacharya opined.[93]

The schools in NEFA became sites of struggle between the Assamese and pan-Indian ethos. In 1953, Hindi replaced Assamese as the medium of instruction.[94] However, Assamese was taught as one of the languages along with Hindi and local languages well into the late 1950s. Both Assamese and Hindi textbooks were used. The students were taught to sing *milangeeti*, the song for unity, in Assamese.[95] Despite the introduction of Hindi, many from NEFA continued to use Assamese as a lingua franca in their contact with the people of Assam.[96] Some became key partners in the journey to reclaim modern Assamese literary history.

Despite the 'devotion and care' of many individuals, the Indianization of NEFA demonstrated many contradictions, of which schools were a classic example, according to Elwin. In his *Philosophy for NEFA*, he described the Tawang monastery as a combination of an 'old fashioned Cathedral school and [a] Basic Education center'.[97] Boys studied in the library, which presented an 'atmosphere of art, religion and learning'. The 'walls are painted with pictures and hung with scrolls. The boys sit on the floor on cushions covered with decorated mats and read on little tables placed in front of them'. Elwin wrote how, by contrast,

> our school looks like a sort of parody. It is housed in a small hut of open cane-work which admits the cold and damp. The boys sit perched on inconvenient benches at silly little desks. The walls of the school are decorated with a few rather bad charts and maps. The teacher, when I was there, did not know a word of the local language and was laboriously trying to impart the elements of Hindi to his pupils. There was nothing of beauty, of art or of their own tradition to inspire the children.[98]

Some students took care of ponies and cattle, some cooked, some practised agriculture, some trained in dancing, art work or the art of printing. When Elwin met some teachers at Rupa, they did not know the local language. They 'had to [speak] in Assamese and get it translated by an interpreter'.[99] The teachers were frequently transferred, which hindered their learning of local languages. Despite apprehensions in many quarters, Elwin's suggestions were taken seriously by senior officials at the helm, one of whom wrote to Kaul, 'I am glad that you agree with the central point of his report.'[100]

Elwin found that Indianization in NEFA was rapid. In some parts, the Indian salutation '*Jai Hind*' was adopted as the name for businesses, shops and other establishments. The significant presence of the Indian state in these remote areas was, in Elwin's opinion, welcomed by most people. He noted that 'although many economic and spiritual links with Tibet remain[ed] in every village', there were also 'expressions of sincere loyalty and appreciation of what the Administration had done'.[101] According to Elwin, relief from the burden of excessive taxation by Tibet and from its monopolistic control over salt and rice had made a significant difference in people's lives.[102]

The introduction of Hindi as a subject in NEFA schools was intended to promote national integration. Schools became laboratories for India's linguistic politics that operated at regional and national levels, though NEFA's experience began differently from that of other parts of India. Yet, the penetration of the Indian state into the farthest north-eastern frontier was a half-done project. Rudimentary anthropological research did not help in any significant understanding of these areas.[103] During a tour of Tawang in 1956, Elwin noted that Indian officials had brought material goods like a jeep and an electric generator to counteract the increasing material civilization that China was spreading in these areas. While these were important, Elwin argued that what was required was the 'strengthening of spiritual bonds' between the Monpas and the Indian officials. This could be done by 'the right people behaving rightly'. Elwin also advised that 'in order that our officers may appreciate the religion of the people with intelligent sympathy, I suggest that they should all make a careful study of Buddhism'. Elwin described the surroundings:

> The alien character of our administrative efforts is impressed on the traveller even before he arrives at Bomdi La by the notices along the road . . . at the entrance to the headquarters he is greeted by a sign-board bearing the distressing American vulgarism—Boom Town Bomdi La. All the notice-boards, even in Tawang and Dirahg Bzong, are in English: even Shillong, where many public notices and directions are in Khasi, does better than that. Then we have Shivaji Bridge at Doimara, where the Sherdukpens have had their camp for many years (surely the Bridge might have been named after a Sherdukpen hero), and Allen's View, Kathing's Point, and even Imti's View.

Elwin also expressed his frustration about the use of terms like 'dialect teacher', 'colony', 'Hindi teacher' and so on. Such usage, Elwin thought, carried an impression that 'development efforts in general are for the benefit of the official staff rather than for the people'.[104]

~

The Indian government's political anxiety about NEFA persisted since the governance of these areas was full of challenges and uncertainties.

Travelling by air in the territory, for instance, was perilous. When Indira Miri took a short trip, in the hope that she would be back in hours, her plane slipped into the mud, and it took 14 days for it to be recovered. In one of his tours to oversee the rehabilitation project after the war in 1962, Rustomji's Dakota 'evidently struck an impenetrable patch of cloud, for visibility was nil, and there was no alternative but to circle, laboriously, to a height of 15,000 feet to avoid crashing into the mountain peaks skirting either side of the narrow gorge of the Siang river'.[105] A visit to NEFA required a permit, much to the annoyance of Indian citizens. The Indian parliamentarian Ram Manohar Lohia defied this and was arrested, causing an uproar in Parliament.

The Indian state lacked the resources, infrastructure and intelligence network to establish a firm presence in NEFA. The Assam Rifles was deployed in the south-eastern part of NEFA as Naga rebels began to be a source of worry. Amidst these uncertainties, an inter-tribe feud over a love affair turned violent. In October 1953, a patrol party of the Assam Rifles, NEFA officials, porters and village headmen reached the remote area of Achingmori along the Subansiri River. Their intention was to establish a civil post and mediate in the feud.[106] They carried with them gifts, which included a valuable commodity—salt. The government believed that airdropping salt in these remote areas—unlike the imperial practice of gifting cigarettes and opium—which added 'some savour to [sic] their simple diet', had paid off in 'winning the confidence and friendship' of many of them.[107] However, the Tagin community saw this patrol party as being in collusion with the rival tribe. The party fell into a trap laid for them. Some 40 of them were massacred, a few escaping to carry back information about this tragic incident some days later.

The handling of this incident was 'a crucial watershed' in the Indian states' approach to NEFA. 'The Assam Rifles were out for blood.'[108] Across the defence establishment and elsewhere, there were calls for revenge against 'tribal barbarity, cunning behaviour, and ingratitude'.[109] Nehru's stand was moderate, and it was supported by the Assam Governor Jairamdas Daulatram, who 'alone remained unmoved by the mad hysteria. The guilty, no question, must be tracked down and punished, but he very properly and firmly insisted that there must be no indiscriminate vendetta against the innocent'.[110] Seen as a serious challenge to the might of the Indian state machinery, and largely out of ignorance of the complexities of tribal social life in India's North-east, this incident 'was overblown in rhetoric as a tribal rebellion' against Indian defence establishments, according to Geeta Krishnatry, who accompanied her husband, Major Surendra Mohan Krishnatry, in the military peace mission into NEFA three years later.[111] Speaking in Parliament on 21 November 1953, Nehru appealed to his fellow parliamentarians not to 'take too exaggerated a view of this incident, serious and tragic as it was'.[112] 'It would have been easy enough for us to take punitive action against these simple, proud and virile people,' Nehru asserted. 'We could have bombed their villages and killed a large number of their people.' Instead, Nehru argued that

> the policy of our Government is not to strike terror or kill and destroy indiscriminately . . . We are confident that we can have the friendship and respect of these simple folk by adopting a firm, clear, and sympathetic policy towards them. By adopting a strong, dignified and imaginative policy we can win their esteem and affection.

Despite these statements, however, the Indian government left no stone unturned to assert its authority and transform the area into a 'war zone'.[113] The places were remote—'even after sending troops by air', it took a 'three weeks' march to get in'.[114] Weeks later, more than a thousand military personnel arrived, and punitive action began, in which five Tagins were killed and sentences of life imprisonment were given to others. According to the historian Bérénice Guyot-Réchard, this incident sent a clear message that if the Indian state tried to impose itself on these areas, it would end up 'antagonising the population and endangering the Indian state's own resilience'.[115]

By the mid-1950s, the increasing alienation of the Assamese language from NEFA was a source of anxiety for the Assamese literary elite who made every effort to express their displeasure.[116] Their anger also stemmed from the fact that for decades the Roman script was in use for the tribal languages in the hill districts of Assam. Nehru, mindful of the increasing resentment of the Assamese elite, in 1955, explained the reasons for his government's decision to introduce the Devanagari script. He explained that 'it is easier to transcribe the sounds of the tribal languages into Nagari'. This would also help the people learn Hindi.[117] The appointment of Hindi speakers as schoolteachers in NEFA was seen as a cause for concern. The press in Assam began to increasingly view the intervention of the Union government in NEFA with suspicion as 'measures were being taken to eliminate Assamese as a medium of instruction, even from the lower classes in the NEFA schools, in spite of protests raised by the tribals of the Frontier'.[118] The press 'was not opposed to the popularization of Hindi as the proposed *lingua franca* of India but was certainly opposed to the way it was sought to be introduced in the NEFA'.[119]

When Hindi was introduced in preference to Assamese, all hell broke loose in Assam. It was seen by many as an attempt to reconfirm Assam's separation from NEFA. 'We favour the learning of Hindi but not at the cost of our own language—Asamese.'[120] An MP from Assam, Hem Barua, pressed in Parliament that 'Assamese is their natural language for inter-tribal communication'. The question was, how crucial was Assamese as the *lingua franca*? The Asam Sahitya Sabha had opened branches in a few parts of NEFA, but its officials, unlike the political leaders, hardly stayed there for more than a few hours at a time. Opinion on the matter was divided. Indira Miri believed that since Assamese was the language of the plains, people with whom the NEFA population had to carry on trade had to learn it out of compulsion. She suggested the use of the Assamese script for NEFA languages to ensure their effective use and standardization. How did the people of NEFA view these developments? The response would have been mixed; some of them expressed their dissatisfaction with the possibility of learning both Assamese and Hindi and made known their preference for Hindi.[121]

For many, NEFA, its rivers and valleys, possessed an untouched beauty which they still retain in part today. Elwin described the Siang, as the Brahmaputra is called there:

> If all the pens that ever poets held were to get to work on it, I doubt if they could digest into words the fascination of this wonderful river, so exquisite, so mysterious, so varied in its charms, at one point flowing through gently sloping woods, at another forcing its way through high gorges.[122]

Yet, for the early twentieth century Assamese speakers, the eastern Himalayas hardly mattered. Well into the mid-1950s, for the average Assamese elite, NEFA was still *terra incognita*. When the Assamese judge Holiram Deka travelled by pony to Bomdila in the early 1950s, he thought his countrymen might be 'legitimately curious' to know what made him 'go to [a] such place'.[123] But things began to change as many Assamese speakers sought to benefit from NEFA's economic opportunities—primarily in the expanding government employment—and others generated compassionate anthropological narratives of NEFA.[124] It is true that the Assamese public considered NEFA as an extension of their material and political landscape, yet they were cautious in the wake of the political crisis arising from the turbulent Nagaland. According to Rustomji, the Assamese feared that the Union government 'would not readily surrender the patronage in appointment, contracts and other fields' and, further, 'was not likely to evince much enthusiasm for NEFA's cultural integration with Assam'.[125] These vast tracts, with the acceleration in the state-building process, were a promised land for jobs and opportunities. There was a significant flow of jobseekers from northern India into NEFA. Of the 8000 government employees, those recruited from Assam represented a little less than a fifth.

The tug of war between the state government and the Governor of Assam further worsened in 1956 with the appointment of S. Fazl Ali, a former Supreme Court judge who had served as the Governor of Odisha, who was disliked even by Elwin. The new Governor, Medhi complained to Nehru, had kept Assam out of the loop in matters of importance. Fazl Ali had headed the States Reorganisation Commission which had rejected Assam's demand that NEFA be made a part of the state.[126]

Over the years, the intricate economic and social linkages between hills and plains, tribals and non-tribals, got disrupted. While mobility across the hills and plains became an integral part of the state-making process, the tribal population was discouraged from adopting Assamese customs, evoking sharp reactions from the Assamese leaders. What did the people themselves want? We do not have conclusive evidence. Hem Barua referred to a number of memorandums submitted by the inhabitants of NEFA in support of the Assamese. This new generation of urban elite from Arunachal, cutting across their ethnic identities, did not break away from the Assamese literary public life. Rather, some of them became a part of it; some took to English, but rarely did they take to Hindi.

The Assamese elite, a section professing left-liberal views, realized that their colleagues from the hills were getting increasingly dissociated from the idea of Assam. Some desperately tried to maintain the traditional associations between the plains and the hills (*bhoiyam* and *pahar*). In 1956, the Assamese movie *Smritir Parash* was released. One of the songs, which was taught to school students in some parts of NEFA, spoke of the rising promise of NEFA. Rather than pursuing hard politics with the Indian state, a section of Assamese fell back on emotive cultural forces in a last-minute attempt to retain NEFA.

Many Assamese considered the central control over NEFA as an attempt to challenge the idea of Assam. Unhappiness and resentment about the Inner Line—which prohibited Assam from gaining from the growing NEFA economy—became obvious. No 'true Indian can be proud of' the Inner Line, grumbled an Assamese litterateur.[127] The Assamese public narrative negotiated the NEFA question cautiously, reiterated that the hill population was not uncivilized and recalled their past intimate relations with the hills. The present state of affairs was blamed on the British: 'The first crack that shook the temple of unity of the hills and plains was caused by the Britishers.'[128]

NEFA's separation from the Assamese imagination was reinforced as the Indian government commissioned an 'authoritative history of NEFA', a task that would otherwise have been proudly undertaken and accomplished by Assamese historians.[129] Earlier, an attempt by the Assam government to establish a research institute in 1956, in line with the Anthropological Survey of India, to study its tribal population, including that of NEFA, had been shot down by the Union government.[130]

The Assamese political leadership was not willing to give up on NEFA easily. Assamese politicians signalled that no one from the plains would be allowed to settle in these areas—a message intended to assuage the hill tribes.[131] The Assamese intelligentsia, to establish their long association with the people of NEFA, quoted the statement of a mid-nineteenth century American Baptist missionary who had written that 'the Assamese language is the common medium of intercourse with the mountain tribes that surround the Valley . . . From their constant intercourse with the Assamese some among them can speak Assamese very well'.[132]

In 1961, a team of leading figures belonging to the Asam Sahitya Sabha made several tours of NEFA.[133] Members of the Sabha, the principal platform of the Assamese literary intelligentsia, met Nehru in Guwahati on 19 May 1961 to express their displeasure about Central interference in the affairs of NEFA and the increasing downgrading of Assamese as the language of instruction there. When the Sabha urged that students from NEFA be taught in the Assamese script, Nehru confronted them: 'Why do you want to limit them (with the Assamese script)?' The Sabha retorted: 'We suggest the Assamese script, Sir, because it is difficult for young tribal boys to pick up two scripts at an early stage of their learning. They are used to their mother tongue and Assamese from their childhood and can learn them both.' Nehru was not convinced and queried, 'Who says this?'[134] Following Nehru's disapproval, the NEFA administration in May 1962 made Assamese an elective subject in NEFA schools and gave preference to Hindi, much to the resentment of the Sabha.[135] The Sabha condemned this promotion of Hindi:

When some people try hard to prove that the inhabitants of the NEFA evince an inordinate preference for Hindi, with which they were never familiar, to Assamese, which they have been using for centuries, that only seems to be either a misrepresentation or an attempt to dress up others' views under some temptation.[136]

However, the march of Hindi was on a firm footing, and Assam's objection was vetoed. In 1962, a young NEFA resident wrote that the students in NEFA had no dislike of Hindi and were proud of learning Hindi rather than the foreigner's tongue, English.[137]

Assam's continued demand for Assamese as the medium of instruction in NEFA found support among those who briefly worked there. One of them was Sitaram Johri, a military official posted in NEFA. Johri had little doubt that 'the medium of instruction in the NEFA schools should be the Assamese [language] . . . unless, of course, the administration is thinking of closing all doors of NEFA leading to Assam'.[138] Though Nehru had announced his government's plan to shift the headquarters of the NEFA administration from Shillong in 1960, it was not until 1974 that this actually happened, marking the cutting of the umbilical cord with Assam. The evolving political fate of NEFA was then still dependent on Assam, as its sole nominee to the Indian Parliament was chosen by Assam, the first of whom was Chow Khamoon Gohain Namshum, nominated in 1952 and 1957. The second nominee, Daying Ering, was chosen on the advice of Assam's chief minister in 1960.[139]

Assamese intelligentsia, political leaders and others remained vocal about the integration of NEFA with Assam through the 1960s.[140] The educationist and parliamentarian Parag Chaliha had summed up the Assamese stand:

> Assamese has been the *lingua franca* among the different tribal groups. We are sorry, however, to disclose, that there has been [a] systematic propaganda from interested quarters in the rest of India against the Assamese people in relation to our Hill brethren . . . It is calculated to isolate the Assamese people from the love and affection

of our tribal brethren, which have been fostered and stabilised by age-old traditions and instil in their place outsiders—who do not belong to the State—so that they might rule unhampered and reap the harvest.[141]

After the war with China, Assamese hopes for control of NEFA continued, and in the troubled years of 1967–68, such hopes were rekindled. In January 1968, speaking from the dais of the Asam Sahitya Sabha, the Assam Governor, Vishnu Sahay, suggested that Assamese be the language of instruction in NEFA and sought the help of the Sabha to achieve this.[142]

~

The story of India's border war of 1962 has been told many times.[143] Here, the purpose is to explain how Assam's northern frontier coped with this crisis. Soon after Independence, the Indian leadership saw early signs of trouble across India's northern borders and understood its implications for the future. In an anxious letter to Nehru on 7 November 1950, Patel warned that the border areas of India in the Assam Himalayas were inhabited by people who 'have no established loyalty to India'.[144] Patel noted that 'throughout history, we have seldom been worried about our North-east frontier. The Himalayas have been regarded as an impenetrable barrier against any threat from the north'. As border disputes between India and China intensified in the early 1950s, Patel's premonition came true. Immediately after World War II, Assam's Governor had moderately increased military presence along the McMahon Line.[145] Two decades later, Assam faced the brunt of being a frontier state.

India's forward policy—the visible presence of government machinery—in NEFA began after 1950. 'With a Chinese presence in Tibet, it became necessary to further strengthen our ties with the hill-people of NEFA and to make known our own presence, in unmistakable terms, up to the international frontier,' recalled Nari Rustomji, NEFA advisor at that time. State-making was, however, a difficult task in this region. The building of roads in the Himalayas was an arduous operation. 'The mere surveying of an alignment is a time-consuming process and scarcity of labour in the hill areas comes in the way of speedy construction. Even after construction is completed, it requires several years for a road to stabilize in the heavy monsoon conditions obtaining in the Himalayan hills.'[146] The development initiatives to enable the penetration of the Indian state in NEFA could hardly meet strategic and military challenges.

The Assamese press had been reporting widely on the Sino-Indian border dispute since 1954, and accounts of the unquiet eastern Himalayas were published. Assam's parliamentarians warned the Union government of the political uncertainty along its northern frontier. Global observers also doubted India's ability to defend the whole of its 3200-kilometre-long northern frontier, given its meagre resources.[147] The north-eastern hill districts had already begun to drift away both because of the policies of the Union government and Assam's own stand. The Indian state responded to this crisis in multiple ways. Towards the end of the 1950s, a number of Chinese deserters—the government being suspicious of their 'actual intention'—were arrested in NEFA and kept in Assam's jails.[148] Meanwhile, in 1959, the Indian Army set up operational headquarters at Jorhat. This colonial-era town was not far away from Longju, the Indian border post that was captured by Chinese troops in August 1959.[149] In April that year, the Dalai Lama had arrived in Assam's tiny north bank town of Tezpur and was greeted by radio commentators, pressmen and Indian officials.[150]

By 1960, China had clearly laid claim to a part of NEFA. The Indian government disputed this, and others too believed the claim was not valid. The anthropologist Fürer-Haimendorf, who worked extensively in these areas during 1944–45, argued that the ethnic communities there, in terms of their agricultural methods, and in material and social structure, corresponded 'closely with many of such Indian hill-tribes as Nagas, Lusheis and Garos', and the latter 'cannot by any stretch of imagination be considered as falling within the cultural sphere of China'.[151] Fürer-Haimendorf noted that in the general matter of living as well as in specific cultural expressions, an Apa Tani or Dafla of the Subansiri area has far more in common with an Ifugao head hunter of the Philippines or a Dayak of Borneo than with a Buddhist Tibetan, and this similarity extends even to matters of world-view and social attitudes.

While Nyishis or Adis are 'as non-Indian as Lolos on the upper Yangtse-kiang', Fürer-Haimendorf warned, accepting Chinese claims of ethnic affinities to determine political allegiance would 'completely disrupt the existing political structures of Asia, for not only India but also numerous other Asian states which contain within their frontier a diversity of ethnic and cultural groups'. Fürer-Haimendorf emphasized that these areas till recently were regarded as 'no man's land' and had never been entered by the Chinese or the Tibetans. However, Indian officials 'have since exercised political control and laid the foundation of an administrative machinery in most of the tribal country south of the Himalayan main range' and so the Indian government 'has thus established the right of *primus occupans* beyond any reasonable doubt', Fürer-Haimendorf argued. Others like the Sinologist from Oxford University, Geoffrey Francis Hudson, saw in the Chinese claim in NEFA 'a persistent desire to put India down, to demonstrate a superiority of strength and will, and to make Delhi give way on an issue on which the prestige of both nations has come to be staked'.[152]

By 1962, the Chinese proposal for a 'Confederation of Himalayan States', which also included NEFA, was well-known.[153] Not just NEFA, Assam's mineral resources had also attracted Chinese attention. During the War, both Japanese and American intelligence had observed that Assam's oil resources could significantly add to Chinese economic opportunities. Indian military officials were aware of China's interest in Assam's oil reserves.[154] Until production began in Ankleshwar oilfield in Gujarat's Cambay basin, Assam had been India's sole commercial producer of crude petroleum; in 1962, Assam still accounted for 60 per cent of India's domestic production.

As the border disputes intensified, Indian officials, in a desire to strengthen their claims, increasingly referred to the colonial tour diaries, annual reports and topographical and geographical survey reports, which were lying dormant for long, as proof of their long-standing presence in the far-flung areas of NEFA.[155] The Indian government decided to push its claim through both civil and military options. In 1960, the Border Roads Organisation was established to expedite road construction. The number of paramilitary posts was enhanced. In April and May 1961, Nehru toured NEFA to see the progress of road construction for defence purposes, and he visited Bomdila.[156] But this did not help to calm the situation, as the Chinese began patrolling along the McMahon Line and making incursions into Indian-administered territory. In June 1962, an acrimonious war of words broke out between the Assamese parliamentarian Hem Barua and Nehru. Barua wanted more information on Chinese 'slanderous propaganda' about Assam's oil towns and also Chinese claims in NEFA.[157] Nehru acknowledged the Chinese refusal to recognize the McMahon Line, but when Barua asked whether China's bolstering of its claims on NEFA and the steady 'military occupations' were a step towards a 'total war on us by China', Nehru answered that he did not think 'any total war is a prospect in view'.[158] Nehru knew that incursions along the frontier could not be wholly prevented, but he was briefed that, in the event of a war, India would have the advantage.[159]

After some months of hostility between the Indian and Chinese military forces, beginning from mid-1962, China's serious intent of taking control of Assam was admitted by the Indian government in October.[160] By then, the Chinese had amassed troops all along the NEFA border, including the Tirap Frontier, where they expected some support from the Naga rebels. Assam received two extra squadrons of fighter bombers on 12 October. 'The Indian government', the *Guardian* in London reported on 28 October, had reluctantly concluded that 'China's goal is not only to wrest control of the border mountains from India but also to bring direct threat to bear on Assam itself'. Two days prior, a national emergency had been declared.[161] Assam was India's main supply line for oil, and more energy could be 'tapped in the area if hydro-electric dams were built on the Himalayan torrents which flow into the Brahmaputra', while Tibet lacked energy resources. The *Guardian* speculated that once they captured Tawang, the Chinese forces would be at the door of Assam in two weeks. As the Chinese began to advance, the Assam government began civil defence of the state, especially in the northern districts. All available jeeps were taken over by the military, and the Home Guard and the Railway Protection Force were formed. Appeals were made to women to help prepare cotton quilts and food packets for the Indian soldiers. Trenches were dug.[162] Meanwhile, Nehru wrote to Chaliha that the Chinese aggression was 'causing us great concern . . . but we shall have to face it with a stout heart'.[163]

On 17 November, the NEFA town of Walong on the eastern frontier, which had an airstrip, was taken over by the Chinese after a bitter battle.[164] This gave the Chinese army direct access to the Brahmaputra Valley and the strategic routes to Burma. More Indian defence posts fell to the Chinese, including Se La. On 18 November, Bomdila, on the border with Tibet, which is only 40 air kilometres from the Assam plains, fell to the Chinese.[165] With the fall of the upper reaches of NEFA, everything went out of control. The Home Ministry sent out instructions to evacuate officials from the cities north of the Brahmaputra, including Tezpur in Assam. They also gave instructions for 'the destruction of the Digboi oil fields and all power plants' in the Brahmaputra Valley.[166] When Bomdila was about to fall, residents from other areas, including the upper reaches, fled, leaving behind their domestic animals, grains and about-to-be-harvested fields.[167] By the evening of 19 November, Tezpur, the headquarters of the Indian Frontier Corps, and frequented by British planters, wore a deserted look. The economist John Kenneth Galbraith, who served as America's ambassador to India in 1961–63, wrote in his diary how on 21 November he 'witnessed the disintegration of public morale'.[168]

Many believed it was only a matter of time before Assam met its grim fate. The *New York Times* ran a front-page headline on 20 November saying 'Chinese Drive into India, Imperiling Assam Plains'.[169] The next day the *Times of India*'s headline read 'Chinese Greed Knows No Bounds: Assam in Peril'.[170] The Chinese troops reached the foothills to the west of Tezpur.[171] On 21 November, many members of Parliament

News of fall of Bomdila in November 1962, during the Sino-Indian War demanded military administration for Assam. Galbraith noted in his diary that this was not agreed to, and 'it was an impressive example of the vitality of Parliamentary rule in India'.[172] Galbraith was told the same day by a 'highly placed leader who had just come back from Tezpur' about rumours of a secret deal between the Chinese and the Pakistanis for the eventual transfer of the Brahmaputra Valley to East Pakistan.[173] This had caused a number of Hindus to flee. Near Tezpur, people in two villages had raised the slogan of 'Pakistan Zindabad' and 'looted some houses and shops'.[174]

After Bomdila fell on 18 November, Nehru wrote two letters to US President John F. Kennedy. In the first letter, he informed Kennedy that 'the Chinese are, by and large, in possession of the greater part of NEFA. Events have moved very fast and we are facing a grim situation in our struggle for survival.'[175] Just hours later, Nehru sent another letter in which he said

> a serious situation has developed in our Digboi oil fields in Assam ... With the advance of the Chinese in massive strength, the entire Brahmaputra valley is seriously threatened and unless something is done immediately to stem the tide, the whole of Assam, Tripura, Manipur and Nagaland would also pass into Chinese hands ... The situation that has developed is, however, really desperate.

Seeking the assistance of fighter aircraft, Nehru stated that 'any delay in this assistance reaching us will result in nothing short of a catastrophe for our country'.[176] These SOSs to the United States remained unknown to the Indian public until 1965.[177] To secure its airspace, India on 19 November also banned flights of Pakistani and Chinese planes over the Mizo hills.[178] Small airfields built during the War helped the Indian government get military aid quickly, including from the US and UK.[179] However, as the newspaper editor Frank Moraes wrote: 'Government caught off-guard militarily, diplomatically and psychologically, gropes like a man in a mist.'[180]

Most Tawang residents were evacuated before the fall of the town.[181] On 21 November, Rustomji was told by many residents at Tezu, another NEFA town, about their 'disillusionment and resentment' at being 'left unprotected and abandoned in the hour of danger'.[182] In another town, Pasighat, residents threatened 'to cut up their leaders in case they deserted the district'.[183] An engineering organization tasked with constructing roads and buildings in NEFA asked people to evacuate, and, as they retreated, they destroyed bridges, roads, stores, camps and their own machinery.[184] Most government officials and planters of the north bank fled, as did a significant number of people who found shelter in relief camps in Tezpur and other places, including educational campuses in Guwahati. On 19 November, the day after Bomdila fell to the Chinese, Brij Mohan Kaul, commander of the Indian Army, was proceeding towards the pass and found the road 'cluttered up with troops and refugees coming back', including Indian and foreign correspondents.[185] After trekking for several days, the evacuees arrived in Assam in the last week of November. Their numbers kept increasing; many arrived with their mules.[186]

Many refugees avoided the newly built paved roads for fear of being caught by the Chinese military. Rather, they followed their traditional routes. When they reached the foothills of Assam and set up camp, they were welcomed by the people of the foothills, with many of whom they had economic and social ties.[187] An estimated 19,000 people fled from NEFA.[188] Those who came from the upper reaches found Assam's warm weather uncomfortable and the language barrier a major problem.[189] At Mangaldai, a camp for the Mompa population came up. The local support to the evacuees was more forthcoming than it had been in 1947. Many in Nagaon converted their homes into evacuee camps. Girls learnt first aid and nursing to help the sick and the injured. A restoration of the civil administration began.[190] Preparations began to house the refugees mainly in the Garo hills, an idea largely welcomed by the residents there.

Even as the Indian defence was giving way, the Chinese population of India were being arrested and sent to a faraway detention camp at Deoli in the desert province of Rajasthan.[191] On a request from the Assam government, on 17 November, the Indian government ordered the internment of all Chinese nationals and people of Chinese origin living in Assam and the bordering districts of West Bengal.[192] A few hundred Chinese families were detained and sent to Deoli. The forefathers of these people had come to Assam and Bengal during the early years of the plantation industry but had soon left their employment as the planters did not honour their contracts. Some of these Chinese families had earned handsomely during the War in the 1940s, supplying food to American forces in eastern Assam. They were fluent in Assamese.[193]

The opinion of communists in India was generally divided on the Sino-Indian border dispute; several senior Indian communist leaders criticized the Chinese frontier policy.[194] As the border conflict grew, they came to be closely watched by Indian intelligence officials. They came under stricter surveillance when China's *People's Daily* published an article voicing the opinion that Indian communists would extend support to the Chinese attack on India.[195] The Indian home minister had warned against the communists on 28 October.[196] There were also orders to arrest all communist leaders. Many of India's, and also Assam's, tallest communist leaders had been known for expressing spirited nationalist political sentiments and were described by Nehru as nationalist communists.[197] However, both the Indian Intelligence Bureau and the American CIA felt that the Indian communists could not be trusted in the event of a Chinese attack. In mid-November 1962, Bishnu Rabha, a well-known name in Assam's cultural world and a major communist leader, the historian Amalendu Guha and several others were arrested under the Defence of India Act, 1962.[198] Officially, the CPI had opposed China's attack on India.[199] But this did not prevent the loyalty of Indian communists from coming under severe scrutiny; legislators in West Bengal censured the CPI members as anti-nationalists.[200]

~

As the Chinese army marched towards the plains of Assam and rumours of the imminent fall of Tezpur spread, the Indian government hastily, and without much thought, instructed the civilian administration to evacuate to the south bank. This coincided with the rapid retreat of the

Indian military; army vehicles dominated almost all roads of the north bank for the next few days.[201]

There was panic in Assam. People felt that 'to be enslaved again is worse than death'.[202] Chief Minister Chaliha appealed to people to join India's territorial army and the National Cadet Corps. The government issued advertisements asking people to grow more food and to buy seeds and fertilizers from its stores at subsidized rates. On the evening of 19 November, Chaliha addressed his people over the radio. He said that the Indian Army was retreating, and Assam was 'in the midst of a great trial'.

> It seems that hard realities of war are coming nearer and we have to be prepared for it . . . I would appeal to every citizen of Assam to face this trial without panic . . . If by chance we become more directly exposed than hitherto, we have to show great determination and patience . . . We will face the emergency with dignity and courage . . . While we trust our army, we must be ready for an extreme crisis; as we all want to die in our motherland, we must have patience, courage, and discipline, we must ensure that we keep the transport system intact.[203]

Some residents of Tezpur, which had a population of 40,000, began to leave on the evening of the 19th, and several thousand crossed the river by the next day.[204] River steamers were commandeered. British families were evacuated to Calcutta. American citizens were advised by their government to leave Assam.[205] But, as the residents of Tezpur fled, the Assam Congress appealed to them not to 'leave their hearths and homes unless necessitated by military reasons'.[206]

On 20 November, the Army Corps headquarters was shifted from Tezpur to Guwahati.[207] From NEFA, 'engineers were fast slipping away'.[208] Skeleton air transport services were utilized to spot the refugees 'streaming into Assam plains'.[209] An order was given to blow up the Tezpur airport, but the ceasefire came in time to save it.[210] Military evacuation created panic among the civilian population: 'It was frightful to see the Border Roads Organization with its heavy trucks and huge

Residents of Tezpur fleeing with all their belongings as the Chinese Army occupied parts of NEFA during the Sino-Indian War, 1962

engineering and earth-moving vehicles cluttering along the roads of Tezpur to the river bank where it monopolized the two available ferries for practically the whole day.'[211] The telephone staff too moved to the south bank.

On the evening of the 20th, still not having received a clear picture from the military, R.K.D. Singh, Darrang's new deputy commissioner, advised the evacuation of women and children. Men went to see their families off but did not return. Rawle Knox, the *Guardian*'s correspondent who was at Tezpur, listened to a public meeting 'attended by a small and listless crowd', where politicians were exhorting people 'to stay in their homes and die under the enemy bombs rather than evacuate', after which they themselves left for safer places.

> Then followed the great civilian exodus from Tezpur. The treasury was emptied; notes were burnt or sent across to Nowgong; coins dumped in tanks; hospitals and jails cleared of the inmates; shops closed; and the civilian staff and even the police started withdrawing from Tezpur following the footsteps of the army.[212]

'A pall of thick smoke hung over the city as government offices got busy in burning documents. By nightfall, Tezpur was a ghost city. The collapse of law and order was complete.'[213] Chaliha conceded that only 'a very small number of urban population stayed on in the town'.[214]

The State Bank of India, India's principal bank in the town, initially threw their currency, worth 3,00,000 pounds in notes and coins, into a nearby lake but gave up 'when the citizenry went diving in'. They then burnt the notes, upon which a small crowd tried 'digging with naked toes into the hot ash to salvage anything worth taking'.[215] 'Most of the receding crowd, who included tribesmen of all kinds' from the Himalayan foothills and 'green-jacketed lunatics' released from the Tezpur asylum, made the journey in the normal Indian way—on foot.[216] 'Harmless' patients from this hospital were handed over to relatives. On the 20th, an estimated 20,000 crossed the river at Tezpur. Many recalled the time the Japanese had been approaching Assam two decades earlier. Evacuation from the eastern-most towns like Digboi also took place.[217] Not everyone fled though. Many—youth, elderly people and women—reassembled to prepare for civil defence. Women learnt to fire rifles.

Did the Chinese have a plan to capture the town which had hosted the Dalai Lama a few years before? A later news item published in the *Indian Express* was of this opinion: 'Reports available here indicate that the Chinese had planned to advance up to Tezpur.'[218] Apparently, the Chinese believed that many Indians in the North-east would go over to their side. There was, however, no substantial proof of this.

Contributions to the National Defence Fund came from traders, tea planters and workers, merchants and professionals, including NEFA residents.[219] Such support took many forms—one cinema owner treated the army to a free show, another individual distributed 50,000 oranges to the thirsty Indian troops. There was a massive expansion of the National Cadet Corps in Assam's schools. While national leaders appreciated the courage and discipline of the residents of Assam, there was widespread public condemnation as political leaders fled Tezpur.

*Jugantar,* the Calcutta-based newspaper, ran a front-page advertisement saying that Bengal would stand by Assam in this hour of crisis.[220] Thousands—15,000 according to the *Indian Express*—

protested before the Chinese consulate in Calcutta.[221] Calcutta-based Hindu organizations like the Bharat Sevashram Sangha arranged relief works.[222] Retired Nepali soldiers settled in Sadiya offered help with arms training and food.[223] The *Assam Tribune* published a pledge: 'We shall not rest till the last Bandit of the Dragon is driven out of the sacred soil of India.'[224]

On the morning of 20 November, B.N. Mullik, the chief of India's Intelligence Bureau, was informed by Army Headquarters that they would be 'withdrawing all troops from both North and South Assam'.[225] Plans for evacuation of Indian government officials from Tezpur met with strong resistance from Chaliha.[226] Home Minister Lal Bahadur Shastri now flew to Assam. When he met the residents of Tezpur on 22 November, they complained that the government did not discharge its responsibility for 'citizen's life and property'.[227] Civil preparedness had already begun on the north bank. Relying on the organizational systems of the Shanti Sena, the volunteer group formed during the Quit India Movement, the local population across several parts of the north bank had already formed resistance groups; some of them quickly learnt the basics of handling arms.

Thousands had begun to flee to Bengal.[228] The rich and the powerful had the privilege of being evacuated quickly. Shastri received complaints that even the chickens of the *burra sahibs* were evacuated.[229] Most European planters left behind their workers, most of them being left without their wages. This immediately sparked off trouble.[230] The tea economy had other worries too. While their everyday operations had been halted as their jeeps were requisitioned by the government, a two-month-long strike by the river steamers in East Pakistan almost emptied the Calcutta auction markets of Assam tea.[231] While the tea-garden workers continued to run their gardens by forming managerial committees,[232] the plantations faced a financial crisis as banks refused to loan them money.[233] The strike by Pakistani workers of the joint Indo-Pakistani steamer line disrupted the outflow of tea from Assam, and there was a steep fall in sales. Desperate, Assam even pleaded that a canal be excavated to connect the Brahmaputra and the Ganga.[234] In the faraway London Stock Exchange, tea shares, especially those of Assam plantations, slumped. Disruption in transport led to the accumulation of tea stocks. As a way out, hundreds of trucks were used to transport these stocks and extra wagons were added to the railways towards the end of November.[235]

On the night of 19 November 1962, Nehru addressed the nation on All India Radio.[236] He spoke in Hindi, followed by English. He told the nation about the defeat of the Indian Army in NEFA. He said:

> Now what has happened is very serious and very saddening to us and I can well understand what our friends in Assam must be feeling, because all this is happening on their doorstep one might say. I want to tell them that we feel very much for them and we shall help them to the utmost of our ability.'

Admitting to the 'overwhelming numbers of the Chinese forces', he assured his countrymen and especially the people of Assam: 'I want to take a pledge to them, here and now, that we shall see this matter to the end and the end will have to be victory for India.' He stressed that 'India is not going to lose this war, however long it lasts and whatever harm it may do us meanwhile.' Sharing the anxiety of the panicked population of Assam, Nehru said,

> Therefore, on this day which has been a sad day for bringing news of reverses and setbacks, I want to send my greetings to the people of Assam, especially to the people of NEFA, and to the rest of India, and to tell them that we must not get worried about this. Sad we must be necessarily, but we must train ourselves and steel ourselves to meet all these reverses and to even make our determination still firmer to do all that we can to repel and throw out the invader from India.

He continued:

> We shall not accept any terms that he may offer because he may think that we are a little frightened by some setbacks. I want to make

that clear to all of you and more especially to our countrymen in Assam, to whom our heart goes out at this moment.

For another few minutes, Nehru castigated China as 'an imperialist of the worst kind', and said the goings-on were 'a menace for the entire world'.

Many in Assam listened to Nehru's speech, which added to their 'growing chronicle of disaster'.[237] One of Nehru's phrases, 'heart goes out', which he frequently used on other occasions too, was immediately noted by many in Assam, including senior Congress leaders. Journalist Kuldeep Nayar, who was the press secretary to Home Minister Shastri, arrived in Assam on 21 November. He noted that 'many Assamese are saying openly that they should join hands with the Chinese and wreak vengeance on "Dilliwallas" for having abandoned the state'.[238] The British journalist Neville Maxwell thought that Nehru's voice 'was old and tired, and his words were dispirited and dispiriting'.[239] A group of Assamese Congressmen wrote to Nehru asking whether his speech was a desertion of Assam to the enemy. Nehru wrote back, 'Our hearts have gone out to all of your people there. I can assure you that there will be no peace till we have rid India and of course, Assam also, of this Chinese menace.'[240] He emphasized that Assam is a 'living part of' India.

Nehru's clarification could not, however, instil a sense of reassurance in the Assamese public narrative. The reason for this is not difficult to explain. Set against the backdrop of the profound psychological effects of the war, though the actual battle lasted only 14 days, the prime minister's speech did not resonate with a section in Assam. Assam's uneven economic growth compared to several Indian states, the widespread perception that it had remained a resource frontier for the Indian economy and the failure of the rising Assamese bourgeoisie to gain a firm foothold in the economic and political trajectory of post-Independence India stoked a sense of deep alienation and disillusionment with the Union government.

~

At midnight on 21 November, China declared a unilateral ceasefire. This unexpected event was largely a result of Russia's diplomatic persuasion and its threat to withdraw the assurance of military support in the event of any attack on mainland China, the *Guardian* reported.[241] The ceasefire led to the immediate withdrawal of the Chinese army from the occupied places, and it was a great relief for Assam, which feared that the Chinese 'could have continued their advance'.[242] But it did not mean an end to anxiety, as an official order still instructed those from other parts of India who were working in Assam to 'send their families home'.[243]

On 5 December, Nehru visited Guwahati and Tezpur, where he addressed well-attended public meetings and spoke to injured soldiers. People greeted him along his way from the airport.[244] In Guwahati, Nehru spoke of how the Chinese attack had 'jolted the people out of lethargy and slackness and infused a new spirit of unity among them'.[245] He commended Assam and NEFA for being brave and acting as the 'shield of India against the Chinese onslaught'. While there

Jawaharlal Nehru at a public meeting in Guwahati on 5 December 1962, on his way to Tezpur after the unilateral ceasefire of China during the Sino-Indian War, 1962

had been some panic, what mattered was how 'the masses face[d] a crisis'. 'You have proved your mettle.' Nehru said that 'in spite of the niggling worries and complaints which have found their way into the newspapers, by and large, the people of NEFA and Assam have risen to the occasion splendidly'. He informed the public that the Chinese army had not yet retreated from Bomdila.

In Tezpur, Nehru declared that 'what has happened on our borders is a historic turning point in the history of the world'.[246] The people of Tezpur, Nehru acknowledged, had gone through 'a special kind of experience when the Chinese were right on your doorstep standing poised to invade at any moment'.[247] It was a highly emotive speech, highlighting the importance of unity, but it also explained the significance of the McMahon Line and India's military strategies for the Himalaya. He also admitted to the recalcitrant behaviour of some government officials in Tezpur.

The ceasefire did not mean an end to the Chinese hostility, as Indian troops continued to face ambushes and firing until 26 November.[248] By early December, China started a fresh campaign to lay claim to Bomdila. As the Chinese withdrew, there was worry that they would leave behind their people to 'turn NEFA area as a base for their nefarious guerilla activities'.[249] 'The Chinese are as much there and in greater number,' a resident of Bomdila reported.[250] A Chinese jet aircraft flew past Assam's eastern towns on 10 December; the Indian government had to lodge a protest.[251]

Even though the ceasefire was declared over a month ago, the actual retreat of Chinese troops was reported only in the last week of December,[252] and in January 1963, the Chinese troops finally retreated from Tawang. When Rustomji arrived there, he reported that 'Monpa tribals from the surrounding areas came streaming in to Tawang, overjoyed that we had kept faith and had not, in the despondency of defeat, forgotten our responsibilities to the Monpa people'. The Chinese began to withdraw their troops north of the McMahon Line a few days later.

In a meeting on 7 December between officials of the defence ministry and the ministry of external affairs, it had been decided to that civil officials would be sent back to select places in NEFA.[253] And by mid-December, India had begun to reoccupy the region. Civilian rescue operations continued along the foothills. The Indian government was worried about Chinese subversive activities in NEFA. In Bomdila, particularly, the Indian state faced a Herculean task. The residents who were returning had to undergo screening 'in order to weed out any unauthorized person, particularly a Chinese fifth columnist'.[254] There were other changes, as the returning evacuees carried home their encounters with a new cultural world. 'The recent upheavals which brought the NEFA tribals in closer contact with the people of the plains, have given them a broader outlook on life.'

While NEFA residents were initially sceptical about returning home, fearing fresh Chinese aggression, they ultimately 'returned to their homes and reverted to their routine chores'. The NEFA administration geared up the machinery to repair the damage done to their morale. Life started to come back to normal. Some prisoners of war escaped and came back to Assam, much to the excitement of the local people.[255] At the end of December, a team of legislators from Assam visited the war-torn NEFA.[256] The government began an initiative for 'small batches of farmers from the plains [to] be allowed to settle in NEFA who in turn will introduce better methods of farming among the tribal people'.[257]

The people who had remained in their homes through the Chinese occupation said that they were not mistreated by the Chinese soldiers, but that the latter had warned that they would be back. While Indian military officials had predicted that the Chinese forces would 'slaughter the whole lot, monks, Monpas and anyone else they found', the Chinese troops behaved differently.[258] In Bomdila, most government properties were destroyed or carted away, including 'hospital and electrical equipment, foodstuffs, harvested crops from five villages and cattle from a government farm'.[259] But while properties of the Indian government were destroyed and the nose of a statue of Rabindranath Tagore in Bomdila was chopped off, the NEFA residents largely escaped hostility.[260] Their food stocks and other household properties remained untouched, though the horses of Dirang residents were taken away by the Chinese army. Good quality roads were constructed in that short period, which the Indian state had failed to do for several years. When Yeshe Dorjee Thongchi, a NEFA resident who eventually became a distinguished Assamese literary figure, returned with his family to their home in a Chinese-occupied village of NEFA, they discovered that the valuables they had hidden inside caves were gone.[261] They knew that only their neighbours could have stolen these, and his mother was able to recover some of them after prolonged negotiations. A leading Assamese cultural personality, Chandradhar Goswami, who headed a non-official delegation sent by the Assam government to enquire into Chinese atrocities in NEFA, reported the absence of any such actions. Rather, his report described the Chinese army's friendliness towards NEFA residents.[262] In some places, the Chinese army extended help in agriculture, village cleanliness and bringing drinking water from a distance. They never failed to show respect to the village elders, Goswami's account stated. However, explosives, unfamiliar to the NEFA residents, caused injuries and death to many, including a friend of Yeshe's, who tried his hand at this 'toy'. While most symbols of the Indian state came under attack, the Chinese troops did not defile the monasteries, and unlike in many war situations, the NEFA women remained safe. Chinese soldiers paid for most items they bought from the villagers.[263] There was no forced labour; roads were constructed with the help of Chinese or Tibetan workers. In some cases, 'fabulous wages' were given 'to tribal folk in a bid to lure them into embracing the Chinese ideology'.[264] The 'Chinese had unloaded [a] maze of Tibetan propaganda material designed to undermine their traditional beliefs and loyalties. They were also reported to have organized a series of talks in the occupied zone as part of their indoctrination drive'.[265] In some places, however, local people suffered as the Chinese retreated, as the People's Liberation Army took possession of food stocks.[266] But, in general, the display of benevolence by the Chinese army, was viewed by NEFA residents in contrast to the Indian state's inability to take care of their needs. The Chinese vacated Bomdila by 6 December and left Tawang, Mechuka and Walong by the end of the month.[267] Subsequently, NEFA's affiliations to the Indian Union grew stronger as the latter showed more willingness to accommodate the former's customs and aspirations.[268]

~

When the Chinese aggression had taken a serious turn in the first week of November, Nehru had just settled, for the time being, a vexatious problem with Assam by sanctioning an enhanced royalty rate for oil, on the advice of his cabinet colleague Morarji Desai.[269] Given the threat of war, work on an ambitious fertilizer and gas project was stopped, and the machinery and assets were diverted to other parts of India.[270] The war made apparent Assam's critical role in the Indian economy. British historian and Tory politician John Grigg wrote,

> The Indian economy is in a dicky enough state, without it being subjected to any further hard knocks. In 1961–62, the trade deficit was 4500 million rupees. If Assam had been lost, the deficit would have been between 5100 and 5200 million rupees. India's development is already an uphill struggle: without Assam it might well have become hopeless.[271]

A month after the Chinese withdrawal, the CIA, warning of a 'continuing possibility that Communist China might invade and occupy Assam', prepared a detailed note on the economic relevance of Assam. This note acknowledged Assam's decreasing significance for India in terms of its petroleum resources: 'The oil facilities in Assam are an integral element of India's economic plans and growth, but the loss of Assam would not affect seriously India's total supply of petroleum', as India depended heavily on imported oil. But, the CIA note went on, these oil facilities would 'be an important addition to Chinese Communist supply capabilities'.[272]

After the war, it did not take very long for the Assamese to recover their confidence. When the new Army general visited Assam in the first week of December 1962, he was told by Chaliha that 'the morale of the Assamese was very high'.[273] There was a feeling among some of the Assamese public that the populace should be trained in arms and weaponry, and Assam be converted into an armed camp.[274] One worried patriot wrote to a newspaper urging an immediate increase in food production: 'The army cannot march on empty stomachs, neither can the citizens of a country work on arms and equipment factories without food.'[275] Other civilians called for austerity. In central Assam, a civil society group appealed to the people to observe every Tuesday as no-fish day as one such measure.[276] The Chinese communist experiment, unlike the Soviet example, had hardly influenced the Assamese intelligentsia. Rather, *Nilachal*, an influential Assamese weekly, published an autobiographical piece on the Dalai Lama in 1964.[277]

The war had weakened Assam's hope of reclaiming NEFA, though many continued to seek the region's integration with Assam and the AICC president promised that it would persuade the Government of India to change its outlook towards NEFA.[278] Nehru's NEFA policy drew serious criticism and his image among the people of NEFA was briefly affected. 'In the popular mind, there has been some ignorance and confusion regarding NEFA—what it denotes? Where exactly it is?' wrote R.N. Haldipur, one of the political officers who later became the state's Governor.[279]

Assamese leaders increasingly realized that their environmental and economic future—floods, soil erosion or need for more hydel power—was closely allied with NEFA's environmental and political stability. In another bid to reclaim NEFA after a tour of the region at the end of 1962, Chaliha called for closer cooperation between NEFA and Assam,[280] and the Assam government tried consistently to build confidence amongst NEFA residents. There were frequent references to the historical linkages between the people of Assam and NEFA, including their commerce and politics. When a group of visitors from Assam saw 'a cannon kept in the courtyard' of the village headmen in NEFA, they quickly concluded that it must have been a gift from the Ahom kings.[281] Ethnic cultural troupes from Assam were sent to perform in NEFA towns. Following the advice of Chaliha's government, several *satra*s, the Assamese Vaishnavite monasteries, tried to popularize Assamese culture among NEFA residents.[282] Demands for the integration of NEFA with Assam gradually became more vocal. There were some who asked for a 'complete reorientation' of NEFA's economy.[283] Unlike most other hill districts of Assam, these areas had remained largely outside the influence of Christian missionaries. Traditional religious forms were deeply rooted, but they slowly made room for modern India's Hindu religious activities. In the mid-1960s, the Indian government invited the Ramakrishna Mission to start its religious and philanthropic work there as part of the Indianization project.

Assamese leaders forcefully expressed their worries about India's fragile borders with China, Burma and East Pakistan. Hem Barua, the Praja Socialist parliamentarian, wrote how 'the north-east frontier needs solidarity and adequate measures of defence against all eventualities'.[284] 'The hounds of war, whoever might unleash them on us, must be resisted and beaten back,' Barua added. On another occasion, he asked for a dismantling of NEFA: 'It is no use trying to preserve the NEFA people as "museum pieces" for the anthropologists.'[285] There was also a growing demand for allowing free trade between Assam and NEFA. Nehru, however, declined, citing strategic reasons.[286]

The popular perception in Assam was that Nehru's India had abandoned the province and its people at a moment of grave crisis in the war with China. The Assamese intelligentsia believed the Indian government's weak border policies on NEFA, founded on Elwin's philosophy, were the root cause of China's military success. 'Of what use is a policy which keeps the very gateways of the country so frail?' asked the *Assam Tribune*.[287] However, Elwin had defenders too; an anonymous writer asserted that 'there is no truer friend of Assam than Dr. Elwin with his much-maligned philosophy for NEFA'.[288]

Questions arose about the loyalty of NEFA's residents to India. The *Illustrated Weekly of India* published photographs of Tawang residents participating in cultural festivities organized by the Chinese army.[289] Nehru had to clarify that 'when the occupying armed forces were there, it was difficult to refuse to do so'.[290] As some politicians sought firm and swift integration of these areas into mainland India,

Nehru said, 'We have to integrate them and we have to bring them nearer in thinking and emotions to the rest of India . . . it is not a sudden process; it may be drawn out over some time.' He remained suspicious of any major move to open up NEFA: 'The first persons who go there are petty shopkeepers intent on making money.' Instead, the Union government planned to bring 'hardy and experienced peasants' into the sparsely populated NEFA, who would act as civilian defence rather than mere food growers.[291] The food and agriculture ministry announced a 'colonization' plan to send 1,00,000 farmers who were knowledgeable about 'advanced techniques of farming' to NEFA. Elwin was against this move, believing that a shocked NEFA population, yet to recover from the Chinese invasion, would oppose any loss of rights in land. Such a move would result in scarcity of land for the tribal people and an increase in moneylending, and the NEFA elite would not trust the government of India anymore. Thus, on grounds 'both of expediency and ethics', this scheme should be abandoned.[292] Assam's Governor advised sending only a 'small number of good farmers', 'quietly and without any fuss', and 'without the people in NEFA getting any impression of a large number coming there'.[293] For the first time, Nehru disagreed with Elwin, but he agreed to send small batches of farmers instead—though he remained cautious about its outcome.[294]

The government was also faced with the task of undoing 'the psychological damage the Chinese occupation forces may have brought on the resident population through various methods including coercion and propagation'. Nehru wrote to the army commanders about the need for gender sensitivity. 'They must be particularly careful in dealing with them, they should not behave [as] superiors but they should [show] courtesy.'[295]

The number of primary schools in NEFA had increased from two in 1947 to 159 in 1962. 'We do not favour shops,' said Nehru, but BCG teams, leprosy eradication units, engineers and soldiers were sent to NEFA. Nehru insisted on continuing with the Inner Line, and more restrictions were imposed on travel of foreigners to Assam.[296] Foreigners went there 'pretending to be specialists, specialists in botany and horticulture and all the rest of it, and subsequently indulged in espionage', said Nehru.

Contrary to the suspicion that they might sympathize with China, the NEFA residents showed an exemplary sense of strategic preparation. They knew those mountains very well, more intimately than the Indian military. When Rustomji visited Apatani villages at Ziro on 25 November, he was given a wide range of strategic advice by villagers—this included the need for the Indian Army to 'quickly position tanks and artillery on all the little hillocks surrounding the Ziro air-strip'. They thought that the Indian government had made a great mistake in letting China get 'puffed up'. 'When a man goes out on a long journey, he takes his umbrella with him in case of rain. He does not wait for the rain to come and then go home to fetch his umbrella,' the NEFA residents argued.[297] Rustomji was told that the Apatani people had always had very great regard and affection for 'our Nehru', but they could not understand what had happened to him of late. 'He seemed to have become *dubla* [weak], and was not hitting back at the Chinese as hard as they had expected.'[298]

It was clear, too, that NEFA residents perceived the retreat of the Indian forces and administrative officials in the face of Chinese aggression as a kind of betrayal. They later complained to a team of Assamese politicians that when the war broke out, 'they all fled away silently [and] we were not told as to what [we] were required to do'.[299] However, the government's relief operations among evacuees did generally help to strengthen ties between the Indian state and the people of NEFA. During a visit to relief camps on the south bank of the Brahmaputra, what struck Rustomji was the 'cheerfulness and sense of gratitude of the evacuees for the little that we had been able to do for them'.[300] With their exposure to the outside, NEFA's tribal leaders began to speak up for their rights. In November 1962, when Rustomji met a group of tribal leaders at Ziro in NEFA, he was told that 'the tribal leaders of NEFA should be periodically called to Shillong for joint consultation regarding matters affecting the common interest of NEFA at this time of crisis'.[301] Such a wish might not have been granted, but this did not stop the people of

NEFA from articulating their political aspirations similar to their counterparts elsewhere in India.

The political history of Assam, illustrated by the events of this chapter and the next, presents one sort of frontier in a tournament of frontiers. Most importantly, the war made the integration of NEFA with Assam unlikely, even while Assam increasingly recognized its dependence on NEFA for resources, including hydropower and timber, which were key to its development.

# 8

# Unfolding Crises in the Highlands

Among the hill districts of Assam was the Mizo hills district (known as Lushai Hills District till 1954), which became a part of Assam province in 1898, but like some others was excluded from direct administration.¹ At Independence, the Mizos were divided about their future links with India. Some preferred to become part of a Crown colony, as discussed in Chapter 1, which they thought would help them become an independent state.² Others wanted to be part of Burma,³ while another faction championed the cause of joining India, being influenced by the Mizo Union, a political organization formed in 1946, which dreamt of shaking off colonial rule and, more importantly, the power of the Lushai chiefs from the Mizo hills. The colonial officials generally considered this party to be fascist in nature.⁴ Defying all speculation, the region remained with India at Independence, 'leading to intense local frustration' among the opponents, with no echo of Independence Day celebrations in the Mizo hills.⁵ Like the Naga National Council, the Mizo Union clarified that they would review their plan to stay with or secede from India after 10 years.⁶ Early in 1949, the discontented Mizos, under the leadership of the Mizo Union, organized a 'civil disobedience movement' which shattered months of calm. A worried Indian government rushed N.K. Rustomji, the advisor to the Assam Governor, to Aizawl, but he merely blamed the communists as being the 'inspiration behind the movement'.⁷ The government enhanced the presence of troops in these hilly areas in the next few months.

When the Indian Constitution was adopted in January 1950, the provisions of its Sixth Schedule were extended to the Mizo hills. The Mizo District Council began to function in 1952, with legislative and executive powers.[8] The district's southern region of Pawi and Lakher continued to enjoy autonomy till another council was inaugurated a year later. More political changes came thereafter when the Assam government, drawing on the popular support of a new generation of urban elite, transferred the powers of the 259 traditional chiefs to village courts.[9] The district—with a mainly rural population of 250,000 in 1961—had a 44 per cent literacy rate, the highest among all districts of Assam. Still, the Mizos did not find any significant share in government jobs. Mizo students were expected to learn the history of Assam broadly framed through the lens of Sir Edward Gait's 1906 volume, where accounts related to the Mizos formed only a tiny part of the larger narrative.[10] As a result, the best-catalogued instance of resentment felt by hill residents against the Assam (and Indian) government was that of the Mizos. On different occasions, Mizo leaders sought support from the Union government to improve their people's living standards.[11]

~

During 1958–59, a severe famine, called *Mautam* in Mizo, gripped this hills district. Most accounts agree that it led to the loss of 5 per cent of the Mizo population.[12] The scarcity of food had been foretold—this catastrophe, repeated every half century or so, was occasioned by a peculiar environmental phenomenon also experienced in other parts of the world.[13] Like the Assam hills, the Mizo hills, too, were gifted with many varieties of bamboo. Bamboo-based culinary practices were widely prevalent. One of the varieties of bamboo—*Melocanna baccifera*, called *mau* or *mautak* in Mizo—witnesses mass synchronous flowering and fruiting, followed by death, every half a century. The fruits contain pear-shaped, avocado-like, green, fleshy seeds that are rich in protein. The *mautak* is a 'running' bamboo, unlike the 'clumping' species, with an extraordinary ability to reproduce and grow, and it produces more than 84 tonnes of fruit per hectare.[14] The plant's rhizomes—underground horizontal stems—help its roots to spread rapidly, intertwining beneath the steep slopes on which the bamboo grows. The shoots mature in a little more than 60 days and form groves that expand quickly—each grove could cover up to 1800 sq. kilometres. The protein-rich seeds of the *mautak* are devoured by wild rats, especially the black rat (*Rattus rattus brunneusculus*), which is the dominant species of rodent in these hills.[15] The plentiful supply of seeds ensures an explosion of the rat population—a single pair of rats producing 14,000 offspring annually.[16] Once the flowering ends and the bamboo dies, these millions of rats begin to attack stocks of grain, mainly rice, leading to a ruthless famine. The Mizos, traditional jhum cultivators, did not produce a significant surplus of grain, and their stocks tended to be fairly lean.[17]

The Mizo hills were virtually in the grip of flowering bamboo of different species and consequent localised famines. With the area's geography standing in the way, India's colonial forestry could not inflict much harm on the bamboo forests of the Mizo hills, unlike elsewhere in the world—similar forests in Japan, for example, were converted into agricultural lands, wiping out species of bamboo that caused rat swarms in the nineteenth century. In 1951, some Mizo elders, many of whom had experienced the 1911 *mautam*, formed an Anti-Famine Campaign Organisation.[18] 'We taught the women to grow more food, and to cook only sufficient food to eat, and save the rest,' recounted a Mizo elder.[19] In February 1956, the Aizawl-based organization forewarned the government about the impending *mautam*. They calculated that the periodic dying of the *muli* bamboo would take place next in 1960, which would be followed by the explosion of the rat population, which would 'eat up the rice crops and cause famine'.[20] While some argued that the plague was the curse of god and any preparation to meet this challenge would be fruitless, the Anti-Famine Campaign resolutely opposed superstition and instead informed people of facts about the famine and of the need to control the rat population.

As bamboo flowering began to spread in 1954, the Anti-Famine Campaign Organisation advised the Assam government on preparedness.[21] They suggested elaborate schemes, including improving transport systems and crop diversification. They also conducted experiments to understand the nature of rat population growth and its relationship to bamboo flowering.[22]

The Mizo press began reporting a localized food shortage in 1955 following a poor harvest the previous year.[23] Some groups of people living in the Mizo hills bordering Myanmar had already threatened to emigrate to the neighbouring country if no relief was forthcoming from the Assam government.[24] These developments alerted the local government officials to the crisis ahead. Official preparations to face the famine began at the local level in 1956. K.G. Iyer, the deputy commissioner of the Mizo hills district, alerting his seniors in Shillong, sought to employ a plant-protection officer and suggested a rat-killing campaign, with a reward of Rs 5 for killing 100 rats and showing their tails as proof.[25] The use of pesticides, such as zinc phosphide, was also advised; posters about these pesticides were distributed. A popular essay on pesticides in the American magazine *Reader's Digest* significantly influenced and shaped the official view.[26] Some parts of neighbouring Manipur had experienced famine due to the depredations of rats; detailed inputs came from the official mycologist there. Officials in the Mizo hills sought further advice from Gauhati University and the Dehradun-based Forest Research Institute. There was broad agreement on the methods to control both rats as well as bamboo flowering.[27] Officials also briefed the touring agriculture minister of Assam about the need to kill rats and destroy bamboo flowers, noting that the apprehended severity of the famine might be lessened by such measures.[28]

The prices of foodstuff began to rise in 1957. In 1958, a Mizo lawmaker authored a detailed report on the need for a famine-relief scheme, road construction and extensive publicity. He stressed that Chaliha's announcement of 1958—that no Mizos would be allowed to starve—would require effective implementation.[29] He pointed out the utmost necessity for the Assam government to distribute a certain quantity of free rice, even if it was costly; further, every Mizo should

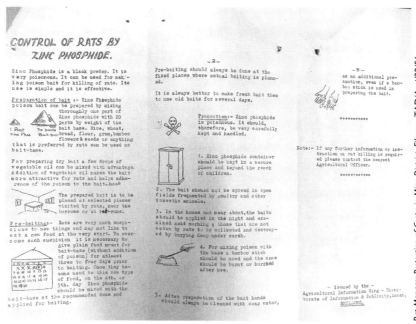

Rat control campaign in Mizo Hills with the use of zinc phosphide by the Assam government

be given the opportunity to earn so that they could buy more rice at a subsidized price.

The prediction of the elders came true only too soon. *Mautam* was flowering everywhere in the Mizo hills by 1958. It coincided with the killing of sparrows by the Chinese, and so, along with the increasing rat population, the higher numbers of locusts and grasshoppers also attacked crops. In May 1958, rat-killing was in full swing, but the food crisis was now apparent. Villagers constructed storage places for rice. The new deputy commissioner proposed that the Mizos should be encouraged to grow maize, potato and *kochu* (taro) as substitutes for rice.[30] In the next few months, rat-killing acquired momentum: 'We used traps and poison—zinc phosphide—and the government paid a bounty of 20 paise for each rat's tail the villagers brought in.'[31] But early in the following year, it was evident that these efforts had failed, as rats began to attack the food stores.[32] In 1959, rats were rampant wherever there was *mautam*.

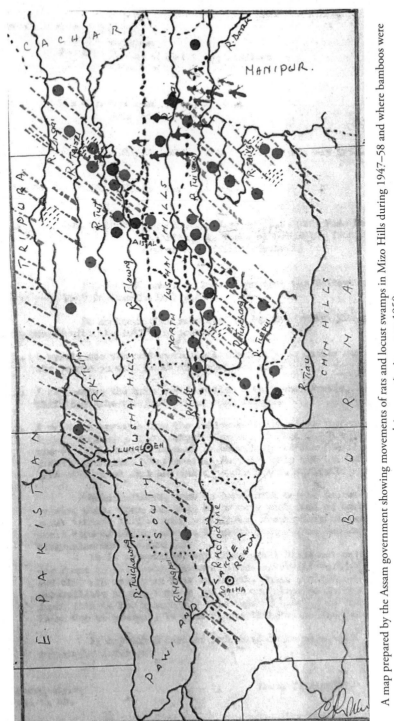

A map prepared by the Assam government showing movements of rats and locust swamps in Mizo Hills during 1947–58 and where bamboos were dying, continuing up to 1958

*Rat Menace: Protection of Crops in Mizo District*, File no. TAD/Agri/22/56, Tribal Areas Department, Agriculture Branch, 1956, Assam State Archives

The government functionaries in Shillong remained largely unaware of this distinctive ecological phenomenon and ignored the experience and forewarning of elders; senior officials scoffed at such warnings as 'superstitious fear'.[33] Meanwhile, the rat population multiplied. Adding to the concerns of Mizos, a plant protection section was removed from the Lushai hills on the understanding that rats were no longer a menace there, inviting the wrath of the Eastern India Tribal Union.[34] A delegation of Mizos met personnel from the Assam administration, who 'sent the deputation back with a warning not to listen to fairy tales'.[35] Unlike villages in the Gangetic basin, settlements in the Lushai hills were 'cut off from each other by deep valleys filled [with] bamboo jungles'.[36]

The connection between rats and the flowering of bamboo had been suggested earlier too, but even then, the government had hardly taken any note.[37] The Assam government dismissed all news of starvation deaths as 'absolutely baseless'.[38] In earlier famines since the late nineteenth century, however, the distressed Mizos had received moderate relief through the combined efforts of the British government and missionaries. This relief helped in part to create a more compassionate image of the colonial government, which was otherwise seen as cruel and hostile to the Mizos.

Drawing from experience, the Mizos had been preparing for the impending crisis. While the Anti-Famine Campaign Organisation had intimated government officials, the Mizo District Council, the legislative body of the Mizo district, had sought a paltry sum of Rs 1.5 million as aid. But the Assam government rejected the concerns as unscientific, dismissing any possible connection between bamboo flowering, the rodent population and famine. A year later in February 1960, as reports of deaths began appearing in newspapers, the Indian government dashed rice supplies by plane and jeep into the Mizo district.[39] Hungry Mizos looted trucks carrying rice from the plains of Assam to Aizawl.[40] A team of Assamese lawmakers—though still unable to see the connection between bamboo flowering and famine—visited the Mizo hills in March 1960, but, by then, it was too late.[41] Officially, arrangements to kill rats were put in place in early 1960. But the

French rat traps were not enough to curb the menace of the exploding rat population. Rat-killing squads were formed, the rodenticide zinc phosphide was distributed through village councils and fumigation of rat holes was undertaken.[42] Seeds and plants were distributed. However, as the monsoon arrived in the Mizo hills, the transportation system virtually collapsed. The Indian Air Force was roped in to drop food, but it could not stop the Mizos from dying of starvation. An official investigation suggested that an estimated 60,000 maunds of rice were required per month, and newspapers reported that 'The quantity of rice sent to the Mizo district was hardly sufficient to meet [the needs of] a fraction of its population'.[43]

Much of the early reluctance to accept the gravity of the situation and the collapse of food security was shaped by the Assamese official and political imagination and also a lack of empathy. The Assam government, which became proactive about the famine in the Mizo hills as late as 1960, came under criticism[44] and appealed to the people to donate freely to their starving neighbours.[45] Official reports were prepared and papers were put in order, but none of it could alleviate the situation. Crime increased as the Mizos battled hunger—the number of people who were convicted in criminal cases increased more than sixfold.[46]

The Mizo Union compelled the Chaliha government to distribute rice to villagers. Officials designated as the 'anti-rat squad' arrived from Jorhat. But seeds could not be distributed in the interiors due to the lack of roads. Of the approximately 1400 kilometres of official roads in the district in 1961, more than 52 per cent were bridle paths; mud tracks constituted the second-most common form of roads.[47] Hem Barua criticized the parliamentarians' lack of concern at the situation: 'People are dying there, and Members are laughing here.'[48] A delegation of the Mizo National Famine Front led by Laldenga met the Governor and the chief minister of Assam on 11 April and sought the setting up of relief camps.[49] While India had sufficient stocks of foodgrains, the Mizo hills lacked an effective transport system. Diplomatic negotiations began with the Burmese government to supply rice from their side. Some supplies were made through Chittagong in East Pakistan. Roads were improved and new ones were built, and a few grain storage buildings were constructed.[50] Hunger forced many to forage for food, but even though rats, part of the Mizo culinary tradition, were plentiful, the absence of rice could not be overcome. Many Mizos had abandoned jhum as they realized that their hard work would go in vain—an estimated half of the area remained fallow in 1959; there was a sudden rise—more than double—in the area officially categorized as forests.[51]

As the famine worsened, Defence Minister Krishna Menon and senior military officials flew over the Mizo district to supervise the airdropping of food. The food scarcity continued well into 1960. The flowering bamboos had died, and the decomposed bamboo groves could have provided excellent manure for a good harvest that year had not the monsoon, unfortunately, been excessive. Most rodents perished as they had no food.[52] Still, in the spring of 1960, the villagers in most places did not cultivate, fearing that rats would eat their crops. A journalist who took an early morning flight in an Indian Air Force Dakota saw 'the bare topped brown hills' which 'presented a gloomy sight with empty houses whose occupants had gone in search of food or work'.[53]

In the face of clamour for rice, Nehru, who believed the famine statistics were 'inappropriate' and had been told that 'there was plenty of fruits' there, exasperatedly wrote to Assam's Governor asking 'why should not fruits and vegetables or something else partly take the place of rice?'[54] A Mizo political delegation met Nehru on 15 July 1960.[55] They drew his attention to both the issues of famine and the rising demand for making Assamese the official language of the state.

Not only were the Assam government's relief efforts half-hearted, but the Union government also remained insensitive to the crisis. An adjournment motion on the Mizo famine moved by the socialist party, including Hem Barua, was not allowed in the Parliament on grounds of lack of evidence. Nehru's response added to the bitterness: 'We should be little chary in accepting these reports from people who are naturally excited about the situation.' Not only was he 'astonished to find the rate at which so-called relief was given there', but he was also sure that the quantity was very big and was more than the normal ration in a "healthy" time when there was rationing ... The real difficulty is not lack of food but the inaccessibility of some particular areas, not of the whole area. The area affected is large; much of it can be reached, but there are certain small parts there which are very difficult of access. Of course, they are being reached, but it is not very easy to reach them.[56]

Writing to Nehru, Assam's finance minister described the 'costly nature of the relief operations ... inaccessible hilly area ... inadequate nature of the state's resources'.[57] Unfortunately, for the next couple of years, the Mizo farmers' crops did not fare well due to forest fires or insect attacks, and starvation deaths continued to be reported till 1963.[58]

While governments remained insensitive, hungry Mizos were supported by the Anti-Famine Campaign Organisation (formed in 1951) and the Mizo Cultural Society (MCS), patronized by the Mizo elites, including government employees. The MCS was outspoken about the Assam government's apathy. One of the participants in the activities of MCS was Laldenga (1927–90), an employee of the Mizo District Council, who was sacked from his job after he participated in an anti-government rally in 1959.[59] Earlier, Laldenga worked as a soldier in the Indian Army. As MCS took to famine-relief works, it changed its name to reflect its objectives, first becoming the Mautam Front in March 1960 and then the Mizo National Famine Front. This rechristening evidently implied the political determination of the Mizos to confront the ineptitude of the Assam government. In 1961, the Mizo National Famine Front, which drew on support from all sections of Mizo society, metamorphosed into the Mizo National Front (MNF), a political party with the goal of self-determination. The MNF soon outpaced the Mizo Union electorally.[60]

Fuelled by the scarcity of food, Mizo political unrest snowballed into an issue the handling of which was beyond the capacity of the Assamese political system, which was already battling challenges in the Naga hills and NEFA and was yet to recover from the trauma of the riots of 1960. In 1960, an estimated 30,000 Indian soldiers were stationed in the Naga hills district alone to tackle the insurgency.[61]

If the earthquake of 1950 had facilitated the intrusion of the Indian state into NEFA, the famine of 1959 alienated the Mizo district from the state machinery of Assam. As the famine relief programme failed, the Mizo Union, which controlled the district council, decided to break away from the Congress.[62] Of the district's three lawmakers in the Assam Legislative Assembly, two belonged to the Mizo Union; they resigned. In October 1962, seven of the 11 legislators of the hill districts elected under the banner of Hill Leaders' Conference resigned to pressure the government on the demand for a separate state. Increasingly, the Mizo people gave voice to the idea of independence for the Mizo hills, which made the government uneasy.[63]

Assam's aggressive language policy had also caused anxiety among the Mizos, and matters reached a head when the Assam government passed The Assam Official Language Act of 1960, which made Assamese the official language.[64] In 1947, many Mizos had dreamt of independence; they increasingly began to regret the decision to stay with India and clamoured for separation from Assam, either as a 'hill state' or as a sovereign country. The Indian press warned the government to pay serious attention to the Mizo crisis 'unless it want[ed] to risk another Naga-type problem on its hands'.[65] A section of unhappy Mizos formed the United Chinland Organisation and called for a separate Chin state spread across adjoining parts of the Mizo hills, including areas in Burma and East Pakistan, and uprooted border demarcation pillars and other identification marks between India and Burma.[66] The construction of a hydropower dam on the river Karnaphuli in East Pakistan in 1962 angered both the Indian government and the Mizos.[67] By 1963, the 'growing independence movement' in the Mizo hills was fairly well known in diplomatic circles,[68] and the Indian government recognized that the Mizo hills were receiving aid from Pakistan.[69] It refused to follow the Naga model of negotiation, even as church leaders sought talks.

The demand for Mizo independence was an unsettling turn of events for the Union government.[70] The Union home secretary arrived in Shillong in October 1962 to take stock of the situation. In the same month, Chaliha wrote to Nehru saying that despite the Mizo district having the highest literacy rate in Assam, it was 'underdeveloped in all respects'. The Assam chief minister placed before the prime minister several proposals for the future of the district, one of them being the withdrawal of the military from the district.[71] Nehru agreed with Chaliha's opinion, and he advised Shastri and Menon, his two key cabinet colleagues, to act accordingly.[72] Both Chaliha and Nehru underestimated the strength of the undercurrent. Nehru told Menon that the Mizo demand for independence 'is not strong at present'. A mutiny among the Mizos in the Assam Regiment in Kashmir was quickly controlled,[73] the unit disbanded and the mutineers imprisoned. In 1963, as the political situation in the Mizo hills deteriorated, Chaliha and Nehru sought to grant clemency to the mutineers, but this was opposed by the Indian defence establishment.

In the next couple of years, the MNF reached out to greater numbers of Mizos and consolidated its organizational structure. Buoyed by this success, it began to plan for a Government of Mizoram (*Mizo Sawrkar*) and drafted a constitution in 1965, which clearly laid down the road map for the future governance of Mizoram.[74] The MNF, learning from the example of Nagaland, was increasingly convinced that powerful defiance of the Indian state would bring them results. In 1965, in a memorandum to Prime Minister Lal Bahadur Shastri, the MNF made it known that the Mizos 'refuse to occupy a place within India as they consider it to be unworthy of their dignity and harmful to the interest of the posterity'.[75] The MNF also told the Indian Prime Minister that 'nationalism and patriotism inspired by the political consciousness has now reached its maturity and the cry for political self-determination is the only wish and aspiration of the people'. They reached out to American and British diplomats for support but without any success.[76] Meanwhile, the Mizo and Assamese leaders drifted further apart. The Mizo hill branch of the Eastern India Tribal Union terminated its association with the Assam government in the mid-1960s for the latter's failure to handle the food crisis.[77]

~

> Tribals, numbering 28 lakhs, are destined to play a decisive role in the political life of the multi-racial state of Assam . . . But they are ill equipped for the new role cast for them . . . Each tribe lives in a world of its own, sealed off against outside social and political influences and currents until recently. They are also deeply suspicious and distrustful of the Assamese of the plains now ruling over the State. The Congress had done very little by way of organisational work or welfare activity amongst them to earn their allegiance. Now the tribes will suddenly jump into the modern complex political life of a democracy, fast becoming conscious of their potential strength.[78]

This prediction from 1951 by an Indian journalist would play out in Assam's politics until the early 1970s. Immediately after Independence, Chief Minister Bardoloi made many promises to the tribal population in Assam, including an assurance of equal rights and socialism.[79] But things began to unfold differently, even as the Indian Constitution envisaged six districts of Assam. Elections to autonomous councils—for the Naga, Lushai, Mikir, North Cachar, Garo, United Khasi and Jaintia Hill districts—were held in January 1952.[80] The autonomous councils encountered many challenges, and tribal elites viewed the actions of the Assam government with apprehension. Having spoken of the tribes in the Naga hills in the past chapter and those in the Mizo uplands in the preceding pages of this chapter, let us now turn to the simmering discontent in the hill closer to the state capital, Shillong.

The state government's attempts to claim revenue from coal and minerals invited the wrath of the Siems, the tribal chiefs. In the mid-1950s, the Assam government collected tax from mines, and this was a source of strong resentment among the Khasi mine owners,[81] who formed the United Khasi-Jaintia Hills Mineral Rights Committee to protest against this. The hill leaders reminded the Assam government that the Sixth Schedule of the Constitution 'granted special privileges to the autonomous districts with regard to minerals but the State government have violated these provisions'.[82] As demand for more cement factories in the Khasi hills intensified, owners of mines and cement factories began negotiations through the Tribal Union.[83] The

United Khasi and Jaintia Hill Districts Tribal Union boycotted the inauguration of the Umtru Hydroelectric Project in 1960. While the Assamese press welcomed this project on the Umtru river in present-day Meghalaya, the Khasis claimed that their land had been taken and that it would benefit only the plains of Assam.[84] The United Khasi and Jaintia Hills Districts Tribal Union wanted to make the powers under the Sixth Schedule an issue in the district council elections. In 1954, the hill leaders gave organized expression to their political aspirations for a separate state within India before the State Reorganisation Committee.[85] The threat of imposition of Assamese in the hills, as discussed in Chapter 6, was looming large.[86] Three years later, in 1957, the Tribal Union swept the elections in the Garo, Khasi and Jaintia hills, the North Cachar hills and the Mizo hills.

In a time of mistrust and poor governance, the occasional state-sponsored initiative like the Hills–Plains Festival could not restore confidence. The second festival held in Shillong as part of the Republic Day celebrations in January 1954—the first had been held in 1947—drew crowds and performers from all communities, but it did not help to dissipate the unrest.[87] Efforts by the Assam government to initiate a literary prize for works on the tribes of Assam, and on themes like decentralization of state power in tribal areas, could not prevent the political landscape of the hills from being reshaped swiftly in response to The Assam Official Language Act of 1960. The angry and apprehensive tribal leaders formed the All Party Hill Leaders Conference (APHLC) in 1960 and sought separation from Assam.[88] The Indian government's announcement of making the Naga district a separate state gave the Mizos hope. An increased share of financial assistance for areas like NEFA, Nagaland and Tripura—which, respectively, received Rs 44, 61 and 36 per capita, compared with the Rs 28 per capita for Assam's hill areas during 1964–65—only strengthened the hill leaders' political conviction.

As discussed in Chapters 5 and 6, the Assam government made its opposition to a separate hill state known before the States Reorganisation Commission in 1954. The 'Government of Assam sees no case for any alteration of the present boundaries of the State', summed up Assam's memorandum before the commission.[89] In return, Assam promised not to 'interfere in any way with tribal rights and customs or to impose the language or culture of any other group of people'. The commission did not betray Assam. But as things moved differently and under new political circumstances, the demand for a separate hill state took a concrete form towards the end of 1960. In August 1960, the hill leaders submitted a lengthy memorandum to Nehru, and also to India's president, cataloguing their displeasure. At the top of the list was the issue of rousing slogans by the Assamese leaders that Assam was for those whose mother tongue was Assamese. The hill leaders pointedly expressed their anxiety that 'their existence as separate and distinct entities of Assam and India is being threatened with extinction'. 'There is no doubt that behind the proposal for declaring Assamese the official language of the State is the motive of the Assamese to assimilate all small tribal communities and to dominate other non-Assamese communities in the state,' they said.[90] For the hill leaders, the only solution was the formation of a separate hill state:

> It is clearly seen that the Hill people of the autonomous districts of Assam will never accept Assamese as the official language of the state now or at any time. On the other hand, it is appreciated that the Assamese community feels equally strong and has gone too far in its agitation to withdraw. The only solution, therefore, is to have a separation.[91]

The Union government had hoped that Chaliha, viewed by the hill leaders as liberal and sympathetic to their aspirations, would find a way to overcome the crisis. Chaliha's cabinet had a minister for tribal welfare, the prominent Garo leader Williamson Sangma. He, however, stayed in this post for a short period; the promulgation of the Language Act led to his resignation. The Assamese intelligentsia were yet to recover from the ghost of the British plan of the early 1940s to make Assam's hill districts a British protectorate separate from India, and they did not make more than token gestures which did not help. In 1961, when the Publication Board of Assam, as mentioned in Chapter 6, proposed to publish books in the Khasi language, the only Khasi member on the board made it clear that the Khasi people were against the idea.[92]

The hill leaders, who had met Nehru several times in Delhi and Shillong, continued to demand a separate state, but the Indian government, worried about further unsettling a politically precarious Assam, refused to give in. Writing to Nichols Roy, who by then was a significant voice in favour of a separate province, Nehru conveyed his opinion that a 'full-fledged state for the Hill areas was not practicable or feasible' and suggested alternatives for them to remain within Assam.[93] While the APHLC appeared amenable, they sought a more concrete plan from the Prime Minister.[94] Between 1960 and 1964, Nehru met the leaders of the APHLC six times, which helped give shape to the contours of political autonomy to the hill districts of Assam. When the APHLC delegates met Nehru on 17 May 1961, much of the discussion was centred around Assamese language, its hegemony and the general apathy of Assamese leaders towards the hills. They reiterated their apprehension about the imposition of the Assamese language. Nehru had to reassure them that 'it was for the hill people to decide the language at the district level and for the hill areas'.[95] He presumed that English would continue but would be replaced by Hindi over a period of time. Nehru recognized that 'an emotional feeling had arisen among the hill people to cut themselves off from Assam'. Many among them worried that unless they learnt Assamese, they would not be entitled to jobs, and this would make them 'second class citizens'.

The hill leaders met Nehru again in Shillong on 21 May 1961. On Assam's language policy, they remained adamant, and when Nehru argued that given the geographical situation, a *lingua franca* was needed, the hill leaders said that broken Hindi would be preferable to broken Assamese. They soon understood that Nehru was unwilling to give in to their demands. They were concerned about the environment in the government offices, where non-proficiency in Assamese would push the tribals to the margins. Rising numbers of educated tribal elite refused to bow to the pressure of the Assamese leadership; political leaders in the hill districts stressed that they had been 'taken advantage of unfairly by the people of the Brahmaputra valley'.[96] In a conciliatory move, Chaliha proposed compulsory learning of hill languages for officials in Assam.

As the war with the Chinese loomed on Assam's northern front, political mobilization for a separate state in the hills gained momentum. The Assam hills district sent only one member to Parliament and eight to the state assembly. A 'Demand Day' on 24 October 1962[97] was a spectacular success and showed the tribal leaders' increasing influence.[98] The general elections in February 1962 had been a key point of consolidation: the APHLC, which contested the elections on the issue of a separate state, had again swept the polls.

As the Naga political experiment resulted in some gains, other hill districts echoed demands for separation from Assam. Recovering from the brutal defeat at the hands of the Chinese and faced with increasing border disputes between East Pakistan and Assam, Nehru, though firm not to concede to the Mizo demand, offered to give more attention to their concerns through a separate wing of his government.[99] In October 1963, Nehru proposed a structure of autonomy, akin to the Scottish pattern of administration, though the plan was dropped eventually. The 'Scottish plan' would ensure that 'the state assembly would not be empowered to pass laws affecting hill areas until these were first examined and passed by representatives from the Hills'.[100] This effective veto power to the legislators of the hill areas on issues affecting their constituents had two clear objectives—maximum possible autonomy for the hills and the preservation of the idea of Assam.[101] A cabinet minister to look after the governance of the hills, a special wing within the Assam secretariat and the appointment of a special committee in the state assembly by the lawmakers from the hills were part of this plan. Nehru, among other things, promised a new hill university. Already existing fissures within the APHLC became more visible on the question of agreeing with Nehru's plan. When, to increase the pressure for a separate hill state, popular demands for the resignation of legislators grew, only seven of the 11 members elected in 1962 resigned.[102] There was growing uneasiness among a section of the Assamese as well.[103] Finally, Nehru's Scottish plan was rejected.

Nehru's death briefly halted these political processes, but his scheme to grant autonomy to the hill tribes was revived by his successor, Prime Minister Lal Bahadur Shastri, in March 1965. The following month, Shastri's government appointed a three-member commission chaired by Hari Vinayak Pataskar, who had been a member of the Constituent Assembly and was then the vice-chancellor of Poona University.[104] The commission was to detail a scheme which would confer 'a full measure of autonomy on the hill areas', while keeping Assam's territorial form intact. When the Pataskar Commission met the APHLC leaders, the latter made it abundantly clear that the future administration of the hill districts should be 'completely separate' from Assam, though they could share a governor, high court and legislative assembly. The APHLC summarized the mood of the hill people before the Pataskar Commission: 'By their many acts of omission and commission they [Assamese leaders] gradually destroyed the fund of goodwill and cooperative spirit which the attainment of independence had generated among the hill people.' Others did not disagree, as a newspaper observed: '[The] hill people's needs were never properly assessed, far less, proper remedies provided. On the contrary, their problems continued to be treated with callous indifference until the Government woke up one day to find things made too hot for it.'[105] The Assam government on its part was against the idea of an independent Mizo state on grounds of national security, but promised further economic development of the Mizo District, while the Mizo District Council boycotted the commission as they were adamant about separation from Assam.

After months of deliberations, the Pataskar Commission submitted its report in March 1966. While stating that economic discrepancies were at the root of the grievances in the hills, the commission did not agree that the hills were economically exploited; rather it reported that the relative contribution of the hill districts to the state revenue was lower in proportion to the population. It also stopped short of proposing any major political autonomy for the hill districts,[106] but it recommended a separate minister, a separate budget, a special commissioner and a development council for the hills.

Two months later in May 1966, the APHLC, which was largely confined to the Khasi and Jaintia hills, rejected the commission's report and called for political mobilization to seek a separate state. The hill leaders argued that, given the new circumstances, the recommendations of the report were 'no longer adequate to meet the situation that had emerged in the hill areas'.[107] By then, the Mizo and Naga crises had grown to present a serious political predicament.

For the Assamese intelligentsia, the report was a welcome relief. 'The wisest course for the Central Government would have been to accept the Pataskar Commission's recommendations and implement them, ignoring the opposition from the APHLC and the Assam Congress,' wrote Birendra Kumar Bhattacharya. The Assam Congress, strikingly absent as an organizational force in the hill areas and generally agreeing with the recommendations of the commission, tried to expand its sphere of influence.[108] After Shastri's death in January 1966, the inexperienced Indira Gandhi had taken over as the Prime Minister. Given her own precarious political situation, and in order to reach the widest political consensus, she formed a Cabinet Committee in June 1966.[109] After weeks of parleying, this committee proposed an idea of a sub-state comprising the hill districts of Assam. There was no such provision in the Indian Constitution, and a constitutional amendment would be required. The hill leaders pointed out that this scheme, given the influence enjoyed by the Assam cabinet and legislature in certain areas, would further enable the domination of the plains over the hills.

In the first weeks of January 1967, the hill leaders intensified their demand for a separate state and began intense lobbying in Delhi.[110] Soon afterwards, the Indian government signalled the formation of a separate hill state, which was to be carved out from the hill districts of Assam. After three days of intense negotiations, ahead of Assamese new year celebrations, Union Home Minister Y. B. Chavan announced, on 13 January 1967, a plan for further reorganization of Assam based on a federal basis.[111] 'Bearing in mind the geography and the imperative needs of security', a regional federation was proposed, composed of 'federating units having an equal status not subordinate to one another'.[112] The units would have their own legislative assemblies and councils of ministers. The federation would have control over subjects of common interest. The Union government thought that all the regions of the North-east would join this federation.

The 13 January proposal was greeted by the tribal population largely as a concession to their demand for a separate hill state. As the hill leaders arrived in Guwahati on their way to Shillong, thousands lined the streets to welcome them.[113] But the proposal sparked opposition from Assamese leaders,[114] many of whom organized themselves on a common platform. A leading public figure termed it an 'unconstitutional declaration',[115] while a celebrated Assamese author denounced it as *Kalanemir Lanka Sambad*—a pointless futuristic proposition.[116] The Assamese elite feared losing Shillong. After Assam's hopes of NEFA's integration with the state were dashed, this came as another shocker. There was also increasing hostility along the Assam–Nagaland border. *Dainik Asam* warned of grim days ahead for Assam and invited its readers to write in expressing disapproval.[117] 'Assam will soon be in the thick of trouble,' the *Times of India* accurately predicted.[118] Chaliha's rivals within the Congress lost no opportunity to challenge him, and the party, riven by mistrust and suspicion, failed to show a spirit of accommodation in that hour of crisis.[119] The angry Congress leadership in Assam [120] shot off a tersely worded letter to the Union home minister: 'Assam Pradesh Congress Committee sits today facing an explosive situation caused by the Union government,' their letter began.[121]

The communist parties—the CPI had recently experienced an ideological split—extended their support for a separate dispensation for the hill districts.[122] In July 1967, Bengali speakers in Cachar expressed their wish to be part of the proposed separate political entity within this federation.[123] The APHLC wanted one unit for all the hill regions, though the Mizo union was in no mood to agree to such a demand.[124]

Thus, the re-creation of Assam's political geography was foregrounded in intense political turmoil. *The New York Times* summed up the anger of the hill people: 'The hill people have contended that they were being exploited by the Assamese majority, who they said, sought to impose their culture and language on them.'[125] Amidst the turmoil came the elections of February 1967, which proved to be a psychological setback for the Congress.[126] Though the Congress secured 73 of the 125 seats in the legislative assembly, this was a significant drop from 1962; and its vote share declined by almost 5 per cent. The Muslim majority areas also saw a decline in Congress success, as Muslim voters, who felt threatened following the deportation of East Pakistanis, tilted towards the communist candidates. Although it won the Mikir hill seats, the Congress was now increasingly seen as dominated by higher castes; it also lost its popularity among the tribal and SC seats in the plains. The APHLC leaders, armed with concessions that seemed to promise some sort of 'equality of status', won all the seats in the Khasi-Jaintia-Garo (KJG) hills. The Congress's political reach in the hills was curtailed by the increasing popularity and influence of the APHLC.

There were several reasons for the Congress's significant loss of popularity in the 1967 state legislative assembly elections. The food crisis of 1966 had seriously eroded its appeal among the urban rich. In its bid to control rising prices, the state government had antagonized business houses and grain traders by pressuring them not to hoard. Government employees, too, were unhappy. The often brutal deportation of Pakistani nationals, more on this in Chapter 9, had caused enormous anxiety among the Muslim population in Assam. Muslim lawmakers had sensed this undercurrent amongst their core electoral supporters, and a worried majority of them threatened to resign from the assembly in June 1965. When the elections took place two years later, the Congress's vote share in the Muslim constituencies declined significantly.[127] Its overall vote share dropped to 43 per cent from 48 per cent in 1962, and contemporary observers noted that this was due to a 'massive withdrawal of support' by the urban middle and lower middle classes, besides Muslim voters.[128]

The Congress's loss largely benefited the communist parties, but it also resulted in moderate gains among urban Hindu voters for the Bharatiya Jana Sangh, which until then had hardly been visible in Assam's electoral landscape despite having contested elections since 1952. Some members of the Jana Sangh were stalwarts in the Assamese cultural world, and the party's political ideas drew significantly from

Assamese cultural history. Scholars and writers like Tirtha Nath Sarma or Prasannalal Choudhury, both of whom contested the elections as Jana Sangh candidates, were charismatic and influential figures in Assamese public life. However, they did not make any major inroads; in the General Elections of 1967, Fakhruddin Ali Ahmed, the future president of India (1974–77), defeated Prasannalal Choudhury in the largely Hindu-dominated seat of Barpeta by a sizeable margin.[129]

The Hindu religious reformist movements, which had since the 1930s gained strength in many parts of northern India,[130] found only moderate resonance in Assam.[131] The mid-1960s also witnessed the rise of the organizational presence of the Vishwa Hindu Parishad (VHP) in the North-east. On the invitation of Shivram Shankar Apte, one of the founders and the first general secretary of the VHP, Hem Chandra Dev Goswami, the Satradhikar (head monk) of the renowned monastery Auniati Satra, participated in the Kumbh Mela of 1966 in Allahabad and also attended the conference of the VHP, where he introduced the audience to the world of Assamese Vaishnavism.[132] The VHP's Assam unit was formed soon thereafter in 1967, and more branches were opened in places mainly populated by Bengali Hindus.[133] The Satradhikar played a key role in the expansion of the VHP's organizational influence. Others from Assam's cultural and literary fields also joined the organization. Several members of the Congress too maintained close relations with the Hindu Mahasabha's office-bearers.[134] Despite this, the Mahasabha could not secure a distinct space in Assam's political life well into the 1960s.

The electoral setback did not stop Prime Minister Indira Gandhi from supporting the cause of the hill leaders. She did not want this stalemate to linger, having successfully passed the Punjab Reorganisation Act, 1966.[135] Several rounds of negotiations took place in the summer of 1967, mostly in Delhi. As Mrs Gandhi backed the reorganization of Assam, the Chaliha-led Congress in Assam opposed it and found support from Morarji Desai, her deputy.[136] The communist parties extended their ideological support to Mrs Gandhi's political standpoint. A contemporary observer noted that the problem of reorganization served as a weapon for her adversaries—'a good stick to beat Mrs. Gandhi with'.[137] In mid-June 1967, several Assamese Congress lawmakers, led by the former chief minister, Bishnu Ram Medhi, rushed to Delhi to make their opinions heard.[138] They cited national security as one of the reasons for their opposition. By now, the idea of a federation had collapsed, and Assam was heading towards further fragmentation.

On 8 and 9 July, as floods swept through Assam, more negotiations took place in Delhi—joined by political leaders of Assam from across party lines, much to the chagrin of the Assamese public.[139] Union Planning Minister Ashok Mehta headed a committee of 11 parliamentarians to sort out the nitty-gritty of the proposed reorganization. As the committee continued to negotiate, a furious APHLC hardened its stance on complete separation from Assam. In Shillong, school buses carried flags of the proposed hill state.[140] Persuaded by Delhi, the Assam Congress, based in part on the Pataskar Commission's recommendations, agreed to grant concessions to the hills but refused to concede any legislative power. Back in Assam, the hill leaders intensified their campaign for a separate state and threatened, but stopped short of launching, 'direct action'.[141] On 30 August 1967, much to the relief of the Assamese leaders, the Mehta Committee submitted its report, rejecting the federal reorganization of Assam and proposing more autonomy—in the form of an autonomous state within Assam, i.e., a 'sub-state'—to the hill districts.[142] The committee's negotiations had ended calamitously,[143] and its recommendations were described by hill leaders as 'both facile and meaningless'.[144] As political differences widened, Mrs Gandhi, weighed down by the severe food crisis and by the Naxalite peasant insurgency in West Bengal, allowed matters in Assam to take their own course for a few months. On 28 December 1967, on a trip to NEFA, Mrs Gandhi declared in Jorhat her government's willingness to concede the hill leaders' demand at the earliest. Any political move to reorganize Assam would require a Constitutional Amendment; as the Congress did not have the required strength in Parliament, Mrs Gandhi began consultations with Opposition parties to secure a consensus.[145]

~

The demand for smaller states in the tribal-dominated areas of India became increasingly loud as the 1960s progressed. Support came from the towering Indian sociologist M.N. Srinivas, among others.[146] The residents of the Assam hill districts had long felt grievances against the Assam government and had written in 1954 to the States Reorganisation Commission seeking spatial reorganization according to ethnic affiliations. A letter from the Mizo hills made known that 'the Assamese people are popularly regarded as bent on imposing their will on the non-Assamese population'.[147] But the commission, advocating the views of the larger states, said that the smaller areas, while requiring the 'fullest consideration', must remain subordinated to 'larger national interests'. The birth of Nagaland in December 1963, and the developments with regard to NEFA, had left Assam with four other hill districts with a population of 1.3 million. Many termed the reorganization as the 'balkanization' of Assam, but the liberal Assamese scholar and novelist Birendra Kumar Bhattacharya wrote, 'The Assamese people will not stand in the way of the Hills tribes achieving their legitimate ambitions.' The eminent author argued that the unhappiness of the hill residents was due to the 'chauvinistic elements' of Assamese society.[148] While he conceded that a growing number of the Assamese increasingly viewed 'the problem of tribal autonomy with earnestness', Bhattacharya appealed for closer rapport between the leaders of the hills and the plains, as well as for lifting of restrictions on social and political intercourse between the hills and the plains.

~

So what ailed Assam's hill districts? In 1960–61, the per capita earnings of residents in these areas were far lower than the other non-hill districts, and it was even worse for the tribal residents.[149] An official enquiry committee agreed in 1966 that Assam's hill districts faced 'acute economic and social problems', which had assumed 'the shape of a political problem of considerable magnitude and complexity'.[150] Apart from the insufficiency of finances allotted for the development in these areas, a significant issue was that of language. In the 1950s, given their high literacy rates and fluency in English, many from the hill areas were preferred in government jobs. White collar jobs also went to the Bengali-speaking population, especially in areas where the public sector had a bigger role to play. This worried the Assamese, and the suggestion that Assamese be made the official language was partly an offshoot of this. As passionate political debates about Assam's reorganization raged, the Asam Sahitya Sabha demanded in mid-1967 that Assam's universities use Assamese as the medium of instruction.[151]

If the Assamese intelligentsia and its leaders insisted on the Assamese language as the glue to unify diverse ethnic groups, which would in turn help in the territorial unity of Assam, others stressed on its untenability. The latter pointed out that Assamese was spoken by less than 1 per cent of the people inhabiting the four hill districts.[152] Their tribal-ness did not bind them together, and the geography stood against any chance of homogeneity. One observer noted that the hill districts 'are like small rooms opening off a central corridor, but with no interconnecting doors'.[153] C.P. Cook, a young research student from Oxford writing for *World Today* in 1968, pointed out that 'the state of Assam, with its capital at Shillong, is in fact a unity in name only: there is a world of difference between the Assamese of the Brahmaputra valley or the thriving commercial town of Gauhati and the many tribes of the inaccessible southern hill districts'.[154] In this context, the Assam Official Language Act of 1960 acted as a prohibitive measure for the hill residents. The Soviet policy of making Russian the national language eventually helped in the creation of many independent nations; the experiment in Assam began to unfold in a somewhat similar way.[155]

Except for the United Mikir and North Cachar hills, the four hill districts were predominantly Christian.[156] If the Mizo hills had the highest Christian population at 86 per cent according to the 1961 Census, one-third of the Garo hills' population were followers of Christianity. In these districts, even those who were not part of the dominant religious faith had a great affinity with their Christian community members. There was a significant increase in conversions to Christianity following World War II—67 per cent between 1951 and 1961—in the hills, especially among the Nagas. This was a result of a combination of factors—besides education and healthcare facilities that continued to be provided by the missionaries, there was a war-induced breaking-down of tribal microcosms, and the Christian missionaries were successful in co-opting indigenous religious practices rather than being antagonistic towards them.[157] The complex tribal languages found a new lease of life when the missionaries introduced the use of the Roman alphabet and published translations of Christian literature in these languages. Christianity was surely a force that brought structural changes in the hill society, serving as a vehicle for a stronger tribal identity and also creating a broad cultural unity.

The Assamese intelligentsia believed that Christianity was the root cause of the alienation of the hill people from Assam. 'Christianity means for a large section of westernised highlanders a gateway to a civilisation supposed to be superior to India,' wrote Birendra Kumar Bhattacharya in 1967.[158] From the late 1950s, church leaders also began to play a proactive role in hill politics, and the Indian government often allowed them to mediate in disagreements, which worried the Assamese Hindu leaders. Meanwhile, the Nagaland Peace Mission, a civil society initiative which came into existence in 1964 with support from the Indian government, was discontinued in May 1966.[159] Reverend Michael Scott, a British citizen and a key member of the mission, who had earlier been involved in South Africa's anti-racial movement and the anti-nuclear-weapon movement in Britain, was expelled from India. During Phizo's years of exile in London, Scott had played a key role in getting 'public opinion in Britain interested in the Naga problem',[160] and he continued to write regularly in the British newspapers on the subject.[161] His writings were seen by the Indian government as 'prejudicial propaganda'.

The hill districts, as we have seen, had suffered due to the closing of transport systems following Partition. The animated trade linkages of the Mizo hills through the waterways with Chittagong port in East Pakistan disappeared. Despite some political initiatives of the Assam government in the post-Partition years, these broken transport linkages could not be revived. The construction of roads, with the exception of village roads, in the hills hardly witnessed any progress after 1950. The flourishing trade in cotton, lac and timber collapsed. Everyday supplies to the interiors of the hills dried up.[162] Exploitation of mineral deposits—limestone in the Khasi reserves or coal in the Garo hills—suffered similarly. With the collapse of the transport system, the mineral trade, too, declined.

The Assam government's record of improving the general economic situation of the hill districts was appalling. A comparison of the per capita expenditure in the plains and hills illustrates this.[163] During 1952–53, these figures were Rs 6.3 and Rs 0.02, and in 1960–61, Rs 5.26 and Rs 2.11 for the plains and hills respectively. The political crisis in the Naga hills compelled the government to moderately enhance the expenditure in the hills, and during 1963–64, the figures stood at Rs 6.65 and Rs 5.34. The per capita income in the plains in 1962–63 was 40 per cent higher than in 1950–51, while the improvement registered by the hill districts during the same period was approximately 4 per cent. The actual per capita incomes for 1962–63 were Rs 301 in the hills and Rs 345 in the plains.[164] If the government revenue earnings from the hills were low, so was the per capita expenditure; compared to Rs 407 in NEFA, only Rs 70 was spent per capita during the Third Five-Year Plan in the hill districts. Despite such acute economic discrepancies, the hills did not fare badly in improving its educational and health facilities, though some of the groundwork for this had already been done by the Christian missionaries. There were 77 hospital beds for every 1,00,000 people in the hills, as against 35 in the plains.[165] Equally striking was the increase in the size of the school-going population and the number of educational institutions. Between 1950–51 and 1963–64, there was a 200 per cent increase in primary schools in the hills, compared to only 59 per cent in the plains. A larger proportion of children of school-going age in the hills were attending primary school than in the plains.

Along with the developing political and cultural binaries between the plains and the hills, a differential economic development model was also taking shape. Many saw serious flaws in this and advised that an integrated plains and hills economic cooperation model held promise.¹⁶⁶ 'Assam would achieve little advantage by organising planning in terms of the two regions, namely, hills and plains,' wrote an economist in 1966.¹⁶⁷ A majority of the Assamese intelligentsia considered the idea of the Sixth Schedule of the Indian Constitution as detrimental to the well-being of the hill population and as one that prevented its integration with the Indian ethos.¹⁶⁸

~

The Mizo dream of political sovereignty took a militant form in 1966. By then, the MNF, with approximately 10,000 members, was well developed and organized, with well-trained, armed volunteers forming its military wing—the Mizo National Army. Hundreds of MNF rebels—some news agencies claimed there were 10,000 of them—had returned from training in East Pakistan weeks earlier.¹⁶⁹ The MNF decided to defy the Indian government and launch an offensive called Operation Jericho.¹⁷⁰ Just weeks after Mrs Gandhi was sworn in as India's third Prime Minister, the government suffered a shock when Mizo rebels raided the treasury and the telephone exchange at Aizawl and overran a security post on the night of 28 February,¹⁷¹ then occupied the main towns and declared independence from India.¹⁷² Except for the police wireless, all systems of communication between the Mizo district and the rest of Assam were snapped by the rebels. The next day, the Union government declared the Mizo district a disturbed area, which allowed the deployment of the military in the aid of the civil administration. Indian troops moved into the district soon after. They cleared roadblocks and repaired bridges. The Mizo rebels declared independence¹⁷³ and made it known that 'India is unworthy and unfit to rule . . . the civilized Mizo people'.¹⁷⁴ The rebels had largely incapacitated road networks, and most areas except for Aizawl were out of reach of the Indian state. More than a hundred officials, including an MNF legislator, were kidnapped.¹⁷⁵ Motor cars were captured. An East Pakistan-based rebel-owned radio station—which aired news bulletins in Mizo—announced that they had captured the interiors and had declared independence.¹⁷⁶ Some retired Mizo military personnel joined the rebels.[177] Mizos working in Shillong had apparently left for their home district days earlier.

The Indian government was outraged by the events. Home Minister G.L. Nanda, who described this incident as 'a campaign by misguided extremist elements in the Mizo National Front to back their demand for independence', made his intention clear, with the backing of Parliament—that he would not tolerate any 'defiance of authority'.[178] The Assam government also demanded stern action; Chaliha called the MNF traitors.[179] When Nanda, speaking in Parliament, said that the Mizo revolt would be 'stamped out', there were cheers. Nanda admitted that the Mizo rebels were receiving aid and training in East Pakistan.[180] An editorial in an Assamese daily called it a national shame and a challenge to national honour.[181] On 28 February itself, the Indian government had indicated that the MNF would be treated with a firm hand.[182]

The MNF continued their attacks for some days, and the Assam government admitted that large parts of the Mizo district were under the control of the rebels.[183] The rebels even broke open prisons and released MNF prisoners. As the situation worsened, the Assam and Union governments worked in tandem to deal with the crisis. The Indian Army, ferried by helicopters, began retaliating from 5 March.[184] Intense fighting between the rebels and the army continued for a few days. On 6 March, the Indian government declared that it had recovered Aizawl.[185] Both Mrs Gandhi and her home minister arrived in Guwahati. The MNF was disbanded, and Chaliha declared Laldenga a traitor.[186] An Assamese cartoon ridiculed the Indian state for falling into a trap orchestrated by the intricate rhythm of the popular 'bamboo dance' of the Mizos.[187]

The Indian Army had been taken unawares by the situation. Lieutenant General Sam Manekshaw, then the general officer commanding-in-chief, Eastern Command of the Indian Army, admitted in June 1966 in Calcutta: 'We were caught with our pants down.'[188] The strong reprisal by the Indian forces shocked the Mizo rebels,[189] as towns and villages of the Mizo hills were bombed.[190] Little was known in the rest of the country about the gravity of the situation. An Assamese newspaper sketchily hinted at a retaliatory air strike by the air force.[191] While Indians remained largely unaware of the air strikes in the Mizo district, the crisis drew global attention. A letter sent by the Mizo Underground Government was published in the London *Times*, which described how the Indian Army and the Air Force had tormented a remote and tiny Indian township. Military strikes in the Mizo hills received widespread publicity in the British press. The foreign secretary of the Mizo rebel government, C.L. Hminga, wrote, 'Mizo people are not such kind of people to submit under the Indian suppressive measures. They are civilized and tough enough and they want nothing else but freedom from Indian rule.'[192] He shared the experience of the Mizos:

> Villages were burnt and villagers were threatened, closed, and their properties were destroyed . . . The regular troops of Indian army are fully armed and much larger in strength . . . the Indian Air Force used Mig21, Hunter, and Vampire jets which dropped bombs, rocketed, and strafed, indiscriminately over the military targets and civilian areas in the suburbs of the town, for three continuous days from 5 March, 1966. Over 195 bombs were dropped on Aizawl town alone. They strafed and rocketed the civilian areas in the suburbs of the town. The business centres in the town were completely gutted and the cost of the damage would not have been less than Rs 300 million or about 15 million pounds.[193]

The Indian historian Ashin Dasgupta, then at the University of Oxford, wrote to *The Times* to say how distressed he was to read this ghastly news. He wrote that a 'large number of people in India are willing and eager to understand the problems of their fellow citizens in the so-called tribal areas of Assam'.[194] Dasgupta told the Mizos that their situation was not unique: 'the citizens of my native city of Calcutta feel far more "exploited" than the villagers of any Mizo village.' In Dasgupta's view, the Mizos had taken a rash step:

> The singularly unfortunate decision by some Mizos was to rush to use arms and although, as Hminga points out, they used only

shotguns, rifles, and daggers, the government had no alternative but to deploy troops against the rebellion. In view of the threatening rains and the very difficult terrain, the army obviously wanted to complete the operations as quickly as possible. I wonder why it did not strike the rebel Mizos that this in fact would happen.

Dasgupta made it known that while there was a great deal of 'sympathy' for Assam's hill residents, 'the entire Indian nation is behind its Government when it comes to a question of rebellion. It is unfortunately a question of survival for India as well'. Days later, *The Times* published a letter from Phizo, then living in London, supporting the Mizos' and Nagas' right to independence: 'would not a secure frontier be better guaranteed by having a friendly neighbour than a people kept in subjugation by force of arms'.[195]

Life in the Mizo hills would not return to normal for the next two decades.[196] The Indian state's retaliation resulted in the rebels going underground, some crossing over to East Pakistan, where[197] they established their military headquarters in the Chittagong Hill Tracts.[198] The rebel government—*Mizo Sawrkar*—functioned from there for another few years. The Pakistani authorities, pursuing a policy of undermining India's administration of the North-east, provided the Mizo rebels with 'funds, arms, training, and advice'.[199] Some rebels 'crossed over to Myitkyina (in Burma) on their onward journey to People's China to attend training classes', reported a Burmese newspaper in 1968.[200] The charismatic Laldenga moved to Britain.[201] In 1969, the Mizo rebels launched attacks on the Indian Army from their base in East Pakistan. The Indian military continued to retaliate: Mizo villages were demolished, and often, Mizo civilians became their targets. About two-thirds of the Mizo population was forced to live in military-controlled settlements, like the American regrouping of strategic hamlets in South Vietnam.[202] An Indian newspaper described the resettlement of Mizo villagers, totalling 82 per cent of the entire Mizo hills population by 1972, as a 'spectacular operation' to 'wipe out the last vestige of rebellion'.[203] Most resettled villages, known as Progressive Protected Villages, were nearer to the main roads and under strict military surveillance. This was a grave blow to the rebels as they could no longer enter villages to raid them for supplies and collect 'tax' from the people. Some of them yielded to the Indian Army, but others continued their guerrilla warfare from East Pakistan. Most villagers in the Mizo hills deeply resented being resettled. Their practice of jhum came to an end as these restricted habitats were not suitable for cultivation.[204] Their resentment sustained the MNF for the next two decades. The Indian government conceded that the situation in the Mizo hills continued to be serious as clashes between the army and the rebels took place at regular intervals.[205]

~

Following Independence, Assam had been plagued by rising unemployment. According to official statistics, there was a five-fold increase in the number of unemployed people between 1951 and 1968.[206] An official register of people looking for jobs at the employment exchange showed an increase of 145 per cent from 1951 to 1966, against the all-India average of 58 per cent.[207] Food shortages were another serious concern, as India's celebrated Green Revolution had no implications for Assam. Through the 1950s, Assam struggled to increase its food production by increasing the area under the plough and introducing some new technology for intensive agriculture. The Japanese method, as it was known, emphasized the use of chemical fertilizers, better-quality seeds and extensive weeding practices. Ammonium sulphate, which was widely used as a nitrogen fertilizer, was sold at a subsidized rate. Assam was far behind in the use of chemical fertilizers (0.90 kg per acre in 1957) compared to states like Bombay and Bihar. There were some genuine challenges to their use, as continuous heavy rains in the state washed away most of the fertilizers in the soil. An official report indicated that soil fertility was 'steadily falling due to continuous cropping'.[208] Crop yield was largely static; with minor fluctuations, the production of rice remained around 1.7 million tonnes annually between 1949 and 1961. Equally grim was the picture of capital investment. During the Third Plan (1961–66),

Assam's share of India's total industrial capital investment was only 1.6 per cent, much less than that of Orissa, West Bengal or Bihar.[209] While India secured managerial control in the tea industry, Assam's approximately 800 plantations and an investment of 500 million pounds were still British-owned, and there was a gradual outflow of British capital to other parts of the globe. An estimated 1500 British citizens still worked in Assam's tea and oil industries. Assam tea, grown on 40 per cent of India's tea acreage, still accounted for 80 per cent of India's tea exports and 19 per cent of India's foreign exchange earnings.[210]

The contribution of tax collected from the tea gardens to the total state tax revenue increased from 15.8 per cent in 1951–52 to 23.4 per cent in 1963–64.[211] It slowly began to decline thereafter as the planters lobbied with the government, expressing their inability to part with their income. Agriculture was still Assam's major source of income despite a fall in its share of gross domestic product from 63 per cent in 1950–51 to 49 per cent in 1965–66. This gap was filled by the concurrent increase in the share of mining, manufacturing and construction. Yet, Assam's factories hardly helped in generating employment. In 1965, factories employed a mere 1.90 per cent of workers in Assam, while the state's income from factories contributed a meagre 2 per cent to the all-India total for 1964–65. From 1951 to 1965, Assam's per capita income rose by just 5 per cent.[212]

Education still followed the colonial pattern, with most youth acquiring general degrees. Industrialization, though limited, temporarily kindled hopes of increased employment opportunities. It helped in the proliferation of vocational and technical institutes training low-skill workers, whose number increased to a thousand in the 1950s—a jump from a single-digit figure in 1942.[213] But in the long run, the industrialization of the 1950s and 1960s hardly benefited the local educated youth, whose situation was no different from their peers in several Indian states. An official estimate indicated that, in 1964, the local share of jobs in existing industries was 27 per cent.[214] The lack of skills or experience among the locals was a commonly cited reason for such a state of affairs.[215] Public sector organizations too were controlled by headquarters that were outside Assam. The ONGC, established in 1956, began drilling operations in 1959. In May 1969, it had 3788 employees, but 90 per cent of the officials in higher-grade posts were born outside Assam.[216] Local youth were recruited largely as manual workers in ONGC. While there was a strong desire for industrialization, this process 'will not be of any help unless arrangement is made to employ local youths', wrote a senior Assamese bureaucrat in 1972.[217]

Drought, food scarcity and famine hit several parts of India severely as weak monsoons, caused by El Niño events from 1963 to 1966, resulted in a 20 per cent decline in food production.[218] Assam too was affected, and early symptoms of starvation, due to crop failure and low government stocks of rice, led to unrest. The *New York Times* reported in 1963 that 'hungry crowds' in Cachar 'looted storehouses'.[219] As floods swept away paddy crops in 1966, sporadic food riots were reported from several urban areas.[220] Starvation loomed large in several localities of western and central Assam, but this grim situation made news when the crisis wreaked havoc in Guwahati.[221] The government blamed the deficit on the cross-border sale of rice for higher profits across East Pakistan and West Bengal.[222] A section of the Assamese intelligentsia thought that demolition of the newly constructed river embankments could be a way to enhance agricultural productivity.[223]

As the food crisis deepened, Mrs Gandhi's government devalued the rupee. She expressed concern that 'there is frustration, agitation, uncertainty. Above all the people are in distress'.[224] Admitting that the food crisis 'will probably be even more difficult during the next few months', she wrote to Chaliha: 'This year's scarcity should not be allowed to impair next year's harvest.'[225] But the fact that much of the food crisis was the result of the government's misguided food policies was eloquently brought out by Assam's economists.[226] The food crisis—with occasional news of starvation deaths—continued well into 1968.[227]

The communist parties demanded that adequate supplies of food be made available to people. They successfully used the crisis to solicit public opinion against the Congress-led government in Assam, which had already faced a backlash from a united Opposition for Assam's deepening political crisis. The anti-government narrative increased the chances of success for separatist views.

~

Assam's prolonged economic and political worries took a violent form early in 1968. As a symbolic resistance to the further territorial reorganization of Assam, 'Assam Unity Day' was observed on 13 January, and the Congress leadership appealed to the Union government not to 'Balkanize or dismember Assam'.[228] This was followed by massive protests; the All Assam Students' Union gave a call for picketing and hartal on 24 January, which was a total success. The Assamese press reported that clashes and violence erupted in many towns.[229] Aircraft were prevented from taking off. In many places, effigies of the Prime Minister were burnt. It was a show of strength for the student organization, which also called for the boycott of Republic Day celebrations.[230] Not everyone, however, joined this strike. A section of students studying in Guwahati, belonging to the Ahom community whose leaders had already begun to articulate their demand for a separate state, appealed to their fellow Ahom students not to join the strike.[231]

Only a handful of officials attended that year's Republic Day celebrations, held in the heart of Guwahati city. A little-known organization called Lachit Sena went on a massive anti-Marwari rampage.[232] At the parade, students and others who proclaimed loyalty to Lachit Sena 'pulled down the national flag'.[233] Widespread looting of shops and wares primarily owned by Marwari traders went on through the afternoon, and a 'number of shops, industrial establishments, petrol pumps and vehicles were set on fire'. The mayhem continued for hours; a people's court was hastily installed near a police station.[234] Curfew was imposed. Home Minister Y. B. Chavan later admitted that the situation 'was getting out of control'.[235] Arson attacks continued the next day and spread to the commercial neighbourhood of Guwahati.

Curfew was imposed, and the state machinery came down heavily on the Lachit Sena. The Assam chief minister blamed the violence and rioting on foreign forces.²³⁶ Traders partially halted their business. For several days, railway wagons were not released by traders, and supplies dried up.²³⁷ Assamese youth stepped in to sell groceries and vegetables. Cleaners of the Gauhati Municipal Board went on strike for a fortnight, and garbage was not cleared. Insurance companies indicated that they would not provide insurance in these conditions, where shops belonging to Marwaris and Bengalis (and also Assamese) were being burnt down. The curfew caused much disquiet among the residents of Guwahati. The celebration of Saraswati Puja was also not allowed. The curfew was lifted after 10 days.

Assam's well-connected Marwari traders and industrialists drew the urgent attention of the Union government and lawmakers to the disturbed situation. Several parliamentarians, including Y.B. Chavan and Balraj Madhok, rushed to Assam. According to Madhok, then the president of the Jana Sangh, the plan to push out non-Assamese Hindus from Assam was a political design to convert Assam into a Muslim-majority state.²³⁸ Opposition legislators also claimed that Assam's Congress leadership and the government had extended their support to these protests and refrained from controlling the disturbances. Some legislators compared the Lachit Sena to the nativist Shiv Sena of Maharashtra.²³⁹

Assam's position as a frontier province, the recent debacle with China and the increasing support from East Pakistan to the Lushai rebels—all were a cause of increasing concern to the Indian establishment. The political situation on the frontier with Burma was also worrying. The situation was debated on in the Parliament for two days, and the Opposition came down heavily on the government. Madhok suggested that a committee of experts on defence and strategic affairs should review aspects of Assam's reorganization, stop illegal infiltration from Pakistan and throw out missionaries from Nagaland and the Mizo hills. Most members criticized the overt regionalism; a member from Madras pointed out that even during the anti-Hindi agitation there, Assamese minorities had been protected by the state. Hirendra Nath Mukherjee, the MP belonging to CPI from West Bengal, blamed the crisis on dissension within the Assam Congress, but he also rued that the name of Lachit Barphukan, the seventeenth century Ahom military commander, was 'being abused and slandered' in the commission of acts of 'such a terribly disgraceful character'.[240]

Was the All Assam Students' Union involved in this incident? Their leaders, as also Home Minister Chavan, made it clear that while the procession was led by students, the violence was committed by outsiders.[241] A government enquiry found that many student protests began without instigation from political parties. The protests started because rice was not available 'at a reasonable rate'. 'The students started beating the shopkeepers, and this was the igniting point.'[242]

Who were these outsiders? The Lachit Sena drew mainly from the urban educated youth who fashioned themselves as champions of Assam's economic sovereignty. The Union government became aware of its presence towards the end of 1967, when posters and leaflets began to appear in Guwahati bearing slogans like 'Assam for Assamese'. The Lachit Sena was a 'mysterious, underground organisation', said the home minister.[243] One poster spelt out its goal: 'To make Assam free from the traitor India and drive out all traitors, exploiters, adulters [*sic*], black-marketeers, Indians for whose existence the Assamese people are suffering and not benefitted at all.' They claimed comradeship with the Naga rebels and sought independence for all of Assam.

The public presence of the Lachit Sena had become noticeable in the first weeks of January 1968. Initially, they served notices on non-Assamese traders and industrialists to quit Assam.[244] One of these read, 'All non-Assamese persons, those who are holding offices irrespective of categories and departments, business, contracts, agencies etc. in Assam should vacate their respective offices and other business affairs including the holding of land or buildings within a reasonable period.'[245] Another notice was issued in the name of the 'Prime Minister' of the 'underground sovereign government of Assam', accusing the Government of India and non-Assamese people of treating Assam as a 'colony'.[246] 'Assam is not getting its due share from its natural resources of oil and tea. Why Assam's crude oil should be taken to Barauni?' the notice asked. Some widely circulated notices, also received by some parliamentarians, read, 'Assam is not part of India; Assam is for Assamese, all the foreigners must get away.'[247]

Non-Assamese merchants had faced challenges in the state through 1966–67, but 1968 was different. It was more than just loss of property. The Assam Merchant Association spelt out the sense of gloom: 'The loss of crores, though very big, can be written off in history with the passage of time, but the future historian alone will be able to assess the real extent of misunderstanding and loss of goodwill.'[248] In 1968, the Federation of Indian Chambers of Commerce and Industry (FICCI) proposed a number of ways to overcome the crisis. One of the suggestions was that the Assamese people should appreciate the role of outside capital for Assam's prosperity; at the same time, FICCI stated that non-Assamese merchants needed to work closely with Assamese traders, who were largely retailers.[249] The local administration highlighted grievances 'about non-employment for young men'.[250] For many traders, this was untenable as their enterprises were 'more or less self-employed; there is not much room for giving employment to others'.

Assam's Opposition did not spare Chaliha for his failure to protect the non-Assamese traders. In fact, many prominent Assamese had sympathies for the Lachit Sena. When asked by Chavan which press printed the widely circulated posters and leaflets, Chaliha answered: 'I know everything, but what can I do? If I have to arrest the people concerned, then many big leaders, very distinguished people would have to be arrested, perhaps at the very end, we shall discover that except for you and me, nobody would be left here.'[251]

~

On 18 February 1968, Mrs Gandhi's government faced a no-confidence motion in the Parliament. The rise of regional movements such as the Lachit Sena, among other issues, was used by the Opposition to criticise her government.[252] But the events of 26 January did not deter Mrs Gandhi from pursuing her political stand on Assam's reorganization. So far, she had not been able to take the Assamese leadership with her. The Asam Sahitya Sabha, which had steadfastly resisted the idea of Assam's territorial reorganization in 1967 and 1968, had at its annual conference on 26–28 January 1968 urged the government to follow the recommendations of the Mehta Committee.[253] Chaliha, too, strongly opposed Assam's further disintegration, including the separation of the Naga hills.[254]

In May 1968, the Union government decided to go ahead with its plan to reorganize Assam. Chavan conceded that matters could take an ugly turn, but he said the process should not be delayed any longer.[255] Notwithstanding threats from Assamese ultra-nationalists and the rise of radical politics in the hills, the internal affairs committee of the Cabinet worked out Assam's reorganization plan, and political shape was given to the state of Meghalaya.[256] Chaliha refrained from consenting;[257] fully backed by his party in Assam, he could still get sufficient support from the Congress Parliamentary Board, which advised Mrs Gandhi not to bypass the wishes of the state government.[258] Morarji Desai threatened to vote against the reorganization if law and order was ceded to the hills. Fakhruddin Ali Ahmed, Mrs Gandhi's cabinet colleague from Assam, threatened to resign as well.[259]

Mrs Gandhi failed to keep her promise to declare Assam's reorganization in the budget session of the Parliament, largely because of her colleagues' opposition. But as she flew to Singapore on 18 May for a bilateral meeting, she expressed hope that 'the gap has been narrowed and when I come back, the matter will be discussed further and a decision taken'.[260] Nine APHLC Assam state legislators resigned on 25 May, sending shock waves through the government. Mrs Gandhi had to cut short her foreign visit.[261] Serious differences within the Union cabinet on the Assam question now became public.[262]

The subsequent parliamentary debate witnessed Mrs Gandhi's ability to secure political support, though she faced strong opposition from the Praja Socialist Party (PSP) and the Jana Sangh. Hem Barua was ruthless in his criticism; he accused the hill leaders of corruption: 'The English educated people in these hill areas want to reap a benefit.' The Jana Sangh, fiercely opposed to the Assam plan, declared 14 July as Asam Day.[263] It demanded the expulsion of Christian missionaries from Assam, NEFA and Nagaland, and it proposed that, rather than an autonomous state, every district council should be converted into a union territory.[264] The APHLC was accused of having 'ramified business interests' in Shillong.

The Chaliha government, backed by the Assam Congress, threatened to resign if law and order was transferred from its jurisdiction.[265] On 27 August, the Assam Legislative Assembly, without any representation from the APHLC, rejected any further reorganization of Assam.[266] Mrs Gandhi, however, continued to gather political support within her party and her cabinet. She overcame the opposition of Desai by coming to his rescue when he got embroiled in a controversy over suspicious trade deals made by his son. She also agreed with the Chaliha government's refusal to transfer law and order to the proposed sub-state.

On 11 September 1968, the Union government declared the creation of an 'autonomous state within the state of Assam' consisting of two districts: Khasi and Jaintia and Garo hills.[267] This was done to ensure that their aspirations did not translate into a rebellion—a few Khasi youths had already joined the Mizo rebels.[268] This sub-state, with all the paraphernalia of a government including legislative autonomy, fell short of APHLC's expectations only in the aspect of the administration of law and order. Shillong remained outside this arrangement. Both APHLC and Chaliha agreed that the arrangement was worth trying out.[269] The Mizo hills and the United Mikir and North Cachar hills were given the choice to opt for this state or remain with Assam. The Assam government would have no veto over the transferred subjects. More importantly, the 16 lawmakers from the hills would form a standing committee with a pre-emptive right to frame laws on these subjects. An administrative structure called the North-Eastern Council, in which all states of the region would have an equal stake, would coordinate development planning apart from looking into external and internal threats. Drawn from Nehru's Scottish Plan, and the Mehta and Pataskar reports, the new arrangement was a largely acceptable framework for growing numbers of elites in the two districts. 'It would have been wholly out of character for a middle-class leadership to follow the insurrectionary path taken by A.Z. Phizo in Nagaland or Laldenga in the Mizo hills,' wrote an observer.[270] The plan was well received among the majority in Assam as well as the APHLC. But many non-tribal residents in the hills were worried by these developments. The non-tribal population of the Garo hills drew up a lengthy memorandum and submitted it to the Indian government, outlining their refusal to be a part of the new scheme.[271] The memorandum described how various legal and political measures adopted by the autonomous district councils had been highly disadvantageous to the non-tribal people.

There was no constitutional precedent for the decision to convert two hill districts of Assam into a sub-state.[272] After winning the general elections of 1967, Mrs Gandhi began to assert her grip on the organizational affairs of her party and government.[273] But this was not enough to get her opponents to accept the idea. Dilip Mukerjee, a senior journalist with the *Statesman*, wrote that Mrs Gandhi privately confided that unless such a political structure was conceded, Assam's hill districts would follow in the steps of Nagaland or the Mizo hills.[274] For politicians across the ideological spectrum and her cabinet colleagues who disagreed, however, Assam's strategic position bordering Pakistan demanded a stronger presence of the state. Bringing about such an amendment to the Constitution was a complex political process, requiring a two-thirds majority vote in both Lok Sabha and Rajya Sabha as well as the consent of at least half of the state legislatures. The Jana Sangh warned that any fragmentation would jeopardise India's unity and security. Others like the PSP worried that the experiment in Assam may result in similar demands from other tribal areas in the country. On the other hand, Jaipal Singh Munda, who fought for the causes of tribals and who had served in the Constituent Assembly, was annoyed that Hem Barua, the socialist MP and poet, was obsessed with 'disintegration and fissiparous tendencies'.[275] But, in fact, as the Assam experiment was taking shape, similar demands led to political violence in the Telangana region of Andhra Pradesh in early 1969.[276]

On 12 November 1968, Mrs Gandhi's cabinet gave approval for the amendment of the Constitution, and on 10 December, the bill was introduced in the Parliament.[277] After two days of debate, this bill was put to vote on 25 March 1969. Mrs Gandhi had by then mustered significant backing across the political spectrum for the amendment, but it failed to get the constitutionally required two-thirds majority, and an embarrassed government withdrew the bill.[278] The bill was reintroduced in the Lok Sabha on 15 April 1969, and this time, the government ensured that it had the required support.[279] On 30 April, the Rajya Sabha passed the bill. The government was able to smoothly complete the required legal procedures, and in the week of Christmas, Meghalaya was born as a state within Assam.[280]

Contrary to the expectations of Mrs Gandhi, however, controversies around the sharing of power soon engulfed this unique constitutional and political experiment of a sub-state.[281] Mahendra Mohan Choudhury, Assam's new chief minister, was in no mood to give way to the hill leaders. Neither was there any serious effort on the part of Assam to reinforce the cohesion needed for sustaining such a complex and delicate arrangement. Friction arose between Assam and Meghalaya over matters of civic administration; for instance, Assam refused to let Meghalaya control the All-India Service officials.[282] The problems in the experiment had implications for other states of India too.[283]

As the fissures widened, an angry Williamson Sangma, the APHLC chairman who would soon become the chief minister of Meghalaya, told the home minister that the 'decision to confer statehood on Manipur and Tripura had completely changed the situation and it was no longer for the present leadership of APHLC to continue to work the existing arrangement without losing the support of the people'. In mid-September 1970, Mrs Gandhi deputed the Union minister of state for home affairs, K.C. Pant, on a whirlwind tour of the North-east. Pant met ministers, governors, lieutenant governors and political leaders. He was convinced that everyone 'favour[ed] an integrated approach to the development and security of the region'.[284]

These developments convinced the Assamese leaders that their hopes of retaining control over the hills were now useless, and their fears soon proved true. On 10 November 1970, Mrs Gandhi wrote to Assam's chief minister conveying her intention to make Meghalaya a full-fledged state separate from Assam.[285] She also announced her government's intention in the Lok Sabha. A panicked Assam government wrote to the Prime Minister expressing the desire to develop an administrative complex in the plains of Assam and sought the Union government's financial assistance to build another capital city, as Shillong would go to Meghalaya.

The reorganization reduced Assam to a fraction of its size at Independence. Further fragmentation was in sight. Union home ministry officials were worried about the growing demand for separate states in the remaining hill districts and the southern district—Mikir hills, North Cachar hills and Cachar. The Mikir and North Cachar hills districts—with less than half a million population thinly spread at an average of 25 persons per square kilometre—had earlier rejected the option of joining Meghalaya. Early in 1970, the political leaders of the two hill districts wrote to Mrs Gandhi expressing the desire for a separate state.[286] For a while, a section of elites in these two districts had been content with the political rewards from the autonomous district councils.[287] Unlike the other hill districts that were seeing disturbances, many from Mikir and North Cachar hills districts had historical connections with the social, cultural and economic networks of the Brahmaputra Valley and beyond,[288] and the power structure in these districts had not produced enough political and social antagonism towards the Assamese leadership. They had previously seen the political movements in the other hills as part of a Christian design. As this situation changed, their own desire for a separate state began to take clear political form.

In Cachar, a largely Bengali-speaking district in the south, the demand for a separate state became loud by the late 1960s. It grew even louder when Gauhati University decided to adopt Assamese as the medium of instruction. Many residents complained that a proposed paper mill in Cachar, intended to harness the rich bamboo forests of the Mizo district, had been moved to the Brahmaputra plains at the behest of the Assam government. Failing a separate Cachar state, they proposed that they be joined with Tripura to make a larger state of Bengali speakers. Mrs Gandhi's government did not accept this demand.[289] 'If Cachar is detached from Assam, the natural course would be to join it with Tripura but even here there is no indication whether the people of the two areas would like to join in a single State,' said a home ministry note.[290]

Meanwhile, as Meghalaya, Manipur and Tripura moved towards becoming full-fledged states, many feared that this would lead to further weakening of Assam, and the strengthening of the claims of others for statehood, including that of the Ahoms. In the mid-1960s, a section of the Ahoms, joined by other ethnic communities, had started a movement (whose origins went back to the late 1940s)[291] for a separate state comprising a couple of districts of Upper Assam. Initially, under the banner of the Ahom Tai Mongolia Rajya Parishad, the movement was renamed *Ujoni Asam Rajya Parisad* in 1970, but it petered out soon after as it failed to get popular backing.[292]

More impactful was the rise of the Plain Tribals Council of Assam, known as PTCA, in 1966–67 as a party representing the tribes of the Brahmaputra Valley. The earlier Tribal League, which had a crucial role in allowing the Bodos and other tribal communities in the Brahmaputra Valley to articulate their political views prior to 1947 and played a prominent part in governance, had virtually disappeared from the political landscape after their debacle in the first general elections in 1952; the League lost the lone seat that it contested for in the assembly.[293] The League had a considerable following among the poor tribals, who then extended electoral support to the Congress, though the communists—RCPI and CPI—were not far behind. Without any significant presence in the political matrix of Assam, the Bodos silently resented being discriminated against or left out of many state-sponsored developmental activities. In the 1960s, that restlessness began to acquire a clear political shape. Their grievance was aggravated by the Assamese leaders' refusal to recognize the multilingual character of Assam and their attempts to absorb the tribal population within the Assamese social system as well as by the failure of the tribal population to hold on to their tiny pieces of landed property.[294] Tribal leaders demanded greater political representation through a reorganization of electoral constituencies and reserved seats so that the tribal voters could play a decisive political role.[295] The Assam government cracked down brutally on PTCA supporters in a public show of strength on 22 May 1968.[296] But the PTCA thrived for years to come—the proof lay in their sizeable presence in various electoral outcomes—and spearheaded the aspirations of the tribal population in the plains for, initially, the 'creation of an autonomous region', which in 1972 metamorphosed into the demand for a separate state of Udayachal (first proposed in 1966).[297]

As political-bureaucratic deliberations on the territorial reordering of Assam came to occupy Central attention in Delhi, political decisions on the fate of the hill districts of Assam were collectively shaped by multiple forces. The Ministry of External Affairs had a role to play, and meetings at the home ministry were joined by officials of the defence ministry. 'The Army Commander should be present at the meetings of the Coordination Committee of the Council dealing with security matters,' India's defence secretary stated.[298] This approach found strong support from the opposition parties in Assam.[299] Border security, development and political contingencies emerged as key issues in these deliberations. However, the views of defence officials did not always prevail. In 1970, though defence officials pushed for making the Mizo hills a union territory, Mrs Gandhi's government was clear that this would have to wait until political normalcy returned,[300] insisting that 'for the present, there need be no change in the position of Mizo hills'.[301]

To give a final touch to Assam's new political destiny, the Union government enacted the North Eastern Council Act in 1971. Expectedly, Assamese leaders opposed the Act, and some of them appealed to Prime Minister Mrs Gandhi saying that it would 'degrade' Assam and reduce it to the 'status of a sub-state'.[302] Assam had already been reduced in size twice after Independence: first in 1951 when, as part of a territorial adjustment, portions of its northern areas were transferred to Bhutan; and second in 1963 when the state of Nagaland was created. However, the Union government cut the hill districts' umbilical cord with Assam for good in 1972. NEFA was reborn as Arunachal, and the Mizo hills as Mizoram, both union territories. The same year, Meghalaya, Manipur and Tripura became states. The name Arunachal was chosen by a senior home ministry official, M.R. Yardi, who was an erudite Sanskrit scholar.[303] Meghalaya had been named by India's leading geographer Shiba Prasad Chatterjee in 1937.[304] The 'balkanization' of Assam was complete.

9

# Atop a Volcano

While the outbreak of military and diplomatic conflict between India and China underlined Assam's vulnerability, the long border with East Pakistan made for further complications. While West Pakistan industrialized fairly rapidly in the 1950s, East Pakistan (a virtual semi-colony of West Pakistan) was marked by rural poverty and a rapidly falling per capita income.[1] As was common earlier, many people continued to seek opportunities in more prosperous areas across the border. The boundary between India and East Pakistan was open and porous, and the passport control fuzzy. A volatile international border threatened by militancy continued to disrupt the movements of goods, services and people. In 1961, the census figures for Pakistan were out before the Indian numbers were available. Left-wing commentators in India noticed 'phenomenal increases' in population in Assam, West Bengal and Tripura compared to a significantly low population growth in East Pakistan during 1951–61. They agreed that the inflow into Assam 'may have largely occurred from Mymensingh, Comilla, and Sylhet'.[2] Many among these migrants had become part of Assam's agrarian economy.

~

The issue of migrants from East Pakistan was raised in public by leading Assamese figures and organisations. In 1962, the spiritual leader and social reformer Pitambar Deva Goswami wrote to Prime Minister Nehru about the imminent threat of Assam being invaded by East Pakistani migrants.[3] As the decadal census exercise began towards the end of 1960, based on feedback received from local enumerators, the Assamese press reported widely on the large-scale inflow of Pakistani nationals into Assam.[4] Several Assamese parliamentarians demanded that the Indian government explain how people from across the border were travelling 'without any valid passports and through unauthorized routes'.[5] Nehru's government denied any large-scale inflow of migrants from Pakistan.[6] However, unlike on previous occasions when the problem had been one of hosting refugees or settling peasants, this time it became an issue of national security. They also raised concerns about the flow of Bengali Muslims into India. Thus, issues of faith and language were linked to that of nationality. Over the next few months, the government began to face increased pressure from the Opposition parties, especially the Jana Sangh. Taken aback, Assam's chief minister, Bimala Prasad Chaliha, proposed 'a barbed wire fence on the border' to assuage the concerns of the Assamese and the national leaders.[7] The reality of the two-nation theory cast a deep shadow on Assamese politics and society, one which has not vanished even after the birth of Bangladesh in 1971.

Census enumeration was completed in the summer of 1961. Despite having no significant political presence, the Opposition parties upped the ante, and some anxieties were expressed in the Parliament. On 7 August 1961, Atal Bihari Vajpayee of the Jana Sangh gave notice for an adjournment motion on 'alleged Pakistani infiltration into Assam',[8] claiming that in the last few years, more than six lakh Muslims from Pakistan had entered Assam. The Speaker asked Nehru to explain this 'planned, large-scale infiltration of Pakistani nationals into Assam'. Nehru admitted that he did not 'know factually how many have come in' and 'would rather wait for further enquiries and further examination in detail for census figures and others'. He, however, assured the Parliament that 'there has been no large-scale infiltration in recent months', describing this as an 'old problem of population flowing over from an over-crowded area to a less crowded area'. He acknowledged that while 'this over-flow has stopped' since Partition, 'it may be that some of it still flows where there is a chance and we are still trying to stop it'. Nehru received support from an unexpected corner. The Opposition MP Hem Barua backed him, saying that 'there has never been any large-scale infiltration of Pakistani nationals into Assam', and 'at present, there are stray cases of inflow of people from East Pakistan'.[9]

The political attention to the problem, already complicated by heightened communal rivalry, compelled the Union government to enhance vigilance on the border from 1961.[10] Shastri, the Union home minister, said that 'such Pakistani infiltrants as are found in Assam are being dealt with under the appropriate law'.[11] The Intelligence Bureau had warned of 'large [scale] "infiltration of Pakistani nationals" into Assam', which the Union government saw as a 'security threat' and subsequently empowered Assam police officials in March 1961 to deport these Pakistani nationals 'who [were] without travel document[s]'.[12]

The publication of the findings of the census of 1961 put the Assam government on the defensive.[13] Senior Congress leaders in the state turned to attack their government. Veteran Congressman Debeswar Sarmah published a booklet explaining how Assam's 'unaccounted population can only be attributed to heavy infiltration of Pak nationals'.[14] Though the numbers he cited were found to be a 'fallacy',[15] panicked senior Assam officials, understanding the implications of such a narrative, concurred that the number was 'considerable'. They proposed 'prosecution and deportation' of those who had entered Assam illegally, 'strengthening of border outposts and check posts' and increasing border patrol. 'Something has to be done to trace the illegal immigrants who have already, more specially recently, entered the state, to prosecute them and to deport them to East Pakistan,' a senior official advised.[16] Next on the official's list of advice was the preparation of a National Register of Citizens. Assam's chief secretary, too, advised the chief minister to take urgent steps to prevent any further entry of migrants from East Pakistan.[17] It is notable that many issues central to the politics of Assam 60 years on had germinated in the late years of the Nehru era.

In April 1962, the Union government confirmed 'a large increase of Muslim population' in Assam's western border districts and conceded that this 'may also be partly due to migration from East Pakistan'.[18] Several lawmakers termed this as a well-planned design by Pakistan to convert Assam into a Muslim-majority state—a dream that had remained unfulfilled since the breakdown of the Cabinet Mission Plan.[19] Home Minister Lal Bahadur Shastri spoke in the Parliament of a 'somewhat large-scale' 'infiltration' from East Pakistan into Assam. Shastri was aware of the complex social and economic situation which shaped India's border areas with Eastern Pakistan.

> The communities on either side are closely knit. There is also the fact of scarcity of labour in that part of the country and, if I might say so, poverty and unemployment in the other area compels them to come to our area and get land for cultivation, and also work in the fields as labourers.[20]

Shastri warned that 'illegal infiltration or any kind of illegal work has to be prevented and stopped'. The senior Congress veteran admitted both the complexity and enormity of the problem. It not only defied an easy solution but also merited a serious response. Though he did not elaborate, he made it clear that steps were being taken by the Union government to stop this process. In Assam, Chaliha had to counter popular fears that Assam would be converted into a Muslim-majority state. An editorial in the *Times of India* dismissed this as a 'baseless fear', and Chaliha insisted that no major influx had taken place,[21] but his party claimed that illegal 'infiltration of Pakistani nationals' into Assam was 'likely to [en]danger' India's security.[22]

In May 1962, the Union government approved an Assam government proposal 'to control and eradicate the problem of illegal infiltration from East Pakistan'—to have additional police staff to patrol the Indo–Pak border, keep a vigil 'against infiltration' from East Pakistan and take 'effective actions against those who after coming to Assam with valid travel documents do not leave the country'.[23] The police would also keep 'thumb and finger impressions and photographs of Pakistani infiltrators'.[24] In official parlance, this administrative mechanism came to be known as the Prevention of infiltration into India of Pakistani Nationals (PIP) project, the details of which were spelt out later with inputs from B.N. Mullik, director of India's Intelligence Bureau (IB). Detection and deportation had entered the official lexicon.

From June 1962, the Indian government began to detect and push back thousands of people from Assam and Tripura to East Pakistan, who they claimed had been entering India without a visa since 1952.[25] In August, the Assam government estimated that one-tenth of Assam's 2.7 million Muslim population had migrated from Pakistan after its formation as an independent country, i.e., after Partition.[26] The East Pakistan district of Comilla officially received 35,000 people who were evicted from India, with about an equal number of those who were not registered in the East Pakistan government records. Jacques Nevard of the *New York Times* reported that 'some of those evicted' from India are 'illegal migrants who have been returned [to East Pakistan] and others are Indian Moslems who have been expelled', though 'what proportion of each is involved is difficult to gauge'.[27]

By April 1964, some 1,30,000 had been pushed out from Assam and Tripura, according to official Pakistani estimates. The Indian estimate was much lower.[28] On paper, these expulsions were 'purely on [grounds of] citizenship', with the burden of proof lying with those evicted, the majority of whom were Muslims. The expulsions set off a 'tinder box of religious antagonism'.[29] In retaliation, many of the evictees 'seized houses and other property' from tribesmen, Hindus and Christians in East Pakistan, forcing hundreds of thousands of them living along the western border of Assam to flee to India.[30] Unconnected subsequent events, such as the theft of a holy relic from Kashmir's Hazratbal Shrine, sparked religious violence against Hindus in East Pakistan. The Pakistan government suggested that this was a reaction against the 'evictions and refugee emigration from Assam and Tripura that inflamed feeling against Hindus'.[31] The *New York Times* reported that 'Moslems killed, maimed Hindus, looting shops, stealing crops and raping women'.[32]

Between January and April 1964, approximately 1,35,000 Hindus fled to West Bengal; many of them were forced to move to central India. A good number came to Assam; one account claimed that an estimated 20,000 came to the Garo hills in January alone, and some of them were rehabilitated in mostly forested lands.[33] In retaliation, Hindus in Calcutta killed Muslims and looted Muslim shops, forcing more than 40,000 Muslims to flee to East Pakistan.[34] The circle of violence continued for weeks. In northern East Pakistan, Christian tribals belonging to the Garo and Hajong communities faced widespread harassment—and by March 1964, 78,000 of these people had moved to Assam.[35] Despite assurances from the Roman Catholic Archbishop of Dhaka and from Pakistan's military ruler Ayub Khan, the tribal people refused to return.

Since 1952, the Indian government had been using legal mechanisms to expel those who were considered unauthorized Pakistani nationals in Assam, Tripura and West Bengal.[36] Doubts had been raised in some quarters about the loyalty of Muslims during the war with China in 1962. Following the expulsions, some Pakistani lawmakers pressed for other 'settlements' as well: 'If India fails to honourably and peacefully settle the Kashmir and Junagadh affairs we will be reverting to our original demand [that] Assam should form part of East Pakistan.'[37] Z.A. Bhutto, Pakistan's minister for power and natural resources in 1962, accused India of pursuing a policy to 'liquidate the minorities living in India'.[38] A Pakistani enquiry commission, known as Jabbar Commission, concluded that 95.8 per cent of Muslims who were evicted from Assam and Tripura were Indian nationals.[39] The Indian government repudiated these claims and produced a counter report.

Concerned about the Assam evictions sparking anti-Hindu riots in East Pakistan, Nehru asked the Ministry of External Affairs to go slow—he believed that enquiries should continue and notices be sent, and only if anyone was 'definitely found to be [a] Pakistani national', 'they should be asked to quit'.[40] Pakistan should also be informed, he said. Nehru expected this to result in many leaving on their own. When Nehru met Pakistani President Ayub Khan in London, the Pakistani leader told him that 'people there [in Pakistan] were excited over the matter', and Nehru felt that 'however justified we might be in expelling them, this led to a chain of events with much more undesirable consequences'.[41] Nehru also received panicked telegrams from some Hindu leaders in East Pakistan who described how the evictions from Assam and Tripura had created trouble for them.[42]

The situation heightened diplomatic tensions between India and Pakistan. Bhutto, now Pakistan's foreign minister, demanded a joint commission to determine the *bona fide* citizenship of the expelled population.[43] The Government of India faced a strong backlash from the Opposition for rendering the minorities in Pakistan vulnerable. The socialist Ram Manohar Lohia and the Jana Sangh's Deen Dayal Upadhyay, heading two different political parties with contrasting political ideologies, issued a joint statement condemning the Indian government for failing 'to fulfil its obligations towards the minorities in Pakistan'. They said this led 'the people understandably [to] become indignant', but appealed 'that this indignation should be directed against the Government and should in no case be given vent to against the Indian Muslims'.[44]

Tired and in poor health by now, Nehru appealed through a radio broadcast for an end to religious strife; he also wrote a letter to Ayub after the arrival of Hindu refugees in India on 19 March 1964.[45] In his reply, Ayub noted that 'no concern or even a word of sympathy [had been expressed] for the thousands of Indian Moslems who have suffered in recent riots in India and have fled in panic to East Pakistan and those who have been forcibly evicted from their homes in Assam and Tripura'.[46] As communal disturbances spread in East Pakistan, the home ministers of India and Pakistan, along with the chief ministers of Assam and West Bengal, met on 7 April 1964.[47] Pakistan insisted that an international tribunal enquire into the evictions, a proposal India did not agree to. As a strategic move, the Indian government agreed to temporarily halt the serving of notices on people, but it was clear that there would be no freezing of the legal process, and that those found to be crossing into India would be deported.[48] The result was the birth of the PIP scheme, mentioned above.

Census statistics had been a powerful tool to propel the political narrative during the deportation drive. These had recorded a higher growth rate for Muslims in Assam between 1951 and 1961 compared to both the gross growth rate of the population of the state and the Muslim growth rate in East and West Pakistan. Officials concluded that 'the magnitude of the rate of growth in each case leaves little doubt that there was a very substantial influx of Hindus and Muslims. The source must be East Pakistan'. They estimated this number at 7.19 lakh but indicated that this was only a conservative estimate.[49] Given the domestic pressure in Assam, the Central government, which settled at a much lower number, agreed that 'this population [needed to go] out as early as possible'.[50] But the Union government was also aware of the precarious humanitarian dimension involved in deportation.

Until 1963, the task of detection, prosecution and deportation of Pakistani nationals was solely done by the same police forces who, prior to Independence, had been tasked with suppressing anti-imperial struggles. They took up the new task of detecting infiltrators with nationalistic zeal rather than dealing with it from a legal and humanitarian perspective, and this traumatized many.[51] The deportations were carried out without any judicial scrutiny.[52] Nehru felt that the government could not 'leave it merely to a police agency which may not perhaps decide quite correctly in some cases'.[53] In December 1963, he suggested a judicial tribunal as a way out,[54] but many felt this would only delay the process of deportation. 'The tribunal would take another fifty years to decide it,' thundered Hem Barua.[55] Nehru was equally concerned by the 'tremendous[ly] vituperative and virulent' public narrative in Pakistan, which claimed that most of those evicted were Indian Muslims. Nehru suggested 'devising some method of enquiry whereby it may be assured that a person who is supposed to be an infiltrant came from Pakistan'.[56] Early in 1964, the Indian government decided to establish tribunals in Assam to bring in some sense of judicial accountability.[57] Their powers and modalities were laid down in September.[58] These tribunals would decide whether or not a person was a foreigner as defined by the pre-Independence era Foreigners Act of 1946.

With the debacle of the war with China haunting Assam, its Congress lawmakers demanded that the India–Pakistan border be sealed, and a tract along it depopulated.[59] The Union government agreed promptly and, in July 1964, proposed that Assam raise a barbed fence along the border, depopulate the area up to two miles from this border and increase financial assistance for border patrolling.[60] 'Dilatory official procedures in Assam and excessive political inhibitions on the part of New Delhi have hindered the eviction process,' wrote the *Times of India*.[61] But home ministry officials were very sure of positive outcomes and effective ground implementation of this scheme. Home Minister Gulzarilal Nanda, speaking in 1964 in a largely Muslim-dominated locality of central Assam, said that it was the duty of every Indian Muslim to take the initiative to identify all infiltrators and hand them over to the government. He warned that it would be better if Pakistani nationals went away of their own accord and 'without our having recourse to various measures'.[62] All these had ripple effects in many parts of Central and Lower Assam.

War broke out between India and Pakistan in the summer of 1965. The short war, fought on India's western frontier, had no clear winner. Assam faced several threats in September 1965; *The New York Times* reported that Pakistan had made three attempts to bomb the city of Guwahati and the newly constructed bridge on the Brahmaputra.[63] Shelling was frequently reported across the border in southern Assam.[64] The threat of another Chinese attack in NEFA too loomed large.[65] The joint steamer companies that operated between Assam and Calcutta through East Pakistan had come to a complete halt. Export of dry fish came to an end in 1965. The long history of the Brahmaputra's role as a central artery of communication between Assam and eastern Bengal had come to an end.[66]

After the war, a more aggressive Pakistani establishment sent some of the deported people back to Assam. Small batches of Hindu refugees, a tiny number with legal documents, also continued to arrive; a nervous government official from Cachar warned that such 'small-scale influx of Pakistani Hindus may lead to large-scale movement to India'.[67] In Assam, suspicious officials believed that many of these people were 'trained and equipped to indulge in anti-national activities against India'. Assam resurrected the largely dormant practice of sending them back; in the first half of 1966, it pushed back more than 7000 such people. In 1967, an estimated 1.7 million migrants from East Pakistan had been served with deportation notices.[68] But the migrant Bengali settlers were not blamed for the scarcity of cultivable land in Assam until the late 1960s. Rather, many amongst the Assamese landowners considered the Chaliha government's deportation policy as a serious threat to their economy.

The large-scale deportations obviously had an impact on electoral politics in Assam in the years to come. The Congress party lost its credibility among Muslim voters, though several of its senior leaders steadfastly opposed the move to deport, recounted B.K. Nehru, the Governor of Assam at the time.[69] Three of them, Dev Kant Barooah, Fakhruddin Ali Ahmed and Moinul Hoque Choudhury, carried considerable clout with the central leadership of the Congress. In the Assembly elections of February 1967, the Congress could win in only 7 of the 16 states where elections took place. In Assam, the Congress performed badly compared to 1962 and vacated space for a leftward swing—a consequence of the unease with the PIP scheme. 'The agitation against this deportation of foreigners was so great that the Government of Assam, while not technically altering its policy, adopted a procedure which made rejection of any trespassers virtually impossible,' B.K. Nehru had written in a secret letter to President V.V. Giri in 1971.[70]

The *modus operandi* of detection and deportation was indeed ruthless. For some Assamese police officials, it was a 'sacred task'.[71] K.P.S. Gill, then the police head of a district, recounted his visits to villages with a predominantly Bengali Muslim population to search for alleged Pakistani nationals. Most villagers initially denied knowledge of such individuals.

> He (Gill) then used to draw himself up to his full height (well over six feet and enhanced by his turban), stroke his moustache, and say in a threatening voice, "Well, then shall I ask my men to search

your homes?" The response was immediate, 'No, Sir, no, Sir. We shall produce them all." And the majority was so produced and escorted back to the frontier . . . (and) placed on trains headed to East Pakistan.[72]

In 1965, the Union government promised that foreign nationals who wanted to be Indian citizens could do so by staying in India for six months.[73] Meanwhile, the Assam government had prepared a register of names of people, Muslims and others, crossing over from Pakistan. Police officials served 'quit India' notices to those whose names were not found in the National Register of Citizens of 1951.[74] In mid-1966, an estimated 71,000 were awaiting deportation, and about half of them had challenged the 'quit India' notices.[75] Many, whose names were recorded in the National Register of Citizens, were still unlucky. One of them was Bhanbhasa Sheikh. When the Assam government questioned his citizenship status, to prove his Indian nationality, Sheikh, who did not have any legal proof of landownership—which was true for the majority of people, given the poor land revenue bureaucracy of the time—produced a receipt of the National Register of Citizens where his name had been recorded. The judicial verdict of 1969, however, went against him—it was ruled that this document was not admissible as legal evidence of citizenship.[76] In 1967, many Hindus who had left or had been evicted from India came back to Assam. Indian officials cited deteriorating economic conditions and increasing clashes between Hindus and Muslims and the dispossession of Hindu landowners in East Pakistan as reasons for the renewed migration.[77] The question posed by Sheikh's case was important—the National Register needed careful verification as it could be a critical determinant of citizenship not for any specific community or group but for all who lived in Assam.

As the deportation drive intensified in 1964–65, 11 Muslim lawmakers from the Congress threatened to resign, and this ruffled the Congress party.[78] During the fourth general elections of 1967, Muslim voters withdrew their support to the Congress in many places. When the Congress Parliamentary Board met in April 1965, it openly criticized the Assam government for its 'weak-kneed' policy of slow eviction and its inability to stop 'infiltration' from East Pakistan.[79] The much-talked-about two-mile depopulated zone remained unimplemented. By the end of the decade, the public narrative had temporarily waned, but deportations continued sporadically; between 1961 and 1969, an estimated 1,92,000 were sent back to East Pakistan.[80] In 1980, when government officials tried to estimate the numbers of those who had come into India from East Pakistan between 1961 and 1971, they reached a figure of 9.67 lakh people, the majority of whom were Hindus.[81]

~

India's diplomatic relations with Pakistan deteriorated further in the 1960s because of the latter's support for the Naga and Mizo rebels. When talks between West and East Pakistan failed and war broke out in March 1971 in East Pakistan, Indian support—military and political—for their independence movement was more than evident.[82] By early April, several hundreds of thousands of civilians were killed by Pakistani forces in East Pakistan. The massive flow of refugees into Indian states soon turned into a major humanitarian crisis. Sydney H. Schanberg of the *New York Times* reported that there was a 'genuine sympathy for the refugees, but the struggle for existence is almost as hard in West Bengal as it is in East Pakistan. And, with more people competing for jobs and land, officials fear the social abrasions will soon appear'.[83] 'The frightened refugees pouring into India from East Pakistan have posed for New Delhi a problem perhaps as serious as any it has faced since independence in 1947,' he wrote.[84]

It went without saying that the Hindu refugees would not go back. It was also clear that if the refugees stayed for a length of time, antagonisms between the hosts and the newcomers were inevitable as they would compete for jobs, land and housing. The Assamese press and government officials were already reporting localized skirmishes—much to the unhappiness of both communities.[85]

Small numbers of refugees had started arriving in the final days of March, and the flow began to swell from mid-April. On 21 April

1971, the Union government said that 2,58,734 refugees had come from East Pakistan so far.[86] Between March and October, an estimated 2,98,000 refugees arrived in Assam, and more would join them in the next few months.[87] They were part of the great exodus of as many as 9.8 million refugees who arrived in India within a short span of 220 days. They walked miles; some fortunate ones used bullock carts, rickshaws or boats.[88] When Tripura was overburdened by the flow of refugees, some were airlifted to Assam by planes provided by the United States.[89] A large majority of them arrived in the border districts of Goalpara and Cachar. The numbers acquired gigantic proportions with the daily arrival of 2000 people on average into Assam, Meghalaya, Tripura and West Bengal; many went to Bihar. In May, the number was as many as 3500 per day.[90] In total, 'the rate of influx has been as high as 1800 persons per hour round the clock from 25 March 1971 to 31 October 1971'.[91]

In May 1971, days before her visit to refugee camps in Assam and Tripura, Indira Gandhi wrote letters to several heads of countries, including President Nixon. Drafted by P.N. Haksar, secretary to the Prime Minister, the letters stated:

> The carnage in East Bengal has naturally disturbed the Indian people deeply. There has been a surge of emotion which we have tried to contain but we find it increasingly difficult to do so in view of the systematic effort on the part of Pakistan to force millions of people to take refuge in our territory.

Mrs Gandhi underlined that the 'two problems—Pakistan's war on the people of East Bengal and its impact on us in the form of millions of refugees—cannot be separated'.[92] The Prime Minister, accompanied by Mahendra Mohan Choudhury and Williamson Sangma, the chief ministers of Assam and Meghalaya respectively, and several top aides, visited one of the makeshift camps in Cachar on 15 May.[93] She was witness to appalling scenes, and her senior officials as well as later historians agree that those sights convinced Mrs Gandhi, who was fluent in Bengali since her days in Shantiniketan, to take a firm decision in favour of military intervention.[94] Speaking at a public event later, she pointed out that 'so massive a migration, in so short a time, is unprecedented in recorded history'.[95] 'These heartrending stories were bound to stir up emotions,' she said, 'specially because the affected people are close to us in experience, culture and other values of life.'[96]

~

The 1971 Bangladesh War gave a new turn to Assam's political history. Mrs Gandhi went to war against Pakistan arguing that the refugee problem had turned serious. These refugees added to the numbers of those who had migrated to and settled in Assam in the previous decades. The Indian government was at first hopeful that the refugees would leave India at the earliest; on 16 May, Mrs Gandhi had said that they would have to return to East Pakistan as soon as possible.[97] But by the 22 May, she changed her stand, saying that 'we cannot send them back to be slaughtered', though her government was not prepared for the enormity of the humanitarian crisis. Refugees squatted in open spaces, and refugee camps were set up in schools and public buildings. Transit refugee camps were established to facilitate their further dispersal. The government fixed a meagre Rs 1.1 as per capita expenditure to feed the refugees. The provision of healthcare, nutrition and medical facilities required coordinated support. Indian officials put to use the experience gathered from 1947. With the aid of international agencies, nutritional programmes were undertaken.

There were political concerns too. Haksar wrote to Mrs Gandhi that the massive inflow of Hindu and Muslim refugees from East Pakistan would lead to great political turbulence. 'Two million fugitives have already crossed into India. They still continue to pour in at the rate of fifty thousand a day,' Haksar told the Chief Justice of India on 13 May 1971.[98] Haksar had no doubt that the refugees would cause social tension and spark religious strife in volatile West Bengal, Assam and Tripura. 'The regions which the refugees are entering are overcrowded and politically the most sensitive parts of India. The situation in these areas can very easily become explosive,' Haksar noted. He knew that the flow of refugees into these poverty-stricken areas would help the communists—'extremist political elements will inevitably gain ground'. Having only partially recovered from the political crisis arising out of the Naxalite movement in Bengal, the Indian government was seriously worried about the communist revolutionaries. By the early 1970s, the Naxalites had begun to infiltrate the poorer communities in the western districts of Assam, sending ripples of concern through the government.[99]

The total number of Bengali Hindus who had come to India between 1947 and February 1971 was estimated by the Indian government at 52,31,000. American political scientist Gary J. Bass wrote, citing Ministry of External Affairs documents, that the sudden rush from March 1971 exceeded that number in a matter of months. According to government estimates, India received 95,16,000 refugees between March and October 1971.[100] A majority of them arrived in West Bengal, and the rest went to Assam, Meghalaya and Tripura. It was unlikely that those who entered Meghalaya would have stayed there; most would have chosen Assam as their next destination. An Indian official communiqué noted that in the first few weeks, the refugees comprised mostly Muslims.[101] But that changed soon, and thereafter, the majority were Bengali Hindus. Officials from the Union Ministry of Home Affairs who visited Assam and West Bengal in May 1971 estimated that Muslims accounted for 5 to 10 per cent of the refugees.[102]

The new refugees were different from those who had arrived between 1947 and 1971. Indian officials believed that the Pakistani government had worked towards a systematic expulsion of Bengali Hindus from Pakistan.[103] Early in June 1971, a team from the World Bank visiting towns and villages of East Pakistan encountered devastation everywhere due to military operations. Some villages had 'simply ceased to exist', and parts of all towns that they visited had been 'razed'.[104] In her press briefings, Mrs Gandhi insisted that the refugees 'belong to every religious persuasion—Hindu, Muslim, Buddhist and Christian',[105] but she also wrote to several of her foreign counterparts that Hindus had fled East Pakistan largely due to the determined anti-Hindu policies of the Pakistani state.¹⁰⁶ The Hindu refugees accused the Pakistani military of having forced them to flee.¹⁰⁷ Statistics prepared by Indian officials estimated that up to 19 July 1971, of the 5.9 million refugees who had entered India, 5.3 million were Hindus.¹⁰⁸ An Australian diplomat who visited refugee camps in Assam in July 1971 found that 90 per cent of the refugees were Hindus.¹⁰⁹

A secret police communiqué noted the 'concern and resentment over large-scale influx of refugees' in the Garo hills, even though many from the community were sympathetic as well.¹¹⁰ Disputes arose over access to local resources, including water. A secret CIA report observed 'growing' hostility towards the refugees.¹¹¹ The Indian Army established a task force to ensure their security. Assam's unease over the influx of refugees became official when Chief Minister M.M. Choudhury called for 'utmost vigilance in maintaining internal peace and security'. He claimed that the refugees were accompanied by 'a number of spies, saboteurs and other anti-social elements'.¹¹² More articulate anti-refugee voices were heard in Meghalaya.¹¹³

The Assam government officially estimated the number of refugees to be 7,50,000, and the people of Assam pointed to their religious background. *Dainik Asam* claimed that the majority were Muslim peasants.¹¹⁴ Migrants were identified as *bhagania*—those who had fled to protect themselves. The government too recognized them as political refugees.¹¹⁵ As the flow of refugees intensified, Indian officials secretly warned the Assam government about the possibility of the return of many Muslims who had recently been evacuated from Assam.¹¹⁶ The Assam government alerted the now largely dormant PIP staff and their wide range of social networks. Up to July 1971, a little under 10,000 earlier deportees were detected as having come back with the new streams of refugees. Officials in Assam were aware that many more would return and were cognizant of who should be kept in the refugee camps, where 'strict vigilance' would be maintained 'both inside and outside the camps'.¹¹⁷ In a secret official document meant for internal discussion, the American intelligence warned that the influx of refugees would seriously imperil the 'political fabric' and economic development in India's North-east. 'These interests India may well consider "vital" and worthy of protection through the "lesser evil" of war,' US security officials noted.[118] The Americans believed that in the event of Pakistan going to war with India, Assam would face a military threat from China as well.[119]

By June 1971, Assam had 139 relief camps.[120] The refugees were asked to register at the nearest police station as per the Foreigners' Act. Some refugees received immunization; most remained malnourished. The Indian Red Cross Society, with the aid of American agencies, was one of the groups supplying food to Assam's relief camps.[121] A few were fortunate to get good care, while the rest languished. Indian officials who visited some camps in Assam and Tripura in June 1971 encountered a 'stinking foul-smell'.[122] Outbreaks of cholera and gastroenteritis were reported. In August, when US Senator Charles H. Percy visited a few camps, he was 'perfectly astounded by the way [the refugees were] cared for'.[123] But most were unlucky. And not all the refugees could be accommodated in camps. P.N. Dhar, one of Mrs Gandhi's closest aides, said that of the 10 million refugees, 3 million could not be housed in camps, and they simply 'melted away into informal labour markets and sweat shops, or became squatters on pavements'.[124] Some others became part of the social milieu.[125] From the camps, the refugees dispersed to other areas, depending on their prescience, social linkages, kinship and family ties and prospects of economic opportunities.

The extraordinary atrocities by the Pakistan Army and the consequent socio-economic tragedies that forced out millions into Assam, West Bengal and other states of India[126] were made worse by the severe economic slowdown in East Pakistan after the 1965 war. The withdrawal of Pakistani industries led to a rise in inflation. In India, home ministry officials were worried about the increasing tensions between Assamese and Bengali people in Assam due to the influx of refugees. The presence of refugees would intensify 'parochial tensions and strains, particularly in Assam where anti-Bengali feeling is deep and wide-spread', a home ministry note said.[127] Haksar agreed and recorded his concerns about the situation in Assam. Assamese student organizations had already asked for the relocation of refugees to other states.[128]

Even though some clashes between Assamese and Bengalis were reported in urban areas, the Assamese, in general, welcomed and celebrated the birth of Bangladesh. The writer Birendra Kumar Bhattacharya praised the linguistic nationalism of the Bengali people in Bangladesh, an idea that had strong resonance in Assam.[129] Several newly formed urban public initiatives collected monetary donations for the general public.[130] Communist leaders who visited the refugee camps urged the Indian government to recognize the government of independent Bangladesh.[131] The large majority of public figures in Assam were moved by the political and humanitarian crisis across the border. Students stayed away from classes and took out processions in support of Bangladesh.[132] Legislators shouted slogans in front of the Assembly in Shillong. For several weeks, the crisis captured front-page attention in Assamese newspapers. Their own difficult political experience with Pakistan galvanized thousands in support of the idea of Bangladesh. The political crisis that would arise from the arrival of refugees was not yet a consequential question. A year later, in 1972, Bhupen Hazarika, participating in the Festival of Political Songs in Berlin, sang to welcome the birth of Bangladesh as a symbol of an anti-fundamentalist, pro-secular and pro-people movement. The massive humanitarian crisis evoked a sympathetic public opinion.[133] Various Hindu Bengali organizations, for instance, the Bangladesh Tran Committee in southern Assam and the West Bengal Economic Development Council, were in touch with the state machinery to ensure that the refugees were accorded social and political support.[134] Several unions, including student organizations, demanded that Bangladesh be recognized by the Indian government.[135]

Provocation came from the Pakistani army on the Assam border in May 1971. One newspaper from West Pakistan threatened to cut off 'Assam from India by force and build a new highway' to China.[136] Having learnt from two previous episodes of war in the last three decades, Assam readied itself for any eventuality. In May 1971, the Pakistani military began to deploy personnel and build bunkers along the frontier with Assam's southern districts.[137] A month later, there were regular reports of bombing and shelling of Assam's border villages by the Pakistani army, which continued until August.[138] The Mukti Bahini forces, the armed and trained group of freedom fighters of Bangladesh which came into existence after March 1971, camped in the border areas of West Bengal, Tripura and Assam; Sylhet, which was a part of Assam before Partition, became one of their strongholds. Mukti Bahini soldiers took shelter in several parts of southern Assam from where they wrested parts of Sylhet and Mymensingh from the control of the Pakistani army. The Indian Army supplied arms and ammunition to the Mukti Bahini across Assam's borders.[139] Police officials in the border states imparted training to Mukti Bahini personnel. As India's military campaign in East Pakistan began in December 1971, 10 divisions of the army were allocated to East Pakistan. Four of these were moved from Assam's highly vulnerable northern frontier with China, across NEFA, which many considered to be a 'calculated risk'.[140]

Indian officials became convinced early on that if Sheikh Mujibur Rahman's Awami League came to power, it would not support the Naga and Mizo rebels staying in East Pakistan. Many believed that the Awami League would help to curb the possible spread of communism in Assam and West Bengal. 'I have received assurance from the National Assembly and Provincial Assembly members that they will not encourage the Nagas or Mizo Hills people to create troubles in our borders,' wrote J.P. Mitter, an eminent leader from Bengal and the Calcutta-based president of the Council for Protection of the Rights of Minorities.[141] Arguing for the need to support the Awami League, Mitter noted that 'if this organization fails to achieve its objective, communism will not only spread in East Bengal, but would be used as a base for disseminating communism in West Bengal and Assam'.[142] Mitter also thought that 'Mujibur Rahman's party is undoubtedly a bulwark against Communism. Bhashani has not much influence now a days.'[143] The decline of Abdul Hamid Khan Bhashani, who was not liked by many Assamese, was a major relief, as Bhashani, once the leading politician from East Pakistan and an inspirational leader of Bengali Muslim peasants in the 1940s, had once demanded a 'One Bengal' comprising Assam, Meghalaya, Tripura and both sides of Bengal.[144]

~

In the early weeks of the refugee crisis, Assam had thought that most refugees would return to Bangladesh in the next few months. The Australian diplomat mentioned earlier reported that the local people in Assam 'accepted the refugees without complaint largely because they had been given to understand [by the Union government] that they would remain no more than six months'.[145] Officials agreed that 'if the refugees stay for any length of time, the pressure for jobs, permanent housing and farming plots will arouse antagonism among the local people who are now their hosts'.[146] Senior Indian diplomats warned that as days passed, the refugees 'would not go back'. 'They would become more and more rooted here,' V.P. Dutt said in a note.[147] D.P. Dhar, Mrs Gandhi's close confidant and India's ambassador to the Soviet Union, despite his optimism about the return of the refugees, said Bangladesh was equally concerned about 'resistance which will be generated amongst the refugees'.[148]

In Assam, the implications of the Bangladesh refugee crisis soon began to unfold. References were made to those who had immigrated to India from East Pakistan in earlier years. For long, the *Times of India* reported, the

> refugees have avoided joining the mainstream life. They lead the life they had in East Bengal. They have opened Bengali medium schools. Many local people treat the evacuees, some of whom have been in Assam for years, as a burden on the State's economy. Relations between the Assamese and the refugees became strained when a section of the Bengali-speaking people demanded that Bengali too should be treated as an official language.[149]

I.G. Patel, finance secretary at that time, noted that 'the Hindus were not to trust Bengali Muslims readily. For Bengali Muslims, India was a land of opportunity'. Patel felt that the Congress party had 'often turned a blind eye to this influx for electoral reasons'. He added, 'This particular outcome of the Bangladesh war was not obvious to us then . . . Pakistan had effectively sealed the borders for ideological reasons. Now that India had a friend in Bangladesh, the borders—

difficult as they were to maintain—became rather porous.' Patel met an economist from Harvard University at a dinner in 1972 who, after giving him a lesson on the economic dynamics of population, told him that as India was now friendly with Bangladesh, 'the historical migration of Bengali Muslims into Assam and India's North-East will be resumed'. Patel conceded that this had never occurred to him.[150]

For the next few years, economic uncertainties surrounded the new nation state of Bangladesh.[151] Most refugees showed little intention of returning, which must have caused concern to Mrs Gandhi's government. On 8 February 1972, she gave a joint statement in Calcutta with Sheikh Mujibur Rahman, the Prime Minister of Bangladesh, where it was announced, 'The Prime Minister of Bangladesh solemnly re-affirmed his resolve to ensure by every means the return of all the refugees who had taken shelter in India since March 25, 1971, and to strive by every means to safeguard their safety, human dignity and means of livelihood.'[152] But a month later, the two prime ministers signed a pact in which this commitment was not honoured.[153] Officials in Assam intensified the search for refugees, but this hardly produced results as many of them were now integrated with the local population. A distressed Assam government communicated to the Union government that a wide variety of reasons—refugees becoming integral to the local economy, their appeal against deportation on compassionate grounds or because they were untraceable, having merged with the local families—had made the process of their return impossible.[154]

As these events were unfolding and anxieties were rising, the much-talked-about PIP scheme remained inoperative between 1971 and 1974. Despite the new circumstance of Bangladesh being a friendly independent nation, detection and deportation of Bangla immigrants resumed in 1974, and several thousands were sent back that year. Days before the Emergency was declared in June 1975, the Assam government sought the urgent intervention of the Union government. Taking a more combative stand against the refugees from Bangladesh, Assam asked for 'adequate powers to deport all Bangalee infiltrators, a clear methodology to combat the influx, and a random sample survey to be conducted by the ministry of home affairs for a proper appreciation of the problem'.[155] The Union government, while admitting in the Parliament that it had intensified deportation, detection and prevention of entry of unauthorized nationals from Bangladesh, was hoping that the other country would play a more active role.[156] Despite demands from Opposition lawmakers from the CPI(M), the Assam government refused to consider such people as refugees and began to describe them as 'illegal immigrants'.

A fresh wave of migration began in mid-1974 as famine—caused by floods, cyclones and damage of crops—gripped northern Bangladesh. By now, there was increased surveillance with border police, watch posts and river patrols equipped with motorboats and arms. The crisis of hunger engulfed Bangladesh from the middle of 1973,[157] and in the famine of 1974, 30,000–40,000 Bangladeshis died of starvation. In neighbouring West Bengal, the *Times of India* reported, 'many villagers are eating weeds and leaves to stave off hunger, and thousands of destitute migrants from the rural areas . . . are swelling the permanent beggar population in Calcutta'. 'Similar stories' were coming from Assam, the newspaper noted.[158]

According to the *Times of India*, 'Some political elements appear to have had a hand in the influx of Hindus, who have come in search of livelihood, though they have come alone, [while] Muslims have brought their families along.'[159] In April 1975, the newspaper reported that 'thousands of people' from famine-stricken northern Bangladesh had arrived in Assam.[160] Both Hindus and Muslims, who escaped in search of food and opportunities, arrived in Assam by rail. 'The immigrants have come through various border routes and from the North Bengal side.' Many were 'provided shelter by the local people', some of whom even organized 'clandestine transit camps'. 'Hundreds of people, including emaciated children and famished women, [were] found begging in the urban areas.' Others spread out to 'sparsely populated tribal areas' or travelled to the farthest point of the northern bank and reclaimed unploughed government land, resisting official attempts to prevent them from settling there. This renewed arrival of migrants in Assam caused widespread dissatisfaction. More importantly, many tried to secure their names on the electoral list.[161] Officials feared the collapse of law and order, and floods had added to their woes. The flow of migrants was estimated at a 'daily influx of several thousands' according to *The Times*.[162] 'More than 20,000 refugees were recently found in a small subdivision in Assam.' Migrants disappeared into 'obscure villages or empty fields'. Assamese public opinion, for instance, in a memorandum from the Asam Sahitya Sabha to the chief minister, expressed serious concern over this migration.[163] The situation in the relief camps was abysmal. A touring journalist from the *Statesman* reported that the 'piercing wail of thousands of children can be heard for hundreds of yards around this relief camp. They are crying because they are hungry and sick'.[164] Mrs Gandhi assured a delegation of Opposition leaders that food supply would be ensured.

How did these refugees, far less welcome than those who came after Partition, survive? In 1975, an organization carried out a survey among a group of more than a thousand refugee families who had moved to the northern boundary of Assam in the Himalayan foothills.[165] They found themselves in a tribal belt amidst Bodo and Santhal settlers, who were either poor agriculturalists or cattle grazers. The refugees had arrived there over several years, and their condition was 'simply pitiable'.

> The pauperized dare-devil refugees have just occupied whatever land they could reach without waiting for permission from the state government . . . they have started cultivating some 1100 out of the 1700 acres reserved for the government veterinary department. Many attempts to evict them have failed because in the absence of any alternative, the refugees would virtually prefer being mowed down by the Government bulldozers rather than face the consequences of eviction. As things stand, the Government has yet to confer settlement rights on these landholders.

Political and economic uncertainties in Bangladesh increased sharply after the assassination of Mujibur Rahman in August 1975. A report prepared by India's Research & Analysis Wing (RAW) in December said that the political leadership of Bangladesh had realized that 'India will no longer tolerate the economic burden that the influx of this large number of refugees would impose upon it'.[166] The Bangladesh government tried its best to control the situation, but, the report said, 'religious antagonism will, however, continue to manifest itself in the form of petty harassment at the local level, reduction of opportunities particularly in government employment and periodic bouts of Islamic and, therefore, anti-Hindu fervor in the majority community.' The report further noted that the minorities in the new nation would remain 'demoralized and insecure' and resort to 'exodus if the degree of pressure mounts'. Any such future exodus would not only place a great 'economic burden' on India, but it would also 'seriously heighten Hindu–Muslim tension in India, particularly in the North eastern region of Bengal and Assam'. Sounding a note of serious caution, the report stated that such a situation would seriously jeopardize 'the basic tenets of our philosophy of secularism'. It warned that

> should an exodus begin, any policy of stopping the refugees at the border by the use of force would be impracticable and we would inevitably be faced with the necessity of accepting these refugees not only on humanitarian grounds, but also due to pressure of public sentiment particularly in West Bengal where the kith and kin of many of these people reside.

Days earlier, a senior official of India's home ministry had advised the governments of border states to 'locate and push back all illegal immigrants from Bangladesh'.[167]

Low-intensity and irregular or sporadic migration, driven by continuous political and economic uncertainties in Bangladesh, continued. 'Assam seems to have become the magnet' for both Hindu and Muslim migrants, reported *The Hindu*.[168] Assam could accommodate only the most unskilled ones, who became part of her rural agrarian economy. By the end of the 1970s, the global outflow from Bangladesh gained rapid momentum. Remittances from migrants significantly contributed to Bangladesh's economy. In 1979, there were reports of Bihari Pakistanis, who had been the primary workforce in East Pakistan's jute and railway industries, waiting to cross over to

India. The BSF was employed to prevent any large-scale migration. *India Today* reported,

> Throughout India's border with Bangladesh, a steady trickle of illegal immigrants flow into India the year round. The rate of infiltration usually depends on the prices of commodities in Bangladesh. In 1979, the BSF pushed back 300 such illegal immigrants from north Bengal alone. The total number may be 10 times higher.[169]

By the end of the decade, the influx of Bangladeshi immigrants into Assam was successfully portrayed as a threat by Hindu leaders.[170] This nationalist mobilization urged the Indian government to declare the immigrant peasants as illegal citizens and demand their deportation from India. The nationalist Assamese press and a section of Hindu political groups began to publicize the adverse effects of migration and its political and economic consequences for Assam.[171] Such opposition to migration acquired a larger legitimacy when the Indian government declared that no illegal migrant population would be allowed to stay in Assam.[172] Nevertheless, Assam continued to receive immigrants from neighbouring Bangladesh—the landless, labouring poor and destitute—who were victims of a wide range of misfortunes, including environmental crisis, social and economic exploitation and discrimination, and whose numbers remain contested.[173]

# 10

# The Battle Continues

Apart from the deeply traumatic crisis of refugees that overwhelmed eastern India, the years between 1968 and 1974 witnessed further turmoil in Assam fuelled by the rising aspirations of her population. These years restaged political events similar to what Assam had witnessed during the mid-1950s and the early 1960s.

By the late 1960s, Assam had 3600 kilometres of embankments along her rivers.[1] Inspired by similar mega-engineering projects in countries like China and America, the government, aided by a vast techno-bureaucracy and planners, undertook the construction of these embankments in the hope of protecting peasants' crops, livestock and other properties from the annual flooding of Assam. Such mechanized anti-flood structures, which regularly fought with local environmental conditions, could hardly withstand the mighty flow of the Brahmaputra and her tributaries. From the mid-1960s, after a decade of experiments in containing rivers to control flooding, embankments began to crumble and river erosion was frequently reported. Despite this crisis, Assam's agricultural economy and prospects of industrialization began to see some hope in the early 1970s. After missing the early initiatives, India's Green Revolution reached Assam's countryside towards the end of the 1960s.[2] A large majority of peasants took to short-duration, high-yielding dwarf varieties of paddy, and some cultivated the Mexican dwarf variety of wheat, which was introduced into large areas of India by American scientist Norman Ernest Borlaug. This brought moderate relief to many families who were on the verge of hunger. Most high-yielding varieties of paddy were introduced during 1966–67. While these varieties were products of global research, they were further improved at the Paddy Research Centre of the newly established Assam Agricultural University. Early dwarf varieties like *Taichung Native I* suffered from many drawbacks, including susceptibility to bacterial blight, and peasants detested this breed. Other varieties were put to the test; they were given local names like *Manohar Sali* and were more popular. The use of fertilizers also slowly became widespread in Assam, seeing a 30-fold increase between 1962 and 1969. Meanwhile, India participated in an international programme to collect rice germplasm. Between 1967 and 1972, supported by a scheme sponsored by American P.L. 480 funds, Assam contributed to the rice gene bank.

In terms of its industrial economy, Assam had not departed much from the colonial pattern. If India's large and medium capital had for the most part deserted Assam, its tea, timber and petroleum industries still formed an enclave economy. There was a significant acceleration in India's industrial production during 1951–65. Several states made remarkable progress, including Tamil Nadu and Gujarat. Though economists generally agreed that there began a significant slowing down of Indian industrial growth from the mid-1960s onwards,[3] state-owned industries represented hope for millions. However, Assam was hardly a beneficiary in the first few decades of India's industrialization.[4] The state's per capita income continued to decline compared to all-India patterns. As we have seen, by the end of the 1960s, the state and Union governments were at loggerheads regarding the construction of a new refinery in Assam, in addition to the ones at Digboi and Guwahati. India had nine working refineries, and two more—including the one at Haldia—were under construction. Sixty per cent of the feed for these refineries was imported in 1969.[5] Indian policymakers suggested that oil refineries should be nearer to the centres of consumption. After two good harvesting seasons during 1967 and 1968, the demand for petroleum products in the country increased, and this boosted the case for another refinery in Assam.[6] Meanwhile, the increasing output of crude oil in Gujarat—the Koyali refinery started in 1965—triggered demands for another refinery there as well. But experts were not in favour of this; they argued it would be more economical to expand an existing refinery rather than set up a new one.[7]

With Assam looking for a way out of her persistent economic woes, political mobilization to compel the Union government to set up the state's third refinery began in the mid-1960s.[8] As India was preparing her Fourth Five-Year Plan, and as new oil fields were being discovered at Lakwa in Upper Assam, there was increasing clamour for another public sector refinery in Assam. A new refinery and petrochemical industry was seen as a potential source of employment, creation of social capital and was considered to be important for the larger well-being of the economy. While lawmakers lobbied in Delhi, Assamese students and the urban population came together under an umbrella organization called the All-Assam Oil Refinery Sangram Parishad.[9] Science and engineering graduates from Assam aspired to play an important role in the oil industry. But the political efforts and massive popular mobilization notwithstanding, the demand was rejected in April 1968 as an expert committee of techno-bureaucrats made it clear that sufficient crude would not be available to operate another refinery and instead suggested a plan to establish a production facility for liquid ammonia, widely used as fertilizer. According to them, crude oil from the Naharkatiya fields could not be refined for high-grade petroleum products. The Guwahati and Barauni (Bihar) refineries were already producing poor-quality products.[10] In agreement with this view was Dev Kant Barooah, the chairman of Oil India Limited (OIL), the charismatic Assamese poet and member of the Congress. Much against the wishes of his fellow politicians from Assam, Barooah, in his speech at the annual meeting of OIL in June 1968, said that often refineries were established in India on the basis of a political decision rather than on sound economic principles.[11]

None of this put to an end to Assam's campaign for another refinery. On 24 March 1969, the day the Indian Parliament took up the very important Constitution Amendment Bill to reorganize Assam, there began a widespread popular public demonstration.[12] Communist and socialist political leaders roped in the urban middle class, collectively represented by students and government employees, in several thousands. Despite the fact that India's petroleum industry was not keen to establish another refinery in Assam, Chaliha's government extended its tactical support to the public clamour for this. It secured support from all political parties in the State Assembly to pass a resolution on 24 March, which was more than symbolic.[13]

Political hopes of a new refinery grew by mid-1969,[14] after the Union government formed another expert committee to investigate its feasibility in April 1969.[15] The Union government's statement that 'we shall do something so that the people of Assam do not feel left out'[16] was seen by Assamese newspapers as an apparent consent to Assam's demand. Public mobilization—led by an alliance of communists and socialist parties—had also intensified by the end of September, with 1,80,000 people being arrested as the demonstrations turned violent.[17] Amongst the arrested, the largest number comprised students, who found in the petroleum industry the biggest hope for their future economic prosperity.

As clashes between Assamese and non-Assamese resurfaced, Mrs Gandhi had to cancel a visit to Assam.[18] She termed the movement 'misconceived and ill-advised'.[19] Chaliha tried to persuade her to initiate a dialogue, but the Union government did not change its stance.[20] On 5 December 1969, though, based on the suggestions of an expert committee appointed to examine the techno-economic feasibility of locating another refinery in Assam, the Prime Minister announced an economic package for Assam, which said that 'the present refining capacity in Assam should be increased by a little over one million tonnes in the Fourth Plan Period either through expansion or the establishment of an additional refinery, as may be found economically feasible'.[21] For another few months, the prospect of another refinery remained fuzzy. Meanwhile, the Indian Oil Corporation (IOC) was asked to prepare a feasibility report for a petrochemicals complex. An angry lawmaker stated that 'unless we agitate about something we do not get it'.[22]

By 1970, Assam's oil fields produced about 3.3 million tonnes of the country's total 6.8 million tonnes per year.[23] This was distributed among three refineries, Barauni getting the highest share of 54 per cent. As exploration intensified, speculation rose. The Guwahati-based refinery could refine only 0.75 million tonnes per annum, while the one at Digboi had a capacity of 0.50 million tonnes.[24] A proposal to moderately enhance the refining capacity of the Guwahati refinery remained inconclusive; the capacity at Barauni was enhanced from 2 million tonnes per annum to 3 million tonnes.

Meanwhile, certain dramatic developments, which had a significant bearing on the multinational oil companies operating in India, unfolded. Making a departure from Nehruvian practices, the government, in 1973, passed the Foreign Exchange Regulation Act (FERA) to enable stricter control on multinational corporations operating in India. A prelude to this came when in 1971, P.C. Sethi, the Union oil minister, deferred the request of BOC, Shell and Esso to increase their oil production output in the country.[25] With the intention of regulating the flow of foreign capital into India, FERA required the MNCs to dilute their holdings in Indian subsidiaries to 40 per cent.[26] BOC, Shell and Caltex had already taken a defensive position in the wake of the discovery of oil by Indian companies, particularly off the Bombay shore. With the birth of the IOC in 1964, through the merger of Indian Oil Company Ltd and Indian Refineries Ltd, the MNCs had been facing competition from Indian capital. Now, they had no option but to silently succumb to the pressure of the nationalization of their holdings in India.[27] Meanwhile, Mrs Gandhi was facing a united and intensified political opposition, except from the CPI. She had outmanoeuvred the dissidents in her own party, known as the Syndicate, and had split the Congress. After some initial hesitancy, Assam remained on her side.[28]

In mid-1970, the Union government asked the expert committee to reassess its position on another refinery for Assam.[29] A successful Assam bandh on 4 September 1970 conveyed the public mood.[30] The Prime Minister now agreed to a third refinery in Assam.[31] A formal announcement for a refinery-cum-petrochemical complex to be established in Assam's western district came on 11 October 1970.[32] An early disagreement on the product outcome was quickly sorted out.

More than a year later in January 1972, Mrs Gandhi, now into her second term, laid the foundation stone of the refinery at Bongaigaon.

~

In November 1970, Mahendra Mohan Choudhury, who had been the general secretary of the Congress during 1956–57, was chosen as the new chief minister of Assam. From the beginning, his opponents within the party challenged him. Though Choudhury refused to bow down to any kind of factionalism, the ground had already been prepared to challenge his power and influence within the party.[33] Mrs Gandhi also considered him as a 'road-block in the way of revamping of the party leadership through the induction of younger and more "progressive" elements at all levels'. While Chaliha had managed to sustain a reasonably liberal outlook towards the minorities despite facing heavy challenges, Choudhury, political commentators predicted, would take a tough stand against the hill people's demand for full statehood.[34]

Assam had by then got an early taste of political radicalism, largely as an offshoot of that in Bengal. A few landlords were killed; the government arrested young radical students from the Gauhati University campus.[35] The Indian government continued to worry about attempts by China and Pakistan to destabilize Assam in the 1970s. The Union government believed that Naga rebels were in contact with these countries. 'China has formulated a strategy of coordinated insurgency in the North-Eastern Region by Nagas, Mizos and other tribal insurgent elements,' the Ministry of Defence warned.[36] The ministry also noted that the insurgents were being helped with finances, arms and weapons and military training and were fed ideological propaganda through radio broadcasts. That East Pakistan had given shelter to Mizo rebels was well-known. The government prepared a white paper on these issues to present in the Parliament. The draft noted that 'China and Pakistan made common cause in fomenting and sustaining tribal insurgency in north eastern India'. Indian intelligence often got information from rebels who were behind bars. Chinese ideological and military support to Naga separatists was a cause for concern: 'They were also put through a musketry test. Lectures were delivered on the tactics of guerrilla warfare, war of Chinese liberation, Vietnam war, Sino-Indian conflict 1962, Mao's thought and the philosophy of communism.'[37] By the early 1970s, the Naga rebels' bonhomie with the Burmese rebels, including the Kachin Independence Army, was also evident. Though the Indian Army's war in Nagaland had come to an end with a ceasefire being declared in 1964, the truce broke down three years later, following which Nagaland experienced an intense period of insurgency and counter-insurgency, an account of which is outside the scope of this book.[38] The slicing of Assam's territory had brought to the fore longstanding disputes over boundaries with new states such Nagaland. As early as 1945 Assam's chief commissioner J.P. Mills had called these disputes a 'sleeping dog' that now seemed to have awakened, leading to serious incidents of violence. Contests over the control of resources, including agricultural land and markets in the foothills, acquired the form of acrimonious and violent political disputes.[39]

Before the 1972 Assam elections, and after months of factionalism within the Assam Congress, Mrs Gandhi removed M.M. Choudhury and made him the Governor of Punjab.[40] The Prime Minister had now begun the practice of nominating her chosen person as the state's chief minister instead of allowing the state party organization to elect one. She had been unhappy with the doubtful position taken by the Choudhury-led Congress government after the Congress split in 1969.[41] The Congress's constant electoral victory in Assam was largely due to the backing of the Assamese-speaking 'bourgeois-landlord' classes. The latter's prosperity and power were dependent, to a great extent, on state patronage. As a political scientist observed, Mrs Gandhi began to mount pressure on the Choudhury-led government and the Assamese power elites by shifting her support to their rivals.[42] These included Assam's linguistic and religious minorities; however, the political and social situations in Assam forced Mrs Gandhi to seek more inclusive alternatives for the post of the chief minister.

In January 1972, Sarat Chandra Sinha—who was not a member of the state legislature then—was Mrs Gandhi's chosen candidate.[43] Sinha, a law graduate from BHU, unlike all his predecessors, was largely an outsider to the social world of the Assamese elites. From that year's election onwards, Mrs Gandhi bypassed the state political leadership and reached out to the masses on her own. None of the state leaders 'has as yet enough independent strength to hope to rise to the top ranks of leadership without her blessings', wrote Norman D. Palmer, the American political scientist. Sinha's party got a massive mandate—95 of the total 114 Assembly seats. The CPI stood firmly behind Mrs Gandhi. The communists and socialists won seven seats. Her rival, the Congress (O), managed only a negligible presence, and the Jana Sangh was not able to make any major breakthrough. The 1972 elections became famous for Indira Gandhi's *garibi hatao*—eliminate poverty—slogan, adopted as part of her government's programme in the previous year.

Sinha's government went ahead with two major decisions that would impact Assam's political landscape for some time to come. The first reduced the upper limit of landholding to 50 bighas. In another move, the Assam Tenancy Act of 1971, which further, and drastically, redefined the rights of landowning classes, was brought into force by the new government in Assam. Many lost their social status, and the rich and privileged families of Guwahati were impacted. But as became apparent in a few years, the actual impact of these laws was partial; most of the large landholders successfully redistributed their properties within their own families. This could be seen in the sudden increase in the number of rich landowners—having more than 50 bighas—by 88 per cent.[44] More on this is discussed in the next chapter.

Political instability ran high in the early '70s. College teachers intensified their demand for autonomy from government control. A large number of colleges, known as non-deficit colleges, were eligible for government budgetary allocation. A teachers' strike had taken place in June 1973,[45] which had temporarily brought the communists and others together. The railway strike of May 1974 badly hit Assam's tea industry.[46] More than a thousand people died in floods that year.

The loss of Meghalaya also meant a loss of crucial control over not only a place of pride for the Assamese but also a key economic resource. The government-owned Assam Cement Limited, commissioned in

Cherrapunji in 1966, was a 'rapidly expanding' industry that had 'upgraded life sharply for the several thousand frequently drenched residents of this little mountain settlement'. Regarded as the place which recorded the world's highest rainfall, Cherrapunji had 'plentiful deposits of limestone and clay'. Gypsum was brought from India's desert state of Rajasthan, and Yugoslavia had extended technical expertise for the plant.[47]

~

In 1971, with the birth of Bangladesh, Bengali pride in their language was at a peak. Assam was one of the states which adopted a three-language formula where Hindi was taught to high school students along with English and the regional language. In Assam, from 1968 onwards, the Asam Sahitya Sabha had already begun to pressure the government and both the universities to adopt Assamese as the language of instruction. The reorganization of Assam became the rallying point for advocating the demand for Assamese as the medium of instruction. Meanwhile, the rumours of the unpublished 1971 Census reports, which allegedly revealed that the numbers of the Assamese speakers had decreased, worried many in Assam.[48] In May 1971, the Asam Sahitya Sabha resolved that within Assam, for administrative reasons, Assamese should be the official language, and Assamese should be the medium of instruction.[49] Gauhati University, in its third decade then, was the symbol of Assamese aspirations. In May 1970, the academic council of Gauhati University decided to adopt Assamese as the medium of instruction, and this came into effect in July 1972. English was retained as a second option. Dibrugarh University followed suit, and colleges in Cachar, Manipur, Nagaland, NEFA and Meghalaya, being affiliated to this university, would also come under this rule.

In Assam, while many shared the aspirations of the Assamese speakers, others underlined that Bengali speakers (*bhasik sankhyalaghu*, a term widely used for them) too had a legitimate right to learn and pursue their academic careers in their mother tongue.[50] The confrontation between the Assamese and Bengali speakers took multiple forms. Assamese-speaking students boycotted classes, even as there was an increasing demand for state support for the Bengali language. In June 1972, the Bengali intelligentsia organized a large group to march in Calcutta, demanding more state investment in the Bengali language.[51] At the same time, the Nepali speakers in Darjeeling sought official recognition of their language. Some non-Assamese speakers, which included several tribal communities, came together under the umbrella of the Linguistic Minorities Rights Committee.[52] Colleges in Manipur, worried about the situation, shifted their affiliation from Gauhati University to Jawaharlal Nehru University, which had been established in New Delhi in 1969.

Allowing English to be an alternative medium of instruction came as a source of huge relief for a small group of Assamese elite and also for the people of the hill states. In Cachar, a largely Bengali-speaking district that was always considered to have more affinity with Bengal, there were rumblings. In their neighbourhood, Bengali speakers had just won a bloody battle and a nation in recognition of their language. Popular mobilization intensified in Cachar to make Bengali a medium of instruction. Under mounting pressure, in March 1972, Gauhati University gave students the option to write their papers in Bengali.[53] But this did not address the problems of Bengali-speaking students in the classroom—and it evoked protests from the Assamese students, who—with the silent backing of a wider public—cited this as an attack on their national and cultural identity. They referred to other Indian states where the switch to the regional language had been much easier. The Assamese students vowed to resist the concession made by Gauhati University. The university's academic council met on 6 June 'in a rather tense atmosphere' and reiterated its position.[54]

As the council's decision became known, there was widespread anger. For the next few days, the university campus 'continued to be a scene of intense agitations and demonstrations'.[55] Bengali-speaking students vacated the campus. The police arrested a few agitating students. On 12 June, the academic council of Gauhati University reconvened in a highly charged atmosphere and under intense scrutiny from the Assamese-speaking student community, and it made Assamese the mandatory medium of instruction, apart from English as an alternative medium.[56] The earlier option of allowing students to write in Bengali was withdrawn. Assamese newspapers expressed a sense of relief.[57]

The government—in consultation with Opposition parties—continued to put pressure on the university to allow Bengali as a medium of instruction in Cachar. 'There was a consensus that, in all fairness, Bengali will have to be used as the medium of instruction in Cachar and that the university should consider the matter most carefully and take an appropriate decision.' Gauhati University had no disagreement with this, but it argued that 'it would be impolitic' to take up this question immediately. The CPI agreed with the idea of Assamese being the medium of instruction, but it proposed that till another university was established in Cachar, teaching should continue in English.[58]

Soon, the issue was out on the streets; it was no longer confined to within the university. If the Bengali Hindus in Cachar remained united, Assamese and Bengali Muslims, in a departure from the earlier history of political solidarity, held meetings together supporting the decision of the university and also rallied against the Bengali Hindus.[59] The university played to the gallery: two languages as mediums of instruction and three languages for answering questions in the examination.

Soon, protests intensified in Cachar, where the refugee crisis was yet to subside entirely, and there was even a demand for making it a union territory. Stray voices were also heard about the Bengalis' willingness to learn Assamese from the school level, provided enough support was given.[60] A major worry for the Bengali community was that it was losing out on employment opportunities. The Bengali speakers in Cachar, increasingly marginalized within the body politic of Assam, did not want to accept defeat. They mobilized, created public opinion, sent out a carefully drafted and less provocative memorandum and continued to demand the inclusion of Bengali as a medium of instruction.[61] Their spirited campaign came to a brief halt when, on 26 October 1972, the Supreme Court declared Gauhati University's decision to declare Assamese as the medium of instruction constitutionally valid. The defenders of Assamese were jubilant.[62]

Across the Brahmaputra Valley, given their modest numbers and complex socio-economic dependency, Bengali and other non-Assamese speakers reacted differently from their Cachar brethren.[63] Support for the Assamese medium came from weaker social groups. The Assam Chah Mazdoor Sangha, the tea garden workers' trade union, was one of them.[64] As violent clashes between the Bengali Hindus (urban petty traders) and Muslims (rural peasantry) spread, an extraordinary political solidarity between the Assamese Hindus and Muslims came to be noticed. A process of *Assamization*, as noted by observers, had begun as early as 1951 when a section of non-Assamese speakers formally declared Assamese as their mother tongue. The 1951 census had enumerated 51 per cent Assamese speakers and 42 per cent Bengali speakers. R.B. Vaghaiwalla, the census superintendent, noted that the decline of the Bengali-speaking population in Assam was a result of 'aggressive nationalism now prevailing in Assam, coupled with the desire of many persons among the Muslims as well as tea garden labour immigrants to adopt Assamese as their mother-tongue in the state of their adoption'.[65]

Depending on the local social composition, political alliances took unlikely forms. For example, Bodos and Hindu Bengalis united in Lower Assam.[66] 'The loud are the linguistic minorities in Assam, [their] voice is up and nobody can check it,' cheered a leader in the Parliament.[67] Some voices could be heard in support of the Bengali speakers in the Brahmaputra Valley too.[68] A number of non-Assamese speakers across Assam, like the members of the Bodo Sahitya Sabha, extended their political support to the Bengali speakers' rejection of Assamese as a medium of instruction.[69]

As pressure from Cachar intensified, on 23 September 1972, the Assam government decided to take a strong stand. The safest option, which had approval from the Union government, was to establish another university in Cachar and also to agree to the announcement of the Gauhati University on Assamese and English being the mediums of instruction.[70] Beyond a separate university, 'no other solution is possible as there is tremendous opposition to Bengali being introduced as an additional medium' wrote Chief Minister Sinha to Indira Gandhi.

Sinha further hinted that for many residents of the Brahmaputra Valley, the other solution was 'the separation of Cachar from Assam'. Indeed, the separation of Cachar was advised by a delegation of the Gauhati University on 23 October 1972.[71]

The idea of their own university, which the Assam government wanted to be fully funded by the Centre, was welcomed by people in Cachar, including its Congress lawmakers.[72] However, this did not go down well with the Assamese speakers, who recalled that the establishment of Gauhati University had faced much opposition from a section of the Bengali intelligentsia. The Asam Sahitya Sabha and the All-Assam Students' Union (AASU), followed by many others, went a step further and opposed both the idea of a separate university for Cachar and that of bilingual instruction in the universities of Assam.[73] An Assam Bandh, called by AASU, was observed on 5 October, and battle lines were drawn.[74] Clashes took place between Bengali Hindus and Assamese. The mayhem that soon followed saw riots, loot, stray incidences of molestation and even the burning of houses in the urban areas of the Darrang district where Bengali Hindus had settled. The death of one young student galvanized emotive politics. As violence spread in the business areas of Assam, a curfew was imposed by the second week of October, and the army had to be deployed.[75] Several people died, including students.[76] It was a major testing ground for student-led political mobilization. The students had extraordinary support and mentoring from their teachers. Violence soon spread to the rural areas of central Assam, and many were killed; in one locality alone, 'four or five villages were reported to have gone into flames'.[77] This was followed by several days of intense picketing by the students. Riots, arson and looting continued for more than a month. Air services came to a halt. On 13 October, eight persons were killed in police firing. A passenger bus was set on fire in Upper Assam. The Assam police took the assistance of the Indian Army to quell the riots.[78] The shock of violence was so extensive that political leaders and officials had to conduct aerial surveys of riot-affected areas of central Assam.[79] The dead, quickly declared martyrs, became symbols of Assamese nationalist political resistance. Bhashani, who by then was a leader of the National

Awami Party of Bangladesh, added to the linguistic passion in Assam by asking for a 'Greater Bengal' in the wake of the political crisis arising from Assam's territorial reorganization.[80]

The violence continued for weeks. Towards the end of October, posters began to appear in Guwahati exhorting the people of Assam to 'liberate the Assamese people from [exploitation by the] Indian people'.[81] That year's Durga Puja, a major religious and cultural event of the Hindu Bengalis, but equally celebrated by the Assamese, remained cheerless and dismal as violence gripped the Brahmaputra Valley. Arson, rioting, house-burning, kidnapping and killing became widespread. Organized mobs raided Bengali-speaking houses. In Jorhat, a prosperous town of Upper Assam, an Assamese person married to a Sylheti-origin Bengali Hindu woman was severely assaulted by their Bengali Hindu neighbours, as he was thought to be a spy for the Assamese.[82]

On 29 October, in a radio speech, Sinha admitted to popular disagreement with the resolution of his government.[83] Sinha, however, made the point that one had to be sensitive to the question of language in Assam, and it would be unwise to force Assamese on the entire population. Assam's historical experience was not a happy one. As pressure mounted and riots continued, the Union government's emissary, Fakhruddin Ali Ahmed, had a discussion with Sinha, and the latter announced on 12 November that the government would not go ahead with the Assembly's resolution. A formal announcement of the end of the agitation was quickly made by AASU.[84] The government withdrew its decision to open a university in Cachar, and it also introduced the compulsory learning of Assamese till high school in non-Assamese schools.[85] At least one political group—Ujani Assam Rajya Parishad (UARP)—protested, saying that the imposition of Assamese was unfair on many smaller linguistic communities and that this would only deepen the fault lines within Assamese society.[86] In Lower Assam, as some colleges did not allow English, community leaders from tribal societies extended their solidarity to the students who remained adamant about not taking instructions in Assamese.[87]

In the winter of 1972, the Indian Parliament was to discuss the *Twelfth Report of the Commissioner for Linguistic Minorities*. This report painted a bleak picture of many smaller languages in the country, including Nepali in Bengal. This was another opportunity for the lawmakers to pay attention to Assam's language troubles. Across India, others too fought forcefully to defend their mother tongues. By then, Assamese Congress members, too, had become more aggressive. 'Could Patna University or Calcutta University provide the facility of mother tongue in all the languages? It is neither practicable nor advisable,' said Tarun Gogoi, who would become Assam's chief minister three decades later.[88] Gogoi added that 'there are those who do not want to merge with the interests of Assam, who do not want Assam University to follow the national policy'. 'UP and Bihar do not allow a linguistic minority to get a job unless they pass this ultra-difficult language test,' complained Samar Guha, a Left MP.[89] Many political leaders foresaw more troubles for India as a whole. It was pointed out that 'Assam is a warning, a serious warning to the entire country and Assam shows how an agreed solution, even an agreed solution reached at a political level can be blown up overnight by the sheer force of physical pressure and violence'.[90]

Back in Assam, the fault lines in the social lives of the Assamese and non-Assamese speakers widened further. Multilingualism and multiculturalism would not be welcomed for the time being. 'The linguistic minorities in every state should learn to merge with the local people and live in peace and harmony with them,' wrote two Assamese students studying in Bombay.[91] Towards the end of 1972, when the Union government decided to establish a university in Meghalaya, which was to be called North-Eastern Hill University (NEHU), Assamese leaders feared that colleges in Cachar would opt for affiliation with this university. Sinha had to persuade Mrs Gandhi not to allow NEHU to have affiliations with colleges from Assam.[92]

The outcome of this language politics had powerful cultural consequences. A section of the elite Assamese already preferred their wards to study in English-medium schools, considered to be a major marker of socio-economic progress. The agitation and the resultant imposition of Assamese by the government led to a boom in privately-run English-medium schools. Several much sought-after elite flagship educational institutes came up, and the fate of government-run Assamese-medium schools was gradually sealed.

~

For several decades, Assam had invested her material resources to develop Shillong as her capital. But with the formation of the state of Meghalaya with its capital in Shillong, there was a need for Assam to choose a new capital. The Assamese elite felt a sense of a loss of treasured memories; for the people of Meghalaya, Shillong represented their valuable heritage. Briefly, as a result of a degree of political understanding between Assam and Meghalaya, the government of the former continued to function from Shillong, but not without some unease. The Assam government formed a committee in 1970 to decide on the new capital of the severely truncated state.[93] The task before the search committee, comprising bureaucrats and engineers, was very difficult. It had four choices: three near Guwahati (Chandrapur, Amchang, Sonaighuli) and one at Silghat in central Assam. But no serious planning had gone into any of these proposals. The Assam government hinted that the choice would depend on how much financial assistance it got from the Union government.[94]

As the proposed choices around Guwahati were prone to 'water-logging during monsoon', plans for draining the low-lying areas into Deepor Beel, which could act as an inland lake-cum-balancing reservoir, were considered. The committee prioritized scenic beauty, which was so much a part of Shillong, now suddenly lost. Many of the sites chosen by the committee reflected this priority: 'The hills are gentle and undulating and offer scope for developing a picturesque hill town'; the plans for the housing of VIPs resembled the 'Greek acropolis'. The Union government, however, thought that the plans were on the extravagant side, exceeding the 200 million rupees it had given for the recent upgrading of Chandigarh, the twin capital city of Haryana and Punjab.

Eventually, Dispur on the eastern fringe of Guwahati city, became the temporary site of the capital until a final selection could be made. Old tea warehouses were renovated to house lawmakers and officials, and space was made for those who sought opportunities in the capital. Most construction works were given to local Assamese entrepreneurs. The legislature building could not match the impressive imperial style of the Shillong legislature. An ancient city, surrounded by hills and the majestic Brahmaputra, Guwahati was still a largely agrarian settlement. Marshy lands and swamps dominated the landscape, dotted with the huts of small peasants and sharecroppers. Most of the agrarian population belonged to Assam's tribal communities with precarious livelihoods. As a result of the communist mobilization of Assam's rural poor in the 1940s, many of those who tilled the lands of the town's rich landlords had defied and humiliated the latter by refusing to pay rent.

During the first two decades after Independence, the economic prosperity of the town progressed only slowly, largely dominated by Assam's cultural elite, both Hindus and Muslims, and the Marwari traders. The latter had made their fortunes from several decades of trade in grain and from the credit markets. Their social life was still confined to the congested colonial market complex. The western fringes of Guwahati received a stream of Hindu refugees from East Pakistan through the 1950s and 1960s. The city was taking the shape of a cosmopolitan society, though with Assamese–Bengali political rivalries as was common elsewhere. 'Anybody who has re-visited Gauhati after a long time must have been struck by the enormous extent the town has grown over the last two decades,' wrote a perceptive observer in 1961.[95]

Mahatma Gandhi had thought that the hill town of Shillong was too far away from the aspirations of the masses. When the foundation stone was laid for the new capital on 2 October 1972, there was some sense of relief that the capital had come back to the plains. The choice of this suburb of Guwahati was not easy, for the Congress camp was divided; a majority favoured Silghat in central Assam. Only in 1969–70 had the city of Guwahati rediscovered its lost ancient glory. The city was mentioned in the ancient Hindu epics and other religious scriptures. Scattered religious structures, integral to the city's landscape and social milieu, bore testimony to its rise and fall over the centuries. During an accidental excavation for a multistorey building in the heart of the city, traces of possible archaeological findings were noticed. Excavations carried out during 1969 and 1970 by a team of scholars from Gauhati University and Pune's Deccan College Postgraduate Research Institute confirmed that they had stumbled upon something bigger. These sites drew wider scholarly attention. An examination of fragments of pottery and the 'stylistic evidence of sculptures' helped archaeologists to conclude that the antiquity of the site could be traced back to the early years of the seventh century AD.[96]

The new capital at Dispur began with modest facilities, but a national daily speculated that this temporary capital would become a permanent one driven by the commercial prospects of Guwahati.[97] The selection of the site also brought back attention to the Lower and Upper Assam controversy. Many pointed out that despite being endowed with an extensive transport network, Guwahati, already burdened by waterlogging and poor sanitation and drainage systems, could 'ill afford to bear the burden of an extra population'.[98] In 1971, this small town had a population of 2,00,000; three decades earlier, it had been a sixth of its size. An urban place of politics, commerce and of vibrant grain trade, Guwahati would soon transform into a chaotic city. Till World War II, this tiny township with an area of less than three square miles was 'essentially a business centre and only a few small-scale industries such as oil mills, rice mills, tool making and repairing etc.'[99] The war, as discussed earlier, introduced dramatic transformation into the town's economic and social life, which was graphically captured in a contemporary verse by Hem Barua, 'Guwahati, 1944'.[100] Things began to change rapidly.

Early in the 1970s, Guwahati was still far from being a machine-driven town; while 162 city buses and 80 auto-rickshaws were officially registered, 640 animal-driven vehicles still jostled for space on the congested roads. More than 5000 bicycles and 3700 cycle-rickshaws ferried its residents. About three-fourths of the houses were electrified; the rest were dependent on kerosene oil lamps. The poor and the wretched managed to secure dilapidated living spaces in the heart of the town—around the main railway station and stadium. 'The spaces below the two flyovers situated near Pan Bazar and the Nehru Stadium have literally become the dwelling place of beggars, vagrants, and lepers. These two places are responsible to a large extent in spreading diseases and emitting obnoxious smell.'[101]

Two modestly ambitious plans, designed between 1965 and 1986, had laid out steps to transform Guwahati into a modern city, but these were largely failures.[102] This was partly because the political and bureaucratic apparatus could not tackle the city's growing population and also due to the fundamental social and ecological features of the city. Writing in 1975, M.S. Prabhakara, the Kannadiga author, journalist and academician, based in Guwahati, noted that there was a 'scramble for new construction'. 'Great hillsides with fantastically contoured profiles are being continuously cut to fill in the low-lying areas . . . a mild shower flooding [the] streets for hours together and, in the rainy season, whole areas under water for weeks or even months together; unimaginably overcrowded city transport,' wrote Prabhakara.[103] There was widespread agreement that Guwahati was characterized by 'little enclaves of opulence and splendour surrounded by the most abject and degrading kind of poverty and filth'.[104]

Midway into Mrs Gandhi's Emergency, Dispur–Guwahati hosted a session of the All India Congress Committee (AICC). There was massive controversy over the misuse of public money and official machinery for this meeting, and there was a hue and cry about the large numbers of tribal residents of the venue area being thrown out.[105] In the outskirts of the city, 'thickly forested bits of flat land', *India Today* reported, were 'touched by some magic wand, converted into a glittering miniature township'.[106] This was one of the last occasions when Guwahati's tribal population was seen in the city's agrarian and rural outskirts. Guwahati, by now, another commentator noted, had 'grown up to become a typical Indian city'. This was also the last major appearance in Assam's public life of Congress president D.K. Barooah, well-known for his deeply undemocratic proclamation 'India is Indira. Indira is India' during the December 1976 Guwahati session of the AICC. Thereafter, he could not secure his position at the centre stage of Assam's politics. The Guwahati session of the AICC did not allow Assamese leaders to play any major role in the political deliberations of the party; the key role was played by the Congress leaders from the states that had been carved out of Assam. However, the session helped to some extent in accommodating the political aspirations of leaders of the ethnic communities.

~

Till the end of the 1960s, Assam was one of the highest-ranking Indian states in terms of net domestic product (NDP), largely sustained by capital investments of the pre-Independence era; it was ranked fifth between 1950 and 1965, but it started sliding thereafter for the lack of any major public investment.[107] For decades, Assam's per capita income, too, had remained high; it was the highest for urban areas among Indian states in surveys done between 1957 and 1964.[108]

Assam's hope for industrialization in the 1970s never took off. As India opened up for more private sector participation in industry, Mrs Gandhi's government insisted that large corporations reach out to less developed areas to establish industries; some did extend the promise of help, but either due to the problems of red tape or political uncertainty, the projects did not get off the ground. The Tatas proposed a synthetic detergent factory at Dhubri in 1970, but the license to set it up could not be obtained till 1975, and the idea was eventually shelved.[109]

There was some silver lining though. The establishment of a petrochemical complex at Namrup, not far from Digboi, the first oil refinery in India, was one of them.[110] But the economic crisis soon took a political form. In August 1974, the *Assam Tribune* carried an editorial titled 'Disappointment in Oil',[111] which blamed the Union government for not allowing Assam to use its oil resources for her own economic development. Questioning the diversion of crude oil to Barauni, it complained, 'Oil is a wasting asset and the only mineral that Assam possesses in considerable quantity.' This did not go down well with officials in Delhi, who considered it as being 'politically motivated'.[112]

They were worried that Assam might refuse to share crude oil with the Barauni refinery.

That Assam's troubles were rooted in a weak economy and were made worse by the Union government's (read India's federal structure) unwillingness to provide economic relief, increasingly found an echo in the voices of the Assamese intelligentsia.[113] This grievance would take multiple forms and would, years later, become part of a very powerful and stimulating Assamese political narrative.[114] A report prepared in 1971 by the Industrial Development Bank of India suggested the pattern of flow of capital: cash outflows—an estimated Rs 130 crore annually—from Assam, by way of remittances of seasonal and semi-permanent workers, business profits, small savings and bank funds, exceeded, in 1968–69, the inflow in the form of loans, grants and all forms of investments. Added to this was an excess of bank deposits over bank credits—in 1970, for instance, against a per capita deposit of Rs 30, the per capita credit was Rs 14.[115] Overall, the report estimated that net outflows exceeded inflows by 9 per cent of the state income, though commodity flows into and out of Assam remained balanced.[116] Many believed that the increasing volume of grants to the North-east was largely to 'freeze, if not reinforce, tribal and sectarian differences'.[117]

A cross-section of officials and policymakers expressed anxiety about Assam's fragile economic order in the 1970s. An estimate carried out in 1971 by two well-known Indian economists suggested that a little less than half of the rural population and 23 per cent of urban dwellers had been poor a decade earlier.[118] The poor were defined as those who did not have access to 2250 calories per person per day. Another official report concluded that the situation had turned grave by 1970–71, when it estimated that—assuming that less than Rs 48 per capita per month designated 'poor'—two-thirds of Assam's population was poor.[119] Employment generation remained sluggish. Between 1961 and 1974, the total number of employed people increased only marginally from 7.4 lakh to 7.7 lakh. During this period, employment in the private sector fell by a fifth, with Assam's share in India's private sector employment falling from 11.51 per cent to 6.85 per cent. Assam's share in India's public sector employment was 2.41 per cent in 1961, and it increased marginally to 2.49 per cent in 1974 (compared to West Bengal's 9.79 per cent and 10.33 per cent for the same period). By the early '70s, unable to get jobs of their choice, a section of educated youth, aided by moderate support from the Assam government, took to plying auto-rickshaws in Guwahati, an official account reported.[120] This situation showed no signs of improvement by the end of the decade.

In 1980, *India Today* carried out an assessment of Assam's economic situation and concluded that, along with its neighbouring states, Assam was 'a chronically ill patient who leaves the doctor scratching his head'.[121] The report further highlighted how six out of 10 families in Assam lived below the poverty line as against the national average of four. Eighty per cent of Assam's food, clothing and heavy and light machinery for small-scale industries were imported from other Indian states. Of India's 15,000 large- and medium-scale industries, Assam had just 21. Assam accounted for 2 per cent of India's foodgrains production. The crop yield had not increased sufficiently; between 1971 and 1977, the per acre yield of foodgrains rose by just 10 per cent, compared with 18 per cent nationally. Fertilizer consumption per hectare of cropped area in Assam was a mere 3 kg compared to 100 kg in Haryana and Punjab. With a per capita income of Rs 852 per annum (at 1980 prices), Assam was one of the poorest Indian states. The state's gross domestic product during this period rose by only 2 per cent—half the national growth rate. Of the approximately 3,00,000 unemployed registered with employment exchanges in the region, only 6000 could find jobs in 1977–78—that is, only 3.5 per cent, against the national average of 13 per cent.[122] Forty per cent of India's villages were electrified; but when darkness fell, electric lights came on in only 10 per cent of Assam's villages.[123] Assam and her neighbours accounted for over 7.5 per cent of India's total area, but only 0.03 per cent of India's total railway lines.[124] Assam had only one branch for a population of 32,000, as against an Indian average of one branch per 20,000 people. As in the earlier decades, Assam's principal items of exports were coal, pulses, jute, tea, timber and oil, and it continued to be heavily dependent on the import of foodgrains and consumer goods.

In 1974, goods alone were transported through an estimated 72,438 wagons of metre-gauge railways.[125]

However, the late 1970s and early 1980s were years of hope for the vast majority of peasants in Assam. The 1970s saw some stability and a moderate rise in foodgrains production. This was mainly due to more areas being brought under cultivation. Between 1970–71 and 1980–81, the area under rice cultivation increased from an estimated 1.9 million hectares to 2.2 million hectares, while production increased from 1.9 million tonnes to 2.5 million tonnes.[126] Mustard and jute were two major crops which helped Assam's peasants improve their lot. Better prices of jute in the late 1970s, which peaked at an 'abnormally high' price during 1984–85, tempted them to assign some portions of their agricultural lands for jute cultivation, which brought them more profit.[127] A major part of the gains went into educating their children, rebuilding their houses and sometimes enhancing their material well-being. But these new-found economic and social opportunities were largely confined to a select few.

~

Before its wounds from the political crisis of 1972 arising from the issue of medium of instruction could heal and before the Assamese speakers (who were by now very much in command of the state's political-bureaucratic machinery) could succeed in guaranteeing the idea of one language in a multilingual social milieu, further troubles arose. The first came when Assam's tribal population living in the plains took to the streets asking for a separate state. Early in December 1972, large numbers of them, united under the banner of Plain Tribals Council of Assam (PTCA), pressed their demand for a separate 'Udayachal' state.[128] The leaders of the PTCA, while announcing this political demand at a press conference in New Delhi on 2 December 1972, claimed that this 'act of disintegration [from Assam] will help strengthen national integration'.[129] The PTCA leaders had met Mrs Gandhi on 30 November and presented a detailed list of grievances against the Assam government and the ruling classes, including the fact that 'they had been forced to learn through the medium of Assamese in colleges and universities'.¹³⁰ They also made it clear that 'it is no longer possible to live in amity with the Assamese'.¹³¹

The next crisis occurred when the Bodos—constituting approximately 4.17 per cent of Assam's total population according to the census of 1971¹³²—declared that they would use the Roman script for their language.¹³³ The momentum for this had been building up over time. The basic grammar and linguistic features of the Bodo language were spelt out from the late nineteenth century onwards.¹³⁴ As early as 1893, the American Baptist missionaries, in their bid to bring education to Assam's hill tribes, had decided to adapt the Roman alphabet for writing tribal languages that did not have scripts.¹³⁵ The Assam government had published a couple of Bodo school textbooks early in the twentieth century in the Roman script, but these were discontinued later.¹³⁶ George Grierson's mammoth *Linguistic Survey of India* had recognized the Bodos as one of the major groups of the Tibeto-Burman language family. More research was published from the 1950s onwards, including studies by anthropologist and linguist Robbins Burling of the University of Pennsylvania and linguist Pramod Chandra Bhattacharya from the Gauhati University, who published their pathbreaking works on the Bodos between 1959 and 1977.¹³⁷ These findings shaped the future linguistic aspirations of the Bodos.

The rise of the modern Bodo language in the twentieth century was sandwiched between the powerful Assamese and Bengali speakers and their linguistic cultures.¹³⁸ But neither of these could fully influence the Bodo language. The first published Bodo book, *Boroni Fisa O Ayen*, was printed in Bengali script in 1915, while the first Bodo literary magazine, *Bibar*, had articles in Assamese, Bodo and Bengali languages, with the Bodo language printed in Assamese script.¹³⁹ Many, like historian Edward Gait and linguist Suniti Kumar Chatterji, predicted that the Bodo language would vanish. Gait warned that the 'Bodo dialects', spoken by more than half a million people in Assam, 'are in their turn giving way to Aryan languages (Assamese and Bengali) and their complete disappearance is only a matter of time'.¹⁴⁰ Speaking several decades later, Suniti Kumar Chatterji concurred that, in most cases, Bodo speakers 'have merged into the Bengali and Assamese speaking masses, Hindu as well as Mussalman, in the area'.[141] The Bodo literary intelligentsia's use of both Assamese and Bengali language in their works was disliked by the Assamese intelligentsia.[142] Leading Bodo intellectuals disapproved of the Assamese view of considering the Bodo language as non-Aryan. *Bibar*, the literary magazine published since 1924, was one of the earliest examples of the Bodo desire to compete with the Assamese and seek a path of progress. *Bibar* made known its displeasure at the Assamese scholars' views on the Bodos.[143] The emerging Bodo intelligentsia could not have ignored the rising political consciousness of their poor agrarian brethren. News of the Bodo tenants' assemblage under the banner of Goalpara Ryot Sabha, a left-leaning platform of the peasants where Hindu and Muslim leaders spoke against the landlords, found space in the first issue of *Bibar*.[144]

In 1952, the Assam government made a small concession to the Bodos, allowing them to read their language in the Roman script up to the primary level. In turn, the Bodo Sahitya Sabha, the literary platform of the Bodo intelligentsia formed in 1952, decided to adopt the Assamese script for the Bodo language. The Bodo political leadership was closely aligned with the Assamese Congress leaders. Also, if schoolgoers learnt their language in the Assamese script, more choices would be available to them later. The mass of the people still used the Bengali, Roman or Assamese script. Meanwhile, not to be defeated by the rising Assamese control of the state machinery, the Bodo intelligentsia now demanded that the Bodo language be made a language of instruction at the primary level.[145] Plans were also afloat for compiling grammar and dictionaries for the Bodo language. The Assam government did not concede, arguing that this would 'adversely affect our common national interests'.[146] Undeterred, the Bodo intelligentsia continued to push their demands for the next few years.

A controversy broke out in 1960 as the question of an official language engulfed Assam. When the 1961 census enumeration was done, unlike in previous years, the Bodo speakers declared Bodo as their mother tongue.[147] Others, like tea-garden workers, followed suit.

An angry Bodo Sahitya Sabha not only made known its hostility to the idea of Assamese as Assam's official language, but it even proposed the adoption of Hindi in its place.[148] As the gulf continued to widen, the first major demand for the Roman script for the Bodo language surfaced in 1964. The idea of a separate state for the tribal people also began circulating around the same time. While several other non-Aryan-language-speaking communities from the Brahmaputra Valley decided to stick to Assamese, this idea began to gain popularity among a group of the Bodo intelligentsia. Experts who consulted leading Indian linguists, including Suniti Kumar Chatterji, helped them to spell out the reasons for their preference for the Roman script over Assamese or Bengali.[149] After several rounds of discussions and examination of the issue by a committee comprising Bodo scholars, the Bodo Sahitya Sabha decided in 1970 to adopt the Roman script. The Sabha made a representation before both the Indian and Assam governments, asking for the teaching of the Bodo language with the use of the Roman script, English as the medium of instruction, and Hindi as the third language. Early in the 1970s, the Bodo language came to be taught in some schools of Lower Assam. This was welcomed by the Sabha, and it was felt that the opportunity to learn the Bodo language should be given to Assamese students too.[150] But many, including the tribal elites, viewed the suggestions to use the Roman script as a tactical move by the Christian missionaries.[151]

In the early 1970s, several factors contributed to unrest among the Bodo population. These included increasing land alienation, which was a consequence, in part, of Assam's urbanization. Well into 1960, only 1 per cent of Bodos lived in towns,[152] a figure which declined to 0.09 per cent by 1971.[153] The growing urban environment was challenging for most tribal communities; despite some modest legal mechanisms, some fell prey to land speculators or had to make way for industries and other enterprises, falling into the trap of complex procedures of the land revenue bureaucracy, while others—foreseeing trouble—silently retreated to rural areas. Independent investigations carried out in the 1970s and later repeatedly referred to rampant land alienation and debt among Assam's tribal population.[154]

For generations, a majority of the Bodos from these areas had laboured under the landlords of Goalpara. Even by the 1970s, there was no significant dent in the powers and position of the latter; neither was there any visible change in the economic well-being of the Bodos and other tribal communities in comparison to that of the Assamese. For instance, among all government employees in Assam in 1975, tribal employees constituted less than 1 per cent despite a mandated 10 per cent share.[155] In the early 1970s, clashes between Bodos and non-Bodos took a violent turn,[156] as a recent delimitation of constituencies had made the Bodos politically irrelevant.[157] The mistrust between the Government of Assam and the Bodo leadership kept growing. These factors had all contributed to the rising linguistic awareness among the Bodos. The 1971 census showed a doubling, in 10 years, of the number of Bodo speakers, which was partly a result of rising language consciousness. Like the Assamese before them, the Bodo literary elites helped shape a standardized form of the language.[158]

Early in 1974, the Bodo Sahitya Sabha introduced, against the wishes of the Assam government, a Bodo textbook in a few Bodo-medium schools.[159] The government retaliated by derecognizing some Bodo-medium schools.[160] The Sabha intensified its political mobilization, and, as public demonstrations began, the government decided to take a tough stand. In September 1974, a couple of Bodo speakers were killed in police firing. This stirred popular Bodo sentiment, and thousands took to the streets. As the Bodo agitation intensified, more deaths took place. Several Bodo protesters died in police firing on 28 September 1974.[161] Clashes continued, and there were more deaths and arrests in November. There were accusations of molestation of Bodo women, which were denied by the government. With continuing clashes between the 'police and the tribal[s]', the numbers of demonstrators swelled, reaching more than 10,000 by November at Bijni in Goalpara, an erstwhile stronghold of the zamindars.[162] The Asam Sahitya Sabha hinted at the possible role of Christian missionaries in instigating the protests. By the end of 1974, 18 Bodo youths had lost their lives, and the Assam government had opened negotiations. Bodo scholars later agreed that the issue of language had truly touched the Bodo masses.

The tragic turn of events, however, received little sympathy from the Assamese press.

With the crisis raging, the Asam Sahitya Sabha had declared that the choice of script for the Bodo language should be dictated purely by academic merit. The following month, the Sabha organized a writers' workshop to discuss the matter. Their meeting was attended by Bodo scholars, and it included Congress ministers.[163] Assamese scholars rejected the proposal to use the Roman script in place of Assamese, arguing that there was no linguistic basis for it. But the Bodo intelligentsia was determined not to succumb to any pressure from Assamese public opinion, and the Roman script was thus adopted. The Sabha still hoped that more Bodo speakers would learn Assamese and decided to prepare Assamese books for Bodo speakers. Maheswar Neog, the president of the Sabha and a noted Assamese scholar, described the Bodo representatives as having 'closed mind[s]'.[164] He and his colleagues rejected the Bodo scholars' claims as not being based on science and not supported by linguistic research. The Bodo literary elites were not willing to bend either—'when we have taken a decision, we will not forgo it,' said Pramod Brahma, one of the key architects of the Bodo demands. As the Asam Sahitya Sabha continued to put pressure on the Bodo literary elite, the Assam government reiterated the essential need for everyone to learn Assamese, further angering the Bodo leaders.[165]

This was the last chance for Assamese leaders to keep their flock together. Still, they adopted a tone of paternalist indignation while negotiating with the Bodo literary elites. Assamese scholars saw nothing wrong in asking the speakers of the minority language to learn the language of the majority.[166] The Bodo speakers, while insisting that the question of script was intrinsically linked to their community's identity, drew attention to the phonetic differences between the Bodo and Assamese languages. They cited Suniti Kumar Chatterji in support of their claim. They argued that the prevalence of compound words in Assamese was a challenge for the Bodo language and also that the Roman script was more technology-friendly.

Early generations of the Bodo intelligentsia and literary elites were, by and large, not averse to the Assamese world; many had equipped themselves in Assamese scholarship and exchanged views and ideas with their fellow Assamese scholars. The distinguished Bodo scholar Bhaben Narzi translated Bodo folktales into Assamese, which was published by Gauhati University even as the language crisis was unfolding. At least a few dozen Assamese scholars, too, were willing to rethink the intellectual orientation of Assamese scholarship towards the emerging branch of tribal studies.

Till the end of 1974, the Indian government followed the stand taken by the Assam government—'Assamese script provides a link among the different tribal languages . . . a common script will help strengthen the many bonds of common interests which have existed for centuries between the communities and will contribute to building a united prosperous state in this sensitive border area.'[167] The PTCA, after a meeting with the Assam government, asked the Bodo leaders to discard their demand for adopting the Roman script.[168] When the Bodo leaders met Mrs Gandhi in March 1975, they reiterated that the Assamese script was difficult to use for Bodos. Unwilling to alienate the Assamese leadership further, she dismissed the claim as being merely 'sentimental'.[169] After further negotiations, the Bodo literary leaders yielded to the persuasion of the Union government and accepted Devanagari as their script. While this formalized the end of the Bodo intelligentsia's structural dependence on the Assamese literary world, the Assamese and the Bodos, in their everyday lives, continued to live and interact with each other across rural Assam. The political and social undercurrents of the months of mass mobilization had a lasting impact on Bodo society, and the uneasy relationship between the Bodo and Assamese intelligentsia would remain visible.

## 11

## Economic and Political Storms

In October 1972, the All India Congress Committee urged the Union government to take over the wholesale trade in food items.[1] This entailed cooperative bodies taking over the Public Distribution System (PDS) through which food was sold at a cheaper rate to the population. The rural rich—in Assam, the rich peasants and *mauzadars*—were aggrieved as they had been the ones who had largely controlled the PDS network thus far. In February 1973, Mrs Gandhi's government took over the wholesale trade of wheat, primarily to ensure a fair price to consumers.[2] States gave in to pressure from the Union government, but the implementation of the nationalization of food procurement was difficult. Farmers were unwilling to cooperate, and some wholesale traders were arrested. The price of wheat went up, black markets proliferated and, with food prices rising globally, the government could not meet its procurement targets. As several states reported food riots, the Prime Minister was attacked by the Opposition. She decided to take a step back. At the Congress Working Committee (CWC) meeting in mid-September 1973 (to which Assam's chief minister, Sarat Chandra Sinha, was a special invitee), it was decided that it would be best to leave rice procurement to the state governments.[3] Mrs Gandhi's government agreed to this, and it also moderately increased the procurement price of paddy. The state governments all refused to take over rice procurement, except for three—among them Assam.

Sinha had announced in the CWC meeting his intention to comply with the Union government's directive, and in November 1973, the Assam government, much against the wishes of the state Congress party, took over the wholesale trade in rice and paddy.[4]

Early in the 1970s, Assam had approximately 663 wholesale dealers, most of them Marwaris. The government aimed to replace these dealers with an equal number of cooperative societies. The wholesale traders, supported by the Jana Sangh, immediately opposed this. Meanwhile, the Prime Minister scrapped her wheat procurement programme.[5] It had lasted just a year and, by all accounts, had dismally failed to meet its own stated objectives. There was no shortfall in rice production in 1974. An estimated 15 million quintals were available for the market, but only 1.7 million quintals were procured by the government, which could feed only one-tenth of the state's population.[6] The price of rice spiralled to more than double the government's fixed rate. The rich stocked rice, fearing scarcity. Assam's rice was needed for sale to the urban population, tea garden workers, agricultural labourers as well as poor peasants who had sold their produce during the harvesting season and needed to buy foodgrains for consumption. Faced with a crisis, the government arranged for the public distribution of 500 g of rice per person per week. Rural areas did not get enough rice through this public distribution system. With restrictions in inter-state trade, dealers could no longer sell rice imported from Punjab. Instead, black marketeers sold imported rice as well as their own local stocks at a much higher price.

This messy situation, further accentuated by a drought-like situation, resulted in food shortages in various parts of Assam.[7] Non-official estimates claimed that 5000 (officially, it was 500) people died of starvation, mostly in Lower Assam.[8] A contemporary observer noted that this starvation was not 'because of insufficient food production but because of the lack of purchasing power among the people'.[9] While estimates of the percentage of poor vary greatly, Assam had a high level of poverty even by the official estimate; three-fourths of her rural population were below the poverty line, and Rs 48 was the per capita income per month in the early 1970s.[10]

By September 1973, there were reports of distress selling of children, desertion of wives and deaths resulting from people eating stuff not fit for consumption.[11] 'Families were struggling to subsist on grass, seeds, and roots.'[12] One agricultural labourer from Goalpara auctioned four of his five children in a weekly market for a paltry sum; another father did not find any customer for his children.[13] In a few places in Lower Assam, hungry peasants raided eateries to get respite from severe hunger.[14]

The state was heading towards a major economic and political crisis, worsened by another major spell of floods in 1974; areas affected by floods trebled compared to 1973.[15] While the prices of rice rose, there was a steep decline in the prices of jute. Most Muslim farmers, being traditional growers of jute, used to buy rice for consumption. As the price of rice increased further, there was a major shift to rice cultivation, which, unlike jute, did not require elaborate manual labour. This left several agricultural labourers suddenly without employment and brought them to the brink of starvation. The journalist M.S. Prabhakara, who had made Guwahati his home for years, went on a tour to investigate the widespread hunger in Lower Assam. He saw hunger everywhere and encountered 'fairly large crowd[s] of hungry and emaciated peasants'. In a marketplace, he was witness to a 'live, command performance' of death from starvation. He saw a 'mother and child' who were 'just [a] bundle of bones'.[16] Severe hunger had forced people to forsake their religious prejudices and food taboos, and many resorted to begging.

As starvation deaths became a subject of heated political debates, a senior minister in the government attributed deaths to people 'eating inedible roots'.[17] One Assamese daily reported on its first page how even stray dogs in Assam's urban areas faced a major crisis, while on another occasion, it described how people had survived for months by eating bamboo shoots.[18] In 1974, when the World Food Conference was underway in Rome, several villages of Lower Assam were affected by a famine that led to hundreds of deaths. These starvation deaths drew international attention.[19] The next year, too, there were 'near-famine conditions in rural areas' of eastern India, reported the *New York Times*.[20]

The food crisis gave rise to oppositional politics[21] in which students took the lead. Contemporary observers agreed on the failure of an established political Opposition to address the issues. 'What has angered the people most of all is the impotence of the established political parties and political institutions. The Assembly meets and passes resolutions. These have become non-events now.'[22] In February 1974, AASU, a leading organization of Assamese students unaffiliated to any major political party and without any direct electoral influence, sought urgent state intervention to redress a wide range of economic grievances. The birth of AASU, in the wake of rising inflation and at a time when there was a significant loss of Congress popularity during the elections held in February 1967, symbolized the growing rise of regional parties and organizations as a result of the general inability of mainstream political parties to engage with local issues.[23] AASU's demands, which largely echoed the Prime Minister Mrs Gandhi's left-wing agenda, included the 'establishment of a socialist economy, nationalization of all foreign capital, and state trading in all food articles'[24], provision of rice to families at a reduced rate and a weekly ration (at a rate lower than what had been fixed by the government) to be provided for every family. They opposed the eviction of peasant settlers in the government-owned Reserved Forests but asked for a halt to the flow of outsiders into Assam. They also demanded an increased pace in Assam's industrialization process, a system of flood control and another large oil refinery in the state.

The students set a deadline for the government and soon afterwards took to the streets when their demands were not implemented. In June 1974, thousands courted arrest.[25] The protests, which had begun in cities, very quickly spilled into rural areas; incidents of looting, arson and attack on local government offices were reported; two youths were shot dead by the police in a place called Bhurbandha.[26] Large areas of the state were put under curfew for several days. The students declared a bandh on 25 June and challenged the government's decision to run public transport that day. The state machinery resorted to arresting students and 'mercilessly' beating up some of them on the residential campus of Gauhati University. This could hardly wean away the popular support from the movement, as the food crisis continued to be grave. While Assam had experienced serious famines in earlier decades following droughts or floods, the origin of the food crisis in the mid-1970s was a result of a grave failure in state initiative in procurement as well as distribution of food grains. Other challenges for the government also awaited. In June 1975, strikes by teachers swept across Assam.

~

The communist mobilization of poor peasants had challenged the Assam government in the 1950s, and the privileges enjoyed by large landowners continued to be eroded over the next two decades. In 1963, the rights of landowners owning rent-free or partially rent-free estates were abolished.[27] By 1972, as mentioned earlier, the government had capped landholdings at 50 bighas.[28] Tea planters, too, had to give up their surplus lands under this provision. Several members of the Congress were for long uneasy about such land reforms and occasionally, as in 1964, advised the government to raise the upper limit,[29] but without success.

Assam's electoral politics after Independence was influenced by rural agrarian relations, and more so from 1967.[30] In the general elections that year, the communists and socialists won several seats as an outcome of years of grassroot-level political mobilization around the tenancy question, which was deeply entrenched in Assam's electoral landscape.[31] Increasing communist popularity worried the Congress government, and in June 1971, the Mahendra Mohan Choudhury government declared its intention to amend the Assam Tenancy Act of 1935 to grant rights of ownership to tenants.[32] Amidst widespread opposition from Assamese landowners, and much to the jubilation of the sharecroppers and their communist organizations, the amended Assam Tenancy Act was implemented in 1973. The law allowed tenants or sharecroppers who had cultivated lands for three consecutive years to legally claim ownership of such lands. This was an extraordinary gain for the sharecroppers. The Sinha-led government ensured the implementation of the Act as its top priority. Sinha, no stranger to the hardships of the Assamese peasantry,[33] publicly warned defiant landowners, but, as expected, there were serious repercussions. There were reports of widespread incidents of eviction of tenants by panicked large landowners in Rural Assam, and there was an increasing preference for wage labour. Angry landowners—typically rich peasants—demanded that the Act be scrapped and tried to scuttle government initiatives.[34] The latter, however, refused to give in, even at the risk of losing its traditional supporters.[35] An official enquiry brought into light widespread malpractices.[36] The government could only partly achieve the intended reallocation of land to small or landless peasants.

Prime Minister Mrs Gandhi's 20-point programme announced in July 1975 gave special emphasis to tenancy reform,[37] and the Emergency left little room for bureaucratic delays in the implementation of land reforms. Special drives were undertaken to expedite the implementation of the reforms, and upbeat sharecroppers hoped to claim occupancy rights through legal means. Official estimates indicate that till 1979, an estimated 2.57 lakh tenants were given the title to lands in Assam.[38] Between 1974 and 1976, an estimated 7.3 lakh bighas of land—acquired through the Ceiling Act—was redistributed among 2,00,000 poor peasant families.[39] This was approximately one-tenth of the total agricultural land in Assam.[40] Most of the beneficiaries were existing sharecroppers.[41] Under the shadow of the Emergency, the government also undertook measures through its otherwise disorganized land revenue bureaucracy to redistribute an estimated half a million acres of land. The total area requisitioned was increased by approximately 4.59 lakh hectares during 1978–80.[42]

These land reforms ushered in a shift in rural agrarian relations.[43] Armed with newfound economic gains, sharecroppers began to show their distinct political consciousness. Both Muslim and Hindu sharecroppers fought protracted legal wars against their Muslim and Hindu landowners respectively. The Muslim sharecroppers intensified their claim for occupancy rights on the land of their Hindu landowners. Their tenancy suits were defended by a number of left-leaning lawyers. Urban or rural rich Assamese families, *inter alia* absentee landowners, now felt threatened. Having been traditional allies of the Congress, they temporarily withdrew their support. In the 1978 Assembly elections, the Congress party, faced with strong opposition from the Assamese large landowners, openly sought the support of Muslim voters. The Congress lost, and a Janata Party-led government came into power in the state, though for a short period. The tussle for occupancy rights also served as a critical ideological apparatus for Assam's agitation against foreigners, which began in 1979. Slowly, the discontent of Assamese large landowners began to metamorphose into an anti-migration sentiment.

While tenancy rights were granted to all sections of sharecroppers, a majority of the gainers were Muslim sharecroppers, some of whom had migrated from Bengal earlier and rented land from Assamese absentee landowners. To understand this, we need to go back to the 1940s when, after Partition, Muslim sharecroppers gained importance in the Brahmaputra Valley's agrarian relations. More and more Assamese landowners showed a preference for Muslim sharecroppers over Assamese Hindu and tribal sharecroppers. The Muslim peasants' skill as jute cultivators and multi-crop producers was well known, and the high price of jute was an incentive for the Assamese landowners. That the migrant Muslim peasants remained beyond any communist mobilization was also a matter of great relief to the absentee landowners. Also, these peasants were without any political leadership, which could have counterpoised the Assamese landowners' nationalist views. The Muslim sharecroppers, therefore, were in great demand, which was fulfilled with their continued migration from East Pakistan.

However, for Assamese landowners, the granting of occupancy rights to their Muslim sharecroppers meant a loss of their privileges. Both the Congress-led Assam government and, later, the Janata Dal government (1978–79) continued with tenancy reforms, posing a threat to the landowners' economic and social interests. This new phase of peasant mobilization, where migrant tenants were at the helm of affairs, realigned the politics of Assam. It was at this crucial juncture that the large landowners started competing with other stakeholders, including the non-Assamese traders, in the state economy. Competition over limited economic resources faced by a new Assamese middle class, deprived of their landed interests, served as the crucial background of the popular mobilization that began in 1979. In subsequent years, both Assamese nationalist mobilization based on anti-migrant sentiments and the ethnic mobilization of the tribal peasantry built on the idea of land alienation came to the forefront of Assam's political landscape.

For decades after Independence, the Congress had extended moderate political support to Bengali Muslim peasants. Following the dissolution of the Muslim League in Assam in March 1948, the political outlook of a large majority of the Muslims continued to be shaped by their community and political leaders from within the Congress as well as by local cultural experiences. As the '50s progressed, more socialists and communists joined to give a new direction to Muslim politics. Yet, the '50s and '60s saw moments of both rapprochement and occasional political polarization. Sporadic but highly localized clashes between Hindus and Muslims continued in rural areas of central and Lower Assam. In July 1958, one such dispute in Nagaon over beef succeeded in further widening communal fissures to turn them into a larger political crisis.[44] Throughout this period, Muslims in Assam, largely rural and agrarian,[45] were battered by political challenges arising out of contestation over their cultural and environmental choices for survival and social life and their increasing enforcement of emerging legal and political frameworks of citizenship. The share of Muslims among Assam's political and professional elite was minuscule, and the bulk of them remained poverty-stricken.

On the economic front, things slowly began to change from the early '70s as there were visible changes in the agrarian economy. Muslim peasants' ability to cultivate both paddy and jute, their increasing adoption of the employment of machinery as well as their understanding of the use of crop diversification all helped. Per hectare use of fertilizer increased.[46] Credit flow into the areas dominated by Muslim peasantry increased. Shops dealing in manure, pesticide and seeds increasingly started appearing in rural Assam. As the net income from both rice and jute became approximately equivalent between the 1970s and 1980s,[47] a few Muslim cultivators could afford to buy more land, reinvesting the profits from their agriculture. Some, including the poorest, like many others across Assam, converted forestlands—

mostly across the floodplains of central Assam—into agricultural lands. Between 1960–61 and 1970–71, the volume of barren land decreased as did the officially marked forested lands.[48] The changes, however, did not benefit everyone equitably; rich peasants and merchants-cum-rural moneylenders gained considerably. The economic condition of the poor peasants did not improve, and signs of economic stratification were visible. The poorest among them continued to join the relentless stream supplying urban labour, often only to become victims of aggressive urban political exclusionism.

The better-off Muslim migrants, moderately benefiting from the new dynamism in the agrarian economy, over the years grew into a microscopic Muslim middle class. They secured government employment or other white-collar jobs. Unlike the Hindu Assamese middle classes or their colonial era predecessors, this new Muslim middle class remained closely tied to their rural world. They struggled to find a space within the larger cultural landscape of Assamese nationality, though Assam was home to many of them. They were identified as *Na-Asomiya*, *Pamua Asomiya* or *Pamua Musalmans* (new Assamese or Assamese Muslim settlers of the river islands). The term 'immigrant' or '*na-Asomiya*' came to be used frequently to describe those people or those whose forefathers had migrated to these areas before Independence. They had already partaken in the vernacular social and literary cultures of Assam; for them, Assamese became a literary language.[49] A distinguished Assamese author recounted hearing Bengali settlers speaking Assamese, in 1953, just like native speakers.[50] Assamese public figures, irrespective of their political outlook, had long advocated the idea that the state's migrant population were welcome to be absorbed into the fold of Assamese nationality; embracing Assamese as their new mother tongue was one of the prerequisites, however. They acknowledged that this process of assimilation would enrich Assamese society.[51] The contributions to the Assamese literary culture of a new generation of writers from amongst the Muslims, who still spoke Bengali at home with their kin, were acknowledged as a proof of this assimilation.[52] Not all such writings exhibited acceptance of the political views of the Assamese; some, like an essay written in 1965, were bold enough to convey the rising concerns of Muslims on issues of illegal immigration and deportation.[53]

The birth of Bangladesh gave a new identity to the battered Muslim population in Assam, at least for a while, as Bangladesh was a friendly nation; many took pride in the fact that it was a nation which was born to defeat the idea of Pakistan. Till the birth of Bangladesh, Muslims who had recently migrated from East Pakistan, or were deemed to have come from there, were often viewed with apprehension.

The Muslims tried to gain a foothold in the contested political landscape of Assam. In the 1972 elections, twice the earlier number of Muslim lawmakers belonging to the Congress party made it to the Assam Legislative Assembly.[54] Buoyed by the moderate agrarian prosperity of the 1960s and early '70s, Assam's Muslim population grew convinced of their political standing, and amid growing unease among cross-sections of voters, the government encouraged patronage to groups like the All-Assam Muslim Parishad, to ensure public support to the Congress party.[55] However, '[t]he Muslim masses [could] no longer [be] hoodwinked into believing that the Congress party is their Great Protector'.[56]

Muslims were always seen by many as Congress loyalists and were also targeted for 'block-voting'. For a very long time, they remained loyal to the Congress party machinery. 'Through an elaborate system of coercion, blackmail, and patronage',[57] they were forced by their community leaders to remain loyal to the Congress in return for their sociopolitical security. However, already by the late 1960s, Muslim voters were increasingly sceptical about the Congress being their saviour.[58] This was evident from the by-election, in February 1975, to the Barpeta constituency, where a seat was vacated by the newly appointed President of India, F.A. Ahmed. The Congress candidate won by a small margin, signalling serious erosion of Congress support among the Muslims. A controversy arose, and the Opposition candidate—called the people's candidate—was arrested; complaints of rigging became widespread. Earlier, in another by-election in Cachar in 1974, the Congress had lost its seat to a CPM candidate. In the elections held in early 1974 for the municipal corporation of Guwahati, the Congress and the CPI had fought together but suffered a severe defeat. Electoral participation was high among the Muslim voters, and their exercise of voting rights gave them the assurance of not being 'branded as Pakistani infiltrators'.[59]

A contemporary observer felt that several factors other than the loss of Muslim votes were responsible for the spectacular setback faced by the Congress: sudden migration into urban areas causing failure in civic amenities, widespread corruption as well as rising dissatisfaction among government employees. Neither did the left benefit. A majority of the Legislative Assembly seats lost by the Congress did not go to any major political party but to the so-called independents. Both the Congress and the left were now ideologically divided. The left had lost its organizational strength; according to one account, its factions were 'hopelessly spilt and scattered, and those that are still active are more interested to tactically undercut one another'.[60]

~

In 1972, Sarat Chandra Sinha became Assam's fifth chief minister, coming to power by displacing many stalwarts. He also secured the blessings of Prime Minister Mrs Gandhi. This was in keeping with her choices in states like Maharashtra (V.P. Naik) or Punjab (Zail Singh), where key leaders from the lower end of caste–class hierarchy headed key state governments. Sinha's arrival was seen as a major threat to the social and political world of the upper-caste Hindus in Assam. Anxious about this change and their displacement, they extended their direct support to popular movements led by the students. The Congress was still the largest party, having the machinery and resources to make its presence visible. The power structure increasingly accommodated ideologically diverse sets of people, limiting the role of upper castes to an extent. Between 1952 and 1977, 35 of the 48 MPs from Assam were Hindus, of whom 10 were Brahmans.[61]

As the 1970s progressed, the Indian state increasingly realized the efficacy of strong-arm methods in quelling popular movements. A prime example of this was the railway strike of May 1974,[62] which Mrs Gandhi's government dealt with a tough hand. In Assam, the government looked at other options, and Sinha tried, with moderate success, to wean away through the political patronage of students belonging to the backward communities from the students' organization. Sinha's government is also remembered and criticized for its methods of seeking political alliances with the castes known as OBCs (Other Backward Classes).[63] Sinha himself was from an OBC background; his predecessors, except one, had been upper-caste Assamese. In Sinha's cabinet, positions were largely assigned to the OBC members. He systematically encouraged organizational space for OBC groups—including the Ahoms, who had ruled Assam before its occupation by the British East India Company in 1826—to propagate their political and social views. Leaders of OBC organizations reached out to Sinha, seeking more opportunities.[64] Though not widely discussed, this political move became a topic of discussion for many and also occasionally attracted scathing attacks in the press.[65] While there was 'very real and highly oppressive dominance of caste Hindus in the politics of Assam', M.S. Prabhakara's astute observation was that the real reason for Sinha's push towards OBC mobilization was 'to ensure yet another section of block voting'.[66]

In fact, as discussed in an earlier chapter, the period between 1967 and the promulgation of the national emergency in 1975 saw several experiments with political permutations and combinations. The Congress party's steady loss of popularity since 1967 compelled it to look for new and assured electoral alliances. Leaders of community and caste groups were wooed, given positions in Central and state governments and other benefits. In Assam, Choudhury's government had already widened its social base; his expansive cabinet was an example of the accommodation of competing social equations. The 1970 mid-term elections was decided by caste, religion and community aspirations. Choudhury's cabinet—50 per cent of whose members belonged to minority groups—was clearly an indication of a new dawn. This took clearer shape when Sinha became the new chief minister in 1972, forming a cabinet much more widely representative than any previous ones. All this greatly worried the higher castes, who were increasingly marginalized in the Congress structure. Unlike in many parts of the Hindi heartland (such as in Bihar), the rich landowners did not dominate the Congress structure in Assam. The backward classes also had a significant presence within the state bureaucracy; of the total Assam government employees in 1971, an estimated 32 per cent belonged to OBCs.[67]

The Congress was able to arrest the decline of its electoral popularity in 1972. This powerful recovery of political space was not only due to Prime Minister Mrs Gandhi's charismatic electioneering but could also be attributed to a wide range of electoral engineering carried out by the Congress party. This involved structural changes in the party organization, taking on board and forging careful electoral alliances with diverse ethnic and religious groups. The results were clear: the Congress party remained in full control of the state machinery; and except for occasional forays by the left and socialist parties, the others hardly succeeded in amassing 6 per cent of the vote share until the 1977 general elections.[68] The left parties—CPI, CPI(M) and RCPI—pushed for the expansion of their electoral presence by trying to mobilize and settle landless peasants, often termed the 'land grab movement'. In the 1972 elections and again in 1978, these parties secured a significant share of votes.[69] The communists, however, could not further expand their political importance as their political views were increasingly perceived as identifying little with the political aspirations of the Assamese nationalists.

By the mid-1970s, ideologically, AASU accommodated diverse sets of political ideas in its schema of agitational programmes. As the Assamese rich landowners had faced increasing resistance from the sharecroppers or poor peasants and the government, resulting in a partial loss of their economic and social privileges, they were looking for an opportunity to strike back and restore their lost privileges. In May 1974, AASU submitted a 21-point charter of demands to the government.[70] Representing the interests of the Assamese nationalist landed gentry, and also drawing their ideological inspiration from the nationalist freedom struggle, they gradually emerged as a rallying point of popular political dissent.[71] Despite their nationalist tone, the AASU charter accommodated demands which appealed to cross-sections of Assamese society. Several demands had a direct bearing upon the Assamese peasantry. For instance, the ASSU urged the government to end the eviction of settlers in the Reserved Forests, to effectively implement the laws that imposed upper limits on landed property ownership and to end continued inflow of migrants to the state. Though the nationalists generally used the word 'outsiders', their anti-migration rhetoric stopped short of clearly mentioning the religious identity of the migrants. The anti-migration movement had acquired a new form, increasingly tilting towards a middle path, focusing on the economic background of migrants and the quantum and nature of state support.

The early 1970s saw a dramatic rise of new electoral fronts, accommodating ethnic and community aspirations of various groups, though they could hardly dent the electoral landscape of the Congress. The UARP, largely representing a section of Assam's underprivileged social groups, could hardly draw support from its own and still powerful conservative gentry in its aim to achieve an Ahom homeland.[72] The traditional gentry were still reluctant to break with their long-term ally, the Congress.[73] The UARP drew upon years of political campaigns initiated by several organizations that had tried to secure political and other privileges as a community, the last one being the Ahom Tai Mongoliya Rajya Parishad, formed in 1967.[74] The Ahoms, unlike many others, experienced politically turbulent times after Independence.[75] Deprived of their historical power in the region by the coming of the British, they were given a share of governance through the legislative reforms of the early twentieth century, but they lost these privileges after Independence. Their grievances against the state apparatus became visible by the 1960s. Their leaders tried to secure benefits by demanding a minority status, by getting elected to the Central or state legislature. These tactics did not succeed in securing for them any spectacular political gains, and their traditional leaders became a part of the Congress machinery for a short period. In the 1950s and early '60s, they continuously sought state patronage for the upkeep of their cultural heritage.[76] The Ahom leadership also spearheaded a separate movement, asking for a 'sovereign independent

Assam', without success.⁷⁷ The People's Democratic Party, a small political party drawn from the left, also experimented with reaching out to cross sections of Assamese society by protesting against Delhi's discrimination against Assam and demanding 'Assam for Assamese'. However, their attempt, too, was a failure. Mrs Gandhi acted swiftly in an attempt to assuage these politico-economic anxieties; the second refinery was granted.

The tribal people of Assam, constituting about a fifth of the population, had also been angered by their economic, political and cultural marginalization post-Independence. The rise of the Plain Tribals Council of Assam (PTCA) was a result of this dissatisfaction. Unlike the UARP, the PTCA had a mass following. Its imperial predecessor, the Tribal League, born in a different political context, had empowered it with political strategies. Mass mobilizations organized by the PTCA deeply polarized the Bodo masses for and against the Congress. In a Bodo short story, 'Jatir Kolongko', the central character Bilisran is treated as an outcast as he is considered a Congress man.⁷⁸

~

Mrs Indira Gandhi's government promulgated Emergency in June 1975. With this, India plunged into a serious political crisis. Mrs Gandhi was aided by one of Assam's most admired political leaders, Dev Kant Borooah. Mild-mannered and an acclaimed poet, Borooah shot to fame as the president of Congress (I) under Mrs Gandhi's shadow. On 14 June 1975, he circulated an appeal to Assam's Congress workers, which presented a list of reasons for the party to remain solidly behind Mrs Gandhi's leadership; it was crucial for the welfare of the nation.⁷⁹ Borooah's defence of the Prime Minister's political actions continued.⁸⁰ It is noteworthy that former AICC presidents, even in the recent past, such as Siddavanahalli Nijalingappa or Shankar Dayal Sharma, were veteran leaders. In contrast, Borooah's political footing at home was weak. This may partly explain the extent of his public rhetoric in praise of Mrs Gandhi.

Soon afterwards, Assam government officials began to rehearse the standard narrative of how all was well. While the reality was different, official accounts, which were full of praise of Mrs Gandhi's authoritarianism, variously said that 'there has been positive improvement of discipline' or of 'discipline, attendance and disposal of business' in all government offices, and that there was 'no report of any abnormal labour relation'.[81] Sinha telegrammed Mrs Gandhi to tell her how he had successfully enforced censorship of the press and was eagerly trying to implement the wishes of her government.[82] His pliant officials, who were warned against 'loose talks', wrote lengthy reports on how to improve Assam's economy and tackle the food crisis.[83] Special task forces, drawn from the state's bureaucracy, were constituted to fast-track Mrs Gandhi's economic programmes.[84] Others discussed the question of enhancing prison capacities; officials of the education department deliberated on the need to increase the number of teaching days, did not allow failed students to be admitted to the same class, nor did they permit student unions to function without approval from the government, and they also barred students with RSS or Naxalite backgrounds from colleges.[85] The lists of things that were not allowed were long. Slogans such as 'hard work, foresightedness, commitment and discipline' or 'catch the corrupt' were coined for public dissemination. The Congress machinery marshalled support for Mrs Gandhi from many quarters, including from tea companies,[86] who were worried about increasing labour protests in their gardens, and the CPI, whose national party backed the Emergency as a fight against capitalists, landowners, black marketers, etc.[87] Like elsewhere in the country, the CPI and the Congress formed joint committees in Assam to supervise economic programmes as well as fight their political opponents.[88] CPI cadres also undertook foot marches in parts of rural Assam in support of land reforms.

The first reaction to the Emergency from the Assamese press was bold defiance. *Dainik Asam*, *Assam Tribune* and others carried a blank editorial in protest.[89] Despite several public figures raising their voices, it did not, however, take long for a section of the press to accede to the pressure, including showering commendation on the leadership of the Prime Minister's son, Sanjay Gandhi, who directed the Youth Congress.[90] However, this did not discourage college teachers in Assam—whose union had a sizeable presence of left-oriented teachers and who were seeking higher wages—from boycotting the organization of examinations. Students extended their support to the teachers' strike. While Assam was largely spared the brutalities of the Prime Minister's authoritarianism, the state machinery came down heavily on individuals. Arrests of traders happened across the state, and political opponents were imprisoned. Emergency-era diktats were forced on people, notably the sterilization programme, a pet project in the Congress-ruled states under the direct supervision of Sanjay Gandhi. Between 1975 and 1977, Assam recorded 3,73,750 sterilizations, 22.88 per 1000 population—exceeding the Central government's target and only being outdone by six states or union territories.[91] Many among those who were forced to undergo this process were unmarried or elderly; some died as a result. Doctors, including medical students, were assigned monthly targets. Others were given motivational targets. The Assam government also stipulated that government employees could not have more than three children. Newly appointed government employees were made to give an undertaking to adopt family planning measures.

Assam's rate of political detention was equivalent to the national average: 179 persons per million population. Amongst those arrested were political opponents of Prime Minister Mrs Gandhi, and teachers, students and trade unionists.[92] Political opponents were put in prison on flimsy grounds, like criticizing the government's sterilization campaign. Assam's home minister, Hiteswar Saikia, directed a district magistrate, despite the latter's unwillingness, to arrest Baneswar Saikia, a senior RCPI leader and head of the College Teachers' Association.[93] A government employee was arrested as he refused to take offerings in a temple from the person who had forced him to undergo sterilization.[94] A Marwari trader was arrested for his refusal to keep government-procured paddy in his godown. A group of engineering students from Guwahati were arrested under the Maintenance of Internal Security Act of 1971 (MISA) when they demonstrated before their principal after being expelled from the examination for using unfair means. Assam did not have large slums to invite razing by campaigners of beautification, but in the summer of 1975, the government evicted tribal settlers from government-owned forest lands.[95] This widespread eviction eroded Sinha's goodwill among the tribal people. Sporadic eviction programmes were undertaken in 1977, and this further undermined his popular support. No one, however, could stop the strong waves of agitational activities amongst the workers in tea gardens.[96]

Assam was one of the few states where the Congress (I) was not routed in the 1977 general elections. The Congress won 10 Lok Sabha seats, securing a little more than half of the total votes polled.[97] The poor performance of the Opposition, which won just three seats, can be attributed to a lower degree of atrocities in Assam during the Emergency than elsewhere in the country and the relative success of the land reforms during this period, the Congress emerging as a party of the poor. Thus, when in June that year, the Acting President of India, B.D. Jatti, dissolved nine state legislative assemblies acting on the advice of the Union cabinet, Assam was not one of them.

The Emergency, however, had silently accelerated the erosion of Muslim support to the Congress and Sinha's government. When Shahi Imam Bukhari spoke at widely attended meetings in Assam in June 1977, he made it clear that the Congress was no longer a trusted ally of the Muslims.[98] Evictions carried out during the rainy season of 1977 had affected several Muslim settlements. Some of this political churning resulted in the formation of Eastern India Muslim Association in 1977.[99] By 1978, the number of Muslim lawmakers in the Assembly was proportional to their numbers. The minority—as the Bengali Muslims came to be described in political vocabulary—would play a significant role in electoral politics in the 1970s. Of the 78 elected parliamentarians from Assam to the Lok Sabha between 1952 and 1977, the electoral fate of 24 was solely decided by minority voters.[100]

Government employees went on strike in January 1978, demanding an increase in their salary. While initially calling their demands 'imaginary',[101] Sinha's government had to finally increase salaries, but the Union government, meanwhile, decreased the central annual grant to Assam. An embattled government, haunted by the excesses of the Emergency, tried to woo popular sentiment by rehabilitating evicted tribal populations and providing free school education to the poor.[102] But this could not prevent the fall of Sinha's government. Unlike the parliamentary elections of 1977, the elections to the State Legislative Assembly in February 1978 saw the Congress losing to the combined Opposition in Assam.[103] Despite this, the Congress did get a fair share of votes from among the tribal voters,[104] but the Muslims largely voted for non-Congress parties.[105] The Janata Party and the left parties won a majority of the seats with large margins. The Janata Party, with its pre-election alliance with the PTCA, could not muster enough numbers to form a government however, and it had to seek support from the CPI(M) (which had contested elections for the first time in Assam) as well as the RCPI.[106] The communists had expanded their political base,[107] and they were rewarded with 20 of the 126 seats in the Legislative Assembly elections of 1978.[108] The communist parties' spectacular success was largely owing to their organizational work amongst poor peasants and other subaltern groups; they won around one-tenth of the total votes polled, while the Janata Party secured approximately one-fourth.

Meanwhile, the Congress party witnessed a split. Most stalwarts in Assam left the Indira faction, including Sinha and the powerful Borooah—though the latter had been responsible for the win in Assam in the 1977 Lok Sabha elections. Mrs Gandhi's faction was left with no known leader. Borooah faded into oblivion as his home turf went haywire. He had courted controversy and invited the wrath of the Assamese intelligentsia earlier too. One of the occasions was in April 1954, when Borooah, speaking in Bengal and most probably playing to the gallery, advocated making Bengali the *rashtrabhasa* (national language) of eastern India.[109]

However, the Congress electoral base had not weakened much; its two factions had collectively secured more votes than the Janata Party. The CPI(M) still did not have a major following in Assam, unlike the RCPI; their cadres spoke Bengali, which remained a matter of concern for many Assamese. After their resounding victories in West Bengal and Tripura, they refused to negotiate with the Janata Party to form the government in Assam. The spread of communist popularity in eastern India—'spreading red between the borders of Burma and the Ganges river'—had already become a cause for worry among Western observers.[110]

The new chief minister, Golap Borbora—who had been imprisoned during the Emergency and had a long stint in the trade union movement—was elected leader of the state Janata Party after days of intense parleying and formed his cabinet in March after consultation with Prime Minister Morarji Desai. This was a new trend in Assam's legislative practice.[111] Borbora's government got a prompt endorsement from the traditional conservative social forces; the powerful Vaishnavite abbot of Garmur congratulated him and welcomed his government as a positive step in India's democratic tradition.[112] The chief minister asked the public to stringently oversee the functioning of his government colleagues and officials. The new government began with two major initiatives: shallow tube well projects to encourage irrigation as well as more state initiatives in the form of loans to small tea producers. Also, school education was made free.[113] The Union government announced plans to construct two gigantic dams upstream on the Brahmaputra and a canal connecting it with the Ganga.[114] Earlier, Morarji Desai had promised the production of more hydropower by harnessing the Brahmaputra. The government had to deal with large-scale land grabbing and land purchases through presumably unethical means and the settlement on forest land by poor migrant Bengalis, which had aggravated religious and ethnic antagonisms, posing political challenges in the days ahead.

Soon after Borbora's government came into power, there were increasing clashes along the Assam–Nagaland border over disputes arising from the reclamation of forest lands at the borders.[115] Borbora promised slackening state regulation in these lands.[116] The border conflicts aggravated in early January 1979, and the political leadership of Assam and Nagaland began an initiative to sort out their boundary disputes. The origin of these disputes was the growing demand for access to lands and resources covering more than 8000 square kilometres of fertile valleys and thick forests. In these areas, the Assam government had allowed new settlers—Nepalis, Assamese and others—to clear, reclaim and settle. A section of Naga villagers was apprehensive of the outcome of such settlement, and this resulted in violent clashes. Border disputes and localized skirmishes had long been part of the Assam and Nagaland story. But these clashes were described as 'brutal, even for a region which has seen many outrages', with modern arms being used against Assamese villagers along the border with Nagaland on 5 January. The *Times of India* reported the death of 50 people the next day, cautioning that this was a conservative estimate. Among the large numbers killed were 'unarmed men, women, and children'.[117] Arson and violence continued for the next few days, and thousands fled in search of safety.[118] Many became homeless; one estimate put the number at more than 2,50,000.[119] Armed clashes took place in March 1979 again, and localized clashes across the foothills, over agricultural lands, continued,[120] adding to the numbers of dead and homeless.

The Janata government saw the writing on the wall, as Assamese dailies persuasively articulated opposition to migration and the control of Assam's economy by non-Assamese and even non-Indians.[121] Influxes from Bangladesh had 'become very acute and no stone should be left unturned to see that this border migration is stopped forthwith', warned the *Assam Tribune*.[122] After the January violence, many within his own party pushed for Borbora's removal. Months later, news of the factionalism within the party came out in the open.[123] Borbora's detractors pressed the Janata Party's high command to replace him.[124] Borbora also soon lost the support of political parties who had helped him to form the government; the communists, whose agitational politics had become increasingly visible, accused the government of leaning towards the Jana Sangh ideology.[125] On 4 September 1979, after 27 months in power, the Borbora ministry lost a vote of no confidence. Another non-Congress government was installed, led by Jogendra Nath Hazarika. Hazarika, a former speaker of the state legislature, led a 17-member breakaway faction of the Janata Dal and was supported by an alliance, which the pundits described as a 'bizarre political animal like the platypus, with parts of the body belonging to various species'.[126]

~

The Borbora government, from the start, had been in the thick of a politically charged atmosphere. They had to deal with localized sporadic communal clashes and workers' strikes. Weeks into its term, the demands for a fertilizer factory in Upper Assam began to acquire political shape; the Union government, however, shelved this idea.[127] An Assamese Congress parliamentarian demanded from the Tea Board of India that all covenanted jobs in his state's tea gardens be given to the youth of Assam.[128] Parallel to this, the AASU leaders, fairly well rooted in Assam's political landscape, also prepared a 14-point charter of demands, with the demand to stop the flow of immigrants into Assam at the top of the list. The other points largely sought economic justice for Assam: industrialization, jobs and better educational infrastructure.[129] The earlier left-leaning political outlook of the student organization had shifted to a more centrist position during the Emergency.[130] After sporadic demonstrations earlier in June, students, largely drawn from colleges and the Gauhati University, demonstrated before the Assembly on 14 June 1978, which led to violent clashes.[131] The students' anger was assuaged by the chief minister's promise of quick action on their charter of demands. In April, when Borbora toured the industrial townships of Upper Assam, many complained of not being able to seek economic opportunities in the oil industries. An anxious Borbora tried to persuade the Union government to appoint an Assamese as the head of Oil India Limited, which he thought could be a way out. A few months later, in September, angry students shut down the oil refinery at Digboi and also demonstrated in the oil fields of the Assam Oil Company for more than three weeks.[132] The oil industry had increasingly become a symbol of exploitation. Many individuals retaliated by demanding higher prices for their lands where drilling was being planned.[133] Others regularly complained of damage to their crops from industrial effluents and fragmentation of their land holdings.[134]

The students were not unjustified in their demands, as contemporary studies by economists have shown. Assam's per capita annual average income in 1980–81 was Rs 1360, lagging far behind most Indian states.[135] This was in sharp contrast to its status in the mid-twentieth century. Economists attributed this sorry state of affairs to Assam's dependence on agriculture, contributing an estimated 50 per cent of the state's domestic product, which had remained stagnant since the middle of the century.[136] Assam's economy largely replicated the economic model of the imperial era, an age of exploitation of raw materials, variously described as an enclave economy or extractive economy. An economist described how Assam was a 'land of poverty in the midst of plenty': 'The present pattern of industrial development of Assam resembles closely the investment made by foreign capitalists on the extractive and plantation industries in underdeveloped countries. The only difference is that the investing parties happen to be not only foreign capitalists but also capitalists from other states.'[137] A memorandum submitted by Borbora's government to the visiting Seventh Finance Commission agreed with the views of economists on the crisis: 'lack of adequate communications, accessibility to markets and low levels of investment. The per capita income, level of savings and investments, spread of infrastructural facilities and special services lag behind many other states.'[138]

Why was there such limited industrialization in Assam despite having so many resources, notably mineral resources? Economists highlighted that contemporary Assam and Gujarat were the two major Indian states with oil reserves, yet there were significant differences in their patterns of utilization. The most scathing criticism was summarized thus: the only 'benefit which Assam is getting at present from drawing out the reserves of its liquid gold are in the form of royalty and sales tax'. As we have seen, the fixing of the royalty rate was also marred by disputes. Producing around 3.6 million tonnes of crude oil annually, Assam had received a royalty of Rs 10 for every tonne, which was revised to Rs 15 in 1972 and then Rs 42 in 1976.[139] After adding other taxes, Assam finally got Rs 54 per tonne on her crude oil, while the Union government earned Rs 991.03 per tonne.[140]

This was an estimated 5 per cent of the price of crude oil in the Middle East. Economists generally agree that existing industries in India that were offshoots of the imperial economy, such as oil in Assam, failed to establish links with the regional economy and, thus, never really took off.

How did this impact an average young resident of Assam? An official inventory of those seeking employment in Assam recorded an astounding figure of 3,20,000 in February 1979, a number that had trebled from that of 1971.[141] Many educated youth took low-paying jobs as teachers in primary schools. India's official parameters of defining its poor kept changing over the decades; yet, a little more than half of Assam's population remained in the poor category, a figure higher than India's national average.

A majority of Assam's urban residents were Bengali or Hindi speakers. In 1971, in the urban areas, Bengali speakers made up 40 per cent and Hindi 15.6 per cent of the total population, while Assamese speakers comprised 38.7 per cent.[142] The quality of everyday life of the Assamese people fell far short of average citizens in many other states. By 1979, only 20 per cent of Assam's villages had electricity, while most villages in Tamil Nadu were electrified.[143] Despite the availability of land, Assam's share in India's total food production during 1977–78 was only 2 per cent, while that of Punjab was 8 per cent. Of the few states behind Assam, Kerala's share was 1.1 per cent.[144]

Meanwhile, the average life span of Indians had risen steadily from 32 in 1941 to 49 years during 1974–75.[145] This was largely due to significant improvements in sanitary conditions and the control of several communicable diseases, including cholera, smallpox, plague and malaria. However, infectious diseases still caused deaths. Malaria, in particular, wreaked havoc and emerged as a larger problem as a strain of *Plasmodium falciparum*, the parasite that causes the deadly cerebral malaria, had developed resistance to the key drug, chloroquine, in Assam.[146] The continued occurrence of cases of smallpox, too, was a major concern.

For the years 1970–71 to 1978–79, Assam's average annual growth rate of per capita income—an important economic indicator to understand the overall economy—was 0.68 per cent compared to the all-India average of 1.49 per cent.[147] If this figure was symptomatic of Assam's uninspiring economic environment, her world of agriculture was equally distressed. During 1975–76, around 34 per cent of Assam's land was under cultivation as compared to Punjab's 82 per cent and Tamil Nadu's 46 per cent.[148] A part of this staggering low rate of acreage was determined by nature but also by the absence of capitalistic features in agriculture. Assam hardly produced any major cash crop, and the market share of jute had declined over a period. How does one explain this sluggish countryside? Post the embankment of the Brahmaputra and its tributaries, the fertility of the farmlands declined rapidly. Over time, rural mercantile capital, essential to maintaining the dynamism of the farming sector, began to dry up.

Agrarian productivity declined to a great degree because of the increasing fragmentation of landholdings, which was the outcome of the increase in population. Assam's rural dwellers—comprising more than three-fourths of its total population—were mostly poor peasants; during 1980–81, approximately 82 per cent [similar to Bengal] of these peasants had no more than 2 hectares of land.[149] Those who had less than 1 hectare of land constituted approximately 60 per cent of the total landholders—a substantial chunk of the population. An estimated one-fourth of the rural agricultural population was officially designated landless. They may have had a small plot of land to build their home but hardly enough to feed themselves. Several Indian states like Gujarat, Punjab, Maharashtra, Andhra Pradesh, Haryana, Karnataka and Madhya Pradesh presented a strikingly different picture, where the major share of agricultural land was owned by large landowners. The average size of landholdings in Assam was only 1.34 hectares compared to the national average of 1.84.

In the early twentieth century, economists had highlighted the limits of the new age of agriculture in Assam. They pointed out that excessive humidity and a generally overcast sky with only short spans of sunshine significantly reduced the photosynthetic efficiency of the high-yielding varieties of seeds.[150] In pockets, the expansion of agriculture had reached its limits. Winter rice was being cultivated in a sizeable area under peasant cultivation for this entire period. Since 1980, Assam had a higher cropping intensity—a formula used by economists to explain the proportion of gross sown area to net sown area—than the all-India average.[151] As the recurrence of embankment failures intensified, peasants took innovative steps to overcome the shortfall in paddy production. In many places, peasants began to produce mustard as their winter crop—the production of mustard almost tripled between 1950 and 2000—and tried their hand at producing summer rice—whose production increased more than 11 times between 1970 and 2000—to be harvested before the onset of the monsoons.[152] Wheat, despite some early attempts, was largely a non-starter; from 2000 hectares of sown area in 1950, it reached around 80,000 hectares in 1980–81 and then began to decline steadily.

~

A British diplomat who visited Assam towards the end of 1978, while taking into consideration the larger political volcanoes that Assam was sitting on, expressed a highly tendentious view about the work culture of the Assamese people. Stating that Assam 'is extremely fertile and its land is easy to cultivate but ease has begotten lassitude', the diplomat made a sweeping and generalized observation: 'Assamese tend to cultivate their culture rather than their land . . .'[153] This was rather a skewed view, which discounted the labouring masses in Assam's villages. However, it is true that Assam's people took pride in their culture, and writers and intellectuals regularly engaged in public debates and discussions. Assam's economic and political storms had compelled the Assamese intelligentsia to take a fresh look at their political and social landscape, and some of the best polemical essays, especially in literary criticism, were produced during the 1970s.[154] These essays took a swipe at the Indian state or at Assamese society's own moral and social crisis while discussing literary cultures or the nature of functioning of economic institutions or social structures. Many writers were trained in the academic disciplines of anthropology, literary criticism, economics, linguistics and history. From their pens came new insights into the making of modern Assam. Their works, ranging through left, liberal and conservative shades of ideas, bore testimony to the diverse and contradictory views held by the Assamese intelligentsia in the 1970s. One such person was the anthropologist Madhab Chandra Goswami. When, in 1971, he was elected as one of the presidents of the annual Indian Science Congress, he chose to speak on the complex but dynamic relations among various social groups, which he summarized as the 'process of tribal integration and absorption into the nuclear Indian society'.[155] He might have, in the fashion of his profession, broadly clubbed these social groups as tribes, peasants and various castes, but, more importantly, he drew attention to the many subtle and continuous transformations that North-eastern societies were undergoing in modern times. In a more conservative tone, Goswami described the caste system as a 'sign of vitality and resilience', saying that it 'indicated continuous growth, development and expansion of the frontiers of social organisation'.[156]

Unlike in the past, Assamese Vaishnavism was no longer exclusively seen through the prism of literary and cultural history. Literary scholars, social scientists and others, often on shared scholarly platforms and across their ideological moorings, studied and debated the many lives of Vaishnavism in Assam's polity, culture and community.[157] They were joined by others in producing a vibrant public intellectual community; for instance, a series of art exhibitions in the 1970s that showcased the finest works of Assamese painters, some self-trained and others who had studied in India's best art institutes, introduced new dynamism into Assamese intellectual life. The Gauhati Artists' Guild, established in 1976, drew hundreds of admirers of new art forms.[158] In addition, theatres, annual book fairs, poetry festivals, etc., continued to influence and inspire minds in the 1970s and later. Much of this cultural and intellectual activity was spearheaded by liberal and left circles in Assam.

The restlessness and promises of the 1970s were captured in prose as well as verse.[159] Several literary works, for instance, *Pita Putra* (1975) by Homen Borgohain—arguably one of the most influential literary figures of Assamese literary canon—brilliantly portrayed the gigantic steps, borne out of political and economic upheavals, which Assamese rural families had taken to overcome social conservatism.[160] People zealously defended their favourite authors, artists or filmmakers, or they criticized those whom they did not admire. Others challenged powerful and established literary journals, publishing their own journals catering to a niche readership to give voice to their ideas and views. Unlike the earlier decades, when Assamese literary thought was largely directed by a single literary journal, the proliferation of such periodicals allowed a larger literary space for experimenting in different genres.[161] Book stores in Guwahati made available classics from across the world, and the promises of revolutionary Europe impressed many.[162] They excitedly looked at global political, economic, technological and cultural developments. The quest for river engineering to tame the Brahmaputra and its floods became a dominant theme in many narratives. If a few remained sceptical of the Chinese political experiments of the previous two decades, others silently translated the works of low-key Chinese dissident poets or classical Chinese verse, including that of Li Pu (701–762 CE) and Tu Fu (713–770 CE), into Assamese.[163] These literary thoughts energized much of Assam's political thinking of the 1970s and even in the later years.

More visible and powerful were women's literary voices. A few steadfastly rose to distinguish themselves as principal architects of modern Assam's social and intellectual world.[164] But only a few were able to carve out a moderately prominent place in the political world. Women's political participation increased from the late 1970s; as their participation in jobs beyond their households had grown and they provided income for their families, they also began to secure a place for themselves in the landscape of political mobilization. In the mid-twentieth century, institutional support for women's education had been lacklustre and the outlook towards it was bleak. An official statement from 1950 made women's place clear: with an 'overwhelming majority of girls attending schools, the education must be such as will make them fit to play socially useful role as mothers of good citizens'.[165] The highly conservative school curriculum for girls—that included domestic science, mothercraft, elementary child psychology, gardening—was not different from what public intellectuals like Boli

Narayan Bora, the Edinburgh-trained Assamese literary figure and a senior engineer in the colonial government, and some others had famously advocated in the 1880s and later.[166] Yet, defying those staid dreams of their government and the orthodoxy, more and more female students broke social barriers.

Assamese women's gradual but remarkable progress in the second half of the twentieth century was the result of a combination of their determination and scattered societal and institutional support, which came slowly. In 1977, Assam's female literary rate was slightly higher (23.52 per cent) than the all-India figure of 22 per cent.[167] Across class and caste, an increasing number of female students were enrolled for school education, though proportionately smaller numbers completed higher degrees. Only 113 of the 2267 students who were enrolled in polytechnics, 917 of the 6711 BSc students and 129 of the 642 MSc students were females—interestingly, this indicated that while the number of women graduates was low, a good proportion of them continued with post-graduate studies.[168] But unlike in several Indian states, there were far fewer female voters compared to male voters, and only a few were nominated as lawmakers.[169] However, on some social indicators, Assam did fairly well among her Indian counterparts. In a survey conducted in 1974 to determine whether women had 'control over dowry or jewels that [they] brought' to their marriage, only 13.59 per cent said that they had no stake in the ownership of these, while approximately 67.71 per cent responded positively.[170] The comparable figures in most Indian states remained far below this.

The 1970s were a time of unhappiness and anger, when the Assamese upper classes, comprising professionals, bureaucrats, rich entrepreneurs, landowners and others, were gripped by resentments against one another as rising peasant and trade union mobilizations seemed to threaten their economic and political opportunities. Also, by the late 1970s, a section of Assamese public intellectuals had developed a fairly sharp critique of the relationship between the state and the Union government. As they articulated their political resentment, in print, in political forums and elsewhere, they remained divided on their political outlook.

For instance, Nibaran Bora—an erstwhile trade unionist, a vocal critic of the Indian government and also the president of Purbanchaliya Loka Parishad (PLP)—wrote a series of essays in Assamese in 1977.[171] These popular essays were illustrative of the political views of many Assamese in the late 1970s. Bora, highlighting the underlying intellectual currents of Assam, equated its relations with the Indian state to those between East and West Pakistan, the culmination of which had been the birth of Bangladesh. Bora spelt out how the Indian state, with inherent flaws in its federal structure, had allowed Indian capital a free hand in exploiting Assam's natural resources while making no significant investment in the state's public infrastructure. He reminded everyone that the Assamese people did not get fair treatment at the hands of the Indian political classes. A fiery orator, Bora underlined this idea of discrimination against Assam by the Indian state by underscoring the state's economic exploitation and political marginalization, and this sentiment was widely shared by public intellectuals. Numerous instances of discrimination—such as lack of employment for Assamese in the newly established public sector industries like the Hindustan Paper Corporation Limited[172]—found their way into popular narratives.

This sense of economic disparity made the Assamese politically restless and took many forms. The Asam Jatiya Parishad and the Purbanchaliya Loka Parishad (PLP) were born during 1977–78, though they had a limited political impact. A majority of such groups strived to remain united under the powerful idea of Assamese nationalism, which often ran counter to the scope of Indian nationalism. Yet, towards the end of the 1970s, a sizeable section of Assamese scholars—despite their furious criticism of Assam's weak political and financial stake in India's federal structure—also highlighted its deep-rooted connections with the rest of the Indian society. 'The first and foremost contribution of Assam seems to be this extension of India's cultural influence in this part of the country,' the folklorist Praphulladutta Goswami wrote compellingly in 1980.[173] He further reminded his fellow Assamese that 'India not only civilized Assam, it also remembered this part of the country with respect and appreciation'. 'Assam had made common cause with the mainland even in the epic days,' another scholar reaffirmed and continued: 'Assam is the country's sentinel in the sensitive east.'[174] Such pendulum-like swings in political temperament were best elucidated by historian Amalendu Guha in 1977 in his *Planters Raj to Swaraj*. He stated Assam's love for both little (Assamese) and great (Indian) nationalisms: 'This two-track patriotism is nowhere so prominently traceable as in the case of Assam.' By the end of the 1970s, these contrasting views on Assam's political, cultural and economic destinies had coalesced under the shadow of Assamese nationalism, and Assam's political life underwent a dramatic transformation.

# 12

# Waves of Popular Protest

The formation of the first non-Congress government in Assam (1978–79), led by Golap Borbora, had raised the hopes of many. They dreamt of greater availability of jobs and lower prices of edible items. However, as we have seen, the short-lived Janata government inherited a turbulent state. Through June 1978, students belonging to the All-Guwahati Students Union and the All-Assam Students' Union (AASU) staged several protests and demonstrations; they demanded that school education be made free (which the government implemented), student scholarships be released every month, rising prices be controlled, the flow of outsiders into Assam be checked, only youth from Assam be employed in government undertakings and that they be allowed to write the Assam Public Service Commission examinations in Assamese for recruitment to coveted government jobs.[1]

The Borbora ministry was deeply troubled and conveyed its concerns to the Union government. When members of India's Seventh Finance Commission visited Assam in June 1978, the Assam government pressed for more funds to be allocated to the state. The student wing of the Janata Party in Assam met Prime Minister Morarji Desai to forewarn him of impending political instability in Assam arising from migration from other states like West Bengal and neighbouring countries.[2] When Desai met Chief Minister Borbora on

24 August 1978, he advocated that the Assam government 'take steps to stop influx into Assam'.³

The political atmosphere was soon charged with anti-outsider rhetoric. In August, a football match in Guwahati, played between the iconic Bengal football team East Bengal and one from Thailand, turned violent after the former won—the Assamese crowd had been supporting the defeated team.⁴ In the same month, AASU reiterated their demands, which included stopping the 'influx of foreign nationals'.⁵ They took to the streets, boycotted classes, and, eventually, on 22 September 1978, they enforced a strike that virtually brought the state to a halt.⁶ As face-offs between the government and students intensified, schools and colleges were closed down in the last week of September.⁷ Students' residences in Gauhati University were vacated.

~

As these events unfolded, India's chief election commissioner, S.L. Shakdher, spoke at a conference of India's chief electoral officers at Ooty, Tamil Nadu, in October 1978. He warned that a large number of foreign nationals had found their way into the electoral rolls of India's north-eastern states, the numbers having grown by 35 per cent during the decade of 1961–71. Shakdher also confirmed what Assam's highest election officer had stated in 1972—that compared to the 'complete indifference and apathy' of the 'general public', the migrant population always showed enthusiasm in the process of electoral rolls revision and updating.⁸ He proposed that the Union government should take steps to identify 'each foreign national' and grant citizenship certificates to 'all eligible persons'.⁹ The chief election commissioner also claimed that political parties had made demands for the inclusion of these names in the electoral rolls. He was only echoing the complaints made by officials and others in Assam in recent years, and weeks later, the Union government confirmed Shakdher's concerns.¹⁰ The fact that there were discrepancies in the voters' list soon found its way into the Assamese popular press, which ensured that the popular anti-migrant narrative remained at the forefront of the Assamese public imagination.

The student organization called for another strike on 12 December 1978, urging the government to take their issues seriously. The two strikes of 1978 helped shape a strong anti-migrant political narrative.[11] For a long time, most migrants had remained content with availing of economic opportunities in the form of agrarian activities. That many of them were now increasingly seen as prospective voters raised the highly politicized subject of citizenship. The names of an estimated 2,00,000 foreigners—mostly from neighbouring Bangladesh—appeared in the electoral list. Many understood that the inclusion of their names in the list would protect them against detection and deportation. Detection of illegal migrants from Bangladesh and their deportation continued into 1979—officially estimated to be 6400 that year.[12] About one-fifth of these deportees were Hindus.

Early in 1979, Assam was in the grip of regular strikes that were joined by the unemployed and recently dismissed workers, temporary teachers and other distressed groups. There were violent clashes in Assam's districts bordering Nagaland and Arunachal, and many Assamese left Arunachal.[13] In March 1979, the deportation of foreign nationals to Bangladesh triggered clashes between Assamese and Bengalis. On 8 March 1979, localized rioting broke out after police allegedly picked up a number of Bengali Hindus from interior Kamrup.[14] Assamese villagers joined lower-level police staff to help identify Bengali residents as foreigners, while the latter banded together to resist the police.[15] As panic struck the Bengali-dominated areas arising from this aggressive round of detection of foreign nationals, a senior official of the Assam government had to pull up the police for 'harassing genuine Indian nationals'.[16] Most political parties opposed such action that took place without having the sanction of Foreigners' Tribunals; the ultra-regionalists like the PLP, on the other hand, rejected the action as a gimmick.[17]

At the completion of a year of the Borbora government in March 1979, an advertisement showcasing the government's work said: 'The problem of continuing influx of population from foreign countries to the State has been taken up in right earnest.'[18] But Borbora's detractors criticized him for not doing enough to deport the foreigners,[19] and on

15 March, beleaguered by dissidence, Borbora informed the Assembly that the number of refugees from Nepal and Bangladesh had assumed 'alarming proportions':[20] 'Influx of foreign nationals has created immense socio-economic, political, linguistic, communal and security problems in Assam which is facing acute unemployment problems and where land is no longer available even for the sons of the soil.' Among Borbora's promised steps to 'deport every foreign national' was the examination of electoral rolls. The Union government concurred with the views of the Assam government,[21] and the proposed measures were cautiously welcomed by the Assamese elite. The *Assam Tribune*—which seemingly voiced the opinions of many upper-class Assamese—grumbled that Borbora's promises were far short of what was needed.[22]

The political situation in Assam changed soon afterwards. On 28 March 1979, Hiralal Patowary, the MP from Mangaldoi, died from a heart attack,[23] necessitating a by-election. The Election Commission announced preparations;[24] draft electoral rolls were published in April 1979, and citizens were allowed to lodge claims for missing names and wrong entries. Officials associated with the process alerted Assamese leaders about the entry of names of many non-citizens. Objections against the inclusion of non-citizens in the electoral rolls, which required the support of enlisted voters from a constituency, poured in. Out of 47,658 such objections in the Mangaldoi constituency, the election officials found 36,780 foreigners, as recounted in the memoirs of an Assamese police official and insider to this development.[25] As this became public knowledge in Assam, a general strike—*bandh*—was called by AASU on 8 June 1979, demanding the deletion of names of foreigners from the electoral rolls and their deportation from India. The strike was hugely successful in the Brahmaputra Valley.[26]

But the final electoral rolls were not published, and the by-election was not held. In July 1979, the Morarji Desai government at the Centre resigned, and Chaudhary Charan Singh, another Janata stalwart, became the Prime Minister supported by the Congress. In August 1979, Charan Singh's government fell, not being able to secure enough political support in the Lok Sabha, and mid-term elections were announced. These were to be held in January 1980, and the Election Commission had to complete the revision of electoral rolls by October 1979. Meanwhile, strong ideological differences within his party coupled with the political aspirations of his opponents, alongside the developments in Delhi, led Chief Minister Borbora to resign on 4 September 1979. Jogendra Nath Hazarika became Assam's new chief minister.

~

The summer of 1979 had seen government employees, teachers and workers protesting in the streets, demanding higher wages, better work conditions and job security. Students in several colleges were on strike. Assam was also hit by a drought,[27] which officially affected 5 million people, approximately a third of the population. In some places, people were forced to travel more than 10 kilometres to collect drinking water.[28] The Election Commission's notification on the revision of electoral rolls came amidst all this.

The state's student leaders were deeply acquainted with the social, cultural and economic dynamics of rural Assam. Many were sensitive to the values of syncretism, but their commitment to freeing Assam of foreigners was stronger as they believed this would lift the state out of its economic distress. At its annual conference from 7 to 10 March, AASU outlined its future course of action. It also elected its new executive committee, headed by Prafulla Kumar Mahanta and Bhrigu Kumar Phukan, both in their 20s, as its president and general secretary. AASU was joined by an umbrella organization, comprising lawyers, litterateurs, other student bodies and government employees, called the Asom Gana Sangram Parishad (AGSP), which came into existence towards the end of August 1979.[29] AASU and the AGSP worked together while maintaining their separate identities. Their work was sustained by the ideological and material support of Assamese speakers across classes. Largely free from the formal and organizational structure of political parties, they were inspired by the vision of Assam as a linguistic state.

Students led the Anti-Foreigners' movement. Some of the AASU executive members

Beginning 6 September 1979, AASU undertook a series of political programmes, which included the boycott of classes. Initially, there were scattered incidents of physical assaults on officials engaged in the revision of electoral rolls. Agitations sprang to life after police stormed a college campus in central Assam. Regular picketing escalated, strikes intensified and the agitation spread, mainly in urban areas of the Brahmaputra Valley. The political resistance to the revision of the voters' list brought together a vast spectrum of the population. An organization of printers—the North Eastern Master Printers' Association—made it known that they would not print the electoral rolls.[30] There were rumours of a demand that no elections be held in Assam before the deletion of the names of foreigners was completed. For a large majority, there was no legal clarity on who a foreigner was; recent refugees were seen as foreigners, and so were non-Assamese traders.

As appeals rose to boycott the election, the Election Commission made it clear that a major revision of the electoral rolls to check the authenticity of citizenship could happen only after the General

Elections.[31] The Hazarika-led Assam government promised to prepare a register of citizens and issue identity cards.[32] In the face of opposition from many Muslim lawmakers, the government promised in October 1979 to establish new Foreigners' Tribunals and reactivate the defunct ones.[33] The *Times of India* urged that 'all this may not be of much avail unless effective steps are also taken to stop further infiltration of aliens into Assam and to deport at least some of those whose foreign nationality has been juridically established beyond question'.[34] The journalist Inder Malhotra, who travelled extensively across Assam in January 1979, noted the widespread disquiet:[35] 'The Assam government is in dispute with the Central Election Commission. The state government wants to strike off the names of illegal immigrants from the electoral rolls. The commission has asked it to desist.'

The government also began filing objections against those who were thought to be foreigners. By November 1979, one account suggests, an estimated 3,46,000 objections were filed claiming that those names should not be in the electoral list. One journalist noted that in the list of those against whom objections were filed, circles were drawn around common Bengali Hindu surnames.[36] Popular accounts gave various figures for the number of foreigners, some suggesting an astounding 3 million. Some of the designated foreigners were pushed into camps near the India–Bangladesh border.[37]

By late 1979, reports of migrants from Bangladesh swelling the border areas or their reclamation of government lands became part of Assam's popular narrative. By then, the street protests were fully in the control of students and youth, united under the banner of the AGSP and AASU, insisting that there should be no elections until the issue of foreigners was settled. Slogans of 'drive out foreign nationals' became a force to unite many against non-Assamese speakers.[38] Most observers realized that India's large political parties had hardly any control over such a mass upsurge. As the popular mobilization acquired momentum, 'every fourth man in Assam became a suspect and remains so in the eyes of the indigenes'.[39] A wide range of official and unofficial accounts converged on the idea that there was an 'illegal' and 'continuous' flow of human population from Nepal and Bangladesh into Assam.[40]

Assam's political situation took a turn for the worse from December 1979. The Assamese leadership was in no mood to hold elections based on electoral rolls they disagreed with. Protests, street demonstrations and strikes continued to dominate Assam's public life. A wide range of people, largely drawn from the Assamese-speaking social world—poor peasants, salaried people, a section of traders and petty industrialists and professionals, formed loose alliances to oppose the election. Some residents of Upper Assam, extending their support to the election boycott, called the protests 'a fierce upsurge, reminiscent of the freedom struggle'.[41] These protesters also reminded everyone that they did not want to see Assam's demography being transformed as it had been in Tripura, where decades of inflow of non-tribals from other areas (particularly East Pakistan) had overwhelmed the local tribal population.

None of this could stop the holding of the General Elections. The Assam government repeatedly asked the Election Commission and Union government for a postponement, but without success.[42] The newspapers reported on a successful general strike on 3 and 4 December 1979, followed by four days of picketing.[43] Support came from traders, government employees and students. By now, Assam's political landscape was truly volatile. The chief minister said that 'there is no use holding the elections here with people of doubtful citizenship',[44] and the Governor endorsed his view.[45] But the Union government was unrelenting, giving an assurance that a National Register of Citizens (NRC) would be prepared soon.[46]

Any individuals or groups suspected of supporting the elections, including oil professionals and public servants in Upper Assam, were attacked. Reports of burning and looting of houses and shops and attacks on trains were frequent. 'Indian Airlines and the Railways have been intimidated and asked to leave the state.'[47] The police resorted to brutal violence; hundreds were killed across Assam within weeks.

Only a handful of political parties dared to participate in electioneering and file nomination papers. Most Congress leaders remained confined to their houses, which were gheraoed.[48] Some like the Congress stalwart Dev Kant Barooah publicly announced that they would not file nominations. On 10 December 1979, when Abida Ahmed, the widow of former president F.A. Ahmed, went to file her nomination in Muslim-dominated Barpeta as a candidate of Indira Gandhi's Congress, a mass of students, teachers, doctors, traders and members of the intelligentsia wearing black badges and carrying black flags marched to the District Collector's office. Police had to open fire to quell the protests, and a teenage student leader, Khargeswar Talukdar, was killed.[49] (Abida was able to smuggle her papers through the mob, but they were eventually rejected.) A spontaneous outpouring of sympathy and anger followed, and the incident sparked a wave of protests. Massive silent processions were taken out in Guwahati.[50] Meanwhile, the CPI and the faction of the Congress opposed to Mrs Gandhi had withdrawn support to the Hazarika government on 8 December, and the government fell on 12 December.[51] President's Rule was imposed—the first of many such spells to come in Assam.

Political developments in Assam shaped the narratives of election campaigns elsewhere in India. Mrs Gandhi made clear her disapproval of the deletion of names of voters from the electoral list. At several campaign meetings, she said that in Muslim-dominated areas, the 'elections would not be fair'.[52] A 'large number of Muslims and tea plantation labourers were removed from the electoral rolls in Assam without following rules', she said in a speech at Visakhapatnam.[53] In Mumbai, Jamiat Ulema-i-Hind had already observed a 10-day protest. Mrs Gandhi also wrote to Syed Abdullah Bukhari, the Shahi Imam of Jama Masjid, saying that 'the forcible eviction of minorities from Assam is indeed a shameful blot on the fair name of our secular society . . . no Indian citizen, regardless of his religious denomination, should be treated as a foreigner and forced to leave the country'.[54] The communist parties objected to the one-sided verifications and demanded that all must be given a chance to present a judicial defence.[55]

In January 1980, amidst resilient popular defiance, General Elections were held in three out of 14 constituencies of Assam, which were dominated by Bengali speakers. Mrs Gandhi came back to power and assumed charge as Prime Minister on 14 January 1980. AASU and the AGSP had given a strike call in the first week of January.[56]

In the first fortnight of January, large-scale communal violence broke out in rural areas of Kamrup between the Assamese and the Bengali-speaking Muslim villagers,[57] which quickly spread to many areas of Lower Assam.[58] Sporadic searches for citizenship certificates were carried out among Bengali families.[59] Some Bengali-speaking Hindu families and other worried linguistic minorities sought refuge in West Bengal.[60] If people from linguistic and religious minorities—many of whom had migrated to Assam from East Bengal during Partition—faced onslaughts, so did their Hindu Assamese neighbours who too fell victim to clashes. There were reports of women being molested by state forces.[61] Protesters—more than 100 according to a non-official estimate—were killed in the oil fields of Upper Assam.[62] Social relations collapsed, and old social and cultural linkages could not stave off violence. Both public narratives and the accounts of journalists got polarized. For months, Assam continued to be tormented by popular agitation, state repression and widespread communal violence. Parts of the state were declared disturbed areas under the Assam Disturbed Area Act of 1955, which allowed even low-ranking police officials to use firearms. Some villagers were made to pay punitive taxes.[63]

In the last week of May 1980, another round of communal violence swept through central and Lower Assam.[64] After being battered by months of political challenges, a social alliance of those who were portrayed as illegal citizens—led by a newly formed student organization of the minorities—began to take shape. A section of them were beneficiaries of the rural economic prosperity of the previous decades, and they refused to bow down to social and economic ostracism in their Hindu Assamese neighbourhood. Prime Minister Mrs Gandhi's support for Assam's religious and linguistic minorities was apparent; she stated that they were 'feeling insecure' and that the ongoing movement was not at all 'a peaceful' one.[65] Student leaders from religious and linguistic minority groups conveyed to the Assam government that they recognized the need to detect and deport migrants from Bangladesh who came after 1971.[66] But this political overture was a brief one; as Mrs Gandhi stood by them, they decided to assert their political rights and took to the streets on 26 May 1980.[67] Religious and linguistic identities united them, and the Assamese villagers were outnumbered. The communal violence of that week deepened the fault line between Muslims and non-Muslims, and communal riots spread rapidly across many parts of central and Lower Assam. These clashes were often determined by local agrarian relations, demographic composition and ethnic, linguistic and religious solidarities, which took several forms. If in one locality a particular religious community was dominant, those belonging to the other faith were attacked, while the opposite occurred in a locality where the converse was the case.[68] Such incidents occurred almost everywhere, including in smaller towns.

~

Economic activities in Assam were hit hard when the transport of crude oil and trade in plywood was blocked early during the anti-foreigner movement. In the 1980s, Assam, Gujarat and Bombay High were the three important sources of India's crude oil. In 1975–76, Assam's share had been a little more than a tenth of India's total crude oil production; this fell to 6 per cent in 1980. The movement's most successful strategy was to block the outflow of crude oil from Assam for several months at a stretch. Across Assam, in most places of oil drilling, refinery, etc., strikes by protesters brought industrial work to a halt. 'At the joint-sector Oil India Limited's pipeline installation at Narengi near Gauhati and at Gauhati refinery, about 150 volunteers [were] carted in shifts every day to squat on the railway tracks and around the controlling valves that guide the flow of crude oil to Barauni refinery in Bihar,' according to one account.[69] The government declared oil supply an essential service. However, the popular upsurge drew strength from both the political economy of the petroleum industry and its cultural symbolism, as by the end of the 1970s, after years of political struggle to assert Assamese ethnic claims on oil and significant economic and social benefits which shaped the rise of a new Assamese elite, oil was no more an abstract economic commodity. Unlike tea, oil was a symbol of Assam's economic prosperity, and it now emerged as a site of political resistance as the supply of crude oil from Assam was repeatedly halted over 13 months during 1980–81. 'We will give blood, not oil,' cried angry and jubilant protesters everywhere. Many picketers—officially seven and unofficially 70—were shot dead on 18 January 1980 in Upper Assam.[70] Early in 1981, the rebels blasted the Assam oil pipeline twice.[71]

Assam's crude oil production dropped from 4.3 million tonnes in 1975–76 to 1.7 million tonnes during 1980–81.[72] Mrs Gandhi tried to brush it off, claiming that the country could do without Assam's oil. However, the blockade affected oil supplies to refineries in Bihar and western Uttar Pradesh. These areas were dependent on the supply of petroleum products, particularly high-speed diesel, from Barauni. The blockade also dealt a crippling blow to the already troubled fertilizer industry. Fertilizer plants dependent on natural gas from Assam oilfields or naphtha from Assam refineries were closed down. The *Times of India* wrote, [Assam] 'ha[s] done enough damage to the country's economy when the rise in oil prices is even otherwise placing an intolerable burden on it'.[73] The strikes in the oil industry 'forced' the Indian government to 'increase imports of refined products to meet its needs at an extra cost of $4 million a day'.[74] These strikes hit the states of Bihar and West Bengal hard, as diesel to run irrigation pumps—these two states accounted for an estimated one-fourth of India's agricultural diesel pumps during 1985–86[75]—was now in short supply. The shortage of kerosene hit many households as well.

With Assam's blockades and strikes, the Union government had to deploy the Army to pump out crude oil lying stagnant in oil fields and transport it to the refinery in Bihar. International observers noted that such blockades gave the Assamese leaders a political advantage, being the 'most important and damaging of the sanction[s] by the agitating student leaders in their long struggle against the central government'.[76] Yet, this form of protest—new in post-Independence India—did not have a long-lasting impact, as India substantially increased its oil output from other sources, primarily from the Bombay offshore field that was established in 1976.[77] India also procured more oil from its new-found friends overseas. In 1980, Iraq promised India 6 million tonnes of crude oil, which was slightly more than the previous year's supply.[78] Russia agreed to increase the supply of both crude oil and oil products to India.[79] In 1981, Lovraj Kumar, the Secretary for the Department of Oil and Natural Gas, declared India's growing confidence in oil exploration and home production. He estimated that India would increase its domestic production from 3,40,000 barrels to 4,40,000 barrels in the next year, and approximately 60 per cent of this production would be from Bombay High. This would mean an 83 per cent fall in the import of crude oil.[80]

~

Ten days after taking charge again as Prime Minister in January 1980, Mrs Gandhi invited the Assam leaders from both AASU and the AGSP for talks.[81] The student leaders met her for the first time in early February 1980. Their delegation arrived in Delhi, 'carrying with it a 119–page memorandum in album form supported by documents, newspaper cuttings including photographs on the current movement in Assam with its analysis', reported an admiring journalist.[82] This rather long document, the logic and language of which echoed the sentiments of an average middle-class Assamese, spelt out the larger context of Assam's agony, its economic situation and its future roadmap.[83] Their demands included the preparation of a register of citizens of Assam based on the previous such government register from 1951, detection of all foreigners who had come to live in Assam since 1951 and their deportation. The document demanded that foreigners without valid documents from the other side of the 'border', which meant Bangladesh, must be 'shot at'.[84]

But the meeting with the Prime Minister did not break the deadlock, and the agitation continued, though the Union government signalled that no election would be held in Assam till the revision of the electoral rolls. The student leaders were given the option of accepting 1967 as the cut-off date for the detection and deportation of illegal citizens, but this was rejected by the student leaders. As one senior bureaucrat recalled,

Student leaders from Assam meeting the Prime Minister Indira Gandhi in New Delhi on 2 February 1980

with her uncanny political sense, [Mrs Gandhi had] decided to start a dialogue [in February 1980] with AASU and invited them for talks. Apparently, there was a feeling that the "AASU boys" would be overwhelmed by the charisma of the Prime Minister, and the issue would be resolved in no time. Soon she was to find that the AASU boys, who were so young . . . were not easily amenable to overtures made at the highest level.[85]

As the year progressed, more people from Assamese urban and rural families, cutting across class and caste lines, joined the popular agitation. Assamese Muslims, who claimed to be descendants of Muslim families that centuries earlier had accompanied the Mughal army, extended their support to the anti-foreigners movement.[86] Assamese public opinion, especially in the urban areas, particularly targeted the poor, in particular Hindi or Bengali speakers. 'Look at this street . . . that beggar, these rickshaw drivers, they are all Bangladeshis. I am a stranger in my own country,' said a young businessman from Guwahati to a visiting journalist in 1983.[87]

The oil blockade had by then caused enough trouble to force Mrs Gandhi to take the Assam crisis seriously. In April 1980, she suggested that the 'family quarrel' should be resolved through 'give and take'.[88] Mrs Gandhi organized an all-party meeting to discuss the Assam imbroglio and to reach a consensus on the date for the identification and deportation of foreigners. She had herself been privy to a series of political negotiations during the Bangladesh war, when millions of refugees from East Pakistan arrived in India. In February 1972, she had persuaded Mujibur Rahman, the Prime Minister of Bangladesh, to take back the refugees who came to India after 25 March 1971.

However, the political and official negotiations did not achieve the desired results. Mrs Gandhi blamed India's far-right political groups and 'foreign powers'[89]; others, like the communist leaders, thought that the CIA was behind the trouble. Political leaders and commentators such as Atal Bihari Vajpayee and Arun Shourie escalated a regional problem into a larger national question, much to the liking of the student leaders of Assam.[90] On 11 January 1981, the BJP organized 'Assam Day' across the country to draw national attention to the political developments in the state.[91] They viewed the issue through the lens of a Hindu–Muslim conflict rather than one of Assam's linguistic aspirations. Assam and her political life became a subject of great interest and curiosity for national and international journalists.

In April 1980, the Union government declared Assam a disturbed area, calling in the military to quell political protests. The Armed Forces (Special Powers) Act of 1958 was applied to maintain public order. The imposition of President's Rule allowed the bureaucracy to take the upper hand. In July 1980, Prime Minister Mrs Gandhi toughened her position on Assam and declared that domestic unrest had weakened India's security.[92]

Between 1980 and 1983, talks with the student leaders continued at the highest level of the Central government. There were relentless backdoor political negotiations, where political leaders and bureaucrats across ideological affiliations played important roles. By the end of 1982, the government and Assam leaders had met for 114 days; during this period, Assam witnessed 239 days of 'some form or other' of agitation, a contemporary account estimated.[93] The student leaders 'were thorough with their homework; were briefed by experienced lawyers, academics of standing and retired civil servants of seniority'. Most discussions, largely overseen by the Prime Minister's trusted bureaucrats rather than perceptive politicians, were 'less of negotiations and more of prepared lectures'.[94] The Assamese leaders stuck to 1951, the benchmark as per the Citizenship Act of 1955, for the identification and deportation of foreigners.[95]

At the peak of the popular mobilization during 1980–82, the functioning of the Assam government remained largely paralysed. A major reason for the success of the protests was that the disruption of the oil economy was imaginatively used as a method of protest. Hundreds of thousands of people, drawn largely from the Assamese-speaking urban and rural population, raised slogans against refugees, outsiders, illegal migrants, etc. The boundaries of these sociopolitical categories remained blurred initially, as those considered outsiders included the Marwari traders, the Bihari labourers, the Nepali workers, the Bengali shopkeepers and the East-Bengali/Pakistani-origin peasants. But by the early 1980s, the term 'outsiders' came to be largely identified with recent settlers from East Pakistan and Bangladesh, and these Bengali-speaking peasants and traders were primarily targeted. Some of them were able to obtain certificates of Indian citizenship through political-bureaucratic connections,[96] but others could not escape the wrath of the protesters. The Marwari traders, despite bearing the brunt in the early days, made a tactical alliance with the movement. Many of them offered financial support or even joined the masses in the streets. Resentment against 'outsiders' erupted in neighbouring Meghalaya too. In October, the non-tribal population—mainly Bengalis—began to face assaults from the tribal majority.[97]

From the beginning, the movement followed a typical pattern of mobilization. A journalist who visited Assam a year after the movement began had this to say:

The AASU, spearheading the agitation, would give the call for a continuous spell of satyagraha all over the state which would paralyse normal life, emptying government offices of its staff, stopping public transportation, halting business. This would be followed by a respite, and then the ritual would repeat itself.[98]

For many, temporary arrest became a matter of social status and a sign of their solidarity with the aims of the student leaders. The arrested would be released after a few hours of detention. But despite the popular backing, not everyone was agreeable to the idea of repeated strikes. The *Assam Tribune*, which broadly supported the movement, published a series of letters to the editor that expressed grave concern about extended periods of suspension of classes and offices not working.

As the popular protests intensified, the ideological rift between left and right was further amplified. While the left's inability to grasp the concerns of Assamese speakers largely alienated them from the popular movement, the right's hostility towards outsiders encouraged religious and ethnic polarization.

This rallying of the larger section of the Assamese around anti-foreigner sentiments pushed Bengali Hindus and Muslims to come together on one platform. The All-Assam Minority Students Union (AAMSU) was formed in March 1980,[99] which articulated Muslim political concerns. Their message was clear: 'purging of "foreigners" will be preceded by a bloodbath', a journalist recorded.[100] With the political crisis of 1974 not forgotten, Assam's tribal population extended partial support to the movement, but they remained wary of the larger aims of the Assamese leadership. Several tribal organizations united under the All-Assam Tribal Protection Action Committee (AATPAC). The Bodo students issued an appeal for a mass upsurge, but they insisted that the political programmes be directed by Bodo students in the Bodo-inhabited areas.[101] As mentioned earlier, as late as 1978, AASU had reiterated their demand for the compulsory use of the Assamese language in schools and offices. The Bodo leaders also feared that the reinforcement of Assamese control in the political system of Assam would meet with adverse reactions. Illustrations of this were many. When AASU tried to enforce the closure of educational institutions in 1980, it did not go without challenge; AAMSU, All-Assam Tribal Students Union and All-Bodo Students Union insisted on the reopening of schools.[102] As the Assamese students, most of whom were Hindus, took an upper hand in directing the political narratives of popular protests, tribal organizations felt left out. In fact, there were numerous instances where they were excluded; in February 1980, when the Union home minister arrived in Guwahati, tribal organizations were debarred from meeting him, which they resented.[103] As they began to feel the pinch and power of Assamese-language speakers, many tribal communities began to feel alienated. These fissures helped Mrs Gandhi, who met the AAMSU leadership during her visit to Assam in April 1980 and followed this by meeting the AATPAC in Delhi in June.[104] Her endorsement had many outcomes.

The All Assam Minority Students Union delegation called on the Prime Minister Indira Gandhi in New Delhi on 10 June 1980

The movement presented no specific charter or programme for bringing political and economic change to Assam. Instead, it focused on two demands that the agitators believed would bring such change: push back foreigners and increase Assam's share in the Union budget. Foreigners were seen as a threat to future Assamese political power besides being contenders for scarce economic opportunities. Assam had bitter memories of the period between 1936 and 1947, when Bengali-speaking politicians had often dominated the political scene. Increased numbers of Bengali-speaking Muslims were seen as a sign of the gradual loss of political control over Assam by the Assamese. For many urban Assamese, as they began to share their feeling of being 'displaced *in situ*', the word 'foreigner' was a symbol of their struggle for existence. Some, though politically passionate, remained somewhat sceptical: 'Today the flame of patriotism is burning in every Assamese heart and the desire to save our motherland has baptized every one of us in the agitational fire,' wrote one of them; yet, he emphatically stated that even if all foreigners were to be deported from Assam, this would bring no economic relief.[105] Others directed their anger at the Union government, which they felt had been unfair to Assam. 'Are we a part of India?' asked an Assamese newspaper.[106]

Political violence took several forms: targets included ideological opponents of the movement, Bengali- or Hindi-speaking traders and workers. Communist leaders or their sympathizers were socially boycotted, abuses were hurled at them and a few were killed. The government, for the most part, used the state machinery to repress protestors, repression becoming part of everyday lore in Assam. The Union government used the same strategy of coercion through the Army as it had done in Nagaland. This further alienated the protesters from the idea of India.

As the agitation in Assam spread and turned violent, scattered counter-demonstrations were organized in West Bengal. The protestors voiced their support for the refugees from East Pakistan, saying they could not be considered illegal immigrants in India. Sporadic retaliation was reported both in West Bengal and in parts of Bihar, where local groups, with support from the Congress or the communist parties, took to blockading the transportation of goods to Assam. Assam was largely dependent on neighbouring states for the import of consumer goods. By early 1980, trucks carrying goods to Assam were blocked by West Bengal in retaliation to the strikes in Assam. This often resulted in the shortage of commodities like salt.

~

How many people in Assam extended their support to the anti-foreigner movement? In 1980, the Delhi-based newsmagazine *India Today*, with its generally moderate views on Assam politics, thought that the agitation had 'absorbed the entire Assamese-speaking Hindu urban middle class and a slice of the agrarian population'.[107] In another instance,

> on 10 April, in spite of an official circular barring all government staff from joining the satyagraha, nearly 95 per cent of the state's 1,10,000 employees turned out at the rallies. While under secretaries and officers above them attended office, those below that rank milled around in front of courts, chanting slogans, violating orders under Section 144 and "getting arrested".[108]

In April, *India Today* reported that the movement was 'fast becoming the stubbornest in the country's history since the Quit India struggle launched against the British rule in 1942'.[109] That month, the government had to withdraw a curfew imposed in Guwahati within six hours as 'milling crowds began storming through barricades'.[110] Support from the Assamese bureaucracy greatly added to the strength of the protestors. *India Today* reported that in Guwahati, an Assamese magistrate had held a Central Reserve Police (CRP) constable by his collar 'as the latter whipped his cane at a crowd of picketers'. Wives and children of officers who continued to attend to duty publicly expressed their loyalty to the various programmes of the movement.

The deputy commissioner of Kamrup, who ordered all the cane-charges in Gauhati during the past fortnight, was caught in an unenviable situation with his wife participating in the picketing. The crowd that has been picketing the road heads leading to the pipeline installation and crude oil pumping station at Narengi includes a fair measure of officers' wives.[111]

Those were moments of crucial importance.

The movement had gained influential friends outside Assam in places like Delhi and Bombay, and the national press began to give it wider publicity. The agitation's strategy and tactics were endorsed by many, including the RSS. Since 1979, Assam's police intelligence had increasingly reported organizational activities of the RSS in the Lower Assam districts.[112] New cadres were given training across Assam. In March and June 1979, Balasaheb Deoras, the third Sarsanghchalak of the RSS, travelled to Assam.[113] He was followed by others, including Rajendra Singh, general secretary of the RSS. The organization spoke for the deportation of Muslim migrants, but it considered the Hindus as victims of India's Partition as well as of atrocities in East Pakistan. Such views, however, found little support among the Assamese protestors. Most refused to differentiate among the foreigners on the basis of religious identity, a contemporary observer noted.[114] The Assam Jatiyatabadi Dal, a key constituent of the AGSP, in their memorandum to the Prime Minister in February 1980, insisted that both Hindu and Muslim migrants were considered foreigners.[115] Journalists who covered the popular agitation reported that the RSS gave organizational support at the grassroots, but their organizational programmes were attended by very few.[116] In an interview given in 1983 to the *Indian Express*, K.S. Sudarshan, the RSS's principal ideologue in Assam, expressed unhappiness about Assam's refusal to make a distinction between Hindus and Muslims.[117]

Except for the BJP and the Janata Dal, no major Opposition party supported the Assamese movement. A key role was played by the BJP, which manifested in 1980. If a section of the student leadership, along with the Assamese upper castes, sympathized with the distinction advocated by the RSS, the idea of class struggles of the kind seen in Bihar resonated with others. Vajpayee, the BJP's top leader, travelled widely in Assam, held discussions with the agitating leaders and spoke eloquently in their defence within and outside the Parliament.[118] The RSS organ, *Organiser*, gave sympathetic publicity to the movement's concerns and strengths,[119] but it added its own ideological explanation. '[The RSS] makes a fine distinction between "refugees", meaning Hindus who ought by rights to be allowed to stay on in "Hindustan", and "infiltrators", who are by implication Muslims,' *India Today* reported in March 1983.[120] In 1980, the organization explained:

> Bharat, it must be remembered, remains the only country in the world, which the displaced Hindus consider as their home and where they can never be considered as foreigners . . . the problem should not be viewed through narrow provincial, language or party interests, but in the light of the needs of national integrity and security.[121]

Mrs Gandhi gauged the reasons for the RSS's organizational support to the popular mobilization, though this was denied by the top RSS functionaries.[122] The RSS had by then an extensive organizational network across the country, with more than 50,000 branches in India, and it took this opportunity to expand its organizational strength in Assam. One report claimed that by early 1983, it had 320 units in Assam.[123]

Failing to appreciate the widespread popular support behind this movement, the national leaders of the CPI and CPI (Marxist), as well as the left-leaning intellectuals, as mentioned earlier, pointed to the role of American intelligence agencies in the Assam crisis.[124] The CIA's involvement remained a part of a tiny section of the Assamese public narrative for quite some time.[125] However, the popular agitation was largely autonomous in origin.

What was the crux of the problem? When Sinha, the former chief minister, was asked this question, he answered, 'The Government of India has to decide who are foreigners and who are citizens and continue deporting foreigners.' He also emphasized that detecting [the] real foreigner is a Herculean task. It is not a question of picking up an Englishman . . . We are the same people, speaking the same language. The Constitution is clear about citizenship rights for anyone who can establish a five year residence and any children born on Indian soil.[126]

Who then was not a citizen in India? So far, the only answer was provided by India's Citizenship Act. Although India's Constitution broadly outlined who could be a citizen, the country's first citizenship law was enacted in 1955, years after the tumultuous Partition. As per this Act, a person who was born in India on or after 26 January 1950 would be an Indian citizen. If a person was born outside India during this period, s/he could become an Indian citizen only if the person's father was a citizen of India by descent. There were more provisions through which one could seek to become an Indian citizen, but these did not apply to a large migrant population.

The complex problem of minorities in East Pakistan and the civil unrest of 1971 in Bangladesh had complicated the issue in India's North-east. Intricate legal and political questions related to citizenship and foreigners took centre stage in the movement's early days.[127] India's political leadership broadly agreed on the distinction between refugees and illegal foreigners. The clamour for the deportation of illegal foreigners on the basis of the register of Indian citizens, known as NRC of 1951, became intense.[128] 'Who, in the world, can be a silent spectator to the process of elimination of the majority by a silent, unarmed, pre-planned invasion of the minority,' wrote Pachu Gopal Baruah, a lawyer.[129]

The diplomatic and legal mechanism of deportation, which had come to a halt in 1979, was re-established in 1982, when religious and linguistic minority settlers were briefly evicted from the government lands.[130] Thin inflows of migrants, mostly Hindus, were reported in mid-1982, as the new military government in Bangladesh began to expropriate the property of 'enemies', which impacted the Hindu minorities.[131] The *Times of India* appealed to the Indian government to 'seek through discreet diplomacy to persuade Dacca to put things right'.¹³² Pressured, the Union government stopped evictions while at the same time providing financial support to those refugees who had come into India between 1961 and March 1971.¹³³

The urban middle-class Assamese, imbued with linguistic and cultural pride, vented economic grievances through participation in popular protests: strikes, bandhs and public curfew were key features of the protests. Students and youth came out to stop the functioning of government offices and the plying of trains. Assamese women drawn from urban and rural families joined hands with student leaders who remained at the forefront of popular demonstrations and shaped political narratives and strategies. Vocal women leaders in rural areas influenced the local initiatives. Lower-rank Assamese police and bureaucracy extended their tacit sympathy to the popular upsurge. This played a major role in sustaining the movement for a longer duration and withstanding state repression.

The movement was largely in the hands of student leaders—both rural and urban, though a majority were still deeply rooted in Assam's rural background, their parents were powerful village elders, and many came from prosperous landed families. Their idealism inspired large numbers; when they delivered their fiery speeches, crowds of both

Women remained in the forefront of the Anti-Foreigners' movement

women and men listened in rapt attention. Most hoped that the decades of economic distress would end with a greater flow of financial support from the Centre. Students across the rural and urban divide had withdrawn from classrooms, the large majority missing class for an entire year in 1980; those who were reluctant were pressured to follow suit. Even younger students listened to the speeches of their leaders, though they might have found it difficult to grasp the nuances

Support came from various professional organizations. A scene from one of the rallies from Guwahati.

Traders joined in large numbers in the movement. A scene from one of the rallies.

of the citizenship debate. The movement remained ideologically nonviolent, but this did not stop the valorization of hatred and a strong anti-minority stand, which often led to localized violence. Left-leaning public intellectuals faced the ire of militant and conservative elements,

Support for the movement came from various communities living in Assam.

Student Unions from Meghalaya extending their support to the movement.

many suffering physical humiliation and intimidation. Occasionally, when there were mass arrests of top-ranking leaders, their combative militant juniors took over. The greatest sufferers from localized militancy were the religious and linguistic minorities. Some closed down their small businesses and moved out of Assam to neighbouring West Bengal.

A scene from the Republic Day celebration organized by AASU in Guwahati in 1980. That year AASU and AGSP called for a boycott of the official Republic Day programme.

Unlike all previous experiences of popular mobilization in Assam, this time, the printed word played a more important role in igniting political aspirations. With an estimated 12 million Assamese speakers, at least six out of every 1000 persons had access to daily newspapers in 1981.[134] Wall graffiti, with slogans or stanzas of popular poems, became a common sight. Cyclostyled hand-outs carrying the news of the movement helped mobilize and sustain local popular support.[135] Some writers expressed their grief and anger in published verse, short stories, novels or short essays.[136]

~

Even as Assamese student leaders and the Union government were busy negotiating a solution, the latter used its resources and political skills to astutely keep the basic demands of the Assamese at bay. This led to further mistrust, with even political parties like the CPI-M describing the Prime Minister 'as the greatest disruptionist of national unity and security'.[137] If in 1981, both the Union government and the Assam leaders tried to seek an answer to the definition of 'illegal' foreigners,[138] and the former was willing to deport those who came after 1966,[139] by the end of 1982, the dispute was mainly about the fate of those who had entered Assam between 1961 and 1971. The Indian government agreed that those who had entered post-1971 would be deported from India—a decision supported by various political groups in Assam,[140] the clandestine understanding being that those who had come between 1951 and 1961 would be given Indian citizenship—it was clear that 1.2 million people could not be dispersed—though there was no official clarity on determining the genuineness of residency.

Early in October 1982, the *Indian Express* reported that another round of negotiations between the Assamese leaders and the Union government had failed over the 'main question of the fate of the 1961–71 entrants from erstwhile East Pakistan'.[141] The report quoted the Assamese leaders as stating that those who had 'crossed over to Assam during 1961–71 should be disfranchised and dispersed to other areas over a period of time'.[142] The then defence minister, R. Venkataraman, a key negotiator, refused to accept a blanket disenfranchisement, and the Union government agreed to the demands for 'constitutional' protection to the 'Assamese people as in the case of Scheduled Castes and Scheduled Tribes'.[143] As these negotiations failed, the Union government at one point also suggested 1966 as the cut-off year for the deportation of all foreign nationals from Assam—while making it clear that those who came to Assam in the wake of the 1965 Indo–Pak war would not be deported.[144] A note of willingness to listen to the hardliners of the movement in Assam now became apparent in Mrs Gandhi's statements. Speaking in Parliament on 7 October, she said that the Assam crisis was 'a very complex, delicate, and emotional matter so far as the people of Assam are concerned and naturally we are all concerned about what happens'.[145] She said that her government could not take any 'hard and fast stand'. While knowing how complex and difficult it would be to deport thousands from India and given Assam's disastrous experience of the mid-1960s, she appeared to be willing for negotiations but 'without causing harm to other people', and that included the minorities in Assam, which she felt had wider implications for the country. Her government also offered to declare all indigenous Assamese enumerated in 1951 as Scheduled Tribes to ensure constitutional protection.¹⁴⁶ This idea was considered objectionable by the Assamese elite and was immediately rejected by the Assamese leaders. Another option before the Union government, offered by Ravindra Varma, a prominent Janata Party parliamentarian, was to grant citizenship to entrants from 1961 to 1971 who had citizenship certificates and to allow tribunals to examine the cases of those who did not have citizenship certificates. This would provide the foundation for broad political consensus leading to the final settlement in 1985.

However, the stalemate did not end immediately. While the negotiations in Delhi on 5–6 January 1983—the 20th round—failed to resolve the crisis, the Union government made clear its intention to go ahead with conducting elections in Assam. The election was scheduled over three days—14, 17 and 20 February—a decision probably taken to help maintain law and order. Election results for Andhra and Karnataka were declared on 7 January, and the Congress defeat forced Mrs Gandhi to seek victories elsewhere. On the same day, the Election Commission announced poll dates for Assam, after a little less than one year of President's Rule. As the Union government tried to get the support of Opposition parties to hold elections (succeeding with the CPM), the Assamese leaders made it clear that the election would be 'squarely and adequately answered'.¹⁴⁷ The Union government decided to delink the negotiations from the holding of polls.¹⁴⁸ The government also hastily, without clarifying the legal and political modalities for the identification of a foreigner, or considering the larger political consequences of such a process, offered to drop from the electoral rolls the names of foreigners and identify those who had come to Assam between 1966 and 24 March 1971 (the Bangladesh Liberation War began on 25 March 1971), but this was rejected by the Assamese student leaders.¹⁴⁹ When the student leaders returned to Guwahati after the failed negotiations, they were arrested, leaving the movement in the hands of the more militant among them.

As Mrs Gandhi's government decided to go ahead with the elections in Assam in February 1983, protests turned violent, and atrocities against religious and linguistic minorities became widespread as they were targeted for their participation in the elections.[150] The worst violence took place between Bengali-speaking Muslim peasants and Assamese-speaking tribal peasants in the central part of the Brahmaputra Valley. Several thousands were reported killed. Assam's otherwise powerful, popular, relatively peaceful and democratic movement against the political and economic policies of the Indian government now drew national and international attention for militant protest and the outbreak of retaliatory violence between Hindus and Muslims, which swept through the Brahmaputra Valley.

~

The holding of elections in Assam in February 1983 was a constitutional requirement after a one-year period of President's Rule. However, it was a tough political and bureaucratic decision, given the general atmosphere of civil unrest. The basic condition for holding elections had not yet been fulfilled—revision of the voters' list. While the government had not undertaken any such revision,[151] equally steadfast were the Assamese leaders in their demand that 'no election should be held to the Assembly or Parliament before the deletion of foreigners' names from the electoral rolls'.[152] While key officials of the Union government knew very well that it was impractical to revise the electoral rolls, senior government officials from Assam nevertheless anticipated the dangers involved in holding the elections.[153] On 28 January, India's Election Commission announced that elections would be held while acknowledging that the 'situation in the State is not absolutely ideal for holding polls'.[154]

The election was officially announced not just to meet constitutional requirements but also to score a political victory. Indira Gandhi's Congress wanted to prove that it could win an election based on the support of ethnic and religious minorities. The consequences were serious not only in terms of the moral erosion of the democratic processes but also in the scoring of an illegitimate political victory. Would it have been possible to defer the elections? Before 1978, there had been talks to extend the provision for President's Rule up to a maximum of three years. Some half-hearted political negotiation took place in November 1982 to amend the Constitution so that President's Rule could be extended beyond one year in Assam.[155] Several Opposition parties, including Janata Party, BJP and Lok Dal, offered conditional support for such an amendment, but the proposal was dropped by December 1982.[156] Mrs Gandhi's government did not have the required numbers to push through the amendment. On 10 February 1983, writing to the American author and her long-time friend, Dorothy Norman, Mrs Gandhi said, 'We can postpone them [elections] by constitutional amendment. But when this idea was put to the Opposition parties, they did not agree to support us and our strength in the Upper House is not sufficient to act by ourselves.'[157] Assam's leading Opposition parties were also staunchly opposed to the continuation of the President's Rule.

The Union government had also allowed executive magistrates in Assam to exercise judicial powers to try and dispose of cases with the right to punish for up to six months.[158] This sparked a power struggle between the judiciary and the executive magistrates. By the last week of January 1983, the law-and-order machinery had become dysfunctional. In Delhi, Mrs Gandhi, reeling under state election defeats, reorganized her cabinet.[159] There was a renewed government repression in Assam, which further consolidated public opinion. Large numbers died in the police firing in the first weeks of February 1983.[160]

When Prime Minister Mrs Gandhi decided to go ahead with the elections, which she knew was 'taking its inevitable course',[161] with the conviction that 'no one has the right to stop the election', there were calls from media houses like *The Hindu*, which cited widespread non-cooperation from Assamese civil servants and appealed that the election be called off.[162] Some leaders in Assam saw the elections as Mrs Gandhi's 'all-out war on the Assamese'.[163] A resident from Shillong wrote in the *Times of India* that with 'the decision to hold elections, the psychological alienation of the indigenous people of the Northeast from the rest of India is complete and the youths have been turned into rebels'.[164] As popular resistance against the elections became strikingly clear, the *Times of India* asserted that 'a situation has arisen which calls for an agonizing reappraisal'. It appealed to Mrs Gandhi, as she embarked on an election campaign in Assam, 'to assess for herself whether anything worthy of being called election can be held in the state at all'.[165] With one more day of the elections yet to be held on 20 February, Vajpayee, at public meetings on 17 and 18 February in Upper Assam, which were attended by AASU leaders, appealed to the people to abstain from voting.[166] However, most political parties other than the BJP and the Janata Party participated in the elections.[167] The left and the socialists formed an alliance.[168] The PTCA also fought the elections.

During election week, AASU declared bandhs, blackouts and janata curfews. The main narratives of the anti-election resistance were spelt out early, but their local implementation took many forms.[169] The anti-election movement established a powerful solidarity, with only the religious and linguistic minorities outside its ambit. A significant section of the urban population—teachers, government employees, lawyers, shopkeepers, traders—opposed the elections. There were no fence-sitters. Resistance against the elections became the symbol of an extraordinary mass upsurge against the state. Learning from the experience of grassroots mobilization of the previous three years, the student leaders planned and instructed their rank and file to resist the election process. In the popular imagination, the Congress party and Mrs Gandhi were successfully portrayed as the worst enemy of the '*Asomiya jati*' (Assamese people). Those who opposed the polls 'dynamited bridges, destroyed roads, wrecked government offices, and kidnapped or killed politicians who refused to obey [the] boycott order'.[170] Political opposition to the poll process soon gave way to violent outbursts. Many owned crude bombs and other weapons. Thirty-six guns were stolen from a Guwahati-based training school.[171] More than 100 agitators died in police firing as they obstructed the election process.

In the face of Assamese employees' absolute refusal to be part of the election process, an estimated 9000 central government employees, including IAS probationers and 248 drivers of the Delhi Transport

Corporation, were airlifted to Assam to run the election machinery.[172] Indian Airlines charged Rs 1.3 crore for airlifting poll officials.[173] Defiant Assam government employees—those in public sector enterprises were also included—faced salary cuts. A perceptive commentator observed that 'Mrs Gandhi's response has resulted in virtually an all-out civil war, with the Government accused of unleashing an "unprecedented terror campaign". She has arrested about a thousand leaders of the anti-election movement, applied strict press censorship, and imposed what amounts to military rule'.[174] Meanwhile, the Assam government restrained several leading newspapers in Assam, as they took a pro-movement stand, from publishing news on the agitation. They were given a reprieve by the Supreme Court of India.[175] In January 1983, in an attempt to assuage popular feelings, a proposal was put forward to shift 'minorities' to those places within Assam where they would be welcomed by their fellow linguistic and religious groups.[176] This hardly had any healing influence.

Mrs Gandhi's election campaign was preceded by widespread violence, including bomb blasts in Guwahati.[177] Unperturbed, she travelled to Assam on 10 February.[178] On the flight, she wrote to Dorothy Norman that it was 'not going to be a pleasant trip'.[179] On the same day, she spoke at several election rallies in Assam. In one that was attended mainly by minority voters, she began with an apology for her poor Bengali, and hence justified her choice to speak in Hindi.[180] This was largely aimed at the migrant Muslim population. She exhorted the electors to defy the boycott call, narrated how negotiations with the leaders of the movement had repeatedly slipped out of her hands despite being on the verge of an agreement, blamed the protestors for violence and assured the Bengali Muslim population of the constitutional safeguards to protect their right to stay in India. She ended her speeches by saying *Khuda hafiz* ('God be with you' in Urdu), interpreted by many as Mrs Gandhi's communal posturing aimed at a section of the electorate.[181] Provocative election speeches by other political leaders, reported in the press, further polarized Assamese Hindus and Bengali-origin Muslims.[182] Anyway, Assam was ready for a showdown 'between a hardline Prime Minister to hold elections and people hellbent on defying her', warned *The Times* on 18 February 1983.[183]

~

The familiar colourful paraphernalia of Indian elections was conspicuous by its absence in Assam in February 1983: 'The usual cacophony of electioneering, is just not there. There are no posters, no graffiti, no banners and no screeching vehicles in most places.'[184] The elections took place amidst serious erosion of civil rights; numerous people were arrested. Slogans on walls issued dire warnings against participating in the elections: 'The national highways would be splattered with [the] blood of those who vote,' warned one such graffiti.[185] Violent clashes took place between the opponents and supporters of the elections, with the former outnumbering the latter, except in some tribal areas where votes were cast in large numbers. In some places, a few election supporters were 'battered to death'.[186] Many polling stations returned empty ballot boxes. In one constituency, only 400 out of 64,000 electors cast their votes. Amongst those who openly defied the call to boycott the elections were Assam's Bengali-speaking Hindu and Muslim voters. Exercising their right to vote could strengthen their position as citizens; after decades of being marginalized, they asserted their political rights, only to invite the wrath of many.

On the morning of 18 February 1983, tragedy unfolded in the Nellie area, a sparsely populated rural settlement on the south bank of the Brahmaputra and 70 kilometres east of Guwahati. In these largely Bengali Muslim-dominated areas, one polling centre registered only 109 votes on 14 February—the average number of electors per polling station was 696. In the legislative constituency of which Nellie was part, less than 2 per cent cast their vote, with the winning candidate securing 714 votes.[187] Eyewitness accounts describe attackers armed with guns, knives, spears and bows and arrows. Victims later told journalists that 'people from other places' had come into their villages and attacked them. Hemendra Narayan, a journalist of the *Indian Express* who happened to be a witness to this ghastly episode, later described what he saw:

> In a desperate dash for survival, the women and children could not keep pace with the men. One by one, they were hacked to death by hundreds of rampaging tribals. They were first hacked with daos. Standing on the other bank of Demal, I could count 22 women lying on the already harvested paddy fields. A woman tried to cross Demal. She was speared.[188]

Narayan further recounted as follows:

> The cries and groans mingled with the cracking of burning that sounded as rapid action bullet fire. Shouting the war cries both groups [were] after the fleeing Muslims. I ran along the bank of Demal. The immigrants ran for their lives, but the hunters were faster. What happened to them is not difficult to guess. The faster must have got them sooner or later. Number of dead? Difficult to say but does it matter . . . Amidst this death and destruction there were however some lucky survivors. As I moved towards the road, I saw a woman in green sari, with three children running towards the west terrified, her cries made unusual sound. She appeared to have forgotten how to cry.

The police officer in charge of the locality reported that 'most of the people who were floating in the river were Muslims'.[189] 'As the daos rose and fell with monotonous precision, the women and children tumbled in heaps in the rice paddies. Mothers were still clutching their babies—both slashed and chopped about like hunks of meat on a butcher's slab.'[190] That night, for most victims, 'the field was their bed, land mattress'.[191]

When a day later, a journalist for the *Guardian* arrived in Nellie, he saw that 'long lines of bodies, some with heads hacked off lay ready for burial . . . as survivors of [the] massacre . . . worked to clear fields of other corpses'.[192] He also came across 'a spear [which] still stood in the ground where it had been hurled. Close by was a beheaded child and a bullet riddled body of a man'. Two days later, local newspapers reported the aftermath of the massacre:

> Nellie and Morigaon townships, as also the adjoining areas, wore a ghastly look with people dumb-stricken and panicky after the nightmare, the like of which [they] have [never] gone through. A large number of spades, sweepers, and *thans* of white cloth, apparently to be used as shrouds, are being rushed to . . . the Nellie area for mass disposal of bodies.[193]

Prime Minister Mrs Gandhi arrived in Nellie on 21 February accompanied by her Cabinet Secretary Krishnaswamy Rao Saheb. Mrs Gandhi, who travelled in a bullet-proof car that was flown in from Delhi to Nellie, was 'visibly shaken' and said that she could 'hardly find words to describe the tragedy'. Mrs Gandhi, who refused to take any responsibility for this violence, also 'flew over rice fields where reporters saw hundreds of corpses . . . but officials did not arrange for her to visit any area where bodies still lay' reported the *New York Times*.[194] The relief camp was crowded with the wounded, with barely a piece of cloth on their bodies. Dead bodies strewn around were still being gathered for burial by those who survived. A child lying dead with its body gashed by injuries from spears and a mother and child lying dead a few feet apart were among the horrific scenes.[195] 'Vultures hovered in the sky and the stench of rotting human flesh filled the air,' another eyewitness account stated.[196]

The remaining weeks of February were extremely turbulent. Nellie's neighbourhood was stricken with panic, as mobs from across ethnic, religious and linguistic backgrounds roamed the streets, with the stronger groups attacking the weaker ones violently, leading to repeated bloodbaths. Daily police intelligence abstracts of these weeks are full of such ghastly incidents. On 19 February in Upper Assam, tea garden workers attacked Assamese villagers. Similar attacks resurfaced in the second week of March.[197]

~

In the neighbourhood of Nellie, apprehending violence, senior police officials regularly visited these Bengali Muslim-dominated areas till 15 February. Most residents of these localities followed their political mentors' urging and cast their votes. This invited the wrath of the neighbouring Assamese (Hindu and tribal) villagers.[198] In secret meetings, it was decided that the election supporters would be socially and economically banished and a fine of Rs 500 would be levied on those who traded with them. On 16 February, a massive crowd of '5 to 6 thousand Muslim people' attacked 'Hindu villages' in a central Assam village, miles away from Nellie.[199] A similar attack was reported the next day; the houses of Hindu villagers were burnt. On 18 February, '2000 Muslims with deadly weapons' attacked and set fire to houses in Assamese villages in Baithalangso, another locality in central Assam. On the same day, 'a large number of Assamese people attacked' a Muslim village and set a few houses on fire. Retaliatory attacks continued throughout the month. On 1 March, 'a group of Assamese, Bengali Hindus and Karbis with deadly weapons attacked and set on fire the houses of Muslims of Dapara . . .'[200]

The massacre of 18 February was repeated with equal ferocity the next day, with more attacks on Muslim families in a few other areas of the district.[201] Muslim villagers also quickly regrouped, consolidated and retaliated. Violence, clashes and house-burnings continued well into March, when the Army was deployed. More corpses were recovered from different parts of Assam. In Nellie, too, clashes continued for another few days leading to the death of 50 more people, in addition to the previous thousands. Government officials were sacked for refusing to toe the government line.

Indeed, as Assam was burning during the months of January to April 1983, widespread communal and ethnic violence spread to different parts. An official commission concluded that 'the magnitude and the complexity of the subject of enquiry can be visualized from the frightening figures of incidents, murders, police firings, public and private losses etc.'[202] Police reported 8019 such incidents. About 2,25,951 people were rendered homeless. There were 1031 incidents related to the burning of bridges and culverts, and 22,436 houses were burned. These were understated figures.²⁰³ The total death toll in the several weeks of unrest remained contested; a CIA report put the figure at 7000.²⁰⁴

The Nellie incident demonstrated a section of the rioters' sadistic and bloodthirsty side. 'We went mad', 'We just couldn't stop', the rioters were quoted by the international press. A massacre of such a scale could hardly generate accurate statistics, as several hundred or more people, labelled as immigrants, were slaughtered by the rioters. According to official estimates, somewhere near 3000 people died; public accounts ranged between 1026 and 8000.²⁰⁵ Whatever the number, it was a sign of serious failure of the state machinery, and it was a cause of concern for the Assamese leaders as well. The victims silently wept.

The mobs of rioters largely comprised poor peasants, petty retailers, daily workers and others across ethnic affiliations. Provocative political speeches, localized conspiracies and strategies and designs for attacks—all played a role in sustaining and spearheading the violence. Ideological and moral support for the pervasive violence came from many quarters. Of the many shades of ideological currents that had inspired the popular upsurge over the past several years, the one that wanted to differentiate between Hindu and Muslim migrants became powerful. The *Assam Tribune* reproduced in its editorial column a quotation from Adolf Hitler: 'The very first essential for success is a perpetually constant and regular employment of violence.'²⁰⁶ A few days later, the paper quoted the Italian dictator Mussolini: 'There is a violence that liberates, and a violence that enslaves; there is violence that is moral and a violence that is immoral.'²⁰⁷ Those who participated in the violence probably did not read these quotes, but their ideologues perhaps did. Yet, those who went on the rampage on 18 February remembered it as their day of 'struggle' (*sangram*). A collective body of the Tiwas, one of the major tribes in Assam, submitted a poorly drafted memorandum to Mrs Gandhi, which condemned this ghastly incident but also created a narrative of their victimization at the hands of new settlers. The massacre of 18 February was presented as retaliation and defence. In the first week of March, the Lalung Darbar—Tiwas were described as Lalungs earlier—demanded that their areas be made free from 'foreigners'.²⁰⁸ This was a localized translation of the central slogan of the movement: detect and deport illegal foreigners. The Lalung Darbar's submission of March 1983 to Mrs Gandhi and its endorsement by the *Assam Tribune* were indicative of the wider sentiment in the state.

Nellie's rise as a thriving agrarian settlement, like many other areas of the Brahmaputra Valley, began in the 1920s and was then further shaped by the Assam government's war-time land settlement of the early 1940s.[209] Before being cultivated, mainly with rice and jute, by the newly arrived Bengali Muslim peasants, who benefitted from a nearby thriving market and good communication networks, these flood-prone areas were frequented by Tiwas, Assamese villagers and others to graze their cattle. In the next four decades, as the population grew and agricultural activities increased, Nellie, like many other parts of Assam, witnessed the unfolding of a new history of volatile land transfer—the most obvious outcome of the rural credit market—from the economically weaker Tiwas to the Muslim peasants. In the 1970s, new Muslim families joined the existing ones who had been uprooted from their earlier areas due to floods and the shifting courses of the Brahmaputra and its tributaries.[210] Many of them had settled on low-lying government lands or on lands bought from the Tiwas or other villagers. Most tribal families, on the other hand, hardly possessed any official legal ownership title, though these lands were in their possession for decades. But even in the early 1980s, Nellie still had some lands that were used by the Tiwas and others.[211] In the early 1980s, according to official statistics, which are the only available source of such an estimate, 12 villages of Nellie locality that were part of the official revenue record had 21,920 bighas of land, of which 10,265 bighas were settled. The rest was still officially under government ownership, which included commons. Of the government-owned areas, one-tenth was water—a source of fish for all—but for the remaining land area, there was intense competition among Muslim, Hindu and tribal communities.[212] In Nellie, the points of contention were manifold, of which one played out critically: the Tiwa population's sense of victimhood at the hands of their industrious Muslim neighbours. The latter, most of whom now spoke Assamese with ease, had secured official legal land titles through a cumbersome bureaucratic process and increasingly asserted control in the local economy.

When the riots occurred in February 1983, the Muslim settlements here were surrounded by tribal and caste Hindu families in a communally charged environment. Frequent exchanges of land did take place on mortgage, one account noted. The attacks of 18 February were preceded by the destroying and burning of land mortgage papers:[213] 'The first thing they did on the day of massacre was to set fire to the mortgage papers.' One account narrated that

> Most of the affected Bangladeshi Muslim families hold 50 to 60 bighas of land bought from the Assamese from 1958 onwards. Most of these Bangladeshi Muslim families hold 15 to 20 bighas of land out of this by way of mortgage. The needy Lalungs and other Assamese pledge their land for 200 to 300 rupees per bigha.

The primary slogan of the movement, i.e., the expulsion of the illegal aliens, took several forms based on local histories and memories.

~

By early 1983, the religious narrative overtook the regional, economic and political character of the anti-foreigner movement, and there was heavy communal, linguistic and ethnic polarization. The social relations between communities—based on economic exchanges or agrarian relations—had been less polarized prior to 1980. During 1981–82, Assam had fewer incidents of high-intensity Hindu–Muslim riots than in other parts of India.[214] American intelligence officials noted that in the wake of the February 1983 violence, 'communal leaders have successfully recast it as a confrontation between predominantly Hindu Assamese and Muslim Bengalis.'[215] This highly communally polarized atmosphere 'provided fertile ground' for the consolidation of Hindu as well as Muslim fundamentalists. The urban Muslims were open to remaining an ally of the Congress in their pursuit of a higher status, but as the communal violence severely demoralized the Muslim poor, the conservative sections within them slowly sought 'solutions to the community's problems through a return to religious orthodoxy and the retention of Islamic personal law rather than through participation in electoral politics'.[216]

In such a communally charged environment, the law-and-order machinery in Assam either failed or took sides. The absence of the police and government machinery was noted by later enquiry commissions. Relief and medical help were scarce. An estimated 2.3 lakh victims fled Assam for West Bengal and Arunachal Pradesh.[217] One account narrates how 10,000 Muslim and Hindu immigrants arrived at a railway station to board trains to West Bengal.[218] Another 3,00,000 people of different religious and ethnic groups took refuge in relief camps and were provided with paltry sums of money. The religious minorities could not escape from humiliation here too, as they were dubbed a 'floating population of doubtful nationality' who were coming to the relief camps 'so that they can be passed off as genuine[ly] affected persons'.[219] The Assamese leaders organized special relief-material collection drives, including 'a fistful of rice everyday' campaign for 10 days, and appealed to organizations to send relief materials in consultation with them.[220]

Historians don't have answers to many questions, but among the facts that cannot be disputed are that senior officials did not arrive there until after a few hours of the mayhem on 18 February. There were serious lapses on the part of the law-and-order agency, and there was a communication lapse. The Tribhuvan Prasad Tewary Commission, which was appointed by the government of Assam in May 1983 to examine the violence of 1983, unmistakably pointed out such wilful lapses. K.D. Tripathi, a senior official of the district under whose jurisdiction was Nellie, deposing before the commission, agreed that 'it was apprehended violent incidents would occur but not [to] such a great extent'.[221] The officer-in-charge of the local police station received reports about 'apprehension of communal clashes at Nellie' and the neighbourhood.[222] On the night of 14 February, 'some Assamese people, about 1000, assembled with deadly weapons at Nellie by beating drums'.[223] This was a signal for people to consolidate their strength and prepare for a dire situation. A senior officer of the Central

Reserve Police Force (CRPF) noticed that 'about 10 thousand people armed with deadly weapons were indulging in rioting at Nellie'.[224] Assam's senior officials were generally aware of the communal tension that prevailed in the larger neighbourhood of Nellie. Despite the high vulnerability, officers were not briefed. 'Mutual distrust became stronger in all the villages,' said one senior police official.[225]

All evidence before the commission indicated that the week prior to that fateful day saw serious deterioration of law and order in the Nellie area. With the elections taking place in Nellie on 14 February, communal tension was already high. Assam's police chief visited the area on the 15th and 'gave instructions' to 'intensify the patrolling and utilize all the resources'.[226] The district magistrate had instructed the people to 'surrender' their arms and ammunition. An officer deposed that 'no information was forthcoming from the people'.[227] Bridges which connected these vulnerable areas were safeguarded by unarmed village defence parties and home guards,[228] and an embankment that acted as a passage to the area was 'found to be cut'.[229] On 16 February, Nellie residents of both communities, apprehending such an attack, sought help from the local police. Meanwhile, communal violence had swept across many parts of central and lower Assam. An inter-community meeting did take place on 17 February in the Nellie area, but none could stop the mayhem. The commission, similar to the findings of another civil society enquiry, found that police officers had implicitly contributed to the tragedy.[230]

~

The Nellie massacre was not an isolated event. Many parts of the Brahmaputra Valley reported widespread communal rioting in the weeks of February 1983, with the worst affected areas being in Nagaon, Darrang and Kamrup. Most places that bore the brunt had a history of disputed land reclamation and fragile social and agrarian relations.[231] Some of these continue to haunt modern memories. One of these was near Gohpur in Darrang, where violent clashes occurred between 11 and 14 February 1983.[232] The riot occurred between the Bodo-speaking tribal population, who were joined by the tea garden workers and Bengali Muslims, and the Assamese-speaking people. Described by a civil society enquiry as 'a mini-war',[233] these clashes led to the loss of more than 100 Assamese lives. The Bodo people, whose political leaning was clearly with the PTCA and who had voted in the elections of February 1983, had been settled in the Reserved Forests since the early 1970s. The widespread demands for land reclamation were joined by other ethnic communities, Assamese or Bengali Muslims.[234] The Forest Department repeatedly tried to evict the settlers. The Bodos imagined these areas as part of a future Udayachal, the dream homeland of Assam's tribal people. The Bodos viewed the Assamese as instrumental in what caused their persecution.

If the communal-ethnic violence in Gohpur and other areas brought out the dynamics of social and economic relations among communities, other areas too saw the unfolding of many fault lines. The situation that developed in Chaulkhowa, a river island in Darrang and an agricultural settlement for Bengal-origin Muslim families, was a telling example of how the contest over resources shaped the nature of clashes between a section of the Hindu Assamese (who laid claims to these lands) and the Muslim families.[235] The spectre of violence in February 1983, between the supporters and opponents of the elections, was the result of class, ethnic and religious contestations.

The 1983 elections led to the loss of 4000 lives, according to a conservative official figure.[236] It was condemned by the larger population as illegitimate, a 'great fraud', though senior officials of the Election Commission found the elections satisfactory[237] and Prime Minister Mrs Gandhi, speaking before her party's lawmakers, defended it on constitutional grounds.[238] A group of election officials brought into Assam wrote in disgust: 'We are some government employees pushed . . . completely against our will for doing "duty" in the great fraud performed in Assam in the name of election.'[239] At least three political parties—Lok Dal, BJP and Janata Party—pleaded before the President of India to dissolve the Legislative Assembly.[240] 'The Government born out of the womb of the "bloody" election shall never be a duly constitutionally . . . elected government,' stated a group of politicians.[241] The Indian government later conceded that Assam's anti-election mobilization had acquired a 'militant and intensified form'.[242] 'As polling day approached, the militancy of the agitation increased. There was large-scale arson and sabotage, the destruction of road bridges, telecommunication installations, and railway tracks with a view to disrupting the movement of election personnel and voters.'[243] By then, both Assam and Punjab had seriously challenged Prime Minister Mrs Gandhi's authority.

Though the *Times of India* wrote that 'deserted booths would have been a far more eloquent testimony to the resentment of the Assamese people than guns and bombs can ever be', it agreed that 'violence cannot detract from the fact that there is very strong opposition to the poll in Assam'.[244] How did the Indian government view this unfolding crisis? This was spelt out on the floor of the Parliament through occasional press briefings by senior ministers. In a nutshell, the main issue was the fate of foreign nationals in Assam who had migrated from East Pakistan or, later, Bangladesh. The discord was about the 'cut-off' date, as it was called, the year until which the migrants would be accepted as Indian citizens by the leaders of the movement. Prime Minister Mrs Gandhi, in her early negotiations with the Assamese leaders, suggested 1971 as this date, which was generally agreed upon by Opposition political parties. Given the humanitarian crisis, this consensus was crucial. The plan was to commence 'work so that the magnitude of the problem could be assessed and talks [could] continue to reach a final decision'. However, the Assamese leaders insisted on 1951 as the cut-off date. The government refused to view the issue from a 'purely legalistic' perspective and wanted a human touch for a 'pragmatic' solution. The government warned that

> the acceptance of the demands of the agitators would mean subjecting the entire population of Assam to scrutiny to determine their status. Such a step would give rise to serious misgivings and grave apprehensions among different communities and groups who have been living in Assam for decades and have been fully a part of its political, economic and social life.[245]

The Lower House of the Parliament, in a rare gesture, suspended its official business, observed two minutes' silence and debated for the day on the Assam crisis. All non-communist political parties castigated the government. Vajpayee, the leader of the BJP, accused the Prime Minister of 'precipitating a bloodbath just to retain political power in the state'.

As the news of the ghastly Nellie massacre reached the global community through extensive reporting,[246] the Indian government 'bought up' copies of *India Today* and *Sunday* and seized imports of *Time* and *Newsweek*, all of which extensively reported on the Assam violence.[247] The Union government also prohibited foreign correspondents from visiting Assam.[248] The international press came down heavily on the Prime Minister. The *Guardian* criticized Mrs Gandhi's government for not taking enough steps to seek 'a solution to the problem of the hundreds of thousands of genuinely illegal immigrants who have somehow slipped on to the electoral register because they support the Congress (I) machine'.[249] It also warned that

> it would be an equal tragedy if the local massacres of an "alien" minority were put down at the price of savage military repression of the local people themselves. India cannot be ruled indefinitely by the subtle shuffling of soldiers from one state to another in order to suppress populist regional revolts.[250]

A young Indian scholar, however, reminded the newspaper that the Assam problem was

> symptomatic of the difficulty of developing a secular culture in a nation of 700 million people, struggling after centuries of colonial domination, to assert its identity in an unbalanced, unfavourable international economic and political order . . . It highlights the magnitude of India's task, of forging one nation among a diverse people, different in caste, religion, language, culture, region and even politics.[251]

The Indian press, too, was scathing in its attack on Mrs Gandhi's government. 'After the Great Calcutta killings in 1946, the Nellie killings in 1983. Nothing so gruesome has disgraced India since the post-partition riots . . . Nellie floodlights the horror in Assam', the *Times of India* said.[252] The *Far Eastern Economic Review* said the elections had finally 'aggravated ethnic tensions' in Assam.[253]

In the summer of 1984, a section of the Assamese civil society independently carried out a probe into the spectacular popular resistance and communal riots, which carried a sense of Assamese victimhood.[254] Till then, the report of the official enquiry, largely boycotted by the student leaders and others, remained 'a closely guarded secret'.[255] Probes and reports aside, the elections left Assam in a vortex of violence and death, with its communities more estranged than ever. Hospitals and public buildings lay destroyed. A Calcutta-based journalist who toured such areas reported 'an eerie silence broken only by the bark of dogs'.[256] The confidence of the people was broken. Violent communal and ethnic clashes metastasized to many parts of Assam, taking a flashing and twirling form in the central and western regions and exposing the deep fault lines in Assamese nationalism.

~

When the election results were declared on 22 February, the *Guardian* carried the news under the caption 'Hollow victory for Gandhi in Assam'.[257] Communal violence still continued, following a similar pattern, with deaths regularly reported. In the Parliament and outside, Prime Minister Mrs Gandhi defended her decision to hold the elections, while expressing her anguish. She made it clear that her government could not arbitrarily throw out Bengali immigrants from Assam. 'Where will they go, which state can we send them to, which country outside will accept them?' the Prime Minister asked.[258]

The new Assam government led by Hiteswar Saikia was voted to power by 17 per cent of the electorate in an election where only 33 per cent exercised their franchise. His government faced a serious crisis of social legitimacy as Saikia's oath-taking ceremony was followed by a widespread boycott of his government. 'As the news of swearing in of the Ministry spread like wildfire, people observed non-cooperation immediately and all activities of city-life came to a grinding halt'.[259] In fact, the social boycott of Saikia's government became a symbol of a new phase of the popular movement. As in previous instances, the leaders of the agitation appealed for a boycott of the Independence Day celebrations on 15 August. The government, on its part, let loose its repressive machinery, leading to sporadic killings. The chief minister's authority was already curtailed by Prime Minister Mrs Gandhi as she retained her government's control 'over much of Assam's internal security forces'.[260]

After February 1983, mass support for the agitational programmes began to thin out. The intensity of popular mobilization had fizzled out after the spring of 1983. The events of early 1983 had created a sense of cluelessness; many were tormented by the violent turn the movement had taken, and it began to lose its unifying appeal. Behind the scenes, the ideological apparatus of the leadership was largely in the hands of a conservative intelligentsia. Globally, Assam was now seen as violent and anti-minority. Saikia, the chief minister, despite the all-out attempt at the social boycott of his government, began to slowly secure his ground. The Assam government also succeeded in dividing the camps of agitators, often communally splitting the ranks of agitation leaders; the prospects of state benefits also lured many away.[261] Backed by the Prime Minister, Saikia acquired full command over his government. At the same time, he denounced the popular sentiment and termed the movement as 'fruitless'.[262]

Meanwhile, Punjab had been flung into a violent political crisis, putting Mrs Gandhi's government into deep trouble.[263] In Assam, too, after a period of ebb, the agitation briefly resurfaced in mid-1984. This was largely an outcome of the Saikia government's determination to correct the electoral rolls in June 1984 without securing any political consensus. Once again, students took to the streets and called for bandhs and picketing.[264] Some of their fellow agitators decided to be more aggressive: bomb blasts were frequently reported in the summer of 1984.[265] The state machinery was in no mood to be lenient; however,

Prime Minister Indira Gandhi laying the foundation stone of the rail-cum-road bridge across the river Brahmaputra at Pancharatna-Jogighopa in Goalpara in 1983.

Prime Minister Indira Gandhi laying the foundation stone of Assam's new capital, Pragjyotishpur, near Guwahati in 1984. This idea was abandoned later.

the repression, which saw the custodial death of a student, could not suppress popular opposition to the Saikia government. The government came down harshly on erring officials and secretly planned to close down the university student residences.[266] Police brutality intensified. In early October 1984, clashes between Hindus and Muslims were reported from Lower Assam. The government made its presence felt by evicting settlers from government lands, including forests.[267] The government set up more tribunals in 1984 to detect and deport illegal immigrants. But these tribunals, headed by retired judges, did not function properly as the rules did not empower the judges effectively. The police were empowered to conduct investigations and arrange for deportations.

In order to prevent illegal immigration, the Union government undertook the construction of a 2200-kilometres-long fence along the border with Bangladesh. The Bangladesh government did not welcome the idea and termed it an 'unfriendly act'.[268] Patrolling along the fluvial India–Bangladesh border was intensified, more border outposts being set up and the average distance between them being brought down to 3.4 kilometres from 5.6 kilometres. More speedboats were deployed on the Brahmaputra. As tension rose across the border, Indian and Bangladeshi troops exchanged gunfire in April 1984. In one instance, Indian troops claimed that Bangladeshi troops had crossed into Assam, filled up trenches that had been dug for the fence and uprooted pillars marking the border. The Bangladesh government contended that the idea of a fence violated a 1974 agreement that banned the construction of 'defence structures' in this border region.[269]

Despite being able to hang on by the skin of its teeth, the Saikia government was unable to quell dissent, and fear haunted Assam's villages. Occasional communal killings, strikes and bomb blasts continued. The *New York Times* reported how, a year later, 'the horror and hate, the tensions and suspicions that fuelled the 1983 killings remain despite the uneasy peace that has settled over the state'. There were brief moments of success for the anti-government strikes, which shut down industries, markets, educational institutions and businesses.

For a long time, the Prime Minister was reluctant to buy peace with the Assamese leaders. The Nellie massacre had adversely affected her global image. In February 1984, she visited Assam and rejected any negotiations. 'If they have anything to say, they can meet state officials,' she said.[270] The unfolding political crisis resulting from Operation Blue Star in Punjab in June, however, brought some relief to the Assamese leaders. They thought that Mrs Gandhi, at this point, could not afford to risk further shrinking her support and would agree to their demands. Negotiations began in July 1984, but they failed to take off.[271] The leaders demanded the dismissal of the Saikia government, but the Prime Minister was in no mood to agree to this. After all, the Congress government had won the elections at the cost of much bloodshed. That was Mrs Gandhi's last visit to Assam before she was assassinated on 31 October 1984.

~

Indira Gandhi's assassination in October 1984 brought about a significant shift in the outlook of the Union government towards the Assam problem. The new Prime Minister, Rajiv Gandhi, according to a section of the Indian press, was keen to prove his willingness to test the principles of democracy, that is, the spirit of accommodation as a way out to resolve India's regional, caste and ethnic disputes. In January 1985, he promised to negotiate with the Assamese leaders.[272] 'The give-and-take of the conference table can yield victories which confrontation cannot.'[273] As a goodwill measure, Rajiv Gandhi persuaded the Assam government to repeal two contentious security regulations in Assam in July.[274] He empowered his associates to offer 'meaningful concessions'. Even though there were no official discussions after 1983, back-channel communications between the Assamese leaders and the Union government continued. India's cabinet secretary, Krishnaswamy Rao Saheb, carried on exploratory negotiations well into the spring of 1985.[275] In March 1985, the task of negotiating on behalf of the Government of India was taken over by Ram D. Pradhan, the Union home secretary.[276] Back-room negotiations between Assamese leaders and the 'skillful drafters' of the Union home ministry were followed by highly publicized meetings with Union ministers.

In Assam, notwithstanding Chief Minister Hiteswar Saikia's unwillingness to negotiate with the AASU leaders, efforts were intensified to look for a way out.[277] Saikia's attempt to create divisions in AASU did not pay off. The Assamese leaders, too, recognized the ground reality—that it was time for a settlement with the Union government. After years of popular protest, the numbers of street agitators had declined, and the outlook of the leaders of the movement also changed.[278]

After a series of negotiations held in Shillong, Pradhan and the AASU leaders reached an agreement on some of the most contentious issues on 30 July.[279] By now, Chief Minister Saikia was also informed that his days were numbered and that he would have to pave the way for a settlement.[280] This was an extraordinary situation in India's democratic experiment. This was followed, on 9 August, by Home Minister S.B. Chavan holding parleys with a wide spectrum of Assam's political factions, including the minorities, in Guwahati. The need to halt unauthorized immigration was not disputed by the Indian government. The previous year, the Election Commission of India, despite the Saikia government's insistence on keeping 1979 as the cut-off year, had suggested that the 1971 electoral roll be considered as the basis for correction.[281] But its implementation was too challenging, given the potential demographic and electoral impact. R.D. Pradhan, who oversaw the final negotiations, had little doubt that the 'issue of infiltration . . . was intimately connected with the future of minorities, especially the Muslims in the Brahmaputra valley'. He felt that the 'Congress party was likely to be adversely affected in case action was taken to expel these infiltrators on a large scale'.[282]

An actual draft was not prepared until a few days before the signing of the agreement. Pradhan wanted to avoid any discussion from which the AASU leaders could retract. At a big rally in Guwahati on 12 August, the Prime Minister announced that 'an accord is in its final stages. There will be no victors. Nor losers'. Saikia caved in finally after he met Rajiv Gandhi. Pradhan recollected, 'Working non-stop for six to seven hours, we completed the work on a draft Memorandum of Understanding on Assam.'[283] Though the AASU leaders would have wished to solicit a larger consensus, Pradhan persuaded them to seize the opportunity and move forward.

Early in the morning of 15 August 1985, the Union government and the leaders of the movement signed the accord, which promised that all immigrants who had arrived in Assam after 1965 would be disenfranchised and immigrants who arrived after 1971 would be deported. The Prime Minister also assured the student leaders that the current state legislature, elected in the disputed poll of 1983, would be dissolved, with a caretaker government in control until fresh elections could be held. This was the biggest victory for the leaders of the movement. Apart from promises to accelerate the economic development of Assam, unspecified 'legislative and administrative safeguards' were also promised by the Central government 'to protect the cultural, social and linguistic identity and heritage' of the Assamese people. Concerning those who had come to Assam post-1965, Home Minister S.B. Chavan clarified that 'though their right to vote will be 'suspended', they will not be harassed in any way and will continue to enjoy other 'legal' and 'constitutional rights'.[284] The accord gave a new twist to India's Citizenship Act, as 25 March 1971—the date of the beginning of the Bangladesh War—was accepted as the cut-off date for the identification of foreigners.[285] The Union government promised to erect a fence along the riverine and open part of the Indo-Bangladeshi border. This officially marked the end of the six-year-long anti-foreigner movement in Assam.

~

Assam, however, could not recover from the deep scars left by the political unrest. The promises made in 1985 were not fulfilled. Even as the accord was signed, many, including R.D. Pradhan, who was the key person behind months of intense political negotiation with the Assamese leaders, understood the impracticality of mass deportation of hundreds of thousands of people and knew that it could not be

Signing of Memorandum of Settlement between the Union government and the All Assam Students Union and the All Assam Gana Sangram Parishad in New Delhi on 15 August 1985

done without setting off further violence.[286] In the euphoria of the moment, political leaders at large, as well as sections of the news media, were unwilling to recognize the complexity of the problem and only expressed relief that the Assam dispute had been 'solved'.[287]

The accord's promises polarized Assam's Hindu and Muslim families again. Muslims in the state were terrified of being disenfranchised and forcibly removed from their land. Most of the poor hardly possessed the right papers. Before the elections in December 1985, the anti-immigrant camp filed more than a million objections to individual voters who had Bengali or Muslim or Nepali names. Thousands of lower-rank officials worked hard to examine these claims. The government produced a list of 10.5 million voters from Assam's population of 23 million. The names of nearly a million voters were dropped from the rolls, most of them because they had immigrated to Assam after 1971. Another 3,00,000 were struck off when the anti-immigrant agitators successfully challenged their eligibility. An estimated 6,00,000 voters wrested their right to get back on the electoral list by proving that they had been living in Assam before 1971.[288]

Disgruntlement had surfaced from the start as a few senior leaders had avoided the accord's signing ceremony. A sizeable section believed that the settlement was a kind of patchwork deal. The settlement's outcomes had two major components: the political part dealt with the question of Indian citizenship and the dissolution of the existing ministry; the other part had loosely defined promises of economic and cultural packages. The settlement made the Muslim population unhappy as they were the ones who were suspected, and their staying in India remained in doubt, at least theoretically. The accord was opposed by several West Bengal-based political organizations. Samar Guha, leader of the Janata Party in West Bengal and a former MP, termed it as 'complete surrender to the forces of coercion' and urged the Assam government to refuse to implement the accord.[289] Bangladesh, while continuing to oppose any barbed wire fencing along the border, commented that the accord 'should not affect' them 'as far as it is an internal affair of India'.[290] On its part, the Indian government sent a high-level Indian emissary to Bangladesh immediately, offering concessions on water-sharing, another contentious matter between the two countries.[291]

~

Days after the signing of the accord, the incumbent Saikia government was dissolved on 19 August to pave the way for holding new elections to the state legislature. Saikia remained in charge of the caretaker government. The elections in December were preceded by a bureaucratic exercise to revise the electoral rolls. Continuous revision of the rolls was mandated by India's election mechanism, but the 1985 exercise was essentially performed to accommodate the promises of the Assam settlement. As this process of revision began, 'more than a million objections were filed' questioning the citizenship status of many residents of Assam.[292]

The process of carving out a space for electoral politics by the Assamese regionalists began in 1984. Two conferences held that year, mainly attended by the Assamese intelligentsia, academics and professionals, laid down the roadmap for such a political party. Their political goals were not very clear at that time. By early 1984, student leaders were also in search of their role in Assam's political life. There were talks of agitating leaders forming a political party and winning elections.[293] Within months of signing the accord, the young student leaders formed a new regional political party, the Asom Gana Parishad (AGP).[294]

Around the same time, in November 1985, the descendants of the Bengal immigrants, battered by the agitation, also formed their own political front. A large section of the Muslims of Assam abandoned the Congress and came under the umbrella of the United Minority Front (UMF), a new political outfit that promised to protect the interests of the linguistic and religious minorities of Assam. The UMF briefly broke into the Congress's electoral support base of the religious and linguistic minorities, tribals, Scheduled Castes and other backward classes.[295]

The elections of December 1985 were held under tight security; 1,00,000 security personnel were deployed. Stalwarts of regional political parties from other Indian states, like the leaders of the Telugu Desam Party, campaigned for the AGP.[296] Several Assamese public intellectuals and scholars openly appealed for a vote for the AGP. The AGP won 63 of the 126 legislative assembly seats, while the Congress won 25 and the UMF won 17.[297] Prafulla Kumar Mahanta, 32 years old then, was sworn in as the new chief minister.

Days before his government assumed charge, Mahanta gave an interview in which he vowed to deport 'illegal immigrants . . . immediately after their detection . . . to their country of origin'.[298] His government's mandate was to deport or disenfranchise 'a million immigrants', the majority of whom were Muslims from Bangladesh. The idea of the deportation of illegal foreigners was not easy to implement, and Bangladesh, from where they were said to have come, did not accept the contention of the Assamese leaders. Besides, the AGP-led Assam government understood that it was not empowered to embark on such an exercise. Passed by the Union government in 1983, the Illegal Migrants (Determination by Tribunal) Act, which stood in the way of the Assam government, gave a brief respite to those who had migrated from East Pakistan/Bangladesh or elsewhere, who, after several decades of living in Assam, were now deeply rooted in Assam's economic, political and cultural processes. Most lived the lives of poor peasants, agricultural workers and daily wage labourers—only a tiny fraction of them pursued other forms of livelihood. A large majority of them had secured political security by ensuring that their names were on the electoral list, yet they remained vulnerable as an immigrant community. Many among them had little tenurial security, and land conflicts intensified in the immigrant-dominated areas. The political contests around the narratives of human flow across the borders refused to die down. Meanwhile, the Union government passed a law in December 1985 changing the scope of who could qualify as a citizen of India.[299] This change, which was spelt out in the Assam Accord, granted citizenship rights to those who came from Bangladesh before 25 March 1971 and were staying in Assam since then.

The new political outfit, largely led by student leaders, was dominated by Assam's upper caste Hindus. Ideologically, they viewed the Congress party's sensitivity to Assam's multi-ethnic social life with apprehension, but they could not afford to abandon the state's intricate multilingual and multi-cultural political landscape. Most AGP members were inexperienced and knew little about the functioning of the state machinery. Once in power, many fell from their pedestals as corruption, including a multi-million-rupee financial scandal, raised its head.[300] Both Prafulla Kumar Mahanta and Assam's Home Minister Bhrigu Kumar Phukan—both of whom had largely 'remained at daggers drawn since the ministry was installed'[301]—resigned on 2 August 1986 but withdrew their resignations soon thereafter.[302] Both Mahanta and Phukan struggled over power-sharing—key to the art of cabinet formation. An embattled government—raging with accusations of corruption and inefficiency—often failed to 'cut much ice in the high-voltage politics' in Delhi to secure political and economic advantages. The political implementation of the Assam Accord, the 'spirit of which seems long ago' disappeared as noted by an observer, was crippled.[303]

Mahanta's government had to lower his aggressive anti-foreigner posture. In a similar vein, Maheswar Neog, the president of the powerful Asam Sahitya Sabha, proposed dual citizenship for Assam's residents as a means to resolve the Assamese identity crisis.[304] Even while attempting to reinforce the idea of the hegemony of Assamese linguistic nationalism, the AGP leadership had, particularly during its eventful second term (1996–2001), established multi-ethnic and multi-religious alliances to stay in power.[305] Like their predecessors, this new generation of Assamese leaders, too, refused to acknowledge an idea of modern Assam that was multilingual. In February 1986, in keeping with their ideological orientation, the Assam government made Assamese a compulsory language for school children across the state.[306] Resistance led to an outbreak of violence in southern Assam in July 1986 in places where on previous occasions, in 1960 and in 1972, serious trouble had erupted on the question of language.[307] Faced with strong opposition from the Bengali-speaking population of the southern districts and the tribal population of Assam, Mahanta's government had to withdraw this policy.[308] The AGP-led Assam government repeated what a section of the Assamese ruling elites had consistently tried to do earlier by imposing the Assamese language on the non-Assamese residents, resulting in political and social crises. The repercussions appeared quite soon: tribal communities demanded their separate homelands, and some eventually got them. Many others, however, though they felt alienated, still clung on to the idea of Assam.

# 13

# Moving towards the Millennium

In the final decades of the twentieth century, Assam continued to contend with multiple challenges. This included conflicting political ideas, environmental challenges, social fault lines and the failed promise of its economy. The works of two anthropologists illustrate the shifting structures of Assamese society.[1] Both these works examined caste, kinship, religion and social structure and provided a window to understanding the wide-ranging transformation in Assam's social and cultural landscape. Both anthropologists noted the significant influence of 'religious egalitarianism' and, more importantly, pointed to a silent transformation within the Assamese social milieu, which had far-reaching consequences. Though older social norms and caste affiliations were falling apart and the larger population had little interest in doctrinal matters, much of the social transformation was confined to the individual level rather than the more extensive social reform.

As more people moved to urban areas in search of livelihood, Assamese traditions were restaged in their new surroundings. For instance, the rural religious institution of *namghar*s, places of worship for Assamese Vaishnavites, became sites for urban social interaction. Religious functions were 'modified and simplified', and people from across castes were welcome. Inter-caste participation in social functions, too, became common, though close communication between lower and higher castes had not fully developed[2] and the spirit of caste often pervaded the 'egalitarian values of Vaisnavism'. Many upper-caste Assamese continued to be influenced by 'rigid caste rules and restrictions',[3] which were also followed by people coming to settle in urban Assam from other parts of India. Caste loyalties had not disappeared, and they were reflected in political aspirations. However, both the anthropologists found greater individual autonomy of choice in all areas of social life—kinship ties, caste ideology and lifestyle.

Dramatic transformations were predominantly witnessed within the Hindu Assamese society, though there were rapid changes among other communities too, including tribal communities, Muslims and Bengali Hindus. Caste discrimination had already entered a new phase by the middle of the twentieth century; either it was challenged, or adjustments were made to remove deep-rooted prejudices. The residential Cotton College in Guwahati, for instance, had since 1915 maintained separate dining arrangements for students from tribal and the so-called lower orders of the Hindu society. But demands for a common dining facility became increasingly loud: 'For years they [students from lower castes] went on agitating for admission into the general dining hall and subsequently secured the consent in writing of all the upper caste boys in the mess,' wrote a college teacher in 1931.[4] However, such examples were not common. Students from the Ahom community were debarred from participating in ritual activities, including Saraswati Puja, a popular religious occasion dedicated to the Hindu goddess of learning.[5] A Calcutta-based anthropologist in the 1930s observed that whereas India's other provinces were undergoing rapid social transformation, Assam was 'less changed'.[6] Inter-ethnic rivalries over land presented other instances of the divisions still rife in Assam society.[7]

Social conservatism was more strongly shielded in such spheres of life as marriages or death rituals; any deviation was highly censured. In 1917, prominent upper-caste families from Jorhat in Upper Assam, following an instance of inter-caste marriage, spoke out against this in a public meeting.[8] Such marriage, they argued, would invite disaster for the *Asomiya jati*, the Assamese people. Though change did begin to come, it was slow: a marriage between an Assamese Brahmin groom and a Kayastha bride in 1935 was an event considered worthy of a newspaper report.[9]

In some places, religious gatherings that included all castes were held.[10] This slow transformation, primarily shaped by the political and cultural awakening in the shadows of India's anti-colonial movement, would shape the aspirations of many underprivileged communities. For instance, in the mid-1950s, spirited members of the lower castes made known their dislike of many practices of social exclusion. A well-attended public meeting in the neighbourhood of Guwahati censured the exclusive practices of a powerful monastery. Referring to the rights conferred by India's Constitution, the meeting challenged the domination of the heads of these monasteries: 'in a democratic system, Satradhikars (the heads of the monasteries) cannot be the masters'.[11] Others took to writing to express their displeasure with the social system. Many became part of dissenting socio-religious organizations. Alongside these ups and downs in Assam's social world, economic and political shifts were also taking place.

~

Assam's tea plantations had been in crisis during World War II. They suffered further setbacks as India attained Independence. The Congress-led Assam government had no sympathy for the planters, having earlier fought against them inside the Legislative Assembly and outside.[12] There was widespread dissatisfaction with the planters for their racial biases and for the intrusion of tea gardens into people's commons. Restrictions on access to grazing grounds caused considerable anguish, and for decades, the residents of the Naga Hills and Mizo Hills had bitterly challenged the planters' encroachment on their jhum lands.[13]

Even before Independence, the Congress-led Assam government, described by an official historian of the Indian tea industry as 'left-wing', compelled the planters (despite their protests) to pay income tax by promulgating the Assam Agricultural Income Tax Act in 1939.[14] Then, in independent India, with the Assam Land (Requisition and Acquisition) Act of 1948, the Assam government took the bold step of acquiring non-cultivated lands lying with the planters. The government promised to allot such acquisitions to landless families in Assam. Most of the tea companies, still owned by Europeans and run by managing agencies, challenged the Act's constitutional validity; however, a long-drawn-out legal battle could not bring them any relief.[15] By 1954, an estimated 1,46,249 bighas of tea estate lands were redistributed amongst poor families, but the promised monetary compensation to the planters remained unpaid for long.[16] More pressure was brought upon the tea estates' landed property when the Assam government enforced the Fixation of Ceiling of Land Holdings Act of 1956. A 'tense atmosphere existed', and, on many occasions, 'trouble was averted by only the narrowest margin', wrote Antrobus, the official historian of the Assam Company.[17] An uncertain political and economic environment—which included the nationalization of the Suez Canal by Egypt's government and the increase in private retail buying of tea in Britain after a brief lull during the war—brought heavy losses to most tea estates.[18] Also, foodgrain supplies to the estates remained elusive; the planters blamed the rising costs of food—which they had to arrange at a concessional price for their workers, whose wages were usually very meagre—for their limited profit.[19]

But there was more. In a sharp departure from the miserable daily wage of 4 annas for a tea garden worker in the 1940s, minimum wages were fixed at a higher rate in 1952. Earlier, workers' strikes had been largely ineffective; while the planters had demanded 'resolute action by government against labour agitators', they increased supplies of liquor to their angry and restless workers to keep them happy. Between 1943 and 1947, the volume of liquor consumed by Assam tea-garden workers more than tripled, from 98,000 gallons annually to 2,96,000 gallons.[20] Heightened political consciousness among the workers, however, brought occasional enhancement of wages and other benefits. The Plantations Labour Act of 1951 introduced tiny benefits for the workers as the planters had to use a small part of their profits for the general well-being of the workers. The planters extracted some concessions in 1958 to reduce excise duty and cess on exported tea.[21] On the other hand, tea-garden workers' living conditions and their rigorous work schedule—hardly acknowledged by the planters except for a few[22]—had not changed fundamentally since the previous century.

In an age of economic nationalism, the Indian government was empowered by a new law in 1953 to appoint members to the powerful Indian Tea Association, fix prices and control tea distribution.[23] In March 1957, A.K. Gopalan, a communist leader, said that 'British capital in the tea industry has proved detrimental to national interests' and asked for its nationalization, but the Union government did not succumb to this pressure. Morarji Desai, the country's Commerce and Industry Minister, insisted that such a 'suicidal' act would only disrupt a significant chunk of foreign investment, and no such attempt was made at the time.[24]

However, Assamese opinion-makers and political leaders remained apprehensive of the colonial-era tea industry. In 1965, Assamese parliamentarian Ajit Kumar Sharma, son of the well-known historian Benudhar Sharma, published a scathing attack on the plantation industry as an exploitative institution. He presented details of the economic layout of the tea industry, the extent of foreign capital investment and a roadmap for the nationalization of this industry.[25] Sharma alleged that many new tea plantation industries had sprung up in Africa from the profits earned in the Assam tea plantations. For instance, Brooke Bond, a familiar name in Assam's tea industry, had set up plantations in Africa and expanded there significantly between 1947 and 1960.[26] Tea production in British Africa had seen a significant jump in a short period,[27] and British capital investment in African tea and coffee production had increased manifold.[28] Assam Company, the oldest joint-stock company that had been producing tea in Assam since 1839, became a part of Assam and African Investments Limited.[29]

By the middle of the century, only a few Indians, among whom only a handful were Assamese industrialists, had secured a place in this economic enterprise. An official enquiry into the running of tea companies revealed that, in 1954, whether it was a sterling or an Indian rupee company, the control of the capital, management and trade was essentially in the hands of non-Indians. Of the 308 tea plantation ventures, 116 were sterling companies; and of the rupee companies,

24 were non-Indian, and another 62 were jointly owned Indian and non-Indian companies. This enquiry concluded that only 11 per cent of the total capital in the tea plantations in Assam was Indian capital, 76 per cent was sterling capital and about 13 per cent non-Indian rupee capital. However, of the 113 crore rupees of capital investment, 35.8 per cent was Indian capital in 1954.[30] Of the three critical elements of the tea industry—production, finance and marketing—the last two were controlled and regulated outside Assam.

A brief period of bonhomie between plantation management and workers followed Independence. However, with a significant rise in Indian capital investment in the industry from the mid-1950s, rapid change took place in the plantation-ownership pattern.[31] Most new owners had earlier experience of the functioning of the tea industry before diversifying into commercial interests like trade in timber or jute. The owners of the managing agencies were mostly Marwari business families; for instance, the British-owned McLeod tea company was taken over by C.L. Bajoria, a Marwari businessman from an orthodox family and an erstwhile shareholder.[32] As Indian entrepreneurs with previous experience in managerial agencies began to buy and own plantations, this became another source of worry for many. The new owners downsized labour; an estimated 10,000 workers were retrenched during 1952–53.[33] According to a confidential note of the Assam government, the workers' unions resisted the 'purchase of the tea gardens by speculators and non-industrialists to safeguard the interest of the labourers'.[34] The government sympathized with the workers; 'no penalties' were imposed on officially illegal strikes.[35]

Much to the dismay of the planters in Assam, the Assam government had imposed new taxes on tea and jute (used for tea chests) in 1954. Hemendra Prasad Barooah, president of the Assam Tea Planters' Association (ATPA), described it as an 'embargo on the freedom of trade and commerce with regard to tea'.[36] The planters faced further trouble in 1959 and again in 1962, when the Assam government began to moderately enhance income tax on tea plantations.[37] The influential tea planters described this increase 'as a great shock to tea companies'. They extensively lobbied to persuade the Assam government to refrain from taking this step.[38] Other states had followed suit and imposed a higher income tax on tea plantations. As pressure from the planters' lobby mounted, in 1964, the Union government appointed a Tea Finance Committee, which advised, despite Assam's opposition, a lower rate of income tax on tea plantations.[39] But the Assam government was not willing to follow such advice; rather, from 1968, the rate of income tax was moderately increased.[40]

The transfer of ownership to Indian-owned companies took time to complete, and several tea companies, like the Namdang Tea Company and the Makum Tea Company, continued to send remittances to England until the 1970s.[41] All through this period, planters did not sell the tea they produced directly to customers. Instead, the standard practice was to auction these products at the Calcutta Tea Auctions centre, established in 1861, the oldest in India and the second oldest in the world. Within India's federal structure, a state could collect sales tax from goods sold, and Bengal remained the primary beneficiary until 1970. A tea auction centre was opened in Guwahati that year, but given the lack of facilities and the absence of buyers, more than three-fourths of the tea produced in Assam continued to be auctioned in Calcutta until the end of the 1970s.[42] The demand for shifting the headquarters of tea companies from Calcutta to Assam to assert the latter's control over the tea industry intensified in the 1970s.[43]

In 1978, the Assam government paved the way for the rise of small entrepreneurs in the tea industry,[44] rolling out financial aid to unemployed youths with up to 7 acres of land to start tea cultivation.[45] Such small-scale cultivation of tea had been prevalent earlier, though to a very small extent. A decade after Independence, when the Indian government investigated the operation of the tea industry, it was found that small-scale tea cultivation with Indian (read Assamese) capital was already in existence. Assam had 173 tea estates that were less than 100 acres (which was still a large area).[46] In 1955, 47 such small tea gardens owned not more than 5 hectares of land each.[47] In 1960, 38 such gardens had a total of 52 hectares of area and produced approximately 5000 kg of tea leaves annually.[48] However, given the nature of the tea industry and the requirement of a complex industrial set-up, such small ventures slowly dried up; by 1970, there were only 17 of them.

In the following decades, with the new initiative, lands in the foothills or other forested landscapes, often owned by the government or privately owned tiny pieces of land, usually assigned for producing non-paddy crops, became part of tea cultivation. Most of these clearances of forested lands were confined to the south banks of Upper Assam. A majority of the people here were familiar with the forests, plants and the agricultural world, but they had very little idea about highly industrialized tea cultivation. This did not deter them, and within a short period, they gained the required expertise. By the turn of the century, an estimated 38,000 such estates were spread over an almost equivalent number of hectares of land. They were 10 times more productive than the plantations of 40 years earlier.[49] Leaves plucked from these plantations were processed in established factories owned by larger estates or those outside the tea-plantation estates. The latter were known as bought leaf factories—numbering over 100, they produced about 38 million kg of tea in 2000, an estimated 8 per cent of Assam's total production.[50]

The quest for increased tea cultivation spread into Assam's loosely governed border areas, primarily covered with forests that provided vital natural resources to the aspiring tribal population. This further intensified contested claims over forested landscapes lying between Assam and Nagaland. The tea cultivators, drawing on examples from their political environment, formed an umbrella organization in 1987, a year after the AGP came to power in the state.[51] Intellectual and technological support came from the Assam Agricultural University, which had earlier played a leading role in developing high-yield variety of seeds suitable for Assam's environment. By 1987, an estimated 44 per cent of the plantations' tea bushes were over 50 years old, after which they became less productive.[52] Coupled with this came the approval, in 1989, from the Tea Board of India, the highest decision-making body on matters of the tea industry, to provide institutional support to non-plantation tea cultivation.[53] More political and bureaucratic support soon followed, including incentives for public lenders to provide finance and the facilitation of land acquisition for such enterprises.[54] The rapid proliferation of tea cultivation away from the plantation model was mainly owing to the new political and economic environment in which a strong sense of Assamese nationalism prevailed.

By 1993, approximately 92 per cent of the lands under small-scale tea cultivation were government-owned, and the rest comprised tiny plots of private agricultural land with varying degrees of lease rights.[55] In 2002–03, their average size was 0.81 hectares.[56] The economic space for this sudden expansion of tea production by petty producers was generally enabled by stagnating exports and profits in the global tea market as well as developments in the Indian market. The rising costs of production compelled some of the more prominent companies like the Tatas and the Hindustan Unilever Limited to slowly withdraw from plantations and diversify into the packaging and retailing of tea.[57] On the other hand, others like McLeod Russel increased their capacities. But the clash between the small tea growers, as they came to be called in official parlance, and the planters witnessed an epic rise, which would affect the growth of Assam's tea industry.

~

As political and economic turmoil engulfed Assam in the last quarter of the twentieth century, the state's flagship mega mammal, the great one-horned rhinoceros, became intertwined with the region's political and cultural agenda. The declaration of Kaziranga as a Reserved Forest in 1905 had been a major step in the protection of this species. The Assam Rhinoceros Preservation Act of 1954 was based on a similar Act passed in the Bengal province before Independence in 1932. Battling many challenges, Kaziranga National Park (KNP) became an exemplary instance of nature conservation in modern India. Once found across the Indus and the Gangetic floodplains, the rhinoceros, along with the lions in the Gir National Park, provided positive stories of the survival of near-extinct animals, largely due to state patronage. By the early 1970s, the rhinoceros was deeply embedded in Assam's sense of regional pride. Apart from a small number in West Bengal and in Nepal, this species of rhinoceros was now unique to Assam. Behind the success story of rhinoceros conservation, several forces had been at play over the decades, including Assam's ecological volatilities, regional cultural aspirations, modern conservation science, state support and many shades of electoral politics.[58] The fluvial environment of the Brahmaputra and the expansive grasslands of the valley created a conducive environment; the collective leadership of early foresters, politicians and conservationists created the institutional framework; and an empathetic agrarian social milieu was equally at work to help the park become a success. KNP was not the lone sanctuary, but it had the highest rhino population.

The last two decades of the century saw the rise of a new kind of environmentalism around the rhinoceros, with the decision to translocate some rhinos from Assam to another suitable habitat in the country to safeguard the future of the species. In March 1984, as Assam's thick cloud of political disquiet slowly began to wane, five rhinos (aged between four and 23 years) from its forests were flown to the Dudhwa National Park in Uttar Pradesh.[59] The new habitat was not much different from their original home, being the swampy and often flooded terai grasslands of Uttar Pradesh. Flown in a large Russian cargo aeroplane, accompanied by veterinarians and wildlife conservationists, this extraordinary journey, now largely forgotten, deserves a special place in Assam's political and environmental history.

The idea of translocating a few one-horned rhinoceroses from the jungles of Assam to a national park in another state had taken shape in the late 1970s. India, Bhutan and Nepal were the exclusive homes for this species of rhinoceros. Estimated to number around 1500 in total, two-thirds of them were to be found in KNP. By the late 1970s, the years of political turbulence in Assam had caused worries about the animal's future. The Wild Life (Protection) Act of 1972 gave the animal full protection, and an international convention prohibited trade in rhinoceros parts. Legal safeguards and state surveillance, however, could not save the animal from being poached as the state experienced political upheaval. According to official accounts, more than 90 rhinos were killed in 1983,[60] which led an angry Indira Gandhi to write to

Saikia, saying she was 'distressed' to learn of this increased poaching and asking him to 'take stern and immediate steps'.[61] Samar Singh, a senior Indian official in the Ministry of Environment, described the situation as 'alarming' in early 1984.[62]

Earlier, in 1979, a team of international conservationists under the banner of the International Union of Conservation of Nature (IUCN) Survival Service Commission recommended that given the increasing chances of poaching, epidemic outbreak, shrinkage of living space and food shortage due to the fast spread of exotic invasive species such as water hyacinth (*Eichhornia crassipes*) and climbing hempweed (*Mikania scandens*), efforts must be made to find an alternative home for the rhinoceros elsewhere in the country.[63] Action was taken on this quickly. In November 1979, the Indian Board for Wildlife agreed to the proposal and identified several such places within the country. R. Schenkel, a global name in rhinoceros conservation, concluded that Uttar Pradesh's Dudhwa was the 'most suitable' for such an exercise. In 1980, preliminary field trials were conducted. Rhinos were tranquilized and shifted to other similar places within Assam.

But Assam was not a cheerful donor. Public opposition to this translocation was clearly visible. Many feared that it was an attempt to deprive Assam of its exclusive position as the home for this animal; they dismissed any ecological arguments for it. When the decision was announced, firebrand Assamese student leaders threatened to 'sabotage the trucks carrying the rhinos', and a senior state forest official admitted that he and his colleagues 'were not happy about the translocation'.[64] In 1982, AASU wrote to Indira Gandhi protesting the idea of translocation. A year earlier, when the Parliament had proposed to amend the Wild Life (Protection) Act of 1972 to make room for translocation, a lawmaker from Assam had protested.[65] Nonetheless, support came from the Assam government, for which the Union government lauded Assam's chief minister, Hiteswar Saikia, for his 'wise and farsighted approach in a matter of national importance'.[66]

The Government of India finally airlifted the rhinos, but by this time, Assam's forested landscapes had undergone a significant transformation. From three game reserves in the 1910s, which were established with the intention to give partial (only hunting of female rhinos was prohibited) protection to the one-horned rhinoceros, Assam came to have several national parks and wildlife sanctuaries by the 1980s—amounting to 5 per cent of her total land. This was possible due to state patronage as well as the increasing role played by conservationists. Some of these flagship national parks came to be embedded in the complex social and cultural history of Assam and produced contested political histories. Manas National Park, situated across the floodplains and the foothills of the eastern Himalayas in Lower Assam, experienced a tumultuous political and ecological period in the late 1980s.[67] Distinct from the Kaziranga National Park in its ecological features, Manas had been formally declared a game sanctuary in 1907, being home to wild buffalo, rhinoceros, bison, tiger, elephant, golden langur, swamp deer, hog deer and barking deer, among other mammals, birds and reptiles.[68] In the late decades of the century, the area got enmeshed with the Bodo political movement.

In 1989, of the 64 million hectares of India's total forest cover, Assam's share was 4 per cent, with 33 per cent of her total geographical area—a fall from 38 per cent in 1971—under forest cover, which did not include the lush tea plantations.[69] Nine other states were ahead of Assam in terms of their share of India's forest cover, but Assam had the highest density of cover among them. As political turbulence engulfed the state, many saw an opportunity to acquire little patches of agricultural land from the government-owned forest lands. Such reclamation, part of peasant communities' relentless quest for cultivatable lands, resulted in a loss of approximately 1500 square kilometres of Assam's forested lands between 1989 and 1993.[70]

Was there any connection between ethnic mobilization and settlements in forests? Soon after the AGP government came into power in 1986, government-owned forest lands re-emerged as one of the sites of contestation. The Assam government briefly pursued a programme of evicting settlers from such forests; many of the evictees belonged to Bodo tribes.[71] Reclamation of government-owned forest lands for cultivation was viewed by peasant communities as a symbol of the fulfilment of a promise of a larger political dream.[72] The AGP government's failure to appreciate the ecological and cultural complexities involved in the process of forestland reclamation and settlements therein played a key role in shaping the political actions of Assam's ethnic tribal communities from the late 1980s. On the other hand, the decline of timberlands helped in awakening public awareness of the need for protection of the environment. Local campaigns against illegal timber logging became widespread.[73]

~

The poor sections of Assam's peasants were constantly in search of new places to settle in as their lands fell victim to moneylenders, river erosion or silting. Unlike the early decades of the twentieth century, when most peasants preferred to annually lease the land they tilled, from the mid-'50s they began to favour permanent settlement (*myadi patta*). During 1960–61, an estimated 55 per cent of peasant-owned land was in the category of permanent settlement.[74] The share of land under annual lease continued to decline over the next few decades, and available land was scarce. This was an important indication of the crisis in available land for the peasant to cultivate. Each year, only a few thousand acres—during 1960–61, an estimated 45,000 acres—were freshly cleared for cultivation.[75] Between 1960–61 and 1997–98, the pace of increase in the net area sown in the plains of Assam had slowed down from 40.95 per cent to 32.88 per cent.[76] Much of the remaining land was not suitable for cultivation, either being swampland or government-designated forested land or simply land beyond the access of the peasants.

We have seen that the benefits of India's Green Revolution largely escaped Assam. The net sown area remained stagnant till the 1980s,[77] but a large section of peasants moved to double cropping. The average landholding size dropped from an estimated 3.6 acres in 1970–71 to 3.4 acres in 1976–77.[78] Sharecropping still remained an integral part of the agrarian landscape. An estimate made in 1970–71 indicated that approximately 16 per cent area, i.e., one-fifth of the total net sown area, was under sharecropping.[79] Assam's per capita fertilizer use of 10.3 kg—considered as a major marker of modern agriculture—was the lowest among the Indian states by the end of the century.[80] The average size of peasant holdings continued to decline from 1.47 hectares during 1970–71 to 1.15 at the close of the century.[81] The use of the high-yielding variety (HYV) of rice only partly took off towards the late 1960s. During 1970–71, a little less than 7 per cent of rice acreage was under HYV, which rose thereafter but largely languished at one-third of the gross cropped area. This was far below the figures in Punjab and Haryana, India's heartland for the Green Revolution, where mechanized farming became widespread.[82] The rice and wheat from these states partly fed Assam in the decades of the '60s and '70s through the infrastructure network of the Food Corporation of India.[83] By the turn of the century, these two states had embraced all available advances in agricultural science and technology. In contrast, most of Assam's cultivators did not have the means to access machines; in 1992, out of India's total 1.2 million tractors used in agriculture, only 700 were in Assam.[84] The use of disc harrows, mould board ploughs, power tillers, planters or levellers was very limited, while seed-cum-fertilizer drills, threshers, reapers and combine harvesters were unheard of. Through 1990–95, Assam's share in India's total tractor sales was 0.2 per cent compared to Uttar Pradesh, Punjab and Haryana's combined share of 37.4 per cent.[85] In this agrarian world, even well-off peasants were unable to take advantage of science and technology, unlike their counterparts in other parts of India.

The increase in Assam's agricultural production was, to a large extent, the result of the significant addition to the total cultivated land area. The area under rice increased from an estimated 1.6 million hectares in 1950 to 4.4 million hectares in 2000. For most of the period from 1960 to 2001, more than 80 per cent of the total acreage was under food crops, with rice alone accounting for more than 75 per cent. Foodgrain production more than doubled during this period. The per acre yield also increased from 1022 kgs in 1970–71 to 1565 kgs in 2000–01. The production of jute had already been affected, and from an estimated 1,01,000 hectares under jute cultivation during 1950–51, it declined once again in the 1990s to reach a low figure of

69,000 hectares during 2000–01.[86] Amidst this turmoil, a section of the peasants, particularly in central and lower Assam, had converted their lowlands for fish farming, or had planted rubber plants in the newly cleared highlands. These new patterns are the result of several factors including the high volatility of India's jute market, anthropogenic modifications of the hydrological characteristics of the valley, the innovation in farming in flooded landscapes and the dawn of capitalist farming in the agricultural sector. Although these developments would have far-reaching socio-economic implications, a detailed discussion of this is beyond the scope of this book.

As we have seen in an earlier chapter, the government's wide range of developmental programmes often posed serious threats to peasant and tribal populations. A government enquiry conducted in 1984 found that an irrigation project undertaken in Dhansiri displaced more than 1000 tribal families; they were 'rendered landless' and 'whatever land remain[ed] after acquisition prove[d] uneconomic'.[87] Most families were not paid compensation, high embankments made nearby lands uncultivable, and even those who received compensation 'had to struggle hard' for several years. Between 1947 and 2000, a wide range of developmental projects forced an estimated 1.9 million people out of their lands. Many of them were from tribal communities.[88]

By the end of the twentieth century, life expectancy in Assam was the lowest amongst the Indian states at 57.3 years, lower than the all-India average of 61.5. A malaria epidemic in 1986 killed hundreds, and repeated waves continued to kill more. Infant mortality was still high, more than 70 per 1000.[89] Assam's capital wealth formation remained among the lowest in India. By all estimates, the century ended with stark indicators of the state's poverty. Consumption expenditure per capita was valued at Rs 465, far below the national average of Rs 579. Most studies point out that, unlike in many Indian states during the period 1960 to 2000, poverty did not decline; rather, it increased marginally.[90] More people—1.3 million—joined the ranks of the poor in the 1990s, including a section of Assam's urban population.[91] However, one study pointed out that while rural Assam in the 1990s was poverty-stricken, Assam's urban areas had lower levels of poverty compared to the rest of India.[92] As a greater number of students joined schools and graduated from college, the queue for government jobs lengthened, largely for lower-level positions. Between 1960 and 1999, the number of state government employees increased six times. In 1974–75, Assam had approximately 2000 industries, which employed 1,06,000 people.[93] A quarter of a century earlier, factory workers had been half this number, which largely remained unchanged for the next quarter century.[94] A very small number of public sector industries came up in this period—largely based on petroleum and other minerals—but did not create a substantial workforce. People's mobility in search of economic opportunities remained very low. In 1961, only 0.3 per cent (19,000) of Assamese speakers lived outside Assam.[95] Their share in the workforce outside Assam grew very sluggishly and reached 1.1 per cent at the close of the century, compared to, say, 8.2 per cent of Tamil speakers or 7.4 per cent of Oriya speakers who lived outside their state.[96]

By the turn of the century, Assam came to have its fourth petroleum refinery. The initial proposal of the Union government to establish this refinery—an outcome of the political agreement between the Assamese leaders and Rajiv Gandhi's government in 1985, as well as the popular demand for a refinery since the mid-'60s—was as a private sector initiative. Assam protested and demanded that this be made a public sector venture.[97] Following the pattern, this new industrial establishment provided a few jobs, and, unfortunately, also resulted in severe environmental distress for elephants.[98] Apart from the large public sector oil industry and private tea industry, a small section of the population earned its livelihood from tiny industrial units. Early in the 1980s, an estimated 10,000 such units produced material largely for internal consumption.[99] State support for these economic activities was limited to monitoring labour welfare through an unsympathetic bureaucratic mechanism and providing meagre financial support and poor infrastructural facilities. Institutional finance was hardly available as state actors could barely influence the financial decisions of the commercial banks. Moreover, most bank loans were not meant for these industries; in 1979, only 34 per cent of loans were given to industries.[100] States like Maharashtra, Tamil Nadu and Uttar Pradesh were far ahead in providing state support to small industries. Financial indicators like credit-deposit ratio—which implies how much the banks are lending compared to their deposits—was 46 per cent in 1980 compared to the all-India average of 67 per cent. This ratio continued to decline. Civil society voices regularly castigated banking institutions for their apathy. Of Assam's total income (gross domestic product) at the close of the century, only 18 per cent came from industry.[101]

In the 1990s, Assam's financial health had improved slightly, as Assam's total official revenue collection increased from an estimated Rs 9380 million during 1985–86 to Rs 33,760 million during 1995–96.[102] This increase was not due to any major enhancement of tax collection in Assam but an increased share from the central taxes of the Union government. For a larger part of the late twentieth century, the government of Assam's total revenue earnings (state sources: sales tax, forest, land, agricultural income tax) were heavily dependent on its share of central excise duties and income tax and financial grants from the Centre (Assam's revenues from central taxes and financial grants contributing not less than 60 per cent of its total revenue during 1980–2000).[103] The per tonne royalty for crude oil was increased from Rs 61 to Rs 192 in 1986 for both Assam and Gujarat.[104]

Well into the 1980s, Assam, still inspired by its vocal and spirited stand in the Constituent Assembly and aware of its failure to generate enough resources to initiate public projects, demanded a greater share in central taxes. The principles of resource sharing—taxes and other financial grants—between the Union and states, usually decided by the Finance Commission, had continuously evolved. States received financial assistance from the Centre for developmental works under various Five-Year Plans. Specific guidelines for this sharing of resources began to take shape between 1965 and 1967. A formula named after its architect, the economist Dhananjay Ramchandra Gadgil, was devised to distribute financial grants by 1969.[105] That year, the Fifth Finance Commission agreed that the needs of Assam, Nagaland and Jammu and Kashmir should be deliberated with special 'care and consideration'.

They would be described as special category states in the financial matrix because of their difficult geography, strategic location, poor state finance and high tribal population, among other factors. The commission hoped that these states would make 'efforts to increase their resources and exercise better fiscal steps'.[106] More states were added to this list later. Of the Union government's total financial assistance, more than 30 per cent—between 1969 and 1974, approximately 40 per cent—would be reserved for these states. The Union government committed to bear 90 per cent of the state expenditure on all centrally sponsored schemes, while the remaining 10 per cent would be given as a loan to the state—unlike the other states, which received funds in the ratio of 30:70. However, the only beneficiaries were the hill districts of Assam, which were then experiencing turbulent political times. This frustrated Assam's political leadership, and in 1979, the State Legislative Assembly passed a resolution against the proposals of the Seventh Finance Commission.[107] This financial arrangement would only encompass all of Assam in October 1990, during the brief tenure of Prime Minister Vishwanath Pratap Singh, who headed a non-Congress coalition minority government.[108]

By the 1980s, most land reform measures—primarily in the form of two legislations, the Assam Fixation of Ceiling on Land Holdings Act of 1956 and the Assam Tenancy Act of 1971—came to a halt for lack of political backing.[109] The victory of the Assamese landed gentry, who had supported the Assamese nationalists to gain electoral power, had a decisive impact on the fate of the Assam Tenancy Act. The economic and social interests of Assamese absentee landlords were defended by the AGP government. In July 1986, Surendra Nath Medhi, the law minister in the AGP ministry, criticized the Act and consolidated public opinion to repeal it. Defending the position of the Assamese landlords, Medhi said that the Act could not be called a 'social legislation'.[110] He condemned the Act for its 'confiscatory' nature and hinted that it had seriously jeopardized the interests of the Assamese landed classes.[111] Simultaneously, the new government promised that each Assamese landless family would be given a patch of land for cultivation.[112] The defeat of the 1971 Act meant the loss of hope for many cultivators, but it gave a fillip to opponents to try and form or find a new platform in the public arena.

~

As Assam entered a new phase of popular protests in 1979, the seeds of another important parallel political development were being sown. Posters and slogans appealing for a 'Bye-Bye to India' or '*Axom Aair Mukti Lage*' (Liberate Mother Assam) began to be infrequently noticed on walls in 1980.[113] No one knew who was behind these calls, nor was there any clarity about their objectives beyond mere symbolism; they were, however, noted by the police. What was little known then was a development, which might have inspired these writings on the walls. In 1979, a few young men and women from urban and rural Assamese families came together in a bid for a sovereign Assam. They believed that in an independent homeland, they would be able to live in dignity, free from the humiliation by 'Hindi'-speaking 'Indians'. Ideologically, they claimed that Assam had the right to be an 'independent sovereign state' and that India's 'occupation' of Assam was illegal. They styled themselves the United Liberation Front of Asom (ULFA).[114] In Assam, they threatened corrupt officials, regularly kidnapped and murdered them and occasionally dictated to the people a list of dos and don'ts. They won instant popularity amongst a section of the urban Assamese elite for whom the political tactics employed by the ULFA appeared to provide better leverage in negotiations with Delhi. In many places, ULFA cadres acted as custodians of moral values. Social punishment was meted out to those seen at odds with their injunctions, including the prohibition of drugs, rhino-poaching, gambling, etc. If a warning issued by ULFA was not heeded, the 'delinquent' was punished publicly, according to a journalist who happened to visit Assam in 1990.[115] At the same time, ULFA (often through its public front of Jatiya Unnayan Parishad) provided textbooks to needy students and built infrastructure like embankments or roads in remote villages where the state did not provide public works. 'Government servants, bank employees, block development officers, tea garden managers, and even policemen were forced to work on the building of roads and embankments while an ULFA girl, a Sten gun slung from her shoulder, along with others supervised them,' reported *India Today*.[116] ULFA compelled locals to provide labour and squeezed out money to finance these works. They received appreciation for their work from Assamese people across class and caste lines, including political leaders and some government functionaries.[117] The rural areas provided them with young cadres, rations and, occasionally, a place to rest and sleep when they were chased by the government forces.

The ULFA cadres were armed with sophisticated weapons originating from China or Burma. 'The power of ULFA flows from the barrels of hundreds of guns at its command,' wrote a journalist who saw 'graffiti and wall-writing' across Assam.[118] Though low-profile and little organized, ULFA struck terror; their 'imagined enemies' were 'agents' of 'colonial India'. The rebels shared their ideological position through a printed mouthpiece named *Swadhinata*, which was aimed at a wide public—rural and urban. Their proclaimed 'number one enemy' was 'Indian State power', which they claimed controlled Assam through 'bureaucrats and capitalists'. Other enemies were 'politicians and various local exploiters', who worked in league to fill their pockets at the expense of Assam. In order to secure support from the working classes, ULFA declared that the 'non-Assamese working class'—who were critical to the everyday functioning of the economy—was not the enemy, but they added that such people must 'adopt Assamese language and culture and aid us in the revolution as true residents of Assam'.[119] A prominent and much sought-after city school, which wanted to discontinue Assamese as a medium of instruction, was closed as the students' organization asked for permission to have a students' union, as was common in government-sponsored public schools.[120]

The ULFA was inspired by groups like the Nationalist Socialist Council of Nagaland (NSCN) and the Mizo rebels. Small groups of these rebels received their early combat training and ideological orientation in north-western Myanmar, from the Kachin Independence Army and the NSCN. More cadres joined these makeshift camps in Myanmar, 'near the Chinese border'. The ULFA had an 'unofficial liaison office' in Yunnan well into the early 2000s.[121] Discreet support also came from the military intelligence of Bangladesh in the 1990s. Rebels also reached out to journalists and international diplomats for moral support.[122] That Assam's political rebels in the 1960s were fully supported by Chinese and Pakistani establishments was well-known to the Indian government.[123] As in the 1960s, East Pakistan had provided support to the Mizo rebels, now, at least from the early 1990s, Pakistan's intelligence forces extended their support to ULFA. The *raison d'etre* this time was to divert attention from a troubled Kashmir; if Assam erupted with more violence, the Indian military would be deployed there in major strength, which would be of advantage to Pakistan's military establishment.[124]

The ULFA boys and girls moved to the difficult hilly and mountainous terrain of western Burma. There they learnt how to use arms and acquired rudimentary training in guerrilla warfare. The earliest hint of ULFA cadres venturing out to Burma for military training came as early as 1981. In the thick of popular unrest and a series of failed negotiations with the Indian government, an MP from Assam disclosed in the Parliament that he had been informed of 'some boys from Assam [who] went to a hideout in Burma to get training'.[125] The same year, a journalist witnessed the circulation of propaganda material on a 'bright future for independent Assam'.[126] Others described Assam's rising political violence as 'urban insurgency'.[127] In March 1983, P.C. Sethi, India's Union home minister, who was concerned that 'lawful authority was systematically sought to be challenged and eroded', drew attention in the Lok Sabha to the display and distribution of posters and leaflets in Assam which carried slogans like 'we shall form our country with the blood of martyrs', 'when Assam will be free' or 'India has no right to rule Assam'.[128]

More young boys and girls undertook risky journeys of several hundred miles over several weeks.[129] Makeshift camps for the rebels came up in remote hilly regions of Bhutan, western Myanmar and Bangladesh. Some of those routes or landscapes were earlier used by other rebels from the Mizo and Naga Hills and Manipur. The exact political accounts of how footholds were gained in these areas are yet to be documented by historians. Depending on India's strategic and diplomatic relations with its neighbours as well as its domestic politics, the rebels negotiated with their hosts. Turbulent political upheavals had rocked the state apparatus in both Bangladesh and Myanmar during those days.[130]

By the late '80s, the rebels gained numerous 'hard core militants and thousands of supporters' and had makeshift 'training camps' in many parts of rural Assam.[131] A journalist who toured Assam in 1990 noticed two things: that the rebels 'enjoy[ed] popular support' and that 'terror [had] gripped traders and businessmen in the state, following widespread incidents of kidnapping and extortion of money'.[132] Most early champions were 'idealistic young intellectuals', who sympathized with the ideal of a just socio-economic system and trusted the narrative of a sovereign Assam free from the 'colonial rule' of India. A tenth of the rebels, one account suggests, comprised women from various social and economic backgrounds.[133] Some of them received rigorous military training, and they endured equal physical hardship, but few were co-opted into the higher echelons of rebel leadership. This, however, did not mean that there was gender discrimination. Even in the 1940s, during India's anti-imperial struggle, women from these areas had participated on an equal footing with men.

Between 1985 and 1990, and increasingly later, the ULFA cadres kidnapped or killed politicians, businessmen, bureaucrats, police officials, engineers and anyone who was seen as inimical to their idea of an ideal society.[134] Robberies at banks and business houses were conducted, and clandestine deals were concluded with tea planters. For the rebels, the tea planters were the last vestige of Assam's history of colonialism. In 1986, the Assam government appealed to these companies to shift their headquarters from Calcutta to Assam, and some did.[135] But by 1990, tea companies like Brooke Bond, Lipton and Doom Dooma, all subsidiaries of Unilever, a British–Dutch company, had either closed their factories or did not participate in auctions as armed rebels intensified their campaign to collect funds.[136] Planters were asked to share their profits to demonstrate the 'active participation of the tea industry in the economic development of Assam'.[137] The planters seldom refused ULFA's demands—'we take away so much and give back so little,' one such voice conceded.[138] A trickle of the tea planters' profits was received by the ULFA, a major part of which was used to buy arms and run training camps outside India.[139]

When Brooke Bond and Lipton did not participate in the auction process in Guwahati, sales declined, and tea prices fell; approximately 13,000 jobs were at stake.[140] Between July 1989 and January 1990, an estimated Rs 150 crores were withdrawn from Guwahati by the tea companies. Brooke Bond and Lipton closed their offices in November 1990. Towards the close of 1990, the Indian government came to the rescue of the tea planters, and some were airlifted out of Assam. There was pressure on the AGP government to act or resign. Inside the gardens, workers and their unions did not share the sentiments of the ULFA rebels; ULFA had demanded ransom even from a garden collectively owned by a cooperative of 52,000 workers.[141]

~

On 10 November, Chandra Shekhar had become India's new Prime Minister. His government had the support of Congress (I) and was not dependent on the AGP (which had been a part of the National Front government led by V.P. Singh) for survival. The Congress (I) had for weeks highlighted Assam's law and order situation and demanded the dismissal of the state government.[142] The pressure from industrial lobbies, too, was loud and clear. So was the denunciation of ULFA by Indian political leaders and the press. 'ULFA has no ideology except a sort of militarised and perverse nationalism,' wrote a well-known Indian journalist.[143] The ULFA 'virtually rules the roost' in Assam, asserted the *Times of India*.[144] The key to this crisis was clear:

> A preferable . . . option would be to institute a package of tough measures to put ULFA on the run, sever its link with the state administration . . . Unless the Central government moves quickly and with single-minded determination to break the back of the United Liberation Front of Assam, the troubled state is bound to go to the way of Punjab and Kashmir.[145]

It was recognized that this needed to be followed by redressing the grievances of the Assamese and introducing a wide range of economic development measures, including the opening of a series of 'downstream units in the state to refine oil'.

Mahanta, the chief minister, who would complete his five-year term on 8 January 1991, met the Prime Minister on 27 November 1990 in New Delhi and also briefed journalists, saying that his government was arresting ULFA cadres. That night, journalists in New Delhi became convinced that 'Assam was heading for Delhi rule'.[146] Early on the morning of 28 November 1990, the AGP government was sacked, and Assam came under President's rule for the fourth time in its history,[147] sharing the same status as Punjab and Jammu and Kashmir. ULFA was declared a banned organization. An official notification summarized ULFA's sins: it was

> creating a deep sense of insecurity among the people by committing other acts like extortion of money, murders of political leaders, police officials, businessmen, and others, threat, intimidation, kidnapping and harassment of people, snatching of fire arms from licenced holders, dacoities, highway robberies, looting of banks, punishment of alleged offenders for social and economic crimes, and forcible occupation of lands and building.[148]

Towards the end of November 1990, the Indian Army unleashed full-scale military operations against the ULFA rebels.[149] Assam was also declared a Disturbed Area. The Armed Forces (Special Powers) Act of 1958, which gave the army the power to maintain public order, was invoked on 28 November 1990. In a move code-named Operation Bajrang, the Indian Army struck deep into the rebels' hideouts.

The ULFA hideouts were largely abandoned by the time the army struck. Among the seized material from these hideouts was an instruction to leave these camps by 19 November.[150] The ULFA had also intensified their money-collection drive, demanding from people contributions to what they described as a 'war fund'. A few of their cadres were killed, and many lower rank cadres were arrested.

But across Upper Assam and other areas, the outlook was gloomy. The ULFA cadres could hardly be differentiated from the others. 'A nagging fear among the people is the unleashing of state repression on the people in the villages of the area, resulting in humiliation and dishonour to the elders and women-folk.'[151] There were also worries of 'retribution and revenge'. Some of these areas had witnessed resistance offered by rebels in the late eighteenth century against state repression, which eventually led to the end of the Ahom rule. Some of the camps were inside dense forests, which army helicopters could not survey, and the others were scattered across Assam's rural and urban milieu. Army raids were conducted in the neighbourhood of the Gauhati University campus after a helicopter survey.[152] For the next few weeks, the army was in full combat with ULFA across the Brahmaputra Valley. People rushed to identify decomposing bodies in mass graves near the camps, where the 'flies and acrid smell' discouraged visitors.[153] 'Some bodies were seen with their hands tied,' a journalist reported.

In the early 1990s, however, the widespread public support for ULFA began to crumble. In 1993, when several senior ULFA leaders were shot dead, there was little to moderate outpouring of public sympathy.[154] Even before this, the ULFA's sway in Assam's politics had not gone uncontested; besides repression from the state and pressure from powerful business houses, a few public intellectuals had voiced their worries. Ideological and organizational confrontation came from others too, one of them being the United Reservation Movement Council of Assam (URMCA).[155] Born in 1986 as an umbrella platform of several organizations representing lower castes, classes and ethnic groups, URMCA held an impressive demonstration in Guwahati in April 1986. It claimed to represent more than two-thirds of Assam's population, and it was seen as an 'omnibus body' for the 'economically backward and exploited'. It asked for 'special provision of reservation in educational, economic and other fronts for the oppressed communities'.[156] The URMCA emerged from years of mobilization among poor peasants and among ethnic communities of Assam who wished for political self-determination.[157] Its rise was viewed with some apprehension; according to an editorial in the *Assam Tribune*, it 'will acquire a political dimension which will not be in the interest of Assam'.[158] Ideologically backed by a communist party, the URMCA ideologically and organizationally contested the principles and goals of the ULFA—the former considered the latter as a representative of Assamese 'chauvinism'.[159] In 1990, a journalist reported seeing signs prohibiting the entry of ULFA supporters in several tribal and OBC villages of Upper Assam, with URMCA supporters manning the entry points to the villages.[160] Away from Assam, the political consolidation of oppressed backward classes had taken a much clearer shape and, to some extent, acted as an ideological inspiration for much that was happening in Assam.

After failed political overtures and earlier military attacks,[161] the ULFA rebels struck again, targeting Congress politicians and intelligence officials. According to official estimates, the ULFA killed 109 persons and kidnapped 95 between January and October 1991, while the army captured more than 5754 ULFA cadres or their supporters during the same period.[162] The military retaliated with 'Operation Rhino' in September 1991.[163] 'An ordeal lies ahead in Assam; it must be faced with forbearance and empathy for the state's people,' a national newspaper warned.[164] By the end of the year, the ULFA declared a ceasefire, but that was not before more than 2500 of its members were arrested.[165] However, this ceasefire was short-lived.

Earlier, in June 1991, the Congress party had come to power in the state after securing one-third of the total votes polled, a marginal improvement from 1985. The ULFA had seized the opportunity during the political transition to abduct dozens, including a Soviet mining engineer, in July. In a deal, the Assam government, led by Hiteswar Saikia, agreed to release senior rebel leaders who had been arrested in November 1990. However, the Soviet engineer was killed, though the press reported that this happened while he tried to escape, and this 'mass amnesty' was swiftly interpreted as 'embarrassing' by international journalists.[166] Some ULFA cadres undertook daring jail escapes.[167] The retaliation by the army had not helped the troubled planters, and clandestine negotiations took place between the planters and the rebels, who were also joined by rebels from other ethnic communities.

This bought temporary peace, as some planters embraced measures that would be viewed favourably by the Assamese elite. In the mid-1990s, the Williamson Magor companies opened a residential school and instituted a literary award. The owner of the company hoped this would be seen as his way 'to put money back into Assam'.[168] From the late 1980s, the Assamese elite began sending their children to Delhi and other places for higher education. Many of them had been city-dwellers for two or three generations, with little or no attachment to the idea of the predominantly rural landscape of Assam. Their numbers grew slowly in the 1990s; but, by the end of the century, they were a sizeable proportion of the population. They hardly shared the social and political aspirations of the ULFA boys and girls.

The army presence in the state was a source of confidence as well as panic and came at a massive cost in human rights. Early in the evening when it began to get dark, most shops in towns would be closed, and no one dared venture out; journalists reported that only troops and government officials would be found on the streets. Sporadic incidents of raids and news of brutal physical assaults by soldiers on rebels and civilians 'left deep wounds' on the Assamese psyche. *Habeas corpus* petitions, through which worried parents sought the whereabouts of their sons, became a part of everyday life for many. The trust between the public and the army collapsed. These unbearable times were captivatingly narrated in several bold Assamese literary works.[169] A section of worried citizens formed an umbrella human rights organization to catalogue and highlight people's trauma.[170]

Not surprisingly, the Congress party lost power in 1996, and the AGP came back to power. Ethnic violence and infighting among the rebels, largely sustained by logistical support from the powers that be, ripped apart Assam's social fabric. State repression and murder of key individuals across ideological leanings became common. Parag Das, a respected journalist who had spent years exploring the reasons for Assam's economic backwardness, was killed in broad daylight in Guwahati in 1996. This sent ripples across Assam, with an increasing number of people voicing support for democratic political norms and strongest disapproval of all forms of violence, as recorded by journalists, literary writers and others.[171] The armed conflict between the ULFA and the Indian government continued; some of the top ULFA leaders remained in exile in Myanmar, Bhutan or Bangladesh. As the Indian government ruthlessly crushed these rebels with the support of these foreign governments, a section of the rebels did not relent, but they retreated from the public imagination. Many of the rebels, however, lost hope. Over time, they questioned their own ideological leanings and were fatigued by their life in the jungles. In the first two decades of the twenty-first century, the Indian government succeeded in bringing most of the key leaders back to India. When the ULFA leaders returned from exile, thousands turned out to see their 'Robin Hoods'.

~

Meanwhile, another group of people who were disenchanted with their situation in Assam sought a different political path. This started from the spring of 1987, when the Bodos began to mobilize their community members.[172] One of the immediate catalysts for this resurgence of political activity among Assam's tribal communities was the large-scale eviction from government lands undertaken by the Assam government since September 1986. These evictions endangered the livelihoods of many, including the poor Bodos, who resolutely resisted them[173] and who were now led by the All Bodo Students Union (ABSU). They had reason to be enthused by political mobilizations of other smaller ethnic communities elsewhere in India, including the burgeoning Gorkhaland movement, which sought a homeland for the Nepalis in the northern districts of West Bengal.

The ABSU had been formed in 1967, and together with the other tribal communities, the Bodos had challenged the domination of the Assamese ruling classes.[174] The Bodo leadership were at odds with the Assamese government ever since they had been thwarted in their choice of a script for the Bodo language in 1974, as described in an earlier chapter. While the earlier demand of the Plains Tribes Council of Assam (PTCA) for a union territory called Udayachal had failed, the United Tribal Nationalists' Liberation Front of Assam

(UTNLFA), a political party born in 1984, demanded that a separate state be carved out of the tribal-dominated areas of the Brahmaputra Valley.[175] Ideologically opposed to the PTCA, this party's birth was an outcome of a divided reaction to the tribal populations living in the Brahmaputra Valley and had the blessings of Prime Minister Indira Gandhi. Their first memorandum to the Prime Minister in 1984 recalled the ordeals of the tribal populations in the political crisis of February 1983 and their grim economic future in an Assam dominated by Assamese speakers.[176] This demand had limited political consequences, but things began to take a serious turn after the AGP government came into power. By 1985, the ABSU parted ways with the PTCA, when the latter formed an electoral alliance with the AGP, seen as antithetical to the Bodo aspirations. In 1986, the Bodo Sahitya Sabha made it clear that the Bodos would prefer Hindi as the third language in educational institutes rather than Assamese.[177] The Assam government had ordered that in non-Assamese-medium schools, Assamese would be compulsory as the third language after English. The votaries of Assamese language endorsed this decision: 'Everybody living in Assam and working in Assam should learn Assamese,' concurred the *Assam Tribune*.[178] Enraged, the ABSU, in 1987, sent a memorandum to Prime Minister Rajiv Gandhi, demanding a separate homeland—a union territory, with limited powers compared to a state in the Indian union, for the tribal population.[179]

Later that same year, the ABSU launched the movement for a separate state called Bodoland and gave calls for strikes in quick succession. The first of these took place in December 1987, and it was followed by a 100-hour strike, which paralysed traffic on the national highways of Lower Assam in March 1988. These strikes effectively challenged the might of the Assam government. As the Bodos across class and religious affinities confronted the powerful state apparatus, they faced retaliation from the AGP-led government, which was determined not to allow another identity movement to prosper. For months, the Bodo student leaders were 'haunted by fear'. While many were arrested, the press reported that 'Bodo menfolk are often found sleeping in the fields or jungles to evade arrest'.[180] Molestations and rapes were also reported, though unmoved officials of the Assam government commented that 'much noise has been created about the mass rape'.[181] Vacant agricultural lands were taken over by non-Bodos.

In the next few years, the highly appealing slogan 'divide Assam fifty-fifty' was found on walls in every public place of Lower Assam. Bodo readers did not rely on Assamese newspapers for news of political developments; the newly launched *Bodoland Times* became the sentinel of the Bodo movement. Unlike in earlier decades, the late 1980s' ethnic-political mobilization received warm and widespread support from Assam's tribal population.

Meanwhile, the AGP government (1986–90) failed to deliver on its promises. Despite their attempts to reach out to a cross-section of Assamese, AGP leaders remained constrained by their ideological moorings, which became evident soon after they formed the government. In February 1986, the AGP government proposed to make the Assamese language compulsory for non-Assamese speakers; however, this faced strong opposition, which was proof of a more self-conscious, articulate and rising tribal population, and the government was forced to withdraw this directive.[182] A series of evictions of tribals and Muslims from the ambiguously demarcated government lands—more informed by ideological prejudices than the prudent governance of land and forests—further alienated the AGP government from the common people.[183]

As a section of the caste-Hindu Assamese, since the coming of the AGP government, reasserted their control over the bureaucracy and other spheres of cultural life, the social and political rift between the Assamese and the tribal population widened. In 1987, Upendranath Brahma, a prominent, soft-spoken Bodo student leader, fell out with the Assamese leaders and decided to work for political awakening among his tribesmen. When Michael Hamlyn, a journalist with *The Times*, spoke to Brahma in 1989, he was told: 'We have to demand a separate homeland for ourselves because we, the tribals, are oppressed economically, culturally, socially and politically by the high-caste Assamese.'[184] The ABSU, led by Brahma, was not alone in voicing such concerns. Speaking in the Parliament in 1986, Samar Brahma

Choudhury, another Bodo leader from the PTCA, echoed this sentiment: 'The tribals are the most unhappy lot in Assam.'[185] His anger was deep-rooted: 'It is the Assamese society which is leading Assam [and] governing Assam' and 'enjoying the maximum government patronage', while 'the tribal people have got a long history of deprivation and criminal neglect'. This strong antipathy to the Assamese became more pronounced in August 1987 when the ABSU published a booklet to answer a series of questions on why they were insisting on splitting Assam equally between the tribals and the Assamese. The answers were forthright: 'the attitude of the Assamese people is anti-tribal; the Assamese people are [exporting] Assamese colonialism in tribal areas and dominating the tribals.'[186] The tribals 'are the original masters of Assam', whereas the 'Assamese have unjustifiably snatched away Assam and its administration through the process of silent aggression', they asserted.

Through long hours of public curfews, bandhs and violence—in some places of the Brahmaputra Valley's north bank, a section of the militant Bodos had outnumbered the non-Bodos, forcing the latter to seek refuge elsewhere[187]—the Bodo political leaders struck at the root of Assam's political and economic structure. Decades earlier, when residents of the hills had protested, there was little strain on the general economy of Assam. This had changed in the late 1980s.

After years of charged political unrest, the Union government began a dialogue. There were several rounds of negotiations between the Bodo leaders and the Union government, starting in 1989.[188] In 1993, the latter agreed to grant limited executive and legislative powers to the areas inhabited by the Bodos. This willingness to devolve power and grant autonomy was half-hearted and only temporarily neutralized the demand for a separate state. Political restlessness amongst the Bodos would continue for many years to come.[189]

While the Bodos demanded a separate state, others like the Koch Rajbongshi, who had once been a ruling dynasty in parts of Lower Assam and northern Bengal, had similar though lesser demands that nonetheless had a crucial bearing on the outcomes of others. From the late 1980s well into the twenty-first century, the leaders of these communities creatively mobilized their followers—and also allowed some form of militancy to take shape—to win political and economic concessions. Years earlier, like the Bodos, the Karbis—whose first newspaper was published by the Christian missionaries in 1949 in the Roman script[190]—demanded the use of Roman script for their literature and language but faced similar police repression.[191] After a period of moderate articulation of political dissent seeking more political empowerment, in 1978, a section of the Karbi and Dimasa leaders demanded a separate state for themselves.[192] Between 1978 and 1981, they succeeded in galvanizing political action in their areas, yet most of their activities remained dormant or confined to petitioning till 1986. In that year, the tribal residents of two hill districts, Karbis and Dimasas, in particular—many Karbi leaders influenced by communist ideologies—demanded more 'legislative and executive powers' so that they could be 'masters of their own destiny'.[193] That year, the Karbi leaders formed the Autonomous State Demand Committee to reach out to a wider population. While they blamed shortfalls in the constitutional arrangements to safeguard their economic and political rights, they also stated that they had been 'suffocate[d] under the grips of the successive Assamese government[s]' and highlighted how 'the Assamese government officials and the Assamese businessmen' siphoned off public funds meant for them 'in the guise of civilizing the tribals'.[194] They pointed out how the various forest laws—made worse by the attitude of the officials and a section of the Assamese intelligentsia, which was similar to that of their colonial predecessors[195]—had increasingly tried to restrict their jhum (shifting method) cultivation in recent decades. Their list of charges against Assamese leaders and officials was rather long but precise, reflecting the deep crisis of extremely slow economic and social development. Similarly worded grievances—asking for roads, education and medical facilities—had been placed before Robert Reid in 1940, then the Governor of Assam.[196] But there had been negligible progress since then. Dams on their rivers were imagined as a source of electricity for the rich elsewhere and a means for controlling floods in the valleys.[197] In 1971, of the 1605 villages in the Mikir Hills District, only three had electricity, only 155 had *pucca* roads and one had a college.[198] An enquiry in 1968 found that many families from among the Karbi tribes 'during the lean months of the year . . . remain half-starved and sometimes they live on fruits of the jungles and wild roots'.[199] Their quest for economic opportunities met many hurdles, including their shrinking access to the forestlands. The districts of Karbi Anglong and North Cachar collectively expanded their net area of cultivation—the only source of livelihood for the majority—between 1951 and 1981–82 by more than four times.[200] However, some of the state-induced strategies to introduce modern agricultural methods in these areas failed, which was primarily a result of a mismatch between two contrasting and competing worlds of agricultural practices and the failure of the government to recognize the differences.[201]

The well-articulated political aspirations of many tribal communities, including the Karbis, paved the way to empower others, including the Bodos, to govern themselves within the framework of the Sixth Schedule of the Indian Constitution. The gains made by other communities, however, were much smaller than those of the Bodos—for instance, in power-sharing arrangement in the legislative domain. Other rewards were more than merely political: for example, the Karbis were able to moderately curtail further decline of their jhum lands.[202] But the political outcomes of such initiatives were not easy for a section of the Assamese ruling elite to swallow, as they realized that their attempts to absorb the tribal populations into their social and cultural structures would not succeed.

~

Assam's economic and political woes did not throttle its cultural aspirations. Among its unique art forms, the Sattriya dance, patronized since the sixteenth century, stands out.[203] However, to understand this, we have to go back a little earlier. A mythological dance form, it originated under the guidance of the Vaishnava saint Sankaradeva and his principal disciple Madhavdeva. Over the centuries, it remained confined within the temple monasteries or sattras. Since the 1950s, alongside the transformations in Assamese society and polity,

Sattriya dance had quietly transformed itself and begun to emerge as an embodiment of Assamese culture and identity. Critical to this transformation were the rising aspirations and power of the Assamese middle classes and Assam's position in the federal nation-state. Towards the late twentieth century, members of the Assamese middle classes—many first-generation engineers, doctors, lawyers, businessmen and members of the elite bureaucracy, who owed their success to educational opportunities—increasingly migrated out of their ancestral villages, out of Assam and outside India in search of better opportunities.[204] This wide network of Assamese speakers held on to their Assamese identity, treasured Assamese culture and facilitated its spread. Sattriya was also promoted as part of the Indian state's efforts to revive the country's indigenous arts and cultures.

Sattriya was transformed earlier in the twentieth century. As anti-colonial nationalist mobilization took root in Assam, the male-dominated Vaishnava dance performances witnessed changes, including increasing participation by women, among whom some rose to positions of leadership. Pitambar Deva Goswami, introduced earlier as a leading Assamese figure in the phase of Gandhian mobilization and also a Sanskritist, is generally credited with introducing radical initiatives in the cultural world of the sattras from the 1920s onwards.[205] In the 1930s, other individuals and organizations took these initiatives forward. Among them was the Shillong-based Prachin Kamrupi Nritya Sangha, which was generally centred around the cosmopolitan cultural milieu of Assam's capital city, Shillong, and was inspired by the nationalist cultural resurgence. These initiatives ensured that the art forms were brought outside the sattras.[206] Their repertoires and performances reached several Indian cities by the 1940s. In parallel, the visibility of women in public performances increased.[207]

The modern rise of Sattriya dance cannot be understood without a reference to the power of Vaishnava texts in the Assamese scholarly traditions, already discussed in an earlier chapter. Vaishnavism and its various performative rituals had deep roots among the Hindus in Assam. The American Baptist missionary, Miles Bronson, much revered by the Assamese literary elite for his support to the Assamese language in the mid-nineteenth century, was amazed by the power of the Vaishnavite texts. 'What is the secret of these books being so popular as to be found in almost [every] house, and on every tongue?'[208] Bronson recognized that Sankaradeva 'struck for the masses'.

Meanwhile, a large number of scholars and art practitioners had begun to highlight the need for Assamese people to take pride in their cultural heritage. It 'will be a pity and shame for us, at least to the people of Assam, if in this very age of self-consciousness, outlook of life, we be so negligent to a cultural heritage of ours of such a significance', wrote one practitioner.[209] An Assamese scholar felt that 'this is by no means indulging in the revivalist sentiment; it leaves room for a scientific approach and research too'.[210] The Assam Sangeet Natak Academy, established in 1952, commenced extensive activities to collect, catalogue and study the Vaishnava musical compositions or Bargeet (literally great songs) that accompany Sattriya dance.[211] Some benefactions came from the zamindars of Goalpara. The songs were recorded, and their origins, subject matter, ragas, instruments, etc. were explored. A team of exponents and scholars under the banner of the Akademi's Bargeet Research Committee explored the possibility of establishing Assam's Vaishnava music as a distinct school of Indian classical music. These early surveys were published in 1957, and scholars outside Assam took notice. More surveys and scholarly publications followed. 'Do Bargeet come under classical music?' asked these scholars. They felt that 'attempts are made in certain quarters to keep Bargeet apart from the hierarchy of classical music under the pretext that they just belong to the bhajan type of music . . . in fact nothing from the point of view of music can come in the way of including it in "classical music"'.[212]

After Independence, India witnessed several movements for a cultural resurgence among its myriad communities. In the search for a distinct political identity in the competitive federal structure of India, linguistic groups refashioned and rediscovered their soul in the literary and cultural spheres and took every opportunity to showcase their art forms in the national space. From 1954 onwards, the Indian government began to organize youth festivals in New Delhi as a part of the nation-building process. In November 1957, in the fourth session of these festivals, which was inaugurated by President Rajendra Prasad and Prime Minister Jawaharlal Nehru, those who presented India's classical dances 'attempted to blend India's ancient folk art with modern dance steps'.[213] A team from Assam performed Sattriya, which had not yet been recognized as a classical dance form. The non-inclusion of Sattriya concerned scholars like Maheswar Neog, who had years of scholarly works on Assamese Vaishnavism behind him. While Assam's Sattriya dance could not be staged officially as being classical, nor was it considered folk in the conventional sense. One commentator described it as 'traditional Manipuri Ras',[214] while another remarked that it was pleasing in its 'cute poses and pretty dresses of women (one of them wore a modern cut blouse), but displayed a certain monotony of movement and gestures'.[215] Neog recounted that this was probably the first occasion when Sattriya was performed in Delhi.[216]

A small group of scholars, including Neog, and performers, who were familiar with other Indian dance forms, continued their engagement with the project of 'resuscitation of sattriya dance style'.[217] Neog was careful not to describe Sattriya as a folk dance. In an introductory essay on Assam's folk dances, he ensured that it was not mentioned.[218] Neog, the university professor, was not an unfamiliar face among Indian classicists. His works had been published in *Proceedings of the All-India Oriental Conference* and the celebrated *Journal of the Music Academy*.[219] Neog had written in 1953 a lengthy introductory essay on the medieval text *Srihasta Muktavali*, of which there was an Assamese rendering;[220] he published a full-length Assamese translation a decade later. This grammar of dance, presumed to be originally written between the fourteenth and sixteenth centuries by Subhaṅkara Kavi, expounded the language of hand gestures in Indian classical dance.[221] Neog's scholarly work added several aspects: it helped in understanding the grammar and details of various rhythms, or *tals*. He was among those scholars who helped establish Sattriya as being central to the sattras, as a living dance form, unlike other Indian classical dances.

In the early years after Independence, Sattriya was still included by the new nation-state among folk dance forms. Sattriya dances, intended 'to heighten the devotion of the worshippers and to display the prowess of the divine Krishna' were 'preserved and practiced by Vaishnava teachers in the Satras', said a publication of the Indian government.[222] Most visitors to Assam carried with them a similar impression. Musicologist Shrikrishna Narayan Ratanjankar highlighted Sattriya's importance among Assam's folk dances.[223] When the great dancer and choreographer Uday Shankar visited Assam in 1954 and appreciated the Naga warrior dance, members of the audience asked him the way to popularize Assam's classical dance among the masses.[224] On another occasion during this tour, he and fellow dancer Amala Shankar recognized the rightful claim of Sattriya as a classical Indian dance form.[225] As the renaissance of Sattriya dance progressed, exponents and scholars continued to have doubts about the classical heritage of the Vaishnava arts. 'Is there a classical theory of rhythm as distinct from Hindustani *tala*?' Neog was asked by an American musicologist.[226]

Between 1955 and 1958, India's national organization for performing arts, the Sangeet Natak Akademi, organized a series of seminars on the country's cultural heritage, and the last one of these was on dances. A team of scholars and performers from Assam, including Neog, presented the classical attributes of Sattirya dance and Ojapali, demonstrating that the recognition of just four schools of classical Indian dance—Bharatnatyam, Kathak, Kathakali and Manipuri—was arbitrary. Only these four enjoyed state patronage, though other dance forms had equal claims. By classical dance, one meant those dance forms which followed authoritative texts including Bharata's *Natyasastra* and Nandikeshvara's *Abhinaya Darpana*. Neog introduced

> Assam's three existing dance styles that had classical patterns—the Nati dance of the Shaiva and Vaishnava temples of Assam, the neo-Vaishnavite Sattra dances, and the Ojapali dances that accompany recitations from the Assamese versions of the Indian epics and puranas—and the singing of the songs of Manasa (Serpent Goddess).[227]

Neog noted that while the first form had almost died out, the Sattriya dance 'although decayed in some regards, carries on a vigorous

Monks from Assam performing Sattriya Dance (Drum Dance), at the All India Dance Seminar, New Delhi, 1958

Monks from Assam performing Sattriya Dance (Chali Nritya) at the All India Dance Seminar, New Delhi, 1958

Monks from Assam performing Sattriya Dance
(Jhumura Nritya) at the All India Dance Seminar, New Delhi, 1958

existence in the sattras . . . and villages of the Brahmaputra valley'. Neog marshalled several texts—*Srihasta Muktavali*, *Tauryatrika-sara*, *Mudra-adhyaya*—to argue that these dance forms, with a grammar of their own, were classical. His fellow artists—all male—from an Upper Assam *sattra* presented a moving performance as Neog spoke.[228] No 'women dancer or actress is allowed in this school, there being no order of nuns in the *sattras*', Neog noted. Most among the viewers were unfamiliar with this dance form, but that did not stop them from applauding the performers.

India's first ever national dance seminar, thus, provided an opportunity to assert claims of national recognition. The seminar suggested the formation of a committee of experts that would study the 'various forms and styles of dance and dance dramas prevalent in different regions'.[229] The committee would also record 'all available authentic texts and film performances', which would help them in preparing a comprehensive report on Indian dances. This committee was essentially appointed to formulate a 'policy of awards to artists in the field of dance and to advise whether the present classification should continue or there should be any further classification or basis for classification'.[230] The committee examined whether the other dance forms had any distinctive features or if they could be 'sub-classified' under the existing four. The committee's views were disappointing. They felt it would be wiser to 'give grants for setting up and conducting schools to develop [the various dance forms], rather than to make any awards at the present stage'. The Akademi was aware of the possible controversy that would erupt from such a stand; yet, broadly agreeing with the experts, it decided to wait 'for a comprehensive collection of all dance forms' in India. A possible storm was averted by adding two more categories: traditional dance forms (which would include Sattriya) and modern Indian dance.

Away from scholarly disputes, by the late 1950s, young women in Assam received help and encouragement to learn Sattriya dance outside the confines of the sattras. Raseswar Saikia Borbayan, a monk from one of the liberal sattras, despite strong opposition from the conservative sections, trained a number of girls in the art.[231] Facilities were set up to teach Sattriya dance outside the sattras. Pradip Chaliha, an early pioneer of taking Sattriya beyond the sattras, established a training school in Upper Assam—Ajanta Kala Mandal—as early as 1951.[232] By the 1960s, Sattriya was a part of the larger urban social milieu. In Guwahati, stage performances of Bihu had Sattriya as a special attraction.[233] State recognition was also visible. In 1963, Maniram Dutta Muktiyar Barbayan, the octogenarian Vaishnavite artist who earlier actively supported the research works of the Bargeet Research Committee, was awarded by the Akademi for Sattriya in the category of 'other traditional dance forms'.[234] Meanwhile, the dramatic transformation of Sattriya into a female-orientated dance form began to take shape from the 1960s. The establishment of training schools in Guwahati, fast emerging as a symbol of the aspiring Assamese urban population, accentuated this process.[235] A small group of urban

Assamese families increasingly considered their daughters' learning this art as a sign of their newfound social status.

Notwithstanding these scholarly initiatives and the increasing public presence of the dance form as being key to Assamese cultural identity, Sattriya was yet to be recognized by India's cultural bureaucracy. This invited the wrath of Assamese scholars, who received sympathy from proponents of other Indian dance forms that too were seeking recognition from the Indian nation-state. The 'need for a proper study of these small schools [Odissi, Kuchipudi, Sattriya etc.] and for their development still looms large. A history of Indian dances still remains a far cry', wrote the influential *Assam Quarterly* in 1967.[236] Nor did the Assam government ignore the new developments surrounding this dance form; an official agreed that Sattriya had 'not yet been able to receive formal recognition as a distinct school of dance' due to a lack of research.[237] To accomplish this, in 1960, it sanctioned a small financial grant to organize a Sattriya dance festival and symposiums in Guwahati that might 'decide the future line of action' to promote and popularise Sattriya.

The 1960s and 1970s witnessed an urban emphasis on the performative aspects of Assamese Vaishnavism, which in varied forms—drama, dance, songs—had been the driving force of religion and culture in Assamese villages for centuries. In the 1960s, Sattriya regularly made forays into the national space as a part of the cultural mosaic.[238] In 1963, when Sattriya dance was performed in Kerala along with other regional dances, the press reported it as the presentation of a tribal dance from Assam.[239] By the late 1960s, Sattriya made its way onto the elite cultural stage of India. A performance by Ritha Devi (a celebrated Odissi dancer, well versed in other classical forms, who was also the granddaughter of Lakshminath Bezbaroa) in 1969 at the Chhandam Dance School in Bombay was one such occasion.[240] Devi and Neog were in correspondence over the need for such performances.[241]

In this period, sattras increasingly began to seek state patronage, and more attempts were made to date the origin of Sattriya to an earlier time and establish it on par with classical dance forms.[242] Several other

Indian dance traditions, like Odissi or Kuchipudi, also waged a struggle to secure recognition among India's classical dances.[243] 'Gestures and poses employed in a sattriya-dance have certain affinities with those of Indian dance-scriptures,' wrote Kapila Vatsyayan.[244] More recognition of Sattriya as a classical form began coming in from Indian dance critics. The Assamese scholars and practitioners saw they were not alone: 'It is only when there was a revival of cultural interest alongside a general national upsurge that dance artists turned their attention to [less recognized dance forms] and brought them to [the] limelight.'[245]

In the early 1970s and more so in the 1980s, there was a full-blown academic assertion of Sattriya as a classical dance. Scholars like Neog proposed that 'the rich tradition of the classical art of India is not completely represented in any one of these [four] forms as some aspects have become attenuated in one school but live in another'.[246] They also noted that since state patronage had declined, smaller numbers were joining the ranks of disciples, and 'for the lack of [a] proper critical outlook', 'which should perhaps be a little conservative', the dance forms had seen many erosions. The dancers were 'taking to cheap and easy bits of the art', and some were infusing 'extraneous elements into the traditional wealth', making it increasingly 'difficult to distinguish between the real and the fake'.[247] Neog highlighted Assam's three different ancient dance forms, of which Sattriya was the last one to evolve. To the critics who asked whether Sattriya had any grammar to ensure its rightful place as a classical dance form, Neog asserted that 'they have a code of their own', their own grammar and codes derived by the process of practice.[248] He assembled a wide range of evidence—travellers' accounts of ancient royal courts, inscriptions, sculptural relics, religious texts—to prove the classical nature of Sattriya.

Meanwhile, under the direct supervision of well-known proponents, more schools were giving training in Sattriya dance in Guwahati and other urban areas by the late '70s.[249] Progress, however, was very slow; in 1973, another leading litterateur lamented that 'all these dance forms await the investigation of scholars and their resuscitation by modern artists'.[250] In 1976, when Kapila Vatsyayan spoke in Guwahati in remembrance of linguist and cultural historian Banikanta Kakati, she referred to Sattriya as an important element of India's classical heritage.[251] Earlier, several of their cultural and literary icons wrote lyrics for songs that expressed the essence of Assamese cultural sensibilities. In this decade, a few among them—Bishnu Prasad Rabha, Jyoti Prasad Agarwala and Bhupen Hazarika—gained popular approval for their enunciation of emancipatory social and political ideas in the lyrics, though not everyone subscribed to their views. The popularity of these songs helped to bring an emotive element into the political actions of the 1980s and even later.

The last quarter of the twentieth century witnessed an increasing body of scholarship on Assamese Vaishnavism, and more authoritative works, including various learning handbooks on Sattriya dance, were published.[252] The sattras, too, worked to reach their rituals to the larger cultural world. Dance commentators were increasingly hopeful of Sattriya being recognized as a classical dance form.[253] Such demands were heartily endorsed by Assam's political leaders.[254] Others, who were opposed to the religious and cultural authority of the sattras, unsuccessfully disputed the nomenclature of this dance form.[255] Sattriya increasingly became a cultural symbol of classical Assam in modern times, as it had transited from being an exclusively male-dominated religious ritualistic art to popular performance. The publication of Sattriya dance grammar, the establishment of professional schools and course curricula and efforts by individual practitioners to train younger dancers took the dance to national and global stages.[256] When in 1994 two celebrated Assamese artists, Indira P.P. Bora and Menaka P.P. Bora, performed Sattriya in Bombay, a critic admiringly wrote that Sattriya had 'acquired a sophistication and contemporary look with female dancers replacing men for the women's roles', adding that the old form had been 'remodelled with classical elements', which gave it 'characteristic beauty, grace and charm'.[257] Alongside this widening appreciation of Assamese culture, the Assamese language began to gain a distinct position in the national perception; for instance, in 1991, the popular health drink Horlicks 'mounted an expensive campaign with different visuals and text' in Assamese along with other Indian languages.[258]

By the turn of the century, many young dancers, drawn from diverse socio-economic backgrounds, had broken out of the layers of social conservatism. Their performances were enhanced with cultural experimentation and innovation; they challenged the orthodox and carried the hope of a new age.[259] These changes coincided dramatically with developments inside the Sangeet Natak Akademi, the organisation responsible for endowing state patronage in the performing arts. In 1998, Bhupen Hazarika, Assam's cultural icon, was elected to head the Akademi. Hazarika, a passionate emissary of Assamese culture, accelerated the bureaucratic procedure to recognize Sattriya as India's classical dance. Finally, with the ceremonial official affirmation of Sattriya as one of India's classical dances in 2000, performers began to enjoy wider recognition and state patronage, which allowed for greater mobility across transnational spaces. This brought some of the social recognition sought by the Assamese middle classes[260] and also significantly contributed to the consolidation of Assamese nationalism, which is increasingly projected and interlinked through Vaishnavism.

# Epilogue

The decades between the early 1940s and the end of the twentieth century, which are the focus of this book, proved to be decisive in the making of modern Assam. Being a frontline province of British India, Assam was deeply affected by the loss and the subsequent re-conquest of Burma by the British, as well as by their bloody battles in defence of Imphal and Kohima. Immediately after the end of World War II in 1945, powerful winds of change began to blow across the subcontinent, culminating in Independence and Partition in 1947. All these events had a long-term impact on the province, which was as much economic and cultural as it was military and political. The early decades of decolonization, as this book has explained, saw the unleashing of a range of new social energies and political forces that soon became critical to the making of modern Assam.

Through the second half of the twentieth century, Assam's development was tied to myriad far-reaching but foreseeable events. The state's impoverished economy and fragile political landscape created the background for the social conflicts and cultural experiments, which marked these decades and often produced results having catastrophic and long-term consequences. Assam directed its energies towards overcoming these frequent challenges but found itself walking a political and social tightrope.

Within a short period following Independence, Assam's territorial outlines—drawn by the erstwhile colonial masters more for bureaucratic and economic convenience than ethnic and linguistic homogeneity—disintegrated. The consequent birth of new states was a welcome development for many, as these significant political experiments in Indian federalism largely fulfilled the political and social aspirations of various ethnic communities. Meanwhile, those who struggled for a cohesive Assamese identity had necessarily to draw from its diverse multilingual, multi-ethnic and religious histories and layered pasts. Alongside, the very complexity and turbulence of Assam's diverse environments—ecological, political and cultural—have denied any singular understanding of the region. The idea of Assam has constantly evolved, with great adjustments having to be made in response to tectonic fractures caused by numerous and varied challenges.

The book illuminates, among other things, three critical developments that have dominated the state's long journey—Assam's continuous sense of grievance against India's federal economic arrangements; its relentless struggle to combat its internal challenges arising from the political, social and economic aspirations of various communities; and, most significantly, the evolving anxieties against those who were considered to be dangerous 'outsiders'. Population mobility, one of the driving forces behind Assam's rise to economic modernity and partly an offshoot of the capitalist desire of imperial Britain, continues to be a highly contested subject and is related to the politics of relentless suspicion and suffering. A passion for language as a marker of identity and a type of identity politics continues to animate disparate sections and classes of Assamese speakers. So does the shifting definition of being an Assamese: who is (or is not) genuinely Assamese has never perhaps mattered more in the all-India setting.

~

How does one write the history of an Indian state after 1947? Rising under the shadow of independent India's political developments, and in the hope of promises sealed in the Indian Constitution, the Republic's constituent states struggled in various ways to participate in the nation-making process. Each followed a different trajectory, so varied were the experiences of colonialism in different regions, especially in the economic and cultural arenas. These experiences prepared the Indian provinces to find their space in the mosaic of India. Thus, a nuanced understanding of the making of modern India after 1947 necessitates a careful understanding of the rise and growth of the Indian states. The history of the Indian nation as seen through the tumultuous experiences of its different regions surely provides a deeper understanding of India in the present times as well. This book amply demonstrates that Assam, like any other major state of the Republic, could be a window to comprehending the enactment of the idea of modern India.

Studying Assam of the post-1947 period brings into view the functioning of an Indian state whose regional identity is subsumed by many layers of cultural and social identities. As this book recounts, Assam's state apparatus took different forms after Independence and came to be controlled mainly by Assamese speakers, though this did not go unchallenged. The more the elites and the ruling classes tried to impose a uniform political-cultural identity on those who lived in the territory, the more elusive their goal became. The Assamization of the state machinery vastly amplified the political turmoil of the 1960s and the 1980s. Yet, Assam was also a state where the aspirations of diverse communities—ethnic, linguistic and religious—were given shape and, sometimes, accomplished. In doing so, multilingualism and multiculturalism discreetly secured a place, despite intermittent periods of political and cultural turbulence.

Assam's ethnic and identity politics has always been an arena for cultural contestation as much as a struggle over economic resources and livelihoods. The interplay between caste, class and ethnicity was on display throughout the last 60 years of the twentieth century. The regional political and cultural consolidation in terms of Assamese speakers and the middle and higher castes importantly impacted caste–tribe relations as well as plains–hills relations. Identity politics flourished on the fertile ground of a broken economy, social inequalities and failed political promises. Political, economic, social and ecological tussles took ethnic and communal forms. The negligible presence of ethnic communities in the power-sharing mechanism facilitated political mobilizations of these groups, inspired by the ideals of social and political improvement and occasionally animated by violence. These communities grew increasingly insulated and alienated from the idea of a pan-Assamese classical cultural past espoused by the Assamese elite. Some others, though belonging to the so-called 'higher castes', fought a weak battle demanding to be recognized as Scheduled Tribes in a bid to gain benefits for their communities.

From Jawaharlal Nehru's time, Assam has refused to flinch from allegiance to the Indian nation-state or its central leadership. During this period, Assamese political leaders, backed by a larger section of civil society, engaged in protracted political negotiations to secure Assam's dignified place in the evolving federal architecture of India. As they bargained with India's national leadership, they themselves faltered in providing similar care to many within the state. While sections of disgruntled residents of Assam joined the ranks of political rebels over the decades, their numbers were relatively small and they received no substantial endorsement from the middle classes of Assamese society at large. Their popular appeal was temporary, and sporadic waves of violence, though severe, did not get wider support. The brief challenge that the political rebels posed fizzled out. An Assam outside India—the dream of a tiny section of its people—never had the traction of a Nagalim or an independent Mizoram; not only was there no leader like Phizo (a comprehensive biography of him is still awaited) or even Laldenga, but also Assam's place in and relationship with India was deeper, stronger and more stable. The rebels' challenge, however, did indirectly contribute to moderate political concessions from the Union government in fiscal, executive and legislative powers. Some of these concessions, primarily inspired by the political principles spelt out by India's constitutional idealism, have, along expected lines, infused many layers of economic and social change among Assam's tribal communities. More may unfold in the future. Nonetheless, by the turn of the century, a section of the population viewed with regret the political disquiet of the bygone decades—which had somewhat tried to correct the state's colonial legacies and mend the fissures in its political and cultural fabric and in the country's federal ecosystem.

Despite several ups and downs post-Independence, Assam and its inhabitants became increasingly integrated into the Indian economy and its political systems. New economic trends became apparent, with the state importing more commodities, and in greater volumes than in the early twentieth century. The importance of its exports, including oil, tea, jute and timber, diminished sharply. Larger secular economic changes, including a shift of the economic centre of gravity from eastern to western India, did not help Assam. Its trade deficit continues to be a drag on its growth. The dream of industrialization, despite some strides since the 1990s, is still elusive as the state has failed to generate an indigenous non-mercantile capitalist class.

As the key indicators of economic development remained stagnant, Assam witnessed a series of political movements seeking decisive state intervention to introduce dynamism into its economy. India's policymakers responded to those demands, but most actions had mixed results. Assam remained underdeveloped, and its index of economic prosperity showed a persistent decline. Official statistics show that Assam did poorly compared to the rest of India, and by the early twenty-first century, it lagged behind most other states in terms of per capita income. Especially worrying is that industries have grown at a slow rate of 0.26 per cent between 2004–05 and 2014–15. Poverty remains a major concern, and the endemic prevalence of corruption increasingly destabilizes systems of public distribution. Land, which was the only source of income for the large majority, is no more a source of promise. Many from the volatile floodplains, tormented by recurring environmental predicaments, have moved out of their villages. The fallout of such mobility, as might be expected, has seen disputes along ethnic and religious lines. An increasing number of people, across castes, ethnic backgrounds and religions—unlike in the previous century—migrate to the rest of India or to other parts of the state in search of livelihood. Though the population of the state increased manifold in the last hundred years, demographers indicate a fall in fertility rates due to many factors, including social and economic conditions.

While Assam's economic future has remained vague, its economic grievances have produced a public narrative of the state as discriminated against by India's federal fiscal arrangement. There is also the perennial anxiety of Assam remaining a resource frontier. Many scholars, writers, lawyers, journalists, teachers and publicists have persuasively described Assam as an example of India's 'internal colonialism'. Though contested, the term does point to uneven levels of development, with Assam substantially behind most Indian states on economic and social indices of development. At the same time, the Union government dreams of reaching out to South-east Asia—a region fast emerging as Asia's economic powerhouse—through the deep-rooted cultural, political and economic corridors provided by Assam and its neighbouring states.

In the last decades of the twentieth century, there were many departures from the experiences of the previous decades, and the rise of a numerically larger middle class comprising a wide spectrum of social and economic backgrounds became significant in the way Assam came to be visualized. Though the growth of the middle classes did not contribute to creating an indigenous class of industrialists and businesspeople, their aspirations and opinions were increasingly important in shaping Assam's cultural and political future. Equally important were the shifts in Assam's social and cultural world. For instance, across rural and urban areas, a growing number of Assamese speakers became increasingly adaptive to multilingualism and multiculturalism. One instance was a visible change in the gastronomic perceptions and attitudes of a wide section of the population; urban culinary codes were increasingly shaped by flavours drawn from the cultural worlds of a range of communities. Another was a new dynamism in the Assamese language, demonstrated by the entry of new words into everyday vocabulary and the elimination of others; in contrast, the lives of some languages spoken by ethnic communities saw many ups and downs. Motifs or designs in textiles that once acted as distinct and exclusive identity markers of ethnic communities have found their place in the way the idea of Assam in the twenty-first century is imagined.

Assam's embracing of these new ways of seeing and imaging itself has led to a slow but growing retreat of social and cultural prejudices. This, however, does not mean that social and economic inequalities have gone away; indeed, some have robustly resurfaced.

The political and social experiences of women, peasants, workers or ethnic communities in Assam, as this book has shown, were equally instrumental in shaping the idea of modern Assam. Much of their role still remains to be examined in detail. For instance, despite the presence of social and cultural barriers, women of all castes, classes and ethnic or religious identities have marked their critical presence in many spheres of public life in modern Assam, especially in the realm of politics. Equally powerful is the voice of women in Assamese literary culture. During the period, some of their gains, which had acquired an institutional form, paved the way for further social and cultural transformation.

Modern Assam was born out of several momentous events that played out from the mid-twentieth century onwards. This book does not necessarily encompass only Assam's tumultuous past, but it highlights promises for Assam's future. Understanding the complicated history with all its surprises, twists and turns would be crucial for dealing with the multiple challenges that confront Assam in the twenty-first century. How will the various historic tussles be resolved? How will the story unfold across the different regions or sectors that make up Assam? Can Assam, placed as it is in a complicated and unstable geostrategic environment, escape from the burden of economic deprivation without causing distress to her environment? Will Assam and other north-eastern states be reluctant partners or eager ones in the transforming idea of India? How far will Assam affect or depart from pan-Indian patterns? Predictions are not a historian's prerogative, but *The Quest for Modern Assam*, I hope, will enable a wider and deeper understanding of Assam today.

# Acknowledgements

This book has been nearly six years in the making. I am indebted to a long list of individuals and institutions who have played a crucial role in helping this book take shape.

Over the years, the New India Foundation (NIF) has become India's leading institutional space providing fellowships to support research on the histories of India after 1947. A fellowship from the NIF allowed me to take time off for writing and the opportunity to travel to libraries and interact with intellectual fellow travellers. I thank all the trustees of the NIF for this opportunity. The team there was helpful throughout the process. Yauvanika Chopra coordinated this work with care and proficiency.

Much of the research was carried out with financial support provided by the Guwahati-based Suryya Kumar Bhuyan Memorial Trust, which generously endowed a chair at the Indian Institute of Technology Guwahati, my workplace. I am grateful to the late Banti Bhuyan, Pradip Kumar Bhuyan and Loya Sinha of the Trust who remained a constant support.

This book could not have been completed without the support, ideas and sustained interest of Ramachandra Guha, the foremost historian of contemporary India and trustee emeritus of the NIF. I learnt and benefited enormously from his generous and meticulous reading of the manuscript. He not only followed the writing of this book closely but also provided key inputs on the structure of the book, drew my attention to several factual inaccuracies that had inadvertently crept in inadvertently and eliminated awkward sentences. My sincere gratitude to him for his faith and trust in this work.

Mahesh Rangarajan read the entire manuscript and his insightful comments helped to further develop and refine my arguments. I am grateful to him for inspiring me to venture into the terrain of contemporary history writing and for our regular and fruitful exchange of ideas throughout the making of this book. An early draft of the manuscript was read by Kalyanakrishnan Sivaramakrishnan, whose detailed comments helped craft some of the core ideas in this book. Their comments were critical as I prepared the final version.

For their belief in the importance of this book and, equally valuable, their generous comments and advice, my gratitude in particular to Rohan D'Souza, Willem van Schendel, Partha Chatterjee, Sunil Amrith and Gunnel Cederlöf. Their feedback and guidance were crucial in helping me understand the workings of the Indian Republic, without which this book would have been much poorer. The final manuscript was read by Jelle J.P. Wouters, Tanmoy Sharma and Aniket De; their comments helped in eliminating inconsistencies and errors.

In Assam, I was fortunate enough to have regular conversations with several scholars who helped me better visualize the modern state. Ranjit Kumar Dev Goswami generously gave his time and resources, shared his ideas, and educated me in Assamese cultural and intellectual history. Prodip Khataniar was an invaluable guide who offered critical help in accessing many little-known aspects of modern Assam. Their support and advice have been indispensable in the making of this book.

A part of the writing for this book was completed at the Centre of South Asian Studies, University of Cambridge, thanks to a Charles Wallace Fellowship. Joya Chatterji, director of the Centre, offered valuable support as did Rachel Rowe, Kevin M. Greenbank and Barbara Row. Kevin and Rachel also helped me access with ease the incredible resources at the Cambridge University library. I would also like to thank Bhaskar Vira, Norbert Peabody, Sanal Mohan, Anjali Bhardwaj Datta, Shuvatri Dasgupta, Salmoli Choudhuri, Rohit Dutta

Roy, Humaira Chowdhury, Trishant Simlai, Saba Sharma and Ankur Barua at the University of Cambridge for listening to my ideas and encouraging me while this work was in progress. The house of Irenee Daly and Donal Lafferty was an extended home for us.

The archives and libraries of the following institutes were the mainstay of this book and I am indebted to their staff: National Archives of India, New Delhi; Abhilekh Patal, National Archives of India, New Delhi; Dr B.R. Ambedkar Central Library and P.C. Joshi Archives at Jawaharlal Nehru University, New Delhi; Nehru Memorial Museum and Library, New Delhi; Central Secretariat Library, New Delhi; British Library, London; South Asian Archive of the Centre of South Asian Studies, University of Cambridge; Library of the Cambridge University; School of Oriental and African Studies library, London; The Bodleian Libraries at the University of Oxford; the libraries of Chicago University, Chicago, Yale University, New Haven and Harvard University, Cambridge MA; Digital Archive of Centre for Assamese Studies, Tezpur University, Tezpur; Assam State Archives, Guwahati; Lakshminath Bezbaroa Library of Indian Institute of Technology Guwahati; Dr Suryya Kumar Bhuyan Library at Cotton University, Guwahati; NE Regional Center Library, the Indian Council of Historical Research, Guwahati; K.K. Handiqui Library, Gauhati University; Department of Assamese, Gauhati University; Department of Historical and Antiquarian Studies, Guwahati; Kamarupa Anusandhan Samiti, Guwahati; Record Room, Special Branch, Assam Police, Kahilipara, Guwahati (research here was conducted during 1997–98); District Library, Guwahati; Assam Legislative Assembly Library, Guwahati; the Assam Tribune Archives, Guwahati; Nanda Talukdar Foundation, Guwahati and Suryya Kumar Bhuyan Archives, North Guwahati.

In particular, the officials and all the staff in the research room of the Assam State Archives, an excellent institution, provided valuable support and advice. I owe special thanks to Nupur Barpatra Gohain, Mukul Das, Arnabjyoti Kashyap, and Nripen Sarma for their untiring support and valuable advice. Special thanks to Nabajyoti Patowary at the Assam Legislative Assembly Secretariat, Naba Kumar Saikia at the library of the Assam Tribune, Pradip Choudhury in the Department of Historical and Antiquarian Studies and James Nye at Chicago University Library..

During the course of my work, I was fortunate to present sections of this work at conferences, seminars and talks held at various institutions including the Department of History, Dibrugarh University; Guwahati College, Guwahati; Indira Gandhi Institute of Development Research, Pune; Indian Institute of Advanced Study, Shimla; Nehru Memorial Museum and Library, New Delhi; the Sasakawa Peace Foundation, Tokyo; Department of History, Harvard University, Cambridge MA; and the Lakshmi Mittal and Family South Asia Institute, Harvard University, New Delhi. I learned much from the seminar audiences and the generous suggestions received there have found place in this book. I express my gratitude to the organizers of these events for inviting me and for the fruitful discussions there.

I was fortunate to be assisted by two excellent editors: Mimi Choudhury read and edited the first draft of my manuscript. Mimi remained a constant support during the writing of this book. Rivka Israel at the NIF was a wonderful and caring editor. Her advice and patience were essential to the finalization of the book. Both have elegantly enhanced the argument, structure, and ideas of the manuscript. Thank you, Mimi and Rivka, for your attention to detail and crucial editorial skills in bringing this book to fruition.

At different stages of my research and writing, I interacted with several scholars whose insights and thoughts shaped this book: they include Gautam Bhadra, Prasenjit Duara, Sugata Bose, Srinath Raghavan, Nandini Sundar, Raziuddin Aquil, Rana P. Behal, A.R. Venkatachalapathy, Maan Barua, Ling Zhang, Anindita Ghosh, Charu Gupta, Dan Smyer Yü, Anindya Sinha, Sripad Motiram, Sahana Ghosh, Mukul Sharma, Kuntala Lahiri-Dutt, Joy Pachuau, Mitul Baruah, Dolly Kikon, Sanjoy Hazarika, Sanjay Barbora, Iftekhar Iqbal and Arnab Dey. I also record my gratitude to Akshaya Mukul, Abhinas Kumar, Koushik Dasgupta, G. Kanato Chophy, Venu Madhav Govindu, Parthasarathi Mandal, Samyak Ghosh, Kasturi Gupta, Aniket Aga, Chitrangada Choudhury and Sarit Chaudhury for their helpful suggestions and guidance. Jairam Ramesh was especially helpful in locating untapped sources. Rimli Barooah provided helpful editorial advice.

Writing the history of a region where I was born and brought up, and spent most of my life, was not an easy task. There was every possibility that I might misjudge in my assessments of its historical development. That risk was partly averted through discussions with those who had first-hand experience of the ups and downs of Assam's tumultuous history. It was a great opportunity to learn from those innumerable conversations in tea shops, bookstores and myriad of other places.

In Assam, Baneswar Saikia, Haidar Hussain and Ramachandra Deka shared their recollections, knowledge and understanding of Assam's fractured past with clarity. I am grateful to them all. I was fortunate to converse with several friends and scholars including Chandan Kumar Sharma, Dambarudhar Nath, Uttam Bathari, Jahnabi Gogoi Nath, Kalyan Das, Gitashree Tamuly, Chandan Kumar Sarma, Hemanta Barman, Santanu Barthakur, Rakhee Kalita Moral, Manoram Gogoi, Monalisha Saikia, Manjil Hazarika, Narayan Sharma, Paresh Malakar and Partha Pratim Hazarika. Their observations helped me frame my questions and I am grateful for their time and effort. Credit must also go to Amarjyoti Mahanta, Debarshi Das, Mrinal Kanti Dutta and Joydeep Baruah for helping me figure out many statistical puzzles related to Assam's economy. Several friends generously shared their rich collections of books and papers for reference and I am thankful to Pranab Swarup Neog, Indibar Deori, Sanjib Kumar Saikia, Jiban Narah, Kalpana Talukdar, Debarati Bagchi, Kanak Chandra Saharia, Bibha Bharali, Bijit Borthakur, Prasun Barman, Baikuntha Rajbongshi, Ankurjyoti Talukdar, James Daimari, Ankur Tamuli Phukan, Bedabrata Gogoi, Prabir Mukhopadhyay, Kishor Goswami, Ayan Sharma, Gautam Kumar Saikia and Anupam Barua. Raktim Thakuria and Ranjan Sarma helped me to procure books that were not available in bookstores.

Jiban Narah has also kindly given permission to quote his verse in the epigraph of this book. Rakhee Kalita Moral and Anindita Kar have kindly translated the texts used in the epigraph from the Assamese. I am grateful to all of them.

For research on this book, I had invaluable assistance from Upasana Devi, Paloma Bhattacharjee, Anusyua Baruah, Ayushi Chauhan and Aditya Ranjan Pathak. Several interns at different stages facilitated research for this work: they include Prabahan Shakya, Abhilash Rajkhowa, Noihrit Gogoi and Ishaana Yasmin Roshid. I am especially grateful to my graduate students with whom I often shared my ideas, and who drew my attention to sources I was unaware of: Prarthana Saikia, Biswajit Sarmah, N.S. Abhilasha, Swagata Mukhopadhya, Namrata Borkotoky, Himalaya Bora, Ajay Sakharam Salunkhe, Rima Kalita, Priyanka Sarma and Upasana Hazarika. This work would not have been possible without the companionship of my PhD students. All of them worked extensively on various aspects of the making of modern Assam. Their research and doctoral work gave me a lot to ponder on during this project. I am especially thankful to Priyanka Sarma and Upasana Hazarika for undertaking the onerous task of proof-reading the notes and bibliography.

It was a privilege to work with my editors at Penguin. Special thanks to Premanka Goswami for his critical interest and continued enthusiasm throughout the writing of this book. Shiny Das and Moutushi Mukherjee ably took this project forward. My thanks to Binita Roy and Shaoni Mukherjee for the first round of copy-editing and to Manali Das for the final version, which was edited with care. I am grateful to Milee Ashwarya, who believed in this project and ensured the book's speedy publication. Aakriti Khurana designed an elegant cover, while Penguin's production team made the transition from manuscript to book seem effortless.

I was fortunate and privileged to be advised by four remarkable physician friends—Rajnish Duara, Mridul Kumar Sarma, Ritankur Borkotoky and Ashim Kharghoria—during this time. Their support took care of the health of my mother and others in the family.

The Indian Institute of Technology Guwahati gave me institutional support as well as time off from teaching. I was fortunate to teach engineering students who helped me understand the value of writing in a way accessible to a non-specialist reader. This book would not have been possible without the creative contributions of my undergraduate students.

My colleagues in the Department of Humanities and Social Sciences have been supportive—both intellectually and otherwise. My historian colleagues John Thomas, Vipul Dutta and Ranu Roychoudhuri were companions on this journey. Liza Das, Anamika Barua and Priyankoo Sarmah always extended their support in various ways.

Ayon Kopil kindly offered to prepare the maps for this book. Dr Narayan Sharma generously shared his personal collection of photographs to be reprinted in this book. I am also grateful to the Sangeet Natak Akademi, New Delhi; Photo Division, Government of India, New Delhi; Department of Historical and Antiquarian Studies, Guwahati; Manuscript Division, K.K. Handiqui Library, Gauhati University; Assam Tribune and Assam State Archives, Guwahati for granting me permission to use material from their collection.

Passages in chapters 3, 5 and 10 of this book are revised versions of what was published in 'Borders, Commodities and Citizens across Mud and River: Assam, 1947–50s', *Studies in History* (2016), 'Imperialism, Geology and Petroleum: History of Oil in Colonial Assam', *Economic & Political Weekly* (2011) and *A Century of Protests: Peasant Politics in Assam since 1900* (New Delhi: Routledge, 2014), respectively.

I started writing the first draft of this manuscript in early 2019 and was able to carry on writing because of a remarkable set of well-wishers, friends and colleagues who stayed the course with me in extraordinary and challenging circumstances. Their support and camaraderie ensured that this project endured I would not want to risk omitting any names and so I refrain from listing them.

My late father would have loved to read this book as he himself had witnessed the major political developments in Assam that this book covers. The love, care, and forbearance of my mother, my parents-in-law, my siblings and their families gave me the strength and courage to persevere.

Banani has remained steadfast in her patience, perseverance, love and care. I owe her much more than what can be expressed in words.

Our son Nizan's determination to help me see the book through was far beyond what one can expect from a young boy. This book owes a great deal to his love and warmth. Meuno's paws never stopped their play on my writing desk and keyboard. They made the long process of writing this book joyful.

Writing a history of contemporary times is a difficult task given the fact that many would-be readers were actual participants in the events described in this book. My narrative and judgements may not meet their intellectual expectations and the readers may come up with alternative evidence or explanations. Imperfections notwithstanding, I sincerely hope this book will provide the readers with a nuanced view of the many histories of contemporary India.

# Timeline (Late Eighteenth Century–2000 CE)

| | |
|---|---|
| 1769–93 | Civil and religious war in Assam leading to the defeat of the Ahom king, who was restored to power with the help of the British East India Company, whose forces arrived in Assam in 1792. |
| 1817–26 | The Burmese army invaded the kingdom of Assam and Cachar. |
| 1824–26 | The first Anglo-Burmese War leading to the occupation of Assam by the British East India Company. The Treaty of Yandabo was signed between the East India Company and the Burmese king in 1826. |
| 1824–38 | The British East India Company completed the task of securing full control of the Ahom kingdom. Guwahati was occupied in July 1824. |
| 1832–54 | The East India Company completed the annexation of Cachar. |
| 1839–67 | Publication of dictionaries and grammars on the Assamese language by British East India Company officials and missionaries. |
| 1834 | The British East India Company government sent a team of scientists to Assam to confirm the presence of the indigenous tea plants in the wild of the state. This was preceded and followed by years of explorations of Assam's natural resources by the officials of the British East India Company in search of botanical and mineral wealth. |
| 1839 | First sale of tea produced in Assam in the London auction market. |
| 1829–39 | Waves of powerful political resistance in the lowlands and hills of Assam and its neighbourhood, challenging the establishment of the British East India company's rule. |
| 1846 | The American Baptist missionaries began the publication of *Orunodoi*, the first printed Assamese magazine from Assam. |

| | |
|---|---|
| 1847 | Introduction of steamer services on the river Brahmaputra, which significantly reduced the time taken to travel between Calcutta and Guwahati. This would greatly facilitate the expansion of the British tea plantations in Upper Assam. |
| 1860 | Beginning of the indentured system of labour contract for the tea gardens in Assam. |
| 1860–63 | Uprisings in the central part of the Brahmaputra valley and in the Jaintia Hills against the taxation and other policies of the British colonial government. |
| 1871–72 | The British Indian Army led punitive expedition to subjugate the chiefs of the Lushai Hills. |
| 1872 | The Garo Hills was annexed to Assam. |
| 1873 | Assamese replaced Bengali as the court language and the language of instruction after the latter was formally introduced as such in 1836. |
| 1873 | The British Indian government introduced the Bengal Eastern Frontier Regulation in 1873. This brought in a system of regulation of people and goods at the foothills through a system of control between the lowlands of Assam and territories lying across the eastern Himalayas and further east. |
| 1874 | Assam was separated from the Bengal government and was made a Chief Commissioner's province by amalgamating Assam proper, Goalpara, Cachar, Sylhet, Naga Hills, Garo Hills and Khasi and Jaintia Hills. |
| 1886 | Introduction of the Assam Land and Revenue Regulation, which would lay down the broad principles on which Assam's lands would be governed. |
| 1890–98 | Lushai Hills was annexed by the colonial government and subsequently made part of Assam. |
| 1891 | Introduction of the Assam Forest Regulation of 1891 to govern the forests in Assam. |
| 1893–94 | Widespread protests against enhancement of land revenue in the ryotwari districts of Assam. |
| 1897 | A major earthquake with an estimated magnitude of 8.15–8.35 on 12 June leading to dramatic environmental changes. |
| 1899 | Formation of the Assam Oil Company, a British joint stock company, to establish an oil refinery at Digboi, near Dibrugarh. |
| 1900 | Publication of *Hemkosh*, a major work on Assamese lexigraphy, by the Assamese scholar Hemchandra Barua. |
| 1901 | Establishment of Cotton College, first college in the province of Assam. The college functioned under the Calcutta University till 1948. |

| | |
|---|---|
| 1911 | The Assam-Bengal Railway connected the Brahmaputra Valley with Calcutta. |
| 1912 | Establishment of the Kamarupa Anusandhan Samiti by a group of Sanskritists, historians and antiquarians to conduct historical and antiquarian investigations on Assam. |
| 1917 | Formation of the Asam Sahitya Sabha signaling the heralding of a new age of Assamese literary nationalism. |
| 1921 | Gandhi's first visit to Assam in August, followed by three more visits in 1926, 1934 and 1946. |
| 1923–29 | Publication of *Asamiya Sahityar Chaneki* (Typical Selection from Assamese Literature) by the University of Calcutta. This work, curated and edited by Hemchandra Goswami, became a landmark in the history of the Assamese literature. |
| 1937 | Formation of the first Assam provincial government led by Syed Mohammed Saadulla of the Assam Valley Muslim Party under the Government of India Act 1935. |
| 1940 | Formation of the Congress ministry led by Gopinath Bardoloi. |
| 1942–44 | After an arduous journey, several million Indian refugees who settled in Burma and were threatened by the Japanese occupation of Burma and the increasing nationalist awakening among the Burmese passed through Assam for their eventual journey to their homes in other Indian provinces. |
| 1944 | Kohima/Imphal battle of World War II. |
| 1946 | Tour of the Gopinath Bardoloi-led committee of India's Constituent Assembly in different parts of Assam on the future of tribals in independent India. |
| 1947 | The Sylhet referendum on 6 and 7 July to decide whether to join with Pakistan was held. |
| 1947 | The Naga Nationalist Council, which was formed in 1946, met Mahatma Gandhi in New Delhi to discuss their future status in independent India. |
| 1948 | The Assam government amended the Assam Land and Revenue Regulation of 1886, which aimed to create statutory provisions protecting property rights in land for tribal people. |
| 1948–51 | The Assam government passed the Assam Adhiars Protection and Regulation Act, Assam State Acquisition of Zamindaries Act, Assam Land (Requisition and Acquisition) Act and Assam Management of Estates Act. All of these acts had a far-reaching impact on agrarian relations in Assam. |
| 1948 | Establishment of Gauhati University. |

| | |
|---|---|
| 1949 | The Mizo Union launched the 'civil disobedience movement'. |
| 1950 | The Government of India enacted the Immigrants (Expulsion from Assam) Act to expel unauthorized migrants from Pakistan into Assam. |
| 1950 | An earthquake of 8.6 in the Richter scale jolted Assam and its neighborhood on 15 August, which reconfigured Assam's topography significantly. |
| 1951–59 | The Anti Famine Campaign Organisation was formed, which finally metamorphosed into the Mizo National Famine Front with a demand for Mizo self-determination. |
| 1952 | Elections held for Naga, Lushai, Mikir, North Cachar, Garo, United Khasi and Jaintia Hill districts Autonomous Council. |
| 1952 | Establishment of the Bodo Sahitya Sabha. |
| 1954 | The Government of Assam enacted the Assam Rhinoceros Preservation Act. The North East Frontier Tract became the North East Frontier Agency, more commonly known as NEFA. |
| 1956 | The enactment of the Assam Fixation of Ceiling on Land Holdings Act, 1956. |
| 1956–57 | Widespread and popular movement demanding the establishment of an oil refinery in Assam. |
| 1957–63 | Separation of the Naga Hills District from Assam administration and the formation of Nagaland. |
| 1959 | The Assam Oil Company formed Oil India Limited to explore oil in Assam. |
| 1958–61 | A famine, known as Mautam, gripped the Mizo hills. Famine in Mizo hills. Birth of the Mizo National Front. |
| 1960–61 | Widespread popular agitation and communal riots as a result of the Assam Official Language Act of 1960. |
| 1961 | Bodo speakers declared Bodo as their mother tongue, indicating the simmering tension over the dominance of Assamese as the official language, followed by demand for the Roman script instead of Assamese. |
| 1962–66 | Implementation of Project PIP (Prevention of infiltration into India of Pakistani Nationals) by the Government of India in Assam and Tripura to deport illegal migrants from East Pakistan. Initiatives were taken to deport the so-called infiltrators from East Pakistan in Assam, followed by communal violence and migration on both sides of the border between India and East Pakistan. |
| 1962 | The Indo–China War and brief occupation of NEFA by China. Several key towns of NEFA fell to the Chinese after 18 October. China declared a unilateral ceasefire on 20 November. |

| | |
|---|---|
| 1962 | The Guwahati Refinery became functional. |
| 1963 | Prime Minister Nehru proposed a structure of autonomy, akin to the Scottish pattern of administration, for Assam's hill districts, though the plan was dropped eventually. |
| 1963 | Completion of the construction of a pipeline to transport crude oil from oilfields in Upper Assam to the refinery in Barauni. |
| 1965 | The Government of India formed a commission, led by Hari Vinayak Pataskar, lawyer and former vice chancellor of the University of Poona, to examine the economic and political situation of Assam's hill areas and to study the question of autonomy to the hill districts of Assam which submitted its report in 1966. |
| 1965 | The trade route between Assam and Calcutta through East Pakistan was disrupted by the Indo–Pak War. Steamer service through the river Brahmaputra came to an end. First master plan for the Guwahati city drawn. |
| 1967 | A committee headed by Ashok Mehta, formed by the Union government, rejected a proposal for federal reorganisation of Assam, and proposed more bureaucratic autonomy for Assam's hill districts. |
| 1966–67 | Food crisis in several parts of Assam due to crop failures and low government stocks of grains. |
| 1966–68 | Formation of the Plain Tribals Council of Assam, which later put forth a demand for the creation of an autonomous region, despite brutal crackdowns by the Assam government. |
| 1966 | Mizo rebels, who had spearheaded a movement for separation of the Mizo Hills from India, launched an armed attack on Aizawl and its neighbourhood. This was followed by the Indian military retaliating against Mizo rebels. |
| 1967 | Formation of the All Assam Students' Union (AASU) and All Bodo Students Union (ABSU). Assam's hill leaders, under the banner of the All Party Hill Leaders Conference, intensified a demand for a separate state by carving out the hill districts of Assam. |
| 1967 | In the election held for the legislative assembly, the Congress's vote share declined by 5 per cent from that of the 1962 election. |
| 1968 | Prime Minister Indira Gandhi proposed the creation of an autonomous state within the state of Assam with two districts: Khasi and Jaintia and Garo hills. There was widespread violence in Guwahati on 26 January in protest against Mrs Gandhi's plan to reorganize Assam. |
| 1969–70 | Archeological excavations in Ambari, Guwahati, leading to a major discovery of antiquities. |

| | |
|---|---|
| 1970 | Death of Chief Minister Bimala Prasad Chaliha and the formation of a new Assam government led by Mahendra Mohan Chaudhury. Establishment of the first Tea Auction Centre in Guwahati. A popular movement demanding establishment of another oil refinery in Assam. A refinery-cum-petrochemical complex was established in the western part of Assam. |
| 1971–73 | Enactment of the Assam (Temporary Settled Areas) Tenancy Act of 1971. Its implementation, after 1973, led to widespread dissatisfaction among the rich Assamese landowners. The upper limit of landholding was reduced further. |
| 1971 | The Government of India enacted the North Eastern Council Act. |
| 1971 | The Bangladesh War of Liberation led to massive inflows of refugees to Assam, Bengal and Tripura. |
| 1972–75 | The Union government decided to take over the procurement of food grains. This set off a series of crises, across the country and in Assam, including black marketing and price rise. Amid this, with a drought-like situation, Assam was on the verge of a food shortage. |
| 1972 | Gauhati University, followed by Dibrugarh University, announced that Assamese will be the medium of instruction in Assam's colleges and university classes. This led to widespread opposition. Cachar, Assam's southernmost district, was rocked by protests against this policy. Violence across Assam on the issue of language. |
| 1972 | Prime Minister Mrs Gandhi started choosing her own chief ministerial candidates instead of state party-elected candidates. Sarat Chandra Sinha became Assam's chief minister. |
| 1972 | Birth of the state of Meghalaya; shifting of Assam's capital from Shillong to Guwahati. |
| 1974–75 | Fresh wave of migration of the destitute from Bangladesh to Assam and its neighbouring states due to famine in northern Bangladesh caused by floods, cyclones and damage of crops. Hunger and famine-like situation in various parts of Assam. The food crisis led to the rise and consolidation of oppositional politics. Students took to the streets; protests spilled from urban to rural areas; and college teachers were on strike. |
| 1974 | Popular movement demanding the Roman script for the Bodo language. NEFA's administrative headquarter was shifted from Shillong to Itanagar. |
| 1975–77 | Years of National Emergency in India, which impacted political life in Assam. A large number of people had to undergo forced sterilization. These years were marked by arrests of political leaders |

|      |      |
|------|------|
|      | and others opposed to the Emergency, agitations among tea garden workers and evictions of tribal and Muslim settlers. |
| 1978 | The first non-Congress government in Assam led by the Janata Party between March 1978 and December 1979; tenancy and land reforms; increasing opposition of Assamese landowners to the Congress party. |
| 1978–89 | Increasing institutional support to increase non-plantation tea cultivation; the Assam government rolled out financial aid to unemployed youth to pave way for rise of small entrepreneurs in the tea industry. |
| 1979 | Announcement for a by-election for a parliamentary constituency and revision of the draft electoral roll, which led to several complaints on names; formation of the Assam Gana Sangram Parishad; wave of protests led by AASU; violent clashes at the Assam–Nagaland border over claims on agricultural lands; no-confidence vote passed against chief minister Golap Borbora. Formation of the United Liberation Front of Asom (ULFA), which demanded an independent sovereign Assam. |
| 1980–81 | Communal polarization deepened and led to incidents of violence in several areas; supply of crude oil from Assam repeatedly halted as a means of political resistance; formation of the All Assam Minorities Students' Union (AAMSU); increased polarization among tribal groups led by students' unions against the dominant narrative of the Assamese nationalist leadership; President's Rule imposed; Armed Forces Special Powers Act of 1958 was imposed in April 1980. |
| 1982 | New environmentalism around rhinoceros amid translocation of rhinoceros from Assam to another Indian state amid local opposition. |
| 1983 | Failure of negotiations between the Government of India and leaders of the Assam movement; announcement of election to the Assam Legislative Assembly in February; popular resistance against election; widespread violence and communal riots; communal riots took place in various parts of Assam. |
| 1984 | Return of communal violence and rioting after a brief break; Mrs Gandhi's assassination and Rajiv Gandhi assumed power as prime minister; negotiations resumed with the leaders of the Assam movement and Government of India. |
| 1985 | End of the Assam agitation and signing of the Assam Accord on 15 August; non-Congress government during December 1985–November 1990 led by the newly formed Asom Gana Parishad. |

| | |
|---|---|
| 1986 | Assamese was introduced as the compulsory language for school education, which was followed by protests and opposition from tribal populations and the Bengali-speaking in southern Assam. A brief spell of malaria epidemic. |
| 1987 | Demand of a separate homeland by All Bodo Students Union (ABSU); increasing popular mobilization demanding a separate state called Bodoland; followed by strikes and violence; increasing political mobilization of ethnic communities. |
| 1990 | The Government of India enhanced oil royalty; President's Rule for the fourth time; Assam was declared a 'Disturbed Area', Armed Forces (Special Powers) Act of 1958 was invoked; ULFA was banned; Operation Bajrang against ULFA. |
| 1991 | Operation Rhino against ULFA. |
| 1993 | Enactment of Bodoland Autonomous Council, 1993 and formation of an interim Bodoland Autonomous Council. |
| 1989–99 | Forest Survey of India, based on satellite data from Landsat, reported increasing loss of forest coverage. |
| 2000 | Recognition of Sattriya as one of India's classical dance. |

# Assam: List of Premiers (1937–50) and Chief Ministers (1950–2001)

| | |
|---|---|
| 1 April 1937–5 February 1938 | Saiyid Muhammad Saadulla |
| 5 February 1938–20 September 1938 | Saiyid Muhammad Saadulla |
| 20 September 1938–17 November 1939 | Gopinath Bardoloi |
| 17 November 1939–25 December 1941 | Saiyid Muhammad Saadulla |
| 25 December 1941–25 August 1942 | Governor's regime |
| 25 August 1942–23 March 1945 | Governor's regime |
| 23 March 1945–11 February 1946 | Saiyid Muhammad Saadulla (care-taker government) |
| 11 February 1946–14 August 1947 | Gopinath Bardoloi |
| 14 August 1947—26 January 1950 | Gopinath Bardoloi |
| 26 January 1947—6 August 1950 | Gopinath Bardoloi |
| 9 August 1950—27 December 1957 | Bishnuram Medhi |
| 28 December 1957—6 November 1970 | Bimala Prasad Chaliha |
| 11 November 1970—30 January 1972 | Mahendra Mohan Chaudhury |
| 31 January 1972—12 March 1978 | Sarat Chandra Sinha |
| 12 March 1978–4 September 1979 | Golap Chandra Borbora |
| 9 September 1979–11 December 1979 | Jogendra Nath Hazarika |
| 12 December 1979–5 December 1980 | President's Rule in Assam |
| 6 December 1980–30 June 1981 | Syeda Anwara Taimur |
| 30 June 1981–13 January 1982 | President's Rule in Assam |
| 13 January 1982–9 March 1982 | Keshab Chandra Gogoi |
| 19 March 1982–27 February 1983 | President's Rule in Assam |
| 27 February 1983–23 December 1985 | Hiteswar Saikia |

| | |
|---|---|
| 24 December 1985–28 November 1990 | Prafulla Kumar Mahanta |
| 28 November 1990–30 June 1991 | President's Rule in Assam |
| 30 June 1991–22 April 1996 | Hiteswar Saikia |
| 22 April 1996–14 May 1996 | Bhumidhar Barman |
| 15 May 1996–17 May 2001 | Prafulla Kumar Mahanta |

# Abbreviations and Acronyms

| | |
|---|---|
| AAGSP | All Assam Gana Sangram Parisad |
| AASU | All Assam Students' Union |
| AAMSU | All Assam Minority Students' Union |
| ABSU | All Bodo Students Union |
| AICC | All India Congress Committee |
| AIR | All India Radio |
| *ALAD* | *Assam Legislative Assembly Debates*, Official Reports |
| AOC | Assam Oil Company |
| APAC | Asia, Pacific and Africa Collections, British Library, London |
| *APIRR* | Assam Police Intelligence Record Room, Kahilipara, Guwahati |
| ASA | Assam State Archives |
| APCC | Assam Pradesh Congress Committee |
| BCG | Bacille Calmette-Guerin, a vaccine for tuberculosis (TB) disease |
| BL | British Library |
| BOC | Burmah Shell |
| BGOI | British Government of India |
| CAD | Constituent Assembly of India Debates, |
| CPI | Communist Party of India |
| CSAS | Center of South Asian Studies, Cambridge University |
| CWC | Congress Working Committee |
| *CWMG* | *Collected Works of Mahatma Gandhi* (New Delhi: Government of India, 1958–94) |

| | |
|---|---|
| *DSR* | *Daily Situation Report*, Office of the Deputy Inspector General of Police, Special Branch, Assam, Kahilipara, Guwahati |
| EIC | British East India Company |
| *FR* | Chief Secretary or Governor's Fortnightly Report |
| GoA | Government of Assam |
| GoI | Government of India |
| GREF | General Reserve Engineer Force |
| IPTA | Indian People's Theatre Association |
| ITA | Indian Tea Association |
| JASB | *Journal of Asiatic Society of Bengal* |
| JUH | Jamiat Ulema-e-Hind |
| KAS | Kamarupa Anusandhan Samiti |
| Lok Sabha Debates | *Lok Sabha Debates*, Official Reports |
| MP | Member of Parliament |
| NAI | National Archives of India, New Delhi |
| NEFA | North-Eastern Frontier Agency |
| NMML | Nehru Memorial Museum and Library, New Delhi |
| NNC | Naga National Council |
| NWFP | North-West Frontier Province |
| NYT | *New York Times* |
| OIL | Oil India Limited |
| PDS | Public Distribution System |
| PHA | *Political History of Assam* |
| PSP | Praja Socialist Party |
| PTCA | Plains Tribes Council of Assam |
| Rajya Sabha Debates | *Rajya Sabha Debates*, Official Reports, |
| RCPI | Revolutionary Communist Party of India |
| RSS | Rashtriya Swayamsevak Sangh |
| SWJN | *Selected Works of Jawaharlal Nehru*, Series 1 and 2 (New Delhi: Jawaharlal Nehru Memorial Fund, 1972–2019) |
| TOI | *Times of India* |
| TOP | *Constitutional Relations Between Britain and India: The Transfer of Power, 1942–47* in 12 vols (London: H.M.S.O., 1970–83). |
| Towards Freedom | *Towards Freedom: Documents on the Movement for Independence in India* (New Delhi: Oxford University Press, 1985–2010), 11 vols. |
| ULFA | United Liberation Front of Asom |
| UMF | United Minority Front |
| URMCA | United Revolutionary Minority Council of Assam |

# Notes

## Prologue

1. Sankardeva, 'Bhagavata: Adi-dasama', in *Sri Sankar Bakyamrita,* ed. Harinaryan Dutta Baruah (Nalbari, Assam: Dutta-Baruah, 1953), 65–68.
2. Bibha Bharali and Banani Chakravarty, eds, *The Languages of Assam: People's Linguistic Survey of India,* vol. 5, part II (Delhi: Orient Blackswan, 2017).
3. For an overview of these rebellions, see, John F. Michell, *The North-East Frontier of India: A Topographical, Political, and Military Report* (Calcutta: Government Printing, 1883); Alexander Mackenzie, *History of the Relations of the Government with the Hill Tribes of the North-East Frontier of Bengal* (Calcutta: Home Department Press, 1884); Richard Gott, *Britain's Empire: Resistance, Repression and Revolt* (London: Verso, 2011).
4. Gunnel Cederlöf, *Founding an Empire on India's North-Eastern Frontiers, 1790–1840: Climate, Commerce, Polity* (Delhi: Oxford University Press, 2013).
5. Captain Francis Jenkins, *Journal of a Tour in Upper Assam, 1838* (MS 95073, Special Collection, School of Oriental and African Studies, University of London), Entry for 10 March 1938.
6. Edward Gait, *A History of Assam* (Calcutta: Thacker, Spink & Co. 1906), 294.
7. Maniram Dewan, *Buranji Vivek-Ratna,* vol. 2 (1838), ed. Nagen Saikia (Dibrugarh: Dibrugarh University, 2002), 224.
8. Gait, *A History of Assam,* 346; Umakanta Duara, 'Maniram Dewan', *Awahan,* vol. 4, ed. Paramananda Majumdar (Guwahati: Publication Board Assam, 2015), 986.

9. 'Tea is the favourite beverage of these tribes and is constantly drunk by them,' wrote John M'Cosh, a medical practitioner employed with the EIC, in 1837. John M'Cosh, *Topography of Assam* (Calcutta: Bengal Military Orphan Press, 1837), 31–32. Also, 'Tea has long been the favourite beverage of the hill tribes, in whose vicinity the shrub is found. The Singphoos have long known and drunk it.' Anyonymous, 'Assam', *Church Missionary Intelligencer*, vol. 1, no. 13 (May 1850), 293.

10. C.A. Bruce, *Report on the Manufacture of Tea, and on the Extent and Produce of the Tea Plantations in Assam* (Calcutta: Bishop's College Press, 1839), 499.

11. In 1836, Purandar Singha wrote to Adam White, political agent to the Bengal government in Assam, how in the event of a tea garden being established in his country, his 'people will learn the process of tea plantation and thus a handsome profit will result to' him. 'Letter from Purandar to White, 13 April, Home Department, Revenue Proceedings, 23 May 1836, nos 2–4', in *Maniram Dewan and the Contemporary Assamese Society*, A.K. Dutta (Jorhat: Anupoma Dutta, 1990), 95.

12. 'Letter from F. Jenkins to N. Wallich, 5 May 1836', *Copy of Papers Received from India Relating to the Measures Adopted for Introducing the Cultivation of Tea Plant in British Possessions in India*, no. 157 (London: His Majesty's Stationery Office, 1839), 70–71.

13. *Further Papers Regarding the Promotion of Tea Cultivation in Upper Assam*, vol. 2, IOR/F/4/1709/69024, September 1837–February 1838, 5 (India Office Records and Private Papers, Asia, Pacific and Africa Collections, British Library).

14. The Singpho Chief Ningroola was one of the first natives from Assam to establish a tea garden; he sold products in the Calcutta market in 1840. (Dutta, *Maniram Dewan and the Contemporary Assamese Society*, 110–11.)

15. Namrata Borkotoky, 'Brewing Trouble or Transforming Nature? Making of Tea Plantations' Environments in Assam' (PhD diss., Indian Institute of Technology, Guwahati, 2021), 50.

16. East India Company, *Statement Exhibiting the Moral and Material Progress and Condition of India during the Year 1859–60*, part II (London: Her Majesty's Stationery Office, 1861), 60.

17. Borkotoky, 'Brewing Trouble or Transforming Nature? Making of Tea Plantations' Environments in Assam', 83.

18. Arupjyoti Saikia, 'Imperialism, Geology and Petroleum: History of Oil in Colonial Assam', *Economic & Political Weekly*, vol. 46, no. 12 (19 March 2011), 48–55; Ditee Moni Baruah, 'Polity and Petroleum: Making of an Oil

Industry in Assam, 1825–1980' (PhD diss., Indian Institute of Technology Guwahati, 2014), 102–09.
19. Historian Amalendu Guha had evaluated that between 1881 and 1901, an estimated Rs 200 million, approximately 15–20 per cent of Assam's income, was invested in the organized sector of the economy in the Brahmaputra Valley of Assam. Amalendu Guha, 'A Big Push Without a Take-off: A Case-Study of Assam, 1871–1901', *Indian Economic and Social History Review*, vol. 5, no. 3 (1968), 204.
20. Tirthankar Roy, *The Economic History of India, 1857–1947* (Delhi: Oxford University Press, 2012), 276.
21. Amalendu Guha, *Planter-Raj to Swaraj: Freedom Struggle and Electoral Politics in Assam, 1826–1947* (Delhi: Indian Council of Historical Research, 1977), Appendix 16, 298.
22. See, for instance, H.K. Barpujari, *North-East India: Problems, Policies, and Prospects since Independence* (Guwahati: Spectrum Publications, 1998); Sanjib Barua, *India against Itself: Assam and the Politics of Nationality* (Philadelphia: University of Pennsylvania Press, 1999); Udayon Misra, *Burden of History: Assam and the Partition—Unresolved Issues* (New Delhi: Oxford University Press, 2017); Yasmin Saikia, *Fragmented Memories: Struggling to Be Tai-Ahom in India* (Durham, N.C.: Duke University Press, 2004); Sangeeta Barua Pisharoty, *Assam: The Accord, the Discord* (Delhi: Penguin, 2019); Mrinal Talukdar, *Assam after Independence* (Guwahati: Nanda Talukdar Foundation, 2017); Uddipana Goswami, *Conflict and Reconciliation: The Politics of Ethnicity in Assam* (Delhi: Routledge, 2014); Sandhya Goswami, *Assam Politics in Post-Congress Era: 1985 and Beyond* (Delhi: Sage Publications, 2020); Monoj Kumar Nath, *The Muslim Question in Assam and Northeast India* (Delhi: Routledge, 2021); Akhil Ranjan Dutta, *Hindutva Regime in Assam: Saffron in the Rainbow* (Delhi: Sage Publications, 2021); Nani Gopal Mahanta, *Confronting the State: ULFA's Quest for Sovereignty* (Delhi: Sage Publications, 2013); Samir Kumar Das, *ULFA: United Liberation Front of Assam: A Political Analysis* (Delhi: Ajanta Publications, 1994); Udayon Misra, *The Periphery Strikes Back: Challenges to the Nation-State in Assam and Nagaland* (Shimla: Indian Institute of Advanced Studies, 2000); Mrinal Talukdar and Kishore Kumar Kalita, *Assam (1945–2020)*, vols 1–7 (Guwahati: Nanda Talukdar Foundation, 2014); Pahi Saikia, *Ethnic Mobilisation and Violence in Northeast India* (Delhi: Routledge, 2011). While not exhaustive, this list demonstrates the increasing importance of studying Assam and its post-colonial journey.
23. See *Further Readings on Assam before 1947* in the Bibliography.

## Chapter 1: The Empire in Disarray

1. Nicholas Mansergh, E.W.R. Lumby and Penderel Moon, eds, *Constitutional Relations Between Britain and India: The Transfer of Power, 1942–47* in 12 vols (hereafter *TOP*) (London: H.M.S.O., 1970–82); Bipan Chandra, ed., *Towards Freedom: Documents on the Movement for Independence in India, 1942* (New Delhi: Indian Council of Historical Research, 2016); Partha Sarathi Gupta, ed., *Towards Freedom: Documents on the Movement for Independence in India, 1943–1944* (Delhi: Oxford University Press, 1997); Bimal Prasad, ed., *Towards Freedom: Documents on the Movement for Independence in India, 1945* (New Delhi: Oxford University Press, 2008); Sumit Sarkar, ed., *Towards Freedom: Documents on the Movement for Independence in India, 1946* (New Delhi: Oxford University Press, 2007); Sucheta Mahajan, ed., *Towards Freedom: Documents on the Movement for Independence in India, 1947*, part I and II (New Delhi: Oxford University Press, 2013–15).
2. Percival Griffiths, *History of the Indian Tea Industry* (London: Weidenfeld & Nicolson, 1967), 174.
3. Angus MacSwan, 'Victory over Japanese at Kohima named Britain's Greatest Battle', Reuters, 21 April 2013, https://www.reuters.com/article/britain-kohima-imphal-nagaland-manipur-w-idINDEE93K04W20130421 (Accessed 2 February 2023).
4. Birendra Kumar Bhattacharya, *Yaruingam* (Guwahati: Lawyer's Book Stall, 1960); Debendranath Acharya, *Jangam* (Guwahati: Publication Board Assam, 1982); Jogesh Das, *Dawar aru Nai* [Clouds Have Gone] (Guwahati: Lawyer's Book Stall, 1955).
5. Srinath Raghavan, *India's War: The Making of Modern South Asia, 1939–1945* (New Delhi: Penguin, 2016), 196–98; Christopher Bayly and Tim Harper, *Forgotten Armies: Britain's Asian Empire and the War with Japan* (London: Penguin, 2005).
6. Sunil S. Amrith, *Crossing the Bay of Bengal: The Furies of Nature and Fortune of Migrants* (Massachusetts: Harvard University Press, 2013), 187–88; *Times of India*, 11 June 1941, 5.
7. Ursula Graham Bower, *Naga Path* (London: John Murray, 1952), 150.
8. Bayly and Harper, *Forgotten Armies: Britain's Asian Empire and the War with Japan*, 268.
9. Gunnel Cederlof, *Founding an Empire on India's North-Eastern Frontiers, 1790–1840: Climate, Commerce, Polity* (New Delhi: Oxford University Press, 2014); Indrani Chatterjee, *Forgotten Friends: Monks, Marriages, and Memories of Northeast India* (New Delhi: Oxford University Press, 2013).

10. Bérénice Guyot-Réchard, 'When Legions Thunder Past: The Second World War and India's Northeastern Frontier', *War in History*, vol. 25, no. 3 (July 2018), 1–33.
11. Raghavan, *India's War: The Making of Modern South Asia, 1939–1945*, 207.
12. Theodore Harold White, ed., *Stilwell Papers: An Iconoclastic Account of America's Adventures in China* (New York: Schocken, 1972), 43.
13. For a description of these routes, see Hugh Tinker, 'A Forgotten Long March: The Indian Exodus', *Journal of Southeast Asian Studies*, vol. 6, no. 1 (March 1975), 1–15; Stephanie Ramamurthy, 'Remembering Burma: Tamil Migrants & Memories' (MPhil dissertation, School of Oriental and African Studies, University of London, 1994), 126–30. Also, Guyot-Réchard, 'When Legions Thunder Past: The Second World War and India's Northeastern Frontier'.
14. R.H. Gribble, *Out of the Burma Night: Being the Story of a Fantastic Journey through the Wilderness of the Hukawng Valley and the Forest Clad Mountains of the Naga Tribes People at the Time of the Japanese Invasion of Burma* (Calcutta: Thacker, Spink & Co., 1944), 22.
15. Ibid.; 'Comments, Notes and Criticisms of Evacuation Scheme: Tamu via Mintha, Narum, Sita, Namtok, Heirok, Wangjing, Imphal and Tamu, Waksu, Lumlong, Sita, Etc.', *V.C. Whyte Papers*, Cambridge South Asian Archives, Centre of South Asian Studies, University of Cambridge, 9.
16. Bayly and Harper, *Forgotten Armies: Britain's Asian Empire and the War with Japan*, 183.
17. For an illustrative map about routes to Assam and Manipur, see Geoffrey Tyson, *Forgotten Frontier* (Calcutta: W.H. Targett, 1945), 21.
18. *Times of India*, 14 July 1942, 5; For an insightful estimation of various numbers, details of refugees' backgrounds, etc., see Michael D. Leigh, *The Evacuation of Civilians from Burma: Analysing the 1942 Colonial Disaster* (London: Bloomsbury, 2014); E. Wood, *Report on the Evacuation of Refugees from Burma to India (Assam) January–July 1942* (Calcutta: Government of India Press, 1942).
19. The lowest figure is 4,50,000 (estimated by H. Tinker in 1975). Tinker, 'A Forgotten Long March: The Indian Exodus'.
20. Archibald Wavell, 'Preface', in *Forgotten Frontier*, Tyson.
21. Acharya, *Jangam*. For an English translation, see Amit R. Baishya, *Jangam: The Movement, a Forgotten Exodus in which Thousands Died* (New Delhi: Vitasta, 2018).
22. *The Times*, 4 December 1942, 5.
23. Robert Reid, *Years of Change in Bengal and Assam* (London: Ernest Benn, 1966), 156.

24. 'Refugees from Burma: Fine work of Indian Navy', *The Times*, 8 May 1942, 3.
25. Reid, *Years of Change in Bengal and Assam*, 158.
26. C.A. Bayly, 'The Nation Within: British India at War 1939–1947', *Proceedings of the British Academy*, vol. 125, (2004), 265–85.
27. Guyot-Réchard, 'When Legions Thunder Past: The Second World War and India's Northeastern Frontier', 8.
28. Ernest Wood, *Report on the Evacuation of Refugees from Burma to India (Assam) January–July 1942*, 28.
29. Ramamurthy, 'Remembering Burma: Tamil Migrants & Memories', 136.
30. Sumit Sarkar, 'Popular Movements and National Leadership, 1945–47', *Economic & Political Weekly*, vol. 17, nos 14–16 (April 1982); B.R. Tomlinson, *The Economy of Modern India* (New Delhi: Oxford University Press, 1993),135–36, also 136n4.
31. Yasmin Khan, *The Raj at War: A People's History of India's Second World War* (London: Bodley Head, 2015), 105–06.
32. Bayly and Harper, *Forgotten Armies: Britain's Asian Empire and the War with Japan*, 186.
33. *Jugantar*, 7 May 1942, 2.
34. Purnakanta Buragohain, *Patkair Sipare No Bochar* (Nine Years Beyond the Patkai) (Dhemaji: Purbanchal Tai Sahitya Sabha, 1993).
35. Khan, *The Raj at War: A People's History of India's Second World War*, 101–102.
36. Government of India, *District Calendar of Events of the Congress Disturbances in Assam (August 1942–March 1943)* (New Delhi: Government of India Press, 1943).
37. Quoted in Bayly and Harper, *Forgotten Armies: Britain's Asian Empire and the War with Japan*, 250.
38. *Times of India*, 15 December 1941, 8.
39. *Times of India*, 21 March 1942, 7.
40. Bayly, 'The Nation Within: British India at War 1939–1947', 268.
41. *Times of India*, 16 June 1942, 5.
42. *Times of India*, 30 May 1942, 7.
43. Dinanath Gopal Tendulkar, *Mahatma: Life of Mohandas Karamchand Gandhi*, vol. 6 (New Delhi: Publications Division, Government of India, 1953), 170; Penderel Moon, *Gandhi and Modern India* (New York: Norton, 1969), 231.
44. Confidential, Chief Secretary to the Government of Assam's Fortnightly Report (hereafter *FR*), 1st half, August 1942; Mahendranath Hazarika, *Biyalisher Biplobot Nagaon* (Guwahati: Publication Board Assam, 1977); Ila Barua, *Bidrohi Asam* (Nagaon: Bijay Prakash Bhawan, 1946); Harendranath

Barua, ed., *Bharatar Mukti Jujat Asam* (Guwahati: Asam Rajyik Mukti Yujaru Abhibartan, 1972); Purna Chandra Sarma, *Mor Ateet Sowarani aru Nagaon Jilat Mukti Sangram* (Nagaon: Sarma Prakash Bhavan, 2022 [1973]).
45. Anil Kumar Sharma, *Quit India Movement in Assam* (Delhi: Mittal Publications, 2007), 69.
46. *FR*, 2nd half, January 1943.
47. Percival Joseph Griffiths, *History of the Joint Steamer Companies* (London: Inchcape & Co. Ltd, 1979), 86.
48. Arun Chandra Bhuyan, *The Quit India Movement: The Second World War and Indian Nationalism* (New Delhi: Manas Publications, 1975), 77; Barua, *Bidrohi Asam*, 29.
49. Birendra Kumar Bhattacharya, *Mrityunjay* (Guwahati: Sahitya Prakash, 1970).
50. Jyotiprasad Agarwala, 'Biyalishor Kahini', in *Jyotiprasad Rachanavali*, ed. Hiren Gohain (Guwahati: Publication Board Assam, 2003), 540–42.
51. Arun Chandra Bhuyan and Sibopada De, eds, *Political History of Assam 1940–47*, vol. 3 (Guwahati: Publication Board Assam, 1999).
52. *FR*, 1st half, 1 November 1942; *Times of India*, 6 December 1945, 7; Griffiths, *History of the Indian Tea Industry*, 385; Rana Pratap Behal, 'Power Structure, Discipline, and Labour in Assam Tea Plantations under Colonial Rule', *International Review of Social History*, vol. 51 (2006), Supplement, 154; Dattatraya Vaman Rege, *Report on an Enquiry into Conditions of Labour in Plantations in India* (Calcutta: Government of India, 1946), 71–72.
53. Bhuyan and De, eds, *Political History of Assam*, vol. 3, 68.
54. Ibid., 69.
55. *FR*, 1st half, November 1943.
56. *FR*, 2nd half, January 1943.
57. Gupta, *Towards Freedom: Documents on the Movement for Independence in India, 1943–1944,* Part 1, 718–19.
58. For details of women's participation and leadership, see Dipti Sharma, *Assamese Women in the Freedom Struggle* (Calcutta: Punthi-Pustak, 1993).
59. *FR*, 1st half, November 1942.
60. Secret Memo No. 1642–C, S.P., Nowgong to DIG, Assam, 28 April 1943, File no.C-6 (10) I of 1943, Special Branch, Assam State Archives (ASA).
61. Bhuyan and De, eds, *Political History of Assam*, vol. 3, 89.
62. 'The Assam Debt Conciliation (Amendment) Bill 1942', in File no. Education and Health_Agriculture_1942_Na_F-1-51_42A, Abhilekh Patal, National Archives of India (NAI).
63. *FR*, 1st half, November 1942; *FR*, 1st half, 1943, 'The District Was Hardly Affected by the Troubles Last Autumn.'

64. 'The Communal situation', secret, 6 January 1943, in *Note on the Communal Situation in India Prepared in the IB Showing Reason for the Absence of Communal Riots during the Year 1942*, Home, Political (Internal), File no. 5/3, 1943, Abhilekh Patal, NAI.
65. *FR*, 1st half, November 1942.
66. 'Letter from H.G. Dennehy, Chief Secretary, Assam to the Secretary, Government of India, Home Department, 11 November, 1942', in *Congress Civil Disobedience Movement 1942–43, Measures to Revival of the Movements*, File no. F-3/2/43, Poll (I), Home Department, Government of India, Abhilekh Patal, NAI.
67. Bhuyan and De, eds, *Political History of Assam*, vol. 3, 105.
68. 'Letter from P.C. Joshi of the CPI Forwarding Memoranda about the Activities of the Communist Party in the Provinces', File no. 7/15/42, Poll (i) KW I, Home Department, Abhilekh Patal, NAI.
69. 'Memo on Our Political-Practical Activity in Assam Valley since August 9', in *Letter from P.C. Joshi of the CPI Forwarding Memoranda about the Activities of the Communist Party in the Provinces*, File no. 7/15/42 Poll (i) KW I, Home Department, Abhilekh Patal, NAI.
70. Amalendu Guha, *Planter Raj to Swaraj: Freedom Struggle & Electoral Politics in Assam 1826–1947* (Delhi: Indian Council of Historical Research, 1977), 224; Arupjyoti Saikia, *A Century of Protests: Peasant Politics in Assam since 1900* (Delhi: Routledge, 2014), 147–48.
71. Gupta, *Towards Freedom: Documents on the Movement for Independence in India, 1943–1944,* Part 1, 53–54.
72. *FR*, 2nd half, December 1943; Bhuyan and De, eds, *Political History of Assam*, vol. 3, 84–87.
73. For details of the police brutalities in different parts of Assam during August and December 1942, see *Situation Reports on the Congress Movement*, File no. 3/16/42–Poll, Political (internal), Home Department, Government of India, 1942, Abhilekh Patal, NAI.
74. Hem Barua, *August Revolution in Assam* (Guwahati: Anu Barua, 1978), 4–9; *Times of India*, 3 September 1942, 5.
75. Dambarudhar Nath, *Satra Society and Culture: Pitambardeva Goswami and History of Garamur Satra* (Guwahati: DVS Publishers, 2012).
76. Tendulkar, *Mahatma: Life of Mohandas Karamchand Gandhi*, vol. 6, 171.
77. Sagar Boruah, 'Profile of a Unique Personality: Pitambar Deva Goswami and His Socio-Political Stance', *Proceedings of the Indian History Congress*, vol. 66 (2005), 842.
78. Keshab Narayan Dutt, *Landmarks of the Freedom Struggle in Assam* (Guwahati: Lawyer's Book Stall, 1958), 107.

79. 'Letter from H.G. Dennehy, Chief Secretary, Assam, to Secretary, Government of India, Home Department, 21 April 1943', in *Proposed Detention Outside Assam of the Satradhikar Goswami of Garamur, Assam, under Defence of India Rule 26 on Account of His Activities Connected with the Congress Civil Disobedience Movement 1942–43*, File no. 44/26/43-Poll (I), Home Department, Government of India, Abhilekh Patal, NAI.
80. *Times of India*, 5 October 1942, 9.
81. Dutt, *Landmarks of the Freedom Struggle in Assam*, 97.
82. Memo of Chief Secretary, Assam, to all Deputy Commissioners, no. C 75/42/58, 4 January 1943 and C/253/92/311, 15 March 1943, ASA, in *Political History of Assam*, vol. 3, eds, Bhuyan and De, 111fn162.
83. 'Letter from H.G. Dennehy, Chief Secretary, Assam, to Secretary, GoI, Home Department, Shillong, 17 June 1943', in *Towards Freedom: Documents on the Movement for Independence in India, 1943–1944*, Part 1, ed., Gupta, 391–92.
84. *FR*, 1st half, November 1942.
85. 'Letter from H.G. Dennehy, Chief Secretary, Assam, to Deputy Commissioner, K & H Hills, Shillong, 8 June 1943', in *Towards Freedom: Documents on the Movement for Independence in India, 1943–1944*, Part 1, ed., Gupta, 382–84.
86. Gupta, ed. *Towards Freedom: Documents on the Movement for Independence in India, 1943–1944*, Part 1, 816.
87. Bhuyan and De, eds, *Political History of Assam*, vol. 3, 131fn223.
88. Louis Mountbatten and Alan Brooke, 'The Strategy of the South-East Asia Campaign', *Royal United Services Institution Journal*, vol. 91, no. 564 (1946), 469–84.
89. Charles F. Romanus and Riley Sunderland, *United States Army in World War II: China–Burma–India Theater: Stilwell's Command Problems*, vol. 2, pt 9 (Washington, D.C.: Center of Military History, United States Army, 1987), 11.
90. Griffiths, *History of the Joint Steamer Companies*, 83.
91. Secret Station List of US Army Forces in India, 1 July 1942, L/WS/1/1292, Asia, Pacific and Africa Collections, BL, in 'British Military Information Management Techniques and the South Asian Soldier: Eastern India During Second World War', *Modern Asian Studies*, vol. 34, no. 2 (May 2000), Sanjoy Bhattacharya, 499.
92. Frank Owen, *The Campaign in Burma* (London: Central Office of Information, 1946), in 'When Legions Thunder Past: The Second World War and India's Northeastern Frontier', Guyot-Réchard, 1–33.
93. Owen, *The Campaign in Burma*.

94. Graham Dunlop, *Military Economics, Culture and Logistics in the Burma Campaign, 1942–1945* (London: Routledge, 2009), 113.
95. Ditee Moni Baruah, 'Polity and Petroleum Making of an Oil Industry in Assam, 1825–1980' (PhD diss., Indian Institute of Technology, Guwahati, 2014), 161.
96. United States of America, *Congressional Records, Proceedings and Debates of the 79th Congress*, first session, vol. 91, part 1 (13 February 1945), 1059–60.
97. Dunlop, *Military Economics, Culture and Logistics in the Burma Campaign, 1942–1945*, 100.
98. *New York Times*, 4 May 1944, 266.
99. Arupjyoti Saikia, *The Unquiet River: A Biography of the Brahmaputra* (New Delhi: Oxford University Press, 2019).
100. Romanus and Sunderland, *United States Army in World War II: China–Burma–India Theatre: Stilwell's Command Problems*, vol. 2, 271.
101. Guyot-Réchard, 'When Legions Thunder Past: The Second World War and India's Northeastern Frontier', 1–33.
102. 'India's Eastern Wall: Preparation of new defences in Assam, man-power from the tea gardens', *The Times*, 6 June 1942, 5.
103. A.H. Pilcher, 'Navies to the 14th Army, 1947', Mss Eur F174/1316 (Asia and Africa Collection, British Library); Hinson Allan Antrobus, *A History of the Assam Company, 1839–1953* (Edinburg: T. and A. Constable, 1957), 229; W.R. Gawthrop, *The Story of the Assam Railways and Trading Company Limited, 1881–1951* (London: Harley Publishing Company for the Assam Railways and Trading Company Limited, 1951), 54.
104. Joe G. Taylor, *Air Supply in the Burma Campaigns* (Alabama: USAF Historical Studies, 1957).
105. *Dainik Assamiya*, 21 August 1946, 1.
106. Dunlop, *Military Economics, Culture and Logistics in the Burma Campaign, 1942–1945*, 55–56.
107. *New York Times*, 25 January 1942, 27.
108. Editorial, 'Welcome signs', *Times of India*, 20 April 1944, 4.
109. *Jugantar*, 7 May 1942, 3.
110. Guyot-Réchard, 'When Legions Thunder Past: The Second World War and India's Northeastern Frontier'.
111. Padmanath Borthakur, *Swadhinata Ranar Sangsparsat* (Dibrugarh: Kaustabh Prakasan, 2006), 198.
112. Bhattacharya, 'British Military Information Management Techniques and the South Asian Soldier: Eastern India during the Second World War', 487.
113. *Times of India*, 2 February 1942, 9; Guyot-Réchard, 'When Legions Thunder Past: The Second World War and India's Northeastern Frontier', 11; *Times of India*, 15 October 1945, 6. This system continued till 1945.

114. Raghavan, *India's War: The Making of Modern South Asia, 1939–1945*, 413–16.
115. *Times of India*, 3 April 1944, 5.
116. *Times of India*, 20 April 1944, 6.
117. *FR*, 2nd half, December 1943.
118. Jelle J.P. Wouters, 'Difficult Decolonization: Debates, Divisions, and Deaths Within the Naga Uprising, 1944–1963', *Journal of North East India Studies*, vol. 9, no. 1 (January–June 2019), 5; Peter Steyn, *Zaphu Phizo: The Voice of the Nagas* (London: Kegan Paul, 2002), 54.
119. Asoso Yonuo, *The Rising Nagas: A Historical and Political Study* (Delhi: Vivek Publication House, 1974), 199; Gordon P. Means and Ingunn N. Means, 'Nagaland—The Agony of Ending a Guerrilla War', *Pacific Affairs*, vol. 39, no. 3/4 (1966), 290fn1.
120. Jangkhomang Guite, 'Representing Local Participation in INA–Japanese Imphal Campaign: The Case of the Kukis in Manipur, 1943–45', *Indian Historical Review*, vol. 37, no. 2 (December 2010), 291–309; Sonthang Haokip, 'Anglo Kuki Relations, 1777–1947 AD' (PhD diss., Manipur University, Manipur, 2011), 258.
121. 'No postponement of I.N.A. trials: Govt's reply to defence body', *Times of India*, 26 October 1945, 3.
122. For eyewitness accounts of the residents of the Naga Hills, see Wabang Moa, 'The Battle of Kohima As the Naga People Saw It', https://www.youtube.com/watch?v=ueM9JK1rhJQ (Accessed 23 May 2021).
123. *The Times*, 29 December 1944, 3.
124. *The Times*, 11 August 1944, 3.
125. William Slim, *Defeat into Victory* (Dehradun: Natraj Publishers, 2014), 334.
126. Tillman Durdin, 'Kohima battle crucial; Japanese forces can be cut off from elements in north', *New York Times*, 28 April 1944, 3.
127. 'Burma Monsoon', *New York Times*, 24 May 1944, 18; 'Monsoon Slows Up Myitkyina Seizure', *New York Times*, 23 May 1944, 1 and 10; 'Long Kohima Battle is seen', *New York Times*, 3 May 1944, 3.
128. For details on the composition of the British Indian Army in wartime, see Kaushik Roy, 'Expansion and Deployment of the Indian Army During World War II: 1939–45', *Journal of the Society for Army Historical Research*, vol. 88, no. 355 (2010), 248–68.
129. Robert Lyman, *Japan's Last Bid for Victory: The Invasion of India 1944* (Barnsley, South Yorkshire: Pen and Sword Military, 2011).
130. Bayly and Harper, *Forgotten Armies: Britain's Asian Empire and the War with Japan*, 388.
131. A.B. Bore, A Report on the Measures of Rehabilitation and Reconstruction undertaken by the Government of India in Naga Hills and Manipur State

in 1944 in order to Repair the Ravages Caused by the Japanese invasion of 1944, 1945, Mss Eur E325/19, Asia, Pacific and Africa Collections, British Library; Guyot-Réchard, 'When Legions Thunder Past: The Second World War and India's Northeastern Frontier', 21; Sima Saigal, *The Second World War and North East India: Shadows of Yesteryears* (New York: Routledge, 2022), 182–83.
132. Guyot-Réchard, 'When Legions Thunder Past: The Second World War and India's Northeastern Frontier', 9.
133. Letter from Secretary, Department of Commonwealth Relations, GoI to Secretary, GoA, No.F.10/44–EI, 28 August 1944, Rehabilitation of the dispossessed population of Manipur State and Naga Hills, Assam, File no. 216/CA (Secret), External Affairs, CA Branch, 1945, Abhilekh Patal, NAI; *Times of India*, 17 June 1944, 1.
134. Assam Relief Measures, Question by Rishang Keishing, *Lok Sabha Debates*, 17 April 1956, column 2392.
135. *FR*, 1st half, 1 February 1943.
136. Katoni Jakhalu, 'Provisional Finance in Assam: A Study of Imperial Provisional Financial Relations, 1874–1947' (PhD diss., North-Eastern Hill University, Shillong, 2001).
137. Reid, *Years of Change in Bengal and Assam*, 156.
138. Revenue receipt increased by 162 per cent, while expenditure increased by 102 per cent. Estimate based on Department of Commercial Intelligence and Statistics, India, *Statistical Abstract for British India 1937–38* (Delhi: Manager of Publications, 1940), Table 111, 280; Government of India, *Statistical Abstract for British India 1946–47* (Delhi: Manager of Publications, 1949), Table 93, Table 206.
139. Expert Committee on Financial Provisions, *Constituent Assembly Debates*, 5 December 1947, vol. VII, Appendix B, 58.
140. *FR*, 2nd half, December 1943.
141. *FR*, 1st half, November 1943.
142. Richard P. Tucker, 'Environmental Scars in Northeastern India and Burma', in *The Long Shadows: A Global Environmental History of the Second World War*, eds, Simo Laakkonen, Richard Tucker and Timo Vuorisalo (Corvallis: Oregon State University, 2017), 117–34.
143. A.V.A. Cant, 'Forestry in Assam', *Nature*, vol. 150, no. 440 (1942), 629.
144. Arupjyoti Saikia, *Forests and Ecological History of Assam, 1826–2000* (New Delhi: Oxford University Press, 2011).
145. Estimate based on Government of Assam, *Progress Report of Forest Administration in the Province of Assam for the Year 1944–45* (Shillong: Assam Government press, 1947).

146. Ibid.
147. 'Secret Note by P. Mason, Joint Secretary, War Department, 9 December 1944', *Question of the Control of the Movement of Foreigners on the Ledo Burma Road,* File no. 111/44, Home Political (External), 1944, NAI.
148. Tim Slessor, *First Overland: London to Singapore by Land Rover* (London: George G. Harrap and Co. Ltd, 1957), Chapter 11, 168–77.
149. Percival Joseph Griffiths, *The History of the Indian Tea Industry* (London: Weidenfeld & Nicolson, 1967), 203.
150. Antrobus, *A History of the Assam Company*, 227.
151. *FR*, 1st half, January 1943.
152. Antrobus, *A History of the Assam Company*, 234.
153. Nirode Kumar Barooah, ed., *Bardoloir Dinalekha: The Diary of Lokapriya Gopinath Bardoloi*, vol. 1, (Guwahati: Publication Board Assam, 2000), 71.
154. *FR*, 2nd half, November 1943.
155. *FR*, 1st half, February 1943, Para. 4, 1. For representative Assamese literary works, see Birendra Kumar Bhattacharya, *Ai* (Guwahati: Lawyer's Book Stall, 1960); Das, *Dawar aru Nai*; Shilabhadra, 'Madhupur Bahudur', in *Shilabhadrar Galpa Samagra: A Collection of Short Stories by Shilabhadra* (Guwahati: Banalata, 2007), 1–14.
156. *FR*, 1st half, February 1943; Anon, 'Judhat Amar Sahajog Kenekoi Bichara Hoi (How our services are secured in the war?)', *Sadiniya Bahni*, 30 July 1943 (Digital Archive, Centre for Assamese Studies, Tezpur University).
157. Hem Barua, 'Guwahati: 1944', in *Hem Baruar Kabita*, Hem Barua (Guwahati: Anwesha, 2014 [1945]), 126–28.
158. Estimate is based on *Assam Directory and Tea Areas Handbook*, 1943 and 1952 (ASA). Tea Board of India, *Assam Directory and Tea Areas Handbook*, 1943 (Calcutta: Tea Board of India, 1943); Tea Board of India, *The Assam Directory and Tea Areas Handbook*, 1952 (Calcutta: Tea Board of India, 1952); Rajendra Prasad, 'Untitled notes, 7 November, 1952', para 2, in *Note Recorded by the President Regarding Certain Problems Facing Assam*, File no. 159 (2)/52, 1952, President Secretariat, Abhilekh Patal, NAI; Also, Saigal, *The Second World War and North East India: Shadows of Yesteryears*, 194.
159. S.R. Deshpande, *Report on an Enquiry into Family Budgets of Industrial Workers in Gauhati, 1947* (Delhi: Manager of Publications, 1947), 1.
160. Antrobus, *A History of the Assam Company*, 237.
161. Letter from Deputy Superintendent of Police, Jorhat to DIG, Assam, Shillong, memo no. B/8571, 2 July 1945, 'Death of an Indian Woman on Account of Alleged Rape Committed by an American Negro Soldier at Jorhat, Assam', File no. 7/48/45.Police/1945, Police, Home Department, Government of India, NAI; *FR*, 2nd half, December 1943.

162. Bhattacharya, *Yaruingam*.
163. Guyot-Réchard, 'When Legions Thunder Past: The Second World War and India's Northeastern Frontier', 25.
164. *FR*, 1st half, December 1943; *FR*, 2nd half, December 1943.
165. *The Times* attributed the valour of the Naga warrior to the 'harvest of seed sown over the course of long years—seed sown of justice, of sympathy, of kindness—by successive generations of British officials'. Editorial, 'Warriors of the Hills', *The Times,* 29 December 1944, 5.
166. *Times of India,* 20 November 1943, 4.
167. David Hotchkiss Price, *Anthropological Intelligence: The Deployment and Neglect of American Anthropology in the Second World War* (Durham, N.C.: Duke University, 2011), 57.
168. Bower, *Naga Path*; Anthony Gilchrist McCall, *Lushai Chrysalis* (London: Luzac & Co Ltd, 1949), 312–20; Correspondence Relating to Plans for the Total Defence Scheme in the Event of the Area Being Overrun, Mss Eur E361/34, India Office Records and Private Papers, Asia, Pacific and African Collections, British Library.
169. *Times of India,* 12 August 1944, 6.
170. *Times of India,* 13 December 1944, 4.
171. *New York Times,* 2 May 1942, 3.
172. *New York Times,* 14 December 1942, 1.
173. *Times of India,* 16 April 1943, 4.
174. *Times of India,* 27 April 1943, 1.
175. 'Jamadar Visati Angami of Chizami village exhibited great courage and leadership, he patrolled ahead of troops in a country strongly held by enemy. Jamadar Prem Bahadur Lama of Kohima commanded platoons of Naga levies to cut enemy lines of communication and clear the Naga hills. Jamadar Unilhu Angami of Kohima Village raised 3000 Naga tribesmen to act as porters and guides for March. He was in charge of a company of Naga levies and led five patrols', *Times of India,* 8 August 1945, 8.
176. *Times of India,* 24 November 1944, 1.
177. 'Opening Address by N.R. Sarkar, Member in Charge of the Department of Education, Health and Lands at the Food Production Conference held at New Delhi on 6 April [1943]', *Grow More Food Campaign: Supply of Papers Regarding Progress and Results to the Secretary of State,* Government of India, Department of Education, Health and Land, File no. 20–34/43–AP, 1943, Abhilekh Patal, NAI. For changing consumption pattern in Bengal during World War II, see S. Bhattacharyya, 'World War II and the Consumption Pattern of the Calcutta Middleclass', *Sankhya: The Indian Journal of Statistics,* vol. 8 no. 2 (1947), 197–200.

178. *Times of India*, 5 November 1943, 5.
179. *Times of India*, 9 August 1943, 5.
180. *FR*, 1st half, November 1943; Estimate based on P.C. Goswami, *The Economic Development of Assam* (Bombay: Asia Publishing House, 1963), 291–92.
181. Jyotiprasad Agarwala, 'Lovita', in *Jyotiprasad Rachanawali*, ed. Hiren Gohain (Guwahati: Publication Board Assam, 2003), 183.
182. Govind Sadashiv Ghurye, *The Aborigines—'So Called'—and Their Future* (Poona: Gokhale Institute of Politics and Economics, 1943).
183. For a detailed and insightful discussion on these proposals, see David R. Syiemlieh, *On the Edge of Empire: Four British Plans for North East India, 1941–1947* (Delhi: Sage Publications, 2014).
184. Robert Reid, *A Note on the Future of the Present Excluded, Partially Excluded and Tribal Areas of Assam*, Calcutta, 1942, Mss Eur F229/44, India Office Records and Private Papers, Asia and Africa Collections, BL.
185. Indian Statutory Commission, *Memorandum submitted by the Government of Assam to the Indian Statutory Commission*, Report of the Indian Statutory Commission, vol. XIV (London: His Majesty's Stationery Office, 1930).
186. Ibid., para. 37, 99–100.
187. Robert Reid, 'The Excluded Areas of Assam', *Geographical Journal*, vol. 103, no. 1/2 (1944), 27.
188. Alexander Mackenzie, *History of the Relations of the Government with the Hill Tribes of the North-East Frontier of Bengal* (Calcutta: Home Department Press, 1884), 55.
189. For further elaboration on this, see Boddhisattva Kar, 'When Was the Postcolonial? A History of Policing Impossible Lines', *Beyond Counter-Insurgency: Breaking the Impasse in Northeast India*, ed. Sanjib Baruah (Delhi: Oxford University Press, 2009), 49–77; Cederlöf, *Founding an Empire on India's North-Eastern Frontiers 1790–1840*; Peter Robb, 'The Colonial State and Constructions of Indian Identity: An Example on the Northeast Frontier in the 1880s', *Modern Asian Studies*, vol. 31, no. 2 (1997), 245–83; David Vumlallian Zou and M. Satish Kumar, 'Mapping a Colonial Borderland: Objectifying the Geo-Body of India's Northeast', *Journal of Asian Studies*, vol. 70, no. 1 (2011), 141–70.
190. Lipokmar Dzuvichu, 'Roads and the Raj: The Politics of Road Building in Colonial Naga Hills, 1860s–1910s', *Indian Economic & Social History Review*, vol. 50, no. 4 (2013), 473–494; Lipokmar Dzuvichu, 'Empire on Their Backs: Coolies in the Eastern Borderlands of the British Raj', *International Review of Social History*, vol. 59, Supplement (2014), 89–112; Joy Pachuau and Willem van Schendel, *The Camera as Witness: A*

*Social History of Mizoram, Northeast India* (Delhi: Cambridge University Press, 2015), Chapter 8, 168–81; Richard Maxwell Eaton, 'Conversion to Christianity among the Nagas, 1876–1971', *Indian Economic & Social History Review*, vol. 21, no. 1 (1984), 1–44; Guyot-Réchard, 'When Legions Thunder Past: The Second World War and India's Northeastern Frontier'.

191. Stephen Legg, 'Dyarchy: Democracy, Autocracy, and the Scalar Sovereignty of Interwar India', *Comparative Studies of South Asia, Africa and the Middle East*, vol. 36, no. 1 (May 2016), 44–65; Guha, *Planter Raj to Swaraj: Freedom Struggle & Electoral Politics in Assam 1826–1947*, 218.
192. Reid, 'The Excluded Areas of Assam', 18–29.
193. For details of this region, see Richard Cockett, *Blood, Dreams and Gold: The Changing Face of Burma* (New Haven: Yale University Press, 2015); John Francis Bowerman, 'The Frontier Areas of Burma', *Journal of the Royal Society of Arts*, vol. 95, no. 4732 (1946), 44–55; Mandy Sadan, *Being and Becoming Kachin: Histories Beyond the State in the Borderworlds of Burma* (Oxford: Oxford University Press, 2013).
194. 'H. Weightman, Secretary, GoI, External Affairs Department to O.K. Caroe, ICS, India Office, 13 October 1943', in *Question of the Future Administration and Constitutional Position of the Present Excluded, Partially Excluded, and Tribal Areas in and on the Border of Assam*, File no. 307–X/43, External Affairs, X Branch, 1943, Abhilekh Patal, NAI.
195. Reid, 'The Excluded Areas of Assam', 27.
196. Reginald Coupland, *The Future of India: The Third Part of a Report on the Constitutional Problem in India Submitted to the Warden and Fellows of Nuffield College, Oxford* (London & New York: Oxford University Press, 1943).
197. 'Confidential Area of Burma', H.J. Mitchell, Chairman, Committee on the Scheduled Area of Burma, 20 March 1942, in *Frontier Areas: Reconstruction; Shan States and Hill Tracts*, IOR/M/4/2803, India Office Records and Private Papers, Asia and Africa Collections, British Library; Also, Syiemlieh, *On the Edge of Empire: Four British Plans for North East India, 1941–1947*, 10–11.
198. 'Wavell to Amery, 10 October and 3 December, [1944], Protection of "Backward Tribes" in the new Indian Constitution', File no. IOR/L/PJ/7/6787, India Office Records and Private Papers, Asia, Pacific and Africa Collections, British Library.
199. L.S. Amery to Lord Wavell, 28 September 1944, India Office, no. 25 in *TOP*, vol. 5, 52–56.
200. Frederick William Pethick-Lawrence, *Fate Has Been Kind* (London: Hutchinson, 1943), 147.

201. J.P. Mills, *A Note on the Future of the Hills Tribes of Assam and the Adjoining Hills in a Self-Governing India* (Shillong: Assam Government Press, September 1945), MSS Eur F236/357, Asia, Pacific and Africa Collections, British Library; Andrew Clow, *The Future Government of the Assam Tribal Peoples* (December 1945), Mss Eur F236/358, Asia, Pacific and Africa Collections, British Library.
202. Colin R. Alexander, *Administering Colonialism and War: The Political Life of Sir Andrew Clow of the Indian Civil Service* (Delhi: Oxford University Press, 2019).
203. Clow, *The Future Government of the Assam Tribal Peoples*. Also, Letter from A.G. Clow to Lord Wavell, no. 191, 23 October 1945, in *Protection of 'Backward Tribes' in the New Indian Constitution*, File 5416/1944, IOR/L/PJ/7/6787: 1944-1946, India Office Records and Private Papers, Asia, Pacific and Africa Collection, British Library.
204. 'Question in the Council of State by the Hon'ble Raja Yuveraj Dutta Singh Regarding Formation of a Frontier Province in Assam by Cutting Out the Hill Districts of the Province, Secretariat of the Governor-General (Reforms)', File no. 23/2/46–R, Abhilekh Patal, NAI.
205. For an overview of public opinion on these proposals in Assam, see 'Reports in the Assam and Bengal Press Regarding the Formation of North East Frontier Province on the Division of Assam. Memorandum by Sir Andrew Clow, Governor of Assam, and by Mr. J.P. Mills Adviser to the Governor, on the Future Assam Tribesmen', File no. Proceedings Nos 316-C.A., 1946 (Secret), Central Asia, External Affairs, Government of India, NAI.
206. 'Statement by Pandit Jawaharlal Nehru, President of Indian National Congress, on the Future of Tribals on the Northeast Frontier with Particular Reference to the History Inhabited by Nagas', File no. 45-NEF/46, 1946, NEF Branch, External Affairs Department, Government of India, PR_000004002118, Abhilekh Patal, NAI.
207. Speech of Sardar V. Patel, *Constituent Assembly of India (Legislative) Debates*, vol. 4, part 1, 20 December 1949, 589.

## Chapter 2: Bumpy Road to Independence

1. Chandan Kumar Sarma, 'Census, Society and Politics in British Assam' (PhD diss., Dibrugarh University, 2018), Chapter 4.
2. Two decades earlier, the Assam Provincial Muslim League (APML), which largely functioned from the district of Sylhet, had tried to seek a political solution to improve the conditions of the Muslim population in Assam. Before the Simon Commission, the APML had asked not only for universal

adult suffrage but also rights for political representation on a 'communal basis'. These political aspirations largely became a reality as things slowly changed after 1937, and the provincial government was formed. Assam Provincial Muslim League, *Memorandum on the Future Constitution of India*, IOR/Q/13/1/1, item 13, E-Assam, 192, 1928 (India Office Records and Private Papers, Asia, Pacific and Africa Collections, British Library). For further discussion on the provincial politics of Assam during 1937 and 1946, see Amalendu Guha, *Planter Raj to Swaraj: Freedom Struggle & Electoral Politics in Assam 1826–1947* (Delhi: Indian Council of Historical Research, 1977); A.C. Bhuyan and S. De, eds, *Political History of Assam, 1940–1947*, vol. 3 (Guwahati: Publication Board Assam, 1999); K.N. Dutta, *Landmarks of Freedom Struggle in Assam* (Guwahati: Lawyer's Book Stall, 1969).
3. *Amrita Bazar Patrika*, 1 February 1941, 8.
4. 'Proceedings of the 2nd Conference of Assam Provincial Muslim League, File no. C/AP/SB No. C-5 (10) (b) 41', in *Gopinath Bardoloi: 'The Assam Problem' and Nehru's Centre*, Nirode K. Barooah (Guwahati: Bhabani Books, 2010), 143fn8.
5. R.J. Moore, 'Jinnah and the Pakistan Demand', *Modern Asian Studies*, vol. 17, no. 4 (1983), 551.
6. Kingsley Davis, *Population of India and Pakistan* (Princeton: Princeton University Press, 1951), 118.
7. Estimate based on *Report on the Land Revenue Administration of Assam for the Years of 1934–1935 & 1944–1945*, Appendix I. (During 1934–35, there was 30,11,523 acres, while it increased to 41,52,088 acres during 1944–45).
8. H.R. Blanford, 'Assam: Progress Report of Forest Administration for the Year 1940–41', *Empire Forestry Journal*, vol. 21, no. 1 (1942), 72–73.
9. C. Macharness, 'Assam: Progress Report of Forest Administration for the Year 1944–45', *Empire Forestry Review*, vol. 26, no. 2 (1947), 320–21.
10. Estimate based on Government of Assam, *Progress Report of Forest Administration in the Province of Assam for the year 1940–41* (Shillong: Government Press, 1942), 2; Government of Assam, *Progress Report of Forest Administration in the Province of Assam for the year 1946–47* (Shillong: Government Press, 1950), 1.
11. *Assam Governor's Fortnightly Report* [hereafter *FR*], 1st half, November 1943.
12. R.B. Vaghaiwalla, *Report: Census of India, 1951*, vol. XII, part I-A, Assam, Manipur and Tripura (Shillong: Superintendent of Census Operations, Assam, 1954), 71.
13. Arupjyoti Saikia, *Forests and Ecological History of Assam, 1826–2000* (Delhi: Oxford University Press, 2011).

14. Jayeeta Sharma, *Empire's Garden: Assam and the Making of India* (Durham, N.C.: Duke University Press, 2013), 92–96.
15. This estimate is based on Government of India, *Indian Agricultural Statistics, 1939–40 to 1942–43*, vol.1 (Delhi: Manager of Publications, 1950), Table V, no. 61, 254–55 and no. 63, 260–61. This figure is a rough estimate only, but it provides an indication.
16. A. Bentinck, S. Dowerah and Keramat Ali, *Report of the Committee to Enquire into the Incidence of Grazing Fees* (Shillong: Assam Government Press, 1927); S.P. Desai, *Report of the Special Officer Appointed for the Examination of Professional Grazing Reserves in Assam Valley* (Shillong: Assam Government Press, 1944).
17. The Line System caused bitter political dissent. In October 1937, the League formally rejected this practice, while the Asom Jatiya Mahasabha—the most vocal organization championing Assamese nationalism—declared rejection of the Line System to be against the interests of the Assamese population. Syed Sharifuddin Pirzada, ed., *Foundations of Pakistan: All India Muslim League Documents, 1906–1947*, vol. 2 (Karachi: National Publication House, 2007), 280; *Deka Asom*, 21 November 1943, 1.
18. 'Resolution of Assam Muslim Association', in *Quaid-i-Azam Mohammad Ali Jinnah Papers Quest for Political Settlement in India, 1 October 1943–31 July 1944*, vol. 10, ed. Z.H. Zaidi (Islamabad: Quaid-i-Azam Papers Project, 2004), 30–31.
19. Speech of Abdul Hamid Khan, 17 March 1944, *Proceedings of Assam Legislative Assembly: Official Report* (Shillong: Assam Government Press, 1944).
20. This estimate is based on Government of Assam, *Report on the Land Revenue Administration of Assam for the Years 1945–46*, Appendix III. The increase between 1941 and 1944 was only 3 per cent.
21. 'Letter from M.A. Rashid to Jinnah, 21 April 1944, Dhubri', in *Quaid-i-Azam Mohammad Ali Jinnah Papers Quest for Political Settlement in India, 1 October 1943–31 July 1944*, vol. 10, ed. Zaidi, 304–06.
22. 'Letter from Jinnah to M.A. Rashid, 16 May 1944, Srinagar', in *Quaid-i-Azam Mohammad Ali Jinnah Papers Quest for Political Settlement in India, 1 October 1943–31 July 1944*, vol. 10, ed. Zaidi, 367.
23. *FR*, 1st half, February 1943.
24. Rajendra Prasad, *India Divided* (Bombay: Hind Kitabs Ltd, 1947), 259.
25. Penderel Moon, ed., *Wavell: The Viceroy's Journal* (Oxford: Oxford University Press, 1973), 41.
26. Robert Reid, 'The Background of Immigration into Assam', *Hindustan Standard*, 19 December 1944, in *India Divided*, ed. Prasad, 260.

27. *FR*, 1st half, November 1943.
28. Moon, *Wavell: The Viceroy's Journal*, 41.
29. C. Rajagopalachari, ed., *Gandhi–Jinnah Talks: Text of Correspondence and Other Relevant Matter* (New Delhi: *Hindustan Times*, July–October 1944).
30. 'Letter from C. Rajagopalachari to M.A. Jinnah, 8 April 1944, *Indian Annual Register*, 1944, vol. 2', in *Indian Nationalist Movement, 1885–1947: Select Documents,* ed. B.N. Pandey (London: Palgrave Macmillan, 1979), 144–45.
31. 'Letter from M.K. Gandhi to M.A. Jinnah, 24 September 1944', in *Gandhi–Jinnah Talks: Text of Correspondence and Other Relevant Matter*, ed. Rajagopalachari, 26–27.
32. *Times of India*, 2 July 1944, 5. For further details on the Gandhi–Jinnah talks of 1944, see Ramachandra Guha, *Gandhi: The Years That Changed the World, 1914–1948* (Delhi: Penguin, 2018), 734–35.
33. 'Letter from M.A. Jinnah to M.K. Gandhi, 25 September 1944', in *Gandhi–Jinnah Talks: Text of Correspondence and Other Relevant Matter*, ed. Rajagopalachari, 29.
34. 'Letter from Lord Wavell to L.S. Amery on the Failure of Gandhi–Jinnah talks, October 3, 1944', in *Constitutional Relations Between Britain and India: The Transfer of Power, 1942–47* (hereafter *TOP*), vol. V, eds, Nicholas Mansergh and Penderel Moon (London: H.M.S.O., 1970–82), 74–75.
35. 'Mr. Jinnah's interview to Representative of the "Daily Worker", London, 5 October 1944', in *Gandhi–Jinnah Talks: Text of Correspondence and Other Relevant Matter*, ed. Rajagopalachari, 79–81.
36. Nirode Kumar Barooah, ed., *Bardoloi Dinalekha: The Diary of Lokapriya Gopinath Bardoloi*, vol. 1 (Guwahati: Publication Board, Assam, 2000), 86; 'Letter from Bardoloi to Rajagopalachari, 14 August 1944, File C-6(4)/44, Assam Police Special Branch', in *Gopinath Bardoloi: 'The Assam Problem' and Nehru's Centre*, Barooah, 171 & 201n23.
37. Barooah, *Gopinath Bardoloi: 'The Assam Problem' and Nehru's Centre*, 173.
38. Ibid., 172–73.
39. N.R. Sarkar, 'Note on the Economic Implications of Pakistan', Appendix III, in *Constitutional Proposals of the Sapru Committee Report,* eds, Tej Bahadur Sapru et al., (Bombay: Padma Publications, 1945), xix. For more on this report, see Bimal Prasad, ed., *Towards Freedom: Documents on the Movement for Independence in India, 1945* (Delhi: ICHR and OUP, 2008), 273–322.
40. Barooah, *Gopinath Bardoloi: The Assam Problem and Nehru's Centre*, 173; '*The Assam Tribune*, 6 October 1944', in Sangeeta Gogoi, 'The Ahom in the Colonial Period: An Ethno Political Study' (PhD diss., Dibrugarh University, 2014), 275.

41. 'Assam without Sylhet has a legitimate claim for free and independent existence in the event of India being divided territorially into Pakistan and Hidustan [*sic*] Zones and that Mahatma Gandhi and Mr. Jinnah should leave the question of Assam without Sylhet to the people of the soil to settle.' Resolution of the Executive Committee of All Assam Ahom Association, 29 September 1944, in *Documents on Ahom Movement in Assam*, ed. Girin Phukon (Moranhat, Assam: Institute of Tai Studies, 2010), xi–xii.
42. N. Bose, 'Purba Pakistan Zindabad: Bengali Visions of Pakistan, 1940–1947', *Modern Asian Studies*, vol. 48, no. 1 (2014), 1–36.
43. Harendranath Barua, ed., *Reflections on Assam cum Pakistan* (Calcutta: H. Goswami, 1944).
44. Gopinath Bardoloi, 'Foreword', in *Reflections on Assam cum Pakistan*, ed. Barua.
45. Prasad, *India Divided*, 251–68.
46. I.A. Talbot, 'The 1946 Punjab Elections', *Modern Asian Studies*, vol. 14, no. 1 (1980), 65–91.
47. Government of India, *Provincial Elections (1945–46), Assam Legislative Assembly; Analysis and Results* (Washington: India Information Services, 1946).
48. 'Voting Percentage: Elections in 1946 to the Provincial Lower Houses', Table 39, Table No. 27, Total Electorate of the Provincial Lower Houses (under 1935 Act), 278, in 'A Study of the System of Representation in India, 1920–46', N.R. Inamdar (PhD diss., Pune University, 1953).
49. Guha, *Planter Raj to Swaraj: Freedom Struggle & Electoral Politics in Assam 1826–1947*, 246–47. Nehru noted the enormous popularity enjoyed by the Congress in Assam: 'There were vast crowds at the meetings and on the wayside, but even more impressive than these crowds was the light in the eyes of the people and a ringing confidence in their voices', in 'Impressions of Assam Tour, 23 December, 1945', *Selected Works of Jawaharlal Nehru* (hereafter *SWJN*), first series, vol. 14, no. 14, 277. Also, M. Tayyebulla, *Karagarar Cithi* (Letters from the Prison) (Guwahati: Publication Board Assam, 1962), 253–55.
50. Candidus, 'Indian political notes: On the eve of polling', *Times of India*, 21 November 1945, 6.
51. N.N. Mitra, *Indian Annual Registrar*, vol. 1, January–June 1947 (Calcutta: Annual Register Office, 1947).
52. 'Whole of Assam for Eastern Pakistan: Demand to be made', *Times of India*, 2 April 1946, 1.

53. Government of India, *Provincial Elections (1945–46), Assam Legislative Assembly; Analysis and Results*, 3; Venkat Dhulipala, *Creating a New Medina: State Power, Islam and the Quest for Pakistan in Late Colonial North India* (New York: Cambridge University Press, 2015).
54. *Times of India*, 13 September 1945, 5.
55. Mitra, 'Indian Annual Register 1946 Jan–June, vol. 1', 23; Government of India, *Provincial Elections (1945–46), Assam Legislative Assembly: Analysis and Results*, 1946; *Times of India*, 2 February 1946, 3.
56. Government of India, *Provincial Elections (1945–46), Assam Legislative Assembly; Analysis and Results*; *FR*, 1st half, December 1945, Political History of Assam, File no. 13, Assam State Archives (hereafter ASA).
57. *Times of India*, 6 March 1946, 7; Gaurishankar Bhattacharjya, *Sabinay Nibedan: An Autobiography* (Guwahati: Sahitya Press, 1999), 603–10.
58. 'All India Muslim League Legislators' Conference, Delhi, 7–9 April 1946', in *Foundations of Pakistan: All India Muslim League Documents, 1906–1947*, vol. 2, ed. Pirzada, 517–18.
59. *Times of India*, 1 February 1946, 3.
60. *FR*, 2nd half, May 1946, in *Towards Freedom: Documents on the Movement for Independence of India, 1946*, ed. S. Sarkar (Delhi: Oxford University Press, 2007), 838.
61. 'Minutes of Meeting between Cabinet Delegation, Field Marshal Viscount Wavell and Mr Gopinath Bardoloi on Monday, 1 April 1946', in *TOP*, vol. VII, no. 35, 76–80; Gopinath Bardoloi, 'A Brief Resume of the Conversation Shri G. Bardoloi had with the Cabinet Mission and Lard Wavell on 1 April 1946', *Assam Congress Committee Papers on Grouping, 1946–47*, File no. 320/1946, Political History of Assam (ASA).
62. Guha, *Planter Raj to Swaraj: Freedom Struggle & Electoral Politics in Assam 1826–1947*, 276.
63. Moon, ed., *Wavell: The Viceroy's Journal*, 233.
64. 'Note of Meeting between Field Marshal Viscount Wavell, Cabinet Delegation, Mr Qaiyum and Sir M. Saadulla on Tuesday, 2 April 1946', in *TOP*, vol. VII, no. 40, 88.
65. 'League Memorandum on Minimum Demands, 12 May 1946', *Foundations of Pakistan*, vol. 2, 532–33.
66. This account is based on 'The Cabinet Mission Plan', in *Speeches and Documents on the Indian Constitution 1921–1947*, vol. II, eds, Maurice Gwyer and A. Appadorai (Delhi: Oxford University Press, 1957).
67. 'Letter from Abell to Mountbatten', in *TOP*, vol. X, no. 234, 27 April 1947, 458.
68. Moon, ed., *Wavell: The Viceroy's Journal*, 271–72.

69. *Jugantar*, 19 May 1946, 3.
70. Arupjyoti Saikia, 'Vernacular for the Nation: Hemchandra Goswami's Typical Selections from Assamese Literature', in *On Modern Indian Sensibilities Culture, Politics, History,* eds, Ishita Banerjee-Dube and Sarvani Gooptu (Delhi: Routledge, 2018).
71. Tayyebulla, *Karagarar Cithi*, 263; David Ludden, 'Spatial Inequity and National Territory: Remapping 1905 in Bengal and Assam', *Modern Asian Studies*, vol. 46, no. 3 (2012), 483–525.
72. Moon, ed., *Wavell: The Viceroy's Journal*, 274.
73. 'Letter from Master Tara Singh to Lord Pethick-Lawrence, 25 May 1946', in *TOP*, vol. VII, no. 380, 697.
74. 'Resolution adopted by the Assam Provincial Congress Working Committee held on 26 May 1946 on the Recommendation of the Cabinet Mission' in *Assam (General)*, vol. 1, 6–A, 1946–47, *Digitized Private Papers, Sardar Patel*, Abhilekh Patal, NAI.
75. 'Assam Congress protest', *Times of India*, 29 May 1946, 3.
76. 'Assam & Bengal', *Times of India*, 5 June 1946, 6.
77. 'Record of Meeting of Cabinet Delegation and Field Marshal Viscount Wavell with Sir F. Burrows on Friday, 24 May 1946', in *TOP*, vol. VII, no. 367, 675.
78. By 1946, both the Bengal Congress and the Hindu Mahasabha, largely backed by Hindu upper classes, campaigned for the partition of Bengal. These leaders thought the partition was preferable than a Muslim-led government in Pakistan. Assam's anti-Cabinet Mission stand was seen as a step closer to the partition of Bengal. Pushpalata Das, 'Bardoloidevar Byaktitat Ebhumuki', in *Gopinath Bardoloi,* ed. Chandraprasad Saikia (Guwahati: Publication Board Assam, 1979), 192–93; Harendranath Barua, 'Gopinath Bardoloi: Ek Chamu Jivani', in *Gopinath Bardoloi*, ed. Saikia, 33; Joya Chatterji, *Bengal Partitioned: Hindu Communalism and Partition, 1932–1947* (Cambridge: Cambridge University Press, 2002), 230–34 and 249.
79. Bhuyan and S. De, eds, *Political History of Assam*, vol. 3, 352–66; Das, 'Bardoloidevar Byaktitat Ebhumuki', 190–99; Tayyebulla, *Karagarar Cithi*, 263–67; 'Memorandum from Tayyebulla, Fakhruddin Ali Ahmed, Omeo Kumar Das, Bijoy Chandra Bhagavati, Harendranath Barua, Pushpalata Das, Hareswar Goswami, Kamakhya Prasad Tripathi, members of the Assam delegation to the Congress Working Committee, 12 June 1946', in *Assam (General)*, vol.1, 6–A, 1946–47, *Digitized Private Papers, Sardar Patel*, Abhilekh Patal, NAI.
80. Quoted in 'Letter from Patel to Mountbatten, 26 April 1947', in *TOP*, vol. X, no. 226, 446.

81. By 1945, the Tribal League, the umbrella organization of tribal populations of the Brahmaputra Valley, came closer to the Congress after years of political alliance with the Muslim League. Amidst this heightened political unrest, Bhimbor Deuri and Rupnath Brahma, both towering leaders of the League and ministerial colleagues in the Saadulla government, joined the Congress Parliamentary Board in July 1946. Bhuyan and S. De, eds, *Political History of Assam*, vol. 3, 316–17, 352–66; Debeswar Sarmah, *Herai Jua Dinbur* (Jorhat: Subarat Sarmah, 1991), 292–302. 'We view the Grouping of Assam with Bengal with grave concern. We, therefore, beg to record our strong protest against this Grouping and to deplore the pretentious claim of the Muslim League to include this Province in its Pakistan Scheme,' opined leaders of the Dimasa-Kachari. Memorandum, Dimasa-Kachari Council of the North Cachar Hills, 13 May 1947, in *Bardoloi Dinalekha: The Diary of Lokapriya Gopinath Bardoloi*, vol. 2, ed. Nirode Kumar Barooah (Guwahati: Publication Board Assam, 2001), 101–02.
82. 'Assam Fights for Freedom and Democracy [Draft Resolutions of Assam Communists]', *Assam Provincial Organising Committee, Communist Party of India*, 1–2; Bhuyan and S. De, eds, *Political History of Assam*, vol. 3, 352.
83. 'Note by Major Wyatt', in *TOP*, vol. VII, no. 373, 684–85.
84. B.N. Rau, 'Outline of an Organisation for the Constituent Assembly, June 5, 1946', in *Framing of India's Constitution: Select Documents*, vol. 1, ed. B. Shiva Rao (Delhi: The Indian Institute of Public Administration, 1967), 360.
85. Speech of Gopinath Bardoloi, 'Motion on matters pertaining to Constituent Assembly', *Assam Legislative Assembly Debates*, 16 July 1946, vol. 2, no. 10, 785–86; M. Tayyebulla, 'Report of Delegation to Congress Working Committee, June 8–10, 1946, Assam Provincial Congress Committee', *Assam Congress Committee Papers on Grouping, 1946–47*, 320/1946, Political History of Assam (hereafter PHA) ASA. This resolution emphasized that the representatives of Assam 'shall frame and settle the Constitution for the Province of Assam', and 'no Group Constitution should be set up for any Group of Provinces', including Assam.
86. 'Motion on Matters Pertaining to Constituent Assembly', *Assam Legislative Assembly Debates*, Official Report, vol. 2, no. 10, 16 July 1946, 785 and 801.
87. Speech of Muhammad Saadulla, 'Motion on Matters pertaining to Constituent Assembly', *Assam Legislative Assembly Debates*, 16 July 1946.
88. Ibid.
89. Harendranath Barua, 'Gana Parisad aru Asom', *Dainik Assamiya*, 5 July 1946, 5–6.

90. 'Telegram from Debeswar Sarma, 30 November, 1946', in *Representations from Assam Legislative Assembly, Constituent Assembly* (December 1946), IOR/L/PJ/10/69 (BL).
91. Several Congress leaders from the Hills, such as J.J.M. Nichols Roy, extended their support to the Cabinet Mission Plan. Das, 'Bardoloidevar Byaktitat Ebhumuki', 194 and 199. Also see, Jogendranath Hazarika, 'Tribals and Their Constitutional Position: A Memorandum to the Members of the Constituent Assembly and the Advisory Committee on behalf of the Twenty-Five Million Souls of Tribal India', F. 10/2–10, April 1947, in *Jinnah Papers*, vol. 1, part 1, no. 370, ed. Zaidi, 641–50. Hazarika, leader of low-caste communities and the editor of *Nayak* (a political journal), demanded that tribals of Assam must be treated as a 'statutory minority' in the future Indian Constitution even if there was a grouping arrangement.
92. For a comprehensive understanding of the Ahom political aspirations, see Yasmin Saikia, *Fragmented Memories: Struggling to be Tai-Ahom in India* (Duke University Press: 2004); Gogoi, 'The Ahom in the Colonial Period: An Ethno Political Study'; Devabrata Sharma, *Asomiya Jatigathan Prakriya Aru Jatiya Janagosthigata Anusthan Samuh* (Jorhat, Assam: Ekalavya Prakashan 2008), 454–55; 'Historically and politically she (Assam) has a tradition behind which is unique and glorious in the History of the far east and bears eloquent testimony to the fact that Assam can never be a digestible part of India,' wrote Padmeswar Gogoi, a distinguished scholar belonging to the Ahom community. Padmeswar Gogoi, 'Future Status of Assam (1945)', in *Documents on Ahom Movement in Assam*, ed. Phukon, 46. Also see 'Resolutions of the Convention of the Assam Tribes both Plain and Hills) Called "The Central Organisation of the Assam Tribes" that met in Shillong, 21–23 March, 1945, Khasi Durbar Hall', in *Documents on Ahom Movement in Assam*, ed. Phukon, 47–48.
93. 'Letter from Surendra Nath Buragohain, President of Ahom Association and Conference of Leaders of the Tribal Communities of Assam to M.A. Jinnah', in *The Ahom in the Colonial Period*, Gogoi, Appendix.
94. Verrier Elwin, 'Assam aboriginals', *Times of India*, 11 July 1946, 6.
95. J.H. Hutton, 'Problems of Reconstruction in the Assam Hills', *Journal of the Royal Anthropological Institute of Great Britain and Ireland*, vol. 75, no. 1/2 (1945), 1–7.
96. Moon, ed., *Wavell: The Viceroy's Journal*, 347.
97. Ibid., 404 and 407.
98. 'Remarks by Pandit Nehru on Grouping and Mr Gandhi on League-Congress Co-operation', in *TOP*, vol. VIII, no. 385, 628; 'Jinnah's Letter

to Viceroy November, 17 1946', in *Framing of India's Constitution*, vol. 1, ed. Rao, 324.
99. Ibid.
100. 'Letter from Abell to Mountbatten, 27 April, 1947', in *TOP*, vol. X, no. 234, 458.
101. 'Letter from Patel to Stafford Cripps, 15 December', in *Sardar Patel's Correspondence*, vol. 3, ed. Durga Das (Ahmedabad: Navajivan Publishing House, 1972), 313–15.
102. Gandhi's conversion quoted in this para is from 'Interview to Assam Congressmen', in M.K. Gandhi, *The Collected Works of Mahatma Gandhi* (hereafter CWMG), vol. 86, no. 295 (Delhi: Publications Division, 1958–1994), 227–30.
103. 'Speech at Prayer Meeting', 16 January 1947, *CWMG*, vol. 86, no. 479, 361.
104. 'Nehru's Confidential Draft for Working Committee, 22 December 1946', in *SWJN*, second series, vol. 1, 31–32.
105. 'Congress Resolution on HMG's Statement, January 5–6, 1947', in *Framing of India's Constitution*, vol. 1, ed. Rao, 353.
106. Quoted in 'Letter from Patel to Viceroy, 26 April, 47' in Grouping of Provinces, File no. 1/21, 1947, *Digitized Private Papers, Sardar Patel*, Abhilekh Patal, NAI.
107. Lionel Carter, ed., *Mountbatten's Report on the Last Viceroyalty, 22 March–15 August 1947*, Part B, 15 April to 6 May (Delhi: Manohar, 2003), 101.
108. Letter from Viceroy, 16 May 1947, New Delhi in Grouping of Provinces, File no. 1/21, 1947, *Digitized Private Papers, Sardar Patel*, Abhilekh Patal, NAI.
109. 'Record of Interview between Mountbatten and Nehru, Viceroy's Interview, no. 51, 11 April, 1947', in *TOP*, vol. X, no. 125, 200. When the Congress agreed to let go of any province that did not want to join the existing Constituent Assembly, Jinnah asked Mountbatten whether the same principle 'would be extended beyond' the two provinces of Punjab and Bengal. Mountbatten accepted it on principle. 'Mr. Jinnah became more and more distressed at the turn the conversation was taking, claiming that [the] Congress was deliberately drawing a red herring across my path, and threatening that in that case he would demand the partition of the province of Assam. I replied that certainly I would grant him the same rights of course as Congress, and if he wishes to put the Muslim majority areas of Assam in Bengal he must let me have his proposals'. 'Record of Interview between Mountbatten and Jinnah, 10 April 1947, Viceroy's Interview, no. 46', in *TOP*, vol. X, no. 116, 186–87.
110. 'Letter from A. Hydari to L. Mountbatten, 5 June', in *TOP*, vol XI, 153–54.

111. Editorial, *Abahon*, vol. 14, no. 7 (1947), 385.
112. *Dainik Assamiya*, 22 August 1946, 3.
113. Joya Chatterji, *Bengal Divided: Hindu Communalism and Partition, 1932–1947* (Cambridge: Cambridge University Press, 1994).
114. Sayed Abdul Maksud, *Maulana Abdul Hamid Khan Bhasani* (Dhaka: Bangla Academy, 1994); Arefin Badal, ed., *Maulana Bhasani* (Dhaka: Dhansiri, 1977). After Partition, Bhashani moved to East Pakistan and remained instrumental in defending the cause of the poor; Williem van Schendel, *A History of Bangladesh* (Cambridge: Cambridge University Press, 2009). Also see M. Rashiduzzaman, 'The National Awami Party of Pakistan: Leftist Politics in Crisis', *Pacific Affairs*, vol. 43, no. 3 (1970), 394–409; Layli Uddin, 'Mobilising Muslim Subalterns: Bhasani and the Political Mobilisation of Peasantry and Lower Urban Classes, c.1947–71' (PhD diss., Royal Holloway, University of London, 2016).
115. Khaliquzzaman Choudhry, *Pathway to Pakistan* (Lahore: Longman, 1961), 261.
116. Maksud, *Maulana Abdul Hamid Khan Bhasani*, 51.
117. Guha, *Planter Raj to Swaraj: Freedom Struggle & Electoral Politics in Assam 1826–1947*, 232–33; Barooah, *Gopinath Bardoloi: 'The Assam Problem' and Nehru's Centre*, Chapter 6; Nirode K. Barooah, *Gopinath Bardoloi aru Assom: Tetia aru Etia* (Guwahati: B.N. Bardoloi, 2010), 156–58.
118. 'Resolution on Government Land, 13 July, 1945', in *Compendium of Government Land Policies: A Compilation from 1937 to 2019,* Government of Assam (Guwahati: Revenue and Disaster Management Department, Government of Assam, 2020), 95–98; Guha, *Planter Raj to Swaraj: Freedom Struggle & Electoral Politics in Assam 1826–1947*, 237.
119. *Abstract of the Assam Police Intelligence Weekly Report* (*APWR*), Assam, 24 March 1946.
120. Speech of Tafazzal Ali, *Bengal Legislative Assembly Proceedings*, 26 July 1946; 85; *Dainik Assamiya*, 18 August 1946, 2; Bimal J. Dev and Dilip Kumar Lahiri, *Assam Muslims: Politics & Cohesion* (New Delhi: Mittal Publications, 1985), 102–03.
121. 'The Assam Muslim League Parliamentary Party has decided for the inclusion of the whole of Assam in Eastern Pakistan', read a telegram from the secretary of the Assam Assembly Muslim League Party sent to the All India Muslim League Working Committee. Whole of Assam for Eastern Pakistan: Demand to be made', *Times of India*, 2 April 1946, 1.
122. *Dawn*, 30 July 1946, 1.
123. Yasmin Khan, *The Great Partition: The Making of India and Pakistan* (New Haven: Yale University Press, 2008); Maksud, *Maulana Abdul Hamid Khan*

*Bhasani*, 51; Chatterji, *Bengal Divided: Hindu Communalism and Partition, 1932–1947*, 231–44.
124. *Dainik Assamiya*, 25 August 1946, 1.
125. *Dainik Assamiya*, 17 August 1946, 1.
126. Ibid.
127. *Jugantar*, 30 June 1947.
128. *FR*, 2nd half, August 1946.
129. *Dainik Assamiya*, 26 August 1946, 1.
130. Ibid.
131. Maksud, *Maulana Abdul Hamid Khan Bhasani*, 51.
132. 'Telegram from G. Bardoloi to Patel, 15 November, 1946', in *Sardar Patel's Correspondence*, vol. 3, ed. Das, 296.
133. *FR*, 1st half, November 1946.
134. *FR*, 2nd half, November 1946.
135. 'Letter from G.E.B. Abell to V. Patel, 15 November, 1946', in *Sardar Patel's Correspondence*, vol. 3, ed. Das, 294–95; 'Letter from V. Patel to Abell, 15 November, 1946', in *Sardar Patel's Correspondence*, vol. 3, ed. Das, 294–95; Guha, *Planter Raj to Swaraj: Freedom Struggle & Electoral Politics in Assam 1826–1947*, 257.
136. *Dawn*, 29 April 1947, 3; *Statesman*, 27 April 1947, 6.
137. Quoted in the *Statesman*, 6 May 1947, 6.
138. 'Eviction policy in Assam: Ex-Premier's Attack', *Times of India*, 21 December 1946, 9.
139. *Dawn*, 13 April 1947, 3. Also, 'Political Situation in Assam', Letter from Syed M. Saadullah to M.A. Jinnah, 16 April 1947, in *Towards Freedom: Documents on the Movement for Independence in India, 1947*, part 1, ed. Sucheta Mahajan (Delhi: Indian Council of Historical Research and Oxford University Press, 2013), 1056–58.
140. Guha, *Planter Raj to Swaraj: Freedom Struggle & Electoral Politics in Assam 1826–1947*, 202–303; Satyendranath Sarma, ed., *Ambikagiri Raychowdhury Rachanavali* (Guwahati: Publication Board Assam, 2009), 489–501.
141. *Dainik Assamiya*, 1 April 1947, 1.
142. *Dainik Assamiya*, 25 April 1947, 1.
143. *CWMG*, vol. 86, 21 October 1946–20 February 1947, 381.
144. Secret Report, Intelligence Bureau, Home Department, 24 March 1947, *Immigration Eviction from Assam of Those who Migrated from East Bengal*, File no 119/46-Part (I), 1946, 18, Abhilekh Patal, NAI.
145. *Times of India*, 21 March 1947, 6.
146. Secret Report, Intelligence Bureau, Home Department, 3 April 1947, in *Immigration Eviction from Assam of Those who Migrated from East Bengal*, 22.

147. 'Viceroy's Personal Report, 2 April 1947', in *TOP*, vol. X, no. 59, 90, and no. 107, 166.
148. *FR*, 2nd half, March 1947.
149. Carter, ed., *Mountbatten's Report on the Last Viceroyalty, 22 March–15 August 1947*, Part B, 15 April to 6 May, 101.
150. *Dawn*, 4 May 1947; 11 May 1947.
151. Attlee, 'Indian Policy, Statement of 3 June 1947, House of Commons', in *TOP*, vol. XI, no. 45, 89.
152. The Muslim League advised leaders in Assam to focus more on the upcoming Sylhet referendum and end the civil disobedience movement. *Western Daily Press*, 7 June 1947, 6. *Dawn*, 7 June 1947, 1; *Times of India*, 12 June 1947, 1.
153. *Times of India*, 10 June 1947, 9.
154. Attlee, 'Indian Policy, Statement of 3 June 1947, House of Commons', in *TOP*, vol. XI, no. 45, para. 13, 92. For further discussion on the Sylhet question in 1947, see Guha, *Planter Raj to Swaraj: Freedom Struggle & Electoral Politics in Assam 1826–1947*, 261–62; Udayon Misra, *Burden of History: Assam and the Partition—Unresolved Issues* (New Delhi: Oxford University Press, 2017), Chapter 4; Anindita Dasgupta, *Remembering Sylhet: Hindu and Muslim Voices from a Nearly Forgotten Story of India's Partition* (Delhi: Manohar, 2014).
155. Attlee, 'Indian Policy, Statement of 3 June 1947, House of Commons', in *TOP*, vol. XI, no. 45, para. 13, 92. According to the Census of India, 1941, Assam had 33.7 per cent Muslim population. Of the districts of Assam, the respective shares were: Sylhet (60.7 per cent), Nagaon (35.2 per cent), Goalpara (46.2 per cent), Darrang (16.4 per cent), Cachar (36.4 per cent) and Kamrup (29 per cent). See P.C. Mahalanobis, 'Distribution of Muslims in the Population of India: 1941', *Sankhya: The Indian Journal of Statistics (1933–1960)*, vol. 7, no. 4 (1946), 429–34.
156. 'Opening Remarks by Mountbatten, Proceedings of a Press Conference held in the Council House, New Delhi, 4 June 1947', in *TOP,* vol. XI, no. 59, 111.
157. Lionel Carter, ed., *Mountbatten's Report on the Last Viceroyalty, 22 March–15 August 1947,* Part B, 15 April to 6 May, 101; 'Record of Interview between Mountbatten and Bardoloi, 1 May', in *TOP*, vol. X, no. 271, 522.
158. 'Letter from Gopinath Bardoloi to Louis Mountbatten, 3 June 1947, IOR, R/3/1/150, Acc. No. 3465', in *Towards Freedom: Documents on the Movement for Independence in India, 1947*, part 2, ed. Sucheta Mahajan, (Delhi: Oxford University Press, 2015), 1893.
159. 'Telegram from L. Mountbatten to Assam Governor, 7 June 1947, no. 1342-S', in *Referendum in Sylhet*, IOR/R/3/1/158, India Office Records and Private Papers, Asia, Pacific and Africa Collections, British Library.

160. 'From F. Burrows to Mountbatten, 20 June 1947', in *TOP*, vol. XI, 278, 536.
161. Joya Chatterji, *Partition's Legacy* (Ranikhet: Permanent Black, 2019), 297.
162. Debarati Bagchi, 'Many Spaces of Sylhet: Making of a "Regional Identity", 1870s–1940s' (PhD diss., University of Delhi, 2015), Chapter 3.
163. For the Sylheti-Nagri script, see Anuradha Chanda, ed., *Script, Identity Region: A Study in Sylhet Nagri* (Kolkata: Dey's Publishing, 2013).
164. Bampfylde Fuller, *Some Personal Experiences* (London: John Murray, 1930), 104.
165. 'Resolution on Re-transfer of Sylhet and Cachar to Bengal', *The Legislative Assembly Debates (Official Reports)*, 23 January 1925 (Simla: Government of India Press, 1925), 151.
166. Memorial from Girish Chandra Roy, a zamindar, and many other zamindars, talookdars and others to the Viceroy and Governor General of India, 10 August 1874, Home Department, Public Branch, September 1874, nos 258–59, NAI, in 'Many Spaces of Sylhet: Making of a "Regional Identity", 1870s–1940s', Bagchi, 93–94.
167. Bagchi, 'Many Spaces of Sylhet: Making of a "Regional Identity", 1870s–1940s', 95.
168. Padmanath Bhattacharya, 'A Note on the Re-union of the District of Sylhet with Bengal', E-Assam-307, 27 October 1928, IOR/Q/13/1/1, item 14, India Office Records and Private Papers, Asia, Pacific and Africa Collections, British Library.
169. Indian Statutory Commission, *Memorandum submitted by the Government of Assam to the Indian Statutory Commission,* Report of the Indian Statutory Commission, vol. XIV (London: His Majesty's Stationery Office, 1930), 98.
170. Government of Assam, *Report on the Annual Land Revenue Administration of the Province of Assam, 1874–75*, para. 116. The Assamese (including both the caste Hindus and tribal) and the Bengalis had 589 and 414 numbers of jobs.
171. C.S. Mullan, *Report on the Census of India, 1931*, Assam, vol. 3, part 2, (Shillong: Assam Government Press, 1932), table X, 181.
172. Jnananath Bora, *Srihatta Bicched* (Calcutta: Samya Press, 1935), Asia, Pacific and Africa Collections, British Library. I am thankful to Debarati Bagchi for drawing my attention to this work.
173. Ibid., 5.
174. Benudhar Rajkhowa, *Notes on the Sylhetee Dialect* (Sylhet: Chandra Nath Press, 1913), 2.
175. Lakshminath Bezbarooa, 'Notes on the Sylheti', *Banhi*, vol. 4, no. 6 (1913).
176. Lakshminath Bezbarooa, 'Sylhet Kar', *Abahaon*, vol. 6, no. 8 (1937).
177. *Jugantar*, 1 July 1947, 3.

178. *Hindustan Times*, 15 June 1947, in *Towards Freedom*, part 2, ed. Mahajan,1903.
179. Mahajan, ed. *Towards Freedom*, part 2, 1894.
180. Letter from R.N. Choudhury to V. Patel, 9 June 1947, in *Towards Freedom*, part 2, ed. Mahajan, 1897.
181. *Jugantar*, 4 July 1947, 6.
182. 'Letter from V. Patel to R.N. Choudhury, 17 June 1947', in *Sardar Patel's Correspondence*, vol. 5, ed. Durga Das (Ahmedabad: Navajivan Publishing House, 1972), 24.
183. 'Letter from V. Patel to Gopinath Bardoloi, 3 July 1947', in *Sardar Patel's Correspondence*, vol. 5, ed. Das, 30.
184. *The Times,* 27 June 1947, 3.
185. *The Times*, 12 April 1947, 4.
186. 'Letter of Nawab of Bhopal to M.A. Jinnah, Secret, Personal, 8 June 1947, Jinnah Papers, vol. 2', in *Towards Freedom,* part 2, ed. Mahajan, 1895–97.
187. Sujit Chaudhuri, 'A "God-sent" Opportunity?', *Seminar*, no. 510 (February, 2002), 61–62.
188. Moon, ed., *Wavell: The Viceroy's Journal*, 233.
189. Notes of A. Clow dated 17 March 1944 quoted in *Constitutional Status of Assam Tribal Areas*, Government of India, External Affairs Department, CA Branch, nos 1–27, File no. 238–CA (Secret), 1945, Abhilekh Patal, NAI.
190. 'Hydari to L. Mountbatten, 5 June 1947', in *TOP*, vol. XI, 153–54.
191. 'Letter from G.N. Bardoloi to Patel, 29 June 1947' in *Sardar Patel's Correspondence*, vol. 5, ed. Das, 27–29.
192. 'Letter from Liaquat Ali Khan to L. Mountbatten, 11 June 1947', in *Referendum in Sylhet*, IOR/R/3/1/158, 25, India Office Records and Private Papers, Asia, Pacific and Africa Collections, British Library.
193. Telegram from Reform Commissioner to Governor's Secretary, Assam, 12 June 1947, 19; Demi official letter from K.V.K. Sundaram, Additional Secretary, Secretariat of the Governor-General (Reforms) to G.E.B. Abell, private secretary to Viceroy, New Delhi, 13 June 1947, in *Referendum in Sylhet*, IOR/R/3/1/158, India Office Records and Private Papers, Asia, Pacific and Africa Collections, British Library, 10.
194. Demi official letter from K.V.K. Sundaram, Additional Secretary, Secretariat of the Governor-General (Reforms) Commission to G.E.B. Abell, private secretary to Viceroy, New Delhi, 18 June 1947, in *Referendum in Sylhet*, IOR/R/3/1/158, India Office Records and Private Papers, Asia, Pacific and Africa Collections, British Library, 25; Letter from Purnendu Kishore Sen Gupta to V. Patel, 15 June 1947, *Sardar Patel's Correspondence*, vol. 5, ed. Das, 25–27.

195. Bagchi, 'Many Spaces of Sylhet: Making of a "Regional Identity", 1870s–1940s'.
196. Sundaram argued that to be eligible to vote a worker needs to work as a 'permanent employee in one or more qualifying tea gardens on not less than 180 days'. Demi official letter from K.V.K. Sundaram, Additional Secretary, Secretariat of the Governor-General (Reforms) to G.E.B. Abell, private secretary to Viceroy, New Delhi, 18 June 1947, in *Referendum in Sylhet*, IOR/R/3/1/158, India Office Records and Private Papers, Asia, Pacific and Africa Collections, British Library, 25.
197. 'Letter from R.N. Choudhury to L. Mountbatten, 4 July, 1947', in *Towards Freedom, part 2*, 1914; V.P. Menon, *The Transfer of Power in India* (Bombay: Orient Longmans, 1957), 388.
198. 'Telegram from Secretary to the Governor of Assam to Reforms, 20 June 1947', in *Referendum in Sylhet*, IOR/R/3/1/158, India Office Records and Private Papers, Asia, Pacific and Africa Collections, British Library, 33.
199. *Jugantar*, 4 July 1947, 5.
200. 'Record of Interview between Rear-Admiral Viscount Mountbatten of Burma and Pandit Nehru, 24 June 1947', in *TOP*, vol. XI, 319, 591.
201. *The Times*, 28 December 1945, 8.
202. *Jugantar*, 3 July 1947, 5.
203. H.A. Antrobus, *A History of the Assam Company 1839–1953* (Edinburgh: T. and A. Constable, 1957), 246.
204. 'Letter from V. Patel to Purnendu Kishore Sen Gupta, 20 June, 1947', in *Sardar Patel's Correspondence*, vol. 5, ed. Das, 27.
205. *Times of India*, 7 July 1947, 1.
206. *Jugantar*, 8 July 1947, 1.
207. Ibid.
208. Ibid.
209. *Jugantar*, 2 July 1947, 6.
210. *Jugantar*, 8 July 1947, 3.
211. *Jugantar*, 2 July 1947, 6.
212. 'Viceroy's Personal Report no.11, 4 July, 1947', in *TOP*, vol. XI, no. 506, 596.
213. *Times of India*, 28 June 1947.
214. 'Letter from A. Hydari to Mountbatten, 11 July, 1947', in *TOP*, vol. XII, 104–05.
215. 'Letter from Pandit Nehru to Rear-Admiral Viscount Mountbatten of Burma, 15 July 1947', in *TOP*, vol. XII, no. 114, 167.
216. 'Minutes of Second Day of First Governor's Conference, 16 April, 1947', in *TOP*, vol. X, no. 158, 269–79.

217. *New York Times*, 8 July 1947, 8; *Aberdeen Press and Journal*, 4 June 1947, 3; *Scotsman*, 21 June 1947, 5
218. Editorial, 'Reshaping India', *The Times*, 24 June 1947, 5.
219. 'Telegram from A. Hydari to Pandit Nehru, 14 July 1947', in *TOP*, vol. XII, no. 107, 155.
220. *New York Times*, 14 July 1947.
221. 'Letter from R. Choudhury to L. Mountbatten', in *Towards Freedom*, part 2, ed. Mahajan, 1924.
222. *Jugantar*, 6 July 1947, 6.
223. 'M.K. Gandhi's Prayer Meeting, New Delhi, 22 July 1947', in *CWMG*, vol. LXXXVIII, 400.
224. 'Letter from Sir A. Hydari to Rear Admiral Mountbatten of Burma, Shillong, 5 June, 1947', in *TOP*, vol. XII, 154.
225. Muhmud Ali, *Resurgent Assam* (Dacca: Nao-Belal Publications, 1967), 80–81.
226. *Jugantar*, 6 July 1947, 6.
227. 'Re-transfer of Sylhet and Cachar to Bengal', Speech of W.A. Cosgrave, January 23, 1925, *The Lesgislative Assembly Debates* (Official Report) (Simla: Government of India Press, 1925), 159.
228. 'Letter from Mountbatten to Pandit Nehru, 20 July, no.181', in *TOP*, vol. XII, 270.
229. 'Clause 3(2)(a) of the Draft India Independence Bill, Viceroy's Conference Paper, VCP, 97, 30 June 1947', in *TOP*, vol. XI, 779–94.
230. 'Muslim League Comments on the Congress Comments on the Indian Independence Bill, Viceroy's Conference paper, VCP, 112, 5 July', in *TOP*, vol. XI, no. 520, 913.
231. 'Congress Comments on the Draft Bill, Mountbatten to Listowel, 3 July 1947', in *TOP*, vol. XI, no. 479, 854.
232. 'Minute 3, Cabinet Meeting, India Burma Committee, 3 July 1947', in *TOP*, vol. XI, 869.
233. *The Times*, 13 September 1947, 7.

## Chapter 3: Birth Pangs

1. 'Letter from Nehru to Mountbatten, 15 July 1947, secret', in *Constitutional Relations Between Britain and India: The Transfer of Power, 1942–47* (hereafter *TOP*), vol. XII, eds, Nicholas Mansergh and Penderel Moon, (London: H.M.S.O., 1970–82), 167–68.
2. 'Letter from Mountbatten to Nehru, 20 July 1947', in *TOP*, vol. XII, 270.
3. '"Terms of Reference of Boundary Commission", Pandit Nehru to Rear-Admiral Viscount Mountbatten of Burma, secret and personal, 12 June

1947', in *TOP*, vol. XI, no. 158, 292–93. Would the commission have a right to deliberate upon the other districts of Assam? According to Hydari, their scope did not go beyond Sylhet; however, Mountbatten had already made it clear that the matter should be decided by the commission itself. 'Confidential Telegram from Mountbatten to Hydari, 24 July 1947', in *TOP*, vol. XII, 321.

4. 'Telegram from A. Hydari to Rear-Admiral Viscount Mountbatten of Burma, 23 June 1947, confidential, no. 314', in *TOP*, vol. XI, 586. On 12 June 1947, Nehru had also written to Mountbatten on the Congress's understanding that, after the referendum, a boundary commission would demarcate the Muslim-majority areas of Sylhet and the adjoining districts. '"Terms of Reference of Boundary Commission", Pandit Nehru to Rear-Admiral Viscount Mountbatten of Burma, secret and personal, 12 June 1947', in *TOP*, vol. XI, no. 158, 292–93.
5. 'Letter from Nehru to Mountbatten, 15 July 1947, Secret', in *TOP*, vol. XII, 168.
6. Ibid.
7. 'Minutes of Viceroy's Forty Seventh Staff Meeting, Item 7, Mountbatten Papers, Secret, no.344, 25 June 1947', in *TOP*, vol. XI, 635.
8. 'Viceroy's Personal Records, no. 10', in *TOP*, vol. XI, no. 369, 682.
9. 'Announcement by the Governor-General, 30 June 1947', in *TOP*, vol. XI, no. 415, 755–56.
10. *Times of India*, 14 July 1947; 'Against June 3 Declaration', *National Herald*, 14 July 1947, in *Towards Freedom: Documents on the Movement for Independence in India, 1947*, part 2, ed. Sucheta Mahajan (Delhi: Oxford University Press, 2015), 1921.
11. 'Against June 3 Declaration', *National Herald,* 14 July 1947, in *Towards Freedom: Documents on the Movement for Independence in India, 1947*, part 2 ed. Mahajan, 1921. Also, Government of India, *After Partition* (New Delhi: Publications Division, 1948).
12. 'Message from C. Radcliffe to G. Abell, 2 August 1947', in *TOP,* 1942–47, vol. XII, 483–84.
13. 'Report of the Bengal Boundary Commission (Sylhet District)', in *Reports of the Bengal Boundary Commission and Punjab Boundary Commission (Radcliffe Awards)*, Government of India (New Delhi: Government of India Press, 1958), 6.
14. 'Memorandum from the Nikhil Cachar Haidimba Barman Samiti to Sylhet Boundary Commission, 21 July 1947, S.P. Mookerjee Papers, File no. 130, Instalments II to IC, NMML', in *Towards Freedom: Documents on the Movement for Independence in India, 1947*, part 2, ed. Mahajan,1926–29.

15. Ashfaque Hossain, 'Historical Globalization and Its Effects: A Study of Sylhet and Its People, 1874–1971' (PhD diss., University of Nottingham, 2009), 262.
16. 'Details of Partition', *New York Times*, 18 August 1947, 7.
17. Hossain, 'Historical Globalization and Its Effects: A Study of Sylhet and Its People, 1874–1971', 263.
18. Government of India, *Reports of the Bengal Boundary Commission and Punjab Boundary Commission*, 9.
19. Government of Assam, *Finance Accounts, 1947–48 and the Audit Report 1948* (Shillong: Assam Government Press, 1949), 21.
20. Sardar V. Patel to Rabindranath Choudhury, New Delhi, 27 August 1947, File no. 7/2, *Digitized Private Papers, Sardar Patel*, PP_000000005023, Abhilekh Patal, NAI, 8.
21. Memorandum from Rabindranath Choudhury to Sardar V. Patel, Home Minister, Government of India, 19 August 1947, File no. 7/2/47, *Digitized Private Papers, Sardar Patel*, Abhilekh Patal, NAI, 33.
22. Rabindranath Choudhury to Sardar V. Patel, Calcutta, 20 December 1947, File no. 7/2, *Digitized Private Papers, Sardar Patel*, PP_000000005055, Abhilekh Patal, NAI, 1.
23. Confidential letter from H.P. Barua, secretary to the Government of Assam, PWD to Secretary to Government of India, PWD, 9 July 1947 in Assam (General), vol. 1, 6–A, 1946–47, *Digitized Private Papers, Sardar Patel*, PP_000000005347, Abhilekh Patal, NAI.
24. Ellen Bal, *They Ask If We Eat Frogs: Garo Ethnicity in Bangladesh* (Leiden: Institute of Southeast Asian Studies, 2007).
25. *Times of India*, 26 April 1947, 7.
26. *Assam Tribune*, 14 December 1949; *Hindustan Standard*, 15 December 1949.
27. Pratap Chandra Goswami, *Jeevan Smriti aru Kamrupi Samaj: A Memoir Dealing with Evolution of the Social Systems of North Kamrup* (Guwahati: Pratul Goswami, 1971), 136–40.
28. Ibid., 131–146; Satyendranath Sarma, ed., *Ambikagiri Raychowdhury Rachanavali* (Guwahati: Publication Board Assam, 1986).
29. *Assam Tribune*, 14 December 1949; *Hindustan Standard*, 15 December 1949; 'Resolution Passed at a joint sitting of the working committee of the Assam Provincial Congress Committee and the Executive Committee of the Assam Congress Parliamentary Party held on 16 December 1949', in *Protests against the Merger of Cooch Behar in West Bengal*, States Department, Political, 1949, File no. 15 (74)-P/49, PP_000005002295, Abhilekh Patal, NAI.

30. Letter from Chief Commissioner, Cooch Behar to A.B. Chatterjee, joint secretary, Government of India, Ministry of States, Demi official no. 103 P, 17 December 1949, in *Protests against the merger of Cooch Behar in West Bengal*, States department, political, 1949, File no. 15 (74)-P/49, Identifer, PP_000005002295, Abhilekh Patal, NAI; Gaurishankar Bhattacharjya, *Sabinay Nibedan: An Autobiography* (Guwahati: Sahitya Press, 1999), 267.
31. 'Minutes of meeting Erskine, A. Abell and Mountbatten, 30 June 1947', in *TOP*, vol. XI, no. 430, 798.
32. Letter from B.R. Medhi, Chief Minister, Assam to J.L. Nehru, Prime Minister, Demi Official, PS.221/52 in File no. PS 221/52 II, *Correspondences Related to Border Troubles*, Chief Minister's Secretariat (ASA).
33. Jawaharlal Nehru, *Selected Works of Jawaharlal Nehru* (hereafter *SWJN*) (New Delhi: Jawaharlal Nehru Memorial Fund, 1984–2019), second series, vol. 5, 128–29; *Times of India*, 12 February 1948, 9; *Times of India*, 8 February 1948, 9.
34. *Times of India*, 12 February 1948, 9; *Times of India*, 8 February 1948, 1, 9.
35. Nehru's cable to Liaquat Ali Khan, *SWJN*, second series, vol. 5, 127–28.
36. Pallavi Raghavan, 'The Finality of Partition: Bilateral Relations between India and Pakistan, 1947–1957' (PhD diss., University of Cambridge, 2012), 148.
37. *Times of India*, 6 February 1950, 5.
38. *Times of India*, 8 November 1948, 5; *Times of India*, 28 October 1948, 1; *Civil & Military Gazette (Lahore)*, 9 November 1948, 3.
39. The Assam government also expressed apprehension about the hoisting of 'white' flags in the border districts of East Pakistan inside Assam. It sent troops to these areas to dispel any sense of its loss of control. Meanings of hoisting of white flags were variously explained: Sarat Chandra Sinha, a Congress MLA and later CM of Assam, claimed that this was a sign of invitation of people from East Pakistan to Assam, whereas Abdul Hashen, another MLA thought that the people had hoisted flags just to chase cholera from the villages. 'Hoisting of white flags in Assam: Reference in Assembly', *Times of India*, 26 March 1948, 8.
40. *Times of India*, 5 September 1965, 1.
41. *Times of India*, 16 March 1948, 6.
42. '*Gloucestershire Echo* – Monday', 19 April 1948.
43. For further details, see D.R. Syiemlieh, 'The Integration of the Khasi States into the Indian Union', in *Making of the Indian Union: Merger of Princely States and Excluded Areas*, eds, S. Nag, T. Gurung and A. Chowdhuri (New Delhi: Akansha Publication House, 2007). Also, see 'Letter from Akbar Hydari to Patel, 16 July 1947, Shillong' and 'Letter from Sir Akbar Hydari

to Nehru, secret and personal letter, secret, 16 August 1947', in *Proposed Agreement with the Federation of Khasi States,* File no. 1947–88/NEF/47, Ministry of External Affairs (NEF branch), Government of India, Abhilekh Patal, NAI; Letter from Hydari to Patel, 15 December 1947, Shillong, *Correpondence with Assam from March 1946 to March 1948, Digitized Private Papers, Sardar Patel,* File no. 3/6, Abhilekh Patal, NAI.

44. 'Position of Assam and Pakistan Activities, Letter from A. Hydari to Patel, 3 March 1948', in *Sardar Patel's Correspondence,* vol. 6, ed. Durga Das (Ahmedabad: Navajivan Publishing House, 1973), 102.
45. Nirode Kumar Barooah, *Bardoloi Dinalekha: The Diary of Lokapriya Gopinath Bardoloi,* vol. 2 (Guwahati: Publication Board Assam, 2001), 4–6.
46. S.K. Chaube, *Hill Politics in North-east India* (New Delhi: Sangam Books Ltd, 1999), 92; Barooah, *Bardoloi Dinalekha,* vol. 2, 39–40.
47. 'Memorandum of Khasi-Jaintia Federated State National Conference to Patel', 7 July 1947, in Assam (general), vol. 1, 6–A, 1946–47, *Digitized Private Papers, Sardar Patel,* PP_000000005347, Abhilekh Patal, NAI.
48. Syiemlieh, 'The Integration of the Khasi States into the Indian Union'.
49. 'Letter from Jairamdas Doulatram to S. Patel, 29 June 1950', in *Sardar Patel's Correspondences,* vol. 9, ed. D. Das (Ahmedabad: Navajivan Publication, 1974), 187.
50. Barooah, *Barodoloi Dinalekha,* vol. 2, 6–19.
51. 'Pakistan asked to withdraw forces from Assam area: Pandit Nehru on eastern border incident', *Times of India,* 8 February 1948, 9.
52. *Times of India,* 9 March 1956, 6; *Times of India,* 10 March 1960, 9; *Times of India,* 19 September 1963, 1; *Times of India,* 31 October 1967, 9; Assam-East Pakistan Boundary: Minister-level conference on Indo-Pakistan Border Questions, in *Signed copy of agreed decisions and procedure to end dispute and incidents along the Indo East Pakistan border area relating to the Indo-Pakistan Minister Level Conference held from the 15th October, 1959 to 22nd October 1959,* File no. 16-I/43(vi)/Pakistan/59, Treaty and Agreement, Home Affairs, 1959, Abhilekh Patal, NAI, 3–5.
53. 'Assam border disputes settled', *Times of India,* 18 June 1955, 10.
54. Ibid.
55. Ibid.
56. Secret Letter from B.R. Medhi to Patel, Demi official no. PS/135/49, 14 October 1950, Shillong, in *Assam Ministerial, September to December 1950,* File no. 3/6, vol. 4, *Digitized Private Papers, Sardar Patel,* Abhilekh Patal, NAI.
57. Government of India, *The Ministry of External Affairs: Report, 1953–54* (New Delhi: Ministry of External Affairs, 1954), para 15.

58. K. Subbaroyan, 'Accord at passport talks in Delhi: Rail route to W. Pakistan to be reopened', *Times of India,* 1 February 1953, 1.
59. R.B. Vaghaiwalla, *Report on the Census of India*, vol. 12, Assam, Manipur and Tripura (Shillong: Superintendent of Census Operations, Assam, 1954), 358–59.
60. These organizations claimed that more than 3,00,000 people had arrived from East Pakistan.
61. *Times of India*, 17 January 1953, 8. Tripura, a princely state, merged with the Union of India in October 1949.
62. Willem van Schendel, *The Bengal Borderland: Beyond State and Nation in South Asia* (London: Anthem Press, 2004).
63. Government of India, *Rehabilitation Retrospect* (New Delhi: Ministry of Rehabilitation, 1957).
64. See Arupjyoti Saikia, 'Jute in the Brahmaputra Valley: The Making of Flood Control in Twentieth-Century Assam', *Modern Asian Studies*, vol. 49, no. 5 (2015), 1405–41.
65. *Assam Gazette*, Part IV, 29 July 1950; *Times of India*, 20 April 1948, 1; *Times of India*, 20 April 1948, 9.
66. *Times of India*, 22 March 1948, 7.
67. Vaghaiwalla, *Report on the Census of India*, vol. 12, Assam, Manipur and Tripura, 356.
68. *The Times*, 31 March 1950, 6; 'Indo-Pakistani agreement: Signature in Delhi, Mr Nehru to visit Karachi', *The Times*, 10 April 1950, 6.
69. Vaghaiwalla, *Report on the Census of India*, vol. 12, Assam, Manipur and Tripura, 359.
70. Secret, Demi-official letter from B.R. Medhi to Sardar Patel, 14 October 1950, Assam Ministerial, File no. 3/6, vol. 4, September to December 1950, *Digitized Private Papers, Sardar Patel*, 1950, Abhilekh Patal, NAI.
71. *Feature Story on Rehabilitation*, Relief and Rehabilitation Department, Assam Secretariat, File no. RHM105/57, 1957 (ASA).
72. P.N. Luthra, *Rehabilitation* (New Delhi: Publications Division, 1972), 17.
73. *Times of India*, 14 February 1950, 3. Revenue Minister Bishnuram Medhi put the figure at 4,00,000. Demographers have not scrutinized these figures. Another study estimated that 0.8 million people migrated to Assam. See Anil Saikia, Homeswar Goswami and Atul Goswami, eds, *Population Growth in Assam: 1951–1991* (New Delhi: Akansha, 2003), 114.
74. Vaghaiwalla, *Report on the Census of India*, vol. 12, Assam, Manipur and Tripura, 356.
75. 'Migration from East Pakistan (1951–1961)', *Economic & Political Weekly*, vol. 13, no. 15 (1961).

76. Vaghaiwalla, *Report on the Census of India*, vol. 12, Assam, Manipur and Tripura, 356.
77. G. Wahed Choudhury, *Pakistan's Relations with India, 1947–1966* (New York: Frederick A Prager, 1968), 193; *The Times*, 10 April 1950, 6.
78. Vaghaivalla, *Report on the Census of India*, vol. 12, Assam, Manipur and Tripura, 356.
79. Malini Sur, *Jungle Passports: Fences, Mobility, and Citizenship at the Northeast India–Bangladesh Border* (University of Pennsylvania Press, 2021); Antara Dutta, *Refugees and Borders in South Asia: The Great Exodus of 1971* (Abingdon: Routledge, 2013); Udayon Misra, *Burden of History: Assam and the Partition—Unresolved Issues* (Delhi: Oxford University Press, 2017); Sanjib Baruah, *In the Name of the Nation: India and Its Northeast* (Stanford: Stanford University Press, 2020), Chapter 2; Anindita Dasgupta, *Remembering Sylhet: Hindu and Muslim Voices from a Nearly Forgotten Story of India's Partition* (Delhi: Manohar, 2014); Anindita Ghoshal, *Refugees, Borders and Identities: Rights and Habitat in East and Northeast India* (Delhi: Routledge, 2020); Moushumi Dutta Pathak, *You Do Not Belong Here: Partition Diaspora in the Brahmaputra Valley* (Delhi: Notion Press, 2017).
80. Vaghaiwalla, *Report on the Census of India*, vol. 12, Assam, Manipur and Tripura, 356.
81. Ibid.
82. Writing in 1921, Gandhi wrote, '[In Assam] trade is controlled by Marwaris and government posts are monopolized by Bengalis', *Collected Works of Mahatma Gandhi [hereafter CWMG]*, vol. 21, 56. Gandhi again came back to this question in 1942. *CWMG*, vol. 76, 69.
83. 'Memorandum on Behalf of Released Employees' Organisation, Sylhet', 21 September 1947, *Assam Refugees*, All India Congress Committee Papers, (1st Instalment) G3/KWI/1947–48 (NMML).
84. *Statesman*, 3 October 1947.
85. Letter from Special Officer, Separation of Office, Government of Assam to Joint Secretary, GoI, Ministry of Home Affairs, New Delhi, Shillong, 22 July 1948, in *Resettlement of released Assam government servants of Sylhet*, File no. 70/1/48/Appointments, 1948, Abhilekh Patal, NAI.
86. Interview with Sucheta Kripalini, see http://www.s-asian.cam.ac.uk/archive/audio/pdf/196d.pdf, Cambridge South Asian Archive, Center of South Asian Library, Cambridge University.
87. 'Demands of Asom Jatiya Mahasabha before the Assam Pradesh Congress Working Committee', *Deka Asam*, vol. 9, no.1 (1949), 1; *Times of India*, 16 May 1949, 6.

88. Government of Assam, Circular, Revenue Department, No. 195.47.188, 4 May 1948 (ASA).
89. Editorial, *Assam Tribune*, 18 July 1949, 3.
90. For an account of India's refugee resettlement programme after 1947, see Ramachandra Guha, *India after Gandhi: The History of the World's Largest Democracy* (New Delhi: Picador, 2007).
91. N.K. Barooah, ed., *Ejon Satyagrahir Rajniti: Gopinath Bardoloi aru Assam, Tetia aru Etiya* (Guwahati: B.N. Bardoloi, 2010).
92. 'Bardoloi to Nehru, 4 March 1948, Assam Secretariat Records', in *Ejon Satyagrahir Rajniti: Gopinath Bardoloi aru Assam, Tetia aru Etiya*, ed. Barooah, 303.
93. 'Refugee problem in Assam: Merger of Manipur, Cooch Behar & Tripura', *Times of India*, 16 May 1949, 6.
94. Ibid.
95. For an idea of Nehru's anxiety on this issue, see Nehru to Gopinath Bardoloi, Chief Minister of Assam, 29 May 1948 in *SWJN*, second series, vol. 6, 118 and Nehru to Bardoloi, 18 May 1949 in *SWJN*, second series, vol. 11, 70–72. Also see, Note by Nehru entitled 'Migration from East Bengal to Assam', 21 July 1948, in *SWJN*, second series, vol. 7, 67–68.
96. 'Letter from Jawaharlal Nehru to Gopinath Bardoloi, May 5, 1950', in *Assam Chief Minister's Correspondences*, ASA.
97. Gyanesh Kudaisya and Tan Tai Yong, eds, *The Aftermath of Partition in South Asia* (London: Routledge, 2002), 145–46.
98. 'Summary of Refugee Rehabilitation Plan' by the *Bengal Rehabilitation Organisation, S.P. Mookherjee Papers* (NMML), File no. 38', in *The Aftermath of Partition*, ed. Kudaisya and Yong, 146.
99. For an idea of these bickering arguments, see Das, ed., *Sardar Patel's Correspondence*, vol. 9.
100. Arupjyoti Saikia, *A Century of Protests: Peasant Politics in Assam since 1900* (New Delhi: Routledge, 2014).
101. 'Patel to G.N. Bardoloi, 3 July 1950', in *Sardar Patel's Correspondence*, vol. 9, ed. Das, 207–208.
102. On 3 July 1950, Patel wrote to Bardoloi about how the latter's view 'betrays lack of a sense of urgency in settling the refugee problem'. Secret and personal, D.O. Number 447/DPM/50, *Assam Ministerial*, May–September 1950, *Digitized Private Papers, Sardar Patel*, 3/6, vol. 3, Abhilekh Patal, NAI.
103. Patel to Bardoloi, 3 July 1950, in *Sardar Patel's Correspondence*, vol. 9, ed. Das, 208; 'G.N. Bardoloi to Patel, 22 June 1950', in *Sardar Patel's Correspondence*, vol. 9, ed. Das, 207.

104. 'Extract of a letter dated 25 April 1950 from Shri Sri Prakasa, Governor of Assam, camp Nowgong to Sardar Patel', enclosure in 'Letter from Patel to Nehru, 3 April 1950', in *Sardar Patel's Correspondence*, vol. 9, ed. Das, 175.
105. 'Letter from Nehru to Gopinath Bardoloi, 7 August 1949', *SWJN*, second series, vol. 12, 263.
106. 'G.N. Bardoloi to Patel, 22 June 1950', in *Sardar Patel's Correspondence*, vol. 9, ed. Das, 206.
107. Ibid., 207.
108. Patel to G.N. Bardoloi, 3 July 1950, in *Sardar Patel's Correspondence*, vol. 9, ed. Das, 183–215.
109. For details, see Saikia, *A Century of Protests: Peasant Politics in Assam since 1900*, 235 and 238.
110. Vaghaiwalla, *Report on the Census of India*, vol. 12, Assam, Manipur and Tripura, 363; Extract of Tour Notes on Minister of Rehabilitation's visit to Assam during the period from 17.1.57 to 23.1.57, in *District wise Scheme for Rehabilitation of Displaced Persons in Assam*, File no 2(30)/56-RHR, RHR, Department of Rehabilitation, 1956, Abhilekh Patal, NAI.
111. 'Condition of refugees in Cachar is desperate: Need for greater care in handling people', *Times of India*, 27 July 1953, 9.
112. *Feature Story on Rehabilitation*, Relief and Rehabilitation Department, Assam Secretariat, File no. RHM105/57, 1957 (ASA).
113. Letter from S.K. Sen, under secretary, GoI, Ministry of Rehabilitation, 25 May 1955, no. CDN/4/97/55 pt IV in File no.2 (30)/56 RHR, 1956, Ministry of Rehabilitation, NAI.
114. 'Record of Interview between Mountbatten and Bardoloi, 1 May 1947', in *TOP*, vol. X, no. 271, 522. Clow also held the same view.
115. Unless otherwise mentioned, the references to railways in Assam prior to 1947 is based on S.B. Medhi, *Transport System and Economic Development in Assam* (Guwahati: Publication Board Assam, 1978).
116. C.N. Vakil, *Economic Consequences of the Partition* (Bombay: Vora & Co., 1950), 58.
117. Government of India, *Indian Railway: One Hundred Years* (New Delhi: Railway Board, 1953).
118. *Amrita Bazar Patrika*, 8 July 1947, 4.
119. 'Marketing Areas in India', vol. V, no. 138, December 1948, *India, Summary of Current Economic Information* (Washington: International Reference Service: U S Department of Commerce, 1948), 7.
120. *Times of India*, 16 December 1947, 5; *The Times of India Directory and Yearbook*, 1952–53, 377.

121. Government of India, *Era of Rapid Change, 1947–1967* (Delhi: Ministry of Information and Broadcasting, 1968), 96–97.
122. Statement by R.A. Kidwai, *Constituent Assembly of India (Legislative) Debates*: Official, part 1, vol. 6, 28 October 1948, 618.
123. P.R.H. Longley, *Tea Planter Sahib: The Life and Adventures of a Tea Planter in North East India* (Auckland: Tonson Publishing House, 1969), 130–31.
124. Karnail Singh, *A Complete Story of the Assam Rail Link Project, with Technical Papers on Important Works* (New Delhi: Ministry of Railways, 1951).
125. Railway Budget for 1947–48, Speech by John Mathai, Minister of Railways and Transport, *The Constituent Assembly of India (Legislative) Debates*, Official Report, vol.1, 20 November 1947, 395.
126. *Statesman*, 11 December 1949, 5.
127. *Economic Weekly*, 18 April 1953, 458.
128. From UK High Commissioner in India, Inward Telegram to Commonwealth Relations Office, 31 March 1950, in *Bengal disturbances, March–December 1950 (Folder 3)* (Government Papers, The National Archives, Kew, 1950).
129. 'Letter from V. Patel to N. Gopalaswamy Ayyangar, 1 December 1949', in Singh, *Assam Rail Link Project*, 153.
130. Michael Kidron, *Foreign Investments in India* (London: Oxford University Press, 1965), 3.
131. *Amrita Bazar Patrika*, 10 July 1947, 5.
132. Amalendu Guha, *Planter Raj to Swaraj: Freedom Struggle & Electoral Politics in Assam 1826–1947* (Delhi: Indian Council of Historical Research, 1977), 270.
133. Estimate based on Tea Board, *Tea Statistics*, 1956, table 1 (iii); Government of India, *Report of the Jute Enquiry Commission*, 1954 (New Delhi: Government of India Press, 1954), Table IV, 12.
134. See n19, Prologue.
135. Vaghaiwalla, *Report on the Census of India, vol. 12, Assam, Manipur and Tripura*, part II-A, Table E, 30.
136. *Times of India*, 3 October 1947, 4.
137. 'Rights of Assam Minorities: Premier's Assurance', *Times of India*, 10 September 1947, 7.
138. B.R. Tomlinson, *The Economy of Modern India: From 1860 to the Twenty-First Century* (Cambridge: Cambridge University Press, 2013), 163. The baseline of 100 is based on the year 1939.
139. Prices of a few commodities for the years 1944 and 1950 were as listed:

|  | 1944 (per maund) | 1950 (per maund) |
| --- | --- | --- |
| Winter rice in husk | 6–0–0 | 8–0–0 |
| Gur | 24–0–0 | 25–0–0 |
| Potato | 17–0–0 | 16–0–0 |
| Mustard oil | 58–12–0 | 97–0–0 |

L.K. Handique, *Annual Report of the Department of Agriculture, Assam for the Years Ending 31st March 1950* (Shillong: Assam Government Press, 1951), 6.
140. *Times of India*, 2 June 1949, 6.
141. Arnab Dey, *Tea Environments and Plantation Culture: Imperial Disarray in Eastern India* (Cambridge: Cambridge University Press, 2018), 49–76.
142. Guha, *Planter Raj to Swaraj: Freedom Struggle & Electoral Politics in Assam 1826–1947*, 189–90. Halem Tea Estate paid £2300 as income tax against £39,664 for the years 1939–41, *The Times,* 8 October 1941, 8.
143. *The English and Scottish Joint Co-Operative Wholesale Society Ltd versus Assam Agricultural Income Tax Commissioner,* Privy Council, Appeal No. 75 of 1946 (From Calcutta), 27 April 1948, https://www.lawyerservices.in/The-English-and-Scottish-Joint-Co-operative-Wholesale-Society-Ltd-Versus-The-Commissioner-of-Agricultural-Income-tax-Assam-1948-04-27 (Accessed 17 April 2023).
144. Estimate based on *Report of the Plantation Inquiry Commission* (1956) Pt. 1, Table VI, 13; S.H. Steinberg, ed., *The Statesman's Year-Book: Statistical and Historical Annual of the States of the World for the Year 1955* (London: Macmillan, 1955), 171.
145. Guha, *Planter Raj to Swaraj: Freedom Struggle & Electoral Politics in Assam 1826–1947,* 270
146. For further details, see Tomlinson, *Economy of Modern India*, 141–42.
147. H.A. Antrobus, *A History of the Assam Company 1839–1953* (Edinburgh: T. and A. Constable, 1957), 240.
148. In November 1948, the Assam government passed the Assam Assessment of Revenue Free Wastelands Grants Act, 1948, which brought the previously revenue-free wasteland grants under assessment, and revenue and other local rates and cesses were levied on them.
149. R.C. Woodford, *Annual Report of the Department of Agriculture, Assam for the Years Ending 31st March 1948* (Shillong: Assam Government Press, 1950).
150. *Times of India*, 7 May 1950, 1.
151. Government of India, 'Drive for Increased Jute Production' Unofficial Note (New Delhi: Press Information Bureau, 10 June 1949); 'Growing More Jute and Cotton', *Economic & Political Weekly* (12 February 1949), 20–21.

152. *Dundee Courier*, 13 December 1949, 4.
153. *The Indian Jute Atlas*, Indian Central Jute Committee, 1959, 14.
154. *Constitutional Assembly Debates*, vol. 9, 8 August 1949.
155. O.H.K. Spate, 'Geographical Aspects of Pakistan Considered', *Geographical Journal*, vol. 102, no. 3 (September 1943).
156. Percival Joseph Griffiths, *A History of the Joint Steamer Companies* (London: Inchcape, 1979), 91.
157. Tariq Omar Ali, *A Local History of Global Capital: Jute and Peasant Life in the Bengal Delta* (Princeton: Princeton University Press, 2018), Chapter 7.
158. 'Letter from Jawaharlal Nehru to Gopinath Bardoloi, April 10 1950', in *SWJN*, second series, vol. 14, part 2, 19. For details of communal disturbance in 1950 in Lower Assam, see Government of Assam, *Outbreak of Communal Violence in Assam in the Year 1950: An Analysis of the Communal Violence in Assam in the Year 1950 on the Basis of the Report of District Authority and Top Most Civil and Police Official to the Mukherjee Commission* (Guwahati: Government of Assam, 2014).
159. 

| Year | Price | Cost | Profit |
|---|---|---|---|
| 1943 | 13.04 | 10.51 | 2.53 |
| 1948 | 22.04 | 19.32 | 2.72 |
| 1953 | 32.46 | 26.14 | 6.32 |

Price per kilogram of tea in annas (1 anna = 0.625 rupee). Source: *Plantation Labour Enquiry Committee Report*, 1956.
160. For the introduction of tapioca (*Manihot esculenta*) in Assam and India, see Alfred W. Crosby Jr, *The Columbian Exchange: Biological and Cultural Consequences of 1492* (Westport, Connecticut: Greenwood Press, 1972); *Natun Asamiya*, 3 January 1954, 3.
161. For an account of trade in horticulture produces of the Khasi and Jaintia Hills bordering Sylhet, see W.W. Hunter, *A Statistical Account of Assam*, vol. 2 (London: Trubner, 1879), 236–37.
162. East India (Industrial Commission, 1916–18), *Minutes of Evidence Taken Before the Indian Industrial Commission, 1916–18*, vol. 5, (London: H.M. S.O., 1919), 453.
163. Government of Assam, *Report on Rural Economic Survey in United Khasi & Jaintia Hills* (Economics and Statistics Department, 1963), 13.
164. Prior to Partition, oranges were sold for Rs 20 to Rs 25 per *luti* (1024 nos). After Partition, they sold for Rs 8 to Rs 16. Prices of betel leaf, which sold for Rs 20 to Rs 25 per *kuri* (2880 pieces), came down to Rs 2 to Rs 3 per *kuri*. Government of Assam, *Report on Rural Economic Survey in United*

*Khasi & Jaintia Hills* (Shillong: Directorate of Economics and Statistics, 1963), 13.
165. The touring members of the Indian Scheduled Castes and Scheduled Tribes Commission who visited these areas in 1954 noted the extreme poverty. Government of India, *Report of the Commissioner for Scheduled Castes and Scheduled Tribes*, vol. 3 (Delhi: Government Printing Press, 1954), 22–35. Also, 'Report on a tour of Assam by Shri H.V.R. Iyengar, Shri P.C. Bhattacharya, Shri H.P. Mathrani and Shri G.R. Garg', in Letter from K.C. Nair, Secretary to the Cabinet, no. 193/CF/49, Cabinet Secretariat, Government of India, New Delhi, 23 August, 1952, paras 8–16, 14–20, in *Flood Situation in Assam*, File no. 199/52, President Secretariat, General Branch, 1952, Abhilekh Patal, NAI.
166. Government of Assam, *Report on Rural Economic Survey in United Khasi & Jaintia Hills*, 12.
167. Speech of P.R. Kyndiah, Government of Meghalaya, *Proceedings of the Meghalaya Legislative Assembly*, 10 December 1974, Shillong.
168. 'Letter from A. Hydari to Patel, 3 March 1948', in *Sardar Patel's Correspondence*, vol. 6, ed. Das, 101–104.
169. 'Cachar lost her road communication with Shillong, which was previously through Sylhet. A jeepable road was built connecting Cachar and Shillong via Jowai and Haflong. Garo hills connection was restored by constructing another road', in *Geography of Assam*, H.P. Das (New Delhi: National Book Trust, 1970), 144.
170. Semi-official letter from B.R. Medhi to Patel, 11 September 1950, File no. *Assam Ministerial, 3/6*, vol. 3, May–September 1950, *Digitized Private Papers, Sardar Patel*, PP_000000005350, Abhilekh Patal, NAI.
171. News of the smuggling of goods across the Indo-Bangladesh border continues to occupy regular attention in the newspapers published from Assam, Meghalaya and Tripura. Also, see Sahana Ghosh, 'Chor, Police and Cattle: The Political Economies of Bovine Value in the India–Bangladesh Borderlands', *South Asia: Journal of South Asian Studies*, vol. 42, no. 6 (2019), 1108–24.
172. Meghalaya's lawmakers perceptively concluded how Partition had continued to inflict miseries on the people. H.S. Lyngdoh, one of the lawmakers, speaking in the Meghalaya Legislative Assembly thus said how it was 'because of the partition of the country . . . economic condition was cut off totally', which resulted in 'immediate closure of trade with Pakistan' and 'loss of agricultural lands' in Pakistan. Speech of H.S. Lyngdoh, *Proceedings of the Meghalaya Legislative Assembly*, 10 December 1974.
173. *Times of India*, 27 June 1948, 3.

174. *Times of India*, 28 July 1948, 7.
175. For further details on this, see Arupjyoti Saikia, *The Unquiet River: A Biography of the Brahmaputra* (New Delhi: Oxford University Press, 2019), Chapter 11.
176. 'Deal firmly with Pakistan: Plea at meeting in Shillong', *Times of India*, 25 November 1952, 7.
177. Joya Chatterji, 'South Asian Histories of Citizenship 1946–1970', *Historical Journal*, vol. 55, no. 4 (December 2012), 1049–71.
178. Prarthana Saikia, 'Citizenship, Nationality and Assam: A Political History since 1947' (PhD diss., Indian Institute of Technology, Guwahati, 2021), Chapter 3.
179. Letter from Bishnu Ram Medhi, Chief Minister, Assam, 26 September 1950 to Patel, secret, D.O. no. PS/135/49, 14 October 1950 in *Assam Ministerial, September–December 1950*, File no. 3/6, *Digitized Private Papers, Sardar Patel*, PP_000000005350, Abhilekh Patal, NAI.
180. Confidential note, in *An Ordinance to Control Influx of Muslims from East Pakistan*, File C 294/48, Home Confidential, 1948, ASA.
181. Secret Letter from Deputy Inspector General of Police, Assam to Chief Secretary, Assam, Memo no. I/C-5 (3) (M) 48/39 Shillong, 25 October 1948 in *An Ordinance to Control Influx of Muslims from East Pakistan*, File no. C 294/48, Home Confidential, 1948, ASA.
182. Speech of Shri Gopalaswami, Minister of Transport and Railways, Government of India, *Parliamentary Debates*, Part 1, official report, vol. 1, 8 February 1950, 314. All references between notes 186 and 190 are from this volume unless otherwise mentioned.
183. Ibid.
184. Niraja Gopal Jayal, *Citizenship and Its Discontents: An Indian History* (Cambridge, MA: Harvard University Press, 2013), 56–63.
185. Speech of Gopalaswami, Minister of Transport and Railways, Government of India, *Parliamentary Debates*, 8 February 1950. The bill was first introduced on 20 December. 1949 but was not taken up for discussion.
186. *Gazette of India*, 24 December 1949, part V, 503.
187. Speech of Shri Gopalaswami Ayyangar, Minister of Transport and Railways, Government of India, *Parliamentary Debates*, 8 February 1950.
188. *Times of India*, 9 February 1950, 10.
189. Speech by D.K. Borooah, *Parliamentary Debates*, Official Report, vol. 1, 8 February 1950 (First Session of Parliament of India, 1950), 329.
190. Speech by A.C. Guha, *Parliamentary Debates*, Official Report, vol. 1, 8 February 1950 (First Session of Parliament of India, 1950), 334.
191. Speech by R.K. Chaudhury, *Parliamentary Debates*, Official Report, vol. 1, 13 February 1950 (First Session of Parliament of India, 1950), 454.

192. 'Petition of Villagers of Bahati, Goalpara to Revenue and Finance Minister, Assam, 18 July 1949', in *Application of the Villagers of Bahati, a Village in Goalpara reg. Anti-Government Activity of some Muslims of Bahati*, Home confidential, File C 559/49, 1949 ASA; *Sadiniya Asamiya*, 20 August 1949, 3.
193. Letter from Nehru to the Chief Ministers, 19 March 1950, *SWJN*, second series, vol. 14, part 1, 416.
194. Taya Zinkin, *Reporting India* (New York: Oxford University Press, 1958), 41–42, 50.
195. Telegram from Nehru to Bardoloi, 13 March 1950, *SWJN*, second series, vol. 14, part 1, 109–10. On the same day, Nehru telegrammed Sri Prakasa, Assam's Governor, expressing how he was 'greatly distressed' and hoped 'Assam Government is giving every help and assistance to sufferers' and 'punishing those who were guilty'. Telegram from Nehru to Sri Prakasa, 13 March 1950, *SWJN*, second series, vol. 14, part 1, 111.
196. 'Extract from a statement made by Pakistan Prime Minister on 28 March 1950 in Constituent Assembly on situation in East Pakistan', Inward Telegram to Commonwealth Relations Office, 28 March 1950, FL 10114/47, India and Pakistan, South East Asia Department, *Bengal Disturbances, March–December 1950 (Folder 3)* (Government Papers, The National Archives, Kew, 1950), http://www.archivesdirect.amdigital.co.uk/Documents/Details/FO_371_84248 (Accessed 2 May 2021).
197. Quoted in Nehru's cable to Liaquat Ali Khan, 11 March 1950, *SWJN*, second series, vol. 14, part 1, no. 65, 107fn2.
198. Letter from Nehru to Rajendra Prasad, 11 March 1950, *SWJN*, second series, vol. 14, part 1, no. 66, 107.
199. 'Some time back it was suggested to you we had better proceed slowly. It seems to me that we should stop all action under it for the present completely'. Letter from J.L. Nehru to G. Bardoloi, 10 April 1950, in *SWJN*, second series, vol. 14, part 2, 18. In May, too, during a press conference, Nehru reiterated the importance of Assam's needs to go slow in this matter, *Times of India*, 23 May 1950, 5. Patel was aware of this development. Amaya Chaliha, 'Chaliha Manuhjan aru Teur Rajniti' (Chaliha, the Man and His Politics) in *Bimala Prasad Chaliha: Remembrance*, eds, Jatin Hazarika and Hari Prasad Chaliha (Guwahati: Bimala Prasad Chaliha Centenary Celebration, 2012), 39.
200. Letter from J.L. Nehru to G. Bardoloi, 10 April 1950, in *SWJN*, second series, vol. 14, part 2, 18.
201. Secret Letter from B.R. Medhi to Patel, Demi official no. PS/135/49, 14 October 1950, Shillong, in *Assam Ministerial, September to December 1950*, File no. 3/6, vol. 4, *Digitized Private Papers, Sardar Patel*, Abhilekh Patal, NAI.

202. E.H. Pakyntein, *Census of India, 1961*, vol. 3, Assam, part 1–A, General Report (Delhi: Manager of Publications, 1964), 256.
203. Vaghaiwalla, *Report on the Census of India*, vol. 12, Assam, Manipur and Tripura, part 1–A, xxxiii–xxiv.
204. Ibid., 146.
205. Ibid., 365.

## Chapter 4: Assam in a Federal India

1. B. Shiva Rao, *The Framing of India's Constitution: Select Documents*, vol. 1 (New Delhi: Indian Institute of Public Administration, 1966), 310. Gopinath Bardoloi, Rev. J.J.M. Nichols Roy, Basanta Kumar Das, Rohini Kumar Choudhary, Omeo Kumar Das, Dharanidhar Basumatari and Akhsay Kumar Das were Congress members, while Saiyid Muhammad Saadulla, Abdul Hamid and Abdul Matin Chowdhury were from the Muslim League. Basanta Kumar Das later became a member from West Bengal. Omeo Kumar Das resigned from the Constituent Assembly in 1947 after his nomination to the Assam ministry. He served as the food and agriculture minister till 1952. *Times of India Directory and Yearbook, 1952–53*, 705.
2. Assam's representatives were Nibaran Chandra Laskar, Dharanidhar Basumatari, Gopinath Bardoloi, J.J.M. Nichols-Roy, Kuladhar Chaliha, Rohini Kumar Chaudhury, Muhammad Saadulla and Abdur Rouf. Arun Chandra Bhuyan and Sibopada De, eds, *Political History of Assam*, vol. 3 (Guwahati: Government of Assam, 1980), 371fn159.
3. *Dainik Asam*, 5 July 1946, 1.
4. For a biographical account of J.J.M. Nichols Roy, see P.R. Kyndiah, *Rev. J.J.M. Nichols Roy, Architect of District Council Autonomy* (New Delhi: Sanchar Publishing House, 1993).
5. Official Report, 22 July 1947, vol. 4, *Constituent Assembly Debates* [hereafter *CAD*] (New Delhi: Lok Sabha Secretariat, 2014), 748–49.
6. Letter from Bijoy Chandra Bhagavati, Kamala Prasad Agarwala, Kamakhya Prasad Tripathi and Mahi Kanta Das to Jawaharlal Nehru, 3 July 1947 in *Assam (General)*, vol. 1, 6–A, 1946–47, *Digitized Private Papers, Sardar Patel*, PP_000000005347, 36–37, Abhilekh Patal, NAI.
7. Letter from M. Tayyebulla to Patel, 5 July 1947, in Ibid.
8. Telegram from Ambikagiri Raychowdhury, President, Assam Jatiya Mahasabha, to Patel, 13 July 1947, in *Assam (General)*, vol. 1, 6–A, 1946–47, *Digitized Private Papers, Sardar Patel*, PP_000000005347, 33–34 Abhilekh Patal, NAI.

9. Sugata Bose, *The Nation as Mother and Other Visions of Nationhood* (Delhi: Penguin, 2017).
10. *Dainik Assamiya*, 10 April 1948, 1; *Assam Tribune*, 2 July 1948, 1; *Dainik Assamiya*, 13 April 1948, 1.
11. Nehru to Bardoloi, 4 July 1948, *Selected Works of Jawaharlal Nehru* [hereafter *SWJN*], second series, vol. 7, 421–22.
12. 'Lakshminath Bezbaroa's letter to Mohan Chandra Mahanta, 10 March 1936, Sambalpur,' in *Patralekha: A Bunch of Letters, etc. Written by Lakshminath Bezbaroa of Assam, to Different Persons and Institutions and by Different Persons and Institutions* ed. Maheswar Neog (Jorhat: Asam Sahitya Sabha, 1968), 39–40.
13. For further details on this, see Gitashree Tamuly, 'Lakshminath Bezbaroa and His Times: Language, Literature and Modernity in Colonial Assam' (PhD diss., Indian Institute of Technology, Guwahati, 2021), Chapter 5.
14. Speech of Kuladhar Chaliha, *CAD*, vol. X, 15 October 1949, 316.
15. Speech of Kuladhar Chaliha, *CAD*, vol. XI, 18 November 1949, 643.
16. *CAD*, 15 July 1947, vol. 1; Constituent Assembly of India, *Reports of Committees*, first series, 1947 (Delhi: Manager of Publication, 1947), 34–41; G. Austin, *The Indian Constitution: Cornerstone of a Nation* (Delhi: Oxford University Press, 1999), 42.
17. *CAD*, 21 July 1947, vol. 1; Constituent Assembly of India, *Reports of Committees*, first series (Delhi: Manager of Publication, 1947), 42–63. On 28 April, Nehru submitted the *Report of Powers Committee*. Constituent Assembly of India, *Reports of Committees*, first series, 1–4.
18. Omeo Kumar Das, *Jiban Smriti* (Guwahati: Publication Board Assam), 1983.
19. Speech of Omeo Kumar Das, *CAD*, vol. 1, 18 July 1947, 660–61.
20. Speech of J.J.M. Nichols Roy *CAD*, vol. 1, 18 July 1947, 662–63.
21. Speech of J.J.M. Nichols Roy, *CAD*, vol. 4, 18 July 1947, 663.
22. Speech of M. Saadulla, *CAD*, vol. 1, 18 July 1947, 670.
23. Speech of Jaipal Singh, *CAD*, vol. 1, 18 July 1947, 672.
24. Letter from Sergeant J.B. Hagjer, RIAF, 16 July 1947, Ambala to Patel in matters of Proportional Representation in the provincial legislature, North Cachar Hills, Assam, in *Assam (General)*, vol. 1, 6–A, 1946–47, *Digitized Private Papers, Sardar Patel*, PP_000000005347, Abhilekh Patal, NAI.
25. *CAD*, vol. 1, 18 July 1947, 674.
26. Aniket De, 'Lineages of Federalism: Race, Empire, and Anti-Colonialism in South Asia' (Draft PhD diss., Harvard University, 2022).
27. Tilak Das, *Assamiyar Jatiya Samashya* (Tezpur: Jiban Chadra Bora and others, 1949).

28. Arupjyoti Saikia, 'History, Buranjis and Nation: Suryya Kumar Bhuyan's Histories in Twentieth-Century Assam', *Indian Economic & Social History Review*, vol. 45, no. 4 (December 2008), 473–507.
29. Girin Phukon, *Assam's Attitude to Federalism* (New Delhi: Sterling Publishers Private Ltd), 62; Amalendu Guha, *Planter Raj to Swaraj: Freedom Struggle & Electoral Politics in Assam, 1826–1947* (Delhi: Indian Council of Historical Research, 1977), 191.
30. Jnananath Bora, 'Bartamanor Ron aru Asom Desh', *Awahan*, vol. 11, no. 2 (1940), 1237–48.
31. 'Memorandum Submitted to the British Parliamentary Delegation by the Asom Jatiya Mahisabha on January 29, 1946', in *Assam's Attitude to Federalism* ed. Phukon, 62.
32. *Assam Tribune*, 4 January 1948, in *Assam's Attitude to Federalism*, ed. Phukon, 62.
33. *Shillong Times*, 7 August 1947, quoted in Ibid.
34. Hiren Gohain, 'Origins of the Assamese Middle Class', *Social Scientist*, vol. 2, no. 1 (1973), 11–26.
35. Kamalakanta Bhattacharyya, a prolific Assamese writer and thinker, for decades prior to Independence wrote on these subjects. Praphulladutta Goswami, *Kamalakanta Bhattacharya Rachnawali* (Guwahati: Publication Board Assam, 1982).
36. *Dainik Assamiya*, 17 April 1948, 1.
37. Jnananath Bora, *Provincialism* (mimeograph, Guwahati, 1955), 2.
38. On 28 April, Nehru submitted the *Report of Powers Committee*. Constituent Assembly of India, *Reports of Committees*, first series, 1–4.
39. Austin, *Indian Constitution: Cornerstone of a Nation*, 244.
40. Speech of Omeo Kumar Das, *CAD*, vol. V, 21 August 1947, 94.
41. Phukon, *Assam's Attitude to Federalism*, 84–107.
42. Rao, *The Framing of India's Constitution: Select Documents*, vol. 4, 506. Members including M. Saadulla, S. Abdul Rouf, Nibaran Chandra Laskar and D. Basumatari met on 23 November 1948 and agreed that Assam would not require an upper house.
43. 'Letter from S.V. Patel to President, Constituent Assembly of India, 8 August 1947', in *CAD*, vol. 5, 243.
44. 'Rupnath Brahma, *Memorandum Submitted to the Sub-Committee on Minorities on the Safeguards for the Plains Tribal People of Assam*', in *The Framing of India's Constitution: Select Documents*, vol. 2, ed. Rao, 370–73.
45. 'Minutes of the Meeting of the Advisory Committee on Fundamental Rights, Minorities, etc., December 30, 1948', in *The Framing of India's Constitution: Select Documents*, vol. 4, ed. Rao, 597–98.

46. K.W.P. Marar, *Report on the Census of India, 1941*, vol. 9, Assam (Delhi: Manager of Publications, 1942), 23; David R. Syiemlieh, 'Sectional President's Address: Colonial Encounter and Christian Missions in North East India', *Proceedings of the Indian History Congress*, vol. 73 (2012), 509–27; Andrew May, *Welsh Missionaries and British Imperialism: The Empire of Clouds in North-east India* (Manchester: Manchester University Press, 2017); John Thomas, *Evangelising the Nation: Religion and the Formation of Naga Political Identity* (Delhi: Routledge, 2015).
47. K.M. Munshi, 'Advisory Committee on Fundamental Rights, Minorities', in *The Framing of the India's Constitution: Select Documents*, vol. 2 ed. Rao, 76.
48. Speech of K.M. Munshi, *CAD*, vol. III, 1 May 1947, 488.
49. Speech of V. Patel, *CAD*, vol. III, 1 May 1947, 502.
50. Speech of M. Saadullah, *CAD*, vol. VII, 24 November 1948, 577–79. Also see Rohit De, 'Cows and Constitutionalism', *Modern Asian Studies*, vol. 53, no. 1 (2019), 240–77.
51. Speech of M. Saadullah, *CAD*, vol. VII, 24 November 1948, 578.
52. Ibid.
53. Otto Niemeyer, *Indian Financial Enquiry Report* (London: His Majesty' Stationery Office, 1936), 11.
54. Phukon, *Assam's Attitude to Federalism*, 110–11.
55. 'Report of the Expert Committee on Financial Provisions of the Union Constitution, Summary of Provincial Suggestions, Appendix B, Annexure III', *CAD*, vol. VI, 4 November 1948, 86.
56. *Expert Committee on Financial Provisions*, Annexure III, Appendix B, Summary of Provincial Suggestions, Part I: (Taxes), 4 November 1948.
57. Speech of Gopinath Bardoloi, *CAD*, vol. IX, 5 August 1949, 229.
58. Rao, ed., *The Framing of India's Constitution: Select Documents*, vol. 4, 405.
59. Speech by R.K. Chaudhuri, *CAD*, vol. IX, 8 August 1949, 254.
60. Speech by Kuladhar Chaliha, *CAD*, vol. VIII, 16 June 1949, 919.
61. Ramachandra Guha, *India After Gandhi: The History of the World's Largest Democracy* (Delhi: Picador, 2007), 109.
62. 'Note by the Central Ministry of Finance on Certain Financial Provisions of the Draft Constitution', in *The Framing of India's Constitution: Select Documents*, vol. 4, ed. Rao, 673.
63. Jogendranarayan Bhuyan, *Sadagar Bholanath Borooah* (Diphu: Diphu Sahitya Sabha, 1993), 39.
64. Jnananath Bora, *Asomot Bideshi* (Calcutta: Sarveswar Bhattacharjya, 1925), 3.
65. 'Speech of Herama Prasad Barua, Council of State Debates', in *Times of Assam*, 16 March 1935. The estimate is based on Government of Assam,

*Report on the Administration of Assam for 1916–17* (Shillong: Assam Secretariat Printing Press, 1918), Table 171, 28.

66. Neil Charlesworth, 'The Problem of Government Finance in British India: Taxation, Borrowing and the Allocation of Resources in the Inter-War Period', *Modern Asian Studies*, vol. 19, no. 3 (1985), 534.
67. P.J. Thomas, *The Growth of Federal Finance in India* (Humphrey Milford: Oxford University Press, 1939).
68. Charlesworth, 'The Problem of Government Finance in British India: Taxation, Borrowing and the Allocation of Resources in the Inter-War Period', 537.
69. Indian Statutory Commission, *Report of the Indian Statutory Commission*, vol. 1 (Calcutta: Government of India, 1930), 353; 'Progress of Income and Expenditure of the Assam government, 1911–12 to 1936–37', in *Economic Development of Assam*, Prabhas Chandra Goswami (Mumbai: Asia Publishing House, 1963), Statement I, 346–47.
70. Indian Statutory Commission, *Memorandum Submitted by the Government of Assam to the Indian Statutory Commission*, Report of the Indian Statutory Commission, vol. XIV (London: His Majesty's Stationery Office, 1930), 363.
71. Eustace Percy, *Report of the Federal Finance Committee* (New Delhi: Government of India Press, 1932), 24.
72. Thomas, *The Growth of Federal Finance in India*, 373.
73. Speech by M. Saadulla, *CAD*, vol. IX, 8 August 1949, 267.
74. Amaresh Bagchi, 'Review Article: Fiscal Federalism—Problems and Possible Solutions', *Indian Economic Review*, vol. 12, no. 2 (1977), 185–211.
75. Niemeyer, *Indian Financial Enquiry Report*, 10.
76. Rana P. Behal, 'Power Structure, Discipline, and Labour in Assam Tea Plantations Under Colonial Rule', *International Review of Social History*, vol. 51, no. 14 (2006), 143. Also see Chapter 3 for further details.
77. This estimate is based on figures provided by 'Accounts Relating to Sea Borne Trade and Navigation in India', in *Report of the Jute Enquiry Commission*, Annexure XIII (New Delhi: Ministry of Finance, Government of India Press, 1954), 209.
78. GoI, *Statistical Abstract for 1946–47* (Delhi: Manager of Publications, 1949), Table 93 and 94, 206–07.
79. Ibid., Table 119 (A), 269.
80. 'Estimate based on Quarterly Bulletins of the Department of Economics and Statistics, Government of Assam', in *Economic Development of Assam*, Goswami, Statement I and II, 347–48.
81. Goswami, *Economic Development of Assam*, Appendix III, 333.

82. Atul Chandra Sarma, 'A Study of Assam Finances: Structure and Trend 1947–48 to 1965–66' (PhD diss., Gauhati University, 1971), Chapter 3, Table 3.1, 99.
83. Ibid., 228.
84. Ibid., Table 5.11 B, 309.
85. Alban Ali and Eric Lambert, *Assam* (Oxford: Oxford University Press, 1946), 17.
86. Anonymous, 'The Scheduled and Tribal Areas', *Indian Journal of Public Administration*, vol. 23, no. 3 (July 1977), 821–36.
87. H.K. Barpujari, *Problem of the Hill Tribes: North-East Frontier: 1873–1962* (Guwahati: Lawyer's Book Stall, 1970), 255–88; Christoph von Fürer-Haimendorf, *Himalayan Barbary* (London: John Murray Publishers Ltd, 1955); Bérénice Guyot-Réchard, *Shadow States: India, China and the Himalayas, 1910–1962* (Cambridge: Cambridge University Press, 2016).
88. A.V. Thakkar and G.N. Bardoloi, 'Joint Report of the Excluded and the Partially Excluded Areas (Other than Assam) and the Northeast Frontier (Assam) Tribal and Excluded Areas Subcommittee, 25 August 1947', in G.N. Bardoloi, *Constituent Assembly of India: Report of the Excluded and Partially Excluded Areas (Other than Assam) Subcommittee*, vol. 1 (New Delhi: Manager of Publications, 1947), para. 2, 51. The third committee on the North-West Frontier Province and Baluchistan was no more relevant for the Constituent Assembly of India due to Partition.
89. Ibid.
90. Illustrations are numerous. For instance, Robert Reid, 'The Excluded Areas of Assam', *Geographical Journal*, vol. 103, no. 1/2 (1944), 18–29.
91. For instance, Jogendranath Hazarika, 'Tribals and their Constitutional Position: A Memorandum to the Members of the Constituent Assembly and the Advisory Committee on behalf of the Twenty-Five Million Souls of Tribal India', Entry no. F. 10/2–10, April 1947, in *Quaid-I-Azam Mohammed Ali Jinnah Papers*, vol. 1, no. 370, part 1 ed. Zaidi, 641–50.
92. G.N. Bardoloi, *Constituent Assembly of India: Northeast Frontier (Assam) Tribal and Excluded Areas Subcommittee*, vol. 2, part 1 (New Delhi: Manager of Publications, 1947) Appendix III, 64.
93. Bardoloi, *Constituent Assembly of India: Northeast Frontier (Assam) Tribal and Excluded Areas Subcommittee*, vol. 2, part 1, 1.
94. Joy L.K. Pachuau, *Being Mizo: Identity and Belonging in Northeast India* (New Delhi: Oxford University Press, 2014), 91–97.
95. The Assam Provincial Congress Committee backed the Mizo Union. Zonunmawia, 'The Formation of the District Council in Mizo hills' (MPhil Thesis, North-Eastern Hill University, 1985), Chapter 3.

96. Bardoloi, *Constituent Assembly of India: Northeast Frontier (Assam) Tribal and Excluded Areas Subcommittee*, vol. 2, part 1, 5.
97. V. Venkata Rao, *A Century of Tribal Politics in North East India* (Delhi: S. Chand, 1976), 161–62; Sajal Nag, Tejimala Gurung and Abhijit Choudhury, eds, *Making of the Indian Union: Merger of Princely States and Excluded Areas* (Delhi: Akansha, 2007), 209–22.
98. Bardoloi, *Constituent Assembly of India: Northeast Frontier (Assam) Tribal and Excluded Areas Subcommittee*, vol. 2, part 1, 32.
99. Ranabir Samaddar, *The Politics of Autonomy: Indian Experiences* (New Delhi: Sage India, 2005), 219; Shibani Kinkar Chaube, *Hill Politics in North-East India* (Delhi: Orient Blackswan, 2012).
100. Bardoloi, *Constituent Assembly of India: Northeast Frontier (Assam) Tribal and Excluded Areas Subcommittee*, vol. 2, part 1, 38.
101. G.N. Bardoloi, *Constituent Assembly of India: Northeast Frontier (Assam) Tribal and Excluded Areas Subcommittee*, vol.2, *(Evidence)* part 2 (New Delhi: Manager of Publications, 1947), 12–13.
102. Ibid., 15.
103. Ibid., 16.
104. Ibid., 39.
105. Ibid., 43. For an account of the relations between the Khamti and the British East India Company, see Alexander Mackenzie, *History of the Relations of the Government with the Hill Tribes of the North-East Frontier of Bengal* (Calcutta: Home Department Press, 1884), 57–63.
106. For details of these treaties, see C.U. Aitchison and A.C. Talbot, eds, *A Collection of Treaties, Engagements, and Sunnuds Relating to India and Neighbouring Countries*, vol. 1 (Calcutta: Foreign Office Press, 1876); Suryya Kumar Bhuyan, *Early British Relations with Assam* (Shillong: Assam Secretariat Press, 1928).
107. Bardoloi, *Constituent Assembly of India: Northeast Frontier (Assam) Tribal and Excluded Areas Subcommittee*, vol. 2, part 2, 48.
108. Ibid.
109. *Posa* was an Ahom-era arrangement of payments to the chiefs of the inhabitants of the hills bordering the Brahmaputra Valley's north; it was also continued by the British colonial administrators. See Chapter 7 for further explanation of *Posa*.
110. Bardoloi, *Constituent Assembly of India: Northeast Frontier (Assam) Tribal and Excluded Areas Subcommittee*, vol 2, part 1, 78.
111. Ibid., 79.
112. Ibid., 79.
113. Ibid., 86.

114. H.Y. Haflangbar, President, Standing Committee Tribal Council, *Memorandum*, in *Constituent Assembly of India: Northeast Frontier (Assam) Tribal and Excluded Areas Subcommittee*, Bardoloi, vol. 2, part 1, Appendix E, 105–09.
115. Bardoloi, *Constituent Assembly of India: Northeast Frontier (Assam) Tribal and Excluded Areas Subcommittee*, vol. 2, part 2, 68.
116. Ibid., 68. All quotes in this para are from this reference.
117. Ibid., 70.
118. Ibid., 75; A. MacDonald Kongor, *Memorandum of Statement of the case of the Hill Tribes of Assam, Particularly the Khasis of the Khasi and Jaintia Hills: Presented to the Sub-Committee of the Advisory Committee of the Constituent Assembly and to the Major Political Parties and to All Authority Concerned*, Shillong, The Hills Union and The Khasi National Durbar, 12 June 1947, File no. 67/48–P.S., Abhilekh Patal, NAI.
119. Bardoloi, *Constituent Assembly of India: Northeast Frontier (Assam) Tribal and Excluded Areas Subcommittee*, vol. 2, part 2, 84.
120. Ibid., 241.
121. For illustrative contrasting views, but of people not interviewed by the Bardoloi Committee, see Bishnuprasad Rava, 'Asomiya Kristi' and 'Asomiya Kristir Chamu Abhas', in *Bishnuprasad Rava Rachana Sambhar*, part II ed. Jogesh Das (Nagaon: Sarveswar Bora, 1997), 1090–1107, 1266–83.
122. '*The Assam Tribune*, January 3, 1948', in *Assam's Attitude to Federalism*, ed. Phukon, 63.
123. Bardoloi, *Constituent Assembly of India: Northeast Frontier (Assam) Tribal and Excluded Areas Subcommittee*, vol. 2, part 2.
124. Abhijit Guha, 'Social Anthropology of B.S. Guha', *Indian Anthropologist*, vol. 48, no. 1 (2018), 1–12; Anonymous, 'Biraja Sankar Guha, 1894–1961', *International Journal of Comparative Sociology*, vol. 3, no. 2 (1962), 277–78.
125. Bardoloi, *Constituent Assembly of India: Northeast Frontier (Assam) Tribal and Excluded Areas Subcommittee*, vol. 2, part 2, 274.
126. Ibid., 241, 279.
127. Ibid., 279–80.
128. A series of scholarship has richly contributed to our understanding of the Naga political question of the twentieth century. For a rich bibliography, see Thomas, *Evangelising the Nation: Religion and the Formation of Naga Political Identity*; Franke, *War and Nationalism in South Asia: The Indian State and the Nagas* (London: Routledge, 2009).
129. *New York Times*, 14 February 1947.

130. Bardoloi, *Constituent Assembly of India: Northeast Frontier (Assam) Tribal and Excluded Areas Subcommittee,* vol. 2, part 1, 181.
131. Telegram from M/S Octavious Steel & Company to C.E. Bernard, secretary, Government of India, Home, no. 655, in *Naga Raids on Certain Tea Gardens in Assam,* File no. 655–668, Foreign Political A, March 1880, Abhilekh Patal, NAI.
132. Telegram from Foreign Secretary, Government of India to Chief Commissioner, Assam, no. 113 IP, 30 January 1880, no. 658, in *Naga Raids on Certain Tea Gardens in Assam.*
133. Guha, *Planter Raj to Swaraj: Freedom Struggle & Electoral Politics in Assam, 1826–1947,* 264.
134. 'Memorandum on the Case of the Naga People for Self-Determination and an Appeal to HMG and the Government of India', in *Constituent Assembly of India: Northeast Frontier (Assam) Tribal and Excluded Areas Subcommittee,* Bardoloi, vol. 2, part 1, 246–49.
135. 'Letter from Lord Pethick-Lawrence to Mountbatten, India Office, 12 April 1947', in *Constitutional Relations Between Britain and India: The Transfer of Power, 1942–47* (hereafter *TOP*), vol. X, eds, Nicholas Mansergh and Penderel Moon (London: H.M.S.O., 1970–82), 219–20.
136. 'Letter from Mountbatten to the Earl of Listowel, Secretary of State, 24 April 1947', in *TOP*, vol. X, 401.
137. 'Burma', *Guardian,* 7 January 1947, 4.
138. Ibid.
139. 'The Visit of Andrew Clow', in Bardoloi, *Constituent Assembly of India: Northeast Frontier (Assam) Tribal and Excluded Areas Subcommittee,* vol. 2, part 1, 245.
140. Both the Bengal Eastern Frontier Regulation and the Chin Hills Regulation gave considerable protection to the Naga Hills. For further details on these laws, see the next section.
141. 'Extracts from the resolutions of the Kohima Tribal Council, 9 April 1947, in Letter from P.F. Adams, Secretary to the Governor of Assam to the Prime Minister, Assam, 7 May 1947', in *Constituent Assembly of India: Northeast Frontier (Assam) Tribal and Excluded Areas Subcommittee,* Bardoloi, vol. 2, part 1, 241.
142. Bardoloi, *Constituent Assembly of India: Northeast Frontier (Assam) Tribal and Excluded Areas Subcommittee,* vol. 2, part 1, 181.
143. Ibid., 182.
144. Ibid.
145. 'Letter from G.N. Bardoloi to the Chairman, Advisory Committee on Fundamental Rights, CAI, 28 July 1947', in *Framing of India's Constitution,* vol. 3, ed. Rao, 684–85.

146. Bardoloi, *Constituent Assembly of India: Northeast Frontier (Assam) Tribal and Excluded Areas Subcommittee*, vol. 2, part 1, 188–189.
147. Ibid., 189.
148. Ibid., 185–86.
149. 'Letter from Hydari to Mountbatten, 11 July 1947', in *TOP*, vol. XII, 104.
150. The draft cable read as follows: 'Benign excellence, Kindly put on record that Nagas will be independent. Discussion with India are being carried on to that effect. Nagas do not accept Indian Constitution. The right of the people must prevail regardless of size', however, it was never despatched. V.K. Nuh, *The Naga Chronicle* (Shillong: ICSSR, 2002), 115; Jelle J.P. Wouters, 'Difficult Decolonization: Debates, Divisions, and Deaths Within the Naga Uprising, 1944–1963', *Journal of North East India Studies*, vol. 9, no. 1 (January–June 2019), 12; *Times of India*, 18 August 1947, 7.
151. Bardoloi, *Constituent Assembly of India: Northeast Frontier (Assam) Tribal and Excluded Areas Subcommittee*, vol. 1, 13–14; Pum Khan Pau, *Indo-Burma Frontier and the Making of the Chin Hills: Empire and Resistance* (London: Routledge, 2019); Anandaroop Sen, 'The Law of Emptiness: Episodes from Lushai and Chin Hills (1890–98)', *Landscape, Culture, and Belonging: Writing the History of Northeast India*, eds, Neeladri Bhattacharya and Joy L.K. Pachau (Delhi: Cambridge University Press, 2019), 226–27.
152. Indian Statutory Commission, *Report of the Indian Statutory Commission*, vol. 1 (London: His Majesty's Stationery Office, 1930), 160.
153. 'Memorandum by the Government of Assam to the Indian Statutory Commission', 99–100.
154. Robert Reid, 'The Excluded Areas of Assam', *Geographical Journal*, vol. 103, no. 1/2 (1944), 18–29; Robert Reid, 'A Note on the Future of the Present Excluded, Partially Excluded and Tribal Areas of Assam', MSS Eur E 278/4, Reid Collection (Asia, Pacific and Africa Collection, British Library).
155. Speech of Edward Cadogan, 10 May 1935, Government of India Bill, House of Commons Debates, Official Report of House of Commons, vol. 301, in https://hansard.parliament.uk/commons/1935-05-10/debates/ a7624730-2cee-406d-a83e-f7d5457f3eb4/SixthSchedule—(Excluded Areas and Partially Excluded Areas).
156. This has been treated extensively in Ornit Shani, *How India Became Democratic: Citizenship and the Making of the Universal Franchise* (Cambridge: Cambridge University Press, 2017), Chapter 6.
157. Shani, *How India Became Democratic*, 218–20; Berenice, *Shadow State*, 84. This will be discussed further in Chapter 7.

158. *Times of India*, 10 September 1947, 7; R.B. Vaghaiwalla, *Census of India, 1951*, Assam, Manipur and Tripura, vol. XII, part II-A (Shillong: Assam Government Press, 1953), Table D-III, 108–110.
159. *Amrita Bazar Patrika*, 9 July 1947, 3.
160. Rao, ed., *The Framing of India's Constitution: Select Documents*, vol. 3, 780.
161. 'Letter from Patel to the President, Constituent Assembly of India, March 4, 1948', in *The Framing of India's Constitution: Select Documents*, ed. Rao, vol. 3, 682.
162. Speech by B. Prasad, *CAD*, vol. IX, 5 September 1949, 1004.
163. Speech of Kuladhar Chaliha, *CAD*, vol. IX, 6 September 1949, 1009.
164. Pushpalata Das, 'Bardoloidevar Byaktitat Ebhumuki', in *Gopinath Bardoloi* ed. Chandraprasad Saikia (Guwahati: Publication Board Assam, 1979), 187–89.
165. Speech of Gopinath Bardoloi, *CAD*, vol. IX, 6 September 1949, 1013.
166. Speech of J.J.M. Nichols Roy, *CAD*, vol. IX, 6 September 1949, 1022.
167. Speech of Jaipal Singh, *CAD*, vol. IX, 6 September 1949, 1019.
168. Speech of A.V. Thakkar, *CAD*, vol. IX, 6 September 1949, 1021.
169. *Times of India*, 7 September 1949, 1; *Amrita Bazar Patrika*, 9 September 1949, 1 and 8.
170. Padmanath Gohainbarua, *Mur Sonwarani* (Guwahati: Publication Board Assam, 1971), 13–19.
171. Dolly Kikon, *Living with Oil and Coal: Resource Politics and Militarization in Northeast India* (Washington: University of Washington Press, 2019).
172. Arupjyoti Saikia, 'Flows and Fairs: The Eastern Himalayas and the British Empire', in *Flows and Frictions in Trans-Himalayan Spaces: Histories of Networking and Border Crossing*, eds, Gunnel Cederlof and Willem van Schendel (Amsterdam: Amsterdam University Press, 2021), 137–63.
173. A. Lushai, 'The Assam Hillman', Letters to the Editor, *Guardian,* 3 March 1948, 4.
174. A. I. Bowman, 'The Assam Hill Man', *Manchester Guardian*, 22 November 1947, 4; Anonymous, 'The Assam Hill Man', *Manchester Guardian*, 20 December 1947, 4; T.P.S. Rajan, 'The Assam Hill Man', *Manchester Guardian*, 31 December 1947, 4; M.P. Khera, 'The Assam Hill Man', *Manchester Guardian*, 9 December 1947, 4.
175. A.I. Bowman, 'The Assam Hill Man', *Manchester Guardian*, 22 November 1947, 4.
176. M.P. Khera, 'The Assam Hill Man', *Manchester Guardian*, 9 December 1947, 4.
177. Christoph von Fürer-Haimendorf, 'The Aboriginal Tribes of India: The Historical Background and Their Position in Present-Day India', *Journal of the Royal Society of Arts*, vol. 98, no. 4832 (1950), 997–1011.

178. Letter from J.P. Mills to E. Hyde 17 May 1940, in *Edgar Hyde Papers*, File C (Bastar), Box VIII, Centre of South Asian Studies Archives, Centre of South Asian Studies, University of Cambridge.
179. 'Review of the Chinese Activities in India, July 1948–June 1949 Prepared by Department of Intelligence Bureau', in File no. 612 (3) CJK/49, 1949, GoI, Ministry of External Affairs, CJK Branch, Abhilekh Patal, NAI.
180. 'The Problem of Hill Tribes, Extract from a note by H.V.R. Iyengar, Letter from H.V.R. Iyengar to K.P.S. Menon, ICS, Secret, 25 October 1949', File no. 147/NEF/49/1949, 1949, Ministry of External Affairs, NEF Branch, Abhilekh Patal, NAI.
181. 'Secret Note for Sheopori by the Indian Embassy Burma, 7 October 1949', File no. 147/NEF/49/1949, Ministry of External Affairs, NEF Branch, 1949, Abhilekh Patal, NAI.
182. *Guardian*, 16 May 1949, 5.
183. B.S. Guha, 'Statement on the Scheduled Tribes, Scheduled Areas and Tribal Areas in the Draft Constitution of India', in *Amendment of Schedules 5 & 6 in the Draft Constitution Concerning the Scheduled Tribes of India*, File no. 8-38/48–A2, Government of India, Ministry of Education, 1948, Abhilekh Patal, NAI.
184. 'Letter from A. Datta, Deputy Secretary, Government of Assam, Medical Department, Tribal Welfare Branch to Deputy Secretary, Government of India, Ministry of Education, no. MTW/14/49/5, 21 January 1950, Shillong', in *Amendment of Schedules 5 & 6 in the Draft Constitution Concerning the Scheduled Tribes of India*.

## Chapter 5: Domestic Woes

1. R.B. Vaghaiwalla, *Report: Census of India, 1951*, vol. XII, part I-A, Assam, Manipur and Tripura (Shillong: Superintendent of Census Operations, Assam, 1954), table 1.51, 102.
2. Ruth Fischer, 'The Indian Communist Party', *Far Eastern Survey*, vol. 22, no. 7 (1953), 79–84.
3. Sugata Bose, *Agrarian Bengal: Economy, Social Structure and Politics* (Cambridge: Cambridge University Press, 1986).
4. The following paragraphs in this section on the communist mobilization are based on Arupjyoti Saikia, *A Century of Protests: Peasant Politics in Assam since 1900* (New Delhi: Routledge, 2014).
5. M.V. Seshagiri Rao, 'A Statistical Study of Labour in the Assam Tea Plantation', *Sankhyā: The Indian Journal of Statistics (1933–1960)*, vol. 7, no. 4 (1946), 446, Table 2.

6. Rana P. Behal, 'Power Structure, Discipline, and Labour in Assam Tea Plantations under Colonial Rule', *International Review of Social History*, vol. 51 (2006), 143–72.
7. Ameer Raza, 'Planning Commission on Implementation of Land Reforms in Assam', in *Implementation of Land Reforms* (Delhi: Planning Commission, 1967), 39.
8. Fischer, 'The Indian Communist Party', 79–84.
9. G.D. Overstreet and M. Windmiller, *Communism in India* (Berkeley: University of California Press, 1959), 236–37.
10. *Second Congress of the CPI: Opening Report by Comrade B.T. Ranadive on the Draft Political Thesis* (n.p.: Communist Party of India, 1948), P.C. Joshi Archive, Jawaharlal Nehru University.
11. Overstreet and Windmiller, *Communism in India*, 272–73; Amit Kumar Gupta, *Agrarian Drama: The Leftists and the Rural Poor in India 1934–1951* (New Delhi: Manohar, 1996); Gangadhar M. Adhikari, *Documents of the History of the Communist Party of India: 1948–1950* (New Delhi: People's Publishing House, 1971).
12. Md. Abdullah Rasul, *A History of the All India Kisan Sabha* (New Delhi: National Book Agency, 1989), 342; Saroj Chakrabarty, *With Dr. B.C. Roy and Other Chief Ministers: A Record upto 1960* (Calcutta: Benson's, 1974), 92–93; Speech of Jawaharlal Nehru, 28 February 1949, *Constituent Assembly of India (Legislative) Debates, Official Report*, vol. II, part 1, 1109.
13. 'Note on the Assam Provincial Communist Party', File no. 55/1949, 'Politburo Resolution on Assam Provincial Committee, 1949', File no. 53/1949, P. C. Joshi Archives, Jawaharlal Nehru University.
14. 'Letter of Soumendranath Tagore to Rabindranath, 1 November 1933, Paris', in *Soumendranath Thakur: Karme O Manane*, ed. Manjula Basu (Kolkata: Tagore Research Institute, 2007), Appendix D, 255–57.
15. Basu, *Soumendranath Thakur: Karme O Manane*, 85–87; Revolutionary Communist Party of India, *Historical Development of Communist Movement in India* (Calcutta: Revolutionary Communist Party of India, 1944), 24–27.
16. 'Revolutionary Communist Party of India, *The Present Situation and the Task of the Party*': *Political Thesis of the Revolutionary Communist Party of India—Adopted at the 4th Conference of the Party held in May 1948* (Calcutta: Bisweswar Bhattacharya, 1948), P.C. Joshi Archives, Jawaharlal Nehru University, 18–19.
17. For a biographical account of Pannalal Dasgupta, see Gouri Sankar Nag, *Pannalal Dasgupta: Story of a Homeless Radical* (New Delhi: Manak Publication Pvt. Ltd, 2018).

18. Pannalal Dasgupta, *Samajtantrabad Ajai Kena* (Kolkata: n.p., n.d.). For a brief overview of the Chinese communists' political experiments, see Rana Mitter, *Modern China: A Very Short Introduction* (Oxford: Oxford University Press, 2008).
19. Basu, *Soumendranath Thakur: Karme O Manane*, 150–55.
20. 'Resolution on Land Settlement & Eviction in Assam', in *Assam Fights for Freedom and Democracy* [Draft Resolutions of Assam Communists], Assam Provincial Organising Committee, Communist Party of India (Guwahati: Assam Provincial Organising Committee, Communist Party of India, n.d.), 48; Assam Provincial Organising Committee, Communist Party of India, *Swadhinotar Ebachar: Communist Partyir Ghosana* (Guwahati: Assam Provincial Organising Committee, Communist Party of India, 1948), 31.
21. Assam Police Abstract of Intelligence, 18 September 1948, ASA; Dipankar Banerjee, *Labour Movement in Assam: A Study of Non-Plantation Workers' Strikes till 1939* ( New Delhi: Anamika Publishers, 2005).
22. *Assam Tribune*, 2 May 1954, 1. Compared to officially reported figure of the occurrence of 56 such incidents in 1952, there were 281 reported incidents in 1953.
23. 'Communist Agitations', Letter from Harold Dennehy, Chief Secretary to the Government of Assam to the Commissioner of Divisions, 14 February 1947, File no. I/A 5/5(F)47, *Assam Police Intelligence Record Room, Special Branch, Kahilipara, Guwahati* (hereafter *APIRR*).
24. *Natun Asam*, 16 March 1949, 1, Centre for Assamese Studies, Digital Archive, Tezpur University.
25. Secret letter from Gopinath Bardoloi to Jawaharlal Nehru, 12 October 1949, New Delhi, unnumbered papers, ASA. The 'Communists have started a vile propaganda for ousting the Government authority in certain places. It is to meet the menace from the Communist that I have to spend my times in tours to explain to the people the position of Government. It is also for these reasons that employment of a larger police force has become necessary to maintain law and order' wrote Bardoloi to Patel; 'Letter from Bardoloi to Patel, 22 June 1950', in *Sardar Patel's Correspondence*, vol. 9, ed. Durga Das (Ahmedabad: Navajivan Publishing House, 1971), 207.
26. File no. I/A-3(6)K/47, *APIRR*; *New York Times*, 21 August 1949, 16.
27. Beltola, a large revenue circle then in the southern neighbourhood of Guwahati, was declared a disturbed area in April 1949 (*Annual Report on the Police Administration of Assam*, 1949, 11). Parts of Sibsagar were also declared as disturbed areas in the mid-1950. Speech by Emran Hussain Chaudhury, 6 October 1950, *Assam Legislative Assembly Debates* (hereafter *ALAD*).

28. *Assam Gazette*, 6 July 1949, Part II, No. c. 260/49; *Natun Asamiya*, 8 September 1950; Government of Assam, *Annual Report on the Police Administration of Assam, 1948* (Shillong: Assam Government Press, 1949), 11.
29. 'Consolidated Report on the Communist Peace Conference and Subsequent Disturbances at Dibrugarh Railway Colony on 15 to 17 July 1949', *Personal File of Bishnu Rabha*, File no. B/128-49, *APIRR*.
30. Jyoti Prasad Agarwala, 'Naliapular Bipod Sanket', in *Jyotiprasad Rachanavali*, ed. Hiren Gohain (Guwahati: Publication Board Assam, 2003), 543–549nn600–601.
31. Entry of 17 July 1949, *Personal Diary of Ajit Kumar Baruah*, Dibrugarh, courtesy, Anupam Baruah, Barbarua, Dibrugarh.
32. 'Police action against communists in Assam: Underground leaders' arrest in surprise raid', *Times of India*, 27 July 1949, 7.
33. Letter from Gopinath Bardoloi to Jawaharlal Nehru, 12 October 1949, New Delhi, unnumbered papers, ASA.
34. 'Patel to Nehru, November 7, 1950', in *Sardar Patel's Correspondence*, vol. 10, ed. Durga Das (Ahmedabad: Navajivan Publishing House, 1974), 339.
35. 'Nehru to Prakasa, 31 January 1949', *Selected Works of Jawaharlal Nehru* (hereafter *SWJN*), vol. 9, second series, 343; Nehru to Sri Prakash, Governor of Assam, 25 March 1949, *SWJN*, second series, vol. 10, 340; 'Extract from the Daily Summary of Information of the Deputy Director, SIB, Assam, 14 November 1949, *APIRR*; 'Note, Secret, B.N. Mullik, Deputy Director, Intelligence Bureau, Ministry of Home Affairs, 18 November 1949', in *Communist Activities on Assam Burma Frontier and in the Tribal Areas of Assam*, File no. 143–NEF/49, 1949, Government of India, Ministry of External Affairs, NEF Branch, Abhilekh Patal, NAI.
36. 'Bardoloi to Patel, 22 June 1950, Guwahati', in *Sardar Patel's Correspondence*, vol. 9, ed. Das, 207.
37. 'Letter from Patel to Jairamdas Doulatram, Assam Governor, 5 June 1950 Dehra Dun', in *Sardar Patel's Correspondence*, vol. 9, ed. Das, 192.
38. 'India plans curbs on reds in Assam: Communist pressure on east brings precautionary step by New Delhi regime', *New York Times*, 9 June 1950, 14.
39. Speech of B.R. Medhi, chief minister, Assam, *ALAD*, 6 October 1950; 'Communism in India and Pakistan; Indian and Pakistani communists in the United Kingdom and Europe, June–October 1950 (Folder 2)' (Government Papers, The National Archives, Kew, 1950).
40. Notification no. c.387/50/6, *Assam Gazette*, 5 July 1950; 'Bishnu Prasad Rabha versus the State, Judgement of Appeal Court, Lower Assam Division, Criminal Appeal no 61 (1) of 1953, File no. B/128-49, *APIRR*.

41. 'Letter from Jairamdas Doulatam, Governor of Assam to Patel, 10 June 1950, Shillong', in *Sardar Patel's Correspondence*, vol. 9, ed. Das, 195.
42. Secret Notes on Communism in India, no. 20, May–June 1950, 19 July, in 'Communism in India and Pakistan; Indian and Pakistani communists in the United Kingdom and Europe, June–October 1950 (Folder 2)' (Government Papers, The National Archives, Kew, 1950), http://www.archivesdirect.amdigital.co.uk/Documents/Details/FO_371_84238 (Accessed 10 March 2021).
43. *Hindustan Times*, 8 September 1950, 6.
44. 'Indian Republic, 29 October 1950', in *Assam Flood Relief and Communist Menace*, File 7E, 1950, *Digitized Private Papers, Sardar Patel*, Abhilekh Patal, NAI.
45. '"Red" menace in Assam increases: Activities on Malayan model basic symptom of economic disorder', *Times of India*, 28 February 1951, 1.
46. *Natun Asamiya*, 31 January 1951; Letter from P.C. Choudhury, IB, SI, Kokrajhar to Superintendent of Police, Goalpara, DIB, 26 July 1952, File no. B-128/49, *APIRR*.
47. Praphulladutta Goswami, *Kencha Patar Kanpani* (Guwahati: LBS, 1991 [1952]), 1–3.
48. Speech by Bishnuram Medhi, Budget Session, 9 March 1951, *ALAD*.
49. *Natun Asamiya*, 24 May 1951, 1.
50. These propaganda materials were proscribed under the Indian Press (Emergency Powers) Act of 1931; *New York Times*, 14 August 1949, 9.
51. *Natun Asamiya*, 31 January 1951, 1.
52. Ibid.
53. *Times of India*, 15 October 1950, 3; *Statesman*, 7 October 1950, 4.
54. *Statesman*, 3 October 1950, 4.
55. '"Red" menace in Assam increases: Activities on Malayan model basic symptom of economic disorder', *Times of India*, 28 February 1951, 1.
56. Haridas Deka, *Jivan aru Sangram*, (Guwahati: LBS, 1992), 54; Tarun Sen Deka, *Mukti Sangramar Adharat Jiban Katha* (Guwahati: R.D. Printers and Publishers, 1993), 132; *Natun Asamiya*, 24 June 1952, 4.
57. Intercepted letter from Bishnu Rabha to Nabin Medhi, Special Jail, Nagaon, May 1953, File no. B/128-49 (*APIRR*); Intercepted letter from Bishnu Rabha to Suren Bhattacharjee, 21 January 1953, Dhubri, File no. B/128-49, (*APIRR*); Editorial, 'Biplabi Communistor Kartyaba', *Lal Nisan*, vol. 2, no. 1 (April 1952). *Lal Nisan* was the official newsletter of the RCPI.
58. Amalendu Guha, ed., 'Personal Reminiscences of Pranesh Biwsas', in *Zamindarkalin Goalpara Zillar Artha Samajik Abastha: Eti Oitihasik Dristipat* (Guwahati: Natun Sahitya Parisad, 2000), 103.

59. 'Statement of Policy of the CPI, All India Conference, Calcutta, 1951', in *Documents of the Communist Movement in India*, vol. 6 (1949–51), ed. Jyoti Basu (Calcutta: National Book Agency Private Limited, 1997).
60. Election Commission of India, *Statistical Report on General Election of 1951 to the Legislative Assembly of Assam* (New Delhi: Government Press, 1952).
61. *Chief Secretary's Fortnightly Report* (hereafter *FR*), 1st half, August 1952; *Natun Asamiya*, 1 November 1952.
62. Lakhyadhar Chaudhury, *Manuh Bichari* (Guwahati: Publication Board Assam, 1992), 85.
63. *FR*, 1st half, September 1957; *FR*, 2nd half, September 1957.
64. Raza, "Planning Commission on Implementation of Land Reforms in Assam', 3.
65. 'Demands of Assam Steamer Workers', *Assam Tribune*, 1 March 1954, 1.
66. *FR*, 2nd half, June 1957.
67. All India Congress Committee, *Zamindari Abolition and Agrarian Reforms: A Summary of the Efforts of the Congress Organisation to Implement the Provisions in the Election Manifesto Regarding Zamindari Abolition* (Delhi: All India Congress Committee, 1948), 32–35; Venu Madhav Govindu and Deepak Malghan, *The Web of Freedom: J.C. Kumarappa and Gandhi's Struggle for Economic Justice* (New Delhi: Oxford University Press, 2016). I am grateful to Venu Madhav Govindu for drawing my attention to these papers.
68. Evidence of Kamakhyaram Baruah, *Agrarian Reforms Committee*, J.C. Kumarappa papers, File no. 17 (14), NMML, 3–4.
69. Evidence of Umakanta Goswami, *Agrarian Reforms Committee*, 4.
70. Evidence of Dinanath Medhi, *Agrarian Reforms Committee*, 7.
71. *All India Congress Committee, Zamindari Abolition and Agrarian Reform: A Summary of the Efforts of the Congress Organisation to Implement the Provisions in the Election Manifesto Regarding Zamindari Abolition*, 13–14. Goalpara had 19 estates and 6,14,710 hectares of land under their ownership.
72. Government of Assam, 'Land Reform Legislation in Other States: Notes from the Government of Assam', *Indian Society of Agricultural Economics, Proceedings of the Thirteenth Conference*, vol. VIII, no. 1 (March 1953), 182–83.
73. *Times of India*, 8 April 1955, 8; Memorial submitted by Prakitish Chandra Barua and seven other zamindars, Gauripur, Goalpara, 1 September 1953 to Rajendra Prasad, President of India in Representations against Assam State Acquisition of Zamindari Bill 1953, File no. 17/114/53, 1953, Judicial, Ministry of Home Affairs, GoI, Abhilekh Patal, NAI.
74. Letter from Tenants of Bijni Raj Estate to Governor of Assam, 28 December 1952, in File 6/52, Revenue (Tenancy) (ASA).

75. Notes on the Items Required by the Sub-Committee of the APCC in their Meeting held on the 8 May 1964, *APCC Papers*, Packet 140, File no. 1, NMML.
76. Frank Ed Moraes, *The Times of India Directory and Year Book Including Who's Who: 1957–58* (Bombay: Times of India Publication); Ashok Mitra and Baldev Raj Kalra, *Census of India, 1961: Land Tenures in India*, vol. 1, part xi-A (i) (Delhi: Government Press, 1962), xxvii.
77. Prabhat Chandra Barua, *Some of the Important Memorials, Representations and Notes by the Zamindars and Raiyats of the District of Goalpara in the Province of Assam, Urging the Transfer of the Permanently Settled Area of Goalpara to Bengal* (Calcutta: Gauripur Raj, 1925), Preface, (Asia, Pacific and Africa Collections, British Library).
78. A.J. Laine, *An Account of the Land Tenure System of Goalpara, with Criticisms of the Existing Rent Law and Suggestions for Its Amendments* (Shillong: Assam Government Printing Press, 1917), 5–7.
79. Arupjyoti Saikia, 'Empire's Nature in the Garo Hills: A Microhistory of India's Environmental Movements', in *Functioning Anarchy: Essays for Ramachandra Guha*, eds, Nandini Sundar and Srinath Raghavan (Delhi: Penguin, 2020), 3–20.
80. Prabhat Chandra Barua, *Nikhil Goalpara Samitir Dwitiya Barshik Adhibesane Pothito* (Gauripur, Assam: Biswakosh Press, 1929), 13.
81. See Chapter 2 for further discussion.
82. Narendra Chandra Dutta, 'Land Reforms in Assam since Independence with Special Reference to the Permanently Settled Areas and the Acknowledged Estates of Bijni and Sidli' (PhD diss., Gauhati University, 1963), Chapter VI, 132.
83. Government of Assam, *Statistical Handbook of Assam, 1978* (Guwahati: Directorate of Economics and Statistics, 1978).
84. In 1968, a special revenue court settled 500 such tenancy cases within a few days of time. *Dainik Asam*, 28 January 1968, 3.
85. Pranesh Biswas, 'Some Aspects of the Assam Government's Agrarian Reform Laws', *All India Kisan Sabha, New Bulletin*, vol. 1, no. 3 (September 1952), 14.
86. Note on the Implementation of Land Reforms Measures, *APCC Papers*, Packet 140, File no. 1, NMML. The Goalpara Tenancy (Emergency Provisions) Act of 1962 gave some breathing space for the tenants to file objections against the discrepancies during the process of recording of rights.
87. Raza, 'Planning Commission on Implementation of Land Reforms in Assam'.
88. Ibid.
89. Assam Land (Requisition and Acquisition) Act, 1948; Assam Fixation of Ceiling on Land Holdings Act, 1956.

90. Rana P. Behal, *A Century of Servitude: Political Economy of Tea Plantations in Colonial Assam* (New Delhi: Tulika, 2014).
91. Gauhati High Court, *Judgement on the Assam Company Ltd. vs The State of Assam and Others*, 6 March 1953, https://indiankanoon.org/doc/1337452/ (Accessed 5 February 2023).
92. Secret, 'Calcutta Special Report, no. 64', 'Reports on Assam, Sikkim and Bhutan' (Government Papers, The National Archives, Kew, 1950), http://www.archivesdirect.amdigital.co.uk/Documents/Details/FO_371_84250 (Accessed 10 March 2021).
93. P.C. Goswami, *Economic Development of Assam* (Bombay: Asia Publishing House, 1963), 116. These rich peasants controlled a little less than 8 per cent of the total landholding.
94. B.R. Saharia, *Assam, 1977: An Exciting Tale of Assam's Triumphant Journey (1947–77) from Backwardness to Modernity* (Guwahati: Director of Information and Public Relations, 1978), 20.
95. Assam State Acquisition of Land belonging to Religious or Charitable Institutions of Public Nature Act, 1959.
96. Mamoni Roisom Goswami, 'Datal Hatir Uye Khowa Haoda' (The Moth Eaten Howdah of the Tusker), in *Upanyas Samagra* (Collected Novels), Mamoni Roisom Goswami (Guwahati: Students Stores, 1998), 125.
97. Note on the Implementation of Land Reforms Measures, *APCC Papers*, Packet 140, F. N. 1, NMML.
98. Ibid.
99. Statement of Revenue Minister, *Proceedings of the Assam Land Reforms Board*, 11 March 1959, NMML.
100. Government of Assam, *Land Settlement Implementation Advisory Committee Enquiry Report* (Shillong: Assam Secretariat, 1971), 51.
101. Saharia, *Assam, 1977*, 20; Government of Assam, *Assam: A Note on the Progress of Implementation of Decisions*, 5. Chapter 11 has more discussion on the implications of the Ceiling Act.
102. 'Kaki Land Reclamation Project Progressing Well', *Assam Tribune*, 27 April 1954, 3. Also see, Planning Commission, *Resettlement Programme for Landless Agricultural Labourers: Case Studies of Selected Colonies* (New Delhi: Planning Commission, 1968), 67–73; Government of Assam, *Report on the Land Revenue Administration of Assam, 1959–60* (Shillong: Government Press, 1961), 6.
103. Jadunath Khaklari, *Kacharir Katha* (Jorhat: Kritinath Khaklari, 1927), 21.
104. Jadab Chandra Khaklari, 'Memorandum of Assam Kachari Jubok Sonmiloni', August 1928–September 1928, in *Assam Memorandum*, IOR/Q/13/1/1 (Asia and Africa Collection, BL).

105. Jayeeta Sharma, *Empire's Garden: Assam and the Making of India* (Durham: Duke University Press, 2011), 222–23; Amalendu Guha, *Planter Raj to Swaraj: Freedom Struggle & Electoral Politics in Assam, 1826–1947* (New Delhi: Indian Council of Historical Research, 1977), 165.
106. Rabi Chandra Kachari, Kameswar Das and Sarveswar Barua, 'Note of Dissent', in *Report of the Line System Committee*, vol. 1, Government of Assam (Shillong: Government Press, 1938), 35.
107. S.P. Desai, 'Resolution on the Line System Committee's Report, 4 November 1939', in *Compendium of Government Land Policies: A Compilation from 1937–2019, Government of Assam* (Guwahati: Revenue and Disaster Management Department, 2020), 52.
108. A.G. Paton, 'Resolution on Land Settlement 13 July 1945', in Government of Assam, *Compendium of Government Land Policies*, 94–96.
109. Guha, *Planter Raj to Swaraj: Freedom Struggle & Electoral Politics in Assam, 1826–1947*, 184.
110. 'Letter from S.M. Matilul Haque, Town Planner, Town and Country Planning Department, Guwahati to Under Secretary, Government of Assam, Town and Country Planning Department, 2 June 1965', in *Exclusion of Certain Areas from the South Kamrup Tribal Belt*, File no. TCP 144/65, Town and Country Planning, ASA.
111. Petition of Dandi Dutta Lahkar and others to Chief Minister, Assam, 20 January 1965, *Exclusion of Certain Areas from the South Kamrup Tribal Belt*.
112. Government of Assam, *Report of the Sub-Committee of Advisory Council of Welfare of Scheduled Tribes (Plains) on Settlement of Land in Tribal Belts and Blocks of Forest Land (1976)*, 52.
113. B.N. Bordoloi, *Constraints of Tribal Development in North East India* (Guwahati: Tribal Research Institute, 1990), 62; B.N. Bordoloi, *Report on the Survey of Alienation of Tribal Land in Assam* (Guwahati: Assam Institute of Research for Tribals and Scheduled Castes, 1999).
114. The tribal belt and block covered approximately 6200 square miles in 1947. The total geographical area in the Brahmaputra Valley is 22,000 square miles. For details, see B.N. Bordoloi, *Transfer and Alienation of Tribal Lands in Assam* (Guwahati: B.N. Bordoloi, 1991), 82–87.
115. Bordoloi, *Transfer and Alienation of Tribal Lands in Assam*, 263–74. Also see Jogendra Kumar Basumatory, *Bhaiyamor Janajatir Bhumi Samachya*, memorandum submitted by Assam Tribal League to the Assam Chief Minister, Dhubri, 1966, ASA.
116. Chandan Kumar Sharma, 'Tribal Land Alienation: Government's Role', *Economic & Political Weekly*, vol. 36, no. 52 (2001), 4794.

117. Arupjyoti Saikia, 'Earthquakes and the Environmental Transformation of a Floodplain Landscape: The Brahmaputra Valley and the Earthquakes of 1897 and 1950', *Environment and History*, vol. 26, no. 1 (2020), 51–77.
118. Bérénice Guyot-Réchard, *Shadow States: India, China and the Himalayas, 1910–1962* (Cambridge: Cambridge University Press, 2017), 97–104.
119. D.R. Mankekar, 'Assam on the Brink of Fresh Calamity', *Times of India*, 17 March 1951, 1. For further details on the government responses to flood relief and steps taken to protect from annual fllods in the 1950s, see, 'Floods and Flood Control in Assam', R.D. Dhir, chief engineer, Central Water and Power Commission, September 1962 & Letter B. Bhagavati, Deputy Minister, Transport and Communications, addressed to the Prime Minister of India regarding Master Plan for flood control in Assam, 17 August 1962, New Delhi, in *Floods in Assam during 1962*, File no. DW-V-502/10/62, 1962, Ministry of Water Resources, GoI, Abhilekh Patal, NAI.
120. 'Floods in Assam abate as weather improves: Great loss of fertile land, crops and cattle', *Times of India*, 20 June 1951, 5.
121. Anonymous, 'Assam Rail Link Project', *Economic Weekly*, vol. 5, no. 16 (18 April 1953), 458.
122. 'Explanatory Memorandum, General Budget, 1947–48', Speech by Finance Minister, 26 November 1947, *Budget for 1947–48 (15th August 1947 to 31st March 1948)*, GoI, Ministry of Finance, 85 in https://dea.gov.in/sites/default/files/BUDGET-1947-48.pdf (Accessed 19 October 2021).
123. The following table gives an idea of the acreage and production of two principal crops of Assam in the 1940s.

| Crops | Acreage (in thousand acres) | | | Production (in thousand tons) | | |
|---|---|---|---|---|---|---|
| | 1936–37 | 1943–44 | 1949–50 | 1936–37 | 1943–44 | 1949–50 |
| Rice | 3763 | 4001 | 4004 | 1209 | 1660 | 1737 |
| Mustard | 393 | 324 | 310 | 56 | 52,350 | 59 |

Computed from Goswami, *Economic Development of Assam*, Table 20, 296 and Table 23, 300; Government of India, *Abstract of Agricultural Statistics of India 1936–37 to 1945–46* (Delhi: Directorate of Economics and Statistics, 1949), Table 2.3, 45.
124. Goswami, *Economic Development of Assam*, Table 23, 300.
125. An estimated 36 per cent of her total expenditure during 1951–56 was spent in various social welfare programmes. Khorshed Alam, 'The Economic Development of Assam since Independence: An Analytical Study' (PhD diss., Gauhati University, 1974), Table 5.1, Chapter 5, 232.

126. The number of school-going students increased from 8610 to 45,387 between 1950 and 1965. Myron Weiner, *Sons of the Soil: Migration and Ethnic Conflict in India* (Princeton: Princeton University Press, 1978), 111.
127. E.H. Pakyntein, *Census of India, 1961: District Census Handbook, The United Mikir and North Cachar Hills district* (Shillong: Superintendent of Census Operations, Assam, 1965), 181.
128. Based on 1948–49 prices. K.N. Raj, 'Some Features of the Economic Growth of the Last Decade in India', *Economic Weekly Annual*, 4 February 1961, Table XVIII, 270; Weiner, *Sons of the Soil: Migration and Ethnic Conflict in India*, 125.
129. Alam, 'The Economic Development of Assam since Independence: An Analytical Study', Chapter 4.
130. Ibid., Chapter 4, Table 4.10, 224.
131. Ibid., Table 5.1, 232.
132. Weiner, *Sons of the Soil: Migration and Ethnic Conflict in India*, Table 4.6, 130.
133. 'Foreign Concerns in Assam', *Assam Tribune*, 10 April 1954, 1.
134. 'Editorial', *Assam Tribune*, 11 April 1954, 4.
135. *Natun Asamiya*, 2 April 1954, 1.
136. Alban Ali and Eric Lambert, *Assam* (Oxford: Oxford University Press, 1946), 17.
137. Government of India, *Report of the Plantation Inquiry Commission 1956*, part 1 (Delhi: Manager of Publications, 1956), 129.
138. E.H. Pakyntein, *Census of India, 1961*, vol. III, Assam, part I-A (Delhi: Manager of Publications, 1964), 404.
139. Government of Assam, *Annual Report on Agriculture, Assam, 1954–55* (Shillong: Government Press, 1955), 41.
140. The prices of edible commodities for 1944 and 1950 were like this: Winter Rice in husk 6–0–0 (1944) and 8–0–0 (1950); Gur: 24–0–0 (1944) and 25–0–0 (1950); Potato 17–0–0 (1944) and 16–0–0 (1950); Mustard Oil 58–12–0 (1944) and 97–0–0 (1950) per maund. Government of Assam, *Annual Report on Agriculture, Assam, 1949–50* (Shillong: Government Press, 1950), 6.
141. B.R. Tomlinson, *The Economy of Modern India: From 1860 to the Twenty-First Century* (Delhi: Cambridge University Press, 1993), 163. The base value of 100 is based on the year 1939.
142. *Times of India*, 14 August 1951, 6.
143. Government of Assam, *Annual Report on Agriculture, Assam 1947–48* (Shillong: Government Press, 1948), 12.

144. Christoph von Fürer-Haimendorf, 'Agriculture and land tenure among the Apatanis', *Man in India*, vol. 26, no. 1 (1946), 20–49.
145. Richard Grove, *Green Imperialism: Colonial Expansion, Tropical Islands Eden and the Origins of Environmentalism, 1600–1860* (Cambridge: Cambridge University Press, 1996).
146. M.D. Chaturvedi and B.N. Uppal, *A Study in Shifting Cultivation in Assam* (Delhi: Indian Council of Agricultural Research, 1953).
147. Nehru to Medhi, May 6, 1953, *SWJN*, second series, vol. 22, 237.
148. P.S. Ramakrishnan and Suprava Patnaik, 'Jhum: Slash and Burn Cultivation', *India International Centre Quarterly*, vol. 19, no. 1 and 2 (1992), 215–20; P.S. Ramakrishnan, 'The Science Behind Rotational Bush Fallow Agriculture System (Jhum)', *Proceedings of the Indian Academy of Sciences (Plant Science)*, vol. 93, no. 3 (July 1984), 379–400.
149. Banerjee, *Labour Movement in Assam: A Study of Non-Plantation Workers' Strikes till 1939*; Guha, *Planter Raj to Swaraj: Freedom Struggle & Electoral Politics in Assam, 1826–1947*, 236–46.
150. Ali and Lambert, *Assam*, 17; T.V. Rama Rao, *India at a Glance: A Comprehensive Reference Book* (Delhi: Orient Longman, 1954), 1032.
151. *New York Times*, 20 November 1954, 21.
152. Hriday Nath Kaul, *K.D. Malaviya and the Evolution of India's Oil Policy* (Bombay: Allied Publishers, 1991).
153. 'Assam Oil Company', *The Times*, 1 June 1928, 24.
154. 'The Burmah Oil Company Limited', *The Economist*, 30 July 1949, 269.
155. Kaul, *K.D. Malaviya and the Evolution of India's Oil Policy*, 20.
156. *New York Times*, 15 November 1953, 4; 'The Burmah Oil Company Limited', *The Economist*, 22 May 1954, 667–68.
157. 'India producing oil: Assam well first in country commercially successful', *New York Times*, 5 March 1954, 31.
158. 'Letter from Secretary, Revenue Department, Government of Assam to the Deputy Commissioner, Lakhimpur, Shillong, 21 January 1954 & Letter from Under Secretary, Revenue Department, Government of Assam to the Deputy Commissioner, Lakhimpur and Sibsagar, 26 August, 1955', in *Oil Committee of Cabinet Papers*, File no. 89/57, 1957, General Branch, Office of the Secretary to the President, President Secretariat, Abhilekh Patal, NAI.
159. 'The Burmah Oil Company Limited', *The Economist*, 25 May 1957, 735–36. In the 1950s, the Digboi refinery refined approximately 3,80,000 tons of crude oil annually, of which Assam consumed an estimated 1,65,000 tons, and the rest was sold in other parts of India. 'Recommendations of the Refinery Location Committee', *Oil Committee of Cabinet Papers*, Annexure IV.
160. Kaul, *K.D. Malaviya and the Evolution of India's Oil Policy*, 20.

161. R.K. Ramadhyani, Secretary, Ministry of Steel, Mines and Fuel, Government of India, 'Formation of a Rupee Company in Participation with Assam Oil Company for Production of Oil in Assam', Summary for the Cabinet, 7 May 1957, *Oil Committee of Cabinet Papers*.
162. *Times of India*, 21 July 1955, 7.
163. Ditee Moni Baruah, 'The Refinery Movement in Assam', *Economic & Political Weekly*, vol. 46, no. 1 (2011), 66; S. Ratnam, Secretary, Expenditure, 'Note', 6 May 1957, Department of Expenditure, Ministry of Finance, in *Oil Committee of Cabinet Papers*, Annexure V.
164. 'Letter from Nehru to Assam governor, top secret, 12 June 1957, no. 459, PMO.57/New Delhi', in *Bishnuram Medhi Papers*, 190 (LL II), NMML.
165. Ibid., 74.
166. Ibid., 75.
167. 'Letter from Malaviya to Medhi, 13 June 1957, no. 191/MMO/56–330', in *Bishnuram Medhi Papers*, 190 (LL II), NMML.
168. 'Letter from Nehru to Assam governor, top secret, 12 June 1957, no. 459, PMO.57/New Delhi', in *Bishnuram Medhi Papers*, 190 (LL II), NMML.
169. 'Letter from Nehru to Fazl Ali, 12 June 1957', no. 459, PMO.57/New Delhi', in *Bishnuram Medhi Papers*, 190 (LL II), NMML.
170. The Refinery Location Committee consisted of Nehru, Malaviya, Krishna Menon, G.B. Pant, Morarji Desai, T.T. Krishnamachari and Swaran Singh along with representatives of the Planning Commission and the Assam government.
171. The text of the committee was like this: 'A refinery if set up in Gauhati might conceivably pay its way', quoted in 'Letter from Medhi to Govind Ballabh Pant, 22 June 1957, CMS 94/57', in *Bishnuram Medhi Papers*, 190 (LL II), NMML; K.N. Kaul, Joint Secretary, 'Note for the Cabinet Committee on Oil', 9 June 1957, Departments of Mining and Fuel, Ministry of Steel, Mines and Fuel, Government of India, para 2, in *Proposal to Establish a New Oil Refinery at Barauni in Behar—Reactions in Assam to the Decision of the Government of India*. Choice for Barauni was based on security, market, transportation facilities and capital investment. Also, 'Letter from Rajendra Prasad, President of India to S. Fazl Ali, Governor of Assam, no. F.89/57, 27 June 1957', in *Proposal to Establish a New Oil Refinery at Barauni in Behar—Reactions in Assam to the Decision of the Government of India*.
172. *Times of India*, 15 September 1955, 7; 'Letter from Abul Kalam Azad, Education Minister, Government of India to Rajendra Prasad, President of India, 24 June 1957', in *Oil Committee of Cabinet Papers*. Also, 'Note for the Cabinet Committee on Oil', Departments of Mining and Fuel, Ministry of Steel, Mines and Fuel, Government of India, para 5, in *Proposal to Establish*

*a New Oil Refinery at Barauni in Behar—Reactions in Assam to the Decision of the Government of India*, File no. 89/57, 1957, General branch, Office of the Secretary to the President, Abhilekh Patal, NAI.
173. Statement of Bishnuram Medhi, 30 August 1956, *ALAD*, vol. 11, no. 18 (1956), 1465.
174. 'The Burmah Oil Company Limited', *The Economist*, 25 May 1957, 735–36.
175. 'The Agreement in Assam', *The Economist*, 14 December 1957, 990–93.
176. 'Formation of a Rupee Oil Company in Assam', Speech of K.D. Malaviya, Minister of Natural Resources, *Lok Sabha Debates*, 18 December 1956, columns 3327–28.
177. *FR*, 1st half, August 1957.
178. 'Speech of Hareswar Goswami', *ALAD*, 17 June 1956, in The Refinery Movement in Assam', Baruah, 67.
179. Letter from S. Fazl Ali, Governor of Assam to Rajendra Prasad, President of India, 17 June 1957, Shillong, *Proposal to Establish a New Oil Refinery at Barauni in Behar—Reactions in Assam to the Decision of the Government of India*. Announcement of Barauni as the site for the refinery had 'produced a profound effect on the minds of not only the people at large but also of the members of the Cabinet who came in a body yesterday to me to say that they had made up their mind to send in their resignations'. A pamphlet, published in June 1957, in defense of a refinery in Assam spelt out the popular attitude: 'Refinery at Gauhati or elsewhere in Assam technically and economically feasible but also profitable'. 'Bulletin of Madarkhat Oil Refinery Action Committee, Assam', in *Proposal to Establish a New Oil Refinery at Barauni in Behar—Reactions in Assam to the Decision of the Government of India*.
180. *FR*, 1st half, June 1957; *FR* 2nd half, June 1957. A public meeting held in Jorhat on 16 June 1957 asserted that 'it is their [of the Assamese] right to get her oil refined in Assam, which would solve considerable unemployment problem in the State'. Quoted in 'Note', no. D 1861-0/57, Office of the Secretary to the President, in *Proposal to Establish a New Oil Refinery at Barauni in Behar—Reactions in Assam to the Decision of the Government of India*.
181. 'Nehru to Medhi, 13 June 1957, no. 1166–PMH/57, New Delhi', in *Bishnuram Medhi Papers*, 190 (LL II) NMML.
182. 'Telegram from Medhi to Nehru, 13 June 1957', in *Bishnuram Medhi Papers*, 190 (LL II), NMML.
183. 'Letter from Medhi to Nehru, 14 June 1957', *Bishnuram Medhi Papers*, 190 (LL II), NMML.

184. *FR*, 1st half, July, 1957.
185. *Assam Tribune*, 28 July 1957, 1.
186. *Assam Tribune*, 30 July 1957, 1.
187. *FR*, 2nd half, July 1957. 'Assam observes unique hartal: Demand for refinery vindicated, normal life at standstill, state creates history in peaceful move', *Assam Tribune*, 30 July 1957, 1.
188. *FR*, 1st half, August 1957.
189. 'Press statement of Nehru, 27 July 1957', in *Bishnuram Medhi Papers*, 190 (LL II), NMML; *The Times*, 15 July 1957; *FR*, 1st half, August 1957.
190. *FR*, 1st half, August 1957.
191. *The Times*, 28 September 1956.
192. '*Natun Asamiya*, Thursday, 20 September 1956', in 'The Refinery Movement in Assam; ed. Baruah, 67.
193. 'Assam's Claims for an Oil Refinery, 27 July 1957, *SWJN*, second series, vol. 38, no. 19, 145.
194. 'Note: Assam Oil Negotiations', 27 November 1957, S.S. Khera, secretary to the Government of India, Department of Mines and Fuel, Ministry of Steel, Mines and Fuel, in *Proposal to Establish a New Oil Refinery at Barauni in Behar—Reactions in Assam to the Decision of the Government of India*; 'Assam Oil Negotiations: Meeting of the Cabinet Held on Wednesday, 27 November 1957, Government of India', in *Proposal to Establish a New Oil Refinery at Barauni in Behar—Reactions in Assam to the Decision of the Government of India*.
195. A final decision to build the new refinery at Guwahati was not made until February 1959, although Assam Chief Minister Bimala Prasad Chaliha insisted that Silghat, in central Assam, should be the preferred location. 'Selection of a Site to Locate the First Refinery in Assam, Meeting of the Cabinet held on Wednesday, 25 February 1959', in *Proposal to Establish a New Oil Refinery at Barauni in Behar—Reactions in Assam to the Decision of the Government of India*.
196. *New York Times*, 2 January 1962, 5. Of the total cost of construction amounting to $33.6 million, the Romanian government lent $11.76 million at 2.5 per cent interest. The Romanian government also provided 50 technicians to build this refinery.
197. Pakyntein, *Census of India, General Report,* vol. III, part I-A, Assam, 404.
198. *New York Times*, 2 January 1962, 5.
199. *Times of India*, 13 June 1959, 1. 'U.K. Government's Offer of Loan for the Pipeline Project of Oil India Limited', Meeting of the Committee of the Cabinet on Oil held immediately after the Cabinet meeting called on Tuesday, 12 May 1959, in *Proposal to Establish a New Oil Refinery at*

Barauni in Behar—Reactions in Assam to the Decision of the Government of India.
200. 'Pipeline Link in India to Assam Is Complete', *New York Times*, 5 April 1963, 92.
201. Ibid.
202. *Times of India*, 27 October 1960, 6; Government of Assam, *Mineral Development in Assam: Symposium Volume* (Shillong: Directorate of Geology and Mining, 1964), 13.
203. *The Times*, 1 June 1961, 11; *The Times*, 2 June 1961, 12.
204. Anonymous, 'Assam Oil Royalty Dispute', *Economic Weekly*, 7 July 1962, 1041–42; Government of Assam, *Memorandum to the Government of India, Ministry of Petroleum, Chemicals and Fertilisers*, 5 May 1980.
205. Ditee Moni Baruah, 'Polity and Petroleum Making of an Oil Industry in Assam, 1825–1980' (PhD diss., Indian Institute of Technology, Guwahati, 2014), 104–08.
206. Anonymous, 'Assam Oil Royalty Dispute', 1041.
207. Government of India, *Report of the Taxation Enquiry Commission 1953–54*, vol. 4, part 3, 47; Government of Assam, *Memorandum to the Government of India, Ministry of Petroleum, Chemicals and Fertilsers*, 5 May 1980; Atul Chandra Sarma, 'Study of Assam Finances Structure and Trend 1947–48 to 1965–66' (PhD diss., Gauhati University, 1971), 182.
208. The new rate was Rs 4.8 per ton, and Assam was expected to get Rs 1.50 crore annually.
209. 'Letter from Nehru to K.D. Malaviya, July 23, 1962', in *SWJN*, second series, vol. 78, no. 137, 194.
210. *The Times*, 2 February 1962, 17.
211. 'Extract from the minutes of the Cabinet meeting, 27 June 1962 in Letter from Nehru to Chaliha', 27 June 1962 in *SWJN*, second series, vol. 77, no. 185, 451n531; 'Letter from B.P. Chaliha to Nehru, 17 July 1962', in *SWJN*, second series, vol. 78, Appendix 3, 713.
212. The revised rate was fixed at Rs 7.50 per metric ton, to be revised after four years. Government of Assam, *Memorandum to the Government of India, Ministry of Petroleum, Chemicals and Fertilsers*, 5 May 1980, 2; Sarma, 'Study of Assam Finances Structure and Trend 1947–48 to 1965–66', 250, n. 1; B.G. Verghese, 'Bounds: Assam in Peril', *Times of India*, 21 November 1962, 1.
213. Anonymous, 'News', *Assam Information*, vol. XI, no. 11 (1960), 12; G.C. Goswami, 'Development of Petrochemical Industries in Assam', in Government of Assam, *Mineral Development in Assam: Symposium Volume* (Shillong: Directorate of Geology and Mining, 1964), 100–15.

214. Promod Gogoi, *Sibsagar Jila Tel Sudhanagar Abhibartanor Prastab Samuh* (Resolutions of Public Meeting Demanding an Oil Refinery in Sibsagar (Sibsagar: Sibsagar Jila Tel Sudhanagar Andolon Samiti, 1966), ASA.
215. Baruah, 'Polity and Petroleum Making of an Oil Industry in Assam, 1825–1980', 2014.
216. Government of Assam, *A Report of the Employment Review Committee on the Employment Position in the Public and Private Sector Industries and Undertakings in Assam, 1969* (Shillong: Government Press, 1969), 10, 36–37.
217. 'We have only driven out the Assamese cultivators from the oil field but we have not cared to know where these people have gone and what happened to them'. Speech of Dulal Barua, *ALAD*, 23 March 1973.
218. Kamrup Jilla Krishak Sabha, *Assam Sarkakar Osorot Mukali Pratibedan* (An Open Report for the Assam government) (Guwahati: Dhireswar Kalita, 1960, pamphlet), in *Memorandum from the Kamrup Jilla Kishan Sabha-Rehabilitation of People Rendered Landless by Acquisition of Land for Oil Refinery, Railways, etc.*, File RSS/225/60, Revenue (s), settlement branch, 1960, ASA.
219. Horace G. Alexander, 'Free India and Her Problems: The North East Frontier', *Guardian*, 26 September 1951, 4.
220. Ibid.
221. *New York Times*, 16 May 1951, 8.
222. 'Memorandum of T. Aliba Imti and Sakhrie to Akbar Hydari, 26 June 1947, Kohima', in *Naga Chronicle*, ed. V.K. Nuh (Delhi: Regency Publications, 2003), 71–74.
223. 'Letter from A. Hydari, Assam Governor to Mountbatten, 11 July 1947', in *Transfer of Power* (hereafter *TOP*) 1942–47, vol. 12, no. 68, 104.
224. For the text of this agreement, see 'Nine Point Agreement with Governor Hydari, 1947', in *Census of India 1961: Demographic and Socio-Economic Profiles of the Hill Areas of North-East India*, B.K. Roy Burman (Delhi: Registrar General, India, 1970), appendix XVIII, LXXVIII.
225. 'Letter from A. Hydari, Governor of Assam to Mountbatten, 11 July 1947', in *TOP 1942–47*, ed. Nicholas Mansergh (London: Her Majesty's Stationery Office, 1983), vol. 12, no. 68, 104–05.
226. 'Memo no. 88–C/47–570–72 Shillong, 22 June 1948', in *Naga Chronicle*, ed. V.K. Nuh, 69.
227. 'Confidential letter from Deputy High Commissioner, UK in India, Calcutta 6 April 1953', in *Naga Tribes of Assam: Agitation for Independence; Petition to the Prime Minister* (Government Papers, The National Archives, Kew, 1953), http://www.archivesdirect.amdigital.co.uk/Documents/Details/FO_371_106853 (Accessed 17 April 2023).

228. Ibid.
229. 'Letter to Ram Manohar Lohia', in *Collected Works of Mahatma Gandhi* (hereafter *CWMG*), vol. 88, entry 423, 395.
230. Quoted in 'Transcript of Talk between Phizo and Indian Prime Minister Morarji Desai, 14 June 1977', in *Nagaland: The Night of the Guerrillas*, Nirmal Nibedon (New Delhi: Lancers Publishers, 1978); Inder Malhotra, 'Desai to Meet Nagas Leader', *Guardian*, 17 May 1977; Gavin Young, 'Naga Battle Will Flare Up', *Guardian*, 19 June 1977, 8.
231. This entire conversation is from 'Interview to Naga Leaders', *CWMG*, vol. 88, pp. 393, 373–74.
232. 'Note on the Naga Independence Movement, Secret', in *Naga Agitation for Independence: Note Prepared by X.P. Division for the Guidance of Our Information Officers in Mission Abroad*, Ministry of External Affairs, X.P. Division, 30 January 1953, File no. N/53/1531/105, Ministry of External Affairs, NEF Branch, GoI, 1953, Abhilekh Patal, NAI.
233. 'Letter from M. Kithan, President, Naga National Council to the Governor General of India, 4 June 1949', in *Request of the Naga National Council to Wait on HE in a Deputation in Connection with Their Political Claim*, File no. 78-GG/49, 1949, Office of the Secretary to the Governor-General, G Branch, Digitized Public Records President Secretariat, Abhilekh Patal, NAI.
234. 'Note by Ministry of Home Affairs', *Declaration of Naga National Council, Federal Government of Nagaland and Naga Army as unlawful*, File no. 14015/4/75–NE, Home Affairs, 1975, Annexure 2, 290, Abhilekh Patal, NAI.
235. 'Letter from J. Doulatram, Assam Governor, to K.P.S. Menon, Ministry of External Affairs', 15 October 1950, in File no. 3/6, *Assam Ministerial*, September to December 1950, vol. 4, Abhilekh Patal, NAI.
236. 'Secret Note on the Naga Independence Movement', in *Naga Agitation for Independence: Note Prepared by X.P. Division for the Guidance of Our Information Officers in Mission Abroad*, Ministry of External Affairs, X.P. Division, 30 January 1953, File no. N/53/1531/105, 1953, Ministry of External Affairs, NEF Branch, GoI, para 10, Abhilekh Patal, NAI.
237. J.H. Hutton, *Tour Diary of Naga Hills District, 1921–1934* (Guwahati: Assam State Archives, 2020), 173.
238. 'India reds stir up tribes on frontier—plan to hold plebiscite', *New York Times*, 16 May 1951, 8; *Agitation of the Naga National Council, Kohima: Proposed plebiscite for the constuitution of an Independent Naga states*, File no. Progs., Nos 24(3)-PA, 1951, Political-A, Ministry of States, GoI, Abhilekh Patal, NAI.

239. B.N. Mullik, *My Years with Nehru, 1948–1964* (Delhi: Allied Publishers, 1972), 300.
240. Ibid., 302.
241. Ibid., 304.
242. Ibid., 302.
243. 'Upliftment of the Tribals', Notes prepared in Shillong by Nehru, 19 October 1972, *SWJN*, second series, vol. 20, 147.
244. 'Nehru to B.R. Medhi, 2 October 1952', in *SWJN*, second series, vol. 19, 200
245. Mullik, *My Years with Nehru, 1948–1964*, 299.
246. 'Confidential letter from Deputy High commissioner, UK in India, Calcutta 6 April 1953', in *Naga Tribes of Assam: Agitation for Independence; Petition to the Prime Minister* (Government Papers, The National Archives, Kew, 1953). http://www.archivesdirect.amdigital.co.uk/Documents/Details/FO_371_106853 (Accessed 5 February 2023).
247. Notes, 'Upliftment of the Tribals', *SWJN*, second series, vol. 20, 145.
248. 'Progress of work during the months of March and April 1951', B.S. Guha, Director, Department of Anthropology, and anthropological adviser to the Government of India, 16 March 1951, *Progress Report in the Department of Anthropology for the year 1950: Question of Publication of Result on Researches Conducted by the Department of Anthropology*, File no. 8–31–A/50–A2, Ministry of Education, GoI, Abhilekh Patal, NAI.
249. I am thankful to Jelle Wouters for drawing my attention to the changing attitude of the colonial officials.
250. 'Secret, Calcutta Special Report', 5.
251. 'Confidential Despatch from P.A. Clutterbuck, High Commissioner of UK to India to Secretary of State for Commonwealth Relations, London, 8 May 1953, Delhi', in *Naga Tribes of Assam: Agitation for Independence; Petition to the Prime Minister* (Government Papers, The National Archives, Kew, 1953). http://www.archivesdirect.amdigital.co.uk/Documents/Details/FO_371_106853 (Accessed 11 May 2020).
252. 'Letter from Inkongmeren, vice president, NNC to the British Prime Minister, Kohima, 5 June 1953', in *Naga Tribes of Assam: Agitation for Independence; Petition to the Prime Minister* (Government Papers, The National Archives, Kew, 1953). http://www.archivesdirect.amdigital.co.uk/Documents/Details/FO_371_106853 (Accessed 11 May 2020).
253. 'Note by B.R. Pearn', 18 June 1953, in Ibid.
254. 'Letter from UK High Commissioner in India to Secretary of State for Commonwealth Relations, 8 May 1953, Commonwealth Relations Office, PA 5/74/2', in *Naga Tribes of Assam: Agitation for Independence; Petition to the Prime Minister*.

255. Bipinpal Das, *Jivanor Bate Bate* (Guwahati: Mediahype Publication, 2016), 85; Bipinpal Das, *The Naga Problem* (Hyderabad: Socialist Party, 1956). Also, Harish Chandola, *The Naga Story: First Armed Struggle in India* (New Delhi: Chicken Neck, 2013), 15–18.
256. 'Medhi to Nehru, 14 May 1953', *Medhi Papers*, NMML.
257. *Report of States Reorganisation Commission* (New Delhi: Government of India Press, 1955), 184.
258. 'Note by Ministry of Home Affairs, Declaration of Naga National Council', *Declaration of Naga National Council, Federal Government of Nagaland and Naga Army as unlawful*, File no. 14015/4/75–NE, Home Affairs, 1975, NAI, Annexure 2, 290.
259. Statement Re. North East Frontier Agency, J.L. Nehru, *Lok Sabha Debates*, House of People, Official Report, 18 August 1955.
260. 'Army called out in Naga Hills District', *Assam Tribune*, 1 February 1956, 1; 'Nagas revolt in India: Troops rushed to quell rising of some tribesmen', *New York Times*, 3 February 1956, 4.
261. Anonymous, 'Unquiet in the North-East', *Thought*, vol. VII, no. 35, 27 August 1955, 16. *Thought* was a magazine launched by Arthur Moore, the erstwhile editor of the *Statesman*.
262. Editorial, *Assam Tribune*, 3 February 1956.
263. 'Meeting the Nagas' Demand: But not with Independence', *Guardian*, 27 April 1956, 9.
264. 'Steady improvement in Naga situation: Mop-up operations proceed satisfactorily', *Times of India*, 27 June 1956, 7.
265. *Times of India*, 17 June 1956, 1.
266. 'Letter from S.M. Dutta, Deputy Director, Intelligence Bureau, Ministry of Home Affairs, Government of India, to Chief Secretary, Assam, No. SA.6/56 (8)-A-I, Subsidiary Intelligence Bureau, Shillong, 27 August 1956', in *Raising of a Naga Militia*, TAD/PL/57/56/1956 (ASA). Dutta referred to similar measures against guerilla warriors from Malaya and Kenya.
267. Speech of Nehru, *Lok Sabha Debates*, 23 August 1956, vol. VII, part II, 1956, in *SWJN*, second series, vol. 34, entry 6, column 170.
268. Mullik, *My Years with Nehru, 1948–1964*, 312–13.
269. 'Nagas Visiting Furkating (Sibsagar) were Purchasing Large Number of Naga Daos from Nepali Blacksmiths', *FR*, 1st half, December 1957.
270. *FR*, 2nd half, January 1957.
271. *FR*, 1st half, August 1957.
272. Visier Meyasetsu Sanyü and Richard Broome, *A Naga Odyssey: My Long Way Home* (Delhi: Speaking Tiger, 2018), 7.

273. 'Meeting with the Nagas' demand but not with independence', *Guardian*, 27 April 1956, 9.
274. For more on this, see Dolly Kikon. *Living with Oil and Coal: Resource Politics and Militarization in Northeast India* (Seattle: Washington University Press, 2019), 51–62, 90–92.
275. 'Naga distrust of the Assamese', *Guardian*, 5 July 1956, 7.
276. Pakyntein, *Census of India, 1961, General Report*, vol. III, part I-A, Assam, 236.
277. 'Socialist criticisms of Naga campaign', *Guardian*, 24 August 1956, 7.
278. Editorial, *Asam Sahitya Sabha Patrika*, nos 2 and 3 (1952), 188.
279. 'Estimate of Annual Grant Received from Assam Government 1959–60', *Asam Sahitya Sabha Patrika*, vol. 19, no. 3 (1960), 71.
280. 'Resolution of Executive Committee of Assam, Shillong, 10 November 1953', in *Asam Sahitya Sabha Patrika*, vol. 13, no. 1 (1954), 69–70.
281. 'Resolutions Adopted in twenty second session of Sabha', no. 4 in Ibid., 64.
282. *FR*, 2nd half, June 1957.
283. *FR*, 1st half, July 1957.
284. *FR*, 1st half, April 1957.
285. 'Our attitude in regard to the Naga Hills District or any other tribal area, in fact, is that we should give them as much as autonomy possible and we should amend the Sixth Schedule by consultation', Speech of Jawaharlal Nehru, *Lok Sabha Debates*, 23 July 1957, vol. 3, column 4819.
286. *FR*, 2nd half, November 1957.
287. *FR*, 1st half, September 1957; *FR*, 2nd half, September 1957.
288. Anonymous, 'Nagas Divided', *Civic Affairs*, vol. 5 (January 1958), 104.
289. 'Report for the Month of June 1958', in *Reports (other than Annual) from Burma*, File B 12 Pr 9/58/1958, Ministry of External Affairs, GoI, Abhilekh Patal, NAI.

## Chapter 6: In Search of the Modern

1. *Hindustan Standard*, 16 September 1947; *Jugantor*, 16 September 1947; *Times of India*, 16 September 1947; Maheswar Neog, ed., *Viswavidyalyour Swapna: The Romance of a University* (Guwahati: Chandra Prakash, 2009).
2. K. Dutta, 'A History of the Cotton College, Gauhati, 1901–1951', in *The Golden Jubilee Volume: Cotton College, 1951–52*, ed. H.K. Barpujari (Guwahati: H.K. Barpujari, 1952), 27–80.
3. H.K. Barpujari, 'A Short History of Higher Education in Assam, 1826–1900', in *The Golden Jubilee Volume: Cotton College, 1951–52*, 1–26.

4. Maheswar Neog, *Visvavidyalaya, Bhasa, Bhasan aru Bhraman* (Guwahati: Gopal Goswami, 1974), 3–4.
5. *Report of the Calcutta University Commission, 1917–19*, vol. IV, part II, section 56.
6. S.K. Bhuyan, 'Assam University', in *Papers Related to the Establishment of Gauhati University in January 1948*, Correspondence of Dr S.K. Bhuyan, A3/3, S.K. Bhuyan Archives, North Guwahati, 189.
7. Neog, *Visvavidyalaya, Bhasa, Bhasan aru Bhraman*, 6; 'The Assamese Students' Welfare League, Bulletin no. 1, 1935', in *Papers Related to the Establishment of Gauhati University in January 1948*.
8. S.K. Bhuyan, 'The University of Assam' (Unpublished manuscript, 1926).
9. Assam Association, 'A Rough Outline of a Scheme of a University in Assam, 1935', in *Viswavidyalyour Swapna: The Romance of a University*, 37–77; M.I. Borah, 'Presidential Address, Assam Student's Conference, Jorhat, 1934', in 'The Assamese Student's Welfare League, Bulletin no. 1, 1935'.
10. A. Banerjee, 'University for Assam', *Modern Review* (December 1935), 708–11.
11. The Assam Legislative Assembly had to send this bill to a Select Committee to scrutinize it further. The 'difference of opinion in the Province regarding the need for a University' was among a wide range of subjects that the committee deliberated on. See 'Question no. 1, Abstracts of Opinions of Gentlemen who were Invited to Advise the Committee, Select Committee on the Assam University Bill, 1941', in *Papers Related to the Establishment of Gauhati University in January 1948*.
12. Neog, *Visvavidyalaya, Bhasa, Bhasan aru Bhraman*, 6; 'The Assam University: Mammoth Protest', in *Sylhet Chronicle*, 29 April 1935, in *Viswavidyalyour Swapna: The Romance of a University*, 17–23; Maheswar Neog, ed., 'The Romance of a University', in *Viswavidyalyour Swapna: The Romance of a University*, 4; 'Speech by Maulavi Abdur Rasheed Chaudhury', 25 March 1941, *Assam Legislative Assembly Debates*, Official Report (hereafter *ALAD*).
13. Gopinath Bardoloi, 'A Case for a University in Assam', in *Lokopriya Gopinath Bardoloi: An Architect of Modern India*, ed. Lily Mazinder Baruah (Delhi: Gyan Publishing House, 1992), 154 and 156.
14. Neog, *Viswavidyalyour Swapna: The Romance of a University*, 11–13, 22; Neog, 'The Romance of a University', 7–9.
15. Maheswar Neog, 'Viswavidyalay Nalage?', in *Gauhati University Papers from Professor Maheswar Neog Memorial Trust*, Digital Archive, Center for Assamese Studies, Tezpur University (Accessed 30 April 2018).
16. Neog, 'Viswavidyalay Nalage?'.

17. *Proceedings of the Board of Trustees*, Assam Provincial Museum, 23 March 1941, Guwahati.
18. S.K. Bhuyan, Note, Officer on Special Duty, Gauhati University, GOA, 28 October 1947, in *Papers Related to the Establishment of Gauhati University in January 1948*.
19. *Assam Tribune*, 30 September 1947, 1.
20. K.K. Handiqui, 'German Academic Ideals', in *Krishna Kanta Handiqui*, ed. A. Sattar (Jorhat: Sahityika, 2008), 55–62; K.K. Handiqui, 'Germanir Gyan Sadhana', in *Krishnakanta Handiqui Rachana Sambhar*, ed. A. Sattar (Jorhat: Asam Sahitya Sabha, 2001), 132–34.
21. Handiqui, 'German Academic Ideals'.
22. K.K. Handiqui, 'First Convocation for Conferring Degrees, Vice-Chancellor's Address', in *Krishna Kanta Handiqui,* ed. A. Sattar, 23.
23. 'Letter from G.N. Bardoloi to S.L. Mehta, October 6, 1947', in *Papers Related to the Establishment of Gauhati University in January 1948*.
24. E.H. Pakyntein, *Census of India 1961, Vol. III, Assam, Part I-A, General Report* (Calcutta: Government of India, 1964), 187; S. Steinberg, *The Statesman's Year Book 1968–69* (London: Macmillan, 1968), 390.
25. D.C. Pavate, *Report of the Gauhati University Enquiry Commission 1962* (Shillong: Assam Government Press, 1962), 20.
26. Jayeeta Sharma, *Empire's Garden: Assam and the Making of India* (Durham: Duke University Press, 2011).
27. Edward Gait, *A History of Assam* (Calcutta: Thacker, Spink & Co., 1906), iii.
28. Alban Ali and Eric Lambert, *Assam* (G. Cumberlege: Oxford University Press, 1946).
29. Anon, *Hints for Europeans Engaged in Commerce and Industry on Their First Arrival in India: With Special Reference to Conditions in Bengal and Assam* (London: Worrall & Robey, 1946).
30. Dimbeswar Neog, *Introduction to Assam* (Bombay: Vora and Co., 1947).
31. Suniti Kumar Chatterji, *The Place of Assam in the History and Civilisation of India* (Guwahati: Gauhati University, 1955).
32. Ibid., 11.
33. Ibid., 82.
34. Lohit Chandra Nayak, *Baṛapeṭā Hitasādhinī Sabhāra Prathama Bacharekiyā Kāryabibaraṇī* (Barpeta: Barpeta Sanatan Dhurma Press, 1897), 2 (Asian and African Collection, British Library).
35. Chandra Nath Sarma, *The Works of Kamarup Anusandhan Samiti* (Guwahati: Kamarupa Anusandhan Samiti, 1920); K.L. Barua, 'Introductory', *Journal of the Assam Research Society*, vol. 1, no. 1 (1933), 1.

36. D. Goswami and S. Kataki, *Report and Conspectus of the Kamarupa Anusandhan Samiti* (Guwahati: Kamarupa Anusandhan Samiti, 1931), 6.
37. S.K. Bhuyan, *Report and Conspectus of the Kamarupa Anusandhan Samiti* (Guwahati: Kamarupa Anusandhan Samiti, 1927), 5.
38. J.P. Mills, 'Assam as a Field for Research', *Journal of the Assam Research Society*, vol. 1, no. 1 (1933), 3.
39. This first major work on the study of ancient inscriptions was not published by Kamarupa Anusandhan Samiti, but rather by its counterpart in Bengal, the Rangapur Sahitya Parisad. See Padmanath Bhattacharya, 'Preface', in *Kamarup-Sasanavali*, comp. Padmanath Bhattacharya (Rangpur: Rangapur Sahitya Parisad, 1931).
40. K.L. Barua, *The Early History of Kamarupa: From the Earliest Times to the End of the Sixteenth Century* (Shillong: Author, 1933); Rajmohan Nath, *The Back-Ground of Assamese Culture* (Shillong: A.K. Nath, 1948).
41. Dimbeswar Sarma, *Kamarupasasanavali* (Guwahati: Publication Board Assam, 1981); Mukunda Madhava Sharma, *Inscriptions of Ancient Assam* (Guwahati: Gauhati University, 1978); Maheswar Neog, ed. *Prachya-Sasanavali: An Anthology of Royal Charters etc. Inscribed on Stone, Copper etc of Kamarupa, Asam (Saumara), Koch-Behar etc from 1205 AD to 1847 AD* (Guwahati: Publication Board Assam, 1974).
42. 'Opening speech of Robert Reid, Governor of Assam, 1941', in *Ancient Treasures of Assam through Assam State Museum,* eds, P.D. Chaudhury and M.C. Das (Guwahati: Assam State Museum, 1959), 2.
43. Museum Reports, 1954–55, *Journal of Indian Museums*, 9.
44. Anonymous, 'Assam: Assam State Museum, Gauhati', *Indian Museums Review, 1961–64*, 3.
45. Chaudhury and Das, *Ancient Treasures of Assam through Assam State Museum*, 3.
46. Aswini Kumar Barkakoty, 'The Growth of Local Self-Government in Assam, 1874–1919' (PhD diss., University of London, London, 1949); Birinchi Kumar Barua, 'A Cultural History of Assam of the Early Period, 400 A.D.–1200 A.D.' (PhD dissertation, University of London, London, 1947); Bhupendranarayan Chaudhuri, 'British Rule in Assam 1845–1858' (PhD diss., SOAS, University of London, 1956); Heramba Kanta Barpujari, *British Administration in Assam, 1825–1845: With Special Reference to the Hill-Tribes on the Frontier* (1949); Pratap Chandra Choudhury, 'The History of Civilisation of the People of Assam to the Twelfth Century A.D.' (PhD diss., University of London, London, 1953). For family history, see Kesav Kanta Borooah, *Baniya Kakatir Bamsawalisara* (Sibsagar: Author, 1913); Phaṇidhara Chalihā,

*Asamara Caliha Kakatibaṃsarabaṃṣavali* (Howrah: Nabar Chandra Dutt, 1909).
47. Benudhar Sarma, *Maniram Dewan: The Biography of Maniram Dutta Barua Dewan* (Guwahati: Asom Jyoti, 1950); Dambarudhar Nath, 'Buranji Sahitya, 1950–1990', in *Asamiya Sahityar Buranji*, vol. 6, ed. Homen Borgohain (Guwahati: ABILAC, 1993), 505–27.
48. Suryya Kumar Bhuyan, 'Presidential Lecture, Historical Session, Asam Sahitya Sabha, 1926', in *Asam Sahitya Sabhar Bhasanavali: A Collection of the Presidential Addresses of the History Section,* eds, Atulchandra Hazarika and Jatindranath Goswami (Jorhat: Asam Sahitya Sabha, 1961), 24.
49. S.K. Bhuyan, *Lachit Barphukan and His Times* (Guwahati: Department of Historical and Antiquarian Studies, 1947), xi.
50. Benudhar Sarma, *Dakhinpat Sattra* (Guwahati: Assam Jyoti, 1967); Sarma, *Maniram Dewan: The Biography of Maniram Dutta Barua Dewan*; Benudhar Sarma, *Shatayoun Sal Ba Swadhinatar Pratham Yudha* (Guwahati: Padma Prakash, 1957); Benudhar Sarma, *Kangrecar Kanciali Rodat: At the Sunny Dawn of Congress* (Guwahati: Asam Jyoti, 1971 [1959]).
51. For instance, Dimbeswar Neog, *History of Modern Assamese Literature from 1826 to 1947* (Allahabad: Ganganath Jha Research Institute, 1955); Dimbeswar Neog, *Asamiya Sahityar Buranji: Prachin, Madhya, Adhunik* (Jorhat: Xuwani Poja, 1950); Birinchi Kumar Barua, *Asamiya Katha Sahitya: Purani Bhag* (Guwahati: LBS, 1950).
52. Maheswar Neog, *Anandaram Dhekiyal Phukan: Plea for Assam and Assamese: With the Complete Text of Observations on the Administration of the Province of Assam, by Baboo Anundaram Dakeal Phookun, Being Appendix J to A. J. Moffat Mill's Report on the Province of Assam, Calcutta, 1854, and A Few Remarks on the Assamese Language and on Vernacular Education in Assam, by a Native, Sibsagor, Asam, 1855* (Jorhat: Asam Sahitya Sabha, 1977).
53. D.N. Bezbarua, *Asamiya Bhasa aru Sahityar Buranji* (Jorhat: D.N. Bezbarua, 1933 [1911]); B.K. Barua, *History of Assamese Literature* (New Delhi: Sahitya Akademi, 1964).
54. Sarbeswar Sarma Kataki, 'Asomiya Prachin Lipi', in *Sarbeswar Sarma Kataki Rachanawali,* ed. L.N. Tamuly, (Guwahati: Publication Board Assam, 2004), 108.
55. Sharma, *Inscriptions of Ancient Assam*, 38.
56. Dinesh Chandra Sen, *Bangabhasa O Sahitya*, vol. 1 (Calcutta: India Publishing House, 1908), 11–12; R.D. Banerji, *The Origin of Bengali Script* (Calcutta: University of Calcutta, 1919), 6. Banerji suggested that 'The modern cursive Odiya script was developed out of the Bengali after the 14th century AD like the modern Assamese'.

57. Lakshminath Bezbaroa, 'Assami Bhasa', *Punya*, vol. 2, nos 1–2 (1898), 22–32; Rabindranath Tagore, 'Bhasa Bisched', *Bharoti* (July 1898), 302–08. See Mandira Das, ed., *Bhasha-Bitarka: Bezbaroa aru Bangar Pandit-Samaj* (Dibrugarh: Dibrugarh University, 2014).
58. Andrew Ollett, *Language of the Snakes: Prakrit, Sanskrit, and the Language Order of Premodern India* (California: University of California Press, 2017).
59. For instance, Gunabhiram Barua, *Asam Buranji, or, The History of Assam* (Calcutta: Author, 1876). For further discussion, see Ranjit Kumar Dev Goswami, 'Towards Aryanization: A Note on Assamese Historiography in the Nineteenth Century', in *Prabandha: A Collection of Essays and Lectures*, Ranjit Kumar Dev Goswami (Guwahati: LBS, 2019), 104–11.
60. 'Assamese is the name of the Aryan language . . . [that] belongs to the Eastern Group of the Indo-Aryan vernaculars.' See George Abraham Grierson, comp. and ed., *Linguistic Survey of India*, vol. 5, *Indo-Aryan Family, Eastern Group*, part 1, *Specimens of the Bengali and Assamese Languages* (Calcutta: Office of the Superintendent of Government Printing, 1903), 393; Banikanta Kakati, *Assamese, Its Formation and Development: A Scientific Treatise on the History and Philology of the Assamese Language* (Guwahati: Department of Historical and Antiquarian Studies, 1941).
61. Debananda Bharali, *Asamiẏa Bhaṣara Maulika Bicara* (Dibrugarh: A.R. & T. Co., 1912), 3.
62. Dimbeswar Neog, *New Light on History of Asamiya Literature: From the Earliest Until Recent Times Including an Account of its Antecedents* (Guwahati: Xuwani Prakas, 1962), 37–45; Beni Madhav Barua, 'Miscellany: The Scribe-Engravers of Indrapala's Second Copper-Plate and Prakrit of Pre-Ahom Times', *Indian Historical Quarterly*, vol. 23, no. 3 (September 1947), 242–47.
63. Kaliram Medhi pronounced his verdict clearly: 'Its origin is to be found in the popular dialects of Assam or of a part of India. It is a branch of the living speech of India, springing from the same source from which Sanskrit itself sprang when it first assumed its literary independence.' Kaliram Medhi, *Asamiya Byakaran aru Bhasatattwa: Assamese Grammar and Origin of the Assamese Language* (Guwahati: LBS, 1999 [1936]), 1.
64. Medhi, *Asamiya Byakaran aru Bhasatattwa: Assamese Grammar and Origin of the Assamese Language*, 1; Dimbeswar Neog, *The Origin and Growth of the Asamiya Language: New Light on the Development of the Asamiya Script, Pre-Historic and Historic Asam* (Guwahati: Xuwani Prakas, 1964), 43.
65. Medhi, *Asamiya Byakaran aru Bhasatattwa: Assamese Grammar and Origin of the Assamese Language*, 40–43.

66. D.C. Sirkar and P.D. Chaudhury, 'Umachal Rock Inscription of Surendravarman', *Epigraphia Indica*, vol. XXXI, pt II (April 1955); Sharma, *Inscriptions of Ancient Assam*, 303–05; P.C. Chaudhury, 'Stone Inscription from Khanikar Gaon Sarupathar', *Journal of Assam Research Society*, vol. XX (1972–73), 3–5. In 1972, a fragment of this inscription was found. The discovery of two more fragments in the subsequent decades gave a complete picture of these inscriptions. H.N. Dutta, *History, Art and Archaeology of Doiyang Dhansiri Valley, Assam* (Guwahati: LBS, 2012), 43–45; Upendra Chandra Goswami, *Asamiya Bhashar Udbhav-Samridhi aru Vikash* (Guwahati: Barua Agency, 1991).
67. T.P. Verma, *Development of Script in Ancient Kamrupa* (Jorhat: Asam Sahitya Sabha, 1976), 31–35.
68. Dimbeswar Neog argued that the 'notion that the Asamiya script . . . developed through Devanagari or through Gupta and Kutil varieties—the two are stages of the evolution of the Brahmi script—is really not borne [out] by facts'. Neog, *Origin and Growth of the Asamiya Language: New Light on the Development of the Asamiya Script, Pre-Historic and Historic Asam*, 97. Also, see Mahendra Bora, *The Evolution of Assamese Script* (Jorhat: Asam Sahitya Sabha, 1981).
69. Golockchandra Goswami, *An Introduction to Assamese Phonology* (Pune: Deccan College Postgraduate and Research Institute, 1966).
70. Golockchandra Goswami, *Structure of Assamese* (Guwahati: Gauhati University, 1982), 5.
71. Mahim Bora, 'Preface to the First Edition', in *Ronga-Jiya*, Mahim Bora (Nagaon: Krantikal, 2000 [1978]).
72. Goswami, *Prabandha: A Collection of Essays and Lectures*, 207.
73. Ibid., 208.
74. Ibid., 208–09.
75. Ibid., 210.
76. Sarma, *Shatayoun Sal Ba Swadhinatar Pratham Yudha*, 'Preface'.
77. L.N. Bezbaroa, 'Presidential Address, Asam Sahitya Sabha, 7th Annual Conference, 1924', in *Bezbaroa Granthavalee*, vol. 2, ed. Atulchandra Hazarika (Guwahati: Sahitya Prakash, 1988), 1867.
78. Goswami, *Prabandha: A Collection of Essays and Lectures*, 210.
79. Pratap Chandra Goswami, *Jeevan Smriti aru Kamrupi Samaj: A Memoir Dealing with the Evolution of the Social Systems of North Kamrup* (Guwahati: Pratul Goswami, 1971), 114–16.
80. Amritbhusan Adhikari, annotated and comp., *Srimannam-Ghosha* (Calcutta: Author, 1911), in *Prabandha: A Collection of Essays and Lectures*, Goswami, 159.

81. Banikanta Kakati, 'Bezbaroa', in *Banikanta Chayanika* ed. Maheswar Neog (New Delhi: Sahitya Akademi, 1981), 132; Goswami, *Prabandha: A Collection of Essays and Lectures*, 159.
82. Goswami, *Prabandha: A Collection of Essays and Lectures*, 210.
83. Ibid.
84. Homen Borgohain and Paramananda Majumdar, comp. and eds, *Jayantee*, vol. 1 (Guwahati: Students' Stores, 2011); Maheswar Neog, *Asamiya Sahityar Ruparekha: An Outline History of Assamese Literature, From the Beginning till Today* (Guwahati: Chandra Prakash, 1987), 321; Tirtha Phukan, 'Jayanti Jugar Sahitya', in *Asamiya Sahityar Buranji*, vol. 6, ed. Homen Borgohain (Guwahati: ABILAC, 1993), 88–100.
85. Maheswar Neog, *Sanchayan* (Delhi: Sahitya Akademi), 34; Ranjit Kumar Dev Goswami, 'Asomiya Kabita, 1951–1971', in *Prabandha: A Collection of Essays and Lectures*, Goswami, 371–79. For a collection of the early poems influenced by romanticism along with others, see Jajneswar Sarma, *Satapatra* (Nagaon: Bijit Barthakur, 2020 [1937]); Nilmani Phookan, ed., *Kuri Satikar Assamiya Kabita* (Guwahati: Publication Board Assam, 1977).
86. Nabakanta Barua, 'Amitakhor, Muktakaru Kathachanda', *Asam Sahitya Sabha Patrika*, vol. 15, no. 2 (1956), 115–20.
87. Mahendra Bora, *Natun Kabita* (Dibrugarh: Banalata, 1956), 11.
88. Ibid., 0.34–0.35; Bora, *Natun Kabita*, 11.
89. For further details, see Nilmoni Phookan, *Kuri Sotikar Asamiya Kabita*.
90. For further discussion, see Gitashree Tamuly, 'Lakshminath Bezbaroa and His Times: Language, Literature and Modernity in Colonial Assam' (PhD diss., Indian Institute of Technology Guwahati, 2021), Chapter 4.
91. For instance, Lakshminath Bezbaroa, *History of Vaishnavism in India and Rasalila of Shri Krishna: The Baroda Lectures* (Calcutta, 1934); Jnananath Bora, 'Kirtana', in *Awahan*, vol. II, ed. Paramananda Majumdar (Guwahati: Publication Board Assam, 2015 [1930]), 1111–13; Atulchandra Hazarika, *Katha Kirtana*, (Guwahati: Barua Agency, 1945); Kaliram Medhi, *Sri Sankardevar Bani* (Guwahati: Duttabarua Publishing, 1949); Maheswar Neog, *Sri Sri Sankardeva* (Guwahati: Chandra Prakash, 2006 [1949]).
92. Goswami, *Prabandha: A Collection of Essays and Lectures*, 154–59; Maheswar Neog, ed., *Banikanta Kakati Rachanawali* (Guwahati: Publication Board Assam, 1991).
93. See, for instance, Ambikagiri Raychowdhury, 'Jati Gothonot Srimanta Sankardeva', in *Ambikagiri Raychowdhury Rachanavali*, ed. Satyendranath Sarma (Guwahati: Publication Board Assam, 2009), 560–562; Hiren Gohain, *Asamiya Jatiya Jibanat Mahapurushiya Paramapara*, vol. 1 (Guwahati: LBS, 1987).

94. L.N. Bezbaroa, *Sankardeva* (Howrah: Banhi Press, 1911); L.N. Bezbaroa, *Mahapurus Sri Sankardeva aru Sri Madhadeva* (Calcutta: Author, 1914).
95. Arupjyoti Saikia, 'Grantha Bisayok Alochana', in *Asamiya Sahityar Buranji*, vol. 5, ed. Ranjit Kumar Dev Goswami (Guwahati: ABILAC, 2015), 790–802.
96. Arupjyoti Saikia, *A Century of Protests: Peasant Politics in Assam* (Delhi: Routledge, 2014), 268–71.
97. Birinchi Kumar Barua, ed., *Mahabharata*, vol. 1*: Adi Parvan* and vol. 2*: Sabha Parvan* (Guwahati: Gauhati University, 1962 and 1963).
98. Rama Saraswati, *Asamīyā Mahābhārata Droṇaparba* (Jorhat: Darpaṇ Press, 1909).
99. Syed Abdul Malik, *Dhanya Nara Tanu Bhal* (Guwahati: Students' Store, 1987).
100. Bharali, *Asamiya Bhaṣara Maulika Bicara*, 23–24; Abdus Sattar, *Sangmisranat Asamiya Sanskriti* (Jorhat: Sahityika, 2017 [1965]).
101. Richard Eaton, *India in the Persianate Age* (London: Penguin, 2019), 384.
102. For details of textbooks and readings prescribed for the students who studied Assamese at the Calcutta University, see Biswanath Rai, 'Kolkota Viswavidyalaye Asomiya Bhasa-Sahitya Charcha: Snatokttar Parjaya', *Ninth Column*, vol. XV, no. XIII (2016), 389–419.
103. See, for instance, Harinarayan Dutta Barua, *Srisankar Bakyamrit* (Nalbari: Dutta Barua, 1953).
104. Tamuly, 'Lakshminath Bezbaroa and His Times: Language, Literature and Modernity in Colonial Assam', Chapter 5.
105. B.K. Barua, *Asomiya Katha Sahitya: Purani Bhag* (Nalbari: Journal Emporium, 1950); Banikanta Kakati, *Purani Asomiya Sahitya* (Calcutta: G. C. Patoway, 1940); Jnananath Bora, *Asamiya Purani Sahitya* (Guwahati: Barua Agency, n.d.).
106. Kakati, *Purani Asomiya Sahitya*, 'Foreword'.
107. Neog, ed., *Banikanta Kakati Rachanavali,* 6; Ranjit Kumar Dev Goswami, 'Banikanta Kakati aru Asomor Boudhik Itihas', in *Prabandha: A Collection of Essays and Lectures*, Goswami, 153. Also, see Bhabananda Dutta, 'Sankari Sadhanar Tatpairya', in *Bhabananda Dutta Rachana Samagra,* eds, Paramananda Majumdar, Samindra Hujuri and Rabindra Kumar Das (Guwahati: Assam Publishing Group, 2020), 289–94.
108. Upen Chandra Lekharu, *Katha-Guru-Carita* (Guwahati: Datta Barua, 1952).
109. Banikanta Kakati and Birinchi Kumar Barua, 'Foreword', in Lekharu, *Katha-Guru-Carita*, vii.
110. Maheswar Neog, *Guru-Carita-Katha: Biographical Account of Vaishnava Saints of Assam, Sankaradeva, Madhavadeva and Others, in Prose, Committed*

to *Writing from Oral Tradition, c. 1758 AD* (Guwahati: Gauhati University, 1987).

111. Suresh Rajkhowa, 'Presidential Address', in *Asam Sahitya Sabhar Bhasanavali: A Collection of the Presidential Addresses of the History Section*, vol. 3, eds, Atulchandra Hazarika and Jatindranath Goswami (Jorhat: Asam Sahitya Sabha, 1961), 146. The use of the term 'Kamarupasasawanali' is in reference to Bhattacharya, *Kamarup-Sasanavali*.

112. Birinchi Kumar Barua, *Ankiya Nat: A Collection of Sixteen Assamese Dramas* (Gauhati: Department of Historical and Antiquarian Studies, 1940); Kaliram Medhi, comp. and ed., *Ankawali* (Guwahati: LBS, 1997 [1950]); S.N. Sarma, *Ankamala: A Collection of Ten Early Assamese Plays* (Guwahati: Gauhati University, 1973).

113. Barua, *Ankiya Nat: A Collection of Sixteen Assamese Dramas*, x.

114. Benudhar Sarma, 'Presidential Address', in *Asam Sahitya Sabhar Bhasanavali: A Collection of the Presidential Addresses of the History Section*, eds, Hazarika and Goswami, 140.

115. Akhil Gogoi and Gitashree Tamuly, *Uribo Para Hale Akou Junjiloheten* (Guwahati: Banalata, 2003), 51–81; Sharma, *Empire's Garden: Assam and the Making of India*; Altaf Mazid, 'Jyotiprasad and Joymoti: The Pioneer and the First Assamese Film', in *Perspectives on Cinema of Assam*, eds, M. Barpujari and G. Kalita, 29–50. (Guwahati: Gauhati Cine Club, 2007), 29–50. Interested readers may see the film, based on footage of the original 1935 film, here: https://www.youtube.com/watch?v=dAYf2y7OTZ8 (Accessed 17 April 2023). The spelling of the film has been used in different ways, i.e., 'Joymati' or 'Joymoti' by the filmmaker. Parthajit Barua, *Jyotiprasad, Joymoti, Indumalati and Beyond: History of Assamese Cinema* (Nagaon: Ajanta Press, 2021), 268.

116. L.N. Bezbaroa, 'Joymoti', in *Bezbaroa Granthavalee*, vol. 2, ed. Hazarika, 1137–74.

117. Ranjit Kumar Dev Goswami, 'Homage to Bezbaroa', in *Prabandha: A Collection of Essays and Lectures*, Goswami, 144.

118. *Times of Assam*, 16 March 1935, 1.

119. To get a sense of the general reception of the film and other challenges, readers can refer to the private papers of Jyotiprasad Agarwalla at http://www.tezu.ernet.in/casms/jyoti.php. Of special relevance for our discussion are *Jyotiprasad Agarwala Personal Papers*, vol. 1 and *Jyotiprasad Agarwala Personal Papers* vol. 3, Digital Library, Center for Assamese Studies, Tezpur University in https://www.tezu.ernet.in/casms/jyoti.php (Accessed 18 January 2018). Also, see Aparna Sarma, 'Close Reading: Joymoti by Jyotiprasad Agarwala', https://www.sahapedia.org/close-reading-joymoti-jyotiprasad-agarwala. (Accessed 18 January 2018).

120. Manoj Barpujari, 'Assamese Cinema: Dreams, Reality and Dichotomies', in *Routledge Handbook of Indian Cinemas,* eds, K. Moti Gokulsing and Wimal Dissanayake (London: Routledge, 2013), 54.
121. 'Draft Letter from Jyotiprasad Agarwala to Political Officer, Mishmi Hills, Sadiya, January 1950, Dibrugarh', in *Jyotiprasad Agarwala Personal Papers*, vol. 3.
122. Apurba Sarma, *Axomiya Chalacitrar San-Pohar* (Guwahati: Aank-Baak, 2014), 20.
123. For a list of production houses of the Assamese cinemas in the 1950s and 1960s, see P.K. Deka, *Satuta Dashakar Asomor Chalachitra* (Guwahati: Rupkar, 2006).
124. Mahesh Chandra Dev Goswami, 'From the pages of The India P.E.N., vol. XI, no. 6 (June 1945)', in *Mahesh Chandra Dev Goswami: Jivan aru Kriti* ed. Prafulla Mahanta (Nagaon: Mahesh Chandra Dev Goswami Smriti Raksha Samiti, 2004), 156.
125. Neog, *New Light on History of Asamiya Literature: From the Earliest Until Recent Times Including an Account of its Antecedents*, 441.
126. Lakshmiram Barooah, comp. and ed., *Sangith Kosha or A Collection of Selected Assamese Songs* (Calcutta: Jahnabi Agency, 1907).
127. Ibid. 442; Birendranath Dutta, *Asamiya Sangitar Aithhya* (Jorhat: Asam Sahitya Sabha, 1977), 82–85.
128. *Assam Tribune*, 4 January 1954, 1.
129. Calcutta 2, 20 March 1947, Programmes for the fortnight March 16-31, *Indian Listener*, vol. XII, no. 6 (7 March 1947), 55.
130. 'Opening of Assam radio station: Sardar Patel's Message', *Times of India*, 2 July 1948, 5.
131. *Indian Listener*, vol. XIV, no. 1 (22 December 1948), 23.
132. H.R Luthra, *Indian Broadcasting* (New Delhi: Publications Division, 1986), 196; Mehra Masani, *Broadcasting and the People* (New Delhi: NBT, 1976).
133. *Akashvani*, vol. XXIV, no. 16 (19 April 1959), 16; *Indian Listener*, vol. XXII, no. 16 (14 April 1957), 13.
134. 'Growth of AIR Network in India, 1947 to 2017' in https://www.indiastat.com/table/media-data/21/all-india-radio-air/450129/48909/data.aspx (Accessed 12 June 2021).
135. Bezbaroa's acclaimed autobiography was translated into Bengali and published by the Akademi in 1957. Lakshminath Bezbaroa, *Amar Jibansmriti* (in Bengali), trans., Arati Tagore (Delhi: Sahitya Academi, 1957).
136. Sahitya Akademi, *Sahitya Akademi Awards: Books and Writers: 1955–1978* (Delhi: Sahitya Akademi, 1990).
137. *Chief Secretary of Assam's Fortnightly Report* (hereafter *FR*), 1 August 1957.
138. *FR*, 1 October 1957.

139. For instance, see *Soviet Desh*, December 1961 (Only the Communist Party's 22nd party congress deliberations were published in this volume), see https://archive.org/details/in.ernet.dli.2015.452903/page/n1/mode/2up [Accessed 9 May 2021].
140. Hemanga Biswas, *Ujan Gang Baiya* (Calcutta: Anustup, 1983).
141. Gogoi and Tamuly, *Uribo Para Hale Akou Junjiloheten,* 161.
142. J.D. Anderson, *A Collection of Kachari Folk-tales and Rhymes* (Shillong: 1895); Benudhar Rajkhowa, *Assamese Demonology* (Calcutta: Patrika Press, 1905), Dibakar Sarma, comp., *Bhanita* (Sibsagar: Author, 1899); Yajnarama Dasa, comp., *Ḍakabhaṇita* (Calcutta: Bijjyan Yantra, 1885); P.R.T. Gurdon, comp. and anno., *Some Assamese Proverbs* (Shillong: Government Printing Press, 1903).
143. 'About Ourselves: A Profile, Department of Folklore Research, Gauhati University', *Bulletin of Folklore Research Department*, vol. 1, no. 1 (1993), 78; K.K. Handiqui, 'Second Convocation for Conferring Degrees, Vice-Chancellor's Address, 1955', in *Krishna Kanta Handiqui* ed. Sattar, 30.
144. Birinchi Kumar Barua, 'Professor Baruar Chithi', in *Birinchi Kumar Barua Rachanavali*, vol. 2, ed. Nagen Saikia (Guwahati: Bina Library, 2015), 1611–81. Barua spelt out a proposal to teach folklore at the Gauhati University in 1947. Birinchi Kumar Barua, 'Scandinavian Desh Samuhot Loka Samskriti Charcha aru Sikhsha Pranali (Study and Teaching of Folklore in Scandinavian Nations), *Dainik Assamiya*, 21 September 1947.
145. Mohini Mohan Brahma and Praphulladatta Goswami, *Bodo Kachari Sola* (Guwahati: Gauhati University Press, 1972).
146. Birendranath Datta, *A Bibliography of Folklore Material of Assam and Adjoining Areas* (Guwahati: Gauhati University Press, 1978); Ankur Tamuli Phukan, 'Scenes of the Obscene: The Lewd, the Rustic and Bihu in Colonial Assam', *Man and Society*, vol. XIV, winter (2017), 150–64.
147. Praphulladatta Goswami, 'The Bihu Songs of Assam', *Eastern Anthropologist*, vol. 3, no. 1, 57–70.
148. *Dainik Asam*, 10 April 1948.
149. Anonymous, 'Guwahatit Rongali Bihur Tindiniya Mahotsava', in *Awahan*, vol. IV, ed. Paramananda Majumdar (Guwahati: Publication Board Assam, 2015 [1932]), 846. For an insightful study on this development, see Ankur Tamuli Phukan, 'Making of a National Festival: Bihu in Colonial and Post-Colonial Assam' (PhD diss., Jadavpur University, 2020).
150. *Dainik Asam*, 13 April 1966.
151. Prosenjit Choudhury, 'Unabimsa Satikar Bidyot Samaj aru Bihu', in *Unois Satikar Asomot Ebhumuki* ed. Prosenjit Choudhury (Guwahati: Bhabani Print and Publications, 2011), 1–16. In 1898, Budhindranath Delihial

Bhattacharya (1865–1945), a clerk with the government and a future tea planter, wished for the government to ban Bihu.
152. Barua, *Asam Buranji, or, The History of Assam*, 280. A similar view was held by his illustrious predecessor; see Haliram Dhekial Phukan, *Assam Desher Itihas Orthat Assam Buranji* (Calcutta: Samacar Candrika, 1829, ed. Jatindra Mohan Bhattacharjee (Gauhati: Mokshada Pustakalaya, 1962), 103–04; Gunabhiram Barua, *Anandaram Dhekial Phukanor Jivan Charitra* (Guwahati: Publication Board Assam, 1992 [1880]), 148; Boli Narayan Bora, 'Bihu', in *Asam-Bandhu, A Monthly Paper Devoted to Assamese Language, Literature and Culture, 1885–1886*, ed. N. Saikia (Guwahati: Publication Board Assam, 1984), 157.
153. Rajani Kanta Bardoloi, *Miri Jiyari* (Barpeta: Barpeta Sonatun Dhurma Press, 1895), 9–17.
154. S.K. Bhuyan, 'Bihu', *Alochani*, vol. 8, no. 7 (1917), 1.
155. L.N. Bezbaroa, 'Bihu', in *Bezbaroa Granthavalee*, ed. Hazarika, 1568–69.
156. Goswami, 'The Bihu Songs of Assam', 69.
157. Sayidur Rahman, 'A Critical Review of Bahagi', *Times of Assam*, 19 May 1923, in *Bahagi: A Collection of Assamese Pastoral Poems and Ballads*, ed. N. C. Bhuyan (Shillong: Assamia Sahitya Mandir, 1963).
158. *Natun Asamiya*, April 1954, 1; *Natun Asamiya*, 13 April 1954, 1.
159. *Natun Asamiya*, 13 April 1954, 1.
160. Tarun Pamegam and party, 'Miri Bihu songs', AIR programmes, East Regional Service, Gauhati, *Indian Listener*, 14 April 1957, 13; 'Bodo Bihu Songs', AIR programmes, East Regional Service, Gauhati, *Akashvani*, Vol. XXIII. No. 15, 13 April 1958, 18.
161. Praphulladatta Goswami, *Bohag Bihu of Assam and Bihu Songs* (Guwahati: Publication Board Assam, 1988), 506.
162. Praphulladatta Goswami, *The Springtime Bihu of Assam: A Socio-Cultural Study* (Guwahati: LBS, 1966), 106.
163. Benudhar Sarma, 'Bihur Purani Jilingoni', in *Bihu Binandia*, ed. Gokul Deka (Tezpur: Gokul Deka, 1971), 1–12.
164. The Assam government notification of the list of public holidays for 1955 did not declare Sankardev Tithi (anniversary) as a public holiday, but government offices remained closed nevertheless (*Assam Gazette*, 24 November 1954).
165. *Sadiniya Asomiya*, 3 March 1945, 1.
166. Goswami, 'From the Pages of The India P.E.N., vol. XI, no. 6 (June 1945)', 154.
167. 'Banikanta Kakati', in Bhaben Barua, 'Jivanar Batat: The Story of a Society', in *Professor Birinchi Kumar Barua Commemoration Volume*, eds,

M. Neog and M.M. Sharma (Guwahati: All India Oriental Conference, 1966), LXI.
168. Bhaben Barua, 'Jivanar Batat: The Story of a Society', in *Professor Birinchi Kumar Barua Commemoration Volume*, eds, Neog and Sharma, XIL.
169. Hiren Gohain, 'Mahaan Upanyasik Birinchi Kumar Barua', in *Hiren Gohain Rachanawali*, vol. 1, eds, Shoneet Bijoy Das and Munin Bayan (Guwahati: Katha Publications, 2009), 426.
170. Hiren Gohain, 'Otihya aru Jivanar Batat', in *Hiren Gohain Rachanawali*, eds, Das and Bayan, 412.
171. This figure is based on Government of India, *Progress of Education in India, 1947–1952* (New Delhi: Manager of Publications, 1954), Table XXII, 112; Government of Assam, *Annual Report on the Progress of Education in Assam During 1962–63* (Shillong: Government Press, 1966), Table IV, 2.
172. See 'Table 2.2' in Robin Jeffrey, *India's Newspaper Revolution: Capitalism, Politics and the Indian-Language, 1977–99* (London: Hurst and Company, 2000), 27; *Report on the Census of India, 1951*, vol. XII, part II-A, Table D 1, 79.
173. Richard F. Nyrop, et al., *Area Handbook for India* (Washington: The American University, 1976), 288.
174. Banikanta Kakati, *The Mother Goddess Kamakhya* (Guwahati: Publication Board Assam, 1989 [1948]).
175. 'Editorial', *Assam Tribune*, 26 March 1954, 4.
176. *Dainik Asam*, 30 August 1947, 1.
177. Ardeshir Ruttonji Wadia, *The Future of English in India* (Calcutta: Asia Publishing House, 1954), 67–68.
178. Government of India, *Report of the State Reorganisation Commission* (New Delhi: Government of India, 1955), 184.
179. Government of India, *Report of the State Reorganisation Commission*, 181.
180. Government of India, *Report of the State Reorganisation Commission*, 186.
181. Letters to the Editor, 'Re-organisation of States', *Assam Tribune*, 8 May 1954, 4; *Assam Tribune*, 7 May, 1954, 3; Government of India, *Report of the State Reorganisation Commission*, 194–95.
182. J.K. Choudhury, 'A Plan for Purbachal: June–July 1948', in *Autonomy Movement in Assam (Documents)*, ed. P.S. Dutta (Delhi: Omsons Publications, 1993), 313–36.
183. Government of India, *Report of the State Reorganisation Commission*, 194–95.
184. *Dainik Assamiya*, 5 July 1947; *Sadiniya Asamiya*, 4 October 1947; *Assam Tribune*, 6 October 1947; *Natun Asamiya*, 19 April 1949; 'Resolution of

Nagaon District Chattra Congress', 27–28 September 1947; All are quoted in Nilamoni Sen Deka, ed., *Asomiya Bhashar Atmapratisthar Sangramar Itihas aru Anannya Prasanga*, Vol. 3 (Guwahati: B.R. Book Stall, 2021), 114–16. In 1954, Ambikagiri Raychowdhury, submitting a memorandum before the State Reorganisation Commission, emphasized the need to make Assamese as Assam's 'regional language' and 'emphatically expressed the view against any proposal for making Assam a bilingual or multilingual state', quoted in *Assam Tribune*, 6 May 1954, 1 and 7. *Assam Tribune*, 5 May 1954, 1 and 8.

185. 'Resolution of Khasi States People Union', 13 July 1948, in *Asomiya Bhashar Atmapratisthar Sangramar Itihas aru Anannya Prasanga*, Vol. 3, ed. Deka, 198.
186. Editorial, *Asam Sahitya Sabha Patrika*, nos 2 and 3 (1952), 188.
187. Maheswar Neog, *The Language Problem of Assam* (Jorhat: Asam Sahitya Sabha, 1961), Appendix B, 52.
188. 'Speech of Bishnuram Medhi', in *ALAD*, 12 June 1957.
189. 'Opinion of Justice H. Deka before the Language Commission', in *Language Commission: Opinions of the Hon'ble Chief Justice and the Other Hon'ble Judges of the Assam High Court, Questionnaire of the Official Language Commission*, File no. un-numbered, Home (Miscellaneous) ASA.
190. K.K. Sinha, ed., *Modern India Rejects Hindi: Report of the All India Language Conference* (Calcutta: Association for the Advancement of the National Languages of India, 1958), iii.
191. Birendra Kumar Bhattacharya, 'The Language of NEFA and National Unity', in *The Outlook on N.E.F.A.*, ed. Parag Chaliha (Jorhat: Asam Sahitya Sabha, 1958), 35. Similar was the view of the Asam Sahitya Sabha. In 1965, the Sabha demanded that until there was a voluntary demand from Assam and other non-Hindi speaking states, Hindi should not be imposed as the country's only official language. 'Resolution of the Executive Committee of the Asam Sahitya Sabha held on 15 February 1965', in *APCC Papers*, Packet 42, File no. 11 (NMML).
192. *Natun Asamiya*, 31 October 1960; *Dainik Assamiya*, 30 August 1947. Many however disagreed with this idea and argued that any such attempt would cause harm to the Assamese literature and language. See, 'Letters to editor', Sriman Prafulla Goswami, *Dainik Assamiya*, 7 July 1947.
193. 'Letter from Jatindra Mohan Goswami, General Secretary, Asam Sahitya Sabha, to Bimala Prasad Chaliha, Chief Minister, Assam, February 5, 1960', in *APCC Papers*, Packet 42, File no. 11 (NMML).
194. 'Letter from Mahendra Mohan Choudhury, President, APCC, to President, Asam Sahitya Sabha, August 10, 1959', in *APCC Papers*, Packet 42, File no. 11 (NMML).

195. 'News of Sahitya Sabha', *Asam Sahitya Sabha Patrika*, vol. 28, no. 1 (1959), 78–79.
196. *Natun Asamiya*, 1 March 1960, 1.
197. *Natun Asamiya*, 4 March 1960, 1.
198. *Natun Asamiya*, 27 May 1960, 1; *Natun Asamiya*, 2 June 1960, 1.
199. *Natun Asamiya*, 7 May 1960, 1.
200. *Natun Asamiya*, 27 May 1960, 1.
201. 'Speeches of Tarun Sen Deka (RCPI) and Birendra Kumar Das (PSP), 29 February 1960', *ALAD*; *Natun Asamiya*, 1 March 1960, 1.
202. *Natun Asamiya*, 8 March 1960, 1; *Natun Asamiya*, 9 March 1960, 1.
203. 'Letter from M.M. Choudhury, President, Assam Pradesh Congress Committee, to President, Asom Sahitya Sabha, 10 August 1959', in *APCC papers*, Packet 42, File no. 11 (NMML).
204. *Assam Tribune*, 11 March 1960, 1.
205. *Natun Asamiya*, 12 March 1960, 1.
206. 'Chaliha's Speech in the *ALAD*', *Natun Asamiya*, 16 March 1960, 1.
207. *Natun Asamiya*, 18 March 1960, 1; *Natun Asamiya*, 19 March 1960, 1.
208. *Natun Asamiya*, 22 March 1960, 1; *Natun Asamiya*, 23 March 1960, 1; *Assam Tribune*, 9 July 1960, 1; *Assam Tribune*, 19 July 1960, 1.
209. *Natun Asamiya*, 23 April 1960, 1; 'Nehru to Chaliha, 25 June 1960', in *Selected Works of Jawaharlal Nehru* (hereafter *SWJN*), second series, vol. 61, 271, fn. 225; 'Copy of the resolution adopted on the question of the Official Language by the Assam Pradesh Congress Committee in its Meeting Held on April 21 and 22, 1960 at Guwahati', in *Sriman Prafulla Goswami Papers*, Packet no. I-III, NMML.
210. *Natun Asamiya*, 3 June 1960, 1; Assam Pradesh Congress Committee, 'A Brief Report on the Recent Disturbances in Assam (Guwahati, July 1960)', in *Sriman Prafulla Goswami Papers*, Packet no. I-III, NMML.
211. *Times of India*, 9 July 1960, 1 and 6.
212. *Natun Asamiya*, 7 June 1960, 1; *Natun Asamiya*, 9 June 1960, 1.
213. *Natun Asamiya*, 26 June 1960; 'Bengalees want Assamese as state language', *Assam Tribune*, 26 June 1960, 1.
214. *Natun Asamiya*, 20 June 1960, 1.
215. *Natun Asamiya*, 24 June 1960, 1; *Assam Tribune*, 24 June 1960, 1.
216. *Times of India*, 7 July 1960, 1.
217. *Times of India*, 8 July 1960, 7.
218. *Indian Express*, 5 July 1960, 1.
219. *Times of India*, 5 July 1960, 1; *Times of India*, 6 July 1960, 1.
220. *Assam Tribune*, 5 July 1960, 1, *Dainik Asam*, 5 July 1960, 1; C.P. Sinha, *Report of the Enquiry Commission into the Police Firing Incident of 4 July 1960* (Shillong: Government of Assam, 1960). This report, which justified

the police firing, was not accepted by the Assam government. *Times of India*, 6 May 1961, 5.
221. 'Curfew-ridden Gauhati: A desolate and dreary picture', *Assam Tribune*, 6 July 1960, 1.
222. 'Curfew extended: atmosphere of gloom pervades', *Assam Tribune*, 6 July 1960, 1.
223. '13 die in Indian riots: 7,000 homes burned in Assam in clashes over language', *New York Times*, 28 July 1960, 3.
224. G. Mehrotra, *Report of the Commission of Inquiry into the Goreswar Disturbances* (Shillong: Assam Government Press, 1961).
225. 'Insanity fair', *Times of India*, 11 July 1960, 6.
226. Mehrotra, *Report of the Commission of Inquiry into the Goreswar Disturbances*.
227. 'Nowgong Enquiry Report by Assam's Additional Chief Secretary A.N. Kidwai', in 'Nehru to G.B. Pant, September 13, 1960', *SWJN*, second series, vol. 63, 188.
228. 'Letter from Bidhan Chandra Ray, Chief Minister, West Bengal to Nehru, August 22 & 23, 1960', in Saroj Chakrabarty, *The Upheaval Years in North-East India: A Documentary In-Depth Study of Assam Holocausts, 1960–1983* (Calcutta: S. Chakrabarty and R. Chakrabarty, 1984), 21.
229. P.C. Goswami, 'Tragedy of Political Tactlessness', *Economic Weekly* (30 July 1960), 1198.
230. Ajit Prasad Jain, 'Report of Delegation of Members of Parliament to Assam, 8 August, 1960', in *Documents on North-East India: Assam (1958 to Modern Times)*, eds, Suresh K. Sharma and Usha Sharma (Delhi: Mittal Publications, 2006), 87.
231. 'FIR of Jadulal Karmakar, Titabor, July 10, 1960', in *Special Police Report from Districts (CID) Cases Arising out of the Language Disturbances*, File no. 574/60, Home (Police), ASA.
232. 'FIR by Tarani Kumar Ghose, Bokakhat, July 25, 1960', in *Special Police Report from Districts (CID) Cases arising out of the Language Disturbances*, File no. 574/60, Home (Police), ASA.
233. Biswas, *Ujan Gang Baiya*, 196–207.
234. 'Speech of Nehru, National Integration Council Committee, Durgapur, May 28, 1961', in *SWJN*, second series, vol. 69, 64.
235. Chakrabarty, *The Upheaval Years in North-East India: A Documentary In-Depth Study of Assam Holocausts, 1960–1983*, 17.
236. *Times of India*, 10 July 1960, 1; *Times of India*, 11 July 1960, 6.
237. Nirad C. Chaudhuri, *The Continent of Circe* (Mumbai: Jaico Publishing House, 1960), 36–37.
238. Prasun Barman, *Assam Upatyakat Bangali* (Guwahati: Assam Publishing Company, 2015).

239. K.C. Chakravarty, 'Assam Disturbances I: Bongal Kheda Again', *Economic Weekly* (30 July 1960), 1193.
240. Anonymous, 'The Assam Debates: A Post Mortem', *Economic Weekly* (10 September 1960), 1366–67; 'Motion Regarding "Situation in Assam", Speech of J.L. Nehru,', *Lok Sabha Debates*, 1 September 1960, column 6220.
241. 'Letter from Nehru to N. Sanjiva Reddy, September 5, 1960', in *SWJN*, second series, vol. 63, 187; 'Letter to Sadiq Ali from Nehru, no. 39, September 23, 1960', in *SWJN*, second series, vol. 63, 190.
242. 'Letter from Nehru to N. Sanjiva Reddy, September 5, 1960', in *SWJN*, second series, vol. 63, 187.
243. 'Nehru supports Assamese as state language', *Assam Tribune*, 18 July 1960, 1; *Times of India*, 18 July 1960, 1.
244. 'Congressmen protest: Premier's charge of inaction', *Times of India*, 18 July 1960, 1; *Assam Tribune*, 18 July 1960, 1.
245. 'Speech of Nehru, Motion Regarding Situation in Assam', in *Lok Sabha Debates*, 1 September 1960, columns 6217–20.
246. 'Nehru to Chaliha, September 24, 1960', in *SWJN*, second series, vol. 63, 192.
247. *Assam Tribune*, 8 July 1960, 1. 'Extract from the Resolution passed by the second All Party Hill Leaders Conference held at Shillong on August 22 & 23, 1960', in *Asomiya Bhashar Atmapratisthar Sangramar Itihas aru Anannya Prasanga, Vol. 6*, ed. Nilamoni Sen Deka, (Guwahati: B.R. Book Stall, 2021), 180–81.
248. 'Resolutions passed by the All Party Hill Leaders Conference of the Autonomous Districts of Assam, Shillong, July 6–7, 1960', in *Report of Delegation of Members of Parliament to Assam*, 8 August 1960, Jain, Appendix vi.
249. Speech of Hynniewta, *Lok Sabha Debates*, 2 September 1960, columns 6537–39.
250. *Assam Tribune*, 6 July 1960, 4; *Natun Asamiya*, 6 July 1960.
251. 'Nehru to Chaliha, May 12, 1961', in *SWJN*, second series, vol. 68, 288–90.
252. Goswami, 'Tragedy of Political Tactlessness', 1198; Jain, *Report of Delegation of Members of Parliament to Assam*, 8 August 1960.
253. 'Hill districts in Assam as separate state: Move gathers momentum', *Times of India*, 17 July 1960, 13.
254. Hitesh Deka, *Mati Kar* (Guwahati: Chandra Prakash, 2013 [1960]); Jain, *Report of Delegation of Members of Parliament to Assam*, 8 August 1960.
255. E.H. Pakyntein, *Report on the Census of India 1961: General Report*, Vol. 3, Assam, Part I-A, 210, Table 8.3.
256. Jain, 'Report of Delegation of Members of Parliament to Assam, 8 August, 1960', 83; N.C. Chatterjee, *Report of Non-Official Commission of Enquiry*

*into the Language Riot in Cachar, 1960, headed by N.C. Chatterjee* (Calcutta: N.C. Chatterjee, 1961); 'Speech of Ranendra Mohan Das, 24 October 1960', *ALAD*.
257. Pakyntein, *Report on the Census of India 1961: General Report*, Vol. 3, Assam, Part I-A, 204.
258. Radhika Mohan Goswami, *Ateet Smriti* (Guwahati: Alok Prakashan, 1989), 95, 104.
259. 'Nehru to Chaliha, June 25, 1960', in *SWJN*, second series, vol. 61, 271.
260. 'Nehru to S.M. Shrinagesh, October 20, 1960', in *SWJN*, second series, vol. 63, 193.
261. 'Proceedings of the Press Conference with the Union Home Minister held at Raj Bhavan, 8 October 1960', *Visit of Union Home Minister in Connection with Language Issue*, Home Confidential, Political Department, Assam Secretariat, PLA 528/60 ASA; Chakrabarty, *The Upheaval Years in North-East India: A Documentary In-Depth Study of Assam Holocausts*, 20.
262. Chakravarti, 'The Assam Disturbances I: Bongal Kheda Again', 1193.
263. D.C. Pavate, *Report of the Gauhati University Enquiry Commission 1962* (Shillong: Assam Government Press, 1962).
264. Ibid., 17.
265. Jain, 'Report of Delegation of Members of Parliament to Assam, 8 August, 1960', 83; Pavate, *Report of the Gauhati University Enquiry Commission 1962*, 11.
266. *Natun Asamiya*, 11 October 1960, 1; 'Speech of Bimala Prasad Chaliha, 10 October 1960', *ALAD*.
267. *Natun Asamiya*, 6 October 1960, 1.
268. *Natun Asamiya*, 10 October 1960; *Assam Tribune*, 10 October 1960, 1; *Assam Tribune*, 12 October 1960, 1.
269. *Natun Asamiya*, 10 October 1960; 'Press Statement of Golap Borbora, General Secretary, Praja Socialist Party', *Natun Asamiya*, 11 October 1970; *Natun Asamiya*, 12 October 1960.
270. *Natun Asamiya*, 12 October 1960, 1.
271. *Natun Asamiya*, 11 October 1960, 1.
272. *Natun Asamiya*, 25 October 1960, 1.
273. *Natun Asamiya*, 31 October 1960, 1.
274. 'Nehru to Ranendra Mohan Das, November 11, 1960', in *SWJN*, second series, vol. 64, 112.
275. 'Record of the Prime Minister's Meeting with the Delegation of the Hill Leaders' Conference, No. 27', in *SWJN*, second series, vol. 69, 117; 'Letter from S.D.D. Nicholas Roy, General Secretary, Council of Action of the All-

Party Hill Leaders' Conference, April 8, 1961, No. 11', in *SWJN*, second series, vol. 68, 763.
276. N.C. Chatterjee, *Report Presented to the Prime Minister of India on the Progress of Rehabilitation of the Riot-Victims in Assam, 1960* (Calcutta: West Bengal Swatantra Party, 1960).
277. Government of Assam, *Report on the Police Administration in the state of Assam for the Year 1961* (Shillong: Assam Government Press, 1964), 3.
278. Rajeswar Prasad, *Days with Lal Bahadur Shastri: Glimpses from the Last Seven Years* (Delhi: Allied Publishers, 1991), 24.
279. *Times of India*, 7 June 1961, 1.
280. Maheswar Neog, *Jivanar Digh aru Bani* (Guwahati: Chandra Prakash, 1988), 472–74; Satich Chandra Kakati, 'The Shastri Formula and the Roy Recipe', in *Assam's Language Question,* ed. Neog, 22–28.
281. 'Pant formula', *Times of India*, 7 June 1961, 7.
282. 'Confidential Note, from D.K. Borooah to Chief Minister, Assam, 19 October 1964', in *Official Language*, File CMS/172/64, CMS, ASA.
283. 'Notification, A.N. Kidwai, Chief Secretary, Government of Assam, 24 July 1964', in *Official Language*, File CMS/172/64, CMS, ASA.
284. 'Confidential Note, from D.K. Borooah, Chairman, Implementation Committee, Assam Official Language Act, 27 July 1964', in *Official Language*, Chief Minister's Secretariat, File CMS/172/64, CMS, ASA.
285. Bodo Sahitya Sabha, 'Public Appeal', *Official Language*, File CMS/172/64, CMS, ASA.
286. E.H. Pakyntein, *Report on the Census of India 1961: General Report*, Vol. 3, Assam, Part I-A, 203.

## Chapter 7: Trouble in the Eastern Himalayas

1. Secret, Calcutta Special Report no. 64, 'Reports on Assam, Sikkim and Bhutan', Government Papers, The National Archives, Kew, 1950. http://www.archivesdirect.amdigital.co.uk/Documents/Details/FO_371_84250 (Accessed 10 March 2021).
2. The hill-dwellers 'to whom we pay tribute live far back on the mountains, they do not molest us after payment', wrote a group of villagers in the north bank of Brahmaputra to Francis Jenkins, the British East India Company official in January 1838. Francis Jenkins, *Journal of a Tour in Upper Assam, 1838,* Entry for 22 January 1838, 3 (Assam State Archives); Swarna Lata Baruah, 'Ahom Policy Towards the Neighbouring Hill Tribes', *Proceedings of the Indian History Congress*, vol. 38 (1977), 249–56; Lakshmi Devi, *Ahom–Tribal Relations: A Political Study* (Guwahati: Lawyer's Book Stall,

1992); Braj Narain Jha, 'Politics of Posa: A Case Study of Pre and Post Independence Scenario in Arunachal Pradesh and Assam', *Proceedings of the Indian History Congress*, vol. 57 (1996), 446–58. Also, see, Jelle J.P. Wouters, 'Keeping the Hill Tribes at Bay: A critique from India's Northeast of James C. Scott's paradigm of state evasion', *European Bulletin of Himalayan Research*, vol. 39, (2012), 41–65; Bodhisattva Kar, 'When was the postcolonial? A history of policing impossible lines', in *Beyond Counter-Insurgency: Breaking the impasse in Northeast India*, ed. Sanjib Baruah (Oxford: Oxford University Press, 2009), 49–77.

3. 'Note on the Posa Paid to the Akas', Correspondence from Deputy Commissioner of Darrang to Personal Assistant to Chief Commissioner of Assam, no. 877 J, 16 February 1884, *Proceedings of the Chief Commissioner of Assam*, Foreign Department, no. 38 (March 1885) (British Library).

4. Yeshe Dorjee Thongchi, *Hanhi aru Sakulor Haihob* (Guwahati: Banalata 2016), 9–10.

5. Deba Prosad Choudhury, 'British Policy on the North-East Frontier of India 1865–1914' (PhD diss., University of London, 1970), 56–101.

6. 'Report on the Sudya Fair', Letter from Colonel Henry Hopkinson, Governor-General's Agent, North East Frontier, and Commissioner of Assam, to the Secretary to the Government of Bengal, Judicial (Political) Department, 6 March 1873, in House of Commons Parliamentary Papers, *Reports on Trade Routes and Fairs on the Northern Frontiers of India* (London: Her Majesty's Stationery Office, 1874), 52–56.

7. Arupjyoti Saikia, 'Flows and Fairs: The Eastern Himalayas and the British Empire', in *Flows and Frictions in Trans Himalayan Spaces: Histories of Networking and Border Crossing*, eds, Gunnel Cederlof and William van Schendel (Amsterdam: Amsterdam University Press, 2022), 137–66; Tansen Sen, *India, China, and the World: A Connected History* (London: Rowman & Littlefield, 2017).

8. M.C. Cooke, 'Gold Thread: Coptis teeta, Wall, and Coptis trifoliam Salisb', *The Pharmaceutical Journal and Transactions* (27 August 1870), 161.

9. Haribilash Agarwala, *Haribilash Agarwala Dangariyar Atmajibani* (Guwahati: Tarunkumar Agarwala, 1967), 40; Jyotiprasad Agarwala, 'Dangariya Haribilash Agarwala', in *Jyotiprasad Rachanavali*, ed. Hiren Gohain (Guwahati: Publication Board Assam, 2003), 878.

10. Alastair Lamb, *The McMahon Line*, 2 vols (London: Routledge, 1966); Carole McGranahan, 'From Simla to Rongbatsa: The British and the "Modern" Boundaries of Tibet', *Tibet Journal*, vol. 28, no. 4 (2003), 39–60; Choudhury, 'British Policy on the North-East Frontier of India, 1865–1914', 102–35; Kyle J. Gardner, *The Frontier Complex: Geopolitics and the*

*Making of the India–China Border, 1846–1962* (Cambridge: Cambridge University Press, 2021), 218–21; Lars-Erik Nyman, 'Tawang: A Case Study of British Frontier Policy in the Himalayas', *Journal of Asian History*, vol. 10, no. 2 (1976), 151–71; Thomas Simpson, *The Frontier in British India: Space, Science, and the Power in the Nineteenth Century* (Cambridge: Cambridge University Press, 2021).

11. Ruth Gamble, 'How Dams Climb Mountains: China and India's State-Making Hydropower Contest in the Eastern-Himalaya Watershed', *Thesis Eleven*, vol. 150, no. 1 (February 2019), 42–67.

12. Sun Yat-sen, *The International Development of China* (New York: G.P. Putnam's Sons, 1922).

13. Letter from L.C. Porter, Secretary, Department of Education, Government of India to the Chief Commissioner, Assam, 5 August 1913, Shimla, no. 59 in *Encouragement of the study of the Chinese language among officers of the Assam administration: Preparation of draft rules for this purpose*, File no. 108–09, Proceedings July 1914, Establishment B, Foreign and Political Department, PR_000004062155, Abhilekh Patal, NAI.

14. Christoph von Fürer-Haimendorf, *Himalayan Barbary* (London: John Murray, 1955), xi.

15. Bérénice Guyot-Réchard, 'Tour Diaries and Itinerant Governance in the Eastern Himalayas, 1909–1962', *Historical Journal*, vol. 60, no. 4 (December 2017), 1023–46.

16. Fürer-Haimendorf, *Himalayan Barbary*, viii.

17. Christoph von Fürer-Haimendorf, 'Primitive Peoples of the McMahon Line Country: Tribal Life in a Territory Now Claimed by China', *Illustrated London News*, 16 January 1960, 92.

18. Ibid.

19. 'Constitutional position of plains areas of the North-East Frontier Tract (Tribal Areas) of Assam- inclusion in normal administration', Note, S.N. Haksar, Joint Secretary, Ministry of External Affairs, *Transfer of the Plains Areas of the Part B Tribal Areas Under the Sixth Schedule of the Constitution to the Government of Assam*, File no 18/51, 1951, Abhilekh Patal, NAI.

20. Amarendranath Pathak, 'Ziro', *Asam Sahitya Sabha Patrika*, vol. 15, no. 1 (1956), 36–47.

21. 'Letter from R.W. Godfrey, Secretary to the Governor of Assam to Secretary, External Affairs Department, GoI, no. 10/sub. 23/46/3–Ad, Shillong, 14 October, 1946', *Tibetan influence in the Northern part of the Subansiri Area*, File no. 85/NEF/46, NEF Branch, External Affairs Department, GoI, Abhilekh Patal, NAI.

22. 'Jairamdas Doulatram, GOA to Manibehn Patel, July 20, 1950, Shillong', File no. xxvi, Letters from Jairamji, *Digitised Private Papers of Sardar Patel*, Abhilekh Patal, NAI.
23. See Chapter 4.
24. Nari Rustomji, *Enchanted Frontiers: Sikkim, Bhutan and India's North-Eastern Borderlands* (London: Oxford University Press, 1971), 123.
25. 'Letter from B.C. Kapur, Secretary to the Government of Assam to Secretary to the GoI, Ministry of Home Affairs, 18 August 1950', no. AAI.40/49 in *Proposal of the External Affairs Ministry to Include in the Indian Foreign Service Cadre Certain Posts in the North-Eastern Frontier Agency at Present Borne on the Indian Civil Administrative Cadre*, File no. F. 1/25/50-A.I.S., A.I.S. section, Ministry of Home Affairs, GoI, Abhilekh Patal, NAI.
26. Nari Rustomji, *Imperilled Frontiers: India's North Eastern Borderlands* (Delhi: Oxford University Press, 1983), 100.
27. Rustomji, *Imperilled Frontiers: India's North Eastern Borderlands*, 98; Clause 17, sub-clause 1 (b) of the 6th Schedule of the Indian Constitution.
28. 'APCC Resolution on Affairs of Part B Tribal Areas, March 1952', quoted in Letter from Bishnuram Medhi to Nehru, 6 March 1952, *Bishnuram Medhi Papers*, Packet no. 190, LL II (102), NMML.
29. 'Letter from Bishnuram Medhi to Nehru, March 9, 1952', *Bishnuram Medhi Papers*, 190, LL II (102), NMML.
30. Ibid.
31. Rustomji, *Imperilled Frontiers: India's North Eastern Borderlands*, 98.
32. R.B. Vaghaiwalla, *Report of the Census of India, 1951, Assam: North-East Frontier Agency, District Census Handbook* (Shillong: Government Press, 1953), ii.
33. Speech of Jawaharlal Nehru, *Lok Sabha Debates*, 22 February 1960, column 2084.
34. Sristidhar Dutta, *Cross-Border Trade of North-East India: The Arunachal Perspective* (Kolkata: Maulana Abul Kalam Azad Institute of Asian Studies, 2002), 38; Bibekananda Agarwala, *The Agarwala Family of Tezpur: A Vignette of the Early Generations* (Tezpur: Devi Prasad Bagrodia, 1998), 18–20. For an account of the development of commerce in the far eastern Himalayas, see Bikram Bora, 'Opening the Gates of Tsangpo: Explorations and Imperial Geo-Politics in the Arunachal Himalayas, c. 1820–c. 1920' (M. Phil dissertation, JNU, 2016), Chapter 4.
35. Ibid., 53.
36. *Times of India*, 11 January 1961, 6. For a discussion on debates surrounding the Inner Line Regulation in the 1950s, see Bérénice Guyot-Réchard, *Shadow States: India, China and the Himalayas, 1910–1962* (Cambridge: Cambridge University Press, 2016), 150–51.

37. Vaghaiwalla, *Report on the Census of India, 1951, Assam: North East Frontier Agency, District Census Handbook*, iv.
38. J.D. Baveja, *Across the Golden Heights of Assam and NEFA* (Calcutta: Modern Book Depot, 1961), 53; R.N. Haldipur, *NEFA: An Introduction* (1966) [digital image], http://www.dspace.cam.ac.uk/handle/1810/243086 (Accessed 21 February 2020).
39. 'Nehru to Jairamdas Doultram, K.L. Mehta, V. Elwin, August 28, 1955', in *Documents on North-East India*, vol. 2, Arunachal Pradesh, eds, Suresh K. Sharma and Usha Sharma (Delhi: Mittal Publications, 2006), 106.
40. Baveja, *Across the Golden Heights of Assam and NEFA*, 53.
41. Rustomji, *Enchanted Frontiers: Sikkim, Bhutan and India's North-Eastern Borderlands*, 288.
42. Government of Assam, *Progress Report of Forest Administration in the Province of Assam, 1950–51* (Shillong: Government Press, 1951), Annual Form No. 24, 90.
43. Assam Saw Mills and Timber Company Limited, *Indian Tariff Board: Evidence Recorded During Enquiry Regarding the Grant of Protection to the Plywood and Tea Chest Industry* (Calcutta: Central Publication Branch, 1928); S. Dutta Choudhury, *Arunachal Pradesh District Gazetteers, Lohit District*, vol. 1 (Shillong: Government of Arunachal Pradesh, 1978), 158; Government of Assam, *Progress Report of Forest Administration in the Province of Assam, 1944–45* (Shillong: Government Press, 1945), 7–8; For a list of timber industries across the Himalayan foothills in Assam, see Government of India, *Large Industrial Establishments in India* (New Delhi: Ministry of Labour, 1958), 270.
44. Vaghaiwalla, *Census, 1951: Assam: North-East Frontier Agency: District Census Handbook*, vi.
45. Statement of J.N. Hazarika, Parliamentary Secretary to the Prime Minister, *Lok Sabha Debates*, 8 May 1953, column 2901.
46. Nehru undertook a longer trip to the tribal areas of Assam in October 1952. He elaborately recounted his experience in Assam with his officials and chief ministers of India. 'Note on Tour of the North East Frontier Areas in October 1952', in *Jawaharlal Nehru: Letters to Chief Ministers, 1889–1964*, vol. 3, ed. G. Parthasarthi (Delhi: Jawaharlal Nehru Memorial Fund, 1987), 147–65.
47. Jawaharlal Nehru, 'Visit to the North-East Frontier Areas, Impressions Given at a Meeting with the Officials of the Ministry of External Affairs, New Delhi, October 26, 1952', in *Selected Works of Jawaharlal Nehru* (hereafter *SWJN*), second series, vol. 20, ed. M. Palat, 155.
48. 'Speech of J. L Nehru, The Sentinels of the Frontier, Tezpur, 21 October 21, 1952', in *SWJN*, second series, vol. 20, 150.

49. J.L. Nehru, 'Foreword' in Verrier Elwin, *A Philosophy for NEFA* (Shillong: North East Frontier Agency, 1957).
50. 'APCC Resolution on the Affairs of the Part B Tribal Areas, March 1952', *Bishnuram Medhi Papers,* Packet no. 190, LL II (102), NMML.
51. *Assam Tribune,* 27 April 1953, 1. Also, 'Resolution of Asom Jatiya Mahasabha and its Significance', Medhi to Nehru, 25 July 1953, *Bishnuram Medhi Papers,* Packet no. 190, LL II (102), NMML.
52. Statement of Jawaharlal Nehru, Written Answer no. 1691, *Lok Sabha Debates,* 11 July 1952, column 1709.
53. Nehru to Medhi, Secret, 'Note on Administration of NEFA', Prime Minister's Secretariat, 24 April 1953, in *Bishnuram Medhi Papers,* Packet no. 190, LL II (102), NMML; Nehru, 'North-East Frontier Areas', note, 24 April 1953, *SWJN*, second series, vol. 22, 235.
54. 'Regarding T.N. Kaul's Note on NEFA', Medhi to Nehru, Shillong, 14 May 1953 in *Bishnuram Medhi Papers,* Packet no. 190, LL II (102), NMML.
55. Ibid.
56. Ibid.
57. Leo E. Rose and Margaret Welpley Fisher, *The North-East Frontier Agency of India* (Berkeley: Institute of International Studies, University of California, 1967), 29.
58. 'Regarding Administration of NEFA', Nehru to Medhi, 20 July 1953, *Bishnuram Medhi Papers,* Packet no. 190, LL II (102), NMML.
59. Speeches by A.K. Chanda, U.C. Patnaik, *Lok Sabha Debates,* 19 February 1954, columns 156–57.
60. 'Notes on a Pilgrimage to Tawang by the Adviser for Tribal Affairs, NEFA, in May–June 1956', in *Dr Elwin's Notes on his visit to Bomdi La and Tawang,* GoI, Ministry of External Affairs, NEFA section, File no. 4/5–NEFA/56, 1956, nos 1–10, Abhilekh Patal, NAI.
61. Reply to Oral Question No. 1524. Statement of Jawaharlal Nehru, *Lok Sabha Debates,* 22 April 1953, columns 2332–33; Bérénice Guyot-Réchard, 'Nation-building or State-making? India's North-East Frontier and the Ambiguities of Nehruvian Developmentalism, 1950–1959', *Contemporary South Asia,* vol. 21, no. 1 (2013), 22–37; Rose and Fisher, *The North-East Frontier Agency of India,* 29.
62. Statement of Jai Sukh Lal Hathi, Deputy Minister of Irrigation and Power, *Lok Sabha Debates,* 1 April 1953, column 1663.
63. Statement of S.A. Khan, Parliamentary Secretary to the Minister of External Affairs Written Answer No. 1311, *Lok Sabha Debates,* 23 December 1953, columns 1611–12.

64. *Times of India*, 24 July 1953, 1.
65. *Times of India*, 19 July 1953, 11.
66. *Times of India*, 27 July 1953, 7. Well-attended and enthusiastic protest meetings were held in many urban areas.
67. Henry M. Gelfand, 'A Critical Examination of the Indian Smallpox Eradication Program', *American Journal of Public Health*, vol. 56, no. 10 (1966), 1638, Table 1.
68. Statement of O.V. Alagesan, Deputy Minister of Railways and Transport, *Lok Sabha Debates*, 17 March 1953, column 1118.
69. Statement by S.A. Khan, Parliamentary Secretary to the Minister of External Affairs, *Lok Sabha Debates*, 15 December 1953, column 1234.
70. *Assam Tribune*, 12 January 1954, 8.
71. Indira Miri, *Moi aru NEFA: A Volume of Reminiscences* (Guwahati: Spectrum, 2003), 1–3.
72. A.P. Borthakur, *Chan Poharat Arunachal: A Book on the Development of School Education and Progress in Arunachal Pradesh (from 1948 to 1986)* (Moranhat: Bulu Barthakur, 2004).
73. Guyot-Réchard, *Shadow States: India, China and the Himalayas, 1910–1962*, 131; Elwin, *A Philosophy for NEFA*, 22.
74. Christoph von Fürer-Haimendorf, *Tribes of India: The Struggle for Survival* (Berkeley: University of California Press, 1982), 28–29. Also see, Christoph von Fürer-Haimendorf, *The Apa Tanis and Their Neighbours: A Primitive Society of the Eastern Himalayas* (London: Routledge and Kegan Paul, 1962), 18–20.
75. Government of India, *Report of the Soil Conservation Reconnaissance Committee for Assam & N.E.F.A.* (Shillong: Government Printing Press, 1957); Yasuyuki Kosaka et al., 'On the Introduction of Paddy Rice Cultivation by Swiddeners in Arunachal Pradesh, India', *Tropics*, vol. 24, no. 2 (1 September 2015), 76–90.
76. Jagdish Lal Dawar, 'Nationalist Discourse and Cultural Hegemony in the North-East, Arunachal Pradesh (NEFA) and Indian Mainstream since 1950s', in *Tribal Studies: Emerging Frontiers of Knowledge*, eds, Tamo Mibang and M.C. Behera (Delhi: Mittal Publications, 2007), 57.
77. Statement of J.L Nehru, Answer to Oral Questions: no. 136, *Lok Sabha Debates*, 27 November 1953, columns 509–10.
78. Statement of J.L Nehru, Answer to Oral Questions: no. 136, *Lok Sabha Debates*, 27 November 1953, column 510.
79. *Assam Tribune*, 8 January 1954, 1.
80. Rose and Fisher, *The North-East Frontier Agency of India*, 29.
81. *Assam Tribune*, 11 January 1954, 1.

82. *Assam Tribune,* 12 January 1954, 1; Statement of A.K. Chanda, *Lok Sabha Debates,* 24 March 1954, columns 2916–17.
83. 'Statement of R.K. Chaudhury', quoted in the Statement of A.K. Chanda, *Lok Sabha Debates,* 24 March 1954, columns 2916–17.
84. *Assam Tribune,* 18 January 1954, 1. Also, *Natun Asamiya,* 26 January 1956, 1.
85. T.N. Kaul, 'A Brief Note on NEFA, Manipur State, Naga Hill District (Kohima) and Lushai Hills' (Secret), 21 April 1953, File 8, Elwin Papers, NMML, in *Savaging the Civilised: Verrier Elwin, His Tribals, and India,* Guha (Delhi: Penguin, 2013), 239.
86. 'Letter from Bishnuram Medhi to Nehru, 9 March 1952', *Bishnuram Medhi Papers,* 190, LL II (102), NMML.
87. Statement of A. K. Chanda, Deputy Minister of External Affairs. Answer to Oral Question No. 495, *Lok Sabha Debates,* 27 February 1954, column 498. Special rules were also formulated for various subsidiary services, like porter, etc., of the NEFA administration. 'Letter from N.K. Rustomji, Adviser to the Governor of Assam to Joint Secretary, Ministry of External Affairs, Government of India, 9 March 1953', in *Fourteen of a Set of Fresh Rules Comprising the Terms of Service Conditions of the Agency Service Corps, NEF Agency,* File no. F. 26 (28) E1/53, Ministry of External Affairs, NEBA section, Abhilekh Patal, NAI.
88. 'Administrative Reform Commission', in *Report of the Study Team on Administration of Union Territories and NEFA,* vol. 1, 1970, 38; Guyot-Réchard, *Shadow States: India, China and the Himalayas, 1910–1962,* 105.
89. Rustomji, *Enchanted Frontiers: Sikkim, Bhutan and India's North-Eastern Borderlands,* 131.
90. Miri, *Moi aru NEFA: A Volume of Reminiscences,* 100–01.
91. Rustomji, *Enchanted Frontiers: Sikkim, Bhutan and India's North-Eastern Borderlands,* 132.
92. Elwin, *A Philosophy for NEFA,* 48–49.
93. B.K. Bhattacharya, 'Nefar Darson [Philosophy of NEFA]', *Ramdhenur Sampadakiya* ed. Birendra Kumar Bhattacharya (Guwahati: Banalata, 2007), 224–25.
94. 'Language Policy in NEFA', Letter from S. Dutt, Ministry of External Affairs, Government of India to A.V. Pai, Secretary to the President of India, 26 September 1959, *Language Policy in NEFA: Minute Recorded by the President Regarding Teaching of Assamese into the Tribal People of NEFA,* File no. 136/59, 1959, Office of the Secretary to the President, General Branch, Abhilekh Patal, NAI. The transition from Assamese to Hindi as a medium of instruction began by imparting education during the first 5

years of 'school years exclusively in tribal dialects written in Devanagari script of reformed and simplified type'.
95. H. Deka, 'Trip to Bomdi La', in *The Outlook on NEFA,* ed. Parag Chaliha (Jorhat: Asam Sahitya Sabha, 1958), 77.
96. '[I]n fact, the Assamese language is, more or less, the lingua franca of considerable areas', admitted Nehru in August 1957, *SWJN*, second series, vol. 39, 229. Rose and Fisher, *The North-East Frontier Agency of India*, 28; Shibani Kinkar Chaube, *Hill Politics in North-east India* (New Delhi: Orient Longman, 1973), 198.
97. Elwin, *Philosophy for NEFA*, 228.
98. 'Notes on a Pilgrimage to Tawang by the Adviser for Tribal Affairs, NEFA, in May–June 1956', in *Dr Elwin's Notes on his Visit to Bomdi La and Tawang*, GoI, Ministry of External Affairs, NEFA section, File no. 4/5–NEFA/56, 1956, nos 1–10, Abhilekh Patal, NAI.
99. 'Notes on a Pilgrimage to Tawang by the Adviser for Tribal Affairs, NEFA, in May–June 1956', in *Dr Elwin's Notes on his Visit to Bomdi La and Tawang*.
100. 'Demi Official Letter from K.L. Mehta, Advisor to Governor, NEFA to T.N. Kaul, Joint Secretary', Ministry of External affairs, Government of India, 21 August 1956, in *Dr Elwin's Notes on his Visit to Bomdi La and Tawang*, GoI, Ministry of External Affairs, NEFA section, File no. 4/5–NEFA/56, 1956, nos 1–10, Abhilekh Patal, NAI.
101. 'Notes on a Pilgrimage to Tawang by the Adviser for Tribal Affairs, NEFA, in May–June 1956', in *Dr Elwin's Notes on his visit to Bomdi La and Tawang*.
102. Elwin, *A Philosophy for NEFA*, 92; 'Notes on a Pilgrimage to Tawang by the Adviser for Tribal Affairs, NEFA, May–June 1956', in *Dr Elwin's Notes on his Visit to Bomdi La and Tawang*, GoI, Ministry of External Affairs, NEFA section, File no. 4/5–NEFA/56, 1956, nos 1–10, Abhilekh Patal, NAI.
103. Illustrative of these works are Raghuvir Sinha, *The Akas: The People of NEFA* (Shillong: Research Department, Adviser's Secretariat, 1962); L.R.N. Srivastava, *The Gallongs: The People of NEFA* (Shillong: Research Department, Adviser's Secretariat, 1962).
104. 'Notes on a Pilgrimage to Tawang by the Adviser for Tribal Affairs, NEFA, in May–June 1956', in *Dr Elwin's Notes on his Visit to Bomdi La and Tawang*.
105. Rustomji, *Enchanted Frontiers: Sikkim, Bhutan and India's North-Eastern Borderlands*, 294.
106. *The Times,* 5 November 1953, 7; Statement of J.L. Nehru, *Lok Sabha Debates,* 21 November 1953, columns 249–56; Guyot-Réchard, *Shadow States: India, China and the Himalayas, 1910–1962,* 120–126; B.M. Kaul,

*The Untold Story* (Delhi: Allied Publishers, 1967), 160–63; Rustomji, *Imperilled Frontiers: India's North Eastern Borderlands*, 131–35; Miri, *Moi aru NEFA: A Volume of Reminiscences*, 64.

107. Rustomji, *Imperilled Frontiers: Sikkim, Bhutan and India's North Eastern Borderlands*, 130.
108. Ibid., 129.
109. Ibid; Kaul, *The Untold Story*, 162.
110. Rustomji, *Enchanted Frontiers: Sikkim, Bhutan and India's North-Eastern Borderlands*, 130.
111. S.M. Krishnatry, *Border Tagins of Arunachal Pradesh* (New Delhi: NBT, 2007), 29.
112. Statement of J.L. Nehru, *Lok Sabha Debates*, 21 November 1953, column 250.
113. Krishnatry, *Border Tagins of Arunachal Pradesh*, 33.
114. Statement of Nehru, *Lok Sabha Debates*, 23 March 1954, column 2792.
115. Guyot-Réchard, *Shadow States: India, China and the Himalayas, 1910–1962*, 125.
116. Maheswar Neog, *Jivanor Digh aru Bani* (Guwahati: Chandra Prakash, 1988), 477; 'Annual Report of the General Secretary, Assam Sahitya Sabha for the Year 1963–64', *Asam Sahitya Sabha Patrika*, no. 3 (1964), 43.
117. J.L. Nehru, 'Note to Jairamdas Doulatram, K.L. Mehta, V. Elwin, Secretary General, Foreign Secretary, Joint Secretary, MEA, Shillong, 28 August 1955', in *SWJN*, second series, vol. 29, 138, para. 23–25.
118. *Chief Secretary of Assam's Fortnightly Report* (hereafter *FR*), 2nd half, May 1957.
119. *FR*, 1st half, June 1957.
120. Birendra Kumar Bhattacharya, 'The Language of NEFA and National Unity', in *The Outlook on NEFA,* ed. Chaliha (Jorhat: Asam Sahitya Sabha, 1958), 35.
121. 'I am told they [the people of NEFA] do not like it and would prefer to read Hindi,' noted Rajendra Prasad, President of India. 'Minute dated 18 September 1859, recorded by the President regarding the teaching of Assamese to the tribal in the NEFA', in *Language Policy in NEFA: Minute Recorded by the President Regarding Teaching of Assamese in to the Tribal People of NEFA*.
122. Verrier Elwin, *The Tribal World of Verrier Elwin: An Autobiography* (New York: Oxford University Press, 1964), 273.
123. H. Deka, 'Trip to Bomdi La, Tourist's Diary', in *The Outlook on NEFA,* ed. Chaliha, 72.
124. Amarendranath Pathak, 'Ziro', *Asam Sahitya Sabha Patrika*, vol. 15, no. 1 (1956), 36–47; Hemalata Bora, 'Seujiya Paharor Maje Maje', in *Hemalata*

Bora Rachanwali, eds, Rubi Bora and Obja Bora Hazarika (Guwahati: Bandhav, 2020 [1962]), 285–330; Lakshesvar Sharma, *Michimi Paharor Ramsina* (Guwahati: Pranita Devi, 1965); Lila Gogoi, *Simantar Mati aru Manuh* (Guwahati: LBS, 1963).

125. Rustomji, *Imperilled Frontiers: India's North Eastern Borderlands*, 99.
126. *Natun Asamiya*, 10 May 1955, 1; *Natun Asamiya*, 11 October 1955, 1; *Natun Asamiya*, 15 December 1955, 1.
127. Padma Barkataki, 'Behind the Inner Line', in *The Outlook on NEFA*, ed. Chaliha, 95.
128. Prafulla Bezbaruah, 'History Yells: The Hills and the Plains of Assam are But One', in *The Outlook on NEFA*, ed. Chaliha, 102.
129. Speech of Jawaharlal Nehru, *Lok Sabha Debates*, 21 December 1960, columns 6709–10. The outcome of this initiative led to the publications of several works. See B.N. Chakravorty, *British Relations with the Hill Tribes of Assam since 1858* (Calcutta: Firma KLM, 1964); L.N. Chakravarty, *Glimpses of the Early History of Arunachal* (Shillong: Research Department, Arunachal Pradesh Administration, 1973).
130. *Establishment of a Cultural Tribal Research Institute in Assam*, Ministry of Education, GoI, File no. 8–13/57.c 1, Abhilekh Patal, NAI.
131. *Natun Asamiya*, 25 January 1954, 1.
132. 'Letter from Miles Bronson to F. James Halliday, Lt-Governor of Bengal, November 13, 1854', in H.K. Barpujari, *The American Missionaries: And North-east India, 1836–1900 A.D.: A Documentary Study* (Guwahati: Spectrum Publications, 1986), 138; Maheswar Neog, 'Arunachalat Asomiya Bhasa', in *Snehar Arunachal: My Hill So Strong*, Maheswar Neog (Jorhat: Asam Sahitya Sabha, 1976), 79–80.
133. 'Report of the General Secretary, Asam Sahitya Sabha', *Asam Sahitya Sabha Patrika*, vol. 20, no. 2, (1961/1962), 65–66.
134. 'Assam Sahitya Sabha's Delegation with the Prime Minister (Appendix 6)', in Maheswar Neog, *Simantar Siksha aru Samskritik Niti or The Educational and Cultural Policies of the North-East Frontier Agency Administration* (Jorhat: Asam Sahitya Sabha, 1962); *Natun Asamiya*, 12 May 1961, 1.
135. *Assam Tribune*, 29 May 1962, 1; Neog, *Simantar Siksha aru Samskritik Niti or The Educational and Cultural Policies of the North-East Frontier Agency Administration*, Appendix 14.
136. Statement Issued by Maheswar Neog, General Secretary, Asam Sahitya Sabha; *Assam Tribune*, 1 June 1962, 1.
137. Tagang Taki, *Ahban: NEFA Adi Mishing Cahtra Samajloi* (Alon: Boken Jiro, 1962), 21.

138. Sitaram Johri, *Where India, China and Burma Meet* (Calcutta: Thacker Spink & Co., 1962), 230.
139. *SWJN*, second series, vol. 64, 119. The first nominee was C.C. Gohain.
140. *Natun Asamiya*, 4 June 1962, 1; *Times of India*, 30 March 1963, 1; Resolution Regarding Administrative Policy in NEFA, Speech by Hem Barua, *Lok Sabha Debates*, 29 March 1963, columns 7048–81.
141. Chaliha, ed. *The Outlook on NEFA*, i.
142. *Dainik Asam*, 29 January 1968, 1; *Dainik Asam*, 30 January 1968, 1.
143. Readers will benefit from a wide range of authoritative accounts on various aspects of this war. Alastair Lamb, *Tibet, China and India, 1914–1950: A History of Imperial Diplomacy* (Hertingfordbury: Roxford Books, 1989); Amit R. Das Gupta and Lorenz M. Luthi, *The Sino-Indian War of 1962: New Perspectives* (New Delhi, Routledge, 2017); Bertil Lintner, *China's India War: Collision Course on the Roof of the World* (London: Oxford University Press, 2018); Neville Maxwell, *India's China War* (London: Jonathan Cape, 1970); Ramachandra Guha, *India after Gandhi: The History of the World's Largest Democracy* (Delhi: Picador, 2007), 301–37; Srinath Raghavan, *War and Peace in Modern India* (London: Palgrave Macmillan, 2010), Chapter 7; Steven Hoffmann, *India and the China Crisis* (California: University of California Press, 2018).
144. 'Patel to Nehru, November 7, 1950', *Sardar Patel's Correspondence*, vol. 10, ed. D. Das (Ahmedabad: Navajivan Publishing House, 1974), 335–41. Historian Srinath Raghavan wrote that this rather long letter was perhaps drafted by G.S. Bajpai, Secretary-General of the Ministry of External Affairs. Srinath Raghavan. 'Sino-Indian Boundary Dispute, 1948–60: A Reappraisal', *Economic & Political Weekly*, vol. 41, no. 36 (2006), 3883.
145. P. Mason, Joint Secretary, GoI, Operations on McMahon Line by Assam Rifles, Secret Memorandum, no. 3999–S/W.1, August 4, 1945', *Operations on McMahon Line by Assam Rifles*, File no. 205 (2), 1945, External Affairs Department, CA Branch, Abhilekh Patal, NAI.
146. Raghavan, *War and Peace in Modern India*, 270.
147. *New York Times*, 19 September 1959, 2; *New York Times*, 8 January 1960, 9; *New York Times*, 20 April 1960, 9.
148. 'Letter from Deputy Adviser to the Governor of Assam to G.C. Phukan, Joint Secretary, Government of Assam, DO CGA/192/57/1, Shillong, 14 March 1958', *Confinement of a Few Chinese Deserters in the State Jails from NEFA*, File no. HJL/22/58 Home Department, Jail Branch (ASA).
149. *New York Times*, 30 August 1959, 11.
150. *New York Times*, 18 April 1959, 4.

151. Fürer-Haimendorf, 'Primitive Peoples of the McMahon Line Country: Tribal Life in a Territory Now Claimed by China'.
152. G.F. Hudson, 'The Frontier of China and Assam: Background to the Fighting', *China Quarterly*, no. 12 (1962), 206; Also, see Klaus H. Pringsheim, 'China, India, and Their Himalayan Border (1961–1963)', *Asian Survey*, vol. 3, no. 10 (1963), 480; George L. Harris, Foreign Areas Studies Division, *U.S. Army Handbook for Nepal (with Sikkim and Bhutan)* (Washington: The American University, 1964), 406.
153. George N. Patterson, 'Recent Chinese Policies in Tibet and Towards the Himalayan Border States', *China Quarterly*, no. 12 (1962), 202; Pringsheim, 'China, India, and Their Himalayan Border (1961–1963)', 491.
154. Kaul, *The Untold Story*, 334–35. Kaul was told by Admiral D. Shankar who was informed by Japanese officials on this.
155. Government of India, *Report of the Officials of the Governments of India and the People's Republic of China on the Boundary Question* (New Delhi: Government of India Press, 1962), 157, 207.
156. 'In Bomdila: Public Meeting'. *SWJN*, second series, vol. 69, 148; *Times of India*, 21 May 1961, 1.
157. Speech by Hem Barua, *Lok Sabha Debates*, 6 June 1962, column 9101.
158. Speech by J.L. Nehru, *Lok Sabha Debates*, 6 June 1962, column 9106.
159. Raghavan, *War and Peace in Modern India*, 270.
160. *The Hindu*, 19 October 1962, 1; Pringsheim, 'China, India, and Their Himalayan Border (1961–1963)', 489–90.
161. P.B. Sinha and A.A. Athale, *History of the Conflict with China, 1962* (New Delhi: Ministry of Defence, Government of India, 1992), 389.
162. *Times of India*, 29 October 1962, 1, 9.
163. 'Nehru to Chaliha, October 20, 1962', in *SWJN*, second series, vol. 79, 39.
164. *Assam Tribune*, 19–20 November 1962; *Times of India*, 17–18 November 1962; Speech of Jawaharlal Nehru, *Lok Sabha Debates*, 19 November 1962, column 2230.
165. 'Bomdi La actually fell into the enemy's hands on the 18th evening, but as the situation was confused a report about it did not reach Delhi until yesterday evening', J.L. Nehru, Statement Re: Situation in NEFA and Ladakh, *Lok Sabha Debates*, 20 November 1962, column 2453; Kaul, *The Untold Story*, 419; *Times of India*, 20 November 1962.
166. D.K. Palit, *War in High Himalaya: The Indian Army in Crisis, 1962* (Delhi: Lancer Publishers, 1991), 341.
167. Lummer Dai, 'Simantar Sakti', in *Lummer Dai Rachanavali* ed. Jayanta Madhab Bora (Guwahati: Publication Board, Assam, 2020), 563.

168. John Kenneth Galbraith, *Ambassador's Journal: A Personal Account of the Kennedy Years* (Boston: Houghton Mifflin Company, 1969), 487.
169. *New York Times*, 20 November 1962, 1.
170. *Times of India*, 21 November 1962, 1.
171. 'In the Kameng Frontier Division of NEFA, the Chinese had reached upto a line generally in an area joining Kalaktang and Chaku. Both these places are on the foot hills'. Sinha and Athale, *History of the Conflict with China, 1962*, 374.
172. Kenneth Galbraith, *Ambassador's Journal: A Personal Account of the Kennedy Years*, 488.
173. Ibid., 492.
174. B.N. Mullik, *My Years with Nehru: The Chinese Betrayal* (Delhi: Allied Publishers, 1971), 443.
175. 'Nehru to Kennedy, 19 November 1962, 8 pm', in *Papers of John F. Kennedy, Presidential Papers*. National *Security Files, Countries, India, Subjects, Nehru Correspondence*, November 1962: 11–19, JFKNSF-111–016. John F. Kennedy Presidential Library and Museum, JFKNSF-111–016–p0010, https://www.jfklibrary.org/asset-viewer/archives/JFKNSF/111/JFKNSF-111–016 (Accessed 17 April 2023).
176. 'Nehru to Kennedy', in *Papers of John F. Kennedy, Presidential Papers, National Security Files, Nehru Correspondence,* November 1962, 11–19, Digital Identifier: JFKNSF-111–016–p0018, https://www.jfklibrary.org/asset-viewer/archives/JFKNSF/111/JFKNSF-111–016; Raghavan, *War and Peace in Modern India*, 308.
177. Maxwell, *India's China War,* 410.
178. *Guardian*, 20 November 1962, 12.
179. *The Times*, 30 October 1962, 12.
180. *Indian Express*, 3 December 1962, 6.
181. *Times of India*, 26 October 1962, 1.
182. Rustomji, *Enchanted Frontiers: Sikkim, Bhutan and India's North-Eastern Borderlands*, 286.
183. Ibid., 287.
184. Nehru's Note for S.S. Khera, Cabinet Secretary, 28 December 1962, *SWJN*, second series, vol. 80, 59; Nehru to A.C. Guha, Member of Parliament, 30 January 1963, *SWJN*, second series, vol. 80, 68; Nehru to Vishnu Sahay, Governor of Assam, 11 December 1962, *SWJN*, second series, vol. 80, 78.
185. Kaul, *The Untold Story*, 420.
186. *Assam Tribune,* 30 November 1962, 1.
187. Thongchi, *Hanhi aru Sakulor Haihob*, 262–65.

188. *Assam Tribune*, 30 November 1962, 1. Others reported a lower number, for instance, an estimated 12,000 by the Guardian. *Guardian*, 28 November 1962, 1.
189. *Jugantar*, 25 November 1962, 5.
190. *Jugantar*, 24 November 1962, 1.
191. *Peking Review*, 28 December 1962, 10–12; For a later remembrance of this, see Liu Chuen Chen, '53 Years of Indo-China War', *India Today*, 20 October 2015; For a gripping fictional account, see Rita Choudhury, *Makam* (Guwahati: Jyoti Prakasan, 2010).
192. Sinha and Athale, *History of the Conflict with China, 1962*, 389; Mullik, *My Years with Nehru*, 425.
193. See 'Chinese community in northeastern Assam', May 1953, https://www.cia.gov/library/readingroom/docs/CIA-RDP80–00810A001300160008–2.pdf.
194. Robert W Stern, 'The Sino-Indian Border Controversy and the Communist Party of India', *Journal of Politics*, vol. 27, no. 1 (1965), 66–86. Communists leaders from other parts of the world also criticized China's policy on the Sino-Indian border issue. At the National Communist and Workers' Party Congress held in Moscow in November 1960, communist leaders from many nations did not support the Chinese border policy. Ajoy Kumar Ghosh, the General Secretary of the Communist Party of India, criticized China's stand on the border issue with India. 'Speech by Ajoy Ghosh at the Conference of Communist and Workers' Parties', *Documents of the Communist Movement in India*, vol. 8, ed., Jyoti Basu (Calcutta: National Book Agency, 1997), 608–28; Communist Party of India, *The India–China Border Dispute and the Communist Party of India: Resolutions, Statements and Speeches, 1959–1963* (Delhi: Communist Party of India, 1963). Also, see Chaowu Dai, 'India's Foreign Policy, the Relationship among Great Powers, and the Sino-Indian Border Dispute', in *The Cold War and China's Neighbor Relationship*, eds, Niu Dayong and Shen Zhihua (Beijing: World Affairs Press, 2004).
195. Mullik, *My Years with Nehru*, 330. I have not read the specific article mentioned in Mullik's account. However, *People's Daily* published a similar article which appealed to Indian communists not to be persuaded by the arguments of Nehru's government on the Indo-China border dispute. Here is one illustration from *People's Daily*. 'Each time the Nehru government stirs up an anti-China campaign, he simultaneously mounts an attack on the Indian Communist Party and progressive forces. But large numbers of Indian Communists and progressives, large numbers of politically conscious workers, peasants, intellectuals and fair-minded people have not been deceived by the

reactionary propaganda of the Indian ruling circles, nor have they knuckled under to their attacks. In the interests of the Indian people, they have, under extremely difficult conditions, stood firm for truth, justice and Sino-Indian friendship and waged unflinching struggles.' The Editorial Department of *Renmin Ribao* [People's Daily], 'More on Nehru's Philosophy in the Light of the Sino-Indian Boundary Question', 27 October 1962, The Sino-Indian Boundary Question (Enlarged Edition) (Peking: Foreign Languages Press, 1962) quoted in History and Public Policy Program Digital Archive, http://digitalarchive.wilsoncenter.org/document/175947, 129–30.

196. *Times of India*, 29 October 1962, 9.
197. 'Nehru to Prafulla Sen, Chief Minister of West Bengal, December 16, 1962', in *SWJN*, second series, vol. 80, 476.
198. Amalendu Guha, 'Memorandum on the Detention and Humiliation of Shri Bishnu Prasad Rabha, 14 June 1963, Office Order by the Deputy Commissioner, Darrang, Assam, January 25, 1963', in *Security Prisoner- Shri Bishnu Prasad Rava*, File no. PLA 186/63, ASA.
199. 'On October 17, the CPI made it clear that the McMahon Line is the border of India. Hence all necessary steps to defend it are justified.' 'Resolution adopted by the secretariat of the National Council of the CPI, New Delhi, October 17, 1962', in *Documents of the Communist Movement in India*, vol. 9 (Calcutta: National Book Agency, 1997), 178; *Statesman*, 18 October 1962.
200. *Jugantar*, 21 November 1962, 1.
201. *Assam Tribune*, 30 November 1962.
202. *Assam Tribune*, 20 November 1962; *Assam Tribune*, 21 November 1962.
203. 'Assam Chief Minister's Appeal to the People', Director of Information and Public Relations, 19 November 1962, Broadcast Talk by the CM, CMS, 258/62/Evacuees ASA; *Jugantar*, 20 November 1962, 5.
204. *Times of India*, 20 November 1962, 1; *Times of India*, 21 November 1962, 1.
205. *Times of India*, 21 November 1962, 1; *Jugantar*, 21 November 1962, 6.
206. 'Press Statement of Sriman Prafulla Goswami, President, 22 November 1962, Assam Pradesh Congress Committee', *Prafulla Goswami Papers*, NMML.
207. Kaul, *The Untold Story*, 420; Sinha and Athale, *History of the Conflict with China, 1962*, 373.
208. Rustomji, *Enchanted Frontiers: Sikkim, Bhutan and India's North-Eastern Borderlands*, 285.
209. Sinha and Athale, *History of the Conflict with China, 1962*, 373.
210. Kuldip Nayar, *Between the Lines* (New Delhi: Allied Publishers, 1969), 238.

211. Ibid., 427–28.
212. Mullik, *My Years with Nehru*, 429.
213. Sinha and Athale, *History of the Conflict with China, 1962*, 372.
214. *Assam Tribune*, 30 December 1962.
215. *Observer*, 25 November 1962, 13.
216. *Observer*, 25 November 1962, 13; Letter from Secretary, Government of Assam, Medical Department to Superintendent, Mental Hospital, Tezpur, Telegram, 24 November 1962, *Shifting of Lunatics from Mental Hospital Tezpur to Ranchi and other Mental Hospitals*, File HFL, 95/61, Home (Jail), ASA.
217. *Jugantar*, 28 November 1962, 2.
218. *Indian Express*, 21 December 1962, 1.
219. *Assam Tribune*, 30 November 1962; *Jugantar*, 27 November 1962, 6; *Assam Tribune*, 30 December 1962.
220. *Jugantar*, 27 November 1962.
221. *Indian Express*, 4 December 1962, 1.
222. Ibid., 2; *Jugantar*, 29 November 1962, 5; *Natun Asamiya*, 31 August 1962, 5.
223. *Jugantar*, 21 November 1962, 5.
224. *Assam Tribune*, 30 November 1962, 1.
225. Mullik, *My Years with Nehru*, 432.
226. Bipin Pal Das, 'Sradheya Chalihadebor Suwaranat', in *Bimalaprasad Chaliha*, ed. C.P. Saikia (Guwahati: Publication Board Assam, 1972), 99.
227. Nayar, *Between the Lines*, 219; Palit, *War in High Himalaya*, 360.
228. *Jugantar*, 23 November 1962, 1.
229. Ibid.
230. Mullik, *My Years with Nehru*, 427; Kaul, *The Untold Story*, 421.
231. *The Times*, 29 November 1962, 19; *Guardian*, 20 November 1962, 13.
232. *Jugantar*, 29 November 1962, 1.
233. *Times of India*, 23 October 1963, 3.
234. *The Times*, 29 November 1962, 19.
235. *Assam Tribune*, 30 November 1962, 1.
236. 'Broadcast to the Nation, 19 November 1962, AIR Tapes NM No. 8596, NM No. 1689, NMML', in *SWJN*, second series, vol. 79, October–November 1962, 454–58; *Jugantar*, 20 November 1962, 1; *Times of India*, 20 November 1962, 1.
237. Maxwell, *India's China War*, 409. The Assam Pradesh Congress Committee agreed that Assam was 'faced with a grim crisis'. Sriman Prafulla Goswami, Press Statement of the President, Assam Pradesh Congress Committee, 22 November 1962, *Prafulla Goswami Papers*, III, subfolder 2, NMML.

238. Nayar, *Between the Lines*, 211.
239. Maxwell, *India's China War*, 409.
240. Nehru to Mahendra Mohan Chaudhary, 'Assam is India', 25 November 1962, in *SWJN*, second series, vol. 79, 494.
241. Victor Zorza, 'An ultimatum from Russia? Why Peking was in a hurry', *Guardian*, 22 November 1962, 1, 20.
242. Rustomji, *Enchanted Frontiers: Sikkim, Bhutan and India's North-Eastern Borderlands*, 292.
243. Quoted in Speech by Hem Barua, *Lok Sabha Debates*, 1962, in *SWJN*, second series, vol. 79, 466.
244. *Jugantar*, 6 December 1962, 1; *Indian Express*, 6 December 1962, 1.
245. Nehru's radio speech, December 5, AIR Tapes, No. 10106, 10107, NM no. 1816 & 1817, 'In Gauhati: Public Meeting', *SWJN*, second series, vol. 80, 575.
246. *Guardian*, 6 December 1962, 12.
247. 'In Tezpur: Public Meeting', *SWJN*, second series, vol. 80, 592. Nehru spoke in Hindi.
248. Sinha and Athale, *History of the Conflict with China, 1962*, 375–76.
249. *Indian Express*, 5 December 1962, 1.
250. *Indian Express*, 9 December 1962, 1.
251. *Indian Express*, 15 December 1962, 1.
252. *Assam Tribune*, 31 December 1962, 1.
253. These places were Ziro, Daporijo, Along, Pashighat, Roing and Tezu. Sinha and Athale, *History of the Conflict with China, 1962*, 380.
254. *Indian Express*, 15 December 1962, 1.
255. *Indian Express*, 7 December 1962, 1.
256. *Assam Tribune*, 31 December 1962, 1.
257. *Indian Express*, 15 December 1962, 1.
258. N. Prasad, 'The Fall of Towang', in *Shadow States: India, China and the Himalayas, 1910–1962*, Guyot-Réchard, 235.
259. *Assam Tribune*, 30 December 1962; *Indian Express*, 1 February 1963, 1.
260. Guyot-Réchard, *Shadow States: India, China and the Himalayas, 1910–1962*, 235–40; Swargajyoti Gohain, *Imagined Geographies in the Indo-Tibetan Borderlands: Culture, Politics, Place* (Amsterdam: Amsterdam University Press, 2020), 26.
261. Thongchi, *Hanhi Aru Sakulor Haihob*, 272.
262. 'Letter from Chandradhar Goswami, 15 January 1963, Non Official delegation of the Assam government', in *NEFA Visit by Social Workers and Organisations*, File no. CMS 189/63, ASA.
263. Guyot-Réchard, *Shadow States: India, China and the Himalayas, 1910–1962*, 235–36.

264. *Indian Express*, 16 December 1962, 1.
265. Ibid.
266. *Indian Express*, 27 December 1962, 1.
267. Sinha and Athale, *History of the Conflict with China, 1962*, 381.
268. For further details, see Guyot-Réchard, *Shadow States: India, China and the Himalayas, 1910–1962*, 251–64.
269. 'Nehru to Chaliha, 4 November 1962', in *SWJN,* second series, vol. 79, 40; 'Nehru to Malaviya, 4 November 1962', in *SWJN,* second series, vol. 79, 40.
270. 'Diversion of Machinery of Assam Fertiliser Factory, Nehru to Kesho Ram, Principal Private Secretary, 14 December 1962', *SWJN*, second series, vol. 80, 79.
271. Lord Alrtincham, 'Mr Nehru's feature', *Guardian*, 22 November 1962, 20.
272. CIA, 'The Economic Significance of Assam', Secret, 17 December 1962, Current Support Brief, https://www.cia.gov/readingroom/docs/CIA-RDP79T01003A001400160001-8.pdf.
273. *Indian Express*, 3 December 1962, 1.
274. *Times of India*, 29 November 1962. The Asam Sahitya Sabha wrote to the Government of India requesting to 'send us as early as possible . . . all the few White Papers containing Notes, Memoranda and Letters exchanged between the Governments of India and China and all other relevant papers' which would help them to publish a book on the war. 'Letter from Maheswar Neog to Secretary, Ministry of External Affairs, GoI, 14 December, 1962' in *Miscellaneous Message from Different Bodies, Individuals etc. on Chinese Aggression*, File no. 4 (1)/62, External Affairs, GoI, Digitised Public Records, Abhilekh Patal, NAI.
275. B.M. Pugh, 'Farming for victory', *Assam Tribune*, 30 November 1962, 4.
276. *Assam Tribune*, 30 December 1962, 3.
277. Dalai Lama, 'Mur Desh Mur Priyajan', *Nilachal*, 2nd Year, no. 1 (1964), 57–104.
278. *Indian Express*, 17 December 1962.
279. Haldipur, *NEFA: An Introduction*, 1966.
280. *Assam Tribune*, 30 December 1962, 1.
281. 'Report on Cultural Tour in NEFA', in *NEFA Visit by Social Workers and Organization*, File no. CMS 189/63, ASA.
282. Bhubanchandra Devagoswami, 'Ziro to Chief Minister, Assam, 2 January 1963', in *NEFA Visit by Social Workers and Organization*, File no. CMS 189/63, ASA.
283. Lakhiprasad Goswami, Leader of the Opposition, Assam Assembly, 'Confidential Report of the Study of Situation in Siang and Subansiri

Divisions of NEFA February 4, 1963', in *NEFA Visit by Social Workers and Organization*.
284. *Statesman*, 11 June 1963, 1.
285. *Statesman*, 9 February 1963, 1.
286. Speech of Jawaharlal Nehru, *Rajya Sabha Debates*, 17 December 1963, column 3675; *The Times of India*, 18 December 1963, 5.
287. Editorial, *Assam Tribune*, 17 December 1962, 4.
288. Anonymous, 'Philosophy of NEFA', *Assam Tribune*, 29 December 1962, 4.
289. *Illustrated Weekly of India*, 20 January 1963, 15.
290. Speech of Jawaharlal Nehru, *Lok Sabha Debates*, 29 March 1963, columns 7065–69.
291. 'A plan to populate NEFA ready: Food output and security, aim', *Times of India*, 3 November 1962, 1.
292. 'Note by K.L. Mehta, Joint Secretary, MEA, December 24, 1962, entry Appendix 23', *SWJN*, second series, vol. 80, 802.
293. 'Nehru to M.J. Desai, Foreign Secretary, 26 December 1962', *SWJN*, second series, vol. 80, 617.
294. Speech of Jawaharlal Nehru, *Lok Sabha Debates*, 29 March 1963, columns 7065–69.
295. Ibid.
296. 'Nehru to Mohanlal Sukhadia, Chief Minister, Rajasthan, December 10, 1962', in *SWJN*, second series, vol. 80, 78.
297. Rustomji, *Enchanted Frontiers: Sikkim, Bhutan and India's North-Eastern Borderlands*, 290.
298. Ibid., 290–91.
299. Lakhiprasad Goswami, Leader of the Opposition, Assam Assembly, 'Confidential Report of the Study of Situation in Siang and Subansiri Divisions of NEFA, February 4, 1963', in *NEFA Visit by Social Workers and Organization*.
300. Rustomji, *Enchanted Frontiers: Sikkim, Bhutan and India's North-Eastern Borderlands*, 289.
301. Ibid., 291.

## Chapter 8: Unfolding Crises in the Highlands

1. Joy Pachuau, *Being Mizo: Identity and Belonging in Northeast India* (Delhi: Oxford University Press, 2014). Years of intense political uneasiness, more especially from 1890 to 1892, preceded the events leading to the incorporation of the Lushai hills into Assam as one of its districts.
2. Willem van Schendel, 'A War within a War: Mizo Rebels and the Bangladesh Liberation Struggle', *Modern Asian Studies*, vol. 50, no. 1 (2016), 75–117.

3. The faction, which supported the idea of unification of the Lushai hills district with Myanmar, was called the United Mizo Freedom Organisation. See 'Letter from President, the Mizo Union, Aizawl, undated, to the Minister of External Affairs, Government of India', in *Agitation by the United Mizo Freedom Organisation for Session of Lushai Hills District to the Union of Burma,* File no. Progs. Nos 40 (49)-OSII, 1948, Overseas-II, External Affairs, GoI, Abhilekh Patal, NAI.
4. 'Letter from A.R.H. Macdonald, Superintendent, Lushai Hills to Secretary to the Governor of Assam, Aizawl, 1 November 1946', in *Political Activities on the Border of the Lushai Hills,* File no. 1240c/46, 1946, ASA.
5. Schendel, 'A War within a War: Mizo Rebels and the Bangladesh Liberation Struggle'; Sangkima, *Mizos: Society and Social Change, 1890–1947* (Guwahati: Spectrum Publications, 1992), Chapter IV.
6. 'Memorandum Submitted to His Majesty's Government by the Mizo Union, 22 April 1947', in Sangkima, *Mizos: Society and Social Change, 1890–1947,* 138; Schendel. 'A War within a War: Mizo Rebels and the Bangladesh Liberation Struggle', Note 24.
7. N.K. Rustomji, 'Report on Communist Activities on the Assam Burma Frontiers', 21 February 1949, in *Reports on Communist activities on Assam-Burma Frontier and in the Tribal Areas of Assam,* File no. 143, NEF/49/1949, Secret. Ministry of External Affairs, NEF branch, GoI, Abhilekh Patal, NAI.
8. J. Zorema, *Indirect Rule in Mizoram: 1890–1954* (Delhi: Mittal Publication, 2007), 155–74.
9. Assam Lushai Hills District (Acquisition of Chief's Rights) Act 1954 in Government of India, *Summary of Legislation in India* (Delhi: Manager of Publications, 1954); Pradip Kumar Bandyopadhyay, *Leadership among the Mizos: An Emerging Dimension* (Delhi: B.R. Publishing, 1985), 2–3.
10. V.L. Nghaka, *History of Assam* (Aizawl: Lalrinlina, 1971 [1966]).
11. Memorandum submitted to the Prime Minister of India on the occasion of his visit to Aizawl on 2 April 1953 by Pawi-Lakher Regional Council, File no. TAD/GA/51 of 1953, Tribal Area Development, General Administration Branch, 1953, ASA.
12. For a seminal study on the Mizo famine, see Sajal Nag, *Pied Pipers in North-East India: Bamboo-flowers, Rat Famine, and the Politics of Philanthropy, 1881–2007* (New Delhi: Manohar, 2008); Also, Sajal Nag, 'Tribals, Rats, Famine, State and the Nation', *Economic & Political Weekly,* vol. 36, no. 12 (March 2001), 1029; C. Rokhuma, *Tam do Pawlin Engnge a Tih?* (The Secret of Famines Found) (Aizawl: Author, 1988); Ken P. Aplin and James Lalsiamliana, 'Chronicle and Impacts of the 2005–09 *mautam* in Mizoram',

in *Rodent Outbreaks: Ecology and Impacts,* eds, Grant R. Singleton, et al. (Los Baños: International Rice Research Institute, 2010), 25.
13. Singleton, Belmain, Brown and Hardy, *Rodent Outbreaks: Ecology and Impacts.*
14. B. Govindan, et al. 'Nutritional Properties of the Largest Bamboo Fruit *Melocanna baccifera* and Its Ecological Significance', *Scientific Reports,* vol. 6, article no. 26135 (2016); K.K. Gupta, 'Flowering in Different Species of Bamboos in Cachar District of Assam in Recent Times', *Indian Forester,* vol. 98, vol. 2 (February 1972), 83–85; M.M. Kumawat, et al., 'Rodent Outbreak in Relation to Bamboo Flowering in North-Eastern Region of India', *Biological Agriculture and Horticulture,* vol. 30, no. 4 (June 2014), 243–52; Xiao Zheng, et al., 'The Bamboo Flowering Cycle Sheds Light on Flowering Diversity', *Frontiers in Plant Science,* vol. 11 (April 2020), 381; Harry George Champion and Shiam Kishore Seth, *A Revised Survey of the Forest Types of India* (New Delhi: Manager of Publications, 1968), 98–101; Alex Shoumatoff, 'Waiting for the Plague', *Vanity Fair,* December 2007, https://www.vanityfair.com/news/2007/12/famine200712 (Accessed 15 August 2021).
15. Ken and Lalsiamliana, 'Chronicles and Impacts of the 2005–09 *mautam* in Mizoram', 21.
16. Rokhuma, *Tam do Pawlin Engnge a Tih?* (The Secret of Famines Found), 128–29; Shoumatoff, 'Waiting for the Plague'.
17. Rokhuma, *Tam do Pawlin Engnge a Tih?* (The Secret of Famines Found), 107–12.
18. Ibid., 120.
19. 'Interview of C. Rokhuma, a Mizo School Teacher, Rodent Control Expert', quoted in Shoumatoff, 'Waiting for the Plague'.
20. Letter from C. Rokhuma, General Secretary, AFCO, Mizo District to Deputy Commissioner, Mizo District, 17 February 1956, Aizawl, *Mizo District: Scarcity of Rice in Article Published in the Hun Thar, a Lushai Weekly,* File no. TAD/CON/29/55, ASA.
21. Rokhuma, *Tam do Pawlin Engnge a Tih?* (The Secret of Famines Found), 124–25; Nag, *Pied Pipers in North-East India: Bamboo-flowers, Rat Famine, and the Politics of Philanthropy, 1881–2007,* 245.
22. Rokhuma, *Tam do Pawlin Engnge a Tih?* (The Secret of Famines Found), 128–35.
23. 'Tampui Mithi', *Hun Thar,* 6 August 1955, quoted in Letter from S.K. Datta, Chief Secretary, Government of Assam (GoA) to Secretary, Tribal Areas Department, GoA, 2 September 1955, Shillong, No. C.66/55/2-Pt, *Mizo District: Scarcity of Rice in Article Published in the Hun Thar, a Lushai Weekly,* File no. TAD/CON/29/55, ASA.

24. 'Extract from a secret report, 13 August 1955', Subsidiary Intelligence Bureau, Ministry of Home Affairs, GoI, 26 August 1955 quoted in Confidential Report, Governor of Assam to Secretary, Tribal Areas Department, memo no. C.66/55/6-Pt, 12 September 1955, *Mizo District: Scarcity of Rice in Article Published in the Hun Thar, a Lushai Weekly*.
25. Letter from K.G. Iyer, DC, Mizo Hills to Secretary, Tribal Areas Development, No.GM.21/56/42, 9 May 1956, *Rat Menace: Protection of Crops in Mizo District*, File no. TAD/Agri/22/56, Tribal Areas Department, Agriculture Branch, 1956, ASA.
26. Peter Farb, 'Biology's New Weapons against Insect Pests', *Reader's Digest*, September 1957.
27. Letter from H.L. Baruah, Professor, Department of Botany to Development Officer, South Mizo District, 20 September 1957, *Rat Menace: Protection of Crops in Mizo District*; Letter from President, Forest Research Institute to Development Officer, South Mizo District, 19 October 1957, *Rat Menace: Protection of Crops in Mizo District*.
28. Development Officer, Lungleh, 'Suggestions of the Precautionary Measures to be Adopted Before the Famine Actually Frowns', 4 December 1957, *Rat Menace: Protection of Crops in Mizo District*.
29. Lalmiwa, Parliamentary Secretary, Tribal Areas Department, 'Mautam', 28 April 1958, 1–7, *Rat Menace: Protection of Crops in Mizo District*.
30. Letter from L.S. Ingty, Deputy Commissioner, Mizo Hills to Secretary, Government of Assam, Tribal Areas Development, Aizawl, 15 May 1958, *Rat Menace: Protection of Crops in Mizo District*.
31. 'Interview of C. Rokhuma, A Mizo School Teacher, Rodent Control Expert', in 'Waiting for the Plague', Shoumatoff.
32. Telegram to Thuamluaia, MLA, Shillong, 10 March, 1959, in *Rat Menace: Protection of Crops in Mizo District*.
33. *Times of India*, 16 February 1960, 8; Rokhuma, *Tam do Pawlin Engnge a Tih? (The Secret of Famines Found)*, 125; Nag, *Pied Pipers in North-East India: Bamboo-flowers, Rat Famine, and the Politics of Philanthropy, 1881–2007*, 245.
34. Letter from President, Eastern India Tribal Union, Mizo District Branch to the Parliamentary Secretary, Tribal Areas Development, 7 March 1959, *Mizo District: Scarcity of Rice in Article Published in the Hun Thar, a Lushai Weekly*, File no. TAD/CON/29/55, ASA.
35. Taya Zinkin, 'Death and Bamboo Flower: Starvation in Lushai Hills', *Guardian*, 17 February 1960, 1.
36. Ibid.
37. Nag, 'Tribals, Rats, Famine, State and the Nation', 1029–33.

38. Quoted by A.M. Thomas, Deputy Minister of Food and Agriculture, *Lok Sabha Debates*, 18 April 1960, column 12235.
39. *New York Times*, 16 February 1960, 4; Speech by Nehru, *Lok Sabha Debates*, 15 February 1960, column 958.
40. *Times of India*, 15 February 1960, 1; Letter from Deputy Commissioner, Mizo District to Deputy Inspector General of Police, CID, Assam, Memo no. 829-30/S.R. 2-60/Crime, Aizawl, 15 March 1960, *Special Report Cases: Mizo Hills District*, File no. HPL 275/60, Home (Police), 1960, ASA.
41. Aplin and Lalsiamliana, 'Chronicle and Impacts of the 2005–09 *mautam* in Mizoram', 25.
42. District Agricultural Officer, Mizo Hills, 'Agricultural Relief Work in the Mizo District', Enclosure in 'Letter from S.R. Barooah, Minister of Agriculture, Assam to R.B. Vagaiwalla, Commissioner, Hills Division, Shillong, Demi official no. 1712, 27 April 1960' in *Mautam in Mizo District*, File no. 268/60/Pt-II, 1960, Chief Minister's Secretariat (hereafter CMS), ASA.
43. *Times of India*, 15 February 1960, 1.
44. 'Famine in Mizo', *Times of India*, 16 April 1960, 6. 'It is crying shame that the Assam government did not rush enough rice to the Mizo district in time and allowed matters to come to a pass where people were dying of starvation,' wrote the *Times of India*.
45. *Natun Asamiya*, 6 March 1960, 1.
46. E.H. Pakyntein, *Report on the Census of India, 1961: Assam, District Census Handbook, Mizo Hills* (Guwahati: Government of Assam, 1965), Table 6.1, 237.
47. Ibid., Table 10.2, 259.
48. Speech of Hem Barua, *Lok Sabha Debates*, 18 April 1960, column 12236.
49. *Times of India*, 15 April 1960, 1.
50. *Times of India*, 19 February 1960, 8.
51. Letter from L.S. Ingty, Deputy Commissioner, Mizo District to R.B. Vaghaiwalla, Secretary, Tribal Affairs Department, GoA, 10 June 1959, *Rat Menace: Protection of Crops in Mizo District*, File no. TAD/Agri/22/56, Tribal Areas Department, Agri Branch, 1956, ASA; Pakyntein, *Report on the Census of India, 1961: Assam, District Census Handbook, Mizo Hills*, Table 3.1, 212.
52. Rokhuma, *Tam do Pawlin Engnge a Tih?* (The Secret of Famines Found), 129.
53. 'Inspection by Mr Menon: Air-Dropping of food', *Times of India*, 16 April 1960, 1.
54. Letter from Nehru to S.M. Shrinagesh, 8 April 1960, *Selected Works of Jawaharlal Nehru* (hereafter *SWJN*), vol. 59, second series, 212; Nehru to

Bimala Prasad Chaliha, Chief Minister, Assam, February 2, 1960, New Delhi, in *Mautam in the Mizo District*, CMS/268/60, 1960, ASA.

55. *Times of India*, 16 July 1960, quoted in *SWJN*, second series, vol. 61, 282, fn. 241.
56. Statement of Nehru, *Lok Sabha Debates*, 18 April 1960, columns 12237–238.
57. Demi Official Letter from F.A. Ahmed to Nehru, 18 February 1961, no. BS/67/60/7, in *Mautam in the Mizo District*, CMS, 268/60/pt-109, 1960, ASA.
58. *Times of India*, 2 July 1963, 9.
59. Chawngsailova, *Ethnic National Movement in the Role of the MNF* (Aizawl: Mizoram Publication Board, 2007), 2–3.
60. In a by-election held in 1963, the MNF won both the seats. Nirmal Nibedon, *Mizoram: The Dagger Brigade.* (New Delhi: Lancer Publishers, 1980), 39.
61. *Observer*, 21 August 1960, 8. This number grew in the 1960s, and by 1974, an estimated 36,000 soldiers were posted in the Naga and Mizo Hills. Trevor N. Dupuy, John A.C. Andrews and Grace P. Hayes, eds, *The Almanac of World Military Power* (New York: R.R. Bowker, 1974), 311.
62. *Times of India*, 16 April 1960, 1.
63. *Times of India*, 11 October 1962, 5.
64. Schendel, 'A War within a War: Mizo Rebels and the Bangladesh Liberation Struggle'.
65. *Times of India*, 31 August 1962, 6.
66. *Times of India*, 24 July 1961, 9.
67. Confidential Note, Office of the British High Commission, Calcutta, 19 July 1963, *India–Pakistan Relations* (Government Papers, The National Archives, Kew, 1963), http://www.archivesdirect.amdigital.co.uk/Documents/Details/FO_371_170637 (Accessed 23 April 2021); *Times of India*, 23 June 1962, 7.
68. 'Eastern India and its Frontier with Pakistan', Confidential Note, Office of the British High Commission, Calcutta, 19 July 1963, *India–Pakistan Relations* (Government Papers, The National Archives, Kew, 1963), http://www.archivesdirect.amdigital.co.uk/Documents/Details/FO_371_170637 (Accessed 23 April 2021).
69. Speech of L.B. Shastri, *Lok Sabha Debates*, 14 August 1963, column 330; 'Letter from Ministry of External Affairs, GoI, to the High Commission of Pakistan in India, New Delhi, March 12, 1966', *Lok Sabha Starred Question no 1172 for 18.4.66 Regarding Headquarters of Mizos in Dacca*, File no. P2/125/41/66, Ministry of External Affairs, Pak I section, GoI, Abhilekh Patal, NAI; *Times of India*, 13 May 1966, 1.

70. *Times of India*, 30 August 1962, 1; *Observer*, 8 September 1963, 6.
71. Nehru to Chaliha, 20 October 1962, *SWJN,* second series, vol. 79, 39
72. Nehru to Shastri, Nehru to Menon, 20 October 1962, *SWJN*, second series, vol. 79, 38–39.
73. The date of this mutiny is not mentioned in Nehru's correspondence. In 1963, when Nehru wrote to Chavan, the Union defence minister, he mentioned the mutiny, which took place 'a year or two ago'. Nehru to Chavan, 9 February 1963, *SWJN*, second series, vol. 81, Entry: 244, 357–58. Also, entries 245 and 248, 358–60.
74. Joy L.K. Pachuau and Willem van Schendel, *The Camera as Witness: A Social History of Mizoram, Northeast India* (Cambridge: Cambridge University Press, 2015), 304.
75. 'Memorandum submitted to the Prime Minister of India by the Mizo National Front General Headquarters, Aizawl, Mizoram on October 30, 1965', in C. Nunthara, *Mizoram: Society and Polity* (New Delhi: Indus Publishing Company, 1996), Appendix, v, 267.
76. Pachau and van Schendel, *The Camera as Witness: A Social History of Mizoram, Northeast India*, 304.
77. *Observer,* 21 August 1960, 8.
78. D.R. Mankekar, 'Tribals' role in Assam: Decisive factor in politics', *Times of India*, 19 March 1951, 1.
79. *Times of India*, 10 September 1947, 7.
80. *Times of India*, 14 November 1951, 5.
81. 'Confidential Fortnightly Report by the Chief Secretary to the Government of Assam', 2nd half, May 1957 in *Fortnightly Reports from the Government of Assam for 1957* (hereafter *FR*), File no. 4/17/57–Poll-II, 1957, Ministry of Home Affairs, Political-II section, Abhilekh Patal, NAI.
82. *FR*, 2nd half, May 1957.
83. *FR*, 2nd half, July 1957.
84. *FR*, 1st half, July 1957.
85. Government of India, *Report of the States Reorganisation Commission* (New Delhi: Government of India Press, 1955), 188.
86. Government of Assam, *Memorandum to the States Reorganisation Commission,* Part 1 (Shillong: Assam Government Press, 1954), 12.
87. 'Speech of Shri Jairamdas Doulatram, Governor of Assam, on the occasion of Inaugurating the Hills and Plains Festival at Shillong on the 26th January 1954', in *Report from Triloki Nath Purwar about Hills Tribes of Assam and talk by Shri S.J. Duncan, Formerly D.C. Naga Hills District with a copy of speech of Shri Jairamdas Doulatram, Governor of Assam, delivered by him on the occasion of inaugurating the Hills and Plains Festival at Shillong*, File

no. 49-G/54, President Secretariat, Abhilekh Patal, NAI; Bérénice Guyot-Réchard, *Shadow States: India, China and the Himalayas, 1910–1962* (Cambridge: Cambridge University Press, 2016), 153, *Natun Asamiya*, 26 January; 27 January; 28 January; 29 January; 30 January 1954.

88. Government of India, *Report of the Commission on the Hill Areas of Assam, 1965–66*, Appendix III, Summary of Discussion Between the Prime Minister and the Hill Leaders, 154; S.R. Bodhi, 'Khasi Political Reality and the Struggle for Statehood: History: Context and Political Processes', in *Handbook of Tribal Politics in India*, eds, Jagannath Ambagudia and Virginius Xaxa (Delhi: Sage Publications, 2021), 399.
89. Government of Assam, *Memorandum to the States Reorganisation Commission*.
90. 'Move for creation of hill state: Tribals prepare ground for renewed agitation', *Times of India*, 29 August 1960, 7.
91. Ibid.
92. Letter from Biswanarayan Shastri to the Chief Minister, Assam, 9 May 1961 in Publication Board, Assam, File no. CMS/134/61, CMS Department, 1961, ASA.
93. Nehru to Nichols Roy, 24 January 1961, *SWJN*, second series, vol. 66, 295.
94. Letter from N. Roy to Nehru, appendix 33b, 13 February 1961, *SWJN*, second series, vol. 66, 640.
95. 'Record of the Prime Minister's meeting with the Delegation of the Hill Leaders', Conference on 17 May 1961, New Delhi', *SWJN*, second series, vol. 69, 117–20.
96. *SWJN*, second series, vol. 69, entry 30, 149–51.
97. *Times of India*, 22 October 1962, 3.
98. *Times of India*, 23 November 1961, 8.
99. *New York Times*, 11 June 1963, 24.
100. Government of India, *Report of the Commission on the Hill Areas of Assam, 1965–66* (Delhi: Ministry of Home Affairs, 1966), 156.
101. Minutes of a meeting of the delegation of APHLC with Nehru, New Delhi, 5 October 1963, in Government of India, *Report of the Commission on the Hill Areas of Assam, 1965–66*, 177–81.
102. *Times of India*, 12 June 1963, 6.
103. K.C. Baruah, *Critical Days of Assam* (Guwahati: K.C. Baruah, 1972), 5–10.
104. Government of India, *Report of the Commission on the Hill Areas of Assam, 1965–66*. The other two members were Shankar Prasad and G.S. Rao.
105. 'Hill people's struggle to be free from exploitation: Period of acute strain ahead as both camps prepare for action Assam', *Times of India*, 27 July 1967, 8.

106. Government of India, *Report of the Commission on the Hill Areas of Assam, 1965–66*, 125–30.
107. Unpublished Notes, Ministry of Home Affairs, GoI, cited in D. Mukerjee, 'Assam Reorganisation', *Asian Survey*, vol. 9, no. 4 (April 1969), 304.
108. 'Political Situation: Adopted in the meeting of Assam Pradesh Congress Committee held on June 7, 1966', *Sriman Prafulla Goswami Papers*, Packet no. I-III, NMML; 'The views formulated by the PCC Executive and Congress Parliamentary Party Executive in the joint meeting held on May 11, 1966, on the recommendations of the Pataskar Commission', *Sriman Prafulla Goswami Papers*, Packet no. I-III, NMML.
109. Mukherjee, 'Assam Reorganisation', 304.
110. *Times of India*, 9 January 1967, 1; *Times of India*, 10 January 1967, 7.
111. *Dainik Asam*, 14 January 1967, 1; Mukherjee, 'Assam Reorganisation', 305; *Times of India*, 14 January 1967, 1.
112. Statement of Union home minister, in 'Assam to be Reorganised Within Six Months', *Times of India*, 14 January 1967, 1. This proposal was welcomed by Swatantra Party, while CPI and PSP opposed it.
113. *Dainik Asam*, 16 January 1967.
114. K.C. Baruah, 'Partition of Assam', *Assam Tribune*, 18 January 1967, in *Critical Days of Assam*, Baruah.
115. K.C. Baruah, 'Reorganisation of Assam', *Assam Tribune*, 25 January 1967, in *Critical Days of Assam*, Baruah, 23.
116. Atul Chandra Hazarika, 'Akou Agini Parikha', *Dainik Asam*, 19 January 1967, 4.
117. *Dainik Asam*, 16 and 17 January 1967, 1.
118. 'New proposal will lead to Assam's disintegration', *Times of India*, 16 January 1967, 7.
119. *Times of India*, 1 June 1967, 8.
120. 'Resolution of Assam Pradesh Congress Executive on Re-organisation of Assam', in *Assam Pradesh Congress Committee, Pradesh Congress on Assam's Reorganisation: A Compilation of Papers, Views, Resolutions and Decisions of Assam Pradesh Congress Committee Taken from Time to Time on the Matters Relating to the Question of Reorganisation of Assam* (Guwahati: Assam Pradesh Congress Committee, 1967), 60–61.
121. 'Memorandum to the Home Minister, May 29, 1967, from Assam Pradesh Congress Committee', in Assam Pradesh Congress Committee, *Pradesh Congress on Assam's Reorganization: A Compilation of Papers, Views, Resolutions and Decisions of Assam Pradesh Congress Committee Taken from Time to Time on the Matters Relating to the Question of Reorganisation of Assam*, 62–64.

122. *Dainik Asam*, 17 January 1967, 1.
123. Ibid., 31 July 1967.
124. Ibid., 18 July 1967.
125. 'Autonomy granted to tribes of Assam', *New York Times*, 14 January 1967, 2.
126. B.K. Bhattacharya, 'Congress Loses in the Cities', *Economic & Political Weekly*, vol. 2, no. 10 (1967), 515–16.
127. K.N. Deka, 'Assam: The Challenge of Political Integration and Congress Leadership', in *State Politics in India,* ed. Iqbal Narain (Meerut: Meenakshi Prakashan, 1976).
128. Ibid., 37.
129. Ahmed secured 60.12 per cent of the total votes polled, while Choudhury secured 39.88 per cent. Election Commission of India, *Statistical Report on General Elections, 1967 to the Fourth Lok Sabha*, vol. 1 (New Delhi: Election Commission of India, 1968), 113.
130. Kenneth W. Jones, *Socio-Religious Reform Movements in British India* (Cambridge: Cambridge University Press, 1990), 184–209.
131. For an insight into the nature of the socio-religious reforms amongst the upper-caste Hindu Assamese population, see *Prachin Kamrupiya Kayastha-Samajar Itibritta,* eds, Harinarayan Dutta Baruah and Saneswar Dutta (Guwahati: Prachin Kamrup-Kayastha Samaj, 2000 [1941]), 99–102. Also, Gaurikanta Talukdar, *Kalitar Vratyodharar Avasyakata* (Guwahati: Sarbeswar Bhattacharya, 1929).
132. Tirthanath Sharma, *Auiniati Satrar Buranji* (Majuli: Auniati Satra, 1975), 231–35.
133. *Dainik Asam*, 28 January 1968.
134. For the early growth of Hindu Mahasabha in Assam, see Radhika Mohan Goswami, *Ateet Smriti* (Guwahati: Alok Prakashan, 1989), 96–98; Also, Anonymous, 'Special Session of the All-India Hindu Mahasabha: Gauhati, 28 December 1926', *Indian Quarterly Register,* vol. 2 (July–December 1926), 354–57. The leaders of the Hindu Mahasabha had particularly spoken out against the increasing settlement of Muslim peasants of Bengali origin in Assam. "Statement of Savarkar, Dadar, Bombay, 8 July 1941 in 'Complaints or representations from organisations representing different communities about matters of communal interest arising in regard to the census enumeration', Home Department, File no. 45/11/41, Public, NAI", in *Religion and Conflict in Modern South Asia* (Cambridge: Cambridge University Press, 2012), Gould, 158, fn. 117.
135. Paul R. Brass, *Language, Religion and Politics in North India* (Cambridge: Cambridge University Press, 1974), 322–25.
136. *Times of India*, 21 June 1967; *Dainik Asam*, 21 June 1967.

137. Mukerjee, 'Assam Reorganization', 306.
138. *Times of India*, 15 June 1967, 9.
139. *Dainik Asam*, 8 July 1967, 1; *Dainik Asam*, 8 July 1967, 1; *Times of India*, 9 July 1967, 1 and 9; *Times of India*, 10 July 1967, 1 and 7; *Dainik Asam*, 10 July 1967, 1.
140. *Dainik Asam*, 11 July 1967, 1.
141. Ibid., 16 July 1967.
142. Ibid., 31 August 1967.
143. Speech of Y.B. Chavan, *Lok Sabha Debates*, 15 November 1967, columns 595–96; *Dainik Asam*, 31 July 1967. Of the 11 members of this committee, only two—W. Sangma and Nichols Roy—belonged to APHLC and the rest were from the Assam Legislative Assembly whose anti-reorganization stand was well known. *Dainik Asam*, 10 July 1967, 1.
144. Anonymous, 'Assam Hills: Search for Autonomy', *Economic & Political Weekly*, vol. 2, no. 36 (1967), 1632–1633.
145. APHLC leaders claimed that except Jan Sangh all Opposition agreed to support a regional federation. *Times of India*, 30 December 1967, 9; *Times of India*, 29 December 1967, 1.
146. M.N. Srinivas, 'Is the Sun Setting?', *Seminar*, no. 90, February 1967, 12–16.
147. 'Joint Memorandum of the Lushai Hills Autonomous District Council and the Mizo Union, to States Reorganisation Commission' in *Memorandum, Resolutions, Letter etc. Against the Demand for Separate Hill State sent to SRC*, CMS/NIL/54, 1954, ASA.
148. Birendra Kumar Bhattacharyya, 'A Separate Assam Hills State: What Does It Mean?', *Economic & Political Weekly*, vol. 2, no. 9 (4 March 1967), 494. The quote from Bhattacharyya on page 325 is also from this essay.
149. R.A. Church, 'Roots of Separatism in Assam Hill Districts', *Economic & Political Weekly*, vol. 4, no. 17 (26 April 1969), 729, Table 2; P.C. Goswami, *Economic Development of Assam* (Bombay, London: Asia Publishing House, 1963), 286, Table 12; Government of Assam, *Draft Third Five-Year Plan, Assam* (Shillong: Government Printing Press, 1960), 7.
150. Tarlok Singh, *Outlays and Programmes for the Hill Region of Assam for the Fourth Plan* (Delhi: Government of India, 1966), 3.
151. *Dainik Asam*, 31 August 1967, 1.
152. Mukerjee, 'Assam Reorganisation', 299.
153. Ibid.
154. C.P. Cook, 'India: The Crisis in Assam', *World Today*, vol. 24, no. 10 (1968), 444–48.

155. Ramachandra Guha, *India After Gandhi: The History of the World's Largest Democracy* (New Delhi: Picador, 2007); G. Kanato Chophy, *Christianity and Politics in Tribal India: Baptist Missionaries and Naga Nationalism* (Delhi: Permanent Black, 2021).
156. A.K. Saikia, *Census of India, Assam, 1971: District Census Handbook, Mikir Hills District* (Shillong: Government of Assam, 1971), 126; A.K. Saikia, *Census of India, Assam, 1971: District Census Handbook, North Cachar Hills District* (Shillong: Government of Assam, 1971), Statement vii, 46.
157. Richard M. Eaton, 'Conversion to Christianity among the Nagas, 1876–1971', *Indian Economic & Social History Review*, vol. 21, no. 1 (1 March 1984), 42–43; Mukherji, 'Assam Reorganization', 299–300; G. Kanato Chophy, *Christianity and Politics in Tribal India: Baptist Missionaries and Naga Nationalism*; John Thomas, *Evangelising the Nation: Religion and the Formation of Naga Political Identity* (Delhi: Routledge, 2017).
158. Bhattacharyya, 'A Separate Assam Hills State: What Does It Mean?', 491, 493–94.
159. The mission consisted of four members: Bimala Prasad Chaliha, Michael Scott, Jayaprakash Narayan and Shankar Rao Deo. *The Times*, 7 May 1966, 8; M. Aram, *Peace in Nagaland: Eight Year Story, 1964–72* (Delhi: Arnold-Heinemann Publishers, 1974); Ranabir Samaddar, ed., *Government of Peace: Social Governance, Security and the Problematic of Peace* (London: Routledge, 2015), 26–28; Namrata Goswami, *The Naga Ethnic Movement for a Separate Homeland: Stories from the Field* (Delhi: Oxford University Press, 2020).
160. 'The Reverend Michael Scott', Secret note, K.S. Puri, under secretary (Naga) Ministry of External Affairs, 13 April 1970, in *Background Note on Angamu Zapu Phizo and Rev. Michael Scott prepared by U.S (Naga) in April 1970*, File NI.102 (42) 70, Ministry of External Affairs, Naga unit, Government of India, Abhilekh Patal, NAI.
161. *The Times*, 12 September 1966, 9.
162. Government of India, *Report of the Commission on the Hill Areas of Assam, 1965–66*, 12.
163. Ibid., Appendix vii, Statement showing capital expenditure of the state of Assam, 189.
164. These figures are at constant prices of 1960–61. Ibid., Table V, 25.
165. Ibid., Table IV, 25.
166. J.N. Sarma, 'Balanced Regional Development: Is It Possible?', *Economic & Political Weekly*, vol. 1, no. 18 (17 December 1966), 757–68.
167. Ibid, 757.

168. *Dainik Asam*, 3 March 1966, 1; *Dainik Asam*, 7 July 1967, 1.
169. Speech of V.C. Shukla, *Lok Sabha Debates*, 23 February 1966, column 1704; *Times of India*, 24 February 1966, 10. Mizo rebels also unsuccessfully tried to take shelter in Burma. *Fortnightly Press Review for the period from August 16 to 31, 1970*, Information Service of India, Rangoon, in *Political Report from Rangoon*, HI/1012 (12) 70, Ministry of External Affairs, Government of India, R & I section, Abhilekh Patal, NAI; *Dainik Asam*, 2 March 1966.
170. Pachau and van Schendel, *The Camera as Witness: A Social History of Mizoram, Northeast India*, 304; Nibedon, *Mizoram: The Dagger Brigade*, Chapter 4; J.V. Hluna and Rini Tochhawng, *The Mizo Uprising: Assam Assembly Debates on the Mizo Movement, 1966–1971* (Newcastle upon Tyne: Cambridge Scholars Publishing, 2012), Chapter 3.
171. *Times of India*, 2 March 1966, 1; *Jugantar*, 2 March 1966, 1 and 5; Statement of G.L. Nanda, Home Minister, *Lok Sabha Debates*, 2 March 1966, column 3426.
172. *New York Times*, 3 March 1966, 10; Nibedon, *Mizoram: The Dagger Brigade*, 59.
173. 'At midnight on Monday (5 March) the Mizos rose in a well-planned revolt, declared their sovereign independence and today are believed to be in virtual complete control of the whole 8000 square mile district, one of the biggest in India', Cyril Dunn, 'Army sent against hill rebels', *Observer*, 6 March 1966, 2.
174. Text of MNF declaration of Independence, in C. Nunthara, *Mizoram: Society and Polity*, 269; Pachuau and van Schendel, *The Camera as Witness: A Social History of Mizoram, Northeast India*, 304.
175. Letter from Superintendent of Police, Special Branch (III), Assam, Shillong to Deputy Secretary to the Government of Assam, Political (B), 23 April 1966 in *Lok Sabha Question Regarding Officials Kidnapped by the MNF rebels in Mizo Hills*, File no. PLB 158/66, Home Confidential, 1966, ASA.
176. *Times of India*, 3 March 1966, 1; *Jugantar*, 3 March 1966, 1; *Dainik Asam*, 2 March 1966, 1.
177. *Dainik Asam*, 2 March 1966, 1.
178. Statement of G.L. Nanda, Home Minister, *Lok Sabha Debates*, 2 March 1966, 3426; *Dainik Asam*, 4 March 1966.
179. *Jugantar*, 6 March 1966, 1.
180. *The Times*, 8 March 1966, 10.
181. *Dainik Asam*, 3 March 1966, 4.
182. 'Statement of Dinesh Singh, Minister of State for External Affairs', *Lok Sabha Debates*, 28 February 1966, 2680.

183. Statement of Chaliha, *Jugantar*, 4 March 1966, 1 and 5.
184. *Jugantar*, 4, March 1966, 1; *Dainik Asam*, 4 March 1966; *Observer*, 6 March 1966.
185. *Jugantar*, 7 March 1966, 1.
186. *Dainik Asam*, 6 March 1966, 1.
187. Ibid., 3 March 1966, 6.
188. This widely referred public acknowledgement is quoted in Bertil Lintner, *Great Game East: India, China, and the Struggle for Asia's Most Volatile Frontier* (New Haven & London: Yale University Press, 2015), 91; Subir Bhaumik, *Insurgent Crossfire: North-East India* (New Delhi: Lancer Publishers, 1996), 151.
189. Schendel, 'A War Within a War: Mizo Rebels and the Bangladesh Liberation Struggle', 75–117.
190. Nibedon, *Mizoram: The Dagger Brigade*, 81. A detailed account of the situation in Mizo Hills in the aftermath of the bombing of Aizwal was prepared by G.G. Swell and S.D.D. Nichols-Roy. The report found that the large areas were 'a heap of rubble of ashes and ashes' due to the bombing. G.G. Swell and S.D.D. Nichols-Roy, *Report on the Mizo Hills Situation* (1966), quoted in Eqbal Ahmad, 'Further notes on South Asia in crisis', *Bulletin of Concerned Asian Scholars*, vol. 5, no. 1, (1973), 32. Benjamin Mark Holt, 'The Long Decolonisation of the Assam highlands, 1942–1972' (PhD diss., University of Leeds, 2021), 208n687.
191. *Dainik Asam*, 7 March 1966, 1.
192. Letter from Hminga, Foreign Secretary, Government of Mizoram, Jungle Camp, 21 March 1966, *The Times*, 1 April 1966, 13.
193. *The Times*, 1 April 1966, 13.
194. *The Times*, 6 April 1966, 13.
195. *The Times*, 13 April 1966, 9.
196. Secret, Fortnightly Press Review for the period 1 to 15.10. 66, Information Service of India, Washington, D. C., *Monthly Political Reports (other than Annuals from Washington)*, File no. HI/191 (78) 66, Ministry of External Affairs, Historical Division, NAI; Pachuau and van Schendel, *The Camera as Witness: A Social History of Mizoram, Northeast India*, 305.
197. *Observer*, 27 March 1966, 5.
198. Schendel, 'A War Within a War: Mizo Rebels and the Bangladesh Liberation Struggle'.
199. Ibid.; J.V. Hluna, 'MNF Relations with Foreign Powers', in *Autonomy Movements in Mizoram*, ed., R.N. Prasad (New Delhi: Vikas Publishing House, 1994), 190; Bhaumik, *Insurgent Crossfire: North-East India*, 145–

49; *Indian Express,* January 19, 1968; 'Record of a meeting between the foreign and commonwealth secretary and the Indian minister of state for external affairs at the ministry of external affairs, New Delhi, 3 December 1968', Document no. 17, confidential, para. 34, in *Record of Secretary of State's discussion in Pakistan* (Government Papers, The National Archives, Kew, 1968), http://www.archivesdirect.amdigital.co.uk/Documents/Details/FCO_37_493 (Accessed 20 August 2020); 'Foreign Involvement in insurgency in North Eastern India', Part II, Mizo Hostilities, paras 25–27, 8, Secret, Ministry of Defence, D (GS-I), in *Foreign Involvement in Insurgency in North Eastern India: Preparation of White Paper on the subject by the Ministry of Defence,* File no. N.II/102 (33) 72, Naga Section, Ministry of Home Affairs, GoI, 1972, Abhilekh Patal, NAI.

200. Quoted in Confidential Letter from K. Hamylton Jones, British Embassy, Rangoon, 16 August 1968, in 'Internal Political Affairs of the [Mizo] Area, 1968 (Folder 2)', (Government Papers, The National Archives, Kew, 1968), http://www.archivesdirect.amdigital.co.uk/Documents/Details/FCO_37_268 (Accessed 6 February 2023).

201. Confidential telegram, 21 April 1967, Commonwealth Office, New Delhi, Telegram no 840, 'Internal Political Affairs of the Mizo Area, 1967–68 (Folder 1)' (Government Papers, The National Archives, Kew, 1967–1968), http://www.archivesdirect.amdigital.co.uk/Documents/Details/FCO_37_267 (Accessed 6 February 2023).

202. *New York Times,* 28 May 1969, 11; Arthur J. Dommen, 'Separatist Tendencies in Eastern India', *Asian Survey,* vol. 7, no. 10 (1 October 1967), 726–39; C. Nunthara, *Impact of the Introduction of Grouping of Villages in Mizoram* (Delhi: Omsons Publications, 1989); C. Nunthara 'Grouping of Villages in Mizoram: Its Social and Economic Impact', *Economic & Political Weekly,* vol. 16, no. 30 (25 July 1981), 1237–40; Nandini Sundar, 'Interning Insurgent Populations: The Buried Histories of Indian Democracy', *Economic & Political Weekly,* vol. 46, no. 6 (5–11 February 2011), 47–57. Also, see Tarlok Singh, *Outlays and Programmes for the Hill Region of Assam for the Fourth Plan* (Delhi: Planning Commission, 1966), 29, 47.

203. *Indian Express,* 7 January 1967, 1; *Nunthara, Impact of the Introduction of Grouping of Villages in Mizoram,* 7.

204. Nunthara, *Impact of the Introduction of Grouping of Villages in Mizoram.*

205. *Times of India,* 21 June 1967, 10.

206. *Dainik Asam,* 11 February 1968, 1.

207. Government of Assam, *Fourth Five-Year Plan of Assam: A Draft Outline* (Shillong: Planning and Development Department, 1968), 29; Government

of Assam, *Assam District Gazetteers: Lakhimpur District* (Guwahati: Government of Assam, 1976), 374.
208. National Council of Applied Economic Research, *Techno-Economic Survey of Assam* (New Delhi, National Council of Applied Economic Research, 1962), 36.
209. These states' share was 17.1, 16.7 and 14.6 per cent, respectively. Government of Assam, *Fourth Five-Year Plan of Assam: A Draft Outline*, 5.
210. *The Times*, 21 November 1962, 10; *Guardian*, 20 November 1962, 1.
211. Atul Chandra Sarma, 'A Study of Assam Finances: Structure and Trend 1947–48 to 1965–66' (PhD diss., Gauhati University), Table 5.11 B, 309.
212. Government of Assam, *Fourth Five-Year Plan of Assam: A Draft Outline*, 8.
213. Computed from Government of Assam, *General Educational Table Relating to Assam, 1942–43* (Shillong: Assam Government Press, 1944), Table IX, 134; Government of Assam, *Education in Assam: Statistical Handbook, 1947–48 to 1960–61* (Shillong: Department of Economics and Statistics, 1962), Table 1, 1.
214. Dilip Kumar Chattopadhyay, *History of the Assamese Movement since 1947* (New Delhi: Minerva Associates, 1990), 101.
215. A senior official of a private sector industry complained that only 'fresh diploma holders without any experience were available'. Government of Assam, *Report of the Employment Review Committee, 1969–70* (Shillong: Assembly Secretariat Press, 1970), 31.
216. Ibid., 10–11.
217. Baruah, *Critical Days of Assam*, 257.
218. Michael Fisher, *An Environmental History of India: From Earliest Times to the Twenty-First Century* (Cambridge: Cambridge University Press, 2018), 188.
219. '80 dead, 200,000 starving in Indian provincial famine', *New York Times*, 27 June 1963, 3; *New York Times*, 12 December 1963, 4.
220. Assam Pradesh Congress Committee, 'Resolution adopted in its meeting held on July 31, 1966: Flood situation', *Assam Pradesh Congress Committee Papers*, Packet no, 160 (1966) NMML; Cachar Ch-Sramik Union, 'Press Statement: Starvation in Cachar garden areas, Effect of the Unprecedented Flood, 21 June 1966', *Assam Pradesh Congress Committee Papers*, Packet no 160 (1966), NMML; *Times of India*, 20 August 1966, 7; *Times of India*, 23 December 1966, 10.
221. Question no. 1710, P.C. Borooah, *Lok Sabha Debates*, 9 August 1966, columns 3505–06; 'Resolutions passed by Guwahati District Congress Committee held on 26 June 1966', *Assam Pradesh Congress Committee Papers*, Packet no 160 (1966), NMML.

222. Official note from Minister, Cooperation, Government of Assam to Chief Minister, Assam, 14 November 1965, in *Food Situation*, Chief Minister's Secretariat, CMS 159/66, 1966, ASA.
223. Resolution adopted in the 3rd annual general meeting of the Nowgong District Journalists Association held on 9 January 1966 in *Food Situation*, Chief Minister's Secretariat, CMS 159/66, 1966, ASA.
224. Text of the Prime Minister's Broadcast, 12 June 1966 in *Correspondence with the Prime Minister*, CMS, 208/66, 1966, ASA.
225. Letter from Indira Gandhi to B.P. Chaliha, chief minister, Assam 15 June 1966 in *Correspondence with the Prime Minister*, CMS, 208/66, 1966, ASA.
226. T.C. Goswami, 'Sarkaror Khadyaniti', *Ramdhenu*, vol. 18, no. 9 (1966), 829–35.
227. *Dainik Asam*, 15 May 1968, 1; Anonymous, 'Food Crisis is Back', *Economic & Political Weekly*, vol. 3, issue 24 (15 June 1968), 898–99; Anonymous, 'Assam Food Crisis: Several Starvation Deaths in Goalpara District', *New Age*, vol. 16, no. 19 (19 May 1968).
228. Mukerjee, 'Assam Reorganization', 308.
229. *Dainik Asam*, 26 January 1968, 1. Also, Speech of D.N. Patodia, *Lok Sabha Debates*, 14 February 1968, column 715.
230. *Dainik Asam*, 28 January 1968, 1; *Dainik Asam*, 26 January 1968, 1.
231. Appeal on behalf of Guwahati-based Ahom Tai Mongoliya students, 16 January 1968, in *Ahom Andolonor Eitihashik Dalil*, vol. 1 ed. Girin Phukon (Maranhat Assam: Institute of Tai Studies and Research, 2012), 150.
232. Chandan Kumar Sharma, 'The Immigration Issue in Assam and Conflicts Around It', *Asian Ethnicity*, vol. 13, no. 3 (April 2012), 295.
233. Y.B. Chavan, Union Home Minister, 'Disturbances in Assam', *Lok Sabha Debates*, 13 February 1968, column 286.
234. Speech by Balraj Madhok, *Lok Sabha Debates*, 14 February 1964, column 735.
235. Disturbances in Assam, *Lok Sabha Debates*, 13 February 1968, column 286.
236. *Dainik Asam*, 29 January 1968, 1.
237. *Dainik Asam*, 3 February 1968, 1.
238. *Dainik Asam*, 4 February 1968, 1 and 8; Speech by Balraj Madhok, *Lok Sabha Debates*, 14 February 1964, columns 734–38.
239. Speech of Hirendra Nath Mukheree, *Lok Sabha Debates*, 1 March 1968, column 756.
240. Speech of Hirendra Nath Mukerjee, *Lok Sabha Debates*, 14 February 1968, column 753.
241. *Dainik Asam*, 2 February 1968, 1.
242. *Ananda Bazar Patrika*, 11 October 1955. It cited the MHA enquiry committee report.

243. Y.B. Chavan, *Lok Sabha Debates*, 13 February 1968, column 302.
244. *Patriot*, 9 January 1968, in 'Assam Reorganization', Mukherjee, 308.
245. Government of Assam, *Education in Assam: Statistical Handbook, 1947–48 to 1958–59*, (Shillong: Department of Economics and Statistics, 1961), Table 1, 1; Government of Assam, *General Educational Table Relating to Assam, 1942–43* (Shillong: Assam Government Press, 1944), Table 1, 3.
246. Speech by Rabi Rai, *Lok Sabha Debates*, 13 February 1968, column 298.
247. Speech by J.B. Kripalani, *Lok Sabha Debates*, 14 February 1964, column 724.
248. *The Eastern Economist*, 28 July 1968, in *History of the Assamese Movement Since 1947*, D.K. Chattopadhyay (Calcutta: Minerva Associates, 1990), 102.
249. Ibid.
250. Speech of Himatsingka, *Lok Sabha Debates*, 14 February 1968, column 707.
251. Quoted in Speech of H.N. Mukherjee, *Lok Sabha Debates*, 14 February 1968, column 755.
252. On 18 February 1968, the Lok Sabha Speaker admitted a no-confidence motion. Reasons given were amongst others 'the encouragement of aggressive regional movements such as Shiv Sena, Lachit Sena, etc.', *Lok Sabha Debates*, 18 February 1968, columns 212–13.
253. Jnananath Bora, Presidential Address, Annual Conference, Assam Sahitya Sabha, in *Asam Sahitya Sabhar Itihas, (1953–1976)* vol. 2, ed. B. Goswami (Jorhat: Asam Sahitya Sabha, 2018), 306; A. Gogoi, *Asomiya Jatiyatabad* (Guwahati: Banalata Publication, 2018), Appendix II; *Dainik Asam*, 28 January 1968.
254. Quoted in Speech of R. Barua, *Lok Sabha Debates*, 14 February 1968, column 721; Jatin Hazarika, *Shadow Behind the Throne, My Tryst with Assam Administration* (Guwahati: LBS, 2016), 39. Hazarika was Chaliha's principal private secretary.
255. *Times of India*, 3 May 1968, 9.
256. *Dainik Asam*, 1 May 1968, 1.
257. *Times of India*, 11 May 1968, 1.
258. *Times of India*, 18 May 1968, 1 and 9; *Dainik Asam*, 26 May 1968, 1.
259. *Dainik Asam*, 14 May 1968, 1.
260. 'Assam reorganization: Cabinet differences narrow down', *Times of India*, 19 May 1968, 9.
261. *Dainik Asam*, 26 May 1968; *New York Times*, 26 May 1968, 8.
262. *Times of India*, 27 May 1968, 1.
263. *Times of India*, 17 June 1968, 1.
264. 'Minute of Dissent of Jan Sangh in Joint Parliamentary Committee', quoted in Speech of Y.V. Chavan, Union Home Minister, *Lok Sabha Debates*, 24 March 1969, column 335.

265. *Dainik Asam*, 31 August 1968, 1; *Assam Tribune*, 31 August 1968, 1.
266. *Dainik Asam*, 28 August 1968, 1.
267. 'India to Create a New State from Assam Areas', *New York Times*, 12 September 1968, 15; *Dainik Asam*, 12 September 1968, 1; *Times of India*, 12 September 1968, 1; *Times of India*, 26 September 1968, 8.
268. *Times of India*, 26 May 1968, 1.
269. *Times of India*, 27 September 1968, 8.
270. Mukerjee, 'Assam Reorganization', 311.
271. Representatives of the Minorities of Garo Hills Autonomous Councils, *Memorandum to the Home Minister of India*, 1967, Digital Archive, Center for Assamese Studies, Tezpur University.
272. Mukerjee, 'Assam Reorganization', 297–311.
273. Inder Malhotra, *Indira Gandhi: A Personal and Political Biography* (Boston: Northeastern University Press, 1991), Chapter 7.
274. Mukerjee, 'Assam Reorganization', 297.
275. Speech of Hem Barua, *Lok Sabha Debates*, 25 March 1969, column 294.
276. P. Raghunadha Rao, *History of Modern Andhra* (New Delhi: Sterling, 1978).
277. *Times of India*, 11 December 1968, 9.
278. *New York Times*, 26 March 1969, 9; *Times of India*, 26 March 1969, 9.
279. *Times of India*, 16 April 1969, 1.
280. *Times of India*, 25 December 1969, 1.
281. B.K. Nehru, *Nice Guys Finish Second* (New Delhi: Viking, 1997), 588.
282. 'Resume of discussions held by MMHA (Shri K.C. Pant) with representatives of State Governments, political parties, etc. in the north-eastern region, Shillong, MHA, 14–15 September 1970', in *Statehood for Manipur, Tripura, Problems of North-eastern Region*, File no. 10/31/SR, vol. 1, 1970, Government of India, Ministry of Home Affairs, Abhilekh Patal, NAI.
283. Balraj Puri, 'A Case for Sub-States', *Economic & Political Weekly*, vol. 5, no. 50 (12 December 1970), 1989–90.
284. 'Secret Note, Ministry of Home Affairs, GoI, undated', in *Statehood for Manipur, Tripura, Problems of North-eastern Region*.
285. 'Letter from Indira Gandhi to M.M. Chaudhury, no. 1197–PMO/70, New Delhi, 10 November 1970', in *Statehood for Manipur, Tripura, Problems of North-eastern Region*.
286. Resolution Passed by the North Cachar Hills District Council, 70th Session, 22 February 1970; Letter from S. Rongpi, President, Mikir Hills Karbi Darbar to Chief Minister, Assam, 21 January 1970; Memorandum to Mrs Indira Gandhi, Prime Minister of India from D.R. Rongpi, Chief Executive Member, Mikir Hills District Council and others, 6 October 1970 in

*Resolutions of Mikir Hills D.C. and N.C. Hills D.C. against amalgamation with Meghalaya*, File CMS 52/70, 1970, ASA.

287. Longkam Teron, *Mikir Janajati* (Jorhat: Asam Sahitya Sabha, 1961), 26–27.

288. *Sabin Alun*, the Karbi folk epic resembling the Hindu epic *Ramayana*, is an illustrative example of these cultural exchanges. Birendranath Datta, Nabinchandra Sarma and Praphulladutta Goswami, *A Handbook of Folklore Material of North-East India* (Guwahati: ABILAC, 1994), 18.

289. Secret, Resume of Discussion held by Mrs Gandhi, Minister of Home Affairs with the Governor of Assam, Nagaland and Lt. Governors of Manipur and Tripura, 22 November 1970, Appendix, III, *Statehood for Manipur, Tripura and Meghalaya and Connected Problems of North-Eastern Region*.

290. 'Secret Note, Ministry of Home Affairs', *Statehood for Manipur, Tripura, Problems of North-eastern Region*, 7.

291. K.V.R. Iengar, 'The Problem of the Hills Tribes', Letter from K.V.R. Iengar to K.P.S. Menon, ICS, 25 October 1949 in *Burmese Goodwill Mission to Assam: Lushai Delegation of UMFO*, File no. 147–NEF/49, Secret, Ministry of External Affairs, NEF Branch, Abhilekh Patal, NAI; Girin Phukon, ed., *Documents on Ahom Movement in Assam* (Moranhut, Assam: Institute of Tai Studies and Research, 2010).

292. *Dainik Asam*, 11 July 1967, 1; Secret letter from P.K. Mahanta, Superintendent of Police, Special Branch, Assam to Chief Secretary, Assam, 5 June 1972 in *Ujoni Asom Rajya Parisad*, PLA 282/72, 1972 Home Confidential, ASA; Amalendu Guha, 'Little Nationalism Turned Chauvinist: Assam's Anti-Foreigner Upsurge, 1979–80', *Economic & Political Weekly*, vol. 15, no. 41/43 (25 October 1980), 1706.

293. Election Commission of India, *Statistical Report on General Election, 1951 to the Legislative Assembly of Assam* (Delhi: Election Commission of India, 1952), 7; Indivar Deuri, *Janagosthiya Samasya: Ateet, Bartaman, Bhabishyat* (Nalbari: Journal Emporium, 2001), 16.

294. U.N. Dhebar, *Report of the Scheduled Areas and Scheduled Tribes Commission, 1960–1961* (Delhi: Government of India Press, 1961), 110, para 11.29.

295. Charan Nazary, *Dream for Udayachal and the History of the Plains Tribals Council of Assam* (Guwahati: NL Publications, 2011), 68–69; Samar Brahma Choudhury, *Janajatir Tej Kiman Ronga* (Kokrajhar: PTCA, 1968), 6–8.

296. Nazary, *Dream for Udayachal and the History of the Plains Tribals Council of Assam*, 70; *Dainik Asam*, 23 May 1968.

297. Letter from Charan Narzary, General Secretary, PTCA to B.K. Nehru, Governor, Assam, 19 May 1970, Goalpara, in *Resolution of Mikir Hills,*

D.C. and N.C. Hills D.C.; 'PTCA Memorandum to Prime Minister of India, 20 May 1967', in Nazary, *Dream for Udayachal and the History of the Plains Tribals Council of Assam*, 195–214.

298. Point 4, Statement of H.C. Sarin, Defence Secretary, GoI, 'Minutes of the Meeting held in Home Secretary's Room to Consider Proposals Relating to Matters Connected with North-eastern Region in the Context of the Decision to Confer Statehood on Manipur, Tripura and Meghalaya, 21 November 1970', in *Statehood for Manipur, Tripura, Problems of North-eastern Region*, Appendix iv.

299. Opinions of Gaurishankar Bhattacharjee and Dulal Barua, Opposition Leaders in Assam in 'Resume of discussions held by MMHA (Shri K.C. Pant) with representatives of State Governments, political parties, etc. in the north-eastern region, Shillong, MHA, 14–15 September 1970', Para 4, in *Statehood for Manipur, Tripura, Problems of North-eastern Region*.

300. 'Resume of the discussion held by PM and MMHA [Union Minister of Home Affairs] with the governor of Assam and Nagaland and Lt. Governors of Manipur and Tripura on 22 November 1970', in *Statehood for Manipur, Tripura, Problems of North-eastern Region*, Appendix III.

301. Ibid., para. 2; Statement of H.C. Sarin, Defence Secretary, GoI, 'Minutes of the Meeting held in Home Secretary's Room to Consider Proposals Relating to Matters Connected with North-eastern Region in the Context of the Decision to Confer Statehood on Manipur, Tripura and Meghalaya, 21 November 1970', in *Statehood for Manipur, Tripura, Problems of North-eastern Region*, Appendix iv.

302. Quoted in 'Centre Urged Not to Implement NEC Act', *Assam Tribune*, 7 February 1971, 1.

303. Ibid., 555.

304. Anonymous, 'Le Plateau de Meghalaya (Garo-Khasi-Jaintia)', *Nature*, vol. 139, (20 March 1937), 489.

## Chapter 9: Atop a Volcano

1. D. Kumar and M. Desai, eds, *Cambridge Economic History of India*, vol. 2, c. 1757–c. 1970 (Cambridge: Cambridge University Press, 1983), 1021–22; Willem van Schendel, *A History of Bangladesh* (Cambridge: Cambridge University Press, 2009).

2. Anonymous, 'Migration from East Pakistan (1951–1961)', *Economic Weekly* (15 April 1961), 612; Pravin M. Visaria, 'Migration Between India and Pakistan, 1951–61', *Demography*, vol. 6, no. 3 (1969), 323–34.

3. 'An Open Letter from Pitambardeva Goswami to Pandit Jawaharlal Nehru, Prime Minister of India, 26 January 1962', cited in *The Majuli Island: Society, Economy and Culture*, Dambarudhar Nath (New Delhi: Anshah Publishing House, 2009), Appendix XIV, 361–65.
4. *Assam Tribune*, 19 April 1961, quoted in 'Speech of P.C. Barooah', *Lok Sabha Debates*, 5 May 1961, column 15695.
5. Written Question no. 1944, P.C. Barooah, *Lok Sabha Debates*, 5 May 1961, column 15695.
6. Speech by J.N. Hazarika, Parliamentary Secretary to the Minister of External Affairs, *Lok Sabha Debates*, 5 May 1961, column 15695.
7. Quoted in 'Speech by Atal Bihari Vajpayee', *Lok Sabha Debates*, 7 August 1961, column 165.
8. Speech by Atal Bihari Vajpayee, *Lok Sabha Debates*, 7 August 1961, column 165.
9. Speech by Hem Barua, *Lok Sabha Debates*, 7 August 1961, column 167.
10. 'The police continued their drive against illegal entry and overstay of Pakistani nationals in Assam and to stop recurrence in future,' wrote the chief secretary of Assam in January 1962. A.N. Kidwai, chief secretary to the Government of Assam (GoA), 'Fortnightly Report for Assam for the first half of January 1962', secret, in *Daily Situation Report received from CID and SIB: Fortnightly Reports*, File no. CMS/350/61, 1961, Assam State Archives, hereafter ASA.
11. Reply to Written Question no. 179, Lal Bahadur Shastri, *Lok Sabha Debates*, 9 August 1961, column 735.
12. 'The Central Intelligence Bureau have reported that the infiltration of Pakistani nationals into Assam without travel documents is still going on at a fairly high rate', Letter from the Under Secretary to the Government of India, Ministry of Home Affairs, New Delhi to the Chief Secretary to the Government of Assam, Home Department, Miscellaneous Branch, Shillong, No. 1/7/61–F.III, dated 22 March 1961, in *White Paper on Foreigner's Issue* (Home & Political Department, Government of Assam, October 2012), Annexure 3A, 53–55.
13. E.H. Pakyntein, Superintendent of Census Operations, Assam, 'Immigration of Muslims into Assam', Confidential report, 7 September 1961 in *Census of Muslims in Assam: With Special Reference to the Check of Infiltration of Pakistanis into Assam*, File no. PLB 143/62, Home Confidential, 1962, ASA.
14. Debeswar Sarmah, *Pakistani Infiltration into Assam* (Jorhat: Debeswar Sarmah, 1962), in *Census of Muslims in Assam: With Special Reference to the Check of Infiltration of Pakistanis into Assam*, 10.
15. 'Note by Assam Governor, V. Sahay, 4 February 1962', in *Census of Muslims in Assam: With Special Reference to the Check of Infiltration of Pakistanis into Assam.*

16. 'File Note of K. Balachandran, Special Secretary, Government of Assam, 18 May 1962', in *Census of Muslims in Assam: With Special Reference to the Check of Infiltration of Pakistanis into Assam.*
17. 'Note from A.N. Kidwai, Chief Secretary, Government of Assam to Chief Minister, Assam, 20 May 1962', in *Census of Muslims in Assam: With Special Reference to the Check of Infiltration of Pakistanis into Assam.*
18. Reply to Written Question no. 201, D.L. Datar, State Minister, Home, GoI, *Lok Sabha Debates*, 26 April 1962, column 1034.
19. Statement of C.K. Bhattacharyya, *Lok Sabha Debates*, 7 August 1961, column 168; A.B. Vajpayee, ibid, column 165.
20. Speech by Lal Bahadur Shastri, *Lok Sabha Debates*, 6 June 1962, column 9255.
21. *Times of India*, 18 June 1962, 6.
22. Quoted in Prafulla Kumar Mahanta, *The Tussle Between the Citizens and Foreigners in Assam* (Delhi: Vikas Publishing House, 1986), 82.
23. Reply to Written Question no. 436, Statement by Datar, Minister of State, Home Affairs, *Lok Sabha Debates*, 4 May 1962, column 2554; File Notes by P.P. Khanna, Deputy Secretary, Ministry of Home Affairs, GoI to R. Venkataraman, Joint Secretary, Ministry of Home Affairs, GoI, 6 October 1971 in *Resettlement of East-West Pakistan Refugees*, vol. 1, File no. 7/371/1971 PMS, NAI. In 1962, 26 patrol posts were approved, and 180 more police watch posts were approved in 1964, of which 80 posts were established till 1967.
24. Cross reference in File no. 37/1/68–62–BS. II quoted in File Notes by P.P. Khanna, Deputy Secretary, Ministry of Home Affairs, GoI to R. Venkataraman, Joint Secretary, Ministry of Home Affairs, GoI, 6 October 1971, in *Resettlement of East-West Pakistan Refugees*.
25. *New York Times*, 8 December 1963, 21.
26. Quoted in Purna Narayan Singha, 'Illegal Immigrants', Letter to the editor, *Times of India*, 18 July 1963, 6; *Times of India*, 5 September 1962, 6; 'Infiltration of Pakistanis from East Pakistan', B.N. Datar, Answer to Oral Question, 4 September 1962, *Rajya Sabha Debates*, 4750. Also, 'Letter from A.N. Kidwai, Chief Secretary, Government of Assam to V. Viswanathan, Secretary', Ministry of Home Affairs, GoI, D.O. No. PLB. 143/62/22, Shillong, 27 June 1962 in *Census of Muslims in Assam: With Special Reference to the Check of Infiltration of Pakistanis into Assam.*
27. Jacques Nevard, 'Ousted Moslems bitter at Indians; hordes driven to Pakistan charge land is seized', *New York Times*, 8 December 1963, 21.
28. *New York Times*, 5 April 1964.
29. Ibid.

30. *New York Times*, 27 February 1964, 16; *New York Times*, 23 February 1964, 6.
31. *The Times*, 20 January 1964, 8.
32. Thomas F. Brady, 'Moslem-Hindu violence flares again: Mass killings and large-scale migrations increase tensions between India and Pakistan', *New York Times*, 5 April 1964.
33. *Times of India*, 31 January 1964, 9; *Times of India*, 10 September 1964, 6.
34. Indian Commission of Jurists, *Recurrent Exodus of Minorities from East Pakistan and Disturbances in India: A Report to the Indian Commission of Jurists by its Committee of Enquiry* (New Delhi: Indian Commission of Jurists, 1965).
35. *New York Times*, 5 April 1964, Section E, 4.; Indian Commission of Jurists, *Recurrent Exodus of Minorities from East Pakistan and Disturbances in India: A Report to the Indian Commission of Jurists by Its Committee of Enquiry* (New Delhi: Indian Commission of Jurists, 1965).
36. Officially, there were 88,705 such people, of which 82,735 were deported between 1952–61. 'Answer to Starred Question no. 98, Statement by Lal Bahadur Shastri, Union Home Minister', *Rajya Sabha Debates*, 7 August 1962, 320–21.
37. 'Statement of Akhtaruddin Ahmad', *National Assembly of Pakistan Debates*, vol.1, 11 March 1963, 183, in *Indo-Pakistan Relations, 1960–1965*, D.C. Jha (Patna: Bharati Bhawan, 1972), 273.
38. 'Statement of Z.A. Bhutto', 19 June 1962', *National Assembly of Pakistan Debates*, vol. 1, 19 June 1962, 176, in *Indo-Pakistan Relations, 1960–1965*, Jha, 274.
39. Government of India, Ministry of Home Affairs, *Study of the Report of the Commission of Enquiry (Jabbar Commission) on Expulsion of Pakistani Infiltrants from Tripura & Assam, India* (New Delhi: Government of India Press, 1964), Preface.
40. 'Deporting Pakistanis', Nehru's Note for Y.D. Gundevia, Commonwealth Secretary, MEA, 8 August 1962, in *Selected Works of Jawaharlal Nehru* (hereafter *SWJN*), ed. M.K. Palat (New Delhi: Jawaharlal Nehru Memorial Fund, 1984–2019) second series, vol. 78, 121.
41. 'Meeting with Ayub', *SWJN*, second series, vol. 78, 125–26.
42. 'Nehru to Shastri, 12 September 1962', *SWJN*, second series, vol. 78, 126.
43. *Times of India*, 27 April 1963, 7.
44. *Organiser*, vol XVII, 20 April 1962, 2.
45. 'Letter from Nehru to Ayub Khan, 19 March 1964', in *SWJN*, second series, vol. 85, 299.

46. Mohammad Ayub Khan, *Speeches and Statements: Field Marshal Mohammad Ayub Khan, President of Pakistan, July 1963–June 1964*, vol. 6 (Karachi: Pakistan Government Publications, 1964), 179; 'Pakistan Agrees to Talk in India; Nehru in Broadcast Appeals for End of Sects' Strife', *New York Times*, 27 March 1964, 3.
47. 'Indo-Pakistan Home Ministers' Conference, New Delhi, April 7–11, 1964', in *Events and Documents of Indo-Pak Relations*, eds, V. Grover and R. Arora (New Delhi: Deep & Deep Publications, 1999); *Times of India*, 11 April 1964, 1; *Times of India*, 13 April 1964, 6; Gulzarilal Nanda's Statement, *Lok Sabha Debates*, 13 April 1964.
48. 'Joint Communiqué by the Home Ministers of India and Pakistan, 11 April 1964', in *Events and Documents of Indo-Pak Relations*, eds, Grover and Arora.
49. E.A. Pakyntein, *Report on the Census of India, 1961, vol. III, Assam, Part 1–A, General Report* (New Delhi: Manager of Publication, 1964), 143–44.
50. Statement of D.L. Datar, Minister of State for Home Affairs, GoI, *Lok Sabha Debates*, 5 September 1962, column 6325.
51. Malini Sur, 'Battles for the Golden Grain: Paddy Soldiers and the Making of the Northeast India–East Pakistan Border, 1930–1970', *Comparative Studies in Society and History*, vol. 58, no. 3 (2016), 804–32.
52. 'Joint Communique by the Home Ministers of India and Pakistan, 11 April 1964, in *Events and Documents of Indo-Pak Relations*, eds, V. Grover and R. Arora.
53. Oral Answer, J.L. Nehru, *Lok Sabha Debates*, 14 August 1963, column 333.
54. Statement by J.L. Nehru, *Lok Sabha Debates*, 16 December 1963, column 4789.
55. Speech by Hem Barua, *Lok Sabha Debates*, 16 December 1963, column 4789.
56. Oral Answer, J.L. Nehru, *Lok Sabha Debates*, 14 August 1963, column 333.
57. Four Foreigners Tribunals were established early in 1964. Statement of Minister of Home, *Lok Sabha Debates*, 4 March 1964, column 3693.
58. Foreigners (Tribunal) Order, 1964, Government of India, Ministry of Home Affairs Order, New Delhi, 23 September 1964.
59. 'With the constant threat of aggression on the northern border by China, a hostile and aggressive attitude on the west and south by Pakistan and violent activities entailing murder, loot, arson, etc. by the Naga hostiles, the state of Assam has been faced with great danger and its security has been seriously threatened.' Assam Pradesh Congress Committee, 'A Memorandum to Gulzarilal Nanda, Minister of Home Affairs, GoI, 15

March 1964', *Sriman Prafulla Goswami Papers*, (I-III), NMML; *Times of India*, 21 March 1964, 6.
60. 'Assam's security', *Times of India*, 8 July 1964, 8.
61. Ibid.
62. *Times of India*, 1964, 3.
63. *New York Times*, 11 September 1965, 1 and 8. Also, *The Times*, 11 September 1965, 6.
64. *Dainik Asam*, 13 August 1965, 1.
65. R.D. Pradhan, *1965 War, The Inside Story: Defence Minister Y.B. Chavan's Diary of India–Pakistan War* (New Delhi: Atlantic, 2007), 130–37.
66. Arupjyoti Saikia, *The Unquiet River: A Biography of the Brahmaputra* (New Delhi: Oxford University Press, 2019).
67. Confidential Letter from S. Khosla, Deputy Commissioner, Cachar, to Chief Secretary, Government of Assam, 13 October 1966, no. SCCL 3/64/III; Month wise Statement of influx of refugees who entered into Assam from East Pakistan during the period from 1 January to 31 October 1966 with and without migration certificate in *Influx of Refugees from East Pakistan*, PLB 389/66, 1966, ASA; *Dainik Asam*, 1 March 1967, 1.
68. Statement of Bimala Prasad Chaliha, Chief Minister, 9 November 1967, *Assam Legislative Assembly Debates* (hereafter *ALAD*).
69. B.K. Nehru, *Nice Guys Finish Second* (New Delhi: Viking, 1997), 543.
70. Extracts from Secret Demi Official Letter no. F-3/11 from B.K. Nehru, Raj Bhavan, Shillong to V.V. Giri, President, Rashtrapati Bhavan, No. F-3/71, 4 June 1971 in *Resettlement of East-West Pakistan Refugees*.
71. Premakanta Mahanta, *Rajbhaganar Pora Kolthokaloi* (Guwahati: Banalata, 2018 [1993]), 56. Mahanta, a senior Assamese police official, oversaw such works on the north bank.
72. Personal reminiscences of K.P.S. Gill quoted in Nehru, *Nice Guys Finish Second*, 542–43 and Sanjoy Hazarika, *Rites of Passage: Border Crossings, Imagined Homelands, India's East and Bangladesh* (New Delhi: Penguin Books, 2000), 59.
73. *Times of India*, 29 April 1964, 1.
74. 'Extract from the interrogation report of case no. 352 (K)/65 and 353 (K)/65 in respect of both Chawna Ali and Amerjan Bibi' and 'Extract from the case no 63 (B)/66 of Abed Ali' quoted in AASU, *Why National Register of Citizens of 1951 Must Be Used to Detect Foreign Nationals in Assam* (Guwahati: AASU, n.d.). Also, see Diganta Oza, ed., *Asam Andolanar Tathyakosh: Data Book on Assam Agitation*, vol. 2 (Guwahati: Implementation of Assam Accord Department, Government of Assam, 2021), 1140–41.
75. *Times of India*, 15 October 1966, 1.

76. *Bhanbhasa Seikh alias Banbasha and Others Versus the Union of India and Others*, second appeal no. 171 of 1967, Judgement and order, Gauhati High Court, October 6, 1969, Gauhati High Court Record Room. I am thankful to Prarthana Saikia for sharing this document. Amalendu Guha, 'Little Nationalism Turned Chauvinist: Assam's Anti-Foreigner Upsurge, 1979–80', *Economic & Political Weekly*, vol. 15, no. 41/43 (25 October 1980), 1711.
77. *Times of India*, 7 July 1967, 6.
78. *Times of India*, 26 June 1965, 7; *Dainik Asam*, 4 August 1965; *Proceedings of the Meeting of the APCC Executive Committee*, 28 June 1965 quoted in K.N. Deka, 'Assam: The Challenge of Political Integration and Congress Leadership', in *State Politics in India* ed. Iqbal Narain (Meerut: Meenakshi Prakashan, 1976), 34.
79. *Times of India*, 22 April 1965, 1.
80. *Sadiniya Nagarik*, 20 December 1980, 1.
81. Government of India, Ministry of Home Affairs, 1980, quoted in Monirul Hussain, 'The Assam Movement: Class, Ideology, and Identity' (PhD diss., Jawaharlal Nehru University, 1993), 384, Table 6 M10.
82. Srinath Raghavan, *1971: A Global History of the Creation of Bangladesh* (Cambridge, Massachusetts: Harvard University Press, 2013); Onkar Marwah, 'India's Military Intervention in East Pakistan, 1971–1972', *Modern Asian Studies*, vol. 13, no. 4 (1979), 549–80.
83. Sydney H. Schanberg, 'Refugees Worry Indian Officials', *New York Times*, 25 April 1971, 10.
84. Sydney H. Schanberg, 'Three Million Links in a Chain of Misery', *New York Times,* 23 May 1971, 205.
85. *Dainik Asam*, 29 April 1971, 1. One such incident in Lumding, a railway town in central Assam, turned violent.
86. *Times of India*, 22 April 1971, 8.
87. GoI, *Statistical Information Relating to the Influx of Refugees from East Bengal into India till 31st October 1971* (Calcutta: Ministry of Labour and Rehabilitation, Department of Rehabilitation, Branch Secretariat, 1971), Forewords and 63.
88. P.N. Dhar, *Indira Gandhi, the 'Emergency', and Indian Democracy* (New Delhi: Oxford University Press, 2000), 155.
89. 'Letter from President Nixon to Indian Prime Minister Gandhi, 28 May 1971', in https://2001–2009.state.gov/r/pa/ho/frus/nixon/xi/45604.htm (Accessed 26 May 2020); On 13 May 1971, the Indian government requested the United States to make available four C-130 transport aircraft and crews to fly refugees from East Pakistan from the over-burdened state

of Tripura to Assam (Telegram 7325 from New Delhi, 13 May; National Archives, RG 59, Central Files 1970–73, REF PAK). The Department of State responded on the same day that the Indian request was receiving urgent consideration, and the Embassy was instructed to ask to what extent India was planning to use its own transport aircraft to participate in the airlift. *The New York Times*, 19 July 1971, 50.

90. GoI, *Statistical Information Relating to the Influx of Refugees from East Bengal till 31st October 1971*, 63.
91. Ibid., Foreword.
92. 'Letter from Mrs Gandhi to President Nixon, 13 May 1971' in https://2001-2009.state.gov/r/pa/ho/frus/nixon/xi/45604.htm (Accessed 26 May 2020).
93. *Times of India*, 16 May 1971, 12; 'Picture Parade', *Assam Information*, vol. 22, no. 4 (July 1971), 22–25; *Dainik Asam*, 16 May 1971.
94. Raghavan, *1971: A Global History of the Creation of Bangladesh*, 77; Dhar, *Indira Gandhi, the 'Emergency', and Indian Democracy*.
95. Indira Gandhi, 'Tragedy in Bangladesh', New Delhi, December 1971, in *The Great Speeches of Modern India* ed. Rudranghsu Mukherjee (New Delhi: Random House India, 2011).
96. *Times of India*, 23 May 1971, 1 and 9; *Dainik Asam*, 23 May 1971, 1.
97. *Times of India*, 17 May 1971, 1.
98. Letter from P.N. Haksar to S.M. Sikri, Chief Justice of India, 13 May 1971, *P.N. Haksar Papers*, Subject File, 227, NMML.
99. 'Letter from Charan Narzary, General Secretary, PTCA to B.K. Nehru, Governor, Assam, 19 May 1970, Goalpara', in *Resolution of Mikir Hills, D.C and N.C. Hills D.C. Against Amalgamation with Meghalaya*, File no. CMS. 52/70, 1970, ASA.
100. GoI, *Statistical Information Relating to the Influx of Refugees from East Bengal into India till 31$^{st}$ October 1971*, Table 1, 1.
101. 'East Bengal Memorandum, 1971, undated, Ministry of External Affairs, WII/121/54/71, vol II', in *The Blood Telegram: Nixon, Kissinger, and a Forgotten Genocide*, Gary J. Bass (New Delhi: Penguin Random House, 2014), 392, note 7.
102. 'Influx of Refugees: Additional Staff Required for Registration, Security and Law and Order in the States of West Bengal, Assam and Tripura', Secret, Intelligence Bureau, Ministry of Home Affairs, GoI, 20 May 1971, in *Resettlement of East-West Pakistan Refugees*.
103. Bass, *The Blood Telegram: Nixon, Kissinger, and a Forgotten Genocide*, 120.
104. Ibid., 132.

105. P.M.'s Statement on Situation in Bangladesh, 24 May 1971, Press Information Bureau, Government of India, *P.N. Haksar Papers*, Subject file 227, NMML.
106. 'Apparently, Pakistan is trying to solve its internal problems by cutting down the size of its population in East Bengal and changing its communal composition through an organized and selective programme of eviction.' Draft of Mrs Gandhi's letter to her foreign counterparts, prepared by P.N. Haksar, 14 May 1971, in *P.N. Haksar Papers*, Subject file 227, NMML. Several international newspapers including *New York Times* (4 July 1971) and *Sunday Guardian* (13 June 1971) reported this. Dhar, *Indira Gandhi, the 'Emergency', and Indian Democracy*, 174–80.
107. R.C. Smith, *Report on Visit to Tripura, Assam and Meghalaya, 6–9 July 1971*, 'Relief for East Pakistan refugees in India, 1971 (Folder 5)' (Government Papers, The National Archives, Kew, 1971), http://www.archivesdirect.amdigital.co.uk/Documents/Details/DO_133_223 (Accessed 17 June 2021).
108. Dharam Deva, Joint Secretary, *Refugee Statistics, 3 July 1971*, Ministry of External Affairs (Pakistan Affairs) in *Visit to India of Dr Henry A. Kissinger, Assistant to President Nixon for National Security Affairs*, File no. WII 121/54/71, vol. 1, AMS, External Affairs, Abhilekh Patal, NAI.
109. R.C. Smith, *Report on Visit to Tripura, Assam and Meghalaya*, 6–9 July 1971.
110. Secret letter from A.K. Das, Superintendent of Police, Special Branch-III, Shillong to Chief Secretary, Assam, 28 May 1971 in *Reports on Operations*-1971, File no. PLB 85/71, Home Confidential, ASA.
111. See 'India: Hostility Toward the East Pakistani Refugees', 15 June 1971, https://www.cia.gov/library/readingroom/docs/CIA-RDP79T00975A 019300030001-4.pdf
112. *Times of India*, 6 June 1971, 9.
113. *Times of India*, 11 July 1971, 11.
114. *Dainik Asam*, 19 September 1971, 1.
115. *Dainik Asam*, 14 May 1971, 1. Partha N. Mukherji, 'The Great Migration of 1971: II', *Economic & Political Weekly*, vol. 9, no. 10 (9 March 1974), 399, 401, 403 and 405–08.
116. 'It is quite likely that a lot of previously deported may re-infiltrate into Assam.' Secret Letter from Deputy Secretary (P.II,), GoI, Ministry of Home Affairs to the Secretary, GoA, Political Department, June 26, 1971, No. 13/65/71–G & Q, *Resettlement of East-West Pakistan Refugees*.
117. Secret Letter from Joint Secretary, Political Department (B), GoA to Deputy Secretary, GoI, MHA, Delhi, 6 August 1971, No. PIB.143/71/64 in *Resettlement of East-West Pakistan Refugees*.

118. Study Prepared in Response to National Security Study Memorandum 133, Washington, 10 July 1971, National Archives, Nixon Presidential Materials, NSC Files, NSC Institutional Files (H-Files), Box H–058, SRG Meeting, South Asia, 7/23/71. Secret, https://history.state.gov/historicaldocuments/frus1969–76ve07/d140 [Accessed 27 May 2020].

119. Speech of Joseph S. Farland, 'Transcript of Conversation among President Nixon, his Assistant for National Security Affairs (Kissinger), and the Ambassador to Pakistan (Farland), Washington, 28 July 1971', *Foreign Relations of the United States, 1969–1976,* vol. E–7, *Documents on South Asia, 1969–1972,* https://history.state.gov/historicaldocuments/frus1969–76ve07/d141 (Accessed 12 September 2020).

120. 'Refugee Statistics, 2 July 1971, Ministry of External Affairs (Pakistan Affairs)', in *Visit to India of Dr Henry A. Kissinger, Assistant to President Nixon for National Security Affairs.* Assam had 2,69,178 refugees by July 1971. West Bengal had 419 camps in July 1971.

121. United States Senate, *Hearing Before the Subcommittee to Investigate Problems Connected with Refugees and Escapees of the Committee on the Judiciary United States Senate, Ninety Second Congress, Second Session,* 2 February 1972 (Washington: US Government Printing Office, 1972).

122. 'Report on the Visit of Border Areas of Assam, Meghalaya and Tripura 1971', in *The Blood Telegram: Nixon, Kissinger, and a Forgotten Genocide,* Bass, 132.

123. 'Press Release USIS, August 1971', in *Supply of Arms to Pakistan,* MEA.W/II 109/13/71 V, Abhilekh Patal, NAI.

124. Dhar, *Indira Gandhi, the 'Emergency', and Indian Democracy,* 158

125. 'Particulars of Persons who came to India from Bangladesh to be Repatriated to Bangladesh', in File no. PLB 313/71, Home Confidential, part 3, 1971, ASA.

126. P.N. Luthra, 'Problem of Refugees from East Bengal', *Economic & Political Weekly,* vol. 6, no. 50 (11 December 1971), 2467, 2469, 2471–72. On Pakistani military atrocities in Bangladesh, see Nayanika Mookherjee, *The Spectral Wound: Sexual Violence, Public Memories, and the Bangladesh War of 1971* (Durham: Duke University Press, 2015); Sarmila Bose, *Dead Reckoning: Memories of the 1971 Bangladesh War* (London: C. Hurst, 2011); Salil Tripathi, *The Colonel Who Would Not Repent: The Bangladesh War and Its Unquiet Legacy* (New Haven: Yale University Press, 2016.); Jahanaraa Imāma, *Ekāttarera Dinaguli* (Dhaka: Sandhānī Prakāśanī, 1986); Yasmin Saikia, *Women, War, and the Making of Bangladesh: Remembering 1971* (Durham, NC: Duke University Press, 2011).

127. 'Influx of Refugees: Additional Staff Required for Registration, Security and Law and Order in the States of West Bengal, Assam and Tripura', Secret,

Intelligence Bureau, Ministry of Home Affairs, GoI, 20 May 1971, in *Resettlement of East-West Pakistan Refugees*.
128. Sangeeta Barooah Pisharoty, *Assam: The Accord, The Discord* (Gurgaon: Penguin Ebury Press, 2019), 40–41.
129. Birendra Kumar Bhattacharya, 'Sheikh Mujiburor Joy Jatrya' (The victory march of Sheikh Mujibur), *Dainik Asam*, 2 April 1971, 4.
130. *Dainik Asam*, 4 April 1971, 1.
131. *Hindustan Standard*, 29 March 1971; *Dainik Asam*, 15 May 1971, 2.
132. *Dainik Asam*, 2 and 3 April 1971.
133. *Dainik Asam*, 1 April 1971, 1.
134. For instance, Telegram from Bangladesh Tran Committee, Karimganj to Prime Minister, India, 25 May 1971; West Bengal Economic Development Council, 'A Memorandum on the Present Bangla Desh Evacuee Problem, 5 June 1971', in *Reports on Operations-1971,* File no. PLB 85/71, Home Confidential, ASA.
135. *Dainik Asam*, 2 April 1971, 1.
136. Telegram from Islamabad to FCO, 2 April 1971, no. 456 in 'Situation between India and Pakistan, 1971 (Folder 1)' (Government Papers, The National Archives, Kew, 1971), http://www.archivesdirect.amdigital.co.uk/Documents/Details/DO_133_201 (Accessed 17 June 2021).
137. Statement of Indira Gandhi, *Lok Sabha Debates*, 2 June 1971; *Times of India*, 23 May 1971, 1; *Jugantar*, 16 May, 26 May, 31 May and 3 June 1971.
138. 'Situation in East Pakistan' from P.N. Goswami, Superintendent of Police, SB, II, Shillong, to Chief Secretary, Assam, 19 August 1971 in *Reports on Operations-1971,* File no. PLB 85/71, Home Confidential, ASA; *Times of India*, 3 June 1971, 1.
139. Barun Das Gupta, 'Memories of Bangladesh Liberation War', *Mainstream*, vol. L, no. 1 (24 December 2011).
140. Marwah, 'India's Military Intervention in East Pakistan, 1971–1972', 566.
141. J.P. Mitter, Strictly Confidential Note to P.N. Haksar, *P.N. Haksar Papers*, Subject File no. 229, NMML.
142. Ibid.
143. Ibid. Also, see Layli Uddin, 'In the Land of Eternal Eid: Maulana Bhashani and the Political Mobilisation of Peasants and Lower-Class Urban Workers in East Pakistan, c. 1930s–1971' (PhD diss., Royal Holloway, University of London, 2015).
144. *Indian Express*, 3 December 1972, 7 and 19 December 1972, 8.
145. Smith, *Report on Visit to Tripura, Assam and Meghalaya*.
146. *New York Times*, 25 April 1971, 10.

147. V.P. Dutt, *India, Pakistan and Bangladesh—The Next* Step, 23 June 1971, quoted in *P.N. Haksar Papers*, Subject File 229, NMML.
148. Letter from D.P. Dhar to P.N. Haksar, undated, in *P.N. Haksar Papers*, Subject File 91, NMML.
149. *Times of India*, 11 July 1971, 11.
150. I.G. Patel, *Glimpses of Indian Economic Policy: An Insider's View* (New Delhi: Oxford University Press, 2002), 145–46.
151. *Time Magazine*, 1 January 1973.
152. *Times of India*, 9 February 1972; Satish Kumar, ed., *Documents on India's Foreign Policy* 1972 (New Delhi: Macmillan, 1975), 213; *Political Notes prepared by the Ministry of External Affairs*, File no. HI/121 (2)72, External Affairs, 1972, Abhilekh Patal, NAI.
153. 'Treaty of Peace and Friendship between the Government of India and the Government of the People's Republic of Bangladesh, 19 March 1972', http://mea.gov.in/bilateral-documents.htm?dtl/5621/ Treaty+of+Peace+and+Friendship (Accessed 1 August 2021).
154. Letter from D.R. Das, Under Secretary, Government of Assam, Political Department (B) to Deputy Secretary, Government of India, Ministry of Home Affairs, Shillong, 22 May 1972 in Government of Assam, *Note on Influx of Refugees from East Bengal into Assam in 1971*, Shillong, 9 July 1971, File PLB/313/71/part, Home Confidential, ASA. 'A considerable number were living with friends & relatives in the interiors and hence is taking time to contact and repatriate them', Letter from P.K. Mahanta, Superintendent of Police, Special Branch, (II), Assam to D.R. Das, Under Secretary, Government of Assam, Political Department (B), 16 May 1972, no. SB. VI/5/410/71/193', in *Note on Influx of Refugees from East Bengal into Assam* in 1971.
155. *Times of India*, 11 June 1975, 10.
156. 'Calling attention to a matter of urgent public importance: Reported recent influx of refugees from Bangladesh into the eastern parts of the country', Speech of Bipinpal Das, Deputy Minister, Ministry of External Affairs, *Rajya Sabha Debates*, 9 May 1975, columns 153–54.
157. *Washington Post*, 29 May 1973, 1, A1.
158. *The Times*, 21 September 1974, 6.
159. *Times of India*, 17 May 1975, 5.
160. A. Sen, *Poverty and Famines: An Essay on Entitlement and Deprivation* (Oxford: Clarendon, 1982); *Times of India*, 5 April 1975, 6; *Times of India*, 15 April 1975, 7; *Dainik Asam*, 1 April 1975, 4.
161. 'Letter from R.A. Mani, Deputy Secretary, Ministry of Home Affairs, Government of India to All State Governments and Union Territory Administrations, 20 August 1975, New Delhi, o.1/ 4011/16 6/75–F.III',

in *Asam Andolonar Tathyakosh: Data Book on Assam Agitation*, vol. 2, ed. Oza, 1074; *Times of India*, 17 May 1975, 5.
162. *The Times*, 8 April 1975, 5.
163. *Dainik Asam*, 22 March 1975, 1 and 4.
164. Quoted in the *New York Times*, 7 November 1974, 12.
165. Association of Voluntary Agencies for Rural Development, *Rehabilitation of Refugees in Angarkata Area, West Kumarikata, Kamrup, Assam* (New Delhi: AAVARD, 1978).
166. Secret Note, N.F. Suntook, Joint Secretary, Cabinet Secretariat, Research and Analysis Wing, 2 January 1976, *Notes from G.S. Misra (Cabinet Secretariat) and of papers on Bangladesh received from Secretary Mr K.R. Narayanan*, File no. PP (JS) 4 (4)/75, P.P. & R Branch, External Affairs, Abhilekh Patal, NAI.
167. Secret Letter from Joint Secretary, Ministry of Home Affairs, GoI to the Chief Secretaries of West Bengal, Assam and Tripura, Meghalaya and Mizoram, 20 December 1975, no 9/18/75–G & Q, *Notes from G.S. Misra (Cabinet Secretariat) and of Papers on Bangladesh received from Secretary Mr K.R. Narayanan*.
168. *The Hindu*, 11 November 1978, 1.
169. See Anonymous, 'Long March by Bihari Pakistanis Stranded in Bangladesh Fizzles out', *India Today*, 15 September 1979.
170. *Organiser*, 21 November 1979, 16, in *The Hindu Nationalist Movement and Indian Politics: 1925 to the 1990s*, Christopher Jaffrelot (New York: Columbia University Press, 1998), 343.
171. 'President's rule in Assam demanded: Jan Sangh resolution on checking Pak infiltration', *Times of India*, 12 August 1963, 7.
172. The Union home minister, Gulzarilal Nanda, speaking in a largely attended public meeting of the Muslim peasants in central Assam, asked the recent migrants to leave Assam. 'No Mercy Will Be Shown to Illegal Infiltrants: Nanda Says It Is Better "To Quit with Grace"', *Times of India*, 19 March 1964, 3. Several years before, Jawaharlal Nehru also signalled that the refugees from East Pakistan must leave India; 'Future Migrants from East Pakistan: "Final Decision Necessary"', *Times of India*, 14 November 1957, 7.
173. Hazarika, *Rites of Passage: Border Crossings, Imagined Homelands, India's East and Bangladesh*; van Schendel, *A History of Bangladesh*, 227.

## Chapter 10: The Battle Continues

1. Government of Assam, *Assam Information,* vol. XIX, no. 1 (April 1968), 19. In 1960, Assam had 2260 kilometres of embankments. By 1978, Assam had

a total 4145 kilometres of embankments, which was 38 per cent of the entire length of the embankments in India. Government of Assam, *Report of the Embankment and Drainage Projects Reviewing Committee, Assam* (Shillong: Department of Public Works, 1960), 25; Government of India, *Report: National Commission on Floods*, vol. 1 (New Delhi: Ministry of Energy and Irrigation, 1980), 108; 'To Review the Flood Control Measures taken up in this State and Assess its Results So Far Obtained', in *First Meeting of Assam Flood Control Board*, File no. DWV-502(6)/63, 1963, Ministry of Water Resources, GoI, Ministry of Water Resources Abhilekh Patal, NAI; Arupjyoti Saikia, *The Unquiet River: A Biography of the Brahmaputra* (New Delhi: Oxford University Press, 2019), Chapter 12.
2. *Times of India*, 20 April 1969, II.
3. Deepak Nayyar, 'Industrial Development in India: Some Reflections on Growth and Stagnation', *Economic & Political Weekly*, vol. 13, no. 31/33 (1978), 1265–78; Sudeep Chaudhuri and Niloy Mukhopadhyay, 'Of Stagnation and Collaboration', *Economic & Political Weekly*, vol. 13, no. 3 (1978), 93–96.
4. National Council of Applied Economic Research, *Techno-Economic Survey of Assam* (New Delhi: National Council of Applied Economic Research, 1962), 97.
5. US Department of the Interior, *Minerals Yearbook, 1969*, vol. 4, *Areas Reports, International* (Washington: US Government Printing Press, 1971), 362.
6. *Times of India*, 18 June 1969, 8.
7. *Times of India*, 7 April 1969, 9.
8. 'Note for Minister, Industries, 25 November 1966', in *Second Refinery in Assam*, CMS, 202/66, 1966, ASA; Sibasagar Jila Tel-Sodhanagar Andolon Samiti, *Sibasagar Jila Tel Sodhanagar Abhibortanor Prastabsamuh* (Sibasagar: Sibasagar Jila Tel-Sodhanagar Andolon Samiti, May 1966), *Second Refinery in Assam*, File no. CMS, 202/66, 1966, ASA.
9. *Times of India*, 25 March 1969, 11.
10. Statement of Ashok Mehta, Minister, Petroleum and Chemicals, *Lok Sabha Debates*, 22 April 1968, column 2124.
11. Dev Kanta Borooah, 'Achievement and Prospects of Oil India in Oil Industry', *Monthly Commentary on Indian Economic Conditions*, vol. 10 (1968), 29–31.
12. *Dainik Asam*, 25 March 1969, 1; *Jugantar*, 25 March 1969.
13. *Dainik Asam*, 25 March 1969, 1; *Times of India*, 25 March 1969, 11; Indira Gandhi, *The Years of Endeavour: Selected Speeches of Indira Gandhi, August 1969–August 1972* (New Delhi: Publications Division, Government of India, 1975), 255.

14. *Times of India*, 12 July 1970, 1.
15. *Dainik Asam*, 5 September 1969, 1; *Dainik Asam*, 11 September 1969, 1.
16. Statement of Triguna Sen, Union Minister of Petroleum, Chemicals and Minerals, *Lok Sabha Debates*, 4 August 1969, column 41.
17. *Times of India*, 20 September 1969, 7; *Times of India*, 16 September 1969, 1; see also *Dainik Asam*, 15, 16, 19, 24, 27 and 30 September 1969.
18. *Times of India*, 22 October 1969, 5.
19. *Times of India*, 24 October 1969, 1 and 14; Gandhi, *The Years of Endeavour: Selected Speeches of Indira Gandhi, August 1969–August 1972*, 254.
20. *Times of India*, 18 October 1969, 7.
21. Gandhi, *The Years of Endeavour: Selected Speeches of Indira Gandhi, August 1969–August 1972*, 255; Statement Regarding Economic Development of Assam, *Lok Sabha Debates*, 5 December 1969, columns 326–27.
22. Speech of R. Barua, *Lok Sabha Debates*, 8 April 1970, column 33.
23. Selected State-wise Production of Crude Oil in India (1970–71, 1975–76, 1980–81, 1985–86 and 1990–91 to 2019–20–up to May 2019) in https://www.indiastat.com/petroleum-data/25/petroleum-production/229/crude-oil-production/379574/stats.aspx (Accessed 10 July 2020).
24. Statement of Raghu Ramaiah, Minister of State, Petroleum and Chemicals, GoI, *Lok Sabha Debates*, 26 August 1968, columns 1545–46.
25. *The Times*, 30 July 1971, 21, col. E.
26. For a short account of the GoI's economic and business policies during Indira Gandhi's regime, see D. Tripathi, *The Concise Oxford History of Indian Business* (New Delhi: Oxford University Press, 2007), 199–200.
27. Due to the new oil exploration and production programme from 1975 onwards, India's oil energy balance stood at 1/3rd import and 2/3rd domestic by 1987. See Ashok Parthasarathi, 'Science and its Applications to Societal Security', *Current Science*, vol. 87, no. 9 (November 2004), 1174–75.
28. For Congress split and Gandhi, see Inder Malhotra, *Indira Gandhi: A Personal and Political Biography* (Boston: Northeastern University Press, 1991), 123–27; Monirul Hussain, 'High Caste to Non-Caste Dominance: The Changing Pattern of Leadership of the Congress Party in Assam', *Indian Journal of Political Science*, vol. 49, no. 3 (1988), 406–07.
29. *Times of India*, 25 August 1970, 1.
30. *Times of India*, 5 September 1970, 7; *Dainik Asam*, 5 September 1970; *Assam Tribune*, 5 September 1970.
31. *Times of India*, 3 October 1970, 1.
32. *Times of India*, 12 October 1970, 1; *Times of India*, 13 October 1970, 1.

33. Satish Chandra Kakakti, 'Mahendramohan Chaudhurir Rajniti', in *Mahendramohan Choudhury,* eds, S. Kakakti, Indira Miri and Ram Goswami (Guwahati: Publication Board, Assam 1984), 57–68.
34. Anonymous, 'After Chaliha in Assam', *Economic & Political Weekly*, vol. 5, no. 45 (November 1970), 1795–96.
35. Secret, Materials for Governor's and Finance Minister's Budget Speech for the year 1972, in File PLB 313/71/part 1972, Home Confidential, ASA; *Times of India*, 9 February 1971, 11; *Assam Tribune*, 24 February 1971, 1.
36. Quoted in Note Prepared by K.S. Puri, Deputy Secretary, NE, 19 June 1972, Ministry of Home Affairs (North-Eastern cell), Secret, para 3, *Foreign Involvement in Insurgency in North Eastern India: Preparation of White Paper on the subject by the Ministry of Defence*, File no. N.II/102 (33) 72, Naga Section, Ministry of Home Affairs, GoI, 1972, Abhilekh Patal, NAI.
37. Ibid.
38. Nirmal Nibedon, *Nagaland: The Night of the Guerrillas* (New Delhi: Lancer Publisher, 1978); Jelle Wouters, *In the Shadows of Naga Insurgency* (New Delhi: Oxford University Press, 2018); Y.D. Gundevia, *War and Peace in Nagaland* (Dehradun: Palit and Palit, 1975); S.C. Dev, *Nagaland: The Untold Story* (Calcutta: Gouri Devi, 1988).
39. Dolly Kikon, *Living with Oil and Coal: Resource Politics and Militarization in Northeast India* (Washington: Washington University Press, 2019).
40. *Dainik Asam*, 29 December 1971, 1; *Dainik Asam*, 30 December 1971, 1; *Dainik Asam*, 31 December 1971, 1; *Assam Tribune*, 30 January 1972, 1; Norman D. Palmer, 'Elections and the Political System in India: The 1972 State Assembly Elections and After', *Pacific Affairs*, vol. 45, no. 4 (1972), 535–55.
41. K.M. Sharma, 'The Assam Question: A Historical Perspective', *Economic & Political Weekly*, vol. 15, no. 31 (1980), 1323. Hussain, 'High Caste to Non-Caste Dominance: The Changing Pattern of Leadership of the Congress Party in Assam', 407.
42. Sharma, 'The Assam Question: A Historical Perspective', 1323. Satish Chandra Kakati, *Smriti Bichitra* (Guwahati: Sahitya Prakash, 1992), 174–75.
43. M.M. Choudhury resigned as the chief minister of Assam on 29 January in New Delhi. There were at least two major contenders for the post of chief minister: Dev Kanta Borooah and M.H. Choudhury. The latter was considered an important voice of Assam's religious-linguistic minorities. On 4 January 1972, the Congress party dissolved the Assam PCC and formed an ad hoc Pradesh Congress Committee and clipped Choudhury's

power. Most members of the PCC belonged to a camp headed by S.C. Sinha, the new ad hoc president. The Pradesh Election Committee, tasked with the selection of candidates for the state assembly election in 1972 was also full of Sinha's nominees. *Times of India*, 30 January 1972, 1; *Times of India*, 5 January 1972, 11; Sharma, 'The Assam Question: A Historical Perspective', 1323.

44. Umananda Phukan, *Agricultural Development in Assam, 1950–1985* (New Delhi: Mittal Publications, 1990), Table 3.2, 28; Indreswar Talukdar, 'Letter to the Editor', *Natun Prithivi* (February 1973) in *Natun Prithivi: A Compilation of Quarterly Journal Natun Prithivi*, ed. Mukut Bhattacharjya, vol. 1 (Guwahati: Reception Committee, 15th biennial conference, Natun Prithivi, 2014), 750–51.
45. *Times of India*, 8 June 1973, 9.
46. Sanghamitra Choudhury, 'The Railway Workers Strike of 1974: Impact in the Eastern and North East Frontier Railway Zones' (PhD diss., North Bengal University, 2019).
47. *New York Times*, 4 August 1972, 11; G. Sara Lyndem, 'Performance of Public Sector Undertakings in Meghalaya' (PhD diss., North-Eastern Hill University, 1990), 43–45.
48. Sharma, 'The Assam Question: A Historical Perspective', 1323. The actual figure was, however, higher than what had been reported in the previous censuses of 1951 and 1961. Amlan Barua and S.B. Roy Choudhury, eds, *Assam State Gazetteer*, vol. 1 (Guwahati: Government of Assam, 1999), 261.
49. 'Minutes of the first executive committee report, Asam Sahitya Sabha, Guwahati, 30 May 1971', in *Asam Sahitya Sabha Patrika*, vol. 28, no. 2 (1971), 72.
50. Ibid.; *Jugantar*, 14 June 1972, 4.
51. *Jugantar*, 15 June 1972, 4.
52. *Times of India*, 15 September 1972, 3.
53. 'When the people of Cachar presented their apprehension to the Government, we informally suggested to the University authorities the need to reconsider their earlier decision in keeping with the spirit of the relevant provisions in the Assam Official Language Act', Letter from Sarat Chandra Sinha, Chief Minister, Assam to K.C. Pant, Union Minister, Home Affairs, State, Shillong, 23 June 1972, *Gauhati University*, File no. CMS 39/72, ASA.
54. 'Letter from Sarat Chandra Sinha, Chief Minister, Assam to K.C. Pant, Union Minister, Home Affairs, State, Shillong, 23 June 1972', *Gauhati University*, File no. CMS 39/72, ASA.
55. Ibid.

56. *Dainik Asam*, 13 June 1972, 1; Kamrupee, 'Cool behind the Noise and Fury', *Economic & Political Weekly* 7, no. 31/33 (August 1972), 1485–88.
57. *Dainik Asam*, 14 June 1972, 4.
58. *Dainik Asam*, 3 June 1972, 6. The CPI's proposal to continue English as the language of instruction was only for Cachar.
59. See, for instance, 'Minutes of Meeting held at Hojai Abdul Hasib High School', Nagaon on 23 June 1972, *Gauhati University*, File no. CMS 39/72, ASA.
60. 'Letter from M.R. Bhattacharjee, Cachar, to Vice-Chancellor Gauhati University, 6 July 1972', *Gauhati University*, File no. CMS 39/72, ASA.
61. See, for instance, 'Resolution of the Coordination Committee of the District Aided High School Teachers' Association of Silchar, Hailakandi and Karimganj, 25 July 1972', *Gauhati University*, File no. CMS 39/72, ASA.
62. *Dainik Asam*, 27 October 1972, 1; *Dainik Asam*, 28 October 1972, 1; *Hindustan Standard*, 4 July 1972; *Times of India*, 27 October 1972.
63. *Dainik Asam*, 29 October 1972, 1, 6.
64. 'Resolution of Assam Chah Majdur Sangha', 2 November 1972, *Gauhati University*, File no. CMS 39/72, ASA.
65. R.B. Vaghaiwalla, *Report of the Census of India, 1951*, vol. XII, Assam, Manipur and Tripura, Part 1–A (Shillong: Superintendent of Census Operations, 1954).
66. 'Minutes of a Meeting of the Guardians and General Public, 6 September 1972, Vidyapith High School, Kokrajhar', *Gauhati University*, File no. CMS 39/72, ASA.
67. Statement of B.K. Daschowdhury, *Lok Sabha Debates*, 29 November 1972, column 255.
68. 'Letter from Amal Kumar Mandal, Biswanath Das, Babul Das, Tapan Das, Harendra Chandra Bose, and Probodh Chakravarty to Chief Minister, Assam, 24 July 1972', *Gauhati University*, File no. CMS 39/72, ASA; 'Letter from Pandu College Students to the Secretary, Pandu College Governing Body', *Gauhati University*, File no. CMS 39/72, ASA.
69. Uddipan Dutta, 'The Role of Language Management and Language Conflict in the Transition of Post-Colonial Assamese Identity' (PhD diss., Gauhati University, 2012), 116.
70. 'Letter from S.C. Sinha to Nurul Hasan, Union Minister of Education, GoI, 18 September 1972, New Delhi', *Gauhati University*, File no. CMS 39/72, ASA.
71. *Dainik Asam*, 24 October 1972, 1, 2.
72. 'Letter from Sarat Chandra Sinha to Indira Gandhi, 6 October 1972', *Gauhati University*, File no. CMS 39/72, ASA; 'Press Release, Assam

Pradesh Congress Committee, September 29', 1972, *Gauhati University*, File no. CMS 39/72, ASA.
73. 'Resolution of 3rd session of Executive Committee of the Asam Sahitya Sabha, September 25, 1972', Letter from Jatindra Nath Goswami, General Secretary, Asam Sahitya Sabha to Chief Minister, Assam, 30 September 1972, *Gauhati University*, File no. CMS 39/72, ASA. 'Letter from Prasanna Narayan Choudhury, General Secretary, Post-Graduate Students' Union, Gauhati University to Members of Academic Council, Gauhati University, 3 June 1972', *Gauhati University*, File no. CMS 39/72, ASA. 'Telegram from DC, Nagaon to Principal Private Secretary to CM, 29 September 1972', *Gauhati University*, File no. CMS 39/72, ASA; *Dainik Asam*, 1 October 1972, 1.
74. *Dainik Asam*, 4 October 1972, 1; *Times of India*, 6 October 1972, 5; *Times of India*, 7 October 1972, 1.
75. *Indian Express*, 7 October 1972, 1; *Indian Express*, 8 October 1972, 1; *Indian Express*, 9 October 1972, 1
76. Officially, 33 people died. Dutta, 'The Role of Language Management and Language Conflict in the Transition of Post-Colonial Assamese Identity', 121.
77. *Indian Express*, 13 October 1972, 1
78. *Times of India*, 9 October 1972, 1; *Times of India*, 15 October 1972, 1.
79. *Jugantar*, 25 October 1972, 5.
80. 'Bhashani's demand for "Greater Bengal"', *Times of India*, 31 October 1972, 9.
81. 'Situation tense in Jorhat', *Times of India*, 29 October 1972, 7.
82. Elu Devi Barua, *Karagarar Diary* (Guwahati: Puthi Prakash, 2001), 90–100.
83. *Dainik Asam*, 30 October 1972, 1.
84. *Times of India*, 13 November 1972, 1.
85. *Assam Tribune*, 12 November 1972, 1.
86. *Dainik Asam*, 1 October 1972, 1, 6.
87. J.K. Basumatary, President, Kokrajhar District Bodo Sahitya Sabha, 'Statement on the Present Crisis of Kokrajhar College, 24 August 1972', in, *Gauhati University*, File no. CMS 39/72, ASA.
88. Speech of Tarun Gogoi, *Lok Sabha Debates*, 29 November 1972, column 222.
89. Speech of Frank Anthony, *Lok Sabha Debates*, 28 November 1972, column 279.
90. Speech of Indrajit Gupta, *Lok Sabha Debates*, 28 November 1972, column 287.
91. Pranab Kumar Bora and Ashok Kumar Saikia, 'Not Chauvinistic: Letter to the Editor', *Times of India*, 5 December 1972, 8. Both these students of D.V. College became IAS officers.
92. *Times of India*, 24 November 1972, 11.

93. This official committee consisted of senior officials of the Assam government: S.K. Mallick et al., 'Report on Site for the New Capital for the State of Assam', in *Central Assistance for Construction of New Capital of Assam, Home Affairs*, File no. 11/9/71–SR, Abhilekh Patal, NAI.
94. Confidential letter from M.M. Choudhury, Chief Minister, Assam to the Prime Minister, India, 24 June 1971, CMS 71/71, *Central Assistance for Construction of New Capital of Assam, Home Affairs,* File no. 11/9/71–SR, Abhilekh Patal, NAI.
95. Parameswar Sarma, 'Gauhati and Its Environs: A Peep Through the Ages', *Assam Quarterly*, vol. 1, no. 1 (January 1961), 5.
96. Z.D. Ansari and M.K Dhavalikar, 'Excavations at Ambari, Guwahati: 1970', in *Ambari Archaeological Site: An Interim Report*, ed. H.N. Dutta (Guwahati: Directorate of Archaeology, Assam, 2006), 13–17.
97. *Times of India*, 26 February 1973, 6.
98. 'Assam Cong[ress] divided on capital issue', *Times of India*, 18 July 1972, 9.
99. S.R. Deshpande, *Report on an Enquiry into Family Budgets of Industrial Workers in Gauhati* (Delhi: Manager of Publications, 1947), 1.
100. Hem Barua, 'Guwahati: 1944', in *Hem Baruar Kabita*, Hem Barua (Guwahati: Anwesha, 2014 [1945]), 126–28.
101. D.B. Chhetry, *Census of India, 1971, Series 3, Assam, Part VI-B, Special Survey Report on Selected Towns, Gauhati* (Delhi: Manager of Publications, 1978), 2.
102. Town and Country Planning Department, Government of Assam, 'Master Plan and Zoning Regulation for Greater Guwahati', *The Assam Gazette (Extraordinary)*, 30 April 1965; Town and Country Planning Department, Government of Assam, 'Modified Final Master Plan and Zoning Regulations for Guwahati', *The Assam Gazette (Extraordinary)* 24 December 1986; A. Das, 'An Evaluation of Guwahati Master Plan: A Sad Story of Missed Opportunities', in *Urban Planning in India*, Amiya Kumar Das (Delhi: Rawat Publications, 2007), 172–86.
103. M.S. Prabhakara, 'Visitations', *Economic & Political Weekly*, vol. 10, no. 8 (22 February 1975), 349 and 351.
104. Ibid., 351. Also, Jugal Das, 'Tahanir Guwahati', *Samjna*, vol. 2, no. 3 (September–October–November 1976), 117–24; Saurabh Kumar Chaliha, 'Sampadakoloi Chithi', in *Saurabh Kumar Chaliha Rachanawali*, eds, Shoneet Bijoy Das and Munin Bayan (Guwahati: Katha Publications, 2008), 557–60.
105. Anonymous, 'Gauhati Gets a Facelift', *Economic & Political Weekly*, vol. 11, no. 47 (November 1976), 1818–19.
106. Sunil Sethi. 'AICC Session Turns Gauhati Flat Land into Miniature Township', *India Today*, 15 December 1976.

107. Krishna Bharadwaj, 'Regional Differentiation in India: A Note', *Economic & Political Weekly*, vol. 17, no. 14/16 (1982), 605–14.
108. Ibid., Table 4–c, 611.
109. 'Letter from S.A. Sabavala, Resident Director, Tata Industries Private Ltd. to Indira Gandhi, 30 July 1973', in *JRD Tata Correspondence*, File no. 38/87/73–PMS, Abhilekh Patal, NAI.
110. *Times of India*, 7 August 1971, 6.
111. Editorial, 'Disappointment in Oil', *Assam Tribune*, 27 August 1974, 4.
112. J.C. Jhuraney, 'Spatial Changes in the Distribution of Employment in the Organised Sector', *Indian Journal of Industrial Relations*, vol. 12, no. 1 (1976), 61–72.
113. T. Misra, 'Assam: A Colonial Hinterland', *Economic & Political Weekly*, vol. 15, no. 32 (9 August 1980), 1357–59 and 1361–64.
114. As an example of this political narrative, see Parag Das, *Swadhin Asomor Arthoniti: Views on Assam Economy in the Light of the Demand for Right to Self Determination as per Provisions of the UN* (Guwahati: Aalibat, 2018 [1995]. On Parag Das's political and economic thoughts, see Sanjib Baruah, *In the Name of Nation: India and Its Northeast* (Stanford: Stanford University Press, 2020), 181.
115. Khorshed Alam, 'The Economic Development of Assam since Independence: An Analytical Study' (PhD diss., Gauhati University, 1974), Appendix II, Table 9, 790.
116. *Draft Outline of the Fifth Five-Year Plan for Assam, 1973*, in 'Visitations', Prabhakar, 349.
117. *Times of India*, 29 March 1974, 4.
118. V.M. Dandekar and Nilakantha Rath, 'Poverty in India - I: Dimensions and Trends', *Economic & Political Weekly*, vol. 6, no. 1 (2 January 1971), 25–27, 29–48, Table 1.5.
119. *Draft Outline of the Fifth Five-Year Plan for Assam*, vol. 1, in 'Visitations', Prabhakar, 349.
120. Anonymous, 'Highlights of Assam's Progress during 1970–71', *Assam Information*, vol. 22, no. 4 (July 1971), 5.
121. Prabhu Chawla, 'Economically, Seven North-Eastern States of India Present a Sorry Figure', *India Today*. 29 February 1980.
122. Government of Assam, *Economic Survey, Assam, 1980–81* (Guwahati: Directorate of Economics and Statistics, 1981), Table 12.16.
123. Chawla, 'Economically, Seven North-Eastern States of India Present a Sorry Figure'.
124. Government of Assam, *Economic Survey, Assam, 1980–81* (Guwahati: Directorate of Economics and Statistics, 1981), Table 9.1.

125. Government of Assam, *Economic Survey, Assam 1974–75* (Guwahati: Directorate of Economics and Statistics, 1975), Table 13.10, 56.
126. Government of India, *Reports of the Agricultural Prices Commission on Price Policy for Crops Sown in 1982–83 Season* (New Delhi: Commission for Agricultural Costs and Prices, 1983), Table 1.2, 89.
127. Government of India, *Reports of the Commission for Agricultural Costs and Prices on Price Policy for Crops Sown in 1987–88 Season* (New Delhi: Commission for Agricultural Costs and Prices, 1988), 135.
128. Charan Narzary, *Dream for Udayachal and the History of the Plains Tribals Council of Assam* (Guwahati: NL Publications, 2011), 95; *Dainik Asam*, 9 December 1972, 1; 'Stir in Assam for Udayachal', *Times of India*, 10 December 1972, 1.
129. *Indian Express*, 3 December 1972, 1.
130. Ibid.
131. *Times of India*, 10 December 1972, 1.
132. K.S. Dey, *General Report: Census of India 1971, Assam*, series 3, Part I-A (New Delhi: Manager of Publications, 1979), Table IX.3, 99.
133. M.S. Prabhakara, 'The Politics of a Script: Demand for Acceptance of Roman Script for Bodo Language', *Economic & Political Weekly*, vol. 9, no. 51 (21 December 1974), 2097, 2099–2102.
134. Sidney Endle, *Outline Grammar of the Kachári (Bārā) Language as Spoken in District Darrang, Assam. With Illustrative Sentences, Notes, Reading Lessons, and a Short Vocabulary* (Shillong: Assam Secretariat Press, 1884).
135. The Assam Missionaries of the American Baptist Missionary Union, *Minutes, Resolutions and Historical Reports of the Third Triennial Conference, 14–22 January Tura, 1893* (Calcutta: Baptist Mission Press, 1893), 27. Similar support came from the Assam government and Welsh missionaries too. Government of Assam, *Report on the Administration of the Province of Assam, 1903–04* (Shillong: Assam Secretariat Printing Press, 1905), vi & 45. Also, see 'Letter from G.A. Small, Acting Director of Public Instruction, Assam to Secretary, Government of Assam, Transferred Departments, 14 June 1929, Shillong, no 9', *Adoption of the Roman Script in India*, Assam Secretariat Proceedings, Education Department, Education A, September 1929, File nos 4–17, ASA.
136. For instance, Government of Assam, *Dimasa Fori Sygangtau: Cachari First Reader* (Shillong: Assam Secretariat Printing Office, 1904); Government of Assam, *Dimasani Forigani: Cachari Second Reader* (Shillong: Assam Secretariat Printing Office, 1904). Similar textbooks were produced for other tribes too. For instance, Reverend J.M. Carvell and Thegkur Pandit, *Mikir, Second book (Arleng Alam: Anggong Akitap)* (Shillong: Government Press, 1904).

137. J. Burton-Page, 'An Analysis of the Syllable in Boro', *Indian Linguistics*, vol. 16 (1955), 334–44; P.C. Bhattacharya, *A Descriptive Analysis of the Boro Language* (Guwahati: Gauhati University, 1977); P.C. Bhattacharya, 'Glimpses from Boro Folksongs', *Indian Linguistics*, vol. 17 (1957), 240–44; Robbins Burling, 'Proto-Bodo', *Language*, vol. 35, no. 3 (July–September 1959), 433–53. Also, D.N. Shankar Bhat, *Boro Vocabulary (With a Grammatical Sketch)* (Poona: Deccan College Postgraduate and Research Institute, 1968).

138. The British official James Drummond Anderson, posted in Assam and known for several scholarly works on the Bodos, also noted that both Assamese and Bengali freely used Bodo words, so much so that 'it has become possible to use Kachari words almost as if they were Assamese words'. Despite their close proximity, there were still pockets of Bodo villages which did 'not speak Assamese at all' well into the late nineteenth century. J.D. Anderson, *A Collection of Kachari Folk-Tales, and Rhymes* (Shillong: Assam Secretariat Print Office, 1895), Preface.

139. Satyendra Kumar Sarma, 'Script Movement Among the Bodo of Assam', *Proceedings of the Indian History Congress*, vol. 75 (2014), 1335–40.

140. Edward Gait, *A History of Assam* (Calcutta: Thacker, Spink & Company, 1906), 6.

141. Suniti Kumar Chatterjee, *Kirata-Jana Kriti* (Calcutta: Royal Asiatic Society of Bengal, 1951), 28.

142. Anonymous, 'Review of Bibar' in *Chetana*, vol. 5, ed. Paramananda Majumdar (Guwahati: Pragjyotish College, 2018 [June 1925]), 564–65.

143. Anonymous, 'Balbar Kichu' in *Bibar: A Collection of Quarterly Magazine (1924–25)*, eds, Phukan Chandra Basumatary, Biswajit Brahma and Kamalakanta Mushaharay (Kokrajhar, Assam: Bodo Publication Board, Bodo Sahitya Sabha, 2019 [1925]), 214–18.

144. 'Editorial', in *Bibar: A Collection of Quarterly Magazine*, eds, Basumatary, Brahma and Mushaharay [1924], 21.

145. 'Memorandum to Assam Chief Minister and Others by Expert Committee on Boro Language and Literature, 25 December 1952, Dhubri', in *Asmoyia Bhasar Atmapratisthar Sangramor Itihash aru Anyanya Prasanga*, ed Nilamoni Sen Deka, vol. 3 (Guwahati: B.R. Book Stall, 2021), 314–15.

146. 'Letter from B.R. Medhi, Assam Chief Minister to Satish Chandra Basumatary, Chairman, Expert Committee on Boro Language and Literature, 20 February 1953', *Asmoyia Bhasar Atmapratisthar Sangramor Itihash aru Anyanya Prasanga*, Deka, 317.

147. E.H. Pakyntein, Superintendent of Census Operations, Assam, 'Memorandum of the Discussion about Law and Order in Connection

with the 1961 Census, Confidential' in *Census of India 1961*, vol. III, Part VIII-A, *Enumeration Administration Report, Assam*, E.H. Pakyntein (Delhi: Government of India Press, 1963), Appendix 42, 130. Even before 1961, there was a demand that the Bodo students should be taught their primary classes in their mother tongue. Speech of Birendra Kumar Das, 29 February 1960, *Assam Legislative Assembly Debates*.

148. Bodo Sahitya Sabha, 'A Statement on the Present Language Issue of Assam and View of Bodos, 3 December 1960', in *Roman (English) Script and Bodo Sahitya Sobha*, comp. and ed. Kanakeswar Narzary (Kokrajhar: Bodo Sahitya Sabha, 1993), 19–21.

149. Sarmah, 'Script Movement Among the Bodo of Assam', 1335–40.

150. 'Editorial', *Asam Sahitya Sabha Patrika*, vol. 28, no. 1 (1971), 7–8.

151. Nirupama Hagzer, 'Bodo Bhasar Lipi Samasya', *Dainik Asam*, 4 April 1971, 5.

152. Computed from E.H. Pakyntein, *Report on Census of India, 1961,* vol. 3, *Assam*, Part II-C, Cultural and Migration Tables, (Delhi: Manager of Publications, 1965), Table C-V, 84.

153. Computed from N.K. Choudhury, *Report on the Census of India, 1971*, Assam, series 3, Part II-C (II), (Guwahati: Director of Census Operations, 1981), Table C-V, Part B, 128.

154. Tarun Khaklari, 'Dakhin Goalparar Janajatiya Samasya', *Natun Prithivi* (February 1972) in *Natun Prithivi: A Compilation of Quarterly Journal Natun Prithivi* ed Bhattacharjya, 121–30; B.N. Bordoloi, *Report on the Survey of Alienation of Tribal Land in Assam* (Guwahati: Assam Institute of Research for Tribals and Scheduled Castes, 1999).

155. Government of Assam, *Statistical Abstract, Assam, 1978* (Guwahati: Directorate of Economics and Statistics, 1979), Table 15.25, 248. As per the 1971 census estimate, of Assam's total population, tribal communities constituted 10 per cent.

156. 'Memorandum to Indira Gandhi, Prime Minister of India, for Containing Law and Order Situation in the Plains Tribal Areas of Assam, 1 September 1973', in Charan Narzary, *Dream For Udayachal and the History of the Plains Tribal Councils of Assam (PTCA, 1967–93)* (Guwahati: N.L. Publication, 2011), 218–24.

157. S.K. Dutta, 'Plains tribals in Assam restive over use of script', *Times of India*, 25 October 1974, 4.

158. Dutta, *The Role of Language Management and Language Conflict in the Transition of Post-Colonial Assamese Identity*, Chapter 5.

159. Bijoy Kumar Daimari, 'The Bodo Movement for the Roman Script', *Proceedings of the North East India History Association*, vol. 8, 1988, 207;

Sujit Choudhury, *The Bodos: Emergence and Assertion of an Ethnic* Minority (Shimla: Indian Institute of Advanced Studies, 2013), 130.
160. S.K. Dutta, 'Plains tribals in Assam restive over use of script', *Times of India*, 25 October 1974, 4.
161. *Dainik Asam*, 29 September 1974, 1.
162. Statement by K. Brahmananda Reddy, Minister of Home Affairs, GoI, *Lok Sabha Debates*, 21 November 1974, columns 225–26.
163. For details of this conference, see Nagen Saikia, ed., *Asamar Lipi Samsya: A Collection of Papers Read at and Proceedings of the Second Writers' Camp* (Jorhat: Asam Sahitya Sabha, 1974). 'Questionnaire regarding Second Writers' Camp: Letter from Nagen Saikia, General Secretary, Asam Sahitya Sabha to Lalit Chandra Doley, 10 October 1974', in *APCC papers*, packet 42, File no. 11 (NMML).
164. Maheswar Neog, 'Script for the Tribal Languages of Assam', in Saikia, *Asamar Lipi Samasya: A Collection of Papers Read at and Proceedings of the Second Writers' Camp*, 75.
165. *Dainik Asam*, 8 November 1974, 1.
166. *Dainik Asam*, 1 October 1972, 4.
167. Statement by K. Raghu Ramaiah, Minister of Parliamentary Affairs, GoI, *Lok Sabha Debates*, 20 December 1974, columns 325–26.
168. *Times of India*, 13 March 1975, 7.
169. 'P.M. on Bodo', *Times of India*, 16 March 1975, 7.

## Chapter 11: Economic and Political Storms

1. *Indian Express*, 10 October 1972, 1.
2. Ashutosh Varshney, *Democracy, Development, and the Countryside: Urban–Rural Struggles in India* (Cambridge: Cambridge University Press, 1998), 96–98.
3. CWC meeting, *Socialist India,* 22 September 1973, 40. This was a mouthpiece of Congress I.
4. Statement of Annasaheb P. Shinde, Minister of State for Agriculture, GoI, *Lok Sabha Debates*, 26 November 1973, column 32; *Assam Tribune*, 12 September 1973, 1; *Assam Tribune*, 20 September 1973, 1; *Assam Tribune*, 3 October 1973, 1.
5. *New York Times*, 29 March 1974, 3.
6. Prabir Baishya, 'Assam-Man-Made Famine', *Economic & Political Weekly*, vol. 10, no. 21 (24 May 1975), 821–22.
7. *Assam Tribune*, 20 September 1973, 1; *Dainik Asam*, 8 September 1973, 1; *Dainik Asam*, 9 September 1973, 1; *Dainik Asam,* 21 September 1973, 1.

8. Baishya, 'Assam-Man-Made Famine'.
9. Ibid., 821.
10. Atikuddin Ahmed, *The Anatomy of Rural Poverty in Assam: A Case Study of Dibrugarh Sub-division* (New Delhi: Mittal Publication, 1987), 10.
11. *Times of India*, 17 September 1973, 5; *Assam Tribune*, 9 October 1973, 1; *Assam Tribune*, 9 October 1973, 1; *Assam Tribune*, 10 October 1973, 1; *Assam Tribune*, 11 October 1973, 1.
12. Bernard Weinraub, 'Large imports appear essential to easing of India's food crisis', *New York Times*, 24 September 1974, 1.
13. *Times of India*, 3 March 1974, 3.
14. *Dainik Asam*, 12 September 1974, 1.
15. Government of Assam, *Economic Survey: Assam, 1974–75* (Guwahati: Directorate of Economics and Statistics, 1975), Chapter IV, Table 4.1, 13.
16. M.S. Prabhakara, 'Death in Barpeta', *Economic & Political Weekly*, vol. 10, no. 10 (8 March 1975), 425.
17. 'Statement of Paramananda Gogoi, Revenue Minister, Government of Assam, Assam Legislative Assembly', *Assam Tribune*, 8 December 1974, 1.
18. *Dainik Asam*, 9 November 1974, 1; *Dainik Asam*, 2 November 1974, 1.
19. *The Daily Telegraph* quoted in *Political Reports etc. (other than Annual Report) from London*, File no. HI/1012(56)/74, Ministry of External Affairs, Abhilekh Patal, NAI.
20. Bernard Weinraub, 'Hunger Grows in big area of East India', *New York Times*, 15 May 1975, 2.
21. *Assam Tribune*, 5 October 1974, 1.
22. B.K. Bhattacharyya, 'Students Fill the Vacuum', *Economic & Political Weekly*, vol. 9, no. 27 (6 July 1974), 1056.
23. David Ludden, *An Agrarian History of South Asia* (Delhi: Cambridge University Press, 1999), 222; Niru Hazarika, *Profile of Youth Organisations in North East India: Assam* (Guwahati: V.V. Rao Institute of Micro Studies and Research, 1998), 1–77; Meeta Deka, *Student Movement in Assam* (New Delhi: Vikas Publishing House, 1996), 226.
24. Bhattacharyya, 'Students Fill the Vacuum', 1056.
25. *Times of India*, 10 June 1974, 1; *Times of India*, 9 June 1974, 1; *Times of India*, 10 June 1974, 1.
26. *Times of India*, 11 June 1974, 1.
27. These estates were known as *nisf-khiraj* (who paid only half of the revenue) and *la-khiraj* (revenue free) estates. Bhumidhar Barman, 'Land Reforms Secure Tenants' Interests', *Times of India*, 22 November 1976.
28. *Times of India*, 6 November 1972, 7.

29. 'Resolutions of the APCC Land Reform Sub-committee', RSS 152/69/5, 30 May 1969, in *APCC Papers* (NMML).
30. This section, which discusses the political and social impacts of the Assam Tenancy Act of 1971, is based on a revision of the author's earlier work. See Arupjyoti Saikia, *A Century of Protests: Peasant Politics in Assam since 1900* (Delhi: Routledge, 2014), 315–20.
31. Election Commission of India, *Statistical Report on General Election, 1967 to the Legislative Assembly of Assam* (New Delhi: Election Commission of India, n.d), 7.
32. *Dainik Asam*, 6 June 1971, 1.
33. Sarat Chandra Sinha, *Andhare Bidara Kad* (Guwahati: Buniyad Publications), 1997.
34. The anger against the Act was mostly visible in Lower Assam. See Saikia, *A Century of Protests: Peasant Politics in Assam 1900*, Chapter 7.
35. *Dainik Asam*, 4 June 1973, 1.
36. Government of Assam, *Enquiry Report on the Allegations Brought by Shri Govinda Kalita, M.L.A., before the House on 19th and 20th May 1971: Regarding Settlement of Lands in and around Gauhati and Other Allied Matters* (Shillong: Assam Secretariat Press, 1971); Monirul Hussain, 'High Caste to Non-Caste Dominance: The Changing Pattern of Leadership of the Congress Party in Assam', *Indian Journal of Political Science*, vol. 49, no. 3 (1988), 408.
37. A. Kohli, *The State and Poverty in India* (Cambridge: Cambridge University Press), 1989, 166–79, 214–17.
38. Government of Assam, *Economic Survey: Assam, 1980–1981* (Guwahati: Directorate of Economics and Statistics, 1981), Chapter IV, Section 4.9.0, 10.
39. Bhumidhar Barman, 'Land reforms secure tenants' interests', *Times of India,* 22 November 1976, 11; 'Landholding Pattern of Assam 1976–1977', available online at http://www.indiastat.com/table/agriculture/2/agriculturallandholdings/153/522927/data.aspx (Accessed 10 May 2021). The upper limit of land holding under the provisions of Assam Fixation of Ceiling on Land Holdings Act of 1956 was fixed at 6.75 hectares through amendments made in 1972 and 1975. Umananda Phukan, *Agricultural Development in Assam, 1950–1985* (New Delhi: Mittal Publications, 1990), 19.
40. Saikia, *A Century of Protests: Peasant Politics in Assam since 1900*, 317.
41. By the end of 1976, of the approximately 2,00,000 people who acquired occupancy rights under the Assam Tenancy Act of 1971, more than half (1,10,000) were sharecroppers. Barman, 'Land Reforms Secure Tenants' Interests'.

42. Government of Assam, *Economic Survey: Assam, 1980–81*, Chapter IV, Table 4.3, 10.
43. Saikia, *A Century of Protests: Peasant Politics in Assam since 1900*, 317–18.
44. Letter from I. Ali, Deputy Inspector General of Police, Administration, Assam, to the Chief Secretary, Assam, 26 August 1958, in File no. HCL 508/58 Home (Police) 1958, ASA.
45. A.K. Saikia, *Census of India, 1971: Assam, A Portrait of Population,* Series-3 (Shillong: Directorate of Census Operations, n.d.), Table 6.6, 104.
46. Anon, *Report on Study on the Increasing Pattern of Uses of Fertilizers, Pesticides and Other Chemicals in the Field of Agriculture in Darrang, Barpeta, Nagaon and Kamrup Districts of Assam* (Guwahati: NEOLAND Technologies, 2003).
47. M.V. Nadkarni and K.H. Vedini, 'Accelerating Commercialisation of Agriculture: Dynamic Agriculture and Stagnating Peasants?', *Economic & Political Weekly*, vol. 31, no. 26 (29 June 1996), A63–A73.
48. Chandrama Goswami, 'Agricultural Land Use in the Plains of Assam', *Economic & Political Weekly*, vol. 37, no. 49 (2002), Table 1, 4892.
49. For an overview of writings of the Muslim authors in Assamese between 1965 and 1990, see S. Islam and M. Kalita, eds, *Ajan: A Selective Collection of Journal Ajan* (Jorhat: Asam Sahitya Sabha, 2007); Jayeeta Sharma, *Empire's Garden: Assam and the Making of India* (Durham: Duke University Press, 2011), 103. Jyotiprasad Agarwala described the settlers from Mymensingh district as *Na-Asomiya*. Jyotiprasad Agarwala, 'Asomiya Dekar Ukti', in *Jyotiprasad Rachanawali*, ed. Hiren Gohain (Guwahati: Publication Board Assam, 2003), 658.
50. Atul Chandra Barua, 'Bhumi aru Jiban: Mantrir Logot Kheti Paridarsan', in *Atulchandra Barua Rachanavali*, vol. 2, ed. Kanaksen Deka (Guwahati: Barua Prakasan, 1996), 340.
51. Jnananath Bora, *Asomot Bideshi* (Calcutta: Sarveswar Bhattacharjya,1925), 63; Ambikagiri Raychowdhury, 'Asambasi Aaan Bhaisakalor Prati: Goane Bhuye Boha Mymmensingia aru Sah Baganor Banua Bhai Sakalor Prati' (An Appeal to the People of Mymmensing who have Settled in Villages and the Workers of the Tea Gardens), *Deka Asom*, vol. 1, no. 1 (1935), 4.
52. Ismail Hussain, *Assamor Char-Chaporir Loka-Sahitya* (Guwahati: Banalata, 2002); Ismail Hussain and Anowar Hussain, eds, *Char Chaporir Jiban Charya* (Guwahati: Natun Sahitya Parisad, 2000); Ismail Hussain, *Char Chaporir Galpa* (Sarbhog, Assam: Natun Sahitya Parisad, 1998); Ismail Hussain, *Asomor Jaitya Jiban aru Abhivasi Asomiya MussalmanI* (Nalbari, Assam: Anamika Granthalay, 1998).
53. Ataur Rahman, 'Anuprabeskakir Samasya' (Problem of Illegal Immigrants), in *Ajan*, eds, Islam and Kalita (April 1965), 3–7.

54. Makhanlal Kar, *Muslims in Assam Politics* (Delhi: Omsons Publication, 1990), 160, 162, Table 4.1, 4.3; Monirul Hussain, 'The Assam Movement: Class, Ideology, and Identity' (PhD diss., Jawaharlal Nehru University, 1989), Table 6, M11, 387.
55. *Times of India*, 5 May 1976, 1.
56. Prabhakara, 'Assam Visitations', *Economic & Political Weekly*, vol. 10, no. 8 (22 February 1975), 351.
57. Prabhakara, 'Death in Barpeta', 423.
58. Anti-Congress-government political speeches were common in public meetings organized by the Jamiat Ulema-e-Hind in Lower Assam, which were largely attended by the Muslim community since the late 1960s. 'Letter from Superintendent of Police, Special Branch, Assam to Chief Secretary, Assam, 17 July 1969' and 'Activities of Jamiat Ulema-e-Hind, in Darrang District', Letter from Superintendent of Police, Special Branch, Assam to Chief Secretary, Assam, 25 February 1969, in *Jamiat Ulema-e-Hind*, File no. PLA 283/67, Political Department, Assam Secretariat, ASA.
59. Prabhakara, 'Death in Barpeta', 425.
60. M.S. Prabhakara, 'Assam: More Elections', *Economic & Political Weekly*, vol. 9, nos 6–7–8 (9 February 1974), 183.
61. V. Venkata Rao, 'Lok Sabha Elections in Assam (1952 To 1977): A Sociological Study', *Indian Journal of Political Science*, vol. 38, no. 4 (1977), 462–75.
62. Stephen Sherlock, *The Indian Railways Strike of 1974: A Study of Power and Organised Labour* (New Delhi: Rupa Publications, 2001).
63. Hussain, 'High Caste to Non-Caste Dominance: The Changing Pattern of Leadership of the Congress Party in Assam', 411.
64. Letter from President, Jorhat Sarucharai Gaon Panchayat OBC Committee, to Chief Minister, Assam, 25 December 1976, in *Matters Related to Tribal Areas Development*, CMS/329/76, 1976, ASA.
65. Homen Borgohain, *'OBC'*, in *Saptam Dasak*, Homen Borgohain (Nalbari: Journal Emporium, 1989), 87–105.
66. Prabhakara, 'Assam Visitations', 351.
67. Government of Assam, *Economic Survey: Assam, 1974–75* (Guwahati: Department of Economics and Statistics, 1975), Table 11.2, 41.
68. Election Commission of India, *Statistical Report on General Elections, 1977 to the Sixth Lok Sabha*, Volume I (New Delhi: Election Commission of India, 1978).
69. The communist parties, consisting of CPI, CPM, FBL, RSP, RCI and SUC, collectively got 8.29 per cent and 11.71 per cent of the votes in the elections held in 1972 and 1978, respectively. Election Commission

of India, *Statistical Report on General Elections, 1972 to the Legislative Assembly of Assam* (Delhi: Election Commission of India, n.d.); Election Commission of India, *Statistical report on General Elections, 1978 to the Legislative Assembly of Assam* (Delhi: Election Commission of India, n.d.).-

70. *Assam Tribune*, 5 May 1974, 1.
71. During 1954–57, nationalists in Assam won a decisive victory over the Indian federal government by changing its policy to establish a refinery in Assam. See D. Baruah, 'The Refinery Movement in Assam', *Economic & Political Weekly*, vol. 46, no. 1 (1 January 2011), 63–69. In the early 1960s, the All Assam Students' Union also spearheaded another movement which led to the acceptance of Assamese as the only official language of Assam.
72. Girin Phukon, *Documents on Ahom Movement in Assam* (Moranhat, Assam: Institute of Tai Studies and Research, 2010), xviii.
73. K.N. Deka, 'Assam: The Challenge of Political Integration and Congress Leadership', in *State Politics in India* ed. Iqbal Narain (Meerut: Meenakshi Prakashan, 1976), 42.
74. Phukon, *Documents on Ahom Movement in Assam*, x.
75. Phukon, *Documents on Ahom Movement in Assam*, ix–xx. Yasmin Saikia, *Fragmented Memories: Struggling to be Tai-Ahom in India* (Durham: Duke University Press, 2004).
76. See, for instance, Speech by Thanuram Gogoi, *Assam Legislative Assembly Debates*, 13 March 1954; *Representation of the All Assam Mohan Deodhai Bailung Sanmilon before the Chief Minister of Assam*, 5 February 1964; *Memorandum to the Chief Minister, Assam on behalf of the All Assam Tai Student's Association*, 25 July 1964; *Representation on behalf of the All Assam Mohan Deodhai Bailung Sanmilon*, 22 March 1965 in Phukon, *Documents on Ahom Movement in Assam*, 57–80.
77. Phukon, *Documents on Ahom Movement in Assam*, xvii; 'Resolutions of a public meeting held at Panidihing and Nitaiphukhuri, Sibsagar, 18 March 1946', Letter from D.R. Chetia to Governor General and Viceroy of India, 24 March 1946, Sibsagar, in *Resolution Passed by Ahom Public of the Sibsagar Sub-Division regarding separate representation in the Provincial Legislature and separation of Assam Province from the British India*, File no. 41/4/46-R, Secretariat of the Governor General (Reforms), Abhilekh Patal, NAI.
78. Mangalsingh Hazawary, 'Jatir Kolonko', in *Baro Chutigalpa Sankalan*, ed. Dharanidhar Owary (Jorhat: Asam Sahitya Sabha,1991), 43–55.
79. 'An appeal from D.K. Borooah, 14 June 1975, Delhi', in *All Matters Relating to Emergency*, File CMS 184/75, 1975, ASA.

80. 'India is as Indira does', *New York Times*, 4 April 1976, 350, 367–70; Ramachandra Guha, *India after Gandhi: The History of the World's Largest Democracy* (Delhi: Picador, 2007), 490.
81. B.K. Bhuyan, Chief Secretary to the Government of Assam, 'Weekly Report for the Week Ending 10 August 1975 and 8 November 1975', in *Weekly Report in Connection with Emergency*, CMS 122/76, 1976, ASA.
82. 'Telex from Chief Minister to Prime Minister, India, 2 July 1975', in *All Matters Relating to Emergency*, File no. CMS 184/75, 1975 ASA.
83. 'Report of the Committee to Suggest Economy Measures During Emergency, 12 July 1975', in *All Matters Relating to Emergency*, File no. CMS 184/75, 1975, ASA.
84. *Link*, 27 July 1975, 24.
85. 'Note Placed by the Education Department Before the Assam Cabinet for Approval, 4 August 1975', in *All Matters Relating to Emergency*, File no. CMS 184/75, 1975, ASA.
86. 'Letter from Managing Director, Kamini Tea Company (Private) Limited, to Chief Minister, Assam, 4 August 1975, Calcutta', in *All Matters Relating to Emergency*, File no. CMS 184/75, 1975, ASA.
87. CPI's views on Assam were eloquently articulated in one such pamphlet which I had consulted—entitled *Jatiya Sangahati Nirapata aru Jaitya Agragotiik Sunichitwa Koribor Karone Supanthi Patrkriyak Nirmul Korak*—issued by several office bearers of the CPI and its various organizational wings of Dhemaji of 28 June 1975 in *All Matters Relating to Emergency*, File no. CMS 184/75, 1975, ASA.
88. *New Age*, 17 August 1975; *Link*, 30 May 1976, 43; *Link*, 2 May 1976.
89. Satish Chandra Kakati, *Smriti Bichitra* (Guwahati: Sahitya Prakash, 1992), 58–63.
90. Sachi Sarma, *Jaruri Avasthat Asomiya Budhijibir Bhumika* (Nalbari: Sree Bhumi Publishing, 1977), 7–8.
91. Christophe Jaffrelot and Pratinav Anil, *India's First Dictatorship: The Emergency, 1975–77* (New Delhi: HarperCollins, 2020), Table 5.4, 193–94; J. C. Shah, *Shah Commission of Inquiry: Third and Final Report* (New Delhi: Government of India Press, 1978), 171–72. Assam's total target fixed by the Government of India was 2,37,300. There were reports of 95 deaths due to sterilization and 21 instances of sterilization of unmarried persons in Assam.
92. Leaders of few political parties, which opposed the Emergency, namely RCPI, RSS, CPI(ML), JEI, CPI(M), Socialist Party and BJS, were arrested. Shah, *Shah Commission of Inquiry: Third and Final Report*, 49.
93. Shah, *Shah Commission of Inquiry: Third and Final Report*, 51–52.

94. Shah, *Shah Commission of Inquiry: Third and Final Report*, 53.
95. *Dainik Asam*, 7 June 1977, 1.
96. 'Secret Note for Minister's use regarding discussion in Rajya Sabha on 28th February 1977 on the Call Attention Notices from Shri Bhupesh Gupta and Shri Sanat Kumar Raha calling his attention to the popular demand for lifting of Emergency and Government's reaction thereto', Ministry of Home Affairs, 12, para 10', *Emergency: Proclamation of Emergency in the Country by the President of India on the 25th June, 1975; and Extension of Emergency to J & K. Copies of Instructions for operation of Emergency,* File no. F 21/92/77–T, Home Affairs, Section I, vol. 1, Abhilekh Patal, NAI.
97. Election Commission of India, *Statistical Report on General Elections, 1977 to the Sixth Lok Sabha,* vol. 1 (New Delhi: Election Commission of India, 1978).
98. *Dainik Asam*, 2 June 1977; 4 June 1977, 1.
99. Kar, *Muslims in Assam Politics*, 186–95.
100. Rao, 'Lok Sabha Elections in Assam (1952 to 1977): A Sociological Study', 462–75.
101. 'Call off strike, Assam CM advises staff', *Times of India*, 2 January 1978, 4.
102. *Dainik Asam*, 13 June 1977, 1.
103. Of the 126 seats, Janata won 53, PTCA won 4, Congress won 26, CPIM won 11, CPI won 5, RCPI won 4, SUCI won 2, CPI (ML) won 1 and Congress (I) won 8 seats. *Assam Tribune*, 12 March 1978, 1.
104. *Guardian*, 23 February 1978, 15.
105. Kar, *Muslims in Assam Politics*, Table 4.7, 165; Hussain, *The Assam Movement: Class, Ideology, and Identity*, Table 6, M11, 387.
106. *Assam Tribune*, 7 March 1978, 1.
107. J.A. Thomson, British High Commission, New Delhi, 'Disaffection in the North East of India', 30 January 1979, para. 6, in *Internal Political Affairs in India: Includes 1978 Diary of Events and Despatch on Disaffection in the North East of India* (Government Papers, The National Archives, Kew, 1979).
108. Election Commission of India, *Statistical Report on General Election, 1978 to the Legislative Assembly of Assam*, 7.
109. *Assam Tribune*, 20 April 1954, 1; *Assam Tribune*, 29 April 1954, 1, *Natun Asamiya*, 20 April 1954, 1
110. *Guardian*, 23 February 1978, 15; British High Commission, New Delhi 'Disaffection in the North East of India', 30 January 1979, para. 6 in *Internal Political Affairs in India: Includes 1978 Diary of Events and Despatch on Disaffection in the North East of India.*

111. *Times of India*, 9 March 1978, 1; *Assam Tribune*, 2 March 1978, 1; *Assam Tribune*, 8 March 1978, 1; *Assam Tribune*, 9 March 1978, 1.
112. *Dainik Asam*, 2 April 1978, 1.
113. *Dainik Asam*, 11 April 1978, 1.
114. *Assam Tribune*, 20 March 1978, 1.
115. *Assam Tribune*, 21 March 1978, 1.
116. *Assam Tribune*, 20 June 1971, 1; See Sumit Mitra, 'Naga warriors go on a rampage, kill unarmed villagers in Assam', *India Today*, 30 December 2014.
117. *Guardian*, 15 February 1979, 8; *Times of India*, 6 January 1979, 1; *Times of India*, 7 January 1979, 1.
118. Secret, *Daily Situation Report*, no. 9, 9 January 1979, Office of the Deputy Inspector General of Police, Special Branch, Assam, ASA; *Times of India*, 11 January 1979, 1.
119. A.M. Zaidi, *Annual Register of Indian Political Parties: Proceedings and Fundamental Text*, 1979 (New Delhi: S. Chand and Company, 1979), 577.
120. Secret, *Daily Situation Report*, no. 244, 1 September 1979, Office of the Deputy Inspector General of Police, Special Branch, Assam, ASA.
121. *Dainik Asam*, 12 March 1978, 1; *Dainik Asam*, 22 March 1978, 1; *Dainik Asam*, 11 August 1978, 1; *Assam Tribune*, 24 August 1978, 1; Editorial, *Assam Tribune*, 28 August 1978, 4.
122. *Assam Tribune*, 23 July 1978, 1.
123. *Times of India*, 7 June 1978, 6.
124. Anon, 'Golap Chandra Borbora Ministry in Assam on its Way Out', *India Today*, 15 August 1979.
125. Arul B. Louis, 'Assam and Arunachal Pradesh CMs' Heads Roll in the Aftermath of Janata Party Breakup', *India Today*, 30 September 1979.
126. Ibid. In the alliance was Congress, Congress (I), Janata (S), Communist Party of India (CPI) and Progressive Democratic front.
127. *Assam Tribune*, 3 August 1978, 1.
128. *Assam Tribune*, 6 April 1978, 1.
129. 'Charter of Demands', in *Asam Andolonae Tahthyakosh–Data Book on Assam Agitation*, vol. 1, ed. Diganta Oza (Guwahati: Implementation of Assam Accord, Government of Assam, 2020), 53.
130. Hussain, *The Assam Movement: Class, Identity and Ideology*, 107–110; Gareth Price, 'The Assam Movement and the Construction of Assamese Identity' (PhD diss., University of Bristol, 1998), 221–22.
131. *Assam Tribune*, 2 June 1978; *Assam Tribune*, 14 June 1978; *Assam Tribune*, 14 June 1978.
132. Notification, J. Hazarika, Secretary to the GoA, Political (A) department, 29 December 1978 in *Law and Order*, File no. CMS, 10/28, 1978, ASA.

133. 'Letter from H.N. Bahuguna to G. Borbora, Chief Minister, Assam, 24 October 1978', in *Oil and Natural Gas Commission (Petroleum and Crude Oil, etc.)*, File no CMS. 196/78 part II, 1978, ASA.
134. 'Letter from B.K. Baruah, Resident Chief Executive to Ghanakanta Dutta and Others, 18 December 1979', in *Oil and Natural Gas Commission (Petroleum and Crude Oil, etc.)*, ASA; Mahendra Chandra Konwar, 'Address of the Reception Committee President', 17th Conference, Ahom Tai Mongoliya Rajya Parishad, 17 and 18 October 1970 in *Ahom Andolonor Eitihashik Dalil*, vol. 1, ed. Girin Phukon (Moranhat, Assam: Institute of Tai Studies and Research, 2012), 144.
135. Atul Kohli, ed., *India's Democracy: An Analysis of Changing State–Society Relations* (Princeton: Princeton University Press, 2015), 157.
136. Atul Goswami, 'Assam's Industrial Development: Urgency of New Direction', *Economic & Political Weekly*, vol. 16, no. 21 (23 May 1981), 953–56; Government of Assam, *Economic Survey of Assam, 1988–89* (Guwahati: Directorate of Economics and Statistics, 1989), Appendix IV-A, 67.
137. Goswami, 'Assam's Industrial Development: Urgency of New Direction'.
138. *Times of India*, 7 June 1978, 6; *Assam Tribune*, 20 March 1978, 1.
139. *Indian Express*, 31 October 1972, 1.
140. Goswami, 'Assam's Industrial Development: Urgency of New Direction'.
141. Government of Assam, *Economic Survey: Assam, 1980–81* (Guwahati: Directorate of Economics and Statistics, 1981), 40.
142. N.K. Choudhury, *Census of India, 1971, Series 3: Assam,* Part II-C (ii) (Guwahati: Director of Census Operations, 1981), Table C-V, 92.
143. Computed from Girilal Jain, ed., *Times of India Directory & Yearbook, 1982* (Bombay: Times of India Press, 1982), 155, 191.
144. Government of India, *Statistical Abstract of India, 1978* (Delhi: Ministry of Planning, 1979), Table 17, 51.
145. Kumudini Dandekar, 'Mortality and Longevity in India, 1901–1961', *Economic & Political Weekly*, vol. 7, no. 18 (1972), Table A, 889; See https://www.censusindia.gov.in/Vital_Statistics/SRS_Life_Table/2.Analysis_2010–14.pdf (Accessed 6 February 2023)
146. *The Times*, 19 June 1978, 5.
147. Figures are based on Rajendra Kumar, *Reserve Bank of India Bulletin*, September 1981 (Bombay: Reserve Bank of India, 1981), Statement 4: Estimates of State Domestic Product (at constant prices), 822. Also see, for larger picture of this growth pattern, Suresh D. Tendulkar and L.R. Jain, 'Economic Growth and Equity: India, 1970–71 to 1988–89', *Indian Economic Review*, vol. 30, no. 1 (1995), Appendix A, Table A.1, 45. I am thankful to Amarjyoti Mahanta for drawing my attention to this work.

148. Government of India, *Statistical Abstract: India, 1978*, new series, no. 23 (New Delhi: Central Statistical Organisation, 1979), Table 15, 44–45.
149. Agriculture Census 2015–16, (Phase-I), All India Report on Number and Area of Operational Holdings, Table 1 (a), 13; D. Bandyopadhyay, 'Land Reforms in India: An Analysis', *Economic & Political Weekly*, vol. 21, no. 25/26 (1986), A50–A56, Annexure 1.
150. Chandrama Goswami, 'Land Use in Assam: A Spatio-Temporal Study' (PhD diss., Gauhati University, 2003), Chapter 3, 78.
151. Goswami, 'Land Use in Assam: A Spatio-Temporal Study', 76.
152. Ibid., 52
153. J.A. Thomson, 'Disaffection in the North East of India', 30 January 1979, para. 6, in *Internal Political Affairs in India: Includes 1978 Diary of Events and Despatch on 'Disaffection in the North East of India'*.
154. Hirendranath Dutta, 'Sahitya Samalochana', *Asamiya Sahityar Buranji*, vol. 6, ed. Homen Bargohain (Guwahati: ABILAC, 1993), 548–60. For illustrative references, see Hiren Gohain, *Sahitya aru Chetana* (Guwahati: Lawyer's Book Stall, 1991 [1977]); Hiren Gohain, *Samaj aru Samalochana* (Guwahati: Lawyer's Book Stall, 1992 [1970]; Hiren Gohain, *Sahityar Satya* (Guwahati: Barua Agency, 1970). Also see, Bhaben Barua, 'Praptaboyskor Samasya aru Asamiya Sanskriti', *Ramdhenu*, vol. 15, no. 7 (1965), 597–608, 673–76.
155. M.C. Goswami, 'Tribe–Peasant–Caste Relations in North-East India', *Proceedings of the 58th Indian Science Congress, Part II: Presidential Address* (1971), 199.
156. Goswami, 'Tribe-Peasant-Caste Relations in North-East India', 218.
157. For instance, see, Hiren Gohain, 'Srimanta Shankar aru Asamor Itihas', in *Bastabar Swapna* (Guwahati: Guwahati Book Stall, 1972), 135–68; Hiren Gohain, *Kirtan Puthir Rasa Bichar* (Guwahati: Lawyer's Book Stall, 1981); Ranjit Kumar Dev Goswami, 'Hara Mohanor Samajik Utsa', *Prabhanda: A Collection of Essays and Lectures* (Guwahati: Lawyer's Book Stall, 2019 [1981]), 33–47; Amalendu Guha, *Vaishnavbadorpara Moamaria Bidhroholoi* (Guwahati: Students Stores, 1993 [1976–79]); Sonaram Chutia, *Asamor Vaishnav Darshanor Swarnarekha* (Guwahati: Srimanta Sankardev Sangha, 1971); Kesavananda Deva Goswami, *Satra Sanskritir Ruprekha* (Dibrugarh: National Library, 1973). Also, see Sivnath Barman, *Sivanath Barman Rachana Sambhar*, vol. 1 (Guwahati: Assam Publishing House, 2021); Anil Roychaudhury, *Asamiya Samaj aru Navabaishnavabad* (Guwahati: Publication Board Assam, 2007). Both Barman and Roychaudhury published their initial works on Assamese Vaishnavism in the 1970s. For bibliographical references on the study of Sankardev and

Assamese Vaishnavism, see Bimal Majumdar, ed., *Descriptive Bibliography of Sankaradeva* (Guwahati: Gauhati University, n.d.).

158. *Dainik Asam,* 25 June 1977, 1.
159. For instance, see Rabindra Sarkar, *Kalantarar Kabita* (Guwahati: Kamrupa Prakashan, 1982); Nilmani Phookan, *Kuri Satikar Asamiya Kabita* (Guwahati: Publication Board Assam, 1977); Homen Bargohain, *Esha Bacharar Asamiya Kabita* (Guwahati: Publication Board Assam, 2000); Bhaben Barua, 'Sonali Jahaj', in *Bhaben Barua Kobita Samagra* (Guwahati: Bandhav, 2018 [1977]); Kabin Phukan, 'Adhunik Asamiya Kabita: Prakriti aru Patbhumi', *Asamiya Sahityar Buranji,* vol. 6, ed. Bargohain, 301–77; Pradip Archarya, 'Asamiya Kabitar Kurita Bachar', *Asamiya Sahityar Buranji,* vol. 6, ed. Bargohain, 377–403.
160. Homen Borgohain, *Pita Putra* (Father and Son) (Calcutta: Sribhumi Publishing Company, 1975).
161. Of these literary magazines, I have consulted four: *Natun Prithivi, Samjya, Sanklap* and *Pada Pradip.* Also, see Kishore Bhattacharya, 'Asomer Bangla o Asomiya Khudra Patrika: Sahityik o Samajik Bhumika', *Ninth Column,* vol. 2, no. 2 (December 2002), 5–8.
162. Saurabh Kumar Chaliha, 'Kitapor Bazar–Panbazar?', in *Saurabh Kumar Chaliha Rachanawali,* eds, Shoneet Bijoy Das and Munin Bayan (Guwahati: Katha Publications, 2008), 654–55.
163. Bhaben Barua, 'Tu Fu r Kobita', *Sanglap,* vol. 1, no. 1 (1971), 6–14; Nilmani Phookan, 'China Kobitaguccha', *Samjya,* vol. 2, no. 3 (September–November 1976), 34–38; Bhaben Barua, *Bhaben Baruar Kobita Samagra* (Guwahati: Bandhav, 2018).
164. For further bibliographical references of the women writers of the twentieth century, see Hem Borah, *Asomiya Sahityalai Mahila Lekhakar Dan* (Golaghat, Assam: Saptabdi Prakashan, 1994); Chitralekha Phukan, *Asomiya Sahitya aru Lekhika* (Guwahati: Lawyer's Book Stall, 1995); Namita Deka, *Swadhinattar Kalar Asomiya Sahityaloi Mohila Lekhokar Avadan* (Guwahati: Bani Mandir, 2013). For autobiographical or biographical accounts of Assamese women writers, see Sheela Barthakur, ed., *Lekhikar Jivoni* (Tezpur: Sadau Asom Lekhika Samaroh Samiti, 1990); Malaya Barua Khound, ed., *Eri Thoi Aha Dinbor* (Guwahati: Lawyer's Book Stall, 1993).
165. Government of Assam, *Assam Marches: A Glimpse into the Educational Progress in Assam, 1948–49–50* (Shillong: n.p, n.d), 6.
166. Boli Narayan Bora, 'Tirutar Bon Ki? (What are the works of Woman?)', in *Mau,* ed. Satyendra Narayan Sarma (Guwahati: Publication Board Assam, 2008 [1886]), 1–7; Ratneswar Mahanta, 'Ghainir Kartabya aru Stree Sikhsa' (Duty of a Wife and Education of Women), in *Asam-Bandhu: A Monthly*

*Paper Devoted to Assamese Language, Literature and Culture*, comp. and ed. Nagen Saikia (Guwahati: Publication Board Assam, 1984 [1885 and 1886]), 355–60, 449–56; Purna Kanta Sarma, 'Stree Sikhsa' (Education of Women), in *Asam-Bandhu: A Monthly Paper Devoted to Assamese Language, Literature and Culture*, comp. and ed. Saikia, 476–80; Ratneswar Mahanta, 'Goanalia Buari', in *Ratneswar Mahanta Rachanwali*, ed. Jogendranarayan Bhuyan (Guwahati: Publication Board Assam, 1977).

167. Government of India, *Selected Educational Statistics, 1977–78* (Delhi: Ministry of Education and Social Welfare, 1978), Table 3.
168. Government of India, *Selected Educational Statistics, 1977–78*, Table 5, 26/15.
169. Government of India, *Selected Educational Statistics, 1977–78*, Table 1, 286 and Table 5, 289.
170. Government of India, *Report of the Committee on the Status of Women in India* (Delhi: Ministry of Education and Social Welfare, 1974), 433, Table 5.3.C.
171. Nibaron Bora, 'Islamabad Banam Dhaka: Delhi Banam Dispur' (Islamabad versus Dhaka: Delhi versus Dispur), *Nagarik*, 15, 22 and 29 December 1977. Priyam Bora, ed., *Mahanayak Nibaran Bora* (Guwahati: Nibaran Bora Smriti Rakshya Samiti, undated), 4–13.
172. *Dainik Asam*, 10 April 1979, 1.
173. Praphulladutta Goswami, 'Assam's Contribution to Indian Culture', in *Assam and the Assamese Mind*, ed. Nagen Saikia (Jorhat: Asam Sahitya Sabha), 1980, 5.
174. Saikia, *Assam and the Assamese Mind*, iv.

## Chapter 12: Waves of Popular Protest

1. *Assam Tribune*, 2 and 3 June 1978, 1.
2. *Assam Tribune*, 18 August 1978, 1.
3. *Assam Tribune*, 26 August 1978, 1. Also, see Golap Borbora, 'Bideshi Bitaron Andolan Bayrtha Kiyo Hoichil', in *Asom Andolon: Pratisruti aru Phalasruti: A Collection of Articles on Assam Movement*, eds, Hiren Gohain and Dilip Bora (Guwahati: Banalata, 2001), 105.
4. *Assam Tribune*, 6 September 1978; Borbora, 'Bideshi Bitaron Andolan Bayrtha Kiyo Hoichil', 109–12.
5. Anjan Sarma, *Asam Andolonor Asampurna Itihas: A Book on the History of Assam Movement* (Guwahati: Powershift, 2018), 318; Manash Kumar Mahanta, *Oitihashik Asom Andolon Juwe Pura Sat-ta Basor: A Text and Experience of Assam Movement* (Guwahati: Olympia Prakashan, 2019), 4–5.

6. *Dainik Asam*, 23 September 1979, 1; *Assam Tribune*, 23 September 1979, 1.
7. *Times of India*, 25 September 1978, 1; *Dainik Asam*, 24 September 1978, 1.
8. Government of Assam, *Report on the Fifth General Election to the Assam Legislative Assembly*, 1972 (Shillong: Election Department, 1974), 6.
9. 'Alien voters "reports disturbing"', *Times of India*, 25 October 1978, 1.
10. Reply to Question no. 456, Statement of Madhu Dandavate, *Rajya Sabha Debates*, 27 November 1978, 72.
11. *Times of India*, 16 January 1979, 9.
12. *Guardian*, 6 October 1979, 7; *Times of India*, 17 January 1979, 9; Assam Pradesh Congress Committee, *Assam's Problem of Foreign Nationals—An Analytical Study* (Guwahati: Congress Bhawan, 1 June 1980); Diganta Oza, ed., *Asam Andolonar Tathyakosh: Data Book on Assam Agitation*, vol. 2 (Guwahati: Implementation of Assam Accord Department, Government of Assam, 2021), 1073.
13. *Dainik Janambhumi*, 6 and 7 January 1979, in *Asam Andolonar Tathyakosh: Data Book on Assam Agitation*, vol. 1, ed. Diganta Oza (Guwahati: Implementation of Assam Accord Department Government of Assam, 2020), 249–50.
14. Secret, *Daily Situation Report*, Office of the Deputy Inspector General of Police, Special Branch, Assam, Kahilipara, Guwahati (hereafter *DSR*) 9 March 1979, para 19, 3–4; 10 March 1979, para 10, 2; *Assam Tribune*, 12 March 1979, 1.
15. T.S. Murty, *Assam, The Difficult Years: A Study of Political Developments in 1979–83* (Delhi: Himalayan Books, 1983), 5.
16. Secret, D.O. Letter from Jatin Hazarika, Secretary, Home and Political Departments, Government of Assam to H.K. Bhattacharjee, DIGP (Border), no. PLB 49/77/16, 23 January 1979, Dispur Guwahati, in *Asam Andolonar Tathyakosh: Data Book on Assam Agitation*, vol. 2, ed. Oza, 1072.
17. *DSR*, 7 March 1979, para 3, 1.
18. *Assam Tribune*, 12 March 1979, 1; *Assam Tribune*, 12 March 1979, 1.
19. T.S. Murty, *Assam: The Difficult Years: A Study of Political Developments in 1979–83*, 5; Sangeeta Barooah Pisharoty, *Assam: The Accord, The Discord* (New Delhi: Penguin, 2019), 24; *Patriot*, 11 March 1979.
20. *Assam Tribune*, 13 March 1979; Murty, *Assam: The Difficult Years: A Study of Political Developments in 1979–83*, 5; Speech of Golap Borbora, *Assam Legislative Assembly Debates*, 16 March 1979; *Assam Tribune*, 16 March 1979.
21. Statement of Dhanik Lal Mandal, State Minister of Home Affairs, *Rajya Sabha Debates*, 16 March 1979.
22. *Assam Tribune*, 19 March 1979.

23. Obituary Reference, *Lok Sabha Debates*, 29 March 1979, column 1.
24. Murty, *Assam: The Difficult Years: A Study of Political Developments in 1979–83*, 5–6.
25. Premkanta Mahanta, *Rajbhaganar Pora Kolthokaloi* (Guwahati: Author, 1994), 99. I am grateful to Prarthana Saikia for sharing with me some of these 'complaints' filed in Darrang District.
26. *Assam Tribune*, 9 June 1979, 1.
27. Murty, *Assam, The Difficult Years: A Study of Political Developments in 1979–83*, 12–13.
28. *Assam Tribune*, 8 June 1979, 1; *Assam Tribune*, 7 June 1979, 1; *Assam Tribune*, 6 June 1979, 1.
29. Murty, *Assam, The Difficult Years: A Study of Political Developments in 1979–83*, 12–13; *Dainik Asam*, 4 September 1979, in *Asam Andolonar Tathyakosh: Data Book on Assam Agitation*, vol. 1, ed., Oza, 93.
30. 'Note Submitted to the Prime Minister by R.V. Sundaramaniam, Advisor to the Governor of Assam, May 1982', in *Report of the Non-Official Judicial Inquiry Commission on the Holocaust of Assam Before During and After Election 1983*, T.U. Mehta (Guwahati: Asom Rajyik Freedom Fighters' Association, 1985), Appendix E; *Dainik Asam*, 27 September 1979, in *Asam Andolonar Tathyakosh: Data Book on Assam Agitation*, vol. 1, ed., Oza, 101; *Assam Tribune*, 28 September 1979, 1.
31. *Dainik Asam*, 19 September 1979, quoted in *Asam Andolonar Tathykosh: Data Book on Assam Agitation*, vol. 1, ed. Oza, 96–97.
32. *Times of India*, 4 December 1979, 19; *Times of India*, 29 December 1979, 15.
33. Girin Phukon and Adil-ul Yasin, eds, *Working of Parliamentary Democracy and Electoral Politics in Northeast India* (New Delhi: South Asian Publishers, 1998), 44.
34. Editorial, 'Testing time in Assam', *Times of India*, 14 December 1979, 8.
35. Inder Malhotra, 'Immigrants crisis hit Assam poll', *Guardian*, 6 October 1979, 7.
36. Sumit Mitra, 'Assam, Meghalaya in the Throes of Widespread Communal Trouble', *India Today*, 15 December 1979.
37. *Times of India*, 29 December 1979, 15.
38. Murty, *Assam, The Difficult Years: A Study of Political Developments in 1979–83*, 19.
39. Keya Dasgupta and Amalendu Guha, '1983 Assembly Poll in Assam: An Analysis of Its Background and Implications', *Economic & Political Weekly*, vol. 20, no. 19 (11 May 1985), 843.
40. Speech of Tarun Gogoi, *Lok Sabha Debates*, 19 March 1979, columns 267–70; 'Calling Attention to Matter of Urgent Public Importance:

Reported Large-Scale Influx of Foreign Nationals into Assam and Neighboring States', Speech of Dhanik Lal Mandal, Minister of State, Ministry of Home Affairs, Government of India, *Lok Sabha Debates*, 19 March 1979, columns 267–68, 270–71, 273; British High Commission, New Delhi, 'Disaffection in the North East of India', 30 January 1979, para. 6, in *Internal Political Affairs in India: Includes 1978 Diary of Events and Despatch on 'Disaffection in the North East of India'* (Government Papers, The National Archives, Kew, 1979) http://www.archivesdirect.amdigital.co.uk/Documents/Details/FCO_37_2151 (Accessed 30 June 2021).

41. *Assam Tribune*, 10 December 1979, 1.
42. *Times of India*, 1 December 1979, 9.
43. *Assam Tribune*, 2, 3, 4, 5 and 6 December 1979.
44. Sumit Mitra, 'Assam, Meghalaya in the Throes of Widespread Communal Trouble', *India Today*, 15 December 1979.
45. *Assam Tribune*, 10 December 1979, 1.
46. *Assam Tribune*, 9 December 1979, 1.
47. Sumit Mitra, 'Assam, Meghalaya in the Throes of Widespread Communal Trouble', *India Today*, 15 December 1979.
48. *Assam Tribune*, 10 December 1979, 1; *Dainik Asam*, 10 December 1979, 1.
49. *Assam Tribune*, 11 December 1983, 1; *Dainik Asam*, 11 December 1983, 1; *Guardian*, 11 December 1979, 7.
50. *Times of India*, 13 December 1979, 1.
51. *Assam Tribune*, 9 December 1979; *Assam Tribune*, 13 December 1979; *Dainik Asam*, 13 December 1979.
52. *Times of India*, 4 December 1979, 19; *Times of India*, 10 December 1979, 9; *Times of India*, 29 November 1979, 9.
53. *Times of India*, 10 December 1979, 9; *Times of India*, 24 December 1979, 8.
54. Letter of Mrs Gandhi to Shahi Imam of Jama Masjid quoted in full in the *Times of India*, 22 November 1979, 5.
55. *DSR*, Report no. 248, 5 September 1979.
56. *Assam Tribune*, 4 January 1979, 1.
57. *DSR*, Report no. 4, 4 January 1980, para 15, 3; Hiren Gohain, 'Cudgel of Chauvinism', *Economic & Political Weekly*, vol. 15, no. 8 (1980), 418–20; Nirupama Bargohain, 'Incidents in North Kamrup', *Economic & Political Weekly*, vol. 15, no. 20 (1980), 878; Vibhuti Patel, 'Another View of Incidents in North Kamrup', *Economic & Political Weekly*, vol. 15, no. 20 (1980), 879; Nirupama Borgohain, 'Nijor Kanok Biswas Nahay', *Saptahik Kalakhar*, vol. 1, no. 6 (26 January–11 February 1980), in *Tejor Akhare Likha*, ed. Hiren Gohain (Guwahati: Student Stores, 2017), 160–72; *Assam Tribune*, 6, 7, 8, 9, 11 and 12 January 1980.

58. *Assam Tribune*, 12 January 1980; *DSR*, no. 5, para 23–25, 5 January 1980.
59. *DSR*, Report no. 4, 4 January 1980, para 15, 3.
60. Sumit Mitra, 'Assam, Meghalaya in the Throes of Widespread Communal Trouble', *India Today*, 15 December 1979; *Amrita Bazar Patrika*, 11 January 1980, 1.
61. *Assam Tribune*, 12 January 1980, 1; Patel, 'Another View of Incidents in North Kamrup'.
62. *Assam Tribune*, 19 January 1980, 1; *Dainik Asam*, 19 January 1980, 1.
63. *Assam Tribune*, 18 January 1980, 1; *Dainik Asam*, 18 January 1980, 1.
64. *DSR*, 26 May 1980, para. 33; *DSR*, 27 May 1980, para 28; *DSR*, 28 May 1980, para. 43; *Dainik Asam*, 27 May 1980.
65. Sumit Mitra, 'Indira Gandhi Gives Belated Recognition, Attention to Growing Tension in Assam', *India Today*, 30 April 1980. In a public meeting held between 30 and 31 January 1981 in Guwahati, the Citizen's Rights Preservation Committee, which brought together Bengali Hindus and Muslims, adopted a resolution 'to take 1971 as base year for detection of foreigners as per national consensus'. 'Secret, Monthly Report to the Governor of Assam', January 1981, in *Monthly Report to the Governor*, File CMS 47/80, CMS Department1980, ASA, 14.
66. *Assam Tribune*, 27 May 1980, 1.
67. *Assam Tribune*, 27, 29 and 31 May 1980; *Dainik Asam*, 27 May 1980, 1; *Dainik Asam*, 28 May 1980, 1; *Dainik Asam*, 29 May 1980, 1; *Dainik Asam*, 30 May 1980, 1; *Dainik Asam*, 31 May 1980, 1; *Dainik Asam*, 1 June 1980; *Dainik Asam*, 2 June 1980, 1; *Dainik Asam*, 3 June 1980, 1; *Dainik Asam*, 4 June 1980, 1; *DSR*, no. 147, 26 May 1980; Tribhuvan Prasad Tewary, *Report of the Commission of Enquiry on Assam Disturbances, 1983* (Dispur: Government of Assam, 1984), 253–54.
68. *DSR*, 27 May 1980, para 29; *DSR*, 28 May 1980, para 44; *Dainik Asam*, 27, 28, and 29 May 1980; *Assam Tribune*, 27 and 28 May 1980. Also, *Dainik Janambhumi*, 27 and 28 May 1980, 2 June 1980 in *Asam Andolonar Tathyakosh: Data Book on Assam Agitation*, vol. 1, ed., Oza, 387–94.
69. *Assam Tribune*, 11 January 1980, 1.
70. *Assam Tribune*, 19 and 21 January 1980.
71. *Times of India*, 7 April 1981; *Dainik Asam*, 7 April 1981, 1.
72. 'Production of Crude Oil (Onshore/Offshore) in India (1970–1971 to 1999–2000)', http://www.indiastat.com/table/petroleum-data/25/crude-oil-production/379574/279376/data.aspx (Accessed 22 May 2020). Also, Ditee Moni Baruah, 'Polity and Petroleum: Making of an Oil Industry in Assam, 1825–1980' (PhD diss., Indian Institute of Technology Guwahati, 2014), 221–22.

73. Editorial, 'Intransigent Still', *Times of India*, 5 April 1980, 6.
74. 'India: Trouble in Assam, 24 April 1980', *National Intelligence Daily*, Thursday 24 April 1980, https://www.cia.gov/library/readingroom/docs/DOC_0005148740.pdf (Accessed 28 September 2020); *Indian Express*, 20 April 1980.
75. Stuti Rawat and Aditi Mukherji, 'Poor State of Irrigation Statistics in India: The Case of Pumps, Wells and Tubewells', *International Journal of Water Resources Development*, vol. 30, no. 2 (April 2014), 5, Table 3.
76. *The Times*, 30 January 1981, 7, col. H.
77. *The Times*, 11 January 1981, 18, col. F. The Central government claimed that the import of crude oil would fall from 3,34,000 barrels to 2,80,000 barrels per day from 1982.
78. *The Times*, 8 February 1980, 18, col. A.
79. *The Times*, 12 December 1980, 24, col. A.
80. In 1981, India was importing 3,34,000 barrels of oil per day. *The Times*, 11 January 1981, 18, col. F.
81. *Assam Tribune*, 20 January 1980, 1.
82. *Assam Tribune*, 2 February 1980, 1 'PM to meet Assam student leaders', *Times of India*, 2 February 1980, 9.
83. 'Memorandum to the Prime Minister of India from All Assam Students Union', 18 January 1980, in *Asam Andolonar Tathyakosh: Data Book on Assam Agitation*, vol. 1, ed., Oza, 803–14.
84. 'Memorandum to the Prime Minister of India from All Assam Students Union', 18 January 1980, in *Asam Andolonar Tathyakosh: Data Book on Assam Agitation*, vol. 1, ed., Oza, 813.
85. R.D. Pradhan, *Working with Rajiv Gandhi* (New Delhi: Indus, 1995), 94.
86. 'Public Coordination Committee of Assamese Muslims, *Leaflet*, 1980', in *Asam Andolonar Tathyakosh: Data Book on Assam Agitation*, vol. 2, ed., Oza, 1153–54.
87. *New Statesman*, 4 March 1983, 1.
88. 'Indira's mission to Assam fails', *Times of India*, 13 April 1980; Editorial, 'Intransigent still', *Times of India*, 15 April 1980, 6.
89. CIA, *India: The Challenge of Communal and Caste Conflict, An Intelligence Assessment*, Secret, August 1983, https://www.cia.gov/readingroom/document/cia-rdp84s00556r000300110002-0, iv. (Accessed 19 March 2020).
90. For Atal Bihari Vajpayee's speeches in the Indian Parliament on the Assam question, see N.M. Ghatate, ed., *Atal Bihari Vajpayee: Four Decades in Parliament*, vol. 1 (Delhi: Shipra Publications, 1998), 444–52. 'Vajpayee urges government to resume talks on Assam', *Hindustan*

*Times*, 19 July 1980, 8. Also, Letter from Ramakrishna Hegde, General Secretary, Janata Party to Indira Gandhi, 31 May 1980 in *Janata Party Papers*, Sub File 375 (a), NMML.
91. *Times of India*, 12 January 1981, 1.
92. *Assam Tribune*, 2 July 1980, 1.
93. Murty, *Assam, The Difficult Years: A Study of Political Developments in 1979–83*, 242.
94. Ibid., 244.
95. 'Letter from Prafulla Kumar Mahanta, President, and Bhrigu Kumar Phukan, General Secretary, AASU, to the Prime Minister of India, 25 June 1980, Guwahati', in *Asam Andolonar Tathyakosh: Data Book on Assam Agitation*, vol. 2, ed., Oza, 1114; 'Letter from Prafulla Kumar Mahanta, President, and Bhrigu Kumar Phukan, General Secretary, AASU, to Zail Singh, Union Home Minister, Government of India, 29 November 1980', in *Asam Andolonar Tathyakosh: Data Book on Assam Agitation,* vol. 2, ed., Oza, 1119.
96. *Assam Tribune*, 17 February 1980, 1.
97. Anonymous, 'Five States in Northeastern Region in Turmoil', *India Today*, 30 November 1979.
98. Sumit Mitra, 'Indira Gandhi Gives Belated Recognition, Attention to Growing Tension in Assam', *India Today*, 30 April 1980.
99. Tooshar Pandit, 'Mrs Gandhi's Velvet Glove and Mailed Fist', *Sunday Special*, 8 June 1980 in *Asam Andolonar Tathyakosh: Data Book on Assam Agitation,* vol.1, ed., Oza, 672; Monoj Kumar Nath, *The Muslim Question in Assam and North East India* (New Delhi: Routledge, 2021), 80.
100. Tooshar Pandit, 'Mrs Gandhi's Velvet Glove and Mailed Fist', 672. The Bengali Hindus and Muslims unitedly tried to defend their political rights during this tumultuous period. In January 1981, the Citizen's Rights Preservation Committee adopted several resolutions, which included asking the Assam government to withdraw 'Quit India notices served illegally to the Indian citizens', 'to stop eviction' and 'to stop harassment on linguistic and religious minorities', amongst others. 'Secret, Monthly Report to the Governor of Assam', January 1981, in *Monthly Report to the Governor*, File CMS 47/80, CMS Department1980, ASA, 14. Also, see note 62.
101. 'Appeal of All Bodo Students Union to Join the Movement', Leaflet, undated, in *Asam Andolonar Tathyakosh: Data Book on Assam Agitation,* vol.1, ed., Oza, 823.
102. *Peoples Democracy*, 7 September 1980, quoted in Suneet Chopra, 'The Assam Movement and the Left: A Reply to Hiren Gohain', *Social Scientist*, vol. 10, no. 11 (1982), 63–70, note 1.

103. *Assam Tribune*, 24 February 1980, 1.
104. *Assam Tribune*, 13 April 1980, *Dainik Asam*, 13 April 1980; Nath, *Muslim Question in Assam and North East India*, 80; Tooshar Pandit, 'Mrs Gandhi's Velvet Glove and Mailed Fist', 672.
105. *Assam Tribune*, 24 February 1980, 1.
106. Quoted in Sumit Mitra, 'Assam, Meghalaya in the Throes of Widespread Communal Trouble', *India Today*, 15 December 1979.
107. Sumit Mitra, 'Indira Gandhi Gives Belated Recognition, Attention to Growing Tension in Assam', *India Today*, 30 April 1980.
108. Ibid.
109. Anonymous, 'Assam Agitation Snowballs into a Crisis of Uncertain Proportions, Threatens to Escalate Even Further', *India Today*, 15 May 1980.
110. Ibid.
111. Ibid.
112. *DSR*, no. 46, 15 February 1979, para 4, 1; *DSR*, no. 4, 4 January 1980, para. 14, 3; *DSR*, no. 5, 5 January 1980, para 18, 3.
113. Tooshar Pandit, 'Is the RSS Active?', *Sunday Special*, 8 June 1980, in *Asam Andolonar Tathyakosh: Data Book on Assam Agitation*, vol. 1, ed. Oza, 676–77.
114. Ibid.
115. 'Memorandum to the Prime Minister of India from Asom Jatiyatabadi Dal, 2 February 1980', in *Asam Andolonar Tathyakosh: Data Book on Assam Agitation*, vol. 1, ed. Oza, 815–18.
116. Shekhar Gupta, *Assam: A Valley Divided* (New Delhi: Vikas Publishing House, 1984), 122.
117. Ibid., 121–22.
118. 'Text of the Statement Issued by A.B. Vajpayee, M.P., President, Bharatiya Janata Party at a Press Conference held at Jaipur on January 11, 1981', in *Asam Andolonar Tathyakosh: Data Book on Assam Agitation*, vol. 3, ed. Oza, 1155, 1161–62.
119. For instance, *Organiser*, 15 June 1980; *Organiser*, 29 June 1980.
120. Chaitanya Kalbag, 'After the Most Bloodstained Election Campaign in Indian History', *India Today*, 31 March 1983.
121. 'A.B.P.S. 1980: Assam Problem', *RSS Resolutions* in http://www.archivesofrss.org/Resolutions.aspx (Accessed 29 September 2020); K.S. Sudarsan, In-Charge, RSS, North East India, *Asamor Bideshi Anuprabeshkarir Samasya Samparkat: Statement on the Problem of Illegal Infiltrants of Assam* (Tezpur: RSS, undated) in *Asam Andolonar Tathyakosh: Data Book on Assam Agitation*, vol. 3, ed. Oza, 1165.

122. Speech of Indira Gandhi, *Lok Sabha Debates*, 1980; Murty, *Assam, The Difficult Years: A Study of Political Developments in 1979–83*, 45.
123. *Statesman*, April (n.d.) 1983, in S. Chakrabarty, *The Upheaval Years in North East India: A Documentary In-depth Study of Assam Holocausts, 1960–1983* (Calcutta: S. Chakrabarty and R. Chakrabarty, 1984), 199. Also, Walter Anderson and Shridhar D. Damle, *The Brotherhood in Saffron: The Rashtriya Swayamsevak Sangh and Hindu Revivalism* (New Delhi: Vistaar Publications, 1987), 215.
124. P. Ramamurti, *Real Face of the Assam Agitation* (New Delhi: Communist Party of India [M], 1980), 8–11; Pauly Parakal, *Secret Wars of CIA* (New Delhi: Sterling Publishers Pvt. Ltd, 1984); Zoya Hasan, 'New Thrust of Imperialism in South Asia', *Social Scientist*, vol. 12, no. 11 (1984), 44. Also for the Soviet views, see 'The Situation in Assam: Western Backing for "Chauvinists and Separatists"', 'Text of report of despatch by "Izvestiya", Aleksandr Ter-Griqoryan, Delhi correspondent, 23 February 1983', *BBC Summary of World Broadcasts,* 5 March 1983; 'Pravda' on Crisis in Assam: 'Foreign Interference in India's Affairs', Text of report of 'Pravda' dispatch by Valentin Korvikov, 4 April 1983, *BBC Summary of World Broadcasts,* 8 April 1983.
125. Hiren Gohain, 'Asomot CIA er Pretalila', *Saptahik Kalakhar*, vol. 1, no. 13 (December 1979) and no. 14 (January 1980) in Hiren Gohain, 'CIA-er Project Brahmaputra aru Amar Andolan', *Saptahik Nilachal*, 11 February 1981.
126. Interview of Sarat Chandra Sinha quoted in Jyoti Jafa, 'Can These Gandhians Provide the Healing Touch?', *Illustrated Weekly of India*, 8 May 1983. Also, Sarat Chandra Sinha, 'Eti Upalabdhi aru Tar Agkatha', in *Asom Andolon: Pratisruti aru Phalasruti: A Collection of Articles on Assam Movement*, eds, Gohain and Bora, 1–6.
127. Anil Roychoudhury, 'Assam: National Register of Citizens, 1951', *Economic & Political Weekly*, vol. 16, no. 8 (21 February 1980), 267–68.
128. AASU, *Why National Register of Citizens of 1951 Must be Used to Detect Foreign Nationals in Assam* (Guwahati: AASU, n.d.); *Assam Tribune*, 24 February 1980, 1; *Assam Tribune*, 24 February 1980, 1.
129. *Assam Tribune*, 12 December 1979, 1.
130. Murty, *Assam, The Difficult Years: A Study of Political Developments in 1979–83*, 181; 'Speedy steps to deport aliens', *Times of India*, 5 April 1982, 1.
131. Murty, *Assam, The Difficult Years*, 179; *Times of India*, 23 July 1982, 1; Taslima Yasmin, 'The Enemy Property Laws in Bangladesh: Grabbing Lands Under the Guise of Legislation', *Oxford University Commonwealth Law Journal*, vol. 15, no. 1 (2015), 121–47.
132. 'Disquieting reports', *Times of India*, 24 July 1982, 8.

133. Murty, *Assam, The Difficult Years: A Study of Political Developments in 1979–83*, 182.
134. Robin Jeffrey, 'Indian-Language Newspapers and Why They Grow', *Economic & Political Weekly*, vol. 28, no. 38 (1993), 2004–2011.
135. See, for instance, 'Sangram', no. 13, 5 March 1981, in *Asam Andolonar Tathyakosh: Data Book on Assam Agitation*, vol. 2, ed., Oza, 1155–56.
136. For a selection of essays and articles written during 1979–85, see Joyashree Goswami Mahanta, *Asom Andolon: Yugamia Cintar Pratifalan*, vols 1–3 (Guwahati: Chandra Prakash, 2014). While the list of literary works is rather long, here are few illustrative works: Sameer Tanti, *Juddhuttarar Kabita* (Guwahati: Lawyer's Book Stall, 1990); P. Bora, *Kotha Manobir Rupkotha* (Guwahati: Shristi Prakashan, 2014); D. Bora, *Kalijar Aai* (Guwahati: Jyoti Prakahsa, 2014); Arupa Patangia Kalita, *Felani* (Guwahati: Jyoti Prakashan, 2003); Homen Borgohain, *Atmanusandhan* (Guwahati: Student's Store, 2003); Mamoni Raisom Goswami, *Sanskar aru Udaybhanur Charitra* (Guwahati: Jyoti Prakashan, 1994); Rita Choudhury, *Ei Samay Sei Samay* (Guwahati: Jyoti Prakashan, 2008); Hiranya Bhattacharjee, *Dharshita* (Guwahati: Guwahati Sadhughar, 2011); and Sanjib Pol Deka, *Asam Andolanar Galpa* (Guwahati: Banalata, 2023).
137. 'Statement of Basava Punniah, Politburo Member of CPI (M)', *Assam: The Difficult Years: A Study of Political Developments in 1979–83*, Murty, 229.
138. *Indian Express*, 1 July 1981, 1.
139. *Indian Express*, 1 August 1981, 1.
140. Statement of Indira Gandhi, *Rajya Sabha Debates*, 7 October 1982, 31; Statement of Nihar Ranjan Laskar, Union Minister of State for Home Affairs, *Rajya Sabha Debates*, 7 October 1982, 23; Statement of P.C. Sethi, *Rajya Sabha Debates*, 7 October 1982, 23; *Indian Express*, 1 October 1982, 1; Prarthana Saikia, 'Citizenship, Nationality and Assam: A Political History Since 1947' (PhD diss., Indian Institute of Technology, Guwahati, 2021), 193–94; Habibullah Wajahat, *My Years with Rajiv: Triumph and Tragedy* (Chennai: Westland, 2020). Habibullah was a senior functionary at the Prime Minister's Office since 1982.
141. *Indian Express*, 2 October 1982, 1.
142. Ibid.; Statement of P.C. Sethi, *Rajya Sabha Debates*, 7 October 1982, 25.
143. *Indian Express*, 2 October 1982, 1; Statement of P.C. Sethi, *Rajya Sabha Debates*, 7 October 1982, 25.
144. *Indian Express*, 11 October 1982, 1.
145. Statement of Indira Gandhi, *Rajya Sabha Debates*, 7 October 1982, 30.
146. *Indian Express*, 11 October 1982, 1.

147. *Times of India*, 6 January 1983, 1; *Assam Tribune*, 6 January 1983, *Dainik Asam*, 6 January 1983.
148. *Times of India*, 5 January 1983, 1.
149. *Dainik Asam*, 6 January 1983, 1.
150. *Indian Express*, 20 January 1983, 1, *Assam Tribune*, 20 January 1983, 1; *Dainik Asam*, 20 January 1983, 1; *DSR*, 16 January 1983, 1; *DSR*, 19 January 1983, 2–8; *DSR*, 20 January 1983, 1–6; *DSR*, 21 January 1983, 1–7; *DSR*, 22 January 1983, 1-3.
151. 'Order by R.K. Trivedi, Chief Election Commissioner, India, 7 January 1983', Annexure F, in *Report of the Non-Official Judicial Inquiry Commission on the Holocaust of Assam Before During and After Election 1983*, Mehta 201.
152. 'Note Submitted to the Prime Minister by R.V. Sundaramaniam', Annexure E, in *Report of the Non-Official Judicial Inquiry Commission on the Holocaust of Assam Before During and After Election 1983*, Mehta, 193.
153. 'Statement of Ramesh Chandra, Chief Secretary, Assam, before the Commission of Enquiry on Assam Disturbances', in *Report of the Commission of Enquiry on Assam Disturbances*, 367; 'Statement of R.V. Subrahmaniam, Adviser to the Governor of Assam', *Report of the Commission of Enquiry on Assam Disturbances*, Tewary, 365–66.
154. 'Press Statement of Election Commission of India, 28 January 1983', in *The Upheaval Years in North East India: A Documentary In-depth Study of Assam Holocausts, 1960–1983*, Chakrabarty, 182.
155. Murty, *Assam, The Difficult Years: A Study of Political Developments in 1979–83*, 224.
156. *Times of India*, 22 February 1983, 8; *Times of India*, 4 October 1982; *Times of India*, 3 November 1983.
157. 'Letter from Indira Gandhi to Dorothy Norman, 10 February 1983, in flight, New Delhi to Assam', in Dorothy Norman, *Indira Gandhi: Letters to an American Friend, 1950–1984* (New York: Helen and Kurt, 1985), 170.
158. Discussion on the Assam Executive Magistrates (Temporary Powers) Act, 1983 (No.1 of 1983) enacted by the President, *Rajya Sabha Debates*, 28 February 1983, 261–62; *Dainik Asam*, 31 January 1983.
159. Chakrabarty, *The Upheaval Years in North East India: A Documentary In-depth Study of Assam Holocausts, 1960–1983*, 182.
160. *Indian Express*, 9 February 1983, 1; *Indian Express*, 11 February 1983, 1; *Indian Express*, 13 February 1983, 1; *Times of India*, 11 February 1983, 1; *Guardian*, 10 February 1983, 8; *DSR*, 2 February 1983, 1; *DSR*, 3 February 1983, 1; *DSR*, 4 February 1983, 1; *DSR*, 8 February 1983, 1; *DSR*, 10 February 1983, 1.

161. 'Letter from Indira Gandhi to Dorothy Norman, 10 February 1983', in Norman, *Indira Gandhi: Letters to an American Friend, 1950–1984*, 170.
162. See '1983: Hundreds die in Assam poll violence', http://news.bbc.co.uk/onthisday/hi/dates/stories/february/20/newsid_4269000/4269719.stm (Accessed 14 June 2020).
163. *Indian Express*, 18 February 1983, 7.
164. Arvind Sethi, 'Assam's Agony', *Times of India*, 15 February 1983, 8.
165. Editorial, 'Cruel choice in Assam', *Times of India*, 11 February 1983, 8.
166. *DSR*, 18 February 1983, 8.
167. Sumanta Sen, 'After Four Strife-Torn Years, Elections in Assam Promises to be a Bizarre Show', *India Today*, 15 February 1983.
168. They included Congress (S), CPI (M), CPI, RCPI, RSP and SUCI. *Ganasakti*, 11 February 1983; 'Statement of CPI (M) in matters of recent election in Assam', *Ganasakti*, 4 March 1983, 3 and 6.
169. Dhruba Bora and Bhabadev Goswami, eds, *Nirbachan Protirodh Sangramar Itihas* (Guwahati: Upendra Nath Gogoi and Debajit Bez Barua, 1983).
170. Sunanda Datta-Ray, 'Fifty battalions fail to halt Assam riots', *Observer*, 20 February 1983, 11.
171. *Assam Tribune*, 1 March 1983, 1.
172. *Indian Express*, 18 February 1983, 1; Dasgupta and Guha, 'Assembly Poll in Assam: An Analysis of Its Background and Implications', 844.
173. *Assam Tribune*, 27 February 1983, 1.
174. Sunanda Datta-Ray, 'Fifty battalions fail to halt Assam riots', *Observer*, 20 February 1983, 11.
175. *Times of India*, 11 February 1983, 1.
176. *Times of India*, 2 January 1983, 1.
177. Chakraborty, *The Upheaval Years in North-East India: A Documentary In-depth Study of Assam Holocausts, 1960–1983*, 183–85.
178. *Indian Express*, 10 February 1983, 1.
179. 'Letter from Indira Gandhi to Dorothy Norman, 10 February 1983', in Norman, *Indira Gandhi: Letters to an American Friend, 1950–1984*, 170.
180. This account is based on Prasar Bharati Archives, https://www.youtube.com/watch?v=FmR39rIGOJI (Accessed 22 November 2020).
181. Wajahat Habibullah, *My Years with Rajiv: Triumph and Tragedy*. When India's Opposition leaders castigated Mrs Gandhi for closing her speech with this phrase, she defended it as a way 'to create a sort of rapport' with the electorate. Speech of Indira Gandhi, *Lok Sabha Debates*, 22 February 1983, column 339.
182. Discussion on Demands for Grants, 1983–84, Ministry of Home Affairs, *Lok Sabha Debates*, 11 April 1983, columns 362–95; *Statesmen*, 22 February

1983, 1; H.K. Barpujari, 'General President's Address: North-East India: The Problems and Policies Since 1947', *Proceedings of the Indian History Congress* 56 (1995), 32; Gupta, *Assam: A Valley Divided*, 35; Mehta, *Report of the Non-Official Judicial Enquiry Commission on Holocaust of Assam*, Annexure T, l; English Translation of Speech of Shri Abdul Ghani Khan Choudhury, Union Railway Minister at Nilbagan, Nagaon, 221–22; Makiko Kimura, *The Nellie Massacre of 1983: Agency of Rioters* (Delhi: Sage Publications, 2015), 85–86.

183. Trevor Fishlock, 'Assam: A furious struggle for survival', *The Times*, 18 February 1983, 12.
184. 'PM rules out Assam poll postponement', *Times of India*, 11 February 1983, 1.
185. Hemendra Narayan, *25 Years On . . . Nellie Still Haunts* (Delhi: Hemendra Narayan, 2008).
186. C. Lokeswar Rao, '14 more die in stir', *Times of India*, 11 April 1983, 1; Trevor Fishlock, '100 die in Assam massacre', *The Times*, 15 February 1983, 1; William Claiborne, '100 die in Assam bow and arrow massacre', *Guardian*, 15 February 1983, 1; *Indian Express*, 15 February 1983, 1; *Indian Express*, 16 February 1983, 1; 'Gandhi's candidate murdered as Assam violence continues', *Washington Post*, 16 February 1983, A23.
187. Election Commission of India, *Statistical Report on General Election, 1983 to the Legislative Assembly of Assam*, 81. Also, see Discussion Regarding Laying of the Report of the Election Commission of India on the General Election to Assam Assembly, *Rajya Sabha Debates*, 2 August 1983, 185–93.
188. *Indian Express*, 19 February 1983, in *25 Years On . . . Nellie Still Haunts*, Narayan. Also, see *Times of India*, 28 February 1983, 1; *Indian Express*, 20 February 1983, 1; *Indian Express*, 21 February 1983, 1.
189. Tewary, *Report of the Commission of Enquiry on Assam Disturbances, 1983*, 280.
190. Ibid.
191. A victim's account quoted in Jabeen Yasmeen, 'Besieged Belonging: "Living on" after the Nellie Massacre' (PhD diss., Indian Institute of Technology, Bombay, 2021), 3. Also, Diganta Sharma, *Nellie, 1983* (Jorhat: Eklabya Prakashan, 2007).
192. Najmul Hasan, 'Election massacre may total 1000', *Guardian*, 21 February 1983, 1.
193. *Assam Tribune*, 21 February 1983, 1.
194. *New York Times*, 22 February 1983, 1; William Claiborne, 'Tremendous Security', *Washington Post*, 26 February 1983, A14; *Indian Express*, 22 February 1983, 1.

195. See https://www.youtube.com/watch?v=a3GZBvYoas4 (Accessed 22 November 2020), Associated Press Archives.
196. *Assam Tribune*, 20 February 1983, 1.
197. *Assam Tribune*, 9 March 1983, 1.
198. Sumanta Sen and Jagannath Dubashi, 'Nellie Massacre: Assam Burns as Ethnic Violence Singes the State', *India Today*, 15 March 1983.
199. Tewary, *Report of the Commission of Enquiry on Assam Disturbances, 1983*, 272.
200. Ibid., 275.
201. *DSR*, 19 February 1983, 6.
202. Tewary, *Report of the Commission of Enquiry on Assam Disturbances, 1983*, 5.
203. Ibid., 6.
204. 'Assam: From Nativism to Communal War' in CIA, *India: The Challenges of Communal and Caste Conflict*, an Intelligence Assessment, 9, https://www.cia.gov/readingroom/docs/CIA-RDP84S00556R000300110002-0.pdf. (Accessed 25 March 2020).
205. When Michael Hamlyn, a journalist from *The Times*, visited Nellie in November 1985, local Muslim populations put the figure at '1026 . . . to be exact'. Michael Hamlyn, 'Villagers reflect on massacre and seek peaceful Assam', *The Times*, 14 November 1985.
206. *Assam Tribune*, 16 February 1983, 4.
207. *Assam Tribune*, 21 February 1983, 4.
208. *Assam Tribune*, 8 March 1983, 1.
209. Government of Assam, *Assessment Report of the South Western Group of the Nowgong District* (Shillong: Assam Government Press, 1932), 13, 51; S.N. Datta, *Report on the Resettlement of the Nowgong District During the Years 1926 (October) to 1932 (January)* (Shillong: Assam Government Press, 1932); Kimura, *The Nellie Massacre of 1983: Agency of Rioters*, 70–72; S.P. Desai, *Report of the Special Officer Appointed for the Examination of Professional Grazing Reserves in Assam Valley* (Shillong: Assam Government Press, 1944), 19–21; *Times of India*, 28 February 1983, 1.
210. 'Petition of Mubarak Ali and Makbul Ali, Kopili Valley, Nagaon to the Conservator of Forests, Assam, 14 February 1956', *Settlement of Land in Nowgong Division*, File no. FOR/155/56, 1957, ASA.
211. Existing writings have emphasized the question of land alienation as central to political conflicts in Nellie and elsewhere in Assam during the February 1983 violence. Kimura, *The Nellie Massacre of 1983: Agency of Rioters*, 74–77; Sanjoy Hazarika, *Rites of Passage* (Delhi: Penguin, 2000), 46.
212. These figures are based on the Statement of K.D. Tripathi, SDO, Marigaon, in Tewary, *Report of the Commission of Enquiry on Assam Disturbances, 1983*, 283.

213. Asghar Ali Engineer, 'Assam: Dirty Hand of RSS', *Illustrated Weekly of India*, 8 May 1983.
214. CIA, *India: The Challenge of Communal and Caste conflict, Secret,* August 1983, 2, Figure 3. For an official account of this sporadic communal violence, see Secret, *Monthly Report to the Governor of Assam,* Government of Assam, Political (A) Department, 21 May 1981 in Monthly Report to the Governor, CMS, CMS/47/80, 1980, ASA.
215. Central Intelligence Agency, *India*: *The Challenge of Communal and Caste Conflict, Secret,* August 1983, 8.
216. Ibid., 3.
217. *Assam Tribune,* 4 March 1983, 1.
218. *Washington Post,* 25 February 1983.
219. *Assam Tribune,* 6 March 1983.
220. *Assam Tribune,* 6 March 1983.
221. Tewary, *Report of the Commission of Enquiry on Assam Disturbances, 1983,* 282.
222. Deposition of Bhadra Kanta Chetia, Officer-in-Charge, Jagiroad Police Station, in Tewary, *Report of the Commission of Enquiry on Assam Disturbances, 1983,* 287.
223. Jahiruddin Ahmed, OC, Nagaon PS, in Tewary, *Report of the Commission of Enquiry on Assam Disturbances, 1983,* 292. Arun Shourie, 'Arun Shourie Turns Up the Most Devastating Evidence on Violence in Assam', *India Today,* 15 May 1983; 'Situation in Assam', Statement of P.C. Sethi, Union Home Minister, *Lok Sabha Debates,* 4 May 1983; *Washington Post,* 5 May 1983.
224. Tewary, *Report of the Commission of Enquiry on Assam Disturbances, 1983,* 263.
225. Statement of M.N.A. Kabir, in *Report of the Commission of Enquiry on Assam Disturbances, 1983,* Tewary, 286.
226. Tewary, *Report of the Commission of Enquiry on Assam Disturbances, 1983,* 281–82.
227. Statement of K.D. Tripathi, Sub-Divisional officer, Morigaon, in Tewary, *Report of the Commission of Enquiry on Assam Disturbances, 1983,* 282.
228. Tewary, *Report of the Commission of Enquiry on Assam Disturbances, 1983,* 285.
229. Ibid., 270.
230. Ibid., 310; Mehta, *Report of the Non-Official Judicial Inquiry Commission on the Holocaust of Assam Before, During and After Election 1983.*
231. Mehta, *Report of the Non-Official Judicial Inquiry Commission on the Holocaust of Assam Before, During and After Election 1983*; Kimura, *The*

*Nellie Massacre of 1983: Agency of Rioters*, 74–76; Tewary, *Report of the Commission of Enquiry on Assam Disturbances, 1983*, 272.

232. Kimura, *The Nellie Massacre of 1983: Agency of Rioters*, 75; Mehta, *Report of the Non-Official Judicial Inquiry Commission on the Holocaust of Assam Before During and After Election 1983*, 169; Tewary, *Report of the Commission of Enquiry on Assam Disturbances, 1983*, 179–82.
233. Mehta, *Report of the Non-Official Judicial Inquiry Commission on the Holocaust of Assam Before, During and After Election 1983*, 165.
234. *Times of India*, 21 February 1983, 1; *Indian Express*, 24 February 1983, 1; *Indian Express*, 25 February 1983, 1.
235. Mehta, *Report of the Non-Official Judicial Inquiry Commission on the Holocaust of Assam Before, During and After Election 1983*, 153; Tewary, *Report of the Commission of Enquiry on Assam Disturbances, 1983*, 179–82; Diganta Sharma, *Chaulkhowa, 1983* (Jorhat: Ekalabya Prakashan, 2012).
236. *Statesman*, 14 September 1983, 1.
237. *Indian Express*, 18 February 1983, 7. On 17 February, the Election Commission of India sent a note to the law ministry which stated, 'It was also known that in the commission's view an ideal situation would have been [to hold the election] when a solution to the main problem of foreign nationals would have been found'. 'EC was against third round of Assam poll', *Indian Express*, 18 February 1983, 1.
238. Ibid.
239. *Assam Tribune*, 1 March 1983, 1.
240. *Assam Tribune*, 2 March 1983, 1.
241. Ibid.
242. Government of India, *Assam Events in Perspective* (New Delhi: Directorate of Advertising and Visual Publicity, 1983), 2.
243. Ibid, 3.
244. Editorial, 'Cruel choice in Assam', *Times of India*, 11 February 1983, 8.
245. Ibid.
246. Rafiq Ahmad, *The Assam Massacre: A Documentary Study* (Lahore: University of the Punjab, 1984).
247. *Washington Post*, 9 March 1983.
248. *Assam Tribune*, 26 February 1983, 1.
249. Editorial, 'Mrs Gandhi flies into a tragedy', *Guardian*, 22 February 1983, 12.
250. Ibid.
251. Peter Ronald deSouza, 'How Assam's tragedy echoes Gandhi's partition dilemma?', *Guardian*, 25 February 1983, 14.
252. Editorial, 'After the carnage', *Times of India*, 22 February 1983, 8.
253. 'Assam's death poll', *Far Eastern Economic Review*, 10 March 1983.

254. Mehta, *Report of the Non-Official Judicial Inquiry Commission on the Holocaust of Assam Before, During and After Election 1983*.
255. 'Tewar[e] Panel Report "A Closely Guarded Secret"', *Assam Tribune*, 19 June 1984, 1.
256. Chakrabarty, *The Upheaval Years in North East India: A Documentary In-depth Study of Assam Holocausts, 1960–1983*, 186.
257. Ajoy Bose, 'Hollow victory for Gandhi in Assam', *Guardian*, 23 February 1983, 6.
258. Speech of Indira Gandhi, *Lok Sabha Debates*, 22 February 1983, Column 340.
259. *Assam Tribune*, 1 March 1983, 1.
260. CIA, 'Indira Gandhi and Assam: A Muddled Response', in *Near East and South Asia Review*, 13 September 1985, in https://www.cia.gov/library/readingroom/docs/CIA-RDP87T00289R000100190001-8.pdf (Accessed 12 May 2020).
261. Shekhar Gupta, 'The Agitation Is Over. It Is Dead and Gone: Sarat Chandra Sinha', *India Today*, 15 September 1983.
262. 'Interview with Hiteswar Saikia', *India Today*, 15 August 1984; K. Sreedhar Rao, *Whither Governance: Reflections of an Assam Civilian* (New Delhi: South Asia Foundation, 2002), 158.
263. Amandeep Sandhu, *Punjab: Journeys Through Fault Lines* (Chennai: Westland, 2019); Gurharpal Singh and Giorgio Shani, *Sikh Nationalism: From a Dominant Minority to an Ethno-Religious Diaspora* (New Delhi: Cambridge University Press, 2022), Chapter 6; Mark Tully and Satish Jacob, *Amritsar: Mrs Gandhi's Last Battle* (Delhi: Rupa Publications, 2021).
264. *DSR*, no. 167, 15 June 1984, paras 6–47; *Assam Tribune*, 15 June 1984, 1, 16 June 1984, 1.
265. *Assam Tribune*, 5 July 1984, 1; *Dainik Asam*, 5 July 1984, 1; *Assam Tribune*, 6 July 1984, 1.
266. *Dainik Asam*, 1 and 2 July 1984; *Assam Tribune*, 8 August 1984; Anonymous, 'Centre Should Not Talk to AASU Alone: Hiteswar Saikia', Excerpts of Interview with Hiteswar Saikia, *India Today*, 15 August 1984.
267. Statement of Dhani Ram Rongphi, Minister, Forests, *Assam Legislative Assembly Proceedings*, 2 April 1984; *Dainik Asam*, 20 August 1984.
268. *New York Times*, 22 April 1984, section 1, 5, 9 May 1984, section A, 5.
269. 'India to proceed with fence on border with Bangladesh', *New York Times*, 16 September 1984, section 1, 3.
270. 'Mrs. Gandhi bars talks with Assam Protesters', *New York Times*, 4 February 1984, 5.
271. Sanjoy Hazarika, 'Assam's activists meet Mrs. Gandhi', *New York Times*, 25 July 1984, 3.

272. 'We have problems in Punjab and in Assam, we are looking towards solving those problems and we are hopeful that we will be able to come in front of you with some good news . . .' Speech of Rajiv Gandhi, *Lok Sabha Debates*, 22 January 1985, column 315; Written Answers, no. 177, Statement of S.B. Chavan, Minister of Home Affairs, *Lok Sabha Debates*, 3 January 1985, column 53; *Assam Tribune*, 5 January 1985; *Assam Tribune*, 6 January 1985; *Dainik Asam*, 7 January 1985; *New York Times*, 6 January 1985; President's Address to both Houses of Parliament, *Lok Sabha Debates*, 17 January 1985, column 8; *Assam Tribune*, 7 January 1985; *Dainik Asam*, 16 January 1985.
273. Pradhan, *Working with Rajiv Gandhi*, 93.
274. *Assam Tribune*, 19 July 1985, 1.
275. *Assam Tribune*, 25 May 1984, 1; Sumit Mitra, 'AASU Leaders' Talks with Union Government Reach Nowhere', *India Today*, 31 May 1985; Mani Shankar Aiyar, *Rajiv Gandhi's India: A Golden Jubilee Perspective, Nationhood, Ethnicity, Pluralism and Conflict Resolution*, vol. 1 (New Delhi: UBSPD, 1998), 88.
276. Pradhan, *Working with Rajiv Gandhi*, 93; 'Statement of R.D. Pradhan', in Aiyar, *Rajiv Gandhi's India: A Golden Jubilee Perspective, Nationhood, Ethnicity, Pluralism and Conflict Resolution*, vol. 1, 88–89.
277. 'Actually, initially, I was reluctant. I must say frankly at that time I was not for the Accord. I told the Governor at that time that as the AASU [All-Assam Students' Union] was now dead, why should we go for the Accord'. Speech of Hiteswar Saikia, in *Rajiv Gandhi's India: A Golden Jubilee Perspective, Nationhood, Ethnicity, Pluralism and Conflict Resolution*, Aiyar, vol. 1, 78.
278. In November 1984, when revision for the electoral roll was in progress for India's General Elections to be held in December 1984—though Assam and Punjab were kept out of this election, a decision largely influenced by the violent experiences of 1980 and 1983—the AASU, despite hesitation in some quarters, did not oppose the move. 'Statutory Resolution Regarding Disapproval of Representation of the People (Amendment) Ordinance and Representation of the People (Amendment) Bill', Statement of A.K. Sen, Minister of Law Justice, *Lok Sabha Debates*, 23 January 1985, columns 190–93; *Dainik Asam*, 8 January 1985, 1; *Assam Tribune*, 20 November 1984, 1. Weeks later, the *Assam Tribune* reported that 'The Assam agitation leaders appear to be keen on reaching out a settlement as the completion of the enumeration process would meet the most important aspect of their demand concerning the foreigners who came to Assam after 1971', *Assam Tribune*, 5 January 1985, 1. On 16 January 1985, the AASU leaders met the Governor of Assam, seeking the prime minister's intervention to resolve the Assam crisis. *Dainik Asam*, 16 January 1985, 1. *Dainik Asam*, 5 January 1985; *Dainik Asam*, 11 January 1985.

279. *Assam Tribune*, 28 July 1985, 1; *Assam Tribune*, 29 July 1985, 1; *Assam Tribune*, 30 July 1985, 1. The *Assam Tribune* reported how the Assam leaders 'who were insisting on a package deal to arrive at a final solution were also found in happy mood' after the Shillong meeting. *Assam Tribune*, 31 July 1985, 1.
280. Pradhan, *Working with Rajiv Gandhi*, 103.
281. *Assam Tribune*, 26 and 27 August 1984, 3; Hemendra Narayan, 'AASU scores on scrutiny issue', *Indian Express*, 13 January 1985, 1.
282. Pradhan, *Working with Rajiv Gandhi*, 94.
283. Ibid., 105.
284. Quoted in K.C. Khanna, 'Minefield of Uncertainties: The Assam Accord and After', *Times of India*, 20 August 1985.
285. Hiteswar Saikia acknowledged that, to him, 'the Accord was good because, for the first time, those who came to Assam right from 1947 to 1971 after the Partition were recognised' as citizens of India. 'Speech of Hiteswar Saikia', in Aiyar, *Rajiv Gandhi's India: A Golden Jubilee Perspective, Nationhood, Ethnicity, Pluralism and Conflict Resolution*, vol. 1, 97.
286. 'Speech of R.D. Pradhan', in Aiyar, *Rajiv Gandhi's India: A Golden Jubilee Perspective, Nationhood, Ethnicity, Pluralism and Conflict Resolution*, vol. 1, 96–97.
287. Pradhan recounted what he told the AASU leaders during the process of negotiations, 'Every time I warned them, even up to the end: "Look, you are making implementation of the Accord progressively more difficult and do not blame me if this Accord is not implemented in the way in which you think it should be implemented. It is not a legal document in that sense. But it is a commitment, a commitment made at a political level. So do not make it far too complex".' 'Speech of R.D. Pradhan', in *Rajiv Gandhi's India: A Golden Jubilee Perspective, Nationhood, Ethnicity, Pluralism and Conflict Resolution*, Aiyar, vol. 1, 96–97.
288. *New York Times*, 4 December 1985; Election Commission of India, *Statistical Report on General Election, 1985 to the Legislative Assembly of Assam*, 3; *The Times*, 7 November 1985, 9.
289. *Times of India*, 18 August 1985.
290. Ibid.
291. CIA, *Assam: A Thumbnail Sketch*.
292. *New York Times*, 6 December 1985, Section A, 2. Also, *Indian Express*, 25 October 1985. For various developments and views of the Union Government during the years 1985 and 1987 regarding the removal of the names of illegal foreigners from the electoral rolls of Assam, see, C.L. Rose, Secretary, Election Commission of India, 'Notes: Election Commission of India', 8 May 1987, in Detection and Deletion of Names of Foreigners

from the Electoral Rolls of Assam, Election Commission of India, Election VII, File no. 23/AS/1/87, 1986, Abhilekh Patal, NAI.
293. Sanjoy Hazarika, 'Peace fragile in Assam a year after carnage', *New York Times*, 26 February 1984, section1, 1; *Dainik Asam*, 9 January 1985, 1; *Dainik Asam*, 10 January 1985, 1.
294. *Times of India*, 13 October 1985, 1; *Statesman*, 14 October 1985; *Indian Express*, 16 October 1985, 1.
295. M. Kar, *Muslims in Assam* (New Delhi: Vikas Publishing House, 1997), Table 7.10, 372; *Statesman*, 20 December 1985, 1; *Hindustan Times*, 26 November 1985, 6.
296. *Dainik Asam*, 4 December 1985, 1.
297. Election Commission of India, *Statistical Report on General Election, 1985 to the Legislative Assembly of Assam*, 156–57; Kar, *Muslims in Assam*, 372, Table 7.6; *Indian Express*, 19 December 1985, 6; *Indian Express*, 20 December 1985, 1.
298. *Washington Post*, 21 December 1985.
299. Motion to Adopt Citizenship (Amendment) Bill, 1985, *Lok Sabha Debates*, 20 November 1985, Columns 309–10; The Citizenship (Amendment) Bill, 1985, *Rajya Sabha Debates*, 2 December 1985, 304–400 and 3 December 1985, 206–33. For details on the Citizenship (Amendment) Act, 1985, see Prarthana Saikia, 'Citizenship, Nationality and Assam: A Political History since 1947' (PhD diss., Indian Institute of Technology, Guwahati, 2021), 213–22.
300. *Times of India*, 15 August 1988, 9; Prasun Sonwalkar, 'Political tremors rocking Assam', *Times of India*, 15 August 1988, 15; Dipak Kumar Sarma, 'Factional Politics in Assam: A Study on the Asom Gana Parishad' (PhD diss., Indian Institute of Technology, Guwahati, 2017), 138–39. News of corruption came to haunt the AGP government again during its second term. See Hiren Gohain, 'The LOC Snowball', *Economic & Political Weekly*, vol. 31, no. 52 (1996), 3347–49; Mrinal Talukdar, *Assam After Independence* (Guwahati: Nanda Talukdar Foundation, 2017), 318–19.
301. *Indian Express*, 1 December 1990, 1.
302. *Times of India*, 4 August 1988, 3.
303. *Times of India*, 15 August 1988, 9;
304. *Times of India*, 12 January 1988, 17; *Assam Tribune*, 23 February 1986, 1.
305. Ruben Banerjee, 'Fragile Victory', *India Today*, 31 May 1996.
306. *Times of India*, 6 May 1986, 8.
307. *Assam Tribune*, 22 July 1986, 1; *Assam Tribune*, 23 July 1986, 1.
308. *Assam Tribune*, 23 July 1986; *Times of India*, 2 February 1986, IV; *Times of India*, 15 June 1986, 9.

## Chapter 13: Moving towards the Millennium

1. Audrey Cantlie, 'Caste and Sect in an Assamese Village' (PhD diss., School of Oriental and African Studies, University of London, 1980). The fieldwork for this was conducted during 1969–71; Kishore Kumar Bhattacharyya, 'Structure and Individual in Assamese Society: A Study of Family, Kinship, Caste and Religion' (PhD diss., Gauhati University, 1990). The fieldwork for this work was conducted in the late 1980s.
2. Bhattacharyya, 'Structure and Individual in Assamese Society: A Study of Family, Kinship, Caste and Religion', 349 and 362.
3. Ibid, 362.
4. B.C. Sengupta, 'Note on the Depressed and Backward Classes of Assam Submitted to the Indian Franchise Commission', quoted in C.S. Mullan, *Report on the Census of India,* 1931, vol. 3, Assam, part 1 (Calcutta: Government of India, 1932), Appendix 1, 213. Also, see Radhika Mohan Goswami, *Ateet Smriti* (Guwahati: Alok Prakasan, 1989), 28; Gitashree Tamuly, 'Lakshminath Bezbaroa and His Times: Language, Literature and Modernity in Colonial Assam' (PhD diss., Indian Institute of Technology Guwahati, 2021), 271.
5. 'Sadou Asam Ahom Chatra Federation-ar Gohari', Ahom Chatrabash, Jorhat, 7 November 1945, in 'Lakshminath Bezbaroa and His Times: Language, Literature and Modernity in Colonial Assam', Tamuly, Chapter 4, 271.
6. H.C. Chakladar, 'Foreword', in *Assam o Bangadesher Bibaha-paddhati*, ed., Bijaybhusan Ghosh Choudhury (Calcutta: Author, 1932).
7. Utsavananda Goswami, *Malou Patharor Buranji* (Jorhat: n.p. 1929).
8. Anonymous, *Asavarna Vivah* (Jorhat: Darpan Press, 1928).
9. *Times of Assam*, 16 March 1935, 1.
10. *Natun Asamiya*, 21 April 1954, 4.
11. *Natun Asamiya*, 1 April 1954, 4.
12. Planters as legislators—though only nine among the approximately 3000 members in 1946—had played a definitive role in Assam's legislative arena, which was a point of contention for the Assamese leaders. Amalendu Guha, *Planter Raj to Swaraj: Freedom Struggle & Electoral Politics in Assam 1826–1947* (Delhi: Indian Council of Historical Research, 1977), 219.
13. Illustrations are numerous from the official archival records of the colonial period. For instance, see W.S. Seton-Karr, Secretary to the Government of India, Foreign Department, 'Note on the late inroads of the Loosais of the Kookie tribe into Sylhet and Cachar, and on the operations undertaken in consequence', 30 April 1869, Shimla, in *Loosai Raids on the Eastern Frontier*

*of Bengal and in Munnipore*, File no. 216–292, 1869, Foreign Department, Political Branch, Abhilekh Patal, NAI.

14. Percival Joseph Griffiths, *The History of the Indian Tea Industry* (London: Weidenfeld and Nicolson, 1967), 564; R.C. Awasthi, *Economics of Tea Industry in India: with Special Reference to Assam* (Guwahati: United Publishers, 1975), 410–12.
15. *Judgement on the Assam Company versus the State of Assam and others,* 6 March 1953, Gauhati High Court, https://indiankanoon.org/doc/1337452/ (Accessed 13 May 2020).
16. Government of India, *India: A Reference Manual* (Delhi: Ministry of Information and Broadcasting, 1955), 478; Indian Tea Association, *Detailed Report of the General Committee of the Indian Tea Association for the Year 1958* (Calcutta: Indian Tea Association, 1959), 48.
17. H.A. Antrobus, *A History of the Assam Company, 1839–1953* (Edinburg: T. and A. Constable Ltd, 1957), 246.
18. Griffiths, *The History of the Indian Tea Industry*, 248–49.
19. 'It has been a very worrying and anxious time for our managers with godowns practically empty and no knowledge of where next week's supplies were to come from . . . they have managed to scrape through without serious labour unrest,' one tea company reported to its shareholders in 1967. 'Williamson Tea Holding Limited', *The Times*, 13 September 1967, 22.
20. Government of India, *Ministry of Commerce Ad Hoc Committee on Tea Questionnaire: Memorandum by the Indian Tea Association* (Calcutta: Central Tea Board, 1950), 65, 105.
21. 'The Assam Frontier Tea Company', *The Times*, 8 August 1958, 13.
22. Oscar Flex, *Assam: 1864*, Translated by Salim Ali (Guwahati: G.L. Publications, 2010).
23. *New York Times*, 10 May 1953, 9.
24. 'Resolution Regarding Nationalisation of Tea Industry', Speech of Morarji Desai, *Lok Sabha Debates*, 22 March 1957, column 486.
25. Ajit Kumar Sharma, *Asomor Chah Udyogat Bideshi Muldhan* (Guwahati: Author, 1966).
26. David Wainwright, *Brooke Bond: A Hundred Years* (London: Brooke Bond Liebig Ltd, 1969).
27. *The Tea & Coffee Trade Journal*, vol. 100–01 (New York: Tea and Coffee Trade Journal Company,1951), 37.
28. Prasad Ranjan Ray, *A Strategy for Rejuvenation of Indian Tea* (Ithaca: Cornell University, 1981); Jonathan Barker, *The Politics of Agriculture in Tropical Africa* (Beverly Hills: Sage Publications, 1984).
29. *The Times*, 11 August 1964, 12.

30. Government of India, *Report of the Plantation Inquiry Commission, 1956*, part 1, Tea (New Delhi: Manager of Publications, 1956), Table IX-A, 27–28, 36.
31. Upendra Nath Bordoloi, *Asomor Arthanaitik Paristhiti: A Collection of Articles on Economic Affairs of Assam* (Guwahati: Gauhati University, 1974), 200–01.
32. Stephanie Jones, *Merchants of the Raj: British Managing Agency Houses in Calcutta Yesterday and Today* (London: Macmillan, 1992), 183.
33. Chief Secretary to the Government of Assam, 'Fortnightly Report for Assam, 1st half of April 1957', in *Fortnightly Report from the Government of Assam for 1957*, File no 4/17/57-Poll.II, Political-II section, Ministry of Home Affairs, Government of India, 1957, Abhilekh Patal, NAI.
34. Ibid, para IV, 2.
35. Government of India, *Report of the Plantation Inquiry Commission, 1956*, 128.
36. 'Welcome recovery of tea industry', *Assam Tribune*, 22 April 1954, 5. Other planters equally resisted the new taxes. The gross profit for the year, after depreciation and interest charges, was £ 4,04, 841, a record for the company. Of this, no less than £ 2,34, 250 is torn from us by the tax collectors. Government's demands, however, do not end with what they seize by direct taxation'. 'Report of the Annual General Meeting of Assam Consolidated Tea Estates', *The Times*, 18 November 1955, 16. Also, 'The Assam Frontier Tea', *The Times*, 11 August 1954, 10.
37. Indian Tea Association, *Report: Indian Tea Association, 1964* (Calcutta: Indian Tea Association, 1964), 33–34; Tea Board of India, *Tea Statistics, 1963–64* (Calcutta: Tea Board of India, 1965), 61.
38. For an insight into the anxieties and various lobbying done by the tea planters to overcome this renewed taxation pressure, see 'Letter from Consultative Committee of Tea Producers Associations to the Secretary, Government of Assam, 16 April 1963' and 'Letter from Secretary, Consultative Committee of Tea Producers Associations to Secretary, Finance Department, Government of Assam, 18 March 1964' in *Assam Agricultural Income Tax and Carriage Tax*, Mss Eur F174/1224: May 1963–Sep 1979 (Asia, Pacific and Africa Collection, BL).
39. Government of India, 'Plantations', *Journal of Industry and Trade*, vol. XV, no. 2 (February 1965), 231.
40. Tea Board of India, *Tea Statistics, 1970–71* (Calcutta: Tea Board of India, 1971), 92.
41. Instances were that of the Namdang Tea Company and Makum Tea Company. 'Letter from Namdang Tea Company Limited and Makum (Assam) Tea Company Limited to Adviser, Makum (Assam) Tea Co. Ltd, Marketing Division, 25 October 1971', Correspondence with the Adviser,

June 1971–August 1972, File Reference Code: GBR/0012/MS JS/12/4/7, Jardine Skinner Archive, Royal Commonwealth Society Collection, Cambridge University Library.
42. Atul Goswami, 'Assam's Industrial Development: Urgency of New Direction', *Economic & Political Weekly*, vol. 16, no. 21 (23 May 1981), 954; Tea Board of India, *Tea Statistics for the Year 1977* (Calcutta: Tea Board of India, 1977), Table 3 (ii), xii; Government of India, *Economic Survey: Assam, 1980–81* (Guwahati: Directorate of Economics and Statistics, 1981), 32.
43. 'Editorial', *Assam Tribune*, 27 July 1978, 4; S.N. Barua, 'Tea Companies and Tea Board', Letters to the Editor, *Assam Tribune*, 2 August 1978, 4; Ratul Borah and Romesh Sarmah, 'Tea Companies', Letters to the Editor, *Assam Tribune*, 11 August 1978. 4.
44. Soneswar Bora, 'Asomot Khudra Chah Kheti: Ek Samajbadi Biplab', in *Cha-Tsing: Souvenir of All Assam Tea Growers Association*, ed. Jatindra Nath Saikia (Golaghat: All Assam Tea Growers Association, 2000), 30–34; J.N. Saikia, 'Gongadhar Saikia: The Versatile Genius with a Towering Personality', in *Gangey: Khyudhra Sah Khetiyokor Pitriswarup Gangadhar Saikiadewor Smarok Grantha*, eds, P. Saikia and R. Borgohain (Golaghat: All Assam Small Tea Growers Association, 2018).
45. 'Assam's scheme to aid poor farmers', *Times of India*, 9 October 1978, 14.
46. Government of India, *Report of the Plantation Inquiry* Commission, 1956, Appendix IX.
47. Tea Board of India, *Tea Statistics, 1956*, Table 1 (iv): Acreage and Production of tea in the tea growing districts of North India classified according to the sizes of the estates, 5.
48. Tea Board of India, *Tea Statistics, 1960*, Table 1 (vi): Area and Production of tea in the tea growing districts of North India and South India classified according to the sizes of the estates for 1959–60, 7.
49. Tea Board of India, *Tea Statistics, 2001*, Table 3 (viii) b: Size wide area and production of tea in India during 2000, 22.
50. Tea Board of India, *Tea Statistics, 2000–2001*, Table 3 (vii): Estimated Production of Cooperative and Bought Leaf Factories in India, 17. In 1998, the number of such factories was 61.
51. Ajit Kumar Bora, 'Introduction of Small Scale Tea Cultivation and Its Impact on Land Use and Socio-economic Condition of the People of Sivasagar District, Assam' (PhD diss., North-Eastern Hill University, 2008), 44.
52. Sharit K. Bhowmik. 'Small Growers to Prop up Large Plantations', *Economic & Political Weekly*, vol. 26, no. 30 (27 July 1991), 1789.
53. Tea Board of India, *Draft Eighth Five-Year Plan for Tea Industry, 1990–91 to 1991–95*, in 'Small Growers to Prop Up Large Plantations', Bhowmik, 1790.

54. 'Small Tea Growers to be Promoted', *Assam Information*, vol. xxxiv (October 1992), 39–40.
55. Parag Kumar Das, *Swadhin Asomor Arthoniti* (Guwahati: Alibat), 2018, Table 10, Statistical Details of Small Tea Cultivators of Assam, 1993, 118–19.
56. Abdul Hannan, 'Farm Size and Trade Relations of Small Tea Growers (STGs) in Assam and North Bengal', *Social Change and Development*, vol. XVI, no. 2 (2019), Table 2.
57. Yujiro Hayami and A. Damodaran, 'Towards an Alternative Agrarian Reform: Tea Plantations in South India', *Economic & Political Weekly*, vol. 39, no. 36 (2004), 3992–97; Deepak K. Mishra, Atul Sarma and Vandana Upadhyay, 'Invisible Chains? Crisis in the Tea Industry and the "Unfreedom" of Labour in Assam's Tea Plantations', *Contemporary South Asia*, vol. 19, no. 1 (2011), 75–90.
58. For further reading on the making of the KNP, see Arupjyoti Saikia, 'The Kaziranga National Park: Dynamics of Social and Political History', *Conservation and Society*, vol. 7, no. 2 (2009), 113–29; Arupjyoti Saikia, 'Rhinoceros in Kaziranga National Park: Nature and Politics in Assam', in *Reframing the Environment: Resources, Risk and Resistance in Neoliberal India*, ed. Manisha Rao (New York: Routledge, 2021), 159–203; Biswajit Sarmah, 'Park, People and Politics: An Environmental History of the Kaziranga National Park' (PhD diss., Indian Institute of Technology, Guwahati, 2021).
59. *Indian Express*, 31 March 1984, 1.
60. Note by Samar Singh, Joint Secretary, Ministry of Environment and Wildlife, GoI, 17 February 1984, in *Rhino Re-introduction Programme from Kaziranga National Park to Dudhwa National Park, UP*, File no. 7–15/79 FRY (WL), vol. iii, RR 3543/94, Ministry of Environment and Forests, Government of India, Abhilekh Patal, NAI.
61. Letter from Indira Gandhi to Hiteswar Saikia, 18 August 1983, New Delhi, no. 641/PMO/83, in *Rhino Re-introduction Programme from Kaziranga National Park, Assam to Dudhwa National Park, UP*.
62. Ibid.
63. Samar Singh and Kishore Rao, 'India's Rhino Re-introduction Programme', in *Rhino Re-introduction Programme from Kaziranga National Park, Assam to Dudhwa National Park, UP*, 5–6.
64. Kunal Verma, 'Rhinos from Pobitara Sanctuary in Assam relocated to Dudhwa National Park in UP', *India Today*, 30 April 1984.
65. Letter from Indira Gandhi to Hiteswar Saikia, 18 August 1983, New Delhi, no. 641/PMO/83, in *Rhino Re-introduction Programme from Kaziranga National Park*.

66. Letter from Digvijay Singh, Lok Sabha MP to Hiteswar Saikia, Chief Minister, Assam, 5 April 1984, in *Rhino Re-introduction Programme from Kaziranga National Park, Assam to Dudhwa National Park, UP*.
67. Sanjoy Hazarika, 'Violence and poaching threaten India wildlife', *New York Times*, 12 September 1989, section C, 4.
68. A.J.W. Milroy, 'The North Kamrup Game Sanctuary, Assam', *Indian Forester*, vol. 42 (1916), 452–64.
69. The 1971 figure is cited from L.C. Sharma, 'India's Forests and Their Potential for the Economy', *Commonwealth Forestry Review*, vol. 51, no. 4 [150] (1972), 307–13.
70. This estimate is based on Government of India, *The State of Forest Report*, 1989 (Dehra Dun: Forest Survey of India, 1989), Table 1.2, 20; Government of India, *The State of Forest Report*, 1993 (Dehra Dun: Forest Survey of India, 1993), Table 1.11, 28.
71. Sandhya Goswami, 'Ethnic Conflict in Assam', *Indian Journal of Political Science*, vol. 62, no. 1 (2001), 134.
72. Anwesha Dutta, 'No Way Out of the Woods: Political Ecology of Extraction, Livelihoods and Conservation in Assam' (PhD diss., Ghent University, 2019); Saba Sharma, 'Territories of belonging: Citizenship and everyday practices of the state in Bodoland' (PhD diss., Cambridge University, 2019).
73. *Natun Dainik*, 21 July 1994, 1.
74. Government of Assam, *Report on the Land Revenue Administration of Assam for the Year 1960–61* (Shillong: Assam Government Press), Appendix I, 14.
75. Ibid., Appendix II, 16.
76. Chandrama Goswami, 'Agricultural Land Use in the Plains of Assam', *Economic & Political Weekly*, vol. 37, no. 49 (2002), Table 1, 4891–93.
77. Reserve Bank of India, *Handbook of Statistics on Indian States, 2018–19* (Mumbai: Reserve Bank of India, 2019), Table 45: State-Wise Pattern of Land Use: Gross Sown Area and Table 46, State-Wise Pattern of Land Use: Net Sown Area, 187–92.
78. Government of Assam, *Economic Survey: Assam, 1976–1977* (Guwahati: Directorate of Economics and Statistics, 1977), Chapter IV, Table 4.2.
79. 'World Agricultural Census, 1970-71'; in *Peasant Agriculture in Assam*, M.M. Das (Delhi: Inter India Publications, 1984), Table 10.1, 159.
80. A combined unit of nitrogen, phosphorous and potassium. Reserve Bank of India, *Handbook of Statistics on Indian States, 2018–19*, Table 81. States like Punjab, Andhra Pradesh and Tamil Nadu had very high figures (161.9, 123.2 and 128.8, respectively).

81. Government of Assam, *Report on Agricultural Census 2010–11 on Number and Area of Operational Holdings* (Guwahati: Directorate of Economics and Statistics, 2014), Table 4, 10.
82. K.C. Talukdar, 'Structural Changes in Assam Agriculture', *Agricultural Economic Research Revenue*, vol. 6, no. 1 (1993), Appendix 1, 'Triennium average area of HYV paddy in different districts of Assam', 50; Government of Assam, *Statistical Hand Book: Assam, 2001* (Guwahati: Directorate of Economics and Statistics, 2001), Table 3.11, 68.
83. Harish Damodaran, *India's New Capitalists: Caste, Business, and Industry in a Modern Nation* (New Delhi: Hachette India, 2018), 260–61.
84. Government of India, *15th Indian Livestock Census 1992*, vol. 1 (New Delhi: Ministry of Agriculture, 1992), 'Number of Tractor, Power & Other Agricultural Implements in Assam (1992), Part 1', in https://www.indiastat.com/table/assam-state/agriculture/number-tractor-power-and-other-agricultural-implem/111386 (Accessed 16 June 2020).
85. Anupam Sarkar, 'Tractor Production and Sales in India, 1989–2009', *Review of Agrarian Studies*, vol. 3, no. 1 (2013), 55–72.
86. Estimates are computed from Table 'Area for Jute in Assam (1950–51 to 1960–61)' and Table 'Area for Jute in Assam (1991–92 to 2000–2001)', https://www.indiastat.com/table/assam-state/jute/area-jute-assam-1950-1951-1960-1961/111334 & https://www.indiastat.com/table/assam-state/jute/area-jute-assam-1991-1992-2000-2001/112824 [Accessed 18 March 2020].
87. B.N. Bordoloi, *Report on the Displacement of Tribals due to Installation of Major Irrigation Project: The Case Study of Dhansiri Irrigation Project in the Darrang District of Assam, Dhansiri Irrigation Project* (Guwahati: Tribal Research Institute, Assam, 1984), 19.
88. Walter Fernandes, 'Internally Displaced Persons and Northeast India', *International Studies*, vol. 50, no. 4 (2013), Table 1, 287–305.
89. Reserve Bank of India, *Handbook of Statistics on Indian States, 2015–16* (Mumbai: Reserve Bank of India, 2016), Table 12.
90. K. Sundaram and Suresh D. Tendulkar, 'Poverty in India in the 1990s: An Analysis of Changes in 15 Major States', *Economic & Political Weekly*, vol. 38, no. 14 (2003), 1385–93.
91. Sundaram and Tendulkar, 'Poverty in India in the 1990: An Analysis of Changes in 15 Major States', 1389–90.
92. Ibid.
93. Government of Assam, *Economic Survey: Assam, 1981–82* (Guwahati: Directorate of Economics and Statistics, 1982), Appendix XIX, 76.

94. Government of Assam, *Statistical Hand Book: Assam, 2001* (Guwahati: Directorate of Economics and Statistics, 2001), Table 11.05, 106.
95. Based on India's census estimate of 1961, in *Sons of the Soil: Migration and Ethnic Conflict in India*, Myron Weiner (Princeton: Princeton University Press, 2015).
96. Government of India, *Census of India, 2001: Language, India, States and Union Territories* (New Delhi: Registrar General, India, 2007), Table C-16, Part A: Distribution of the 22 Scheduled Languages - India/ States/ Union Territories - 2001 Census, 20–27.
97. Memorandum to Rajiv Gandhi, Prime Minister, India, from All Assam Oil Refinery Sangram Parisad, 26 June 1987, in *Assam Fights for Public Sector Oil Refinery, with 3 Million Tonnes Initial Capacity*, Guwahati, 29 November 1987.
98. P.K. Sarma, et al., 'A Geo-Spatial Assessment of Habitat Loss of Asian Elephants in Golaghat District of Assam', *Gajah*, vol. 28 (2008), 25–30; Maan Barua, 'The Political Ecology of Human–Elephant Relationships in India: Encounters, Spaces, Politics' (PhD diss., Oxford University, 2013).
99. Government of Assam, *Economic Survey: Assam, 1980–81*, 33.
100. Ibid.
101. Reserve Bank of India, *Handbook of Statistics on Indian States, 2015–16* (Mumbai: Reserve Bank of India, 2016), Table 16 and 31, 42, 115.
102. Reserve Bank of India, *Handbook of Statistics on State Government Finances*, 2004 (Mumbai: Reserve Bank of India, 2004) Table 5, 13–15.
103. Parag Dutta, 'A Study of State Finances and Fiscal Reforms in Assam Post Reform Experiences and Challenges' (PhD diss., Indian Institute of Technology Guwahati, 2012), Table 3.2: Percentage of contribution of different sources of revenue receipt of the state during 1990–91 to 2009–10, 54; Government of Assam, *Economic Survey: Assam*, 1981–82 (Guwahati: Directorate of Economics and Statistics, 1982), Appendix xxxiv: 91.
104. *Assam Tribune*, 12 June 1986, 1; Reserve Bank of India, *Report on Currency and Finance, 1986–1987*, vol. 1 (Bombay: Reserve Bank of India, 1987), 88.
105. R. Ramalingom and K.N. Kurup, 'Plan Transfers to States: Revised Gadgil Formula: An Analysis', *Economic & Political Weekly*, vol. 26, no. 9/10 (1991), 501–06. Also, see Nikhil Menon, *Planning Democracy: How A Professor, An Institute and An Idea Shaped India* (Delhi: Penguin, 2022), 208–10.
106. Government of India, *Report of the Fifth Finance Commission, 1969* (New Delhi: Manager of Publications, 1969), Chapter 6, 64.
107. Speech of Satish Agarwal, Union Minister of Finance, Government of India, *Lok Sabha Debates*, 4 May 1979, columns 78–79.

108. File no. 12/1/2005–FR, Financial Resource Division, Planning Commission, Government of India, quoted in Govind Bhattacharjee, 'The Reality of Special Category States', *Economic & Political Weekly*, vol. 49, no. 40 (2014), 56, note 10.
109. This section draws from Arupjyoti Saikia, *A Century of Protests: Peasant Politics in Assam since 1900* (Delhi: Routledge, 2014), 325–26.
110. Surendra Nath Medhi, 'Is the Assam Tenancy Act of 1971 a social legislation?', *Assam Tribune*, 24 July 1986, 4.
111. The suggestion put forward by the law minster had raised considerable debate. Durlav Chandra Mahanta, 'Ejan Sahakarmir Dristit Shri Sailen Medhi', in *Sailen Medhi: Byktitwa Aru Samaj Chinta*, ed. Yamini Phukan (Guwahati: 80th Birthday Celebration Committee, 2009), 36–37.
112. *Assam Tribune*, 27 July 1987, 1.
113. Secret, *Daily Situation Report*, Special Branch, Assam Police (hereafter *DSR*) no. 5, 5 January 1980; *DSR*, no. 13, 13 January 1980, para 14, 3.
114. An extensive body of work has thrown light on the political trajectory of the ULFA. This includes N.G. Mahanta, *Confronting the State: ULFA's Quest for Sovereignty* (Delhi: Sage Publications, 2013); S. Baruah, *Durable Disorder: Understanding the Politics of Northeast India* (New Delhi: Oxford University Press, 2007); Samir Kumar Das, *ULFA: United Liberation Front of Assam: A Political Analysis* (Delhi: Ajanta Publications, 1994); Manoj Kumar Nath, *ULFA: Seujiya Sapon, Tejranga Itihasa* (Guwahati: Aank Baak, 2013); Rajeev Bhattacharyya, *Rendezvous with Rebels: Journey to Meet India's Most Wanted Men* (Delhi: HarperCollins, 2014); Mrinal Talukdar, *ULFA* (Guwahati: Nanda Talukdar Foundation, 2011); Sanjoy Hazarika, *Strangers of the Mist: Tales of War and Peace from India's Northeast* (Delhi: Penguin, 1994); Sanjib Baruah, *Beyond Counter-insurgency: Breaking the Impasse in Northeast India* (Delhi: Oxford University Press, 2009); Hiren Gohain, 'Extremist Challenge and Indian State: Case of Assam', *Economic & Political Weekly*, vol. 31, no. 31 (August 1996), 2066–68; and Hiren Gohain, 'Chronicles of Violence and Terror: Rise of United Liberation Front of Asom', *Economic & Political Weekly*, vol. 42, no. 12 (March 2007), 1012–18.
115. S.N.M. Abdi, 'Rising Militancy', *Illustrated Weekly of India*, vol. 111, no. 18 (6 May 1990), 22–25.
116. Uttam Sengupta and Shekhar Gupta, 'Assam in Turmoil: Government Struggles Hopelessly to Establish Semblance of Authority', *India Today*, 15 September 1990.
117. 'ULFA is also trying to usher in social reforms which are laudable,' said Prafulla Kumar Mahanta. Abdi, 'Rising Militancy'.

118. Abdi, 'Rising Militancy'. For reports of ULFA and China connection, see, K. Ajay, 'China accused of engineering tribal battles', *South China Morning Post*, 24 December 1986, 18; Lintner, *Great Game East: India, China and The Struggle for Asia's Most Volatile Frontier*, 185.
119. Editorial, *Swadhinata*, in 'Rising Militancy', Abdi.
120. *Assam Tribune*, 28 May 1986, 1.
121. Bertil Lintner, *Great Game East: India, China and the Struggle for Asia's Most Volatile Frontier* (New Delhi: HarperCollins, 2015), 193 and 197.
122. *Hindustan Times*, 13 September 2020, 1.
123. *Foreign Involvement in Insurgency in North Eastern India: Preparation of White Paper on the Subject by the Ministry of Defence,* File no. NII/102/33/72, secret, Ministry of Home Affairs, Government of India, Naga Unit section, 1972, Abhilekh Patal, NAI.
124. Lintner, *Great Game East: India, China and The Struggle for Asia's Most Volatile Frontier*, 192. Lintner came to this conclusion based on his conversation with the ULFA leaders.
125. Speech of Santosh Mohan Dev, *Lok Sabha Debates*, 21 December 1981, column 419.
126. Sabita Goswami, *Along the Red River: A Memoir* (New Delhi: Zubaan, 2013), 90; Sabita Goswami, *Mon Gangar Tirot* (Guwahati: Assam Book Hive, 2017), 98.
127. For instance, a geologist employed with Oil India Limited was killed in 1980. Hameeduddin Mahmood, 'Assam Agitation Takes a Violent Turn as Congress (I) Forms Govt. at the Centre', *India Today*, 15 February 1980; 'Urban insurgency in Assam', *Times of India*, 2 May 1981, 1.
128. Speech of P.C. Sethi, *Lok Sabha Debates*, 14 March 1983, column 425, 427.
129. For an eyewitness account of such journeys, see Kaberi Kochari Rajkonwar, *Issa Anissa Swotteo Kisu Katha* (Guwahati: Alibat, 2013).
130. Lintner, *Great Game East: India, China and The Struggle for Asia's Most Volatile Frontier*, 188–91.
131. Sanjoy Hazarika, 'Indian Army Fights Rebels in Assam', *New York Times*, 29 November 1990, Section A, 3. Life inside such training camps has been described in several fictionalized, some closer to autobiographical, accounts. See Raktim Sarmah, *Borangga Nang* (Guwahati: Cambridge India, 2006); Anurag Mahanta, *Aoulingor Jui* (Guwahati: Nilay Prakash, 2014). Also, see Anurag Mahanta, *Kongliyangor Maat* (Guwahati: The Panagea House, 2015).
132. 'These boys are very nice. They clean toilets and arrange their own beds. They are prepared to cook food too. They do not expect to be served food

when they return late at night after their work is over. They eat happily whatever is kept aside for them in a plate. They have no bad habits; ULFA boys do not gamble or drink', was the view of one rural woman. Abdi, 'Rising Militancy'.
133. Rakhee Kalita Moral, 'The Woman Rebel and the State: Making War, Making Peace in Assam', *Economic & Political Weekly*, vol. 49, no. 43/44 (2014), 66–73.
134. For details, see Uddipan Dutta, *Creating Robin Hoods: The Insurgency of the ULFA in Its Early Period, Its Parallel Administration and the Role of Assamese Vernacular Press (1985–1990)* (New Delhi: WISCOMP, 2008).
135. *Assam Tribune*, 21 April 1986, 1.
136. Sanjoy Hazarika, 'Tea Factories Shut After Threats by Militants', *New York Times*, 25 November 1991, section 1, 17.
137. 'Letter from T.C. Dutta, commander, District Committee, ULFA', in *Business Maharajas*, Gita Piramal (New Delhi: Penguin, 2011), 289.
138. Darbari Seth, head, Tata Tea, in *Business Maharajas*, Piramal, 261–62; Uttam Sengupta, 'ULFA Threatens Assam Tea Industry', *India Today*, 31 July 1990.
139. *New York Times*, 14 February 1991, Section A, 13.
140. *Times of India*, 28 December 1990.
141. *Assam Tribune*, 28 November 1990, 1, 8.
142. *Indian Express*, 27 November 1990.
143. *Times of India*, 27 December 1990.
144. Editorial, 'Central rule for Assam', *Times of India*, 29 November 1990, 12.
145. Editorial, 'Insurgency in Assam', *Times of India*, 17 November 1990, 8.
146. *Indian Express*, 28 November 1990, 1.
147. *Times of India*, 29 November 1990, 1; *Indian Express*, 29 November 1990, 1; *Associated Press*, 28 November 1990; *Independent* (London), 29 November 1990, 11.
148. Quoted in the *Indian Express*, 29 November 1990, 1. Statement of M.M. Jacob, Minister of State, Ministry of Parliamentary Affairs and Minister of Home Affairs (State), *Lok Sabha Debates,* 22 August 1991, column 143.
149. Sanjoy Hazarika, 'Indian Army Fights Rebels in Assam', *New York Times*, 29 November 1990, Section A, 3; H. K. Barpujari, 'General President's Address: North-East India: The Problems and Policies since 1947', *Proceedings of the Indian History Congress*, vol. 56 (1995), 39.
150. *Assam Tribune*, 30 November 1990, 1.
151. Ibid, 1, 6.
152. *Assam Tribune*, 2 December 1990, 1.
153. 'Fierce fighting at Saraipung, Jawan and ULFA man killed', *Assam Tribune*, 6 December 1990, 1.

154. Udayon Misra, 'No Tears for the Liberators', *Economic & Political Weekly*, vol. 28, no. 32/33 (7 August 1993), 1635–36; Barpujari, 'General President's Address: North-East India: The Problems and Policies since 1947', 40–41.
155. Shekhar Pathak, 'Assam in Turmoil, Government Struggles Hopelessly to Establish Semblance of Authority', *India Today*, 15 September 1990.
156. 'Special provision of reservation demanded', *Assam Tribune*, 22 April 1986, 1.
157. Ranoj Pegu, *Federal Asom Kiyo?* (Why a federal Assam?), a pamphlet issued by URMCA, 1987, in *Asomiya Jatiyotabadi*, ed. Akhil Gogoi (Guwahati: Banalata, 2018), Appendix 9.
158. Editorial, 'URMCA Stir', *Assam Tribune*, 24 April 1986, 4.
159. Abdi, 'Rising Militancy'. The Communist Party referred here was known as the CPI (Marxist-Leninist)'s Bhaskar Nandi group.
160. Pathak, 'Assam in Turmoil, Government Struggles Hopelessly to Establish Semblance of Authority'.
161. Kaushik Roy, *Military Thought of Asia: From the Bronze Age to the Information Age* (New Delhi: Routledge, 2020), 191.
162. Reply to written answers, no. 254, Statement of S.B. Chavan, Union Minister of Home Affairs, *Lok Sabha Debates*, 9 December 1991, column 65; Government of India, *Annual Report, 1991–1992, Ministry of Home Affairs* (New Delhi: Departments of Internal Security, States and Home),12–13.
163. Ajoy Bose, 'Sweep by army in Assam after separatist group kills hostage', *Guardian*, 17 September 1991, 8; Diganta Khargharia, 'Indian Army Captures 100 Guerrillas in Assam Operation', *United Press International*, 16 September 1991; *Statesman*, 6 November 1991.
164. 'Assam at flashpoint', *Times of India*, 10 September 1991, 14.
165. Answer to Written Question no. 504, Statement of M.M Jacob, Union Minister of State, Ministry of Home Affairs, *Lok Sabha Debates*, 25 November 1991, column 261.
166. Ruben Banerjee, 'Hiteswar Saikia Takes Calculated Risk to Buy Peace in Assam', *India Today*, 31 July 1991; Derek Brown, 'All separatists freed in Assam hostage deal', *Guardian*, 10 July 1991, 11; 'Kidnapped Russian Killed in Eastern India', *Agence France Presse*, 9 July 1991; Sanjib Baruah, 'The State and Separatist Militancy in Assam: Winning a Battle and Losing the War?', *Asian Survey*, vol. 34, no. 10 (1994), 873.
167. 'Jailbreaks unnerve Assam gov[ernment]', *Times of India*, 30 June 1991, 4.
168. Piramal, *Business Maharajas*.
169. Dhurbajyoti Bora, *Kalantarar Gadya* (Guwahati: Students' Stores, 1997); Arupa Patangia Kalita, *Felani* (Guwahati: Jyoti Prakashan, 2003); Monalisha Saikia, *Shankhaninad* (Guwahati: Banalata, 2015). For a discussion on the literary works, see Amit Baishya, *Contemporary*

*Literature from Northeast India: Deathworlds, Terror and Survival* (New Delhi: Routledge, 2019).

170. Formed towards the end of 1991, the Manab Adhikar Sangram Samiti played a leading role in highlighting the many lives lost to human rights violations during these days. *Times of India*, 12 December 1991, 6.
171. For instance, see Saurabh Kumar Chaliha, 'Paragaloi Bidai', in *Saurabh Kumar Chaliha Rachanawali,* eds, Shoneet Bijoy Das and Munin Bayan (Guwahati: Katha Publications, 2008), 533–36.
172. *Assam Tribune*, 4 March 1987; *Dainik Asam*, 23 March 1987; *Dainik Asam*, 14 June 1987; *Assam Tribune*, 21 June 1987; Pahi Saikia, *Ethnic Mobilisation and Violence in Northeast India* (Delhi: Routledge, 2011).
173. *Dainik Asam*, 5 June 1987; *Dainik Asam*, 10 June 1987; *Dainik Asam*, 13 June 1987.
174. Sanjib Baruah, *India against Itself: Assam and the Politics of Nationality* (Philadelphia: University of Pennsylvania Press, 1999), 183–92.
175. *Assam Tribune*, 27 June 1987.
176. 'Memorandum to Indira Gandhi, Prime Minister of India, by United Tribal Nationalists' Liberation Front of Assam, 2 May 1984', in *Autonomy Movement in Assam,* ed. P.S. Dutta (New Delhi: Omsons Publications, 1993), 180–82.
177. *Assam Tribune*, 8 April 1986, 1.
178. Editorial, 'Assamese in schools', *Assam Tribune*, 4 April 1986, 4.
179. ABSU, 'A Memorandum to Rajiv Gandhi, Prime Minister of India, 22 January 1987, Kokrajhar in *Autonomy Movement in Assam,* ed. Dutta, 221–38.
180. 'Identity crisis gains momentum', *Times of India*, 17 March 1988, 17.
181. Statement of a district official quoted in Prasun Sonwalkar, 'Tribal girls' rape in maze of inquiries', *Times of India*, 2 March 1988, 7; *Assam Tribune*, 2 March 1988, 1.
182. M. Kar, *Muslims in Assam Politics, 1946–1991* (New Delhi: Vikas Publishing House, 1997), 404; Achintya Bhattacharjya, *Bortaman Asomor Tribal Samasya* (Guwahati: Ganasakti, 1988), 9.
183. *Dainik Asam*, 3 March 1987, 1; *Dainik Asam*, 11 March 1987, 1; *Dainik Asam,* 20 March 1987, 1; *Dainik Asam*, 8 June 1987, 1; *Assam Tribune*, 4 March 1987, 1; 'Speech of Binoy Khungur Basumatary', *Assam Legislative Assembly Debates*, 2 March 1987; 'Statement of Chintamani Panigrahi, Minister of State, Ministry of Home Affairs', *Rajya Sabha Debates*, 3 March 1987; 'Memorandum on behalf of the United Minorities Front, Assam, in the matter of problems faced by the people belonging to Linguistic, Religious and Ethnic Minorities of Assam, 30 April 1987' in *Muslims in Assam*, Kar, 454–57, Annexure E.

184. Michael Hamlyn, 'Separatist revolt in Assam spawns spiral of violence', *The Times*, 16 March 1989, 10. Also, see Ramesh Menon, 'Corrupt AGP Government Loses Support, Fails to Live Up to People's Expectations', *India Today*, 15 September 1988; Uddipana Goswami, *Conflict and Reconciliation: The Politics of Ethnicity in Assam* (New Delhi: Routledge, 2014), 8.
185. Speech of Samar Brahma Choudhury, *Lok Sabha Debates*, 11 April 1986, columns 404–05.
186. ABSU, 'Divide Assam Fifty-Fifty: Fifty-Three Questions and Answers', 22 August 1987, in *Autonomy Movement in Assam*, ed. Dutta, 240–41.
187. *Times of India*, 29 June 1989, 7; *Times of India*, 4 September 1989, 24; *Times of India*, 23 April 1989, 11.
188. *Times of India*, 23 April 1989; Farzand Ahmed, 'All-Bodo Students' Union, Assam Govt Meet Fails to Check Violence', *India Today*, 30 September 1989.
189. Baruah, *India Against Itself: Assam and the Politics of Nationality*, 192.
190. Rasing Pator, comp., *Birta: The First Karbi Newspaper, Vol 1, 1949–1956* (Diphu, Assam: Author, 2010).
191. Borsing Rongpher, *Karbi Anglongar Rajnoitik Itihas* (Diphu: Phu Phu Publication, 2020), 68–75; Uttam Bathari, 'Managing Diversity: The Case of the Karbi-Dimasa Autonomy Movement', in *Troubled Diversity: The Political Process in Northeast India*, ed. Sandhya Goswami (Delhi: Oxford University Press, 2015), 141–64.
192. Rongpher, *Karbi Anglongar Rajnoitik Itihas*, 94–95.
193. 'Memorandum to the Prime Minister of India by Autonomous State Demand Committee for Creation of Autonomous State for Karbi and N C Hills Districts', 16 September 1986', in 'The Movement for an Autonomous State Comprising Two Districts Karbi Anglong North Cachar Hills of Assam in the Larger Context of Re-organization of Assam', Parimal Ch. Acharjee (PhD diss., Gauhati University, 2005), Appendix II.
194. Ibid.
195. E.H. Pakyntein, *District Census Handbook, United Mikir and North Cachar Hills, Census of India, 1961, Assam* (Guwahati, 1965), 23; P.C. Goswami and P.D. Saikia, 'Problems of Agricultural Development in Tribal Areas', *Indian Journal of Agricultural Economics*, vol. XXV, no. 3 (1970).
196. Note on conversation with Khorsing Teron MLA, 28 October 1940 with Robert Reid, SDO, Golaghat in *Notes by Robert Reid, Governor of Assam—Tour Notes of Subdivisional Officer, Golaghat, 1939–42*, Governor's secretariat, File no. 122–C/42, 1942, ASA.
197. Letter from Sampat Iyengar, Project Officer, Umtru Electric Project to R. T. Rymbai, Special Officer, Tribal Areas Development, Assam, 14 December

1954, in *Hydro Electric Development in Mikir Hills*, File no. 566/54, 1954 Planning & Development Department, ASA.

198. A.K. Saikia, *District Census Handbook, Mikir Hills District, Census 1971, Series, Assam* (Guwahati: Government of Assam, 1972), 1, 6–7.

199. B.N. Bordoloi, *District Handbook of the United Mikir and North Cachar Hills of Assam* (Shillong: Tribal Research Institute, 1972), 17.

200. Estimate based on Pakyntein, *District Census Handbook, United Mikir and North Cachar Hills*, Table 3.1, 318; Government of Assam, *Statistical Handbook of Assam, 1989* (Guwahati: Directorate of Economics and Statistics, 1989), Table 3.01, 68–71.

201. An official thus wrote about the Karbis' ways of agriculture: 'The modern technique of cultivation or animal husbandry are not within their knowledge.' Government of Assam, *Report on The Small and Marginal Farmers and Landless Agriculturalists Development Agency: Mikir Hills* (Shillong: Directorate of Evaluation, 1973), Preface.

202. Between 1976 and 2011, there was a marginal increase of 9000 hectares of area under jhum in Karbi Anglong district. Niangpi Guite, 'Impact of Jhum Cultivation on Forest Cover in Karbi Anglong District of Assam' (PhD diss., North-Eastern Hill University, 2013), Chapter III, Table 3.3.

203. 'Questions around Ram Vijay: Sattriya in a Monastic Tradition: Interview with Sri Narayan Chandra Goswami', in *Performing the Ramayana Tradition: Enactments, Interpretations, and Arguments*, eds, Paula Richman and Rustom Bharucha (Delhi: Oxford University Press, 2021), 250–53; Sunil Kothari, ed., *Sattriya: Classical Dance of Assam* (Mumbai: Marg, 2013); Mallika Kandali, *Sattriya: The Living Dance Tradition of Assam* (Guwahati: Publication Board Assam, 2014); Mallika Kandali, *Nrityakala Prasanga aru Sattriya Nritya* (Guwahati: N.L. Publication, 2012); Arshiya Sethi, 'An Overlay of the Political: The Recognition of Sattriya', *Seminar*, no. 676 (December 2015), https://www.india-seminar.com/2015/676/676_arshiya_sethi.htm; Bhabananda Barbayan, 'The Legacy of Sattriya Dance, Drama and Music', *Nartanam: A Quarterly Journal of Indian Dance*, vol. XVI, no. 2 (2016), 49–98; Pitambar Dev Goswami, *Satriya Utsabor Porisoi aru Tatporjyo* (Dibrugarh: Kaustubh Prakashan, 2002).

204. Other nations in South Asia encountered similar experiences. See, for instance, Willem van Schendel, *A History of Bangladesh* (Cambridge: Cambridge University Press, 2009), 227.

205. Dambarudhar Nath, *Satra, Society and Culture: Pitambardeva Goswami and History of Garamur Satra* (Guwahati: DVS Publishers, 2012), 120–208; Sagar Boruah, 'Profile of a Unique Personality: Pitambar Deva Goswami

and His Socio-Political Stance,' *Proceedings of the Indian History Congress*, vol. 66 (2005), 835–44.
206. A.C. Hazarika, *Shillongor Puroni Asomiya Somaj* (Guwahati: Hazarikas, 1993), 30–31, 96–97; Sunil Kothari, *Sattriya: Classical Dance of Assam*, 12; Atulchandra Hazarika, *Manchalekha: A History of the Assamese Stage from 1468–1967* (Guwahati: Lokendranath Medhi, 1967), 210–22.
207. *Natun Asamiya*, 23 April 1956, 1.
208. Miles Bronson, 'Letter to the Editor, *Friend of India*, 25 May 1855', in *American Baptist Missionaries and North East India, 1836–1900*, ed. H.K. Barpujari (Guwahati: Spectrum Publishers, 1986), 142.
209. K.N. Das, 'The Music of Assam', *Journal of the Madras Music Society*, vol. XXI, nos I–IV (1950), 180.
210. Maheswar Neog and Keshav Changkakati, *Rhythm in Vaishnava Music of Assam* (Guwahati: Assam Sangeet Natak Akademi, 1962).
211. 'The Constitution: Assam Sangit Natak Academy (The Assam Kala Parisad)', Letter from Jairamdas Doulatram, Governor of Assam to Rajendra Prasad, President of India, 9 April 1953, in *National Academy of Dance, Drama and Music, Establishment of Sangeet Natak Akademi*, File no. 22-G/52, 1952, Abhilekh Patal, NAI.
212. Ibid., 16.
213. Ajudhyanath Dhar, 'Youth to Fore', *March of India*, vol. IX, no. 12 (December 1957), 39, in *4th Inter University Youth Festival Report*, File no. D 7/1957/NA/F/13/69/1957, Ministry of Education, Government of India, Abhilekh Patal, NAI.
214. Quoted in Maheswar Neog, *Jivanar Digh Aru Bani: The Warp and Woof of Life* (Guwahati: Chandra Prakash, 2009), 282.
215. Ibid.
216. Ibid.
217. *Diary of Maheswar Neog*, Entry for 1 January 1959, Professor Maheswar Neog Memorial Trust, Digital Library, Department of Assamese, Tezpur University; 'Interview with Jatin Goswami, Sattriya exponent', in https://www.youtube.com/watch?v=1tkWYGcNR5Y (Accessed 13 May 2021).
218. Maheswar Neog, 'Assam', *Marg*, vol. 13, no. 1 (December 1959).
219. M. Neog, 'Different Religious Cults of Assam Before the Advent of Neo-Vaisnavism', *Proceedings and Transactions of the All India Oriental Conference*, vol. 18 (1955), 427–35.
220. M. Neog, 'The Hastamuktavali of Subhankara', *Journal of the Music Academy*, vol. XXIV, nos I–IV (1953), Appendices, 1–24. Maheswar Neog, ed., *Srihastamuktavali* (Guwahati: Publication Board Assam, 1964).

221. Neog, ed. *Srihastamuktavali*, 29.
222. Government of India, *Folk Dances of India* (New Delhi: Publications Division, 1956), 6.
223. *Natun Asamiya*, 25 April 1954, 1.
224. *Assam Tribune*, 10 April 1954, 6; Neog, *Jivanar Digh Aru Bani*, 287.
225. Neog, *Jivanar Digh Aru Bani*, 410.
226. 'Letter from Alain Danielou to M. Neog, 2 October 1958, Chennai', in *Maheswar Neog Private Papers, Vol. 1*, Professor Maheswar Neog Trust, Digital Library, Department of Assamese, Tezpur University.
227. Maheswar Neog, 'The Classical Dance Tradition in Assam', in *Aesthetic Continuum: Essays on Assamese Music, Drama, Dance and Paintings*, ed. Maheswar Neog (New Delhi: Omsons Publication, 2008).
228. Neog was accompanied by a team of artists from a Sattra. Neog, *Jivanar Digh Aru Bani*, 415.
229. Sangeet Natak Academi, *Dance Seminar Recommendations*, 1958 (New Delhi: Sangeet Natak Academi, 1958), https://archive.org/details/dli.ministry.11750 (Accessed 6 February 2023).
230. Sangeet Natak Academi, *Annual Report, 1958–59* (New Delhi: Sangeet Natak Academi, 1959), 12.
231. Nrityacharya Jatin Goswami speaking on Rakheswar Saikia Borbayan, in https://www.youtube.com/watch?v=ckS7LugGcDs (Accessed 14 May 2021); Kothari, ed., *Sattriya: Classical Dance of Assam*, 111.
232. Pradipjyoti Mahanta, 'Pradip Chaliha (1918–2004)', in *Katha Barenya 100: A Collection of the Profiles of 100 Luminaries in the field of art and literature of Assam*, eds, Soneet Bijay Das and Munin Bayan (Guwahati: Katha, 2006), 136–37; Kothari, ed. *Sattriya: Classical Dance of Assam*, 111.
233. Bhupen Barua, 'Guwahatir Mukoli Manchat Pratam Rongali Bihu', *Katha*, vol.1 (January 2004), 17; *Natun Asamiya*, 16 April 1956.
234. See https://sangeetnatak.gov.in/sna/citation_popup.php?id=822&at=2 (Accessed 12 April 2020).
235. Pragjyoti Kala Parishad (1962) and Sangeet Sattra (1968). Kothari, ed. *Sattriya: Classical Dance of Assam*, 113; Jatin Goswami, 'Rasheswar Saikia Barbayan: Kamalabari Sattrar Para Sangeet Sattraloi', in *Sattriya Nrityar Saphura Meli: Adhyapak Raeshwar Saikia Barbayan,* ed. Niren Kakati (Guwahati: Sangeet Sattra, 2022), 14–15.
236. Maheswar Neog, 'The Heritage of Fine Arts in Assam', *Assam Quarterly*, vol. 4 (1967), 32.
237. 'Steps for Popularising Assamese Dances', Letter from R. Baruah, Deputy Director of Information and Publicity, Cultural Affairs, Government of Assam to Secretary, Education (PTM), 24 April 1961; *Festival of Satria*

*Dances of Assam*, File no. ETP/49/60, Education (PTM) Department, GoA, 1960, Assam State Archives.

238. Hazarika, *Manchalekha: A History of the Assamese Stage from 1468–1967*, 228–30.
239. 'Colourful dances of Assam: tribal theme', *Times of India*, 14 December 1963, 9.
240. *Times of India*, 10 August 1969.
241. 'Letter from Ritha Devi to M. Neog, 31 August 1968', in *Maheswar Neog Private Papers, Vol. 1*, Professor Maheswar Neog Trust, Digital Library, Department of Assamese, Tezpur University.
242. S.N. Sarma, *The Neo-Vaishnavite Movement and the Satra Institution of Assam* (Guwahati: Gauhati University, 1966), 170.
243. For Kuchipudi, see Rumya S. Putcha, 'Between History and Historiography: The Origins of Classical Kuchipudi Dance', *Dance Research Journal*, vol. 45, no. 3 (2013), 91–110; Janaki Bakhle, *Two Men and Music: Nationalism in the Making of an Indian Classical Tradition* (New York: Oxford University Press), 2005; Anurima Banerji, *Odissi Dance: Paratopic Performances of Gender and State* (Kolkata: Seagull Books, 2018).
244. Kapila Vatsyayan, *Traditions of Indian Folk Dance* (New Delhi: Clarion Books, 1987), 260.
245. M. Neog, ed. *Sattriya Dances of Assam and Their Rhythms* (Guwahati: Publication Board Assam, 1973), 5.
246. Ibid., 5.
247. Ibid., 28.
248. Natya Shodh Sansthan, Calcutta (NSS), *An Interview of Shri Maheswar Neog*, https://archive.org/details/dni.ncaa.NSS-AC_190A_76B_NSS_DIGN_75–AC/NSS-AC_190A_76B_NSS_DIGN_75–AC_SIDE_A.mp3 (Accessed 2 May 2021).
249. *Dainik Asam*, 13 April 1978, 3.
250. C.P. Saikia, 'Introduction', in *Sattriya Dances of Assam and Their Rhythms*, ed. Maheswar Neog (Guwahati: Publication Board Assam, 1973).
251. Kapila Vatsyayan, *A Study of Some Traditions of Performing Arts in Eastern India: Margi and Desi Polarities* (Guwahati: Gauhati University, 1981).
252. Suresh Chandra Goswami, *Asomor Natya Nrittya Kala* (Guwahati: Authors Book Stall 1979); Ghanakanta Bora, *Sattriya Nritya (Mati Akhara)* (Guwahati: LBS, 1993); Jatin Goswami, *Sankari Nrityar Mati Akhara* (Guwahati: Srimanta Sankaradeva Sangha, 1997); Jaganath Mahanta, *Sattriya Nrityar Hastaputhi* (Guwahati: Forum for Sankardev Studies, 2000).
253. Sunil Kothari, 'Dance festival at Bhopal', *Times of India*, 27 August 1984.

254. 'Statement of Hiteswar Saikia, Chief Minister, Assam, 22 October 1992', quoted in 'Time to Elevate Satriya Dance', *Assam Information*, vol. 44 (October 1992), 33.
255. Jatin Goswami, 'Few Important Information Regarding New Edition', in Suresh Chandra Goswami, *Sankari Natya-Nritya Kala: A Book on Dramas and Dances of Shri Shri Sankardev* (Guwahati: Banphul, 2014); *Telegraph*, 22 April 2001.
256. For a list of practitioners, with many having undergone years of training in other Indian classical dances, of this period, see Kothari, ed. *Sattriya: Classical Dance of Assam*, 110–41. For illustration of a course curriculum to teach Sattriya in the 1960s, see Goswami, *Sankari Natya-Nritya Kala: A Book on Dramas and Dances of Shri Shri Sankardev*, 135–36.
257. N. Hariharan, 'Ritual with sophistication', *Times of India*, 30 June 1994, 8.
258. Robin Jeffrey, *India's Newspaper Revolution: Capitalism, Politics and the Indian-Language Press, 1977–1999* (London: Hurst and Company, 2000), 52.
259. Devika Saikia, 'A Comparative Study of Two Classical Dance Forms of India: Bharatnatyam and Sattriya' (PhD diss., Dibrugarh University, 2010), 128–36; Shilpi Goswami, 'From Ritual to Performance: A Study of the Sattriya Performance Traditions of Assam as Intangible Heritage with a Special Reference to the Kamalabari Group of Sattras' (PhD diss., Tezpur University, 2015).
260. Georgie Pope, 'Mobilising Assamese Vaishnavite Performance Practices' (PhD diss., King's College London, 2019).

# Glossary

| | |
|---|---|
| Ankiya Nata | Vaishnavite one-act theatrical performance |
| Bandh | General strike |
| Bhagania | Refugee |
| Bhaona/Bhawana | Vaishnavite theatrical performance |
| Bhasik Sankhyalaghu | Linguistic minorities |
| Bhoiyam | Plain or lowlands in contrast to hills or highlands |
| Bideshi | Foreigners |
| Bigha | A traditional unit of land measurement and approximately equivalent to approximately one-third of an acre, that is, 0.33 acres. |
| Buranji | Ahom or Assamese royal chronicles |
| Carita | Biographies of Assamese Vaishnavite saints |
| Dewani rights | The right to collect revenue |
| Garibi hatao | Get Rid of Poverty |
| Haat | a market, often in rural areas, organized on fixed days at regular intervals |
| Hartal | Strike |
| Jajmani | Socio-economic and ritual arrangements between families of different castes in India |
| Janata | Public |
| Jati | Nationality |
| Jatiya Swahid | National Martyr |
| Jhum | Shifting cultivation |
| Khuda hafiz | May God protect you. |
| Killas | Forts |

| | |
|---|---|
| Koibarta | As fishermen were called in Assam and other parts of eastern India |
| Manya bhasa | Standard variety of a language, and the reference in this work for the modern Assamese language |
| Maund | Unit of measurement approximately equivalent to 40 kilograms |
| Mautam | Famine in Mizoram, mainly caused by the flowering of bamboos |
| Mauzadar | A fiscal officer of revenue unit |
| Mishmi Teeta | A small, stemless perennial evergreen herb grown mainly in the eastern Himalayas. Known for its bitter taste, this bacteriostatic herb's rhizomes have long been used for medicinal use in China and India. |
| Muslim National Guard | The paramilitary affiliate of the Muslim League |
| Na Asamiya/ Pamua Asamiya/ Pamua Musalman | Terms to describe Muslim migrants native to Bengal, who had merged with Assam's sociocultural milieu. |
| Nadiyal | Fishermen |
| Namghar | Place of worship for the Assamese Vaishnavites |
| Ojapali | A folk performance tradition from Assam, performed by a small troupe led by a master called *Oja* and his associates named *pali*. The performance revolves around a narrative largely based on the Ramayana, the Mahabharata, and the *Puranas* and involves choral singing, dancing, hand gestures, and the use of cymbals. |
| Pahar | Hills |
| Paik/Pyke | Individuals under the Ahom kings. Their duty was to render physical labour to the king and state at fixed periods of the year. |
| Posa | The Ahom government's scheme obliging the inhabitants of the foothills to annually supply goods to the highland communities. In return, the hill tribes had to refrain from raiding the Ahom territory. |
| Pucca | Concrete/metalled road |
| Puthi | Manuscript, often indicating a work of religious nature |
| Rashtrabhasa | Language of the nation |
| Ryotwari | One of the principal methods of revenue collection in British India, where the ryots (peasants) inherited their land directly from the state and also paid revenues directly to the state. |

| | |
|---|---|
| Sadhu bhasa | Standard language |
| Sangram | Movement |
| Sarbajanin | Universal; for everyone. |
| Sarkari | Official |
| Satradhikar | Head of a Vaishnavite monastery |
| Syiem | Chieftain of the Khasis |
| Tadvob | Derivative words from Sanskrit |
| Tatsom | Words that are used in similar forms in Sanskrit |
| Tala | Traditional rhythmic pattern in classical Indian music. |
| Thana | Police station |
| Ujaniya | Residents of Upper Assam |

# Further Readings on Assam before 1947

Acharyya, N.N. *The History of Medieval Assam: From the Thirteenth to the Seventeenth Century*. New Delhi: Omsons Publications, 1992.

Ahmed, Khan Choudhury Amanatullah. *Koch Biharer Itihas* (A History of Cooch Behar). Cooch Behar: Cooch Behar State, 1936.

Antrobus, H.A. *A History of the Assam Company, 1839–1953*. Edinburgh: T. and A. Constable, 1957.

Banerjee, Anil Chandra. *The Eastern Frontier of British India, 1784–1826*. Calcutta: A. Mukherjee & Company, 1964.

Barooah, Nirode K. *David Scott in North-East India, 1802–1831: A Study in British Paternalism*. New Delhi: Munshiram Manoharlal, 1970.

Barpujari, Heramba Kanta. ed. *Political History of Assam*. vol.1. Guwahati: Publication Board Assam, 1999.

Barpujari, Heramba Kanta. *Assam in the Days of the Company: 1826–1858: A Critical and Comprehensive History of Assam during the Rule of the East-India Company from 1826–1858*. Guwahati: Lawyer's Book Stall, 1963.

Barpujari, Heramba Kanta. ed. *The Comprehensive History of Assam*, vols 1–5. Guwahati: Publication Board of Assam, 1990–93.

Barua, Birinchi Kumar. *A Cultural History of Assam*. Guwahati: Lawyer's Book Stall, 1969.

Barua, Kanaklal. *Early History of Kāmarupa*. Guwahati: Lawyer's Book Stall, 1966.

Baruah, Ditee Moni. 'Polity and Petroleum Making of an Oil Industry in Assam, 1825–1980'. PhD diss., Indian Institute of Technology Guwahati, Guwahati, 2014.

Baruah, S.L. *A Comprehensive History of Assam*. New Delhi: Munshiram Manoharlal, 1985.

Baruah, S.L. *Last Days of Ahom Monarchy: A History of Assam from 1769 to 1826*. New Delhi: Munshiram Manoharlal, 1993.

Baruah, Sanjib. 'Clash of resource use regimes in Colonial Assam: A nineteenth-century puzzle revisited'. *Journal of Peasant Studies* 28, no. 3 (2001): 109–24.

Basu, Nirmal Kumar. *Assam in the Ahom Age, 1228–1826: Being Politico-Economic and Socio-Cultural Studies*. Calcutta: Sanskrit Pustak Bhandar, 1970.

Behal, Rana Pratap. *One Hundred Years of Servitude: Political Economy of Tea Plantations in Colonial Assam*. New Delhi: Tulika Books, 2014.

Bhadra, Gautam. *Iman O Nishan*. Kolkata: Subarnarekha Publishers, 2018.

Bhattacharjee, Jayanta Bhusan. *Cachar Under British Rule in North East India*. New Delhi: Radiant Publishers, 1977.

Bhuyan, Suryya Kumar. *Tungkhungia Buranji: A Chronicle of the Tungkhungia Kings of Assam*. Guwahati: Department of Historical and Antiquarian Studies, 1932.

Bhuyan, Suryya Kumar. *Anglo-Assamese Relations, 1771–1826: A History of the Relations of Assam with the East India Company from 1771 to 1826, Based on Original English and Assamese Sources*. Guwahati: Lawyer's Book Stall, 1949.

Bhuyan, Suryya Kumar. *Atan Buragohain and His Times: A History of Assam, from the Invasion of Nawab Mir Jumla in 1662–63, to the Termination of Assam–Mogul Conflicts in 1682*. Guwahati: Lawyer's Book Stall, 1957.

Bhuyan, Arun Chandra, and Sibopada De. *Political History of Assam*, vols 2-3. Guwahati: Publication Board Assam, 1999.

Blurton, T. Richard. *Krishna in the Garden of Assam: The History and Context of a Much-Travelled Textile*. London: British Museum, 2016.

Borthakur, Achyut Kumar. *The Administration of Justice in Assam (1826–1874)*. New Delhi: Manohar, 2019.

Cederlöf, Gunnel. *Founding an Empire on India's North-Eastern Frontiers, 1790–1840: Climate, Commerce, Polity*. New Delhi: Oxford University Press, 2014.

Chakravarty, Archana. *History of Education in Assam 1826–1919*. Delhi: Mittal Publications, 1989.

Chakravorty, Birendra Chandra. *British Relations with the Hill Tribes of Assam since 1858*. Calcutta: Firma K.L. Mukhopadhyay, 1964.

Chatterjee, Indrani. *Forgotten Friends: Monks, Marriages, and Memories of Northeast India*. New Delhi: Oxford University Press, 2013.

Chophy, G. Kanato. *Christianity and Politics in Tribal India: Baptist Missionaries and Naga Nationalism*. Delhi: Permanent Black, 2021.

Choudhury, Pratap Chandra. *Assam–Bengal Relations from the Earliest Times to the Twelfth Century A.D.* Guwahati: Spectrum Publications, 1988.

Choudhury, Pratap Chandra. *The History of Civilization of the People of Assam to the Twelfth Century A.D.* Guwahati: Department of Historical and Antiquarian Studies in Assam, 1959.

Choudhury, R.D. *Archaeology of the Brahmaputra Valley of Assam: Pre-Ahom Period.* Delhi: Agam Kala Prakashan, 1985.

Choudhury, R.D. *The Sculptures of Assam.* Guwahati: Assam State Museum, 1987.

Chowdhuri, Prasenajit. *Socio-Cultural Aspects of Assam in the Nineteenth Century.* New Delhi: Vikas House, 1994.

Dasgupta, Anindita. *Remembering Sylhet: Hindu and Muslim Voices from a Nearly Forgotten Story of India's Partition.* New Delhi: Manohar, 2014.

Deka, Meeta. *Student Movements in Assam.* New Delhi: Vikas Publishing House, 1996.

Dey, Arnab. *Tea Environments and Plantation Culture: Imperial Disarray in Eastern India.* Cambridge: Cambridge University Press, 2018.

Dihingia, Hemeswar. *Assam's Struggles against British Rule, 1826–1863.* New Delhi: Asian Publication Services, 1980.

Dutt, Keshab Narayan. *Landmarks of the Freedom Struggle in Assam.* Guwahati: Lawyer's Book Stall, 1969.

Dutta, Anuradha. *Assam in the Freedom Movement.* Calcutta: Darbari Prokashan, 1991.

Gait, Edward. *A History of Assam.* Calcutta: Thacker, Spink and Co., 1906.

Gogoi, Padmeswar. *The Tai and the Tai Kingdoms with a Fuller Treatment of the Tai-Ahom Kingdom in the Brahmaputra Valley.* Guwahati: Department of Publication, Gauhati University, 1968.

Gohain, Hiren. 'Origins of the Assamese Middle Class'. *Social Scientist*, 2, no. 1 (1973): 11–26.

Gohain, U.N. *Assam under the Ahoms.* Jorhat, Assam: U.N. Gohain, 1942.

Goswami, Priyam. *Assam in the Nineteenth Century: Industrialisation & Colonial Penetration.* Guwahati: Spectrum Publications, 1999.

Goswami, Priyam. *Indigenous Industries of Assam: Retrospect and Prospect.* New Delhi: Shipra Publications, 2005.

Goswami, Surendra Kumar. *A History of Revenue Administration in Assam, 1228–1826 A.D.: A Detailed History of the Revenue System of the Ahom Rulers.* Delhi: Spectrum Publications, 1986.

Guha, Amalendu. *Medieval and Early Colonial Assam: Society, Polity, Economy.* Calcutta: K.P. Bagchi, 1991.

Guha, Amalendu. *Planter Raj to Swaraj: Freedom Struggle & Electoral Politics in Assam, 1826–1947.* New Delhi: Indian Council of Historical Research, 1977.

Hazarika, B.B. *Political Life in Assam during the Nineteenth Century.* Delhi: Gian Publishing House, 1987.

Kalita, Bharat Chandra. *Military Activities in Medieval Assam.* Delhi: Daya Publishing House, 1988.

Kar, Bodhisatva. 'Framing Assam Plantation Capital, Metropolitan Knowledge and a Regime of Identities, 1790s to 1930s'. PhD diss., Jawaharlal Nehru University (JNU), New Delhi, 2007.

Kour, Kawal Deep. *A History of Intoxication: Opium in Assam, 1800–1959.* New Delhi: Manohar, 2019.

Lahiri, Nayanjot. *Pre-Ahom Assam: Studies in the Inscriptions of Assam between the Fifth and the Thirteenth Centuries AD.* New Delhi: Munshiram Manoharlal, 1991.

Lahiri, Rebati Mohan. *The Annexation of Assam, 1824–1854.* Calcutta: Firma KLM, 1994.

Ludden, David. 'Investing in Nature around Sylhet: An Excursion into Geographical History'. *Economic & Political Weekly* 38, no. 48 (2003): 5080–88.

Mahanta, Aparna. *Journey of Assamese Women, 1836–1937.* Guwahati: Publication Board Assam, 2008.

May, Andrew J. *Welsh Missionaries and British Imperialism: The Empire of Clouds in North-East India.* Manchester: Manchester University Press, 2017.

Misra, Sanghamitra. *Becoming a Borderland: The Politics of Space and Identity in Colonial Northeastern India.* New Delhi: Routledge, 2011.

Misra, Tilottoma. *Literature and Society in Assam: A Study of the Assamese Renais[s]ance, 1826–1926.* Guwahati: Omsons Publications, 1987.

Misra, Tilottoma. *Ramnabami-Natak: The Story of Ram and Nabami.* New Delhi: Oxford University Press, 2007.

Misra, Udayon. *Burden of History: Assam and the Partition—Unresolved Issues,* New Delhi: Oxford, 2017.

Nag, Sajal. *The Uprising: Colonial State, Christian Missionaries and Anti-Slavery Movement in North-East India, 1908–1954.* New Delhi: Oxford University Press, 2016.

Nath, Dambarudhar. *History of the Koch Kingdom, 1515–1615.* Delhi: Mittal Publications, 1989.

Nath, Jahnabi Gogoi. *Agrarian System of Medieval Assam.* New Delhi: Concept Publishing Company, 2002.

Neog, Maheswar. *Early History of Vaisnava Faith and Movement in Assam: Sankaradeva and His Times.* Guwahati: Department of Publication, Gauhati University, 1965.

Neog, Maheswar. *Socio-Political Events in Assam Leading to the Militancy of the Māyāmariyā Vaisnavas*. Calcutta: K.P. Bagchi & Company, 1982.

Purkayastha, Sudeshna. *Indigenous Industries of Assam, 1870–1925*. Kolkata: K.P. Bagchi, 2005.

Rappaport, Erika Diane. *A Thirst for Empire: How Tea Shaped the Modern World*. Princeton, New Jersey: Princeton University Press, 2017.

Reid, Robert Neil. *History of the Frontier Areas Bordering on Assam, 1883–1941*. Shillong: Assam Government, 1942.

Saikia, Arupjyoti. *A Century of Protests: Peasant Politics in Assam since 1900*. New Delhi: Routledge, 2014.

Saikia, Arupjyoti. *Forests and Ecological History of Assam, 1826–2000*. Delhi: Oxford University Press, 2011.

Saikia, Arupjyoti. *The Unquiet River: A Biography of the Brahmaputra*. New Delhi: Oxford University Press, 2019.

Saikia, Mohini Kumar. *Assam–Muslim Relation and Its Cultural Significance*. Golaghat, Assam, Luit Printers, 1978.

Saikia, Rajen. *Social and Economic History of Assam 1853–1921*. New Delhi: Manohar, 2000.

Saikia, Yasmin. *Fragmented Memories: Struggling to be Tai-Ahom in India*. Durham and London: Duke University Press, 2004.

Sarma, Satyendranath. *A Socio-Economic & Cultural History of Medieval Assam: 1200 A.D.–1800 A.D.* Guwahati: Bina Library, 2001.

Sharma, Jayeeta. *Empire's Garden: Assam in the Making of India*. Durham: Duke University Press, 2011.

Sharma, Manorama. *Social and Economic Change in Assam: Middle Class Hegemony*, New Delhi: Ajanta Publications, 1990.

Sword, Victor Hugo. *Baptists in Assam: A Century of Missionary Service, 1836–1936*. Guwahati: Spectrum Publications, 1992.

Syiemlieh, David R. *British Administration in Meghalaya: Policy and Pattern*. New Delhi: Heritage Publishers, 1989.

Zou, David Vumlallian, and M. Satish Kumar. 'Mapping a Colonial Borderland: Objectifying the Geo-Body of India's Northeast'. *Journal of Asian Studies* 70, no. 1 (2011): 141–70.

# Select Bibliography

Abdi, S.N.M. 'Rising Militancy'. *Illustrated Weekly of India* 111, no. 18 (1990): 22–25.

Acharjee, Parimal Chandra. 'The Movement for an Autonomous State Comprising Two Districts Karbi Anglong North Cachar Hills of Assam in the Larger Context of Re-Organization of Assam'. PhD diss., Gauhati University, Guwahati, 2005.

Acharya, Debendranath. *Jangam*. Guwahati: Publication Board Assam, 1982.

Agarwala, Bibekananda. *The Agarwala Family of Tezpur: A Vignette of the Early Generations*. Tezpur: Devi Prasad Bagrodia, 1998.

Agarwala, Haribilash. *Haribilash Agarwalla Dangariyar Atmajibani*. Guwahati: Tarunkumar Agarwalla, 1967.

Amritbhusan Adhikari, annotated and comp., *Srimannam-Ghosha* (Calcutta: Author, 1911) reprint, edited by Bhaba Prasad Chaliha and Rabindra Narayan Chaudhury. Guwahati: Publication Board Assam, 2010.

Ahmed, Atikuddin. *The Anatomy of Rural Poverty in Assam: A Case Study of Dibrugarh Sub-Division*. Delhi: Mittal Publications, 1987.

Aitchison, C.U., and A.C. Talbot. eds. *A Collection of Treaties, Engagements, and Sunnuds Relating to India and Neighbouring Countries*, vol. 1. Calcutta: Foreign Office Press, 1876.

Aiyar, Mani Shankar. *Rajiv Gandhi's India: A Golden Jubilee Perspective, Nationhood, Ethnicity, Pluralism and Conflict Resolution*, vol. 1. New Delhi: UBSPD, 1998.

Alam, Khorshed. 'The Economic Development of Assam since Independence: An Analytical Study'. PhD diss., Gauhati University, Guwahati, 1974.

Alexander, Colin R. *Administering Colonialism and War: The Political Life of Sir Andrew Clow of the Indian Civil Service*. New Delhi: Oxford University Press, 2019.

Ali, Alban, and Eric Lambert. *Assam*. Oxford: G. Cumberlege, Oxford University Press, 1946.

Ali, Mahmud. *Resurgent Assam*. Dacca: Nao-Belal Publications, 1967.

Ali, Tariq Omar. *A Local History of Global Capital: Jute and Peasant Life in the Bengal Delta*. Princeton: Princeton University Press, 2018.

All India Congress Committee. *Zamindari Abolition and Agrarian Reforms: A Summary of the Efforts of the Congress Organisation to Implement the Provisions in the Election Manifesto Regarding Zamindari Abolition*. Delhi: All India Congress Committee, 1948.

Allen, B.C. *Census of India, 1901. Volume IV-A, Assam, Part II, Tables*. Shillong: Assam Secretariat Printing Office, 1902.

Amrith, Sunil S. *Crossing the Bay of Bengal: The Furies of Nature and the Fortunes of Migrants*. Cambridge, Massachusetts: Harvard University Press, 2013.

Anderson, J.D. *A Collection of Kachari Folk-Tales and Rhymes*. Shilong: Assam Secretariat Print Office, 1895.

Anon. 'Review of Bibar'. *Chetana*, vol. 5, edited by Paramananda Majumdar, pp. 564–65. Guwahati: Pragjyotish College, 2018 (June 1925).

Anon. 'Assam Rail Link Project'. *Economic Weekly* 5, no. 16 (18 April 1953): 458.

Anon. 'Assam: Assam State Museum, Gauhati'. *Indian Museums Review*, 1961–64: 3.

Anon. 'Assam'. *Church Missionary Intelligencer* 1, no. 13 (May 1850): 291–300.

Anon. 'Balbar Kichu'. In *Bibar: A Collection of Quarterly Magazine (1924–25)*, edited by Phukan Chandra Basumatary, Biswajit Brahma and Kamalakanta Mushaharay, pp. 214–18. Kokrajhar, Assam: Bodo Publication Board, Bodo Sahitya Sabha, 2019 (1925).

Anon. 'Biraja Sankar Guha, 1894–1961'. *International Journal of Comparative Sociology* 3, no. 2 (1962): 277–78.

Anon. 'Special Session of the All-India Hindu Mahasabha: Gauhati, 28 December, 1926'. *Indian Quarterly Register* 2 (July–December 1926): 354–57.

Anon. 'After Chaliha in Assam'. *Economic & Political Weekly* 5, no. 45 (1970): 1795–96.

Anon. 'Asomot Bideshi Kakot'. *Abahan* 3, no. 2 (1931): 249–50.

Anon. 'Assam Hills: Search for Autonomy'. *Economic & Political Weekly* 2, no. 36 (1967): 1632–33.

Anon. 'Books in Assamese'. *Indian Literature* 1, no. 1 (1957): 137–49.

Anon. 'Editorial'. *Abahan* 3, no. 3 (1931): 369–74.

Anon. 'Five States in Northeastern Region in Turmoil', *India Today,* 30 November 1979.

Anon. 'Food Crisis Is Back'. *Economic & Political Weekly* 3, no. 24 (1968): 898–99.
Anon. 'Gauhati Gets a Facelift'. *Economic & Political Weekly* 11, no. 47 (1976): 1818–19.
Anon. 'Khadya Samasya Samadhanot Bigyan'. *Ramdhenu* 17, no. 9 (1965): 895–96.
Anon. 'Migration from East Pakistan (1951–1961)'. *Economic Weekly* 13, no. 15 (1961): 612.
Anon. 'News of Sahitya Sabha'. *Asam Sahitya Sabha Patrika* 28, no. 1 (1959): 78–79.
Anon. 'The Scheduled and Tribal Areas'. *Indian Journal of Public Administration* 23, no. 3 (July 1977): 821–36.
Anon. *Hints for Europeans Engaged in Commerce and Industry on Their First Arrival in India: With Special Reference to Conditions in Bengal and Assam*. London: Worrall & Robey, 1946.
Anon. *No, They Are Not Foreigners, They Are Citizens*. Silchar: Fariadi, 1980.
Ansari, Z.D., and M.K. Dhavalikar. 'Excavations at Ambari, Guwahati: 1970'. In *Ambari Archaeological Site: An Interim Report*, edited by H.N. Dutta, p. 1317. Guwahati: Directorate of Archaeology, Assam, 2006.
Antrobus, H.A. *A History of the Assam Company, 1839–1953*. Edinburgh: T. and A. Constable Ltd, 1957.
Aplin, Ken, and James Lalsiamliana. 'Chronicles and Impacts of the 2005–09 Mautam in Mizoram'. In *Rodent Outbreaks: Ecology and Impacts*, edited by Grant Singleton, Steve Belmain, Peter Brown and Bill Hardy, pp. 13–47. Los Baños: International Rice Research Institute, 2010.
Aram, M. *Peace in Nagaland: Eight Year Story, 1964–72*. Delhi: Arnold-Heinemann Publishers, 1974.
Asam Sahitya Sabha. 'Minutes of the First Executive Committee Report, ASS, Guwahati, 30 May, 1971'. *Asam Sahitya Sabha Patrika* 28, no. 2 (1971): 72.
Assam Legislative Assembly. *Report on the Select Committee on the Assam (Temporarily Settled) Tenancy Bill 1970*. Shillong: Assam Legislative Assembly, 1971.
Assam Rural Infrastructure and Agricultural Services Society. *Report on Study on the Increasing Pattern of Uses of Fertilizers, Pesticides and Other Chemicals the Field of Agriculture in Darrang, Barpeta, Nagaon and Kamrup Districts of Assam*. Guwahati: NEOLAND Technologies, 2003.
Association of Voluntary Agencies for Rural Development. *Rehabilitation of Refugees in Angarkata Area, West Kumarikata, Kamrup, Assam*. New Delhi: AAVARD, 1978.

Bagchi, Debarati. 'Many Spaces of Sylhet: Making of a "Regional Identity", 1870s– 1940s'. PhD diss., University of Delhi, New Delhi, 2015.
Baishya, Amit R. *Contemporary Literature from Northeast India: Deathworlds, Terror and Survival*. New York: Routledge, 2019.
Baishya, Amit R. *Jangam: The Movement, a Forgotten Exodus in which Thousands Died*. New Delhi: Vitatsa, 2018.
Baishya, Prabir. 'Man-Made Famine'. *Economic & Political Weekly* 10, no. 21 (1975): 821–22.
Bakhle, Janaki. *Two Men and Music: Nationalism in the Making of an Indian Classical Tradition*. New York: Oxford University Press, 2005.
Bandyopadhyay, D. 'Land Reforms in India: An Analysis'. *Economic & Political Weekly* 21, no. 25/26 (1986): 50–56.
Banerjee, Dipankar. *Labour Movement in Assam: A Study of Non-Plantation Workers' Strikes till 1939*. New Delhi: Anamika Publishers, 2005.
Banerji, Anurima. *Dancing Odissi: Paratopic Performances of Gender and State*. Kolkata: Seagull Books, 2018.
Banerji, Rakhal Das. *The Origin of Bengali Script*. Calcutta: University of Calcutta, 1919.
Barbayan, Bhabananda. 'The Legacy of Sattriya Dance, Drama and Music'. *Nartanam: A Quarterly Journal of Indian Dance* XVI, no. 2 (2016): 49–98.
Bordoloi, B.N. *Report on the Displacement of Tribals due to Installation of Major Irrigation Project: The Case Study of Dhansiri Irrigation Project in the Darrang District of Assam, Dhansiri Irrigation Project*. Guwahati: Tribal Research Institute, Assam, 1984, p. 19.
Bardoloi, Gopinath. *Constituent Assembly of India: Report of the Northeast Frontier (Assam) Tribal and Excluded Areas Subcommittee*, vol. I–II. New Delhi: Government of India Press, 1947.
Bardoloi, Rajani Kanta. *Miri Jiyari*. Barpeta: Barpeta Sonatun Dhurma Press, 1895.
Barkakoty, Aswini Kumar. 'The Growth of Local Self-Government in Assam, 1874–1919'. PhD diss., University of London, London, 1949.
Barker, Jonathan. *The Politics of Agriculture in Tropical Africa*. Beverly Hills: Sage Publications, 1984.
Barman, Prasun. *Assam Upatyakat Bangali*. Guwahati: Assam Publishing Company, 2015.
Barman, Sivnath. *Sivanath Barman Rachana Sambhar*, vol. 1. Guwahati: Assam Publishing House, 2021.
Barooah Pisharoty, Sangeeta. *Assam: The Accord, the Discord*. New Delhi: Penguin Random House, 2019.

Barooah, Lakshmiram. compiled and ed. *Sangit Kosh or a Collection of Selected Assamese Songs.* Jahnabi Agency, 1907.

Barooah, Nirode K. *Bardoloi Dinalekha: The Diary of Lokapriya Gopinath Bardoloi,* vol. 1 & 2. Guwahati: Publication Board Assam, 2000–01.

Barooah, Nirode K. *Gopinath Bardoloi: 'The Assam Problem' and Nehru's Centre.* Guwahati: Bhabani Print and Publications, 2010.

Barooah, Nirode K. ed. *Bordoloi Dinalekha: The Diary of Lokapriya Gopinath Bardoloi.* Vol. 1 and 2. Guwahati: Publication Board Assam, 2000.

Barooah, Nirode K. *Gopinath Bardoloi aru Assaom: Tetia aru Etia.* Guwahati: B.N. Bardoloi, 2010.

Barooah, Siba Prasad. *A Brochure on Assamese Literature and Culture.* Guwahati: Bani Sahitya Mandir, 1956.

Barpujari, Heramba Kanta. ed. *The Golden Jubilee Volume: Cotton College, 1951–52.* Guwahati: H.K. Barpujari, 1952.

Barpujari, Heramba Kanta. *The American Missionaries and North-east India, 1836–1900 A.D.: A Documentary Study.* Guwahati: Spectrum Publications, 1986.

Barpujari, Heramba Kanta. 'British Administration in Assam (1825–1845) with Special Reference to the Hill-Tribes on the Frontier'. PhD diss., University of London, London, 1949.

Barpujari, Heramba Kanta. 'General President's Address: North-East India: The Problems and Policies Since 1947'. *Proceedings of the Indian History Congress* 56 (1995): 1–73.

Barpujari, Heramba Kanta. *North-East India: Problems, Policies, and Prospects since Independence.* Guwahati: Spectrum Publications, 1998.

Barpujari, Heramba Kanta. *Problem of the Hill Tribes: North-East Frontier: 1873–1962.* Guwahati: Lawyer's Book Stall, 1970.

Barpujari, Heramba Kanta. *Uttar Purbanchalar Samasya Aru Rajniti.* Guwahati: G.L. Publications, 1999.

Barthakur, Padmanath. *Swadhinata Ranar Sangsparsat.* Dibrugarh: Kaustabh Prakasan, 2006.

Barthakur, Sheela. ed. *Lekhikar Jivoni.* Tezpur: Sadau Asom Lekhika Samaroh Samiti, 1990.

Barua, Amlan, and S.B. Roy Choudhury. eds. *Assam State Gazetteer,* vol. 1. Guwahati: Government of Assam, 1999.

Barua, Bhaben. 'Tu Fu r Kobita', *Sanglap* 1, no. 1 (1971): 6–14.

Barua, Bhaben. 'Jivanar Batat: The Story of a Society'. In *Professor Birinchi Kumar Barua Commemoration Volume,* edited by M. Neog and M.M. Sharma, pp. XIIV-IXIV. Guwahati: All India Oriental Conference, 1966.

Barua, Bhaben. *Bhaben Barua Kobita Samagra.* Guwahati: Bandhav, 2018 (1977).

Barua, Birinchi Kumar. ed. *Mahabharata Adi Parva*. Vol. 1. Guwahati: Gauhati University, 1962.

Barua, Birinchi Kumar. ed. *Sabha Parvan*. Vol. 2. Guwahati: Gauhati University, 1963.

Barua, Birinchi Kumar. 'A Cultural History of Assam of the Early Period: 400 A.D.–1200 A.D'. PhD diss., University of London, London, 1947.

Barua, Birinchi Kumar. *Asamiya Katha Sahitya: Purani Bhag*. Guwahati: LBS, 1950.

Barua, Birinchi Kumar. *Asomiya Katha Sahitya: Purani Bhag*. Nalbari: Journal Emporium, 1950.

Barua, Birinchi Kumar. *History of Assamese Literature*. New Delhi: Sahitya Akademi, 1964.

Barua, Birinchi Kumar. *Jivanar Batat*. Calcutta: Banhi Press, 1944.

Barua, Birinchi Kumar. *Professor Baruar Chithi*. Guwahati: Lawyer's Book Stall, 1968.

Baruah, Ditee Moni, 'Polity and Petroleum: Making of an Oil Industry in Assam, 1825–1980'. PhD diss., Indian Institute of Technology Guwahati, 2014.

Baruah, Ditee Moni. 'The Refinery Movement in Assam'. *Economic & Political Weekly* XLVI, no. 1 (2011): 63–69.

Barua, Gunabhiram. *Anandaram Dhekial Phukanor Jivan Charitra*. Guwahati: Publication Board Assam, 1992.

Barua, Harendra Nath. *Reflections on Assam cum Pakistan*. Calcuttà: H. Goswami, 1944.

Barua, Harendra Nath. ed. *Bharatar Mukti Jujat Asam*. Guwahati: Asam Rajyik Mukti Yujaru Abhibartan, 1972.

Barua, Hem. *Hem Baruar Kabita*. Guwahati: Anwesha, 2014 (1945).

Barua, Hem. *August Revolution in Assam*. Guwahati: Anu Barua, 1978.

Barua, Ila. *Bidrohi Asam*. Nagaon: Bijay Prakash Bhawan, 1946.

Barua, K.L. 'Introductory', *Journal of the Assam Research Society* 1, no. 1 (1933): 1.

Barua, Khanindra Chandra. *Critical Days of Assam*. Guwahati: K.C. Barua, 1972.

Barua, Maan. 'The Political Ecology of Human–Elephant Relationships in India: Encounters, Spaces, Politics'. PhD diss., Oxford University, Oxford, 2013.

Barua, Prabhat Chandra. *Nikhil Goalpara Samitir Dwitiya Barshik Adhibesane Pothito*. Gauripur, Assam: Biswakosh Press, 1929. Digital Archive, Centre for Assamese Studies, Tezpur University.

Baruah, Lily Mazinder. ed. *Lokopriya Gopinath Bardoloi: An Architect of Modern India*. Delhi: Gyan Publishing House, 1992.

Baruah, Sanjib. *India against Itself: Assam and the Politics of Nationality*. Philadelphia: University of Pennsylvania Press, 1999.

Baruah, Sanjib. *Durable Disorder: Understanding the Politics of Northeast India*. New Delhi: Oxford University Press, 2005.

Bass, Gary J. *The Blood Telegram: Nixon, Kissinger and a Forgotten Genocide*. New York: Vintage Books, 2014.

Basu, Jyoti. ed. *Documents of the Communist Movement in India*. Calcutta: National Book Agency, 1997.

Basu, Manjula. *Saumyendranath Thakur: Karme O Manane*. Kolkata: Tagore Research Institute, 2007.

Bathari, Uttam. 'Managing Diversity: The Case of the Karbi-Dimasa Autonomy Movement'. In *Troubled Diversity: The Political Process in Northeast India*, edited by Sandhya Goswami, pp. 141–64. New Delhi: Oxford University Press, 2015.

Baveja, J.D. *Across the Golden Heights of Assam and NEFA*. Calcutta: Modern Book Depot, 1961.

Bayly, Christopher, and Tim Harper. *Forgotten Armies: Britain's Asian Empire and the War with Japan*. London: Penguin Books, 2005.

Behal, Rana P. *One Hundred Years of Servitude: Political Economy of Tea Plantations in Colonial Assam*. New Delhi: Tulika Books, 2014.

Behal, Rana P. 'Power Structure, Discipline, and Labour in Assam Tea Plantations Under Colonial Rule'. *International Review of Social History* 51, no.14 (2006): 143–72.

Bentinck, A., S. Dowerah, and Keramat Ali. *Report of the Committee to Enquire into the Incidence of Grazing Fees*. Shillong: Assam Government Press, 1927.

Bezbaroa, Lakshminath. 'Assami Bhasa'. *Punya* 2, nos 1–2 (1898): 22–32.

Bezbaroa, Lakshminath. 'Editorial'. *Banhi* 21, no. 2 (1932). In *Bezbaroa Granthavali*. Vol. 3, edited by Jatindranath Goswami. Guwahati: Sahitya Prakash, 2005.

Bezbaroa, Lakshminath. 'Presidential Address: Asam Sahitya Sabha, 1924'. In *Bezbaroa Granthavalee: Complete Works of Lakhinath Bezbaroa*. Vol. 2. edited by Atul Chandra Hazarika. Guwahati: Sahitya Prakash, 1988.

Bezbaroa, Lakshminath. *Amar Jibansmriti*. Translated by Arati Tagore. New Delhi: Sahitya Akademi, 1957.

Bezbaroa, Lakshminath. *Lakshminath Bezbaroa Rachanawali*. Vol. 2. edited by Atul Chandra Hazarika. Guwahati: Sahitya Prakash, 1988.

Bezbaroa, Lakshminath. *Mahapurus Sri Sankardeva aru Sri Madhaveva*. Howrah, Calcutta: Author, 1914.

Bezbaroa, Lakshminath. *Sankardeva*. Howrah: Banhi Press, 1911.

Bezbarua, D.N. *Asamiya Bhasa aru Sahityar Buranji*. Jorhat: D.N. Bezbarua, 1911.

Bharadwaj, Krishna. 'Regional Differentiation in India: A Note'. *Economic & Political Weekly* 17, no. 14/16 (1982): 605–14.

Bharali, Bibha, and Banani Chakravarty. eds. *Languages of Assam: Peoples Linguistic Survey of India*. Vol. 5. Part 1. Delhi: Orient Blackswan, 2017.

Bharali, Debananda. *Asamiya bhaṣara maulika bicara*. Ḍibrugaṛh: A.R & T. Co, 1912.

Bhat, D.N. Shankara. *Boro Vocabulary: With a Grammatical Sketch*. Pune: Deccan College Postgraduate and Research Institute, 1968.

Bhattacharjee, Govind. 'The Reality of Special Category States'. *Economic & Political Weekly* 49, no. 40 (2014): 48–56.

Bhattacharjee, Hiranya. *Dharshita*. Guwahati: Guwahati Sadhughar, 2011.

Bhattacharjya, Achintya. *Bortaman Asomor Tribal Samasya*. Guwahati: Ganasakti, 1988.

Bhattacharjya, Gaurishankar. *Sabinay Nibedan: An Autobiography*. Guwahati, Sahitya Press, 1999.

Bhattacharya, Birendra Kumar. *Yaruingam*. Guwahati: Lawyer's Book Stall, 1960.

Bhattacharya, Padmanath. *Kamrup-Sasanavali*. Rangpur: Surendrachandra Roy Chowdhury, 1931.

Bhattacharya, Pramod Chandra. 'Glimpses from Boro Folksongs'. *Indian Linguistics* 17 (1957): 240–44.

Bhattacharyya, Birendra Kumar. 'A Separate Assam Hills State: What Does It Mean?' *Economic & Political Weekly* 2, no. 9 (1967): 491–94.

Bhattacharyya, Birendra Kumar. 'Congress Loses in the Cities'. *Economic & Political Weekly* 2, no. 10 (1967): 515–16.

Bhattacharyya, Birendra Kumar. 'Students Fill the Vacuum'. *Economic & Political Weekly* 9, no. 27 (1975): 1056–57.

Bhattacharyya, Birendra Kumar. *Mrityunjay*. Guwahati: Sahitya Prakash, 1970.

Bhattacharyya, Kisor Kumar. 'Structure and Individual in Assamese Society: A Study of Family, Kinship, Caste and Religion'. PhD diss., Gauhati University, Guwahati, 1990.

Bhattacharyya, Rajeev. *Rendezvous with Rebels: Journey to Meet India's Most Wanted Men*. Delhi: HarperCollins, 2014.

Bhattacharyya, S. 'World War II and the Consumption Pattern of the Calcutta Middleclass'. *Sankhyā: The Indian Journal of Statistics (1933–1960)* 8, no. 2 (1947): 197–200.

Bhaumik, Subir. *Insurgent Crossfire: North-East India*. New Delhi: Lancer Publishers, 1996.

Bhaumik, Subir. *Troubled Periphery: The Crisis of India's North East*. New Delhi: Sage Publications, 2009.

Bhuyan, Arun Chandra, and Sibopada De. eds. *Political History of Assam, 1940–47*. Vol. 3. Guwahati: Publication Board Assam, 1999.

Bhuyan, Arun Chandra. *The Quit India Movement: The Second World War and Indian Nationalism*. New Delhi: Manas Publications, 1975.

Bhuyan, Jogendranarayan. *Sadagar Bholanath Borooah*. Diphu: Diphu Sahitya Sabha, 1993.

Bhuyan, Suryya Kumar. 'Bihu'. *Alochani* 8, no. 7 (1917): 1–4.

Bhuyan, Suryya Kumar. *Lachit Barphukan and His Times: A History of the Assam-Mogul Conflicts of the Period 1667 to 1671 AD*. Guwahati: Department of Historical and Antiquarian Studies, 1947.

Bhuyan, Suryya Kumar. *Report and Conspectus of the Kamarupa Anusandhan Samiti for 1925–26 and Part of 1926–27*. Guwahati: Kamrup Anusandhan Samiti, 1927.

Biswas, Hemango. *Ujan Gang Baiya*. Edited by Moinak Biswas. Kolkata: Anustup, 2012.

Bodhi, S.R. 'Khasi Political Reality and the Struggle for Statehood: History: Context and Political Processes'. In *Handbook of Tribal Politics in India*, edited by Jagannath Ambagudia and Virginius Xaxa, pp. 394–410. Delhi: Sage Publications, 2021.

Bodo Sahitya Sabha. 'A Statement on the Present Language Issue of Assam and View of Bodos'. In *Roman (English) Script and Bodo Sahitya Sobha*, compiled and edited by Kanakeswar Narzary, pp. 19–21. Kokrajhar: Bodo Sahitya Sabha, 1993.

Bora, Ajit Kumar. 'Introduction of Small Scale Tea Cultivation and Its Impact on Land Use and Socio-Economic Condition of the People of Sivasagar District, Assam'. PhD diss., North-Eastern Hill University, Shillong, 2008.

Bora, Bikram. 'Opening the Gates of Tsangpo: Explorations and Imperial Geo-Politics in the Arunachal Himalayas, c. 1820 – c. 1920'. M.Phil diss., Jawaharlal Nehru University, 2016.

Bora, Boli Narayan. 'Tirutar Bon Ki (What Are the Works of Woman?)'. In *Mau*, edited by Satyendra Narayan Sarma, pp. 1–7. Guwahati: Publication Board Assam, 2008 (1886).

Bora, Boli Narayan. 'Bihu'. In *Asam-Bandhu* 1, no. 5 (1885), edited by N. Saikia, pp. 152–57. Guwahati: Publication Board Assam, 1984.

Bora, Dhurbajyoti. *Kalantarar Gadya*. Guwahati: Students' Stores, 1997.

Bora, Dilip. *Kalijar Aai*. Guwahati: Jyoti Prakash, 2014.

Bora, Ghanakanta. *Sattriya Nritya (Mati Akhara)*. Guwahati: LBS, 1993.

Bora, Hemalata. 'Seujiya Paharor Maje Maje'. In *Hemalata Bora Rachanwali*, edited by Rubi Bora and Obja Bora Hazarika, pp. 285–330. Guwahati: Bandhav, 2020 (1962).

Bora, Jayanta Madhab. ed. *Lummer Dai Rachanavali*. Guwahati: Publication Board Assam, 2020.

Bora, Jnananath. *Asomiya Purani Sahitya*. Guwahati: Barua Agency, n.d.
Bora, Jnananath. *Asomot Bideshi*. Calcutta: Sarveswar Bhattacharjya, 1925.
Bora, Jnananath. *Provincialism*. Guwahati, mimeograph, 1955.
Bora, Jnananath. *Srihatta Bicched*. Calcutta: Samya Press, 1935.
Bora, Mahendra. *The Evolution of Assamese Script*. Jorhat: Asam Sahitya Sabha, 1981.
Bora, Mahim. *Ronga-Jiya*. Nagaon: Krantikal, 2000.
Bora, P. *Kotha Manobir Rupkotha*. Guwahati: Shristi Prakashan, 2014.
Bora, Soneswar. 'Asomot Khudra Chah Kheti: Ek Samajbadi Biplab'. In *Cha-Tsing: Souvenir of All Assam Tea Growers Association*, edited by Jatindra Nath Saikia, pp. 30–34. Golaghat: All Assam Tea Growers Association, 2000.
Borah, Hem. *Asomiya Sahityalai Mahila Lekhakar Dan*. Golaghat, Assam: Saptabdi Prakashan, 1994.
Bordoloi, B.N. *Constraints of Tribal Development in North East India*. Guwahati: Tribal Research Institute, 1990.
Bordoloi, B.N. *Report on the Survey of Alienation of Tribal Land in Assam*. Guwahati: Assam Institute of Research for Tribals and Scheduled Castes, 1999.
Bordoloi, B.N. *Transfer and Alienation of Tribal Land in Assam: With Special Reference to the Karbis of the Karbi Anglong District*. Guwahati: B.N. Bordoloi, 1991.
Bordoloi, Upendra Nath. *Asomor Arthanaitik Paristhiti: A Collection of Articles on Economic Affairs of Assam*. Guwahati: Gauhati University, 1974.
Bore, A.B. *A Report on the Measures of Rehabilitation and Reconstruction undertaken by the government of India in the Naga Hills and the Manipur State in 1944 in order to repair the ravages caused by the Japanese invasion of 1944*. New Delhi: Government of India, 1945.
Borgohain, Homen, and Paramananda Majumdar. eds. *Jayantee*. Vol. 1. Guwahati: Students' Stores, 2011.
Borgohain, Homen. *Asamiya Sahityar Buranji*. Vol. 6. Guwahati: ABILAC, 1993.
Borgohain, Homen. *Saptam Dasak: A Collection of Articles*. Nalbari: Journal Emporium, 1989.
Borgohain, Homen. *Esha Bacharar Asamiya Kabita*. Guwahati: Publication Board Assam, 2000.
Borkotoky, Namrata. 'Brewing Trouble or Transforming Nature? Making of Tea Plantations Environments in Assam'. PhD diss., Indian Institute of Technology Guwahati, Guwahati, 2021.
Barpujari, Manoj. 'Assamese Cinema: Dreams, Reality and Dichotomies'. In *Routledge Handbook of Indian Cinemas*, edited by K. Moti Gokulsing and Wimal Dissanayake, pp. 51–62. Oxon: Routledge, 2013.

Borooah, Gunabhiram. *Assam Buranji, or, the History of Assam*. Calcutta: Gunabhiram Borooah, 1876.

Borooah, Kesav Kanta. *Baniyākākatira Baṁśāwalisāra*. Assam: Kesav Kanta Borooah, 1913.

Borthakur, A.P. *Chan Poharat Arunachal: A Book on the Development of School Education and Progress in Arunachal Pradesh (from 1948 to 1986)*. Moranhat: Bulu Barthakur, 2004.

Boruah, Sagar. 'Profile of a Unique Personality: Pitambar Deva Goswami and His Socio-Political Stance'. *Proceedings of the Indian History Congress* 66 (2005): 835–44.

Bose, Neilesh. 'Purba Pakistan Zindabad: Bengali Visions of Pakistan, 1940–1947'. *Modern Asian Studies* 48, no. 1 (2014): 1–36.

Bose, Sugata. *Agrarian Bengal: Economy, Social Structure and Politics, 1919–1947*. Cambridge, UK: Cambridge University Press, 1987.

Bose, Sugata. *The Nation as Mother and Other Visions of Nationhood*. New Delhi: Penguin Random House, 2017.

Bower, Ursula Graham. *Naga Path*. London: John Murray, 1950.

Brahma, Mohini Mohan, and Prafulladutta Goswami. eds. *Bodo Kachari Sola*. Guwahati: Gauhati University Press, 1972.

Bronson, Miles. 'Letter to the Editor: Friend of India'. In *The American Baptist Missionaries and North-East India (1836–1900 A.D.)*, by H.K. Barpujari, pp. 156–58, Guwahati: Spectrum Publications, 1985.

Buragohain, Purnakanta. *Patkair Sipare Na-Basar*. Dhemaji: Purbanchal Tai Sahitya Sabha, 1993.

Burling, Robbins. 'Proto-Bodo'. *Language* 35, no. 3 (1959): 433–53.

Burton-Page, J. 'An Analysis of the Syllable in Boro'. *Indian Linguistics* 16, (1955): 334–44.

Cantlie, Audrey. 'Caste and Sect in an Assamese Village'. PhD diss., SOAS, University of London, London, 1980.

Carter, Lionel. ed. *Mountbatten's Report on the Last Viceroyalty, 22 March–15 August 1947*. New Delhi: Manohar Publishers and Distributors, 2003.

Cederlöf, Gunnel. *Founding an Empire on India's North-Eastern Frontiers, 1790–1840: Climate, Commerce, Polity*. New Delhi: Oxford University Press, 2014.

Chakrabarty, Saroj. *The Upheaval Years in North-East India: A Documentary In-Depth Study of Assam Holocausts, 1960–1983*. Calcutta: S. Chakrabarty and R. Chakrabarty, 1984.

Chakravarty, K.C. 'Assam Disturbances: Bongal Kheda Again'. *Economic Weekly* 12, no. 31 (1960): 1193–95.

Chaliha, Parag. ed. *The Outlook on NEFA*. Jorhat: Asam Sahitya Sabha, 1958.

Chalihā, Phaṇidhara. *Āsāmara Calihā Kākati Baṃśara Baṃśāvalī*. Howrah: Nabar Chandra Dutt, 1909.
Chaliha, Saurabh Kumar. 'Paragoloi Bidai'. In *Saurabh Kumar Chaliha Rachanawali*, edited by Shoneet Bijoy Das and Munin Bayan, pp. 533–36. Guwahati: Katha Publications, 2008.
Chaliha, Saurabh Kumar. 'Sampadakoloi Chithi'. In *Saurabh Kumar Chaliha Rachanawali*, edited by Shoneet Bijoy Das and Munin Bayan, pp. 557–60. Guwahati: Katha Publications, 2008.
Chaliha, Saurabh Kumar. 'Purani Panbazar'. *Katha* 1 (January 2004): 13–14.
Champion, Harry George, and Shiam Kishore Seth. *A Revised Survey of the Forest Types of India*. New Delhi: Manager of Publications, 1968.
Chanda, Anuradha. *Script Identity Region: A Study in Sylhet Nagri*. Kolkata: Dey's Publishing, Maulana Abul Kalam Azad Institute of Asian Studies, 2013.
Chandola, Harish. *The Naga Story: First Armed Struggle in India*. New Delhi: Chicken Neck, 2013.
Chandra, Bipan. ed. *Towards Freedom: Documents on the Movement for Independence in India, 1942*. New Delhi: Indian Council of Historical Research, 2016.
Charlesworth, Neil. 'The Problem of Government Finance in British India: Taxation, Borrowing and the Allocation of Resources in the Inter-War Period'. *Modern Asian Studies* 19, no. 3 (1985): 534.
Chatterjee, Indrani. *Forgotten Friends: Monks, Marriages, and Memories of Northeast India*. New Delhi: Oxford University Press, 2013.
Chatterjee, N.C. *Report of the Non-Official Commission of Enquiry into the Language Riot in Cachar*. Calcutta, 1961.
Chatterjee, N.C. *Report Presented to the Prime Minister of India on the Progress of Rehabilitation of the Riot-victims in Assam, 1960*. Calcutta, 1960.
Chatterjee, Shiba P. 'Le Plateau de Meghalaya (Garo-Khasi-Jaintia)'. *Nature* 139 (1937): 489.
Chatterji, Joya. 'South Asian Histories of Citizenship, 1946–1970'. *The Historical Journal* 55, no. 4 (2012): 1049–71.
Chatterji, Joya. *Bengal Divided: Hindu Communalism and Partition, 1932–1947*. Cambridge, UK: Cambridge University Press, 2002.
Chatterji, Joya. *Partition's Legacies*. Albany: SUNY Press, 2021.
Chatterji, Suniti Kumar. *Kirata-Jana-Kriti*. Calcutta: The Asiatic Society, 1951.
Chatterji, Suniti Kumar. *The Place of Assam in the History and Civilisation of India*. Guwahati: Gauhati University, 1955.
Chattopadhyay, Dilip Kumar. *History of the Assamese Movement since 1947*. Calcutta: Minerva Associates, 1990.
Chaube, Shibani Kinkar. *Hill Politics in Northeast India*. New Delhi: Orient Blackswan, 2012.

Chaudhuri, Bhupendranarayan. 'British Rule in Assam, 1845–1858'. PhD diss., University of London, London, 1956.
Chaudhuri, Nirad C. *The Continent of Circe: Being an Essay on the People of India*. Bombay: Jaico Publishing House, 1960.
Chaudhuri, Sudeep, and Niloy Mukhopadhyay. 'Of Stagnation and Collaboration'. *Economic & Political Weekly* 13, no. 3 (1978): 93–96.
Chaudhury, Lakhyadhar. *Manuh Bichari*. Guwahati: Publication Board Assam, 1992.
Chaudhury, P.C. 'Stone Inscription from Khanikar Gaon Sarupathar'. *Journal of Assam Research Society* 20 (1972–73): 3–5.
Chaudhury, P.D., and M.C. Das. *Ancient Treasures of Assam Through Assam State Museum*. Guwahati: Directorate of Museums, Assam, 1984.
Chawngsailova. *Ethnic National Movement in the Role of the MNF*. Aizawl: Mizoram Publication Board, 2007.
Chhetry, D.B. *Census of India, 1971. Series 3, Assam. Part VI-B. Special Survey Report on Selected Towns, Gauhati*. Delhi: Manager of Publications, 1978.
Chophy, G. Kanato. *Christianity and Politics in Tribal India: Baptist Missionaries and Naga Nationalism*. New Delhi: Permament Black, 2021.
Chopra, Suneet. 'The Assam Movement and the Left: A Reply to Hiren Gohain'. *Social Scientist* 10, no. 11 (1982): 63–70.
Choudhry, Khaliquzzaman. *Pathway to Pakistan*. Lahore: Longmans, 1961.
Choudhury, Bijaybhusan Ghosh. ed. *Assam o Bangadesher Bibaha-paddhati*. Calcutta: Author, 1932.
Choudhury, N.K. *Census of India, 1971, Assam, series 3, Part II-C (II): Social and Cultural Tables*. Delhi: Manager of Publications, 1981.
Choudhury, Pratap Chandra. 'The History of Civilisation of the People of Assam to the Twelfth Century A.D'. PhD diss., University of London, London, 1953.
Choudhury, Prosenjit. 'Unbimsa Satikar Bidyat Samaj Aru Bihu'. In *Unois Satikar Asomot Ebhumuki*, by Prosenjit Choudhury, pp. 1–16. Guwahati: Bhabani Print & Publications, 2011.
Choudhury, Rita. *Ei Samay Sei Samay*. Guwahati: Jyoti Prakashan, 2008.
Choudhury, Rita. *Makam*. Guwahati: Jyoti Prakasan, 2010.
Choudhury, Sanghamitra. 'The Railway Workers Strike of 1974: Impact in the Eastern and North East Frontier Railway Zones'. PhD diss., North Bengal University, Siliguri, 2019.
Choudhury, Sujit. *The Bodos: Emergence and Assertion of an Ethnic Minority*. Shimla: Indian Institute of Advanced Studies, 2013.
Church, R.A. 'Roots of Separatism in Assam Hill Districts'. *Economic & Political Weekly* 4, no. 17 (26 April 1969): 729.

Chutia, Sonaram. *Asamor Vaishnav Darshanor Swarnarekha*. Guwahati: Srimanta Sankardev Sangha, 1971.

Communist Party of India, *The India–China Border Dispute and the Communist Party of India: Resolutions, Statements and Speeches, 1959–1963*. Delhi: Communist Party of India, 1963.

Constituent Assembly of India. *Constituent Assembly Debates: Official Report.* Vols I–XII, New Delhi: Lok Sabha Secretariat, 1948.

Constituent Assembly of India. *Reports of Committees of the Constituent Assembly, First Series, 1947*. Delhi: Manager of Publication, 1948.

Cook, C.P. 'India: The Crisis in Assam'. *World Today* 24, no. 10 (1968): 444–48.

Cooke, M.C. 'Gold Thread: Coptis teeta, Wall., and *Coptis trifolia*, Salisb'. In *Pharmaceutical Journal and Transactions*, edited by Jacob Bell, p. 161. London: John Chruchill, 1870.

Coupland, R. *The Indian Problem: Report on the Constitutional Problem in India.* New York: Oxford University Press, 1944.

Crosby, Alfred W. Jr, *The Columbian Exchange: Biological and Cultural Consequences of 1492*. Westport, Connecticut: Greenwood Press, 1972.

Dalton, E.T. 'Notes on Assam Temple Ruins'. *Journal of Asiatic Society of Bengal* 24, no. 1 (1855): 1–24.

Dalton, E.T. *Descriptive Ethnology of Bengal*. Calcutta: Office of the Superintendent of Government Printing, 1872.

Damodaran, Harish. *India's New Capitalists: Caste, Business, and Industry in a Modern Nation.* India: Hachette India, 2018.

Dandekar, Kumudini. 'Mortality and Longevity in India, 1901–1961'. *Economic & Political Weekly* 7, no. 18 (1972): 889–92.

Dandekar, V.M., and Nilakantha Rath. 'Poverty in India - I: Dimensions and Trends'. *Economic & Political Weekly* 6, no. 1 (1971): 25–48.

Das Gupta, Amit R. and Lorenz M. Luthi, *The Sino-Indian War of 1962: New Perspectives*. New Delhi: Routledge, 2017.

Das Gupta, Barun. 'Memories of Bangladesh Liberation War'. *Mainstream* 50, no. 1 (2011).

Das, Bipinpal. 'Sradheya Chalihadebor Suwaranat'. In *Bimalaprasad Chaliha*, edited by C.P. Saikia, p. 99. Guwahati: Publication Board Assam, 1972.

Das, Bipinpal. *Jivanor Bate Bate*, Guwahati: Mediahype Publications, 2016.

Das, Bipinpal. *The Naga Problem*. Hyderabad: Socialist Party, Central Office, 1956.

Das, Durga. ed. *Sardar Patel's Correspondence*: *1945–1950.* Ahmadabad: Navajivan Publishing House, 1971–1974.

Das, H.P. *Geography of Assam*. New Delhi: National Book Trust, 1970.

Das, Jogesh. *Daawar Aru Nai*. Guwahati: Lawyer's Book Stall, 1955.

Das, Jugal. 'Tahanir Guwahati'. *Samjna* 2, no. 3 (September–October–November 1976): 117–24.
Das, K.N. 'The Music of Assam'. *Journal of the Madras Music Society* XXI, Parts I–IV, (1950): 143–80.
Das, Lakhinath, Debendranath Changkakoti and Maheswar Neog. 'Bargeet aru Sashtrya Sangeet'. *Asam Sahitya Sabha Patrika* 16, no. 1 (1957): 41–48.
Das, M.M. *Peasant Agriculture in Assam: A Structural Analysis.* New Delhi: Inter-India Publications, 1984.
Das, Mandira. ed. *Bhasha-Bitarka: Bezbaroa aru Bangar Pandit-Samaj.* Dibrugarh: Dibrugarh University, 2014.
Das, Omeo Kumar. *Jiban Smriti.* Guwahati: Publication Board Assam, 1983.
Das, Parag Kumar. *Swadhin Asomor Arthoniti.* Guwahati: Aalibaat, 2018.
Das, Pushpalata. *Report of Employment Review Committee, 1969–70.* Guwahati: Assam Legislative Assembly, 1970.
Das, Samir Kumar. *ULFA: United Liberation Front of Assam: A Political Analysis.* Delhi: Ajanta Publications, 1994.
Das, Shoneet Bijoy, and Munin Bayan. eds. *Saurabh Kumar Chaliha Rachanawali.* Guwahati: Katha Publications, 2008.
Das, Tilak. *Asamiyar Jatiya Samashya.* Tezpur: Jiban Chadra Bora and Others, 1949.
Das, Yajnarama. *Daka Bhanitā.* Calcutta: Bijjnana Yantre, 1885.
Dasgupta, Anindita. 'Denial and Resistance: Sylhetti Partition "Refugees" in Assam'. *Contemporary South Asia* 10, no. 3 (2001): 343–60.
Dasgupta, Keya, and Amalendu Guha. '1983 Assembly Poll in Assam: An Analysis of Its Background and Implications'. *Economic & Political Weekly* 20, no. 19 (1985): 843–53.
Datta, Birendranath. *A Bibliography of Folklore Material of Assam and Adjoining Areas.* Guwahati: Gauhati University, 1978.
Datta, S.N. *Report on the Resettlement of the Nowgong District During the Years 1926 (October) to 1932 (January).* Shillong: Assam Government Press, 1932.
Dayong, Niu and Shen Zhihua. eds. *The Cold War and China's Neighbor Relationship.* Beijing: World Affairs Press, 2004.
De, Aniket. 'Lineages of Federalism: Race, Empire, and Anti-Colonialism in South Asia'. PhD diss., Harvard University, Cambridge, Massachusetts, forthcoming.
De, Rohit. 'Cows and Constitutionalism'. *Modern Asian Studies* 53, no. 1 (2019): 240–77.
Deka, K.N. 'Assam: The Challenge of Political Integration and Congress Leadership'. In *State Politics in India,* edited by Iqbal Narain, pp. 30–50. Meerut: Meenakshi Prakashan, 1976.

Deka, Meeta. *Student Movement in Assam*. New Delhi: Vikas Publishing House, 1996.

Deka, Namita. *Swadhinattar Kalar Asomiya Sahityaloi Mohila Lekhokar Avadan*. Guwahati: Bani Mandir, 2013.

Deka, P.K. *Satuta Dashakar Asomor Chalachitra*. Guwahati: Rupkar, 2006.

Deka, Sanjib Pol. *Asam Andolonar Galpa*. Guwahati: Banalata, 2023.

Department of Commercial Intelligence and Statistics, India. *Statistical Abstract for British India, with Statistics Where Available, Relating to Certain Indian States for the Year 1928–29 to 1937–1938*. Delhi: Manager of Publications, 1940.

Desai, S.P. *Report of the Special Officer Appointed for the Examination of Professional Grazing Reserves in Assam Valley*. Shillong: Assam Government Press, 1944.

Deshpande, Shantaram Ramkrishna. *Report on an Enquiry into Family Budgets of Industrial Workers in Gauhati*. Delhi: Manager of Publication, 1947.

Dev, S.C. *Nagaland: The Untold Story*. Calcutta: Gouri Devi, 1988.

Dey, Arnab. *Tea Environments and Plantation Culture: Imperial Disarray in Eastern India*. Cambridge, UK: Cambridge University Press, 2018.

Dev, Bimal J., and Dilip Kumar Lahiri. *Assam Muslims: Politics & Cohesion*. New Delhi: Mittal Publications, 1985.

Dev Goswami, Pitambar. *Satriya Utsabor Porisoi aru Tatporjyo*. Dibrugarh: Kaustabh Prakashan, 2002.

Dey, K.S. *General Report: Census of India 1971, Assam*, series 3, Part I-A. New Delhi: Manager of Publications, 1979.

Dhansiri Irrigation Project. *Report on the Displacement of Tribals due to Installation of Major Irrigation Projects: The Case Study of Dhansiri Irrigation Project in the Darrang District of Assam*. Guwahati: Tribal Research Institute, Assam, 1984.

Dhar, P.N. *Indira Gandhi, the 'Emergency', and Indian Democracy*. New Delhi: Oxford University Press, 2000.

Dhekial Phukan, Holiram. *Assam Desher Itihas Orthat Assam Buranji*. Guwahati: Mokshada Pustakalaya, 1962 (First published by Samacar Candrika, Calcutta in 1829).

Dhulipala, Venkat. *Creating a New Medina: State Power, Islam, and the Quest for Pakistan in Late Colonial North India*. Cambridge, UK: Cambridge University Press, 2015.

Dommen, Arthur J. 'Separatist Tendencies in Eastern India'. *Asian Survey* 7, no. 10 (1967): 726–39.

Dunlop, Graham. *Military Economics, Culture and Logistics in the Burma Campaign, 1942–1945*. London: Routledge, 2009.

Dutta Baruah, Harinarayan, and Saneswar Dutta. eds. *Prachin Kamrupiya Kayastha-Samajar Itibritta*. Guwahati: Prachin Kamrup-Kayastha Samaj, 2000 (1941).

Dutta, A.K. *Maniram Dewan and the Contemporary Assamese Society*. Jorhat: Anupoma Dutta, 1990.

Dutta, Akhil Ranjan. *Hindutva Regime in Assam: Saffron in the Rainbow*. Delhi: Sage Publications, 2021.

Dutta, Anwesha. 'No Way Out of the Woods: Political Ecology of Extraction, Livelihoods and Conservation in Assam'. PhD diss., Ghent University, Ghent, 2019.

Dutta, Birendranath. *Asamiya Sangitar Aitihya*. Jorhat: Asam Sahitya Sabha, 1977.

Dutta, H.N. *History, Art and Archaeology of Doiyang Dhansiri Valley, Assam*. Guwahati: LBS Publications, 2012.

Dutta, Hirendranath. 'Sahitya Samalochana'. In *Asamiya Sahityar Buranji*, vol. 6, edited by Homen Bargohain, pp. 548–60. Guwahati: ABILAC, 1993.

Dutta, Keshab Narayan. 'Editorial'. *Asam Sahitya Sabha Patrika* 2 (new series), no. 3 (1952, 1874 saka): 188.

Dutta, Keshab Narayan. *Landmarks of the Freedom Struggle in Assam*. Guwahati: Lawyer's Book Stall, 1958.

Dutta, Narendra Chandra. 'Land Reforms in Assam since Independence with Special Reference to the Permanently Settled Areas and the Acknowledged Estates of Bijni and Sidli'. PhD diss., Gauhati University, Guwahati, 1963.

Dutta, Parag. 'A Study of State Finances and Fiscal Reforms in Assam Post Reform Experiences and Challenges'. PhD diss., Indian Institute of Technology Guwahati, Guwahati, 2012.

Dutta, Partha Sarathi. ed. *Autonomy Movement in Assam (Documents)*. Delhi: Omsons Publications, 1993.

Dutta, Sristidhar. *Cross-border Trade of North-East India: The Arunachal Perspective*. Kolkata: Maulana Abul Kalam Azad Institute of Asian Studies, 2002.

Dutta, Uddipan. 'The Role of Language Management and Language Conflict in the Transition of Post-Colonial Assamese Identity'. PhD diss., Gauhati University, Guwahati, 2012.

Dutta, Uddipan. *Creating Robin Hoods: The Insurgency of the ULFA in Its Early Period, Its Parallel Administration and the Role of Assamese Vernacular Press, 1985–1990*. New Delhi: WISCOMP, Foundation for Universal Responsibility of His Holiness the Dalai Lama, 2008.

Eaton, Richard M. 'Conversion to Christianity among the Nagas, 1876–1971'. *Indian Economic and Social History Review* 21, no. 1 (1984): 1–44.

Election Commission of India. *Report on General Election, 1967 to the Legislative Assembly of Assam*. New Delhi: Election Commission of India, 1968.

Election Commission of India. *Statistical Report on the General Election, 1972 to the Legislative Assembly of Assam*. New Delhi: Election Commission of India, 1972.

Election Commission of India. *Statistical Report on General Election, 1983 to the Legislative Assembly of Assam*. New Delhi: Election Commission of India, 1983.

Elwin, Verrier. *The Tribal World of Verrier Elwin: An Autobiography*. New York: Oxford University Press, 1964.

Endle, Sidney. *Outline Grammar of the Kachári (Bārā) Language as Spoken in District Darrang, Assam: With Illustrative Sentences, Notes, Reading Lessons, and a Short Vocabulary*. Shillong: Assam Secretariat Press, 1884.

Farb, Peter. 'Biology's New Weapons against Insect Pests'. *Reader's Digest*, September 1957.

Fernandes, Walter. 'Internally Displaced Persons and Northeast India'. *International Studies* 50, no. 4 (2013): 287–305.

Fisher, Michael. *An Environmental History of India: From Earliest Times to the Twenty-First Century*. Cambridge: Cambridge University Press, 2018.

Flex, Oscar. *Assam: 1864*, translated by Salim Ali. Guwahati: G.L. Publications, 2010.

Franke, Marcus. *War and Nationalism in South Asia: The Indian State and the Nagas*. London: Routledge, 2009.

Fuller, Bampfylde. *Some Personal Experiences*. London: J. Murray, 1930.

Fürer-Haimendorf, Christoph von, 'Agriculture and land tenure among the Apatanis'. *Man in India*, 26, no. 1 (1946): 20–49.

Fürer-Haimendorf, Christoph von, *Himalayan Barbary*. London: John Murray, 1955.

Fürer-Haimendorf, Christoph von. 'The Aboriginal Tribes of India: The Historical Background and Their Position in Present-Day India'. *Journal of the Royal Society of Arts*, vol. 98, no. 4832 (1950): 997–1011.

Fürer-Haimendorf, Christoph von. *Himalayan Barbary*. London: John Murray, 1955.

Gait, Edward. *A History of Assam*. Calcutta: Thacker, Spink & Company, 1906.

Galbriath, John Kenneth. *Ambassador's Journal: A Personal Account of the Kennedy Years*. Boston: Houghton Mifflin, 1969.

Gandhi, Indira. 'Tragedy in Bangladesh'. In *The Great Speeches of Modern India*, edited by Rudranghsu Mukherjee. Noida: Random House India, 2011.

Gandhi, Indira. *The Years of Endeavour: Selected Speeches of Indira Gandhi, August 1969– August 1972*. New Delhi: Publications Division, 1975.

Gandhi, Mohandas K. *Collected Works of Mahatma Gandhi*. New Delhi: Publication Division, Ministry of Information and Broadcasting, 1958–1994.

Gardner, Kyle J. *The Frontier Complex: Geopolitics and the Making of the India–China Border*, 1846–1962. Cambridge: Cambridge University Press, 2021.

Gawthrop, W.R. *The Story of the Assam Railways and Trading Company Limited 1881–1951*. London: Harley Publishing, 1951.

Gelfand, Henry M. 'A Critical Examination of the Indian Smallpox Eradication Program'. *American Journal of Public Health* 56, no. 10 (1966): 1638.

Ghatate, N.M. ed. *Atal Bihari Vajpayee: Four Decades in Parliament*. Vol. 1. Delhi: Shipra Publications, 1998.

Ghosh, S. 'Everything Must Match: Detection, Deception, and Migrant Illegality in the India–Bangladesh Borderlands'. *American Anthropologist* 121 (2019): 870–83.

Ghosh, Sahana. 'Chor, Police and Cattle: The Political Economies of Bovine Value in the India–Bangladesh Borderlands'. *South Asia: Journal of South Asian Studies* 42, no. 6 (2019): 1108–24.

Ghurye, G.S. *The Aborigines—'So Called'—and Their Future*. Poona: Gokhale Institute of Politics and Economics, 1943.

Gogoi, Akhil. *Asomiya Jatiyotabad*. Guwahati: Banalta, 2018.

Gogoi, Lila. *Simantar Maṭi aru Manuh*. Guwahati: LBS, 1963.

Gogoi, Sangeeta. 'The Ahom in the Colonial Period: An Ethno Political Study'. PhD diss., Department of History, Dibrugarh University, Dibrugarh, 2014.

Gohain, Hiren, and Dilip Bora. eds. *Asom Andolon: Pratisruti aru Phalasruti: A Collection of Articles on Assam Movement*. Guwahati: Banalata, 2001.

Gohain, Hiren, ed. *Jyotiprasad Rachanavali*. Guwahati: Publication Board Assam, 2003.

Gohain, Hiren. 'Chronicles of Violence and Terror: Rise of United Liberation Front of Asom'. *Economic & Political Weekly* 42, no. 12 (March 2007): 1012–18.

Gohain, Hiren. 'Extremist Challenge and Indian State: Case of Assam'. *Economic & Political Weekly* 31, no. 31 (August 1996): 2066–68.

Gohain, Hiren. 'Mohan Upanyasik Birinchi Kumar Barua'. In *Hiren Gohain Rachanawali*, vol.1, edited by Shoneet Bijoy Das and Munin Bayan, pp. 426–28. Guwahati: Katha Publications, 2009.

Gohain, Hiren. 'Otihya aru Jivanar Batat'. In *Hiren Gohain Rachanawali*, vol.1, edited by Shoneet Bijoy Das and Munin Bayan, pp. 412–25. Guwahati: Katha Publications, 2009.

Gohain, Hiren. *Asomiya Jatiya Jeevanat Mahapurushia Parampara*. Guwahati: Aalibaat Publication, 1987.

Gohain, Hiren. *Bastabar Swapna*. Guwahati: Guwahati Book Stall, 1972.

Gohain, Hiren. *Kirtan Puthir Rasa Bichar*. Guwahati: Lawyer's Book Stall, 1981.

Gohain, Swargajyoti. *Imagined Geographies in the Indo-Tibetan Borderlands: Culture, Politics, Place.* Amsterdam: Amsterdam University Press, 2020.

Gohainbarua, Padmanath. *Mur Sonwarani.* Guwahati: Publication Board Assam, 1971.

Goswami, Atul. 'Assam's Industrial Development: Urgency of New Direction'. *Economic & Political Weekly* 16, no. 21 (1981): 953–56.

Goswami, Chandrama. 'Agricultural Land Use in the Plains of Assam'. *Economic & Political Weekly* 37, no. 49 (2002): 4891–93.

Goswami, Chandrama. 'Land Use in Assam: A Spatio-Temporal Study'. PhD diss., Tezpur University, Tezpur, 2003.

Goswami, D., and S. Kataki. *Report and Conspectus of the Kamarupa Anusandhan Samiti for 1927–28 to 1929–30.* Guwahati: Kamarupa Anusandhan Samiti, 1931.

Goswami, G.C. 'Development of Petrochemical Industries in Assam'. In *Mineral Development in Assam: Symposium volume,* by Government of Assam. Shillong: Directorate of Geology and Mining, 1964.

Goswami, Golockchandra. *An Introduction to Assamese Phonology.* Pune: Deccan College Postgraduate and Research Institute, 1966.

Goswami, Golockchandra. *Structure of Assamese.* Guwahati: Gauhati University, 1982.

Goswami, Jatin. *Sankari Nrityar Mati Akhara.* Guwahati: Srimanta Sankaradeva Sangha, 1997.

Goswami, Kesavananda Deva. *Satra Sanskritir Ruprekha.* Dibrugarh: National Library, 1973.

Goswami, Mahesh Chandra. 'From Everywhere in India'. *The India P.E.N.* XI, no. 6 (June 1945), in *Mahesh Chandra Dev Goswami: Jivan aru Kriti*, edited by Prafulla Mahanta, pp. 155–56. Nagaon: Mahesh Chandra Dev Goswami Smriti Raksha Samiti, 2004.

Goswami, Mamoni Roisom. 'Datal Hatir Uye Khowa Haoda (The Moth Eaten Howdah of the Tusker)'. In *Upanyas Samagra* (Collected Novels), by Mamoni Roisom Goswami, pp. 1–166. Guwahati: Students Stores, 1998.

Goswami, Namrata. *The Naga Ethnic Movement for a Separate Homeland: Stories from the Field.* New Delhi: Oxford University Press, 2020.

Goswami, Prahas Chandra. 'Tragedy of Political Tactlessness'. *Economic Weekly* 12, no. 31 (1960): 1195–98.

Goswami, Prahas Chandra. *Economic Development of Assam.* Bombay: Asia Publishing House, 1963.

Goswami, Praphulladutta. 'The Bihu Songs of Assam'. In *The Eastern Anthropologist* 3, no. 1 (1949): 57–70.

Goswami, Praphulladutta. *Bohag Bihu of Assam and Bihu Songs*. Guwahati: Publication Board Assam, 1988.

Goswami, Praphulladutta. *Springtime Bihu of Assam: A Socio-Cultural Study*. Guwahati: Lawyer's Book Stall, 1966.

Goswami, Pratap Chandra. *Jeevan Smriti aru Kamrupi Samaj: A Memoir Dealing with Evolution of the Social Systems of North Kamrup*. Guwahati: Pratul Goswami, 1971.

Goswami, Radhika Mohan. *Ateet Smriti*. Guwahati: Alok Prakasan, 1989.

Goswami, Ranjit Kumar Dev. *Prabandha: A Collection of Essays and Lectures*. Guwahati: LBS, 2019.

Goswami, Sabita. *Along the Red River: A Memoir*. New Delhi: Zubaan, 2013.

Goswami, Sabita. *Mon Gangaor Tirot*. Guwahati: Assam Book Hive, 2017.

Goswami, Sandhya. 'Ethnic Conflict in Assam'. *Indian Journal of Political Science* 62, no. 1 (2001): 123–37.

Goswami, Sandhya. *Assam Politics in Post-Congress Era: 1985 and Beyond*. Delhi: Sage Publications, 2020.

Goswami, Shilpi. 'From Ritual to Performance: A Study of the Sattriya Performance Traditions of Assam as Intangible Heritage with a Special Reference to the Kamalabari Group of Sattras', PhD diss., Tezpur University, 2015.

Goswami, Suresh Chandra. *Asomor Natya Nrittya Kala*. Guwahati: Authors Book Stall, 1979.

Goswami, Suresh Chandra. *Sankari Natya-Nritya Kala: A Book on Dramas and Dances of Shri Shri Sankardev*. Guwahati: Banphul, 2014.

Goswami, T.C. 'Sarkaror Khadyaniti'. *Ramdhenu* 18, no. 9 (1966): 829–35.

Goswami, Uddipana. *Conflict and Reconciliation: The Politics of Ethnicity in Assam*. Delhi: Routledge, 2014.

Gould, William. *Religion and Conflict in Modern South Asia*. Cambridge: Cambridge University Press, 2012.

Government of Assam, *A Report of the Employment Review Committee on the Employment Position in the Public and Private Sector Industries and Undertakings in Assam, 1969*. Shillong: Government Press, 1969.

Government of Assam, *Annual Report on Agriculture, Assam, 1949–50*. Shillong: Government Press, 1950.

Government of Assam, *Annual Report on Agriculture, Assam, 1954–55*. Shillong: Government Press, 1955.

Government of Assam, *Assam Marches: A Glimpse into the Educational Progress in Assam, 1948–49–50*. Shillong: n.p, n.d.

Government of Assam, *Assessment Report of the South Western Group of the Nowgong District*. Shillong: Assam Government Press, 1932.

Government of Assam, *Draft Third Five-Year Plan, Assam*. Shillong: Government Printing Press, 1960.

Government of Assam, *Education in Assam: Statistical Handbook, 1947–48 to 1960–61*. Shillong: Department of Economics and Statistics, 1962.

Government of Assam, *Education in Assam: Statistical Handbook, 1947–48 to 1958–59*. Shillong: Department of Economics and Statistics, 1961.

Government of Assam, *Finance Accounts, 1947–48 and the Audit Report 1948*. Shillong: Assam Government Press, 1949.

Government of Assam, *General Educational Table Relating to Assam, 1942–43*. Shillong: Assam Government Press, 1944.

Government of Assam, *Outbreak of Communal Violence in Assam in the Year 1950: An Analysis of the Communal Violence in Assam in the Year 1950 on the Basis of the Report of District Authority and Top Most Civil and Police Official to the Mukherjee Commission)*. Guwahati: Government of Assam, 2014.

Government of Assam, *Progress Report of Forest Administration in the Province of Assam, 1950–51*. Shillong: Government Press, 1951.

Government of Assam, *Report on The Small and Marginal Farmers and Landless Agriculturalists Development Agency: Mikir Hills*. Shillong: Directorate of Evaluation, 1973.

Government of Assam. *Annual Report on Agriculture, Assam 1947–48*. Shillong: Government Press, 1948.

Government of Assam. *Assam District Gazetteers: Lakhimpur District*. Guwahati: Government of Assam, 1976.

Government of Assam. *Backwardness to Modernity*. Guwahati: Director of Information and Public Relations, Government of Assam, 1978.

Government of Assam. *Compendium of Government Land Policies: A Compilation from 1937 to 2019*. Guwahati: Revenue and Disaster Management Department, Government of Assam, 2020.

Government of Assam. *Dimasa Fori Sygangtau: Cachari First Reader*. Shillong: Assam Secretariat Printing Office, 1904.

Government of Assam. *Dimasani Forigani: Cachari Second Reader*. Shillong: Assam Secretariat Printing Office, 1904.

Government of Assam. *Economic Survey, Assam 1974–75*. Guwahati: Directorate of Economics and Statistics, Assam, 1976.

Government of Assam. *Economic Survey, Assam 1976–77*. Guwahati: Directorate of Economics and Statistics, 1977.

Government of Assam. *Economic Survey, Assam 1979–80*. Guwahati: Directorate of Economics, 1980.

Government of Assam. *Economic Survey, Assam 1980–81*. Guwahati: Directorate of Economics and Statistics, 1981.

Government of Assam. *Economic Survey, Assam 1981–82*. Guwahati: Directorate of Economics and Statistics, Assam, 1982.

Government of Assam. *Economic Survey, Assam 1984–85*. Guwahati: Directorate of Economics and Statistics, 1985.

Government of Assam. *Enquiry Report on the Allegations Brought by Shri Govinda Kalita, M.L.A., before the House on 19th and 20th May, 1971 regarding Settlement of Lands in and around Gauhati and Other Allied Matters.* Shillong: Assembly Legislative Assembly Secretariat, 1971.

Government of Assam. *Fourth Five Year Plan of Assam: A Draft Outline*. Shillong: Planning and Development Department, 1968.

Government of Assam. *General Educational Table Relating to Assam, 1942–43*. Shillong: Department of Education, 1944.

Government of Assam. *Progress Report of Forest Administration in the Province of Assam for the year 1944–45*. Shillong: Assam Government Press, 1947.

Government of Assam. *Report of the Embankment and Drainage Projects Reviewing Committee, Assam*. Shillong: Department of Public Works, 1960.

Government of Assam. *Report of the Land Revenue Administration of Assam for the Year 1934–35*. Shillong: Assam Secretariat Printing Office, 1936.

Government of Assam. *Report of the Land Revenue Administration of Assam for the year 1944–45*. Shillong: Assam Secretariat Printing Press, 1946.

Government of Assam. *Report on Agricultural Census 2010–11 on Number and Area of Operational Holdings*. Guwahati: Directorate of Economics and Statistics, Assam, 2014.

Government of Assam. *Report on Rural Economic Survey in United Khasi & Jaintia Hills*. Shillong: Department of Economics and Statistics, 1963.

Government of Assam. *Report on the Administration of Assam for 1916–17*. Shillong: Assam Secretariat Printing Office, 1918.

Government of Assam. *Report on the Land Revenue Administration in the Province of Assam for the year 1874–75*. Shillong: Secretariat Press, 1875.

Government of Assam. *Report on the Land Revenue Administration of Assam for the year 1960–61*. Shillong: Assam Government Press, undated.

Government of Assam. *Report on the Police Administration in the state of Assam for the year 1961*. Shillong: Assam Government Press, 1964.

Government of Assam. *Statistical Handbook, 1947–48 to 1958–59*. Shillong: Department of Economics and Statistics, Government of Assam, 1961.

Government of Assam. *Statistical Handbook, Assam, 2001*. Guwahati: Department of Economics and Statistics, 2001.

Government of India, *Abstract of Agricultural Statistics of India 1936–37 to 1945–46*. Delhi: Directorate of Economics and Statistics, 1949.

Government of India, *Assam Events in Perspective*. New Delhi: Directorate of Advertising and Visual Publicity, 1983.

Government of India, *Progress of Education in India, 1947–1952*. New Delhi: Manager of Publications, 1954.

Government of India, *Report of the Officials of the Governments of India and the People's Republic of China on the Boundary Question*. New Delhi: Government of India Press, 1962.

Government of India, *Report of the Soil Conservation Reconnaissance Committee for Assam & N.E.F.A*. Shillong: Government Printing Press, 1957.

Government of India, *Statistical Abstract for 1946–47*. Delhi: Manager of Publications, 1949.

Government of India, *Statistical Abstract: India, 1978*, new series, no. 23. New Delhi: Central Statistical Organisation, 1979.

Government of India. 'Report of the Bengal Border Commission (Radcliffe Award)'. *The Gazette of India (Extraordinary)*, 1947.

Government of India. *15th Indian Livestock Census 1992: Part 1-Livestock*. New Delhi: Department of Agriculture and Cooperation, 2000.

Government of India. *Agriculture Census 2015–16, (Phase-I): All India Report on Number and Area of Operational Holdings*. New Delhi: Agriculture Census Division Department of Agriculture, Co-Operation & Farmers Welfare, 2019.

Government of India. *District Calendar of Events of the Congress Disturbances in Assam, August 1942–March 1943*. New Delhi: Government of India Press, 1943.

Government of India. *Indian Museums Review, 1961–64*. New Delhi: Ministry of Scientific Research and Cultural Affairs, Government of India, 1966.

Government of India. *Recurrent Exodus of Minorities from East Pakistan and Disturbances in India*. New Delhi: The Indian Commission of Jurists, 1965.

Government of India. *Report of the Commission on the Hill Areas of Assam, 1965–66*. Shillong: Directorate of Information and Public Relations, 1966.

Government of India. *Report of the Jute Enquiry Commission*. New Delhi: Government of India Press, 1954.

Government of India. *Report of the States Reorganisation Commission*. Delhi: Government of India Press, 1955.

Government of India. *Report: National Commission on Floods*. Vol. 1. New Delhi: Ministry of Energy and Irrigation, 1980.

Government of India. *Reports of the Agricultural Prices Commission on Price Policy for Crops Sown in 1982–83 season*. New Delhi: Commission for Agricultural Costs and Prices, 1983.

Government of India. *Some Aspects of Operational Land Holdings in India, 2002–03. NSS Report No. 492*. New Delhi: National Sample Survey Organisation, Ministry of Statistics and Programme Implementation, 2006.

Government of India. *Statistical Abstract for the year 1946–47*. New Delhi: Manager of Publication, 1949.

Government of India. *Statistical Abstract, India, 1978, new series, no. 23*. New Delhi: Department of Statistics, Ministry of Planning, Government of India, 1979.

Government of India. *Statistical Information Relating to the Influx of Refugees from East Bengal into India till 31st October, 1971*. Calcutta: Ministry of Labour and Rehabilitation, 1971.

Government of India. *Study of the Report of the Commission of Enquiry (Jabbar Commission) on Expulsion of Pakistani Infiltrants from Tripura and Assam*. New Delhi: Ministry of Home Affairs, Government of India Press, 1964.

Government of India. *The State of Forest Report, 1989*. Dehradun: Forest Survey of India, 1989.

Government of India. *The State of Forest Report, 1993*. Dehradun: Forest Survey of India, 1993.

Government of India, *Report of the Plantation Inquiry Commission: Part 1*. New Delhi: Government of India Press, 1956.

Government of India, *Report of the Fifth Finance Commission*. New Delhi: Finance Commission of India, 1969.

Govindan, Balaji, Anil John Johnson, Sadasivan Nair Ajikumaran Nair, Bhaskaran Gopakumar, Karuna Sri Lakshmi Mallampalli, Ramaswamy Venkataraman, Konnath Chacko Koshy and Sabulal Baby. 'Nutritional Properties of the Largest Bamboo Fruit *Melocanna Baccifera* and Its Ecological Significance'. *Scientific Reports* 6 (2016): 1–12.

Govindu, Venu Madhav, and Deepak Malghan. *The Web of Freedom: J.C. Kumarappa and Gandhi's Struggle for Economic Justice*. New Delhi: Oxford University Press, 2016.

Granville, Austin. *The Indian Constitution: Cornerstone of a Nation*. Oxford: Oxford University Press, 1966.

Gribble, R.H. *Out of the Burma Night: Being the Story of a Fantastic Journey through the Wilderness of the Hukawng Valley and the Forest Clad Mountains of the Naga Tribes People at the Time of the Japanese Invasion of Burma*. Calcutta: Thacker Spink & Co., 1944.

Grierson, George Abraham. ed. *Linguistic Survey of India, Vol. V, Indo-Aryan Family Eastern Group, Part-I, Specimens of the Bengali and Assamese Languages*. Calcutta: Office of the Superintendent of Government Printing, 1903.

Griffiths, Percival Joseph. *A History of the Joint Steamer Companies*. London: Inchape & Co., 1979.

Griffiths, Percival Joseph. *The History of the Indian Tea Industry*. London: Weidenfeld & Nicolson, 1967.

Grove, Richard H. *Green Imperialism: Colonial Expansion, Tropical Island Edens and the Origins of Environmentalism, 1600–1860*. New Delhi: Oxford University Press, 1995.

Grover, V., and R. Arora. eds. *Events and Documents of Indo–Pak Relations*. New Delhi: Deep & Deep Publications, 1999.

Guha, Abhijit. 'Social Anthropology of B.S. Guha: An Exploration'. *Indian Anthropologist* 48, no. 1 (2018): 1–12.

Guha, Amalendu. *Vaishnavbadorpara Moamaria Bidhroholoi*. Guwahati: Students' Stores, 1993.

Guha, Amalendu. 'A Big Push Without a Take-off: A Case-Study of Assam, 1871–1901', *Indian Economic and Social History Review* 5, no. 3 (1968): 199–221.

Guha, Amalendu. 'Little Nationalism Turned Chauvinist: Assam's Anti-Foreigner Upsurge, 1979–80'. *Economic & Political Weekly* 15, no. 41/43 (1980): 1699–1720.

Guha, Amalendu. *Goalpara Zillar Artha Samajik Abastha: Eti Oitihasik Dristipat*. Guwahati: Natun Sahitya Parisad, 2000.

Guha, Amalendu. *Medieval and Early Colonial Assam: Society, Polity, Economy*. Kolkata: K.P. Bagchi & Company, 2012.

Guha, Amalendu. *Planter Raj to Swaraj: Freedom Struggle & Electoral Politics in Assam 1826–1947*. New Delhi: Indian Council of Historical Research, 1977.

Guha, Ramachandra. *Gandhi: The Years that Changed the* World, *1914–1948*. Delhi: Penguin, 2018.

Guha, Ramachandra. *India after Gandhi: The History of the World's Largest Democracy*. Delhi: Picador, 2007.

Guha, Ramachandra. *Savaging the Civilized: Verrier Elwin, His Tribals, and India*. Delhi: Penguin, 2013.

Gundevia, Y.D. *War and Peace in Nagaland*. Dehradun: Palit and Palit, 1975.

Gupta, Amit Kumar. *Agrarian Drama: The Leftists and the Rural Poor in India 1934–1951*. New Delhi: Manohar, 1996.

Gupta, K.K. 'Flowering in Different Species of Bamboos in Cachar District of Assam in Recent Times'. *Indian Forester* 98, no. 2 (1972): 83–85.

Gupta, Partha Sarathi. ed. *Towards Freedom: Documents on the Movement for Independence in India, 1943–1944*. Delhi: Oxford University Press, 1997.

Gupta, Shekhar, and Uttam Sengupta. 'Assam in turmoil, government struggles hopelessly to establish semblance of authority'. *India Today*, 15 September 1990.

Gupta, Shekhar. 'The agitation is over. It is dead and gone: Sarat Chandra Sinha'. *India Today*, 15 September 1983.

Gurdon, P.R.T. *Some Assamese Proverbs*. Shillong: Government Printing Press, 1903.

Guyot-Réchard, Bérénice. 'Tour Diaries and Itinerant Governance in the Eastern Himalayas, 1909–1962'. *The Historical Journal* 60, no. 4 (2017): 1023–46.

Guyot-Réchard, Bérénice. 'When Legions Thunder Past: The Second World War and India's Northeastern Frontier'. *War in History* 25 (2018): 328–60.

Guyot-Réchard, Bérénice. *Shadow States: India, China and the Himalayas, 1910–1962*. New York: Cambridge University Press, 2017.

Habibullah, Wajahat, *My Years with Rajiv: Triumph and Tragedy*. Chennai: Westland, 2020.

Haldipur, R.N. 'NEFA - An Introduction'. *Bulletin of Tibetology* 3, no. 2 (1966): 72–83.

Hannan, Abdul. 'Farm Size and Trade Relations of Small Tea Growers (STGs) in Assam and North Bengal'. *Social Change and Development* 16, no. 2 (2019): 78–99.

Haokip, Sonthang. 'Anglo Kuki Relations: 1777–1947 AD'. PhD diss., Manipur University, Imphal, 2011.

Hayami, Yujiro, and A. Damodaran. 'Towards an Alternative Agrarian Reform: Tea Plantations in South India'. *Economic & Political Weekly* 39, no. 36 (2004): 3992–97.

Hazarika, A.C. *Shillongor Puroni Asomiya Somaj*. Guwahati: Hazarikas, 1993.

Hazarika, Atul Chandra. *Jatiya Sangeet*. Shillong: Chapala Book Stall, 1949.

Hazarika, Atul Chandra. *Katha Kirtana*. Guwahati: Barua Agency, 1945.

Hazarika, Atul Chandra. *Manchalekha: A History of the Assamese Stage from 1468–1967*. Guwahati: Lokendranath Medhi, 1967.

Hazarika, Jatin. *Shadow Behind the Throne: My Tryst with Assam Administration*. Guwahati: Lawyer's Book Stall, 2016.

Hazarika, Mahendranath. *Biyalisher Biplabot Nagaon*. Guwahati: Publication Board Assam, 1977.

Hazarika, Niru. *Profile of Youth Organisations in North East India: Assam*. Guwahati: V.V. Rao Institute of Micro Studies and Research, 1998.

Hazarika, Sanjoy. *Rites of Passage: Border Crossings, Imagined Homelands, India's East and Bangladesh*. Delhi: Penguin, 2000.

Hazarika, Sanjoy. *Strangers of the Mist: Tales of War and Peace from India's Northeast*. New Delhi: Penguin, 1994.

Hluna, J.V. 'MNF Relations with Foreign Powers'. In *Autonomy Movements in Mizoram*, edited by R.N. Prasad, pp. 189–202. New Delhi: Vikas Publishing House, 1994.

Hluna, J.V., and Rini Tochhawng, *The Mizo Uprising: Assam Assembly Debates on the Mizo Movement, 1966–1971*. Newcastle upon Tyne: Cambridge Scholars Publishing, 2012.

Hossain, Ashfaque. 'Historical Globalization and Its Effects: A Study of Sylhet and Its People, 1874–1971', PhD diss., University of Nottingham, Nottingham, 2009.

Hudson, G.F. 'The Frontier of China and Assam: Background to the Fighting'. *China Quarterly*, no. 12 (1962): 203–06.

Hunter, W.W. *A Statistical Account of Assam*. Vol. II. London: Trübner & Co., 1879.

Hunter, W.W. *A Comparative Dictionary of the Languages of India and High Asia with a Dissertation*. London: Trubner, 1868.

Hussain, Ismail. *Assamor Char-Chaporir Loka-Sahitya*. Guwahati: Banalata, 2002.

Hussain, Monirul. 'High Caste to Non-Caste Dominance: The Changing Pattern of Leadership of the Congress Party in Assam'. *Indian Journal of Political Science* 49, no. 3 (1988): 402–17.

Hussain, Monirul. 'The Assam Movement: A Sociological Study'. PhD diss., Jawaharlal Nehru University (JNU), New Delhi, 1989.

Inamdar, N.R. 'A Study of the System of Representation in India, 1920–46'. PhD diss., Savitribai Phule Pune University, Pune, 1953.

Indian Central Jute Committee. *The Indian Jute Atlas*, Calcatta: Indian Central Jute Committee, 1959.

Indian Statutory Commission. *Memorandum submitted by the Government of Assam to the Indian Statutory Commission, Volume XIV*. London: His Majesty's Stationery Office, 1930.

Indian Tea Association. *Detailed Report of the General Committee of the Indian Tea Association for the year 1958*. Calcutta: Indian Tea Association, 1959.

Jaffrelot, Christophe. *The Hindu Nationalist Movement and Indian Politics: 1925 to the 1990s*. New York: Columbia University Press, 1998.

Jaffrelot, Christophe, and Pratinav Anil. *India's First Dictatorship: The Emergency, 1975–1977*. Noida: HarperCollins, 2020.

Jaffrelot, Christophe. *The Hindu Nationalist Movement and Indian Politics 1925 to the 1990s: Strategies of Identity-Building, Implantation and Mobilisation (with Special Reference to Central India)*. London: Hurst, 1996.

Jakhalu, Katoni. 'Provisional Finance in Assam: A Study of Imperial Provisional Financial Relations, 1874–1947'. PhD diss., North-Eastern Hill University, Shillong, 2001.

Jayal, Niraja Gopal. *Citizenship and Its Discontents: An Indian History*. Cambridge, Mass.: Harvard University Press, 2013.

Jeffrey, Robin. 'Indian-Language Newspapers and Why They Grow'. *Economic & Political Weekly* 28, no. 38 (1993): 2004–11.
Jeffrey, Robin. *India's Newspaper Revolution: Capitalism, Politics and the Indian-Language Press*. New York: St Martin's Press, 2000.
Jha, D.C. *Indo–Pakistan Relations, 1960–1965*. Patna: Bharati Bhawan, 1972.
Jhuraney, J.C. 'Spatial Changes in the Distribution of Employment in the Organised Sector'. *Indian Journal of Industrial Relations* 12, no. 1 (1976): 61–72.
Johri, Sitaram. *Where India, China and Burma Meet*. Calcutta: Thacker Spink & Co., 1962.
Jones, Stephanie. *Merchants of the Raj: British Managing Agency Houses in Calcutta Yesterday and Today*. London: Palgrave Macmillan, 1992.
Kakati, Banikanta. 'Bezbarooa'. In *Banikanta-Chayanika*, edited by M. Neog, p. 132. New Delhi, Sahitya Akademi, 1981.
Kakati, Banikanta. *Assamese, Its Formation and Development: A Scientific Treatise on the History and Philology of the Assamese Language*. Guwahati: Department of Historical and Antiquarian Studies, 1941.
Kakati, Banikanta. *Purani Asomiya Sahitya*. Calcutta: G.C. Patowary, 1940.
Kakati, Banikanta. *The Mother Goddess Kamakhya*. Guwahati: Publication Board Assam, 1989 (1948).
Kakati, Niren. ed. *Sattriya Nrityar Saphura Meli: Adhyapak Rashewar Saikia Barbayan*. Guwahati: Sangeet Sattra, 2022.
Kalita, Arupa Patangiya, *Felani*. Guwahati: Jyoti Prakashan, 2003.
Kamrupee. 'Cool behind the Noise and Fury'. *Economic & Political Weekly* 7, no. 31/33 (1972): 1485–88.
Kandali, Mallika. *Nrityakala Prasanga aru Sattriya Nritya*. Guwahati: N.L. Publication, 2012.
Kandali, Mallika. *Sattriya: The Living Dance Tradition of Assam*. Guwahati: Publication Board of Assam, 2014.
Kar, Boddhisattva. 'When Was the Postcolonial? A History of Policing Impossible Lines'. In *Beyond Counter-Insurgency: Breaking the Impasse in Northeast India*, edited by Sanjib Baruah, pp. 49–79. New Delhi: Oxford University Press, 2009.
Kar, Makhanlal. *Muslims in Assam Politics*. Delhi: Vikas Publishing House, 1997.
Kakati, Satish Chandra. *Smriti Bichitra*. Guwahati: Sahitya Prakash, 1992.
Kaul, Brij Mohan. *The Untold Story*. Bombay: Allied Publishers, 1967.
Kaul, H.N. *K.D. Malaviya and the Evolution of India's Oil Policy*. New Delhi: Allied Publishers, 1991.
Khaklari, Jadunath. *Kacharir Katha*. Jorhat: Kritinath Khaklari, 1927.

Khan, Mohammad Ayub. *Speeches and Statements: Field Marshal Mohammad Ayub Khan, President of Pakistan, July 1963–June 1964*, vol. 6. Karachi: Pakistan Government Publications, 1964.

Khound, Malaya Barua. ed. *Eri Thoi Aha Dinbor*. Guwahati: Lawyer's Book Stall, 1993.

Kikon, Dolly. 'Disturbed Area acts: Intimacy, anxiety and the state in Northeast India'. PhD diss., Stanford University, Stanford, California, 2013.

Kikon, Dolly. *Living with Oil and Coal: Resource Politics and Militarization in Northeast India*. Seattle: University of Washington Press, 2019.

Kimura, Makiko. *The Nellie Massacre of 1983: Agency of Rioters*. Delhi: Sage Publications, 2015.

Kohli, Atul. *The State and Poverty in India*. Cambridge: Cambridge University Press, 1989.

Kohli, Atul. ed. *India's Democracy: An Analysis of Changing State–Society Relations*. Princeton: Princeton University Press, 2014.

Kosaka, Yasuyuki, Bhaskar Saikia, C.K. Rai, Komo Hage, Haruhisa Asada, Tag Hui, Tomo Riba and Kazuo Ando. 'On the Introduction of Paddy Rice Cultivation by Swiddeners in Arunachal Pradesh, India'. *Tropics* 24, no. 2 (1 September 2015): 76–90.

Kothari, Sunil. ed. *Sattriya: Classical Dance of Assam*. Mumbai: Marg, 2013.

Kshurav, N.S. *Soviet Yuktarastar Communist Partyir Karjyasuchi Samparke*. (Translation in Assamese, pamphlet), Soviet Desh, 1961.

Kudaisya, Gyanesh, and Tan Tai Yong. *The Aftermath of Partition in South Asia*. London: Routledge, 2000.

Kumar, Dharma, and Meghnad Desai. eds. *Cambridge Economic History of India*. Vol. 2. New York: Cambridge University Press, 1983.

Kumar, Satish. ed. *Documents on India's Foreign Policy* 1972. New Delhi: Macmillan, 1975.

Kumawat, M.M., K.M. Singh, R.S. Tripathi, T. Riba, S. Singh, and D. Sen. 'Rodent outbreak in relation to bamboo flowering in north-eastern region of India'. *Biological Agriculture & Horticulture* 30, no. 4 (2014): 243–52.

Kuri, Pravat Kumar. *Tenancy Relations in Backward Agriculture: A Study in Rural Assam*. Delhi: Mittal Publications, 2004.

Kyndiah, P.R. *Rev. J.J. M. Nichols Roy, Architect of District Council Autonomy*. New Delhi: Sanchar Publication House, 1993.

Laakkonen, Simo, Richard Tucker, and Timo Vuorisalo. eds. *The Long Shadows: A Global Environmental History of the Second World War*. Corvallis, Oregon: Oregon State University Press, 2017.

Lahkar, Bibhuti P., Jayanta K. Baruah, Nirupam Hazarika and Pranjit K. Sarmaet. 'A geo-spatial assessment of habitat loss of Asian elephants in Golaghat District of Assam'. *Gajah* 28 (2008): 25–30.

Laine, A.J. *An Account of the Land Tenure System of Goalpara, With Criticisms of the Existing Rent Law and Suggestions for its Amendments*. Shillong: Assam Government Printing Press, 1917.

Lama, Dalai. 'Mur Desh Mur Priyajan'. *Nilachal*, April 1964: 57–104.

Lamb, Alastair. *Tibet, China and India, 1914–1950: A History of Imperial Diplomacy*. Hertingfordbury: Roxford Books, 1989.

Leigh, Michael D. *The Evacuation of Civilians from Burma: Analysing the 1942 Colonial Disaster*. London: Bloomsbury, 2014.

Lintner, Bertil. *Great Game East: India, China and the struggle for Asia's most volatile frontier*. Noida: HarperCollins Publishers India, 2012.

Long, James. *Returns relating to Publications in the Bengali Language, in 1857: Selections from the Records of the Bengal Government*. Vol. xxxii. Calcutta: General Printing Department, 1859.

Longley, Philip R.H. *Tea Planter Sahib: The Life and Adventures of a Tea Planter in North East India*. Auckland: Tonson Publishing House, 1969.

Ludden, David. *An Agrarian History of South Asia*. Delhi: Cambridge University Press, 1999.

Lyman, Robert. *Japan's Last Bid for Victory: The Invasion of India, 1944*. South Yorkshire: Casemate Publishers, 2011.

Macharness, C. 'Assam: Progress Report of Forest Administration for the year 1944–45'. *Empire Forestry Review* 26, no. 2 (1947): 320–21.

Mackenzie, Alexander. *History of Relations of the Government with the Hill Tribes of the North-East Frontier of India*. Calcutta: Home Department Press, 1884.

Mahajan, Sucheta. ed. *Towards Freedom: Documents on the Movement for Independence in India, 1947*, Part 2. New Delhi: Oxford University Press, 2015.

Mahajan, Sucheta. ed. *Towards Freedom: Documents on the Movement for Independence in India, 1947, part 1 and 2*. New Delhi: Oxford University Press, 2013–2015.

Mahanta, Durlav Chandra. 'Ejan Sahakarmir Dristit Shri Sailen Medhi'. In *Sailen Medhi: Byektitwa aru Samaj Chinta*, edited by Yamini Phukan, pp. 36–37. Guwahati: 80th Birthday Celebration Committee, 2009.

Mahanta, Jaganath. *Sattriya Nrityar Hastaputhi*. Guwahati: Forum for Sankardev Studies, 2000.

Mahanta, Joyasree Goswami. *Asom Andolon: Yugamia Cintar Ek Pratifalan*. Vols 1–3. Guwahati: Chandra Prakash, 2015.

Mahanta, Mitradev. 'Geeti Satadal'. In *Mitradev Mahanta Rachanavalee*, edited by Nagen Saikia, pp. 30–36. Jorhat: Premananda Trust, 2012.

Mahanta, Nani Gopal. *Confronting the State: ULFA's Quest for Sovereignty*. Delhi: Sage Publications, 2013.

Mahanta, Pradipjyoti. 'Pradip Chaliha (1918–2004)'. In *Katha Barenya 100: A Collection of the Profiles of 100 Luminaries in the Field of Art and Literature of Assam*, edited by Soneet Bijay Das and Munin Bayan, pp. 136–37. Guwahati: Katha, 2006.

Mahanta, Prafulla Kumar. *The Tussle between the Citizens and Foreigners in Assam*. New Delhi: Vikas Publishing House, 1986.

Mahanta, Premakanta. *Rajbhaganar Pora Kolthokaloi*. Guwahati: Banalata, 2018 (1993).

Mahanta, Ratneswar. 'Ghainir Kartabya aru Stree Sikhsa' (Duty of a wife and Education of Women)'. In *Asam-Bandhu: A Monthly Paper Devoted to Assamese Language, Literature and Culture*, compiled and edited by Nagen Saikia, pp. 355–60, pp. 449–56. Guwahati: Publication Board Assam, 1984 (1885 and 1886).

Mahanta, Ratneswar. 'Goanalia Buari'. In *Ratneswar Mahanta Rachanwali*, edited by Jogendranarayan Bhuyan. Guwahati: Publication Board Assam, 1977.

Mahmood, Hameeduddin. 'Assam agitation takes a violent turn as Congress(I) forms govt at the Centre'. *India Today*, 15 February 1980.

Majumdar, Paramananda. ed. *Awahan*. Vol. II. Guwahati: Publication Board Assam, 2019.

Maksud, Syed Abul. *Maulana Abdul Hamid Khan Bhashani*. Dhaka: Bangla Academy, 1994.

Malhotra, Inder. *Indira Gandhi: A Personal and Political Biography*. New Delhi: Hay House Publishers, 2014.

Malhotra, Inder. *Indira Gandhi*. Delhi: Directorate of Advertising and Visual Publicity, Government of India, 1975.

Mansergh, Nicholas, and Penderel Moon. eds. *The Transfer of Power 1942–47*. Vols 1–12. London: Her Majesty's Stationery Office (HMSO), 1970–1983.

Marar, K.W.P. *Census of India, 1941, Volume XI, Assam*. Delhi: Manager of Publications, 1942.

Marwah, Onkar. 'India's Military Intervention in East Pakistan, 1971–1972'. *Modern Asian Studies* 13, no. 4 (1979): 549–80.

Maxwell, Neville. *India's China War*. London: Jonathan Cape, 1970.

May, Andrew. *Welsh Missionaries and British Imperialism: The Empire of Clouds in North-east India*. Manchester: Manchester University Press, 2017.

Mazid, Altaf. 'Jyotiprasad and Joymoti: The Pioneer and the First Assamese Film'. In *Perspectives on Cinema of Assam*, edited by M. Barpujari and G. Kalita, pp. 29–50. Guwahati: Gauhati Cine Club, 2007.

McCall, Anthony Gilchrist. *Lushai Chrysalis*. London: Luzac, 1949.

McDuie-Ra, Duncan. 'The India–Bangladesh Border Fence: Narratives and Political Possibilities'. *Journal of Borderlands Studies* 29, no.1 (2014): 81–94.

Medhi, Kaliram. *Asamiya Byakaran aru Bhasatattwa*. Guwahati: Publication Board Assam, 1936.

Medhi, Kaliram. *Sri Sankardevar Bani*. Guwahati: Duttabarua Publishing, 1949.

Mehra, Masani. *Broadcasting and the People*. New Delhi: National Book Trust, India, 1976.

Mehrotra, G. *Report of the Commission of Inquiry into the Goreswar Disturbances*. Shillong: Assam Government Press, 1961.

Mehta, K.L. 'Record of the Prime Minister's Meeting with the Delegation of the Hill Leaders' Conference on 17th May, 1961'. In the *Selected Works of Jawaharlal Nehru, Second Series*, Vol. 69, edited by Sri S. Gopal, p. 117. New Delhi: Jawaharlal Nehru Memorial Fund, 2016.

Mehta, T.U. *Report of the Non-Official Judicial Enquiry Commission on Holocaust of Assam*. Guwahati: Asom Rajyik Freedom Fighters' Association, 1985.

Menon, Nikhil. *Planning Democracy: How a Professor, an Institute and an Idea Shaped India*. New Delhi: Penguin, 2022.

Menon, P.M., K.G. Sivawamy, and M.V. Mathur. *Report of the Plantation Inquiry Commission, 1956. Part I*. Delhi: Manager of Publications, 1956.

Menon, V.P. *The Transfer of Power in India*. Princeton: Princeton University Press, 1957.

Ministry of Rehabilitation (Government of India). *Rehabilitation Retrospect*. New Delhi: Ananda Press, 1957.

Miri, Indira. *Moi aru NEFA: A Volume of Reminiscences*. Guwahati: Spectrum, 2003.

Mishra, Deepak K., Atul Sarma, and Vandana Upadhyay. 'Invisible Chains? Crisis in the Tea Industry and the "Unfreedom" of Labour in Assam's Tea Plantations'. *Contemporary South Asia* 19, no. 1 (2011): 75–90.

Misra, Tilottoma. 'Assam: A Colonial Hinterland'. *Economic & Political Weekly* 15, no. 32, (1980): 1357–64.

Misra, Udayon. 'No Tears for the Liberators'. *Economic & Political Weekly* 28, no. 32–33 (1993): 1635–36.

Misra, Udayon. *The Periphery Strikes Back: Challenges to the Nation-State in Assam and Nagaland*. Shimla: Indian Institute of Advanced Studies, 2000.

Mitra, Ashok, and Baldev Raj Kalra. *Census of India, 1961, Land Tenures in India. Vol. 1, part xi-A (i)*. Delhi: Government Press, 1962.

Mitra, N.N. *Indian Annual Register, 1946. January–June*. Vol. I. Calcutta: Annual Register Office, 1947.

Mitra, Sumit. 'AASU leaders' talks with Union government reach nowhere'. *India Today*, 31 May 1985.

Moon, Penderel. ed. *Wavell: The Viceroy's Journal*. Oxford: Oxford University Press, 1973.

Moon, Penderel. *Gandhi and Modern India*. New York: Norton, 1969.

Moral, Rakhee Kalita. 'The Woman Rebel and the State: Making War, Making Peace in Assam'. *Economic & Political Weekly* 49, no. 43–44 (2014): 66–73.

Mountbatten, Louis, and Alan Brooke. 'The Strategy of the South-East Asia Campaign'. *Royal United Services Institution Journal* 91, no. 564 (1946): 469–84.

Mukerjee, Dilip. 'Assam Reorganisation'. *Asian Survey* 9, no. 4 (1969): 297–311.

Mukherjee, S.K. 'The Reorganization of Assam and the Bodo Movement'. In *Reorganization of North-East India Since 1947,* edited by B. Datta Ray and S.P. Agrawal. New Delhi: Concept Publishing Company, 1996.

Mukherji, Partha N. 'The Great Migration of 1971: II'. *Economic & Political Weekly* 9, no. 10 (1974): 399–408.

Mullan, C.S. Census *of India, 1931, Vol. III, Assam, Part I-Report.* Delhi: Government of India Press, 1932.

Mullik, B.N. *My Years with Nehru.* Bombay: Allied Publishers, 1971.

Nadkarni, M.V., and K.H. Vedini. 'Accelerating Commercialisation of Agriculture: Dynamic Agriculture and Stagnating Peasants'. *Economic & Political Weekly* 31, no. 26 (1996): A63–A73.

Nag, Gouri Sankar. *Pannalal Dasgupta: Life Story of a Homeless Radical.* New Delhi: Manak Publications Pvt. Ltd, 2018.

Nag, Sajal, Tejimala Gurung, and Abhijit Choudhury. eds. *Making of the Indian Union: Merger of Princely States and Excluded Areas.* New Delhi: Akansha, 2007.

Nag, Sajal. 'Tribals, Famine, Rats, State and the Nation'. *Economic & Political Weekly* 36, no. 12 (2001): 1029–33.

Nag, Sajal. *Pied Pipers in North-East India: Bamboo-flowers, Rat Famine, and the Politics of Philanthropy, 1881–2007.* New Delhi: Manohar, 2008.

Narayan, Hemendra. *25 years on- Nellie still haunts: Assam '83: A journalist's travels.* Delhi: Hemendra Narayan, 2008.

Nath, Dambarudhar. 'Buranji Sahitya (1950–90)'. In *Asamiya Sahityar Buranji,* vol. 6, edited by Homen Borgohain, pp. 505–26. Guwahati: ABILAC, 1993.

Nath, Dambarudhar. *Satra Society and Culture: Pitambardeva Goswami and History of Garamur Satra.* Guwahati: DVS Publishers, 2012.

Nath, Dambarudhar. *The Majuli Island: Society, Economy and Culture.* New Delhi: Anshah Publishing House, 2009.

Nath, Manoj Kumar. *ULFA: Seujiya Sapon Tejranga Itihasa.* Guwahati: Aank Baka, 2013.

Nath, Monoj Kumar. *The Muslim Question in Assam and Northeast India* (Delhi: Routledge, 2021).

National Council of Applied Economic Research. *Techno-Economic Survey of Assam.* New Delhi: National Council of Applied Economic Research, 1962.

Nayak, Lohit Chandra. *Baṛapeṭā Hitasādhinī Sabhāra Prathama Bacharekiẏā KāryaBibaraṇī*. Barpeta: Barpeta Sanatan Dhurma Press, 1897.

Nayar, Kuldip. *Between the Lines*. New Delhi: Allied Publishers, 1969.

Nayyar, Deepak. 'Industrial Development in India: Some Reflections on Growth and Stagnation'. *Economic & Political Weekly* 13, no. 31/33 (1978): 1265–78.

Nehru, Braj Kumar. *Nice Guys Finish Second*. Delhi: Penguin Publishers, 2012.

Nehru, Jawaharlal. 'Foreword'. In *A Philosophy for NEFA* by Verrier Elwin, pp. xi–xii. Shillong: North East Frontier Agency, 1959.

Nehru, Jawaharlal. 'Telegram to Jairamdas Doulatram'. In *Documents on North-East India: Arunachal Pradesh*, edited by S.K. Sharma and Usha Sharma, p. 108. New Delhi: Mittal Publications, 2006.

Nehru, Jawaharlal. *Selected Works of Jawaharlal Nehru*, First and Second Series. New Delhi: Jawaharlal Nehru Memorial Fund, 1984–2019.

Neog, Dimbeswar, *History of Modern Assamese Literature from 1826 to 1947*. Allahabad: Ganganath Jha Research Institute, 1955.

Neog, Dimbeswar. *Asamiya Sahityar Buranji: Prachin, Madhya, Adhunik*. Jorhat: Xuwani Poja, 1950.

Neog, Dimbeswar. *Introduction to Assam*. Bombay: Vora and Co., 1947.

Neog, Dimbeswar. *New Light on History of Asamiya Literature*. Guwahati: Xuwani Prakash, 1962.

Neog, Dimbeswar. *Origin and Growth of the Asamiya Language*. Guwahati: Xuwani Prakas, 1964.

Neog, Maheswar, and Keshav Changkakati. *Rhythm in the Vaishnava music of Assam*. Guwahati: Bargit Research Committee, Asam Sangeet Natak Akademi, 1962.

Neog, Maheswar. ed. *Banikanta Kakati Rachanawali*. Guwahati: Publication Board, Assam, 1991.

Neog, Maheswar. *Snehar Arunachal: My Hill So Strong*. Jorhat: Asam Sahitya Sabha, 1976.

Neog, Maheswar. 'Different Religious Cults of Assam before the advent of Neo-Vaisnavism'. *Proceedings and Transactions of the All India Oriental Conference* 18, (1955): 427–35.

Neog, Maheswar. 'Script for the Tribal Languages of Assam'. In *Asamar Lipi Samsya: A collection of papers read at and proceedings of the second writers' camp,* edited by Nagen Saikia, p. 75. Jorhat: Asam Sahitya Sabha, 1974.

Neog, Maheswar. 'The Classical Dance Tradition in Assam'. In *Aesthetic Continuum: Essays on Assamese Music, Drama, Drance and Paintings*, edited by Maheswar Neog. New Delhi: Omsons Publications, 2008.

Neog, Maheswar. 'The Heritage of Fine Arts in Assam'. *Assam Quarterly* 4, (1967): 13–32.

Neog, Maheswar. *Anandaram Dhekiyal Phukan: Plea for Assam and Assamese: with the Complete Text of Observations on the Administration of the Province of Assam, by Baboo Anundaram Dakeal Phookun, Being Appendix J to A.J. Moffat Mills' Report on the Province of Assam, Calcutta, 1854, and A Few Remarks on the Assamese Language and on Vernacular Education in Assam, by a Native, Sibsagor, Asam, 1855.* Jorhat, Assam: Asam Sahitya Sabha, 1977.

Neog, Maheswar. *Asamiya Sahityar Ruparekha.* Guwahati: Chandra Prakashan, 1962.

Neog, Maheswar, compiled and ed. *Patralekha: A Bunch of Letters, etc. Written by Lakshminath Bezbaroa of Assam, to Different Persons and Institutions and by Different Persons and Institutions.* Jorhat: Asam Sahitya Sabha, 1968.

Neog, Maheswar. *Banikanta Rachanavali.* Guwahati: Publication Board Assam, 1991.

Neog, Maheswar. ed. *Prachya-Sasanavali: An Anthology of Royal Charters etc. Inscribed on Stone, Copper etc of Kamarupa, Asam (Saumara), Koch-Behar etc from 1205 AD to 1847 AD.* Guwahati: Publication Board Assam, 1974.

Neog, Maheswar. ed. *Srihastamuktavali.* Guwahati: Publication Board Assam, 1964.

Neog, Maheswar. ed. *Viswavidyalyour Swapna: The Romance of a University.* Guwahati: Chandra Prakash, 2009.

Neog, Maheswar. *Hastamuktavali of Subhankara.* Jorhat: Asam Sahitya Sabha, 1980.

Neog, Maheswar. *Jibanor Digh aru Bani.* Guwahati: Chandra Prakash, 1988.

Neog, Maheswar. *Sanchayan.* Delhi: Sahitya Akademi, 1971.

Neog, Maheswar. *Simantar Siksha Aru Samskritik Niti or The Educational and Cultural Policies of the North-East Frontier Agency Administration.* Jorhat: Asam Sahitya Sabha, 1962.

Neog, Maheswar. *The Language Problem of Assam.* Jorhat: Asam Sahitya Sabha, 1961.

Nibedon, Nirmal. *Nagaland, the Night of the Guerrillas.* New York: Lancers Publishers, 1978.

Nichols Roy, S.D.D. 'A New Hill State in the North East'. In the *Selected Works of Jawaharlal Nehru, Second Series, Vol. 68,* edited by Sri S. Gopal, p. 763. New Delhi: Jawaharlal Nehru Memorial Fund, 2016.

Niemeyer, Otto. *Indian Financial Inquiry Report.* Delhi: Manager of Publications, 1936.

Norman, Dorothy. *Indira Gandhi: Letters to an American Friend, 1950–1984.* New York: Helen and Kurt, 1985.

Nuh, V.K. ed. *The Naga Chronicle.* New Delhi: Regency Publications, 2016.

Nunthara, C. *Impact of the Introduction of Grouping of Villages in Mizoram.* Delhi: Omsons Publications, 1989.

Nyrop, Richard F. *Area Handbook for India*. Virginia: University of Virginia, 1975.
Ollett, Andrew. *Language of the Snakes: Prakrit, Sanskrit, and the Language Order of Premodern India*. California: University of California Press, 2017.
Overstreet, G.D., and M. Windmiller. *Communism in India*. Berkeley: University of California Press, 1959.
Owary, Dharanidhar. *Baro Chutigalpa Sankalan*. Jorhat: Asam Sahitya Sabha, 1991.
Oza, Diganta. *Asam Andolonar Tahthyakosh: Data book on Assam agitation*. Vol. 1. Guwahati: Government of Assam, 2020.
Oza, Diganta. *Asam Andolonar Tahthyakosh: Data book on Assam agitation*. Vols 2–3. Guwahati: Government of Assam, 2021.
Pachuau, Joy L.K., and Willem van Schendel. *The Camera as Witness: A Social History of Mizoram, Northeast India*. Cambridge: Cambridge University Press, 2015.
Pachuau, Joy L.K. *Being Mizo: Identity and Belonging in Northeast India*. New Delhi: Oxford University Press, 2014.
Pakyntein, E.H. *Census of India, 1961, Vol. III, Assam, Part 1-A-General Report*. New Delhi: Manager of Publication, 1964.
Pakyntein, E.H. *District Census Handbook, Mizo Hills*. Guwahati: Government of Assam, 1965.
Palit, D.K. *War in High Himalaya: The Indian army in Crisis, 1962*. London: C. Hurst & Co., 1991.
Palmer, Norman D. 'Elections and the Political System in India: The 1972 State Assembly Elections and After'. *Pacific Affairs* 45, no. 4 (1972): 535–55.
Pandey, Bishwa Nath. ed. *The Indian Nationalist Movement, 1885–1947: Select Documents*. London: Macmillan, 1979.
Parakal, Pauly V. *Secret Wars of CIA*. New Delhi: Sterling, 1984.
Parliament of India. *Report of Delegation of members of Parliament to Assam, August, 1960*. New Delhi: Lok Sabha Secretariat, 1960.
Patel, I.G. *Glimpses of Indian Economic Policy: An Insider's View*. New Delhi: Oxford University Press, 2002.
Pathak, Amarendranath. 'Ziro'. *Asam Sahitya Sabha Patrika* 15, no. 1 (1956): 36–47.
Pathak, Moushumi Dutta. *You Do Not Belong Here: Partition Diaspora in the Brahmaputra Valley*. Delhi: Notion Press, 2017.
Patir, Lily. 'Agricultural Intensification and Socio-Economic Change in North East India: A Case Study of the Nishi (Social-Change, Tribe, Migration)'. PhD diss., State University of New York at Stony Brook, New York, 1985.

Pator, Rasing, complied., *Birta: The First Karbi Newspaper, Vol. 1, 1949–1956*. Diphu, Assam: Author, 2010.

Patterson, Maureen L.P. 'The Science behind Rotational Bush Fallow Agriculture System (Jhum)'. *Journal of Asian Studies* 28, no. 4 (1969): 743–54.

Pavate, D.C., *Report of the Gauhati University Enquiry Commission 1962*. Shillong: Assam Government Press, 1962.

Percy, Eustace. *Report of the Federal Finance Committee*. New Delhi: Government of India Press, 1932.

Pethick-Lawrence, F.W. *Fate Has Been Kind*. London: The National Book Association, Hutchinson & Co., 1943.

Phookan, Nilmani. 'China Kobitaguccha'. *Samjya* 2, no. 3 (September–November 1976): 34–38.

Phookan, Nilmani. *Kuri Satikar Asamiya Kabita*. Guwahati: Publication Board Assam, 1977.

Phukan, Chitralekha. *Asomiya Sahitya Aru Lekhika*. Guwahati: Lawyer's Book Stall, 1995.

Phukon, Girin. *Assam: Attitude to Federalism*. New Delhi: Sterling Publishing Private Limited, 1984.

Phukon, Girin. ed. *Documents on Ahom Movement in Assam*. Moranhat, Assam: Institute of Tai Studies and Research, 2010.

Phukan, Tirtha. 'Jayanti Jugar Sahitya'. In *Asomiya Sahityar Buranji*, Vol. 6, edited by Homen Borgohain, pp. 62–76. Guwahati: ABILAC, 1993.

Phukan, Umananda. *Agricultural Development in Assam, 1950–1985*. New Delhi: Mittal Publications, 1990.

Phukan, Yamini. ed. *Sailen Medhi: Byktitwa Aru Samaj Chinta*. Guwahati: 80th Birthday Celebration Committee, 2009.

Piramal, Gita. *Business Maharajas*. New Delhi: Penguin, 2011.

Pirzada, Syed Sharifuddin. *Foundations of Pakistan, All-India Muslim League Documents, 1906–1947, Volume II (1924–1947)*. Karachi: National Publishing House Limited, 2007.

Planning Commission, *Resettlement Programme for Landless Agricultural Labourers: Case Studies of Selected Colonies*. New Delhi: Planning Commission, 1968.

Pope, Georgie. 'Mobilising Assamese Vaishnavite Performance Practices', PhD diss., King's College London, 2019.

Prabhakar, M.S. 'Death in Barpeta'. *Economic & Political Weekly* 10, no. 10 (1975): 423–25.

Prabhakar, M.S. 'Visitations'. *Economic & Political Weekly* 10, no. 8 (1975): 349, 351.

Pradhan, R.D. *1965 War, the Inside Story: Defence Minister Y.B. Chavan's Diary of India–Pakistan War*. New Delhi: Atlatic, 2007.

Pradhan, R.D. *Working with Rajiv Gandhi*. New Delhi: Indus, 1995.

Prasad, Bimal. ed. *Towards Freedom: Documents on the Movement for Independence in India, 1945*, Delhi: Indian Council of Historical Research and Oxford University Press, 2008.

Prasad, Niranjan. *The Fall of Towang, 1962*. New Delhi: Palit & Palit, 1981.

Prasad, Rajendra. 'Foreword'. In *Sankaradeva: Vaisnava Saint of Assam*, by B.K. Barua. Guwahati: Assam Academy for Cultural Relations, 1960.

Prasad, Rajendra. *India Divided*. Bombay: Hind Kitabs Ltd, 1947.

Prasad, Rajeshwar. *Days with Lal Bahadur Shastri: Glimpses from the Last Seven Years*. New Delhi: Allied Publishers, 1991.

Price, David H. *Anthropological Intelligence: The Deployment and Neglect of American Anthropology in the Second World War*. Durham, NC: Duke University Press, 2008.

Puri, B.N. *Studies in Early History and Administration in Assam*. Guwahati: Gauhati University, 1968.

Puri, Balraj. 'A Case for Sub-States'. *Economic & Political Weekly* 5, no. 50 (1970): 1989–90.

Putcha, Rumya S. 'Between History and Historiography: The Origins of Classical Kuchipudi Dance'. *Dance Research Journal* 45, no. 3 (2013): 91–110.

Raghavan, Srinath. *1971: A Global History of the Creation of Bangladesh*. Cambridge, Massachusetts: Harvard University Press, 2013.

Raghavan, Srinath. *India's War: The Making of Modern South Asia, 1939–1945*. London: Penguin Books, 2016.

Rahman, Sayidur. 'A Critical Review of Bahagi'. *Times of Assam*, 19 May 1923. In *Bahagi, a collection of Assamese Pastoral Poems and Ballads*, edited by N.C. Bhuyan. Shillong: Assamia Sahitya Mandir, 1963 (First published in 1920).

Rajagopalachari, Chakravarti. *Gandhi–Jinnah Talks: Text of Correspondence and Other Relevant Matter, July–October, 1944*. New Delhi: Hindustan Times, 1944.

Rajkhowa, Benudhar. 'Presidential Lecture: Historical Session, Asam Sahitya Sabha, Dhuburi, 1926'. In *Asam Sahitya Sabhar Bhasanavali: A collection of the presidential addresses of the history section,* edited by Atul Chandra Hazarika and Maheswar Neog. Jorhat: Asam Sahitya Sabha, 1961.

Rajkhowa, Benudhar. *Assamese Demonology*. Calcutta: Patrika Press, 1905.

Rajkhowa, Benudhar. *Notes on the Sylhetee Dialect*. Sylhet: Chandra Nath Press, 1913.

Rajkonwar, Kaberi Kochari. *Issa Anissa Swotteo Kisu Katha*. Guwahati: Alibat, 2013.

Ramakrishnan, P.S. 'The science behind rotational bush fallow agriculture system (jhum)'. *Proceedings of the Indian Academy of Sciences (Plant Science)* 93, no. 3 (July 1984): 379–400.

Ramakrishnan, P.S., and Suprava Patnaik, 'Jhum: Slash and Burn Cultivation'. *India International Centre Quarterly*, vol. 19, no. 1 and 2 (1992): 215–20.

Ramalingom, R., and K.N. Kurup. 'Plan Transfers to States: Revised Gadgil Formula: An Analysis'. *Economic & Political Weekly* 26, no. 9–10 (1991): 501–06.

Ramamurthy, Stephanie. 'Remembering Burma: Tamil migrants and memories'. MPhil diss., SOAS, London, 1994.

Ramamurti, P. *Real Face of the Assam Agitation.* New Delhi: Communist Party of India (M), 1980.

Rao, B. Shiva. ed. *The Framing of India's Constitution: Select Documents.* Vol. 1. New Delhi: Indian Institute of Public Administration, 1966.

Rao, B. Shiva. ed. *The Framing of India's Constitution: Select Documents*, Vol. 2. New Delhi: Indian Institute of Public Administration, 1967.

Rao, B. Shiva. ed. *The Framing of India's Constitution: Select Documents.* Vol. 3. New Delhi: Indian Institute of Public Administration, 1967.

Rao, B. Shiva. ed. *The Framing of India's Constitution: Select Documents.* Vol. 4. New Delhi: Indian Institute of Public Administration, 1968.

Rao, P. Raghunadha. *History of Modern Andhra.* Delhi: Sterling, 1978.

Rao, T.V., Rama, and G.D. Binani. *India at a Glance: A Comprehensive Reference Book on India.* Bombay: Orient Longmans, 1954.

Rao, V. Venkata. 'Lok Sabha Elections in Assam (1952 to 1977): A Sociological Study'. *Indian Journal of Political Science* 38, no. 4 (1977): 462–75.

Rao, V. Venkata. *A Century of Tribal Politics in North East India.* Delhi: S. Chand, 1976.

Rasul, Md. Abdullah. *A History of the All India Kisan Sabha.* Calcutta: National Book Agency, 1989.

Rava, Bishnuprasad. *Bishnuprasad Rava Rachana Sambhar: Part II.* Edited by Jogesh Das. Nagaon: Sarveswar Bora, 1997.

Ray, Prasad Ranjan. *A Strategy for Rejuvenation of Indian Tea.* Ithaca: Cornell University, 1981.

Reid, Robert Neil. *Years of Change in Bengal and Assam.* London: Benn, 1966.

Reserve Bank of India. *Handbook of Statistics on Indian States, 2015–16.* Mumbai: Reserve Bank of India, 2016.

Reserve Bank of India. *Handbook of Statistics on Indian States, 2018–19.* Mumbai: Reserve Bank of India, 2020.

Richman, Paula, and Rustom Bharucha. eds. *Performing the Ramayana Tradition: Enactments, Interpretations, and Arguments.* New Delhi: Oxford University Press, 2021.

Robb, Peter. 'The Colonial State and Constructions of Indian Identity: An Example on the Northeast Frontier in the 1880s'. *Modern Asian Studies* 31, no. 2 (1997): 245–83.

Rokhuma, C. *Tam do pawl in engnge a tih? (The Secret of Famines Found.) The Activities of the Anti-Famine Campaign Organisation Mizoram on Mautam Famine 1959.* Aizawl: Gosen Press, 1988.

Romanus, Charles F., and Riley Sunderland. *Stilwell's Command Problems: China–Burma Theatre.* Vol. II. Washington D.C.: Office of the Chief of Military History, 1956.

Romanus, Charles F., and Riley Sunderland. *United States Army in World War II: China-Burma-India Theater: Stilwell's Command Problems*, pt. 09, v.02. Washington, D.C.: Center of Military History, United States Army, 1987.

Rongpher, Borsing. *Karbi Anglongar Rajnoitik Itihas.* Diphu: Phu Phu Publication, 2020.

Rose, Leo E., and Margaret Welpley Fisher. *The North-East Frontier Agency of India.* Berkeley: Institute of International Studies, University of California, 1967.

Roy Burman, B.K. *Report: Census of India 1961: Demographic and Socio-Economic Profiles of the Hill Areas of North-East India.* Delhi: Registrar General, India, 1970.

Roy, Asim. *The Islamic Syncretistic Tradition in Bengal.* Princeton: Princeton University Press, 2014.

Roy, Prasad Ranjan. 'A Strategy for Rejuvenation of Indian Tea'. PhD diss., Cornell University, Ithaca, New York, 1981.

Roychaudhury, Anil. *Asamiya Samaj aru Navabaishnavabad.* Guwahati: Publication Board Assam, 2007.

Raychowdhury, Ambikagiri. 'Asomot Sangeet Charcha'. In *Ambikagiri Raychowdhury Rachanavali*, edited by Satyendranath Sarma, pp. 844–46. Guwahati: Publication Board Assam, 2009.

Roychowdhury, Ambikagiri. 'Jati Gothonot Srimanta Sankardev'. In *Ambikagiri Raychowdhury Rachanavali*, edited by Satyendranath Sarma, pp. 560–62. Guwahati: Publication Board Assam, 2009.

Rustomji, Nari K. *Enchanted Frontiers: Sikkim, Bhutan and India's North-Eastern Borderlands.* Bombay: Oxford University Press, 1971.

Rustomji, Nari K. *Imperilled Frontiers: India's North-Eastern Borderlands.* New Delhi: Oxford University Press, 1983.

Saharia, B.R. *Assam, 1977: An Exciting Tale of Assam's Triumphant Journey (1947–77) from Backwardness to Modernity.* Guwahati: Directorate of Information and Public Relations, 1978.

Sahitya Akademi. *Sahitya Akademi Award: Books and Writers, 1955–1978.* Delhi: Sahitya Akademi, 1990.

Sahni, Jogendra Nath. *Indian Railways: One Hundred Years, 1853 to 1953.* New Delhi: Ministry of Railways (Railway Board), Government of India, 1953.

Saikia, Anil, Homeswar Goswami, and Atul Goswami. eds. *Population Growth in Assam, 1951–1991 with Focus on Migration*. New Delhi: Akansha Publishing House, 2003.

Saikia, Arupjyoti. 'Earthquakes and the Environmental Transformation of a Floodplain Landscape: The Brahmaputra Valley and the Earthquakes of 1897 and 1950'. *Environment and History* 26, no. 1 (2020): 51–77.

Saikia, Arupjyoti. 'History, Buranjis and Nation: Suryya Kumar Bhuyan's Histories in Twentieth-Century Assam'. *Indian Economic & Social History Review* 45, no. 4 (December 2008): 473–507.

Saikia, Arupjyoti. 'Rhinoceros in Kaziranga National Park: Nature and Politics in Assam'. In *Reframing the Environment: Resources, Risk and Resistance in Neoliberal India*, edited by Manisha Rao, pp. 159–203. New York: Routledge, 2021.

Saikia, Arupjyoti. 'The Kaziranga National Park: Dynamics of Social and Political History', *Conservation and Society* 7, no. 2 (2009): 113–29.

Saikia, Arupjyoti. 'Vernacular for the Nation: Hemchandra Goswami's Typical Selections from Assamese Literature'. In *On Modern Indian Sensibilities Culture, Politics, History*, edited by Ishita Banerjee-Dube and Sarvani Gooptu. Delhi: Routledge, 2018.

Saikia, Arupjyoti. 'Empire's Nature in the Garo Hills: A Microhistory of India's Environmental Movements'. In *A Functioning Anarchy: Essays for Ramachandra Guha,* edited by Nandini Sundar and Srinath Raghavan, pp. 3–20. Delhi: Penguin Random House, 2021.

Saikia, Arupjyoti. 'Flows and Fairs: The Eastern Himalayas and the British Empire'. In *Flows and Frictions in Trans Himalayan Spaces*, edited by Gunnel Cederlof and William van Schendel, pp. 137–66. Amsterdam: Amsterdam University Press, 2022.

Saikia, Arupjyoti. 'Grantha Bisayok Alochana'. In *Asamiya Sahityar Buranji*, Vol. 5, edited by Ranjit Kumar Dev Goswami, pp. 790–802. Guwahati: ABILAC, 2015.

Saikia, Arupjyoti. *A Century of Protests: Peasant Politics in Assam since 1900*. New Delhi: Routledge, 2014.

Saikia, Arupjyoti. *Forests and Ecological History of Assam*. New Delhi: Oxford University Press, 2011.

Saikia, Arupjyoti. *The Unquiet River: A Biography of the Brahmaputra*. New Delhi: Oxford University Press, 2019.

Saikia, C.P. 'Introduction'. In *Sattriya Dances of Assam and Their Rhythms,* edited by Maheswar Neog. Guwahati: Publication Board Assam, 1973.

Saikia, Chandraprasad. ed. *Gopinath Bardoloi*. Guwahati: Publication Board Assam, 1979.

Saikia, Devika. 'A Comparative Study of Two Classical Dance Forms of India: Bharatnatyam and Sattriya'. PhD diss., Dibrugarh University, 2010.

Saikia, J.N. 'Gongadhar Saikia: The Versatile Genius with a Towering Personality', In *Gangey: Khyudhra Sah Khetiyokor Pitriswarup Gangadhar Saikiadewor Smarok Grantha*, edited by P. Saikia and R. Borgohain. Golaghat: All Assam Small Tea Growers Association, 2018.

Saikia, Monalisha. *Shankhaninad*. Guwahati: Banalata, 2015.

Saikia, Nagen. *Asamar Lipi Samsya: a collection of papers read at and proceedings of the second writers' camp*. Jorhat, Asam Sahitya Sabha, 1974.

Saikia, Nagen. ed. *Birinchi Kumar Barua Rachanavali*, vol. 2. Guwahati: Bina Library, 2015.

Saikia, Pahi. *Ethnic Mobilisation and Violence in Northeast India*. New Delhi: Routledge India, 2011.

Saikia, Rajen. *Social and Economic History of Assam (1853–1921)*. New Delhi: Manohar, 2001.

Saikia, Yasmin. *Fragmented Memories Struggling to be Tai-Ahom in India*. Durham, N.C.: Duke University Press, 2004.

Saikia, Yasmin. *Women, War, and the Making of Bangladesh: Remembering 1971*. Durham, N.C.: Duke University Press, 2011.

Samaddar, Ranabir. ed. *The Politics of Autonomy: Indian Experiences*. New Delhi: Sage Publications, 2005.

Sandhu, Amandeep. *Punjab: Journeys Through Fault Lines*. Chennai: Westland, 2019.

Sangeet Natak Akademi. *Annual Report, 1958–59*. New Delhi: Sangeet Natak Akademi, 1959.

Sangeet Natak Akademi. *Dance Seminar Recommendations*. New Delhi: Sangeet Natak Academi, 1958.

Sangkima. *Mizos: Society and Social Change, 1890–1947*. Guwahati: Spectrum Publications, 1992.

Sanyü, Visier Meyasetsu. *A Naga Odyssey: My Long Way Home*. New Delhi: Speaking Tiger, 2017.

Sapru, Tej Bahadur. *Constitutional Proposals of the Sapru Committee*. Bombay: Padma Publications, 1946.

Sara Lyndem, G. 'Performance of Public Sector Undertakings in Meghalaya'. PhD diss., North-Eastern Hill University, Shillong, 1990.

Saraswatī, Rāma. *Asamīyā Mahābhārata Droṇaparba*. Jorhat: Darpaṇ Press, 1909.

Sarkar, Anupam. 'Tractor Production and Sales in India, 1989–2009'. *Review of Agrarian Studies* 3, no. 1 (2013): 55–72.

Sarkar, Rabindra. *Kalantarar Kabita*. Guwahati: Kamrupa Prakashan, 1982.

Sarkar, Sumit. ed. *Towards Freedom: Documents on the Movement for Independence in India 1946, Part 1*. New Delhi: Oxford University Press, 2007.

Sharma, Ajit Kumar. *Asomor Chah Udyogat Bideshi Muldhan*. Guwahati: Author, 1966.
Sarma, Anjan. *Asam Andolonor Asampurna Itihas*. Guwahati: Bhabani Books, 2018.
Sarma, Apurba. *Axomiya Chalaccitrar San-Pohar*. Guwahati: Aank-Baak, 2014.
Sarma, Atul Chandra. 'A study of Assam finances structure and trend, 1947–48 to 1965–66'. PhD diss., Gauhati University, Guwahati, 1971.
Sarma, Benudhar. 'Bihur Purani Jilingoni'. In *Bihu Binandia*, edited by Gokul Deka, pp. 1–12. Tezpur: Gokul Deka, 1971.
Sarma, Chandan Kumar. 'Census, Society and Politics in British Assam'. PhD diss., Dibrugarh University, 2018.
Sarma, Chandra Nath. *The Works of Kamarupa Anusandhan Samiti*. Guwahati: Kamarupa Anusandhan Samiti, 1920.
Sarma, Dimbeswar. *Kamarupasasanavali*, Guwahati: Publication Board Assam, 1981.
Sarma, J.N. 'Balanced Regional Development: Is It Possible?', *Economic & Political Weekly* 1, no. 18 (1966): 757–69.
Sarma, J.N. *World Agricultural Census, Assam, 1970–71*. Guwahati: Directorate of Economics and Statistics, 1975.
Sarma, Parameswar. 'Gauhati and Its Environs: A Peep through the Ages'. *Assam Quarterly* 1, no. 1 (January 1961): 5–13.
Sarma, Purna Chandra. *Mor Ateet Sowarani aru Nagaon Jilat Mukti Sangram*. Nagaon: Sarma Prakash Bhavan, 2022 (1973).
Sarma, Purna Kanta, 'Stree Sikhsa' (Education of Women)'. In *Asam-Bandhu: A monthly paper devoted to Assamese language, literature and culture*, compiled and edited by Nagen Saikia, pp. 476–80. Guwahati: Publication Board Assam, 1984 (1885 and 1886).
Sarma, Sachi. *Jaruri Avasthat Asomiya Budhijibir Bhumika*. Nalbari: Sree Bhumi Publishing, 1977.
Sarma, Satyendranath. ed. *Ambikagiri Raychowdhury Rachanavali*. Guwahati: Publication Board Assam, 2009.
Sarma, Satyendranath. *The Neo-Vaisnavite Movement and the Satra Institution of Assam*. Guwahati: Gauhati University, 1966.
Sarma Kataki, Sarbeswar. 'Asomiya Prachin Lipi'. In *Sarbeswar Sarma Kataki Rachnawali: The Complete Works of Sarbeswar Sarma Kataki*, edited by Laxmi Nath Tamuly, pp. 91–127. Guwahati: Publication Board, Assam, 2004.
Sarmah, Biswajit. 'Park, People and Politics: An Environmental History of the Kaziranga National Park'. PhD diss., Indian Institute of Technology Guwahati, 2021.

Sarmah, Satyendra Kumar. 'Script Movement Among the Bodo of Assam'. *Proceedings of the Indian History Congress* 75 (2014): 1335–40.
Sattar, Abdus. *Krishna Kanta Handiqui.* Jorhat: Sahityika, 1978.
Secombe, T.L. *Statement Exhibiting the Moral and Material Progress and Condition of India during the year 1859–60, part II.* London: Her Majesty's Stationery Office, 1861.
Sen, Amartya. *Poverty and Famines: An Essay on Entitlement and Deprivation.* Oxford: Clarendon Press, 1982.
Sen, Dinesh Chandra. *Bangabhasa or Sahitya.* Vol. 1. Calcutta: Hemchandra Sen, 1896.
Sen, Tansen. *India, China, and the World: A Connected History.* London: Rowman & Littlefield, 2017.
Sen Deka, Nilamoni. ed. *Asomiya Bhashar Atmapratisthar Sangramar Itihas aru Anannya Prasanga.* Vols 1–8. Guwahati: B.R. Book Stall, 2021.
Sethi, Arshiya. 'An Overlay of the Political: The Recognition of Sattriya', *Seminar*, no. 676 (December 2015).
Shah, J.C. *Shah Commission of Inquiry: Third and Final Report.* New Delhi: Government of India Press, 1978.
Shani, Ornit. *How India Became Democratic: Citizenship and the Making of the Universal Franchise.* Cambridge: Cambridge University Press, 2017.
Sharma, Anil Kumar. *Quit India Movement in Assam.* Delhi: Mittal Publications, 2007.
Sharma, Aparna. 'Close Reading: Joymoti by Jyotiprasad Agarwala'. *Sahapedia.* 16 April 2020, https://www.sahapedia.org/close-reading-joymoti-jyotiprasad-agarwala (accessed 12 February 2022).
Sharma, Benudhar. 'Presidential Address'. In *Assam Sahitya Sabhar Bhasanavali: A Collection of the Presidential Addresses of the history section, Jorhat,* edited by Atul Chandra Hazarika and Maheswar Neog, p. 146. Jorhat: Asam Sahitya Sabha, 1961.
Sharma, Benudhar. *Dakhinpat Satra.* Guwahati: Assam Jyoti, 1967.
Sharma, Benudhar. *Kangrecar Kanciali Rodat.* Guwahati: Asom Jyoti, 1959.
Sharma, Benudhar. *Maniram Dewan.* Guwahati: Asom Jyoti, 1950.
Sharma, Benudhar. *Shatayoun Sal Ba Swadhinatar Pratham Yudha.* Guwahati: Padma Prakash, 1957.
Sharma, Chandan Kumar. 'Tribal Land Alienation: Government's Role'. *Economic & Political Weekly* 36, no. 52 (2001), 4791–4795.
Sharma, Chandan Kumar. 'The immigration issue in Assam and conflicts around it'. *Asian Ethnicity* 13, no. 3 (2012): 287–309.
Sharma, Devabrata. *Asomia Jatigathan Prakriya Aru Jatiya Janagosthigata Anusthan Samuh.* Jorhat: Ekalavya Prakashan, 2008.
Sharma, Diganta, *Nellie, 1983.* Jorhat: Eklabya Prakashan, 2007.

Sharma, Dipti. *Assamese Women in the Freedom Struggle*. Calcutta: Punthi-Pustak, 1993.

Sharma, Jayeeta. *Empire's Garden: Assam and the Making of India*. Durham: Duke University Press, 2011.

Sharma, K.M. 'The Assam Question: A Historical Perspective'. *Economic & Political Weekly* 15, no. 31 (1980): 1321–24.

Sharma, L.C. 'India's forests and their potential for the economy'. *Commonwealth Forestry Review* 51, no. 4 (1972): 307–13.

Sharma, Lakshesvar. *Michimi Paharor Rangsina*. Guwahati: Pranita Devi, 1965.

Sharma, Mukunda Madhab. *Inscriptions of Ancient Assam*, Guwahati: Gauhati University, 1978.

Sharma, S.K., and Usha Sharma. eds. *Documents on North-East India: Assam (1936–1957)*. Vol. 4. New Delhi: Mittal Publications, 2006.

Sharma, Tirthanath. *Auiniati Satrar Buranji*. Majuli: Auniati Satra, 1975.

Sherlock, Stephen. *The Indian Railways Strike of 1974: A Study of Power and Organised Labour*. New Delhi: Rupa Publications, 2001.

Shoumatoff, Alex. 'Waiting for the Plague'. *Vanity Fair*, 1 April 2008.

Shrikant, L.M. *Report of the Commissioner for Scheduled Castes and Scheduled Tribes* 1953: Third Report. Delhi: Manager of Publications, 1954.

Singh, Charan. *Agrarian Revolution in Uttar Pradesh*. Lucknow: Prakashan Shakha, Soochna Vibhag, Government of Uttar Pradesh, 1957.

Singh, Gurharpal, and Giorgio Shani, *Sikh Nationalism: From a Dominant Minority to an Ethno-Religious Diaspora*. New Delhi: Cambridge University Press, 2022.

Singh, Karnail. *A Complete Story of the Assam Rail Link Project*. New Delhi: Ministry of Railways, Government of India, 1951.

Singh, Tarlok. *Outlays and Programmes for the Hill Region of Assam for the Fourth Plan*. New Delhi: Government of India, 1966.

Sinha, Sarat Chandra. *Andhar Bidara Kad*. Guwahati: Buniyad Publications, 1997.

Sinha, K.K. ed. *Modern India Rejects Hindi Report of All India Language Conference*. Calcutta: Association for the Advancement of the National Languages of India, 1959.

Sinha, P.B., and A.A. Athale. *History of the Conflict with China, 1962*. New Delhi: History Division, Ministry of Defence, Government of India, 1992.

Sinha, Raghuvir. *The Akas: The People of NEFA*. Shillong: Research Department, Adviser's Secretariat, 1962.

Sirkar, D.C., and P.D. Chaudhury. 'Umachal Rock Inscription of Surendravarman'. In *Epihraphica Indica*, Vol. XXXI, Part II, 1955.

Slessor, Tim. *First Overland: London to Singapore by Land Rover*. London: George G. Harrap and Co. Ltd, 1957.

Slim, William. *Defeat into Victory: Battling Japan in Burma and India, 1942–1945*. New York: Cooper Square Press, 2000.

Srinivas, M.N. 'Is the Sun Setting'. *Seminar*, no. 90 (February 1967): 12–16.

Srivastava, L.R.N. *The Gallongs: The People of NEFA*. Shillong: Research Department, Adviser's Secretariat, 1962.

Steinberg, S.H. ed. *The Statesman's Year-Book 1968–69: The One-Volume Encyclopedia of All Nations*. London: Palgrave Macmillan, 2016.

Steinberg, S.H. ed. *The Statesman's Year-Book: Statistical and Historical Annual of the States of the World for the Year 1955*. London: Macmillan, 1955.

Stracey, P.D. *Progress Report of Forest Administration in the Province of Assam, 1950–51*. Shillong: The Assam Government Press, 1961.

Sundar, Nandini. 'Interning Insurgent Populations: The Buried Histories of Indian Democracy'. *Economic & Political Weekly* 46, no. 6 (2011): 47–57.

Sundaram, K., and Suresh D. Tendulkar. 'Poverty in India in the 1990s: An Analysis of Changes in 15 Major States'. *Economic & Political Weekly* 38, no. 14 (2003): 1385–93.

Sur, Malini. 'Battles for the Golden Grain: Paddy Soldiers and the Making of the Northeast India–East Pakistan Border, 1930–1970'. *Comparative Studies in Society and History* 58, no. 3 (2016): 804–32.

Sur, Malini. *Jungle Passports: Fences, Mobility, and Citizenship at the Northeast India–Bangladesh Border*. Philadelphia: University of Pennsylvania Press, 2021.

Syiemlieh, David R. *On the Edge of Empire: Four British Plans for North East India, 1941–1947*. New Delhi: Sage Publications, 2014.

Tagore, Rabindranath. 'Bhasha-Bicched'. *Bharati* 22 (July 1898): 302–08.

Talukdar, Gaurikanta. *Kalitar Vratyodharar Avasyakata*. Guwahati: Sarbeswar Bhattacharya, 1929.

Talukdar, K.C. 'Structural Changes in Assam Agriculture'. *Agricultural Economics Research Review* 6, no. 1 (1993): 37–50.

Talukdar, Mrinal, and Kishore Kumar Kalita. *ULFA*. Guwahati: Nanda Talukdar Foundation, 2011.

Tamuli Phukan, Ankur. 'Making of a National Festival: Bihu in Colonial and Postcolonial Assam'. PhD diss., Jadavpur University, Kolkata, 2020.

Tamuli Phukan, Ankur. 'Scenes of the Obscene: The Lewd, the Rustic and Bihu in Colonial Assam'. *Man and Society* XIV, 2017: 150–64.

Tamuly, Gitashree, and Akhil Gogoi. *Uribo Para Hale Akou Junjiloheten*. Guwahati: Banalata, 2003.

Tamuly, Gitashree. 'Lakshminath Bezbaroa and His Times: Language, Literature and Modernity in Colonial Assam'. PhD diss., Indian Institute of Technology Guwahati, 2021.

Tanti, Sameer. *Juddhuttarar Kabita*. Guwahati: Lawyer's Book Stall, 1990.

Tata Services Limited, *Statistical Outline of India, 1980*. Bombay: Tata Services, Department of Economics and Statistics, 1980.

Taylor, Joe G. *Air Supply in the Burma Campaigns*. Washington: USAF Historical Studies, 1957.

Tayyebulla, M. *Karagarar Chithi*. Guwahati: Publication Board Assam 1962.

Tea Board of India. *Tea Statistics for the year 1977*. Calcutta: Tea Board of India, 1979.

Tea Board of India. *Tea Statistics for the year 2000–2001*. Calcutta: Tea Board of India, 2002.

Tendulkar, D.G. *Mahatma: Life of Mohandas Karamchand Gandhi*. Vols 1–8. Bombay: Vithalbhai K Jhaveri and D.G. Tendulkar, 1951–1954.

Tendulkar, Suresh D., and L.R. Jain. 'Economic Growth and Equity: India, 1970–71 to 1988–89'. *Indian Economic Review* 30, no. 1 (1995): 19–49.

Teron, Longkam. *Mikir Janajati*. Jorhat: Asam Sahitya Sabha, 1961.

Tewary, Tribhuvan Prasad. *Report of the Commission of Enquiry on Assam Disturbances, 1983*. Dispur: Government of Assam, 1984.

Thomas, John. *Evangelising the Nation: Religion and the Formation of Naga Political Identity*. New Delhi: Routledge, 2015.

Thomas, P.J. *The Growth of Federal Finance in India*. Humphrey Milford: Oxford University Press, 1939.

Thongsi, Yeshe Dorje. *Hahni aru Sakulor Haihob*. Guwahati: Banalata, 2016.

Ṭikekara, Aruṇa. *The Cloister's Pale: A Biography of the University of Mumbai*. Bombay: Popular Prakashan, 1984.

Tomlinson, Brian Roger. *The Economy of Modern India: From 1860 to the Twenty-First Century*. Cambridge: Cambridge University Press, 2013.

Tripathi, Dwijendra. *The Concise Oxford History of Indian Business*. New Delhi, New York: Oxford University Press, 2007.

Tully, Mark, and Satish Jacob. *Amritsar: Mrs Gandhi's Last Battle*. Delhi: Rupa, 2021.

Tyson, Geoffrey. *Forgotten Frontier*. Calcutta: W.H. Targett & Co., 1945.

Uddin, Layli. 'In the land of eternal Eid: Maulana Bhashani and the political mobilisation of peasants and lower-class urban workers in East Pakistan, c.1930s–1971'. PhD diss., Royal Holloway, University of London, London, 2015.

United States Senate. *Hearing before the subcommittee to investigate problems connected with refugees and escapees of the Committee on the Judiciary United States Senate, Ninety Second Congress, Second Session February 2, 1972*. Washington DC: U.S. Government Printing Office, 1972.

Vaghaiwalla, R.B. *North-East Frontier Agency: District Census Handbook*. Bombay: Municipal Printing Press, 1954.

Vaghaiwalla, R.B. *Report: Census of India, 1951: Volume XII*, Assam, Manipur and Tripura, Part 1-A. Shillong: Superintendent of Census Operations, Assam, 1954.

Vakil, C.N. *Economic Consequences of Divided India: A Study of the Economy of India and Pakistan*. Bombay: National Information & Publications, 1950.

van Schendel, Willem. 'A War within a War: Mizo Rebels and the Bangladesh Liberation Struggle'. *Modern Asian Studies* 50, no. 1 (2016): 75–117.

van Schendel, Willem. *History of Bangladesh*. New York: Cambridge University Press, 2009.

van Schendel, Willem. *The Bengal Borderland: Beyond State and Nation in South Asia*. London: Anthem, 2005.

Varshney, Ashutosh. *Democracy, Development, and the Countryside: Urban–Rural Struggles in India*. Cambridge: Cambridge University Press, 1998.

Vatsyayan, Kapila. *A Study of Some Traditions of Performing Arts in Eastern India: Margi and Desi Polarities*. Guwahati: Gauhati University, 1981.

Verma, Kunal. 'Rhinos from Pobitara Sanctuary in Assam Relocated to Dudhwa National Park in UP'. *India Today*, 30 April 1984.

Verma, T.P. *Development of Script in Ancient Kamrupa*. Jorhat: Asam Sahitya Sabha, 1976.

Visaria, Pravin M. 'Migration between India and Pakistan, 1951–61'. *Demography* 6, no. 3 (1969): 323–34.

Wadia, Ardeshir Ruttonji. *The Future of English in India*. Bombay: Asia Publishing House, 1954.

Wainwright, David. *Brooke Bond: A Hundred Years*. United Kingdom: Brooke Bond Liebig, Ltd, 1970.

Weiner, Myron. *Sons of the Soil: Migration and Ethnic Conflict in India*. Princeton, NJ: Princeton University Press, 1978.

White, Theodore Harold. ed. *Stilwell Papers: An Iconoclastic Account of America's Adventures in China*. New York: Schocken Books Inc., 1972.

Wood, E. *Report on the Evacuation of Refugees from Burma to India (Assam), Jan–July 1942*. Calcutta: Government of India, 1942.

Woodford, R.C. *Annual Report of the Department of Agriculture, Assam for the years ending 31$^{st}$ March 1948*. Shillong: Assam Government Press, 1950.

Wouters, Jelle. *In the Shadows of Naga Insurgency*. Delhi: Oxford University Press, 2018.

Yasmeen, Jabeen. 'Besieged Belonging: "Living on" after the Nellie Massacre'. PhD diss., Indian Institute of Technology Bombay, Mumbai, 2021.

Yasmin, Taslima. 'The Enemy Property Laws in Bangladesh: Grabbing Lands under the Guise of Legislation'. *Oxford University Commonwealth Law Journal* 15, no.1 (2015): 121–41.

Yonuo, Asoso. *The Rising Nagas: A Historical and Political Study*. Delhi: Vivek Publishing House, 1974.

Zaidi, A.M. ed. *Annual Register of Indian Political Parties: Proceedings and Fundamental Text, 1979*. New Delhi: Indian Institute of Applied Political Research, 1980.

Zaidi, Z.H. ed. *Quaid-i-Azam Mohammad Ali Jinnah Papers*. Islamabad: National Archives of Pakistan, 1993–2005.

Zheng, Xiao, Shuyan Lin, Huajun Fu, Yawen Wan and Yulong Ding. 'The Bamboo Flowering Cycle Sheds Light on Flowering Diversity'. *Frontiers in Plant Science* 11 (2020): 381.

Zinkin, Taya. *Reporting India*. London: Chatto & Windus, 1962.

Zou, David Vumlallian, and M. Satish Kumar. 'Mapping a Colonial Borderland: Objectifying the Geo-Body of India's Northeast'. *Journal of Asian Studies* 70, no. 1 (2011): 141–70.

# Index

**A**

*Abahon*, 61
Acharya, Debendranath, 5
Advisory Committee on Fundamental Rights, Minorities and Tribal and Excluded Areas, 124
Advisory Committee on Fundamental Rights of Citizens, Minorities, and Tribal Areas and Excluded Areas, 134
Agarwala, Jyotiprasad, 30
Agrarian Reforms Committee (ARC), 171
Ahom Association, 48, 138
Ahom community, 496
Ahom rule, end of, 519
Ahom Sabha, 47
Ahom Tai Mongolia Rajya Parishad, 350, 419
Ajanta Kala Mandal, 534
Akademi's Bargeet Research Committee, 529
All Assam Ahom Association, 47
All-Assam Bengali Conference, 252
All Assam Manipuri Congress, 76
All-Assam Minority Students Union (AAMSU), 453
All Assam Music Conference, 234
All-Assam Muslim Parishad, 415
All Assam Oil Refinery Action Committee, 189, 190
All-Assam Oil Refinery Sangram Parishad, 379
All-Assam Students' Union (AASU), 389, 437
All-Assam Tribal Protection Action Committee (AATPAC), 453
All-Assam Tribal Students Union, 454
All Bodo Students Union (ABSU), 454, 522
formation of, 522
All-Guwahati Students Union, 437
Allied war, 8
All India Congress Committee (AICC), 8, 54, 395, 406
on January 1947, 60
All-India Hindu Mahasabha, 30
All India Language Conference, 244
All India Radio (AIR), 234
All India Spinners' Association, 8

All India Village Industries Association, 8
All Party Hill Leaders Conference (APHLC), 246, 320
All-Tribes Naga Conference, 209
American Baptist missionaries, xxxii, 400
American Baptist missionary, 528
American Foster Wheeler Corporation, 192
*Amish o Niramish Aahar,* 53
*Amrita Bazar Patrika,* 152
Anglo-American Imperialists, 269
Anglo-Burmese War (1824–26), 33, xxv, xxviii
Anglo-Kuki War (1917–19), 20
Anglo-Persian Oil Company, 187
Anthropological Survey of India, 56, 143, 160, 280
anti-colonial struggle, xxxiii
anti-eviction movement, 68
Anti-Famine Campaign Organisation, 309, 310, 313, 316
anti-nuclear-weapon movement, 332
anti-racial movement, 332
Antrobus, H.A., 26
Ao Nagas, 207
*A Philosophy for NEFA,* 268
*A Plea for Sanskrit as National Language,* 121
Arbitral Tribunal (1947), 81
Armed Forces (Special Powers) Act of 1958, 451, 518
Asam Sahitya Sabha, 208, 243, 246, 277, 280, 344, 389, 494
Asom Gana Parishad (AGP), 492
Asom Gana Sangram Parishad (AGSP), 441
*Asomiya jati,* 496

Asom Jatiya Mahasabha, 54, 58, 66, 93, 95
Asom Sangrakhini Sabha, 54
Assam
  in 1947, xix
  agricultural economy and industrialization in 1970, 377
  Ahom dynasty, xxiv
  Assam Bengal Railway, 8
  British diplomat visited, 431
  China haunting, 360
  Congress leadership, 54–56
  crude oil extraction in 1881, xxxi
  economic activities in, 447
  economic and political storms, 406–436
  economy and political systems, 543
  encouragement to learn Sattriya dance, 534
  environmental conditions of, xxii–xxiii
  ethnic and tribal communities, 27
  export, xxxii
  in a federal India, 116–160
  financial health, 511
  first non-Congress government in, 437
  and India's Union government, relationship between, xx
  Jawaharlal Nehru on, xix
  jute cultivation, xxxii
  landscape, xxii
  land settlement programmes, 41
  languages in, xxiii
  material resources to develop Shillong, 392
  Muslim League in, 62
  Muslim population as per 1941 Census, 40

Index 841

petroleum deposits in Upper
  Assam, xxxi
Plain Tribals Council of, 350
political crisis of 1972, 399
political developments in, 445
political landscape in 1980, xxi
President's Rule, 466
pro-Pakistan movement in, 62
protest in, 437–494
requisition of private properties,
  30
rivers in, xxiii
Seventh Finance Commission
  visited, 437
tea plantations crisis during World
  War II, 497
tea planters' role in World War
  II, 17
tea production started in the
  1830s, xxix
Tibet earthquake, xix
unemployment, xxi
'united, xx
universities in, 211–212
Assam Adhiar Rights and Protection
  Act of 1948, 163
Assam Agricultural Income Tax Act
  (1939), 497
Assam Agricultural University, 378,
  502
Assam, 'balkanization' of, 351
Assam Bengal Railway, 16, 101
  American technology in, 16
  MRS in, 16
Assam–Bengal relationship, 83
Assam Cement Limited, 384
Assam Chah Mazdoor Sangha, 388
'Assam Day,' 451
Assam Disturbed Area Act (1955),
  446

Assamese–Bengali cultural war, 250
Assamese, Bengali settlers speaking,
  414
Assamese cinema, 232
Assamese cultural
  tribal elites' anger against, xx
Assamese Muslim peasants, public
  meeting of, 66
Assamese script, 224
Assam Expulsion Act, 113
Assam Fixation of Ceiling on Land
  Holdings Act of 1956, 512
Assam Forest Regulation of 1891, 42
Assam Jatiyatabadi Dal, 457
Assam Land (Requisition and
  Acquisition) Act, 1948, 97, 175,
  497
Assam Legislative Assembly, 169, 202
Assam Legislative Council, 70
Assam Maintenance of Public Order
  Act of 1947, 165
Assam Management of Estates Act,
  172
Assam Merchant Association, 344
Assam Official Language Act, 256,
  317, 320
Assam Official Language Bill, 251,
  254
Assam Oil Company, xx
  formation, xxxi
  found oil in 1953, xx
  refinery, xxxi
  second oil refinery in 1961, xx
Assam Oil Company (AOC), 186
Assam Provincial Congress
  Committee, 54, 81
Assam Provincial Hindu Mahasabha,
  81
Assam Provincial Muslim League, 40,
  44

Assam Public Service Commission, 437
*Assam Quarterly,* 535
Assam Rail Link, 101, 102
Assam (Sylhet) Referendum Offence Ordinance, 76
Assam Regiment, 23
Assam Rhinoceros Preservation Act of 1954, 503
Assam Rifles, 23, 168, 201, 275
Assam Sangeet Natak Academy, 529
Assam Saw Mills and Timber Company, 265
Assam's Official Language Implementation Committee, 256
Assam State Acquisition of Zamindaris Bill, 172
Assam State Museum, 219
Assam Tea Company, 75
Assam Tea Planters' Association (ATPA), 500
Assam Tenancy Act (1971), 384, 410, 512
Assam to Kunming gasoline pipeline construction, 13
*Assam Tribune,* 94, 123, 241, 266, 271, 421
Assam Trunk Road, 14
'Assam Unity Day,' 341
Assam University Day, 213
Assam War Fund, 23
Aung San-led Burma Independence Army, 2
Auniati Satra, 328
Austrian Communist Party, 162
'*Axom Aair Mukti Lage,*' 513

## B

'Backward Tracts,' 34
Balipara Frontier Tract, 140
'Balkanize or dismember Assam,' 341
Bamunia, 224
Bangiya Sahitya Parishad, 218
Bangladesh Liberation War, 466
Bangladesh, migration in, 373
Bangladesh Tran Committee, 369
Bangladesh War, 365
Banikanta Kakati Memorial Lecture, 217
Barauni refinery, 190, 397
Bardoloi Committee, 135–137
  met Naga leaders, 144, 148
Bardoloi, Gopinath, 8, xviii
Bargeet Research Committee, 534
Barphukan, Lachit, 221
Barua, Amulya, 64
Barua, Harendranath, 55
Barua, Kanaklata, 9
Battle of Imphal, 2, 19
Battle of Kohima, 2
Bengal Boundary Commission, 79, 80
Bengal Eastern Frontier Regulation (1873), 33, 150
Bengali settlers, Assamese peasants and Nepali grazers, clashes between, 66
Bengal Provincial Tea Company, xxix
*bhaona/bhawana,* 232
*Bharati,* 222
Bhashani, 44
"Bhatiali," 253
Bhattacharya, Birendra Kumar, 27
Bhattacharya, Padmanath, 70
Bhuyan, Nakul Chandra, 239
Bihu, 534
  Bohag, 238, 239
  celebration of, 238
  Mishing, 239
  programme, Latasil, 239
Birla, G.D., 6
Biswas, Hemanga, 236

*Bodoland Times,* 524
Bodo Sahitya Sabha, 257, 388, 401–403
*Bongal Kheda Andolan,* 249
Bora, Jnananath, 71
Border Roads Organisation, 285
*Boroni Fisa O Ayen,* 400
Bose, Subhas Chandra, 2
Bower, Ursula, 3
Brahmaputra
    cultivation area, 41
    Valley, land reclamation, 44
'Britain's greatest battle ever,' 2
British East India Company, 69, 139, 232
British Empire, rice bowl of, 2
British Government of India (BGOI), 5
    imposed Excess Profits Tax, 25
    organized food production conference, 29
British rule, 33
Brooke Bond, 499, 516
Bruce, Robert, xxviii
Buragohain, Purnakanta, 6
    at China–Burma border outpost, 6
Burma
    British authority collapse in, 4–5
    civilian escapees from, 5–6
    evacuees from, 6
    Japanese conquest of, 13
    Japanese military occupation of, 19
Burma Frontier Service, 31
Burmah Oil Company, 85, 195, 196
Burmah Shell (BOC), 187
Burmese wars (1817–26), xxiv

## C

Cabinet Mission arrangement, 60
Cabinet Mission Plan, 53
    collapsed on May 1947, 61
Cachar States Reorganization Committee, 243
Calcutta
    Assamese students in, 213
    Inter-Dominion conferences, 95
Calcutta Tea Auctions centre, 501
Caltex, 187
Ceiling Act, 411
Census Report (1951), 91
Central Election Commission, 443
Central Reserve Police (CRP), 456
Central Reserve Police Force (CRPF), 478–479
Central Sales Act (1956), 196
Chaliha, Bimala Prasad, 353
Cherideo Purbut Tea Estate, 175
Chinese aggression, 301
Chinese liberation, war of, 383
Chin Hills Regulation (1896), 150
Chin Regiments, 159
Choudhury, Mahendra Mohan, 348, 382
Choudhury, Rabindranath, 81
Churchill, Winston
    resignation of, 36
'civil disobedience movement,' 307
Clow, Andrew, 9, 37
College Teachers' Association, 422
Committee on Minorities, 124
Communist Party of India (CPI), 11, 47, 76, 163
Congress Socialist Party (CSP), 170
Congress Working Committee (CWC), 57, 406
*Constituent Assembly Debates,* 119
Constituent Assembly, formation of, 116
Constitution Amendment Bill, 379

'coolie-*bat*', 253
*Coptis teeta,* 259
Cotton College, 18
  establishment of, 211
Cotton, Henry, 211
Coupland Plan, 35
C.R. formula, 46

**D**
*Dainik Asam,* 326, 367, 421
*Dainik Assamiya,* 55, 90, 118, 122
*Datal Hatir Uye Khowa Haoda,* 171, 176
*Dawn,* 66
Defence of India Act (1962), 290
'Demand Day,' 323
Desai, Morarji
  in hydropower production, 425
Devanagari script, 277
Dibrugarh
  American army camps in, 13–14
Digboi oil refinery, 15, 165
'Disappointment in Oil,' 396
*Do Bigha Zamin,* 233
Doom Dooma, 516
Douglas C-47 military transport aircraft, 17
Drafting Committee, 116, 127–129
Dudhwa National Park, 504

**E**
earthquake, in Brahmaputra, 180
East Bengali Muslim peasants, 67
eastern Himalayas, trouble in, 258–306
Eastern India Muslim Association, 423
*Eastern Pakistan: Its Population, Delimitation, and Economics,* 47

East India Company (EIC), 139, xxv, xxvi
  concern of, xxvi
  officials' preference for Bengali, xxxii
*Economic Weekly,* 102
Election Commission of India, 488
El Niño events, 340
Elwin, Verrier, 56, xix
'Excluded Areas,' 34

**F**
Federal Finance Commission, 131
Federated State National Council, 141
Federation of Indian Chambers of Commerce and Industry (FICCI), 344
Fifth Finance Commission, 511
Finance Commission, 133
Fixation of Ceiling of Land Holdings Act of 1956, 498
Food Corporation of India, 508
food crisis of 1966, 327
Foreigners Act (1946), 114
Foreign Exchange Regulation Act (FERA), 381
Francis Kingdon-Ward, 268
Fuller, Bampfylde, 70

**G**
Gadgil, Dhananjay Ramchandra, 511
Gandhian Vinoba Bhave, 250
Gandhi, Indira
  AASU's demands and, 409
  announced 20-point programme, 411
  assassination, 487
  Emergency, 395
  *garibi hatao,* 384
  on massacre of 18 February, 475

on military intervention, 364–365
in Nellie, 473
and P.N. Dhar, 368
promulgated Emergency, 420
and Sarat Chandra Sinha, 416
visit to refugee camps in Assam, 364
on wholesale trade of wheat, 406
Gandhi, Mahatma
21-day fast, 13
on Hindu–Muslim unity, 59
Gargaya, 224
Garo community, in Bengal's Mymensingh district, 82
Garo Hills, xxvi
Gauhati Artists' Guild, 432
Gauhati University
Act, 211
adopt Assamese as medium of instruction, 385
establishment of, 214
General Reserve Engineer Force (GREF), 17
"Gentlemen, Assam retires," 59
*Geographical Journal,* 106
Ghurye, G.S., 31
Gir National Park, 503
Goalpara
new townships in, 98
zamindars of, 172–174
Goalpara Ryot Sabha, 401
Goalpara Tenancy Act of 1929, 174
Goswami, Golok Chandra, 224
Goswami, Pitambar Deva, 11
Government of India Act (1935), 34, 121, 131, xxxiii
grazing fees, collections of, 43
Great Calcutta Killings (1946), 64, 89, 483
Green Revolution, 376, 377, 507, 508

Griffiths, Percival, 2
Griffith, William, xxix
Gross, Anthony, 27
'Grow More Food' campaign, 29, 43, 45, 176, 182, 185
"grow more Moslems"', 45
*Guardian,* 157
guerrilla warfare, 338, 383, 515
Guha, Biraja Sankar
education of, 143
Gujarat University, 242
Guwahati
economic and cultural centre, 18
military camps in, 4
new townships in, 98
Pethick-Lawrence visited, 36
refinery, 192
'Guwahati, 1944,' 394
Guwahati–Barauni pipeline, 194
Guwahati Cotton College, 70
Guwahati University Students' Advisory Board, 183

**H**
Handiqui, K.K., 215–216
Hazarika, Bhupen, 236, 538, xxi
Hazarika, Jogendra Nath, 426, 441
high-yielding variety (HYV), 508
Hills–Plains Festival, 320
Hindu Assamese society, 496
Hindu Mahasabha, 109, 138
Hindu–Muslim tension, in India, 375
Hindustani Talimi Sangh, 269
Hindustan National Guard, 76
Hindustan Paper Corporation Limited, 435
Hindustan Unilever Limited, 503
*Hints for Europeans,* 217
*History of Assamese Literature,* 53

'Hollow victory for Gandhi in Assam,' 483
Horlicks, 537
Hutton, J.H., 31, 57
Hydari, Akbar, 69

**I**

Illegal Migrants (Determination by Tribunal) Act, 493
*Illustrated Weekly of India,* 303
Immigrants (Expulsion from Assam) Act, 113, 114
Imperial Legislative Assembly, 70
Imphal
   Allied army in, 22
India Independence Bill (1947), 79
Indian Administrative Service, 264
Indian Board for Wildlife, 505
Indian Constitution, Sixth Schedule, xviii
Indian Frontier Administrative Service (IFAS), 271
Indian Independence Bill, 78
Indian National Army (INA), 2
Indian National Trade Union Congress, 75, 104
Indian Oil Corporation (IOC), 380
Indian People's Theatre Association (IPTA), 165, 236
Indian Rebellion (1857), xxix
Indian Red Cross Society, 368
Indian Statutory Commission, 31, 70, 131, 150
Indian Tea Association (ITA), 6, 26, 97
India's Citizenship Act, 459, 489
*India Today,* 456
Indo-Aryan languages, evolution of, 223
Indo-China War (1962), 196

Indo-Pakistan Boundary Disputes Tribunal, 85
Indo-Pakistan War, 100
Industrial Development Bank, 397
Industrial Policy Resolution, 104
Instrument of Accession, 86
International Union of Conservation of Nature (IUCN) Survival Service Commission, 505
*Introduction to Assam,* 217

**J**

Jabbar Commission, 357
Jaintia Hills Districts Tribal Union, 320
*jajmani* system, 83
Jamiat Ulema-e-Hind (JUH), 11, 49
*Jana Gana Mana,* 118
Japan
   bombing Burma, 1
   and the British Indian Army (1944) battle, xvii
   occupied Burma in 1942, xvii
Japanese
   forces
      in Burma, 2–3
      occupied Rangoon, 2
   in Kohima, 20
   and Nagas, 20
   raids on eastern Assam, 18
   troops attacked the Naga Hills, 29
*jati,* 230
'Jatir Kolongko,' 420
'jatiya sangeet,' 118
*Jayantee,* 227
Jenkins, Francis, xxix
jhum cultivation, 143
*Jivanar Batat,* 240
Joint Steamer Company, 13
Joshi, P.C., 11

*Journal of the Assam Research Society,* 218
*Journal of the Music Academy,* 530
*Joymoti,* 232
*Jugantar,* 293
Jute, export of, 132

## K

Kachin Independence Army, 383, 514
Kaitheli, 224
Kaki Land Reclamation Project, 177
*Kalanemir Lanka Sambad,* 326
Kamarupa Anusandhan Samiti (KAS), 218
Kataki, Sarbeswar Sarma, 222
*Katha-guru-carita,* 230
Kaziranga National Park (KNP), 503
Khan, Abdul Hamid, 44
Khasi and Jaintia Hills, xxvi
Khasi Jaintia Federated State National Conference, 86
Khasi-Jaintia-Garo (KJG) hills, 327
Kohima Convention, 209
Koyali refinery, 379
Kumbh Mela (1966), 328
Kunzru, Hridya Nath, 6

## L

Lachit Sena, 341, 343
'land grab movement,' 418
'*larke lenge Pakistan*', 64
Latasil Bihu programme, 239
Leach, Edmund, 27
Ledo Road, 25
Line System, 43
*lingua franca,* 37, 145
Linguistic Minorities Rights Committee, 386
*Linguistic Survey of India,* 400
Lipton, 516

London School of Economics, 235
*Lovita,* 30
Lushai Hills, xxvi
Lushai Hills Total Defence Scheme, 28

## M

Mahanta, Prafulla Kumar, 493
Maintenance of Internal Security Act of 1971 (MISA), 422
Makum Tea Company, 501
Manas National Park, 506
*Manchester Guardian,* 157
Manipur
    Allied forces poisoned water bodies in, 22
Maniram Dutta Barbhandar Barua, xxviii
Marwari traders, in Assam's frontier hills, 33
massacre, of 18 February, 474
*Mautam,* 308
McLeod tea company, 500
McMahon Line, 260, 282, 285
Meghalaya
    statehood on 1972, xx
Mehta Committee, 329, 345
Memorandum of Settlement, signing of, 490
Meston Award, 131
Meston Committee, 130
'military emergency,' 65
military expenditure and inflation, 6
Military Railway Service (MRS), 16
Mills, J.P., 36
*Miri Jiyori,* 238
Mishing Bihu, 239
*Mission to Moscow,* 12
Mizo Cultural Society (MCS), 316
Mizo hills, military strikes in, 336

## 848          Index

Mizo National Army, 334
Mizo National Famine Front, 314, 316
Mizo National Front (MNF), 316, 335
Mizoram
    statehood on 1972, xx
*Mizo Sawrkar,* 337
Mizo Union, 136
Mizo Union and Chaliha government, 314
Montagu–Chelmsford Reforms, 212
Mountbatten, Lord Louis, 60
'Mrityur Sesh Muhurtat Abedan,' 255
Mughal empire, xxv
Mukti Bahini forces, 369–370
Munshi, K.M., 125
Murari Chand College, 211
Muslim League, 7
Muslim National Guard, 67, 76

### N
Naga Hill Administration, 38
Naga Hills, xxvi
Naga Hills Jhum Regulation, 185
Naga hills, political crisis in, 209
Naga Hills Tuensang Area, 209
Nagaland
    Peace Mission, 332
    statehood on 1963, xx
Naga National Council (NNC), 38, 134, 146, 198, 199, 307
    and Constituent Assembly, 200
    letter to the British high commissioner, 203
Naga Nationalist Council, 148
Naga Special Police squads, 208
Namdang Tea Company, 501
*namghars,* 495
*Namghosha,* language of, 226

National Army Museum, 2
National Book Trust, 235
National Cadet Corps, 293
National Defence Fund, 293
Nationalist Socialist Council of Nagaland (NSCN), 514
National Register of Citizens (NRC), 115, 362, 444
*Nature,* 24
Naxalite movement, 366
Nehru, Jawaharlal, xviii, xxxiv
    in Guwahati, 250
    hill leaders met, 322
    Liaquat Agreement, 91
    met Ayub Khan, 357
    speech, Assam listened to, 296
    visited Guwahati and Tezpur, 297
Nellie massacre, 479, 482, 487
Nepali cattle grazers, 43
Niemeyer Award, 132
Nikhil Cachar Haidimba Barman Samiti, 81
*Nilachal,* 302
Nine Point Agreement, 198
Noakhali communal violence, 89
Noakhali riots, in East Bengal, 64–65
North Eastern Council Act, 351
North-Eastern Hill University (NEHU), 391
North-East Frontier Agency (NEFA), 200, 261, 263, xix
    'advanced techniques of farming' to, 304
    Assamese language from, 276
    Assamese speakers, 278
    census in, 264
    environmental and political stability, 302
    first Assamese to join, 269
    Indianization in, 273

Indianization of, 270
Marwari traders, 264
Medhi and, 267
*Philosophy for,* 272
primary schools in, 304
schools in, 272
North-East Frontier Tracts (NEFT), 261
North West Frontier Province, 59
North-West Frontier Province (NWFP), 50, 134
'no truck with India,' 202

**O**

Official Language Commission, 244
Oil and Natural Gas Commission, 197
Oil India Limited (OIL), 195, 196, 379
*O Mor Aponar Desh,* 118
Operation Bajrang, 518
Operation Blue Star, 487
Operation Jericho, 334
'Operation Rhino,' 520
Other Backward Classes (OBC), 417
Otto Niemeyer Committee, 126

**P**

Pakistani Nationals (PIP) project, 356, 358
Pakistan (Control) Ordinance, 110
'Pakistan Zindabad' slogan, 288
Pal, Bipin Chandra, 69, 72
Parisad, Gana Sangram, 256
Parshuram Kund, Gandhi's ashes in, 270
'Partially Excluded Areas,' 34, 160
Partition Award, xviii
Pataskar Commission, 324–325
Patel, Vallabhbhai, 81, xxxiv

Patharia Hill Reserved Forest, 85
People's Democratic Party, 420
Percy Committee, 132
Permanent Settlement of Bengal (1793), xxvii
Phukan, Ananda, 64
Phukan, Bhrigu Kumar, 493
*Pita Putra,* 432
Plain Tribals Council of Assam (PTCA), 350, 399, 420, 522
Plantation Inquiry Commission, 170
*posa* system, 258
Prachin Kamrupi Nritya Sangha, 528
Pragjyotishpur, 241
Praja Socialist Party (PSP), 345
*Proceedings of the All-India Oriental Conference,* 530
Progressive Protected Villages, 337
provincial autonomy, 121
Provincial Constitution Committee, 123
Public Distribution System (PDS), 406
punitive tax, 12
Punjab Reorganisation Act (1966), 328
*Purani Asamiya Sahitya,* 230
Purbanchaliya Loka Parishad (PLP), 435

**Q**

Quit India Movement, 1, 7, 173

**R**

Radcliffe Commission award, 85
Radcliffe, Sir Cyril, xviii
Railway Protection Force, 286
Ramakrishna Mission, 6
Rangoon, air raid in, 2
Rat-killing squads, 314

Raychowdhury, Ambikagiri, 58, 95
*Reader's Digest,* 310
*Reflections on Assam cum Pakistan,* 47
Reform Commission, 74
Reid, Robert, 31, 32
    proposed to combine frontier areas of Assam and frontier areas of Burma, 34
*Report of the Union Constitution Committee,* 119
*Report on the Constitutional Problem in India,* 35
*Report on the Principles of a Model Provincial Constitution,* 119, 121
Research & Analysis Wing (RAW), 374
Revolutionary Communist Party of India (RCPI), 11, 64, 164
    activists arrested, 168
Rourkela Hindustan Steel Plant, 194
*ryotwari* system, 162, xxvii

**S**

Saadulla, Muhammad, 7
Sadiya and Balipara Frontier Tracts, 152
Sadiya Frontier Tract Jhum Land Regulation, 265
Sahitya Akademi, 235
Saikia, Hiteswar, 483
    unwillingness to negotiate with AASU leaders, 488
*Sangeet Kosha,* 234
Sangeet Natak Akademi, 531, 538
Sankardeva's teachings, 229
*Sankardeva tithi,* 239
Sarkar Committee, 126–127
Sarkar, Nalini Ranjan, 29, 126
*satradhikar,* 66

School of Oriental and African Studies, 36
'Scottish plan,' 323
Second Anglo-Burmese War, 34
Seventh Finance Commission, 428, 512
Shell Oil, 188
shelter camps, 5
Shillong
    government functionaries in, 313
    new townships in, 98
Shillong Refugee Aid Society, 92
Simla Conference of 1914, 260
Simon Commission, 70, 145, 178
Singapore Radio, 18
Singha, Purandar, xxviii
Sinha, Sarat Chandra, 416
Sino-Indian border, 283
Sino-Indian border dispute, 290
Sino-Indian conflict 1962, 383
*Siraj,* 233
Sixth Schedule
    adoption of, 156
    of the Constitution, 152, 153
*Smritir Parash,* 279
Socialist Party of India, 204
'social legislation,' 512
*Soviet Desh,* 236
*Srihatta Bicched,* 71
Standard Vacuum Oil, 188
Standstill Agreement, 106
State Language Day, 246–247
State Reorganisation Committee, 320
*Statesman,* 168
States Reorganisation Commission, 279, 320, 330
Steel Brothers & Company, 26
*Swadhinata,* 514
Sylhet

Hindu population of, 72
merger with Pakistan, 78
Muslim leadership, 73
Nagri script, 69
referendum, 69, 77, 142
referendum in, xviii
reunion with Bengal, 70
strained relationship with
 Assamese intelligentsia, 71–72
Sylhet Boundary Commission, 82

**T**

Tagore, Dwarkanath, xxix
Tagore, Saumyendranath, 164
Tea Board of India, 502
tea, export of, 132
Tea Finance Committee, 501
tea gardens, tax collection from, 339
Tezpur, American army camps in, 13–14
*The Aborigines—'So-Called'—And Their Future,* 31
The Assam Debt Conciliation Act, 10
*The Future of India,* 35
'The Hump,' 15
*The Naga Problem,* 204
*The Naked Nagas,* 155
*The Origin and Development of the Bengali Language,* 217
Third Round Table Conference, 131
Thongchi, Yeshe Dorjee, 258
Tibeto-Burman languages, 33, 224
*Times of India,* 57, 95, 98, 168, 248
Tirap Frontier, 285
Tribhuvan Prasad Tewary Commission, 478
*Twelfth Report of the Commissioner for Linguistic Minorities,* 391
'Two Nation Theory,' 35

**U**

*ujaniya* Asamiya, 226
Ujani Assam Rajya Parishad (UARP), 390, 419, 420
Umtru Hydro Electric Project, 191
Unclassed State Forests (USF), 41
Undesirable Immigrants Bill, 110
unfolding crises, in highlands of Assam, 307–351
Union Constitution Committee, 123
Union Powers Committee, 123
United Chinland Organisation, 317
United Khasi-Jaintia Hills Mineral Rights Committee, 319
United Liberation Front of Asom (ULFA), 513
 cadres armed with sophisticated weapons, 514
 demanded ransom from garden, 517
 kidnapped and killed between January and October 1991, 520
 moved to western Burma, 515
 and Nationalist Socialist Council of Nagaland, 514
United Minority Front (UMF), 492
United Reservation Movement Council of Assam (URMCA), 519
United Tribal Nationalists' Liberation Front Assam (UTNLFA), 522–523
Upper Assam
 cut down of trees, 24
 no-rent movement in, 8
Upper Shillong Farm
 establishment of, 185
'urban insurgency,' 515
US naval base
 Japanese attack on, 13

## V

Varendra Anusandhan Samiti, 218
Viceroy's Commissioned Officers (VCO), 29
Vietnam war, 383
Vishwa Hindu Parishad (VHP), 328

## W

'war fund,' 518
war preparations, 15
Watch and Ward Scheme, 28
Wavell, Viceroy, 35
West Bengal, 'chicken-neck' corridor in, 100
West Bengal Economic Development Council, 369
Wild Life (Protection) Act of 1972, 504, 505
World Food Conference, 408
*World Today*, 331
World War II, 1–2

## Y

*Yaruingam*, 27
'*Yeh azaadi jhoothi hai*,' 164